Industrial Products Handbook

Industrial Products Handbook

VOLUME 2

edited by
JOHN J. McKETTA
The University of Texas at Austin
Austin, Texas

Marcel Dekker, Inc. New York • Basel • Hong Kong

Library of Congress Cataloging-in-Publication Data

Industrial products handbook / edited by John J. McKetta.
p. cm.
Articles excerpted from: Encyclopedia of chemical processing and design.
Includes bibliographical references and index.
ISBN 0-8247-8709-9 (v. 1). -- ISBN 0-8247-8706-4 (v. 2)
1. Chemical engineering--Handbooks, manuals, etc. I. McKetta, John J. II. Encyclopedia of chemical processing and design.
TP151.I53 1993
660--dc20 93-2240
CIP

The publisher offers discounts on this book when ordered in bulk quantities. For more information, write to Special Sales/Professional Marketing at the address below.

This book is printed on acid-free paper.

Marcel Dekker, Inc.
270 Madison Avenue, New York, New York 10016

Current printing (last digit):
10 9 8 7 6 5 4 3 2 1

PRINTED IN THE UNITED STATES OF AMERICA

Preface

We feel there is a need for a handbook covering in extensive detail the various, mainly chemical products of major industrial use. Each product is presented by a world expert in that particular area in such a manner that it is easily understood and applied. Each professional practicing engineer involved in the design, manufacture, and application of industrial products should have a copy of this book on his or her working shelf.

The handbook is conveniently presented in alphabetical order. Volume 1 covers product design and applications from abrasives through essential oils; Volume 2 continues with ethylene-propylene elastomers and proceeds through plastic fiberglass and platinum group metals. An upcoming Volume 3 will cover the rest of the alphabet. Whenever possible, shortcut methods of calculations involving product design and applications are included, along with nomographic methods of solutions. In the front of the book are two convenient sections that will be very helpful to the reader. These are (1) conversion to and from SI units and (2) cost indexes that will enable the reader to update any cost information.

As editor, I am grateful for all the help I have received from the great number of authors who have contributed to this book. I am also grateful to the huge number of readers who have written to me with suggestions of products to be included.

John J. McKetta

Contents of Volume 2

Contents of Volume 1

Contributors

G. H. Amberg Senior Research Engineer, Fuels Division, Chevron Research Company, Richmond, California

M. R. Barusch Manager, Lubricating Oil Additives Division, Chevron Research Company, Richmond, California

G. David Baskin U. S. Department of the Interior, Bureau of Mines, Washinton, D. C.

R. C. Berg Manager, Detergent Processes (Retired), Process Division, UOP, Des Plaines, Illinois

A. L. Bisio Engineering Advisor, Exxon Research and Engineering Company, Clinton, New Jersey

Philip G. Blakey Vice President, Electronic Gases, Airco, Murray Hill, New Jersey

Terry L. Blevins Senior Technologist, Fisher-Rosemont Systems Division, Fisher Controls International, Inc., Austin, Texas

Heinz P. Bloch Engineering Associate, Exxon Chemical Company, Baytown Olefins Plant, Baytown, Texas

Grant F. Carruth, Ph.D., P.E. Owens-Corning Fiberglas, Granville, Ohio

Raymond A. Chartier Olin Research Center, Olin Corporation, New Haven, Connecticut

R. L. Chiang, Ph.D. Research Associate, Advanced Separations Systems, Air Products and Chemicals, Inc., Allentown, Pennsylvania

Chun H. Cho, Ph.D. Senior Technical Consultant, Process Instrumentation Business Unit, Fisher Controls International, Inc., Marshalltown, Iowa

A. M. Chreitzberg Program Manager of Utility Load Leveling, ESB Incorporated, Yardley, Pennsylvania

Carl E. Coats Composite Polymers Division (Retired), Ashland Chemical, Inc., Columbus, Ohio

Gabriel J. Cordova Manager, Process Control, John Brown E&C Inc., Stamford, Connecticut

Myron D. Dalluge Senior Technical Service Representative, Polyester Development, Composite Polymers Division, Ashland Chemical, Inc., Columbus, Ohio

Al Di Cara, Jr. Director of Plant Operations, Ungerer & Company, Bethlehem, Pennsylvania

T. R. Dillman Vice President, Research and Development and Engineering, Alcoa Separations, Pittsburgh, Pennsylvania

Robert N. DiNapoli Vice President/Principal, Merlin Associates, Inc., Atlanta, Georgia

James B. Doe Research Associate, Technology Center, ESB Incorporated, Yardley, Pennsylvania

George T. Doyle Project Manager, John Brown E&C Inc., Stamford, Connecticut

Charles W. Drake, P.E. Executive Vice President, Process MDS Inc., Houston, Texas

E. J. Duwell Research Manager, Industrial Abrasives Division, 3M Company, St. Paul, Minnesota

R. L. Englund Technical Manager, Automotive Trades Division, 3M Company, St. Paul, Minnesota

Lawrence M. Fodor, Ph.D. Technical Manager, Research and Development, Phillips Petroleum Company, Bartlesville, Oklahoma

T. J. Fowler, Ph.D. Distinguished Fellow, The Chemical Group, Monsanto Company, St. Louis, Missouri

V. Ganapathy Heat Transfer Specialist, ABCO Industries, Abilene, Texas

Larry H. Gasper, M.S., P.E. Staff Engineer, Process Engineering, Ciba-Geigy, Greensboro, North Carolina

Jacob M. Geist, Ph.D., P.E. President, Geist TEC, Geist Technology and Engineering Company, Allentown, Pennsylvania

Om P. Goyal Senior Technical Advisor, Special Projects, Refinera Isla, Curaçao, Netherlands Antilles

H. Tracy Hall Professor Emeritus, Department of Chemistry and Chemical Engineering, Brigham Young University, Provo, Utah

James R. Hancock Director, Engineering Services, H. C. Price Co., Bartlesville, Oklahoma

W. D. Harris, Ph.D. Professor Emeritus, Department of Chemical Engineering, Texas A & M University, College Station, Texas

Frederick G. Harrison Director of Chemical Operations, Waters Chromatography: Division of Millipore, Cambridge, Massachusetts

Herold I. Hertanu Manager, Corporate Computer Engineering, John Brown E&C Inc., Stamford, Connecticut

Harry Isacoff Corporate Director, Technical Services, International Flavors and Fragrances (U.S.), New York, New York

John O. Izatt, P.E. Consultant, Houston, Texas

Fred C. Jahnke Senior Staff Engineer, Texaco Inc., White Plains, New York

N. S. Johary Chief Executive, Atul Industries Ltd., Atul, District Bulsar, Gujarat State, India

A. H. Jorgensen Zion Chemicals USA, Inc., Louisville, Kentucky

Vinayaka Kahol Himachal Pradesh State Industrial Development, Ltd., Shimla, Himachal Pradesh, India

Sergio D. Kapusta, Ph.D. Senior Research Chemist, Shell Development Company, Houston, Texas

Joseph R. Kenton Senior Research Chemist (Retired), Phillips Petroleum Company, Bartlesville, Oklahoma

C. B. Khanpara Chief Executive, Bharat Pulverizing Mills P. Ltd., Bombay, India

Emil O. Kindschy Staff Engineer, Manufacturing Department, Shell Oil Company, Houston, Texas

M. A. Knight, Jr. President, Maurice A. Knight Company, Akron, Ohio

Walter E. Kunze Group Vice President, Research and Development, Construction Technology Laboratories, Portland Cement Association, Skokie, Illinois

M. J. Kwasowski Manager, Manufacturing and Technical Support, Owens-Corning Fiberglas Corporation, Waxahachie, Texas

Rong C. Lin Bureau of Foods, Food and Drug Administration, Washington, D.C.

Kenneth J. Lisant Director of Advanced Research, Petrolite Corporation, St. Louis, Missouri

J. Roger Loebenstein, Ph.D. Commodity Specialist, Division of Mineral Commodities, Bureau of Mines, U.S. Department of Interior, Washington, D.C.

G. N. Long, Ph.D. Director of Product Development, Research and Development Department, UOP, Des Plaines, Illinois

Stanley L. Lopata Chairman of the Board, Carboline Company, St. Louis, Missouri

J. H. Macpherson, Jr. Vice President, Fuels and Asphalts Research Department, Chevron Research Company, Richmond, California

Irving Malkin Manager, ELTECH Systems Corporation, Affiliate of Diamond Shamrock Corporation, Fairport Harbor, Ohio

Edward T. Marshall Exxon Chemical Company (Retired), Short Hills, New Jersey

Reynold W. Martin II, P.E. Senior Staff Engineer, General Foods Corporation, Central Engineering, Dover, Delaware

E. Owen McBride McBride Engineers, Houston, Texas

Philip G. McCracken, Ph.D. Production Technical Director (Retired), Ciba-Geigy Agricultural Division, Greensboro, North Carolina

Charles W. McKetta, Ph.D. Associate Professor of Forest Economics/ Management, University of Idaho, Forest Resources Department, Moscow, Idaho

John J. McKetta, Ph.D., P.E. The Joe C. Walter Professor of Chemical Engineering, The University of Texas at Austin, Austin, Texas

I. K. Miller, Ph.D. Research Fellow, E. I. du Pont de Nemours and Company (Retired), Wilmington, Delaware

William A. Mod Research Associate (Retired), Dow Chemical Company, Freeport, Texas

Gregory M. Moelter Senior Research Associate, Celanese Fibers Company, Charlotte, North Carolina

Bennet R. Mogul Chief Chemist, Vulcan Materials Company, Chattanooga Division, Chattanooga, Tennessee

Malcolm G. Murray, Jr., P.E. Owner, Murray & Garig Tool Works, Baytown, Texas

Ernest O. Ohsol, Sc.D., P.E. Consulting Chemical Engineer, and Chairman, Unipure Corporation, Houston, Texas

R. J. Pellet, Ph.D. Senior Research Associate, Texaco Research and Development, Beacon, New York

R. D. Picht Manager, Process Engineering, Alcoa Separations, Rockford, Illinois

G. Frank Phillips Consultant, Research and Development, Dr Pepper—Seven-Up Company, Dallas, Texas

Douglas M. Queen Douglas M. Queen, Inc., Consultant on the Construction Industry, New Canaan, Connecticut

Syed Qutubuddin, Ph.D. Assistant Professor, Departments of Chemical Engineering and Macromolecular Science, Case Western Reserve University, Cleveland, Ohio

J. A. Rabo, Ph.D. Senior Fellow (Retired), Research and Development Department, UOP, Des Plaines, Illinois

J. Albert Rolston, P.E. Consulting Engineer, Rolston and Associates, Granville, Ohio

Alvin J. Salkind Vice President—Technology, ESB Incorporated, Yardley, Pennsylvania

Paul A. Sanders Research Associate, "Freon" Products Laboratory, E. I. du Pont de Nemours & Co., Wilmington, Delaware

Steven M. Seelinger, P.E. Manager, Mechanical Engineering, BASF Corporation, Parsippany, New Jersey

Avilino Sequeira, Jr., P.E. Senior Research Consultant, Research and Development, Texaco, Inc., Port Arthur, Texas

Raymond B. Seymour Professor and Coordinator of Polymer Research, Department of Chemistry, University of Houston, Houston, Texas

Walter Lee Sheppard, Jr., P.E. President, C.C.R.M. Inc., Havertown, Pennsylvania

Stephen M. Sinker Development Associate—Technical Specialist, Celcon Acetal Copolymer, Hoechst Celanese Corporation, Summit, New Jersey

C. V. Smalheer Staff Assistant, Literature, to Vice-President of Research and Development, The Lubrizol Corporation, Cleveland, Ohio

Richard Steele Vice President and Technical Director, Celanese Fibers Company, Charlotte, North Carolina

Robert C. Talbot Marketing Consultant, HETRON Resins, Composite Polymers Division, Ashland Chemical, Inc., Columbus, Ohio

L. E. Tedrow Senior Engineer, Mobil Oil Corporation (Retired), Fairfax, Virginia

B. R. Tegge, Ph.D. Senior Engineering Associate, Exxon Chemical Company, Linden, New Jersey

B. V. Vora Associate Director for Petrochemicals, Process and Systems Development Department, UOP, Des Plaines, Illinois

James L. Walker President, Metaloil Refining Corp., Houston, Texas

Guy E. Weismantel President, Weismantel International, Kingwood, Texas

Warren E. White, Jr., P.E. President, FutureSoft Engineering, Houston, Texas

Joseph F. Wilson Research Scientist (Retired), Phillips Petroleum Company, Bartlesville, Oklahoma

Arnold C. Witte Research Consultant, Research and Development, Texaco, Inc., Port Arthur, Texas

Richard A. York Senior Engineer, Manufacturing Department, Shell Oil Company, Houston, Texas

Ronald D. Young Staff Chemical Engineer, Tennessee Valley Authority, Muscle Shoals, Alabama

Adam Zanker, Ch.E., M.Sc. Senior Research Engineer, Haifa Oil Refineries, Ltd., Haifa, Israel

Abel A. Zelnick Chief Piping Engineer (Retired), Badger Engineers, Cambridge, Massachusetts

Conversion to SI Units

To convert from	To	Multiply by
acre	square meter (m^2)	4.046×10^3
angstrom	meter (m)	1.0×10^{-10}
are	square meter (m^2)	1.0×10^2
atmosphere	newton/square meter (N/m^2)	1.013×10^5
bar	newton/square meter (N/m^2)	1.0×10^5
barrel (42 gallon)	cubic meter (m^3)	0.159
Btu (International Steam Table)	joule (J)	1.055×10^3
Btu (mean)	joule (J)	1.056×10^3
Btu (thermochemical)	joule (J)	1.054×10^3
bushel	cubic meter (m^3)	3.52×10^{-2}
calorie (International Steam Table)	joule (J)	4.187
calorie (mean)	joule (J)	4.190
calorie (thermochemical)	joule (J)	4.184
centimeter of mercury	newton/square meter (N/m^2)	1.333×10^3
centimeter of water	newton/square meter (N/m^2)	98.06
cubit	meter (m)	0.457
degree (angle)	radian (rad)	1.745×10^{-2}
denier (international)	kilogram/meter (kg/m)	1.0×10^{-7}
dram (avoirdupois)	kilogram (kg)	1.772×10^{-3}
dram (troy)	kilogram (kg)	3.888×10^{-3}
dram (U.S. fluid)	cubic meter (m^3)	3.697×10^{-6}
dyne	newton (N)	1.0×10^{-5}
electron volt	joule (J)	1.60×10^{-19}
erg	joule (J)	1.0×10^{-7}
fluid ounce (U.S.)	cubic meter (m^3)	2.96×10^{-5}
foot	meter (m)	0.305
furlong	meter (m)	2.01×10^2
gallon (U.S. dry)	cubic meter (m^3)	4.404×10^{-3}
gallon (U.S. liquid)	cubic meter (m^3)	3.785×10^{-3}
gill (U.S.)	cubic meter (m^3)	1.183×10^{-4}
grain	kilogram (kg)	6.48×10^{-5}
gram	kilogram (kg)	1.0×10^{-3}
horsepower	watt (W)	7.457×10^2
horsepower (boiler)	watt (W)	9.81×10^3
horsepower (electric)	watt (W)	7.46×10^2
hundred weight (long)	kilogram (kg)	50.80
hundred weight (short)	kilogram (kg)	45.36
inch	meter (m)	2.54×10^{-2}
inch mercury	newton/square meter (N/m^2)	3.386×10^3
inch water	newton/square meter (N/m^2)	2.49×10^2
kilogram force	newton (N)	9.806

To convert from	To	Multiply by
kip	newton (N)	4.45×10^3
knot (international)	meter/second (m/s)	0.5144
league (British nautical)	meter (m)	5.559×10^3
league (statute)	meter (m)	4.83×10^3
light year	meter (m)	9.46×10^{15}
liter	cubic meter (m^3)	0.001
micron	meter (m)	1.0×10^{-6}
mil	meter (m)	2.54×10^{-6}
mile (U.S. nautical)	meter (m)	1.852×10^3
mile (U.S. statute)	meter (m)	1.609×10^3
millibar	newton/square meter (N/m^2)	100.0
millimeter mercury	newton/square meter (N/m^2)	1.333×10^2
oersted	ampere/meter (A/m)	79.58
ounce force (avoirdupois)	newton (N)	0.278
ounce mass (avoirdupois)	kilogram (kg)	2.835×10^{-2}
ounce mass (troy)	kilogram (kg)	3.11×10^{-2}
ounce (U.S. fluid)	cubic meter (m^3)	2.96×10^{-5}
pascal	newton/square meter (N/m^2)	1.0
peck (U.S.)	cubic meter (m^3)	8.81×10^{-3}
pennyweight	kilogram (kg)	1.555×10^{-3}
pint (U.S. dry)	cubic meter (m^3)	5.506×10^{-4}
pint (U.S. liquid)	cubic meter (m^3)	4.732×10^{-4}
poise	newton second/square meter ($N \cdot s/m^2$)	0.10
pound force (avoirdupois)	newton (N)	4.448
pound mass (avoirdupois)	kilogram (kg)	0.4536
pound mass (troy)	kilogram (kg)	0.373
poundal	newton (N)	0.138
quart (U.S. dry)	cubic meter (m^3)	1.10×10^{-3}
quart (U.S. liquid)	cubic meter (m^3)	9.46×10^{-4}
rod	meter (m)	5.03
roentgen	coulomb/kilogram (c/kg)	2.579×10^{-4}
second (angle)	radian (rad)	4.85×10^{-6}
section	square meter (m^2)	2.59×10^6
slug	kilogram (kg)	14.59
span	meter (m)	0.229
stoke	square meter/second (m^2/s)	1.0×10^{-4}
ton (long)	kilogram (kg)	1.016×10^3
ton (metric)	kilogram (kg)	1.0×10^3
ton (short, 2000 pounds)	kilogram (kg)	9.072×10^2
torr	newton/square meter (N/m^2)	1.333×10^2
yard	meter (m)	0.914

Bringing Costs up to Date

Cost escalation via inflation bears critically on estimates of plant costs. Historical costs of process plants are updated by means of an escalation factor. Several published cost indexes are widely used in the chemical process industries:

Nelson-Farrar Cost Indexes (*Oil and Gas J.*), quarterly
Marshall and Swift (M&S) Equipment Cost Index, updated monthly
CE Plant Cost Index (*Chemical Engineering*), updated monthly
ENR Construction Cost Index (*Engineering News-Record*), updated weekly

All these indexes were developed with various elements, such as material availability and labor productivity, taken into account. However, the proportion allotted to each element differs with each index. The differences in overall results of each index are due to uneven price changes for each element. In other words, the total escalation derived by each index will vary because different bases are used. The engineer should become familiar with each index and its limitations before using it.

Table 1 compares the CE Plant Index with the M&S Equipment Cost

TABLE 1 *Chemical Engineering* and Marshall and Swift Plant and Equipment Cost Indexes since 1950

Year	CE Index	M&S Index	Year	CE Index	M&S Index
1950	73.9	167.9	1971	132.3	321.3
1951	80.4	180.3	1972	137.2	332.0
1952	81.3	180.5	1973	144.1	344.1
1953	84.7	182.5	1974	165.4	398.4
1954	86.1	184.6	1975	182.4	444.3
1955	88.3	190.6	1976	192.1	472.1
1956	93.9	208.8	1977	204.1	505.4
1957	98.5	225.1	1978	218.8	545.3
1958	99.7	229.2	1979	238.7	599.4
1959	101.8	234.5	1980	261.2	659.6
1960	102.0	237.7	1981	297.0	721.3
1961	101.5	237.2	1982	314.0	745.6
1962	102.0	238.5	1983	316.9	760.8
1963	102.4	239.2	1984	322.7	780.4
1964	103.3	241.8	1985	325.3	789.6
1965	104.2	244.9	1986	318.4	797.6
1966	107.2	252.5	1987	323.8	813.6
1967	109.7	262.9	1988	342.5	852.0
1968	113.6	273.1	1989	355.4	895.1
1969	119.0	285.0	1990	357.6	915.1
1970	125.7	303.3	1991	361.3	930.6
			1992	358.2	943.1

TABLE 2 Nelson-Farrar Inflation Refinery Construction Indexes since 1946 (1946 = 100)

Date	Materials Component	Labor Component	Miscellaneous Equipment	Nelson-Farrar Inflation Index
1946	100.0	100.0	100.0	100.0
1947	122.4	113.5	114.2	117.0
1948	139.5	128.0	122.1	132.5
1949	143.6	137.1	121.6	139.7
1950	149.5	144.0	126.2	146.2
1951	164.0	152.5	145.0	157.2
1952	164.3	163.1	153.1	163.6
1953	172.4	174.2	158.8	173.5
1954	174.6	183.3	160.7	179.8
1955	176.1	189.6	161.5	184.2
1956	190.4	198.2	180.5	195.3
1957	201.9	208.6	192.1	205.9
1958	204.1	220.4	192.4	213.9
1959	207.8	231.6	196.1	222.1
1960	207.6	241.9	200.0	228.1
1961	207.7	249.4	199.5	232.7
1962	205.9	258.8	198.8	237.6
1963	206.3	268.4	201.4	243.6
1964	209.6	280.5	206.8	252.1
1965	212.0	294.4	211.6	261.4
1966	216.2	310.9	220.9	273.0
1967	219.7	331.3	226.1	286.7
1968	224.1	357.4	228.8	304.1
1969	234.9	391.8	239.3	329.0
1970	250.5	441.1	254.3	364.9
1971	265.2	499.9	268.7	406.0
1972	277.8	545.6	278.0	438.5
1973	292.3	585.2	291.4	468.0
1974	373.3	623.6	361.8	522.7
1975	421.0	678.5	415.9	575.5
1976	445.2	729.4	423.8	615.7
1977	471.3	774.1	438.2	653.0
1978	516.7	824.1	474.1	701.1
1979	573.1	879.0	515.4	756.6
1980	629.2	951.9	578.1	822.8
1981	693.2	1044.2	647.9	903.8
1982	707.6	1154.2	622.8	976.9
1983	712.4	1234.8	656.8	1025.8
1984	735.3	1278.1	665.6	1061.0
1985	739.6	1297.6	673.4	1074.4
1986	730.0	1330.0	684.4	1089.9
1987	748.9	1370.0	703.1	1121.5
1988	802.8	1405.6	732.5	1164.5
1989	829.2	1440.4	769.9	1195.9
1990	832.8	1487.7	797.5	1225.7
1991	832.3	1533.3	827.5	1252.9
1992	824.6	1579.2	837.6	1277.3

Index. Table 2 shows the Nelson-Farrar Inflation Petroleum Refinery Construction Indexes since 1946. It is recommended that the CE Index be used for updating total plant costs and the M&S Index or Nelson-Farrar Index for updating equipment costs. The Nelson-Farrar Indexes are better suited for petroleum refinery materials, labor, equipment, and general refinery inflation.

Since

$$C_B = C_A(B/A)^n \tag{1}$$

Here, A = the size of units for which the cost is known, expressed in terms of capacity, throughput, or volume; B = the size of unit for which a cost is required, expressed in the units of A; n = 0.6 (i.e., the six-tenths exponent); C_A = actual cost of unit A; and C_B = the cost of B being sought for the same time period as cost C_A.

To approximate a current cost, multiply the old cost by the ratio of the current index value to the index at the date of the old cost:

$$C_B = C_A I_B / I_A \tag{2}$$

Here, C_A = old cost; I_B = current index value; and I_A = index value at the date of old cost.

Combining Eqs. (1) and (2),

$$C_B = C_A(B/A)^n(I_B/I_A) \tag{3}$$

For example, if the total investment cost of plant A was $25,000,000 for 200-million-lb/yr capacity in 1974, find the cost of plant B at a throughput of 300 million lb/yr on the same basis for 1986. Let the sizing exponent, n, be equal to 0.6.

From Table 1, the CE Index for 1986 was 318.4, and for 1974 it was 165.4. Via Eq. (3),

$$\begin{aligned} C_B &= C_A(B/A)^n(I_B/I_A) \\ &= 25.0(300/200)^{0.6}(318.4/165.4) \\ &= \$61,200,000 \end{aligned}$$

JOHN J. McKETTA

Ethylene–Propylene Elastomers

Introduction

It has been a goal for many years to prepare elastomers from simple olefins such as ethylene and propylene. Structural variation achievable with such polymers gives desirable properties, particularly oxidative and thermal stability. Introduction of limited functionality permits vulcanization. However, a preparative scheme for such elastomers could not be found until Professor Karl Ziegler and his co-workers learned how to polymerize simple olefins to high molecular weight polymers with coordinated catalysts. The basic Ziegler discovery, applied to the low pressure polymerization of ethylene, was expanded by Professor G. Natta and others to the preparation of numerous polymers including ethylene–propylene elastomers.

Ethylene–propylene elastomers are available in two types:

Copolymers which can be vulcanized only with free radical cross-linking agents such as peroxides.
Terpolymers which can be vulcanized with sulfur-type curing agents.

Copolymers have the ASTM designation EPM and terpolymers are designated EPDM. Both materials provide unsurpassed resistance to ozone exposure and weathering.

Historical Background

Subsequent to the discoveries by Professors Ziegler and Natta, additional studies were carried out by research teams the world over. These established optimum conditions of synthesis and vulcanization and the relationship between structural properties and performance. This research work was responsible for the rapid development of ethylene–propylene elastomers as shown in Fig. 1. Limited quantities of ethylene–propylene elastomers were distributed to the rubber industry in the United States as early as January 1961. The first commercial elastomer, an ethylene–propylene copolymer manufactured by Exxon Chemical, became available in September 1961. Sulfur curable ethylene–propylene terpolymers were fully commercialized in December 1963. The present United States and overseas suppliers of EPM–EPDM elastomers and the trade names used by each are shown in Tables 1 and 2. Typical sizes of these EPM–EPDM elastomer plants are about 25–50 kton/yr. Typical 1979 prices for the products are in the range of 60 to 75¢/lb depending on the elastomer grade, ethylene and diene content, etc., but excluding oil and carbon black content if so extended.

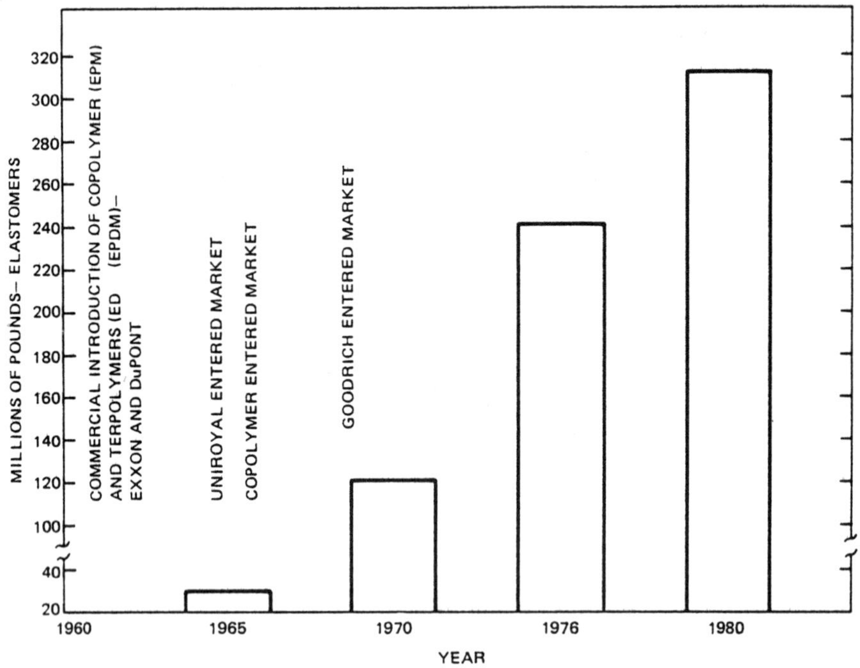

FIG. 1. Annual consumption of EP-type elastomers in the United States.

Catalyst Synthesis

The best catalysts for the synthesis of ethylene–propylene elastomers are those obtained by the reaction of aluminum alkyl catalysts with hydrocarbon-soluble vanadium compounds or alkyl esters of vanadic or chlorovanadic acid. Other transition metals such as niobium, titanium, and chromium can be substituted for vanadium. Similarly, beryllium, zinc, and alkali metals can be used as replacements for aluminum. However, the elastomers obtained from aluminum- and vanadium-base catalysts are by far the best as regards elastomeric properties and the absence of crystalline homopolymer fractions.

The preferred catalysts are essentially homogeneous, yielding copolymers of minimum crystallinity and polyethylene or polypropylene contents. When hydrocarbon-insoluble vandium compounds are used, the resulting elastomers have a broad compositional and molecular weight distribution. Moreover, some of the insoluble fractions of these elastomers contain crystallinity of both polyethylenic and polypropylenic nature. This heterogeneity in the polymer may be attributed to the existence in the insoluble catalysts of two or more types of active sites with different reactivity ratios. Consequently, the elastomeric properties of copolymers prepared from hydrocarbon-insoluble vanadium compounds are poor.

At least one of the reagents employed as the catalyst must contain a halogen (as is the case for propylene homopolymerization but not for the homopolymerization of ethylene). However, halogen-free catalyst components can be used if the catalyst preparation and/or the polymerization

TABLE 1 EP Elastomers Suppliers: United States

Supplier	Plant Location	Trade Name	Grade Slate Emphasis, EP Products Type and (Diene)
Copolymer Rubber and Chemical	Addis, Louisiana	EPsyn	Terpolymers (ENB)
Du Pont	Beaumont, Texas	NORDEL	Terpolymers (1,4-Hexadiene)
Exxon Chemical	Baton Rouge, Louisiana	VISTALON	Copolymers and terpolymers (ENB)
B. F. Goodrich Chemical	Orange, Texas	EPCAR	Copolymers and terpolymers (ENB)
Uniroyal	Geismar, Louisiana	ROYALENE	Copolymer and terpolymers (ENB/DCPD)

TABLE 2 EP Elastomer Suppliers: Except United States

Supplier	Plant Location	Trade Name	EP Product Type
Montedison	Ferrara, Italy	DUTRAL	Copolymer and terpolymers (ENB)
Bunawerke Huls	Marl, Germany	BUNA AP	Copolymer and terpolymers (ENB)
Esso Chimie	N.D. Gravenchon, France	VISTALON	Copolymer and terpolymers (ENB)
Dutch State Mines	Beek, Holland	KELTAN	Terpolymers (ENB and DCPD)
International Synthetic Rubber	Grangemouth, Scotland	INTOLAN	Terpolymers (ENB and DCPD)
Sumitomo Chemical Co.	Anegasaki, Japan	ESPRENE	Terpolymers (ENB and DCPD)
Japan Synthetic Rubber Co.	Yokkaichi, Japan	NIHON	Terpolymers (ENB and DCPD)
Mitsui Petrochemical Inds.	Ichiham, Japan	MITSUI	Copolymer and terpolymers (ENB and DCPD)
Rumania	Pitesti, Rumania	ROMTER	Terpolymers (ENB and DCPD)
USSR	Russia	SKEP or SKEPT	Terpolymers (ENB and DCPD)

reactions are carried out in the presence of a halogen-containing hydrocarbon solvent.

The catalyst can be prepared either in the presence (prereduced) or in the absence of olefins and then introduced into the polymerization reactor, or it may be formed *in situ* by separately introducing the catalyst components into the reactor. Initial catalyst activity is high but it decreases with increasing residence time.

Polymerization temperatures and pressures may be chosen within a wide range. Generally, temperature varies between +20 and 40°C and the pressure between 1 and 20 atm. The synthesis may be carried out with the polymer either in solution or in suspension. If a solution process, the reaction media will consist of an aliphatic, aromatic, or halogenated hydrocarbon which contains the dissolved elastomer.

The reactivities of ethylene and propylene are quite different. Hence, the monomer composition in the liquid phase differs significantly from that of the feed from which it is formed. It is essential that the composition in the liquid phase be kept constant with time in order to obtain an elastomer of constant composition. Therefore, close control over reactor mixing and temperature is essential.

Ethylene–Propylene Copolymer

Ethylene–propylene copolymers (EPMs) are made from the olefins ethylene and propylene. The sequence distribution and the ratio of monomers in the polymers can be varied depending upon the properties desired. In general, having the most alternating distribution of monomers in the polymer provides the most amorphous or least crystalline polymer. When the polymers are amorphous, crystallinity is not developed upon stretching. Therefore, the tensile strength of gum vulcanizates is low. Nevertheless, vulcanizates with

TABLE 3 EPM Vulcanization and Compound Techniques

Ingredient	Function
Peroxides:	Cross-linking agents. Normally used at 0.01 mol (2.0–3.0 phr)
DiCup	
Vulcup R	
Varox	
Coagents:	Improve efficiency of vulcanization. Minimizes chain scission
Sulfur (0.3 phr)	
EDMA (1.0 phr)	
TAC (1.5 phr)	
Ricon (1.0–3.0 phr)	
SR 350 (1.5–2.0 phr)	
Coupling and wetting agents (0.5–1.0 phr):	Enhance stress-strain behavior with mineral fillers
Vinyl silane	
Acrylic silane	
Carbowax	

sufficient tensile strength for most rubber goods applications can be obtained by incorporating carbon black or other reinforcing fillers.

EPMs are vulcanized through free radicals produced most generally from peroxides such as dicumyl peroxide or ditertbutyl peroxide. While the polymers can be cured with just peroxide, better physical properties are obtained when a small amount of sulfur, ethylene dimethacrylate, or other co-agent is also included in the formulation. The co-agent regulates free radical generation and modifies the nature of the cross-linking. It also improves the efficiency of the cross-linking reaction *per se*. Typical EPM vulcanization and compounding techniques are summarized in Table 3.

When compounding EPM, it is critical to avoid the use of acidic additives which can degrade the peroxide. Also, unsaturated materials, which could preferentially react with the peroxide, should be avoided or kept to a minimum.

Ethylene–Propylene Terpolymers

In order to obtain unsaturated elastomers that can be vulcanized with traditional sulfur recipes, a suitable diene or triene is introduced as a comonomer. The amount of unsaturation in commercial terpolymers is usually low (1–2 mol%), the amount of unsaturation being only that required to provide sites for sulfur vulcanization.

Numerous studies have shown that the termonomer should:

Contain at least two olefin units; only one of which should be polymerizable, with the other being suitable for vulcanization with sulfur.

Be relatively uniformly distributed along the main chain.

Exhibit a high copolymerization rate while not interfering with the polymerization of ethylene and propylene.

The residual olefin unit following polymerization should be pendant to the main chain to minimize chain cleavage. Termonomers should also be low in molecular weight so as to provide a favorable unsaturation to weight ratio. Diolefins having the same reactivity in both double bonds cannot be used unless the introduction of branching is desired. Similarly, acyclic conjugated dienes such as butadiene provide poor ozone resistance. Conjugated dienes lead to catalyst deactivation and significant formation of homopolymer.

A large number of diolefins, both linear and cyclic, have been examined as third monomers for EPDMs. Despite the numbers that can in principle be used, only three are used commercially: ethylidene norbornene, dicyclopentadiene, and 1,4-hexadiene.

The distinguishing characteristic of EPDM elastomers is that the unsaturation is always in the side chain pendant to the main or backbone chain as shown in Fig. 2 for ethylidene norbornene and in Fig. 3 for 1,4-hexadiene. Consequently, any oxidation or chemical reaction with residual unsaturation present after vulcanization can have only a limited effect upon the properties of the elastomer.

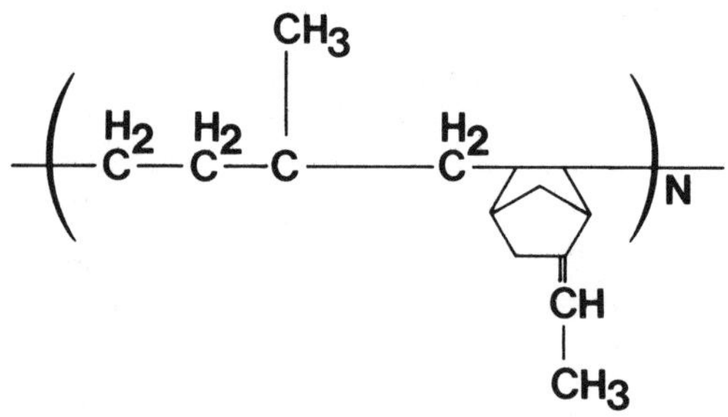

FIG. 2. Ethylene–propylene ethylidene norbornene.

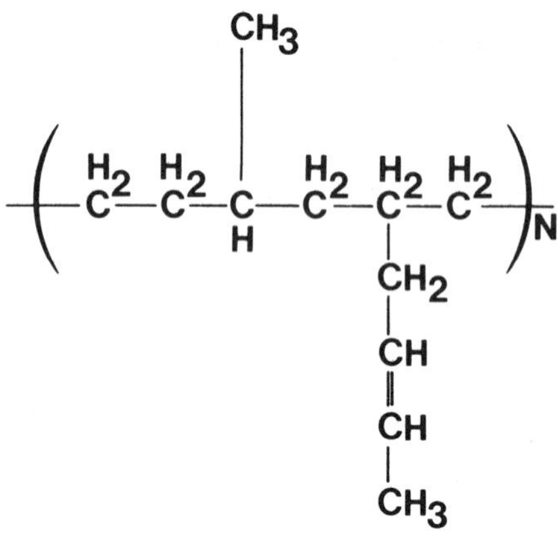

FIG. 3. Ethylene–propylene 1,4-hexadiene.

The elastomer molecular parameters that are significant for grade definition are: Mooney viscosity (an empirical measure of molecular weight), molecular weight distribution, ethylene content, and diene type and concentration (as indicated by the speed of cure). Typical EPDM types are shown in Table 4.

Terpolymers react with sulfur during vulcanization in a manner similar to the reaction of sulfur during the vulcanization of natural rubber. The vulcanization reactivity of the side chain double bond is, however, dependent upon the chemical groups adjacent to it. Typical EPDM cure systems are given in Tables 5 and 6.

TABLE 4 Vistalon EPDM Types

	2504	3708	5600	6505
Mooney viscosity	Low	Medium	High	Medium
Molecular weight distribution	Broad	Broad	Medium-Broad	Medium-Narrow
Ethylene content	Medium	High	Medium-High	Medium
Cure speed	Medium	Medium	Medium-Fast	Ultra Fast

TABLE 5 General Purpose EPDM Cure Systems[a]

Cure System A	Cure System B	Cure System C	Cure System D
1.5 Sulfur 0.5 MBT 1.5 TMTDS	2.0 Sulfur 1.8 MBT 0.8 TMTDS 0.08 TDEDC (80%) 0.8 DPTTS	1.5 Sulfur 0.5 MBT 3.0 TMTDS	1.5 Sulfur 2.0 MBTS 0.8 TMTDS 0.8 ZDEDC
Medium cure rate Good heat resistance Fair compression set Good scorch resistance Nonblooming in steam Low cost	Fast cure rate High tensile strength Fair compression set Nonblooming in press and steam	Fast cure rate High tensile strength Good heat resistance Good compression set Good scorch resistance Nonblooming in steam Low cost	Medium cure rate Good scorch resistance Nonblooming in press and steam Low cost Fair compression set

[a]BAPFR-4 = Bromobutyl alkylated phenol formaldehyde resin.
Di-cup 40 = Dicumyl peroxide.
DPTTS = Dipentamethylene thiuram tetrasulfide.
DTDM = 4,4′-Dithiodimorpholine.
MBT = Mercaptobenzothiazole.
MBTS = Benzothiazyl disulfide.
TDEDC = Tellurium diethyl dithiocarbamate.
TMTDS = Tetramethyl thiuram disulfide.
ZDBDC = Zinc dibutyl dithiocarbamate.
ZDEDC = Zinc diethyl dithiocarbamate.
ZDMDC = Zinc dimethyl dithiocarbamate.

Vulcanizate Properties

Like the general purpose rubbers, ethylene–propylene elastomers show good mechanical and dynamic properties and are quite superior in important properties such as resistance to ozone, chemical attack, and heat. A comparison of the physical properties of EPDM, natural rubber, and SBR vulcanizates is given in Table 7. The beneficial properties of EPDM vulcanization are shown in Table 8.

Ethylene–propylene elastomers are virtually impervious to ozone degradation. Extensive tests have shown that vulcanizates are unaffected after years of exposure to ozone at concentrations as high as 100 ppm. In even more severe tests, vulcanizates which were stretched 50% and exposed to an ozone concentration of 2000 ppm for 10 days showed no signs of cracking. This inherent resistance to ozone, combined with superior resistance to degrada-

TABLE 6 Special Purpose EPDM Cure Systems[a]

Cure System E	Cure System P	Cure System R
0.3 Sulfur 3.0 TMTDS 2.0 DTDM 3.0 ZDMDC 3.0 ZDBDC	0.32 Sulfur 9.0 Di-cup 40C	5.0 Hypalon 40 15.0 BAPFR-4
Medium cure rate	Fast cure rate	Slow cure rate
Best (nonperoxide) heat aging	Excellent heat resistance	Best development of properties at high temperature curing
Best (nonperoxide) compression set resistance	Excellent compression set resistance	Excellent heat resistance
Excellent scorch resistance	Nonblooming in press and steam	Excellent compression set resistance with high temperature cures
Slight bloom in steam	Care must be taken in steam vulcanization to remove oxygen	Nonblooming in press cures Nonrecommended for steam cures

[a]See Table 5 for the key to abbreviations.

tion by ultraviolet radiation and the extremes of atmospheric temperature, make ethylene–propylene elastomers quite suitable for use outdoors.

No great difference exists between the mechanical–dynamic properties of EPM and EPDM vulcanizates, apart from the fact that peroxide vulcanization binds the chains with C—C bonds while in sulfur vulcanization polysulfidic cross-links are obtained. Sulfur cross-links are also obtained in copolymers when the curing recipe involves both peroxide and sulfur. However, EPM and EPDM vulcanizates do differ quite markedly in their resistance to ozone and to aging. In terpolymer aging, cross-linking reactions generally prevail over degradation reactions in the initial state of exposure to high temperature, although the behavior depends on the specific vulcanization system employed. In Fig. 4 the effect of cure systems on the elongation retention of terpolymers after aging is shown.

Ethylene–propylene elastomers offer excellent resistance to acids, alkalis, and hot detergent solutions. A summary of the chemical resistance of EPDM vulcanizates is given in Table 9. EPM and EPDM vulcanizates are resistant to salt solutions, oxygenated solvents, synthetic hydraulic fluids, and animal fats. Ethylene–propylene vulcanizates have only limited resistance to hydrocarbon solvents such as toluene and automotive gasoline. However, the good retention of physical properties after exposure to these hydrocarbons has

TABLE 7 Comparison of Physical Properties[a]

	EPDM	Natural Rubber	SBR
Specific gravity	0.86	0.93	0.94
Tensile strength	G-E	E	G-E
Dynamic properties	G-E	E	G
Color stability	E	G-E	G-E
Electrical properties	E	G	G
Resistance to:			
Weather	E	F	F
Ozone	E	P	F
Heat	E	F	F-G
Low temperature	G-E	G-E	F-G
Chemicals	E	G	G
Abrasion	G-E	G-E	G
Tearing	G	G-E	F
Compression set	G	E	E
Gas permeation	P-F	P-F	P-F
Oils	P	P	P
Flame	P	P	P

[a]E = excellent, G = good, F = fair, P = poor.

made EPDM vulcanizates useful where the exposure to hydrocarbons is not prolonged. Some mechanical properties of EPMs and EPDM vulcanizates are markedly influenced by the ethylene content and also by the regularity of the distribution of monomer sequences. High ethylene content polymers are stiffer at room temperature and therefore present higher elastic moduli and hardness at the same cross-link density. Furthermore, the possibility of crystallization occurring when the polymer is stretched, permits higher tensile strengths to be obtained. However, too high an ethylene content or a nonhomogeneous sequence distribution can worsen the dynamic properties and tension set.

TABLE 8 EPDM Vulcanizate Properties

Ozone resistance	Excellent
Oxidation and heat resistance	Excellent
Weather resistance	Excellent
Physical properties and abrasion resistance	Good
Chemical resistance	Excellent
Electrical properties	Excellent
Low temperature flexibility	Very good
Moisture and steam resistance	Excellent
Mineral oil resistance	Some
Compound cost	Low

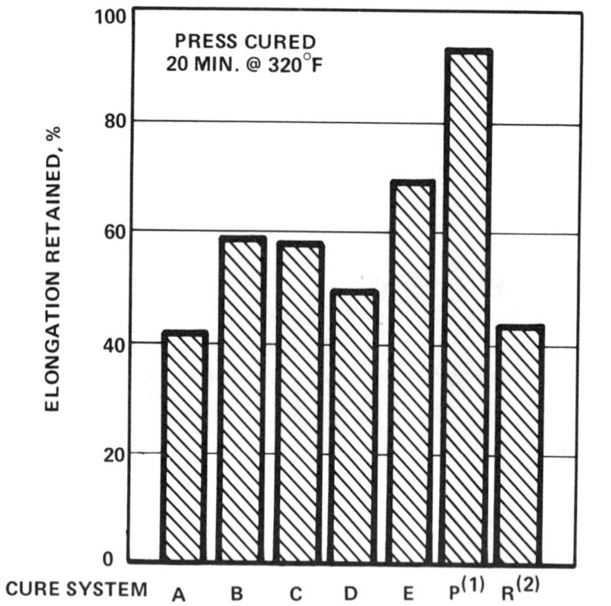

FIG. 4. Vistalon 2504. Effect of cure system on elongation retention after air aging for 7 d at 257°F.

Properties are also influenced by the degree of unsaturation. The higher the unsaturation, the higher is the maximum cross-link density that can be attained. Terpolymers with a higher degree of unsaturation yield vulcanizates with a lower compression set. However, compression set also depends on cross-link type and is lower in vulcanizates containing mainly monosulfidic bonds. With the same vulcanization recipe, EPDMs with a higher degree of unsaturation contain a higher fraction of monosulfidic cross-links than less unsaturated ones at the same cure rate.

The possibility of controlling both the concentration and type of cross-linking by adjusting the level and type of unsaturation as well as the changes possible by modifying vulcanization recipes is specific to EPDMs and distinguishes them from highly unsaturated elastomers.

TABLE 9 EPDM Chemical Resistance

	72-h Immersion at 212°F:			
	Volume Change (%)	Tensile Strength Retained (%)	Elongation Retained (%)	Hardness Change (parts)
ASTM No. 1 oil	+62	103	94	−30
ASTM No. 3 oil	+108	60	71	−42
Dioctyl phthalate	+7	107	89	−3
Distilled water	+1	112	84	0
Hexane[a]	+55	55	53	−25
Hydrochloric acid (10%)	+14	116	91	−3
Methyl ethyl ketone[a]	−5	72	65	+5
Perchloroethylene	+73	68	68	−35
Skydrol 500	−5	110	65	+5
Sodium chloride (25%)	0	118	94	−1
Sodium hydroxide (10%)	+2	121	92	+1
Tide (1%)	+1	115	91	+1
Toluene	+92	47	53	−40

[a]72-h immersion at bp of test liquid rather than at 212°F.

Polymerization Processes

The manufacture of EPMs and EPDMs involves four major operations:

Polymerization
Diluent recovery and purification
Propylene recovery and purification
Finishing

A typical EPM-EPDM process flow sheet is shown in Fig. 5.

The reaction occurs in the polymerization section, and it is here that the properties of the polymer are fixed. The monomers, diluent and catalyst feedstreams, the reactor system, the deashing system (to remove the residual catalyst residues from the polymer), and the water slurry system (to remove the unreacted monomers and diluent from the polymer and carry the product to finishing) are included in the polymerization section of the plant.

The reaction diluent serves as the carrier for the polymer and the monomers. The diluent is dried and purified in this section. Facilities for the recovery of unreacted diene are also generally included in the process.

Unreacted propylene is purified, dried, and recycled to the reactor in the

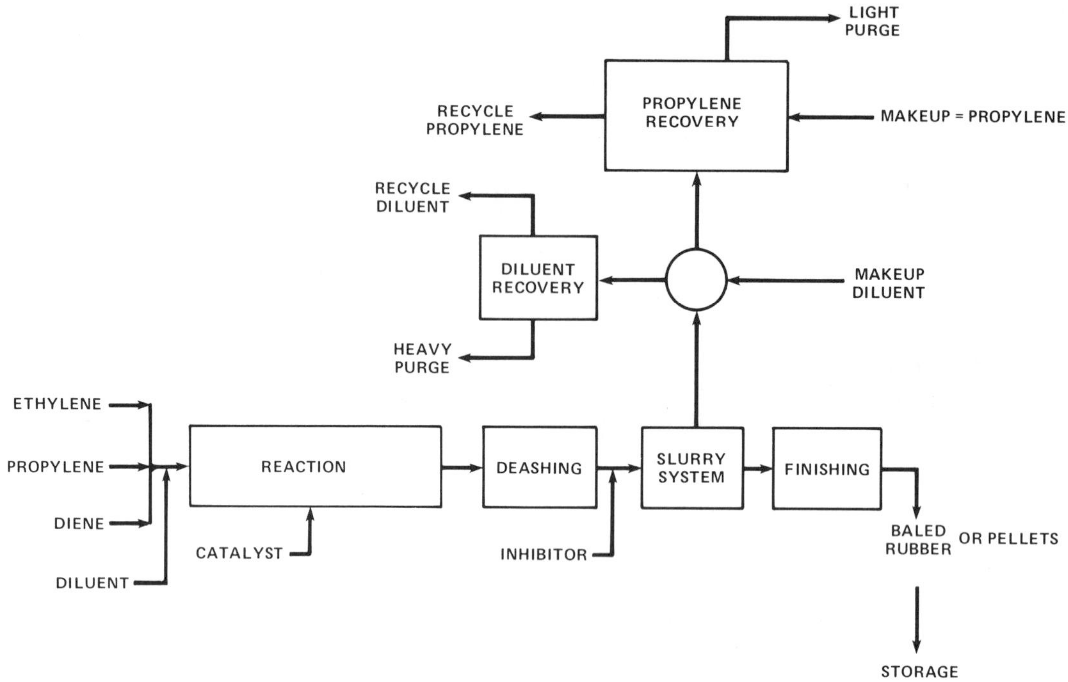

FIG. 5. Simplified flow plan of EPM–EPDM process.

propylene recovery section. Propylene conversions are always lower than ethylene coversions in EPDM polymerization, and recycle of propylene is therefore required. Unreacted ethylene is usually not recycled since ethylene conversion per pass is high. Purge streams for control of impurity level may also be provided in both the diluent and propylene recovery and purification sections of the process.

In the finishing area, the polymer is processed to a form acceptable to the customer. EPMs and EPDMs are sold in bale, crumb, and pellet forms.

The control of the EPM–EPDM polymerization reaction and the stringent product quality specifications require the use of a reaction diluent. Many diluents are proposed in the EPM–EPDM patent literature and are used by various manufacturers. The diluents can be any inert hydrocarbon liquid which does not interfere with the catalyst system and may include aliphatic, alicyclic, aromatic, and chlorinated hydrocarbons. Specific patent references include pentane, heptane, isooctane, cyclopentane, cyclohexane, benzene, toluene, carbon tetrachloride, trichloroethylene, and tetrachloroethylene. Such diluents as propane, iso and normal butane, propylene, and methyl chloride, in which the products are not completely soluble, have also been proposed. This latter class of diluents offers the advantage of a low viscosity, slurry type reaction because of their poor solvent characteristic for the EPM–EPDM elastomers.

Availability, purity, and cost are primary factors in affecting the selection of a diluent. Diluent losses are low in a well-designed plant. Nevertheless, diluent cost cannot be neglected.

The viscosity of the reaction medium containing polymer is also important. Viscous liquid cements reduce effective reactor mixing and heat transfer. This places a limitation on the maximum polymer concentration which can be achieved. The viscosity of the polymerization liquid is a function both of the solvent viscosity, the solubility of the polymer,and the polymer molecular weight. Amorphous EPM–EPDM polymers can be considered to be liquids having critical miscibility points with a solvent. In a good solvent, the relatively high solution viscosity corresponds to molecules in an extended state. In general, polymer concentrations in an EPM–EPDM process are rather low compared to other polymer processes, making diluent recycle mandatory. The diluent must be removed from the polymer in an economic manner. Typically, the diluent is separated from the polymer by steam stripping; therefore, the higher boiling diluents are more difficult and more costly to separate from the polymer. Other conceivable process problems involve:

Purification of the reaction diluent. This is a primary concern with any process using Ziegler-Natta catalyst.

Coordination catalyst systems are quite sensitive to impurities and poisons in the diluent.

Catalyst poisons may be divided into several classes. Some, such as water, alcohol, and other polar organic compounds, kill the catalyst. Others do not necessarily stop the reaction, but are polymerized into products of no use in EPM–EPDM elastomers, such as low molecular weight olefins. The major effect of these poisons is to reduce catalyst utilization and monomer conversion.

Reactor control is a complex problem. It is complicated by the significant time lag between the polymerization reaction and available rubber samples used to follow reactor operations. Reactor holding time is important and can vary due to reactor feed rate changes or the formation of fouling polymer.

Heat transfer is possible either by feed prechilling or by the use of an autorefrigerated reactor. In an autorefrigerated reactor the heats of polymerization and agitation are dissipated by boiling the reaction medium. In this case the polymer concentration is not limited by heat transfer, but by the viscosity of the solution/slurry.

The methods and equipment used in carrying out the various operations depend upon the technical expertise of the individual manufacturers and have not been disclosed. However, apart from the polymerization step, the most likely differences between processes of different manufacturers involve principles of engineering rather than principles of chemistry.

TABLE 10 Vistalon EPDM Application Areas

Automative	Windshield weatherstrips, sponge seals, radiator/heater hoses, bumpers, mounts, brake hoses, vacuum tubing, tire components
Electrical	Power cable/medium high voltage insulation, cable jacketing, filler, connectors
Industrial hoses	Steam, welding, drain, garden hoses
Building/construction	Sealing gaskets, sheeting, insulations
Miscellaneous	Appliance, conveyor belts, shoe soles, tires, tire valves, plastic blends, etc.

TABLE 11 Reasons for Growing Use of EPDM in Auto Hose

Cost competitiveness
Availability
Heat resistance
Moderate oil resistance

TABLE 12 EPDM Use in Auto Hose

	Present	
Hose	Tube	Cover
Power steering	CR, NBR	CR, CSM[b]
Air conditioning	NBR	CR[b]
Power brake	CR[b]	CR[b]
Vacuum brake	SBR, CR[b]	CR[b]
Fuel line	ECH, NBR	ECH, CR[b]
Emission control	ECH, NBR	ECH, CR[b]
Air injection	EPDM	EPDM
Coolant, (radiator, heater)	EPDM	EPDM

[a]CR = Chloroprene, CSM = hypalon, ECH = Epichlorohydrin, NBR = Nitrile butadiene.
[b]Feasible to use EPDM.

Applications

The application areas for EPM and EPDM are summarized in Table 10. Major application areas for EPMs and EPDMs are mechanical goods, weather stripping, window seals, drain hoses, and heater hoses. The largest outlet for EPM and EPDMs is in automotive parts that are exposed to high temperatures; here its aging and weathering properties are excellent for window channels, weather stripping, boots and covers, radiator and air-conditioning hoses, body seals, bumper and insulator gaskets and mountings, etc. Table 11 summarizes the reasons for the growing use of EPDM in auto hose. A wide variety of hoses are used in a car, as shown in Table 12.

A. L. BISIO
B. R. TEGGE

Fertilizer Components: Ammonium Nitrate

The commercial production of large quantities of ammonium nitrate for agricultural purposes in the United States began after World War II when the ammonia, nitric acid, and ammonium nitrate plants used to manufacture chemicals during the war were converted to nitrogen fertilizer manufacture [1, 2]. The first crystalline ammonium nitrate offered for sale was not satisfactory because of its tendency to cake and absorb moisture from the air. However, the value of ammonium nitrate as a low-cost fertilizer and the availability of the decommissioned plants provided the stimuli which eventually led to the solution of the problem through prilling and the use of anticaking agents. From that point, the industry has grown to an estimated yearly production of 8,724,000 short tons in 1981 (see Table 1). In recent years, usage has slowed due to the increasing use by farmers of anhydrous ammonia and dry urea, which are more economical sources of agricultural nitrogen. Another competitive product is the urea-ammonium nitrate solution, which is favored by some farmers because of certain conveniences in handling that it offers.

In 1980, ammonium nitrate was produced by 55 different manufacturers in solid form in 79 different plants and in aqueous solution form, for use in urea-ammonium nitrate liquid fertilizer, in 48 plants [4].

Processes

All ammonium nitrate is produced by the reaction of anhydrous ammonia and nitric acid. Anhydrous ammonia is the fundamental feedstock for an ammonium nitrate plant since the nitric acid is formed by the catalytic oxidation of ammonia to nitric acid. All existing processes for the production of dry ammonium nitrate have four basic steps: (1) neutralization of nitric

TABLE 1 United States Capacity and Production of Ammonium Nitrate [3] (thousand short tons)

	1960	1970	1975	1980	1981
Capacity	4,084	8,387	8,460	10,773	10,582
Production:					
Agriculture:					
Solid	1,572	3,315	3,321	3,397	3,450
Liquid[a]	1,253	2,092	2,438	3,581	3,581
Total	2,825	5,407	5,759	6,978	7,031
Industrial	297	954	1,041	1,574	1,693
Total	3,122	6.361	6,800	8,552	8,724
Pricing ($/short ton)	—	59.97	185.93	171.36	195.50

[a]Ammonium nitrate in nitrogen solutions.

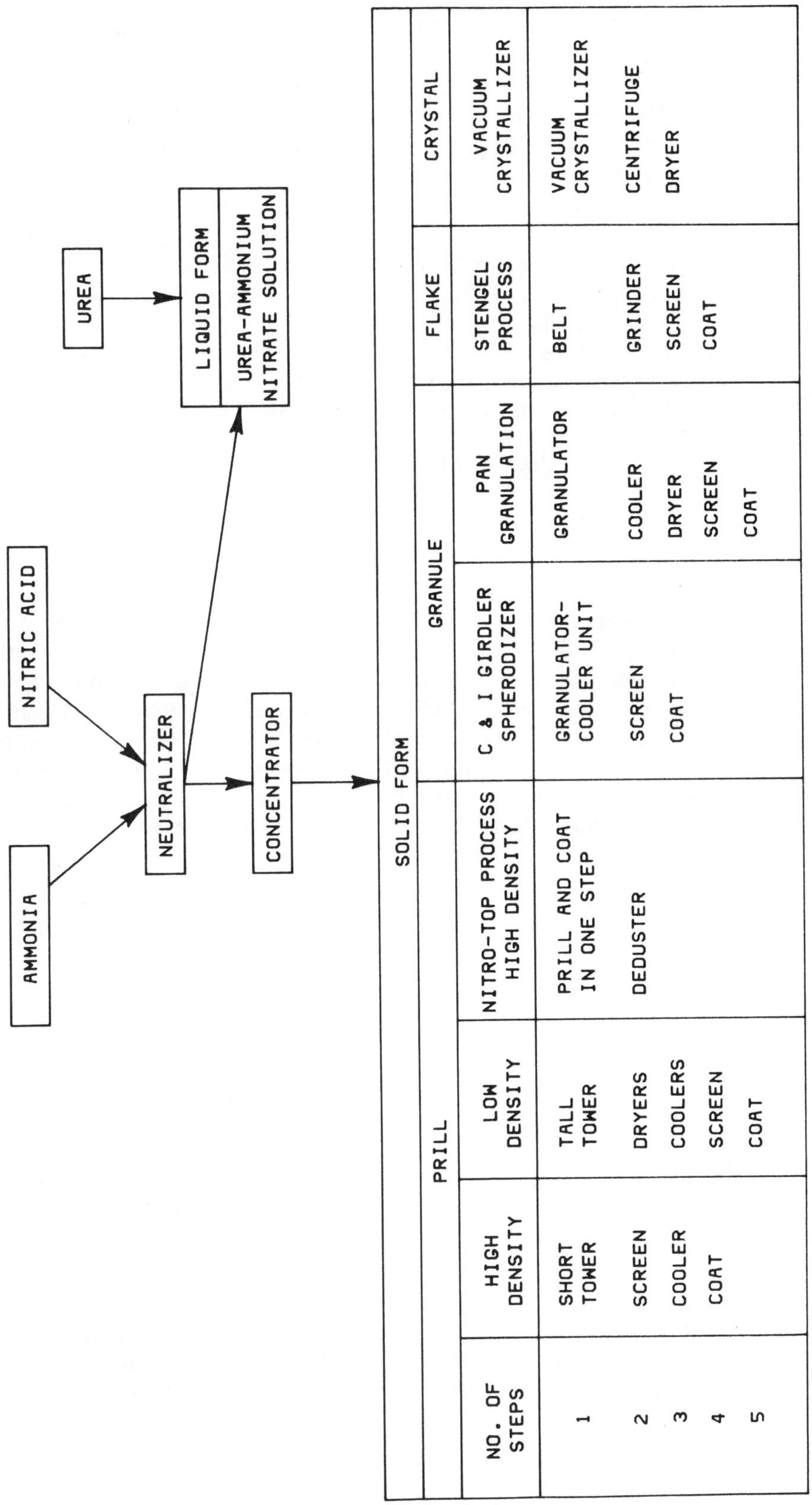

FIG. 1. Schematic of ammonium nitrate processes.

acid with anhydrous ammonia to form an aqueous solution of ammonium nitrate, (2) concentration of the ammonium nitrate solution, (3) formation of solid ammonium nitrate, (4) drying, cooling, and coating to prevent caking.

The major differences between the processes occur in the third step—the formation of the solid product. Variations in this step result in four fundamental forms of the product: prills, flakes, granules, and crystals. Prills account for an estimated 90% of production and are produced in both high and low density forms. Because high density prills are more economical to produce and their properties are suitable for agricultural use, they make up the large majority of production. Low density ammonium nitrate is used in the explosives industry because its high porosity allows the absorption of fuel oil which is a necessary component of blasting agents, although some pulverized high density material is used in slurry explosives.

Figure 1 summarizes the various ammonium nitrate processes.

Prilling Processes

Neutralization

Ammonium nitrate is produced in the neutralizer from the exothermic reaction (37.4 kcal/mol) of 57% nitric acid and anhydrous ammonia. The heat generated concentrates the solution to 78–83%, depending upon the reactor conditions. The two reactants enter the neutralizer through spargers with the ammonia to acid feed ratio controlled in one of three ways: (1) pH control of the ammonium nitrate solution at the exit point from the neutralizer, (2) metering the ratio of the flow of the two reactants using ammonia as the independent variable, or (3) pH control of the steam condensate from the neutralizer. The solution is agitated by circulating it through a pipe loop below the neutralizer. The pressure in the neutralizer is maintained by controlling the steam flow from the neutralizer, a portion of which is utilized to heat the primary concentrator.

Concentration

Most prill production is high density material which requires concentration of the ammonium nitrate solution to near 99.8%. Low density prills are prepared from a concentrate that is about 96%.

In high density processes (see Fig. 2), the ammonium nitrate solution leaving the neutralizer is concentrated in an air-swept, falling film evaporator using steam heat. To keep the final concentrate in a molten form, a temperature of about 182°C is maintained. Ammonium nitrate slowly decomposes under these conditions with the loss of ammonia and an increase in acidity of the resulting molten concentrate. This problem is remedied by addition of ammonia to the concentrate to maintain a pH of approximately five. The concentrate flows by gravity to a small vessel and then is pumped to the top of

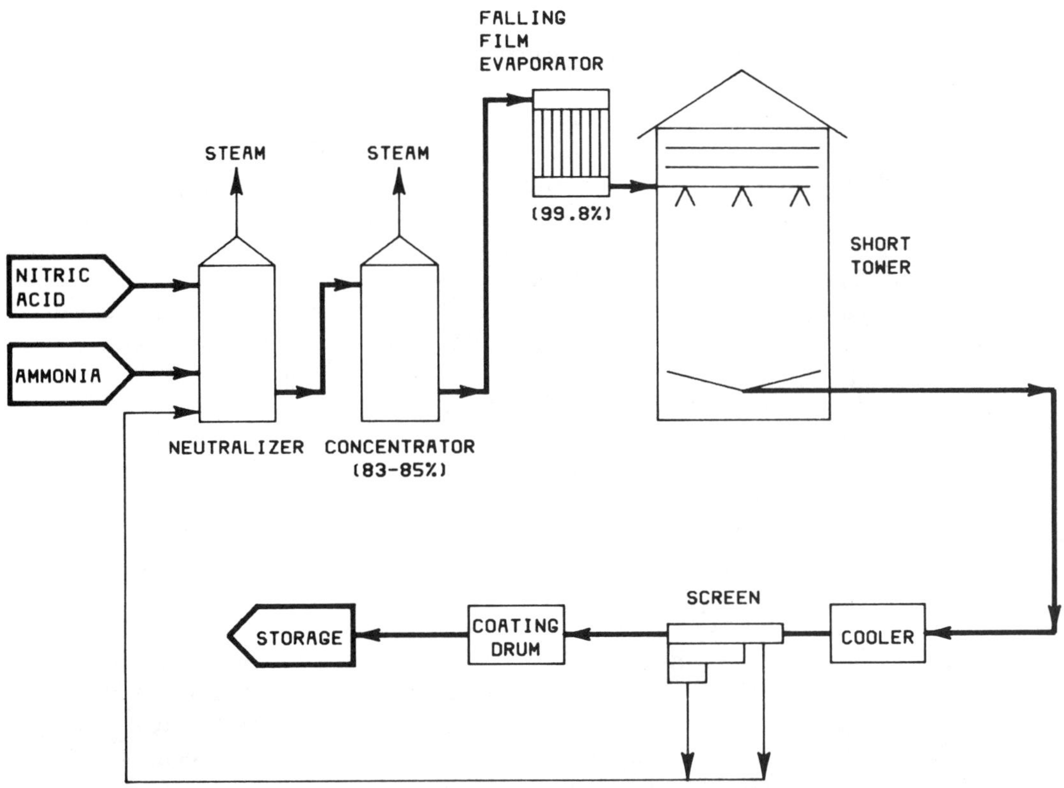

FIG. 2. High-density prilling process.

the prilling tower. One variation on equipment layout locates the concentrator on top of the prilling tower, thereby reducing the amount of hot concentrate in the system by omitting some piping.

In low density prilling processes (flow sheet similar to Fig. 2 but with exceptions as noted in text), the ammonium nitrate solution is concentrated to about 96%. Low pressure steam generated in the neutralizer may be used for initial concentrator heat duty with the final heat supplied by plant steam. The 96% ammonium nitrate solution leaving the secondary concentrator is pumped to a surge tank or directly to the prilling tower without the use of a falling film evaporator as in the high density case. The solution is maintained at 128°C or above to prevent solidification.

Prilling

The third step of the process, prilling, is accomplished by dropping liquid in air under conditions which allow the formation and solidification of free-falling spheres by evaporation and cooling. The conditions of this step must be chosen so that the prills will develop sufficient mechanical strength to resist breakage or distortion by the time they strike the bottom of the tower. The most important variable in this regard is the distance through which they fall.

Prilling a 99.5–99.8% ammonium nitrate melt requires a free-fall distance of 35–85 ft and results in the formation of high density prills. The hot melt is fed from the concentrator into a network of piping and spray nozzles in the top of the prilling tower. The liquid droplets fall from the nozzles countercurrently through air which enters the tower at ambient temperature. Air is forced through the tower by fans located at the bottom or is sucked into the base of the tower by exhaust fans mounted on top. The prills are transferred from the bottom of the tower to a rotary drum cooler where they are cooled in either ambient or refrigerated air. The prills are not exposed to a separate drying step, but trace quantities of moisture evaporate from the prills upon cooling. Fines from the cooler and concentrator carried over by the air are collected in a wet scrubber and returned to the neutralizer. The cooled prills are screened and the over- and undersize material are dissolved in water and pumped to the neutralizer. Specification prills are coated with a coating agent in a rotary drum tumbler. The high density product has a typical bulk density of 0.99–1.04 g/cm^3, or 62–65 lb/ft^3, compacted.

The formation of low density prills from a 96% ammonium nitrate melt requires a tall tower which has a free-fall distance of 160 to 220 ft. This increased distance is required to insure prill solidification. The reduction of the moisture content in the prills to 0.10–0.14% requires extended drying time. Applying excessive heat too fast to the prills can destroy the prill structure by exploding the prill with exiting steam. The moisture content of prills leaving the dryer section is typically 0.25–0.35% and the prill temperature is 55–60°C. Low density prills require additional drying and, therefore, a drying section is interposed between the tower and the cooling section in Fig. 2. The temperature and relative humidity of air used varies with the season of the year, but the use of chilled and dehumidified air is usually required in the latter portion of the drying section. Prills leaving the cooling section are, typically, 25–29°C and contain 0.10–0.14% moisture. The temperature of the prills must decrease monotonically to ambient conditions to avoid cycling the prills through crystalline phase transitions, because such cycling can lead to prill fracture.

Ammonium nitrate fines, from the air passed through the dryers and coolers, and the over- and undersized prills are collected, dissolved in water, and returned to the concentrator. The clean air is exhausted to the atmosphere. The low temperature at which 96% ammonium nitrate melt is prilled in contrast to the high temperature needed to prill a 99.5% melt can eliminate the need to scrub the prill tower exhaust air.

Low density prills contain a network of interconnecting voids which is the cause of the low density. The typical bulk density of these prills is 0.78–0.82 g/cm^3, or 49–51 lb/ft^3, compacted.

In the prilling processes just described, it is possible to control the diameter of the prills by applying a sonic vibration to the concentrate in the spray header at the top of the prilling tower. In such systems [5-8] the ammonium nitrate concentrate is fed under low pressure and at low velocity through orifice plates into a quiescent zone while mechanically applying a constant frequency of vibration to the concentrate. For a given orifice size, the vibration frequency can be chosen to produce prills of the desired diameter.

Coating

In both high and low density processes, a suitable coating agent is applied to the cool prills in a rotary drum. In a single component system using kaolin clay or diatomaceous earth, the coating is proportionally metered to the coating drum with prills. In a two-component coating mixture, such as kaolin clay and a surfactant, the mixture can be fed to the drum as a preblended mix, or the ingredients can be charged individually to the drum. In one method, clay is metered onto a weigh belt. The surfactant additive, in powder form, is metered onto the moving bed of clay. The uncoated ammonium nitrate prills are fed to a second weigh belt and the materials on both belts drop into a revolving coating tumbler where the mixture is agitated until the coating agent adheres to the prills.

The Nitro-Top Process

The only other process which produces prilled ammonium nitrate is the Nitro-Top Process, developed by Fisons. A flow sheet and detailed process description may be found in Ref. 9. In the process, prills are formed from a 99.7% melt and coated in one step in a 23-ft tower. The bottom 6 ft of the tower contains coating dust which is fluidized with air. Two distinct clay phases exist in the tower: a dense clay phase in the bottom and a lean phase, approximately 10–16 ft in height, in the upper portion of the tower. As a molten droplet of ammonium nitrate falls from the spray nozzle, a coating of dust collects on each prill and a hard shell is formed. The partly solidified prills pass into the dense dust phase where solidification is completed. The temperature of the ammonium nitrate droplet is initially about 170°C and the dust and air temperature is about 50°C. Most of the heat within the bed is removed via water-cooled surfaces within it. Acceptable coating agents include talc, kaolin, and montmorillonite clays.

Solution Processes

As shown in Table 1, the use of ammonium nitrate in solution form has been increasing steadily in recent years. These solutions are usually mixtures of ammonium nitrate and urea, and they presently represent a majority of the ammonium nitrate used agriculturally.

In solution processes the ammonium nitrate is produced simply by the neutralization of nitric acid with anhydrous ammonia. Therefore, the discussion of the neutralization step in the section on prilling processes above adequately describes the comparable portion of a solution plant. Beyond that point the process is a mixing operation in which the aqueous ammonium nitrate is combined with an aqueous solution of urea. Nevertheless, solution plants can be complex operations because they frequently begin with natural gas and produce all the chemicals necessary in the process from it. Anhydrous ammonia is produced from the natural gas by well-known methods with the formation of by-product carbon dioxide, which is reacted with a portion of the ammonia to produce urea. A second portion of the ammonia is oxidized to nitric acid which is then neutralized with a third portion of the ammonia to form the ammonium nitrate solution. The urea and ammonium nitrate streams are then mixed to form the final product which typically contains 32% nitrogen. A typical analysis is 46.7% ammonium nitrate, 33.6% urea, and 19.7% water.

Other Processes

Although the prill is the most important dry form in which ammonium nitrate is produced, other forms have been produced through the years and still make up a small amount of present production. The processes in which these forms are produced are used to produce other products in addition to ammonium nitrate, such as mixed grades of fertilizers containing different combinations of nitrogen, phosphorus, and potash. Except where noted, these processes all utilize a feed concentrate prepared in ways similar to that described in the section on prilling.

The Spherodizer Granulation Process

This process granulates by the repeated buildup of layers on small seed particles. A flow sheet for this process is given in Ref. 11. An ammonium nitrate melt (99.5%) is pumped through a spray system inside a rotating drum onto a rolling bed of small particles of ammonium nitrate. As the particles become coated with the hot ammonium nitrate, a slight drop in surface temperature causes the ammonium nitrate to crystallize. The net result is a gradual buildup of ammonium nitrate on the surface of the seed and an increase in granule size. The granulation step takes place in the front section of the rotating drum and cooling occurs in the exit end. A dam, or retaining ring, located in the drum retains a sufficient bed of granules to allow the particles to build up several layers of ammonium nitrate per pass. Granules overflow into the cooling section of the drum and are cooled by passing atmospheric air countercurrently to the flow of solids. The cool granules are transported to a screening section where oversized and undersized granules are separated from the product. Crushed oversized and all of the undersized granules are recycled to the granulation section as seed. The ratio of recycle to product is kept at about 2:1. The granular product is coated with 1.2 to 2.0% of clay and is two to three times harder than prills, which is an advantage in bulk blending fertilizer operations.

Pan Granulation

This process forms granules in a rotating inclined pan by the agglomeration of smaller particles or by layer-by-layer buildup. A flow sheet for this process is given in Ref. 12. This process is primarily used for production of mixed grade fertilizers, but small amounts of ammonium nitrate have been prepared by this method. The hot ammonium nitrate solution is sprayed onto a cascading bed of undersized ammonium nitrate particles on a rotating, inclined pan to produce well-rounded granules. The concentration of ammonium nitrate charged to the pan can vary slightly, providing other variables in the process are adjusted in order to achieve granulation. Selection of the correct recycle ratio is essential for optimum granulation. A recycle ratio of 1.5–2:2 is used when the recycle temperature is about 60°C and 2.5:1 when the temperature is about 71°C. A pan angle of inclination of about 65°, a rotation of 14–16 r/min, and a bed depth of about 16 in. gives good granulation. The product from the pan is cooled, dried in drum-type vessels, and screened. The crushed oversized and fines are fed back to the pan. Specification product is coated in a drum tumbler and sent to storage. Variations of this basic process have been described [13, 14].

Stengel Process [15]

This process produces high density ammonium nitrate in the form of flakes. A process flow sheet is given in Ref. 16. It is reported that one of the advantages of this process is its simplicity of requiring one piece of equipment to neutralize and concentrate nitric acid and ammonia to 99.5+% ammonium nitrate. Some of these savings, however, are absorbed in the more elaborate equipment and exotic metallurgy required in the ammonia and acid preheat stages. Ammonia and nitric acid are charged continuously into the top of a vertical packed reactor and flow downward into a separator unit, where preheated air removes the water vapor. The moisture content of the molten ammonium nitrate at this point is about 0.2% and the melt temperature is near 200°C. The melt is then fed to continuous steel cooling belts, where it solidifies and then passes into a breaker which breaks the sheet into flakes about 2 in. in diameter. The flakes are then further reduced in size by grinders, screened, and the over- and undersized material recycled.

Vacuum Crystallization [17, 18]

This process was developed in about 1947. A process flow sheet is given in Ref. 18. Ammonium nitrate is produced by the partial neutralization of nitric acid with gas-phase anhydrous ammonia in cylindrical tanks operated in parallel and at atmospheric pressure. A solution with a pH of 0.7 is produced in the first reactor section and flows continuously to an adjusting tank where additional ammonia is added to bring the pH to 6.4. The heat of reaction allows water to boil in both neutralizing steps, resulting in a 56% solution leaving the second neutralizer. This solution is concentrated to 79% in four forced-circulation vacuum concentrators. The liquor leaves the concentrators at 60°C and the concentration is about 1% under saturation.

Supersaturation is induced in the solution by continuous evaporation and cooling in a vaporizer section as it flows to the crystallizer, where the product is removed continuously by air lifts.

Handling

There are three problems that must be dealt with in handling solid ammonium nitrate: caking, safety hazards, and prill degradation. The first of these problems, caking, has already been touched upon in the discussion of prilling processes where methods of applying anticaking agents to prills were described. Ammonium nitrate is hygroscopic and, left in contact with moist air, will adsorb water on its surface [1, 2, 19]. The moist prills then stick to each other and form large agglomerates. An early method used to make prills nonhygroscopic was to apply 0.5–1.0% of petrolatum or asphaltum to the surface of the prills. This generated an explosion hazard, however, since ammonium nitrate is a strong oxidizer and can react violently with organic matter [2, 20]. Recognizing this hazard, regulator agencies banned the use of such anticaking agents. New inorganic anticaking agents, based upon diatomaceous earth, kaolinite, or other clays, were developed. Such agents are effective when applied in 3–5% concentration. This quantity of inert material reduces the effectiveness of ammonium nitrate as a component in explosives, however. Therefore, new two-component systems [21, 24], based upon kaolin clay and alkylarylsulfonates, which were effective at only 1.0–1.5%, were developed. The organic matter in these compositions is low enough so that explosion hazards are minimal and regulations allow their use [25]. Organic compounds other than alkylarylsulfonates can also be used [26–28].

The two-component coating systems are used to coat both agricultural and industrial prilled ammonium nitrate. The amount of coating applied and the ratio of inert to additive used are different for each product. Prills intended for agricultural use require more coating than those used to make blasting agents because they are stored longer (up to 1 year). Agricultural prilled ammonium nitrate is coated with 2.0–3.5% inert, such as kaolin clay, and 0.02–0.06% additive. Explosive grade product contains only 0.6–1.2% clay and 0.06–0.12% additive. High density prills normally have poorer clay adhesion properties because of smooth and glossy surfaces which reduce the amount of coating which can be applied.

The safe handling of ammonium nitrate can be accomplished by observing three rules: (1) avoid confinement, (2) avoid overheating, and (3) avoid contact with organic matter. These points are addressed by codes and regulations issued by the National Fire Protection Association; the U.S. Departments of Transportation, Labor, and Treasury; The Environmental Protection Agency; and various state and local air pollution agencies [29–34]. By compliance with these regulations, the ammonium nitrate industry has operated safely for the past 30 years.

Ammonium nitrate can be heated safely under the proper conditions as evidenced by the manufacturing processes where it is handled in molten form at 182°C. At this temperature, the exothermic dissociation into ammonia and nitric acid occurs at a modest rate. As the temperature increases to 250°C and then to 300°C, two more decomposition reactions occur:

$$NH_4NO_3 \text{ (solid)} \xrightarrow{180^\circ C} NH_3 \text{ (gas)} + HNO_3 \text{ (gas)} + 41 \text{ kcal/mol}$$

$$NH_4NO_3 \text{ (solid)} \xrightarrow{250^\circ C} N_2O \text{ (gas)} + 2H_2O \text{ (gas)} - 10 \text{ kcal/mol}$$

$$NH_4NO_3 \text{ (solid)} \xrightarrow{300^\circ C} N_2 \text{ (gas)} + \tfrac{1}{2}O_2 \text{ (gas)} + 2H_2O \text{ (gas)} + 28 \text{ kcal/mol}$$

Therefore, normal temperature excursions encountered in routine handling in warehouses, hopper cars, and retail sales outlets do not present problems.

The third handling problem, prill degradation (granules and flakes are similarly affected), has its basis in the crystalline morphology of ammonium nitrate. Five crystal forms exist, referred to as Phases I–V, having transition temperatures between the various phases at −18, 32, 84, and 125°C. Phase IV is the stable phase between −18 and +32°C which includes normal ambient conditions. When a prill is heated above 32°C, it undergoes a transition to Phase III with an accompanying volume expansion of 3.6%. The same prill, when cooled to below 32°C, returns to Phase IV with a contraction of 3.5%. Such expansion and contraction stresses the prill and can result in fracturing. Repeated cycles will weaken even the stronger prills and will ultimately result in extensive degradation to powder known as "sugaring." Similar results are experienced if thermal cycling through the −18°C transition temperature occurs. Thermal cycling conditions are frequently encountered in routine handling of ammonium nitrate. For instance, on summer days temperatures above 32°C are common with the following night temperature below 32°C. Prills stored in warehouses or, more commonly, in transit under these conditions will thermal cycle. The fundamental method to cope with this problem is through human diligence to avoid exposing prills to thermal cycling.

Some ammonium nitrate manufacturers use modifiers to stabilize the crystal against phase changes. A mixture of less than 0.5% boric acid, ammonium sulfate, and ammonium orthophosphate added to molten ammonium nitrate is one such effective modifier [35–43].

Uses

The two large uses of ammonium nitrate are in agriculture and explosives, with consumption being 85 and 15% of total production, respectively. Ammonium nitrate is an ideal source of nitrogen in agriculture because it contains both the reduced (NH_4^+) and oxidized (NO_3^-) forms of the element, both of which are available to growing plants. Since the high density prill is the more economical to produce, it is used almost exclusively in agriculture when the dry form is desired.

Nitrogen solutions, which contain both ammonium nitrate and urea, account for more than half of the total ammonium nitrate used in agriculture. Although the solutions are more expensive, they allow the farmer to apply seed, fertilizer, and other agricultural chemicals simultaneously and in close proximity to each other. Anhydrous ammonia has also replaced large quantities of ammonium nitrate because of its higher nitrogen content and better economics.

The reason that anhydrous ammonia will not completely supplant ammonium nitrate is that it can be applied only prior to or during planting season or while crops are very small. Since some crops require fertilization during the growing season, ammonium nitrate will continue to be used in that application.

As an explosive, ammonium nitrate is most widely used in the coal industry. The majority of ammonium nitrate consumed in this application is primarily low density prills containing 5.6% fuel oil. The low density prill is used because it has a high porosity which facilitates oil absorption. Typical low density prills have an available pore volume of 0.14 cm^3/g and an average pore diameter of about 24 μm. Such mixtures are referred to as blasting agents and are considered to be low explosives. They are typically used by placing them in a bore-hole along with a small quantity of a high explosive which serves as a booster. Detonation of the charge sets off a rapid oxidation of the fuel oil by the ammonium nitrate resulting in the explosive formation of gaseous products (CO_2, H_2O, and N_2).

Ammonium nitrate is also used in gelled slurry explosives. This material is a high explosive and is prepared by forming a slurry of combinations of different ingredients. Nearly all of them contain ammonium nitrate, aluminum powder, organic matter, and suitable gelling agents in a saturated aqueous solution of ammonium nitrate. After this material has gelled, it too is detonated by the use of a high explosive booster. Slurry explosives are used in mining operations also, but mainly where the formations to be fractured are wet, very dense, or strong, as in hard rock mining.

References

1. *Preparation of Ammonium Nitrate for Use as a Fertilizer*, U.S.D.A. Technical Bulletin No. 912, June 1946.
2. *Ammonium Nitrate—Its Properties and Fire and Explosion Hazards*, U.S. Department of the Interior, I.C. No. 7463, June 1948.
3. *Fertilizer Trends—1982*, National Fertilizer Development Center, Tennessee Valley Authority, Muscle Shoals, Alabama.
4. *Fertilizer Trends—1979*, National Fertilizer Development Center, Tennessee Valley Authority, Muscle Shoals, Alabama.
5. J. W. Cramer (Armour and Co.), U.S. Patent 3,274,642 (September 27, 1966).
6. Montecatini, British Patent 826,815 (January 20, 1960).
7. C. G. DeHaven and R. O. Welty (Phillips Petroleum Co.), U.S. Patent 2,968,833 (January 24, 1961).
8. J. A. Delaloye and J. D. Stafford (Phillips Petroleum Co.), U.S. Patent 2,931,067 (April 5, 1960).

9. G. Drake, *Production of Ammonium Nitrate*, Paper Presented before the Fertilizer Society of London, October 25, 1973.
10. *Large-Scale Production of Urea-Ammonium Nitrate Solution*, Technical Bulletin, Pullman-Kellogg, Houston, Texas.
11. R. M. Reed and J. C. Reynolds, *Chem. Eng. Prog., 69*(2), 62–66 (1973).
12. R. S. Meline, I. W. McCamy, J. L. Graham, and T. S. Sloan, *J. Agr. Food Chem., 16*(2), 235–240 March-April, 1968).
13. R. A. Shurter, Jr., and A. P. Miller (Commercial Solvents Corp.), U.S. Patent 3,211,522 (October 12, 1965).
14. O. Shauli (Norsk Hydro AS, Norway), U.S. Patent 4,008,064 (February 14, 1977).
15. L. A. Stengel (Commercial Solvents Corp.), U.S. Patent 2,568,901 (September 25, 1957).
16. A. S. Hester, J. J. Dorsey, and J. T. Kaufman, *Ind. Eng. Chem.*, *46*, 622–632 (1954).
17. P. Miller and W. C. Salmon, *Ind. Eng. Chem., 40*, 154–160 (1948).
18. W. C. Saeman, I. W. McCamy, and E. C. Houston, *Ind. Eng. Chem., 44*, 1912–1915 (1952).
19. *Fertilizer Grade Ammonium Nitrate*, Manual A-10, Manufacturing Chemists' Association, Washington, D.C.
20. "The Texas City Disaster," *Nat. Fire Prot. Assoc. Q., 41*(1), 25–27 (1947).
21. J. F. Wilson, V. C. Vives, and J. C. Hillyer (Phillips Petroleum Co.), U.S. Patent 3,116,185 (December 31, 1963).
22. J. F. Wilson, J.C. Hillyer, and V. C. Vives (Phillips Petroleum Co.), U.S. Patent 3,201,354 (August 17, 1965).
23. J. W. Putt, U.S. Patent 2,773,896 (December 11, 1956).
24. J. J. Jasnosz (Petrochemicals Co.), U.S. Patent 4,001,378 (January 4, 1977).
25. *Code of Regulations*, U.S. Department of Transportation, Title 49, Part 173.182(a).
26. H. H. Ender (Union Carbide Corp.), U.S. Patent 3,190,775 (June 25, 1965).
27. R. E. Baarson, M. R. McCorkle, and D. T. Oklsen, *Anti-Caking of Hygroscopic Salts and Multi-Component Fertilizers with Fatty Chemical Conditioning Agents*, Paper Presented before the Division of Fertilizer and Soil Chemistry, American Chemical Society Meeting, September 14–16, 1959.
28. R. V. Coates, M. F. Curtis, G. J. Harris, and P. S. Smith (Fisons Fertilizers, England), U.S. Patent 3,533,776 (October 13, 1970).
29. *Storage of Ammonium Nitrate*, Bulletin 490, National Fire Protection Association.
30. *Code of Federal Regulations*, U.S. Department of Transportation, Title 49, Parts 171–179.
31. *Code of Federal Regulations*, U.S. Department of Treasury, Title 27—Alcohol, Tobacco and Firearms Regulations—Blasting Agents.
32. *Code of Federal Regulations*, U.S. Department of Labor, Title 29, Part 1910.109—Occupational Safety and Health Administration Regulations for Explosive and Blasting Agents.
33. *Manufacturing, Storage, Transportation and Use of Explosives and Blasting Agents*, Bulletin 495, National Fire Protection Association.
34. *Code of Federal Regulations*, Environmental Protection Agency, Title 40, Chapter 1, Subchapter N, Part 418.
35. M. L. Brown, A. W. Green, and L. Blanton, *J. Org. Food Chem., 16*(3), 373–377 (1948).
36. M. L. Brown, A. W. Green, and L. Blanton (Mississippi Chemical Corp.), U.S. Patent 3,317,276, (May 2, 1967).

37. H. Diekmann and K. Opp (Badische Anilin und Soda-Fabrik Aktiengesellschaft), U.S. Patent 3,171,716 (March 2, 1965).
38. R. F. McFarlin and D. E. Brown (U.S.S. Agri-Chemicals), U.S. Patent 3,428,414 (February 18, 1969).
39. R. F. McFarlin and J. G. Stites (Monsanto Chemical Co.), U.S. Patent 3,030,179 (April 17, 1962).
40. O. P. Mollerstedt and E. S. Ljungaverk (Fosfalbolaget, Sweden), U.S. Patent 3,639,643 (February 1, 1972).
41. E. J. Griffith (Monsanto Co.), U.S. Patent 3,148,964 (September 15, 1964).
42. E. D. Guth (Phillips Petroleum Co.), U. S. Patent 2,943,928 (July 5, 1960).
43. R. Folck-Manas, D. J. Newman, and S. Atkins (Chemical Construction Corp.), U.S. Patent 3,649,173 (March 14, 1972).

LAWRENCE M. FODOR
JOSEPH F. WILSON

Fertilizer Components: Ammonium Sulfate

Ammonium sulfate was an important source of synthetic nitrogen fertilizer even before commercial production of synthetic ammonia began in the early part of this century, because it was available as a by-product of town-gas works and coke ovens. It continues to be an important nitrogen source in the United States today. However, because of the large increase in use of higher analysis nitrogen fertilizers such as urea, ammonium nitrate, and anhydrous ammonia, its percentage contribution to total fertilizer nitrogen usage decreased from about 5.3% in 1965 to about 2.1% in 1980. In some parts of the United States, particularly in the northwest, the sulfur content of the soils is normally low. If this problem becomes more widespread, ammonium sulfate might become as valued for its sulfur content as for its nitrogen content.

Over 95% of the ammonium sulfate used in the United States is for fertilizer. Approximately 2 to 4% is used in liquid cattle feed supplements and the remainder is used in fireproofing and firefighting mixtures, tanning, fermentation, and various chemical applications. [1–3].

TABLE 1 Production Statistics for Ammonium Sulfate in the United States [4] (thousands short tons)

Production	1970	1975	1976	1977	1978	1979	1980	1981
Synthetic[a]	1894	2106	2010	2264	2449	2363	2136	2139
Coke-oven by-product	595	489	497	470	428	455	398	384
Total	2489	2595	2507	2734	2877	2818	2534	2523

[a] Includes by-product from chemical operations as well as prime product.

United States production data for ammonium sulfate are shown in Table 1. Coke-oven production has decreased from about 23.9% of total production in 1970 to about 15.2% in 1981. In 1978, about 46 companies in the United States produced ammonium sulfate. The five largest producers were Allied Chemical Corp., Dow Badische Co., Occidental Petroleum Corp., Nipro, and Valley Nitrogen Producers, and they accounted for about 65% of United States production capacity.

Processes

There are three general methods for making ammonium sulfate.

1. The reaction of ammonia or ammonia containing gas with sulfuric acid or solutions containing sulfuric acid:

$$2NH_3 + H_2SO_4 \longrightarrow (NH_4)_2SO_4 + 67.7 \text{ kcal/g-mol}$$

2. The reaction of calcium sulfate with ammonium carbonate:

$$NH_3 + H_2O \longrightarrow NH_4OH + 8.3 \text{ kcal/g-mol}$$

$$2NH_4OH + CO_2 \longrightarrow (NH_4)_2CO_3 + H_2O + 22 \text{ kcal/g-mol}$$

$$(NH_4)_2CO_3 + CaSO_4 \longrightarrow (NH_4)_2SO_4 + CaCO_3 + 3.9 \text{ kcal/g-mol}$$

3. The reaction of ammonia or ammonia containing gas with sulfur dioxide and oxidation of the diammonium sulfite product to ammonium sulfate:

$$2NH_3 + SO_2 + H_2O \longrightarrow (NH_4)_2SO_3 + 61.2 \text{ kcal/g-mol}$$

$$(NH_4)_2SO_3 + \tfrac{1}{2}O_2 \longrightarrow (NH_4)_2SO_4 + 67.5 \text{ kcal/g-mol}$$

Aqueous ammonium sulfate solutions are obtained from these reactions and these are processed to recover crystalline product. When a saturated solution of a crystallizable salt such as ammonium sulfate is cooled or supercooled, it is metastable just before solid crystal nuclei form. After nuclei are formed the solution is labile or unstable and crystals will grow from each nucleus if additional metastable liquid is supplied. Metastable conditions are affected by pH, temperature, impurities, crystal surface area, and agitation. Uniformly sized crystals are produced in a crystallizer when the supply of metastable liquid feed is kept constant and when the number of new nuclei formed is equal to the number of crystals removed. Production rates are normally held constant; therefore, the average crystal size is a function of the nucleation rate. Crystallization is discussed in detail in Volumes 14 and 15 of this *Encyclopedia.*

Various improvements have been made in processes and equipment over the years with the objective of improving the size, size distribution, and shape of the recovered crystalline ammonium sulfate to make it easier to handle, store, and use. These are discussed in detail in the section describing the coke-oven by-product processes. There are also granulation processes available for increasing the ammonium sulfate particle size when crystal growth is restricted because of equipment limitations or the presence of crystal growth inhibitors.

In one granulation process the fine ammonium sulfate solid, containing 2 to 3% moisture, is passed through a set of rotating compacting rolls which compress the feed into a continuous sheet about 1/8 in. thick. This material is dried to a moisture content of about 0.1% and is then passed through serrated steel granulator rolls where the dried compacted material is reduced in size [2]. The flat, irregular-shaped particles are screened and the undersized particles are recycled to the process. The oversized granules are broken into smaller particles and then recycled to the process.

In another process a mixture of fine solid ammonium sulfate particles and small moist crystals of ammonium sulfate are passed through a blunger [6, 7]. This equipment consists of a long tube with a shaft running through the middle to which are attached a number of paddles. When the shaft is rotated, the paddles mix the small moist crystals and the dry recycle material, causing them to stick together to form granules because of the tackiness of the saturated mother liquor present. The moist granules emerging from the blunger are dried in a rotary drier. When the moisture is removed, the particles in each individual granule are cemented together by crystallization of the ammonium sulfate that was present in the mother liquor phase. The dried granules are screened, and the undersize and oversize materials are reprocessed.

Particle size can also be increased by moistening fine particles of ammonium sulfate in a drum granulator with liquids such as a lignosulfonate solution or ammonium phosphate solution and drying the resulting granules [8, 9]. Also, a mixture of fine ammonium sulfate and fly ash can be moistened with a solution of ammonium sulfate followed by pelleting and drying [10].

1. Reaction of Ammonia and Sulfuric Acid

The three main sources of feed for the preparation of ammonium sulfate by the reaction of ammonia and sulfuric acid are:

A. Coke oven by-product
B. Pure ammonia and sulfuric acid
C. By-product from chemical manufacturing

Prior to 1921, when the first domestic synthetic ammonia plant started production, the principle source of ammonium sulfate in the United States was from the coking of coal. Bituminous coking coal contains about 1.5% nitrogen. About 15–20% of this nitrogen is converted to ammonia during the coking operation. This ammonia is often recovered from the coking gases as ammonium sulfate, and from 21 to 28 lb can be produced per ton of coal. The requirements of the steel industry govern the production of coke, but at the present time about 15.2% of the ammonium sulfate produced in the United States is derived from coking operations.

A large and expanding source of ammonium sulfate is that produced as by-product of chemical processes such as caprolactam and acrylonitrile production. Another source is from waste sulfuric acid pickle liquor from steel production [11].

A. Coke Oven By-Product

Three different processes are used for the production of ammonium sulfate from coke oven gas. These are:

1. The saturator process
2. The ammonia absorption process
3. The controlled crystallization process

Each of these processes utilizes the neutralization reaction of sulfuric acid and ammonia. However, they vary in effectiveness in controlling the size and quality of the ammonium sulfate crystals [2, 12, 13]. All three processes use the same methods for removal of mother liquor: washing, neutralizing the excess sulfuric acid, and drying.

The saturator process is the oldest of the three methods used for producing ammonium sulfate. It is also the least efficient and is no longer used much in the United States. Neutralization and crystallization occur in the same reactor and there is no way to control crystal size or size distribution. It involves the reaction, at about 140°F, of the ammonia-containing gas with sulfuric acid in a reactor called a saturator. The acid concentration is maintained between 2 and 5% by the continuous controlled addition of concentrated sulfuric acid. Ammonium sulfate crystals precipitate from the supersaturated solution, settle to the bottom of the saturator, and are pumped to a centrifuge where the mother liquor is removed. They are rinsed with water and then with aqueous ammonia to neutralize residual sulfuric acid. The crystals are then dried in a drum dryer, using heated air, until the moisture content is reduced to about 0.1%, cooled to ambient temperature, and sent to storage.

An undesirable characteristic of this process is that deposits of ammonium sulfate coat the bottom and sides of the saturator after it has been in operation a short while, and it is necessary to interrupt operations occasionally to dissolve them. This is done by increasing the acid concentration to 10–15%. The ammonium bisulfate that is formed is more water soluble and the deposits dissolve.

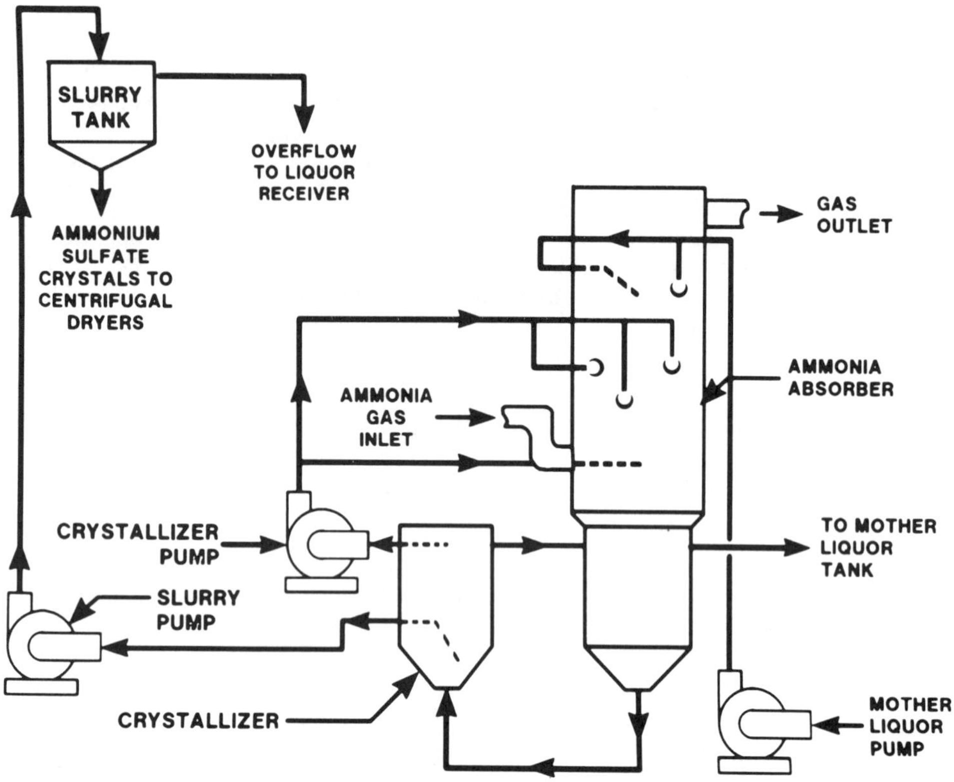

FIG. 1. Ammonia absorption process.

The ammonia absorption process for making ammonium sulfate is an improvement over the saturator process because it uses separate reactors for the neutralization and crystallization steps and permits some control over crystal size. In addition, ammonium sulfate does not deposit on the bottom and sides of the crystallizer.

This process involves the use of an unpacked spray-type absorber, a crystallizer tank, and related equipment (Fig. 1). The ammonia-containing gas is charged to the bottom of the absorber and is scrubbed with a countercurrent spray of saturated ammonium sulfate solution containing 3 to 6% sulfuric acid. The ammonium sulfate product solution is sent to the crystallizer tank. Part of the solution is recirculated to the absorber and part is sent to a mother liquor tank where concentrated sulfuric acid is added continuously to maintain the free acid content in the desired range. This refortified solution is recycled to the absorber. Crystal slurry is removed continuously from the bottom of the crystallizer tank and is pumped to the slurry tank. The clear solution that separates is collected in a liquor receiver and is recirculated to the absorber. The crystal slurry that is removed from the bottom of the slurry tank is sent to a continuous centrifugal dryer. After the crystals are dried to 0.1% moisture content, they are screened, cooled, and sent to storage.

The highest quality ammonium sulfate crystals are produced using the controlled crystallization process. This is similar to the ammonia absorption process except that a vaporizer is incorporated in the crystallizer and water can be removed under controlled conditions. Crystal size control is achieved by varying the circulation rate and the crystal concentration.

The sulfuric acid content of the nearly saturated ammonium sulfate solution that is circulated through the absorber is maintained at about 6%. The absorber effluent is sent to the circulating system of the crystallizer where crystallization takes place because of the cooling and concentrating effects of the vaporizer. Smaller crystals remain suspended in the circulating liquid and the larger crystals settle to the bottom and form a slurry. The slurry is removed and processed as previously described.

The dust-free, rice-size crystals produced by this process are free flowing and are more resistant to breakage than the product prepared by the two previously discussed processes. In addition, they are more resistant to caking during storage, and the larger and more uniform sized crystals are easier to spread evenly on a field when applied alone or in fertilizer blends.

B. Prime Product

In the past, when the demand for ammonium sulfate in the United States began to exceed the supply available from coke ovens, additional product was prepared by reacting synthetic ammonia and pure sulfuric acid. This pure product is called prime ammonium sulfate. In the 1950s prime product accounted for the majority of the ammonium sulfate produced in the United States, but today it amounts to only a small fraction of total production. The same types of neutralizing and crystallizing equipment are used for these feeds as are used with coke-oven gas.

A spray tower ammoniation process is used in Japan to produce dry ammonium sulfate powder. In this process, sulfuric acid is sprayed into a tower filled with ammonia gas. Dry ammonium sulfate powder is formed because the heat evolved by the reaction evaporates the water that is present [2, 12]. Water vapor and excess ammonia are removed from the tower and separated in a column. Recovered ammonia is returned to the process. The ammonium sulfate powder is continuously removed from the bottom of the tower and sent to storage. It is used for the preparation of dry mixed fertilizer formulations. If desired, the powdered product can be granulated or compacted to produce larger particles.

C. Chemical By-Product

A large portion of the ammonium sulfate produced in the United States is derived from various chemical process by-product streams. A few of these processes are briefly described below.

Large quantities of caprolactam are used in the United States to prepare nylon 6. One process for preparing caprolactam is

$$\underset{\text{Cyclohexanone}}{C_6H_{10}O} + \underset{\text{Hydroxylamine sulfate}}{\tfrac{1}{2}(NH_3OH)_2SO_4} \xrightarrow[\text{Aqueous ammonia}]{NH_4OH} \underset{\text{Cyclohexanone oxime}}{C_6H_{11}NO} + \underset{\text{Ammonium sulfate}}{\tfrac{1}{2}(NH_4)_2SO_4} + \underset{\text{Water}}{2H_2O}$$

$$\underset{\text{Cyclohexanone oxime}}{C_6H_{11}NO} \xrightarrow[H_2SO_4 \cdot SO_3 \text{ (Fuming sulfuric acid)}]{\text{Beckmann rearrangement}} \underset{\text{Caprolactam–sulfuric acid mass}}{C_6H_{11}NO \cdot H_2SO_4}$$

$$\underset{\text{Caprolactam–sulfuric acid mass}}{C_6H_{11}NO \cdot H_2SO_4} \xrightarrow[\text{Aqueous ammonia}]{2NH_4OH} \underset{\text{Caprolactam}}{C_6H_{11}NO} + \underset{\text{Ammonium sulfate}}{(NH_4)_2SO_4} + \underset{\text{Water}}{2H_2O}$$

Ammonium sulfate is a by-product from the preparation of hydroxylamine sulfate, cyclohexanone oxime, and the neutralization of the caprolactam reaction mixture, and a total of 4.5–5 lb is produced per pound of caprolactam.

Acrylonitrile, an intermediate in the production of acrylic fibers, is prepared by reacting propylene, an excess of ammonia, and oxygen:

$$CH_3{-}CH{=}CH_2 + NH_3 + 1\tfrac{1}{2}O_2 \longrightarrow CH_2{=}CHCN + 3H_2O$$

The excess ammonia in the reaction mixture is neutralized with aqueous sulfuric acid, and from 1 to 3 lb of ammonium sulfate is produced per pound of acrylonitrile.

Acrylamide, used for polymer production, is prepared from acrylonitrile:

$$CH_2{=}CHCN + H_2O \xrightarrow[H_2SO_4]{} CH_2{=}CHCONH_2 \cdot H_2SO_4$$

$$CH_2{=}CHCONH_2 \cdot H_2SO_4 \xrightarrow[2NH_4OH]{} CH_2{=}CH{-}CONH_2 + (NH_4)_2SO_4 + 2H_2O$$

Neutralization of the acrylamidium hydrogen sulfate solution with ammonium hydroxide yields acrylamide and ammonium sulfate.

Ammonium sulfate crystals are recovered from the various ammonium sulfate solutions using a crystallizer equipped with a vaporizer (air stripping or vacuum). These are the same types of crystallizers previously described in the controlled crystallization process.

2. Reaction of Calcium Sulfate with Ammonium Carbonate

The idea of manufacturing ammonium sulfate by the reaction between calcium sulfate and ammonium carbonate was first used at a plant in Austria in 1809, and the ammonium sulfate product was then reacted with sodium chloride to produce ammonium chloride. This early ammonium sulfate process was not successful enough to be used generally, and it was more than

100 years before an economical commercial process was developed by Badische Anilin und Soda Fabrik in Germany. Two plants were built and operated in Germany during World War I [14].

This production method is still used in parts of the world where sulfuric acid is expensive and where a supply of calcium sulfate is available, such as in England, France, Germany, and India.

The various reactions involved in this process were shown previously. The saturated ammonium carbonate solution used in the process is prepared by dissolving carbon dioxide in ammonium hydroxide solution. Carbon dioxide is available as a by-product of the process for making hydrogen (from hydrocarbon feeds) for the synthesis of ammonia. The conversion in the last reaction is about 95% after 5 h if the gypsum is ground fine enough for at least 95% of it to pass through a 120-mesh screen and if the reaction temperature is kept at 70°C.

It is desirable to use slightly more than the theoretical amount of ammonia to precipitate iron impurities. The reaction mixture is filtered to separate calcium carbonate and unreacted calcium sulfate from the ammonium sulfate solution. The addition of certain carboxylic or sulfonic acid salts is reported to facilitate removal of very fine precipitate in this filtration step [15].

3. Reaction of Ammonia with Sulfur Dioxide

A number of methods have been reported over the years for processing sulfur-containing stack and flue gases to reduce air pollution while also producing ammonium sulfate. Some of these processes will probably become economically attractive in the future because the value of the ammonium sulfate product will help defray the cost of pollution abatement.

The Marino process (Fig. 2) is reported to be a low cost desulfurization technique even for small-scale units [16, 17]. It involves the reaction of an aqueous ammonia solution with sulfur dioxide in a reactor-crystallizer open to the atmosphere to prepare crystalline ammonium sulfite as shown previously.

Ammonium sulfite crystals are centrifuged from the crystallizer effluent and are oxidized to ammonium sulfate in a rotary dryer. In a similar process it is claimed that the oxidation step can be done on either the ammonium sulfite solution or on the crystalline solid [18].

Microcrystalline particles of ammonium sulfate are produced by passing a mixture of sulfur dioxide, oxygen, water, and ammonia through a bed of vanadium pentoxide catalyst particles at 200–450°C and 0.1–5 atm pressure [19]:

$$SO_2 + \tfrac{1}{2}O_2 + H_2O + 2NH_3 \xrightarrow[\substack{200\text{–}450^\circ C \\ 0.1\text{–}5\ \text{atm}}]{V_2O_5} (NH_4)_2SO_4 + 128.7\ \text{kcal/g-mol}$$

In the Piritas Espanolas (PE) process the sulfur dioxide in the stack gas is absorbed in a basic organic solvent such as a toluidine or a xylidine [20]. The sulfite is oxidized by air and the organic sulfate is decomposed with ammonia:

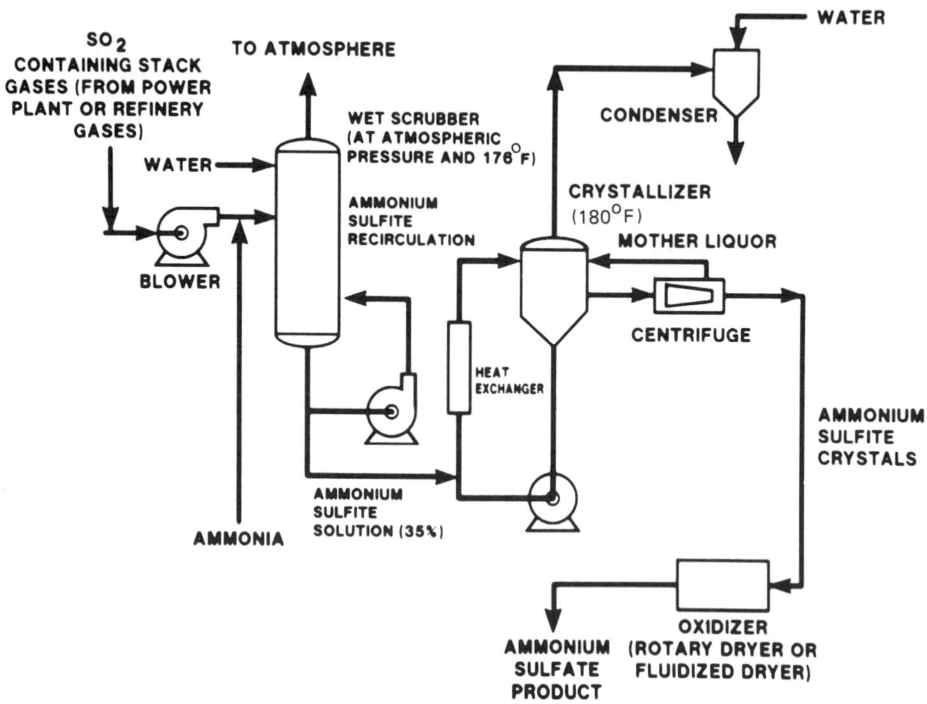

FIG. 2. Marino process for pollution control.

$$2C_7H_7NH_2 + SO_2 + H_2O \longrightarrow (C_7H_7NH_3)_2SO_3$$

$$(C_7H_7NH_3)_2SO_3 + \tfrac{1}{2}O_2 \longrightarrow (C_7H_7NH_3)_2SO_4$$

$$(C_7H_7NH_3)_2SO_4 + 2NH_3 \longrightarrow 2C_7H_7NH_2 + (NH_4)_2SO_4$$

The ammonium sulfate is recovered by centrifuging and drying. A more recent variation of this process uses an amine in the absorber which is a stronger base than ammonia and also uses an alcohol solvent to facilitate precipitation of the ammonium sulfate crystals [21].

Product Specifications

The ammonium sulfate product is usually checked for nitrogen content, sulfur content, free acidity, moisture content, and screen size distribution. The producers usually guarantee that their product will meet the following specifications:

1. A sulfur content of 23.8% minimum
2. A nitrogen content of 20.5–21.0% minimum
3. A maximum sulfuric acid content of 0.05%
4. A maximum moisture content of 0.1%
5. Free flowing

TABLE 2 Ammonium Sulfate Particle Size Distribution

Screen Size U.S. Standard	Ammonia Absorber Product	Controlled Crystal Product	Granulated Product
+6	0	0	2
−6+8	0	1	23
−8+30	22	97	73
−30	78	2	2

There will be some variation in ammonium sulfate crystal size depending on the method of production. Rice-shaped crystals, as obtained in the controlled crystallization process, are preferred for bulk blending and for aerial application. Typical particle-size distributions for three different types of ammonium sulfate are shown in Table 2.

Handling and Storage

Ammonium sulfate can be stored and shipped without experiencing caking problems if proper attention is paid to certain of its physical and chemical properties and the handling and storage conditions. The particles should be relatively uniform in size and free of fines. All equipment should be designed to minimize crystal breakage with the resulting formation of additional fines. It is also important that the crystals be free of acid and their moisture content should not exceed about 0.1%. When the humidity is high, it is important to cool the product emerging from the dryer to ambient temperature, using dry air, before it is stored or shipped in bagged or bulk form. This eliminates the problem of product caking caused by the condensation of water when the warm moist air cools below its dew point.

If caking is still a problem, it may be necessary to use a coating agent such as diatomaceous earth or an anticaking agent such as an alkylnaphthalene sulfonate salt or a fatty acid. Finally, the product should be stored in a weatherproof structure.

References

1. *Chemical Economic Handbook*, SRI International, Menlo Park, California.
2. F. Sedlack, in *Fertilizer Nitrogen* (V. Sanchelli, ed.), Reinhold, New York, 1964.
3. "Forest Fires: Fighting with Chemicals," *Chem. Eng. News*, *49*(35), 4 (August 30, 1971).
4. *Fertilizer Trends*, 1982 ed., Tennessee Valley Authority.
5. *Current Industrial Reports*, Series M28B, U.S. Department of Commerce.

6. S. P. Robinson (Phillips Petroleum Co.), U.S. Patent 2,631,084 (March 10, 1953).
7. W. A. Lutz and W. T. Marston (Door-Oliver), U.S. Patent 2,867,523 (January 6, 1959).
8. K. A. E. Blackmore (Georgia-Pacific Corp.), U.S. Patent 3,725,029 (April 3, 1973).
9. M. A. Barber (Reserve Oil and Gas Co.), U.S. Patent 3,738,821 (June 12, 1973).
10. R. W. Richardson, U.S. Patent 3,923,489 (December 2, 1975).
11. W. Tiddy (Allied Chemical and Dye Corp.), U.S. Patent 2,511,306 (May 28, 1946).
12. C. J. Pratt and R. Noyes, *Nitrogen Fertilizer Chemical Processes*, Noyes Development Corp., Pearl River, New York, 1965.
13. J. F. Holt and P. J. Farley, "Ammonium Sulfate Trends," *Chem. Eng. Prog., 64*(5), 54–58 (May 1968).
14. G. I. Higson, "The Manufacture of Ammonium Sulfate from Anhydrite," *Chem. Ind.* (September 8, 1951).
15. D. J. M. O'Sullivan and B. B. Pearce (Imperial Chemical Industries), U.S. Patent 3,085,857 (April 16, 1963).
16. A. C. Marina, Canadian Patent 939,115 (January 1, 1974).
17. "Clean-Air Route Has Made-in-Mexico Label," *Chem. Eng.*, pp. 58–59 (January 22, 1973).
18. C. M. Ambrossi, West German Patent 2,313,177 (September 19, 1974).
19. A. Vian-Ortuno, C. Iriarte-Fernandez, and C. Melches-Serrano, U.S. Patent 2,912,304 (November 10, 1959).
20. A. Vian-Ortuno and A. Crespi-Gonzalez, U.S. Patent 2,970,039 (January 31, 1961).
21. R. L. Grimsley and R. L. Every (Continental Oil Co.), U.S. Patent 3,472,618 (October 14, 1969).

JOSEPH R. KENTON

Fertilizers, Mixed

Definition

"Mixed fertilizers" is the designation for fertilizers that contain two or all three of the major plant nutrients—nitrogen, phosphorus, and potassium. These nutrients are expressed as N for nitrogen, P_2O_5 for phosphorus or phosphate, and K_2O for potassium, which usually is referred to as potash.

The term "compound fertilizer" is used widely in Europe and some other parts of the world to designate these NP and NPK fertilizers. Another term "complex fertilizer" has some usage to designate products from nitric phosphate or ammonium phosphate processes.

Types of Mixed Fertilizers

The production pattern for finished mixed (NPK) fertilizers in the United States has evolved to three main systems. These are:

Granulation
Bulk blending
Fluid fertilizers—liquids (solutions) and suspensions

Granulation

In granulation processes for mixed (NPK) fertilizers, the ingredients in the formulation are combined and formed into discrete granules by a combination of chemical reactions and physical means. The main chemical reactions involve the neutralization of acids (or acidic components) with ammonia. Heat and moisture are the primary driving forces for granulation. Heat is provided by chemical reactions, and in some cases by the addition of steam. Moisture present in the ingredients of the formulation, or added as water or steam, together with heat that causes dissolution of some components, provide the plasticity (liquid phase) needed for granulation.

The object of granulation of NPK fertilizers is to combine the materials so that each granule contains reasonably uniform proportions of the fertilizer nutrients.

Bulk Blending

A bulk-blended fertilizer is one consisting of a mechanical mixture of fertilizer materials. As referred to here, bulk blending is defined as a physical mixing process for granular fertilizer materials (simple or binary) in small plants that are located near the point of use of the blended products.

Grades of Mixed Fertilizers

In the United States and most other countries, the mixed fertilizers are marketed as $N–P_2O_5–K_2O$ grades. These have a range of ratios from about 1:4 to 3:1 ($N:P_2O_5$). Some common grades include 6–24–24, 8–16–16, 14–14–14, and 20–10–10. Bulk blends are sometimes marketed as a given amount of N, P_2O_5, and K_2O per ton or larger batch. State regulatory agencies monitor production and shipments in efforts to ensure that fertilizers sold are within established tolerances for the specified individual nutrients.

The important secondary nutrients—sulfur, calcium, and magnesium—are often included in mixed fertilizers with no additional cost. In the 1980s efforts are being made in some countries to add charges for sulfur that is high in cost.

When micronutrients such as Fe, Cu, Zn, Mn, B, and Mo are included (in fractional percentages), charges are assessed.

Fertilizer Production Patterns

The fertilizer industry in the United States and world has evolved and developed markedly during its 140-year history since Liebig. Its greatest development has occurred since about 1945, with production spreading to many developing countries. The United States fertilizer industry is organized basically into separate segments for production and marketing of nitrogen, phosphate, or potash intermediates and products. There is some overlapping, but the large basic complexes produce predominately N, P, or K products. The finished NP or NPK fertilizers are usually prepared in small- or medium-sized plants near the markets. Ammonium phosphates are mainly produced near the phosphate rock mines.

Nitrogen fertilizer production complexes are located near natural gas sources. Nearness to markets is another important consideration, as are transportation alternatives. Locations on waterways facilitate domestic shipments by low-cost barge and export shipments via oceangoing vessels.

The major United States phosphate production centers are near the phosphate rock mines in Florida, North Carolina, and western areas of Idaho, Utah, and Wyoming. There is a substantial economic advantage for upgrading phosphate rock (28–32% P_2O_5) to wet-process acid (52–54% P_2O_5), triple superphosphate (TSP, 44–46% P_2O_5), diammonium phosphate (DAP, 18–46–0), and monoammonium phosphate (MAP, 11–52–0) for long-distance shipment to regional or local plants that produce finished granular or fluid fertilizers.

Most of the potash used in the United States was mined near Carlsbad, New Mexico, until the early 1960s, when the deposits in Saskatchewan, Canada, came into production. In 1981 the Canadian mines supplied more than 70% of the potash consumed in the United States. Major United States potash corporations built mining and processing operations there, but several of these have been taken over by the Government of Saskatchewan.

Most finished fertilizers in the United States are processed in regional or local plants comparatively near the markets. Production and marketing techniques for the three main systems—granulation, bulk blending, and fluids—are described later [2].

Most finished fertilizers in Europe, Asia, and Latin America are produced at major production complexes, located mainly to facilitate receipt of raw materials and shipment of products to the markets. Locations that allow shipment by water are highly preferred. Major raw materials and intermediates—such as phosphate rock, phosphoric acid, nitric acid, and ammonia—are often shipped to these complexes from domestic or outside sources.

In Europe, and to a considerable extent in Asia and Latin America, the finished granular NPK fertilizers are produced as "complex fertilizers" by nitric phosphate or ammonium phosphate processes. These comparatively high-investment process systems are located at major centralized fertilizer production centers, rather than near the markets. Production capacity is 50 to 100 tons/h or more, often in multitrain units [5]. Grades include 14–14–14, 22–11–11, and 10–20–10 by nitric phosphate processes that are based on the acidulation of phosphate rock with nitric acid [6]. Complete NPK grades made by ammonium phosphate processes include 17–17–17 and 11–22–22.

The inclusion of urea in formulations allows higher analysis grades such as 19–19–19 and 14–28–14. The ammonium phosphate–urea system allows production of the highest analysis grades possible with available fertilizer materials [8].

The ammonium phosphate produced in the United States is essentially all as N–P_2O_5 grades 18–46–0 for DAP and 10–50–0 or 11–52–0 for MAP. Most of the large production is used in bulk blending, but increasing quantities of MAP are being used in formulating suspensions. Large tonnages of DAP (18–46–0) are exported by United States producers [9, 10].

The proportion of finished NPK fertilizers produced in the United States by ammoniation-granulation processes reached a maximum of about 80% during the early 1960s. Since that time, there has been a decreasing trend in granulation as the production of bulk blends and fluid fertilizers continues to increase. By 1980 the granular NPK fertilizers accounted for only about 30% of total finished mixed fertilizers.

The practice of physically mixing granular N, P, and K intermediates (bulk blending) started in the North Central States in the mid-1950s. Growth was spectacular, and more than 5000 blending units were in operation by 1970; about 5500 are believed to be in operation in 1982.

Production of liquid fertilizers started in California in 1923. Growth was slow for the next 25 years and had reached only 22,000 tons in that state in 1953. In 1955, 147 companies were reported to be manufacturing liquids. Growth was rapid in the 1960s, the number of plants increasing from 355 in 1959 to more than 1700 in 1968. The number of plants increased spectacularly to about 2800 in 1971. By 1981 the total of fluid NPK plants in the United States had stabilized at about 3200 [1].

Table 1 shows the estimated percentage of United States fertilizers marketed as granular, bulk blended, and fluid mixtures in 1981 [11].

The average total plant food content (N, P_2O_5, and K_2O) of mixed fertilizers in the United States rose from 13% in 1880 to 15% in 1910, and to 20% in 1940. The total nutrient content averaged 40% in 1970 and about 44% in 1981.

United States consumption of N, P_2O_5, and K_2O in all fertilizers jumped from 1.8 million tons in 1940 to 16 million tons in 1970 and 23.5 million tons in 1981—about a thirteenfold increase in 40 years. Nutrient consumption in 1982 dropped to 21.5 million tons because of the adverse farm economy. Consumption of the individual major nutrients in 1982 is given in Table 2.

TABLE 1

	Percent of Total Fertilizers	Percent of Total Mixed Fertilizers
Granular NPK's	16.6	28.6
Bulk blends	31.5	54.3
Fluids (liquids and suspensions)	9.9	17.1

TABLE 2 Nutrient Consumption, United States (1982) (in million tons) [12]

N	11.1
P_2O_5	4.8
K_2O	5.6

The total fertilizer consumption in the United States in 1982 was 50 million tons of material (21.5 million tons of total nutrients) with a value of about 8.5 billion dollars. Mixed fertilizers accounted for about 58% of the total fertilizers used in the United States in 1982 [12] and an estimated 64% of the world total in 1981.

Production of Granular Mixed Fertilizers

The earliest mixed fertilizers in the United States were based on waste materials from the meat-processing industry. In 1913, about 42% of the nitrogen in United States fertilizers was supplied by these wastes; in 1981 the proportion was about 0.5%. The first mineral-mixed fertilizers were in powdered form and caked badly. Analysis was low, such as 6–8–4 and 2–10–7 ($N–P_2O_5–K_2O$). The practice of producing fertilizers in granular form, which was already popular in Europe, did not develop to any appreciable extent in the United States until the dependable and comparatively simple TVA (Tennessee Valley Authority) ammoniation-granulation process was developed and demonstrated in 1952. This versatile process became widely used, and more than 60% of United States fertilizers were prepared this way during the 1960s [13].

Materials Used

The use of N, P_2O_5, and K_2O intermediates in local plants for production of solid mixed fertilizers started in the United States and Europe with use of potash, calcium cyanamide, sodium nitrate, guano or other solid nitrogen materials, and ordinary superphosphate (OSP) to produce low-grade pulverized mixtures. Ammoniating solutions came on the scene later and gave more versatility in fixing lower cost nitrogen. Ammonium sulfate became available as supplemental nitrogen, mainly as by-product material. With the advent of granulation in the United States in the early 1950s, the use of intermediates became more important. Granulation had started as early as the mid-1930s in Europe, and by 1950 it was quite popular in some countries. In the United States, anhydrous ammonia became more practical and economical to transport. Nitrogen solutions containing free ammonia were used to ammoniate locally produced OSP (20% P_2O_5) and shipped-in TSP (46% P_2O_5) that became an important intermediate for upgrading the phosphate content. Higher analysis granular products with better handling, storage, and application properties were produced. Sulfuric acid was used to promote granulation and allow greater fixing of ammonia, and later wet-process phosphoric acid (53–54% P_2O_5) came into use in moderate amounts as an intermediate to provide higher analysis grades. Secondary nutrients (S and Mg) and micronutrients (Zn, Cu, B, Mo, Fe, Mn, etc.) were added as needed [3].

Equipment and Operating Technique

In the United States, the TVA ammoniation-granulation process and equipment (rotary cylinder or drum) that originated in 1952 were widely adopted. Within a year, about 50 plants of this type were in operation. By 1962 there were 164 plants in the United States known to be using this process, and 200 or more local and regional granulation plants of this type were estimated to be in operation by the mid-1960s [3]. The rotary drum-type granulation equipment is by far the most widely used because of its versatility in combining the mixing, ammoniation, and granulation in a single unit. Other types of granulators, including pug mills, spray drums, and inclined pan granulators, are used to a lesser extent.

The ammonium phosphate "boom" in the middle 1960s and the growth of bulk blending and liquid fertilizer production slowed the growth in local granulation plants, and the number declined. However, the 100 or so plants of this type in operation in 1982 accounted for nearly 30% of the total production of mixed fertilizer in the United States.

The granulation system has several important advantages, including those listed below.

A variety of NPK grades of various ratios can be produced with economical formulations. Secondary and micronutrients can be readily added to produce special grades.

Recycle ratios are low, and grades can be changed more easily than in large complex plants.

Investment in basic production facilities is comparatively low, and fewer costly auxiliary and support facilities are required than for a large complex.

Operation can be seasonal, if desired, with use of a small crew of local operating personnel that do not require a high level of training.

Ownership can be local with obvious advantages in marketing of products due to personal acquaintance with customers and their preferences.

Some typical formulations for several grades of granular fertilizers that are produced in NPK granulation plants are shown in Table 3.

A schematic diagram of a typical local granulation plant of the type used in the United States is shown in Fig. 1.

Such plants include storage bins for several solid intermediate materials and tanks for ammonia, nitrogen solution, and acids. In most plants the solid materials are moved from ground-level bins by front-end loader and elevated to a cluster hopper. The components used are batch weighed in the propor-

TABLE 3 Some Typical Formulations for Grades of Granular Fertilizers

Materials used	Grade ($N–P_2O_5–K_2O$) (lb/short ton)				
	10–10–10	12–12–12	5–20–20	6–24–24	10–20–10
Ammonia	—	—	126	60	—
N solution, 44.8%N[a]	360	408	—	96	457
Ammonium sulfate, 20.5% N	196	294	—	—	—
Diammonium phosphate, (18–46–0)	—	—	—	180	—
Ordinary superphosphate, 20% P_2O_5	1020	400	316	—	420
Triple superphosphate, 46% P_2O_5	—	346	754	864	709
Potassium chloride, 60% K_2O	334	400	668	800	334
Sulfuric acid	70	140	128	—	76
Steam	—	—	—	150	—

[a]25% NH_3, 69% ammonium nitrate, 6% H_2O.

tions required in the formulation and fed collectively at a fairly steady rate to the ammoniator-granulator. Some plants use individual feeders for the solid components. Ammonia or nitrogen solution and sulfuric acid are sparged beneath the bed in the rotary drum. When phosphoric acid is used, it is sprayed onto the bed in the granulator. Magnetic flow meters and automatic rotameters are commonly used for controlling the rate of feed of the liquids. The formulations are devised to provide the proper balance of heat, moisture, and total fluid phase in order to allow good granulation. They are balanced to ammoniate properly and to produce the desired grade.

Material from the granulator flows into a direct fuel-fired rotary dryer and then into a rotary, countercurrent cooler. Rotary dryers in granulation plants in the United States are heated by gas-fired or fuel oil-fired burners. Coal-fired combustion chambers are used in a few countries. Use of coal fuel was being evaluated as an economy measure by several companies in the United States in the early 1980s.

The rotary coolers in NPK granulation plants use ambient air in countercurrent flow. A number of plants recycle cooler exhaust air as secondary air to the dryer to conserve energy and to simplify dust collection. A single dust collection system and fume scrubber serve both the cooler and dryer. The cooled material is screened to separate the desired product size (usually about −6+12 mesh), oversize is crushed, and undersized fines are recycled to the granulator. The product may be treated with a surface conditioner to minimize caking. Products are usually stored in bulk prior to bagging and shipment [14]. There are some variations in equipment and operating technique, such as elimination of the dryer by using a pipe reactor for melt granulation as described later. NPK granulation plants usually produce from 15 to 30 tons/h. They are comparatively simple and flexible in operation, and allow the use of a variety of materials in formulations.

Bulk movement of granular NPK fertilizers in spreader trucks and tote boxes became common in the mid-1970s, and by 1980 a number of plants were moving 60 to 75% or more of their production in bulk. This practice is an effort to incorporate some of the advantages and economy of bulk blending in moving granular-mixed fertilizers to customers.

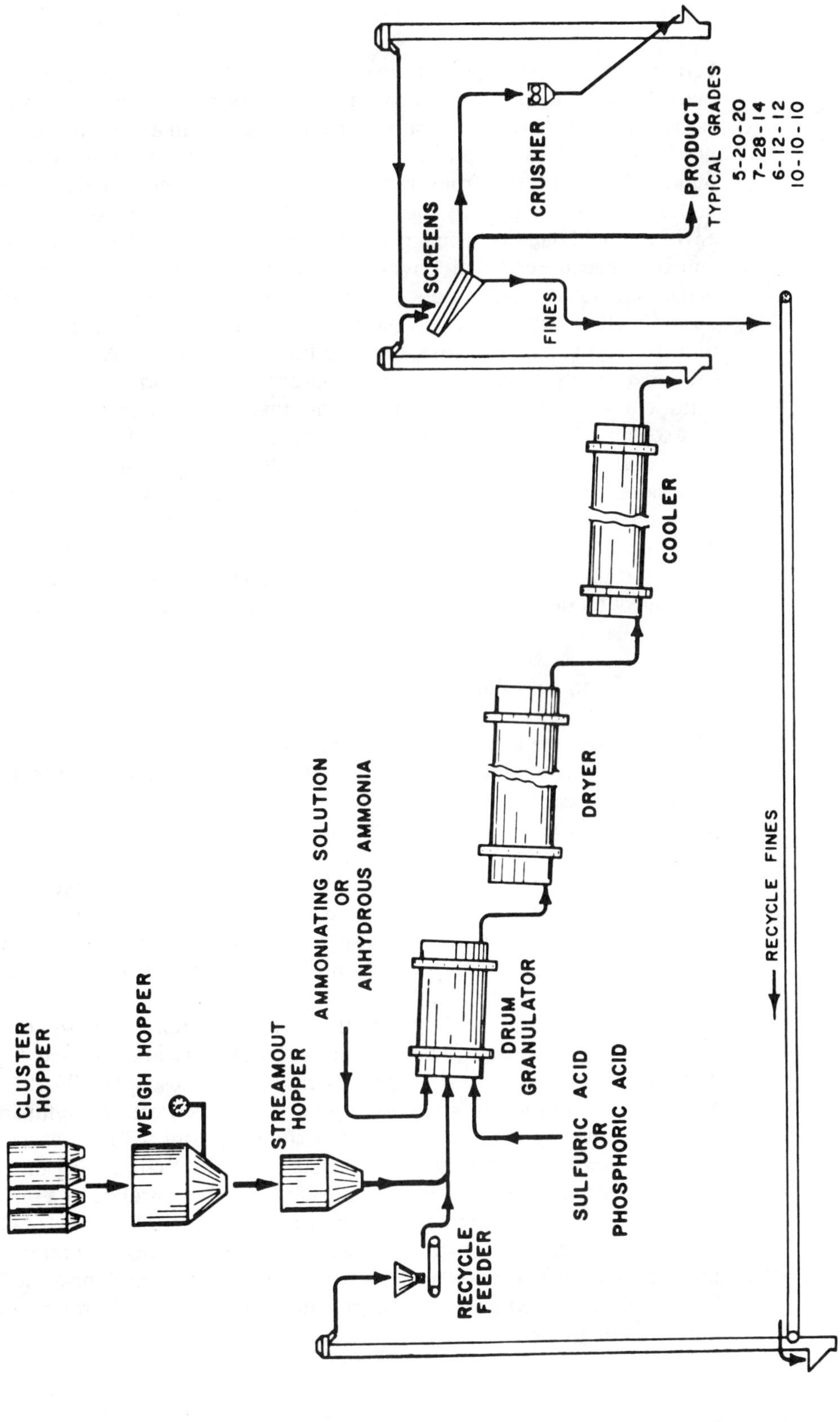

FIG. 1. Typical granulation plant in the United States.

Environmental Problems

Perhaps the greatest problem facing local granulation plants in the 1970s was meeting required regulations to avoid atmospheric and stream pollution. The earlier plants were usually located in rural or suburban areas, but neighborhoods eventually grew up nearby. It became more important to control and remove dust and fumes from stack effluents, and the need to avoid dumping liquid wastes into streams increased. With continuing intense interest in environmental factors, good control of all aqueous effluents and stack emissions became essential. Environmental problems resulted in some plants being shut down and production consolidated at other more favorable locations. It was found that changes in formulations and in operating techniques could greatly decrease dust and fume problems. TVA and industry showed in early tests that use of wet-process phosphoric acid instead of sulfuric acid greatly decreased fumes and dust. A more effective and lower cost scheme is melt granulation by use of a pipe reactor for simultaneous ammoniation of phosphoric and sulfuric acids (discussed later).

Engineering firms and equipment manufacturers have devised simpler and more effective dust and fume control equipment; these joint efforts have made it easier to deal with environmental problems. The development of bag filters and their operating technique, which allowed their use for very effective collection of dust in fertilizer plants, was a major accomplishment.

Energy-Saving Pipe Reactors

TVA has taken the lead in the development and industrial use of comparatively simple pipe reactors for neutralization of sulfuric and/or phosphoric acids with ammonia. The efficient use of heat of reaction saves a large proportion of the energy required in production of granular fertilizers. In production of mixed (NPK) granular fertilizers, the pipe-cross reactor (PCR) is used as shown in Fig. 2. The phosphoric and sulfuric acids required in formulations are fed through opposing pipes into the main branch of the pipe reactor where ammonia is added. Reaction is rapid, and the heat of reaction evaporates a large part of the water to produce a melt that discharges onto the bed in the granulator [15, 16].

The sulfuric acid (H_2SO_4) fed to the PCR is neutralized to ammonium sulfate, $(NH_4)_2SO_4$. The phosphoric acid (H_3PO_4) is ammoniated to an NH_3:H_3PO_4 mole ratio near 1.0 (monoammonium phosphate, $NH_4H_2PO_4$). For smooth operation it is important that water is fed with the anhydrous ammonia entering the PCR in the proportion of about 0.3 lb of water per pound of ammonia. Magnetic flow meters are best for controlling the feed rates of H_2SO_4 and H_3PO_4. The ammonia feed rate is controlled by a turbine meter or an armored rotameter whith remote readout. All of the H_2SO_4 is neutralized in the PCR, since this greatly decreases evolution of fumes from the granulator that occurs when H_2SO_4 reacts with potassium chloride (KCL). Part of the H_3PO_4 required in the formulation may be fed to the rotary drum ammoniator-granulator.

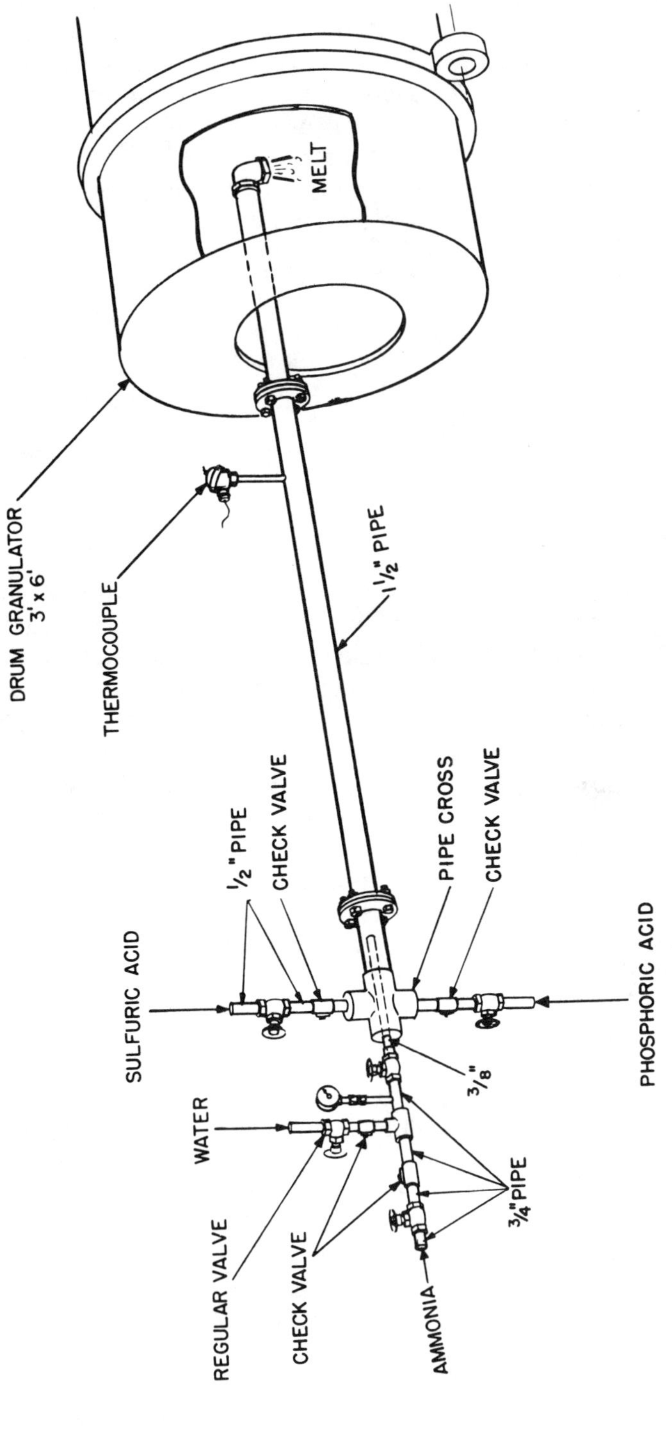

FIG. 2. TVA pilot plant pipe-cross reactor.

Proper reaction temperature is 280 to 340°F, and is controlled by the proportion of water or scrubber solution fed with the anhydrous ammonia. Evaporation of water is very efficient because of the intense heat of reaction of ammonia with the acids in the confined reaction space in the PCR. Most NPK grades do not require drying after granulation, and several plants using the PCR completely eliminated use of a dryer. The very vigorous reaction provides good mixing of reactants during their short residence in the PCR.

Corrosion is severe because of the presence of partially neutralized H_2SO_4 near the feed end of the PCR. The use of Hastelloy C-276 for the entire PCR ensures satisfactory service life.

Some key information concerning design and operation of the PCR is given below.

Size of PCR. 6- to 8-in. pipe size, 9- to 10-ft long (Hastelloy C-276).
Reaction rate. Heat flux of 500,000 to 800,000 Btu/in.^{2} of pipe cross-sectional area; optimum (600,000).
PCR skin temperature. Maximum of 300°F to control corrosion.
Production rate for NPK granular fertilizers using a PCR. 20 to 35 tons/h.

If monoammonium phosphate (MAP) or NPK grades based on MAP are produced, only phosphoric acid is neutralized. Otherwise, the operation is about the same as just described. Type 316L stainless steel is suitable for construction of the pipe reactor if no sulfuric acid is fed. Commercial plant tests have been made in use of the pipe reactor in production of granular diammonium phosphate, and this work is continuing.

The Tennessee Valley Authority (TVA) holds U.S. patents on the pipe reactors and their operation. Royalty-free licensing is available to the industry for a very small one-time issuance fee. This is TVA's practice to promote wide use of its key developments.

About 35 plants using the PCR were in operation in the United States and other countries in 1982. The need for burning fuel for drying the granular products is greatly decreased or eliminated in all plants.

Granulation Practices in Other Countries

In continental Europe, less use is made of local granulation plants than in the United States, although several plants of this general type that are at least regional in nature are utilized in France, Germany, and Spain. In other countries, such as The Netherlands, Italy, and Belgium, the local plant concept is not practiced and several grades of finished NPK fertilizers of complex types are produced in larger centralized plants. Nitric phosphate plants of comparatively large size have been used rather extensively in Europe, and ammonium phosphate-based systems came into use in the 1970s.

In the United Kingdom there is substantial practice of the regional or local granulation-plant concept, although there are also large major producers. There is considerable practice of blending granular intermediates in preparation of final varieties of grades in large granulation plants.

Production of granular mixed fertilizers is practiced widely in several Central and South American countries. Several years ago the Eirich pan granulator was introduced, and this system proliferated for mechanical granulation with moisture. In programs to modernize existing plants, as well as in new plants, rotary drum-type granulators are being installed. In larger complex plants, the spray-drum granulator (Spherodizer) is used quite extensively, but this type of granulator is not being installed in new facilities.

Production in Asia is primarily of complex NPK fertilizers at large production complexes. Ammonium phosphate-based grades predominate and have become more prevalent in Japan since about 1970. Considerable amounts of ammonium chloride are used in finished granular fertilizer formulations in Japan [2].

Bulk Blending

History and Growth

A blended fertilizer may be described as one consisting of a mechanical mixture of fertilizer materials. The practice of bulk blending of granular fertilizers has grown rapidly in the United States, particularly since the early 1960s. This practice started in Illinois in 1947; growth was slow, reaching only 200 units in the United States by the mid-1950s. In 1981, bulk blending accounted for about 53% of the total mixed fertilizers used in the United States (16.7 million tons of material).

Key factors in the rapid growth of bulk blending were convenience in ability to provide a variety of plant food ratios or grades (or prescription amounts of N, P, and K), economy due to handling in bulk, and custom services provided by the blender. The blender is the retail dealer in the streamlined bulk–blending–marketing system, and he usually transports the fertilizer to the farms and applies it when needed. Typical blending plants produce and market only 2000 to 6000 tons per year on a seasonal basis. Capital investment in blending units is comparatively low ($250,000 to $300,000), but most blenders have about an equal investment in application equipment [17].

Blending plants operate on a seasonal basis, and usually the operators have supplemental business enterprises or they provide additional farm services to which the success of such plants is largely attributed. These services may range from soil sampling to establish a basis for fertilizer needs, to the service of applying the fertilizers to the soil. Farmers generally are willing to pay for the application service since there are many other demands for farm labor.

Intermediates Used in Bulk Blending

The granular or prilled intermediates most commonly used in bulk-blending plants in the United States are urea, ammonium nitrate, diammonium phosphate (18–48–0), triple superphosphate, and potassium chloride. Lesser amounts of ammonium sulfate, granular ordinary superphosphate, and potassium sulfate are used. Operating experience and TVA studies have pointed out some combinations of materials that are incompatible and should be avoided [18]. These include urea with unammoniated superphosphate and, of course, urea with ammonium nitrate. Secondary and micronutrients, herbicides, and pesticides can be suitably provided in bulk blends if proper care is taken [19]. Equipment used for transport of the intermediates in bulk must keep the material dry and avoid spillage.

Equipment and Operating Technique

There are varied arrangements of equipment in the thousands of plants throughout the United States. The most popular type of blending plant layout is shown in Fig. 3. This type of plant has a horizontal rotary mixer at ground level. In a variation, the rotary mixer may be elevated to allow discharge directly into spreader trucks.

The key equipment is prefabricated by a number of equipment manufacturers in a variety of types. The basic system is quite simple, as indicated by the diagram in Fig. 4. Typically, the blending operation involves receipt of the intermediate granular components in bulk by railroad car or truck, storage of the intermediates separately in bins, weighing of the granular components in desired proportions, and mixing to obtain essential uniformity. The weighing and mixing operations are combined in some types of equipment such as the ribbon mixer mounted on weigh scales. The most popular type of rotary mixer usually receives preweighed batches of the granular intermediate components. Weigh hoppers are used in some plants while other plants weigh front-end loaders with their scoop loads of material. The mixing or blending step usually requires only 1 to 2 min, so high hourly rates of production are achieved.

The entire cycle of weighing, mixing, and discharging may be automated. The weight of each component of the blend is punched on a card which is fed into a control mechanism that is set to repeat the cycle for the desired number of batches. Once started by a push button, operation continues until the entire consignment has been prepared. Rotary mixers are available with capacities of 1 to 6 tons per batch and ribbon blenders with 1 to 4 tons, so high hourly capacity of 15 to 30 tons/h can be obtained with simple but ingenious arrangements.

Problems in Bulk Blending

Bulk blending is a simple type of practice and can provide uniform mixtures in almost any desired proportions. Blends can be prepared to provide a given weight of N, P, and K rather than specific grades. However, unless proper materials are used and specific practices are followed, segregation can occur and nonuniform blends will then be delivered and applied to the farm. The factors involved and the precautions that are necessary have been thoroughly described by Hoffmeister et al. of TVA [29]. The main requirements are the use of granular materials with a well-matched range of particle size and the

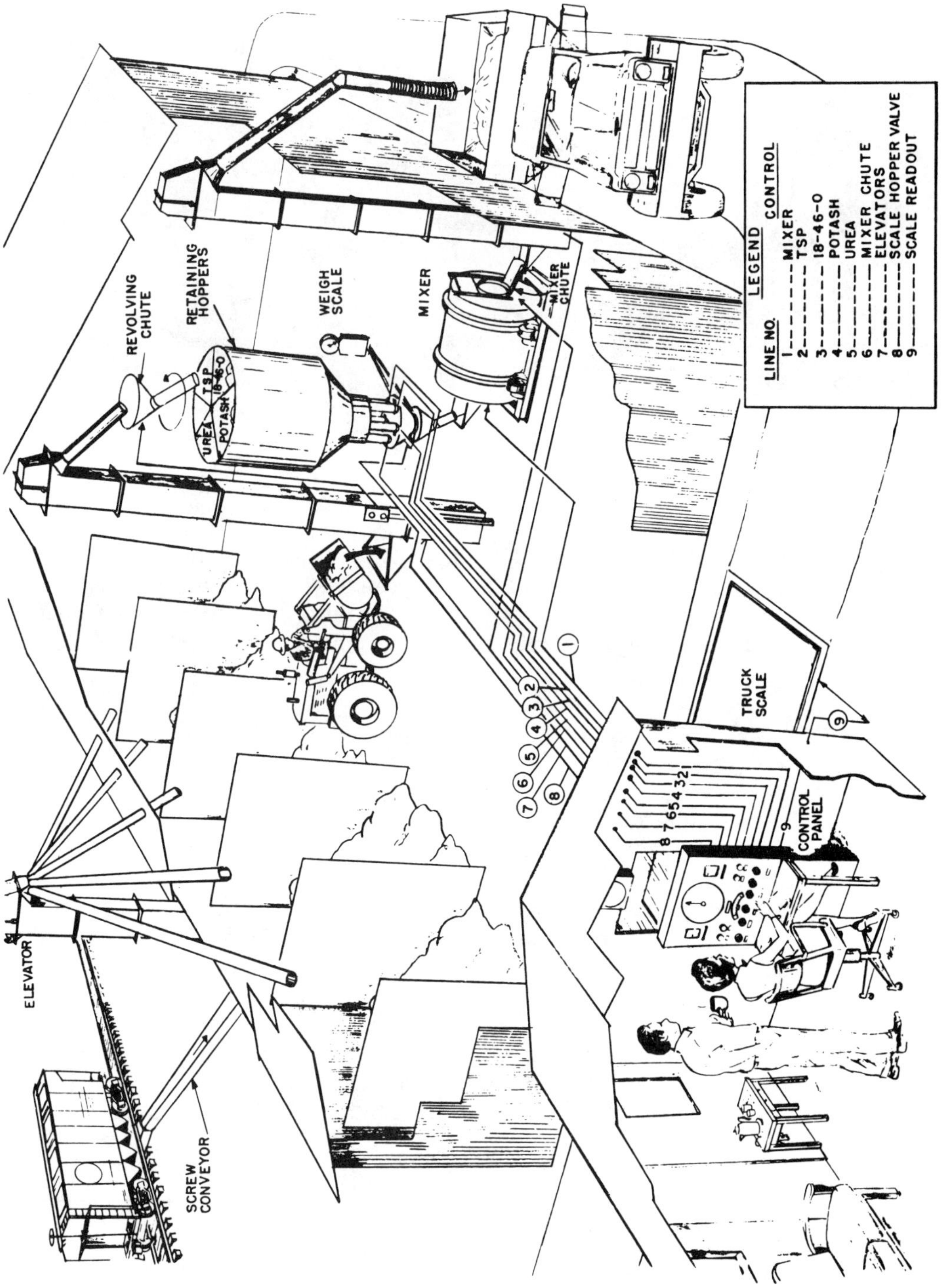

FIG. 3. Bulk-blending plant layout.

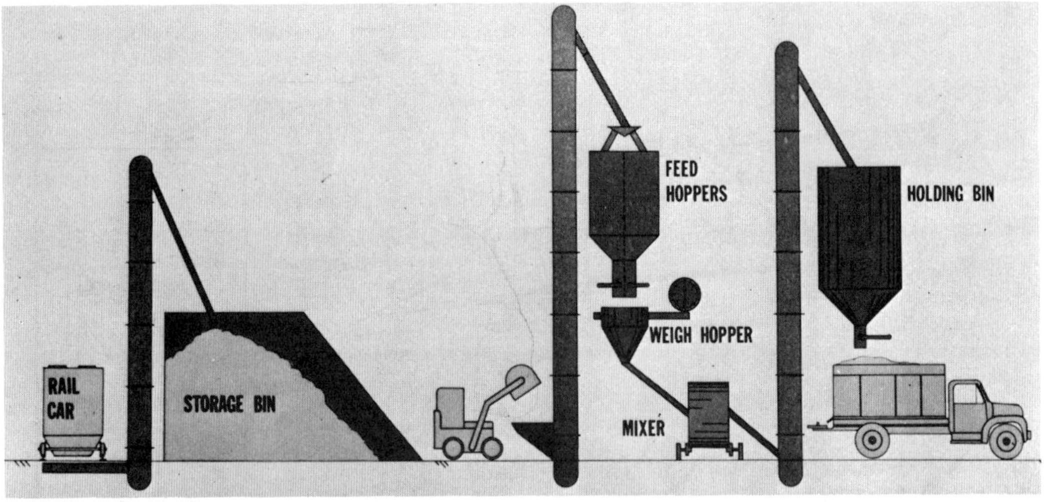

FIG. 4. A bulk-blending plant, simple concept.

handling of the mixture after blending in ways that will minimize segregation. It is quite easy to obtain a uniform blend by use of proper materials, but maintaining this uniformity on the way to the farm and onto the soil involves precautions. Shape and density of the granules are much less important factors than is matching the particle size [17].

Practice in Other Countries

Although bulk blending has increased spectacularly in the United States and now accounts for more than one-half the mixed fertilizers, this practice has not been very widely adopted in other countries. Canada uses this system quite extensively, but there is limited practice of this concept in the United Kingdom or in Brazil and other South American countries. Several blending plants were built in the Caribbean area. In Korea, ammonium phosphate and potash are cogranulated and additional nitrogen is provided by blending with prilled urea.

In one bulk-blending operation in England, an annual output of about 15,000 tons was reached in the second year of operation at a single well-located plant. The goal of 50,000 tons was reached in the fifth year [4].

Fluid Fertilizer

Fluid fertilizers are of three types—liquids, suspensions, and slurries. Properly prepared, *liquids are clear solutions* that remain essentially free of any precipitates for extended periods. The liquids usually have a brown or green color derived from the wet-process acid used in their preparation. Clear liquid fertilizers of comparatively high analysis and high quality are dependent on ammonium polyphosphates in the intermediates used in their preparation. TVA researchers, starting in the late 1940s, pioneered in the development of polyphosphates and processes for preparation of liquid fertilizers of high quality [1].

Suspension fertilizers have substantial proportions of plant nutrients suspended in a finely divided state in the liquid. About 2% of a gelling type of clay is added to enhance suspending properties. *Slurry fertilizers do not have extended suspending properties*. They are not nearly so popular as suspensions, since they should be used as soon as is practical after preparation. Slurries usually are prepared by acidulation of phosphate rock with nitric and sulfuric or phosphoric acids, followed by ammoniation of the slurry.

Growth and Popularity of Fluid Fertilizers

Fluid fertilizer use in the united States was only 27,000 tons in 1954 but increased to nearly 16 million tons by 1980. This tonnage included anhydrous and aqua ammonia and nitrogen solutions applied directly, and accounted for nearly one-third of total fertilizers used.

Fluid-mixed fertilizers (6 million tons) accounted for 17% of the United States total of mixed fertilizers in 1981, continuing the steady increase from 12% in 1970. The main fluid-fertilizer activity is in the United States, but there is substantial production in France and a few plants in Canada, Mexico, Belgium, Brazil, the Soviet Union, South Africa, and the United Kingdom.

The market continues to expand for fluids because of the increased practice of direct application of ammonia and nitrogen solutions, and the continuing growth in popularity of suspensions. One manufacturer of fluid fertilizer production and application equipment reported sales to 23 countries in 1981 [1].

The dominant features of the fluid production and marketing system are the simplicity of mixing facilities and the ease of handling. Also, fluid fertilizers can be applied uniformly at rates greater than an acre per minute with standard high flotation-type equipment. As farm mechanization increased, fluids became more popular. Uniform application, ease of adding pesticides and micronutrients, greater homogeneity, fewer dust problems, and adaptability to irrigation systems are some of the incentives for greater use of fluids. Custom application by dealers or farmer application with dealer-owned equipment constitute additional advantages [20, 21].

There were about 300 fluid fertilizer plants in the United States in 1950, and 750 in 1960. The number increased to 1200 in 1965 and more than doubled to 2700 by 1970. The total in 1974 was 2800 mixed fluid plants, which increased further to 3000 in 1976 and to about 3200 in 1980. Total nutrient consumption as mixed fluids was only 143,000 tons ($N + P_2O_5 + K_2O$) in 1960. This increased sharply to 823,000 tons of nutrients in 1970 and to about 1,300,000 tons in 1975. Total nutrient content of mixed fluids ($N + P_2O_5 + K_2O$) was estimated to be about 28% in 1960. Growth of the higher analysis suspensions resulted in an increase to about 34% plant food content in 1974, and to about 35.2% total plant food content in 1981. The total tonnage of mixed (NPK) fluids increased to about 5 million tons of fluid fertilizer materials. The 1.8 million tons of nutrients as mixed fluid fertilizers in 1981 accounted for about 7.5% of total nutrients applied in the United States, or 17% of total nutrients in mixed fertilizers [1].

These statistics may not seem to be very impressive among total fertilizers, but growth of fluids certainly has been impressive.

T. P. Hignett, in his Sixth Francis New Memorial Lecture in 1969, gave a good assessment of advantages for liquids [22].

> Liquid fertilizers are dependably free-flowing. They are well adapted to handling and application by mechanized, labor-saving methods. Precise metering and placement and uniform distribution are easier with liquids than with solids. Liquids are homogeneous, free from dustiness or caking, and unaffected by hygroscopicity. They are fully water soluble. With liquids, there are no sacks to lift, open, and dispose of; there is little delay in refilling applicators. Liquid fertilization may be combined with irrigation or with application of herbicides or pesticides.

Clear Liquid (Solution) Fertilizers

TVA pioneered the development of liquid and suspension fertilizers. Development of polyphosphate liquid intermediates (11–33–0 and later 11–37–0) in the early 1960s led to clear liquid grades of higher analysis with good storage properties. The polyphosphates sequester (hold in solution) the plant food elements and impurity contents for extended periods of storage. The base liquids are shipped to local plants and used to produce NPK grades such as 8–8–8, 8–16–8, and 7–21–7 [23]. In 1971, TVA developed a very simple process for production of high-polyphosphate liquids by use of a pipe reactor in which ammonia reacts with superphosphoric acid of low (20 to 30%) polyphosphate content almost instantaneously. The heat of reaction drives off most of the water and forms a polyphosphate melt that is processed to 10–34–0 or 11–37–0 grade liquids of high quality with about 75% of the P_2O_5 as polyphosphate. Investment is quite low [24]. The polyphosphate liquid is often shipped to local plants for use in the preparation of finished NPK liquid grades.

The pipe reactor used in this application is much like the pipe-cross reactor described earlier. The reaction tube is made of 4-in. 316L stainless steel pipe, and the length ranges from 16 to 18 ft. An inverted U configuration is often used. Stainless steel construction is suitable since no sulfuric acid is used. A magnetic flow meter is used for controlling the feed rate of H_3PO_4, and an armored rotameter or turbine meter for anhydrous liquid ammonia. In this application the liquid ammonia must be vaporized before entering the pipe reactor. Since the wet-process superphosphoric acid (70% P_2O_5) is essentially anhydrous, the reaction temperature is high (650 to 700°F). Combined water is driven off at this high temperature to provide a reaction melt with 75% or more of the P_2O_5 as polyphosphate. A chemical scale builds up inside the pipe, and this provides corrosion resistance. Periodic removal of scale is necessary.

After rapid development in pilot-plant studies, TVA introduced the simple pipe-reactor system for production of high-polyphosphate liquid fertilizers in 1971. Broad and intense interest by the United States liquid fertilizer industry developed quickly, and 135 commercial units of this type were documented in 1979. Since wet-process superphosphoric acid (68–70% P_2O_5) of low polyphosphate content (20–35%) is used, the absence of free water to be evaporated results in the much higher temperature of 650–700°F. At this temperature, additional polyphosphate is rapidly formed so that 75–80% of the P_2O_5 in the melt is polyphosphate [25].

Suspensions

In the late 1950s and early 1960s there were substantial efforts to break through the grade (solubility) ceiling imposed by liquid (solution) fertilizers of good quality. A main effort was through fluids that contained a large part of their nutrient content as finely divided solids. In the early years such fertilizers were commonly referred to as slurries. Later the term suspension came into use for higher analysis fluids that were much more dependable in storage, handling, and application. It may be well here to differentiate the terms "suspension" and "slurry."

Suspension fertilizers are fluid mixtures of solid and liquid materials in which the solids do not settle rapidly and which can be redispersed readily with agitation to give a uniform mixture. Certain types of clay are added as suspending agents. The suspension is fluid enough to be pumped and applied to the soil in application equipment commonly available for liquid fertilizers with little alteration of the equipment.

Slurry fertilizers are fluid mixtures of solid and liquid materials in which the solids settle rapidly in the absence of agitation to form a firm layer which is difficult to resuspend. Continuous agitation is required to ensure a uniform mixture that can be pumped and applied to the soil.

The use of base suspensions presumably began when TVA shipped the first car of 12–40–0 in January 1963. Continuing research, development, and demonstration work with industry during the next two decades led to suspensions reaching a status in the United States approaching that of clear liquids (solutions) by 1980. About 45% of all fluid fertilizer plants in 1982 produced suspensions as part or all of their production [1].

Here are some important advantages for suspensions:

The practical limit in concentration is much higher than for clear liquids (solutions), particularly when potash is a component. Solubility is not a limiting factor. When the $K_2OP_2O_5$ ratio is 1:1, the suspension concentration (14–14–14) is twice that of clear liquids.

Adequate proportions of secondary and micronutrients can be readily incorporated, as can pesticides, herbicides, etc.

Materials commonly used in formulating suspensions are generally lower in cost and more widely available than those required for clear liquids [26].

The growth of suspensions was spurred in the mid-1970s by the development of equipment and technique for ready incorporation of solid intermediates such as MAP, DAP, and nitrogen materials as major components in formulations [27]. These solid intermediates were available in unlimited quantities and were substantially lower in cost than high-grade wet process acid and polyphosphates required for high analysis liquids (solutions) [28]. Suspensions are likely to continue to grow, and because of important advantages, may ultimately dominate the fluid segment of the United States industry. Slurries, on the other hand, have essentially disappeared from the market.

Production of Suspensions

Since about 1975, there has been an upswing in use of solid intermediates in the production of NPK suspensions. The main solid materials used are urea, potash, granular DAP (18–46–0), granular MAP (10–54–0), and nongranular MAP (11–52–0). There is considerable use of 11–55–0 granular ammonium phosphate (15% of the P_2O_5 as polyphosphate) introduced by TVA. Ammonia and wet-process phosphoric acid are optional materials.

A typical local mix plant for preparation of suspensions from solid materials and ammonia is shown in Fig. 5. The main features of the plant are the large recirculating pump and the high-intensity mixer. Many plants of this type have annual production greater than 3000 tons of NPK suspensions—such as 11–33–0, 20–10–10, and 7–21–21—and their production rate is about 20 tons/h. Cost studies show that suspensions made from solid materials can be produced about as economically as bulk blends of comparable grades [28].

Future for Fluid Fertilizers

Development of the suspension segment of the United States fluid fertilizer industry, which can use lower cost materials such as solid MAP or DAP and TVA base suspensions 13–38–0 and 9–32–0 as intermediates, helped make fluids cost competitive with dry mixtures. This, plus the demonstrated advantages for fluids, gave rise to a sharp increase in use of suspensions in the late 1970s. There will be an increased use of lower cost solids to produce suspensions along with further improvements in suspension application equipment for row or starter fertilizer application. The narrowing of the retail price gap between fluids and dry fertilizers coupled with advantages to the farmer, such as overall convenience, relieving critical labor constraints, and making better use of limited investment capital, suggest that the use of fluids will continue to grow more rapidly than the total market.

Growth of suspensions will continue higher than for clear liquid (solution) mixtures because of their lower cost and the increasing impurities content of wet-process acid that will make production of high-grade clear liquids more difficult and expensive.

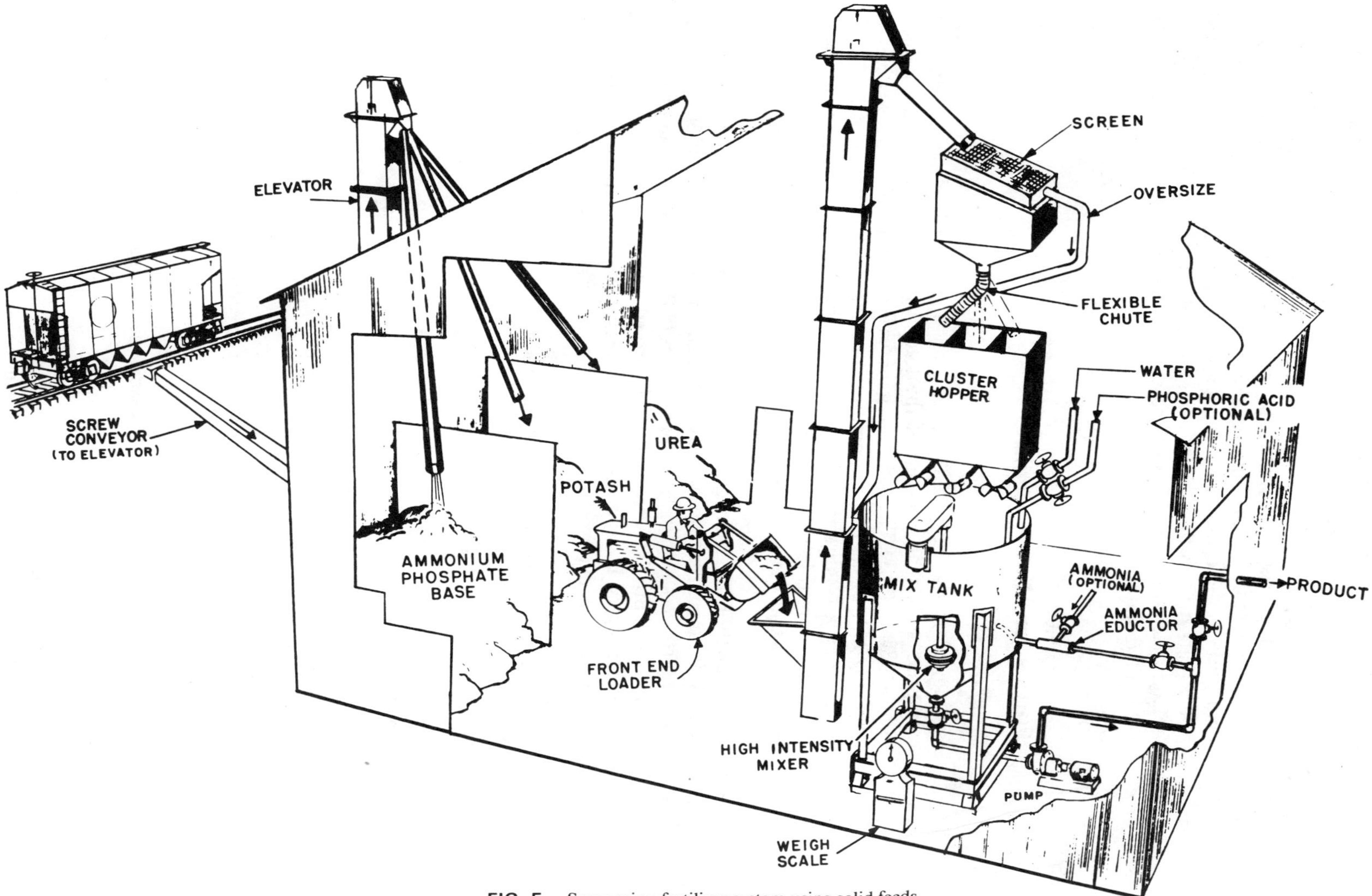

FIG. 5. Suspension fertilizer system using solid feeds.

Advantages of fluid fertilizers, including the lower investment for production facilities, ease of preparation and incorporation of additives, convenience of handling, and high reliability of fluid application systems, will contribute to the continued strong growth of fluid fertilizers in the United States market. Growth will continue in several other countries, but fluids will not approach the status of this dynamic segment of the fertilizer industry in the United States.

Future for Mixed Fertilizers

As viewed in the early 1980s, mixed fertilizers are likely to continue to comprise more than one-half of the total nutrients applied in the United States (58% in 1982). The continuing increase in popularity and lower cost of applying anhydrous liquid ammonia and urea-ammonium nitrate (UAN) solution (31% N) directly will continue to erode the proportion of nitrogen applied as mixed fertilizers. The proportion of mixed fertilizers used in the world is likely to decrease only slowly below the 64% of total nutrients applied in 1982.

Production and use of granular mixed NPK fertilizers in the United States are likely to continue to decrease gradually below the level of 30% of total mixed fertilizers held in 1981. Bulk blends (54% in 1981) and fluid fertilizers (17% in 1981) are likely to continue in growth to higher percentages of total mixed fertilizers. The growth of fluids is likely to be at a higher rate, especially for suspensions that were the only type of fertilizers showing real growth in the early 1980s.

The growth of both bulk-blending and fluid fertilizers will continue to be slow throughout the world.

References

1. *Fluid Fertilizers*, Tennessee Valley Authority, Muscle Shoals, Alabama, 1984, Chap. I.
2. R. D. Young, *Production of Compound Fertilizers from Intermediates in Local Plants* (TVA Circular Z-30), Tennessee Valley Authority, Muscle Shoals, Alabama, September 1971, pp. 5–12.
3. Ref. 2, pp. 12–20.
4. Ref. 2, pp. 34–35
5. R. D. Young and C. H. Davis, "Phosphate Fertilizers and Process Technology," in *The Role of Phosphorus in Agriculture*, American Society of Agronomy, Crop Science Society of America, and Soil Science Society of America, Madison, Wisconsin, 1980, pp. 204–210.
6. *Fertilizer Manual*, International Fertilizer Development Center and United Nations Industrial Development Organization, 1979, pp. 203–210.
7. Ref. 6, pp. 263–265.

8. R. G. Lee, M. M. Norton, and H. G. Graham, "Urea-Ammonium Phosphate Production Using the TVA Melt-Type Granulation Process," in *Proceedings of the 24th Annual Meeting of the Fertilizer Industry Round Table 1974*, Washington, D.C., 1975, pp. 79–86.
9. R. D. Young, G. C. Hicks, and C. H. Davis, "TVA Process for Production of Granular Diammonium Phosphate," *J. Agr. Food Chem., 10*, 442–447 (November-December 1962).
10. R. D. Young and G. C. Hicks, "Production of Monoammonium Phosphate in a TVA-Type Ammonium Phosphate Granulation System," *Commer. Fert. 114*(2), 26–27 (1967).
11. Unpublished TVA data.
12. *Commercial Fertilizers*, USDA Crop Reporting Board, Washington, D.C. (November 1982).
13. L. D. Yates, F. T. Nielsson, and G. C. Hicks, "TVA Continuous Ammoniator for Superphosphates and Fertilizer Mixtures, Part I," *Farm Chem., 117*, 38, 41, 43, 45, 47, 48 (July 1954); "Part II," *Ibid., 117*, 34, 36–38, 40–41 (August 1954).
14. F. P. Achorn and J. S. Lewis, *Producing Granular Fertilizers* (TVA Circular Z-18), Tennessee Valley Authority, Muscle Shoals, Alabama, May 1970.
15. *Pipe-Cross Reactor—Technical Update* (TVA Circular Z-95), Tennessee Valley Authority, Muscle Shoals, Alabama, June 1979.
16. F. P. Achorn and D. G. Salladay, "Pipe-Cross Reactor Eliminates the Dryer," *Farm Chem., 139*(7), 34, 36, 38 (July 1976).
17. T. P. Hignett, *Bulk Blending of Fertilisers: Practices and Problems* (Proc. No. 87), The Fertiliser Society of London, 1965.
18. G. Hoffmeister, "Compatibility of Raw Materials in Blended Fertilizers—Segregation of Raw Materials," in *Proceedings of the 12th Annual Meeting of the Fertilizer Industry Round Table 1962*, Washington, D.C., 1963, pp. 83–88.
19. R. D. Young, "Providing Micronutrients in Bulk-Blended, Granular, Liquid, and Suspension Fertilizer," *Commer. Fert., 118*(1), 21–24 (1969).
20. Y. C. Smith and J. E. Culp, "Service Sells Fluid Fertilizers in Texas," *Fert. Solutions, 22*(6), 86, 88, 90, 92, 94 (November-December 1978).
21. *Application of Fluid Fertilizers* (TVA Circular Z-6), Tennessee Valley Authority, Muscle Shoals, Alabama, April 1970.
22. T. P. Hignett, *Trends in Technology* (Proc. No. 108), Fertiliser Society of London, 1969.
23. E. O. Huffman and E. L. Newman, "Polyphosphates are Revolutionizing Fertilizers. Part IV, Behavior and Outlook," *Farm Chem., 133*(2), 28–30, 32 (1970).
24. R. S. Meline, R. G. Lee, and W. C. Scott, "Use of a Pipe Reactor in Production of Liquid Fertilizers with Very High Polyphosphate Content," *Fert. Solutions, 16*(2), 32–45 (March-April 1972).
25. F. P. Achorn, H. L. Kimbrough, and F. J. Myers, "Latest Developments in Commercial Use of the Pipe-Reactor Process," *Fert. Solutions, 18*(4), 8–9, 12, 14, 16, 20–21 (July-August 1974).
26. H. L. Balay, "Savings Big Attraction for Using Solids in Suspensions," *Fert. Solutions, 21*(2), 86, 88, 90, 92 (March-April 1977).
27. *Phosphorus Potassium, 95*, 41–42 (May-June 1978).
28. H. L. Balay and D. G. Salladay, "Producing and Marketing Suspensions from Solids," *Custom Applicator, 9*, 36–38, 40, 43 (February 1979).
29. G. Hoffmeister, S. C. Watkins, and J. Silverberg, "Bulk Blending of Fertilizer Material: Effect of Size, Shape, and Density on Segregation," *J. Agric. Food Chem., 12*, 64–69 (January-February 1964).

RONALD D. YOUNG

Fiberglass

Fiberglass is the technical term applied to products composed of fibers made from glass. The ability to fiberize glass arises from two unique properties of a glass, i.e., the continuous variation of its viscosity with temperature and the high surface tension of molten glass. The word "fiberglass" has evolved to apply to a wide range of products from continuous filament yarns used in reinforcements and the textile industry to wool or noncontinuous fibers used for insulation purposes [3].

These two types of glass fiber differ in their manufacture. Continuous filament fibers are produced by dropping molten glass through a metal bushing with numerous holes and then attenuating the resulting streams by pulling the fibers by winding on a spindle [2]. This type of process is very sensitive to glass purity, and in some operations the glass is manufactured on one facility, then distributed as "marbles" to the filament operations in another facility, the purpose being material control.

Noncontinuous fiber production differs primarily in the method of fiber attenuation; that being accomplished by interaction with a high velocity jet of air, steam, or a gas flame. The requirements of the process on the glass are somewhat less stringent; in fact, some types of mineral fibers are produced in certain areas using slag as the base material. The bulk of this article is concerned with the noncontinuous fiber or "wool" process, beginning with glass formulation.

Glass

Glass is primarily silica, more specifically a solution of various oxides in a silica matrix. Figure 1 contrasts a glass to an SiO_2 crystal on a molecular level. The highly ordered structure of silica is responsible for the high viscosity and difficulty of melting of this material. Other oxides added to the silica lattice serve to weaken network bonding, reducing the viscosity and the required energy to "melt." Pure silica melts at about 3100°F whereas glass, by definition, has no melting point.

Figure 2 illustrates some of the fundamental properties and characteristics of glass as related to producing glass fiber. A plot of the log of viscosity vs temperature reveals a characteristically continuous curve lacking inflection points. The change in viscosity with temperature is reversible along the curve. The location and slope of the curve is determined by glass composition and may be controlled by the addition or deletion of oxides to the solution. Three properties of a glass will be discussed that must be critically controlled in the fiber-forming processes. They are viscosity, the liquidus, and durability.

Viscosity is defined as resistance to flow. Glass viscosity greatly affects the fiber-forming operation, as all processes specify a certain viscosity range. Viscosity also has a profound effect on the amount of energy required to melt

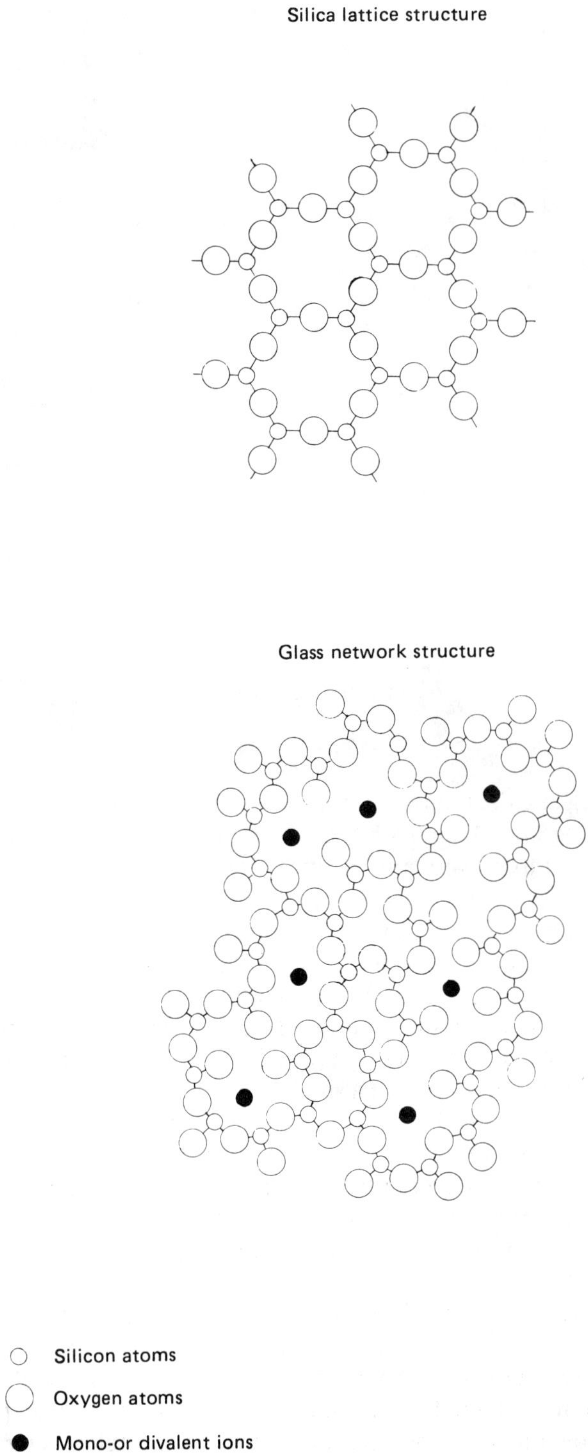

FIG. 1. Comparative network structure representation of a silica crystal and a typical glass.

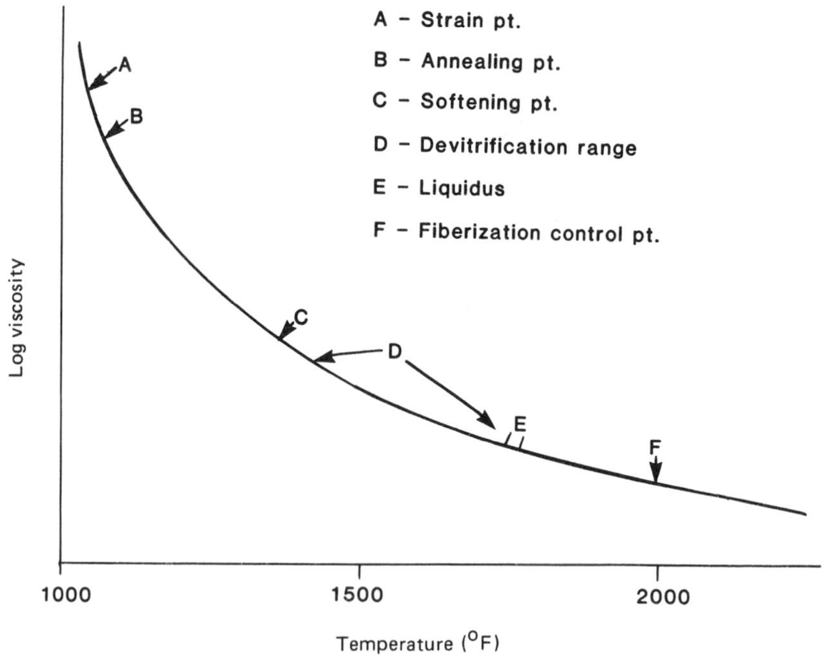

FIG. 2. Typical glass characteristic curve.

the glass, the temperature range within which the glass must be handled, and the rigidity of the fiber itself. As mentioned above, glass viscosity is controlled by composition, and formulations will specify levels of various oxides depending upon what specific properties are desired. Viscosity is so sensitive to composition that variations in raw materials can produce drastic changes in viscosity. Raw material quality assurance and consistency is therefore a necessary step in the overall manufacture.

Because of its effect on the fiberizing process, the viscosity must be closely monitored. The property is usually measured by heating a sample of glass to a desired temperature in a small furnace, then submerging a spindle in the melt and measuring the torque required to rotate the spindle. The torque is related to the viscosity of the glass. A control point is selected near the fiberization viscosity, and comparison is made to the viscosity calculated from the measurement. Deviations are noted and corrected by formulation changes. Some common raw materials and their effects on viscosity are noted in Table 1.

The liquidus is the temperature at which crystal formation can occur if the glass is allowed to remain at this temperature for a certain period of time. There is a range of temperatures (devitrification range) that extends from the softening point to the liquidus within which crystal formation can occur. Below the softening point, however, ion mobility is restricted so as to make crystal formation insignificant. Crystalline phases are unstable above the liquidus. The importance of liquidus point is obvious: the devitrification temperature must be far enough below the fiberizing temperature to prevent

TABLE 1 Effect of Some Oxides on Glass Properties[a]

Oxide	Viscosity	Liquidus[b]	Durability: Water	Durability: Acid
SiO_2	+	±	+	+
Al_2O_3	+	±	+	+
CaO	−	±	+ (slight)	+ (slight)
MgO	− (slight)	±	+ (slight)	+ (slight)
B_2O_3	−	±	+ (slight)	−
Na_2O	−	±	−	+ (slight)

[a]A "+" indicates that addition of the specific oxide will increase or raise the property in question.
[b]The typical effect on liquidus varies with % composition. Smaller amounts of these oxides may tend to lower the liquidus. After a certain point, however, further addition may serve to raise the liquidus point.

formation of crystalline inclusions in the glass fibers which can weaken them. Liquidus is also determined by glass composition.

As applied to glasses used for fiberizing, durability is defined as resistance to chemical attack. This, too, is a function of glass composition and is especially important because of the extremely high surface area in a fibrous glass product. While compatibility with binders is a primary requirement, because of the large surface area subject to attack, even seemingly harmless agents such as water can be of significant concern. Durability is normally reported in a manner similar to corrosion in metals; as a weight loss after a specified period of time.

The data in Table 1 show the effects of some commonly used oxides on the three properties discussed above. Other additives to a batch formulation include compounds called fluxes which assist in defoaming in the melter and oxidizers which aid in elimination of any organic components. The latter are usually nitrates or sulfates.

A particular batch formulation is selected based on its viscosity, liquidus, the durability of its fibers, other desired end-use properties, and cost. Selection of a formulation is usually a tradeoff between batch cost and energy required to melt; these two variables are often at odds. A glass is usually designed with a specific end product in mind. Other glass properties of interest include density, refractive index, color, and strength. Further treatment of these properties is beyond the scope of this article.

Batch Mixing and Transport

Figure 3 shows a typical batch mixing process. Controls in the batch mixing area begin with raw material specification and testing. In light of previous discussions regarding the effect of composition on viscosity, an acceptable glass might be possible, for example, only if the boron content of a certain raw

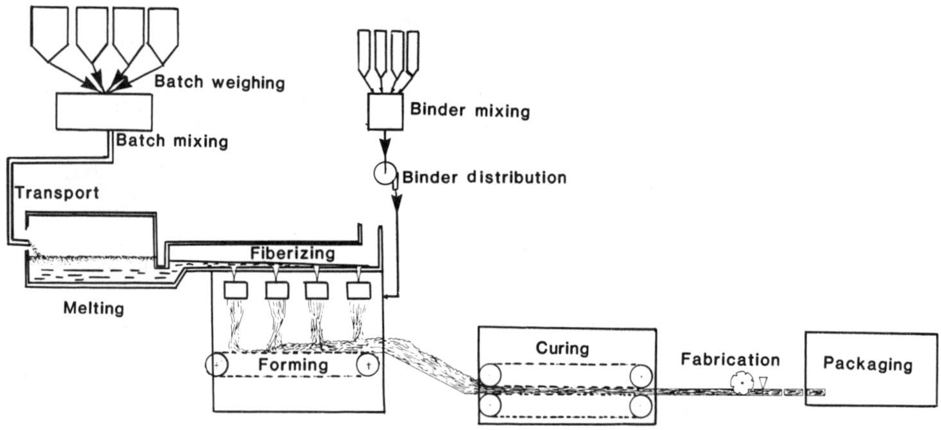

FIG. 3. Schematic of a noncontinuous glass fiber production process (wool).

material is within a specific range. Material outside this range must either be rejected or other formulation changes made to compensate for the anomaly.

It is for this latter reason that the batch mixing system must be flexible in addition to being reliable and accurate. To insure consistent formulation and production, raw ingredients are weighed sequentially and combined into a batch mix. The mixture is then mechanically blended to insure a uniform distribution before transporting to the melter. Transport methods in use include mechanical conveying and pneumatic conveying.

Melter Operation

Figures 4 and 5 illustrate schematically two types of melters in wide use throughout the industry.

Recouperative-type furnaces utilize natural gas or oil as the source of energy. Batch is melted by the heat imparted by the burner flame, a process known as surface melting. Thus the primary design criteria for capacity of such a furnace becomes the surface area of glass exposed to the burners. Heat is recovered from the exhaust gases and used to preheat the combustion air. Even with this measure, however, efficiencies rarely exceed the 20% range, and combustion gases exhausted to the atmosphere can be an environmental concern, forcing the need for equipment primarily to filter out the entrained batch dust prior to discharge.

Electric melters have eliminated the need for a heat recovery system because the batch layer or "blanket" also provides insulation to trap heat in the melt. This type of melter operates on the principle that the resistivity of glass is a function of temperature, varying from nearly infinite at room temperature to some smaller, finite value at melting temperatures [1]. The

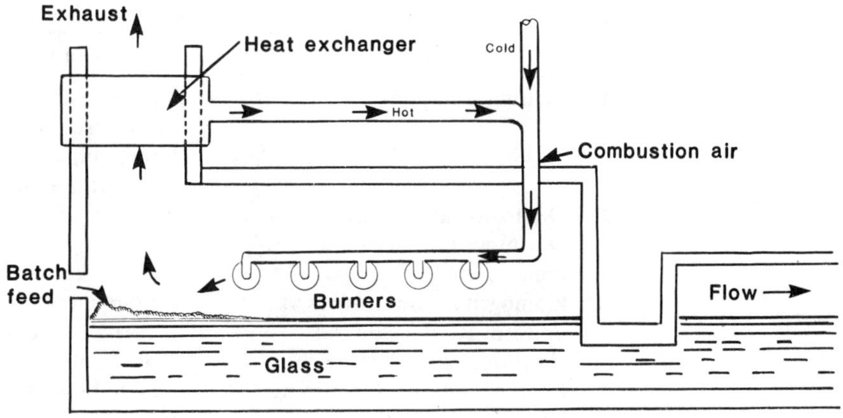

FIG. 4. Recuperative-type melter.

glass is heated by its own resistance to the applied current. The actual melting takes place under glass and the capacity of such a melter is dependent upon the kW (power) applied. The energy conversion efficiency of these types of furnaces can run as high as 65%. Environmental issues are generally less significant on electric melters because of the lack of the high exhaust volumes present with recuperative melters.

Other melter designs found in use are hybrids; part gas/oil, part electric. Selection of a particular design depends upon fuel availability, physical space limitations, economics, and, to some extent, the local environmental laws and regulations.

Controls are necessary to assure that batch is fed into the melter at a rate equal to the desired pull (throughput or glass flow rate out) plus melting losses (dusting and outgassing). A uniform, consistent glass level in the furnace is mandatory to maintain thermal gradients and the pull rate. In electric furnaces the batch crust thickness must be maintained at a specified level and

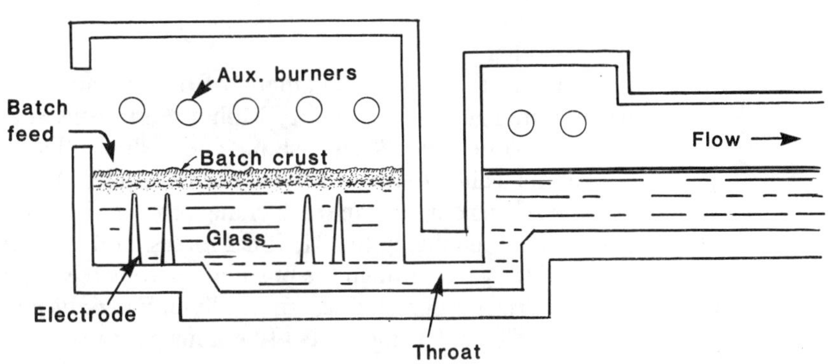

FIG. 5. Electric-type melter.

TABLE 2

Stage	Controls/Variables
1. Melting (solution)	Type of glass (liquidus) Particle size of raw materials Energy input Temperatures underglass
2. Degassing (arises from decomposition of carbonates, etc.)	Addition of fluxes
3. Homogenization (insures uniform RI, density, and eliminates unmelted batch).	Employment of bubblers and currents to control thermal gradients
4. Glass conditioning (attaining a uniform glass at proper temperature for fiberizing)	Length of forehearth Flow rates Heat loss controlled by additional burners

is controlled by the power fed to the melter and by the pull. Spreader devices are employed to distribute the batch evenly over the crust surface to assist in control of level.

The melting operation can be resolved into four stages, the latter two taking place in a region downstream of the melter called the forehearth. At each stage, different variables or mechanisms are used to control the process (Table 2).

The end objective of the melting operation is to deliver a glass of uniform composition, specific viscosity, and temperature, and at a constant flow rate to the fiberizer.

Fiberizing Operations (Wool)

Types of processes used to fiberize glass into wool products vary within the industry [3, 5]. The newest type of operation is the rotary-type process discussed here.

Refer to Fig. 3 for a schematic of the overall fiberizing operation. The force behind glass flow is gravity. Molten glass drops into a fiberizer through a flow control device called a bushing. The bushing is basically a sized hole lined with a metal alloy to which current can be applied. The subsequent heating or cooling of this device imparts a change to the viscosity of the surface of the glass stream, changing the frictional forces, and allowing more or less "slippage" of the glass through the bushing, thereby regulating flow.

A fiberizer is depicted schematically in Fig. 6. Its purpose is to turn liquid glass into fibers. The method of fiberizing glass involves dropping the molten glass through a bushing into a rotating assembly called a spinner. The spinner can be described as a flat metal cylinder with a solid base and a perforated wall

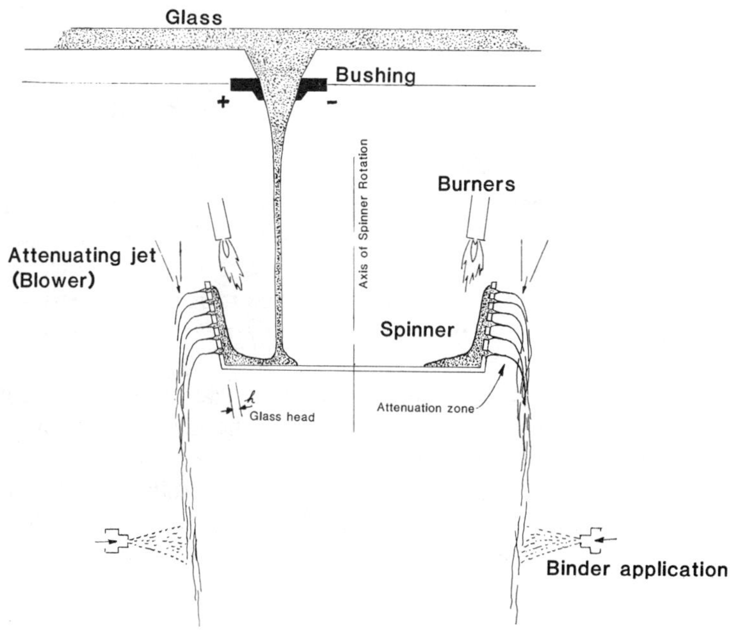

FIG. 6. Typical rotary fiberizer schematic.

(Fig. 6). The spinner is continually heated and rotates at a velocity which causes the molten glass to migrate from the bottom up the sides by centrifugal force. The glass is forced through the holes in the spinner wall by the same force and exits the spinner as thick fibers. These "primary" fibers are attenuated to the desired diameter by drag forces provided by a high velocity jet of air or steam which also directs the fibers downward where they are cooled, sprayed with binder, and collected on a moving conveyor.

There are generally several fiberizer assemblies per forehearth, and collection of fibers is facilitated by providing suction through perforations in the collecting conveyor. The fiberglass "pack" is then transported out of the fiber-forming area to curing and fabrication operations.

Process control throughout the fiber-making operation is geared toward producing a good quality fiber, as this is the key to obtaining a finished product with the required thermal and physical characteristics. Two properties that are routinely monitored are fiber diameter and fiber length. Of the two, control of fiber *diameter* is more critical as far as thermal properties are concerned; length relates more to pack strength and resilience. The behavior of glass in the spinner is an important consideration in controlling fiber properties. Perhaps the most critical item is the maintainence of a specific head of glass against the spinner walls. This assures equal usage (and wear) of all holes. Since fiber diameter is a function of thoughput per hole which is dependent upon hole diameter, an understanding of fiberizing physics is necessary to effect proper spinner design [4].

Glass head h can be described by

$$h \sim \frac{\nu F l}{\rho^2 r \omega^2 d^4 N}$$

where glass of viscosity ν and density ρ flows at rate F through spinner of radius r, wall thickness l with N holes of radius d, and rotational velocity ω. Dependence upon the viscosity, and its relation to the temperature of delivery to the spinner, has been discussed previously. Again this point to good control of raw materials and the batch mixing and melting processes; the glass must reach the spinner at the fiberizing temperature at a predetermined viscosity. Note the effect of hole size ($h \sim d^{\frac{1}{4}}$). This stems from the appearance of the cross-sectional area term (πd^2) twice in the derivation: once in relation to the frictional forces and again in the flow per unit area component. Nearly all spinner alloys that are economical are attacked by molten glass at a rate which is highly temperature dependent. Attack is most prevalent where the largest surface area is exposed to glass flow, i.e., the holes. Hole diameter changes with spinner age, and it is therefore necessary to have the capability to replace spinners on a regular basis. This frequency will be determined by the maximum hole size that will produce an acceptable fiber at process settings within a specified range.

Fiber diameter is also dependent upon the amount of attenuation exerted on the primary fibers. Glass exits the spinner and is attenuated by both centrifugal and drag forces provided by a high velocity jet of air or steam emanating from an assembly known as a blower. Variations within the jet stream coupled with temperature gradients in the vicinity and uneven hole wear (therefore varying throughputs per hole) give rise to the production of a range of fiber diameters and lengths from a particular fiberizer assembly. Careful design and maintainence of the blower system is critical to the control of fiber quality. Other controls relate to the amount of heat applied to the spinner to maintain operating temperature. A partial list of variables affecting the fiberizing process appears in Table 3. In addition to blower design and spinner replacement capability, fiberizer design must include adequate cool-

TABLE 3 Some Fiberizing Process Variables

Glass viscosity
Glass temperature
Glass flow rate (pull)
Number of spinner holes
Hole diameter
Rotation rate of spinner
Temperature of spinner
Attenuation jet velocity and distribution
Glass head in spinner
Temperature distribution in attenuation zone

ing for moving parts. A good design will also provide for measurement/monitoring of some critical process items: pull, glass stream and spinner temperatures, firing system monitoring, and attenuating jet control.

Binders

A binder is applied to the fibers before they are collected into a "pack." The binder upon curing will provide a basis for product integrity and dimensional stability. Some desirable properties of a binder are listed in Table 4. Main components generally include:

1. A resin, most frequently a phenol-formaldehyde or urea-formaldehyde thermosetting polymer. This is the bonding portion of the binder. Desirable properties include low cost, stability (shelf-life), water solubility, and environmental effects.
2. Coupling agents, usually silane-type compounds provide moisture resistance by bonding to both the glass and the organic resins.
3. Additives for pH control insure stability during application and provide proper conditions for cure. They also serve to neutralize alkalinity at the glass fiber surface, thereby affecting product durability.
4. Specialty additives such as dyes for product color and dust suppressants.

A binder solution is usually applied to the fibers through spray tips. The binder must have the proper surface tension to allow wetting of the fibers and subsequent flow to fiber junctions. Small droplets at the junctions will cure upon application of heat, forming a bond between individual fibers which is manifested in the aggregate as pack resilience. Care must be exercised in order that cure takes place only at higher temperatures, and not from exposure to the forming environment. This can be controlled by adjustments made to the resin formulation.

TABLE 4 Desirable Binder Properties

Water soluble
Shelf-life
Low cost
Cure point (temperature much higher than forming temperatures)
Good wetting to fibers
Nonflammable
Noncorrosive
Thermally stable when cured
Water resistant when cured

The most common systems in use for binder mixing are volumetric batch-type systems in which the ingredients are sequentially charged into a mixing tank where agitation and pH adjustment take place. The mixture then passes onto a surge tank for distribution. Level control devices include bubblers, differential pressure cells, and capacitance probes. The thermosetting nature of the binder presents special build-up problems, and any instrumentation in contact with the binder must be maintained. This becomes an important factor in the selection of devices used to measure pH and solids content (or refractive index) of the binders; e.g., standard industrial grade instrumentation can be used only with a flushing system. Some limited success has been experienced with the use of metering pumps (positive displacement) for mixing binder. Maintainence costs are generally higher with this type of system, however, because of the build-up problems.

Positive displacement metering pumps have also found use in binder distribution to the individual fiberizer units. However, distribution is most commonly accomplished by a centrifugal pump through a flow control device, then to a set of spray tips for application to the glass fibers. Flowrators, control valves, and mass flow meters have found widespread use in this application, replacing a simple ball valve and pressure gauge system. Selection of instrumentation must again take into account the build-up problem; output from the device should not drift as the sensor builds-up or plugs. Ease of cleaning and maintainence should be an installation prerequisite. In many instances, the distance from the binder mixing area to the forming area is considerable. Binder distribution systems in this case are staged utilizing surge tanks, recirculating lines, and additional pumps.

Forming and Curing Process

The glass fibers now coated with binder are collected by suction onto a perforated conveyor at the bottom of a semienclosed "hood," the purpose of which is fiber containment. The fibers are deflected mechanically to distribute them evenly across the forming conveyor, allowing a more even cure and uniform product.

Design and selection of the suction fans are based on the desired throughput of the process. Downstream of the fans, the forming exhaust gases are scrubbed or otherwise treated before discharge to the atmosphere; however, there exist systems in which part of the exhaust gases are recycled to the forming process. The benefits of such a system include reduced energy usage and environmental emissions.

From the forming area the pack is transported through a curing apparatus, most commonly a forced convection-type oven in which heated air is passed through the pack to advance the resin. Study of the temperature–time relationship involved reveals that a significant portion of the energy expended goes into driving off water in the binder. For this reason, moisture content of the uncured pack is important and must be maintained at a level that permits complete elimination in the oven, yet high enough to prevent cure at ambient temperatures during the forming process. Control is gained by manipulation of binder dilution.

During the thermosetting process, the pack must be held at the desired thickness of the finished product. This is accomplished by the utilization of top and bottom perforated conveyors or a series of heated rollers. By definition, the curing process is not reversible, and proper cure of the binder will lend resiliency and dimensional stability to the product. Improper cure, however, can lead to problems with product odor, moisture absorption, and performance. It is therefore highly desirable to monitor and control curing temperatures, air flows, and moisture.

Product thickness is controlled in the curing operation by adjustment of the gap between the top and bottom conveyors or rollers. This also provides some control of product density; however, this property is normally varied by maintaining a constant glass pull and raising or lowering the speed of the conveyors from the forming section through the packaging operation. Consequently, more fibers or fewer fibers are laid down per square foot.

Postcuring Operations

After the curing process, the pack is usually passed over a purging or cooling section which draws ambient air through the product to eliminate curing gases and brings the pack temperature down to a level where it can be safely handled. The mechanics of this step vary widely from one operation to the next.

Fabrication of the material depends upon the end use of the product. The cured pack has stiffness and integrity and can be trimmed, slit, and chopped to whatever widths and lengths are required. Again, hardware variation between facilities is considerable; however, trimming and slitting is generally done with circular saw blades and the length dimension controlled by a chopper similar to those used in the paper industry (a hydraulic or pneumatically actuated blade). Any other modifications such as facing application are performed at this point.

Packaging operations will not be discussed in detail due to their diversity. Packaging depends upon the nature of the product and customer requirements, but generally takes the form of a roll-up or a bagger-type operation. Considerations include product compression, ventilation, package weight and dimensions, intended storage conditions, and cost.

References

1. A. G. Pincus and G. M. Dikea, *Electric Melting in the Glass Industry*, Books for Industry, New York, 1976.
2. K. L. Loewenstein, *The Manufacturing Technology of Continuous Glass Fibers*, Elsevier, New York, 1973.
3. J. G. Mohr and W. P. Rowe, *Fiberglass*, Van Nostrand Reinhold, New York, 1978.
4. R. D. Mhaskar and Y. T. Shah, "Stability Analysis of Glass Fiber Spinning," *Glass Technol., 18*(5), 152–158 (October 1977).
5. Roesengarth and Hager, U.S. Patent 2,234,087; J. H. Thomas, U.S. Patent 2,192,944 (1940); Slayter, U.S. Patent 2,431,205 (1947); Stalego, U.S. Patent 2,609,566 (1952); St. Gobain, U.S. Patent 3,215,514 (1965).

M. J. KWASOWSKI

Flavors and Spices (see also Essential Oils)

Introduction

Definition

Flavor is a "distinctive taste; savor," according to the *American Heritage Dictionary of the English Language* [1] or "that quality of something which affects the sense of taste or gratifies the palate: savor; the blend of taste and smell sensations evoked by a substance...in the mouth," according to *Webster's Third New International Dictionary* [2].

There are few, if any, items of food or drink which could be said to be completely without flavor. Large quantities of human effort have gone into making foods and beverages more flavorful–wines and cheeses date back to very early days of mankind.

Many of our most characteristic flavors were developed before there was any underlying theory to explain their creation–the flavor of roast beef, roast pork, bleu cheese, beer. Other flavors existed in nature–raspberry, orange, cherry–without knowledge of which chemical constituents made up the flavor.

It is only in recent years that a sophisticated flavor industry has developed. From small organizations importing vanilla beans, extracting cola nuts or cocoa nibs, and grinding spices, have come large flavor factories making artificial chemicals for use as flavors and sophisticated reaction, enzyme-derived, extracted, and encapsulated flavors.

The line between "flavors" and other ingredients is not clear. Cocoa contributes flavor and is used in flavors, but is considered a food. Monosodium glutamate, disodium inosinate, and disodium guanylate are flavors but are treated separately from a legal and labeling point of view as "flavor enhancers."

Flavors are additives that create or improve flavor of food, tobacco, or other products when used at levels of 0.01–2% depending on the strength of the flavor and level desired in the end product.

Flavor—Taste and Odor

There are four generally recognized taste sensations: sweet, sour, salt, bitter. All the other nuances of flavor are related to odor or aroma in conjunction with the taste sensations.

Overview

This article includes two sections on flavor technology. The section on classical flavor technology highlights the processes which have built the flavor industry–compounding (blending) and extraction–and type of products manufactured–essential oils, oleoresins, essences, resinoids, extracts.

The processes involved in classical flavor technology can be deceptively simple. Yet, each ingredient and the final product must be evaluated subjectively (by taste or smell) to determine its suitability for use. What is supposedly the same pure chemical from different suppliers may be totally different in a flavor formula where minor impurities may have a major impact on the end product.

Under nonclassical flavor technology are included items such as hydrolyzed vegetable protein, monosodium glutamate, soy sauce, enzyme-derived flavors, and reaction products. Other items, such as cocoa, coffee, and tea, might reasonably have been included, but are not.

It is frequently desirable to have a normally liquid flavor in solid form. The section on encapsulation of flavors and powdered flavors deals with this.

Pollution control for the above is discussed in a separate section. Finally, information on the common herbs and spices is provided along with some information on processing.

Classical Flavor Technology

Analytical/Synthesis/Creation

Flavors are generally intended as an imitation of a food found in nature or as it is after processing. Therefore, a logical approach to creating flavors is to analyze natural products to determine the specific chemicals responsible for flavor.

This is done by analyzing for all chemicals present in a natural product and submitting samples of the pure chemicals isolated to someone who can make a judgment as to potential use in flavors. The person who makes that judgment is a flavorist or flavor chemist. The analytical job is made easier by the use of modern gas chromatography, spectral analysis, and mass spectrometry.

Those chemicals that have merit in flavors are synthesized. Based on projected costs for the chemical, a determination can be made as to whether its cost/use justifies the additional efforts to manufacture.

Flavor creation is normally the province of flavorists or flavor chemists. Flavorists have by experience of tasting and smelling different combinations of chemicals learned to create flavors having a particular nuance that might be requested by a customer. For example, a strawberry flavor may be requested that is wild, fresh, cooked, or jamlike in flavor and suitable for use in beverages, yogurt, candy, or dessert. Thus, both the type of flavor required and the end use must be weighed in creating a flavor.

Compounding

Compounding or blending is at the heart of the traditional flavor business. The necessary equipment may range from a portable mixer attached to a 55-gal stainless steel drum to large stainless tanks with fixed agitators.

Order of addition of ingredients may be critical. The diluent (vegetable oil, propylene glycol, ethanol) is charged to the tank. The key flavor chemicals are then added and mixed until a uniform solution results.

Flavors frequently have 15–30 separate ingredients. Sometimes subformulas are involved. A subformula may be used for the following reasons:

1. Special processing is required (e.g., extraction)
2. It is desirable to weigh certain chemicals separately for accuracy
3. Standard items made in larger quantities are to be incorporated

Quality control is complex, particularly when several suppliers of a given ingredient are available. Modern analytical equipment can be used to assay purity. The final judgment has to be a subjective one.

Extracts

Extraction of botanicals has a long history. Cola nuts, vanilla beans, coffee beans, and cocoa nibs are some products that are extracted for flavor use. After extraction, the extract is normally concentrated by vacuum distillation to yield the final extract.

Selection of solvents is empirical, based on product quality as well as yield, within the limitation of food purity of final product. The solvent or mixture of solvents is generally referred to as the "menstruum" in flavor manufacturing.

The final solvent used must be ethanol, propylene glycol, glycerin, or some other food-grade solvent. Ethanol–water mixtures are frequently used.

Most flavor extraction is done by the percolation technique. The botanical to be extracted is chopped or ground. A tank or drum with a perforated plate acting as a false bottom is lined with cloth. The ground botanical is either placed onto the cloth-lined bottom directly or is placed in a cloth sack. The tank is then filled with solvent. The solvent can be still or recirculated with a pump. Duration of extraction is 3–5 days with a menstruum of 40–50% ethanol by volume.

A typical percolation procedure is as follows [3]:

1. Chop or grind botanical
2. Charge percolation tank with botanical
3. Fill tank with menstruum
4. Let stand 3 days
5. On the fourth day, begin to draw off extract slowly as additional menstruum is added to maintain level
6. Extract is drawn off until flow is negligible and additional menstruum is consumed
7. Percolator is charged with water
8. After 24 h, draw off water extract until volume of water extract is equal to the total alcoholic extract
9. Blend alcohol and aqueous extracts and package

Many variations are possible in the above procedure. Each manufacturer has his own process. Batch countercurrent extractions are possible when flavor volume justifies the capital required.

Concentration of the extracts is possible to produce "folded extracts." This can be done by using an extract as the menstruum or by distillation. If distillation is the method of choice, a relatively nonvolatile solvent such as propylene glycol or glycerin is sometimes added to protect the concentrate from scorching.

Oleoresins

Oleoresin is a term applied to flavor extract when a pure, low boiling solvent is used to recover volatile and nonvolatile flavor constituents from botanicals with complete removal of the solvent.

The botanical is mixed with part of the solvent during grinding to minimize loss of volatiles by keeping the plant material cool. Extraction can be done in the same type of percolator described under "Extracts." Extracts are concentrated by vacuum distillation with solvent recovery. The concentrate is then purified of water and solvent by addition of ethanol followed by distillation [3].

Nonclassical Flavor Technology

Hydrolyzed Vegetable Protein

Hydrolyzed vegetable protein (HVP) is made by hydrolyzing or digesting protein from soybeans, corn, wheat, or another vegetable source. The protein is selected according to availability, cost, and end use application (e.g., beef, chicken, veal, pork flavors for use in soup, gravy, dry mix, canned, or other end use).

HVP is made by hydrolysis of protein with hydrochloric acid, followed by neutralization with sodium hydroxide, cooling, filtration, and concentration. Product is available as a liquid at about 40% solids, paste at 85% solids, or as a powder [4–6].

Flavor of HVP will be a function of proteins used, degree of hydrolysis, exposure to heat during processing, and aging before filtration.

Concentration of HVP is normally done in vacuum pan evaporators. Powdered HVP is prepared by spray drying or vacuum drying.

Autolyzed Yeast

Autolyzed yeast has many of the same end uses as HVP. It has a brothy, meaty character suitable for soup, gravy, and other meat flavor applications. Commercial autolyzed yeast is made from *Saccharomyces cerevesiae*. Both bakers yeast and brewers yeast are strains of this species of yeast.

Much development work has been done to use the by-product yeast from the brewing industry, although yeast can be grown specifically for autolyzed yeast flavors.

Yeast is autolyzed by heating the cells to 40–60°C. This temperature is high enough to kill the yeast cells without inactivating the cell enzymes. The enzymes then attack the protein and nucleic acids present in the cell to produce peptides, polypeptides, amino acids, nucleotides, and nucleosides. The flavor ingredients can then be washed out of the cell with the insoluble cellular material separated by centrifugation [13].

Other variations include plasmolysis and hydrolysis. In plasmolysis, salt is added to rupture the cells by osmotic pressure differences. In hydrolysis, hydrochloric acid is used to rupture the cells.

The yeast extract is separated from the cell bodies by counter-current washing with three or four centrifugal separators. The yeast extract (5–8% solids) may be polish filtered or further treated to meet the particular flavor standard.

The extract is concentrated under vacuum either in batch vacuum pans, in continuous systems, or combined continuous and batch systems. The product may be concentrated to 80% solids if a paste is desired or dried to a powder in a spray dryer or vacuum oven. Spray drying is very difficult, and special equipment is needed to cope with the extreme hygroscopicity of autolyzed yeast.

Monosodium Glutamate, Nucleic Acids

Monosodium glutamate (MSG) has wide usage as a "flavor enhancer" compatible with a wide range of end products—soups, gravies, dry mixes.

MSG can be produced by [14]:

1. Extraction from natural sources—flour, corn, soybeans, peanuts, molasses
2. Fermentation—conversion of glucose and urea or ammonia by bacteria
3. Chemical synthesis from acrylonitrile

Most MSG is made by fermentation. One of the advantages of fermentation is that the L-glutamic acid optical isomer is produced rather than the racemic mixture produced synthetically. The L-glutamic acid isomer is useful as a flavor enhancer while the D-isomer is not.

The nucleic acids, 5′-inosinic (IMP), and 5′-guanylic acids (GMP) are useful as flavor enhancers in a way similar to MSG. They are often used in combination with MSG in food.

IMP and GMP can be produced from ribonucleic acid present in yeast. Yeast cells are ruptured by heat treatment and osmotic effects of salt. Enzymes are then applied to cleave the cell RNA into its component nucleic acids. This product can be concentrated and dried. IMP can also be made by chemical phosphorylation of inosine [14].

Soy Sauce

Soy sauce is selected as an example of the class of reaction or enzyme-derived flavors. There are two pathways to an end product which may be called soy sauce (although the flavors are different):

1. Acid hydrolysis of ground soy flakes and wheat by refluxing with hydrochloric acid followed by neutralization and aging in hardwood tanks
2. Fermentation or enzyme hydrolysis of protein followed by aging and filtration [7]

The latter process has been practiced in Japan and the Far East for 1000 years. A plant was recently opened in the United States for the manufacture of soy sauce by the Japanese process.

In the fermentation process, defatted soybean flakes and wheat are heat treated to pasteurize and gelatinize starches. The solids are adjusted to the proper moisture, spread onto a belt conveyor, and innoculated with pure cultures of mold. The mold culture is grown on sterilized wheat and soy.

The innoculated grains are spread onto perforated propagating beds. Warm moist air flows through these beds during a 3-day fermentation period. The enzymes elaborated by the mold cultures hydrolyze proteins to peptides and amino acids and the starches into sugars.

After the mold fermentation period, the fermented grains are charged to yeast fermentation tanks. A brine solution and pure yeast cultures are added. An aerated fermentation continues for 6 months. During this fermentation, hydrolysis of proteins and starches continues. At the same time, sugars are converted to alcohols by the yeast.

As the fermentation progresses, lactobacillae take over, producing lactic and other organic acids. The alcohols and acids react to form the esters which are important constituents of many flavors.

After fermentation, the soy sauce is recovered by filtration and/or pressing. The filter cake is sold for animal feed [8].

Enzyme-Derived Flavors

Soy sauce is a well-documented case of enzyme-derived flavors. Many food flavors are derived from enzymes and/or microorganisms—cheese, cabbage, cucumber, yogurt, Japanese natto, Indonesia Tempeh, and certain meat products such as Lebanon bologna [9].

With the advent of highly purified enzymes it has been possible to apply concentrated enzymes directly to increase flavor strength or improve flavor. In the dairy area this has been done with cheese, milk fat, and yogurt; in other areas this technology has been applied to rice, soybean milk, fish, and apple wine [10].

This technology has been used extensively in the cheese area. An entire new industry has grown up to manufacture enzyme-modified cheese. The advantages of enzyme-modified cheese are:

1. It can be used directly as a flavor in snacks, casseroles, macaroni and cheese, and cheese dips.
2. It can be used in processed cheese to replace some aged cheese with unaged cheese to reduce costs.

The technology for producing enzyme-modified cheese is highly proprietary. The key to successful manufacture of this product lies in selecting a battery of enzymes to engender necessary flavor and rigidly controlling conditions (i.e., temperature, time, pH) so that the enzymes are effective.

The technology used for cheese can be applied to related products—butter, cream, milk.

Reaction Products

In reaction products, concentrated flavors are made by blending precursors of flavor chemicals and heat treating the reactants. This area of flavors developed from observation of how natural flavors are made. For example, roast beef flavor is developed when raw beef is roasted. This flavor is strongest where the beef is exposed to the highest heat—on the surface—and near surface beef fat.

By analogy, one could attempt to make a natural or artificial beef flavor by reacting protein and fat at high temperatures. Many flavors are indeed manufactured by this approach. Protein–fat, amino acids–fat, amino acids–sugar, protein–sugar–fat, etc. are systems developed to produce flavors. The carbonyl-amine Maillard reaction is used in many reaction products. Heat is normally required for these reactions to proceed. This can be done in open or closed kettles or by reflux.

Other flavors can be made by analogies similar to that of roast beef.

Powdered Flavors

Flavors in powder form are necessary for many applications—dry mixes (gravy, casseroles, gelatin, pudding), snacks, dry beverages, or for handling reasons when a user of flavor prefers to handle a powder rather than a liquid.

Powdered flavors can be produced by encapsulation and drying (homogenization followed by spray drying, for example) or by "plating," i.e., blending of liquid or pastes into solids.

Spray Drying

In spray drying an emulsion of flavor oil, carrier (normally a polymer such as dextrin, gum arabic, starch, gelatin), and water is prepared. This is normally done by addition of the carrier to water (hot or cold, depending on the carrier), dispersion of carrier, addition of the flavor oil, mixing, and homogenization.

Homogenization may be done by simple mixing (least adequate procedure), high shear mixing (either with in-tank homogenization equipment such as Effenbach, Premier, Gifford-Wood mills, or special agitator blades on a conventional shaft), sonic homogenizers, or valve-impactor type such as the Manton-Gaulin homogenizer.

The purpose of homogenization is to reduce oil droplet diameter to 1–3 μm. Smaller oil droplet diameters result in lower oil loss in spray drying, minimize separation of oil during drying, and minimize surface oil that can lead to less shelf stability due to oxidation.

A typical spray drying formulation for 20% oil—a common level in the flavor industry—follows:

77	parts flavor oil
308	parts gum arabic
615	parts water
1000	parts total

Water levels vary for different types of carriers and are selected based on the type of spray dryer to be used. Most standard spray dryers cannot handle a viscosity much above 120 cP. Spray drying solids level is normally 30–40%.

There is a wide range of spray dryer designs available and any type of spray dryer could, of course, be constructed to a particular design. Spray-dried flavors have been produced on all standard types of dryers. There are three common types of spray systems:

1. Centrifugal wheel or disk
2. Single fluid (pressure)
3. Two-fluid (air atomization)

Dryer air flow can be either laminar or turbulent. In standard dryers the centrifugal wheel atomizer is normally coupled with turbulent air flows in a dryer that has a height-to-diameter ratio of roughly 1/1. Such a dryer is shown in Fig. 1.

The single fluid and two fluid nozzles are generally coupled with laminar air flow towers with a height-to-diameter ratio of roughly 5/1.

Dryer temperatures range from inlet air temperatures of 300–500°F to outlet temperatures of 160–230°F. Temperatures are set depending on properties of the flavor oil, hygroscopicity of carrier, and type of dryer.

Particle size of the dried powder is a function of dryer design and atomization conditions. The latter can be varied by changing the revolutions per minute of the centrifugal disk or the nozzle diameter in pressure or two fluid atomization. Most flavors are in the range of 50–100 μm in particle size.

There are many spray-dried flavors sold that are not based on flavor oils, but on flavor solids. These include fruit juices, flavors containing hydrolyzed

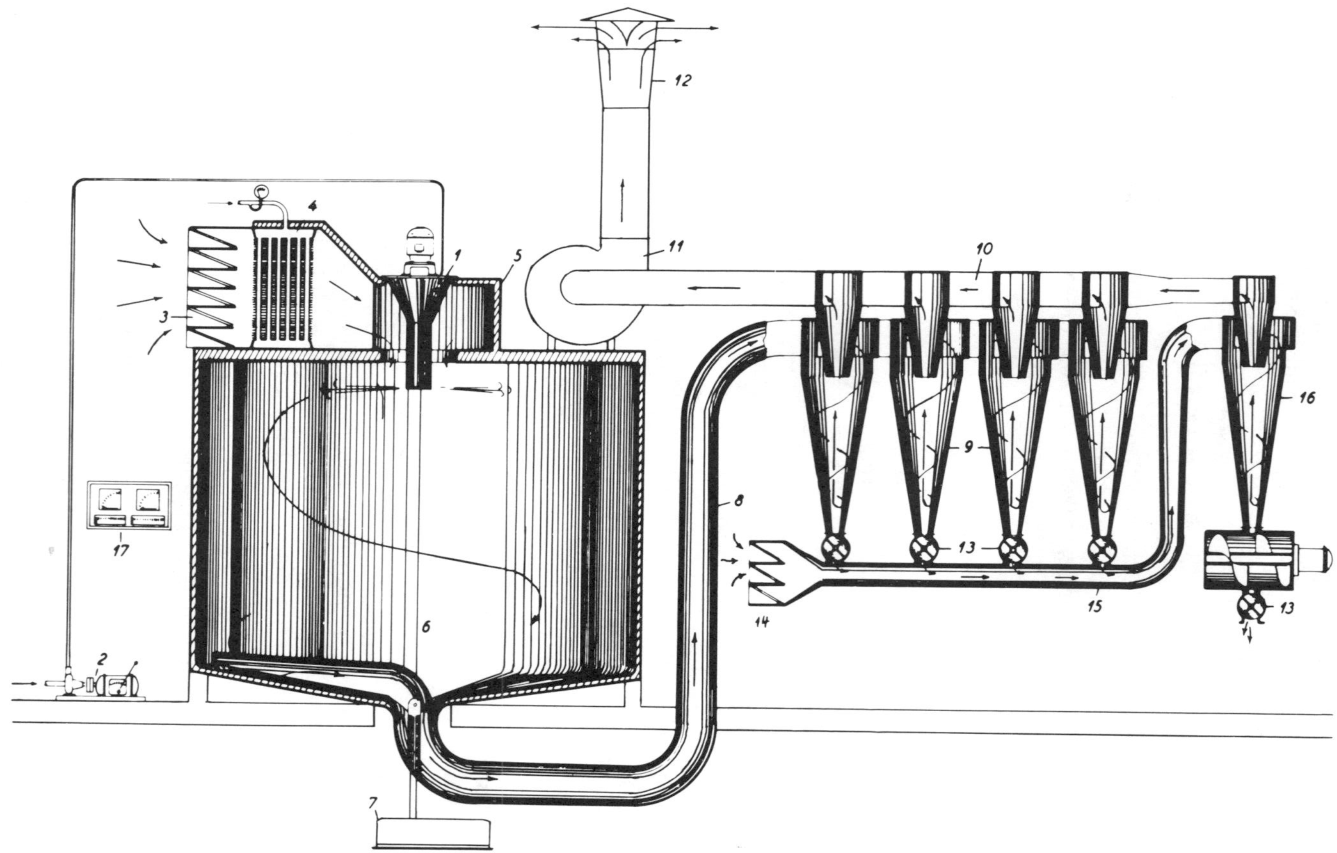

FIG. 1. Anhydro spray dryer with centrifugal wheel atomization. (1) Centrifugal wheel atomizer. (2) Feed pump, positive displacement. (3) Inlet air filters. (4) Steam air heater (can be direct fired gas, indirect fired oil, electric, or combinations thereof). (5) Hot air distributor. (6) Cylindrical drying chamber with a nearly flat bottom. (7) Pneumatic powder collector and discharger. (8) Powder conveying duct. (9) Primary collection cyclones, single or multiple depending on dryer capacity. Multiple cyclones are in parellel. (10) Exhaust air duct (include H_2O vapors and small percent of powders and odors). (11) Exhaust fan. (12) Exhaust stack. (13) Rotary powder discharge valves. (14) Powder cooling air filter. (15) Powder cooling conveying duct. (16) Final collection cyclone and whirl trap. (17) Control panel. Note: A wet scrubber or other pollution control device is normally inserted between No. 11 and 12. Heat escaping out the stack can also be recovered by use of a heat exchanger between No. 12 and No. 3 to close the loop. (Courtesy Anhydro, Inc.)

vegetable protein, and flavors containing sugar. In these cases, homogenization is not necessary. Drying conditions relate to flavor effects at the different temperatures and hygroscopicity of the flavor powder.

Dryers designed to handle hygroscopic flavor materials frequently use rotary air brooms or air curtains to keep the chamber walls clear, powder cooling after drying, and dehumidification of dryer air.

Each type of product is a special case. Products containing sugar may dry well, but sugar-containing products at low pH, e.g., fruit juices, may dry considerably less well in a given system. Frequently, a nonhygroscopic carrier must be used to facilitate spray drying.

Freeze Drying

Freeze drying processes have been well developed for the coffee industry. However, drying costs are considerably higher than for spray drying, especially for comparatively low volume products such as flavors.

In freeze drying the product—coffee, tea, flavor emulsion—is prepared at the highest possible solids level. This product is then frozen either by freezing in place or by freezing dropwise in liquid refrigerant. Once in the freeze-drying chamber, vacuum is applied to reduce the chamber pressure to less than 100 μm. While under vacuum, temperatures are gradually increased until all moisture is evaporated.

For many products, greater flavor retention is observed than in conventional dryer operations. There are particular advantages when it is desirable to retain a certain shape or texture—freeze-dried strawberries, for example.

The texture advantage may work against quality in a flavor because the product normally has to be milled to achieve the particle size normally required for a powdered flavor.

''Plating'' or Blending

"Plating" or blending is a time-honored and inexpensive way to prepare powdered flavors. The simplest kind of blending is powder–powder blending. In that case, two or more powdered ingredients are blended to uniformity. For example, a chocolate flavor may be made by blending vanillin (a synthetic vanilla flavor) and cocoa powder. In this case the particle size of the vanillin would have to be reduced by milling before or after blending to be compatible with cocoa powder which is quite fine (about 200 mesh). However, the blending operation is not complex. Simple ribbon- (Fig. 2) or screw-type (Fig. 3) (Nauta, etc.) blenders are adequate. The major variable to be determined is mixing time for each blender size (which will increase with size).

For more complex blending procedures, e.g., blending of pastes onto powders, higher power blenders are required. Vee blenders (Fig. 4) with high shear dispersion bars, high shear ribbon blenders (Litteford-Lodige, Day Turbulent, etc.), are necessary.

Since ingredients may be of different particle size, milling is sometimes necessary. The simplest type of hammer mill may be suitable for easy-to-grind

FIG. 2. Ribbon blender. (Courtesy J. H. Day Co.)

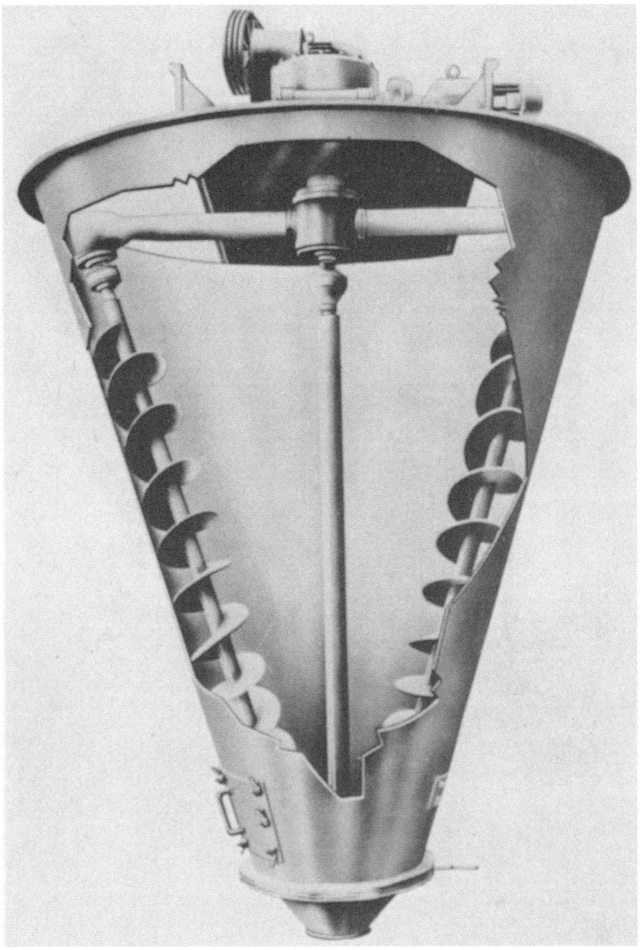

FIG. 3. Nauta blender. (Courtesy J. H. Day Co.)

powders, while air-fed or chilled mills may be necessary for heat-sensitive or sticky products.

Spices, for example, are sometimes ground in mills chilled with carbon dioxide "snow" or liquid nitrogen to minimize degradation of oil.

Pollution Control

Pollution problems and control procedures for the flavor industry will be similar to those of other industries except that odor intensity is high for flavor chemicals in general and volumes are low in comparison to the chemical processing industry in general.

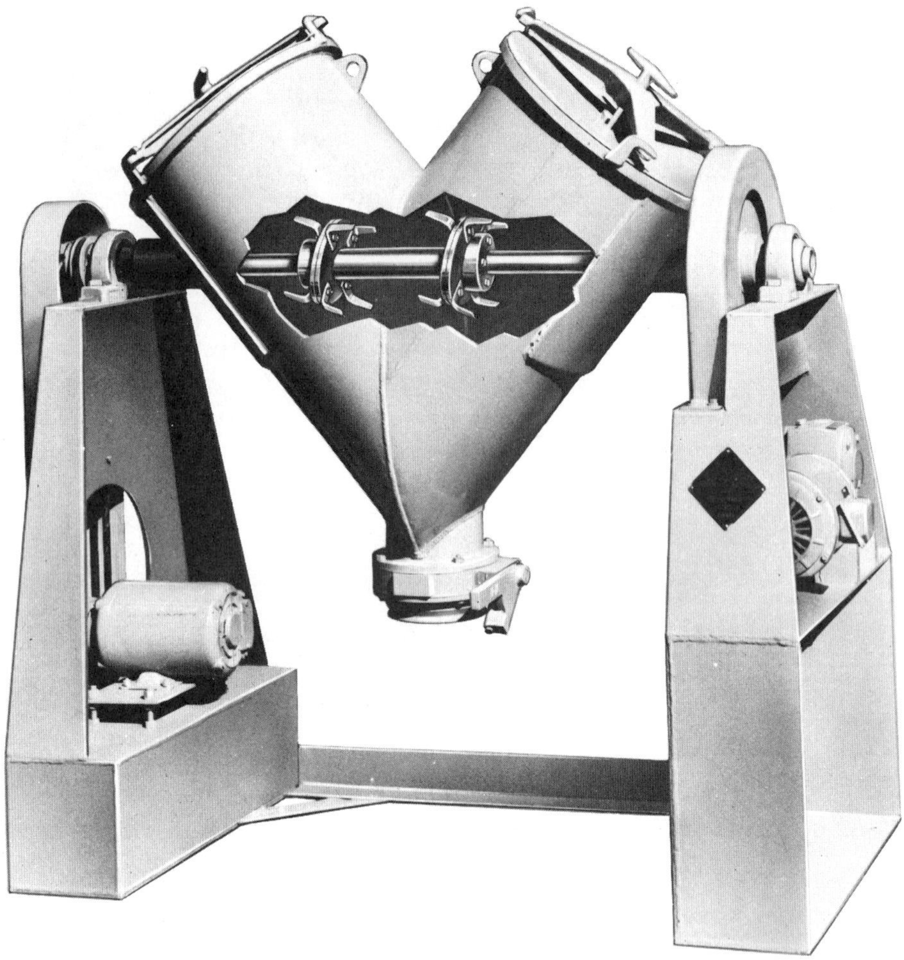

FIG. 4. Vee blender. (Courtesy Patterson-Kelley Co.)

Most flavor processing is batch rather than continuous. Many different flavors must be made in the same equipment. Therefore, pollution control is also related to avoiding cross-contamination of flavors.

The key to pollution control of flavors is containment. Highly odorous materials must be handled in closed vessels as much as possible. Good manufacturing practices must be strictly enforced—minimize spills, clean up promptly, use spot ventilation as required.

Good general room ventilation coupled with spot ventilation over specific pieces of equipment is vital. Some or all of the exhaust should be further treated.

Any standard pollution control method can be used. However, carbon filters are quite effective in dealing with flavor exhausts which can be high in odor level yet low in mole fraction of flavor chemicals. Methyl mercaptan, as a worst case example, is detectable by smell in parts per billion in air.

Some chemicals are absorbed more irreversibly or in greater quantity than others. Design of weight of carbon beds, number of sections, and maximum air flow must be based on data generated for a given percentage removal of the worst case items involved.

When carbon filters are exhausted, they must be recycled by incineration to destroy all odors. A temperature of 1400–1800°F is required.

Scrubbing of air exhaust can also be valuable, especially when the pollution control system is specific to a given process so that air flow is limited. Scrubbing is more effective when a scrubbing solution exists that is very effective in inactivating odorous chemicals irreversibly. It is very important that the waste from the scrubbing system be truly neutral in odor and cannot be reactivated on addition to the general chemical waste or sewage disposal system.

Incineration is another tool. This is most effective when the exhaust is concentrated. The main application in the flavor area for incineration lies in spray drying exhausts. The exhausts can be incinerated to 1400–1800°F to completely combust the odorous materials. Some of this heat can be recovered to provide the hot air needed for drying. For the flavor industry, this must be indirect means rather than direct use of the incinerated air.

For those operations generating dust, it is desirable to retain as much of the solid materials as possible in the product since it represents good material. In spray drying this is accomplished by use of a series of cyclones. It is more difficult in powder blending. The air stream is normally cleaned with baghouses and scrubbers. Generally product collected in a baghouse is lost unless very large volumes of powder are involved to justify separate baghouse systems for the different classes of flavors.

Spices

Spices are flavoring materials that come from plant material—bark, rhizomes, fruits, seeds, buds. Generally, spices have an essential volatile oil and a bitter, astringent, or pungent nonvolatile component. Herbs are flavoring materials that are derived from plant leaves. A third grouping—actually vegetable—is often included because of its importance to the flavor industry—onion and garlic.

This list of spices is very long. The major spices are discussed below by category. Export volumes of certain spices are shown in Table 1. United States imports of spices are shown in Table 2.

Pungent Spices

This category includes pepper (white and black), capsicum-peppers, and ginger.

Pepper world exports were 268,000,000 lb in the 1980s [11].

Pepper, as with most spices, is grown in tropical areas.

TABLE 1 Exports of Specified Spices and Flavoring Materials by Major Producing Countries 1974–80 (in metric tons) (U.S. Department of Agriculture)[a]

Item and Country	1974	1975	1976	1977	1978	1979	1980
Black and white pepper:							
Brazil	15,491	17,944	19,986	17,099	29,505	25,186	31,964
India	28,569	24,399	17,813	25,892	19,370	20,545	26,795
Indonesia	15,188	14,525	29,481	30,856	37,090	24,986	29,345
Madagascar	2,241	3,461	2,958	3,748	1,137	2,570	[c]
Malaysia[b]	28,933	29,873	34,850	26,795	30,780	36,118	30,709
Sri Lanka	337	96	10	635	1,205	876	945
Vanilla beans:							
Comoros	161	211	124	230	240	170	13
French Polynesia	11	15	7	9	3	3	1
Indonesia	54	237	334	410	389	17	77
Madagascar	1,353	858	1,101	1,713	1,459	437	424
Mexico	15	1	—	8	2	1	[c]
Reunion	9	8	20	12	9	23	8
Uganda	—	—	—	1	—	[c]	[c]
Ginger:							
Fiji	1,248	1,416	1,089	1,815	1,845	1,854	1,496
India	4,770	3,670	4,835	5,453	11,219	14,586	7,022
Jamaica	355	286	535	215	174	133	150
Nigeria	630	664	1,928	2,198	1,759	[c]	[c]
Sierra Leone	210	150	547	541	447	[c]	[c]
Taiwan	6,617	6,697	6,668	7,981	9,726	9,503	10,768
Cloves:							
Madagascar	5,069	22,254	4,739	3,653	14,767	13,513	4,229
Sri Lanka	428	157	478	1,224	471	793	1,208
Tanzania	3,665	7,516	7,242	5,906	1,238	[c]	[c]
Cinnamon:							
Madagascar	412	123	120	276	143	[c]	[c]
Seychelles	1,304	1,100	1,204	[c]	570	483	[c]
Sri Lanka	7,669	4,501	6,794	5,740	6,532	6,980	7,939
Cassia:							
India	1,360	775	817	574	338	188	610
Indonesia	3,000	3,006	4,526	5,192	8,637	10,891	14,576
Taiwan	674	333	485	390	370	103	278
Nutmeg:							
Grenada	1,048	2,037	2,699	2,983	1,973	2,303	1,801
Indonesia	5,031	5,378	5,505	5,372	5,822	6,518	6,501
Sri Lanka	124	132	296	152	395	328	261
Trinidad & Tobago	57	43	51	15	20	33	77
Mace:							
Grenada	144	162	432	222	267	333	302
Indonesia	1,094	1,209	1,258	938	1,248	1,188	1,376
Pimento (allspice):							
Jamaica	2,629	1,757	1,993	2,350	3,015	1,830	1,909
Turmeric:							
India	10,560	8,515	14,830	8,922	7,514	23,969	11,320
Cardamom:							
Guatemala	1,472	1,700	1,883	3,662	4,651	3,444	5,007
India	1,814	1,579	1,634	2,056	2,551	2,453	3,085
Sri Lanka	147	334	162	84	149	179	164

[a]Source: Foreign trade statistics of the respective countries.
[b]Sarawak only.
[c]Data not available.

TABLE 2 United States: Imports of Specified Condiments, Seasonings, and Flavoring Materials, 1980 and 1981 (U.S. Department of Agriculture)[a]

Condiments and Flavoring Materials[b]	1980 Metric tons	1980 1,000 dollars	1981 Metric tons	1981 1,000 dollars
Allspice (pimento)	734.6	1,266.0	813.5	1,436.9
(ground)	0.5	0.3	2.0	3.3
Anise seed	534.0	1,041.7	524.2	1,266.0
Basil	562.4	556.1	744.9	684.2
(other than crude)	2.8	13.6	3.2	17.0
Capers	657.6	2,681.1	757.5	3,709.7
Capsicum or red peppers:				
Anaheim and ancho	712.0	1,264.9	796.0	1,530.4
Other	4,339.1	5,239.9	4,350.9	5.321.5
(ground)	118.5	214.0	171.7	383.4
Caraway seed	3,101.7	3,964.7	3,031.2	3,162.3
Cardamom seed	119.7	777.6	83.7	491.0
Cassia	9,056.0	8,705.9	8,173.1	9,466.8
(ground)	34.2	62.5	269.4	245.5
Celery seed	2,083.7	1,361.9	2,040.9	1,371.0
Cinnamon	877.5	1,667.9	844.4	1,418.2
(ground)	23.4	52.2	44.2	115.6
Cloves	955.0	8,093.9	944.2	8,096.3
(ground)	[c]	0.3	0.3	1.9
Coriander	3,879.6	1,491.7	4,663.4	1,852.8
Cumin seed	3,625.6	5,381.0	4,726.6	6,115.0
Curry and curry powder	191.0	622.6	221.0	749.5
Dill seed	417.9	414.9	537.7	498.8
Fennel seed	1,186.8	969.1	1,416.0	1,268.3
Garlic (dehydrated)	131.9	251.2	118.9	155.7
Ginger	4,078.3	3,391.4	4,324.5	3,859.8
(ground)	92.4	103.6	54.1	66.0
(sweet)	58.8	106.3	54.7	110.2
(candied)	251.1	438.5	181.8	460.6
Laurel (bay) leaves	359.2	648.3	394.0	654.1
(other than crude)	1.9	5.0	1.5	3.0
Mace	210.7	461.1	261.8	532.4
(ground)	2.4	2.6	5.2	10.0
Marjoram	303.9	311.5	343.0	371.6
(other than crude)	—	—	10.9	11.7
Mint leaves	147.2	230.0	214.7	301.1
(manufactured)	53.8	226.0	34.3	175.5
Mustard seed	29,448.4	8,251.5	35,091.2	10,984.8
(ground)	1,290.8	2,076.4	1,123.8	1,806.9
(other)	1,143.0	2,104.5	1,118.2	2,169.8
Nutmegs	2,040.0	4,086.8	2,170.3	3,525.6
(ground)	13.7	40.1	32.2	80.3
Onions (dehydrated)	41.4	63.1	99.6	101.7
Origanum leaves	2,749.1	4,896.7	3,067.9	5,118.7
(other than crude)	89.5	119.3	56.3	68.9
Paprika[d]	3,520.2	6,285.8	4,499.5	7,668.0
Parsley	167.8	159.0	137.9	145.4
(manufactured)	22.7	69.4	44.6	132.5
Pepper, black	29,643.9	50,778.1	28,563.4	36,327.9
Pepper, white	3,193.8	7,690.4	2,503.1	4,455.0
(black and white ground)	11.4	40.8	50.7	153.3

TABLE 2 *(continued)*

Condiments and Flavoring Materials[b]	1980 Metric tons	1980 1,000 dollars	1981 Metric tons	1981 1,000 dollars
Poppy seed	2,660.9	1,910.9	2,842.1	2,336.2
Rosemary	311.4	229.1	267.0	185.0
(other than crude)	0.8	4.6	1.8	8.8
Sage	1,926.2	6,115.6	1,481.7	4,827.6
(ground or rubbed)	27.0	83.9	14.8	56.3
Savory	73.8	132.4	54.1	60.5
(other than crude)	0.1	1.8	0.2	0.9
Sesame seed	31,571.4	33,559.9	37,954.0	35,202.3
Tarragon	27.2	330.5	29.6	286.5
(other than crude)	7.8	26.3	6.9	35.1
Thyme	581.0	1,244.0	577.9	1,043.6
(other than crude)	3.4	10.2	10.3	25.4
Turmeric	1,549.2	1,182.9	1,862.5	1,129.6
Vanilla beans	343.0	18,615.5	640.2	31,248.2
Mixed spices	982.8	1,790.7	847.0	1,860.2
Total	152,346.9	203,919.5	166,308.2	206,962.1

[a]All values refer to FOB country of origin. Source: U.S. Department of Commerce, Horticultural and Tropical Products Division, FAS, USDA, March 1982.
[b]Unground, unless otherwise specified.
[c]50 kilograms or less.
[d]Ground and unground.

In 1981 the United States imported 28,563 metric tons of black pepper and 2503 metric tons of white pepper representing $36,327,900 and $4,455,000, respectively. This is the largest spice import in dollar volume [12].

The sharp pungent taste of pepper is caused in large part by the alkaloids piperine and piperidine and the resin chavicine.

Pepper is produced from berries which are picked green for black pepper or ripe for white pepper. For black pepper, the berries are piled into heaps where they ferment and then they are spread out to dry in the sunlight. For white pepper the ripe berries are washed and macerated to remove the hull. The dehulled berries are then dried in the sunlight.

The dried peppercorns are ground to yield the familiar pepper product. Grinding normally occurs in the importing country because the ground product has a short shelf-life.

Capsicum peppers are used in paprika and cayenne powder. The nonvolatile pungent ingredient is capsaicon. Ginger is the washed and dried rhizome of a plant. The nonvolatile pungent chemical is zingerone.

Phenolic Spices

This category includes allspice and clove. Allspice is a dried berry. The spice has about 4% volatile oil, primarily eugenol. Clove is a dried flower bud. The spice contains 14–21% volatile oil, again mostly eugenol.

Other Spices

Cinnamon

Cinnamon and cassia represent two distinct spices, but are closely related and are used interchangeably. Cassia cinnamon is a dried bark. The volatile oil is 80–95% cinnamic aldehyde, cinnamyl acetate, small amounts of cinnamic acid, benzaldehyde, methyl salicylaldehyde, methyl orthocoumoraldehyde, salicylaldehyde, salicylic acid, and coumarin [3].

Cinnamon is widely used in baking for its sweet aromatic qualities.

Mace and Nutmeg

Mace and nutmeg are recovered from the same plant. Both have similar flavor characteristics.

When the nutmeg first is harvested and husked, mace, which covers the nutmeg kernel, is removed and dried separately.

Nutmeg contains up to 15% volatile oil, mace 14%. Nutmeg contains 24–30% fixed oil, mace 30% or more.

Turmeric

Turmeric, the powdered rootstock of *Curcuma longa* of India, is used for color (yellow) and flavor. The aroma is peppery, the taste aromatic and bitter.

Turmeric is used in flavoring meat and egg dishes and as a coloring agent in mustard.

Aromatic Seeds

These include anise, caraway, cardamom, celery, coriander, cumin, dill, fennel, foenugreek, mustard, poppy, and sesame.

Mustard seed is the most important commercially with 35,091 metric tons imported into the United States in 1981. (Mustard is also grown in Montana, California, and other parts of the United States.) Sesame seed was imported at 37,954 metric tons in 1981 [12].

There are three principal kinds of mustard seed—white, brown, and black. Commercial mustard flours are manufactured by grinding and blending the different kinds of seeds [3].

Herbs

Herbs include basil, chervil, bay, marjoram, mint, oregano, parsley, rosemary, sage, savory, spearmint, tarragon, thyme, valerian root, and zedoary root.

Oregano was imported into the United States at 3067 metric tons in 1981.

Sage was imported at 1482 metric tons in 1981. These were the two herbs imported in largest volume [12].

Herbs are dried leaves of the various named plants. Each has its characteristic volatile oil, in most cases representing 1–3% of the herb by weight.

Vegetables

Garlic and onion, although vegetables, are frequently lumped with the other spices because of their high flavor potency.

Garlic is cultivated world wide. The volatile oil is about 0.1%, consisting of di- and tri-sulfides [3]. Garlic powder is made by dehydrating garlic in a tunnel dryer and grinding the dried garlic.

Onion is a bulb as is garlic. Onion also contains a volatile oil in very small amounts, primarily consisting of disulfides. Onion powder is made by grinding dried onions. Onions are grown in many regions of the United States with significant portions of the industry in California and Oregon.

Processing of Spices

Most spice processing occurs in the country of origin. This includes harvesting, sometimes washing, fermenting, and drying. Processing is usually of the simplest type because labor is inexpensive.

There has been a tendency in recent years to locate more advanced processing facilities in the country of origin. This has been in part because of raw material cost and labor cost advantages and partly for geopolitical and geoeconomic reasons.

Normally grinding is done in the country of sale to minimize the flavor degradation that results when spices are ground and the spice oils are exposed to air. Spice grinding has been done in the past with hammermills, pulverizers, and similar mills. The product is screened to the various sizes specified.

In recent years, technology has been developed for grinding spices with liquid nitrogen or carbon dioxide snow. This takes away the heat generated in grinding to minimize loss of volatile oils during grinding.

Oleoresins

Oleoresins are prepared from many spices. As discussed previously, oleoresins are extracts made with a pure, low boiling solvent followed by complete removal of the solvent.

The advantages of oleoresins are that they are more concentrated than the spice itself and are in a fluid or semifluid form for ease of handling in liquid systems.

While the volatile or essential oils from the spices are important, the nonvolatile pungent chemicals present in many spices are crucial to the flavor. Exhaustive extraction with an excellent solvent (usually immiscible in water) is required. The type of equipment required is similar to that discussed under "Extracts."

References

1. W. Morris (ed.), *The American Heritage Dictionary of the English Language*, American Heritage Publishing Co., New York, 1969, p. 500.
2. P. B. Gove (ed.), *Webster's Third New International Dictionary of the English Language*, G. & C. Merriam Co., Springfield, Massachusetts, 1964.
3. J. Merory, *Food Flavorings—Composition, Manufacture, and Use*, 2nd ed., AVI Publishing Co., Westport, Connecticut, 1968.
4. A. E. Goossens, "Protein Foods—Flavors and Off-Flavors," *Food Eng. 54*, 59–60 (October 1974).
5. C. Manley, "A Study of the Volatile Compounds and Chemical Reactions of Hydrolyzed Soybean Protein," Ph.D. Thesis, University Microfilms, Ann Arbor, Michigan, 1969.
6. L. Trauberman, "Flavor Protein Hydrolysates," *Food Eng., 32*, 47–49 (October 1960).
7. J. C. Cowan, "Soybeans," in *Kirk-Othmer Encyclopedia of Chemical Technology*, 2nd ed., Wiley-Interscience, New York, p. 611.
8. J. V. Ziemba, "Authentic Soy Sauce Brewed in Wisconsin," *Food Eng., 54*, 58–60 (February 1974).
9. E. W. Seitz, *Flavor Production by Microorganisms*, Presented at Fifth International Fermentation Symposium, Berlin, 1976.
10. E. W. Seitz, "Industrial Application of Microbial Lipases: A Review," *J. Am. Oil Chem. Soc., 51*, 12–16 (1974).
11. "Flavors and Spices," in *Chemical Technology: An Encyclopedic Treatment, Vol. 7, Vegetable Food Products*, Barnes and Noble, New York, 1975.
12. *Spices*, Foreign Agriculture Circular, U.S. Department of Agriculture, Foreign Agricultural Service, Washington, D.C., April 1982.
13. A. R. Acraman, "Processing Brewers Yeasts," *Process Biochem., 1*, (September 1966).
14. H. Oeda, "Amino Acids (MSG)," in *Kirk-Othmer Encyclopedia of Chemical Technology*, Vol. 2, 2nd ed., Wiley-Interscience, New York, pp. 198–212.

REYNOLD W. MARTIN II

Forest Products: Economics of Timber Supply

Wood as a Raw Material

Wood is a traditional feedstock for fiber and chemical products. As the availability of petroleum hydrocarbons declines, many engineers look to renewable biomass as a technically feasible replacement. Technical feasibility does not imply economic feasibility nor does the renewability of a resource necessarily enhance its economic suitability as a raw material.

The physical or chemical properties of individual woody plant cells give fiber products their utility. Cells are elongated, hollow, and flexible. After mechanical or chemical separation these fibers can be woven or matted into paper, and glued or pressed into board. Chemically, all woods are composed of polysaccharides (alkali soluble hemicellulose and insoluble cellulose), lignin, and other carbohydrates such as volatile oils and tannin. The chemical engineer can use pyrolysis, hydrogenation, and hydrolysis to produce phenols, alcohols, polyols, ketones, acids, and consumable yeasts, glucose, and vanillin.

Woody cell structures and chemical proportions vary by tree species, genetics, geographic region, location within the tree, and growth conditions. Trees are commercially classified as softwoods (mostly conifers) and hardwoods (predominantly porous wood angiosperms). Softwoods tend to have longer, more uniform pliable cells, less lignin, more resinous extractives, and lower alkaline solubility. Both are widely used for nonsolid wood products, but suitability varies by product.

Variation in raw materials affects production. Producers can either specify and purchase an appropriate feedstock or modify their process to use available or cheaper materials. Given time, foresters can manage for desirable feedstock traits. The matching of raw material demands to biological potentials is an economic process.

Demands for Wood

World consumption of forest products is estimated at 85 billion ft^3/yr. Half is burned as fuel in developing countries. Industrial nations process the remainder into construction and consumer goods. The average annual United States wood use is 14.8 billion ft^3 (hardwoods 3.5, softwoods 11.3) for numerous competing uses. It is sawn (48%), pulped (33%), sliced (10%), burned (5%), and otherwise processed (4%). The United States is generally self-sufficient in hardwoods, but is a net importer of softwood lumber and pulp, averaging 1.2 billion ft^3/yr. While wood consumption has been stable since 1950 (increasing only 0.6%/yr), pulp uses (including chemical) have risen 2.5%/yr, displacing round, split, and fuelwood uses. Sawnwood consumption is subject to an unstable 5–7 yr building cycle which peaked in 1973 and 1979. Pulp consumption of roundwood is more stable, but feedstock types vary with changes in the availability of sawmill residuals.

Wood pulp products are predominantly fiber based. The industry annually produces 62–77 million tons of paper and board output. Woodpulp provides 77% of the feedstocks, using 82 million equivalent cords of roundwood per year of which 73% is softwood. The rest is from wastepaper and other sources. Wood chips for pulping come from timber grown as pulpwood (60%), plus tops, logging residuals, and sawmill residuals (40%). Pulpwood use is concentrated in the South (64%). The West (21%) and North (16%) are minor pulpwood regions in comparison. Except for gum naval stores (rosins and turpentines), wood chemicals are usually produced from pulp or pulping by-products.

Pulp or chemical processes must compete for roundwood because standing timber is sold to its highest valued use. Use value is derived from end product selling prices by subtracting the costs of conversion, marketing, transportation, and harvesting. Pulp products have low values when compared with solid wood products. Their proportionately high manufacturing costs create low derived values and limit pulp feedstocks to nearby lower grade timber.

For wood chemicals there are competing alternative feedstocks, principally fossil hydrocarbons, which limit the choice of wood as a raw material. Feedstock preference depends on existing plant flexibility and relative raw material prices. While rising petroleum prices in the early 1980s caused a brief increase in rayon production and wood fuel use (residential and cogeneration), methanol and ethanol hydrolysis from wood still required subsidies, with other forms of biomass such as corn or urban waste economically more preferred. To date in the United States, wood renewability has been a minor consideration in its use as a replacement raw material.

Economic Supplies of Wood

Timber supply comes from existing mature inventories and investments in replacement timber stands. The world's closed or commercial forests cover 6.4 billion acres, 19% of its land area. Standing inventory is 12.6 trillion ft^3 of timber worldwide, but 75% of the 42 billion ft^3 annual harvest is from softwood forests in North America, Europe, and the USSR. Alarms about global deforestation are not based on timber supply as the current industrial use of wood could be maintained by 3% of the available forest area.

The United States commercial forest land base is 487.7 million acres containing 456 billion ft^3 of softwoods and 255 billion ft^3 of hardwoods (Table 1). The dominant timber supply regions are the Pacific Northwest, the Southeast, and Canada.

Western forests are characterized by public ownership (68%) with large but declining old growth inventories and maturing private second growth. These are softwood forests of Douglas fir, hemlock, true firs, ponderosa pine, lodgepole pine, spruces, and a mix of larches, white pines, and cedars in order of abundance. Hardwoods such as aspen, cotton wood, and alder are of minor importance.

Southern forests are 91% privately owned mixed second growth. The dominant species are the short leaf pines, longleaf and other pines, red and black oaks, white oaks, gums, hickories, and other hardwoods. The inventory balance leans to hardwoods (52%). A 2% forest arcreage decline over 25 yr is offest by a 67% increase in softwood inventories.

Nontimber goals and conservative management often reduce the productivity of public ownerships although federal forest management expenditures are relatively high. This is reflected in low rates of inventory turnover (annual harvest/inventory) (Table 2). Industrial lands are higher quality and more

TABLE 1 United States Commercial Forest Character, 1976–1977 (in billion ft^3)[1]

Region	Softwoods			Hardwoods		
	Growing Stock	Annual Growth	Annual Removal	Growing Stock	Annual Growth	Annual Removal
Pacific Coast	219.1	2.9	4.0	16.9	0.5	0.1
South	97.1	6.2	4.5	104.9	4.5	2.1
Rocky Mountains	94.9	1.6	0.8	4.9	0.1	—
North	44.6	1.6	0.7	128.6	4.2	2.0
Totals	455.7	12.3	10.0	255.3	9.3	4.2

intensively managed but inventories are being reduced. Nonindustrial private holdings have been characterized as nontimber oriented and undependable timber suppliers, but their supply price responsiveness is higher, and they exceed public land productivity when measured on like sites.

Since wood is bulky, the 283 United States pulp or integrated mills are located closer to feedstock markets than product markets. Harvest and hauling costs are 40% of produced steam value and 15–20% of fiberboard or chemical values. Northwestern whole tree chipping costs $16–19/BDU (a 200 ft^3 box) to harvest and $0.14/BDU/mi to haul; southern pine roundwood costs $34–49/cord to harvest and haul 30 mi.

Large installations are necessary to achieve economies of scale in plants which convert low grade material to low valued products. A 35-ton/d steam plant costs $0.5 million to build, a 500-ton fiberboard plant $45 million, and a 1500-ton chemical plant $130 million. The capital and labor requirements lead to high industrial concentration ratios (eight companies produce 45% of the output). These costs dominate the investment cash flows.

Several factors temper raw material costs. Stumpage value, the value of standing timber, is derived from the value of the end product. The mill delivered price can be calculated and the costs of handling, transport, taxes, etc. bid backward to the owner of timber. Pulpwood average stumpage prices run $9.80–11.70/cord (less than 25% of delivered value) in southern pines and $5–7/cord in northern softwoods. These prices have been stable over the last two decades when adjusted for inflation.

Since transportation charges limit supplier options, low grade timber markets become localized. Residuals from western old growth harvests have few alternative uses. In the South there are more local suppliers than mills, a market condition leading to lower and more stable feedstock prices. However, a new plant or expansion of an existing plant increases demand pressure, and hence prices, in localized stumpage markets. Competition occurs mainly at overlap of mill feedstock areas and depends on the transport rate, relative value of final products, and conversion efficiency.

Wood processing firms attempt to control feedstock price or availability by long-term management agreements with small owners or by creating self-sufficiency with timberland purchases. These integration strategies vary inconclusively throughout the industry.

The primary timberlands investment criterion is the profitability of

TABLE 2 Softwood Timber Production by Ownership Class, 1976–1977 [1]

Owner	Inventory (billion ft^3)	Annual Growth (billion ft^3)	Annual Removal (billion ft^3)	Turnover Rate (%)
Forest Service	207.7	2.5	2.0	1.0
Other public	50.9	1.1	0.8	1.6
Industrial	74.4	2.9	3.6	4.8
Private	122.7	5.9	3.6	2.9
Totals	455.7	12.4	10.0	2.2

holding the land asset. This depends on each acre's site productivity, existing inventory, location, workability, tax environment, regulatory constraints, and price expectations. The asset value can be affected by management which changes the cash flows from the land over time. Forest valuation procedures convert potential cash flows to wealth which is used in two basic investment decisions: to determine timberland market price in sales or purchases, or for owned lands to identify the management regime which maximizes the value of the land in production by that owner. In the competitive market for timberland, these two values will be identical.

Land's biological potential is measured by yield functions which estimate the net volume (V) of wood available for harvest at any point in time as a function of site quality (S), stand density (D), and age (A). The Schumacher function [2]

$$\ln(V) = \beta_0 + \beta_1 S + \beta_2 A^{-1} + \beta_3 \ln(D) \tag{1}$$

is a simple yield equation used to represent even-aged (clearcut) stand regimes which are common in softwood and pulp grade hardwood plantations. The beta coefficients are empirically developed constants which will be unique for each timber species or forest region. The sigmoidal appearance of yield in natural stands (see Curve A, Fig. 1) comes from vigorous growth after establishment with increasing competition as trees begin to reach merchantable sizes. Transformation of yield into a dynamic stand value function is required for financial analyses. Typically unit harvesting costs decline while log grades and values increase with tree size. Some sawtimber stumpage prices increase faster than inflation.

A more intensive management alternative such as fertilization at age 20 would create another yield function such as Curve B of Fig. 1. Intensive

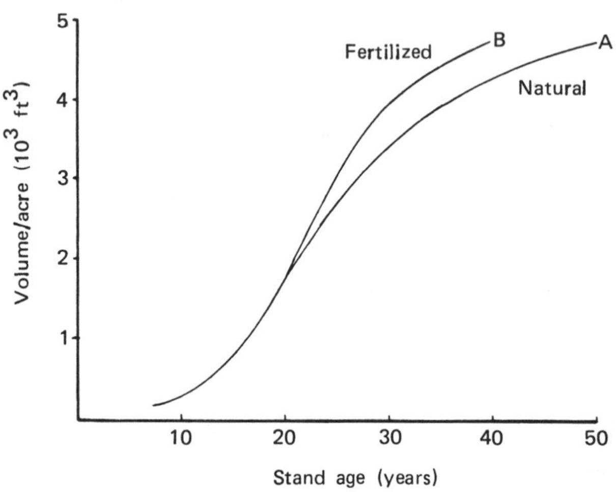

FIG. 1. Loblolly pine yields under two management intensities (site index = 90, fully stocked) [3].

management opportunities include site preparation, brush and pest control, spacing control (thinning), genetic improvement, fertilization, etc. using fire, mechanical, biological, and chemical treatments.

Producers who want to maximize fiber yield use intensive practices and long rotations (cycles from forest establishment to harvest). Single rotation volume eventually peaks due to mortality (at age 90 in Curve A), but the yield over multiple successive rotations on the same acre is maximized when each stand is harvested at its highest possible average annual yield (at age 30 in Curve B). Although this produces the most fiber from an acre over time and is required by law for many public forests, extra treatment costs and extended capital holding costs (the discount rate) are often greater than the value of the technologically feasible yield which they create. The most profitable timber investments have less intensive, even shorter, rotations.

Private firms test for after tax, financially optimal investment levels, and rotation lengths regardless of the loss of biological potential. The regime is selected which produces the largest wealth measured by net present value (NPV) of expected cash flows which varies by cost and timing of treatments, growth responses, and values and timing of harvest entries. The updated Faustmann formula is a discrete form for the common bare land, multiple rotation case.

$$\text{NPV}=\sum_{t=0}^{r} \frac{C_0 Q_t \left(\frac{1+g}{1+i}\right)^t}{1-\left(\frac{1+g}{1+i}\right)^r} \tag{2}$$

where t = time from planting (0) to rotation end (r)
C = cash flow/unit of treatment or harvest (+ or – in year 0 terms)
Q = quantity of treatment or harvest at t
g = rate of cost or price change (adjusted for inflation)
i = risk adjusted discount rate (adjusted for inflation)

The continuous form is found in Hyde [4] or Jackson [5].

This approach recognizes that stumpage prices can increase faster than inflation ($g>0$). Real price increases counteract the negative effect of the discount rate on long-term capital investments and have made timberland investments more appealing. Using prices from like competitive sales in the same market area automatically adjusts for the alternative products which can be manufactured from the same size bole. The use of artificial raw material transfer prices for owned timber can distort valuation estimates.

Federal tax advantages under IRS code 631a&b make timber investments more favorable. The maximum tax rate on timber capital gains is 28% compared with 46% on ordinary income. Since 1981, tax credits and 7-yr regeneration amortization have offset ordinary income. In addition, most states also grant timber a preferential tax status.

Once individual stand investments have been analyzed, mill input requirements, stand age class distribution, growth, and economic fluctuations are matched in a harvest scheduling algorithm. Classical sustained yield even flow systems require perfect age class distributions and assume that constant annual growth enables constant timber consumption. Conceptually simple, these systems are unachievable in dynamic ecosystems and inappropriate for fluctuating economic conditions.

Simulation algorithms can model the forest's responses to management alternatives and policy changes. Programs such as SIMAC, TREES, and ECHO contain a low cost binary search routine which can assign large inventories of already prioritized stands to feasible cutting periods. Optimization algorithms such as linear, goal, and dynamic programming select management regimes for individual stands as well as assign their priority and timing for an assured optimal harvest flow under sets of operating constraints. Such programs are data intensive and require explicit definitions of all possible permutations of cutting units, management regimes, and cutting periods. The basic model I approach selects between predetermined alternative regimes of investment intensity and harvest periodicity for each cutting unit in an objective function such as [2]

$$\text{maximize NPV} = \sum_{i=1}^{n} \sum_{k=1}^{m} C_{ik} X_{ik} \tag{3}$$

where X_{ik} = number of acres of unit i assigned to regime k
C_{ik} = discounted cash flow/acre of unit i under regime k

subject to operating constraints such as:

Available cutting unit acreage
Harvested acres in a period
Harvest volume flow targets
Period cash flow targets
Impacts on other forest resources

A typical matrix for a forest-sized problem will exceed 10,000 columns. Newer programs such as FORPLAN, MUSYC, and MAX-MILLION are capable of assessing numerous yield trajectories for the same stands and simultaneous harvest scheduling across several forest outputs. Most of these programs are available in nonproprietory versions; see Clutter et al. [2] for references.

Timber production by economic criteria insures that supplies of pulp and chemical feedstocks will be available although prices will vary. Public harvests will continue to decline in the West due to increasing alternative use emphasis rather than changes in holdings or productivity. A public switch to economic operating criteria would reduce timber sales after a two-decade inventory adjustment spike and reduce management intensity. Softwood lumber supplies from the Canadian West will decline over the next 20 yr, but pulpwood and chip imports could increase. Southern and other private forest lands are increasing in value, and management intensity is generally increasing with rising stumpage prices.

Declining United States construction demands may abate the rapid rise in sawtimber stumpage values (3.8%/yr > inflation for Douglas fir) which would make fiber uses more competitive, but suppliers in all regions are promoting international markets. Alaska and the Pacific Northwest are looking to the Pacific rim and Southern Europe where expected log and chip deficits will maintain competitive pressures on domestic fiber feedstocks. The relative price of petroleum hydrocarbons is currently too low to expect more than marginal replacement by forest biomass feedstocks.

Bibliography

Goldstein, I. S. (ed.), *Organic Chemicals from Biomass,* CRC Press, Boca Raton, Florida, 1981.

Goldstein, I. S., Holley, D. L., and Deal, E. L., "Economic Aspects of Low-Grade Hardwood Utilization," *For. Prod. J., 28* (8), 53–56 (1978).

Haygreen, J. G., and Bowyer, J. L., *Forest Products and Wood Science: An Introduction,* Iowa State University Press, Ames, Iowa, 1982.

Kollmann, F. F. P., Kuenzi, E. W., and Stamm, A. J., *Pinciples of Wood Science and Technology. Vol. II. Wood-Based Materials,* Springer-Verlag, New York, 1975.

Sjostrom, E., *Wood Chemistry: Fundamentals and Applications,* Academic, New York, 1981.

Ulrich, A. H., *U.S. Timber Production, Trade, Consumption, and Price Statistics 1950–80,* USDA Forest Service. Misc. Pub. No. 1408, August 1981.

References

1. USDA, Forest Service, *An Analysis of the Timber Situation in the United States 1952–2030,* Forest Resource Report #23, U.S. Government Printing Office, Washington, D.C., December 1982.
2. J. L. Clutter, J. C. Fortson, L. V. Pienaar, G. H. Brister, and R. L. Bailey, *Timber Management: A Quantitative Approach,* Wiley, New York, 1983.
3. C. W. McKetta, 1983.
4. W. F. Hyde, *Timber Supply, Land Allocation, and Economic Efficiency,* Johns Hopkins University Press, Baltimore, Maryland, 1980.
5. D. H. Jackson, *The Microeconomics of the Timber Industry,* Westview Press, Boulder, Colorado, 1980.

CHARLES W. McKETTA

Gaskets, Gasket Materials

Designing a tight metal-to-metal joint is a difficult if not impossible task. Machining of the surfaces, even though done with accurate equipment, will still leave some roughness and tiny clearances (perhaps only several millionths of an inch) through which a liquid under pressure can leak. Highly polished metal surfaces can be made to be leakproof, but this is expensive. For this reason a packing (gasket) of a compressible material which deforms under load is used to fill the irregularities between flange faces so they are sealed against leakage. The gasket maintains a tight seal between the flange faces. Pipe flanges, manways, and practically all jointing devices in refineries, chemical plants, and power plants require the use of gaskets in one form or another. Additionally, the use of gasketed joints makes the task of assembly and disassembly much simpler.

For a gasket to seal properly, several factors must be considered: (a) the gasket material, (b) the flange material, (c) the flange face finish, and (d) the bolting material.

Gasket Materials

Gaskets are made of many diverse materials including the following:

Cork
Rubber (both natural and synthetic)
Cork and rubber
White asbestos (chrysotile)
Blue African asbestos (crocidolite)

Elastomers (synthetic rubbers):

SBR (styrene–butadiene)
CR (chloroprene, Neoprene)
Buna-N (nitrile, NBR)
Fluorocarbon (Viton)
Hypalon (chlorosulfonated polyethylene)
Silicones
EPDM (ethylene–propylene diene monomer)

Plastics

Teflon (PTFE, polytetrafluoroethylene)
Kel-F
Phenolic resins

Metals are also used for gasket materials where conditions warrant. Grafoil (a graphite material) and metallic gasket materials of carbon steels and stainless steels such as 304, 304L, 316, 316L, 321, and 347 are often used where high temperatures and/or corrosive materials are present.

There are also gaskets made of aluminum, copper alloys (cupronickel), Alloy 20, Hastelloys, Monels, Inconels, Incoloys, and many others. There is no end to the various materials that may be utilized for gaskets, provided they can be sufficiently compressed to provide the seal required.

Selecting the proper gasket material for a particular application depends on the following:

1. The pressure of the process fluid or gas to be contained
2. The temperature of the process fluid or gas to be contained
3. The chemical resistance of the gasket material to the corrosive characteristics of the process fluid or gas to be contained

Table 1 lists some nonmetallic gasket meterials and their characteristics.

A "rule of thumb" for the selection of gasket materials has evolved from many years of field experience. It is based on multiplying the operating pressure by the operating temperature (Table 2).

Asbestos Gaskets

Asbestos is the most commonly used gasket material. It consists of two types: white chrysotile and Blue African (crocidolite). Both have about the same temperature limitations. They consist mostly of magnesium silicate with 14% water of crystallization; thus, hydrated magnesium silicate. Asbestos is usually compounded with a binder such as SBR or NBR and other synthetic rubbers into sheets which are then cut into required flange gaskets. These synthetic rubber binders determine the chemical resistance of the gasket.

Although asbestos has been and still is the commonest type of gasket specified, asbestos gaskets and fillers are being phased out of specifications by some engineering companies because of its carcinogenic qualities. Manufacturers of asbestos gaskets are observing special handling procedures to diminish and avoid the formation of asbestos dust in the working environment. Many are now manufacturing substitutes for asbestos gaskets which may possibly have lower temperature limits.

Spiral-Wound Gaskets

These are made of springlike preformed metal strips into a special chevron shape. These strips are alternately spiral-wound with asbestos or another type of filler. The gasket density is determined by the compactness of the windings and fillers and may be designed for the specified flange closures.

A cross section of a typical spiral-wound gasket is shown in Fig. 1. The

TABLE 1 Gasket Materials

Material	Comments	Temperature Limit (°F)
Natural rubber	Good resistance to mild acids, alkalies, salts, and chlorine solutions; not suitable for oils, solvents, and strong acids	−65 to 200
SBR(styrene-butadiene rubber)	Good resistance to abrasives, mild alcohols, organic acids, and dilute alkalies; not suitable for oils, gasoline, and solvents	−65 to 250
CR (chloroprene, Neoprene)	Suitable for nonaromatics, oils and fuels, moderate acids, alkalies, and salt solutions; unsuitable for aromatic and chlorinated hydrocarbons and strong oxidizing acids	−60 to 250
Buna-N rubber (nitrile, NBR)	Resistance to abrasion, heat, oils, and solvents, aromatic and aliphatic hydrocarbons, petroleum oils and gasolines, caustics and salts, dilute acids; unsuitable for chlorinated hydrocarbons, ketones and esters, and strong oxidizing agents	−60 to 250
Fluorocarbons (Viton)	Good resistance to oils, fuels, chlorinated solvents, aliphatic and aromatic hydrocarbons, and strong acids; unsatisfactory with amines, esters, ketones, and steam	−40 to 450
Hypalon (chlorosulfonated polyethylene)	Good resistance to alkali, acid, and salt; resists weathering, ozone, oils, sunlight, diesel fuels, kerosene; unsuitable for aromatics and chlorinated hydrocarbons, chromic and nitric acid	−50 to 275

(*continued*)

TABLE 1 *(continued)*

Material	Comments	Temperature Limit (°F)
Silicones	Suitable for sunlight and ozone; unsuitable for steam, aliphatic and aromatic hydrocarbons	−150 to 500
Grafoil	A graphite material, excellent resistance to many acids, alkalies, organic compounds, salt solutions, heat transfer fluids; not good for oxidizing agents; will sublimate at temperatures over 6000°F	Up to 6000
PTFE (Teflon)	Suitable for severe corrosive services	−90 to 500
Asbestos	White is used for general purposes; Blue African usually specified for acid service	700 to 1000 depending on the binders and formulation
Asbestos millboard	Used in gaskets as a filler for metal jacketed design gaskets; as a gasket in low pressure/high temperature applications	Up to 900

TABLE 2

Material	Maximum Temperature of Materials (°F)	Maximum $P \times T$
Rubber	200	15,000
Vegetable fiber	250	40,000
Solid fluorocarbon	450	75,000
Asbestos cloth, rubberized	500–600	125,000
Compressed asbestos	650–1000	250,000
Metal gaskets	Depends on metal	Over 250,000

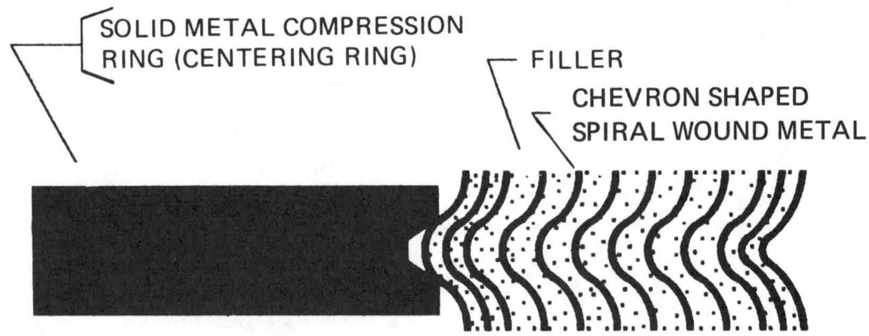

FIG. 1

solid compression ring is usually of carbon steel and serves as an antiblowout device and compression stop which centers the gasket within the flange bolts on the raised face of the flanges. It also serves as a limit stop during bolt-up of the flanges to prevent crushing of the gasket. Sometimes an inner ring is specified. This protects against excessive heat, minimizes erosion of the flange facings, reduces fluid turbulence, and prevents material build-up between the flange bore and the gasket i.d. (See Fig. 2.)

The cross section of the spiral-wound gasket is such that compressing it results in a springlike action by the metal strip. Under compression the metal acts as a seal, and the filler compressing under the bolt load fills the imperfections of the flange face. This gasket thus has a resiliency which is critical for temperature and pressure cycling, joint relaxation, vibration, and shock.

To help in warehousing and identification, the spiral-wound gaskets have been color-coded to indicate the metal utilized. This color is painted on the compression (centering) ring on the o.d. edge. The filler material used for the spiral-wound gasket has also been color-coded, with a minimum of four

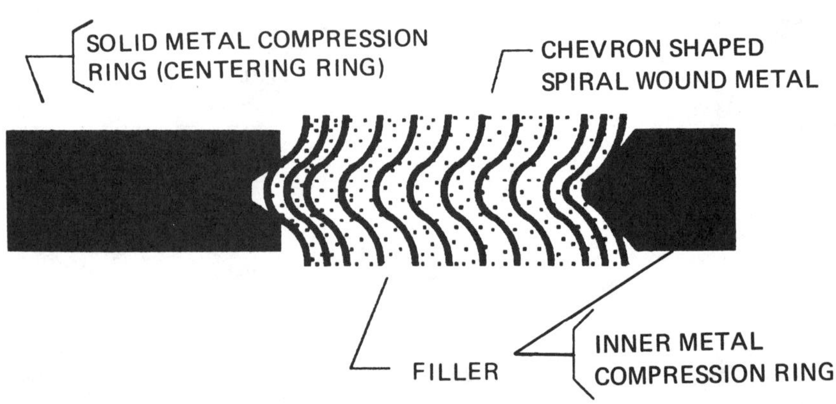

FIG. 2

TABLE 3 Spiral-Wound Gaskets: Recommended Maximum Temperatures and Standard Color Codes

Material	Temperature (°F)	Color Code
Metallic windings:		
304SS	1000	Yellow
316LSS	1400 to 1500	Green
347SS	1400 to 1500	Blue
321SS	1400 to 1500	Turquoise
Monel	1500	Orange
Nickel	1400	Red
Titanium	2000	Purple
Alloy 20	1400 to 1500	Black
Inconel	2000	Gold
Carbon steel	500	Silver
Hastelloy B	2000	Brown
Hastelloy C-276	2000	Beige
Incoloy	2000	White
Phosphor bronze	500	Copper
Nonmetallic fillers:		
Canadian asbestos	1000 to 1200	No stripe
Blue African asbestos	1200 to 1300	Light blue stripe
PTFE	500	White stripe
Ceramic	2300	Light green stripe
Graphite	900 (oxiding atmosphere) 6000 (neutral or reducing atmosphere)	Gray stripe

stripes approximately equally spaced on the outer edge of the metal centering ring. Standard colors for the metals and fillers, together with temperature limitations, are shown in Table 3.

Gasket Selection Criteria

The choice of the various types of gasket materials depends on several factors: (a) The material of the gasket, its compatibility with the process fluid so that it will not swell or dissolve nor corrode the flange surface or bolting. (b) The gasket's resistance to temperature and pressure. (c) The flange surface finish. (d) The gasket's density, i.e., when a rubber gasket is specified, its Durometer hardness is usually specified. This is especially true when glass-fiber-reinforced flanges are used. (e) The gasket must also have a high coefficient of friction to be held properly between the flanges. (f) Other considerations are vibration and thermal cycling, effect of heat aging and hardening, stress relaxation, and the frequency of joints dismantling.

Flange Materials and Flange Finish

The flange types used most often in refinery and chemical plants are flat-face cast iron, raised-face carbon steel, stainless steels and alloys, and ring joints. There are others such as tongue and groove (large and small), also male and female. Each pair must somehow confine the gasket and prevent it from creeping out of the confined space.

Sketches of flange types are shown in the "Flanges" article, Vol. 22. (See also "Avoiding Oversized Flame Problems," *Chemical Engineering*, November 16, 1981.)

The ASME/ANSI B16.5 Code (1981) specifies in paragraph 6.3.4 that "the finish of contact faces of pipe flanges and connecting end flanges of fittings shall be. . .either a serrated-concentric or serrated spiral finish having a pitch of 24 to 40 grooves per inch (.06 to 1 mm) shall be used. The cutting tool employed shall have an approximate radius of 0.06 inch (1.6 mm) or larger. The resultant finish shall have a 125 to 500 microinch (3.2 to 12.5 mm) roughness."

When not specified, the finish required for the flange may be as described above. Sometimes the piping engineer may specify "Stock Finish" which would give an AARH of 250 to 500 μin. To seal a joint, the gasket is compressed and flowed into the surface irregularities by bolt pressure. The filling of these irregularities is most necessary for gases, which have no surface tension, while other fluids having surface tension may not require complete void filling. In any case, the pressure exerted upon the gasket must be greater than that of fluid pressure attempting to leak past it.

Concentric serrations for flange finishes are recommended for hard-to-hold gases, fluids, and vacuum. Spiral or phonographic serrations can lead to leakage because of the path in the serrations.

When soft gaskets are used, the flange finish should be at least in the 250 to 500 μin. range. This finish allows the gasket to comply with the irregularities and, owing to bolt pressure, seal them. For the smoother finishes such as 125 μin. and lower, metal gaskets are recommended. These are spiral wound with various fillers, metal gaskets, and metal-jacketed gaskets.

Listed below are some recommended finishes for various fluids and gaskets.

Spiral-wound gaskets are recommended for practically all pressure classes:

500 μin., general purpose, 150 and 300 lb pressure classes
250 μin., general purpose, 400 lb and above pressure classes
125 μin., hydrogen, hazardous materials, and difficult-to-contain fluids
80 μin., for vacuum service*

*Some gasket manufacturers recommend that 125 μin. should be the minimum finish for vacuum service and that the serrations be concentric. They also state that 250 μin. should be the maximum finish. When finishes are smoother than 125 μin., an inordinate amount of bolt pressure must be induced to hold the hard-to-contain fluids. Smooth finishes may also allow the

Table 4 shows various gaskets in cross section and recommended flange finishs in microinchs, AARH.

Ring-Type Gaskets

These come in oval and octagonal shapes as shown in Table 4 for "Solid Metal Gaskets." They should be made of a material suitable for the service conditions. It is recommended that the rings be of a hardness lower than the flanges to assure tight joints when gaskets are placed. It is recognized, however, that this is sometimes not possible with some alloys. (See Fig. 3.)

Bolt Loading

There are three main forces acting on a gasket: (a) the hydrostatic end force, (b) the internal fluid pressure/design pressure, (c) the compressive bolt load . (See Fig. 4.)

(a) The hydrostatic end force is always present and acts to separate the flanges when the system is pressurized
(b) The internal pressure acts on that gasket portion exposed to the internal fluid pressure which tries to blow the gasket out of the joint or leak pass it
(c) The compressive bolt load is the application of the initial force that causes the gasket to flow into the flange surface irregularities regardless of operating conditions

---

spiral-wound gasket to slide radially. The gasket manufacturers state that the recommendations are based on experience and feedback from the field.

A great deal of exploratory testing of all types of gaskets has been and is being performed by the Varysburg Gasket Research Laboratory. A report "Gasket Leakage Behavior Trends" by H. D. Raut, A. Bazerqui, and L. March in the WRC Bulletin 271 reports on tests performed. Here are some of the conclusions reported on spiral-wound gaskets, both asbestos-filled and graphite-filled, which contradict some of the recommendations by gasket manufacturers.

1. For both spiral-wound asbestos-filled and graphite-filled gaskets, no definite correlation was found between surface finish and sealing capability.
2. Spiral-wound graphite-filled gaskets generally were found to seal better than spiral-wound asbestos-filled gaskets.

A caution is added to the above. The above conclusions only indicate trends in the tests that were run and should not be generalized beyond the conditions of the test parameters. Meanwhile, the gasket industry recommendations should be followed, based, of course, on the piping engineer's experience.

TABLE 4 Gasket Seating Surface Finishes

Gasket Description	Gasket Cross Section	Flange Surface Finish, μin. AARH	Comments
Flat nonmetallic (all materials)	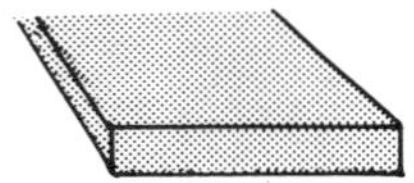	500–750	
Flat metallic[a]		63	This type is used where flanges are smooth; since they are not resilient, sufficient bolt force must be used to make the metal deform to the flange face; used for ammonia fittings, valve bonnets, tongue and groove joints, etc.
Corrugated metal	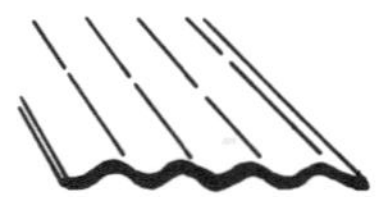	63	This type is also used for smooth-faced flanges; made of thin corrugated metal, it is suitable for low pressure with low bolt loads; it is used for large diameter flanges for combustion gases and high temperature; temperature limits depend on the metal used
Corrugated metal with soft filler		125	Same as above
Metal-jacketed gaskets	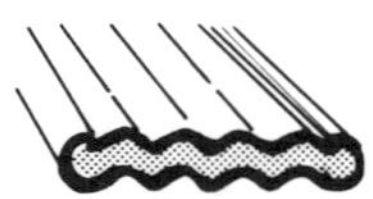 	63–80	The metal-jacketed gasket has a filler material enclosed in the metal jacket; it is used for smooth-faced flanges and in applications with temperatures as high as 1650°F; it is used a great deal in heat exchanger and valve bonnet applications; the lap of this gasket type is the side

			which must act as the primary seal when compressed; it is usually used in confined contact faces; the corrugated metal jacket produces multiseals on the face of the flange and is suitable for temperature cycling and conditions
Solid metal:		63	Solid metal gaskets require smooth plain flange faces and high bolting forces to provide a seal; the force must be high enough to metal flow into the imperfections of the flange gasket surface; consequently, the gasket hardness should not exceed that of the flange material; all solid metal gaskets require smooth flange finishes of 63 μin. maximum and should not exceed 125 μin.
Profile	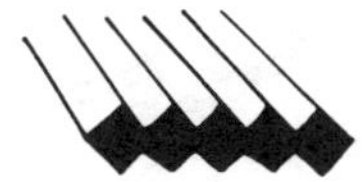		In order to obtain a high seating stress it has been found that the bolt area to gasket area may have to be in the ratio 2 : 1. This may sometimes not be possible in all cases, and usage suggests a serrated or profile gasket to obtain the necessary seating load on the gasket
Serrated	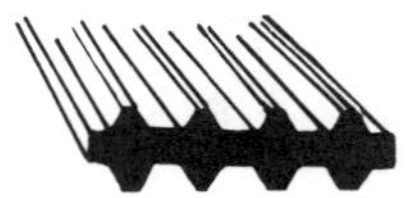		
Profile gasket with metal jacket	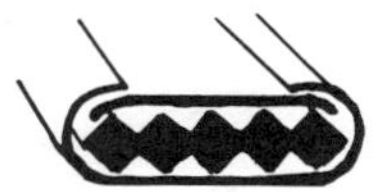 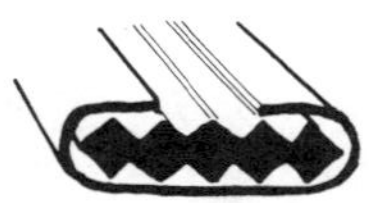		
Round cross-section solid	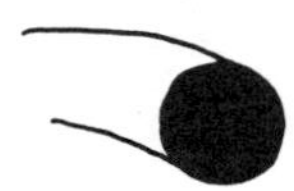		These are from solid metal for high temperature and high pressure services

(continued)

TABLE 4 *(continued)*

Gasket Description	Gasket Cross Section	Flange Surface Finish, μin. AARH	Comments			
			Recommended Metals and Hardnesses for Temperature Conditions			
			Metal	Maximum hardness Brinell 200 kg	Rockwell "B"	Maximum service temperature (°F)
Oval ring type	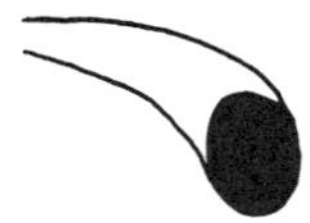					
Octagonal ring type	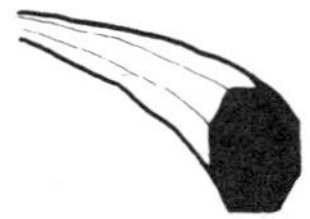		Soft iron	90	56	1000
			Low carbon steel	120	68	1000
			(7.6Cr–½Moly)	130	72	1200
			Type 410— (11–13Cr)	170	86	1300
Delta type			304SS (18Cr–8Ni)	160	83	Depending on service conditions
Bridgeman			316SS (18Cr–12Ni)	160	83	
			347SS (18Cr–10Ni)	160	83	
Lens type			Monel	125	70	
			Nickel	120	68	
			Copper	[b]	[b]	
Hollow metal:		32	These are specialty type gaskets suitable for particular situations. The hollow metal O-rings may be obtained vented for high pressure uses and pressure filled for high temperature uses. The C-type may be used in vacuum services and high pressure applications. They are used in grooves with smooth finishes.			
O Ring	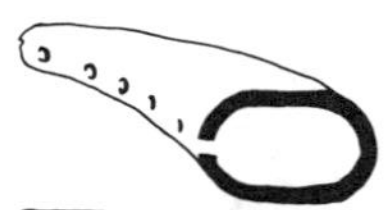					
C Seal						
V Seal						
Spiral wound		80–500	See discussion under "Spiral-Wound Gaskets"			

[a]Solid metal washer-type gaskets require extremely high seating stresses to seal. This usually necessitates a bolt area to gasket area greater than a ratio of 2 : 1. If this is not possible, it is preferred to use a profiled or serrated gasket to achieve the necessary seating load on the gasket.

[b]Hardness as agreed upon.

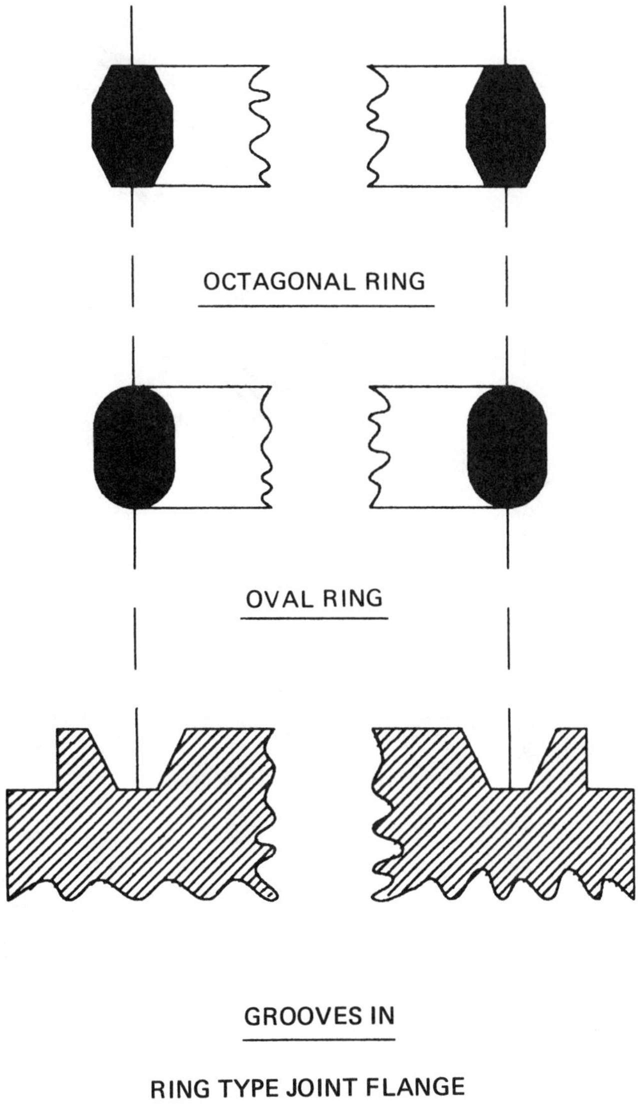

FIG. 3

ASME UPVC Division 1, Appendix 2 and Gaskets

The ASME Unfired Pressure Vessel Code Seating Section VIII, Division 1, Appendix 2, states that "the minimum load applied to the gasket is a function of the design pressure, the gasket material, and the effective gasket or contact area to be kept tight under pressure." This minimum initial load for proper gasket seating is termed y. It is expressed in pounds per square inch and is independent of the internal pressure. This initial loading is applied at atmo-

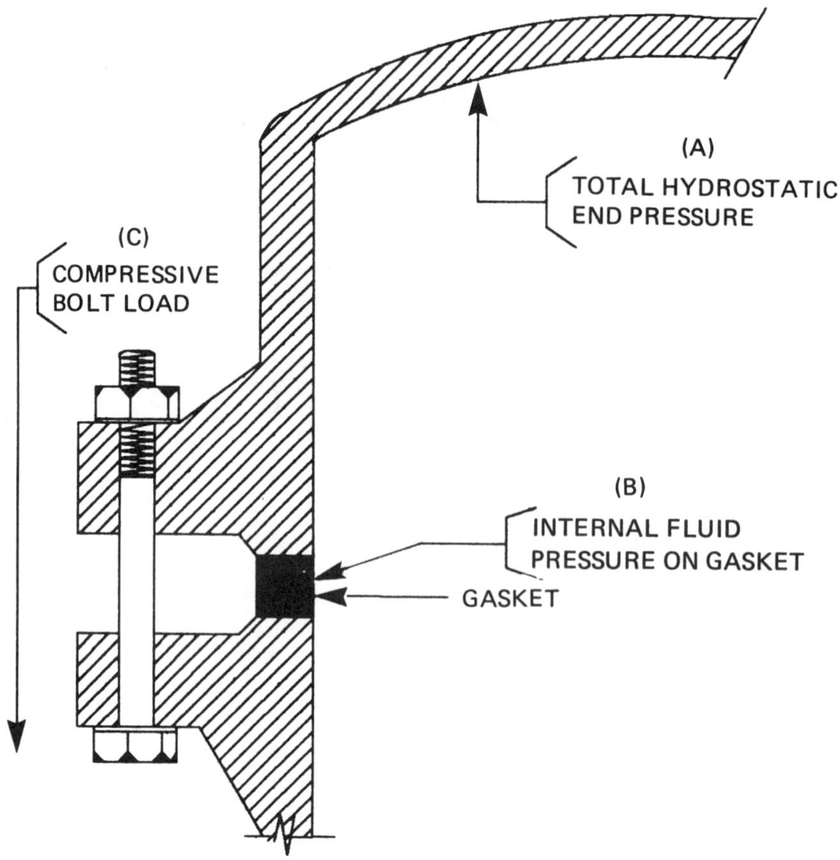

FIG. 4

spheric temperature and pressure when assembling the flanges in the absence of internal pressure and is considered sufficient to seat the gasket.

Besides the gasket seating stress y, the gasket factor m must also be considered. Its value is a function of the gasket material and its construction. It is the ratio of the residual unit stress on the gasket (in pounds per square inch) to the internal pressure (in pounds per square inch). This is a constant for a particular gasket material and construction. The result must be higher than unity or leakage may occur. (See Table 5.)

The minimum initial bolt load W_{m2} may be determined from

$$W_{m2} = 3.14bGy$$

where b is the effective gasket or joint-contact surface seating width in inches and G is the diameter in inches at the location of the gasket load reaction. (See Table 6.)

The required bolt load (W_{m1}) for operating conditions may be found:

$$W_{m1} = H + H_p = 0.785G^2P + (2b + 3.14GmP)$$

where H = total hydrostatic end force, lb
H_p = total joint contact surface compression load, lb
P = design pressure, lb/in.^{2}

When W_{m1} and W_{m2} are determined, then the minimum required bolt area A_m is calculated:

$$A_{m1} = \frac{W_{m1}}{S_b} \qquad A_{m2} = \frac{W_{m2}}{S_a}$$

where S_a = allowable bolt stress at ambient temperature, lb/in.^{2}
S_b = allowable bolt stress at operating temperature, lb/in.^{2}
$A_m = A_{m1}$ if $A_{m1} \geq A_{m2}$
$A_m = A_{m2}$ if $A_{m2} \geq A_{m1}$

A_m is the total actual cross-sectional area of the bolts taken as the greater of A_{m1} or A_{m2}, in square inches.

The bolt may then be selected when the actual bolt area A_b is equal to or greater than A_m.

A_b = (the number of bolts) × (minimum cross-section area of the bolts, square inches)

From this the maximum unit load (S_g max) on the gasket bearing surface is equal to the total maximum bolt load in pounds divided by the actual seating area of the gasket in square inches.

$$S_g \max = \frac{A_bS_a}{0.7854[(\text{o.d.} \times 0.125)^2 - (\text{i.d.})^2]} \quad \text{for spiral-wound gaskets}$$

$$= \frac{A_bS_a}{0.7854[(\text{o.d.})^2 - (\text{i.d.})^2]} \quad \text{all other gasket types}$$

When a stress greater than S_a is to be used for passing a hydrostatic test, the actual prestress pressure test value should be used as S_a in the above equations.

Some suggested stress values for spiral-wound gaskets with fillers (S_g max) are

Canadian or Blue African asbestos	25,000 lb/in.^{2}
TFE-Filled	13,000
Grafoil	20,000

TABLE 5 Gasket Materials and Contact Facings[a]

Gasket Factors(m) for Operating Conditions and Minimum Design Seating Stress (y)

Note: This table gives a list of many commonly used gasket materials and contact facings with suggested design values of m and y that have generally proved satisfactory in actual service when using effective gasket seating width b given in Table 6. The design values and other details given in this table are suggested only and are not mandatory.

Gasket Material		Gasket Factor m	Minimum Design Seating Stress y (lb/in.^{2})	Sketches and Notes	Refer to Table 6: Use Facing Sketch	Refer to Table 6: Use Column
Self-Energizing types: O Rings, Metallic. Elastomer. Other gasket types considered as self-sealing		0	0	—	—	—
Elastomers without fabric or a high percentage of asbestos fiber:					1(a, b, c, d), 4, 5	II
Below 75 Shore Durometer		0.50	0			
75 or higher Shore Durometer		1.00	200			
Asbestos with a suitable binder for the operating conditions	$\frac{1}{8}$ thick	2.00	1600			
	$\frac{1}{16}$ thick	2.75	3700			
	$\frac{1}{32}$ thick	3.50	6500			
Elastomers with cotton fabric insertion		1.25	400			
Elastomers with asbestos fabric insertion.	3-ply	2.25	2200			
With or without wire reinforcement	2-ply	2.50	2900			
	1-ply	2.75	3700			
Vegetable fiber		1.75	1100			
Spiral-wound metal, asbestos filled	Carbon stainless or	3.00	10000		1(a, b)	

Corrugated metal, asbestos inserted, or corrugated metal, jacketed, asbestos filled	Soft aluminum	2.50	2900			
	Soft copper or brass	2.75	3700			
	Iron or soft steel	3.00	4500			
	Monel or 4–6% chrome	3.25	5500			
	Stainless steels	3.50	6500			
Corrugated metal	Soft aluminum	2.75	3700		1(a, b, c, d)	
	Soft copper or brass	3.00	4500			
	Iron or soft steel	3.25	5500			
	Monel or 4–6% chrome	3.50	6500			
	Stainless steels	3.75	7600			
Flat metal, jacketed, asbestos filled	Soft aluminum	3.25	5500	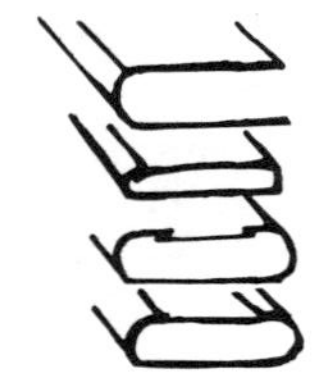	1a, 1b, 1c*, 1d*, 2*	
	Soft copper or brass	3.50	6500			
	Iron or soft steel	3.75	7600			
	Monel	3.50	8000			
	4–6% chrome	3.75	9000			
	Stainless steels	3.75	9000			
Grooved metal	Soft aluminum	3.25	5500		1(a, b, c, d), 2,3	
	Soft copper or brass	3.50	6500			
	Iron or soft steel	3.75	7600			
	Monel or 4–6% chrome	3.75	9000			
	Stainless steels	4.25	10100			
Solid flat metal	Soft aluminum	4.00	8800		1(a, b, c, d), 2, 3, 4, 5	I
	Soft copper or brass	4.75	13000			
	Iron or soft steel	5.50	18000			
	Monel or 4–6% chrome	6.00	21800			
	Stainless steels	6.50	26000			
Ring joint	Iron or soft steel	5.50	18000		6	
	Monel or 4–6% chrome	6.00	21800			
	Stainless steels	6.50	26000			

[a]Reprinted with permission of ASME.
*The surface of a gasket having a lap should be against the smooth surface of the facing and not against the nubbin.

TABLE 6 Effective Gasket Width[a,b]

	Facing Sketch Exaggerated		Basic Gasket Seating Width, b Column I	Column II
1a				
1b*	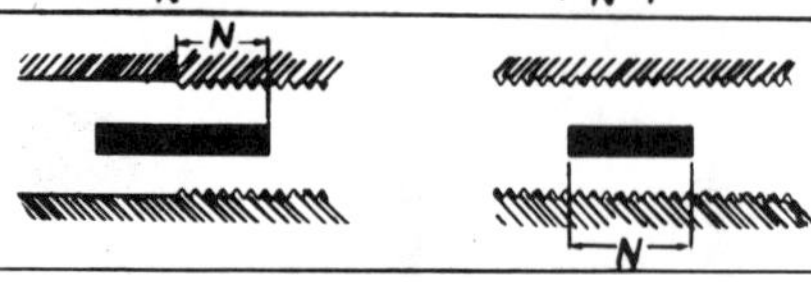		$\frac{N}{2}$	$\frac{N}{2}$
1c	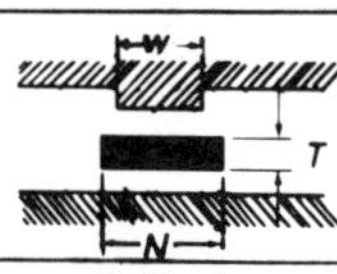	$w \gtreqless N$		
1d*	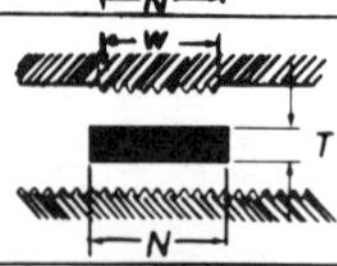	$w \gtreqless N$	$\frac{w+T}{2}; \left(\frac{w+N}{4} \text{ max}\right)$	$\frac{w+T}{2}; \left(\frac{w+N}{4} \text{ max}\right)$
2	1/64″ Nubbin 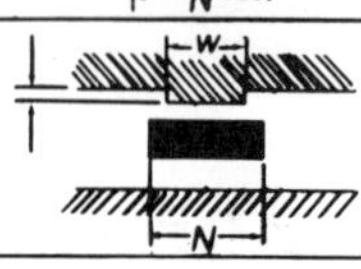	$w \leqq \frac{N}{2}$	$\frac{w+N}{4}$	$\frac{w+3N}{8}$
3	1/64″ Nubbin 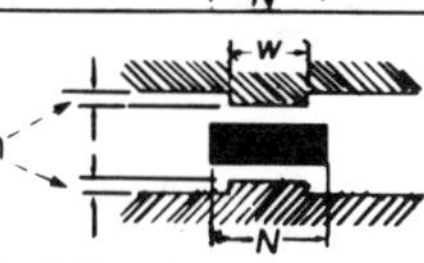	$w \leqq \frac{N}{2}$	$\frac{N}{4}$	$\frac{3N}{8}$
4*	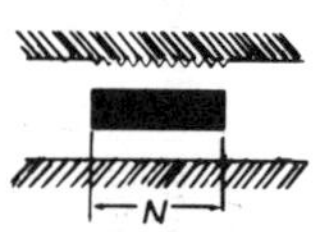		$\frac{3N}{8}$	$\frac{7N}{16}$
5*	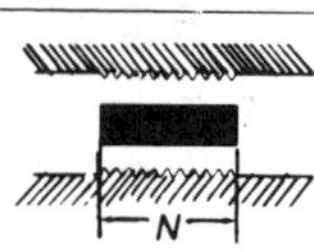		$\frac{N}{4}$	$\frac{3N}{8}$
6	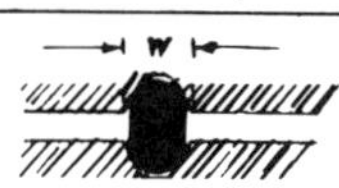		$\frac{w}{8}$	

TABLE 6 *(continued)*

Effective Gasket Seating Width, b

$$b = b_0 \text{ when } b_0 \leqq \frac{1}{4} \text{ in.}$$

$$b = 0.5\sqrt{b_0} \text{ when } b_0 > \frac{1}{4} \text{ in.}$$

Location of Gasket Load Reaction[c]

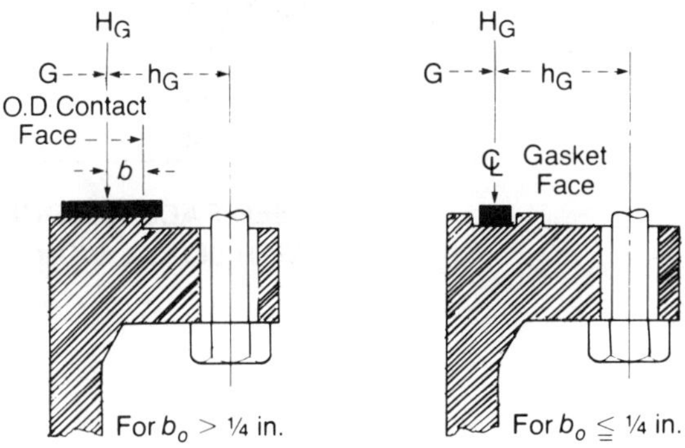

[a]Reprinted with permission of ASME.
[b]Where serrations do not exceed 1/64 in. depth and 1/32 in. width spacing, Sketches 1b and 1d shall be used.
[c]The gasket factors listed only apply to flanged joints in which the gasket is contained entirely within the inner edges of the bolt holes.

The ASME Unfired Pressure Vessel Code previously mentioned is titled "Rules for Bolted Flange Connections With Ring Type Gaskets." This code is mandatory, and the bolt calculations lead to the design of flanges. These calculations for flange design are seldom required unless standard flanges cannot be utilized.

Example of Calculations

20 in., 300 lb RF WN (weldneck) Flange (ANSI B16.5) using a spiral-wound asbestos-filled gasket

Temperature: 400°F
Pressure: 630 lb/in.^{2}gauge

From flange dimensions (ANSI B16.5) and also Table 7 (Bolting Data for Standard Flanges)

Flange o.d.: 30.5 in.
Raised face o.d.: 23 in.
Bolt circle o.d.: 27 in.
Bolt holes: 24, $1\frac{3}{8}$ in. diameter
Bolts: $1\frac{1}{4}$ in. diameter (from Table 9)
Bolts A193B7/A1942H Nuts

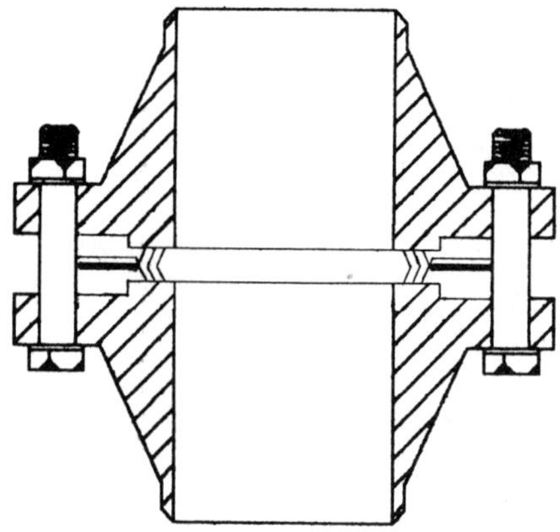

RAISED FACE WELDNECK FLANGE
WITH SPIRAL WOUND GASKET

From dimensions of spiral-wound gaskets (API 601, Table A-4)

Gaskets i.d.: 20.69 in.
Gaskets o.d.: 22.75 in.
Centering ring o.d.: 25.75 in.

$m = 3$, $y = 10{,}000$ (from Table 6 for spiral-wound asbestos-filled carbon, stainless steel, or Monel gasket)

To Find N

22.75″	o.d. gasket
−0.125″	For spiral-wound gasket
22.625″	o.d. (corrected)
−20.6875″	i.d. gasket
1.9375″	Nominal width of gasket

$$N = 1.9375/2 = 0.96875$$

$$b_o = \frac{N}{2} = \frac{0.96875}{2} = 0.48438$$

Since 0.48438 is greater than 1/4 in., then

$$b = \frac{\sqrt{b_0}}{2} = \sqrt{\frac{0.48438}{2}} = 0.3479$$

To Find G

22.75″	o.d. gasket
−0.125″	For spiral-wound gasket
22.625″	
−0.696″	$2b = 2\,(0.34798)$
21.929″	G

To Find Minimum Bolt Load for Operating Conditions

$$W_{m1} = \frac{3.14G^2P}{4} + (2b \times 3.14GmP)$$

$$= \frac{3.14(21.929)^2 630 \text{ lb/in.}^2}{4} + 2(0.34798)(3.14)(21.929)(3)630 \text{ lb/in.}^2$$

$$= 237{,}819.7 \text{ lb} + 90{,}572 \text{ lb}$$

$$= 328{,}391 \text{ lb}$$

To Find Gasket Seating Bolt Load

$$W_{m2} = 3.14bGy$$

$$= 3.14(0.34798)(21.929)10{,}000$$

$$= 239{,}609 \text{ lb}$$

To find the required cross-sectional area of bolts at operating temperature:

$$A_{m_1} = \frac{W_{m_1}}{S_b}$$

$$= 328{,}391/25{,}000^*$$

$$= 13.1 \text{ in.}^2$$

To find the required cross-sectional area of bolts at atmospheric temperature:

$$A_{m2} = \frac{W_{m2}}{S_a}$$

$$= 239{,}609/25{,}000^\dagger$$

$$= 9.6 \text{ in.}^2$$

To find actual stress:

$$S_g = \frac{A_b S_a}{0.785[(\text{o.d.} - 0.125)^2 - (\text{i.d.})^2]}$$

*From bolt strength Table 8 for A193 B7 bolts 2½ in. and under at 400°F.
†From bolt strength Table 8 for A193 B7 bolts 2½ in. and under at −20 to 100°F.

TABLE 7 Bolting Data for Standard Flanges

Nominal Pipe Size (in.)	150 lb/in.^{2} Series: Diameter of Flange (in.)	Number of Bolts	Diameter of Bolts (in.)	Bolt Circle (in.)	300 lb/in.^{2} Series: Diameter of Flange (in.)	Number of Bolts	Diameter of Bolts (in.)	Bolt Circle (in.)
$\frac{1}{4}$	$3\frac{3}{8}$	4	$\frac{1}{2}$	$2\frac{1}{4}$	$3\frac{3}{8}$	4	$\frac{1}{2}$	$2\frac{1}{4}$
$\frac{1}{2}$	$3\frac{1}{2}$	4	$\frac{1}{2}$	$2\frac{3}{8}$	$3\frac{3}{4}$	4	$\frac{1}{2}$	$2\frac{5}{8}$
$\frac{3}{4}$	$3\frac{7}{8}$	4	$\frac{1}{2}$	$2\frac{3}{4}$	$4\frac{5}{8}$	4	$\frac{5}{8}$	$3\frac{1}{4}$
1	$4\frac{1}{4}$	4	$\frac{1}{2}$	$3\frac{1}{8}$	$4\frac{7}{8}$	4	$\frac{5}{8}$	$3\frac{1}{2}$
$1\frac{1}{2}$	$4\frac{5}{8}$	4	$\frac{1}{2}$	$3\frac{1}{2}$	$5\frac{1}{4}$	4	$\frac{5}{8}$	$3\frac{7}{8}$
$1\frac{1}{2}$	5	4	$\frac{1}{2}$	$3\frac{7}{8}$	$6\frac{1}{8}$	4	$\frac{3}{4}$	$4\frac{1}{2}$
2	6	4	$\frac{5}{8}$	$4\frac{3}{4}$	$6\frac{1}{2}$	8	$\frac{5}{8}$	5
$2\frac{1}{2}$	7	4	$\frac{5}{8}$	$5\frac{1}{2}$	$7\frac{1}{2}$	8	$\frac{3}{4}$	$5\frac{7}{8}$
3	$7\frac{1}{2}$	4	$\frac{5}{8}$	6	$8\frac{1}{4}$	8	$\frac{3}{4}$	$6\frac{5}{8}$
$3\frac{1}{2}$	$8\frac{1}{2}$	8	$\frac{5}{8}$	7	9	8	$\frac{3}{4}$	$7\frac{1}{4}$
4	9	8	$\frac{5}{8}$	$7\frac{1}{2}$	10	8	$\frac{3}{4}$	$7\frac{7}{8}$
5	10	8	$\frac{3}{4}$	$8\frac{1}{2}$	11	8	$\frac{3}{4}$	$9\frac{1}{4}$
6	11	8	$\frac{3}{4}$	$9\frac{1}{2}$	$12\frac{1}{2}$	12	$\frac{3}{4}$	$10\frac{5}{8}$
8	$13\frac{1}{2}$	8	$\frac{3}{4}$	$11\frac{3}{4}$	15	12	$\frac{7}{8}$	13
10	16	12	$\frac{7}{8}$	$14\frac{1}{4}$	$17\frac{1}{2}$	16	1	$15\frac{1}{4}$
12	19	12	$\frac{7}{8}$	17	$20\frac{1}{2}$	16	$1\frac{1}{8}$	$17\frac{3}{4}$
14	21	12	1	$18\frac{3}{4}$	23	20	$1\frac{1}{8}$	$20\frac{1}{4}$
16	$23\frac{1}{2}$	16	1	$21\frac{1}{4}$	$25\frac{1}{2}$	20	$1\frac{1}{4}$	$22\frac{1}{2}$
18	25	16	$1\frac{1}{8}$	$22\frac{3}{4}$	28	24	$1\frac{1}{4}$	$24\frac{3}{4}$
20	$27\frac{1}{2}$	20	$1\frac{1}{8}$	25	$30\frac{1}{2}$	24	$1\frac{1}{4}$	27
24	32	20	$1\frac{1}{4}$	$29\frac{1}{2}$	36	24	$1\frac{1}{2}$	32

Nominal Pipe Size (in.)	900 lb/in.^{2} Series: Diameter of Flange (in.)	Number of Bolts	Diameter of Bolts (in.)	Bolt Circle (in.)
$\frac{1}{2}$	$4\frac{3}{4}$	4	$\frac{3}{4}$	$3\frac{1}{4}$
$\frac{3}{4}$	$5\frac{1}{8}$	4	$\frac{3}{4}$	$3\frac{1}{2}$
1	$5\frac{7}{8}$	4	$\frac{7}{8}$	4
$1\frac{1}{4}$	$6\frac{1}{4}$	4	$\frac{7}{8}$	$4\frac{3}{8}$
$1\frac{1}{2}$	7	4	1	$4\frac{7}{8}$
2	$8\frac{1}{2}$	8	$\frac{7}{8}$	$6\frac{1}{2}$
$2\frac{1}{2}$	$9\frac{5}{8}$	8	1	$7\frac{1}{2}$
3	$9\frac{1}{2}$	8	$\frac{7}{8}$	$7\frac{1}{2}$
4	$11\frac{1}{2}$	8	$1\frac{1}{8}$	$9\frac{1}{4}$
5	$13\frac{3}{4}$	8	$1\frac{1}{4}$	11
6	15	12	$1\frac{1}{8}$	$12\frac{1}{2}$
8	$18\frac{1}{2}$	12	$1\frac{3}{8}$	$15\frac{1}{2}$
10	$21\frac{1}{2}$	16	$1\frac{3}{8}$	$18\frac{1}{2}$
12	24	20	$1\frac{3}{8}$	21
14	$25\frac{1}{4}$	20	$1\frac{1}{2}$	22
16	$27\frac{3}{4}$	20	$1\frac{5}{8}$	$24\frac{1}{4}$
18	31	20	$1\frac{7}{8}$	27
20	$33\frac{3}{4}$	20	2	$29\frac{1}{2}$
24	41	20	$2\frac{1}{2}$	$35\frac{1}{2}$

400 lb/in.² Series				600 lb/in.² Series			
Diameter of Flange (in.)	Number of Bolts	Diameter of Bolts (in.)	Bolt Circle (in.)	Diameter of Flange (in.)	Number of Bolts	Diameter of Bolts (in.)	Bolt Circle (in.)
$3\frac{3}{8}$	4	$\frac{1}{2}$	$2\frac{1}{2}$	$3\frac{3}{8}$	4	$\frac{1}{2}$	$2\frac{1}{4}$
$3\frac{3}{4}$	4	$\frac{1}{2}$	$2\frac{5}{8}$	$3\frac{3}{4}$	4	$\frac{1}{2}$	$2\frac{5}{8}$
$4\frac{5}{8}$	4	$\frac{5}{8}$	$3\frac{1}{4}$	$4\frac{5}{8}$	4	$\frac{5}{8}$	$3\frac{1}{4}$
$4\frac{7}{8}$	4	$\frac{5}{8}$	$3\frac{1}{2}$	$4\frac{7}{8}$	4	$\frac{5}{8}$	$3\frac{1}{2}$
$5\frac{1}{4}$	4	$\frac{5}{8}$	$3\frac{7}{8}$	$5\frac{1}{4}$	4	$\frac{5}{8}$	$3\frac{7}{8}$
$6\frac{1}{8}$	4	$\frac{3}{4}$	$4\frac{1}{2}$	$6\frac{1}{8}$	4	$\frac{3}{4}$	$4\frac{1}{2}$
$6\frac{1}{2}$	8	$\frac{5}{8}$	5	$6\frac{1}{2}$	8	$\frac{5}{8}$	5
$7\frac{1}{2}$	8	$\frac{3}{4}$	$5\frac{7}{8}$	$7\frac{1}{2}$	8	$\frac{3}{4}$	$5\frac{7}{8}$
$8\frac{1}{4}$	8	$\frac{3}{4}$	$6\frac{5}{8}$	$8\frac{1}{4}$	8	$\frac{3}{4}$	$6\frac{5}{8}$
9	8	$\frac{7}{8}$	$7\frac{1}{4}$	9	8	$\frac{7}{8}$	$7\frac{1}{4}$
10	8	$\frac{7}{8}$	$7\frac{7}{8}$	$10\frac{3}{4}$	8	$\frac{7}{8}$	$8\frac{1}{2}$
11	8	$\frac{7}{8}$	$9\frac{1}{4}$	13	8	1	$10\frac{1}{2}$
$12\frac{1}{2}$	12	$\frac{7}{8}$	$10\frac{5}{8}$	14	12	1	$11\frac{1}{2}$
15	12	1	13	$16\frac{1}{2}$	12	$1\frac{1}{8}$	$13\frac{3}{4}$
$17\frac{1}{2}$	16	$1\frac{1}{8}$	$15\frac{1}{4}$	20	16	$1\frac{1}{4}$	17
$20\frac{1}{2}$	16	$1\frac{1}{4}$	$17\frac{3}{4}$	22	20	$1\frac{1}{4}$	$19\frac{1}{4}$
23	20	$1\frac{1}{4}$	$20\frac{1}{4}$	$23\frac{3}{4}$	20	$1\frac{3}{8}$	$20\frac{3}{4}$
$25\frac{1}{2}$	20	$1\frac{3}{8}$	$22\frac{1}{2}$	27	20	$1\frac{1}{2}$	$23\frac{3}{4}$
28	24	$1\frac{3}{8}$	$24\frac{3}{4}$	$29\frac{1}{4}$	20	$1\frac{5}{8}$	$25\frac{3}{4}$
$30\frac{1}{2}$	24	$1\frac{1}{2}$	27	32	24	$1\frac{5}{8}$	$28\frac{1}{2}$
36	24	$1\frac{3}{4}$	32	37	24	$1\frac{7}{8}$	33

1500 lb/in.² Series				2500 lb/in.² Series			
Diameter of Flange (in.)	Number of Bolts	Diameter of Bolts (in.)	Bolt Circle (in.)	Diameter of Flange (in.)	Number of Bolts	Diameter of Bolts (in.)	Bolt Circle (in.)
$4\frac{3}{4}$	4	$\frac{3}{4}$	$3\frac{1}{4}$	$5\frac{1}{4}$	4	$\frac{3}{4}$	$3\frac{1}{2}$
$5\frac{1}{8}$	4	$\frac{3}{4}$	$3\frac{1}{2}$	$5\frac{1}{2}$	4	$\frac{3}{4}$	$3\frac{3}{4}$
$5\frac{7}{8}$	4	$\frac{7}{8}$	4	$6\frac{1}{4}$	4	$\frac{7}{8}$	$4\frac{1}{4}$
$6\frac{1}{4}$	4	$\frac{7}{8}$	$4\frac{3}{8}$	$7\frac{1}{4}$	4	1	$5\frac{1}{8}$
7	4	1	$4\frac{7}{8}$	8	4	$1\frac{1}{8}$	$5\frac{3}{4}$
$8\frac{1}{4}$	8	$\frac{7}{8}$	$6\frac{1}{2}$	$9\frac{1}{4}$	8	1	$6\frac{3}{4}$
$9\frac{5}{8}$	8	1	$7\frac{1}{2}$	$10\frac{1}{2}$	8	$1\frac{1}{8}$	$7\frac{3}{4}$
$10\frac{1}{2}$	8	$1\frac{1}{8}$	8	12	8	$1\frac{1}{4}$	9
$12\frac{1}{4}$	8	$1\frac{1}{4}$	$9\frac{1}{2}$	14	8	$1\frac{1}{2}$	$10\frac{3}{4}$
$14\frac{3}{4}$	8	$1\frac{1}{2}$	$11\frac{1}{2}$	$16\frac{1}{2}$	8	$1\frac{3}{4}$	$12\frac{3}{4}$
$15\frac{1}{2}$	12	$1\frac{3}{8}$	$12\frac{1}{2}$	19	8	2	$14\frac{1}{2}$
19	12	$1\frac{5}{8}$	$15\frac{1}{2}$	$21\frac{3}{4}$	12	2	$17\frac{1}{4}$
23	12	$1\frac{7}{8}$	19	$26\frac{1}{2}$	12	$2\frac{1}{2}$	$21\frac{1}{4}$
$26\frac{1}{2}$	16	2	$22\frac{1}{2}$	30	12	$2\frac{3}{4}$	$24\frac{3}{8}$
$29\frac{1}{2}$	16	$2\frac{1}{4}$	25	—	—	—	—
$32\frac{1}{2}$	16	$2\frac{1}{2}$	$27\frac{3}{4}$	—	—	—	—
36	16	$2\frac{3}{4}$	$30\frac{1}{2}$	—	—	—	—
$38\frac{3}{4}$	16	3	$32\frac{3}{4}$	—	—	—	—
46	16	$3\frac{1}{2}$	39	—	—	—	—

TABLE 8 Maximum Design Stresses for Bolting Materials (See ANSI B31.3 Appendix A, Table 2 for a complete listing of materials and temperatures to 1500°F) (stresses are in KSI)

Material	ASTM Spec	Grade	Size Range	−20 to 100°F	200°F	300°F	400°F	500°F	600°F	650°F	700°F	750°F
				Carbon Steel								
	A675	45		11.2	11.2	11.2	11.2	11.2	11.2	11.2	11.0	10.2
	A675	50		12.5	12.5	12.5	12.5	12.5	12.5	12.5	12.1	11.1
	A675	55		13.7	13.7	13.7	13.7	13.7	13.7	13.7	13.2	12.0
	A675	60		15.0	15.0	15.0	15.0	15.0	15.0	15.0	14.3	12.9
	A307	B		13.7	13.7	13.7	13.7	13.7				
	A325			19.3	19.3	19.3	19.3	19.3	19.3	19.3	—	—
				Alloy Steel								
5Cr	A193	B5	4 in. and under	200	20.0	20.0	20.0	20.0	20.0	20.0	20.0	20.0
Cr–Mo	A193	B7	$2\frac{1}{2}$ in. and under	25.0	25.0	25.0	25.0	25.0	25.0	25.0	25.0	23.6
Cr–Mo	A193	B7	Over $2\frac{1}{2}$ in. to 4 in.	23.0	23.0	23.0	23.0	23.0	23.0	23.0	23.0	22.2
Cr–0.2Mo	A193	B7M	$2\frac{1}{2}$ in. and under	20.0	20.0	20.0	20.0	20.0	20.0	20.0	20.0	20.0
Cr–Mo–V	A193	B16	$2\frac{1}{2}$ in. and under	25.0	25.0	25.0	25.0	25.0	25.0	25.0	25.0	25.0
Cr–Mo–V	A193	B16	Over $2\frac{1}{2}$ in. to 4 in.	22.0	22.0	22.0	22.0	22.0	22.0	22.0	22.0	22.0
				−325 to 100°F	200°F	300°F	400°F	500°F	600°F	650°F	700°F	750°F
				Stainless Steel								
304 Soln Trtd	A193	B8,CL.1		18.8	15.6	14.0	12.9	12.1	11.4	11.2	11.0	10.8
316 Soln Trtd	A193	B8M,C1.1		18.8	16.1	14.6	13.3	12.5	11.8	11.5	11.3	10.8
304 Strn Hrd	A193	B8,CL.2	Up to $\frac{3}{4}$ in.	25.0	15.6	14.0	12.9	12.1	11.4	11.2	11.0	10.8
304 Strn Hrd	A193	B8,CL.2	$\frac{3}{4}$ in. to 1 in.	20.0	15.6	14.0	12.9	12.1	11.4	11.2	11.0	10.8
304 Strn Hrd	A193	B8,CL2	Over 1 to $1\frac{1}{4}$ in.	18.8	15.6	14.0	12.9	12.1	11.4	11.2	11.0	10.8
304 Strn Hrd	A193	B8,CL2	Over $1\frac{1}{4}$ to $1\frac{1}{2}$ in.	18.8	15.6	14.0	12.9	12.1	11.4	11.2	11.0	10.8
316 Strn Hrd	A193	B8M,CL.2	Up to $\frac{3}{4}$ in.	22.0	22.0	22.0	22.0	22.0	22.0	22.0	22.0	20.0
316 Strn Hrd	A193	B8M,CL.2	$\frac{3}{4}$ to 1 in.	20.0	20.0	20.0	20.0	20.0	20.0	20.0	20.0	20.0
316 Strn Hrd	A193	B8M,CL.2	Over 1 in. to $1\frac{1}{4}$ in.	18.8	16.2	16.2	16.2	16.2	16.2	16.2	16.2	16.2
316 Strn Hrd	A193	B8M,CL.2	Over $1\frac{1}{4}$ in. to $1\frac{1}{2}$ in.	18.8	16.1	14.6	13.3	12.5	12.5	12.5	12.5	12.5

To find the actual cross-sectional area of bolts (from ANSI B16.5): 1 1/4 in. diameter bolt has root thread area of 0.929 in.^{2} (see Table 9 for alloy steel bolts).

Since the material is an alloy bolt (ASTM A193 B7), diameter less than 2 1/2 in., A_b = actual cross-sectional area of one bolt from above 0.929 in.^{2}. But there are 24 bolts compressing the gasket, therefore:

A_b = 0.929 in.^{2} (1 bolt area) × 24 = 22.296 in.^{2} (actual total cross-sectional root area of bolts)

$$S_g = \frac{22.296^2 \text{ in. } (25{,}000 \text{ lb/in.}^2)}{0.785[(22.75 - 0.125)^2 - (20.69)^2]}$$

$$= \frac{557{,}500}{0.785[511.890625 - 428.0761]}$$

$$= \frac{557{,}500}{0.785(83.814525)}$$

$$= 8471.85 \text{ lb/in.}^2$$

Since 8471.85 lb/in.^{2} is within the allowable stress limits (25,000 lb/in.^{2}) for spiral-wound gaskets with asbestos filler, the gasket is okay to use.

It is very unusual for the above calculations to be performed since standardization has been established for many flanges and gaskets. The piping engineer specifies the flanges and gaskets compatible with the process fluid, temperature, and pressure, and which have served satisfactorily on previous jobs. Many gasket manufacturers will perform this calculation upon request.

Notation Used in Calculations

A_b	actual total cross-sectional root area of bolts or section of least diameter under stress (in.^{2}) (see Table 9 depending on bolting material)
A_m	total required cross-sectional area of bolts, taken as greater of A_{m_1} or A_{m2} (in.^{2})
A_{m_1}	total required cross-sectional area of bolts required for operating conditions (in.^{2})
A_{m2}	total required cross-sectional area of bolts required for gasket seating (in.^{2})
b	effective seating width (in.)
$2b$	joint-contact-surface pressure width (in.)
b_0	basic gasket seating width (in.)
G	diameter (in.) of location of gasket load reaction. When $b_0 \leq 4$ in., G = mean diameter of contact face (in.). When $b_0 > 4$ in., G = o.d. of gasket contact face minus $2b$ (in.)
m	gasket factor
N	used to determine the basic gasket seating width b_0 based upon the possible contact width of the gasket
P	design pressure (lb/in.^{2})
S_a	allowable bolt stress at atmospheric temperature (lb/in.^{2})

TABLE 9 Data for Use with Machine Bolts and Cold Rolled Steel Stud Bolts: Load in Pounds on Bolts and Stud Bolts when Torque Loads Are Applied

Nominal Diameter of Bolt (in.)	Number of Threads (per in.)	Diameter at Root of Thread (in.)	Area at Root of Thread ($in.^2$)	Stress: 7,500 $lb/in.^2$		Stress: 15,000 $lb/in.^2$		Stress: 30,000 $lb/in.^2$	
				Torque (ft-lb)	Compression (lb)	Torque (ft-lb)	Compression (lb)	Torque (ft-lb)	Compression (lb)
$\frac{1}{4}$	20	0.185	0.027	1	203	2	405	4	810
$\frac{5}{16}$	18	0.240	0.045	2	338	4	675	8	1,350
$\frac{3}{8}$	16	0.294	0.068	3	510	6	1,020	12	2,040
$\frac{7}{16}$	14	0.345	0.093	5	698	10	1,395	20	2,790
$\frac{1}{2}$	13	0.400	0.126	8	945	15	1,890	30	3,780
$\frac{9}{16}$	12	0.454	0.162	12	1,215	23	2,430	45	4,860
$\frac{5}{8}$	11	0.507	0.202	15	1,515	30	3,030	60	6,060
$\frac{3}{4}$	10	0.620	0.302	25	2,265	50	4,530	100	9,060
$\frac{7}{8}$	9	0.731	0.419	40	3,143	80	6,285	160	12,570
1	8	0.838	0.551	62	4,133	123	8,265	245	16,530
$1\frac{1}{8}$	7	0.939	0.693	98	5,190	195	10,380	390	20,760
$1\frac{1}{4}$	7	1.064	0.890	137	6,675	273	13,350	545	26,700
$1\frac{3}{8}$	6	1.158	1.054	183	7,905	365	15,810	730	31,620
$1\frac{1}{2}$	6	1.283	1.294	219	9,705	437	19,410	875	38,820
$1\frac{5}{8}$	$5\frac{1}{2}$	1.389	1.515	300	11,363	600	22,725	1,200	45,450
$1\frac{3}{4}$	5	1.490	1.744	390	13,080	775	26,160	1,550	52,320
$1\frac{7}{8}$	5	1.615	2.049	525	15,368	1,050	30,735	2,100	61,470
2	$4\frac{1}{2}$	1.711	2.300	563	17,250	1,125	34,500	2,250	69,000

Data for Use with Alloy Steel Stud Bolts:
Load in Pounds on Stud Bolts when Torque Loads Are Applied

Nominal Diameter of Stud (in.)	Number of Threads (per in.)	Diameter at Root of Thread (in.)	Area at Root of Thread ($in.^2$)	Stress: 30,000 $lb/in.^2$ Torque (ft-lb)	Stress: 30,000 $lb/in.^2$ Compression (lb)	Stress: 45,000 $lb/in.^2$ Torque (ft-lb)	Stress: 45,000 $lb/in.^2$ Compression (lb)	Stress: 60,000 $lb/in.^2$ Torque (ft-lb)	Stress: 60,000 $lb/in.^2$ Compression (lb)
$\frac{1}{4}$	20	0.185	0.027	4	810	6	1,215	8	1,620
$\frac{5}{16}$	18	0.240	0.045	8	1,350	12	2,025	16	2,700
$\frac{3}{8}$	16	0.294	0.068	12	2,040	18	3,060	24	4,080
$\frac{7}{16}$	14	0.345	0.093	20	2,790	30	4,185	40	5,580
$\frac{1}{2}$	13	0.400	0.126	30	3,780	45	5,670	60	7,560
$\frac{9}{16}$	12	0.454	0.162	45	4,860	68	7,290	90	9,720
$\frac{5}{8}$	11	0.507	0.202	60	6,060	90	9,090	120	12,120
$\frac{3}{4}$	10	0.620	0.302	100	9,060	150	13,590	200	18,120
$\frac{7}{8}$	9	0.731	0.419	160	12,570	240	18,855	320	25,140
1	8	0.838	0.551	245	16,530	368	24,795	490	33,060
$1\frac{1}{8}$	8	0.963	0.728	355	21,840	533	32,760	710	43,680
$1\frac{1}{4}$	8	1.088	0.929	500	27,870	750	41,805	1,000	55,740
$1\frac{3}{8}$	8	1.213	1.155	680	34,650	1,020	51,975	1,360	69,300
$1\frac{1}{2}$	8	1.338	1.405	800	42,150	1,200	63,225	1,600	84,300
$1\frac{5}{8}$	8	1.463	1.680	1,100	50,400	1,650	75,600	2,200	100,800
$1\frac{3}{4}$	8	1.588	1.980	1,500	59,400	2,250	89,100	3,000	118,800
$1\frac{7}{8}$	8	1.713	2.304	2,000	69,120	3,000	103,680	4,000	138,240
2	8	1.838	2.652	2,200	79,560	3,300	119,340	4,400	159,120
$2\frac{1}{4}$	8	2.088	3.423	3,180	102,690	4,770	154,035	6,360	205,380
$2\frac{1}{2}$	8	2.338	4.292	4,400	128,760	6,600	193,140	8,800	257,520
$2\frac{3}{4}$	8	2.588	5.259	5,920	157,770	8,880	236,655	11,840	315,540
3	8	2.838	6.324	7,720	189,720	11,580	284,580	15,440	379,440

S_b	allowable bolt stress at design (operating temperature; lb/in.^{2})
S_g	actual unit stress at gasket bearing surface (lb/in.^{2})
W	flange design bolt load (lb)
W_{m_1}	minimum required bolt load for operating conditions (lb)
W_{m2}	minimum required bolt load for gasket seating (lb)
Y	minimum gasket seating stress (lb/in.^{2})
o.d.	outside diameter of gasket (in.)
i.d.	inside diameter of gasket (in.)

Following are ASME/API gasket standards:

ANSI B16.21 Nonmetallic Flat Gaskets for Pipe Flanges. These standards cover full face, self-centering ring, and small flat ring raised-face gaskets, large male and female, and large tongue and groove gaskets; small male and female, also small tongue and groove faced flanges. Gaskets for the following types of flanges are dimensioned: ANSI B16.1—Cast Iron; ANSI B16.5—Steel Pipe; ANSI B16.24—Bronze Flanges, API 605—Large Diameter Carbon Steel Flanges; MSS-SP44 Steel Pipe Line Flanges; MSS-SP51 Corrosion Resistant Flanges.

ANSI B16.20 STANDARD is for *Ring-Joint Gaskets and Grooves for Steel Pipe Flanges*.

API STANDARD 601 deals with *Metallic Gaskets for Raised Face Pipe Flanges* and *Flanged Connections (double jacketed corrugated and spiral wound)*. Dimensions are given for ANSI B16.5, API-605, and MSS-SP44 Flanges.

Installing Gaskets

1. The flange surface where the gasket sits must be clean and free of all scratches, pits, or cracks and tool marks, and especially radial scratches across the grooves.
2. The gasket should be inspected to be sure it is the one specified.
3. All bolts, studs, units, and washers should be cleaned and inspected for any damaging signs of pitting and galling.
4. Nut facings, bolts, or studs should be well lubricated. Graphite and oil is recommended for most; for high temperature, use some antiseize compounds. These lubricants will help achieve the necessary bolt stress required for flange tightening.
5. For raised face installations, insert the bolts in the lower half of the flanges, then slip the gasket in, insert the remaining bolts, and hand-tighten. If the flanges are grooved, insert the gasket in the groove; if necessary to prevent its falling out, apply a dab of some grease that is compatible with the process fluid to hold it in place until the bolts or studs are tightened.
6. In tightening bolts, follow the procedure known as "the sequential order." Preliminary tightening should be no more than 30% of the recommended

bolt stress. If the sequence is not followed, there is a possibility of cracking the flanges and crushing the gasket.

7. Increase the torque to approximately 50 to 70% of the required stress.
8. When the above is completed, do a clockwise rotational torque, checking the torque until the required bolt stress has been achieved.
9. In many cases, low yield bolting materials, such as common carbon steel bolts, may be specified. Upon hydrostatic testing, which is one and a half times the design pressure, flanges may be found to leak since the bolt stress has been exceeded. Appendix S of the ASME Section VIII, Division 1, Pressure Vessel Code states that in order to pass the hydrostatic test, bolts may be stressed to higher values. With ordinary carbon steel bolts, the yield point of the material may be exceeded. If this occurs, it is recommended that high tensile bolts and nuts should be used to pass the hydrostatic test satisfactorily.

   When the hydrostatic test is passed, the tensile stress on the bolts should be relieved to 50% of the allowable bolt stress and the high tensile bolting material replaced by the specified bolting material. After replacement, these bolts should be stressed to the allowable stress for the operating conditions. Then the previously specified bolting-up procedures may be continued.

   In high temperature situations, the bolt stress may be relaxed due to the creep of the bolt material. When this occurs and the bolt material is in the upper end of its stress range, it is possible for flange leakage to occur in time. It is therefore suggested that a bolt in this situation be prestressed to the required bolt stress at operating conditions to assure a leak-free joint.

   Differences in thermal expansion between the materials of the bolts and the flanges may vary the bolt stress. One of the solutions to this problem is the use of conical spring washers on the bolts. These will maintain a constant stress on the bolts.

   Tables of allowable bolt stresses for different materials are given in most gasket manufacturers' catalogs.

Sources

ASME Pressure Vessel Code Section VIII
Appendix 2
Appendix 3

PVRC Gasket Test Program
H. D. Raut and G. F. Leon
Varysburg Gasket Laboratory, New York

General Dynamics Electric Boat Division
Groton, Connecticut
ASME 1977 Energy Technology Conference

G. Blick, "Bending Moments and Leakage at Flanged Joints," *Petroleum Refiner*, 1950

H.D. Raut, A. Bazerqui, and L. Marchand, *Gasket Leakage Behavior Trends*, WRC Bulletin 271

K. Granek and F. W. Heckenkamp, "Spiral-Wound Gaskets—Panacea or Problem," *Chemical Engineering*, March 23, 1981

Flexatallic Gasket Company
Parker Seals
Sepco Metallic Gaskets
Garlock, etc.
Lamons Metal Gasket Co., *Gasket Handbook*, 1980

Glossary of Trademarks

Viton: E. I. du Pont de Nemours & Co. trademark for a series of fluoroelastomers based on the copolymer of vinylidene fluoride and hexafluoropropylene

Hypalon: E. I. du Pont de Nemours & Co. trademark for chlorosulfonated polyethylene, a synthetic rubber

Teflon: E. I. du Pont de Nemours & Co. trademark for tetrafluoroethylene (TFE) polymers. The name also applies to fluorinated ethylene–propylene (FEF) resins

Kel-F: 3M Company trademark for a series of fluorocarbon products

Grafoil: High Temperature Materials, Inc. trademark for pure flexible graphite tape

Hastelloy: Haveg Industries, Inc. trademark for a series of high-strength, nickel-base, corrosion-resistant alloys

Monel: Huntington Alloy Products Division, International Nickel Co., Inc., trademark for a large group of corrosion-resistant alloys

Inconel: Huntington Alloy Products Division, International Nickel Co., Inc., trademark for a group of corrosion-resistant alloys

Incoloy: Huntington Alloy Products Division, International Nickel Co., Inc., trademark for a group of corrosion-resistant alloys

Buna-N: Buna Chemische Werke, Schkopan, Germany, trademark for butadiene–acrylonitrile copolymer

Neoprene: E. I. du Pont de Nemours & Co. trademark

ABEL A. ZELNICK

Grease Manufacture

General Technology of Greases

Lubricating greases that are marketed today are complex products. They consist of a thickener, a fluid lubricant, and additives to enhance certain properties of the grease. The thickener may be any of a number of materials that include soaps, such as those formed by the saponification of a fatty material with an alkali; nonsoap chemical compounds, such as those based on a urea derivative; and inorganic materials, such as those made from certain clays (i.e., montmorillonite). The success of a thickener to form a grease depends on one or more of the following: (1) the solvency of the fluid medium for the thickener and the solubility of the thickener in the fluid, (2) the attractive forces between the thickener and the fluid, (3) the capillary forces that hold the fluid within the network of thickener particles (or fibers), and (4) the mechanical interlocking of the fiber network of the thickener itself.

For a thickener system to be effective in a grease, it must have the proper fiber structure. With the aid of an electron microscope, the soap fibers can be photographed and studied. As discussed later, the type of fiber structure developed greatly affects the properties of the finished grease, and processing conditions are the key to forming the desired fiber structure. Figures 1, 2, and 3 show the typical fiber structure for three of the more widely used grease thickeners. As noted, the micrograph (Fig. 1) for the sodium soap grease shows a thick, rope-like fiber structure; the micrograph (Fig. 2) for the calcium soap grease shows a short, very dense fiber structure; and the micrograph (Fig. 3) for the lithium soap grease shows a long, twisted fiber structure.

The fluid lubricant most commonly used to formulate greases is an oil derived from petroleum. Either paraffinic or naphthenic oils can be used, and these can be either a single viscosity component or a blend of low and high viscosity components. Most soaps are more soluble in a naphthenic oil, whereas a paraffinic oil is inherently more resistant to oxidation. As a general rule the composition of the fluid lubricant is selected on the basis of the thickener used and the performance characteristics required, and a blended base oil is often used. Synthetic base oils can also be used, including synthetic hydrocarbons, such as poly-α-olefins and dialkylbenzenes; organic esters, such as dibasic acid esters and polyol esters; polyalkylene glycols; and various silicone fluids. Due to their higher cost, synthetic base oils are usually used in specialty greases where extreme low temperature or high temperature performance characteristics are required.

Additives are used to modify and improve certain properties of the grease. The principal types of additives used are antioxidants, rust and corrosion inhibitors, extreme pressure (EP)-antiwear-lubricity agents, and solid fillers. Antioxidants are used to protect the grease during storage and to extend the service life at elevated temperatures. Common types of antioxidants used include various amines, substituted phenols, and metal carbamates. Rust and

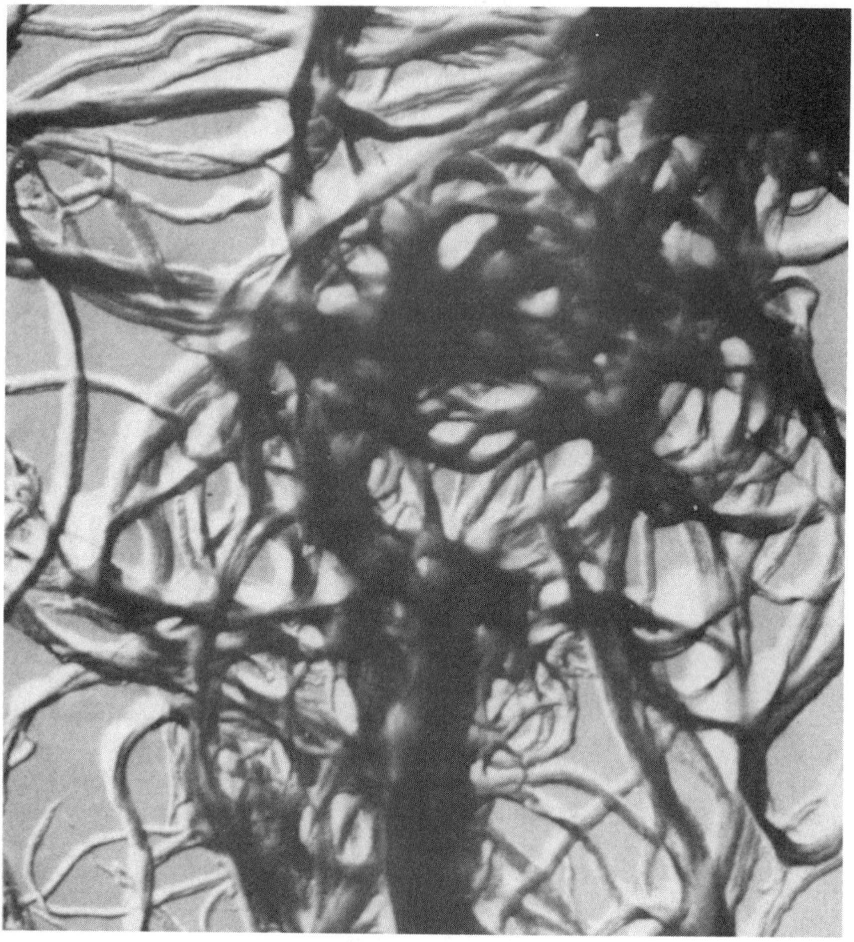

FIG. 1. Electron micrograph of sodium soap grease (8000×).

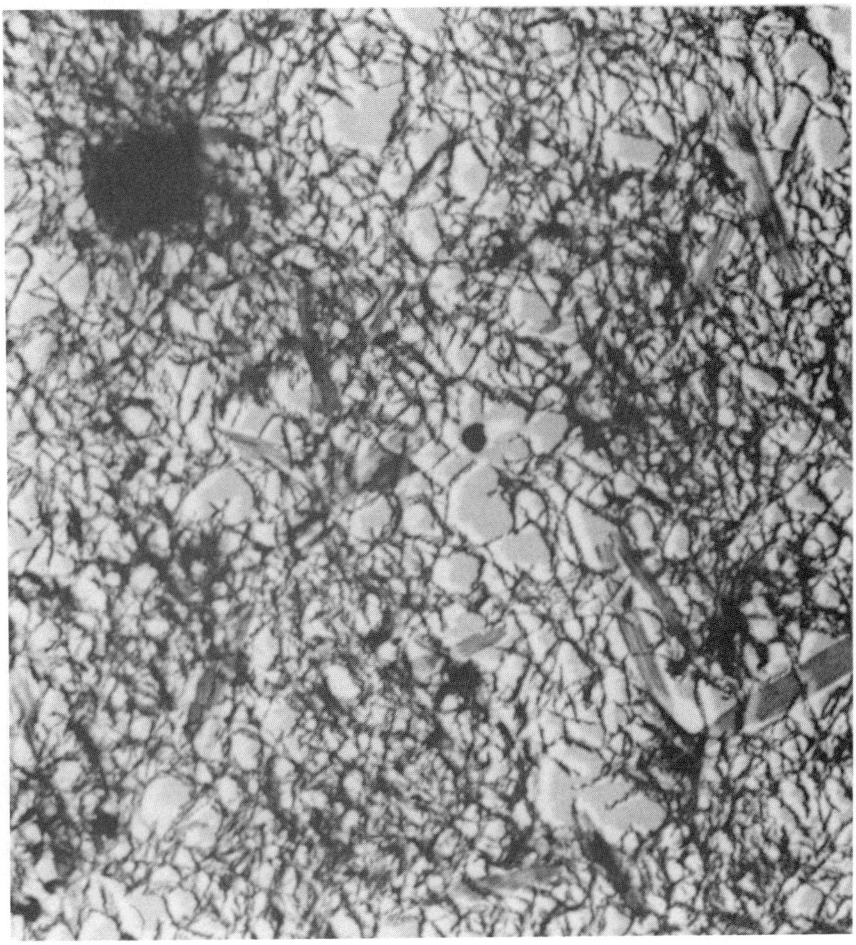

FIG. 2. Electron micrograph of calcium soap grease (8000×).

corrosion inhibitors provide protection from rusting in the presence of water and inhibit the grease from attacking certain metals such as copper, steel, and bronze. Such inhibitors include various sulfonates, fatty amine derivatives, amine phosphates, benzotriazoles, and mercaptothiodiazoles. EP additives function to extend the loads that can be carried by the lubricant film; antiwear additives reduce wear under boundary lubrication; and lubricity agents reduce and smooth friction under conditions of low sliding speeds. EP-antiwear-lubricity additives include materials such as sulfurized fatty oils, dithiocarbamates, zinc dialkyldithiophosphates, chlorinated paraffins, and various sulfur/phosphorous compounds. Solid fillers are used to improve grease performance under adverse conditions. The more commonly used fillers are graphite, molybdenum disulfide, and various powdered metals such as lead, copper, and zinc.

The single most distinguishing property of a grease is its consistency, which is defined as the depth in tenths of a millimeter, that a standard cone

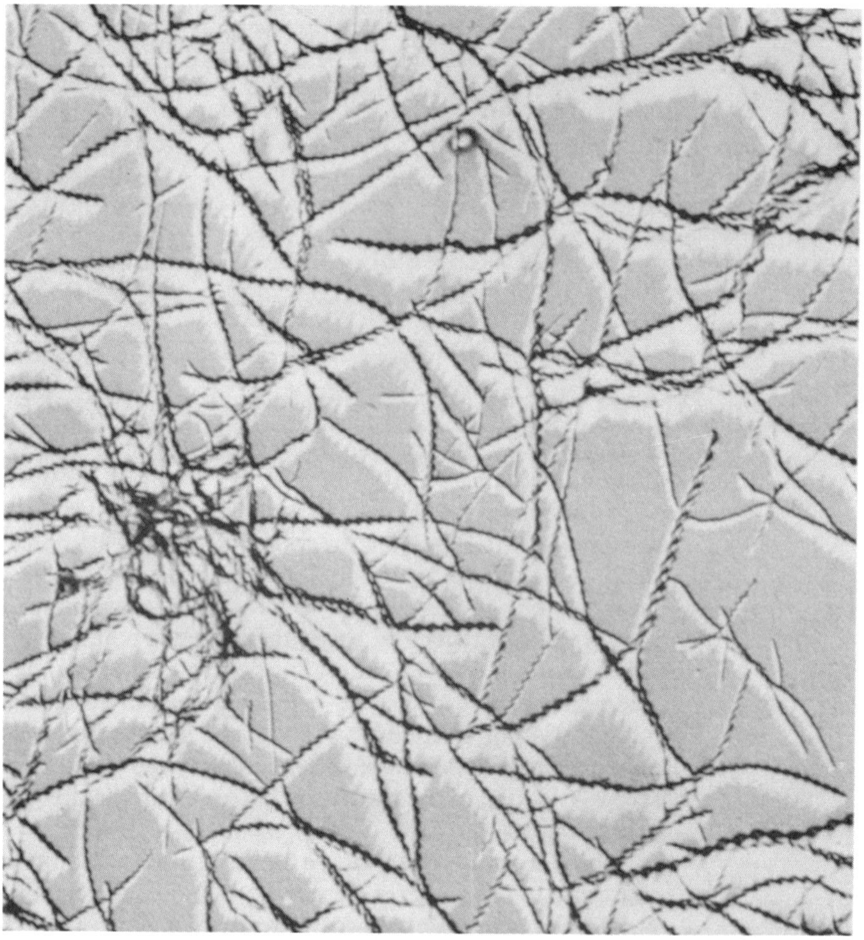

FIG. 3. Electron micrograph of lithium soap grease (8000×).

penetrates the sample under prescribed conditions of weight, time, and temperature. In order to obtain a uniform sample, the grease is worked 60 strokes in a prescribed worker before running the penetration. Based on worked penetration, the National Lubricating Grease Institute (NLGI) has devised a classification system for greases using defined consistency numbers ranging from 000 (very soft) to 6 (very hard). Each consistency number has a range of 30 penetration units with a 15 penetration-unit range between each number. This classification system is shown in Table 1. The classification number is commonly referred to as the grade and is used when specifying and discussing greases.

Another important property of a grease is the dropping point. Greases do not have a sharp melting point, but upon heating, become softer until at some point they become essentially fluid and no longer function as a thickened lubricant. To determine the dropping point of a grease, a sample is placed in a test cup that contains a small orifice and is heated at a uniform rate. The dropping point is reported as the temperature when the first drop of material falls from the lower end of the cup. Dropping points are useful in characteriz-

TABLE 1 NLGI Classification of Greases

NLGI Grade	Penetration Range
000	445–475
00	400–430
0	355–385
1	310–340
2	265–295
3	220–250
4	175–205
5	130–160
6	85–115

ing greases as each type of soap thickener exhibits a particular dropping point range. Table 2 shows the typical dropping point range for the commonly used grease thickeners.

As a general rule, greases cannot be used at temperatures above their dropping points. However, the dropping point by itself does not establish the maximum usable temperature for a grease as other factors, such as oxidation, must also be considered. The recommended maximum usable temperature for a grease is usually well below the dropping point, as indicated in Table 2. The maximum usable temperature generally indicates the temperature limit where the grease can be used without frequent relubrication. With frequent relubrication or continuous lubrication, the maximum usable temperature can be raised. Extended use at temperatures above 350°F will usually result in severe oxidation of the petroleum base oil such that frequent relubrication is necessary.

There are many other grease properties that are important. These include resistance to softening (shear stability), flow characteristics (greases are non-Newtonian materials whose viscosity is a function of shear rate), water resistance, antiwear, oxidation stability, high-temperature bearing life, and low temperature properties. All of these can be defined by specific tests that are described in the ASTM Standard Methods of Tests and will not be discussed here.

TABLE 2 Dropping Point and Maximum Usable Temperature of Greases

Thickener Type	Dropping Point (approximate) (°F)	Maximum Usable Temperature (°F)
Calcium, water stabilized	210–220	175
Aluminum	220–230	175
Calcium, anhydrous	275–285	225
Sodium	340–350	250
Lithium	385–395	275
Complex soap	Above 450	350
Nonsoap, Polyurea	Above 450	350
Organo-clay	Above 500	350

Types, Characteristics, and Usage of Greases

As noted in an earlier paragraph, greases can be classified as to the type of thickener used. The following will discuss greases classified as soap thickened, complex soap thickened, and nonsoap thickened. A type, characteristic, and usage summary is shown in Table 3.

Soap Thickened Greases

Soaps that are used in the manufacture of greases are made by reacting a long-chain fatty material with an alkali. Soap thickened greases include aluminum soap greases, sodium soap greases, calcium soap greases, and lithium soap greases. Aluminum soaps are made by reacting aluminum hydroxide with a fatty acid such as stearic acid, but most grease manufacturers use a preformed aluminum di-stearate soap. The finished grease is characterized by having a smooth, gel-like appearance, a low dropping point, good water resistance, and greater thixotropic behavior (softening or hardening dependent on shearing rate) than most other greases. Usage of this type of grease has greatly decreased, but it is still used on some older-designed equipment to lubricate slow-speed bearings, particularly those under wet conditions.

Sodium soaps are made by reacting sodium hydroxide with a tallow-derived triglyceride or fatty acid. The finished grease is characterized by having a rough, fibrous appearance, a moderately high dropping point, very poor water resistance, and good adhesive (cohesive) properties. Sodium greases are widely used today in various industrial and automotive applications, such as in rolling contact bearings.

Calcium soaps are made by reacting calcium hydroxide (lime) with either 12-hydroxystearic acid (derived from caster oil) or with a tallow-derived triglyceride. The grease made from the castor oil derivative is usually referred to as an anhydrous calcium grease, whereas the grease made from the tallow derivative is referred to as a water-stabilized calcium grease. The water-stabilized grease contains up to 2 wt.% water which aids in the formation of the soap fibers. Both greases are characterized by having a smooth, buttery appearance and good water resistance. The dropping point of the anhydrous grease is higher than the dropping point of the water-stabilized product, as indicated in Table 2. Calcium greases are widely used for bearing lubrication in the presence of water and as a general purpose railroad rail lubricant.

Lithium soaps are made by reacting lithium hydroxide with a fatty acid, primarily 12-hydroxystearic acid. The finished grease is characterized by having a smooth and buttery to slightly stringy appearance, a high dropping point, good resistance to softening and leakage, and moderate water resistance. Lithium greases represent over 60% of the United States grease market and are used throughout the automotive and industrial market as a chassis lubricant, wheel bearing grease, and a ball and roller bearing grease.

TABLE 3 Type, Characteristics, and Usage of Greases

Type	Characteristics	Usage
	Soap Thickened	
Aluminum	Smooth, gel-like appearance Low dropping point Good water resistance Softening/hardening tendencies greatly dependent on shear rate	Lubricate low-speed bearings Wet applications Usage decreasing
Sodium	Rough, fibrous appearance Moderately high dropping point Poor water resistance Good adhesive (cohesive) properties	Older industrial equipment where relubrication is frequent Rolling contact bearings
Calcium	Smooth, buttery appearance Low dropping points Good water resistance	Bearings in wet applications Railroad rail lubricant
Lithium	Smooth, buttery to slightly stringy appearance High dropping point Resistant to softening and leakage Moderate water resistance	Automotive chassis lubricant Automotive wheel bearings General industrial grease Thread lubricants for the oil drilling industry
	Complex Soaps	
Aluminum complex	Smooth, slight gel-like appearance Dropping points above 450°F, Good water resistance Resistant to softening Shorter life at high temperature	Steel mill roll neck, rolling, and plain bearings
Calcium complex	Smooth, buttery appearance Dropping points above 450°F Good water resistance Inherent EP or load-carrying capabilities	High-temperature industrial and automotive bearing applications
Lithium complex	Smooth, buttery appearance Dropping points above 450°F Resistant to softening and leakage Moderate water resistance	Automotive wheel bearings High-temperature industrial service including various roller-element bearing applications
	Nonsoap Thickeners	
Polyurea	Smooth, slightly opaque appearance Dropping points above 450°F Good water resistance Oxidation resistant Less resistant to softening and leakage	Industrial roller-element bearings Automotive constant-velocity joints
Organo-clay	Smooth and buttery appearance Dropping points above 500°F Resistant to leakage Good water resistance	High temperature bearings with frequent relubrication Steel mill roll neck bearings

Complex Soap Greases

A complex soap is usually described as a soap wherein the soap is formed by cocrystallization of two or more compounds, one being a long-chain fatty acid as used to form a normal soap and the other being a complexing agent as represented by a short-chain organic acid. Complex soap thickened greases include aluminum complex, calcium complex, and lithium complex greases. All of these complex greases exhibit very high dropping points, usually above 450°F. This single property enables these greases to be used in high-temperature applications that would exclude use of their noncomplex soap counterparts discussed above.

Aluminum complex thickeners are made by reacting an organoaluminum compound, such as aluminum isopropoxide, with a fatty acid, such as stearic acid, and a cyclic acid, such as benzoic acid. The finished grease is characterized by having a smooth, slightly gel-like appearance, excellent resistance to softening, and good water resistance, but relatively shorter life at high temperatures than the other complex greases.

Calcium complex thickeners are made by reacting calcium hydroxide with a fatty acid, such as 12-hydroxystearic acid, and acetic acid. Calcium complex greases have a smooth, buttery appearance, good water resistance, and inherent extreme pressure or load-carrying capabilities.

Lithium complex thickeners are made by reacting lithium hydroxide with a fatty acid, such as 12-hydroxystearic acid, and either a dicarboxylic acid, such as azelaic acid, or the dimethyl ester derivative of the dicarboxylic acid. The finished grease has properties very similar to those of a regular lithium grease except for its improved high temperature properties related to the increased dropping point. Lithium complex greases are therefore finding wide application as high temperature wheel and roller bearing greases and as general purpose industrial greases.

Nonsoap Greases

Nonsoap thickened greases are those that utilize a chemical (nonsoap) thickener or an organo-clay thickener. One of the more commonly used chemical thickeners is polyurea. A polyurea thickener is made by reacting a diisocyanate with a diamine and a monoamine. A tetraurea is formed which can then be used to thicken a base oil to form a grease. Polyurea greases are generally smooth, but somewhat opaque, exhibit dropping points near 500°F, and have very good resistance to oxidation. They are widely used to lubricate all types of industrial roller-element bearings but are particularly effective in lubricating ball bearings used in electric motors.

Organo-clay thickeners used to make greases are referred to as organophilic bentonites. Two varieties of bentonites are used, montmorillonite and hectorite. For a clay to be effective as a grease thickener, it must first be treated with a suitable quaternary ammonium salt, such as dimethyldioctadecyl ammonium chloride, which causes the clay surfaces to be oleophilic. In making a grease, the clay is mixed with a lubricating oil, and a dispersant, such as acetone or propylene carbonate, is added. As the clay platelets separate, the oil coats each platelet, thereby forming a stable gel structure. It is usually necessary to increase the separation of the clay platelets by mechanical means, such as by using a mill, a mechanical device used to disperse grease thickeners and described further in the section on kettle processing.

Clay greases are smooth-textured greases with good heat resistance since the thickener will not melt. They have excellent resistance to water and exhibit good resistance to leakage. However, they are more sensitive to additives than are soap-thickened greases, and many additives can affect the surface coating of the clay, causing the grease to de-gel and become fluid. Clay greases are often used in high-temperature applications, such as furnace door bearings, kiln car wheel bearings, and bearings on shafts extending through furnaces, as well as certain low-temperature applications, such as steel mill roll neck bearings where high resistance to water washout is needed.

Processes for Manufacturing Greases

There are three basic steps used in the manufacture of all soap thickened greases. These are (1) reacting a fatty material with an alkali to form a soap, (2) dehydrating and conditioning the soap, and (3) incorporating and dispersing the oil and additives to form a finished grease. The following three processes are representative of those used to manufacture greases.

Kettle Process

Traditionally, the manufacture of greases has been done as a batch process carried out in large kettles. Typical examples of modern greases kettles are shown in Figs. 4 and 5. Such kettles generally range in capacity from 10,000 lb (approximately 1450 gal) to 50,000 lb (approximately 7000 gal). As can be seen from the schematic photograph shown in Fig. 5, a counterrotating stirrer with wall scrapers is often used to aid mixing and heat transfer. These stirrers rotate at speeds in the range of 5 to 60 r/min and require drives in the range of 50 to 100 hp. A jacket suitable for heating with either steam or hot circulating oil is used to supply the heat required. A vapor recovery system is used to handle the fumes and by-products formed during manufacture.

A typical kettle procedure consists of manually charging the fatty material, alkali, and a portion of the base oil to the kettle through a hatch located in the lid of the kettle. The saponification reaction is carried out at about 180 to 200°F. Most saponification reactions occur readily at this temperature, and it is usually necessary to allow only about an hour before continuing. After completing the saponification step, the mixture is dehydrated. The time required to complete the dehydration is dependent on the amount of water present. The water vapor and fumes formed during the dehydration step are collected by a vapor recovery system and treated as necessary before being released to the atmosphere.

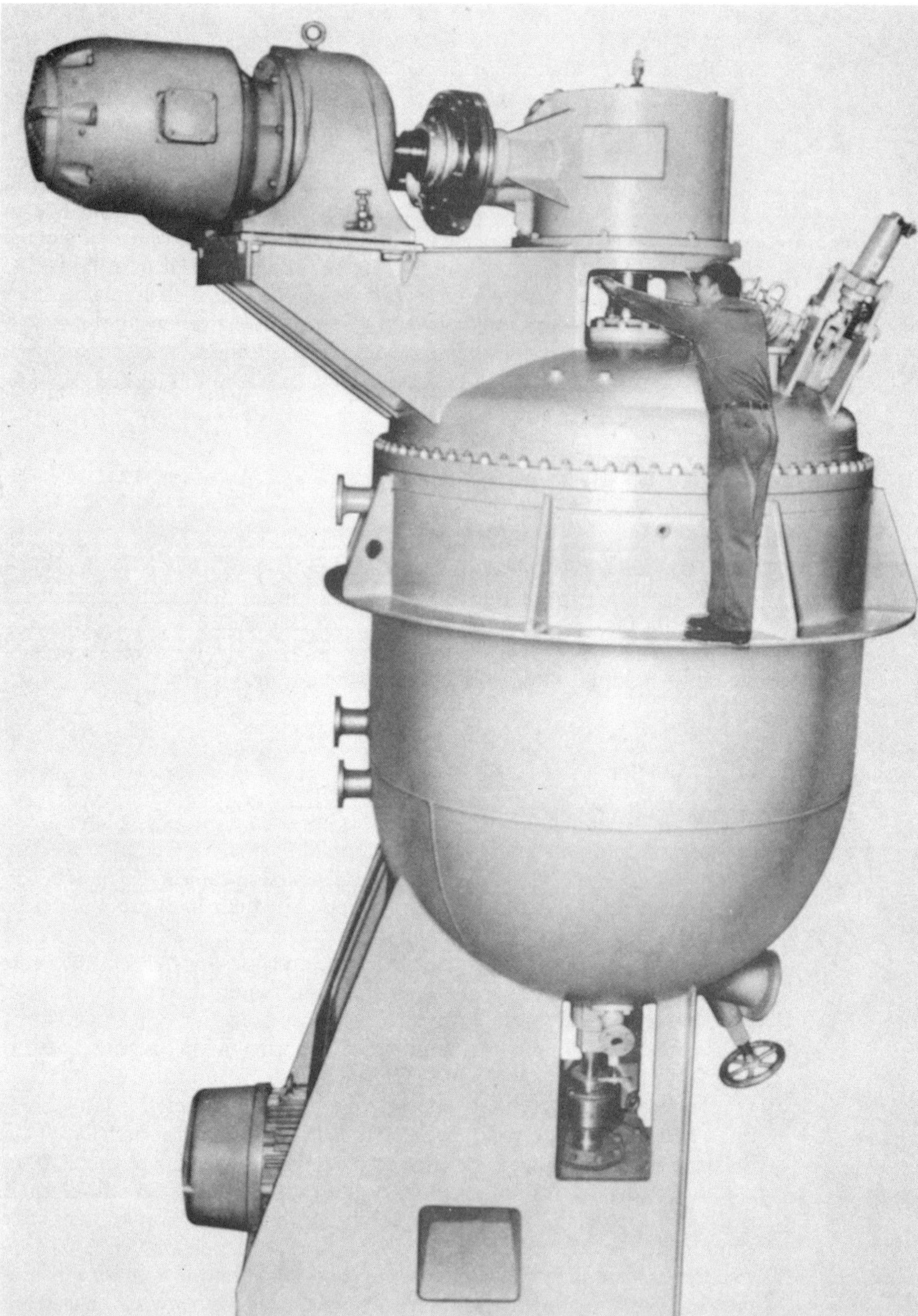

FIG. 4. Closed top, 1450 gal grease kettle.

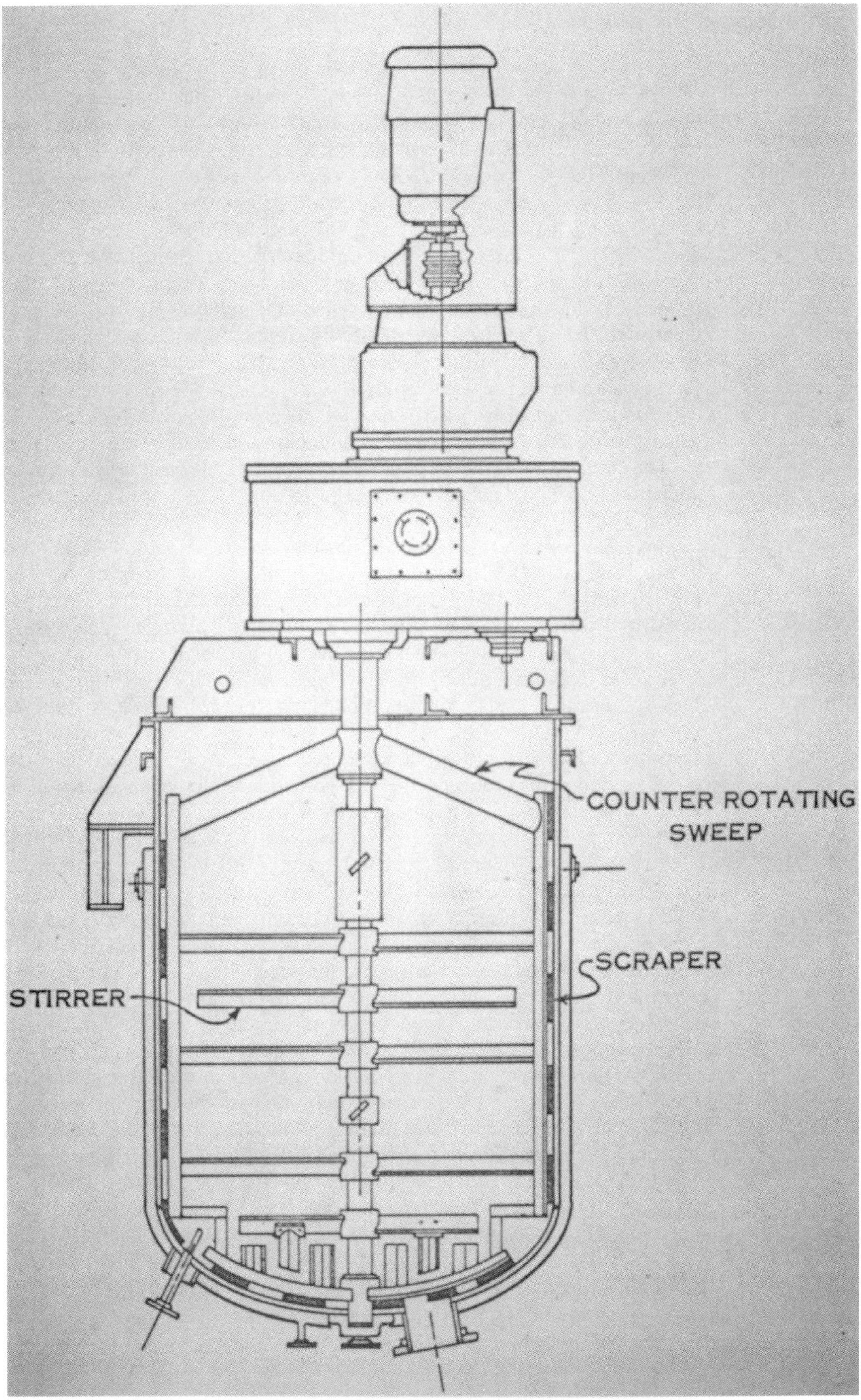

FIG. 5. Schematic of a modern grease kettle.

Once the water is removed, it is possible to begin heating the batch to an elevated temperature as required to condition or form the desired soap structure. Sometimes additional oil is needed during this step to help disperse the soap. The top temperature used is a function of the type of soap being processed. For example, anhydrous calcium soaps are heated to about 275°F, sodium soaps are heated to about 330°F, and lithium soaps are heated to about 395°F. After the soap reaches the required top temperature, it is held there for a certain period of time in order to condition the soap fibers properly. Following the conditioning step, the soap is cooled, usually at a rate determined by the nature of the soap, as the remaining oil is gradually added.

Stirring is used throughout the processing cycle, but especially during the final oil addition as it is very important that the soap be dispersed uniformly without forming soap gels. After the oil has been added and the grease cooled, usually below 200°F, any required additives are added.

The consistency of the grease is determined by running a penetration test and, if required, the consistency is adjusted by adding more cut-back oil. Sometimes it is necessary to further disperse the soap which can be done by milling. This operation consists of passing the grease through a shearing device, such as that represented by a colloid mill or a homogenizer. A colloid mill is a high energy shearing device consisting of an annular 0.003 to 0.05-in. opening between a rotating cone and stationary cylindrical cone through which the grease is passed. The homogenizer applies high mechanical energy to a grease by pumping the grease through a restricted orifice using a high-pressure, positive displacement pump. The purpose of using either of these milling devices is to insure full dispersal of the soap fibers. This results in a significant hardening of the grease, sometimes changing the penetration as much as 100 points or more. Once the consistency has been adjusted to the required grade range, the grease is drawn from the kettle into the desired containers.

Successful kettle manufacture is largely an art based on the skill and knowledge of the greasemaker. Very often he must make adjustments in holding times and heating or cooling rates. Thus it is necessary that the greasemaker observe each step of the process and make changes as required. Batch processing is time consuming, requiring anywhere from 9 to over 24 h, depending on the type of grease being made, for completion of a single batch of grease. Once the grease has been drawn from the kettle, the kettle must be cleaned thoroughly before starting the next batch. Cleaning is necessary to avoid contamination, either from the additive system used or from the soap used. Many soaps are not compatible with one another, and the mixing of different soap-thickened greases must be avoided. Cleaning can also be time consuming as it usually requires that the kettle be water or oil washed.

Many processing variables can affect the finished grease. Alkalinity or acidity of the soap is an important factor as it may affect the performance of the grease or its storage characteristics. The oil-to-fat ratio used in the charge can affect the thickening characteristics of certain soaps. The rate of oil addition, either during the heating cycle or during the cooling cycle, can have a pronounced effect on the yield. Yield is defined as the amount of thickener required to produce a grease of a given consistency. A good or high yield would indicate having the least amount of thickener for the desired consistency. The development of soap fibers is similar to crystallization phenomenon and can be greatly affected by the cooling rates used. Also, the top temperature used during the batch is critical for most soaps. If the temperature is too low, the desired soap structure will not be formed; if the temperature is too high, the soap will become soluble in the base oil and will not form the required fiber structure. All of these variables must be considered for each grease system and each optimized to give the desired characteristics in the finished grease.

Contactor Process

In an effort to increase the efficiency of batch processing, the Stratco contactor was developed. It is a pressure reactor used for the formation of a soap concentrate which can be further processed by adding additional oil to produce a finished grease. Figure 6 shows the essential parts of the contactor. High dispersion mixing is achieved by using a rotating impeller operating in conjunction with stationary vanes which produces a zone of intense mixing and circulation. Material is pulled down through the center of the contactor by the impeller, reversed, and then forced up through the annular space. An internal heating coil is used to effect heat transfer and create a continuous flow path for the soap concentrate.

The manufacturing process used for the contactor is very similar to that described previously for the kettle. Ingredients required for saponification are charged to the contactor through the top manway. After all of the ingredients have been charged, the manway is sealed, agitation is established by turning on the bottom mixer, and heat is applied to the internal heating coil. The contents are heated very rapidly under pressure to the required top temperature. The pressure is then released and the contents cooled by adding the required cut-back oil. As an alternative, the soap may be pumped from the contactor to a receiving kettle for adding the cut-back oil and additives. Use of a contactor greatly reduces heating times and shortens the reaction time. For example, batch cycle times when using a contactor to manufacture lithium soap greases are reported to be 5 to 7 h as compared to 9 to 12 h when using a conventional kettle.

Processing variables affecting the contactor process are similar to those described for the kettle process. The most critical variable is the top temperature used during the heating cycle.

Continuous Process

During the mid-1960s, the first fully continuous process was commercialized for the production of greases. A flow diagram of that process* is shown in

*The continuous grease process is a licensed process available from Texaco Development Corporation.

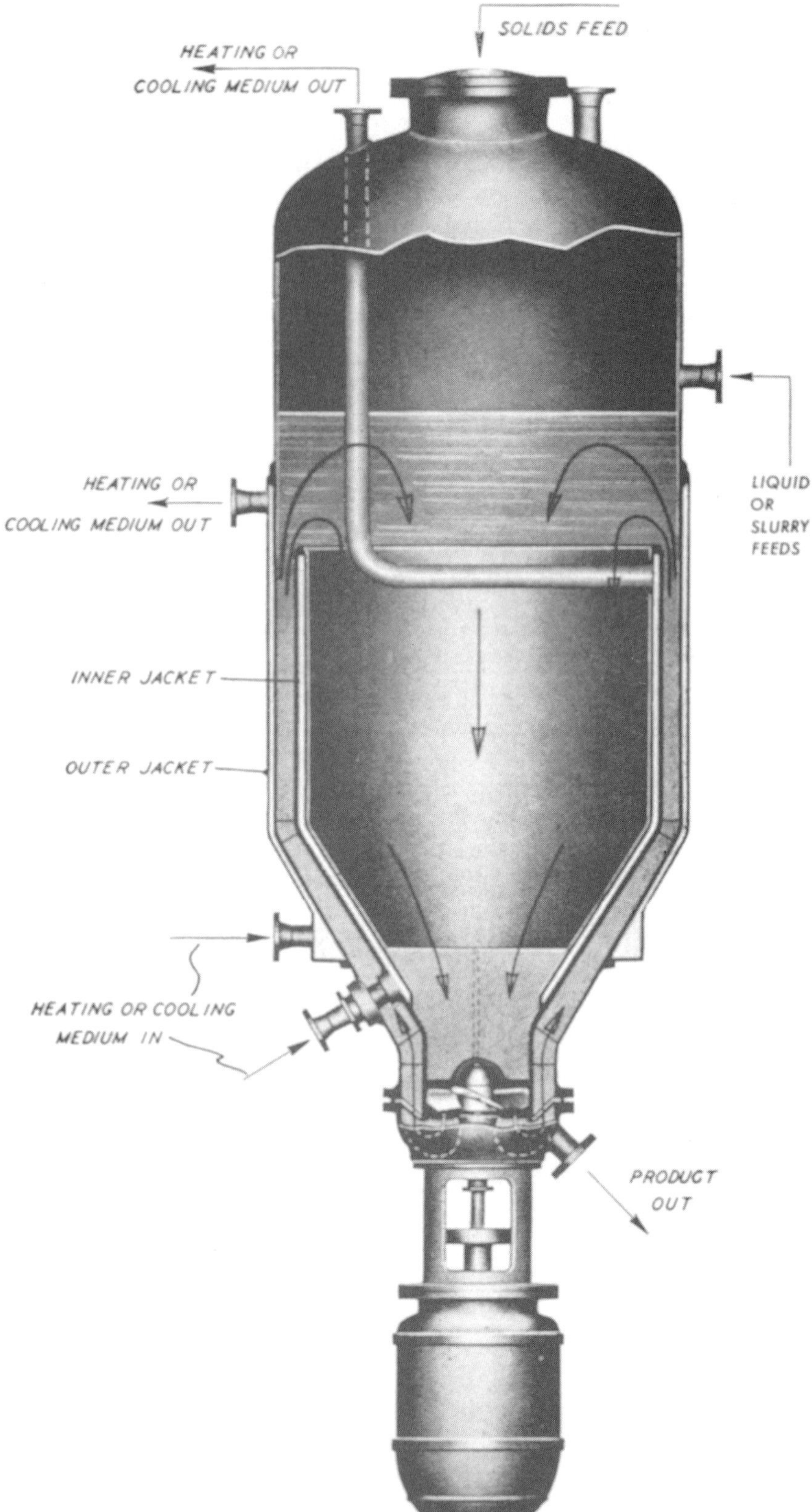

FIG. 6. Stratco contactor.

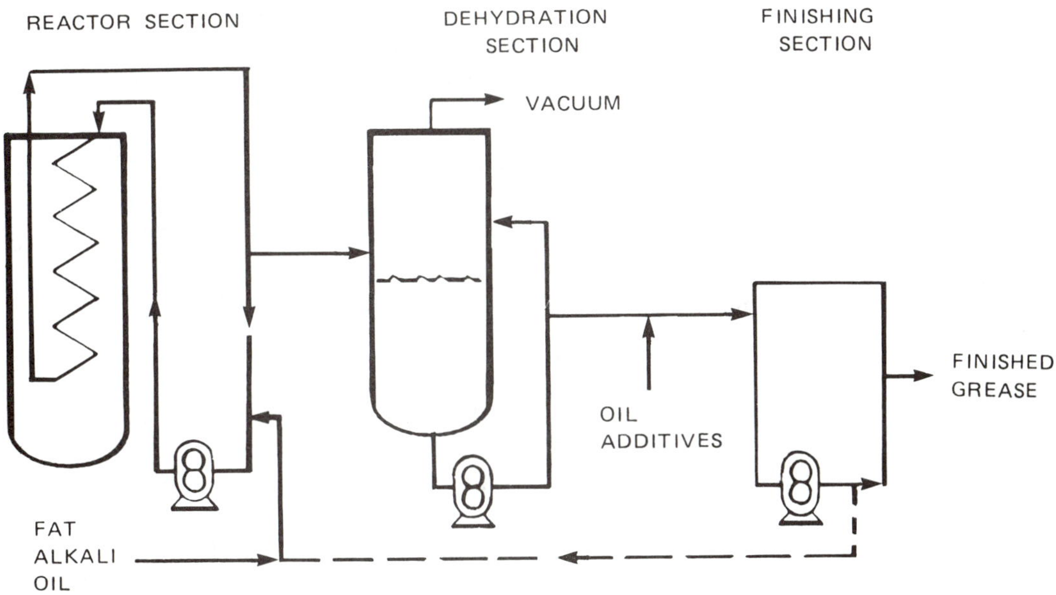

FIG. 7. Flow diagram of the Texaco continuous grease process.

Fig. 7. The process consists of three sections—the reactor section, the dehydration section, and the finishing section. A fatty material, an alkali, and a diluent oil are metered into the reactor section where saponification occurs. The reactor consists of a pipe coil jacketed by a larger section of pipe. Either steam or circulating hot oil can be used to supply the required heat. Normally the reactor is operated at a temperature of about 300 to 330°F and at a pressure as required to prevent vaporization of the water present. Because of the small volumetric capacity, residence time in the reactor section is short, usually about 1 to 3 min.

The stream from the reactor enters the dehydration section which is operated under a vacuum. Before entering the flash chamber, the soap mixture passes through a heat exchanger to regain the heat-of-vaporization losses resulting from the pressure differential between the reactor and dehydration sections. Heat is added in the flash chamber itself either by using electric strip heaters mounted externally on the vessel or by using a jacketed vessel heated with circulating hot oil. Typically the operating temperature in the flash chamber is about 370°F. A recycle pump is used to pump the soap base through a shearing valve to provide for multipass dispersion of the soap fibers being formed. The volumetric holdup in the dehydration section is about 40 gal, which gives a residence time of about 15 min.

The soap base from the dehydration section enters the finishing section where it receives more oil and additives as needed. The soap base-oil-additive mixture is recycled through a closed loop which also includes a shearing valve. The function of this section is to produce a smooth uniform product with the desired consistency. The consistency of the finished grease is con-

TABLE 4 Comparison of Continuous and Batch Grease Processing (Basis: Plant for manufacturing 10 million lb/yr of lithium, calcium, and sodium soap greases)

	Continuous Process	Batch Process
Investment cost factor	1.0	2.0
Direct labor, man-h per 10,000 lb grease	1.4	4.9
Heating load, Btu/h	1,500,000	3,000,000
Cooling water, gal/min	140	200
Electrical, kW/h	120	380

tinuously monitored by an on-line controller, noted as a consistometer,* which measures and controls the consistency of the finished product by increasing or decreasing the amount of oil being added. The residence time in the finishing section is short, usually less than 1 min. The finished grease from the unit is routed to product storage tanks from which the grease is filled into packages.

Variables related to the continuous process are as follows. In the reactor section the key variables are temperature, pressure, and recycle ratio. Residence time could also be a factor but is usually high enough for commercial units so as not to be critical. The recycle ratio is designed to maintain turbulent flow through the reactor coil. This ensures adequate contact between the fatty material and the alkali to obtain complete saponification. The pressure is critical as it must be kept above the vaporization pressure of water to ensure that the water present remains in a liquid form. In the flash chamber the most important variables are temperature and recycle ratio. The proper temperature of the soap base must be maintained in order to form the desired fiber structure. The recycle ratio is critical in order to obtain the required dispersion of the soap fibers as they are being formed. In the finishing section the recycle ratio is critical because it greatly affects how well the soap base and final cut-back oil are mixed. Sufficient mixing must be provided to obtain a smooth, homogeneous grease. Inadequate mixing could cause the finished grease to contain as undispersed soap gels which can plug filter screens used in filling operations as well as those used by customers in centralized lubrication systems.

Because of its compact size and versatility, the continuous process offers several advantages over a batch process. These are summarized in Table 4. The investment cost factor for the continuous process is estimated as half that for the batch process. Manpower requirements are less for the continuous process as well as are heating, cooling, and electrical requirements. These advantages enable a plant based on the continuous process to manufacture greases with a greatly reduced operating cost.

*Instrument licensed by Texaco Development Corporation.

Grease Applications and Future Trends

There is no one universal grease suitable for all applications. As already discussed under the section on the general grease types and usage, each grease has certain properties that enable it to be used successfully. It is therefore necessary to analyze carefully the specific application and then choose a grease whose properties match the required performance criteria. Table 5 illustrates several typical grease applications and the key grease properties required.

The items in Table 5 relate to the composition of the grease. In addition to composition, the consistency is also important. Most applications can be met with a No. 2 grade grease. If low temperature properties are critical, a No. 1 or 0 grade grease may be required. However, softer grade greases generally give higher leakage and poorer water resistance. Therefore, all factors must be considered to select the right grease for a specific application.

It has been projected that the United States lubricant market will remain fairly constant over the next decade, with little or no growth expected. Lithium soap greases will continue to be the largest volume products, with a continued decrease in the use of sodium and calcium soap greases. The complex grease market will continue to grow as the demand for high dropping point products increases. Of these, it is anticipated that lithium complex greases will show the greatest amount of increase, although aluminum complex and polyurea greases will continue to find wide application in the industrial market. Synthetic greases should also become more cost effective and find wider market acceptance.

TABLE 5

Application	Key Properties
Automotive wheel bearings	Low leakage and bleed resistance Moderate EP properties Rust and oxidation resistance Extended life at high temperatures Compatibility with seals
Automotive chassis grease	Fretting and wear protection Water resistance Compatibility with seals
Ball and roller bearings	Long life at high temperatures Rust and oxidation resistance Good low temperature properties Leakage resistance
Heavily loaded bearings	High EP and load-carrying capabilities Low wear Corrosion resistance Relatively high base oil viscosity

Bibliography

Boner, C. J., *Manufacture and Application of Lubricating Greases*, Reinhold, New York, 1954.

Green, W. B., and Witte, A. C., "Continuous Grease Manufacture," *Lubrication*, *55*(1), (1969).

Green, W. B., and Witte, A. C., *Continuous Grease Manufacture,* Paper Presented at the 1972 National Fuels and Lubricants Meeting of the National Petroleum Refiners Association.

Graham, S. D., and Meyer, D. W., "Today's Decision in Grease Manufacturing—Kettles vs. a Contactor," *NLGI Spokesman*, September 1984.

NLGI Lubricating Grease Guide, National Lubricating Grease Institute, 1984.

Ruge, I. W., "Lubricating Greases—Characteristics and Selection," in *Handbook of Lubrication*, Volume II, CRC Press, 1984.

ARNOLD C. WITTE

Herbicides

Introduction

A weed may be described as an unwanted plant at a given time and place. A herbicide is a chemical product that can be used to destroy or inhibit the growth of a weed.

Herbicide manufacture in the United States is a relatively small segment of the overall chemical industry. The annual value of shipments is about $2.5 billion of the total $211 billion sales of the industry.

However, as a percent of profits, these pesticides are significant contributors. Profit margins from the herbicides can be several times the average 5% of the industry.

Because of the high profit potential of herbicide chemicals, there is a very high level of research directed at safer and better products. The spectrum of biological activity is becoming very narrow. That is, the product can be very selective to weeds with a high level of safety to the crop. Greater emphasis is placed on fate in the environment and in safety to humans.

History

The use of herbicides began in ancient times. The Romans, after conquering the Carthagenians, plowed salt into their fields to prevent the growth of their crops. From the mid-nineteenth century up to World War II, a variety of compounds was used to control weeds. These included iron sulfate, sulfuric acid, sodium arsenic, sodium chlorate, and petroleum oils. Some products showed some selectivity, but gave considerable crop damage.

In 1945, 2,4-D (2,4-dichlorophenoxyacetic acid) was introduced as a product to control broadleaf weeds while allowing grass-like plants to grow. This product could be used on lawns and in wheat, barley, rice, corn, and sugarcane to control many broadleaf weeds. Selectivity was not ideal, but even today this product has a very high consumption.

Beginning in the early 1960s, newer, better products began appearing. Today, products are available to control both broadleaf and grass pests in most agricultural, industrial, and home and garden applications.

Rates of application have been drastically reduced from 50–200 lb/acre for the old inorganic products down to 1–3 lb/acre for most common products today. Many newer products just entering the market, or about to enter, have rates of 0.05 to 0.1 lb/acre.

A major historical event to the herbicide manufacturing industry was the Federal Insecticide, Fungicide and Rodenticide Act (FIFRA) passed in 1947 and its revision in 1972. The Environmental Protection Agency (EPA) administers this act which states that products must be safe and effective. The rates, method of application, and the target crops are specified in detail.

Characteristics of Herbicide Manufacture

Herbicide manufacture can be divided into two major segments:

1. Chemical manufacture
2. Formulation and packaging

Manufacture of herbicide-active substances is mainly limited to the 12–15 major chemical companies that screen, test, and develop labels for the active ingredients. The financial requirements are very substantial. The minimum outlay for this activity is probably $25,000,000/year on an ongoing basis.

Formulation and packaging, on the other hand, is a very diverse industry with many manufacturers in many parts of the country.

Formulation is the conversion of the active ingredient to a form or condition that can be used directly by the customer, i.e., the farmer.

Formulators may have labels of their own, whereby they market products under license or after patent expiration, or they may contract to formulate and package for the patented owner of a product. The formulators usually use lower cost labor and do not have the overheads of the major companies. In addition, they may be located nearer the point of use so that freight savings may be significant.

Chemical Manufacture

Because herbicides are biologically active compounds and because they are regulated under FIFRA, some special needs exist that are not necessarily present in the manufacture of other types of chemicals. Some of these follow.

Product Containment

The final products must be contained in such a way that surrounding vegetation is not damaged. Since 1–2 lb/acre per year normally affects vegetation, this requires a major effort.

Pesticide Effluent Guidelines

Herbicide manufacturers are regulated not only by priority pollutant and organic chemicals effluent guidelines but also by pesticide effluent guidelines. The maximum amount of herbicide leaving in wastewater is very low, in some cases down to 0.25 lb/d with 5 to 40 lb/d being typical. Thus, any herbicide manufacturing or formulation facility will have rather extensive wastewater treatment operations.

Label Requirement

A label to sell a herbicide is received after a very long, expensive, and uncertain process. The label covers minimum assay and limits to the impurities that may be tolerated. Because of the uncertainty of registration, the materials used in the registration tests are seldom from commercial production units.

When a commercial process is finally developed, it may be by a different synthesis route or may contain different or changing levels of impurities. A slight change in registration may be possible, but it is necessary that the commercial product be in agreement with registration.

Formulation and Packaging

Types of common formulations are:

Emulsifiable concentrates
Wettable powders
Flowables (aqueous suspensions)

Pellets
Tablets
Impregnated granules
Coated granules
Wettable dispersible granules
Impregnated wax bars

A description of the various types of formulations is beyond the scope of this article, but almost all contain a dispersant and a wetting agent. Depending on needs, it may be necessary to add other items such as clays, binders, suspension agents, electrolytes, viscosity builders, etc. All ingredients must come from an EPA approved list of inert ingredients.

The formulation must be acceptable from many standpoints including:

Storability (shelf life)
Compatibility with other products
Trouble-free application, i.e., no lumps to plug spray nozzles

Packaging must meet several criteria which include:

Package integrity throughout the distribution chain
Labeling must meet EPA requirements
Should be easy for customer to handle

A formulation facility has many of the characteristics of the chemical manufacturing site and, in addition, must put a high degree of attention to worker exposure since there is, in general, more hand labor involved.

Design of the facility must provide for changeover between products to avoid product cross contamination. The facilities may be used for other types of products, i.e., insecticides or fungicides. A herbicide contaminating an insecticide or a herbicide contaminating a growth regulator could prove disastrous.

Classification of Herbicide

Herbicides are classified by several methods. Major ones are:

Selective or total kill
Preemergence or postemergence
Contact or systemic
Mode of action, i.e., destruction of chlorophyll, interruption of photosynthesis, overstimulation of growth
Organic or inorganic
Chemical classification of organics

Chemical Classification

The herbicides of economic importance can be divided into categories according to their general chemical classification. Those compounds with similar chemical structure also show similarities in herbicidal activity. The classifications are somewhat arbitrary and do not fully cover each compound used in the market. However, they do describe the similarities of compounds within a group.

A summary of the estimated production volumes and sales values of the major compounds is shown in Table 1. Annual production of all types of organic herbicides is estimated at about 700 million lb/yr with a value of over $2.5 billion.

Amides

The amides compose the largest volume group of herbicides used in the United States market. The group contains a variety of chemical types ranging from the H-substituted acetamides to the substituted benzamides. Most of the amides are applied as preemergence or preplant herbicides. A few, like propanil and butachlor, are applied postemergence.

The principal products in terms of annual production and sales are the α-halo H-substituted acetamides. The group includes acetochlor, alachlor, butachlor, diethatyl ethyl, metolachlor, and propachlor. These chloroacetamides account for 85% of the amide herbicides.

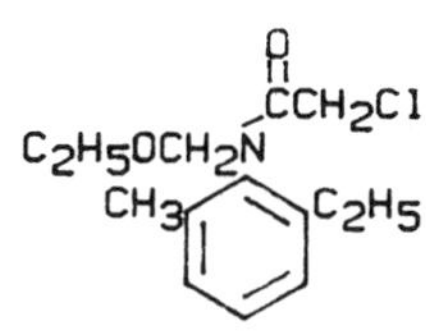
ACETOCHLOR

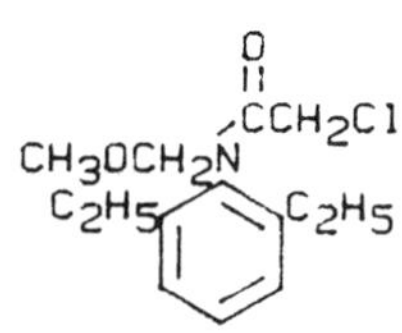
ALACHLOR

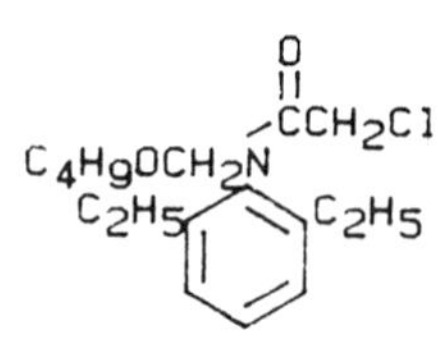
BUTACHLOR

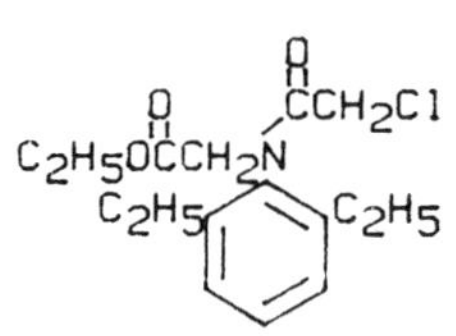
DIETHATYL ETHYL

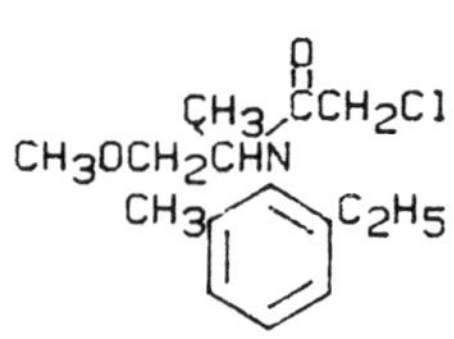
METOLACHLOR

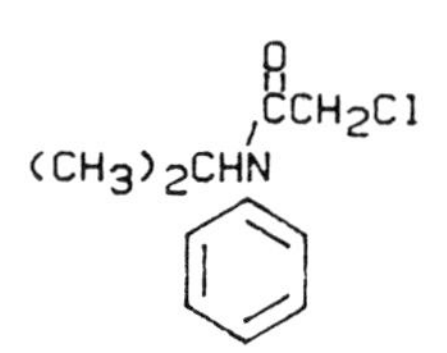
PROPACHLOR

Manufacture of these compounds usually consists of reacting a substituted aniline with a ketone or alcohol followed by reaction with an acetyl chloride:

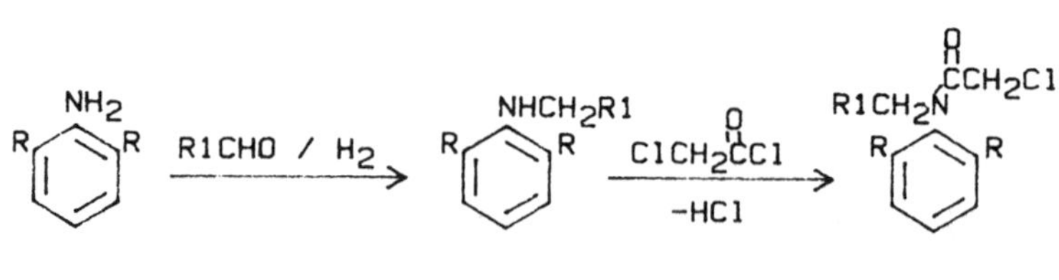

TABLE 1 Herbicide Volumes

	Production Estimates (million lb/yr)	Sales Revenues (million $/yr)
Amides:		
Alachlor	100	270
Metolachlor	50	175
Propachlor	8	25
Acetochlor	5	20
Butachlor	3	15
Diethatyl ethyl	1	5
Propanil	15	30
Naptalam	10	30
Pronamide	2	10
Diphenamid	2	10
Total amides	200	600
Triazines:		
Atrazine	75	115
Cyanazine	25	70
Propazine	10	20
Simazine	5	10
Prometon	1	5
Metribuzin	8	120
Hexazinone	1	15
Total triazines	115	355
Dinitroanilines:		
Trifluralin	45	175
Pendimethalin	10	60
Oryzalin	4	20
Benefin	4	20
Total dinitros	65	275
Ureas/sulfonyl ureas/uracils:		
Linuron	10	80
Diuron	6	30
Flumeturon	3	15
Chlorsulfuron	0.2	50
Sulfometuron methyl	0.05	10
Bromacil	4	30
Terbacil	1	10
Total ureas	25	230

TABLE 1 *(continued)*

	Production Estimates (million lb/yr)	Sales Revenues (million $/yr)
Carbamates/Thiocarbamates:		
Butylate	45	120
EPTC	12	30
Molinate	4	12
Vernolate	4	8
Pebulate	3	6
Triallate	1	5
Diallate	0.5	2
Total carbamates	70	180
Chlorophenoxies:		
2,4-D	60	80
2,4,5-T	8	20
MCPA	5	10
MCPB	1	2
Total phenoxies	75	110
Carboxylic acids:		
Glyphosate	10	150
Dicamba	10	70
Chloramben	8	40
Endothal	4	25
Picloram	2	25
Dalapon	7	10
Diclofop-methyl	2	30
Fluazifop-methyl	2	20
Total carboxy acids	45	370
General:		
Bentazon	10	150
Paraquat	7	70
Acifluorfen	3	45
Sethoxydim	1	20
Total	21	285
Other herbicides	50–100	150–300
Total all herbicides	666–736	2550–2700

The synthesis can be carried out solvent-free or in a solvent which is later used in the formulated product.

The substituted anilines are produced by the reaction of aniline (or toluidine) with ethylene under pressure (using a catalyst). Conversion of the substituted aniline to the chloroacetanilide product is straightforward and overall yields can exceed 90%.

The principal products, alachlor and metolachlor, account for 80% of the total amides supplied to the United States market. They are produced in large dedicated units, usually starting from the substituted anilines, 2,6-diethyl aniline or 2-methyl-6-ethyl aniline.

Other significant amides include propanil, naptalam, pronamide, and diphenamide. Propanil is made by the following scheme:

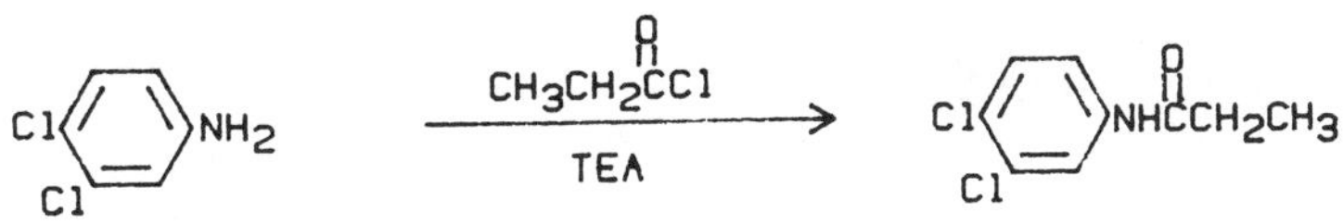

3,4-DICHLOROANILINE PROPANIL

The other amides are usually produced from the reaction of an acid or acid chloride with an amine. The active ingredients are liquids or low melting solids. They are typically formulated as emulsifiable concentrates in aromatic solvents or as low concentration granules.

Triazines

The triazines are the second largest group of herbicides used in the United States. Most of the triazines are soil applied preemergence herbicides. The compounds are absorbed through the roots and translocate through the plant leaves and meristems. They are herbicidally active by inhibiting photosynthesis.

The principle triazines are the 1,3,5 symmetrical triazines, accounting for over 90% of the total production for the group. Significant *s*-triazines include atrazine, cyanazine, simazine, propazine, prometon, and prometryn.

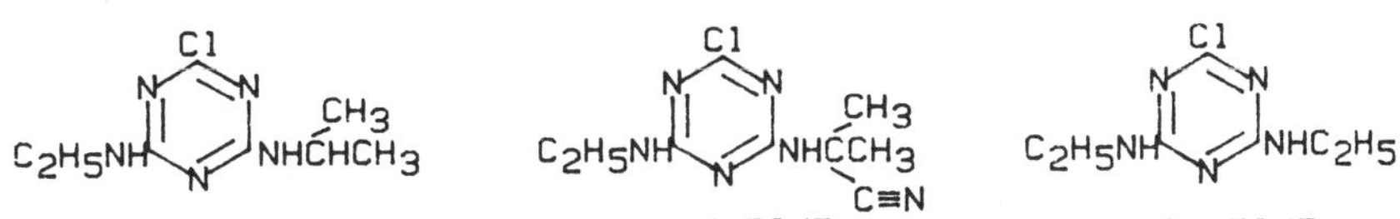

ATRAZINE CYANAZINE SIMAZINE

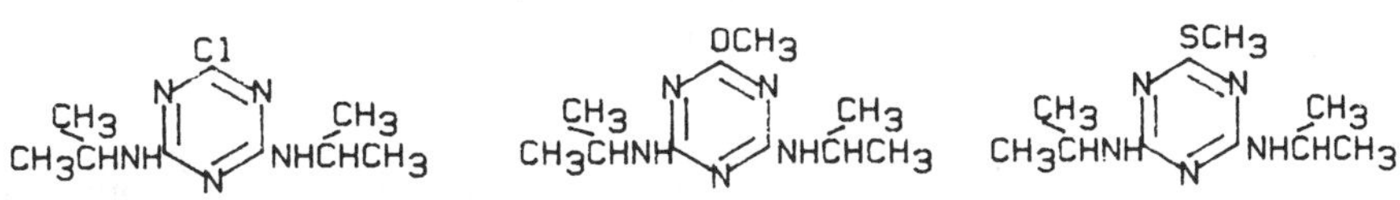

PROPAZINE PROMETON PROMETRYN

The triazines are manufactured by substitution of lower amines, alcohols, and mercaptans to cyanuric chloride. The reaction is carried out in an organic solvent with an acid acceptor. The family or triazines are made:

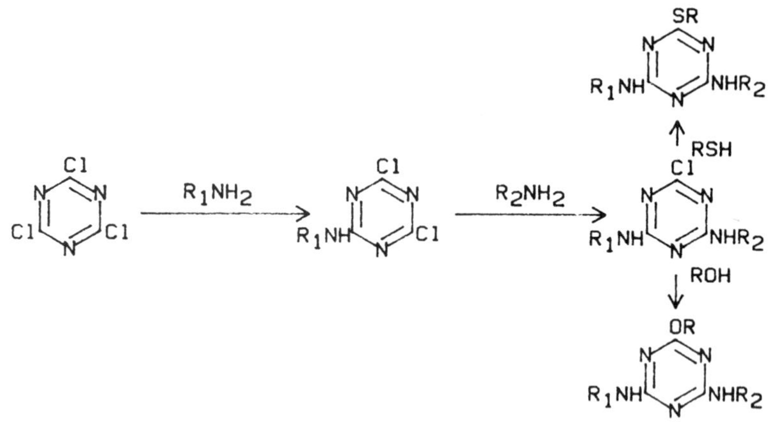

The cyanuric chloride intermediate is made by the reaction of HCN with chlorine:

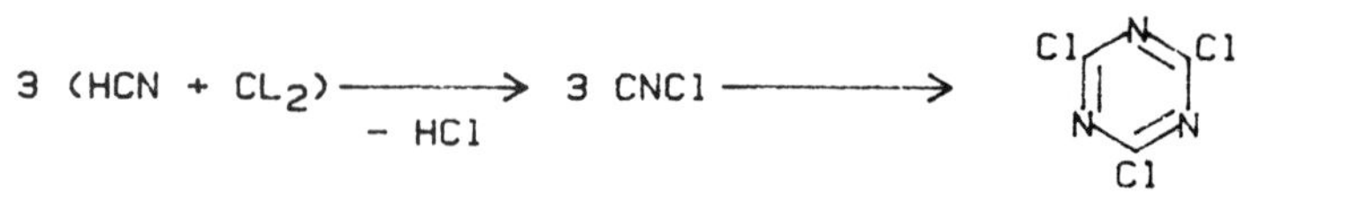

Yields for the triazine reactions are high with an overall yield of product from HCN above 90%. The assay of the technical materials is typically above 97% active ingredient.

The other triazines include metribuzin and the *s*-triazine hexazinone. Metribuzin is the major nonsymmetrical triazine. The technical material can be manufactured from thiocarbazide and a keto acid:

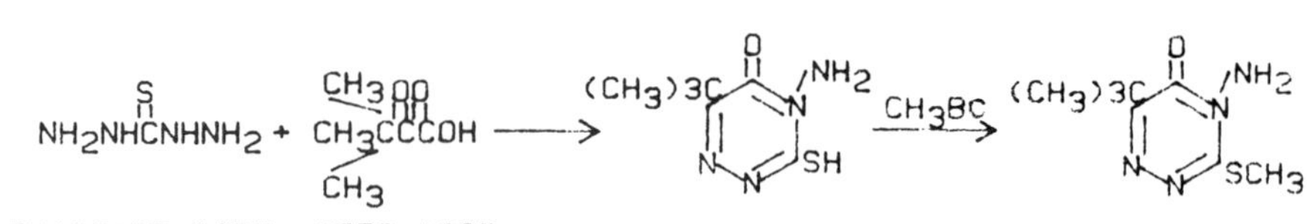

All the commercial triazines are solids at room temperature and are formulated as powders or liquid suspensions.

Carbamates/Thiocarbamates

Many of the carbamates are soil-applied herbicides. The compounds enter the plant through the root system or coleoptile and translocate to inhibit the normal plant metabolism. A few carbamates are foliar applied and are used as postemergence herbicides.

The principal products in the group are the thiocarbamates, accounting for over 90% of the carbamate compounds. The group includes butylate, EPTC, vernolate, molinate, pebulate, diallate, and triallate.

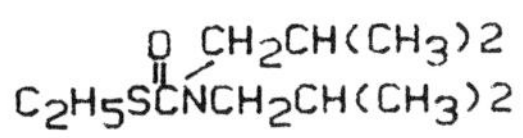

BUTYLATE

EPTC

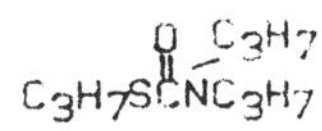

VERNOLATE

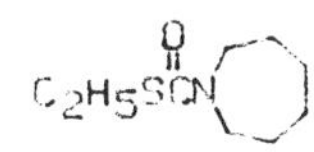

MOLINATE

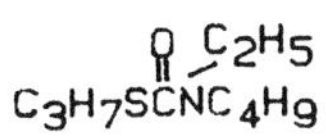

PEBULATE

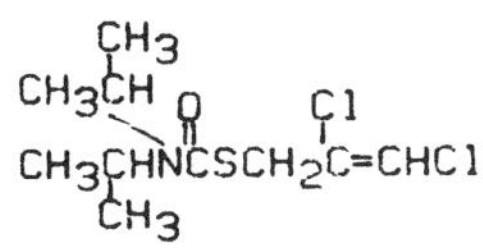

DIALLATE

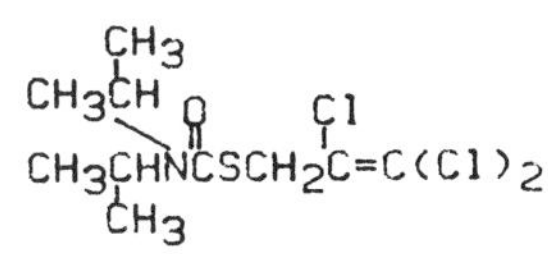

TRIALLATE

They are typically soil applied, being relatively volatile, especially in wet soils. The herbicide is usually incorporated in the top 5 to 7 cm of the soil surface.

Manufacture of most thiocarbamates involves the use of phosgene, reacted with mercaptans and amines in various sequences:

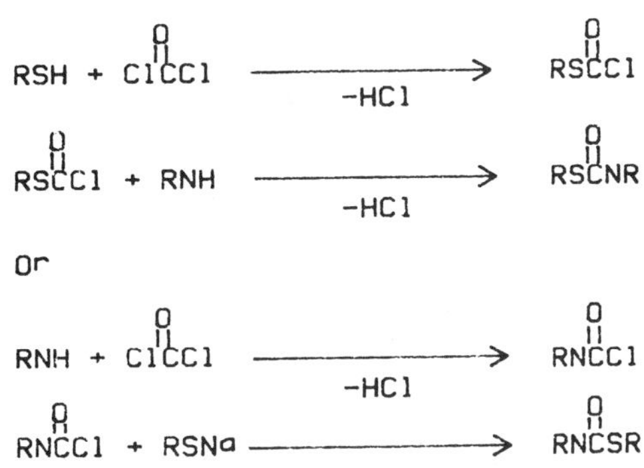

A safener is added to the thiocarbamates butylate and EPTC. The safener is a dichloroacetamide that permits the use of these products on otherwise susceptible plants (especially corn).

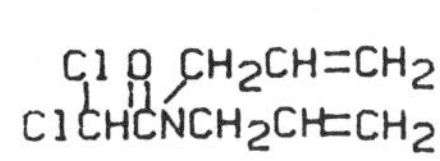

R-25788

The safener permits the plant to degrade the toxic metabolite, thiocarbamate sulfoxide, more rapidly.

The chlorinated thiocarbamates, diallate and triallate, are produced using carbonyl sulfide:

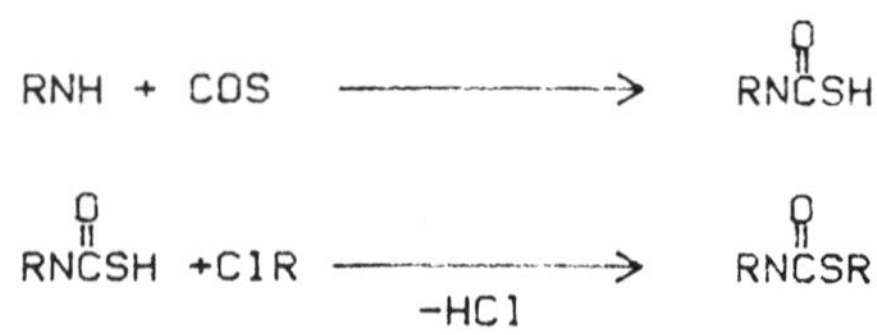

The thiocarbamates are liquids at room temperature and are formulated as emulsifiable concentrates or low concentration granule products.

Dinitroanilines

The dinitroanilines are important grass herbicides in the broadleaf crops. They are typically applied preemergence and require soil incorporation for their herbicidal activity. Most dinitroanilines affect the growth process associated with seed germination. The compounds are only slightly absorbed by the plant and do not translocate.

The principal dinitros used in the United States market are trifluralin, pendimethalin, oryzalin, and benefin.

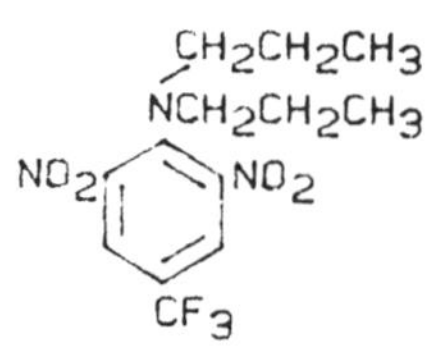

TRIFLURALIN

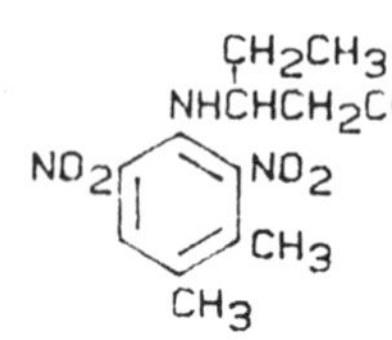

PENDIMETHALIN

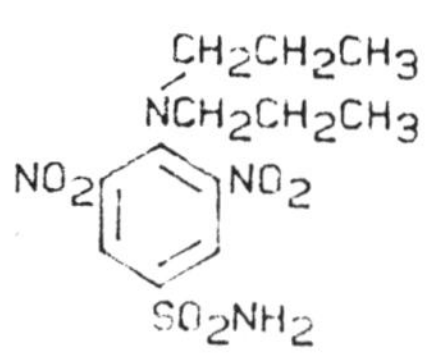

ORYZALIN

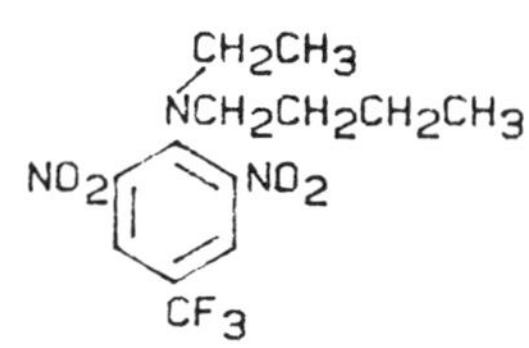

BENEFIN

Manufacture of most of the dinitros involves the reaction of an aliphatic amine with a 2,6-dinitrochlorobenzene. Trifluralin, the largest volume dinitro compound, accounts for 75% of the total group consumption in agriculture. It is made:

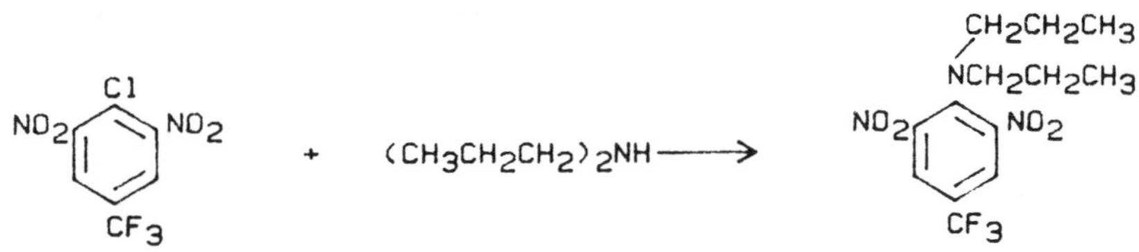

2,6-DINITRO 4-TRIFLUORO METHYL CHLOROBENZENE — DI-N-PROPYLAMINE — TRIFLURALIN

The principal raw material, dinitrobenzotrifluoride, is made:

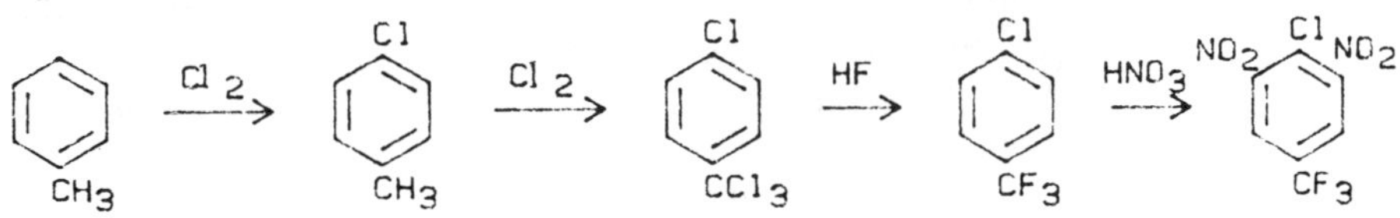

The second largest volume dinitro herbicide, pendimethalin, is made from *p*-chloro-*o*-xylene and *sec*-butyl amine:

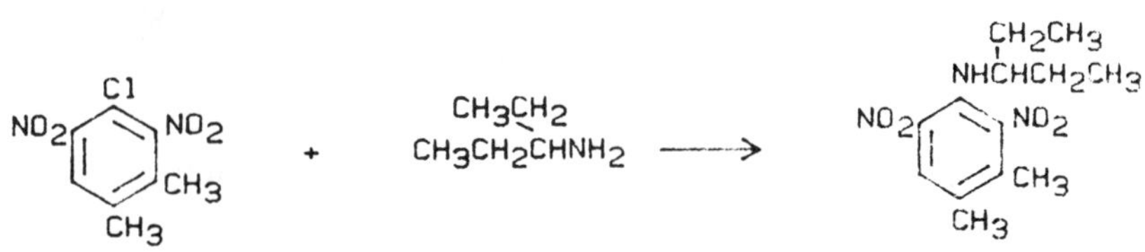

2,6-DINITRO-3,4-DIMETHYL CHLOROBENZENE — N-(1ETHYLPROPYL) AMINE — PENDIMETHALIN

The dinitroanilines are low melting solids, usually formulated as emulsifiable concentrates or low concentration granules.

Chlorophenoxies

The chlorophenoxies have been used extensively for the control of broadleaf weeds in cereal crops, turf, and rangeland. The compounds can be absorbed through the root or foliage and translocate throughout the plant, depending upon the growth status. The herbicides cause abnormal growth response affecting respiration, food reserves, and cell division.

The principal compounds in the group are 2,4-D and 2,4,5-T with their various esters and salts.

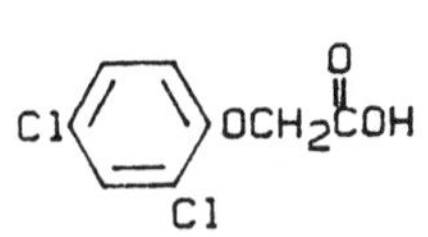

2,4-D

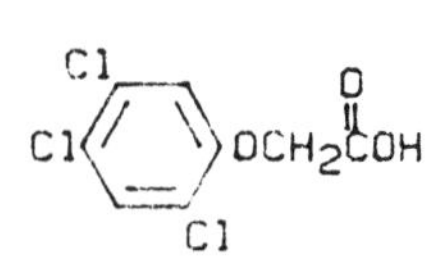

2,4,5-T

2,4-D is produced by the following reaction sequence:

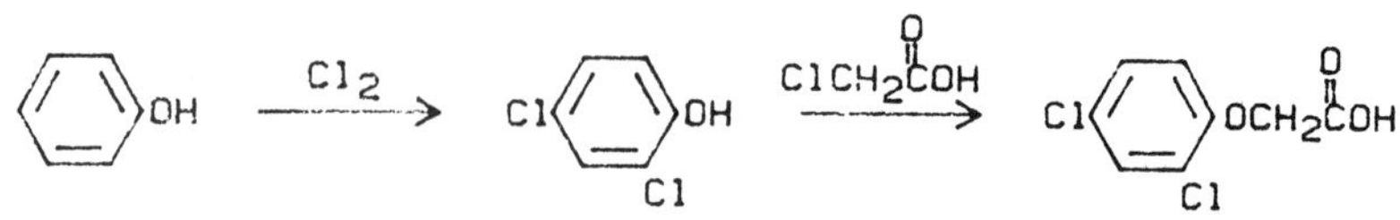

PHENOL 2,4-DICHLOROPHENOL 2,4-D

2,4-Dichlorophenol is produced by the direct chlorination of phenol, usually in a solvent. Chlorination is carried out at low temperature to avoid the manufacture of the 2,6 isomer. The yield of 2,4-D is improved if excess sodium dichlorophenolate is used in the reaction. The unreacted phenol is stripped off and recycled. The process benefits from the use of the purest possible 2,4-dichlorophenol, giving a higher quality product and lower consumption of the chloroacetic acid.

2,4,5-T is made in a similar fashion to 2,4-D using 2,4,5-trichlorophenol.

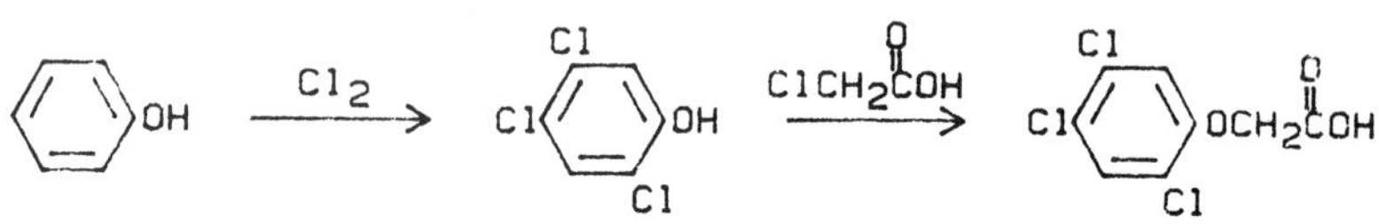

PHENOL 2,4,5-TRICHLOROPHENOL 2,4,5-T

An important side reaction in the manufacture of 2,4,5-T is the condensation of two molecules of the phenol:

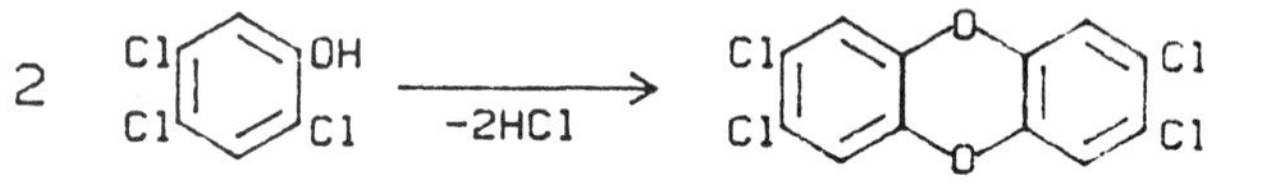

2,3,7,8-TETRACHLORO DIBENZO DIOXIN

The toxicity of the "dioxin" necessitates that the level of this by-product in the final product be very low.

Similar in chemical structure and herbicidal activity are MCPA and its analogs MCPB and MCPP.

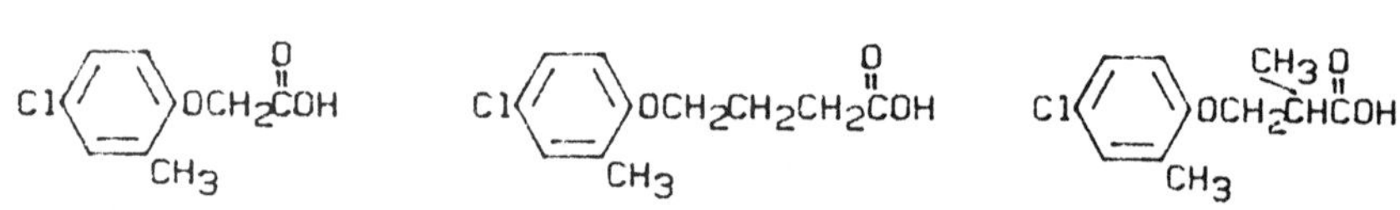

MCPA MCPB MCPP

The materials can be manufactured from either 4-chloro-2-methylphenol or the direct chlorination of the 2-methylphenoxy acid:

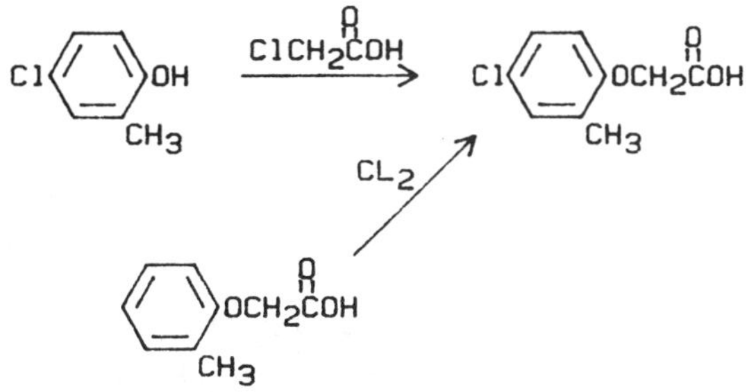

The chlorophenoxies are high melting solids. They are formulated as soluble powders, aqueous solutions, and emulsions depending on the compound reacted with the phenoxy acid, forming the ester or salt.

Ureas/Sulfonyl Ureas/Uracils

Ureas. The urea herbicides are generally soil applied, and they control many broadleafs and grasses. They are absorbed through the roots and translocate to the upper parts of the plant where they inhibit photosynthesis. The principal urea herbicides are linuron, diuron, and fluometuron.

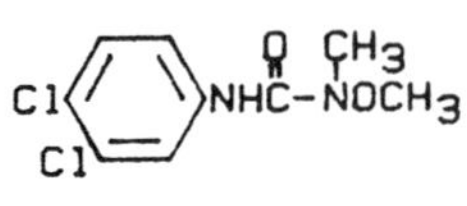

LINURON

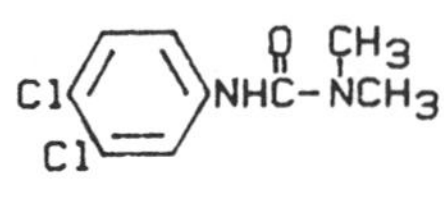

DIURON

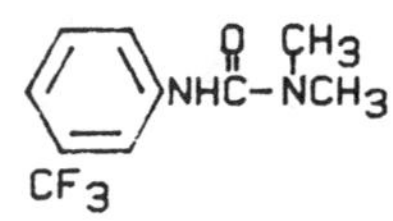

FLUOMETURON

The ureas are produced by the reaction of phosgene with an aniline compound to give an isocyanate intermediate. The product is subsequently formed by the reaction with an aliphatic amine:

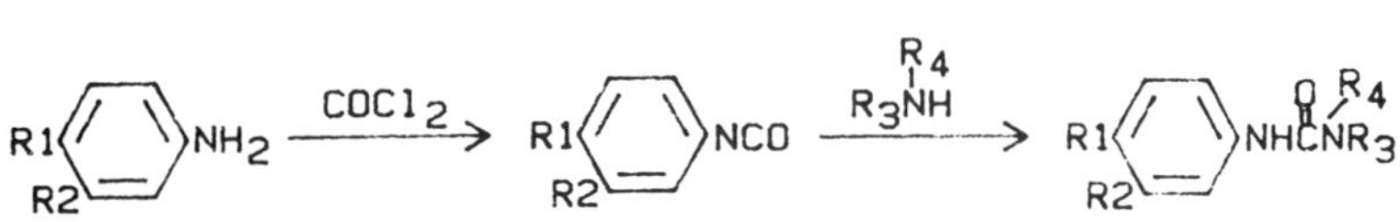

ANILINE ARYL ISOCYANATE UREA

Manufacture of linuron is shown in the following scheme:

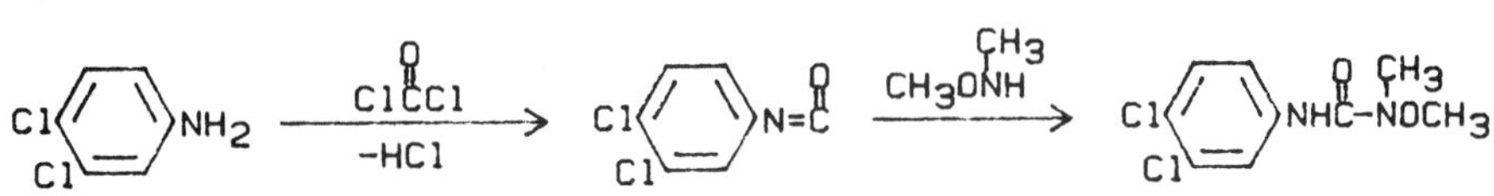

3,4-DICHLORO ANILINE 3,4-DICHLORO PHENYL ISOCYANATE LINURON

The aromatic isocyanates have higher boiling points than their aliphatic counterparts and can be produced in an organic solvent from phosgene and an aniline. The production of the aliphatic isocyanate requires specialty equipment since the high temperature requires correspondingly high pressures for the volatile aliphatics.

Sulfonyl Ureas. The sulfonyl ureas are a potent new class of herbicides, effective at extremely low use rates. Application can be pre- or postemergence. The compounds are absorbed foliar and through the plant root system, translocating throughout the plant. Inhibition of cell division is thought to be the primary herbicidal activity. The sulfonyl ureas include chlorsulfuron, sulfometuron methyl, and metasulfuron methyl:

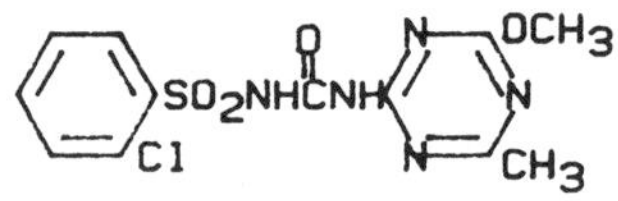

CHLORSULFURON

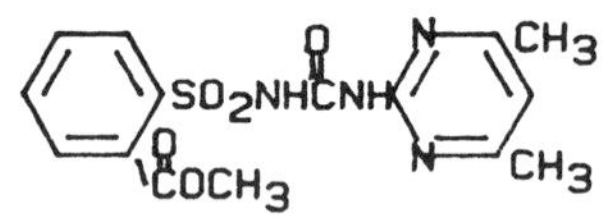

SULFOMETURON METHYL

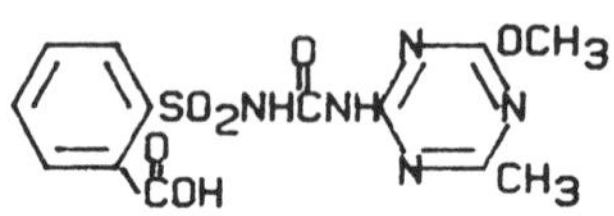

METASULFURON METHYL

Manufacture of chlorsulfuron is similar to the other urea compounds, with phosgene being used to form the urea bond. The sulfonamide is converted to the isocyanate followed by reaction with the amine compound:

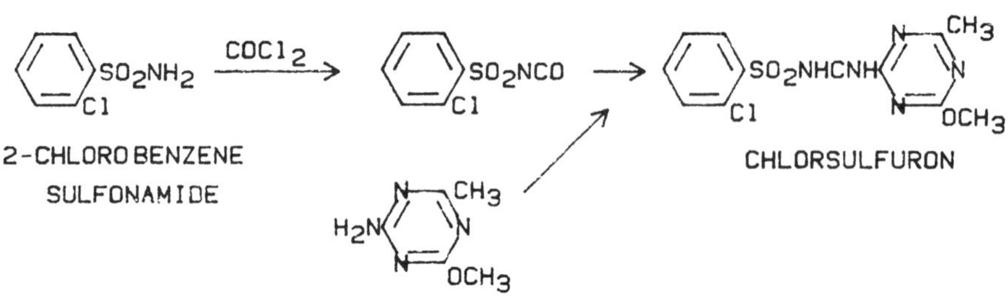

2-AMINO-4-METHOXY-6-METHYL-1,3,5-TRIAZINE

Uracils. The third class of general urea compounds is the uracils, bromacil and terbacil. The compounds are typically soil applied with similar herbicidal activity to the urea.

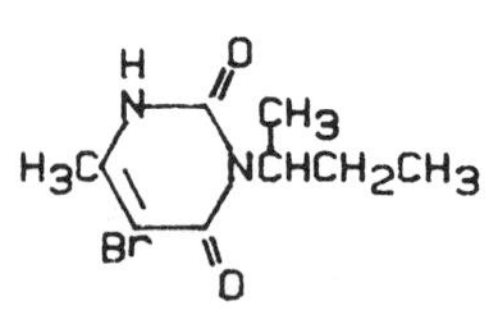

BROMACIL

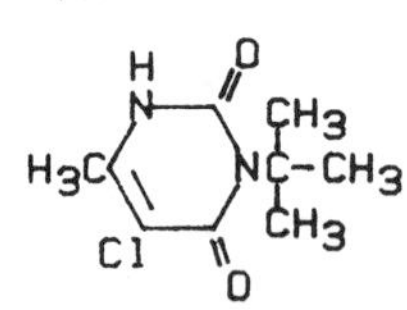

TERBACIL

The compounds are made by the reaction of an amide with an isocyanate:

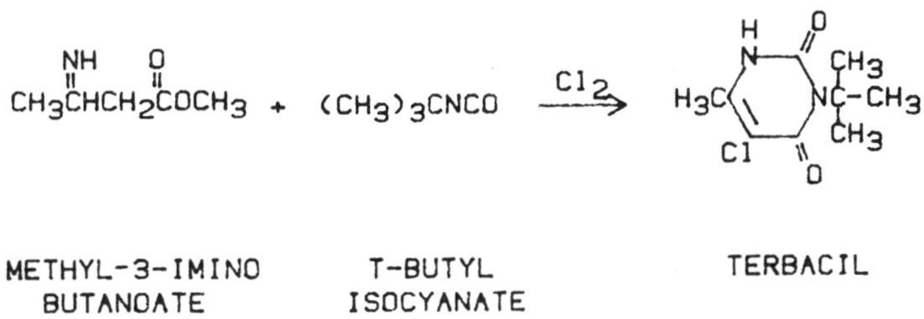

The ureas are high melting solids with low solubility in most solvents. The products are usually formulated as wettable powders or liquid suspensions.

Carboxylic Acids

The carboxylic acids are a general class of compounds with varied herbicidal activity. They are used both pre- and postemergence, applied to both soil and foliage. The compounds include glyphosate, dicamba, picloram, chloramben, endothall, dalapon, diclofop-methyl, and fluazifop-butyl.

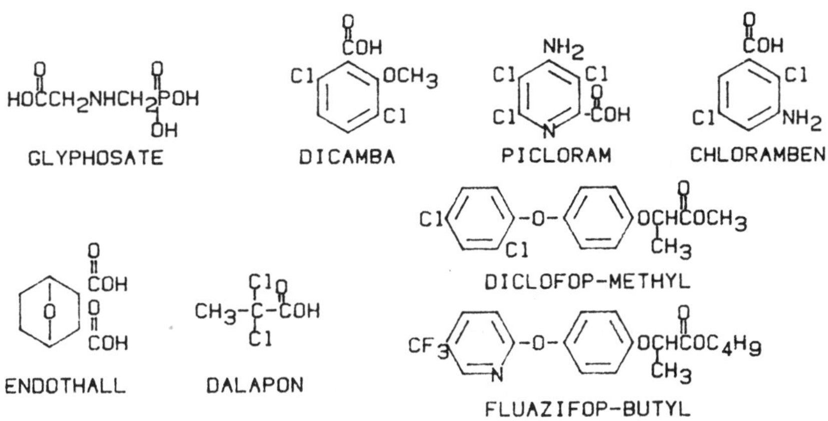

The principle carboxylic acid compound is glyphosate, a nonselective foliar-applied herbicide. It is made by the following reactions:

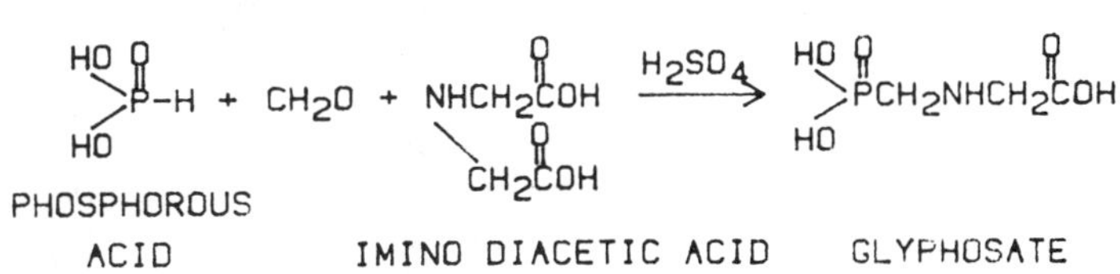

Also important are the phenoxy propionate postemergence compounds, diclofop-methyl and fluazifop-butyl. They can be made by the following scheme:

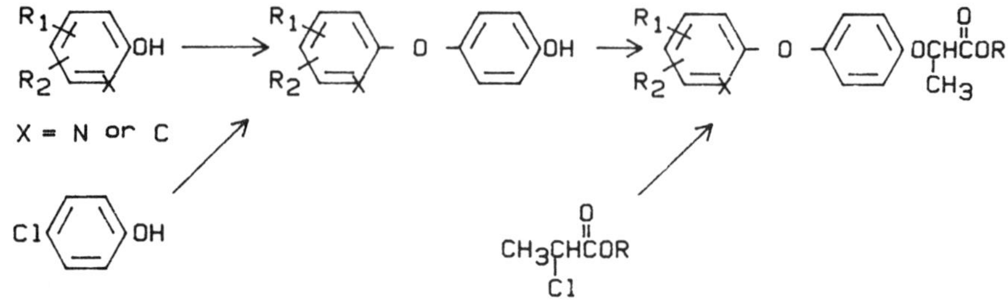

4-CHLOROPHENOL α-CHLOROPROPIONIC ESTER

General Compounds

Several compounds that do not appear in the general classifications are significant herbicides in terms of volume or annual sales. Notable are paraquat, bentazon, acifluorfen, and sethoxydim.

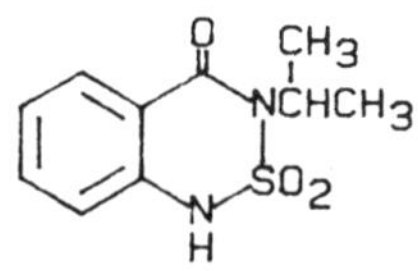

BENTAZON

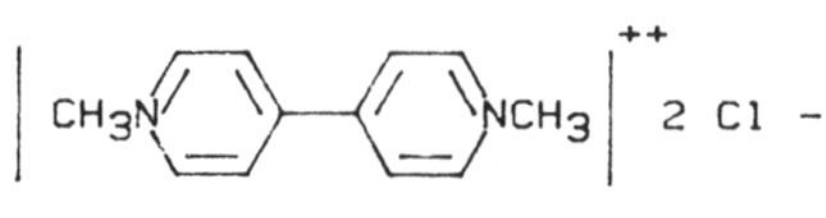

PARAQUAT

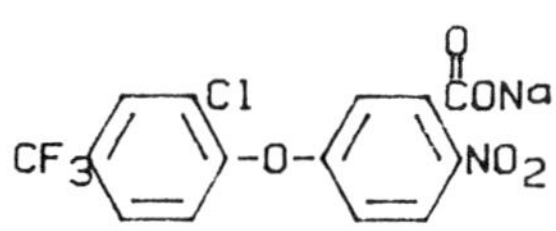

ACIFLUORFEN

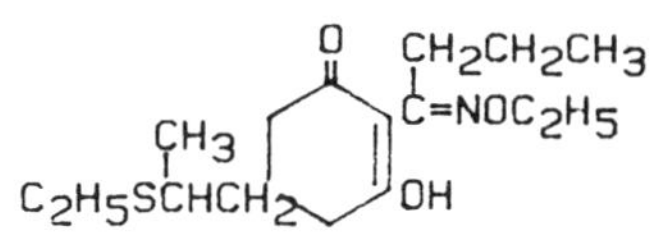

SETHOXYDIM

These compounds are postemergence herbicides, applied to the foliage of target plants.

Bibliography

Anonymous, *Farm Chemical Handbook*, Meister, Willoughby, Ohio, 1985.

Beste, C. E., *Herbicide Handbook*, 5th ed., Weed Society of America, Champaign, Illinois, 1983.

Greer, J. D., and Johnson, O. H., *Marketing Research Report on Herbicides*, Stanford Research Institute, Menlo Park, California, 1980.

Melnikov, N. N., *Chemistry of Pesticides*, Springer-Verlag, New York, 1971.

Sanders, H. J., *Chem. Eng. News*, p. 20 (August 3, 1981).

Sittig, M., *Pesticide Process Encyclopedia*, Noyes, Park Ridge, New Jersey, 1977.

Spencer, E. Y., *Guide to the Chemicals Used in Crop Protection*, 7th ed., Canadian Governmental Publishing Center, London, Ontario, 1981.

Storck, W. J., *Chem. Eng. News*, p. 35 (April 9, 1984).

Trewhitt, J., and Bluestone, M., *Chem. Week*, p. 34 (April 3, 1985).

Worthing, C. R., and Walker, S. B., *The Pesticide Manual*, 7th ed., British Crop Protection Council, Lavenham Press, Lavenham, Suffolk, 1983.

PHILIP G. McCRACKEN
LARRY H. GASPER

Inhibitors: Corrosion

Introduction

An inhibitor is a substance that retards the rate of a chemical reaction, i.e., the opposite of a catalyst. A corrosion inhibitor, then, is a substance which, when added in small concentrations to an environment, decreases the rate of attack by the environment on a metal. Corrosion inhibition has become, together with corrosion-resistant alloys, barrier coatings, and electrochemical protection systems, one of the foremost methods for combating metallic corrosion. There are many systems in which the use of corrosion inhibitors is the simplest and most economical approach to corrosion control.

The number of corrosion inhibitors used in various applications is surprisingly large, and the mechanisms of inhibition are diverse. Therefore, in order to make intelligent use of them we must, first of all, identify those problems that can be effectively solved by the use of inhibitors. In addition, the possibility of adverse effects of the inhibitor on the process or on other parts of the system must also be considered. All this requires some understanding of the principles of corrosion and inhibitor action, and of the economics of inhibitor application.

A detailed discussion of all the different aspects of corrosion inhibition is outside the scope of this article, which is intended as an introduction to the subject. The reader is referred to the vast published literature on inhibition (some of which is listed at the end of this article) to answer specific questions.

Corrosion

In a broad sense, corrosion can be characterized as "the destructive attack of an engineering material (metal, ceramic, plastic) by chemical or electrochemical reaction with its environment." The overwhelming importance of metals in our economy many times obscures the fact that nonmetals are also susceptible to corrosive attack.

Chemical corrosion results from a direct reaction between a corrosive (e.g., chlorine, either in the gas phase or dissolved in a solvent, such as trichlorethylene) and a material (such as steel):

$$Cl_2 + Fe \longrightarrow FeCl_2 \tag{1}$$

Electrochemical corrosion reactions occur in a conductive electrolyte (normally an aqueous solution) and are mediated by electron transfer between the corrosive (e.g., hydrogen ions or dissolved oxygen) and the metal:

$$2H^+ + 2e^- \longrightarrow H_2 \tag{2}$$

or

$$\tfrac{1}{2}O_2 + H_2O + 2e^- \longrightarrow 2HO^- \tag{3}$$

and

$$Fe \longrightarrow Fe^{2+} + 2e^- \tag{4}$$

Equation (4) is an "anodic" reaction: the metal is oxidized from the metallic to the 2+ state, generating Fe^{2+} ions in the solution and two electrons. Equations (2) and (3) are the most common "cathodic" reactions in acid and alkaline (or neutral) solutions, respectively. Each of these reactions may in turn be composed of several elementary steps, and may be followed by further transformation of the reaction products (e.g., precipitation of iron oxides or hydroxides on the metal surface, etc.).

There are many alternative methods of expressing the corrosion rate of a metal, such as weight loss, weight loss per unit area and unit time (e.g., milligrams per square decimeter per day, or mdd), rate of penetration (e.g., mils per year, or mpy), or current density (e.g., $\mu A/cm^2$ or mA/ft^2). The last two are preferred since they make comparison of corrosion rates easy and independent of specimen shape.

The rate of electrochemical reactions depends exponentially on the potential of the electrode where the reaction takes place, Φ, measured with respect to a reference potential, Φ_0 (see "Electrochemical Engineering: Theory" and "Corrosion: Cathodic and Anodic Protection" in this *Encyclopedia*). Defining the overpotential by $\eta = \Phi - \Phi_0$, the reaction rate, expressed as a current, is

$$i = i_0 \exp(b\eta) \tag{5}$$

or, rearranging and converting to decimal log,

$$\eta = \beta \log(i/i_0) \tag{6}$$

where i_0 is the value of i at $\phi = \phi_0$ (i.e., $\eta = 0$), called the exchange current density, and β is a constant. A "polarization diagram" is a graphical representation of Eq. (6) for both the anodic and the cathodic components of a corrosion reaction. Figure 1 illustrates a theoretical diagram for a corroding metal in acid solutions. Polarization diagrams are useful for analyzing the influence of inhibition on electrochemical corrosion.

The three components of the corrosion cell are: (1) the corrosive (e.g., oxygen or hydrogen ions); (2) the metal to be corroded; and (3) an electrical circuit to transfer the electrical charges between the anodic and cathodic

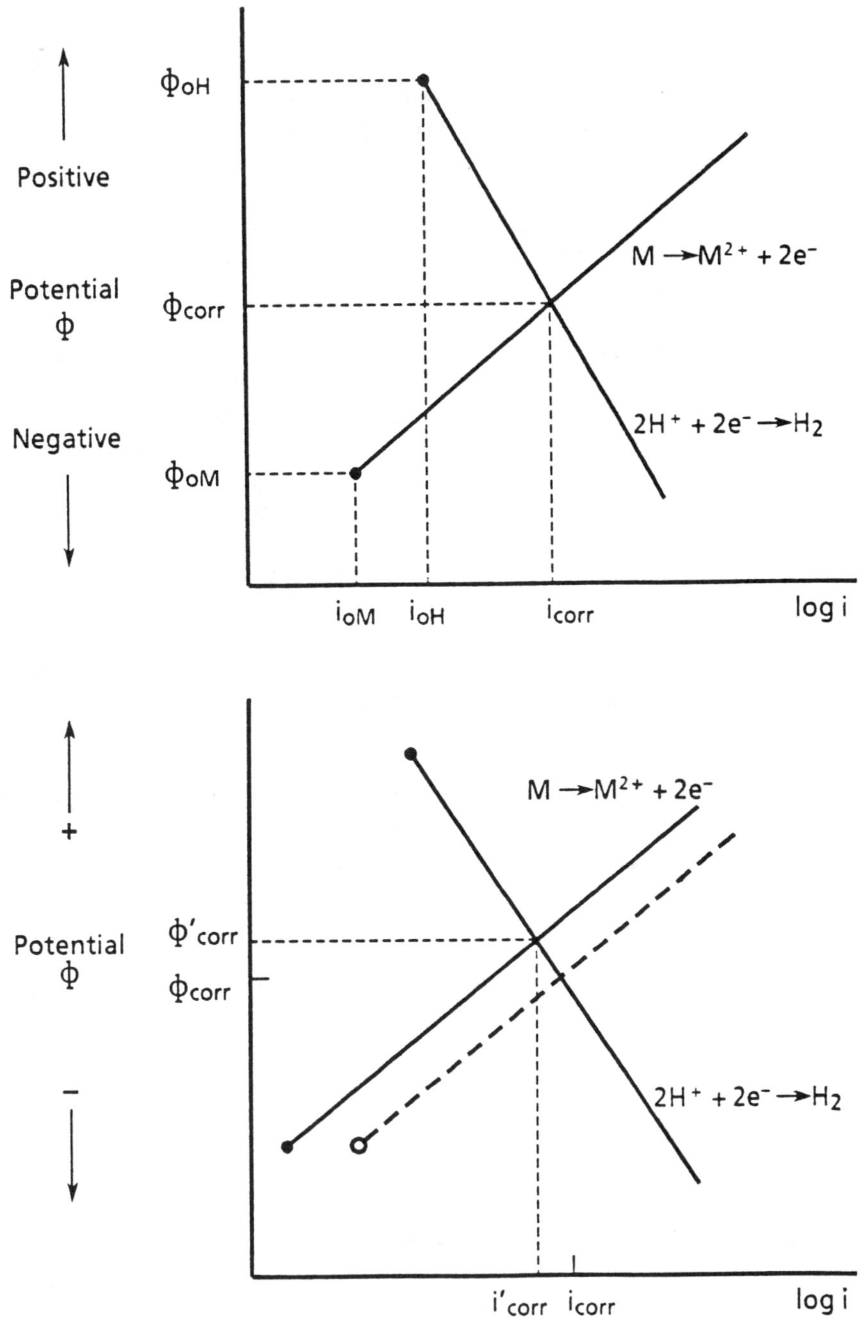

FIG. 1. Theoretical polarization diagram, potential vs log of current density, for a metal M corroding in an acid solution. Φ_{corr} = corrosion potential. i_{corr} = corrosion current density. Φ_{0M} and Φ_{0H} = standard potential for the M/M^{2+} and H^+/H_2 redox couples, respectively. i_{0M} and i_{0H} = exchange current densities, i.e., current at $\Phi = \Phi_0$.

reaction sites, i.e., the metal itself for electrons and a conductive electrolyte for ionic transport.

The overall rate of the corrosion process is limited to that of the slowest "rate-limiting" step. In order to retard the rate of the reaction, any of the steps may be inhibited. However, the effectiveness of inhibition will be maximized if the rate-limiting step is preferentially affected. Identifying this step in a complex corrosion situation is one of the first challenges in designing an effective inhibition program.

In aerated, neutral solutions, such as cooling water or boiler water, the main cathodic reaction is oxygen reduction, Eq. (3). The corrosion rate is normally limited by availability of oxygen to the metal surface, which is proportional to the concentration of dissolved oxygen in the solution. In strongly acidic systems, on the other hand, the main cathodic reaction is hydrogen ion reduction, Eq. (2), which is usually limited by the catalytic activity of the metal surface. Under some circumstances the corrosion rate may be limited by other factors, e.g., by the rate of metal dissolution (on corrosion-resistant alloys protected by a thin passive film) or by the electrical resistance of the cell (in distilled water).

Obviously, the type of inhibitors used in each case should reflect the differences in the limiting step of the corrosion process.

Classification of Inhibitors

The most convenient system to classify inhibitors is by their mechanism of inhibition. This approach has some limitations when dealing with substances which function by mechanisms we do not yet understand. However, it is very successful in the large majority of cases.

Historically, inhibitors have been classified as "anodic" or "cathodic," depending on which component of the corrosion reaction they preferentially retard. Figure 2 illustrates the effect of preferential inhibition of the anodic (a) or the cathodic (b) reactions on the polarization diagram of Fig. 1. In both cases, the corrosion rate decreases and the corrosion potential shifts either in the negative or the positive direction, respectively. In most cases, however, both partial reactions are affected to some extent, resulting in "mixed" inhibition.

Most inhibitors seem to fall into two categories: 1) those which act on the metal surface and improve its corrosion resistance, called "barrier layer formers"; and 2) those that modify the corrosivity of the environment, which in turn may be subdivided into "pH neutralizers" and "scavengers." A third group, "miscellaneous" inhibitors, does not fit neatly into either of the above two definitions.

Barrier Layer Formers

These inhibitors have the ability to interfere with the corrosion reactions by depositing a barrier layer between the metal surface and the environment.

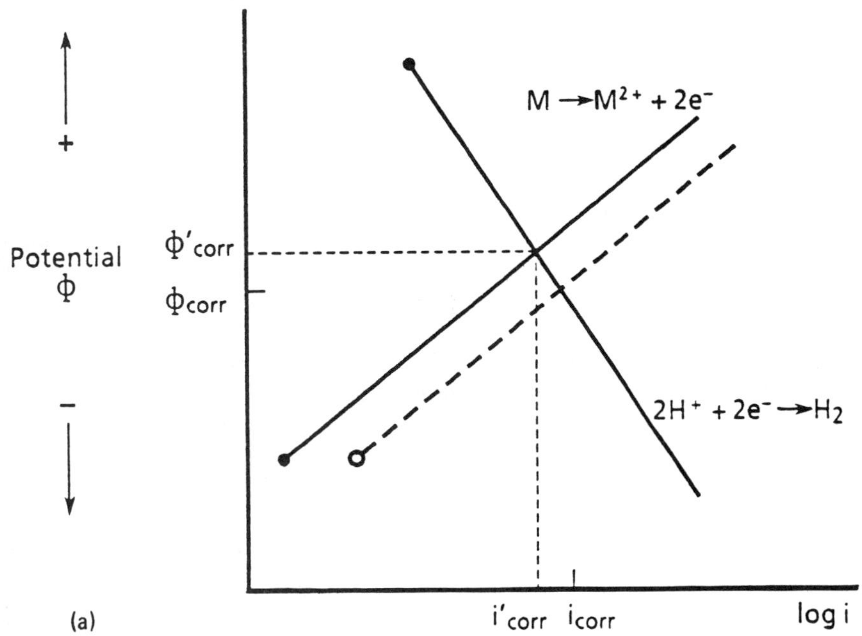

FIG. 2a. Influence of preferential inhibition of the aniodic reaction on the theoretical polarization diagram of Fig. 1. Φ'_{corr} corrosion potential of inhibited system. Φ_{corr} = original corrosion potential. i'_{corr} = corrosion current density of inhibited system. i_{corr} = original corrosion current density.

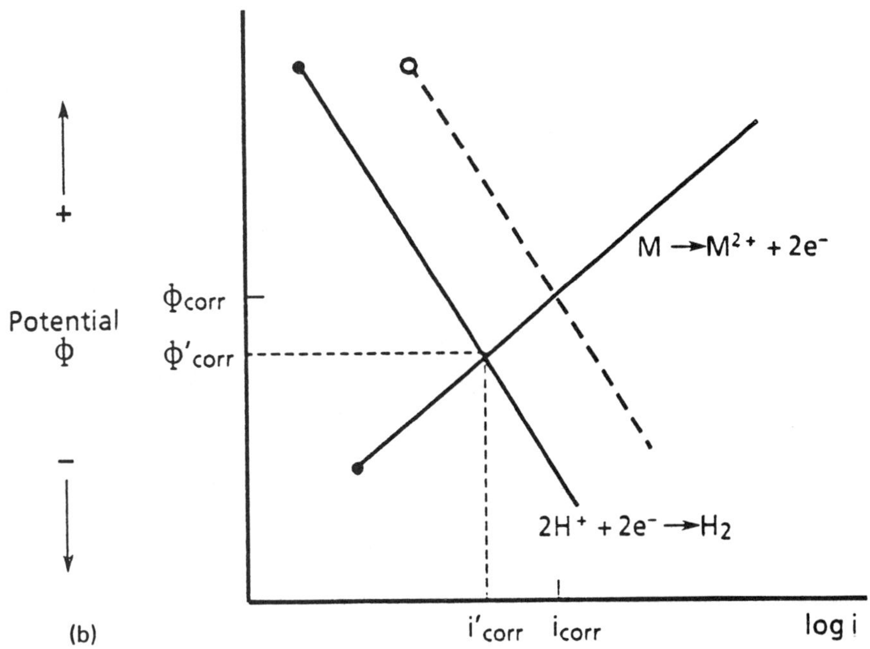

FIG. 2b. Influence of preferential inhibition of the cathodic reaction on the theoretical polarization diagram of Fig. 1.

They have been the most extensively used and studied, becoming almost synonymous with corrosion inhibitors. Several different types can be distinguished within this category.

Adsorption Film Formers

These inhibitors adsorb on the metal surface and interfere with the corrosion reaction on the adsorption site. The interference may be purely physical (blockage of the surface) or may involve an electrochemical interaction between the adsorbate and one or more components of the corrosive system (e.g., cathodic poisons). Materials such as acetylenic alcohols, organic nitrogen compounds (quinoline, piperazine, other aromatic amines, quaternary ammonium salts, etc.), and inorganic substances (sulfides, arsenic, tin, etc.) are known to function through this mechanism in strongly acid solutions. Table 1 gives some examples of film-forming inhibitors. Organic film formers are adsorbed on metals due to interactions (e.g., electrostatic attraction, π-electron bonding, etc.) between the metal and one or more "active" groups on the adsorbate. These groups usually contain a nitrogen atom (amines, imines, ammonium salts), multiple C—C bonds (acetylenic alcohols), or C=O bonds (organic acid salts, formaldehyde). In addition, the size and configuration of the molecule are also important in determining the extent of blocking of the surface.

These inhibitors are most effective when they interfere with one of the steps of the cathodic hydrogen ion reduction. For instance, arsenic salts deposit on the steel surface a thin film of elemental arsenic, which is an extremely poor catalyst for hydrogen ion reduction. The rate of the cathodic reaction, and hence the corrosion rate, can be reduced by several orders of magnitude.

Adsorption inhibitors are generally not very effective in neutral solutions, where the main cathodic reaction is the reduction of dissolved oxygen. Some organic compounds, notably benzotriazole and related compounds, are

TABLE 1 Film-Forming Adsorption Inhibitors

Inhibitor	Metals	Systems
Imidazoline	Fe, steel	Acids (HCl, dilute H_2SO_4, CO_2, organic)
Quaternary ammonium	Fe, steel	Acids (HCl, dilute H_2SO_4, CO_2, organic)
Acetylenic alcohols	Steel	Acids
Formaldehyde	Fe, steel	Acids (HCl, dilute H_2SO_4, CO_2, organic)
Na_2S, NaI	Fe, steel	Acids (HCl, dilute H_2SO_4, CO_2, organic)
As_2O_3, Na_3AsO_4	Fe, steel	Acids (HCl, dilute H_2SO_4, CO_2, organic)
Rosin amine	Fe, steel	Acids (HCl, dilute H_2SO_4, CO_2, organic)
Pyridine	Fe, steel	Acids (HCl, dilute H_2SO_4, CO_2, organic)
Mercaptobenzothiazole	Fe, Cu	Aerated water
Benzothiazole	Cu	Aerated water, acids
Aliphatic, aromatic amines	Fe, steel	Acids

effective on copper alloys, although the mechanism of interaction may involve the formation of an insoluble compound layer instead of a simple adsorption film. Imidazoline, sodium benzoate, and sodium mercaptobenzothiazole are somewhat effective on steel. However, a "conversion layer former" would be preferred for this application.

Conversion Layer Formers

Instead of simply adsorbing on the metal surface, these inhibitors react chemically either with the metal or with some component of the solution, forming a more or less thick layer of an insoluble compound that isolates the metal from the environment. Formation of these scales may also adversely affect other processes, such as heat transfer or fluid flow.

Phosphates and their related compounds (phosphonates, polyphosphates) are the best known and most widely used, especially in cooling water systems. They form insoluble iron phosphate layers that provide a significant degree of protection, partly by decreasing the availability of oxygen to the corroding surface and partly by increasing the electrical resistance of the corrosion cell. Silicates, chromates, and to some extent carbonates can be used on metals such as steel, copper, and aluminum. Table 2 gives more examples of this type of inhibitor.

Passivating Inhibitors

These inhibitors function by shifting the electrochemical potential of the metal into a region where a stable, insoluble, thin film of metal oxide or hydroxide is formed which effectively protects the metal from further attack. Figure 3 shows a polarization diagram typical of iron and its alloys in aqueous solutions. The development of a stable oxide, referred to as "passivation," is associated with a sharp decrease in the corrosion current (rate). Passivators are useful in neutral solutions, and in many cases the presence of dissolved oxygen enhances their effectiveness. Chromates are the best known examples. They form a mixed iron oxide/chromium oxide film on steels that is very effective in protecting the metal. Other examples of passivating inhibitors are nitrites, nitrates, and molybdates. In addition to steel, aluminum and

TABLE 2 Scale-Forming Inhibitors

Inhibitor	Metal	System
$Ca(HCO_3)_2$	Steel	Fresh water
$Ca(OH)_2$, CaO, $ZnSO_4$	Fe, Zn, Cu	Fresh water
Phosphates, polyphosphates	Fe, Zn, Cu, Al	Boilers
Na_2SiO_3	Fe, Zn, Cu	Fresh water
NaH_2PO_4	Steel	

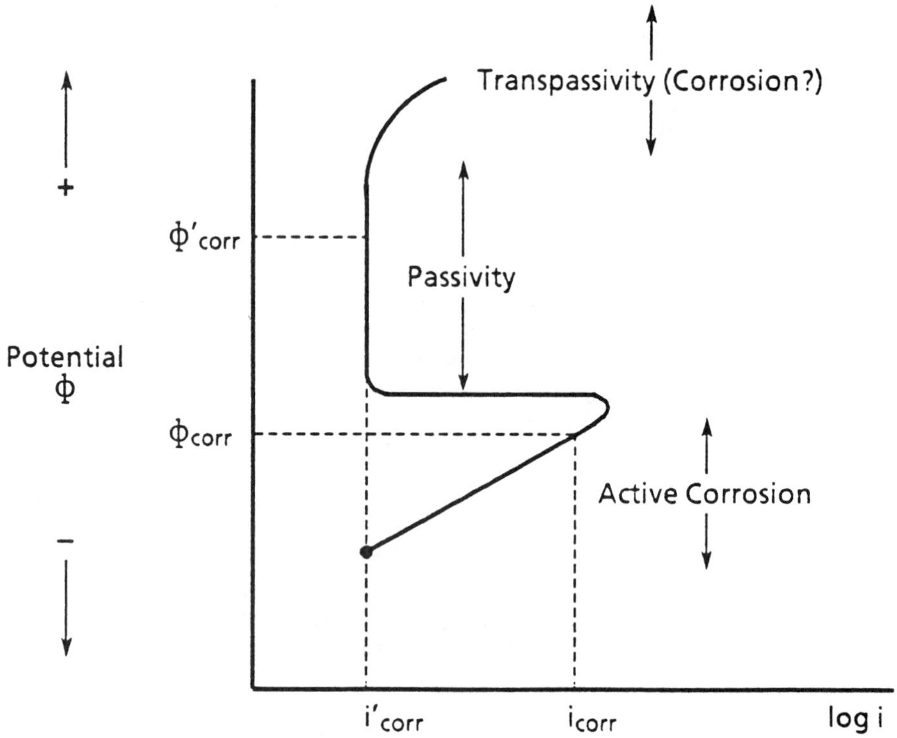

FIG. 3. Theoretical anodic polarization diagram for a passivating metal in aqueous solutions, showing areas of active corrosion, passivity, and transpassivity. Φ_{corr}, i_{corr} = initial corrosion potential and current. Φ'_{corr}, i'_{corr} = corrosion potential and current after addition of passivating inhibitor (e.g., chromate).

copper alloys may also be protected by using these inhibitors. Table 3 gives a partial listing of systems where passivating inhibitors have been successfully applied.

The main advantages of passivating inhibitors are their low cost and the relatively large degree of protection they afford even at low concentrations. However, they present some serious toxicity problems, in particular chromates and nitrites. They are best suited for closed systems where the risk of an accidental release into the environment is low.

Water can also be used as a passivating inhibitor in nonaqueous solutions, especially with highly reactive metals such as titanium or aluminum. A small amount of water (usually less than 1%) favors the formation of a protective

TABLE 3 Passivating Inhibitors

Inhibitor	Metal	Conditions	Systems
Na_2CrO_4	Fe, Al	pH > 8	Cooling water, drilling muds
$NaNO_2$	Fe, Al, Ni	pH > 6	Cooling water
$NaNO_3$	Fe	—	Cooling water
$(NH_4)MoO_4$	Fe	—	—

film that prevents catastrophic corrosion failures, such as stress corrosion cracking. The best known examples of this application are the systems ammonia/carbon steel, methanol/titanium, and chlorinated hydrocarbons/aluminum or titanium.

Environment Modifiers

The most straightforward approach to corrosion control is to eliminate the corrosive from the environment. Without a cathodic reaction, the anodic metal dissolution reaction also stops. The two most common corrosives in aqueous systems are, as mentioned earlier, hydrogen ions and dissolved oxygen. Therefore, the two most common types of environment modifier inhibitors are "pH neutralizers" and "oxygen scavengers." However, the method is also useful for other corrosives, such as HCl or Cl_2. It is most effective in closed circuits, where once eliminated the corrosive is not replenished, although in some cases it is also used in "once-through" flow systems.

Neutralizing Inhibitors

In neutral solutions at room temperature the concentration of hydrogen ions is relatively low. Therefore, hydrogen ion reduction represents a minor corrosion threat when compared with, e.g., oxygen reduction. However, at higher temperatures the concentration of hydrogen ions (due to water dissociation) and their diffusivity increase considerably, and hydrogen reduction may become a significant contributor to the corrosion reaction. Even at lower temperatures, certain chemical reactions (for instance, the dissociation of "weak" acids, such as carbonic or formic) provide a constant source of hydrogen ions, making the environment much more corrosive than what a simple pH measurement would indicate.

Neutralizing inhibitors reduce the concentration of hydrogen ions in the environment. A partial list of these inhibitors is shown in Table 4. This approach to inhibition has been particularly successful in closed circuit systems operating at high temperatures, such as boilers. Ammonia or organic amines are normally added to the feedwater to reduce the free hydrogen ion concentration. Most of the volatile or vapor-phase inhibitors (methylamine,

TABLE 4 Neutralizing Inhibitor

Inhibitor	System
Ammonia	Boilers, cooling water, fresh water, vapor phase
MEA, DEA	Glycol cooling systems
Borate	Glycol cooling systems (automobile coolants)
CaO	Fresh waters
Cyclohexylamine	Vapor-phase inhibition
Cyclohexylamine carbonate	Vapor-phase inhibition
Amylamine benzoate	Vapor-phase inhibition

morpholine, cyclohexylamine) are neutralizing inhibitors with a high vapor pressure.

Basic materials, such as sodium carbonate, sodium hydroxide, and ammonia, are used in the chemical industry to prevent corrosion by acidic contaminants such as carbon dioxide, hydrogen sulfide, hydrogen chloride, organic acids, etc. For example, ethylene glycol and other related compounds (di- and triethylene glycol, glycerol, etc.) are commonly used in cooling or dehydration systems. However, they are susceptible to oxidation at high temperatures, with formation of very corrosive organic acids. Sodium borate or sodium phosphate buffers are added in order to maintain the pH of the glycol in the 7 to 8 range, thus reducing both the tendency of the glycol to oxidize and the corrosivity of any oxidation products that may form.

Scavengers

The most common scavenging inhibitors are used in boilers or in water injection systems to remove dissolved oxygen from the feedwater. Mechanical methods (e.g., gas stripping) are also used to reduce the dissolved oxygen concentration. However, chemical reaction with the scavenging inhibitor is the most effective method to remove traces of oxygen (down to a few ppb). The two most widely used oxygen scavengers are hydrazine and sulfite ions (in the form of sodium sulfite, ammonium sulfite, sodium metabisulfite, or sulfur dioxide). The overall chemical reactions in each case are

$$4N_2H_4 + O_2 \longrightarrow 4NH_3 + 2H_2O + 2N_2 \tag{7}$$

$$2SO_3^{2-} + O_2 \longrightarrow 2SO_4^{2-} \tag{8}$$

Both scavengers need a catalyst in order to produce practical scavenging rates at ambient temperatures. Even though the hydrazine reaction is intrinsically "cleaner," the higher cost of hydrazine, its environmental sensitivity, and the lack of an efficient catalyst limit its application to high-pressure boilers. Transition metal ions (Co^{2+}, Mn^{2+}, Ni^{2+}) or free radical initiators can be used to catalyze the sulfite reaction. The most common problem responsible for low scavenging rates arises from inactivation of the catalyst, e.g., by precipitation with sulfide ions present in the solution or by complexing with EDTA (added to soften the feedwater).

Other scavenging inhibitors are used to eliminate HCl or Cl_2 contaminants from chlorinated hydrocarbons. Amines, dioxane, or ethylene oxide can react with HCl, rendering it inactive.

Miscellaneous Inhibitors

This type of inhibitor interferes with processes that ultimately result in corrosion, even though they are not corrosive *per se*. For instance, scale inhibitors are used in boiler feedwater or in oil production to prevent formation of deposits, e.g., of calcium sulfate or calcium carbonate, on the metal surface. These deposits may have an adverse effect on the process (e.g., heat transfer or fluid flow). In addition, the microenvironment formed under the deposits may be significantly more corrosive than the bulk solution, e.g., due to overheating, concentration of the solution, lowering of the local pH, etc. Therefore, eliminating the deposits also eliminates the corrosion problem. Similarly, antifouling compounds used to prevent the growth of marine organisms on a ship haul may also prevent corrosion under these deposits.

Biocides (formaldehyde, quaternary ammonium salts, etc.) are added to many water systems to prevent the growth of a variety of bacteria, in particular the sulfate-reducing bacteria. These organisms metabolize sulfate ions with production of hydrogen sulfide, which is very corrosive toward steel and copper alloys. These inhibitors are particularly important in seawater cooling or injection systems.

Economics of Inhibition

An effective inhibition program should be both technically sound and economically competitive. Some of the questions that the corrosion engineer must answer are: What is the necessary level of corrosion control? How much inhibitor will be required to maintain that level? Which is the best inhibitor for this particular corrosion problem, and what is the best application method? What size storage tanks, pumps, pipes, etc. should be used?

The cost of inhibition, including both capital expenditures and maintenance costs, should be compared not only to the cost of corrosion, but also to that of alternative corrosion control methods, such a cathodic protection or corrosion-resistant alloys. Some of the factors influencing inhibitor selection and cost will be discussed.

Inhibition Efficiency

The most convenient way of comparing corrosion inhibitors is on the basis of their "inhibition efficiency," which is the percentage that corrosion rates are lowered in their presence, i.e.:

$$\%E = \frac{R_0 - R_i}{R_0} \times 100 \qquad (9)$$

where R_0 and R_i are the background (uninhibited) and inhibited corrosion rates, respectively. In practice, inhibition efficiencies as high as 90 to 99% are common, and an even higher protection may be necessary in highly corrosive systems. The efficiency of an inhibitor is affected, among other things, by its concentration and the temperature, pressure, and composition of the environment.

Effect of Concentration

An economic analysis of inhibition should consider not only the cost of the chemical, but also the inhibition efficiency and the amount of chemical necessary to maintain that efficiency. Inhibitor concentrations are usually expressed in parts of inhibitor, by weight, per million parts of solutions, or ppm. The total amount of chemical required for a particular application can be calculated simply by multiplying the desired concentration times the total volume of fluids to be inhibited.

Figure 4 shows schematically the variation of the corrosion rate of a metal with the concentration of two types of inhibitor. For film-forming inhibitors the efficiency is assumed to be directly proportional to the degree of coverage of the metal surface. The equilibrium coverage is related to the bulk concentration of inhibitor through an "adsorption isotherm," such as the Langmuir isotherm:

$$\theta = \frac{K_a C}{1 + K_a C} \tag{10}$$

where θ is the fractional surface coverage, K_a is a constant, and C is the inhibitor concentration. This isotherm is very often used to describe the adsorption of film-forming inhibitors on metals, although it implies a reversi-

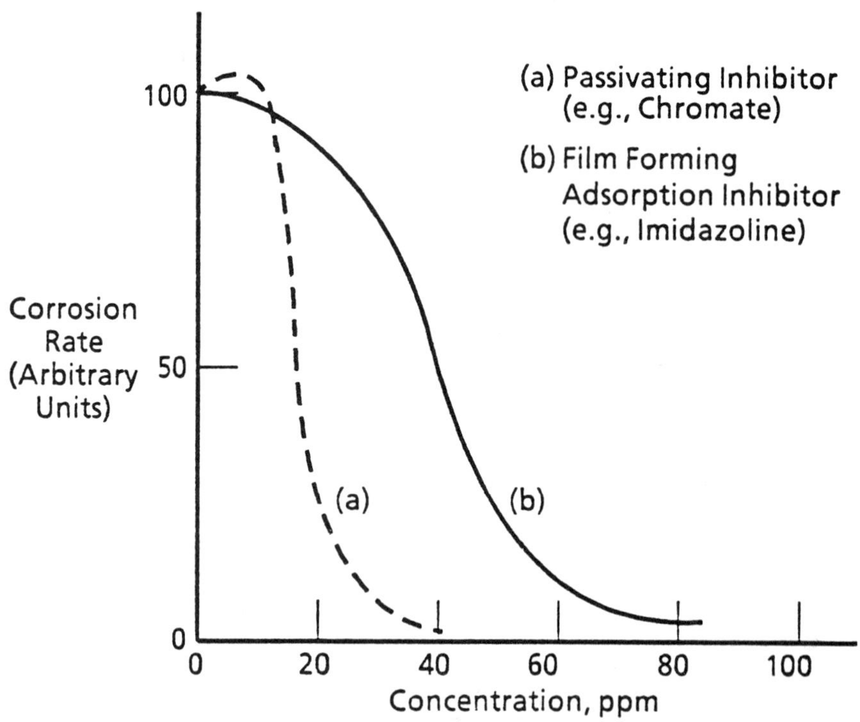

FIG. 4. Schematic diagram of the dependence of metal corrosion rate on concentration of two different inhibitors.

ble adsorption which is not necessarily observed. More complicated expressions that take into account the formation of chemical bonds between the inhibitor and the metal, and the interaction between adsorbed molecules, could also be used.

Even though in most cases the corrosion rate decreases continuously with concentration, a point of diminishing returns may be reached beyond which the cost of inhibition (which is directly proportional to the amount of chemical used) increases faster than the efficiency of the inhibitor. Figure 4 can therefore be used to optimize the inhibitor concentration.

In some cases the use of more than one inhibitor results in an enhancement of the efficiency over that achieved using a single inhibitor, a process called "synergism." Many commercial inhibitor formulations combine chemicals in order to maximize their efficiency. For instance, potassium iodide enhances the inhibition efficiency of many film-forming amines in acid solutions.

Effect of Temperature

The rate of corrosion, as that of all chemical reactions, generally increases with temperature. Exceptions to this rule arise, e.g., from the formation of a more protective scale or from the reduced solubility of a corrosive (oxygen, carbon dioxide) at higher temperatures. The tendency of inhibitors to adsorb on metal surfaces decreases with temperature. Scale-forming inhibitors may be less effective because of the greater solubility of the protective deposits. Thermal stability of the inhibitors is also an important consideration, e.g., most organic compounds are unstable at very high temperatures.

On the other hand, the efficiency of oxygen scavengers increases with temperature due to an increase in the reaction rate. Since most commercial inhibitor formulations contain a mixture of substances, the temperature coefficient of corrosion should be determined for each particular case.

Effect of Pressure

The main effect of pressure (up to a few thousand $lb/in.^2$) on corrosion rates is to increase the solubility of gaseous corrosive, and therefore the corrosivity of the environment. In most cases, pressure has a very minor influence on inhibition efficiency, although it may affect the solubility of the inhibitor.

Effect of Solution Composition

Several examples of the influence of solution composition on inhibitor efficiency have already been mentioned, e.g., the deactivation of oxygen scavenger catalysts by dissolved sulfide ions or EDTA. In general, the composition of the solution may affect the solubility or the reactivity of one of the components of the inhibition system, or it may interfere with one of the steps of the inhibition reaction.

For example, divalent cations may precipitate phosphates, silicates, or organic molecules such as sulfonates, reducing their effective concentration in the solution. Chromates cannot be used in sulfide-containing solutions because they would be lost by reduction. In addition, the solubility of inhibitors in aqueous solutions may decrease with electrolyte concentration (the so-called "salting-out" effect).

Chloride ions are strongly adsorbed on metallic surfaces, and may interfere with the adsorption of chromates or of film-forming amines. Chlorides, sulfates, and other anions can also disrupt the oxide–hydroxide films produced by passivating inhibitors, resulting in severe forms of localized corrosion.

Methods of Application

The use of the correct application method is as important to the success of an inhibition program as the choice of the right chemical. The most common methods follow.

Continuous Application

This method is used in once-through flow systems, for instance, in water supplies, oil field injection water, oil and gas production, once-through cooling water systems, etc. Inhibitors are injected, using a chemical injection pump, either neat or dissolved in a suitable solvent. The method allows for a precise control of dosage.

Another form of continuous inhibition application is the use of capsules, sticks, or pellets that may slowly release the inhibitor by continuous dissolution.

Batch Treatment

In this method, a quantity of inhibitor is added at one time to provide protection for an extended period. Additional inhibitor may be necessary to compensate for losses of inhibitor, e.g., through leaks, decomposition, or continuous reaction with a corrosive. The most familiar examples of batch treatment are cooling systems (e.g., automobile radiators) or boilers.

Batch treatments are also used in oil and gas producing wells. In this case, some type of film-forming inhibitor is applied periodically (normally monthly or biweekly) from a more or less concentrated solution. The frequency of application is determined by the persistency of the inhibitor. One variation of this technique is the so-called "Squeeze Treatment" in which the inhibitor is actually squeezed into the formation, and produced back together with the formation fluids (oil, gas, and brine).

Coatings

Many of the pigments used on coatings are also corrosion inhibitors. The best known coating inhibitors are zinc chromate and lead oxide (red lead), which act as passivators for steel. Zinc oxide is a neutralizing inhibitor, while metallic zinc actually cathodically protects the underlying metal.

Problems in Inhibitor Application

The application of corrosion inhibitors may have adverse effects on the process in which they are to be used. A careful examination of the nature of the inhibitor may prevent most of these problems.

Foams and Emulsions

Foams and emulsions are both dispersions of one phase in another: a gas in a liquid and two immiscible liquids, respectively. Because of their polar nature, some inhibitors behave as detergents or surfactants, stabilizing the dispersions under agitation and resulting in a loss of process control. The solutions are similar to both problems: add a demulsifier or antifoaming agent, use another inhibitor, or inhibit with slugs during equipment shutdown.

Creation of New Corrosion Problems

Some inhibitors may actually increase the corrosion rate of certain components of a system containing dissimilar metals. For instance, some amines protect steel but severely attack copper alloys. At low concentrations and particularly in the presence of chloride ions, chromates and other passivating inhibitors may induce severe localized corrosion problems (pitting). Cathodic poisons, such as sulfide ions or arsenic compounds, may increase the tendency of steel to absorb atomic hydrogen, thus increasing the risks of blistering or hydrogen embrittlement (a very dangerous form of failure).

The only solution to these problems is to investigate the interaction of the inhibitor with all the metallic components of a system.

Interference with the Process

It has already been mentioned that scale formers may interfere with both heat transfer and fluid flow.

Toxic Effects

Toxic effects must be considered in processes where the inhibitors may somehow contaminate the environment, in particular in food processing equipment, potable water supplies, etc.

Conclusions

The purpose of this article is to give an introduction to the complicated field of corrosion inhibition. The general aspects presented should provide the background for making an intelligent approach to corrosion control. However, because of the large number of chemicals available, the variety of possible corrosion problems, and the possibility of adverse effects, each situation should be carefully analyzed to determine the best choice of inhibitor and application method. Some of the practical considerations in inhibitor use are:

1. Minimum concentration of inhibitor needed.
2. Adverse effects of solution components.
3. Effectiveness under varied exposure conditions: temperature, pressure, velocity, pH. Time dependence of corrosion rate.
4. Adverse effects of inhibitor on product or process.
5. Effect on other metals present in the system. Tendency to induce pitting, cracking, etc.
6. Hazards in handling: toxicity, explosions, etc.
7. Cost.

Bibliography

In addition to the Bibliography on corrosion given in the "Corrosion" article and the References given in the "Corrosion: Cathodic and Anodic Protection" article of this *Encyclopedia,* the following are recommended.

On Corrosion:

Brasunas, A. De S., and Hammer, N. E. (eds.), *NACE Basic Corrosion Course,* NACE, Houston, 1970.
Pourbaix, M., *Lectures on Electrochemical Corrosion,* Plenum, New York, 1973.
Scully, J. C., *Fundamentals of Corrosion,* Pergamon, Oxford, 1966.
Tomashov, N. D., *Theory of Corrosion and Protection of Metals,* Macmillan, New York, 1965.
Uhlig, H. H. (ed.), *Corrosion Handbook,* Wiley, New York, 1948.
Uhlig, H. H., *Corrosion and Corrosion Control,* Wiley, New York, 1963.

On Corrosion Inhibition:

Bergman, J. I., *Corrosion Inhibitors,* Macmillan, New York, 1963. An update of this book has been edited by C. C. Nathan, NACE, Houston, 1973.
Butler, G., *Corrosion and Its Prevention in Water,* Reinhold, New York, 1966.
Cooling Water Treatment Manual, TPC Publication No. 1, NACE, Houston, 1971.
James, G. V., *Water Treatment,* Technical Press, London, 1965.
Ranney, M. W., *Corrosion Inhibitors, Manufacture and Technology,* Noyes, Park Ridge, New Jersey, 1976.
Rozenfeld, I. L., *Corrosion Inhibitors,* McGraw-Hill, New York, 1981.

Articles on Corrosion Inhibition:

Dean, S. W., Derby, R., and von dem Bussche, G. T., "Inhibitor Types," in *CORROSION 81,* NACE, Toronto, 1981, Paper 253.
Donahue, F. M., and Nobe, K., "Theory of Organic Corrosion Inhibitors," *J. Electrochem. Soc., 112,* 886 (1965).
Hackerman, N., and Schmidt, H., "The Role of Adsorption from Solution in Corrosion Inhibitor Action," *Corrosion, 5,* 237 (1949).
Kaesche, H., and Hackerman, N., "Corrosion Inhibition by Organic Amines," *J. Electrochem. Soc., 105,* 191 (1958).
Oakes, W. D., "Historical Review of Inhibitor Mechanisms," in *CORROSION 81,* NACE, Toronto, 1981, Paper 248.
Proceedings of the 6th European Symposium on Corrosion Inhibitors, University of Ferrara, Italy, 1985. These symposia have been held every 5 years since 1960.

SERGIO D. KAPUSTA

Insulation

The greater the insulation thickness, the lower the heat loss but the greater the capital expenditure. What is the optimum thickness?

The charts in this article show how to estimate the optimum thickness of one layer of an insulator for both stagnant and turbulent air conditions. They are based on neglecting the resistances caused by both the metal and the inside film at the inner wall.

Atmospheric Film Coefficient

A convenient method for computing heat losses from an exposed surface to air is to use a combined coefficient that represents both the convection and radiation transfer of heat. Its value varies depending on the following factors:

1. The type and position of the surface: flat or cylindrical (vertical, horizontal, or sloped).
2. Wind velocity. Forced convection heat transfer is greater than natural heat transfer.
3. Temperature difference between the outer surface and the ambient air.

The standard combined film coefficient of convection and radiation in the air film on the insulator (Btu/h·ft^2·°F) may be modified into the following equation:

$$h = \frac{\tau_1}{\tau_2}(a + b\Delta t_0) \tag{1}$$

where τ_1 is a dimensionless factor depending on the surface (Table 1). τ_2 is given in Fig. 1. It depends on wind velocity and the outside temperature difference, Δt_0. It approaches unity for still air. a and b are constants: a = 1.2 Btu/ft^2·°F·h, and b = 0.0048 Btu/ft^2·°F·h.

TABLE 1 The Surface Factor, τ_1

		45° Slope		Horizontal	
	Vertical	Upperside	Underside	Upperside	Underside
Flat	1.250	1.440	1.065	1.625	0.875
Cylindrical	1.187	1.100		1.000	

Insulation Thickness

The combined radiation and convection heat loss from an outer surface to the atmosphere must be balanced against the rate of heat flow through the insulation. Therefore, for a given heat-transfer area, the equation for heat flow can be written as

$$q = K\Delta t_i/X = h\Delta t_0 \tag{2}$$

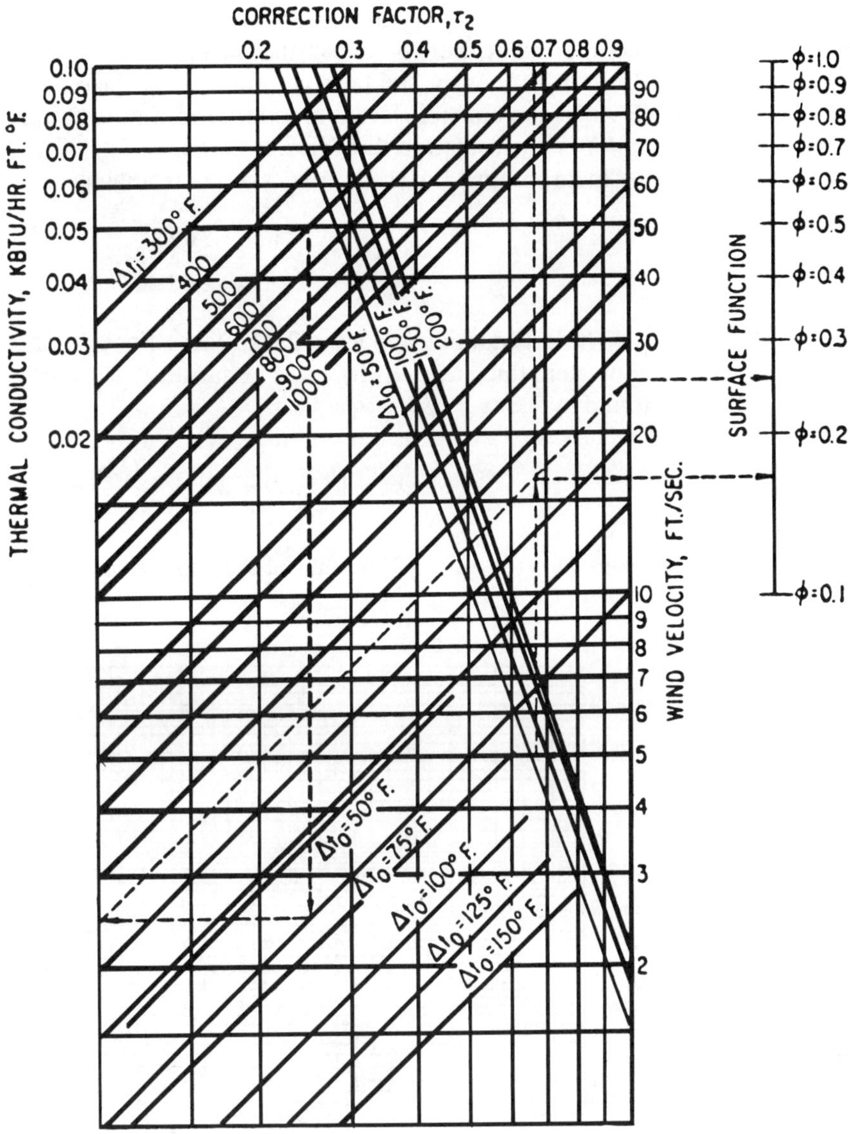

FIG. 1. Estimating the surface function.

where q is the rate of heat flow through or from the insulation, Btu/h·ft^2, K is the thermal conductivity of the insulator at the average temperature, Btu/h·ft·°F, Δt_i is the fluid temperature minus the outer surface temperature, °F. Δt_0 is the outer surface temperature minus atmospheric temperature, °F, and X is the insulation thickness, ft.

Incorporating Eq. (1) in Eq. (2) and rearranging:

$$\tau_1 X = \frac{\tau_2 K \Delta t_i}{\Delta t_0 (a + bt_0)} \tag{3}$$

The last equation applies to flat surfaces. For cylindrical arrangements, an equivalent thickness, X_e (ft), must be substituted for the actual thickness. It is found by

$$X_e = 1.513(D + 2X) \log \frac{(D + 2X)}{D} \tag{4}$$

where D is the outside diameter of the cylindrical surface, ft.

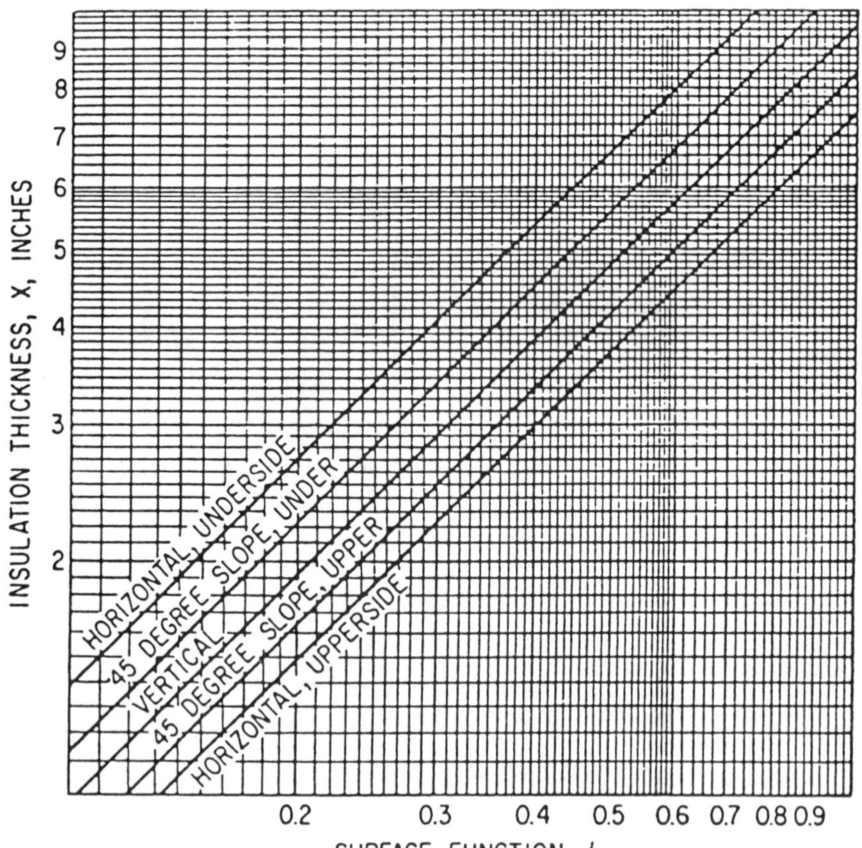

FIG. 2. Insulation thickness for flat surfaces.

The right-hand side of Eq. (3) can be estimated from Fig. 1 regardless of the shape and orientation of the insulated surface. It will be called the surface function. It has the dimensions of length and allows an estimation of the insulation thickness for different surfaces using Fig. 2.

Example 1. Find the insulation thickness on the vertical walls of a furnace if the temperature of air, surface, and fluid are 85, 150, and 650°F, respectively. The insulating material has a thermal conductivity of 0.05 Btu/h·ft·°F (at 400° F).

Step 1. Estimate the surface function from Fig. 1 by drawing a horizontal line from $K = 0.05$ to $\Delta t_i = 500$, then drop vertically to $\Delta t_0 = 65$. Draw a horizontal line back to the left axis and extend a line parallel to the 45° slope reference lines terminating at the wind velocity base line.

Step 2. Draw a horizontal line from the terminating point in Step 1 to the surface function line and read $\phi = 0.26$ for still air. If the air is turbulent, the function will shift to a lesser value. For a wind velocity of 5 ft/s and $\Delta t_0 = 65$, follow the example line on Fig. 1 and read $\tau_2 = 0.67$ and $\phi = 0.167$.

Step 3. Estimate the insulation thickness from Fig. 2 as a function of the surface position. If the air is still, the thickness on the vertical walls is 2.5 in.

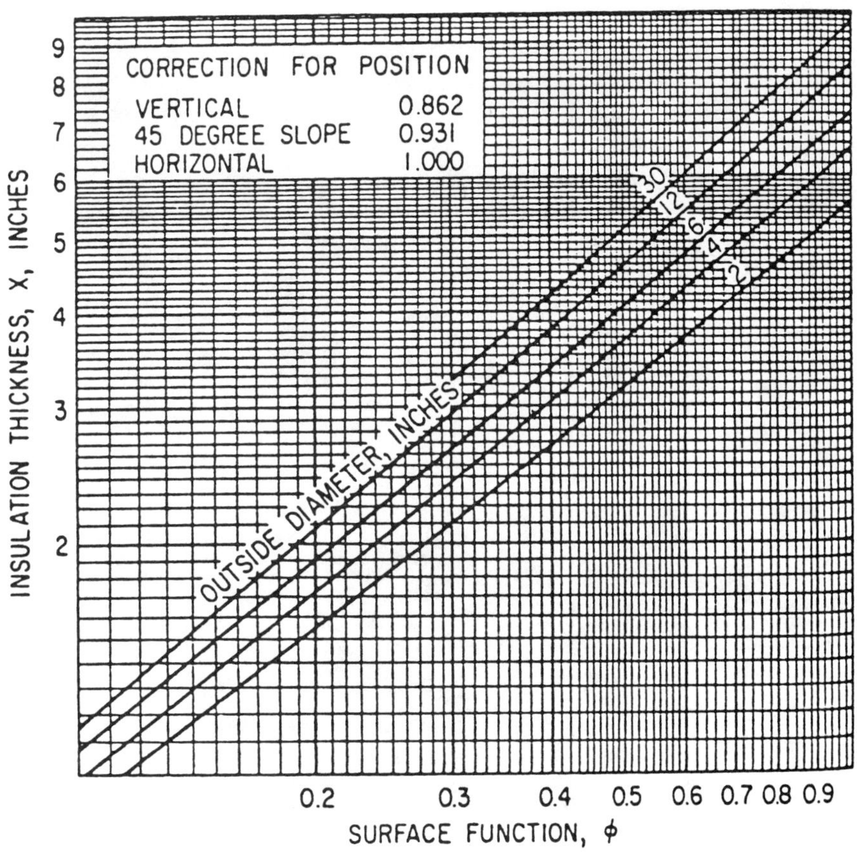

FIG. 3. Insulation thickness for cylindrical surfaces.

TABLE 2 Insulation Thickness for Different Surfaces

	Vertical (in.)	Horizontal Upperside (in.)	Horizontal Lowerside (in.)
Flat	2.5	1.95	3.5
Cylindrical	1.8	2.14	2.14

Example 2. A 3½-in. vertical pipe (D = 4 in.) carrying a fluid at 650°F is to be insulated. If the surface temperature and the thermal conductivity of the insulator are 150°F and 0.05 Btu/h·ft·°F, what is the insulation thickness?

Estimate the surface function from Fig. 1. It will be the same as indicated in Example 1. Then find the insulation thickness from Fig. 3 and multiply it by the correction factor for its position. That is, $\phi = 0.26$ if the air is still and the thickness = 2.14 (0.862) = 1.84 in.

Table 2 compares the insulation thickness for different surfaces estimated under the same conditions of the last two examples ($\phi = 0.26$).

Optimum Insulation Thickness

The cost of a thermal insulator as well as its moisture resistance and thermal, chemical, and mechanical properties must be considered in selecting any insulating material.

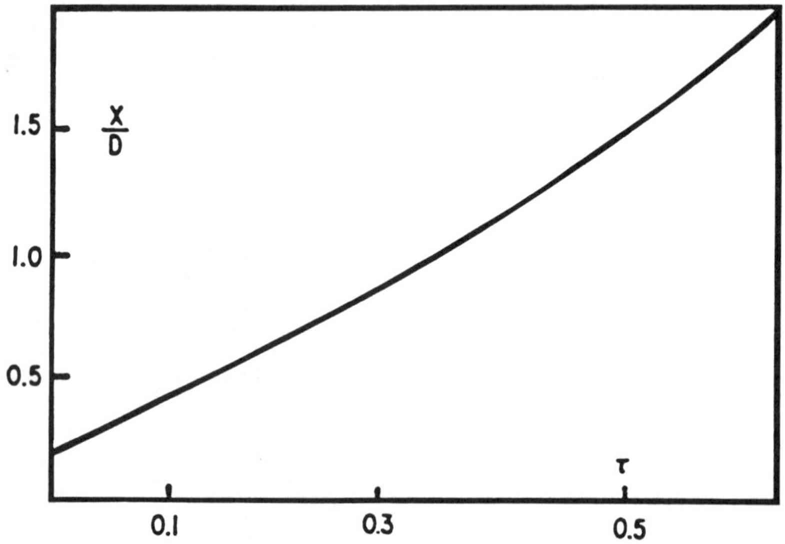

FIG. 4. Patton factor for pipes.

The total annual cost of insulation is the sum of the cost of heat energy lost and fixed charges. A plot of costs versus the insulation thickness will determine the most economical thickness. A dimensionless factor can be used to calculate insulation thickness, depending on the ratio of insulation thickness to pipe diameter (Fig. 4) in the following equation:

$$\tau = \frac{2}{D}\left\{\sqrt{\frac{tC_hK\Delta t_0}{fC_i(10)^6}} - \frac{K}{h}\right\} \tag{5}$$

where t is the operating time in hours per year, C_h is the annual cost of heat loss per million Btu, C_i is the installed cost of insulation per cubic foot, and f is the fraction of the installed cost depreciated annually.

The unknown surface temperature in the last equation can be easily found in parallel with the optimum thickness by trial and error. Still better, it is possible to plot Δt_0 vs X obtained from Figs. 1, 2, and 3 and from Eq. (5) on the same graph and find the point of intersection. The recommended procedure is as follows:

1. Make a rough guess at the surface temperature and select two other points, say 25 to 50° above and below this value.
2. Find the corresponding insulation thickness for each of the three points by two ways, first from Figs. 1, 2, and 3, and then from Eq. (5).
3. Plot these points with Δt_0 for the X-axis and the insulation thickness for the Y-axis and connect them with two smooth curves. The intersection of the two curves indicates the optimum thickness.

Example 3. Find the optimum insulation thickness on the vertical pipe given in Example 2. The following data are available: Cost of heat loss, C_h = \$2.0/million Btu; cost of installation, C_i = \$4; depreciation fraction, f = 0.1; operating time, t = 8000 h/yr.

The steps to calculate the given example are indicated in Table 3. The points are plotted in Fig. 5. At the intersection of the two curves, Δt_0 = 92°F and the optimum thickness is 0.875 in. (1 in.).

TABLE 3 Estimate of Optimum Thickness

Assumed Surface Temperature (°F)	Δt_0	ϕ (Fig. 1)	X (Fig. 2)	h (Eq. 1)	τ (Eq. 5)	X (Fig. 4)
135	50	0.385	2.55	1.710	0.144	0.625
160	75	0.215	1.58	1.853	0.179	0.75
185	100	0.140	1.12	1.995	0.209	0.875

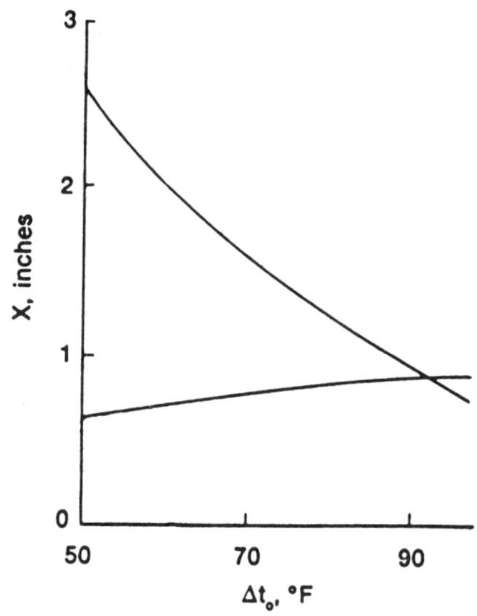

FIG. 5. Graphic solution to Example 3.

Critical Insulation Thickness

In certain instances the heat loss from an insulated pipe may exceed that from an uninsulated one. In these systems the insulator has a relatively high thermal conductivity and its resistance to heat flow is insufficient to compensate for the additional heat loss resulting from the increased exposed area. The heat loss increases to a maximum, then it decreases with an increase in thickness. The thickness of the insulator which corresponds to the maximum heat loss is called the critical insulation thickness (X_{cr}, ft). It is verified by

$$(D + 2X_{cr}) = 2K/h \tag{6}$$

The excessive heat loss will be avoided if X_{cr} does not exist. Substituting $X_{cr} = 0$ and Eq. (1) for h, then rearranging:

$$\Delta t_0 = \left(\frac{2}{\tau_1 b}\right)\left(\frac{\tau_2 K}{D}\right) - \left(\frac{a}{b}\right) \tag{7}$$

Figure 6 represents the last equation to estimate either the minimum surface temperature of a certain insulator or the maximum thermal conductivity.

Example 4. A horizontal pipe is insulated with asbestos. The following data are available:

air velocity = 6.2 ft/s
pipe outside diameter = 1.35 in.
thermal conductivity, $K = 0.135$ Btu/ft·°F·h

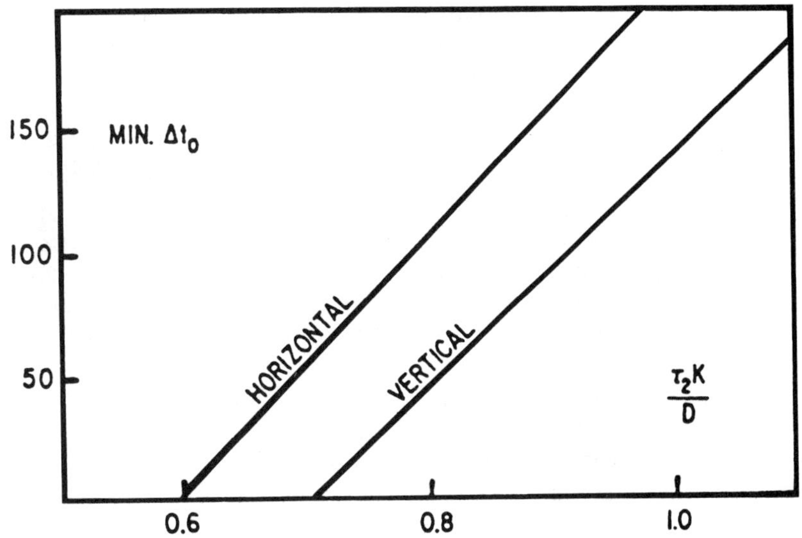

FIG. 6. Minimum surface temperature for pipes.

Assuming $\Delta t_0 = 100$, then $\tau_2 = 0.66$ at 6.2 ft/s (from Fig. 1).

$$K\tau_2/D = (0.135)(0.66)(12)/1.35 = 0.79$$

From Fig. 6, $\Delta t_0 = 100°F$.

High Temperature

Ceramic fiber blankets have been used for several years to line fired heaters. Usually, the blankets are installed in heaters by impaling them on stainless steel studs.

If clean fuels are fired, such as natural gas or even Number 2 oil, ceramic fiber blankets are installed on type 310 stainless steel studs. Layers are overlapped to prevent heat leaks and the stud pattern is devised to support the blanket over the expected life of the lining.

If heavy fuel oil is fired, alloy studs with washers are provided and protected with ceramic fiber putty to prevent corrosion by metal slags. When high sulfur fuels are fired, the shell interior walls should be protected with a high-temperature coating of sodium silicate or coal-tar epoxy. Another method is to apply a thin layer of insulation to the exterior of the vessel to maintain the vessel's wall temperature safely above the dew point. A third approach is to impale a thin sheet of aluminum or alloy sheet steel on the studs at the midpoint of the ceramic insulation to reduce the flow of sulfur-containing gases to the vessel's i.d.

When firing dirty fuels, always specify a blanket lining of high-purity ceramic. If a back-up blanket containing iron is used, it will fail very quickly from chemical attack.

In reformers and cracking furnaces firing at temperatures above 2000°F, ceramic cups are used instead of alloy clips to retain the blanket. The alloy stud tip is recessed about 1 ½ in. into the lining. The cup is filled with ceramic fiber putty to protect the stud from the furnace temperature and to lock the retainer securely to the anchor.

In furnace areas which will experience high hot gas erosion or even water washing, ceramic fiber linings can be used by installing a ¼- or ½-in. layer of wet ceramic fiber blanket to the furnace's hot face. The blanket will become hard and rigid when the furnace is force dried with hot gases or when firing takes place. A blanket applied as just described should be able to withstand hot erosive gases flowing in excess of 200 ft/s. Other methods have not been so successful because if a wire mesh is used, the gas flow is changed, causing small areas of turbulence which tend to pull out the fibers and eventually crater the lining.

Energy Savings

Ceramic linings can reduce energy costs in high-temperature process furnaces. As an example, a process furnace was lined with 9 in. of refractory brick. The face temperature of the brick was 2000°F and the shell temperature was designed for 200°F with an ambient temperature of 80°F. After a few years in service, hot spots developed on the shell raising its average temperature to 325°F. The furnace was relined with 6 in. of ceramic blankets. The average shell temperature fell to less than 200°F. From a cost standpoint, the furnace was lined with 6000 ft^2 of ceramic insulation. At a gas cost of $2/million Btu, the fuel savings were $47,000/yr. The insulation paid for itself in 1 year.

In another small fired heater, castable refractory was originally installed for a design refractory face temperature of 1600°F and a furnace shell temperature of 220°F. After several years of operation, the original castable spalled and cracked, resulting in a shell temperature of 300°F. A 4-in. ceramic refractory blanket was installed that dropped the furnace shell temperature to less than 200°F and reduced heat losses 55%.

Tank Insulation

Sprayed-on rigid urethane foam can provide more than energy savings to hot oil tanks. The cost of steam can more than justify this type of insulation, but the added benefits are: better temperature control of the oil which improves its handling and reduces pumping costs, less corrosion inside the tank roof because of condensation, and reduced tank painting cost. One refiner reduced the heat loss from a 120-ft by 48-ft No. 6 fuel oil tank from 1.5 to 0.2 million Btu/h by applying 2 in. of urethane foam to the tank. To protect the foam, two coats of neoprene, each 2 mils thick, were applied over the foam to inhibit weathering and sunlight degradation.

The uninsulated tank has a heat loss of 71.4 Btu/h·ft^2 through the roof and 38.6 Btu/h·ft^2 through the wall at an average temperature of 50°F. After insulation was applied, the wall heat loss dropped to 5.1 Btu/h·ft^2. The roof loss fell to 3.0 Btu/h·ft^2.

Approximate insulation and coating cost in 1985 was $60,000, but it cost $15,000 to repaint the tank. The payout for the insulation is about 4 years and, in addition, there is no need to repaint the tank every 8 years as was previously done.

As fuel costs increase, the economics of tank insulation change significantly.

This material appeared in *Hydrocarbon Processing Equipment Design Handbook, 1982*, and is repeated with the permission of the editor.

Bibliography

Barrows, G. L., "Save Energy with Ceramic Fiber Insulation," *Hydrocarbon Process.*, p. 187 (October 1977).

Curt, R. P., "A New Approach to Economic Insulation Thickness," *Hydrocarbon Process.*, p. 137 (March 1976).

El Kabbani, A. S., "Insulation Thickness Estimate Simplified," *Hydrocarbon Process.*, p. 145 (March 1970).

Hackman, L. E., and Chambers, H., "New Refractories Solve Old Problems," *Hydrocarbon Process.*, p. 259 (November 1978).

Howell, B. T., and Seymour, R. L., "Protect Reformer Walls Against Burn Out," *Hydrocarbon Process.*, p. 147 (March 1977).

Polastri, F., "Nomographs Find Pipe Insulation Thickness," *Hydrocarbon Process.*, p. 231 (November 1971).

Seebold, J. G., "Reduce Control Valve and Combustion Noise," *Hydrocarbon Process.*, p. 97 (March 1972).

Soderlind, C., "Tank Insulation Can Pay Off," *Hydrocarbon Process.*, p. 122 (July 1973).

Thomas, D. E., James, R., and Sparks, C. R., "Some Plant Noise Problems and Solutions," *Hydrocarbon Process.*, p. 149 (October 1972).

JOHN J. McKETTA

Insulation, Calcium Silicate

Calcium silicate, as its name indicates, is a chemical combination of lime and silica. Like any other cement, it is a self-setting cement reinforced with a fiber but it can stand temperatures as high as 1200°F without any noticeable damage. Because of such intrinsic properties as low density, high area covering capacity, absence of toxicity, and low thermal conductivity, it has become a choice of drier, annealing, heat exchanger, and preheater manufacturers. Its lower labor and handling costs, and clear and streamlined operations have made it still more popular with sophisticated industries such as food processing and pharmaceuticals.

Fundamentally speaking, in all insulating materials the property of insulation is associated with the dead air pores entrapping still air, which prevents loss of heat due to convection. However, in some cases, heat is also preserved by reflecting most of the heat. Thus, depending upon the way by which heat loss is prevented, insulating materials are classified in four different groups: reflective, fibrous, cellular, and granular (Fig. 1). Calcium silicate and other chemical insulating materials belong to the last group.

Why Choose Calcium Silicate?

Various factors are taken into consideration before choosing a type of insulation. Sometimes the product may have good insulating properties but it is very difficult to use, or breakage is very high, or sometimes its behavior at elevated temperature is highly undesirable because of thermal changes occurring in the insulation. Some of the factors which are generally taken into consideration before making any decision are described below.

Temperature Range

Calcium silicate has a higher fusion point than any other insulating material available in this range, and it has been found to be most suitable from 1000 to 1200°F. This 100% inorganic self-setting material does not lose strength or burn or fuse at this high temperature.

Thermal Changes

Thermal change occurring at elevated temperature is another important factor which is generally taken into consideration. If there are too many thermal changes, which are generally permanent, a material may not be chosen in spite of the fact that it has very good insulating properties. In calcium silicate, maximum linear shrinkage at 1200°F has been found to be 2%, which is nominal.

FIG. 1. Top: Granular-type material. Bottom: Cellular-type material.

Thermal Conductivity

This is the most important factor in choosing the right type of material. Calcium silicate enjoys a very good reputation among other available insulating materials, not only because of its low bulk density and ease of handling, but particularly because of its superior insulating property.

Table 1 depicts the thermal conductivity of various well-known insulating

TABLE 1

Material	Maximum Working Temperature (°F)	Density (lb/ft^3)	Thermal Conductivity ($Btu/in/ft^2/°F/h$)
1. Fibrous aluminium silicate	2300	3–10	0.31 at 300°F 0.82 at 1000°F
2. Fibrous potassium titanate	2200	15–18	0.33 at 300°F 0.53 at 1000°F
3. Mineral fiber rock	1800	16–24	0.50 at 400°F 0.75 at 1000°F
4. Calcium silicate	1200	11–18	0.42 at 300°F 0.66 at 1200°F
5. Glass, cellular	800	9–18	0.55 at 300°F 1.04 at 800°F
6. Mineral fiber fill	1200	10–12	0.26 at 100°F 0.65 at 600°F
7. Magnesia, 85%	600	11–12	0.44 at 300°F 0.46 at 400°F

materials having almost the same bulk density and the same maximum working temperature range as calcium silicate.

The fact that calcium silicate is best among insulating materials having the same working temperature, range, and bulk density is further proved by studying a graph of the different temperatures vs the thermal conductivity of various insulating materials (Fig. 2).

Mechanical Strength

Breakage during transportation and at the time of installation has a definite bearing on the cost of material, and thus affects the final selection of a material. In the case of calcium silicate, in spite of the presence of millions of microscopic intercellular spaces, strength is quite adequate to ensure safe transportation and easy installation. The minimum crushing strength of calcium silicate preformed insulation is 60 lb/in^2. Because of its cementing properties, it does not lose strength after coming in contact with water. Its strength shows a nominal decrease from 60 to 35 to 40 lb/in^2 after immersion in water for 18 h. Thus breakage during stacking or storing at the site is reduced. Flexural strength of 35 lb/in^2 also ensures quite safe installation.

Also, there is no breakage loss as such because even the damaged pieces can be reutilized after crushing as a loose filler for filling joints. It can also be molded after the addition of certain binders.

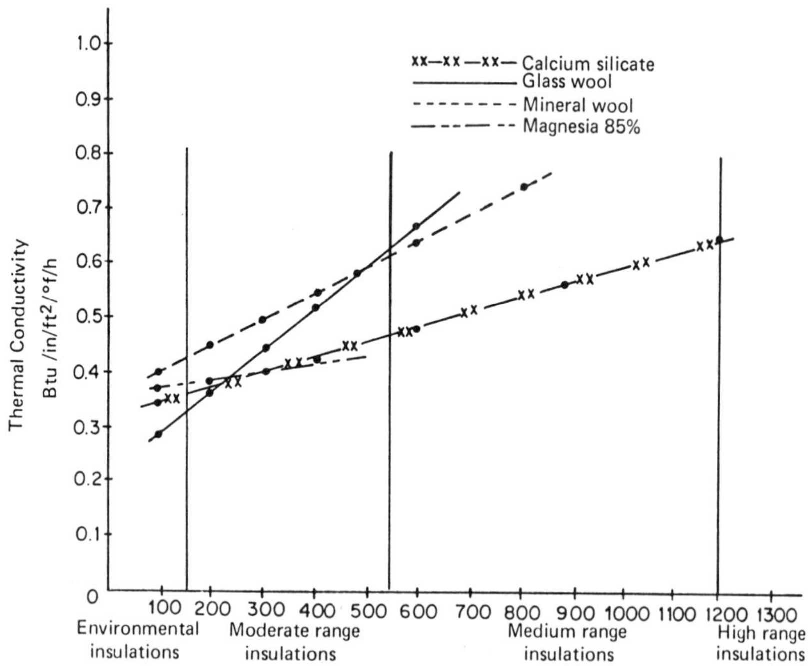

FIG. 2. Comparative insulation properties of different insulating materials.

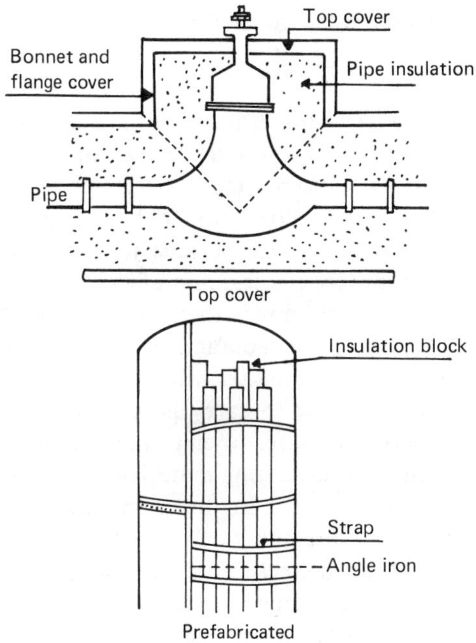

FIG. 3. Installation of insulation materials.

Design Limitation

The paste formed after the reaction and after mixing the reinforcing agent can be fabricated to obtain any design which is possible by molding.

Effect of Atmosphere

This inorganic material, containing about 69% silica, possesses great resistance to atmospheric changes. Even frequent sudden temperature changes do not affect the texture or insulating property of the material. Continuous high temperature also does not cause much damage. It is an excellent insulating material for use in the presence of inflammable gases.

Installation Limitations

The most generally available forms of calcium silicate molded insulations are slabs, pipe sections, and curved legs. Thus it provides easy installation for straight-walled furnaces, curved pipes, and for any other special equipment. Only fabrication is needed. Blocks are held in close contact with the face of the furnace to be insulated by means of wires spaced at 6 or 9 inches. All the joints etc. are filled with powder made of broken pieces of calcium silicate blocks mixed with the binder.

A diagrammatic representation of an installation is shown in Fig. 3.

Economics and Efficiency

Economics and efficiency of the material are fully dependent upon the cost of applied insulation and the cost of the energy it preserves, and this depends upon the various factors connected with the nature of the operation, namely the surface temperature to be maintained, the specified heat loss, and the temperature of the surface to be insulated. Let us see how it makes the operation economical and efficient.

As is well known, there are three modes of transmitting heat: conduction, convection, and radiation. Heat losses due to conduction are associated with the property of matter, whereas convection losses are due to the faculty of the moving matter to carry heat energy. Heat radiation losses are due to the property of matter to emit and absorb different rays.

In most insulating materials, heat losses are controlled by reducing those due to convection. In fibrous materials a strange phenomenon exists where the thermal conductivity and heat losses increase with a decrease of bulk density or with an increase of surface area up to a limiting value. Verschool et al. suggested that this phenomenon is associated with the "free air." It does not exist in this material because here the insulating property is associated with the millions of dead microscopic pores entrapped between the microgranules of calcium silicate. This results in minimizing the heat losses due to convection. To stress this, we calculated the heat losses of 3.5 inch thick materials—calcium silicate, glass wool, and mineral wool—at different temperatures, following H. Parnham's method. The values obtained are plotted in Fig. 4.

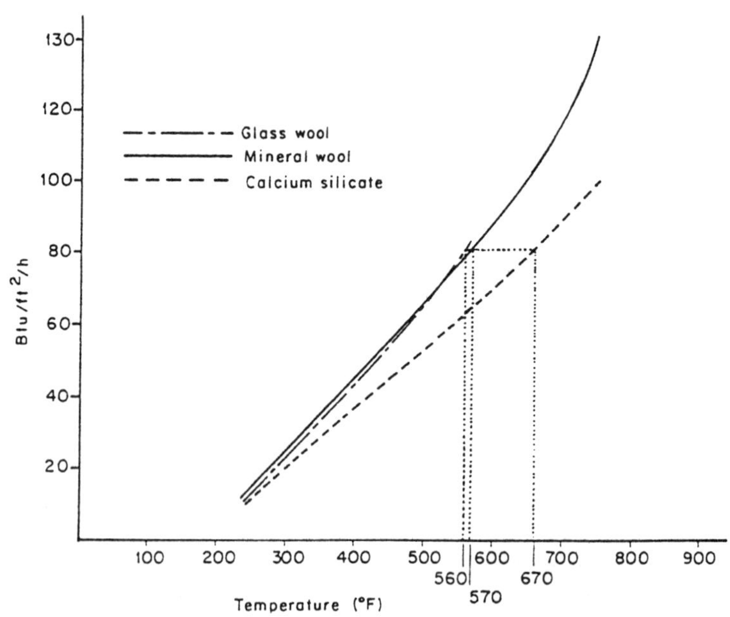

FIG. 4. Calculated heat losses (3.5 inch lining) vs temperature.

By applying the usual formula, we can calculate the thickness equivalent of each material needed to produce the same effects (same heat losses, etc.). After comparing the values we find that a calcium silicate slab will produce the same effects as a far thicker slab of glass wool or mineral wool. Thus it makes the operation most economical and efficient because heat losses in a calcium silicate insulation slab at 670°F would be the same as would be produced by glass wool at 560°F or by mineral wool at 570°F. An example of how use of

TABLE 2

1. Value of fuel (coal)	10 paise/lb ($11.65/1000 lb[a])		
2. Hours of operation	8,100 h/yr		
3. Heat content of the fuel	12,000 Btu/lb		
4. Average exposure temperature of still air	80°F		
5. Operating temperature	350°F		
6. Efficiency of combustion	80%		
7. Estimated cost of installed insulation/100 ft²	*Thickness (inches)*	*Cost (Rs.)*	*Cost ($)*[a]
	1	706.17	82.27
	$1\frac{1}{2}$	1,062.16	123.74
	2	1,414.34	164.77
	$2\frac{1}{2}$	1,765.55	205.69
	3	2,113.76	246.25
8. Amortization period	5 yr		
9. Installed cost/year/100 ft²	*Thickness (inches)*	*Cost (Rs.)*	*Cost ($)*[a]
	1	141.24	16.45
	$1\frac{1}{2}$	212.43	24.79
	2	282.87	32.95
	$2\frac{1}{2}$	353.11	41.14
	3	422.75	49.25
10. Heat cost/h/100 ft²	*Thickness (inches)*	*Heat loss (Btu/h)*	
	0 (bare surface)	3,235	
	1	116	
	$1\frac{1}{2}$	77.3	
	2	58.0	
	$2\frac{1}{2}$	46.4	
	3	38.6	
	$3\frac{1}{2}$	33.1	
11. Value of heat lost. Cost of heat loss/year/100 ft² in rupees (heat lost/ft²/h/yr) (price/lb × 100): heat content × efficiency	*Thickness (inches)*	*Cost (Rs.)*	*Cost ($)*[a]
	0	28,440.00	3,313.26
	1	978.75	114.02
	$1\frac{1}{2}$	489.38	57.01
	2	390.50	45.49
	$2\frac{1}{2}$	325.48	37.92
	3	279.29	32.54

[a]Based on July 15, 1977, exchange rate: 1 Rs. = $0.1165.

TABLE 3 Total Cost (see Fig. 5)

Thickness (inches)	Cost of installation and fuel (Items 9 and 11 of Table 2)	Cost (Rs.)	Cost ($)[a]
0	0 + 28,440	28,440.00	3,313.26
1	141.23 + 978.75	1,119.98	130.48
$1\frac{1}{2}$	212.43 + 489.38	701.81	81.76
2	282.87 + 390.50	673.37	78.48
$2\frac{1}{2}$	353.11 + 325.48	678.59	79.06
3	422.75 + 279.29	702.04	81.79

[a]Based on July 15, 1977, exchange rate: 1 Rs. = $0.1165.

this material makes a furnace more efficient and economical is presented in the example given in Table 2.

From the data the optimum insulation thickness is found to be 2 inches, and we can analyze how economical and efficient operation is made by the use of this material (Table 3 and Fig. 5).

Figure 6 shows the decrease in the cold face temperature with increasing thickness of insulation when the hot face temperature is 752°F (400°C).

Conclusion

After studying the various aspects of this insulating material, we can very safely say that it is probably one of the most economical and efficient

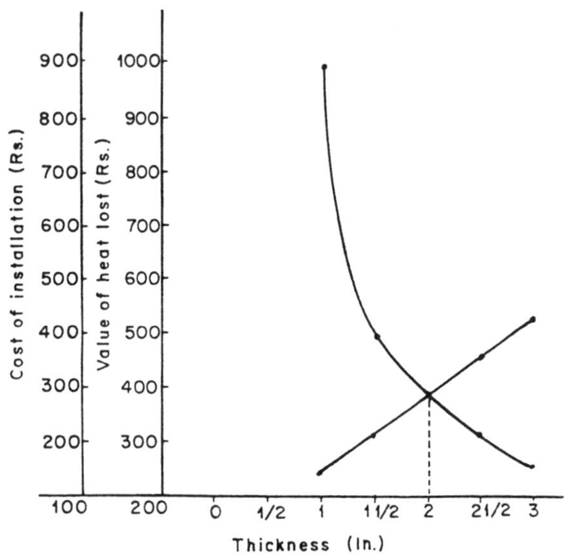

FIG. 5. Cost of installation/value of heat loss vs thickness. The optimum thickness is 2 inches.

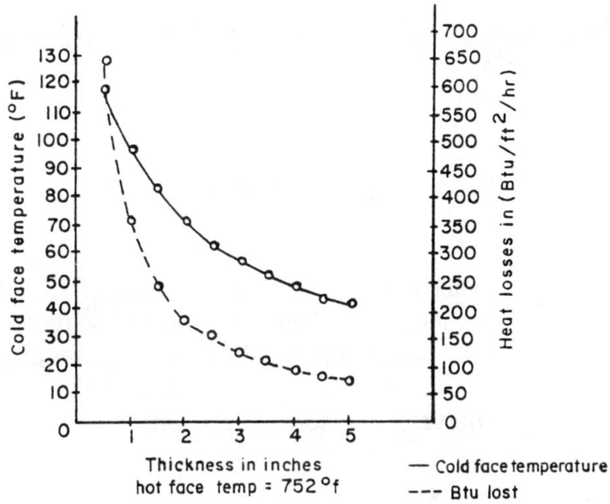

FIG. 6. Decrease in cold face temperature with thickness of insulation at a hot face temperature of 752°F.

insulating materials, and one which is suitable for various operations where temperatures up to 1200°F are encountered.

This material appeared in *Chemical Age of India*, *26*(4), 285–290 (1975).

Bibliography

ASTM 552.

ASTM C-303; ASTM C-533.

ASTM C-489.

ASTM C-517.

British Standard Specification 3958, Part 2.

Ceramic Data Book, Cahner, Chicago, 1974, Section 6.

Coldery, J. M., and Purton, M. J., "Application of Thermal Analysis Investigation on Calcium Silicate," *J. Appl. Chem.*, *8*, (1968).

Lead, P. S., "Calcium Silicate as High Temperature Insulating Material," *Chem. Eng. World*, *7*(1), 65 (1971).

Parnham, H., "Calculations of Heat Losses, Temperature Gradients, and Junction Temperatures in Refractory Walls and Structures," *Refract. J.*, *1967*, 380–390 (November).

Perry, J. W., *Chemical Engineer's Handbook*, 4th ed., McGraw-Hill, New York, 1963.

Shah, H. V., and Mehta, D. J., "Calcium Silicate Moulded Insulation," *Indian Chem. Manuf.*, *1968*, 15–17 (August).

Shah, H. V., and Mehta, D. J., "Calcium Silicate Moulded Insulation," *Res. Ind.*, *14*(2), 62–65 (1969).

Verschoor, V. D., and Creobler, P., *Heat Transfer by Gas Conducting and Radiation in Fibrous Insulation*, Presented at the Annual Meeting of the American Society of Mechanical Engineers, November 1951.

VINAYAKA KAHOL

Insulation and Heat Loss Calculation

Part 1. Computer Method

Determination of heat-transfer coefficients for air, water, and steam flowing in tubes and calculation of heat loss through multilayered insulated surfaces have been simplified by two computer programs.

The programs, written in BASIC, have been developed for the IBM and equivalent personal computers.

Heat Transfer Coefficients

This program estimates the heat-transfer coefficients when air, water, or steam flow inside tubes and pipes. Inputs are simply the flow, pressure, tube or pipe, i.d., and temperature.

Thermal and transport properties of the fluid are not needed. For saturated steam, the saturation temperature is computed by the program; therefore, no reference to the steam tables is necessary.

The heat-transfer coefficient for flow inside tubes is given by

$$h_i = 2.44 W^{0.8} F / d^{1.8} \tag{1}$$

Equation (1) is derived from the basic relationship

$$\mathrm{Nu} = 0.023 \mathrm{Re}^{0.8} \mathrm{Pr}^{0.4} \tag{2}$$

where $\mathrm{Nu} = h_i d/12k$, $\mathrm{Re} = 15.2W/d/\mu$, $\mathrm{Pr} = C_p/k$, and $F = k^{0.6} C_p{}^{0.4}/\mu^{0.4}$.

TABLE 1 Heat-Transfer Coefficient Nomenclature

Nomenclature	Program Symbol	Description and Units
C_p	—	Specific heat, Btu/lb·°F
d	D	Tube, pipe i.d., in.
F	F	Factors defined in Eq. (2)
h_i	H	Heat transfer coefficient, Btu/ft²·h·°F
k	—	Thermal conductivity, Btu/ft²·h·°F
Nu	—	Nusselt number
P	P	Pressure, lb/in.²abs
Pr	—	Prandtl number
Re	—	Reynolds number
T	T	Temperature, °F
W	W	Flow, lb/h
μ	—	Viscosity, lb/ft·h

TABLE 2 Equations for Factor F

Air:
$F = 0.17718 + 0.00003952(T - 400)$
Water:
$F = 10^{(-1.318+0.214 \log T)}$
Saturated steam:
$F = 0.172 + 0.079X - 0.007297X^2 + 0.000257X^3$
where:
$X = 0.01P$, $T = 115P^{0.225}$
Superheated steam:
If $P < 200$: $F = 0.244 + 0.000132(T - 327)$
If $P \geqslant 200$: $F = 0.343 + 0.071X - 0.043Y - 0.058XY + 0.028X^2 + 0.041Y^2$
where:
$X = 3.33 \log P - 10$ and $Y = 0.005T - 4$

Table 1 gives definitions of the terms in the preceding equations. The factor F has been evaluated for the various fluids and is presented in Table 2. For engineering purposes, the results for air could be used for flue gases as well.

The program listing is shown in Fig. 1.

To illustrate the use of the program, four examples are worked with the results shown in Fig. 2.

```
5 PRINT"HEAT TR COEFFTS FOR AIR,WATER,STEAM IN TUBES/PIPES"
1Ø PRINT" "
15 PRINT"IF STEAM IS IN SATURATED CONDITION,INPUT Ø FOR TEMPERATURE "
2Ø PRINT" "
25 INPUT"MEDIUM-AIR  OR WATER OR STEAM?=";M$
27 PRINT" "
3Ø INPUT"FLOW/TUBE-LB/H,TEMP-F,PRESSURE-PSIA,TUBE ID-IN=";W,T,P,D
35 PRINT" "
4Ø IF M$="STEAM" THEN 7Ø
5Ø IF M$="AIR" THEN F=.17718+3.952E-Ø5*(T-4ØØ):GOTO 11Ø
6Ø F=1Ø^(-1.318+.214*LOG(T)):GOTO 11Ø
7Ø IF T=Ø THEN 1ØØ
8Ø IF P<2ØØ THEN F=.244+.ØØØ132*(T-327):GOTO 11Ø
9Ø X=1.434*LOG(P)-1Ø:Y=.ØØ5*T-4:F=.343+.Ø71*X-.Ø43*Y-.Ø58*X*Y+.Ø28*X*X+.Ø41*Y*Y:
GOTO 11Ø
1ØØ X=.Ø1*P:F=.172+.Ø79*X-.ØØ7297*X*X+.ØØØ257*X^3:T=115*P^.225
11Ø H=2.44*W^.8*F/D^1.8
115 PRINT"RESULTS"
12Ø PRINT" "
13Ø PRINT"HEAT TR COEFFICENT-MEDIUM =";M$
14Ø PRINT" "
15Ø PRINT"FLOW-LB/H=";W;"TEMP-F=";T;"TUBE ID-IN=";D;"PRESS-PSIA=";P
16Ø PRINT" "
17Ø PRINT"HT TR COEFFT-BTU/FT2HF=";H
175 PRINT" "
18Ø END
```

FIG. 1. Heat-transfer coefficients program listing.

```
HEAT TR COEFFTS FOR AIR,WATER,STEAM IN TUBES/PIPES
IF STEAM IS IN SATURATED CONDITION,INPUT Ø FOR TEMPERATURE
MEDIUM-AIR  OR WATER OR STEAM?=? AIR
FLOW/TUBE-LB/H,TEMP-F,PRESSURE-PSIA,TUBE ID-IN=? 45Ø,235,2Ø,1.778
RESULTS
HEAT TR COEFFICENT-MEDIUM =AIR
FLOW-LB/H= 45Ø TEMP-F= 235 TUBE ID-IN= 1.778 PRESS-PSIA= 2Ø
HT TR COEFFT-BTU/FT2HF= 19.598Ø2
```

Air

```
HEAT TR COEFFTS FOR AIR,WATER,STEAM IN TUBES/PIPES
IF STEAM IS IN SATURATED CONDITION,INPUT Ø FOR TEMPERATURE
MEDIUM-AIR  OR WATER OR STEAM?=? WATER
FLOW/TUBE-LB/H,TEMP-F,PRESSURE-PSIA,TUBE ID-IN=? 5ØØØØ,45Ø,1ØØØ,2.9
RESULTS
HEAT TR COEFFICENT-MEDIUM =WATER
FLOW-LB/H= 5ØØØØ TEMP-F= 45Ø TUBE ID-IN= 2.9 PRESS-PSIA= 1ØØØ
HT TR COEFFT-BTU/FT2HF= 2Ø12.ØØ3
```

Water

```
HEAT TR COEFFTS FOR AIR,WATER,STEAM IN TUBES/PIPES
IF STEAM IS IN SATURATED CONDITION,INPUT Ø FOR TEMPERATURE
MEDIUM-AIR  OR WATER OR STEAM?=? STEAM
FLOW/TUBE-LB/H,TEMP-F,PRESSURE-PSIA,TUBE ID-IN=? 56ØØ,Ø,45Ø,2.Ø67
RESULTS
HEAT TR COEFFICENT-MEDIUM =STEAM
FLOW-LB/H= 56ØØ TEMP-F= 454.6431 TUBE ID-IN= 2.Ø67 PRESS-PSIA= 45Ø
HT TR COEFFT-BTU/FT2HF= 265.3379
```

Saturated steam

```
HEAT TR COEFFTS FOR AIR,WATER,STEAM IN TUBES/PIPES
IF STEAM IS IN SATURATED CONDITION,INPUT Ø FOR TEMPERATURE
MEDIUM-AIR  OR WATER OR STEAM?=? STEAM
FLOW/TUBE-LB/H,TEMP-F,PRESSURE-PSIA,TUBE ID-IN=? 56ØØ,5ØØ,45Ø,2.Ø67
RESULTS
HEAT TR COEFFICENT-MEDIUM =STEAM
FLOW-LB/H= 56ØØ TEMP-F= 5ØØ TUBE ID-IN= 2.Ø67 PRESS-PSIA= 45Ø
HT TR COEFFT-BTU/FT2HF= 228.34Ø7
```

Superheated steam

FIG. 2. Results for heat-transfer coefficient program.

Example 1. Air at a flow rate of 450 lb/h, 20 lb/in.^{2}abs, and 235°F flows in a tube of 1.77 in. i.d. Estimate the heat-transfer coefficient.

After keying in the program listing, feed the input data in the RUN mode. The data are fed in the order: MEDIUM = AIR, FLOW/TUBE, TEMP, PRESSURE, and TUBE ID; 450, 235, 20, and 1.778.

The resulting heat-transfer coefficient, 19.59 Btu/ft^2·h·°F, is printed out as shown in Fig. 2.

Example 2. Determine the heat-transfer coefficient for 50,000 lb/h of water flowing in a 2.067 in. i.d. pipe at a temperature of 450°F and a pressure of 100 lb/in.^{2}abs.

Data input is the same as Example 1 except the medium is now WATER. The resulting coefficient of 2012 Btu/ft^2·h·°F is shown in Fig. 2.

Example 3. In this example the heat-transfer coefficient is determined for 5600 lb/h of saturated steam at 450 lb/in.^{2}abs flowing through a 2.9 in. i.d. pipe.

The medium is STEAM. For the temperature, use a value of zero. This will cause the program to calculate the saturation temperature. The results show the saturation temperature is 455°F, and the heat-transfer coefficient is 265 Btu/ft^2·h·°F.

Example 4. The same conditions as in Example 3 are used for this example except steam is superheated at a temperature of 500°F. In this case the steam temperature is entered in the appropriate place.

The result of this example is 229 Btu/ft^2·h·°F.

Insulation Heat Loss

The second program calculates the heat loss through multilayered insulated surfaces and predicts the temperature profile through the layers. The program can handle any number of layers.

Required input date include: number of layers, layer thickness, thermal conductivity of layers, ambient temperature, hot face temperature, casing emissivity, and wind velocity.

Thermal conductivity data must be obtained for any two known temperatures.

The program will evaluate the thermal conductivity at the operating temperature.

The heat loss from the exterior insulation surface is given by the two basic equations:

$$Q = 0.173\epsilon \times 10^{-8}[(t_s + 460)^4 - (t_a + 460)^4] + 0.296(t_s - t_a)^{1.25} [(V + 69)/69]^{0.5} \quad (3)$$

and

$$Q + K_m(t_{p+1-i} - t_{p+2-i})/L_i \quad (4)$$

TABLE 3 Insulation Heat Loss Nomenclature

Nomenclature	Program Symbol	Descriptions and Units
ϵ	J	Casing emissivity
K_m	G	Thermal conductivity of layer, Btu·in./ft·h·°F
L_i	A(27) to A(26 + p)	Thickness of each layer, in.
p	P	Total number of layers
Q	Q	Heat loss, Btu/ft²·h
t_a	H	Ambient temperature, °F
t_h	A	Hot face temperature, °F
t_s	A(p + 1)	Casing temperature, °F
t_i	A(2) to A(p)	Intermediate temperatures, °F
t_m	T	Mean layer temperature, °F
V	V	Wind velocity, ft/min

Using the two equations to solve for the temperature results in

$$t_{p+1-i} = t_{p+2-i} + QL_i/K_m \tag{5}$$

K_m is calculated at the mean layer temperature t_m using the linear relationship

$$K_m = a + bt_m \tag{6}$$

In the above equations, i is the layer number. See Table 3 for definition of the terms in the preceding equations. Figure 3 shows the problem arrangement for a system with three insulation layers.

A trial-and-error logic is used to solve for the heat loss and the temperature profile. A quick convergence logic is used to speed up the iterative procedure.

The complete program listing is given in Fig. 4.

After the input data are obtained, the procedure starts by assuming the surface temperature. A starting point is

$$t_s = t_a + 200 \tag{7}$$

With the assumption, the program calculates the heat transfer Q from Eq. (3).

Next, the temperature drop ΔT in each layer is assumed. To start, it is

$$\Delta T = (t_h - t_s)/p \tag{8}$$

Then:

$$t_{p+1-i} = t_{p+2-i} + \Delta T \tag{9}$$

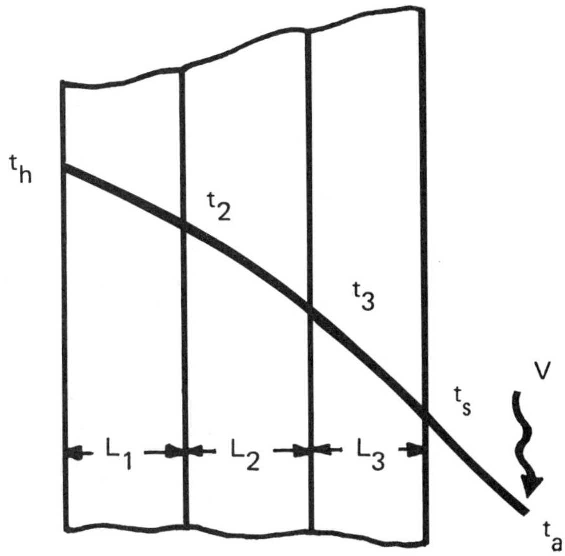

FIG. 3. Heat loss problem.

```
10  PRINT"INSULATION PERFORMANCE"
20 DIM A(60)
30 INPUT"number of layers,hot face temp,ambient temp,wind vel in fpm,surf emiss=
";P,A(1),H,V,J
35 PRINT"thermal conductivity data in BTU in/ft2h F"
40 FOR I=1 TO P
50 INPUT "starting from hot face-name,thick,temp 1,cond 1,temp 2,cond 2 =";A$,L,
M,K,N,O
60 A(26+I)=L:A(41+I)=(K-O)/(M-N):A(34+I)=K-A(41+I)*M:A$(I)=A$
70 NEXT I
80 A(P+1)=H+200:U=A(1)
90 Z=A(P+1)-H
100 X=(U-A(P+1))/P
110 W=.01*(A(P+1)+460):Y=.01*(H+460)
120 Q=.173*J*(W^4-Y^4)+93.6*(W-Y)^1.25*SQR((V+69)/69)
130 FOR I=1 TO P
140 A(P+1-I)=A(P+2-I)+X
150 T=.5*(A(P+1-I)+A(P+2-I)):G=A(35+P-I)+A(42+P-I)*T
160 R=A(P+2-I)+Q*A(27+P-I)/G
170 IF ABS(R-A(P+1-I))<3 GOTO 190
180 A(P+1-I)=.5*(R+A(P+1-I)):GOTO 150
190 NEXT I
200 IF ABS(A(1)-U)<3 GOTO 220
210 Z=.5*Z:A(P+1)=A(P+1)+SGN(U-A(1))*Z:GOTO 100
215 PRINT" "
220 PRINT"   RESULTS"
225 PRINT"TEMP -deg F:NAME:THICKNESS,IN"
230 FOR I=1 TO P+1
240 PRINT A(P+2-I),A$(P+2-I),A(28+P-I)
250 NEXT I
255 PRINT" "
260 PRINT"HEAT LOSS -BTU/ft2h=";Q
265 PRINT" "
270 PRINT"AMB TEMP=";H;"WIND VEL-FPM=";V;"EMISS=";J
275 PRINT" "
280 END
```

FIG. 4. Insulation heat loss program listing.

TABLE 4 Input Data for Fired Heater (example)

Number of layers = 2
Hot face temperature = 1800°F
Ambient temperature = 80°F
Wind velocity = 440 ft/min (5 mi/h)
Surface emissivity = 0.9
Thickness of layer 1 (starting from hot face) = 4 in.
Thermal conductivity at 1600°F = 1.7 Btu·in./ft²·h·°F
Thermal conductivity at 1400°F = 1.4 Btu·in./ft²·h·°F
Thickness of layer 2 = 4 in.
Thermal conductivity at 1000°F = 0.9 Btu·in./ft²·h·°F
Thermal conductivity at 600°F = 0.5 Btu·in./ft²·h·°F

K_m is then calculated at the average layer temperature, t_m, by the relation

$$t_m = 0.5(t_{p+1-i} + t_{p+2-i}) \tag{10}$$

derived from Eq. (6). The coefficients a and b are estimated from the input data on each insulation layer.

From Eq. (5), t_{p+1-i} is calculated, and from Eq. (4), Q is calculated. If t_{p+1-i} from Eqs. (8) and (9) are equal, the program proceeds. If not equal, t_{p+1-i} is corrected by averaging the two values and recalculaging t_m from Eq. (10). If t_{p+1-i} from Eqs. (8) and (9) are equal, the hot face temperature, t_h, is printed out. Actually, the program will print out t_h if the two values are within 3°F.

The assumed t_s is corrected quickly because the correction factor is halved each time a correction is made. The first trial value is $t_s \pm 200$, the next is $t_s \pm$

```
INSULATION PERFORMANCE
number of layers,hot face temp,ambient temp,wind vel in fpm,surf emiss=? 2,1800,
80,440,.9
thermal conductivity data in BTU in/ft2h F
starting from hot face-name,thick,temp 1,cond 1,temp 2,cond 2 =? lay 1,4,1600,1.
7,1400,1.4
starting from hot face-name,thick,temp 1,cond 1,temp 2,cond 2 =? lay 2,4,1000,.9
,600,.5
   RESULTS
TEMP -deg F:NAME:THICKNESS,IN
 137.0313                      0
 1338.142     lay 2            4
 1802.481     lay 1            4

HEAT LOSS -BTU/ft2h= 191.4249

AMB TEMP= 80 WIND VEL-FPM= 440 EMISS= .9
```

FIG. 5. Results of heat loss example.

100, and so forth. The program then prints out the results: temperature in °F for each layer, thickness of each layer, heat loss through the layers, ambient temperature, wind velocity, and emissivity.

Example. To illustrate the use of the program for the heat loss and layer temperatures, the profile is calculated for a fired heater with two layers of insulation. Input data are shown in Table 4.

The program is first key in. In the RUN mode, the screen asks for the data in the same order as they are to be fed in. The results of the example are shown in Fig. 5.

The hot face temperature calculated may not be exactly equal to the input temperature. This is due to the error margin used for the program iteration. In the case of the example, the calculated value is 1802.481°F. This is very close to the input value of 1800°F.

Part 2. Rapid Nomographic Method

The heat loss from insulated piping is a function of several variables:

$$\alpha = \frac{(t_1 - t_a)}{\left[\left(r^2 \ln \frac{r_2}{r_1}\right) \Big/ k + 1/f\right]} \tag{11}$$

Often, the insulation thickness, t, is decided by limiting the heat loss to a particular value. Then solving for $t(r_2 - r_1)$ becomes difficult because the expression in the denominator involves r_1 and t. Estimating Q, given r_1 and t, is less difficult.

However, both types of problems can be solved by Fig. 6 which takes into account the effect of outside film coefficient f. This coefficient generally varies from 1.5 to 2.5 Btu/ft^2·h·°F. Table 5 gives f values for typical situations.

The surface temperature t_s is obtained from

$$(t_s - t_a) = Q/f \tag{12}$$

Example. Determine the thickness of insulation to limit heat loss to 60 Btu/ft^2·h in a 3-in. NPS pipe. Pipe temperature t_1 is 580°F; t_a, the ambient temperature, is 80°F. Insulation K value is 0.5 Btu/ft^2·h·°F/in. and outside film coefficient is 2.0 Btu/ft^2·h·°F. What is the surface temperature of the insulation?

For the solution, connect $(t_1 - t_a) = 500$ with $Q = 60$ and extend to cut line 1 (dashed lines) at A. Connect $f = 2.0$ with point A and extend to cut line 2 at B. Connect B with $K = 0.5$ to cut line 3 at C. The horizontal from C and the vertical from pipe size 3 intersect the curve corresponding to $t = 2.5$ in. Hence 2.5, or the next standard size of insulation.

From Eq. (12), $(t_s - t_a) = 60/2 = 30$. Hence $t_s = 30 + 80 = 110$°F.

The effect of using a different thickness of insulation and the corresponding heat loss can easily be calculated. For example, using 2.0-in. thick insulation, we see that (solid lines) $Q = 78$ Btu/ft^2·h and surface temperature increases to $(78/2 + 80) = 119$°F.

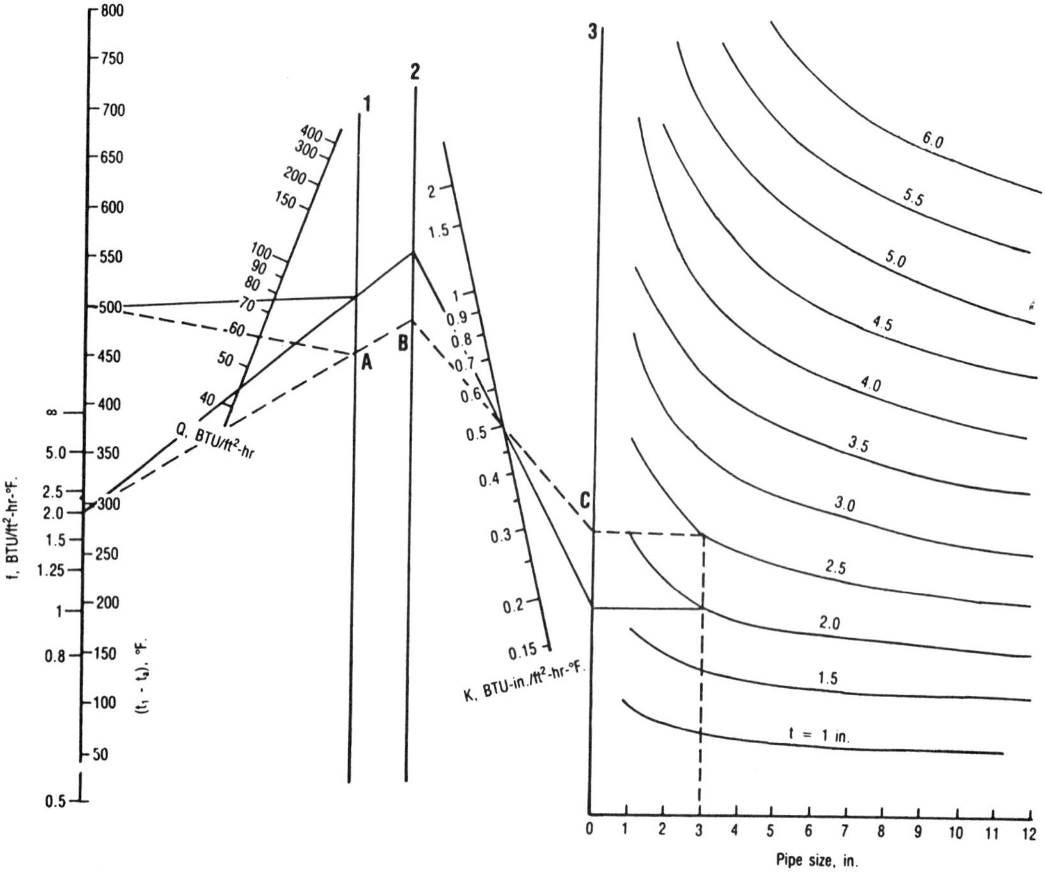

FIG. 6. Heat loss in insulation.

Life Cycle Costing

Life cycle costing is a method of evaluating the cost of owning and operating the system over the life of the equipment.

The following expressions aid evaluation of the life cycle cost (see Table 6 for nomenclature):

$$TCC = CCO + CC \tag{13}$$

TABLE 5 Values of f[a]

Still air	1.2–1.8
7.5 mph wind	2.0–4.0
15 mph wind	3.5–5.0

[a]Btu/ft²·h·°F. For preliminary estimates, use 2.0.

TABLE 6 Nomenclature

C_a	Annual cost of operation, $
CC	Fixed or capital cost, $
C_e	Cost of energy, $/10^6 Btu
CCO	Capitalized cost of operation, $
e	Escalation factor
i	Interest rate
N	Life of the plant in years.
f	Outside film coefficient, Btu/ft²·h·°F
Q	Heat loss, Btu/ft²·h
t_a, t_s, t_1	Ambient, surface, and pipe temperatures, °F
TCC	Total capitalized cost, $
K	Thermal conductivity of insulation, Btu/ft²·h·°F/in.
L	Length of pipe, ft

where

$$CCO = C_a\left(\frac{l+e}{l+i}\right)\left[\frac{1-\left(\frac{l+e}{l+i}\right)^N}{1-\left(\frac{l+e}{l+i}\right)}\right] \tag{14}$$

The alternative with the lowest TTC is the best, as shown by the following.

Example. In choosing between the 2.0 and 2.5-in. thickness of insulation, the plant engineer has the following data:

Length of pipe: 1,000 ft
Cost of energy: $4/10^6 Btu
Interest and escalation factors are 0.15 and 0.08 (15% and 8%).
Cost of insulation for 2.5-in. insulation including labor is $8,000; for 2.0 in. it is $5500.
Annual period of operation is 8000 h. Life of equipment is 20 yr.

For the solution, calculate the annual dollar value of the heat loss, C_a:

$$C_a = N\pi\left(\frac{d+2t}{12}\right)L\alpha C_e/10^6$$

For 2.5-in. thickness:

$$C_a = \pi\left(\frac{3.5+5}{12}\right) \times 1000 \times 60 \times 4 \times 8000/10^6 = \$4256$$

Capitilized cost of operation, CCO:

$$CCO = 4256 \times \frac{1.08}{1.15}\left[\frac{1-\left(\frac{1.08}{1.15}\right)^{20}}{1-\left(\frac{1.08}{1.15}\right)}\right] = \$47{,}062$$

Total capitalized cost, $TCC = 47{,}062 + 8000 = \$55{,}062$. Similarly, for the 2.0-in. thickness, $TCC = \$59{,}639$.

The 2.5-in. thickness is better in the long run, though its initial cost is higher.

If the plant runs for only 1000 h during the course of a year, the same calculations yield $TCC = \$13{,}883$ for 2.5 in. and \$12,266 for 2.0 in.

When the period of operation is less, a lower investment is adequate.

In this way, alternatives may be evaluated without elaborate studies.

This material appeared in *Oil and Gas Journal*, April 25, 1983, and August 19, 1985, and is reprinted with the permission of the editor.

Bibliography

Ganapathy, V., *Applied Heat Transfer*, Pennwell, Tulsa, Oklahoma, 1982.
Turner, W. C., and Malloy, J. F., *Thermal Insulation Handbook*, McGraw-Hill, New York, 1981, pp. 40–45.

V. GANAPATHY

Ion-Exchange Agents

Introduction

An ion-exchange agent is an essentially insoluble material containing ions that can be interchanged stoichiometrically for ions of the same sign when in contact with electrolyte in aqueous solution. Ion-exchange agents (which may exchange cations, anions, or both) may be thought of as reservoirs of exchangeable ions.

The ion-exchange process is reversible. For example, in water softening the cation exchange is

$$2NaR + CaCl_2(aq) \rightarrow CaR + 2NaCl$$

The exchanger in the Na^+ form exchanges for Ca^{2+} ions. The exhausted exchanger can be regenerated with sodium chloride solution, and is converted back to the Na^+ form. It is this property that makes the exchange agent so useful. It can be used repeatedly without losing efficiency. In this way a relatively small volume of exchange agent can be used to treat large volumes of electrolyte solutions.

Ion-exchange agents are used [1–12] in water softening, in water demineralization, in chemical processes, for separation in analyses, in chemical syntheses, in medical research, in pharmaceutical industry, in mining, in agriculture, in hydrometallurgy, in electrolytic cells, in pollution control, etc.

At present, synthetic organic polymers are the most efficient and widely used ion exchangers. A wide variety of resins or polymers with different properties has been developed, and they are either commercially available or have been described in the literature. The latest development involves the replacement of the hydrocarbon matrix with a perfluorocarbon matrix.

Typical Exchanger

A typical ion-exchange agent consists of an inert hydrophobic matrix, a three-dimensional network of hydrocarbon or fluorocarbon chains. The matrix contains interlocking channels or pores of varying diameters. Attached to the matrix and essentially evenly distributed throughout are functional groups, and attached to these fixed groups, to satisfy electric charges, are the exchangeable counterions. The polymer is made hydrophilic by introducing the ionic functional group. The groups can be introduced before, during, or after polymerization.

The polymer should be insoluble but able to swell to a limited extent. The degree of cross-linking must be controlled. Linear, noncross-linked polyelectrolytes are soluble. Polymers which are too highly cross-linked cannot swell. The mobility of the counterion in such a polymer is so low that ion exchange no longer occurs.

Porosity determines the size and the rate of diffusion of the molecule or ion that may enter the matrix or structure and is related to the degree of cross-linking. The polymer has essentially no appreciable porosity until it is swollen in a suitable solvation medium. Cross-linked polymers swell to a well-defined and reproducible degree in the appropriate system.

The conditions of polymerization of the styrene–divinylbenzene polymer determines whether a gel or a macroreticular polymer is obtained. Gels contain from 2 to 12% divinylbenzene as the cross-linking agent. The macroporous [13–15] exchangers are polymers having considerably larger pores than the more conventional gel-type exchangers. They possess pore diameters up to several thousand angstroms and surface areas greater than 100 m^2/g. They exhibit very little volume change in solvation if prepared with a sufficient degree of cross-linking. Pores [15] may be varied in both size and uniformity, depending upon the solvent system. Small volume changes occur on transfer from a highly polar to an essentially nonpolar solvent system. Much larger molecules may enter the polymer structure by virtue of its porosity. Due to the cross-linking, high selectivity for one ion with respect to another is realized. Disadvantages of macroporous polymers are

1. Poor regeneration efficiency
2. Lower exchange capacity
3. Higher regeneration costs

Various interpolymer [17, 18, 20] systems have been developed where entanglement reduces swelling. Cross-linking may occur during or subsequent to the reaction.

Cation-Exchange Exchangers

In 1935 Adams and Holmes [19] discovered the ion-exchange properties of a phenol–formaldehyde condensate polymer. The polymers [19] acted as exchangers only from solutions of high pH since phenols are very weak acids. Later $-SO_3H$, a strong acid group, was introduced either by sulfonation of the polymer after polymerization or by substituting phenolsulfonic acid for phenol in the preparation. The resulting exchanger was effective at all pH's and could be used in the H^+ form.

In 1944 d'Alelio [22] patented the first successful ion-exchange polymer. It was a carboxylic acid exchanger prepared by copolymerizing a cross-linking agent, e.g., ethylene dimethacrylate, with a vinyl acid, e.g., acrylic acid, $CH_2{=}CHCOOH$. Later he introduced the most successful [22, 28] polymer of all by cross-linking. He formed a cross-linked aromatic resin by copolymerizing styrene with divinylbenzene and subsequently sulfonating with concentrated H_2SO_4. He introduced one sulfonic acid group into each benzene ring.

By the end of 1945 Dow Chemical Co. introduced commercially the sulfonated polystyrene exchanger under the trade name Dowex 50 [25]. It was the first exchanger to be produced in spherical form.

The most common cation [21, 24] exchangers with fixed functional groups are strong acid polymers with sulfonic acid groups and weak acid polymers with the carboxylic acid group; $-SO_3^-$ and $-COO^-$.

Other cation exchangers have been developed with different properties and acid strengths. These polymers or resins carry phosphonic, phosphinic, arsenic, and selenonic acid groups; $-PO_3^{2-}$, $-HPO_2^-$, $-AsO_3^{2-}$, and $-SeO_3^-$.

Ion exchangers which contain two or more different types of fixed functional groups are called "bifunctional" or "polyfunctional," Polymers carrying functional groups with high selectivities for certain counterions have been prepared.

The most widely used weak acid cation exchangers are prepared by copolymerizing an organic acid, acrylic or methacrylic acid, with divinylbenzene, ethylene dimethacrylate, or a similar compound with two vinyl groups. Bifunctional [23] exchangers containing both carboxylic acid and sulfonic acid groups by sulfonation of acrylic and methacrylic acid polymers have been prepared.

Specific Exchangers

Cation exchangers with specific [26, 27] selectivity for certain cations have been made by introducing functional groups which form strong complexes, chelates, with these cations. Polymers with chelating iminodiacetic acid groups are available. Resins specific for K, Zn, and transition metals have been developed.

Anion Exchangers

The first anion-exchange agent was made by Adams and Holmes [19] by use of *m*-phenylene diamine condensed with formaldehyde.

Anion [28–40] exchangers were developed exclusively with synthetic organic polymers. In 1948 Rohm and Haas introduced IRA-400 [34], a strongly basic anion exchanger. Anion exchangers have been prepared with weak base amino groups, $-NH_3^+$ and NH_2^+, and quaternary ammonium groups as well as with strong base quaternary phosphonium groups and tertiary sulfonium groups.

The most important anion exchangers are cross-linked polystyrenes into which strong or weak base groups have been introduced by chloromethylation and subsequent amination.

Amphoteric Ion-Exchange Agents

Ion exchangers that contain both acidic and basic functional groups are called amphoteric. Many ion exchangers of this type, the so-called "snake-cage" polyelectrolytes, have been prepared. The polymers are used for separation by "ion retardation." The exchanger is prepared by polymerization of the monomeric counterions within the polymer.

In most applications the exchangers used are gels in the form of small particles, 0.1 to 1 mm in diameter. Exchangers having higher porosity or particular mechanical properties are needed for certain applications. Highly porous macroreticular ion exchangers have been made by a variation of the conventional pearl-polymerization technique. The spherical beads have wide pores sizes (up to 400 Å) and large surface areas.

General Physical Properties [1–12]

Ion exchangers are produced and sold as granules or spheres (beads) of the proper size and uniformity to meet the requirements. Bead size is controlled by polymerization conditions and by screening. Products are sold in particle sizes ranging from 400 to 16 mesh. The finest materials are used for laboratory chromatography, while the larger products are used in applications involving high flow rates or slurries.

Physical Stability

The exchangers should be strong enough to resist degradation (breakage) by the forces they encounter. Factors affecting physical degadation are methods of handling, small diameter spheres, exceptional high flow rates, frequent pumping or agitation, depth of resin bed, osmotic shock due to change in solution concentration, and resulting volume change. Recommended quality control tests to evaluate stability, attrition, and osmotic shock should be used. Screening tests should be performed to determine if any physical weakness exists. Microscopic examination of particles for internal cracks and broken particles is helpful.

Density

In the water swollen state, a typical specific gravity for ion exchangers is about 1 to 1.4. Bulk density ranges from 35 to 60 lb/ft^3 for wet products. As normally loaded into a column, exchangers contain about 30–40% void volume.

Bed Expansion

Backwashing an ion-exchange column to remove dirt impurities, remove fine exchanger particles, and reduce pressure drop is normal procedure. Flow rate above a certain minimum causes particle fluidization of the bed, resulting in bed expansion. This value is measured at a specific cross-sectional flow rate and temperature.

Pressure Drop

The pressure drop through an exchanger bed is dependent upon the particle shape, size, uniformity, compressibility, flow rate, and fluid viscosity. Data are available at various flow rates and particle sizes at 25°C.

General Chemical Properties [1–12]

Some of the general chemical properties of importance are exchanger capacity, swelling equilibria, ionic equilibria, kinetics, and chemical stability.

Capacity

Exchanger capacity is the total number of functional groups available for exchange, and it is expressed on a dry-weight, wet-weight, or wet-volume basis. The dry-weight capacity is expressed in milliequivalents per gram. For styrene–divinylbenzene copolymers, the theoretical weight capacity is about 5.43 meq/g. For the polymer containing 8 wt.% DVB and 4 wt.% ethylstyrene, the capacity is slightly lower—5.35 meq/g. On a wet basis it is expressed as the meq/g wet exchanger and takes into account water uptake of the exchanger.

For the cross-linked polyacrylic acid exchanger the dry-weight capacity is about 9.0 meq/g, and for the styrene-type anion exchangers with methylene trimethyl ammonium groups the capacity is 2.5 to 4.0 meq/g.

For technical application and design purposes, the number of exchangeable counterions in an exchange column and the size of the column are more pertinent. Technical volume capacity is defined as the number of iongenic groups per unit volume of packed bed. It is given in equivalents per liter of a fully swollen bed. Other units used are equivalents per cubic foot of bed and pound of CaO or $CaCO_3$ per cubic foot. Care should be exercised to make sure that the capacities used in column calculations are in the proper units. Volume occupied by a specific amount of ion exchanger depends upon the ionic form of the resin or polymer, composition of the solution with which the exchanger is in contact, etc. (the experimental conditions). This value is somewhat high since the bed usually contracts when being treated with electrolyte solutions or solvents other than water. Volume capacity depends upon the water content of the exchanger, and hence on the degree of cross-linking in the case of styrene-type polymers. A weekly cross-linked polymer swells more, and thus has a lower capacity per unit volume. Of more theoretical importance is the capacity in milliequivalents per gram of solvent in the polymer or per milliliter of swollen gel. The concentration of fixed ionic groups refers to the particular state of the resin under the given experimental conditions, thus it is a variable.

The apparent or effective capacity, expressed in terms of the counterions, is more practical and depends on experimental conditions.

Operating capacity is a measure of the useful performance obtained under a specific set of operating conditions in a column. It is determined by total capacity of the polymer, level of regeneration, composition of solutions treated, polymer specificity (selectivity) for one ion with respect to another, flow rate through the column, temperature, particle size, and other factors.

Swelling Equilibria

Various theories [16] for swelling, sorption, and ion-exchange equilibria are presented in the references. Ion-exchange agents are able to sorb the solvents in which they are placed. The ion exchanger usually expands or swells, but only to a limited degree. An equilibrium is attained beyond which swelling does not occur. Swelling equilibrium is a balance of opposing forces. Solvent retention capacity is a reproducible quantity dependent upon the ion-exchange capacity, counterion, functional group, kind of solvent, composition of the solution, extent of cross-linking of the polymer, relative humidity, and temperature. Polymer volume changes with conversion to ionic forms of different degrees of hydration. For a sulfonic-acid-type cation exchanger, there is a volume change with monovalent ion species: $Li^+ > Na^+ > K^+ > Cs^+ > Ag^+$. With polyvalent ions, hydration is reduced by cross-linking action, thus, $Na^+ > Ca^{2+} > Al^{3+}$. Swelling is favored by high capacity of the polymer, strong solvation of the functional group, large and strongly solvated counterions, low valence of counterions, complete dissociation in the polymer, and low concentration of the external solution.

Water vapor sorption isotherms of the sulfonated styrene-type cation exchanger show that water uptake at low relative humidity is almost independent of the degree of cross-linking. At high relative humidity, the exchangers take up much more water and the degree of cross-linking has a pronounced effect.

Ionic Equilibria

Ion-exchange reactions are reversible. By treating an exchanger with an excess of electrolyte solution, the exchanger can be converted to the desired form:

$$RA^+ + \underset{\text{Excess}}{B^+} \longrightarrow RB^+ + A^+$$

If a limited quantity of solution B^+ is present, a reproducible equilibrium is established depending upon the properties of A^+ and B^+ and upon the selectivity of the exchangers. Since the reaction is reversible, the equilibrium can be approached from either side:

$$RA^+ + B^+ \rightleftarrows RB^+ + A^+$$

The selectivity coefficient $K_A{}^B$ for this reaction is given by

$$K_A{}^B = \frac{\overline{m}_B \cdot m_A}{\overline{m}_A \cdot m_B}$$

where m and $\overline{m}$ refer to ionic concentrations in solution and resin, respectively. A corrected selectivity coefficient may be obtained by multiplying the selectivity coefficients by the activity coefficients at equilibrium in solution and in the polymer, respectively.

Several theories [41–44] of factors contributing to equilibria have been proposed. A more refined treatment [45] includes both an activity coefficient term for chemical interaction and a swelling term. Other factors, such as formation of ion pairs, complex ions, solubilization, and salting out, influence equilibrium.

The effects of the coion and neutral molecules have been taken into consideration.

Kinetics

The ion-exchange process involves diffusion through the film of solution in contact with the exchanger and diffusion within the particle itself. For example, a counterion A leaving the active functional group within the exchanger must migrate through the particle into the solution. Simultaneously, a counterion B must migrate the other way and occupy the site left by counterion A. Through agitation, the concentration in the solution is leveled out. Agitation affects neither the interior of the exchanger nor the film adhering to the surface of the exchanger. Thus, there are two rate-determining steps:

1. Interdiffusion within the exchanger itself—particle diffusion
2. Interdiffusion in the adhering film—film diffusion

Film diffusion is rate controlling at low concentration while particle diffusion is controlling at high concentration. Film diffusion control is favored by high capacity, low degree of cross-linking, small particle size, low concentration, poor agitation, and preference of the ion exchanger for the counterion which is taken up from solution.

Overall exchange rates may be influenced by a change in solvent nature and content, particle size, temperature, and functional group. Exchange rates are more rapid in water systems and become increasingly slower with less polar solvents. This is true because solutes are more highly ionized in the more polar solvents and exchangers are, at the same time, more highly swollen.

The importance of the rate at which ion exchange takes place lies in the fact that it determines the portion of equilibrium capacity which may be used in a practical situation, such as in a column. It influences equipment size.

Stability

Ion exchangers should not be operated beyond their chemical limitations. Exchangers are degraded slowly by oxidation which may be induced catalytically. Certain metal ions, for example, iron, manganese, and copper, should be minimized in oxidizing solutions. Strong oxidizing agents will rapidly degrade a polymer matrix and should be avoided. With cation hydrocarbon base exchangers the attack is first on the backbone of the matrix. With anion exchangers the attack is first on the functional group.

Limits of thermal stability are imposed by the strength of the C—N bond in the case of anion exchangers. The strength is sensitive to pH; i.e., a low pH enhances stability. The quaternary ammonium salts are the least stable, with a maximum temperature of 50°C recommended for hydroxide cycle operation. The tertiary amines are the most stable, with good performance being maintained up to 100°C. Cation exchanger stability is also dependent upon pH. The stability of the C—S bond decreases with a lower pH. Cation exchangers containing the sulfonic acid functional group are not recommended for use above 150°C in the presence of water. The salt form of anhydrous exchangers is stable up to a temperature of at least 250°C, where depolymerization begins.

Attack by gamma radiation can cause simultaneous reactions such as polymerization, depolymerization, oxidation, and rupture of the carbon-sulfur or carbon-nitrogen bonds. Some of the observed results include gas evolution, bead swelling, weight loss, and appearance of weak acid capacity. In spite of these limitations, hydrocarbon matrix exchangers serve important functions in fuel processing, fission product recovery, and waste decontamination in the nuclear industry.

Limits of the fluorocarbon exchangers are similar because the limit is imposed by the thermal stability of the functional group, not the matrix; however, the chemical stability is better because of the matrix.

Ion-Exchange Membranes

An ion-exchange membrane may be defined as any ion-exchange material, irrespective of its geometric shape, which can be used as a separation wall between two solutions. In addition to acting as a barrier it possesses the chemical and electrochemical properties of an ion exchanger. High electric conductivity and a difference in permeability for counterions, coions, and neutral molecules are perhaps the most important properties. When in contact with electrolyte solutions of low or moderate concentrations, the counterions enter the membrane and have little difficulty in passing from one solution to the other. Coions have difficulty in passing. The membrane is permselective for counterions and approaches the behavior of an ideal semipermeable membrane. In solutions of higher concentration, the Donnan exclusion is less effective and permselectivity is reduced.

Two types of ion-exchange membranes have been used: "homogeneous" and "heterogeneous." "Homogeneous" membranes are coherent ion-exchanger gels in the form or shape of disks, ribbons, tubes, films, etc. Their structure is the same as the usual ion-exchange polymers or resins. "Heterogeneous" membranes [46] are fine ion-exchange particles embedded in an inert hydrophobic thermoplastic binder. They are usually in the form of films or sheets. The advantage of "heterogeneous" membranes is their mechanical strength. Their disadvantages are

1. Ion-exchange particles must be in contact
2. High electric resistance
3. Repeated swelling and shrinking breaks the bond with the thermosplastic binder, leading to reduced selectivity, lower current efficiency, and leakage through the membrane

With the development of "homogeneous" membranes with greatly improved mechanical stability, "heterogeneous" membranes have lost their appeal.

The early membranes produced were fragile, brittle, and difficult to handle because the osmotic pressure of the counterions was sufficient to break the molecular network. The membranes were 1 to 2 mm thick. Homogeneous [47–50] membranes are made by introducing high concentrations of iongenic groups into cross-linked sheets of polystyrene and polymerizing between glass plates in the presence of a woven supporting cloth of glass, polypropylene, etc. This is followed by sulfonation or chloromethylation and quaternization with a tertiary amine. In addition, polymers prepared in the presence of a large amount of nonpolymerizable diluent were utilized in the preparation of ion-exchange membranes.

In the 1960s and early 1970s, fluorocarbon-based cation-exchange membranes known as Nafion [51–55] were developed and introduced commercially. The membranes are permselective. Nafion consists essentially of polymer chains of tetrafluoroethylene several units in length joined by a perfluorinated vinyl segment having a pendant group containing some ether linkages, and a terminal acid group which provide the cation-exchange capacity.

The excellent chemical, mechanical, and thermal properties of Nafion make it a prime candidate for the membrane of a chloralkali electrolytic cell because of the following characteristics:

1. It can be extruded into a film
2. It can withstand a operating temperature of 100°C
3. It can withstand an oxidizing atmosphere of wet chlorine and hypochlorite on one side and a reducing atmosphere of H_2 and caustic on the other
4. It has a useful life of several years
5. It produces low salt caustic

The early Nafion membrane's performance in the chloralkali cell was not entirely satisfactory, and this led to increasing efforts to develop an outstanding membrane.

Several approaches were taken. The sulfonic acid functional group was replaced with the carboxylic acid group. Bilayer [56] or composite membranes were developed with different equivalent weight sulfonic acid films laminated together. Bilayer [58] membranes with the carboxylic acid groups on one side and sulfonic acid groups on the other were developed by lamination. Bilayer membranes have been prepared by surface treating [57] a sulfonic acid group membrane to give a very thin layer or film of —COOH functional groups on one side and a relatively thick (a few mils) sulfonic acid film on the other.

The purposes of the bilayer membranes were to reduce polarization in cells, to resist fouling by organic ions, to enhance permselectivity for univalent ions relative to ions of higher valence, to reduce membrane electrical resistance, and to increase current efficiency.

The Japanese have been very active in this area. Asahi Chemical Industry Co., Asahi Glass Co., and Tokyamo Soda Co. [60] have developed fluorocarbon membranes for the chloralkali cell. The properties of the membranes are presented in the literature [59, 61–64].

Early published reports giving the properties of the fluorocarbon base ion-exchange membranes indicated that the selectivity of the membranes, expressed as current efficiency, was determined by hydration of the functional group. The relationship between equivalent weight and hydration was contained in these reports. Efforts to improve the current efficiency of the sulfonic functional membrane by increasing the equivalent weight, decreasing the number of functional groups, and by using other functional groups, such as sulfonamide and carboxylic acid, decreased hydration.

Another polymer system [65] having a lower useful equivalent weight and a lower hydration regardless of the functional group was developed by Dow Chemical. This was done by making polymers having a shorter pendant group connecting the functional site to the polymer backbone, Results showed the polymer to be considerable less hydrated than other membranes with a longer pendant group, with the same functional group, and with the same equivalent weight. In cell operation the new single film membrane gave higher current efficiencies with lower equivalent weight at the same caustic concentration than the longer pendant group membrane of higher equivalent weight and the same functional group. The same held true for sulfonic/sulfonic composite membranes and for sulfonic/carboxylic membranes.

Some of the producers of ion-exchange agents are listed in Table 1, and ion exchangers available are presented in Table 2.

TABLE 1 Producers of Ion-Exchange Agents

Company	Country	Trade Name
Asahi Chemical Industries Ltd.[a]	Japan	
Asahi Glass Co., Ltd.[a]	Japan	Flemion
Bayer	FRG	Lewatil
Bio Rad Laboratories	USA	Aminex
Chemolimpex	Hungary	
Dia Prosim	France	
Dow Chemical	USA	Dowex
Du Pont[a]	USA	Nafion
Duolite International, S.A.	France	
Duolite International, Ltd.	Great Britain	
Kuraray Chemical Co., Ltd.	Japan	
Ljubljana	Yugoslavia	
Mitsubishi Chemical Industries, Ltd.	Japan	
Mobay Chemical Corp.	USA	
Montedison	Italy	
Permutil	Great Britain	
Rohm & Hass	USA	Amberlyts
Sumitomo Chemical Co., Ltd.	Japan	
Sybron Chemicals, Inc.	USA	
Tokyama Soda Co., Ltd.[a]	Japan	
Tokyo Organic Chemical Industries, Ltd.	Japan	

[a]Producers of ion-exchange membranes.

TABLE 2 Ion Exchangers Available

Strong acid cation	Gel type	DVB-styrene
Strong acid cation	Macroporous	DVB-styrene
Weak acid cation		Acrylic acid-DVB
Strong base anion	Gels Type 1	DVB-styrene
	Type 2	DVB-styrene
Strong base anion	Macroporous Type 1	DVB-styrene
	Type 2	DVB-styrene
Weak base anion		
Mixed exchangers strong acid and strong base		

Some Uses of Ion-Exchange Agents

Water Treatment [69]

Water softening is the major use of ion exchangers. Hard water contains principally Ca and Mg ions which cause scale formation in power plant boilers, pipe lines, and cooking utensils. They cause undesirable soap precipitates or scums as well as a waste of soap. In water softening, hard ions (Ca and Mg) are exchanged for soft ions (Na) of like sign on the exchanger. Hard water is passed through a bed of strong acid cation exchanger in the sodium form and is softened. The spent exchanger is regenerated by passing a fairly concentrated (6–20%) solution of NaCl through the bed. After washing the NaCl solution out of the bed, the cycle is repeated.

Softening Brackish Water

Brackish water containing up to about 8 g/L (0.5 lb/ft^3) dissolved solids can be softened by using a strong acid cation exchanger. This requires using beds in series with countercurrent flow regeneration. A large excess of salt regenerant is applied to the second unit in the series. Hardness leakage (hardness left on the exchanger from the preceding regeneration) increases with an increase in total dissolved solids concentration. With low total dissolved solids (in the 5–8 mg/L range), a weak acid cation exchanger may replace the second strong acid cation exchanger bed in the system. This exchanger will remove all the Ca and Mg present in the effluent from the strong acid cation exchanger bed. Regeneration of weak acid exchangers can be accomplished in two steps: first, HCl to rid the bed of hardness, and then NaOH to neutralize the acid.

Demineralization

Demineralization [66, 71] is used for treatment of feedwater to high pressure boilers; for treating process cooling water; for treating process water for various chemical, pharmaceutical, and food applications; and for producing high purity [67] water for the electronics and other industries. Demineralization is a process for removing dissolved solids (ionic impurities) from water. Demineralization by ion exchange involves both cation and anion exchangers.

Either a fixed bed series system or a mixed bed system can be used. For series operation, water is first passed through a bed of strong acid cation exchanger that is in the H^+ form to exchange the cation in solution for H^+ ions. The effluent is then passed through a column or bed of anion exchanger in the hydroxide form to replace anions in solution with OH^-. The H^+ ions from the cation exchanger neutralizes the hydroxide from the anion exchanger. The net effect is the removal of electrolytes and a yield of deionized water.

In the mixed bed system, raw water is passed through an intimately mixed bed of cation and anion exchangers where both types of exchange take place simultaneously. The H^+ ion is neutralized by OH^- as soon as it leaves the cation exchanger. The choice of system depends upon the quality of water desired, operating and capital economics, and the composition of the raw water. In the mixed bed system the exchangers are separated prior to regeneration.

Strong acid exchangers require a higher acid concentration than do weak acid exchangers.

The use of either a gel or a macroporous anion exchanger depends upon the organic content of the water. Macroporous anion exchangers are used to treat water which has a high level of organics. The ability of macroporous anion exchangers to handle organics without a loss of capacity due to fouling overcomes their lower operating capacity.

Waste Treatment—Radioactive

Ion exchangers have been used to remove trace amounts of radioactive materials from water before discharge to the environment. Synthetic organic cation and anion exchangers based on the styrene-DVB matrix are used in a mixed bed system.

Condensate Polishing

Removal of particulate matter and dissolved solids from utility power plant condensate [68] can be accomplished in a high flow deep-bed filter demineralizer. Mixed bed ion exchangers are utilized as the filter and demineralizer.

Nitrite Removal

Strong base anion exchangers in the chloride form are used for the selective removal of nitrates from nitrate polluted waters.

Dealkalization [70]

In many industries it is necessary to remove the hardness and alkalinity from raw water before the water is used in a process. Several processes involving ion exchangers are used for softening and dealkylizing water.

Ion exchangers frequently replace acids, alkalis, and metal catalysts in hydrolysis, inversions, esterifications, hydrations [73] or dehydrations, polymerizations, hydroxylations, and epoxidation reactions as acid-free catalysts. Perfluorinated ion exchangers [72] in the hydrogen form are useful acid catalysts for a variety of synthetic applications.

Another use of ion exchangers is in catalytic distillation [74] in which the reaction and extractive distillation is carried out in a single unit.

Purification

Ion exchangers are used in processes for removing contaminating acids, alkalis, salts, or mixtures from nonionized or slightly ionized organic substances. Their use is feasible in aqueous, semi-aqueous, and nonaqueous solvents. Ion exchangers are applicable to organic or inorganic compounds; e.g., removal of formic acid from 50% formaldehyde solution, removal of amines from methanol, removal of iron from steel pickling operation, purification of aluminum bright-dip baths containing 75–80% phosphoric acid, and removal of iron chloride complex with an anion exchanger.

Metal Extraction [81], Separation, Concentration, and Recovery

Ion exchangers are used to recover small amounts of desired solute from large quantities of contaminants by selectively separating and concentrating the solute. For example, recovering uranium [79, 80] from leach solution by using a strong base anion exchanger, and recovery of Cu with a strong acid cation exchanger in the H^+ form. Nickle can be recovered from rinse water by using a strong acid cation exchanger. The precious metals gold [77, 78], platinum, and silver can be recovered in the form of metal complexes on anion exchangers.

Ion Exclusion [75, 76]

Ion exclusion is a process permitting the separation of ionized substances from nonionized or slightly ionized organic or inorganic substances when both are present in aqueous or semi-aqueous solutions. An advantage is the ability to purify contaminated substances inexpensively using water as the regenerating medium. Examples are glycerin–salt separation, sucrose–salt separation, separation of mineral acids from acetic acid, separation of salts from alcohols, and separation of salts from high molecular weight amines.

Ion Retardation

Ion retardation is a separation [82] process utilizing an amphoteric ion exchanger (i.e., having both cation and anion groups within the matrix). Absorbed ion pairs are weakly held and may be displaced by water as the regenerant. Ion retardation is used to separate salts from organic solutes and may be used to separate mixtures of inorganics and highly ionized electrolytes.

Desiccation [83]

Strong acid cation exchangers in the dry state are useful as desiccants. The sodium or potassium form of exchangers is most satisfactory for reusable applications. Ion exchangers show their greatest capabilities in drying such hydrophobic solvents as hydrocarbons and chlorinated hydrocarbons. Regeneration of the exchangers is accomplished at bed temperatures of 275–325°F with air, nitrogen, or natural gas as a purge.

References

1. F. C. Nachod and J. Schubert (eds.), *Ion Exchange Technololgy*, Academic, New York, 1956.
2. J. A. Kitchener, *Ion Exchange Resins*, Wiley, New York, 1957.
3. F. Helffrich, *Ion Exchange,* McGraw-Hill, New York, 1962.
4. R. Kunin, *Ion Exchange Resins*, Kreiger, Huntington, New Jersey, 1972.
5. J. A. Murinsky and Y. Marcus (eds.), *Ion Exchange and Solvent Extraction*, Vols. 1–9, Dekker, New York, 1960–1985.
6. J. E. Salmon and D. K. Hale, *Ion Exchange—A Laboratory Manual*, Academic, New York, 1959.
7. K. D. Dorfner, *Ion Exchangers—Properties and Applications*, Ann Arbor Science Publishers, Ann Arbor, Michigan, 1973.
8. G. H. Osborn, *Synthetic Ion Exchangers*, Chapman and Hall, London, 1955.
9. O. Samuelson, *Ion Exchangers in Analytical Chemistry*, Wiley, New York, 1953.
10. *Ion Exchange and Its Applications, Papers Read at the Confernce, London Univ., 5th–7th April 1954*, Society of Chemical Industry.
11. C. Calmon and H. Gold (eds.), *Ion Exchange and Pollution Control*, Vols. 1 and 2, CRC Press, 1979.
12. *Ion Exchange in the Process Industries, Papers Read at the Conference Held at Imperial College of Science and Technology, London S. W. 7, 16th–18th July 1969*. Society of Chemical Industry.
13. M. Mindick and J. Svars, U.S. Patent 3,549,862 (1970), to Dow Chemical Co.
14. R. Kunin, E. F. Meitzner, J. A. Oline, S. A. Fisher, and N. Frisch, "Macroreticular Sulfonic Acid Cation Exchange Resin—Characterization of Amberlyst 15," *Ind. Eng. Chem., Prod. Res. Dev., 1*, 140 (1962).
15. R. Kunin, "Pore Structure of Macroreticular," in *Ion Exchange in the Process Industry, Papers Read at the Conference Held at Imperial College of Science and Technology, London S.W. 7, 16th–18th July 1969*, Society of Chemical Industry.

16. W. G. Lloyd and T. Alfrey Jr., *J. Polym. Sci.*, *62*, 503 (1962).
17. M. J. Hatch, U.S. Patent, 3,041,292 (1962), to Dow Chemical Co.
18. R. M. Wheaton and M. J. Hatch, in *Ion Exchange*, Vol. 2 (J. A. Marinsky and Y. Marcus, eds.), Dekker, New York, 1969.
19. B. A. Adams and E. L. Holmes, *J. Soc. Chem. Ind.*, *54*, 1–6T (1935).
20. G. R. Stroh, U.S. Patent 2,515,142 (1950), to American Cyanamid Co.
21. W. L. Evers, U.S. Patent 2,518,420 (1950), to Rohm and Haas.
22. G. F. d'Alelio, U.S. Patents 2,230,111 and 2,366,007 (1944), to General Electric Co.
23. A. H. Ferris, U.S. Patents 2,678,306 and 2,678,307 (1954), to Rohm and Haas.
24. G. W. Bodamer, U.S. Patent 2,597,438 (1952), to Rohm and Haas.
25. W. C. Bauman, J. R. Skidmore, and R. H. Osmin, "Dowex 50—A New High Capacity Cation Exchange Resin," *Ind. Eng. Chem.*, *40*, 1350 (1948).
26. H. P. Gregor, M. Taifer, L. Citeral, and E. I Becker, *Ind. Eng. Chem.*, *44*, 2834 (1953).
27. A. Shogseid, U.S. Patent 2,592,350 (1952), to Norsk Hydro-Electrick KV.
28. G. F. d'Alelio, U.S. Patent 2,366,008 (1944), to General Electric Co.
29. J. C. H. Hwa, U.S. Patent 2,597,493 (1952), to Rohm and Haas.
30. J. C. H. Hwa, U.S. Patent 2,597,494 (1952), to Rohm and Haas.
31. W. C. Bauman and G. B. Hensted, U.S. Patent 2,601,202 (1952), to Dow Chemical Co.
32. W. C. Baman and R. McKeller, U.S. Patent 2,614,099 (1952), to Dow Chemical Co.
33. G. W. Bodamer, U.S. Patent 2,597,439 (1952), to Rohm and Haas.
34. C. H. Burney, U.S. Patents 2,591,373 and 2,591,574 (1952), to Rohm and Haas.
35. R. M. Wheaton and W. C. Bauman, *Ind. Eng. Chem.*, *43*, 1088 (1951).
36. R. M. Wheaton and D. F. Harrington, U.S. Patent 2,642,117 (1953), to Dow Chemical Co.
37. R. E. Anderson, "A Contour Map of Anion Exchange Resin Properties," *Ind. Eng. Chem., Prod. Res. Dev.*, *3*, 85 (1964).
38. E. L. McMaster, U.S. Patents 2,616,872 and 2,632,001 (1953), to Dow Chemical Co.
40. M. J. Hatch, J. A. Dillon, and H. B. Smith, *Ind. Eng. Chem.*, *48*, 1812 (1959).
41. W. C. Bauman and J. Eichhorn, "Fundamental Properties of a Synthetic Cation Exchange Resin," *J. Am. Chem. Soc.*, *69*, 2832 (1947).
42. G. E. Boyd, J. Schubert, and A. W. Adamson, "The Exchange Adsorption of Ions from Aqueous Solution by Organic Zeolites—Ion Exchange Equilbria," *J. Am. Chem. Soc.*, *69*, 2818 (1947).
43. H. P. Gregor, "A General Thermodynamic Theory of Ion Exchange Process," *J. Am. Chem. Soc.*, *70*, 1293 (1948).
44. H. P. Gregor, "Biggs-Donnan Equilibria in Ion Exchange Resin," *J. Am. Chem. Soc.*, *73*, 642 (1951).
45. E. Glueckauf. *Proc. R. Soc.*, *A214*, 207 (1952).
46. G. W. Bodamer, U.S. Patent 2,681,300 (1954), to Rohm and Haas.
47. J. L. Eisemann, E. T. Roach, and A. Sciaszlig, U.S. Patent 3,607,706 (1971), to Ionics, Inc.
48. W. K. Chen, U.S. Patent 3,247,133 (1966), to American Machine and Foundary Co.
49. Y. Mizutani and M. J. Nishemeira, *J. Appl. Polym. Sci.*, *14*, 1847 (1970).
50. M. Seko, H. Mujauchi, and O. Asahi, in *Ion Exchange Membranes* (D. S. Flett, ed.), Horwood, 1983.
51. D. J. Connally and W. F. Franklin, U.S. Patent 3,282,875 (1966), to E. I. du Pont de Nemours Co.
52. W. R. Wolfe, British Patent 1,184,321 (1970) to E. I. du Pont de Nemours Co.

53. W. G. Grot, G. E. Munn, and P. N. Walmsley, *Perfluorinated Ion Exchange Membranes*, Presented to 141st National Meeting, The Electrochemcial Society, Houston, May 7–11, 1972.
54. D. J. Vaughan, "Nafion: An Electrochemcial Traffic Controller," *DuPont Innovation*, *4*(3), 10–13 (1973).
55. D. C. England, U.S. Patent 4,138,426 (1979), to E. I. du Pont de Nemours Co.
56. H. Ukihashi et al., U.S. Patent 4,116,888 (1978), to Asahi Glass Co.
57. M. A. Seko, A. Yomujama, and S. Ogawa, "Chloralkali Electrolysis Using Perfluorocarboxylic Acid Membranes," in *Ion Exchange Membranes* (D. S. Flette, ed.), Horwood, 1983.
58. M. Seko, U.S. Patent 4,178,218 (1979), to Asahi Chemical Industry Co.
59. Takamatsu and A. Eisenberg, *J. Appl. Polym. Sci.*, *24*, 2221–2235 (1979).
60. T. Sata, K. Montani, and Y. Ohashi, "Perfluorinated Ion Exchange Membrane, Neosepta-F and Its Properties," in *Ion Exchange Membranes* (D. S. Flett, ed.), Horwood, 1983.
61. A. Eisenberg and H. L. Yeager, *ACS Symp. Ser.*, (February 23–26, 1982).
62. S. C. Yeo and A. Eisenberg, *J. Appl. Polym. Sci. 21*, 875–898 (1977).
63. "X-R Perfluorosulfonic Acid Membrane," *Du Pont News Bull.*, October 1963.
64. M. Seko, *Ind. Eng. Chem.*, *Prod. Res. Dev.*, *4*, 286–292 (1976).
65. B. R. Ezzell, W. P. Carl, and W. A. Mod, Untitled Paper Presented at the AIChE National Meeting, Houston, March 1985.
66. S. B. Applebaum, *Demineralization by Ion Exchange*, Academic, New York, 1968.
67. T. Mottershead, "Production and Use of High Purity Water," in *Microelectronics Industries Ion Exchange Technology* (D. Naden and M. Streat, eds.), Horwood, 1984, pp. 25–49.
68. J. T. McNulty, "Anion Exchange Resin Kinetics in Mixed Bed Condensate Polishing," *Ion Exchange Technol.*, 1984.
69. J. Brown and N. J. Ray, "Ion Exchange in Water Purification—Where Do We Stand?" *Ion Exchange Technol.*, 1984.
70. *Dealkylation Handbook of Water Conditioning*, Beta Laboratories, Philadelphia.
71. E. Zanganiaric and G. H. Beasley, "Deionization of Boiler Feed Water: Silica Removal by Countercurrent Regenerated Anion Exchange," *Ion Exchange Technol.*, 1984.
72. "Nafion Membranes and Related Versatile Heterogeneous Catalysts," *Aldrich Chem. Co. Bull., 18* (1), (1985).
73. N. Neir, "Direct Hydration of Propylene to Isopropyl Alcohol," *Ion Exchange Technol.,* 1984.
74. "Catalytic Distillation with a Very Broad Reach," *Chem. Week*, September 11, 1985.
75. R. M. Wheaton and W. C. Bauman, "Ion Exclusion—A Unit Operation Utilizing Ion Exchange Materials," *Ind. Eng. Chem.*, *45*, 228 (1953).
76. D. W. Simpson and W. C. Bauman,"Concentration Effects of Recycling in Ion Exclusion," *Ind. Eng. Chem.*, *46*, 1958 (1954).
77. B. R. Green and R. H. Potgieter, "Unconventional Weak Base Ion Exchange Resin Useful for the Extraction of Metals, Especially Gold," *Ion Exchange Technol.*, p. 626 (1984).
78. A. Mehmert and W. A. M. Teriele, "The Recovery of Gold from Cyanide Liquors by a Counter Current Contactor Using Ion Exchange," *Ion Exchange Technol.,* p. 637 (1984).
79. S. Gonzales-Luque and M. Streat, "The Recovery of By-product Uraniums from Wet Phosphoric Acid Solutions Using Selective Ion Exchange Resins," *Ion Exchange Technol.*, p. 679 (1984).

80. S. Belfer, E. Korngold, and Y. Egozy, "Uranium Recovery from Phosphoric Acid with Selective Resins," *Ion Exchange Technol.*, p. 736 (1984).
81. J. Martins, C. Costa, J. Loureiro, and A. Rodriques, "Recovery of Tungsten from Hydrometallurgical Liquors by Ion Exchange," *Ion Exchange Technol.*, p. 715 (1984).
82. M. J. Hatch and J. A. Dillon, "Acid Retardation—A Simple Method of Separating Strong Acids from Their Salts," *Ind. Eng. Chem. Prod. Res. Dev.*, *2*, 253 (1963).
83. C. E. Wymore, "Sulfonic-Type Cation Exchange Resins as Desiccants," *Ind. Eng. Chem.*, *Prod. Res. Dev.*, *1*, 173 (1962).

WILLIAM A. MOD

Ion-Exchange Design Considerations (see also Ion-Exchange Agents)

Scope

The purpose of this article is to describe how ion-exchange resins can be effectively utilized in process applications. Information on common ion-exchange processes, methods of operations, general types of equipment, and key process design considerations should aid in determining the applicability of ion exchange to a process need. Requirements for properly functioning ion-exchange equipment and the necessary support facilities are presented.

It is assumed that in considering the use of ion-exchange resin: (1) the overall processing operation has been evaluated to determine the most advantageous location to obtain the desired results; (2) composition of the liquid to be treated has been defined as completely as possible; and (3) all conditions of the liquid (such as pH, temperature, and clarity) are known in order to determine the applicability of ion-exchange resins in the liquid treatment process.

Selection of Ion-Exchange Operation

Ion-Exchange Processes

Deionization

The most widely used application of ion-exchange technology is the removal of dissolved salts from a liquid process stream. This process is distinguished by the combined use of acidic form cation-exchange resins and basic form anion-exchange resins for the removal of dissociated salt molecules. Hydrogen form cation resins exchange the dissociated cation portion of salt molecules for hydrogen ions, and the corresponding acids are formed. Basic form anion resins adsorb the acid or exchange the anionic portion of the molecules for hydroxide ions, which subsequently react with the hydrogen ions to produce water and a deionized product.

Ion Replacement

In contrast to deionization processes where dissolved salts are removed from the process liquid, ion replacement processes modify the ionic composition of the process liquid. The common practice of ion-exchange water softening (in which divalent ions, such as calcium and magnesium ions, are exchanged for sodium ions) is an example of ion replacement. Applications involving the exchange of sulfate, nitrate, or bicarbonate ions for chloride ions are also practiced. Other ion replacement processes are possible but are limited by the relative resin selectivity and mass action equilibrium relationship between the ionic compounds and the ion-exchange resins used.

Selective Sorption

This process can be employed in separating weakly dissociated acids from more highly dissociated acids or their salts. The separations are dependent on the preferential sorption order of anions by the ion-exchange resin and are determined by ionic strengths, valencies and sizes, the ionic species involved, and the properties of the ion-exchange resin.

Two relatively weakly ionized acids may also be separated by this technique. This occurs when the salt form of the resin is derived from an acid whose ionization constant is greater than one of the weak acids but less than the other.

Strong acids can be preferentially removed from solutions containing other electrolytes by using weakly basic anion-exchange resin. The acids are adsorbed by the weakly basic resin through a neutralization reaction; neutral salts are unaffected by this mechanism.

Complex Formation

A variety of resins have been developed with high specificity for an ion or group of ions. These highly specific resins have been developed with compounds known to have chelating or complexing properties. The specificity of these resins offers possibilities of application in areas where conventional ion-exchange resins are inoperable. Separation of similar heavy metals is possible, removal of trace quantities of heavy metals from alkali or alkaline earth metals can be accomplished, and alkaline earth metals may be separated from alkali metal solutions. These resins are also effective in polar and nonpolar solvent separations.

Chromatographic Separation

Ion-exchange chromatography is a process which allows separation of the components in a liquid according to the different rates of migration of the constituents through an ion-exchange resin column.

The affinities of nonionized compounds on ion-exchange resins depend on several factors, including subtle differences in the resin's structure. With liquid chromatographic techniques, large affinity differences are not needed to accomplish effective separations.

The methods in which ion-exchange resin are employed in chromatographic separations are similar to those used in adsorption or partition chromatography. Since the properties of ion-exchange resins are different from those of adsorbents (such as activated carbon or alumina), some differences in operating techniques must be accommodated.

To obtain useful separations in most chromatographic operations, it is essential that an equilibrium is attained at all points within the resin column. The rate at which equilibrium is accomplished is usually much slower than in adsorption chromatography where the adsorption is confined to the surface.

The largest industrial use of ion-exchange resin for chromatographic separation is the fractionation of isomers from liquid solutions containing glucose and fructose. A simulated moving-bed equipment technique is utilized to accomplish the separation.

Ion Retardation

This process employs a resin containing both anionic- and cationic-exchange sites. The resin will exchange both anions and cations from a liquid solution; the ions are held so weakly that they are displaced by rinsing with water. Separation is possible because certain ions are held more tightly than others.

Ion retardation is also used to separate an electrolyte from a nonelectrolyte. The electrolyte penetrates the resin matrix and is retarded, while the nonelectrolyte passes through the resin column. Large organic molecules that cannot enter the resin beads can be separated from ionic substances.

Ion Exclusion

This process is similar to ion retardation in that nonionized, or only slightly ionized, organic or inorganic substances can be separated from ionized materials. Ion exclusion uses the Donnan exclusion principle. When passed through a column of resin, the ionized substances are not adsorbed by the exchanger. The nonelectrolyte substance is unaffected by Donnan potentials and is free to distribute itself between the aqueous external and pore solutions. When rinsed with water, the resin columns first elute the ionic and then the nonionic constituents. Conventional ion-exchange resins are used in the ion exclusion processes; the process is dependent upon the physical and chemical properties of the resin employed.

Methods of Operation

The liquid–solid contact necessary for ion exchange can be accomplished in many ways. Some of these methods are practical only when there is a specialty use for the ion-exchange resin. In most applications, however, the choice of operational methods centers around two concerns: (1) should the resin be in a packed or fluidized bed, and (2) should the liquid to be treated and the regenerant solution contact the resin in the same direction or in opposite directions.

Fixed Bed vs Fluidized Bed

The performance of an ion-exchange resin is limited by kinetic, equilibrium, and mechanical factors. These effects are minimized by using ion-exchange resins in fixed (packed) beds.

The fixed bed provides an exchange zone and an actual exchange front to be set up in the column. Kinetic factors associated with mass transfer of ions between a liquid and the ion-exchange resin and mechanical factors (such as axial dispersion and column wall effects) are predictable when using column processes. Their effects on ion-exchange processes are minimized by proper column design and operation of the resin column. The result is a general domination of the efficiencies of ion-exchange processes by equilibrium controlled factors. This is desirable since ion-exchange processes are designed to take advantage of the equilibrium conditions possible between the constituents of a liquid and the ion-exchange resin.

Fluidized (unpacked) beds of an ion-exchange resin are used where suspended solids are present in a liquid to be treated and when it is not practical or desirable to remove the solids.

Complete contact of the liquid and the ion-exchange resin is the primary design concern of fluidized-bed operation. The process trades the need for low filterable solids in the liquid to be treated for some adverse effects of kinetic and equilibrium factors. These factors must be minimized to make the trade desirable.

In general, only the service step is accomplished in a fluidized bed. The regeneration (displacement of material from the resin) is performed on the ion-exchange resins when it is in a packed bed.

Cocurrent vs Countercurrent

In standard operations, both the regenerant solution and the liquid being processed are passed downflow through a resin column. The efficiency of the regenerant utilization is relatively poor because of equilibrium factors; the resin remains partially in the unregenerated form. During service, the purity of the treated liquid is dependent on the regenerated state of the resin at the bottom of the column.

To obtain the highest regenerant efficiencies and the purest effluents, the

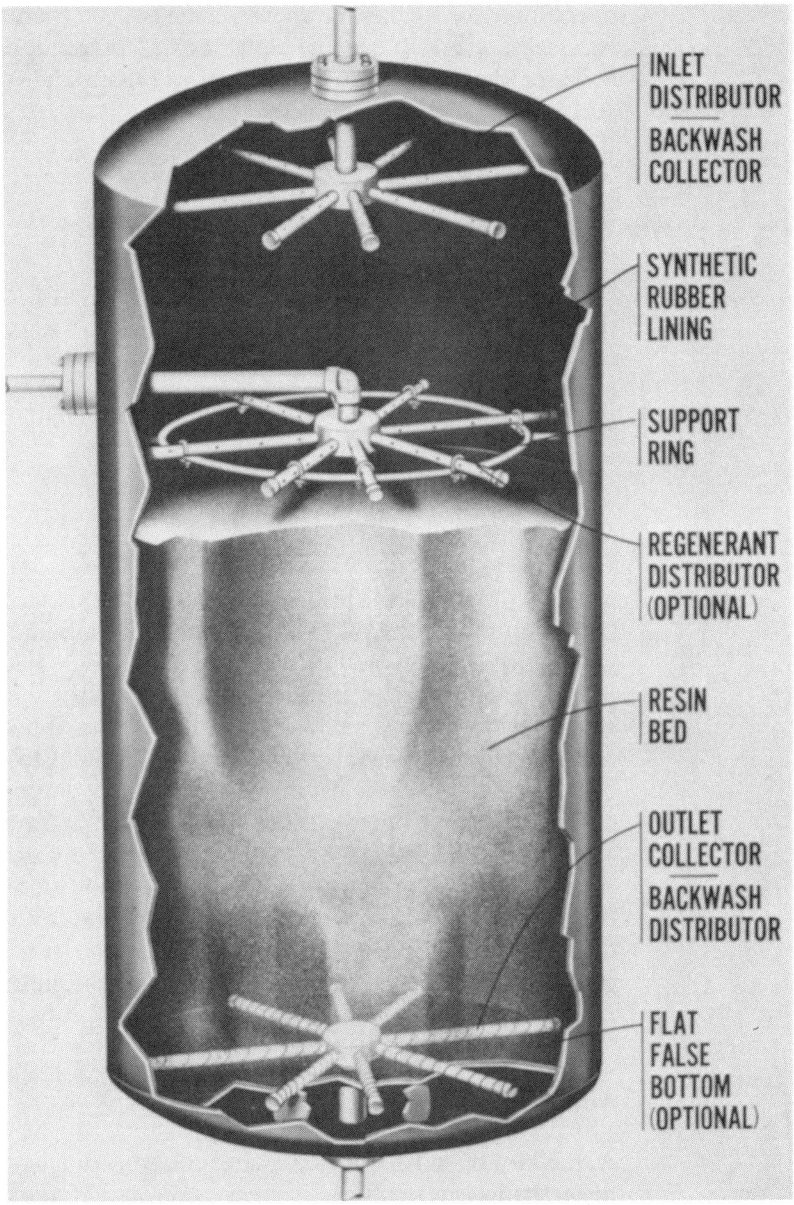

FIG. 1. Typical cation or anion exchanger showing internal distribution systems.

regenerant solution and the liquid to be treated are passed through an ion-exchange column in opposite directions. This countercurrent technique allows the liquid to contact the most highly regenerated resin last, so there is little or no leakage. To maximize a countercurrent system, the resin must not fluidize during the regeneration; if fluidization occurs, resin mixing will result and most of the advantages of this type of operation will not be realized.

Countercurrent ion-exchange processes provide not only higher purities of treated liquids but also result in higher chemical efficiencies than cocurrent operations. As regeneration levels increase, the chemical efficiencies of the two techniques will become equal. For all practical ranges of regeneration, however, the countercurrent method will maintain its advantage of effluent purity.

Types of Equipment

For the effective utilization of an ion-exchange resin, the equipment in which the resin is placed must be designed to take advantage of the special characteristics of that resin. There are many equipment designs in which ion-exchange resins are used for processing operations. Major types of equipment are described below.

Single and Multiple Columns

Much of the appeal of the ion-exchange process stems from the simplicity of a single column operation and the numerous configurations that are possible with the wide variety of ion-exchange resins (Fig. 1). A typical ion exchanger is a vertical cylindrical pressure vessel with a resin support–liquid collection system at the bottom and a distribution system above the resin bed. Externally, the unit is provided with a valve manifold to permit operation and backwashing, introducing the chemical, and rinsing of the resin. Some designs have been outgrowths of standard filtration equipment.

The use of a strong acid cation exchanger followed by a weak base or strong base anion exchanger is the basis for deionization. Three or more beds can be used to achieve either operating economy or a greater degree of deionization. Different properties of ion-exchange resins can be utilized by placing single units in various configurations for multiple bed systems.

Mixed Beds

A standard mixed-bed ion-exchange column contains a mixture of hydrogen form strong acid cation-exchange resin and hydroxide form strong base anion-exchange resin (Fig. 2). When a liquid is passed through a fixed bed of the resin mixture, a degree of deionization is achieved that is difficult to accomplish with individual resin beds in series. This high degree of purity is achieved because the mixture of resin converts the deionization process to a reaction in which the only product is water.

$$(R^-)H^+ + (R^+)OH^- + NaCl \rightarrow (R^-)Na^+ + (R^+)Cl^- + H_2O$$

While the resins do not have to be completely regenerated to give a high quality effluent (since essentially no back reaction occurs), it is necessary that the resins be intimately mixed.

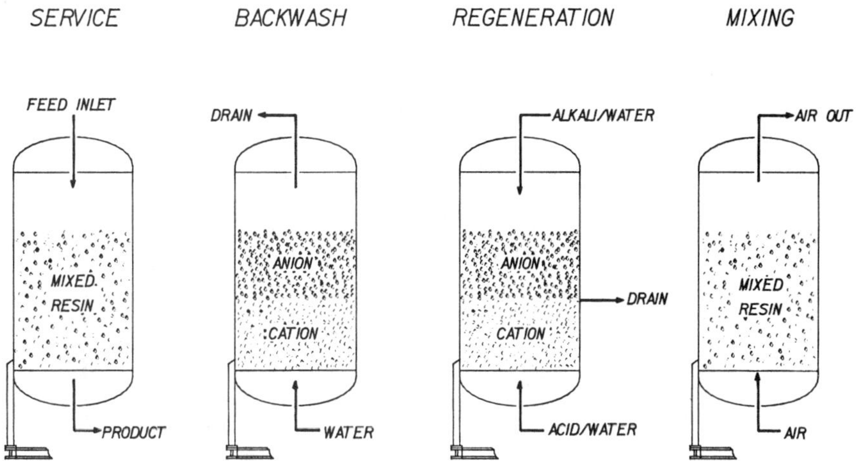

FIG. 2. Mixed bed operation.

When the mixture is exhausted, the two resins are separated into layers by backwashing; hydraulic separation occurs because anion-exchange resins have a lower density than cation-exchange resins. The resins are regenerated in place, simultaneously rinsed, and remixed by air before being returned to service.

Although the basic concept of the mixed bed is simple, practical operation can be difficult to achieve. Properly designed distribution manifolds, air mixing techniques, and the elimination of chemical traps are essential for optimum performance.

Continuous Ion Exchangers

A large number of continuous and semicontinuous ion exchangers have been developed over the years; two types have found commercial acceptance—pulsed columns and fluidized beds. Ion-exchange resin in the pulsed columns are pulsed in a loop containing zones for service, regeneration, and rinse; the zones are separated by valves. In the fluidized bed design, the column is divided vertically into chambers; resin is transferred from chamber to chamber down the column without interruption of feed flow (Fig. 3). The ion-exchange resin is fluidized by an upward flow of liquid from which ions are to be exchanged. The number of chambers and the volume of resin in each chamber depend upon the kinetics of ion exchange for the particular system. As the resin moves countercurrently to the liquid flow, the residence time of all resin particles within the column is the same regardless of differences in particle size or settling rate. The transfer of resin continues from chamber to chamber separately and consecutively until the top chamber is empty. Regenerated resin is then transferred from an external elution column to the top chamber.

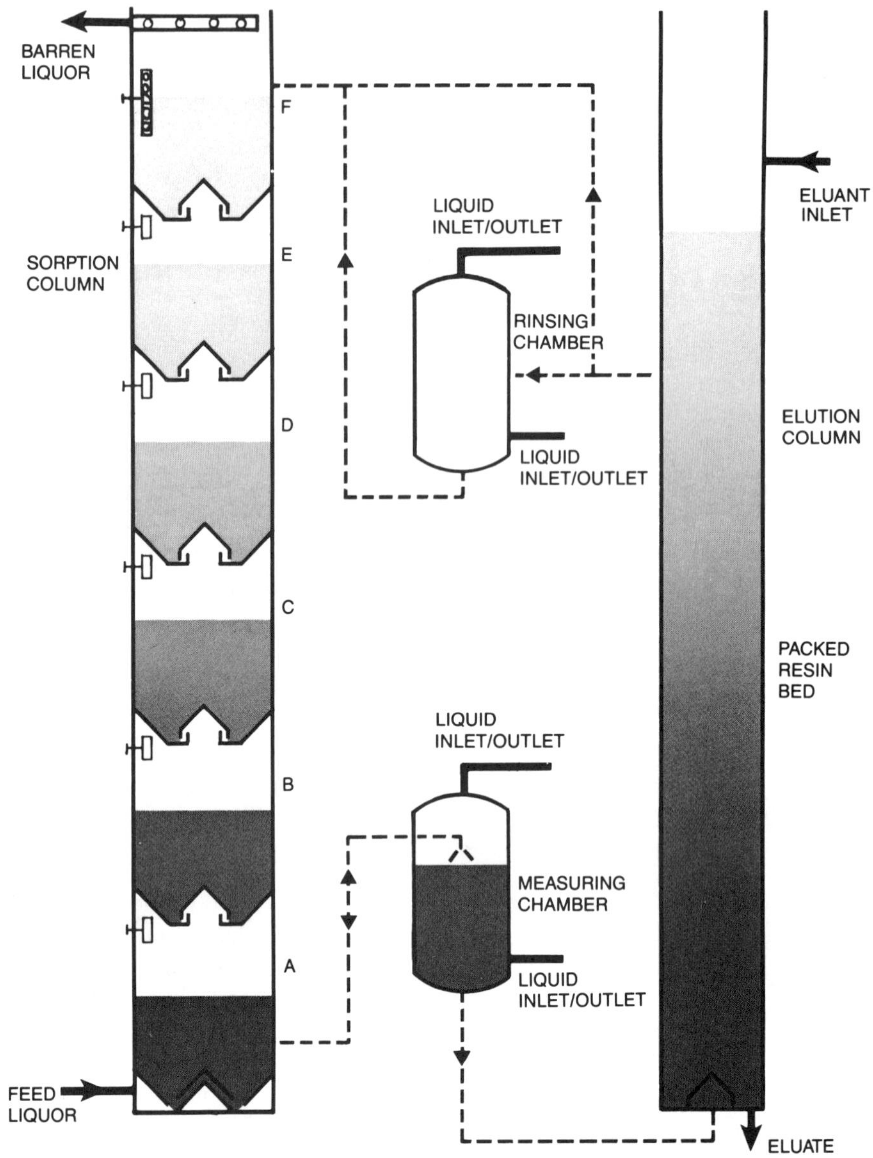

FIG. 3. Typical arrangement of Himsley continuous fluidized bed system.

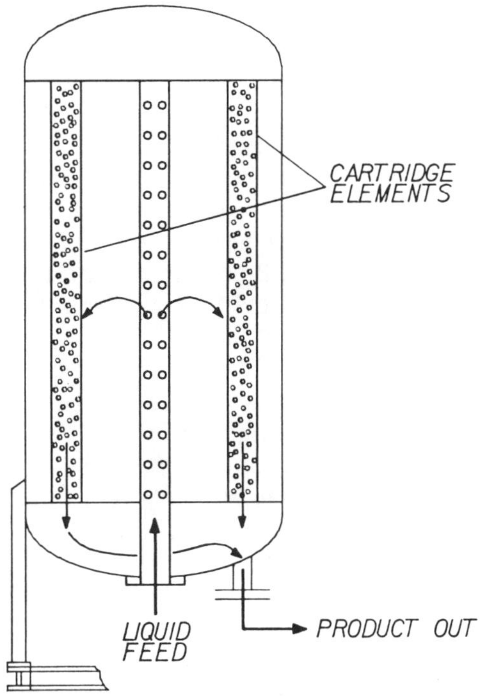

FIG. 4. Ion-exchange unit with powdered mixed resins in cartridge elements.

Resin Precoat Filters

This equipment typically uses tubular cartridge elements in a specially designed vessel (Fig. 4). Ion-exchange resin which has been ground into powder is precoated on the elements to form a uniform layer of media. Liquid is treated until the resin precoat is exhausted. The spent resin is then removed and usually discarded. The elements are again precoated with the ground resin, and the filter is readied for operation. This equipment eliminates the need for regenerant chemicals, since none are required. Liquid disposal is simplified since only the resin must be disposed. The ion-exchange resin must perform in a cost-effective manner to make this type of equipment desirable.

Simulated Moving Bed

Fractionation of a mixture of components can be accomplished by continuous simulated moving-bed chromatographic equipment. The individual components in aa mixture are selectively adsorbed by the ion-exchange resin in the column according to their respective affinities for the media. Thus, if a mixture of Components A and B and their solvent is passed through a column of ion-exchange resin that exhibits a stronger bond for Component A than for B, a longer retention time will be exhibited by A than by B, and a separation can be effected.

Continuous separation of A from the mixture of A and B is accomplished by introducing a mixture of A and B into the fluid stream continuously circulating in a closed loop of the system. As the internal recirculating flow carries the A and B mixture downstream from its introduction point through the resin, A is adsorbed, allowing B to move downstream ahead of A. After a period of time, the B component will progress through one column section and proceed to the succeeding section. The feed stream position will then be advanced to the next column section to maintain the feed position between the advancing B component and the A component lagging behind. In this manner, feedstock is continuously separated into a Component A rich product stream and a Component B by-product stream. The by-product stream is removed downstream of the feed position and the product stream is removed upstream of the feed position. The process results in a stabilized profile that continuously circulates through the vessel.

A simulated moving-bed system maintains the ion-exchange resins in a series of discrete segments contained in a vessel or vessels. The number of feed/desorbent/product/by-product distribution and collection points is determined by the separation curve for the components to be fractionated, as well as the required purity of the components.

Process Design Considerations

For ion-exchange system sizing, the quantity of liquid to be processed in a period of time must be determined. The processing rate is often expressed in gallons per day or pounds per day. Continuous ion-exchange systems are normally sized on this basis. However, for fixed-bed ion-exchange operation where service must be interrupted periodically to regenerate the ion-exchange material chemically, the processing rate can be determined as follows:

$$\text{Processing rate} = \frac{\text{quantity to be processed}}{\text{time period minus regeneration time}}$$

Equipment must be sized such that the service time is sufficient to allow a unit in regeneration to be completed prior to the exhaustion of the usable capacity of the unit in service. The service time of a single unit in a multiple unit system is usually designed for a service time which exceeds the sum of the regeneration time required for all of the units in service. Systems can be designed where multiple units are regenerated simultaneously, and appropriate reductions in the service time requirement can be made. However, this adds additional units to the multiple unit system.

Having determined the required feed processing rate per fixed-bed ion exchanger and the required length of the service period, the exchange or adsorption load to each unit for a service period can be calculated. For continuous ion-exchange equipment, the load is calculated on the basis of exchange load per unit time.

The capacity of an ion-exchange material to remove a given component or components normally must be determined experimentally. Fortunately, data for commonly used ion-exchange resins applied to water treatment and some purification applications have been determined and are often published by the various ion-exchange-resin manufacturers. When using published information, some caution should be used when applying the data. The operating capacity of ion-exchange materials is dependent not only on the composition of the process fluid being treated, but also on such process variables as the concentration of the components to be removed, process flow contact rate, regenerant chemical concentration, regenerant chemical contact time with the ion-exchange resin, service endpoint criteria, chemical rinse water characteristics, method of capacity calculation (load corrections for service leakage), and operating temperatures. Most published data have been determined at ambient operating temperatures, service flow rates of 2 gpm/ft^3 of resin, and feed with dissolved solids in the 200–500 ppm as $CaCO_3$ range. The most common difference in reported data results from service endpoint criteria differences and the method employed to calculate capacities. Operation of the service cycle to high exchange capacity loading often improves reported capacities, but has an adverse impact on service leakage of the components to be removed.

Service leakage data are often reported on an average leakage basis. However, service operation must be terminated in many applications when service leakages exceed a fixed quality limit. In other cases, where the system effluent goes to storage and is mixed or where the effect of service leakage is based upon the accumulation of service leakage components, it is possible to use the average leakage values. Often it is good practice to design for an average leakage that is at least 20% lower than the maximum leakage limits imposed by the application.

Design data for ion-exchange processing of various aqueous chemical streams can be obtained from the data bases developed by the various equipment manufacturers. These data are seldom published or readily available to the end user.

Ion-exchange operating capacities are affected by the rate of mass transfer between the process fluid and the ion-exchange resin. For strong acid or strong base-type resins, published data provide reliable designs up to flows of 4 gpm/ft^3, where the ion-exchange load concentration does not exceed 750 ppm as $CaCO_3$ of ion exchangeable solids. Ion-exchange media volume determined by the service length requirements will often limit the volumetric flow rate to less than 4 gpm/ft^3. For some system designs where the ion-exchange load is low, ion-exchange media volumes must be increased to meet the recommended flow per unit volume limitations. Service cycle times are then increased above the minimum required. The 4 gpm/ft^3 limit can be exceeded; however, a reduction in operating capacity can occur and must be taken into consideration when sizing the system.

Like all unit operations, ion exchange has limitations. The properties of ion-exchange resin are difficult to use when nonaqueous liquids contain so little water that ionic movement or dissociation is impaired. It is also difficult to use resin when the high viscosity of a liquid adversely affects the diffusion processes that control ion-exchange reactions.

Ion-exchange processes, while useful for concentrating specific solutes, are not the complete solution to waste treatment problems. The regenerant chemical waste produced by ion-exchange processes normally contains the concentrated waste component previously removed. The waste stream must be disposed of or, optimally, recycled back to the process.

Due to mass action equilibrium restrictions between the ion-exchange resin and the solution to be treated, ion-exchange processing of high electrolyte content streams is somewhat restricted. Processes involving metal complex formation, chelation, or ion exclusion are often viable. Deionization of solutions with high electrolyte content is not normally practical.

The potential problem of bacteriological growth in ion-exchange equipment must be considered when designing ion-exchange processes. The growths can contaminate product streams or, in some cases, plug the ion-exchange beds, creating excessive pressure drop or bed channeling difficulties. The problem can be severe for process streams rich in nutrients. A variety of techniques, such as temperature control, chemical treatment, and recirculation flows, can be used to control bacteriological growth problems.

Ion-exchange resins can be fouled by a variety of materials, such as iron, metal salts, certain organic compounds, and particulate materials. In many cases the effects can be controlled with appropriate pretreatment of the process stream or resin cleanup methods.

In most applications, ion-exchange resin has a useful service life measured in years; however, the stability of ion-exchange resin is affected by temperature. The combined effects of temperature, the presence of oxidizing agents, and heavy metals which catalyze organic reactions can rapidly degrade the useful life of ion-exchange resins. Temperature limitations for ion-exchange resins vary with resin type and application.

Requirements for Equipment Design

Process concepts need to be translated into equipment designs. Detailed hardware design information is beyond the scope of this article; however, several general equipment design considerations are discussed below.

Tanks and Vessels

Typically, a tank diameter which will allow service operation at flows that will exceed 2 gpm/ft^2 of tank area and not exceed 12 gpm/ft^2 are acceptable. Once the vessel diameter has been determined, the ion-exchange media bed depth can be calculated (media volume divided by area = bed depth). The resin bed depth in a fixed-bed ion-exchange unit usually should exceed 30 in. and be limited to a maximum depth of 96 in. High flows per unit area and deep ion-exchange resin depths may result in high pressure drops. Pressure losses across a resin bed are normally limited to 10–20 lb/in.^{2} Large pressure losses can, in combination with exchange media volume changes (resulting from ionic or osmotic changes), cause physical damage to the exchange media, the exchanger, and the internals of the exchanger.

Many industrial ion-exchange systems use vertical cylindrical pressure vessels of steel construction; stainless steel and fiberglass tanks are also commonly used. In addition, spherical, conical, and compartmented vessels are used for special processes.

The use of interior coating or linings in an ion-exchange tank is dictated by the chemicals that are used to regenerate the resins or the nature of the liquid being processed. Rubber or polyvinyl chloride linings are commonly used where acids and alkalis are needed for regeneration; epoxy, phenolic, and galvanized coatings are routinely used where operating condition are less aggressive.

Most fixed-bed ion exchangers are designed for in-place backwashing of the ion-exchange media to remove suspended material that may be filtered from the process stream during the service cycle. To accommodate this requirement, a free space in the tank above the ion-exchange resin must be provided and equal to 75–100% of the ion-exchange resin depth.

Piping and Valves

Ion-exchange equipment is commonly constructed with PVC, stainless steel, or lined carbon steel flanged piping. Consideration should be given to the specific environment present where the ion-exchange equipment is to be installed. Lined carbon steel pipe is commonly used on large equipment or where severe service conditions are expected.

Selection of valves suitable for the intended service is especially important. Most of the ion-exchange system sequencing is accomplished by valve manipulation. Valves and valve operators must be selected to provide reliable valve closure during all anticipated operating conditions. For automated systems, particular attention should be given to ensure fail–safe valve operation for power, control air, and system control interruptions. Valve operators which provide for prompt valve sequencing response, while avoiding flow surges or water hammers, are required to prevent equipment damage. Valve operators with some form of actuator speed control are desirable.

Often there are trade-offs between durability, operating manpower requirements, maintenance requirements, and ease of operation versus cost. Selection of components which are compatbile with existing equipment can reduce the spare parts required and simplify maintenance procedures.

Exchange Media Support

Several design concepts are available for supporting the ion-exchange resin. These include flat false bottom designs, dished tank bottom designs with graded gravel media support beds, and dished tank bottom designs with sloped collection laterals.

From a performance standpoint, flat bottom designs are preferred; however, graded gravel media support beds are less expensive and can be used in many applications. Dished bottom designs without graded media support are normally not used unless complete exchange media removal is regularly required in the operation.

Flow Distribution

For optimum operation of fixed-bed ion-exchange equipment, it is essential that liquid passing through the ion-exchange media maintains a plug flow distribution pattern. This necessitates the use of well-designed liquid flow distributors for all inlet and outlet process flow streams. Perforated pipe spargers are preferred and are normally provided in hub-radial or header lateral configurations (Fig. 5). Header lateral designs provide more consistent results, particularly where large flow turndown ratios are encountered. The less expensive hub-radial sparger designs are often acceptable for small diameter tanks. There are many other distribution and collection designs, but the hub-radial and the header lateral designs are the most widely used.

Flow distribution spargers must be constructed of materials suitable for the chemical and temperature environment in which the equipment will be operated. In many cases, PVC (polyvinyl chloride) or CPVC (chlorinated polyvinyl chloride) plastics are adequate. In other cases where greater mechanical strength is required, various corrosion-resistant metal alloys, such as 316 stainless steel or Hastalloy C, may be used.

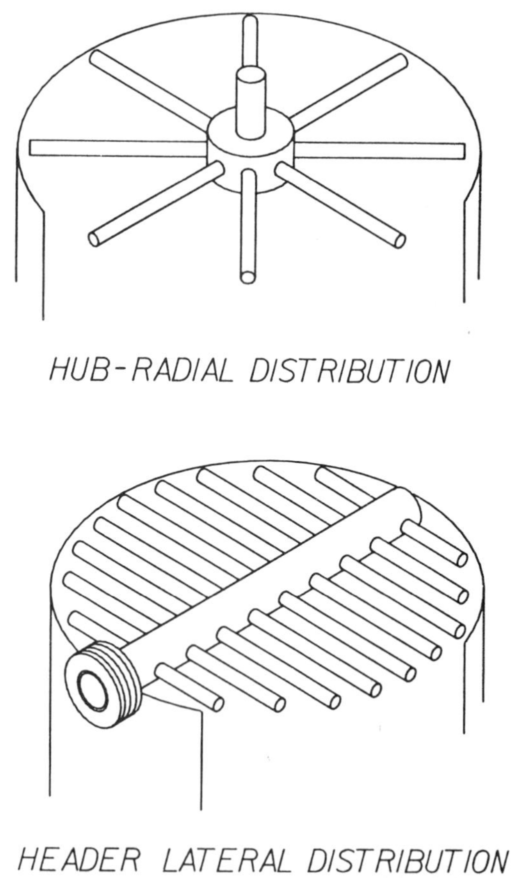

FIG. 5. Standard types of distribution.

Automation and Instrumentation

While ion-exchange equipment can be designed for manual operation, most equipment is designed for partial or completely automated operation. Equipment control schemes span a range of sophistication and cost. Large complex systems typically use state-of-the-art microprocessor based controls. Less complex systems may use electromechanical sequencing mechanisms.

Similarly, control and monitoring instrumentation may be tailored to individual needs. Manual testing procedures can be used to monitor product quality and regenerant chemical concentrations where suitable manpower is available. For complex systems, on-line monitoring and data recording instrumentation are normally used.

As the sophistication of controls and instrumentation increases, so does the need for routine maintenance to ensure proper operation of the ion-exchange system.

Safety Considerations

In addition to protecting pressure vessels and piping from overpressurization, special precautions are required for chemical handling equipment. The strong acid and strong base chemicals used in the regeneration of ion-exchange equipment are hazardous to personnel and corrosive to equipment not compatible with these chemicals. Block and bleed valve arrangements for concentrated chemical lines in conjunction with interlocked controls on automated equipment must be used to prevent improper chemical dilution.

Although ion-exchange resins are compatible with a wide range of chemicals, resins are degraded by strong oxidizing agents. Nitric acid and other strong oxidizing agents can cause explosive reactions when in contact with ion-exchange resins. Consideration must be given to the chemical compatibility of the particular resins and the liquid being processed.

Ion-exchange resins typically undergo volume changes when the ionic form or the external solution concentration is varied. Resins which have been dehydrated and are subsequently wetted undergo considerable volume changes. The mechanical forces resulting from the osmotic pressures causing these volume changes can and have ruptured containment vessels when proper design practices have not been followed.

Support Facilities

Planning for processes involving ion-exchange treatment methods must include support facilities for operation of the ion-exchange processing equipment. Poorly planned support facilities can cause interruptions in the otherwise successful operation of ion-exchange equipment.

TABLE 1 Typical Space Requirements[a]

System	Tank Diameter (in.)	Tank Straight Side (in.)	Height (ft)	Square Feet
Two-bed deionizer	20	72	8	32
	36	96	$11\frac{1}{2}$	52
	60	96	12	138
	96	96	14	240
Mixed-bed deionizer	20	72	8	24
	36	96	$11\frac{1}{2}$	45
	60	96	12	96
	96	96	14	160

[a]Does not include auxiliary equipment or operating access space.

Space Requirements

It is often necessary to make space requirement estimates for installation of ion-exchange equipment in new or existing facilities. Both overall equipment height and floor space requirements must be considered (Table 1).

The total ion-exchange equipment height must take into account the tank straight side requirement, the depth of the exchanger tank heads, the top and bottom piping requirements, and the vessel support structure to determine the overall equipment height. It must be determined if any building height or installation site access limitations restrict the dimensions of the completed equipment.

Ion-exchange systems are normally shipped as partially assembled packages to reduce field installation cost. Field assembly requirements are greater for large equipment. Ion-exchange vessels larger than 12.5 ft in diameter usually must be constructed at the installation site due to shipping limitations.

Most ion-exchange equipment is designed for indoor installation. Outside installations are occasionally used where ambient temperatures are sufficiently warm to avoid heat tracing and freeze protection considerations. Space requirements for chemical handling equipment and waste treatment systems must be considered separately. For complex processing systems, equipment suppliers should be consulted.

Utilities

Electrical service considerations are similar to requirements for other chemical processing equipment (Table 2). The electric service must accommodate the need for controls, pumps, blowers, and compressors. Some systems may require electrical service to operate immersion heating equipment. Contingency planning for electrical power losses is especially important where valve closures are required or product degradation within the processing equipment is a concern.

Many systems are dependent on control air for system operation (Table 3). As with the electrical services planning, contingency planning must be done to ensure that any interruption in the air supply is accommodated in a safe and orderly manner. Often the system control designs overlook the possibility of instrument and operating air losses.

In addition to the need for instrument and control air supplies, air pressure may be used for tank purging and air mixer scour operations. Blowers may be required for mixing ion-exchange resin in mixed-bed equipment.

Generally, the need for steam is for caustic chemical dilution water heating or process liquid heating. Steam may also be useful for sanitization purposes, although the temperature sensitivity of ion-exchange materials limits this use. Low pressure steam is usually adequate and preferred.

Auxiliary water sources may be required to perform the chemical regeneration steps for the ion-exchange system. This is especially true where the process fluid contains valuable nonaqueous components which should not be discharged to waste disposal systems. Chemical steps involving caustic solutions must use hardness free water to avoid precipitation of calcium or magnesium solids. Equipment which is regenerated countercurrent to the direction of the service flow must use cation free water for cation exchangers and deionized water for anion exchangers.

Special displacement fluids occasionally are required for displacement of process fluids which react adversely with water and are used prior to regeneration steps. Air displacement of the process fluid is used in special situations, but is not generally recommended. Air displacement can displace only interstitial process liquid, but is not effective in displacing process liquid which is held within the ion-exchange resin. Process liquid held within the exchanger material must ultimately be diffused from the media by a displacing liquid.

Chemicals—Handling and Storage

Provisions must be considered to handle the chemicals used in ion-exchange operations conveniently and safety. Normally, these chemicals are shipped and received in a bulk and concentrated form. Chemicals can be supplied in carboys, bags, drums, or tank truck or railcar containers. These bulk liquids or solid chemicals are then stored at the plant site for eventual use.

Concentrated chemicals must be diluted from the commercially available concentrations to 5 to 10% by weight prior to use in the ion-exchange processing equipment. Two methods are commonly used to accomplish the necessary dilution. In some cases, chemicals are diluted to an intermediate concentration, usually 20% by weight, and subsequently educted into the ion-exchange equipment; often, single batch tanks are used for dilution and storage of intermediate solution concentrations. In other cases these chemicals may be pumped into a flowing dilution stream at a mixing tee and used for regeneration of the ion-exchange resin.

TABLE 2 Electrical Consumption: Volt-Ampere

System	Maximum Flow (gpm)	Power for Control		Power for Rinse Recirculation		Power for Chemical Mix	
Two-bed deionizer	50	720	1 ϕ	240	1 ϕ	120	1 ϕ
	100	720	1 ϕ	720	3 ϕ	150	1 ϕ
	200	720	1 ϕ	720	3 ϕ	150	1 ϕ
Mixed-bed deionizer	50	720	1 ϕ	240	1 ϕ	120	1 ϕ
	100	720	1 ϕ	720	3 ϕ	120	1 ϕ
	200	720	1 ϕ	720	3 ϕ	150	1 ϕ

TABLE 3 Air Consumption: Cubic Feet per Minute

System	Maximum Flow (gpm)	Air for Controls	Air for Mixing
Two-bed deionizer	50	0.06	—
	100	0.10	—
	200	0.27	—
Mixed-bed deionizer	50	0.06	25[a]
	100	0.10	50[a]
	200	0.22	100[a]

[a]Use 20 min/operating cycle for mixing period.

Operating instructions and automated controls must be designed to prevent introduction of regenerant chemicals into the liquid being processed. Precautions must be taken to avoid excessive temperatures due to heat of hydration during chemical dilution steps.

Regenerant Waste Management

In most cases, regenerant wastes may be safely discharged to local waste treatment facilities following pH adjustment to a neutral pH. Regenerant waste neutralization is best accomplished in batch-holding tanks. Ion-exchange systems produce chemical wastes of abruptly changing flows, variable composition, pH buffering capacity, and chemical demand. This makes continuous neutralization methods difficult to control. Continuous neturalization may be practical where ion-exchange streams are a minor portion of the load to a large waste treatment facility. Batch neutralization holding volume capacity should be sufficiently large so as to accommodate upset conditions.

In extreme cases where toxic materials have been concentrated into the ion-exchange media, toxic materials containing regenerant wastes may need to be segregated for on-site destruction, process recycle, or off-site disposal.

R. D. PICHT
T. R. DILLMAN

Kerosene and Jet Fuels

Kerosene is a refined petroleum fraction used for lighting, heating, cooking, and as fuel for diesel engines, tractors, rockets, jet engines, and as a base for insecticides. For a very long time it was largely used for household lighting and known as lamp oil.

Kerosene is recovered from crude oil by distillation. Its percent yield varies from crude to crude. Its consumption has been declining due to increasing urbanization, electrification, and a growing number of substitutes such as LPG, solar energy, and other conventional and nonconventional energy sources. Table 1 shows the decreasing annual recovery of kerosene

TABLE 1 Percent Annual Recovery of Kerosene from Crude Oil in the United States [1]

Year	% of Crude
1964	2.9
1968	2.7
1973	1.7
1974	1.3
1977	1.2
1978	1.0
1979	1.0
1980	1.0
1981	0.9
1982	0.9
1983	0.9
1984	0.9
1985	0.9

from crude oil in the United States—an indication of relatively decreasing consumption pattern. Consumption of kerosene as compared to other petroleum fractions is less in developed countries than in developing and underdeveloped countries.

Specifications of various grades of kerosene are established mutually by government and petroleum refiners.

Properties

Kerosene exhibits its approximate composition in the range of C_{12}–C_{16}, boiling normally between 150 and 235–315°C. The properties of kerosene drawn from Arabian heavy and light crudes differ substantially in yield, sulfur, cycloparaffins, and aromatic content (see Table 2). Illuminating kerosene is a straight-run distillate from paraffinic or mixed base crudes and a solvent-treated distillate from aromatic crudes. Fuel Oil No. 1 kerosene is a straight-run distillate treated for stability, the detailed specifications of which are given in Table 3.

For use in lamps, a highly paraffinic oil is desired because aromatics and naphthenes give a smoky flame. In order to avoid atmospheric pollution, sulfur content must be low. A minimum flash point of 100°F (38°C) is desirable to reduce explosion hazards.

TABLE 2 Properties of Kerosene Obtained from Arabian Crude [2]

Properties	From Arabian heavy	From Arabian light
Cut range, °C	150–235	150–235
Yield, vol.%	12.2	18.4
Specific gravity	0.787	0.788
Sulfur, wt.%	0.19	0.092
Paraffins, vol.%	58.0	58.9
Cycloparaffins, vol.%	23.7	20.5
Aromatic material, vol.%	18.3	20.6
Freezing point, °C	−53	−55
Smoke point, mm	26	26
Aniline point, °C	59	56
Viscosity, mm^2/s (= cSt):		
at 34°C	4.74	5.09
at 38°C	1.12	1.13

Recovery and Yields

Kerosene is separated as a sidestream from a primary distillation tower operating at atmospheric pressure and with a bottoms temperature of 370–400°C. This sidestream necessarily contains some lighter materials required to be removed by steam stripping. Up to 10% of the stream may be stripped and returned to the tower. If too much light material is left in the sidestream, kerosene will not meet the flash safety specifications. Since jet fuels boil within the kerosene cut-range, the two types of products are obtained from selected crudes in a blocked operation (see Fig. 1). The yield of kerosene in a refinery can be manipulated to as low a level as nothing and as high as 15–25% of crudes.

TABLE 3 Specifications for No. 1 Fuel Oil (ASTM D 396-79) [3]

Density at 15°C, maximum, g/cm^3	0.8495
Distillation point, °C:	
10%, maximum	215
90%, maximum	288
Flash point, minimum, °C	38
Pour point, maximum, °C	−18
Water and sediment, maximum, vol.%	0.05
Carbon residue on 10% bottom, maximum, %	0.15
Viscosity at 38°C, kinematic, mm^2/s (= cSt):	
Minimum	1.4
Maximum	2.2
Corrosion, copper strip, maximum number	3
Sulfur, maximum, wt.%	0.5

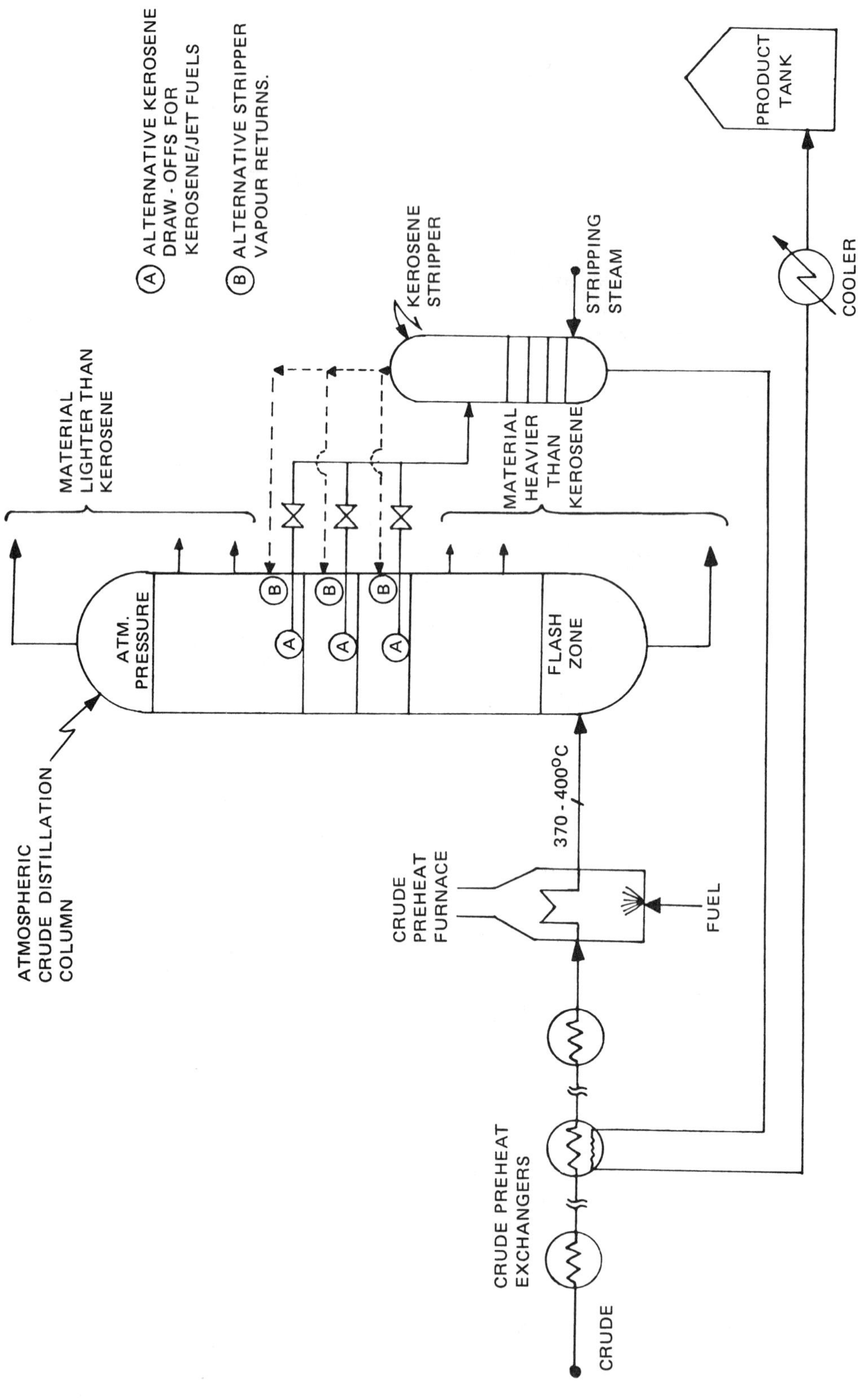

FIG. 1. Atmospheric distillation of crude: kerosene as a sidestream.

Application of hydrocracking for refinery product upgrading helps generate premium quality kerosene—low in sulfur and nitrogen. Typical yields for steam cracking of kerosene are given in Table 4.

Table 5 gives an idea of United States refinery yield and domestic deliveries as a percent of crude processed and petroleum products consumed.

Aromatics in Kerosene

Certain crudes, including most Indian crudes, yield kerosene with high aromatic materials. Middle East and the majority of United States crudes are low in aromatics. Although aromatics themselves are high valued products, their presence in kerosene is undesirable because of their smoky combustion behavior.

Identification of Aromatics

The analysis of kerosene (bp 150–250°C) by conventional gas chromatography is not suitable because of the wide temperature range. This fraction contains many individual hydrocarbons with different structures [6].

Aromatic hydrocarbons are separated from saturated hydrocarbons by adsorption chromatography and fluorescent indicator adsorption.

Vacuum rectification of kerosene on a column with 20 theoretical plates separates two narrower fraction (bp 150–200 and 200–250°C). Qualitative determination of the composition of the 150–200°C fraction is carried out on a squalene capillary column at 110°C and of the 200–250°C fraction at 130°C after prior separation of the paraffinic and cycloparaffinic compounds from the aromatic hydrocarbons. Stuckey [7] described a rapid method using gas chromatography in two stages which gave excellent separation of saturated and aromatic hydrocarbons on 1,2,3-tris(2-cyanoethoxypropane) and the separation of the aromatic hydrocarbons achieved on Silicon DC-550.

Removal of Aromatics

The removal of aromatics from kerosene can be accomplished by the conventional SO_2 extraction process. However, removal can be improved by using a C_6 light hydrocarbon reflux and through closer attention to design and operational aspects. The process can be simulated on a computer by developing a rigorous method for handling multistage multicomponent extraction calculations.

The Edeleanu Process is based on the higher solubility that liquid SO_2 exhibits for aromatic hydrocarbons in comparison with its solubility for paraffins and naphthenes.

Kerosene feed is initially dried and cooled to extraction temperature by heat exchange with a raffinate solution before it passes from the extractor to a

TABLE 4 Typical Yield for a Steam Cracker with Kerosene Feed [4]

Product	%
Hydrogen	0.62
Methane	11.52
Acetylene	0.14
Ethylene	23.02
Ethane	4.76
Propadiene	0.32
Propylene	14.83
Propane	0.56
1,3-Butadiene	4.43
Butene	1.80
Isobutene	1.73
n-Butane	0.05
Isobutane	0.16
Cyclopentene	1.51
Pentadiene	0.99
Cyclopentane	0.11
Pentene	1.88
Pentane	0.35
Hexane:	
To 93°C	16.05
>93°C	15.17
H_2S + C from CO	0.22

regeneration system in which SO_2 is boiled off The extract solution from the bottom of the column passes to a second regeneration system. The SO_2 recovered from both the extract and raffinate streams is collected and recycled back to the top of the extractor (see Fig. 2). The limits of aromatic concentration in the extract at various operating temperatures for typical feed-stocks are given in Fig. 3 [8]. At the usual operating temperatures, 20–30 vol.% of paraffins and naphthenes is lost in the extract, thus reducing the yield of kerosene.

TABLE 5 United States Refinery Yields and Domestic Deliveries of Kerosene (1979 estimates) [5]

	10^6 m^3 [a]	%
Refinery yields	10.7	1.2 of crude processed
Domestic deliveries	11.0	1.0 of petroleum products consumed

[a]To convert m^3 to bbl, multiply by 6.29.

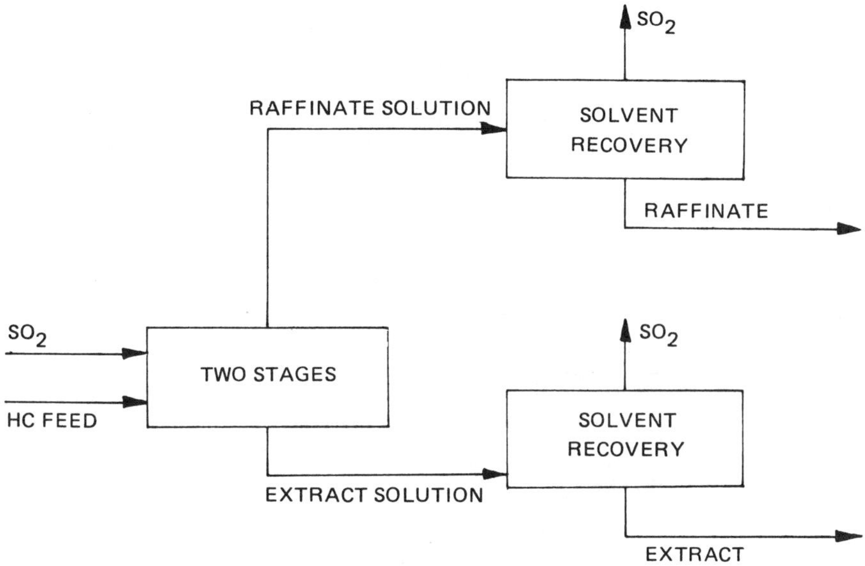

FIG. 2. The conventional SO_2 extraction process for treating kerosene removes the aromatics with the extract stream.

The modified scheme is presented in Fig. 4. The hydrocarbons constituting the reflux stream will displace the saturates (paraffins/naphthenes of the kerosene range) present in the extract solution. Thus, the loss of paraffinic/naphthenic hydrocarbons of the kerosene range is minimized and an extract richer in aromatics is produced.

To estimate the success of the extraction operation, it is important to predict the liquid–liquid equilibria. For this purpose, the multicomponent

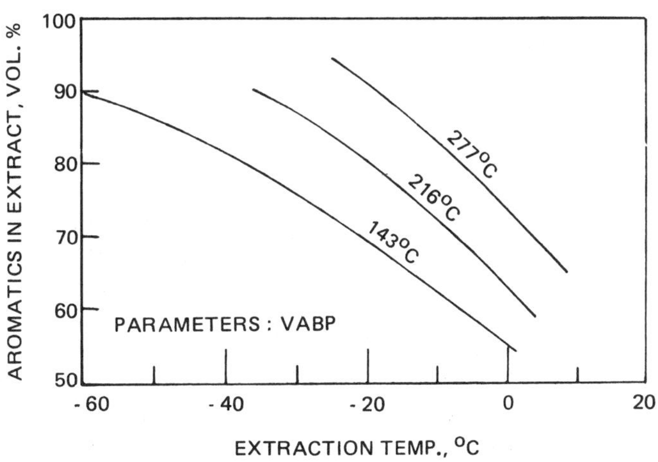

FIG. 3. Lower extraction temperatures give a higher aromatic concentration in the extract.

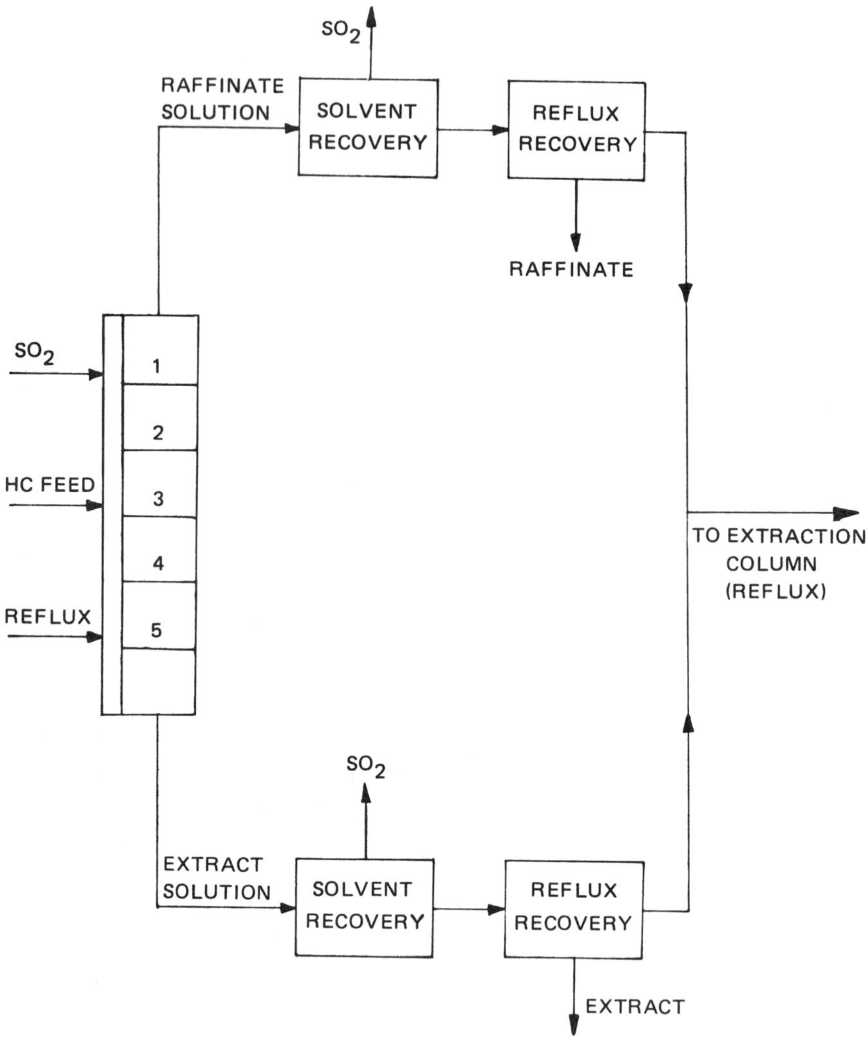

FIG. 4. Incorporation of a recycle stream increases the yield of treated kerosene for a given quality.

liquid equilibrium model developed by Black and Hartwig [9] and adopted by Hutton [10] is used. It is possible to estimate the equilibrium data for any ternary system comprising aromatic–paraffin–SO_2 by using corrections based on the carbon number and Z number (hydrogen deficiency) of the hydrocarbons. The Z number is defined as $Z = \mathrm{H} - 2\mathrm{C}$, where, H and C are number of hydrogen and carbon atoms, respectively, in the hydrocarbon molecule.

In one experiment [11], the feed was chosen as the 140–240°C kerosene fraction of Nahorkatiya-Moran crude. This had an aromatic content of 40.6 wt.% and a smoke point of 14 mm. The extraction temperature was taken as −10°C. By increasing the reflux ratio from 0.5 to 1.5, the aromatic content of the extract increased form 94 to 99.8%.

TABLE 6 Comparison of Conventional and Modified Kerosene Extraction Processes [11]

	Conventional		Modified
Number of ideal stages	2	2	5
Rates, mol/h:			
Feed	1.0	1.0	1.0
Solvent	3.5	5.0	9.0
Reflux	—	—	1.0
Yields, wt.%:			
Raffinate	44.33	44.53	65.68
Extract	55.67	55.47	34.32
Aromatics, content, wt.%			
Raffinate	11.72	7.27	10.33
Extract	63.60	67.36	98.55

As shown in Table 6, the modified process gives a yield of 66% as compared to 45% in the conventional extraction process for the comparable quality of raffinate. The extract of the modified process is more valuable as a feedstock for making petrochemicals, since solvents will be richer in aromatics.

Comparison with Wide Cuts and Aviation Gasoline [12]

From the fuel standpoint, kerosene is compared with wide cuts and aviation gasoline for properties related to aircraft operation and safety. The most widely used types of wide cuts are NATO F-40 typified by CGSB 3-GP-22h and ASTM D1655 Jet B and NATO F-34 typified by CGSB 3-GP-23h and ASTM D1655 Jet A and Jet A-1.

Volatility Characteristics

The three main volatility factors relating to flammability are flash point, vapor pressure, and distillation. These are compared in Table 7. Aviation gasoline is the most volatile, wide-cut fuel less volatile, and kerosene the least volatile of the three fuels. The flash point of kerosene fuels can be used as an indication of the maximum temperature for safe handling. This property is not particularly meaningful for wide-cut fuels or aviation gasoline.

Ignition

For kerosene, the minimum energy requirement is 0.2 mJ, which occurs with a mixture of 100–150 mg of hydrocarbon/L of air. The ignition energy at 50°F required to ignite wide-cut fuel is about 1.3 mJ whereas 18 mJ is required to

TABLE 7 Comparative Volatility Characteristics of Kerosene as an Aviation Fuel[a] [12]

Properties	Wide cuts	Kerosene	Aviation Gasoline
Distillation:			
Initial boiling point, °F	(142)	(131)	(108)[b]
10% recovered, °F	(216)	400 max	167 min
20% recovered, °F	290 max	(382)	—
40% recovered, °F	—	—	167 max
50% recovered, °F	370 max	450 max	221 min
90% recovered, °F	470 max	(473)	275 min
Final boiling point, °F	(456)	550	338 max
Flash point, °F	(below 0)	105 min[c]	(below −40)
Reid vapor pressure, lb:			
Minimum	2.0[d]	(0.1)	5.5
Maximum	3.0	(0.2)	7.0

[a]Figures in parentheses are typical values.
[b]Aviation gasoline distillation as percent evaporated.
[c]3-GP-23, flash point, 103°F minimum.
[d]Minimum RVP, no requirement in ASTM Jet B, optional in 3-GP-22 h.

ignite kerosene. The extra energy required for kerosene mists or sprays is related to the need to provide energy to vaporize its less volatile droplets. Energy requirements for ignition vary from a minimum of 0.2 mJ under ideal vapor conditions to 30 or 40 mJ for a kerosene spray at 0°F. This small amount of energy is readily available through sparks caused by poor electrical connections, improper grounding, faulty switches or relays, broken electrical wires, or from friction sparks under crash landing conditions.

Fuel Effect on Aircraft Operation

Fluidity characteristics of aviation fuels are given in Table 8. Aviation gasoline and wide-cut fuels have better low temperature properties than kerosene.

TABLE 8 Comparative Fluidity Characteristics of Kerosene as an Aviation Fuel[a] [12]

Property	Wide cuts	Kerosene	Aviation Gasoline
Freezing point, °F max	−72[b]	−58[c]	−72
Viscosity, cSt at −30°F	(2.2–3.43)[d]	15 max (5.3–13.5)[e]	(1.18–1.40)[f]

[a]Figures in parentheses are typical values.
[b]Jet B freezing point is −58°F, which is also optional for 3-GP-22 h.
[c]Jet A-1 freezing point. Jet A calls for −40°F.
[d]Range of four values presented in Ref. 13.
[e]Range of 63 samples presented in Ref. 13 with an average of 9.38.
[f]Data from Ref. 14.

TABLE 9 Comparative Inherent Cleanliness Properties of Kerosene as an Aviation Fuel[a] [12]

Property	Wide cuts	Kerosene	Aviation Gasoline
Specific Gravity, 60/60°F	0.751–0.802	0.775–0.840, 15 max	(0.705)
Viscosity, cSt at −30°F,	(2.2–3.43)	(5.3–13.5)	(1.18–1.40),
WSIM[b]	75 min[c] (80–95)	75 min[c] (80–95)	not used
Water reaction interface rating, max	1 b	1 b	1 b

[a]Figures in parentheses are typical value.
[b]Water Separation Index Modified (WSIM).
[c]Specification requirement in 3-GP-22 h and 23 h ASTM D1655 does not have a WSIM requirement for either Jet B or Jet A-1. Values in parentheses are considered typical for fuels purchased under any of the specifications.

Contamination of fuel by undissolved water causes fuel filter and transfer valve freezing, resulting in fuel starvation. The inherent cleanliness properties of fuels are compared in Table 9, and the specification requirements for contaminant control in Table 10.

Other Operational Considerations

For aircraft maintenance purposes, kerosene is favored over wide-cut fuel because fuel tank purging to reduce the air/vapor mixture to below the lean inflammability limit is more easily accomplished. Carbon buildup on engine components is greater with kerosene than with wide-cut fuel, and with certain

TABLE 10 Comparative Specification Requirements for Contaminant Control

Property	Wide cut	Kerosene
Total solids:[b]		
Delivery to aircraft	2 mg/IG max (<1 mg/IG)	2 mg/IG max (<1 mg/IG)
Delivery to bulk storage	10 mg/IG max	10 mg/IG max
Undissolved water, ppm	(30 max)[c]	(30 max)[c]
Fuel system icing inhibitor, vol.%	0.10–0.15[d]	–

[a]Figure in parentheses are typical values.
[b]Specification requirement in 3-GP-22 h and 23 h. No requirement in ASTM D1655 for either Jet B or Jet A-1, but most airlines use limits of 1–4 mg/gal.
[c]Not a specification requirement, 30 ppm max is the general accepted level.
[d]Optional in 3-GP-22 and 23. A general additive clause in the ASTM specification would permit its use.

TABLE 11 Relative Hazard Associated with Product Switching during Aircraft Fueling [12]

	Product in Aircraft Tank[b]	Product Being Loaded[a] Wide Cut	Wide Cut Plus ASA-350	Kerosene	Kerosene Plus ASA-350
(a)	Wide cut	H	M	H	M
(b)	Wide cut plus ASA-350	H	M	H	M
(c)	Kerosene	H	M	M	L
(d)	Kerosene plus ASA-350	H	M	M	L
(e)	Combination wide cut and kerosene[b]	H	M	H	M
(f)	Combination wide cut and kerosene plus ASA-350	H	M	H	M

[a]Relative hazard. Low (L): Tank vapors nonflammable and low charge levels on entering fuel. Medium (M): Either tank vapors are nonflammable or charge on entering fuel is reduced to a low level. High (H): Flammable tank vapors and high charge levels on entering fuel.
[b]The fuel in an aircraft tank should not be considered to be of one type until three successive fuelings of the same type of product have occurred or the aircraft tank has been drained and one fueling with the desired product has occurred. If absolute assurance is required, a sample of the product from the aircraft tank must be sent to a laboratory for analysis.

sensitive engines this may lead to increased maintenance requirements. The higher volatility of wide-cut fuel also increases its ability to relight in flight compared with kerosene. A gallon of kerosene contains about 3–4% more Btu's than a gallon of wide-cut fuel, while a pound of wide-cut fuel contains, on the average, 0.5% more Btu's than a pound of kerosene.

The relative hazards associated with product switching during aircraft fueling are shown in Table 11.

Kerosene reduces the overall fire hazard in a potentially survivable crash compared to wide-cut gasoline [12].

Evaporation Characteristics of Spraying in Air Streams

The design of premix-prevaporization combustors is hampered by lack of knowledge on the rate of evaporation of kerosene fuel sprays when they are injected into a flowing air stream, spray parameters such as mean drop size (SMD), and drop size distribution and air-flow properties such as pressure, temperature, and velocity, all of which influence the overall rate of spray evaporation [15].

One of the earliest experimental studies on spray evaporation, carried out by Sacks [16], determined the evaporation rate of kerosene issuing from a 0.0228 flow number swirl atomizer into a slowly moving air stream flowing inside a 54-mm diameter tube. A schematic diagram of the test installation is shown in Fig. 5. A rotary blower supplied air to a turbojet combustor.

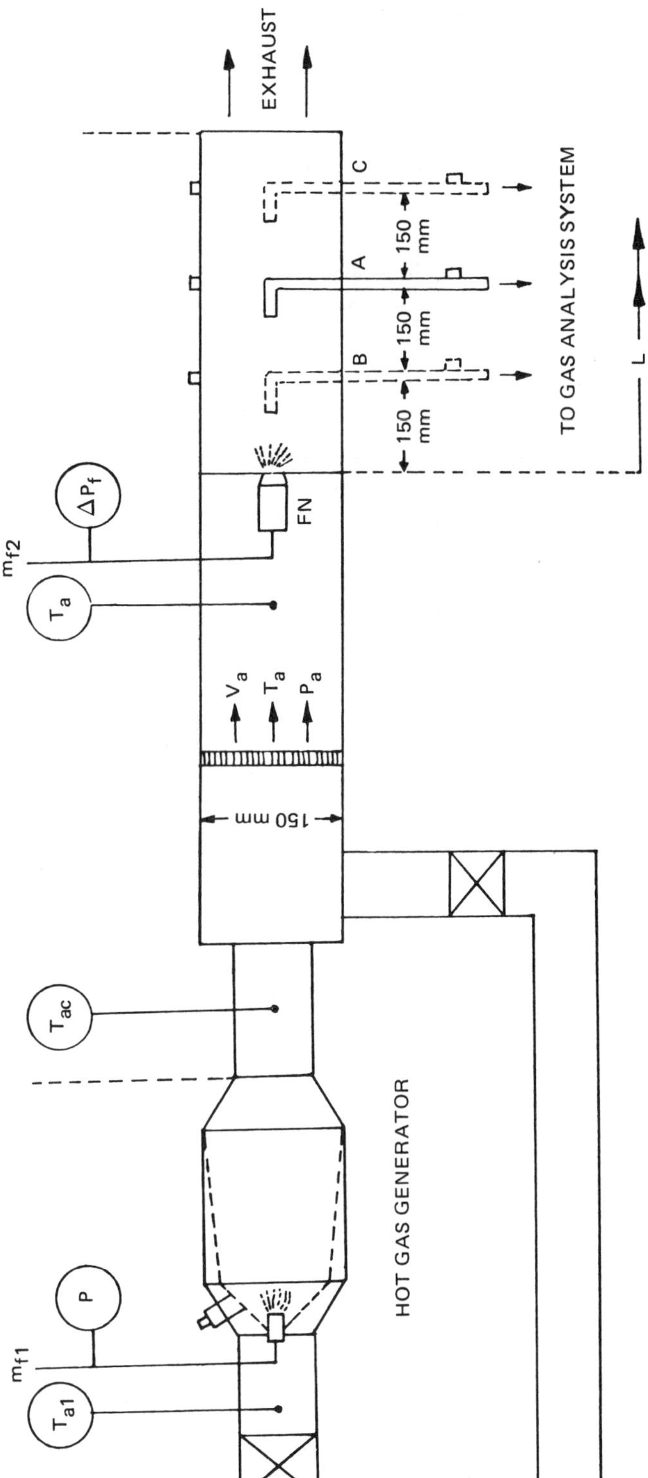

FIG. 5. Schematic layout of the test installation: spray evaporation.

Aviation kerosene, supplied to specification D.ENG.R.D. 2494 (specific gravity = 0.795), was injected into the flowing air stream through a number of interchangeable pressure atomizers.

Effect of Air Temperature

An increase in air temperature raises spray evaporation rates considerably at all velocities. The evaporation rate increases almost linearly with temperature from 288 to 428 K. At higher temperatures the effect is less marked.

Effect of Air Velocity

An increase in air velocity also increases the evaporation rate, although the effect is much less pronounced than that of temperature. Moreover, an increase in air velocity increases the relative velocity between the air and the fuel, which in turn increases the heat transfer rate. Both a reduction in spray drop size and an increase in heat transfer rate tend to promote spray evaporation.

Effect of Axial Distance from the Fuel Injector

An increase in axial distance from the atomizer increases the spray residence time, which in turn enhances spray evaporation.

Effect of Atomizer Fuel Injector Pressure

One effect of an increase in fuel pressure is to reduce the mean drop size and thereby increase the fuel surface area and hence the spray evaporation rate quite considerably.

Effect of Atomizer Flow Number

For a given fuel flow, an increase in the flow number reduces the evaporation rate due to a fall in fuel injection pressure and hence of the fuel surface area.

Correlation of Spray Evaporation

The parameter $N/(100 - N)$ correlates well with the following empirical relationship, as shown in Fig. 6.

$$\frac{N}{(100 - N)} = 3.37 \times 10^{-6}\left[\frac{T_a}{1000}\right]^{4.32}\left[\frac{V_a}{100}\right]^{1.71}[\Delta P_f]^{0.56}[FN]^{-4.32}[L]^{1.57}$$

The above expression is similar to that derived by Bahr [17].

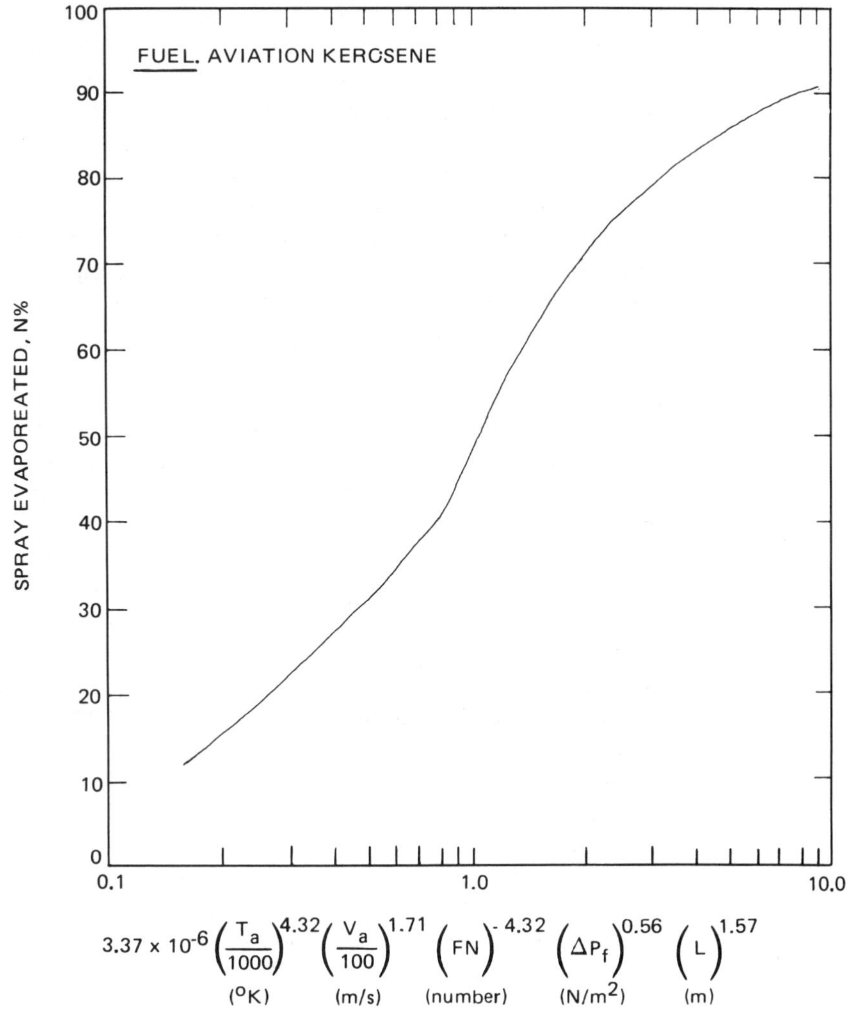

FIG. 6. Correlation of percentage fuel spray evaporated in a constant area duct for aviation kerosene injected from a swirl atomizer.

The rate of evaporation of aviation kerosene sprays injected from swirl-type pressure atomizers into air flowing in a constant area duct is given to a reasonable order of accuracy by the relationship. Thus, spray evaporation rates increase with increases in air velocity, air temperature, fuel injection pressure, and axial distance from the injector, and with a reduction in atomizer flow number. The most significant factors influencing spray evaporation are air temperature and mean drop size.

Ignition Energy Requirements

Measurements of minimum ignition energy [15] must be obtained under controlled conditions of fuel–air ratio, fuel drop size, and fuel velocity.

Ignition performance is improved by an increase in spark energy. The only experimental study that satisfies these conditions is due to Subba Rao and Lefebvre [18]. Their experiments were conducted using capacitance spark of 100 μs duration. However, more recent work by Ballal and Lefebvre [19] has shown that the optimum spark duration varies appreciably with operating conditions, and that for all measurements of minimum ignition energy, the optimum spark duration must first be ascertained. Minimum ignition energy is defined as the total electrical energy dissipated from the weakest spark that will ignite a flammable mixture when the spark gap is set at the quenching distance and the spark duration is the optimum value.

The apparatus employed is shown schematically in Fig. 7. It is fitted with glass side walls in order to allow the ignition process to be visually observed and photographed. Aviation kerosene, suppled to specification D.ENG.R.D. 2494, is sprayed coaxially in the direction of the air stream through interchangeable atomizers fitted on the pipe-axis upstream of the convergent entry duct. Fuel injection pressure is measured on a gauge mounted close to the atomizer. Spark energies are measured by connecting two probes to the electrode tips and feeding their output into a two-channel oscilloscope.

This type of electrode is adopted and used in all subsequent measurements of minimum ignition energy. Drop sizes are measured over the entire range of air and fuel flows.

The total amount of energy liberated in a spark discharge is of importance to ignition. In any given mixture of strength and flow conditions there is one particular value of spark duration for which the rate of energy release is an optimum for ignition. It follows that the smallest amount of energy required to effect ignition at the optimum spark duration must represent the true minimum ignition energy.

Ignition energies are measured for various spark durations at two different levels of mean drop size (SMD) under constant conditions of air velocity and fuel–air ratio. Figure 8 shows that optimum spark duration (t_{sopt}) increases with an increase in SMD. In a liquid fuel–air mixture flowing at atmospheric pressure and temperature, the most important parameters affecting $E_{\min}$ are SMD, air velocity, and fuel–air ratio. An increase in air velocity increases $E_{\min}$. Spark energy is only effective in overcoming the adverse effects of an increase in velocity when the spray drop size is small.

Analysis of the data obtained in this investigation suggests that the most effective method of increasing the rate of fuel evaporation is by improved atomization, but in mixtures weaker than stoichiometric, an increase in fuel–air ratio is also beneficial. At higher levels of spark energy, a smaller proportion of fuel–air appears in a form which contributes to fuel evaporation.

Combustion System

An atmospheric pressure combustion system burning kerosene fuel in a simple baffle-swirler with an aerodynamic flow pattern was evaluated over a wide range of air flows and with a limited amount of air preheat [20].

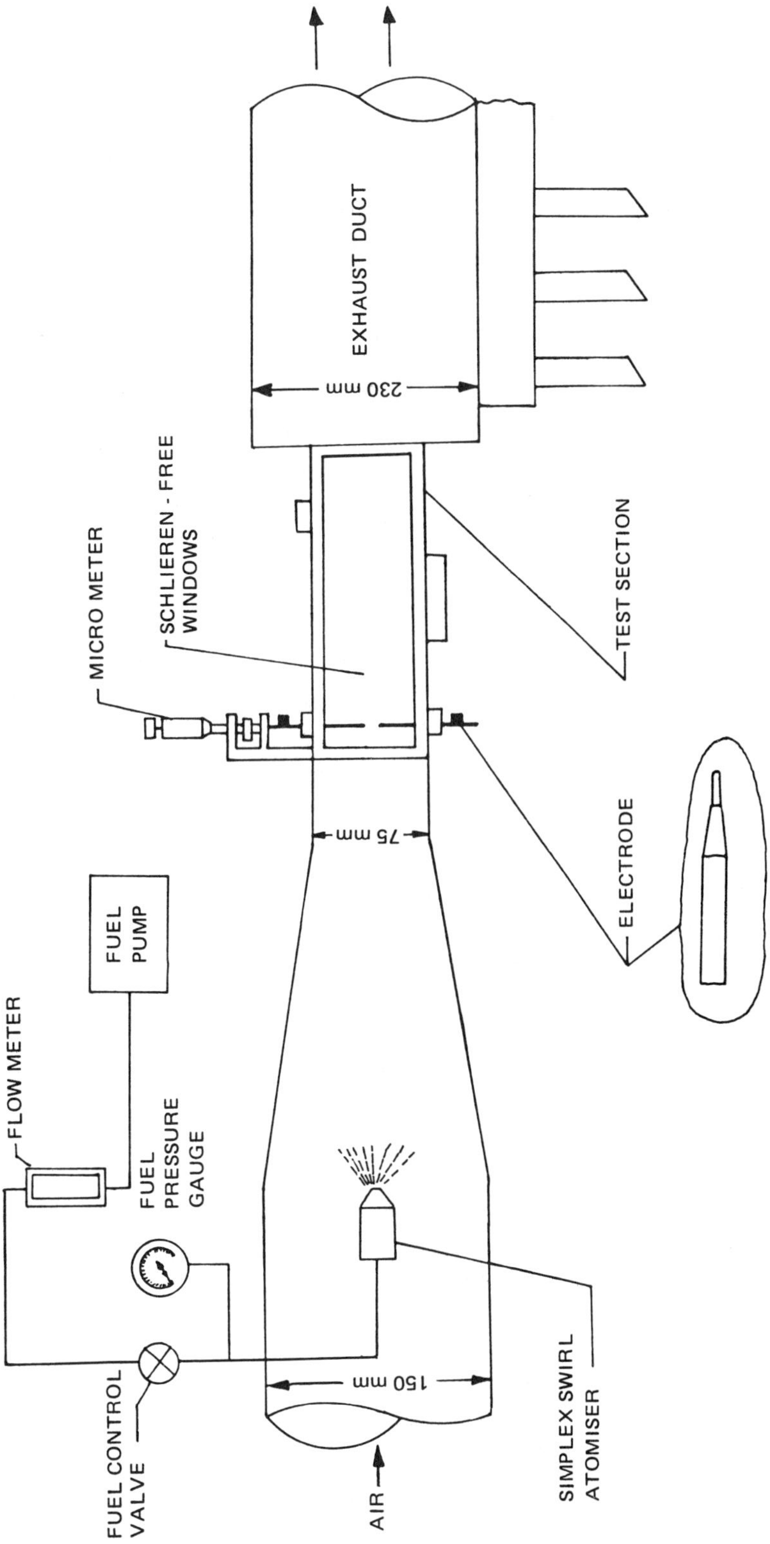

FIG. 7. Schematic diagram of experimental setup: ignition energy requirements.

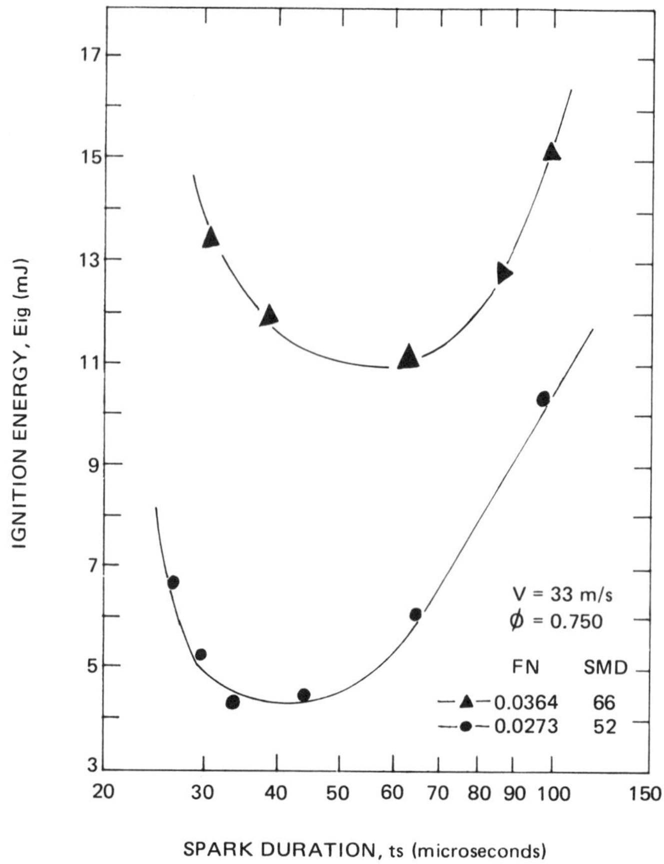

FIG. 8. Measurements of ignition energy at various values of spark duration.

Combustion Aerodynamics

The design of a combustor is based on an idealized flow model in which a three-dimensional, parallel, uniform flow is superimposed upon a system of ring vortices to give a spherical stagnation stream line enclosing a ring vortex. To obtain higher thermal loadings and shorter flame lengths than were possible with any simple combustor, the "baffle-swirler" design was devised.

The layout of the baffle-swirler combustor is shown in Fig. 9. This combustor has an annular air swirler to increase vortex strength behind the baffle and to supply additional air directly into the burning zone. A wider and more closely controlled spray cone angle and a loose stainless steel radiation liner was set around the main combustion section to protect the walls against the higher temperature anticipated.

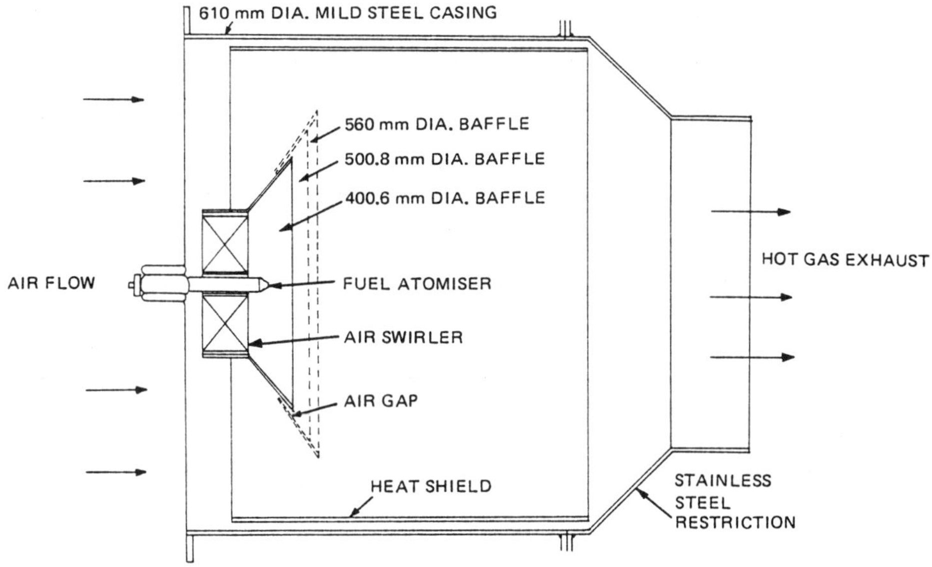

FIG. 9. Layout of baffle-swirler combustor for kerosene.

Combustion Efficiencies

Losses due to unburnt hydrocarbons were very low at both entry temperatures (315 and 425 K) even at low fuel air ratios (0.46 to 3.3 kg/s), except at the lowest air flows. The increasing unburnt hydrocarbon levels at weak mixtures for 0.46 kg/s and 315 K suggest that some fuel has in fact penetrated the recirculation zone and the impinged fuel is unable to evaporate and subsequently burn. Generally, however, the trend under normal conditions is for unburnt fuel losses to diminish with increasing heat release.

Because of the consistently high combustion efficiency and the absence of any marked deterioration in combustion intensity as the air throughput is increased, it has not been possible to assign any clear limit of operation to this type of combustor except possibly that set by excessive flame length at high temperature rise conditions of peak combustion intensity as the percentage pressure drop is increased.

To maintain high combustion efficiency in this type of aerodynamic flow system, correct fuel atomization and placement are essential.

Long-Term Biodegradability

The biodegradability of textile chemicals by conventional biology treatment systems is of vital concern to the textile industry because most waste treatment plants depend on biological respiration for the generation of sludge and ultimate removal of organic contamination from the waste stream. A particu-

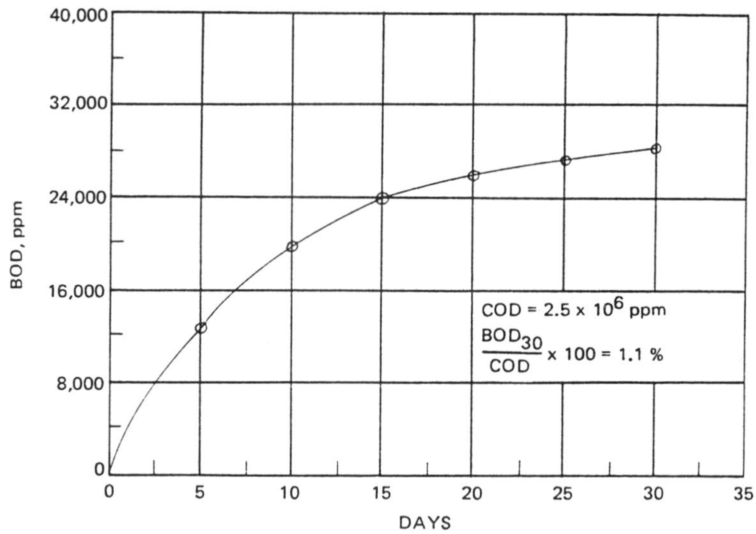

FIG. 10. Biodegradation of textile chemical kerosene.

lar textile chemical does not have to be biodegradable to be removed by a biological treatment plant [21].

Biodegradation of Kerosene as a Textile Chemical

The data presented for kerosene are taken from a 30-d sampling period. Biochemical oxygen demand (BOD) studies compared with the chemical oxygen demand (COD) of the sample are shown in Fig. 10. This compound is very resistant to biodegradation, using only 1.1% of its total COD in 30 days. Over 95% of kerosene seems to remain unchanged after incubation with an active biomass for 30 days. This stability is illustrated by the detectable odor of kerosene in fish taken from streams where kerosene has been discharged. When kerosene is treated in a biological waste treatment plant, a large portion of the solvent may be removed by evaporation. Both the sun and weather conditions influence the quantity of solvent removed. The sludge also removes solvent by adsorption and gravity. Both of these processes may remove the kerosene from the waste. If the waste contains large fractions of solvents, it is better to optimize the physical treatment system which treats 95% of the kerosene rather than the biological system which only treats 1 to 5% of the solvent. The biological process is complex and sensitive to pH, temperature, loading, and many chemicals.

Supply–Demand

The price of kerosene is inelastic. The demand for kerosene is also inelastic, whether it is used as a principal fuel and illuminant in developing countries or as a jet fuel in industrialized countries. There are few substitutes for kerosene for either use because of its relatively low cost.

Posted kerosene prices are given in Table 12, and the United States supply/demand picture is shown in Table 13.

TABLE 12 Comparative Product Prices (United States cents per United States gallon of kerosene) [22]

	Exxon, Aruba, 7/3/80	Shell, Curacao, 31/3/80	Shell, Pulau Bukom, Singapore, 12/2/80	Shell, Bandar, Mahshahr, 26/2/80	Caltex, Bahrain, 19/5/80
Average turbine kerosene	—	—	96.0	105.5	99.5
Kerosene	103.0[a]	103.5[b]	96.7[c]	100.5[c]	98.8[b]
	—	—	95.7[b]	99[b]	—

[a]Dual purpose.
[b]Regular.
[c]Premium.

TABLE 13 United States Supply/Demand Picture (supply-demand in thousands of barrels per day) [23]

	July 1980	July 1981	Percent Change
Kerosene jet fuel	36,100	36,963	+2.39
Kerosene	14,750	13,146	−10.87

Symbols

K	constant
SMD	mean drop size (μm)
t_s	spark duration
T_{sopt}	optimum spark duration
E_{ig}	minimum ignition energy, with $t_s = t_{sopt}$ (mJ)
ϕ	equivalence ratio
V	air velocity
FN	atomizer flow number ((L/h)(N/m)$^{0.5}$)
L	axial distance downstream of fuel injector (m)
N	percentage of spray evaporated
P	pressure (N/m^2)
T	temperature (°K)
ΔP_f	atomizer pressure drop (N/m^2)
ΔT	temperature difference between drop and air (°K)

Subscript

a	air
f	fuel

The author appreciates the suggestions received from Mr V. K. Garg, Technical Assistant, Tecnagement Consultant, New Bombay, India.

References

1. *Basic Petroleum Data Book*, API Refining Department, Washington, D.C., 1980.
2. *Oil Gas Journal*, p. 99 (March 29, 1976).
3. *Annual Book of ASTM Standards*, American Society for Testing and Materials, Philadelphia, Pennsylvania, 1980, Parts 23, 24, and 29.
4. *Oil Gas Journal*, p. 106 (April 17, 1968).
5. *Petroleum Statement, Monthly: Crude Petroleum, Petroleum-Products, and Natural Gas Liquids*, December 1979, DOE/EIA-0109 (79/12), U.S. Department of Energy, Washington, D.C., May 5, 1980.
6. D. I. Papazova and M. C. Pankova, *State Economic Corporation "Neftochim,"* Science and Research Institute, Bourgas, Bulgaria.
7. C. L. Stuckey, *J. Chromatogr. Sci*., *9*, 575 (1971).
8. W. F. Wilkinson, J. R. Ghublikian, and P. Obergfell, "The SO_2 Extraction Process for Aromatic Recovery," *Chem. Eng. Prog.*, *49*(5), 257–262 (1953).
9. C. Black and G. M. Hartwig, *Chem. Eng. Prog. Symp. Ser.*, *81*(63), 65 (1967); *88*(64), 66 (1968).
10. A. E. Hutton and C. D. Holand, "Use of Field Tests in the Modeling of a Liquid–Liquid Extraction Column," *Chem. Eng. Sci.*, *26*, 919–936 (1972).
11. S. J. Chopra and P. K. Mukhopadhyay, *Hydrocarbon Process*., February 1978.
12. R. B. Whyte and L. Gardner, Fuels and Lubricants Laboratory, Division of Mechanical Engineering, National Research Council of Canada, Ottawa, Ontario, Canada, K1A 0R6.
13. *Aviation Fuels, 1963, Petroleum Products Survey, No. 34*, U.S. Department of Interior, Bureau of Mines, April 1964.
14. M. Smith, *Aviation Fuels*, Foules, Ottawa, Canada, 1971.
15. K. V. L. Rao and A. H. Lefebvre, *Combust. Flame*, *26*, 303–309 (1976).
16. W. Sacks, *The Rate of Evaporation of a Kerosene Spray*, Note 7, National Aeronautic Establishment of Canada, 1951.
17. W. Bahr, *Evaporation and Spreading of Iso-octane Sprays in High Velocity Airstreams*, NACARM.E. 53 I 14 (November 1953).
18. H. N. Subba Rao and A. H. Lefebvre, "Ignition of Kerosene Fuel Sprays in a Flowing Air Stream," *Combust. Sci. Technol*., *8*, 95–100 (1973).
19. D. R. Ballal and A. H. Lefebvre "The Influence of Spark Discharge Characteristics on Minimum Ignition Energy in Flowing Gases," *Combust. Flame*, *24*, 99–108 (1975).
20. G. F. Pearce, A.R.L. Mechanical Engineering Notes, Library of Maraven, S.A., Venezuela.
21. J. J. Porter and E. H. Snider, *J. Water Pollut. Control Fed.*, *48*(9) (1976).
22. *Petroleum Economist*, June 1980.
23. *The Oil Daily (New York)*, July 22, 1981.

OM P. GOYAL

Liquefied (Cryogenic) Gases

In the absence of a precise terminology, let us adopt this arbitrary definition of "cryogenic gases": A cryogenic gas is one that can be liquefied or solidified only at temperatures below −100°F. The five gases covered in this article all fall into this class: oxygen, which boils at −297°F under atmospheric pressure; nitrogen (−320°F); carbon dioxide (sublimes at −109°F); argon (−303°F); hydrogen (−423°F). Table 1 lists boiling point and other properties for these gases.

What is special about handling these five cryogenic gases in the plant? The greatest peculiarity is that these gases are often supplied and stored as cryogenic liquids, and require special designs, equipment, and materials to handle them safely. Oxygen and hydrogen are special cases, in that one fiercely promotes combustion and the other is highly flammable. Thus the safety concerns for these two gases are compounded.

This article addresses four key areas: specification, storage, handling in the liquid state, and handling in the gaseous state. Some decisions in these areas may be outside an engineer's control, but it is important to understand what the options are, how the choices are made, and where the potential hazards lie. In any case, it is recommended that for any application of these gases, a competent supplier or consultant be involved in technical decisions.

Specifying Cryogenic Gases

Before handling any cryogenic gas, the engineer has to decide: What purity? In what volume? Gas or liquid state? Supplied how? Here is a look at these choices, and some guidelines for how to specify a cryogenic gas.

Purity Requirements

Commercial-grade liquefied industrial gases are pure enough for most chemical-process-industries applications, but there are instances when higher purity is required. For example, a catalyst used to react nitrogen with another gas may be sensitive to low concentrations of oxygen.

Minimum purity specifications are recommended by the Compressed Gas Association (a United States trade association). Typically, the purity of gases as-shipped is better than these specifications show, but the as-stored purity may be reduced if there is any contamination during transfer into the storage facility. (As-stored purity should still be at or above specifications.)

How Volume Affects Supply Options

The volume and peak demand of gas required for a particular application influence the mode of supply.

TABLE 1 Key Properties of Air, O_2, N_2, Ar, H_2, and CO_2

	Air	Oxygen	Nitrogen	Argon	Hydrogen	Carbon Dioxide
Molecular weight	28.96	32.00	28.01	39.95	2.02	44.01
Color/odor	None	None	None	None	None	Pungent
Specific gravity (air = 1)	1	1.11	0.97	1.38	0.070	1.53
Density, lb/ft^3 (70°F, 1 atm)	0.075	0.083	0.072	0.103	0.0052	0.114
Boiling point, °F (normal, 1 atm)	−317.9	−297.3	−320.4	−302.6	−423.0	−109.3[a]
Heat of vaporization, Btu/lb	88.3	91.7	85.6	70.1	191.7	296.6[a]
Critical pressure, atm	NA	50.1	73.5	48.3	13.0	72.9
Critical temperature, °F	NA	−181.1	−232.4	−188.1	−400.0	87.9
Heat capacity, C_p	0.24	0.22	0.25	0.12	3.42	0.20
Viscosity, μP (77°F)	184.7	206.4	178.0	226.4	89.4	15.0
Thermal conductivity, Btu/h·ft^2·°F (32°F)	0.0139	0.0142	0.0139	0.0098	0.0973	0.0085

[a]Carbon dioxide sublimes rather than boils.

Monthly consumption has the greatest effect. A user who needs only 5000 std ft^3 of oxygen* per month is better off with compressed-gas cylinders, while a user who needs 5 million std ft^3 per month should consider liquid or pipeline supply.

Demand patterns include seasonal fluctuations—usually predictable—and variations in loading caused by plant startup or shutdown. Peak loads are not always apparent, though. For example: If nitrogen is used to blanket the vapors in a storage tank, there is a considerable increase in demand at sunset. Why? As the tank cools down, nitrogen flows into the headspace to maintain storage pressure. The rate depends on the cooling rate of the vapors in the tank. Here, the difference between minimum and maximum nitrogen demand is considerable and perhaps unexpected.

Security of supply or storage capacity. The quantity of gas that should be held in storage depends on the reliability of supply., If the gas is shipped on request from a gas producer's facilities, storage should allow for reorder leadtime—two to five days' supply is usually enough.

In addition to these factors, the engineer must decide whether the gas should be supplied in gaseous or liquid form. If the gas is to be used as a coolant (for example, carbon dioxide in a food-freezing application), it should be supplied as a liquid because both the low temperature and the latent heat of vaporization can be put to use. If the end use requires a gaseous state, the gas can be supplied either as a gas or a liquid. When supplied as a liquid, it will, of course, have to be vaporized before use.

Delivery Options

Here are the six most common modes of supplying cryogenic gases, and guidelines for when each is likely to be most practical.

Compressed-gas cylinders are best for small-volume (or one-time) applications, such as pilot-plant testing. As a rough guideline, users who need less than 50,000 std ft^3 of gas per month should check out compressed-gas cylinders. The standard cylinder has a capacity of about 270 std ft^3 at a cylinder pressure of 2265 lb/in.^{2}gauge, but other cylinder sizes are available. In the case of carbon dioxide, the 1800-lb/in.^{2}gauge standard cylinder holds 50 lb (437 std ft^3). The cost of gas in cylinders is rather high per unit volume, and is usually based on a price per cylinder consumed plus a rental fee for the cylinders themselves.

Liquefied-gas cylinders (commonly known as liquid cylinders) are portable, vacuum-insulated cryogenic containers for liquid oxygen, nitrogen, and argon. These require less handling than gas cylinders (because they are larger) and less capital investment than bulk-liquid stations. Thus they bridge the gap between these two delivery options, and should be considered for applications to 100,000 std ft^3 per month. Liquid cylinders can deliver either gas or liquid at pressures to 230 lb/in.^{2}gauge, but normal operation is at about 125 lb/in.^{2}gauge. The capacities of these vessels range from 3630 std ft^3 for nitrogen to 4500 std ft^3 for oxygen. As with compressed-gas cylinders, users pay for the number of cylinders used plus a rental fee for cylinders held on-site.

*Standard conditions for gas are 70°F, 1 atm.

Compressed-gas trailers are often called tube trailers. These trailers have capacities up to 125,000 std ft^3. Such trailers supply gas at pressures to 2640 lb/in.^{2}gauge—thus the gas can be used for applications such as high-pressure purging or autoclave pressurization. In most cases, tube trailers are delivered full and remain on-site as storage vessels until empty. This requires a large standing area with clear access—a typical tube trailer is 23 ft long. The cost of the gas is based on the amount delivered, plus a rental—or demurrage—fee for the trailer. In most cases, nitrogen tube trailers are not specified for permanent facilities unless the application requires the high pressure.

Bulk liquefied gas is the most common delivery option after compressed-gas cylinders. Liquefied gas can be delivered by road in trailers with capacities to 4500 gal, or in railcars with capacities to 17,000 gal. Storage is on-site in a vessel specially designed for the gas (which we will describe later). Typically vessels hold 500–11,000 gal of liquefied gas at pressures to 250 lb/in.^{2}gauge; vessels that provide only liquid operate at only 25–75 lb/in.^{2}gauge, to reduce vapor losses. Table 2 shows how to convert lb to gal to std ft^3 for gases as stored as liquids.

Gas suppliers usually provide storage tanks (plus vaporizers and other equipment if needed), and charge a monthly rental and maintenance fee. Because of this cost, a bulk liquid supply is usually considered economical only when usage is 50,000 std ft^3 per month or more.

On-site cryogenic production. Oxygen and nitrogen can be produced in on-site air-separation units, which are economical if volumes are at least 8 million std ft^3/mo for nitrogen or 15 million std ft^3/mo for oxygen. These, units may be owned by either the user or the supplier. If the unit is supplier-owned, the contract is usually a take-or-pay arrangement, where a monthly fee provides a specified amount of gas—used or not—over a contract period of 7–15 years.

Pipeline supply grids link several users with a centralized separation plant or plants. Examples of such grids are: a complex around Baton Rouge, Louisiana (H_2, N_2, O_2); one at the Houston Ship Channel (N_2, O_2); and one in Teesside, UK (N_2, O_2). Pipeline supply, like supplier-owned on-site production, is usually on a take-or-pay basis.

TABLE 2 Volume of Gas per Unit Weight and Volume of Liquid

	Liquid Weight		Gas Volume		Liquid Volume	
	lb	kg	std ft^3 [a]	Nm^3 [b]	gal	L
Oxygen	1.0	0.454	12.08	0.317	0.105	0.398
Nitrogen	1.0	0.454	13.80	0.363	0.148	0.561
Argon	1.0	0.454	9.67	0.254	0.086	0.326
Hydrogen	1.0	0.454	192.0	5.047	1.693	6.408
Carbon dioxide	1.0	0.454	8.74	0.229	0.118	0.447

[a]Measured at 1 atm and 70°F.
[b]Normal cubic meter, measured at 1 atm and 0°C.

Storing Cryogenic Gases

Having decided on a particular supply option, the user needs to store the gas and deliver it to its point of use in the plant. This section covers storage vessels and related equipment, except for compressed-gas cylinders (see Refs. 1 and 2 for information on cylinder handling). In general, the gas supplier will be responsible for the storage and supply system—including vaporizers, regulators, and strainers. But the user needs to know how these devices work, where potential hazards lie, and how these hazards can be minimized.

Storage Tanks for N_2, O_2, and Ar

Storage vessels for these three atmospheric gases are essentially identical, except for special fittings on the fill lines that allow only the desired gas to be pumped in. These tanks are designed for the extremely low temperatures and resulting high volatility of liquefied gases. Vertical and horizontal tanks are available.

Cryogenic storage tanks are typically installed on reinforced-concrete pads, and require low-voltage power plus steam or hot water if a heating medium is needed for vaporization. Pressure regulators usually do not require plant or instrument air, because these regulators normally use the stored gas itself. This saves one utility, and also assures that instrument lines do not freeze up due to wet air. Cryogenic tanks are protected with both safety valves and bursting disks [3, 4] which are designed to relieve tank pressure even if the tank is heated quickly by a surrounding fire.

Figure 1(a) shows a schematic view of a cryogenic tank, with all of the valving and piping. The vessel is like a large vacuum flash in that it has two shells, with a partial vacuum between them. The inner shell conforms to Section VIII (Div. 1) of the ASME Boiler & Pressure Vessel Code—internal working pressure is usually 100–175 lb/in.^{2}gauge—and is made of a nonembrittling alloy such as nickel steel, 304 stainless steel, or an aluminum alloy. The outer shell is carbon steel, with no ASME Code stamp because external design pressure is less than 15 lb/in.^{2}gauge.

The space between the shells is filled with insulation, usually a form of perlite (expanded volcanic ash), and evacuated to 10–100 mmHg. (Evacuated perlite is much less conductive than common insulation materials. Its thermal conductivity is about 90×10^{-5} Btu/h·ft^2·°F, compared with about 2400×10^{-5} for foamglass and 1000×10^{-5} for polyurethane foam.) To ensure that the inner cold does not embrittle the carbon-steel outer jacket, the piping that exits from the outer shell is usually 306 or 315 stainless steel. This steel is also used for the piping between the shells.

How Cryogenic Tanks Operate

Figures 1(b), 1(c), and 1(d) break up the piping and valving of Fig. 1(a) into three key systems: filling, pressurizing, and economizing. Let us look at each of these individually to see how the liquefied gas is stored and held in storage.

Filling. A storage tank usually holds liquid at 100–175 lb/in.^{2}gauge. Maintaining the plant's supply of high-pressure liquid while the tank is being filled requires a dual-filling technique.

Figure 1(b) shows how liquefied gas is pumped from the transport vessel

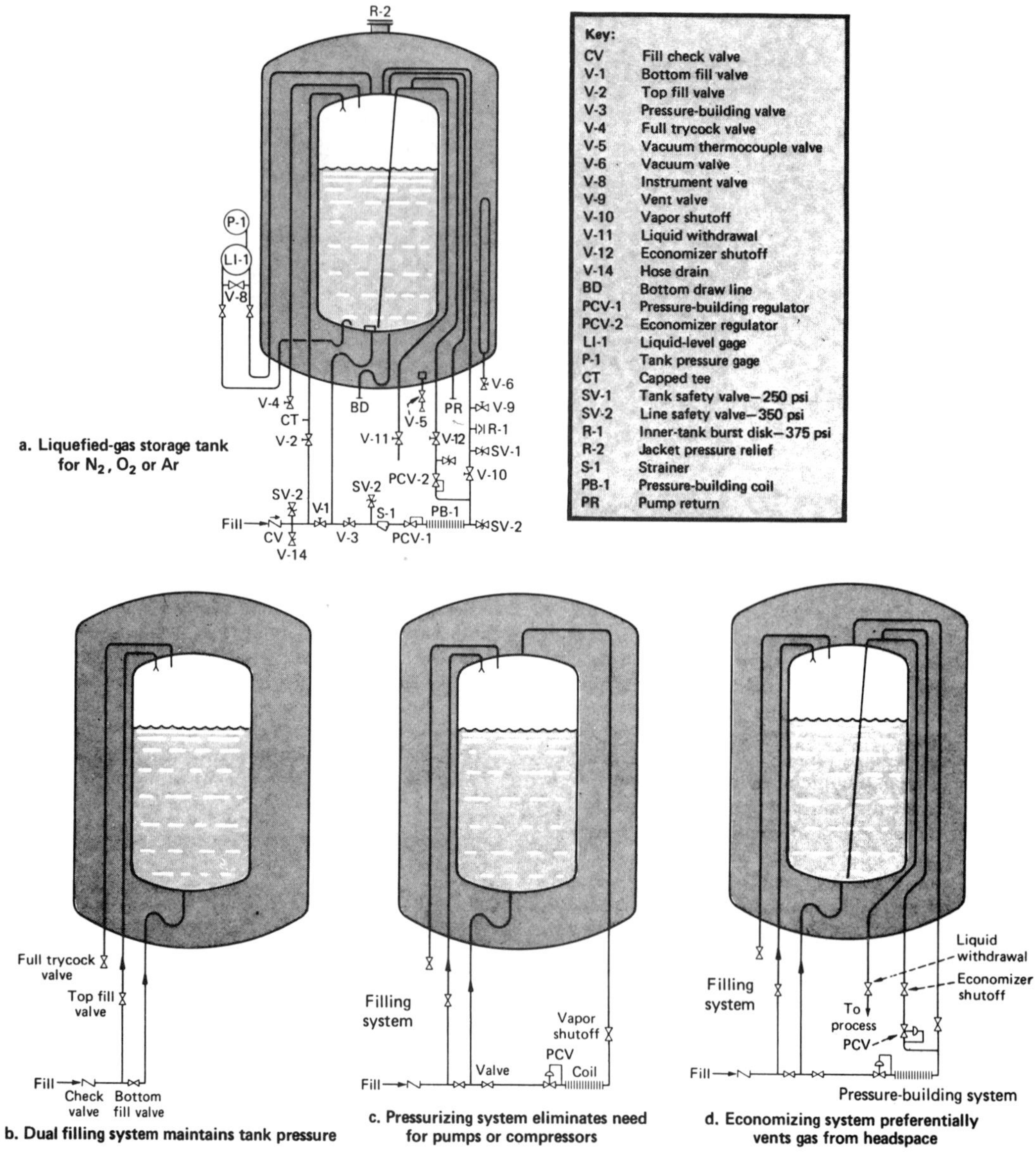

FIG. 1. Storage tank and component parts.

into the tank through a check valve, then through two valves into both the top and bottom of the tank. Why? If liquefied gas were pumped into the bottom only, the headspace in the tank would be compressed, and eventually tank pressure would rise and open a relief valve. This would waste some of the gas. On the other hand, pumping liquid into the top of the vessel only would condense some of the headspace vapors, reducing the tank pressure below normal and affecting plant supply. With dual filling, tank pressure stays normal. When the tank nears capacity, the person loading the tank opens the trycock valve, in a 1/4-in. line, to allow a bit of liquid to exit. When liquid starts to come out of the valve, filling is stopped. This leaves about 5–10% headspace in the tank.

Pressurizing. Figure 1(c) shows the automatic pressurizing system, which provides an output pressure to 250 lb/in.^{2}gauge from a standard tank without a pump or compressor. When the tank pressure falls below the desired output pressure, the regulator opens, and hydrostatic head forces liquid through a valve to the pressure-building coil. Here the liquid is vaporized and returned to the headspace of the tank, causing a pressure buildup. High-pressure liquid can then be delivered through the diptube and the liquid-withdrawal valve in Fig. 1(d).

Economizing. Heat leaking into the storage tank vaporizes some of the liquid, which could cause a loss of gas to the atmosphere through the pressure-relief system. To minimize this loss, cryogenic tanks include an economizing system, as shown in Fig. 1(d). The backpressure control valve (regulator) is set to open when tank pressure rises slightly above the desired pressure. This breaks the liquid siphon on the diptube and causes gas to leave the tank via the liquid-withdrawal valve until tank pressure returns to normal operating limits. The system saves by preferentially taking gas from the top rather than liquid from the bottom of the tank. In typical operation, a tank equipped with an economizer will not vent any gas for 3–5 days of no demand. Once the tank reaches the venting pressure, normal evaporation loss is about 0.3% of the liquid content per day if there is still no process demand.

Storage Receiver for Carbon Dioxide

Carbon dioxide is stored as a liquid at a temperature of 0°F and a pressure of 295–305 lb/in.^{2}gauge. Its typical storage vessel is a skidmounted horizontal tank, which is usually installed complete with valves and a small compressor. The vessel (Fig. 2) is carbon steel (ASME Code design), wrapped with polyurethane foam and covered by a metal or vinyl jacket.

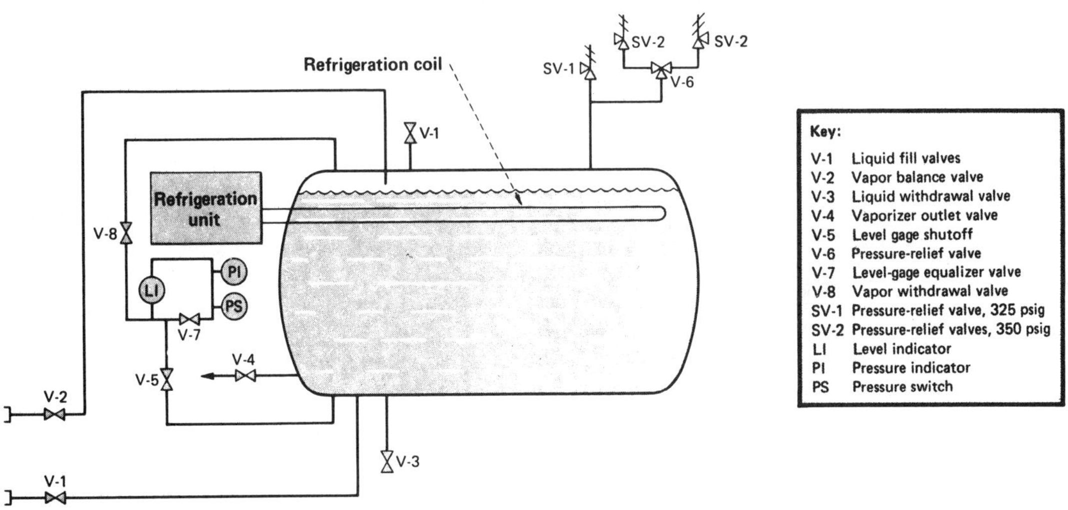

FIG. 2. Carbon-dioxide storage receiver is a complete, skidmounted package.

Unlike atmospheric-gas storage systems, carbon-dioxide storage receivers are designed never to vent—except via the relief system in an emergency. An air-cooled refrigeration unit (using Freon 12 or 22) automatically cools the tank's contents when the pressure rises to 300 lb/in.^{2}gauge. When the pressure drops back to 280 lb/in.^{2}gauge, the cooling automatically stops.

A pressurizing system, similar to that described for atmospheric-gas storage tanks, maintains tank pressure during carbon-dioxide withdrawal. This system is very important because a significant drop in pressure would lower the temperature of the tank contents and create a risk of embrittling the carbon-steel vessel wall.

Carbon-dioxide storage vessels are filled, using a vapor-return system, via valves V1 and V2 in Fig. 2. The relief valves on the tank are set at 325 and 350 lb/in.^{2}gauge, with two valves at 350 lb/in.^{2}gauge for extra safety. Standard carbon-dioxide receivers range in size from 4 to 60 tons capacity. A typical 30-ton receiver has a 3–5-hp compressor that pulls about 6 A of 440 V power. Other utilities are required for the vaporizer system: steam, cold water, or additional electric power, depending on the method of vaporization used.

Hydrogen Storage Tanks

Delivery and storage of liquid hydrogen is essentially the same as for oxygen, nitrogen, and argon. But there are differences because the boiling point of hydrogen is so low: more insulation and stainless-steel vacuum-insulated hoses for transferring hydrogen from the transport vessel to the tank. These measures prevent excessive vaporization.

Liquid-hydrogen tanks operate at pressure of 100–120 lb/in.^{2}gauge (lower than other liquid tanks), again to prevent excessive vapor loss. This pressure range also ensures that the hydrogen does not reach its critical pressure (191 lb/in.^{2}gauge). It is important to prevent air from ever contacting liquid hydrogen, because air will liquefy if it contacts the hydrogen, creating an explosion hazard because the condensed air may be oxygen-enriched.

Location of Liquid Storage Tanks

The guidelines for tank location depend on the particular gas to be stored. However, it is generally recommended that storage facilities be located outdoors, because indoor accumulations of any cryogenic gas may lead to such hazards as fire, explosion, or asphyxiation. Any leakage—particularly of liquid—will result in cold gas that can creep and accumulate in low spots, such as trenches, drains, or underground work areas. Storage of oxygen and hydrogen involves greater hazards, so their locations are more critical.

Liquid oxygen. Oxygen is not flammable, but it supports combustion. More importantly, it supports combustion more strongly than air does. Atmospheres with more than 21% oxygen lower the ignition temperatures of air-flammable materials, and may cause combustion of materials not normally flammable in air. Thus, liquid-oxygen storage vessels must be located well away from flammable materials and sources of ignition.

Figure 3 illustrates the recommended minimum separation between people, roads, various materials, and a bulk-liquid-oxygen storage tank [12]. When it is not possible to achieve the recommended distances, a firewall should be installed. This wall must be designed to protect the uninsulated portions of the tank, associated pipework, and controls. It should be high enough to block the line of sight between the oxygen tank and a hazardous exposure—a building, a storage tank, or a pipe with flammable contents.

Liquid hydrogen. Hydrogen storage facilities should be located only in open spaces, because hydrogen/air mixtures in confined spaces could explode. Any protective barrier or firewall should be a single wall—not ever a 360° enclosure—and diversion trenches should be used to prevent hydrogen spills from carrying to possible ignition sources nearby. Any flammable materials near the tank should be contained in nonflammable enclosures with water (spray or deluge) protection.

All electrical equipment should conform to Class I, Group B or Groups C and D (National Electrical Manufacturers' Association classification) when completely sealed, and pressurized with inert gas or dry air. All metal parts on

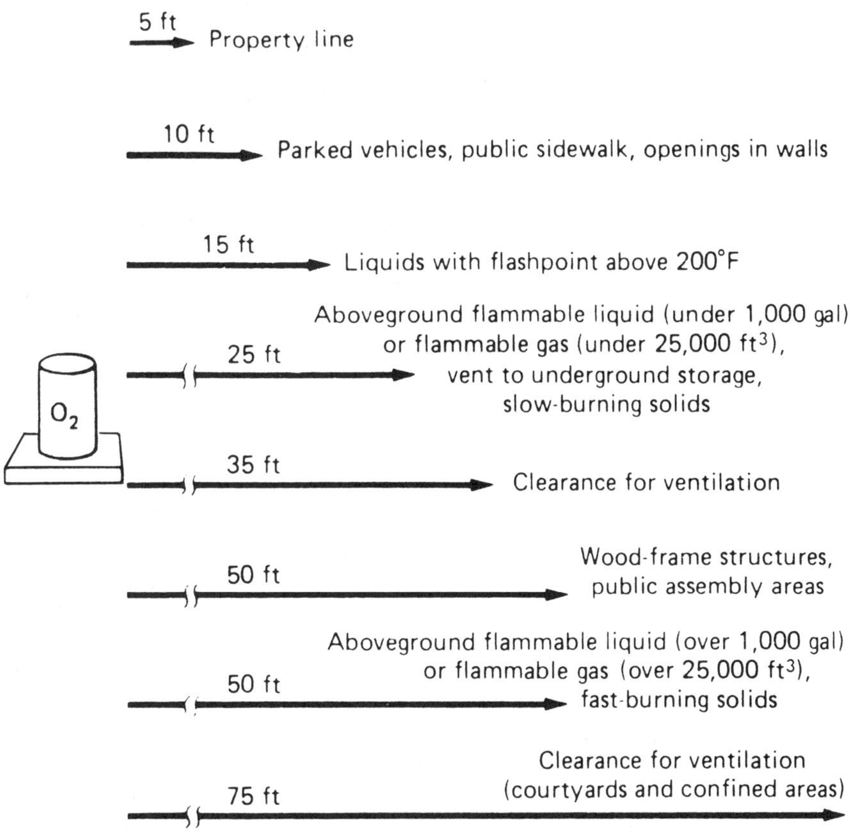

FIG. 3. Minimum recommended distance from liquid-oxygen storage tank.

operating machines, conduits, and controls should be grounded. More-detailed specifications for liquid hydrogen storage can be found in a National Fire Protection Association (NFPA) publication [6].

Vaporization

When a plant has an application for the cold temperature and latent heat capacity of a cryogenic gas, the gas may be removed from storage in the liquid state and vaporized as part of a cooling step—this is discussed later in this article. Cryogenic gases are usually used in the gaseous state, requiring some means of vaporization.

Ambient-air vaporizers pass the liquefied gas through finned tubes, usually constructed of aluminum or 304 stainless steel with extruded-aluminum fins. Natural convection of ambient air heats and vaporizes the gas at an operating pressure up to 450 lb/in.^{2}gauge. The standard unit is rated at 5000 std ft^3/h, based on 70°F ambient temperature and 70% relative humidity in 8-h continuous duty. The vaporizer should be conservatively sized for winter conditions, because condensing moisture from the air can freeze on the tubes, reducing their heat-transfer capability to about 55% of nominal capacity (in the northern United States). For duties greater than 5000 std ft^3/h, two or more vaporizers may be installed in parallel.

Other vaporizer designs are available for applications where ambient-air vaporizers are inadequate: Forced-draft, heated-air forced-draft, and water-deluge vaporizers provide greater heat input per unit transfer area. If vaporization demand is still higher, higher-temperature heat sources may be necessary. For example: Water at 50°F is sufficient for vaporizing carbon dioxide, but an electrical heater is usually used, as its heat can also be applied to pressure building.

How much energy does it take to vaporize cryogenic gases? Table 3 shows the energy required to produce 10,000 std ft^3/h of 70°F gas for the five gases discussed in this article.

TABLE 3 Energy Required to Produce 10,000 std ft^3/h of 70°F Gas from Liquid

Gas	Delivered (Btu/h)	kW	Steam (lb/h)[a]	Air (std ft^3/min)[b]
Oxygen	142,000	41.6	133	14,200
Nitrogen	134,400	39.5	126	13,400
Argon	123,000	36.1	115	12,300
Hydrogen	89,000	26.4	84	8,900
Carbon dioxide	171,000	50.2	160	17,100

[a] 100 lb/in.^{2}gauge saturated steam with outlet temperature of 150°F.
[b] Temperature drop 10°F through vaporizer.

A special safety feature that should be part of every vaporizer system is a low-temperature cutoff switch. If vaporizer capacity is exceeded, or the heat source is lost, such a switch—installed downstream of the vaporizer—will close a valve in the liquid line. This prevents liquefied gas from entering the process lines (designed for gases), which could otherwise result in embrittlement and fracture,. The low-temperature switch is typically set at −20°F for an ambient-air vaporizer and 40°F for a steam vaporizer. It is designed to require manual resetting before the system can recommence gas supply.

Handling in the Liquid State

The five cryogenic gases present some similar hazards in the liquid state due to their low temperature and high volatility. Here is some general information about the hazards of oxygen, nitrogen, carbon dioxide, argon, and hydrogen, along with guidelines for how to protect personnel and equipment.

Worker Protection

The extreme cold of cryogenic liquids will cause "cold burns" when unprotected skin touches uninsulated pipes or surfaces. Immediate treatment is required—immersion of affected areas in 105–115°F water is the accepted first-aid procedure. Valves in liquid lines should have extended stems to prevent cold burns and to keep them from freezing.

Protective clothing should be worn when working around cryogenic liquids. These garments should include: insulated gloves made of leather, rubber, or asbestos; a face shield or goggles; loose-fitting clothing, with trouser bottoms outside the shoes so that no liquid can collect in them.

Piping Materials

Selection of correct piping materials is critical because cryogenic temperatures can cause brittle fatigue and lead to failure. This problem is most serious with ferrous metals. On the other hand, nonferrous metals such as copper and aluminum alloys, which are less susceptible to brittle fatigue, are more likely to fail in a fire than ferrous metals because of their relatively low melting points. If a pipe does melt down or fracture, the resulting leak can lead to a more serious fire if hydrogen or oxygen is released. In practice, nonferrous metals are used for most cryogenic-liquid applications. Table 4 shows the lowest temperatures at which various common materials resist embrittlement.

TABLE 4 Temperature Limits below Which Metals Can Embrittle

Material	Minimum Operating Temperature
Carbon steel	240 K (−28°F)
Aluminum-killed steel	220 K (−64°F)
2% Nickel steel	210 K (−82°F)
3% Nickel steel	170 K (−154°F)
9% Nickel steel	70 K (−373°F)
Monel, 18/8 stainless steel, copper, aluminum and alloys	<10 K (−442°F)

Liquid Transfer

If the cryogenic gas is to be used as a liquid, then it must be transferred from storage to end use in a liquid state. All such transfer piping should be insulated (for anything but very short pipe runs) because transfer of liquefied gas in uninsulated lines may vaporize substantial quantities of liquid.

In the case of liquid nitrogen, vacuum-jacketed piping should be considered for continuous-flow service over distances greater than 150 ft. Similarly, liquid hydrogen typically requires vacuum-jacketed lines because of its extremely low boiling point. For the "inert" cryogenic gases—nitrogen, carbon dioxide, and argon—polyurethane foam insulation is generally enough for short runs. Fluorocarbon foams are recommended for liquid-oxygen piping.

A potential hazard in liquefied-gas handling is caused by too-rapid cooldown during startup. Startup should be gradual, because the first liquid that hits the warm downstream piping will vaporize; pressure can build to dangerous levels if too much liquid vaporizes. For example, pressures to 600 lb/in.^{2}gauge can be generated from a 30-lb/in.^{2}gauge liquid-storage unit if warm lines are filled too quickly. Because of the potential for liquid-to-gas expansion, the liquid-handling system must have pressure-relief valves in runs where liquefied gas can be trapped; for example, between a shutoff valve and a control valve.

Pipe joints should not be soft-soldered; silver solder is recommended instead. When insulating any pipe network for liquid nitrogen, argon, or hydrogen, the insulation must be fitted airtight. As the boiling points in Table 1 show, these gases can condense air, causing an oxygen-rich liquid to accumulate in the insulation. This is a major fire hazard, and has been suspected as the cause of more than one explosion. If the insulation is applied tightly, it prevents the condensation of air.

Liquid Pumps

A pump is required if the liquid (or vaporized gas) is needed at a pressure higher than can be supplied by the storage tank (and vaporizer) alone. Generally, a positive-displacement or centrifugal pump should be used (centrifugal for high-flow, low-pressure). Liquid oxygen is the most difficult of the cryogenic gases to pump safely, since it is essential that no foreign matter contact the oxygen, and that clearances be maintained between impeller piston and pump body, and between motor and stator. Bronze and aluminum are the preferred material of construction for moving parts, while stainless steel and aluminum are preferred for pump bodies.

Handling in the Gaseous State

Nitrogen, argon, and carbon dioxide require no special handling except the standard considerations of pressure drop and flow control. We will cover their few peculiarities last in this article. Handling oxygen or hydrogen, however, presents specific hazards. These will now be discussed in much greater detail.

Oxygen

Oxygen gas poses a great potential hazard because it promotes combustion so vigorously. The following recommendations and data are a general outline of oxygen-handling techniques, not a comprehensive guide. The data, by the very nature of their measurement in the lab, are not exact. Thus each application for gaseous oxygen should be examined by qualified personnel to eliminate any potential hazards.

One item that deserves special mention is enriched air—air with more than the usual 21% oxygen. If an air stream has an oxygen content above 28–30% by volume, it supports ignition and combustion as oxygen would. Thus, enriched air with more than 28% oxygen should be treated in the same manner as pure oxygen.

Ignition temperatures and sources. Oxygen affects the flammability limits, ignition temperatures, and combustion rates of materials. Table 5 shows

TABLE 5 Oxygen Enhances the Combustion of Common Hydrocarbons

	Minimum for Ignition					
	Temperature (°F)		Energy (mJ)		Flammability Limits (% by vol.)	
Combustible	Air	O_2	Air	O_2	Air	O_2
Methane	999	—	0.30	0.003	5.0–15	5.1–61
n-Butane	550	532	0.25	0.009	1.8–8.4	1.8–49
n-Hexane	437	624	0.288	0.006	1.2–7.4	1.2–52
Acetone	869	—	1.15	0.002	2.6–13	2.6–60
Benzene	1040	—	0.22	—	1.3–7.9	1.3–30
Gasoline (100/130)	826	600	—	—	1.3–7.1	1.3
Trichloroethylene	788	745	—	18	10.5–41	7.5–91

how—for ignition and flammability limits of some common hydrocarbons. In these examples, oxygen substantially reduces ignition energy, but has little effect on minimum ignition temperature. (Ignition energy is the minimum spark energy that will cause ignition.) Oxygen also broadens the range of concentrations over which hydrocarbon mixtures will burn.

In addition to enhancing the combustion of normally flammable materials, oxygen atmospheres also enable some normally nonflammable materials to burn. Examples: carbon and stainless steels, cast iron, aluminum, zinc, and polytetrafluoroethylene (PTFE). Materials that will not ignite in solid form, not even in oxygen, include bronze, silver, nickel, asbestos, and copper—although copper in a finely divided form will ignite.

A source of ignition may include one or more of the following:

1. Direct heat from an open flame, cigarette, static or live electrical discharge, welding or cutting operations—in effect, any "normal" fire hazard.
2. A rupture in an oxygen line that left a piece of jagged metal exposed—the high velocity of oxygen escaping from such a rupture can ignite the edges of the metal. (This reinforces the need for adequate pressure relief in oxygen lines.)
3. Dynamic effects such as the movement of small particles in an oxygen pipe. At sufficient velocity, such particles can cause a spark with enough energy to ignite pipework or other system components.
4. Temperature rise due to adiabatic compression, which can be caused by rapid opening and closing of valves, by oscillating flows, or by sudden pressurization. Such an ignition mechanism is thought to be limited to high-pressure (6000 lb/in.^{2}gauge) oxygen systems, and should not be a problem when supply is directly from liquid storage.
5. Flammable materials—such as grease or paint—in the oxygen system will ignite inside the pipework or components.

Piping for oxygen gas. All possible ignition sources should be considered in the design of an oxygen piping system. The chosen design should depend first on safety, and only then on cost of materials and allowable pressure drop. Since fast-moving oxygen and particles can be an ignition source itself, there are maximum recommended velocities (actual ft/s) for oxygen in steel and aluminum piping. Figure 4 shows these velocities for oxygen at temperatures of 70°F or less. If the oxygen is warmer, then maximum velocities are lower. Copper and Monels have no specified velocity limits.

Routing oxygen pipe requires special precautions:

1. The possibility of mechanical damage (for example, from dropped construction materials) should be minimized.
2. Oxygen pipes should not pass underneath pipes or vessels that contain flammable liquids.
3. If lines containing flammable materials must be adjacent to the oxygen line at some point (for example, if all lines converge at a reactor entrance), the pipe joints or flanges should not be adjacent.

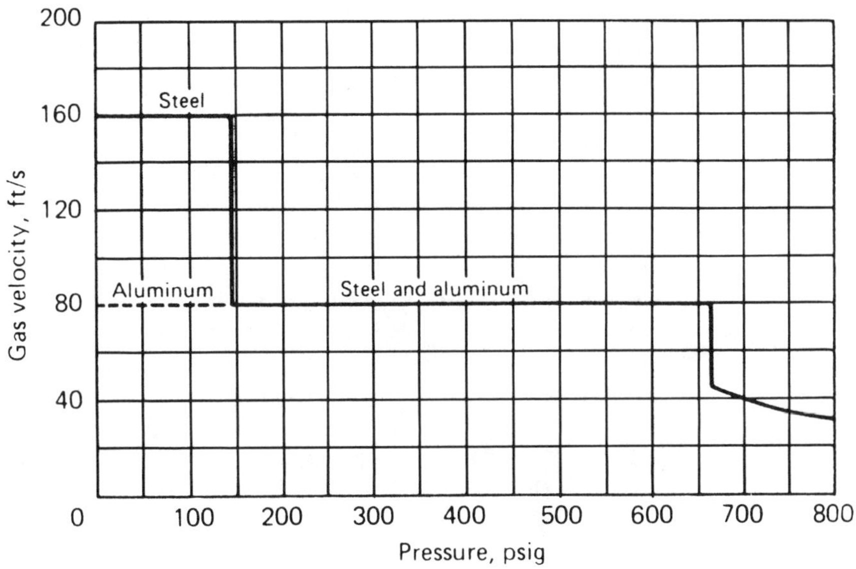

FIG. 4. Maximum allowable pipe velocities for 70°F dry oxygen.

4. Oxygen lines should be identified clearly: either color coded or marked to show gas and direction of flow.
5. Oxygen lines should be routed at least 2 in. from electrical cable and conduit.
6. All oxygen pipe should be bonded to the ground unless the pipe is cathodically protected. (Cathodic protection will not work if the pipe is grounded).

If it is necessary to put oxygen pipe underground, it should be buried at least 4 ft deep and rest in stone-free loose earth or sand. No flammable fluid should run in the same trench. If the line must run underneath a roadway or other heavy-traffic area, a pipe-within-a-pipe system is recommended. The outer pipe in this case needs to be vented. For all underground oxygen pipe, the location should be clearly indicated aboveground. No valves should be located underground.

Materials of construction for oxygen gas. Underground joints should be welded, brazed, or silver-soldered, not flanged. In all oxygen pipe, under- and aboveground, pipe-jointing compounds should be avoided if possible. The few sealants considered suitable for oxygen lines are fluorinated hydrocarbons, such as PTFE. Gasket materials acceptable for oxygen service are PTFE, Teflon (TFE) polychlorotrifluoroethylene (PCTFE), and polyimide filled with 15% graphite. Compressed-asbestos fiber with a PTFE binder can also be used. In choosing a gasket, some allowance must be made for cold flow (in TFE, for example) to ensure leak-tight joints, but care must also be taken to make sure that no gasket material protrudes into the oxygen stream, as this could cause ignition.

All of these materials are limited to certain temperature and pressure ranges, and it is essential that the material chosen be compatible with the specific service. For example: In an application where oxygen is injected into a hot gas stream (900°F), the oxygen line at the injection point should be made of a high-ignition-temperature metal such as an Inconel or Hastelloy.

No hydrocarbon oil or grease should *ever* be used on oxygen components. If some lubricant must be used, then fully fluorinated hydrocarbons based on chlorotrifluoroethylene and perchloroethers are acceptable.

Materials for the moving components in oxygen systems must meet stricter requirements than piping materials. Control valves, regulators, and other flow-impeding devices are subjected to a greater degree of turbulence and higher velocities as oxygen flows through their various restrictions. For oxygen valves, the choice of materials depends on the operating pressure. Above 2500 $lb/in.^2$gauge, copper-based alloys or Monel should be used for body and trim. Below 2500 $lb/in.^2$gauge, stainless-steel components can be used if velocities are low enough. Valve seats may be pure PTFE, but reinforced PTFE reduces cold-flow problems. In specific applications, other fluorocarbons and polyimide/graphite compounds can also be acceptable seat materials—factors that affect this choice are oxygen temperature and pressure, as well as the mechanical strength of the particular elastomer. Packings are generally PTFE.

Instruments, too, must conform to specifications for oxygen service. Pressure gauges must be marked "Oxygen—use no oil" and should be tested only with clean water or oil-free air. No particular materials are required for oxygen instruments, but orifice plates should be made of brass or bronze.

Cleaning oxygen systems. All instruments and other oxygen components must be kept clean to operate safely. Because cleanliness is so important, three levels are specified [7].

Class A: For materials in contact with impure oxygen (enriched air below 28% O_2) and for components in process branch lines that contain other gases, such as nitrogen.

Class AA: For fixed surfaces in contact with pure oxygen, including orifice plates and pipes.

Class AAA: For moving surfaces in contact with pure oxygen. This most stringent requirement covers components such as pressure regulators and flow-control valves.

The purpose of cleaning is to remove potential ignition sources and flammable materials from areas where they may contact oxygen; this means removing particulate matter, fibers, condensible hydrocarbons, and solvent-soluble organic residues. The basic steps are: clean with an agent such as trichloroethylene or an H_3PO_4/HF mixture, rinse away the cleaning agent, inspect to assure cleanliness, dry out the system.

When installing an oxygen system, there is usually a choice between purchasing all components precleaned or cleaning some of the components *in situ* after installation. Generally, components other than piping should be precleaned, marked as such, and sealed in plastic bags until installation. But piping may be purchased precleaned or cleaned *in situ* by pumping a variety of solvents through the system and monitoring the cleanliness of the exiting solvents.

There are pros and cons to either approach. Precleaning is easier and more easily inspected, but contaminants could enter the system during assembly. *In situ* cleaning removes any such contamination, but the work is difficult to inspect, branched systems are hard to clean thoroughly, and solvents could possibly be retained in low points of the system. In practice, the choice of methods depends on the particular system and work environment. After installation, whether or not the equipment has been cleaned *in situ*, the oxygen-handling system should be pressure tested and purged with oil-free, dry nitrogen.

Overall oxygen-system safety. After the safety of the oxygen-handling system itself is assured, the safety of the overall plant and process must also be considered. The key step: an automatic, reliable oxygen-shutdown system. Such a system ensures that no oxygen enters the process during shutdown or purge, eliminating possible fire or explosion hazards. As an example of why such a system must be automatic and carefully designed, consider this situation: Suppose that oxygen is being used to enrich an air stream for an oxidation reactor. The air is supplied by a blower, which is also used without enrichment to purge the oxidation chamber during shutdown. Here are some hazards that could be built into such a system, and ways of avoiding them.

1. If oxygen flow is coupled only to air flow, an enriched-air purge (instead of the expected air purge) will enter the oxidation chamber after shutdown. Contact of this oxygen-rich stream with hot metal components could lead to a fire. This situation can be avoided by coupling oxygen flow to the process and to the air flow.
2. If the oxygen shutoff system can be tripped only by failure of the air-blower motor, then oxygen flow could continue without any air flow for a short time if the link between blower and motor fails. Such a situation is more hazardous than the last, because pure oxygen will now enter the oxidation chamber. The problem can be avoided by linking oxygen shutoff to both the air flow (via a pressure switch or a differential-pressure cell) and the blower motor.
3. Instant shutoff of oxygen flow may be hazardous, since it creates a fuel-rich atmosphere in the oxidation chamber. Apart from emergency shutoff, oxygen flow should be reduced gradually to keep fuel from escaping unreacted out of the oxidation chamber.
4. If the oxygen supply is shut off automatically, the oxygen that remains in the piping can constitute a hazard if it empties into the process stream. Avoiding this problem requires special venting or valving.

Figure 5 illustrates the interlocks and safety features in an oxygen line that has a nitrogen purge system. Note the double-block-and-bleed arrangement of the shutoff valves. This is essential because it provides a positive shutoff, not only instantaneously but over a prolonged period of time. At the oxygen-

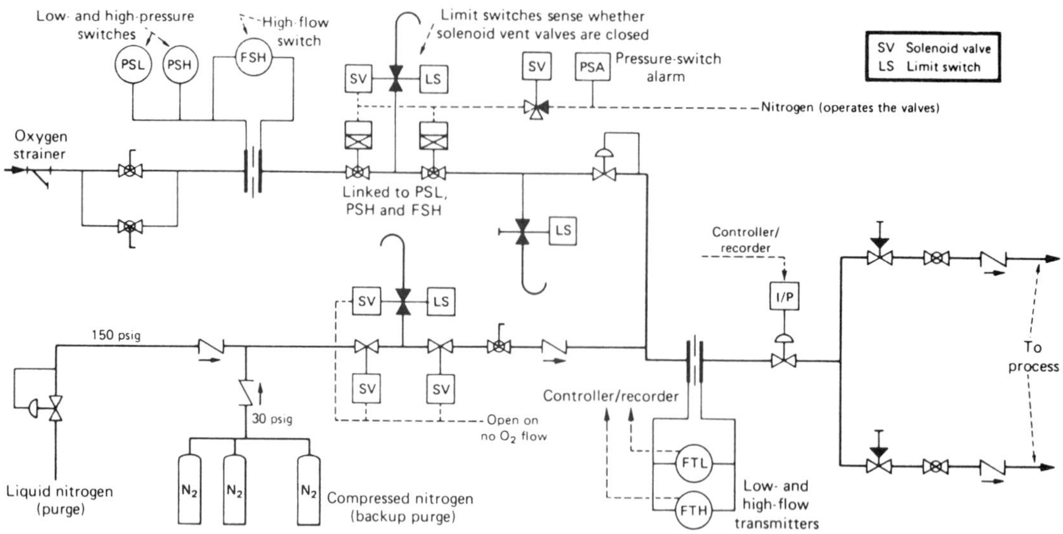

supply end, a high-pressure cutoff switch assures that oxygen does not enter the system at too high a velocity. (Figure 4 shows that maximum recommended velocity is lower for higher pressures.) The low-pressure and high-flow switches back each other up in sensing oxygen-line fractures. All valves, with the exception of the vent valves, fail closed. All of the vents should be directed away from work areas, and should be supplied with bug screens to prevent blockage.

Check valves prevent oxygen from backing up into the nitrogen purge system, and an alarm warns when nitrogen pressure falls below oxygen pressure. Note also that the first valve in each nitrogen line should be cleaned for oxygen service (Class AA).

The main valves in the oxygen system are fitted with limit switches. These sense whether a valve is actually closed—an improvement over systems that merely sense whether a valve-closing signal has been sent. Before oxygen can flow, all of the limit and pressure switches must be in the proper positions. This prevents oxygen from escaping through a partially open vent valve, for example.

The system includes an emergency nitrogen purge that can flush oxygen out of the lines and maintain gas flow enough to prevent process gas from entering the system. Backup for the 150-lb/in.^{2}gauge vaporized nitrogen is provided by cylinders of compressed nitrogen—the backup automatically cuts in when nitrogen pressure falls below 30 lb/in.^{2}gauge.

Operation and maintenance of oxygen systems. Other safety precautions that should be exercised include: monitoring of oxygen in the atmosphere, if the oxygen is being used in a confined space (at a pump underground, for example); high and/or low process-temperature trips; low-level alarm on the oxygen storage tank.

Maintenance of oxygen-handling systems is not unusual except that spark-free tools are recommended and cleanliness is required at all times. Clean maintenance means wearing clean clothing and not allowing grease or oil to contaminate system components (this precludes the use of barrier creams on hands). As mentioned before, all parts should be cleaned and sealed in plastic bags until the moment of installation.

If hotwork (such as cutting or welding) is to be carried out on an oxygen line or on a vessel connected to an oxygen line, the oxygen system must be purged before any work can start. In addition, oxygen should be physically sealed off from the work area by the use of line blinds or by breaking the oxygen line. Valves alone should never be relied on for shutting off oxygen to hotwork areas.

Hydrogen

The potential hazards of handling hydrogen can be illustrated by comparing its combustion properties with those of more-familiar methane and gasoline. Table 6 lists the relevant properties of these flammables (remember that these values are not absolute limits but rather the limits determined in the lab). How do these properties affect the handling of hydrogen?

1. Hydrogen has higher diffusion and buoyant velocities than either methane or gasoline. Thus it forms an explosive mixture with air more rapidly but also disperses more rapidly. However, cold hydrogen gas from a liquid-hydrogen spill may disperse more slowly.
2. Liquid hydrogen will leak more readily than methane or gasoline because it is less viscous, but as gas its "leakage potential" is similar to methane's.

TABLE 6 A Comparison of Properties That Affect Combustion

Property	Hydrogen[a]	Methane	Gasoline
Molecular weight	2.016	16.043	107
Boiling point, °K (1 atm)	20.3	111.6	310–478
Critical pressure, atm	12.8	45.4	24.5–27
Expansion factor (liquid-to-vapor)	845	649	156
Limits of flammability in air, vol.%	4.0–75	5.3–1.5	1.0–7.6
Limits of detonatability in air, vol.%	18–59	6.3–14	1.1–3.3
Minimum ignition energy, mJ	0.02	0.29	0.24
Autoignition temperature, °K	858	813	501–744
Burning velocity, cm/s	265–325	37–45	37–43
Diffusion coefficient, cm^2/s	0.61	0.16	0.05

[a]Properties refer to *para*-hydrogen; hydrogen also exists in an *ortho* state. As a gas, it is 3 : 1 *ortho:par* at room temperature. In liquid form, it is almost completely *para*. Chemical properties are identical but physical properties differ for the two forms.

3. The ignition energy of hydrogen is much lower (0.02 mJ minimum). For comparison: a static charge generated in the human body may produce 10 mJ.
4. Hydrogen has a rate of flame propagation five times as high as methane's; thus a hydrogen ignition is more likely to become an explosion.

As with any flammable gas, all possible ignition sources should be eliminated. Electrical installations should be Class I, Group B (as for liquid hydrogen). Any enclosures where hydrogen is being used should be well-ventilated, with 20–60 air changes per hour. As an added precaution, a hydrogen detector should be installed in any confined area where hydrogen is used, but care must be taken to make sure that the detector element (a hot wire, for example) is itself not an ignition source—the detector should be intrinsically safe.

Any moving machinery in hydrogen areas should be nonsparking and totally enclosed. As with oxygen, spark-resistant tools (bronze alloy) are recommended. Clothing worn in hydrogen areas should be static resistant, and conductive-soled shoes are recommended.

Hydrogen fires. Flames from a hydrogen fire are almost invisible in daylight; thus the fire hazard of hydrogen is compounded because flames may spread unnoticed to other flammables.

When a fire is noticed, the first remedy should be shut off the hydrogen flow—by an automatic and/or remote control system. What if the flow cannot be cut off? The situation could easily get out of control: It is difficult to extinguish a hydrogen fire; if the fire is extinguished but the hydrogen continues to leak, it may start another fire or explosion if it reaches a second ignition source. Such a scenario shows why the shutoff system is necessary.

Nitrogen, Carbon Dioxide, and Argon

When handling nitrogen or argon for inerting, the key problem is to keep them free of air or other contaminants. This can be difficult if a process stream that the gas ties into is at a higher pressure than the inerting gas. In such a case, a check valve in the purge line may be insufficient protection—a case in point involved chlorine gas that crept down a nitrogen line past a check valve and into a nitrogen storage tank.

To prevent this from happening, a double-block-and-bleed valve system (as illustrated in Fig. 5 for oxygen) or twin lift-check valves should be installed in the inert-gas line.

Carbon dioxide is peculiar in that it can flash from liquid to both gas and solid simultaneously.

Here is an example of a problem that this property can cause: Suppose that liquid carbon dioxide is transferred from a storage receiver, where it is held at 300 lb/in.^{2}gauge and 0°F, to a 100-lb/in.^{2}gauge end use. Opening the liquid valve will create snow in the line if the line has not yet been pressurized—the carbon dioxide goes directly to solid snow from vapor. This snow can plug the lines and valves and regulators. This problem is avoided by pressurizing the line to 100 lb/in.^{2}gauge, using carbon dioxide gas from the headspace of the storage receiver, before allowing any liquid to flow.

General References

Compressed Gas Association, *Handbook of Compressed Gases*, 2nd ed., Reinhold, New York, 1981.

Cryogenics Safety Manual, British Cryogenics Council, London, 1970.

Hord, J., *Is Hydrogen Safe?*, Cryogenics Division, Institute of Basic Standards, National Bureau of Standards, Boulder, Colorado.

Hydrogen, CGA Pamphlet G-5, Compressed Gas Association, New York.

Safe Handling of Compressed Gases, CGA Pamphlet P-1, Compressed Gas Association, New York.

References

1. "Safe Storage and Handling of Compressed Gases," *Plant Eng.*, April 19, May 17, and June 14, 1979.
2. Compressed Gas Association, *Handbook of Compressed Gases*, 2nd ed., Reinhold, New York, 1981.
3. *Safety Relief Device Standards—Compressed Gas Storage Containers*, CGA Pamphlet S-1.3, Compressed Gas Association, New York.
4. *Frangible Disc Safety Device Assembly*, CGA Pamphlet S-3, Compressed Gas Association, New York.
5. *Fire Protection Handbook*, Vol. 4, National Fire Protection Association, Boston, 1979, Section 50.
6. Ref. 5, Section 50B.
7. *Equipment Cleaned for Oxygen Service*, CGA Pamphlet G-4.1, Compressed Gas Association, New York.

PHILIP G. BLAKEY

Liquefied Natural Gas, Economics

Over 20 years of safe and efficient operation has established liquefied natural gas (LNG) as an economically viable method of energy transport. LNG projects are known to be highly capital intensive. Billions of dollars are needed for the required liquefaction, shipping, and regasification facilities.

Several past articles have provided techniques for estimating capital investment associated with these facilities [1–3]. Once the capital investment has been determined, estimates can be made of annual operating costs and annualized capital-related charges to arrive at net cost of service (COS) between liquefaction and regasification. The potential netback to the gas producer for the raw gas prior to liquefaction can then be estimated for a given regasified fuel value at the market site.

The results of a parametric analysis of LNG cost of service as a function of project capacity and trade distance indicate that there is little incentive in terms of reduced COS in developing LNG projects with capacities much in excess of 1000 MMSCFD. This is particularly true as the trading distance increases.

For a typical 3900 nautical mile trade, doubling the project capacity from 250 to 500 MMSCFD requires an increase in total investment of $800 million, from $1.5 billion to $2.3 billion. But it reduces unit COS by 21%, $4.21 to $3.32/MSCF. Doubling project capacity from 1000 to 2000 MMSCFD, however, requires an increase in project investment of $2.7 billion, from $3.6 billion to $6.3 billion. This results in only a 12% reduction in unit COS, $2.70 to $2.41/MSCF.

Savings in unit COS for projects with capacities greater than 1500 to 2000 MMSCFD appear very marginal. There may, however, be circumstances, such as the exploitation of costly remote offshore and arctic onshore reserves, which will require large-scale utilization in excess of 1000 MMSCFD in order to economically justify development.

Netback Price

Most LNG import prices (ex regasification) are related in some manner to the equivalent price in terms of heating value of crude oil and/or light fuel oil. This has resulted in regasified LNG prices (1982)* of $5.50 to $5.75/MMBtu in Europe and $6.25 to $7.00/MMBtu in Japan.

The early 1983 drop of 15% in posted OPEC crude oil prices will result in some proportionate reduction in LNG import price. The exact amount will depend on the terms of the particular contract.

Figure 1 estimates gas netback price delivered to the liquefaction plant as a function of the regasified LNG market price for various capacity LNG

*The costs can be updated by using Cost Indexes.

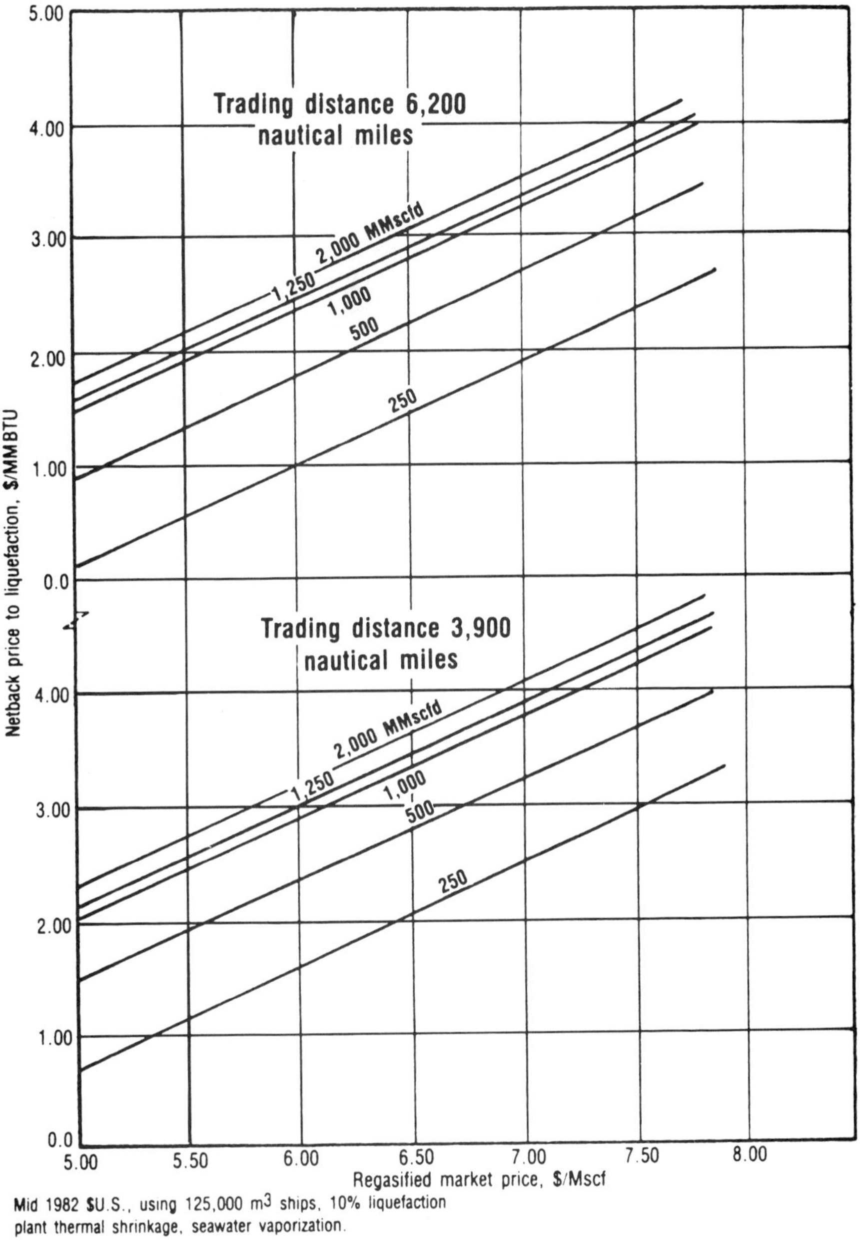

FIG. 1. LNG netback price.

projects, assuming a 3900 nautical mile trade route. Data are also presented for a 6200 nautical mile route. Both sets of cost data assume a liquefaction plant thermal shrinkage of 10%.

Thus, a netback price prior to liquefaction equivalent to \$2.50/MMBtu (1982) might be expected for a 1000 MMSCFD, 3900 nautical mile import project to Europe. For a similar project to the Japanese market, a netback price close to \$3.30/MMBtu appears possible.

Increasing the trading distance to 6200 nautical miles reduces the netback price to \$1.90/MMBtu for the European market and \$2.75/MMBtu for the Japanese market.

These gas netback prices are on a delivered basis to the LNG plant. They must accommodate costs associated with field development, gathering, and transport to the LNG plant.

Economic Sensitivity

Because of the generalized nature of the analysis, the sensitivity of the unit COS to changes in erected plant or ship cost, capital recovery factor, liquefaction plant operating cost, and ship fuel cost was studied (Table 1). Sensitivity in shipping costs varies with shipping distance, owing to the increased number of ships needed and increased capital investment.

For a given LNG project, the area of greatest uncertainty is the cost of the liquefaction plant.

TABLE 1 Sensitivity Analysis

	Project Capacity (MMSCFD)				
	250	500	1000	1250	2000
	Incremental Cost (\$/MSCF)				
+10% erected plant cost:					
Liquefaction	0.22	0.16	0.13	0.12	0.11
Shipping[a]	0.04–0.29	0.04–0.29	0.04–0.29	0.04–0.29	0.04–0.29
Regasification	0.09	0.06	0.04	0.04	0.03
Total project	0.35–0.60	0.26–0.51	0.21–0.46	0.20–0.45	0.18–0.43
+1% capital recovery factor:					
Liquefaction (20–21%)	0.10	0.07	0.06	0.05	0.05
Shipping[a] (16–17%)	0.02–0.14	0.02–0.14	0.02–0.14	0.02–0.14	0.02–0.14
Regasification (18–19%)	0.05	0.03	0.02	0.02	0.01
Total project	0.17–0.29	0.12–0.24	0.10–0.22	0.09–0.21	0.08–0.20
+1% operating cost:					
Liquefaction (4–5%)	0.07	0.05	0.04	0.03	0.03

	Trade Distance (nautical miles)					
	1600	3900	6200	8500	10,800	13,000
Ship fuel cost ±\$6/bbl oil equivalent[a]	0.02	0.03	0.05	0.07	0.08	0.10

[a] Varies with shipping distance.

A cost over-run of 20% in the LNG plant erected cost could add from \$0.25 to \$0.50/MSCF to the cost of the LNG product, depending on the size of the project.

An increase in the liquefaction plant operating charges from 4 to 5% of the erected plant cost increases the landed LNG cost by \$0.03 to \$0.07/MSCF, depending on the project. A variation in the cost of ship fuel of \$6/bbl oil equivalent, on the other hand, results in an incremental COS differential of \$0.02 to \$0.10/MSCF, depending on the trade distance.

Analysis Basis

Annual operating and capital-related costs have been calculated as percentages of facility capital investment based on information derived from more detailed financial analyses.

All cost data are given in terms of constant 1982 dollars with no allowances for inflation.

Plant investments were developed for LNG projects with nominal capacities of 250 to 2000 MMSCFD. Shipping investments were developed for trade distances of 1600 to 13,000 nautical miles for ships of 125,000 and 165,000 m^3 capacity.

Trade distances were adjusted to yield an even number of ships based on the design criteria given in Table 2. Typical shipping distances for various LNG trade routes are given in Table 3.

Investment costs for the liquefaction plant are based on typical processing conditions for a sulfur-free gas without extensive LPG recovery, marine, or infrastructure facilities.

Conventional and proven technology is also assumed for all plant facilities.

Storage costs are based on conventional double wall, single-containment tank designs with internal pumps. Storage requirements are minimal in terms of total installed capacity. They do not account for unusual shipping or weather conditions such as ice and fog or extreme peakshaving loads during regasification.

TABLE 2 LNG Shipping Criteria

Ship size, m^3	125,000 and 165,000
Average speed, knots	18.5
Port time, h (each end)	36
Annual operating days	340
Average boiloff, %/d	0.125
Capacity utilized, %	98
LNG properties:	
Gas–liquid ratio, MSCF/m^3	21.01
Specific gravity	0.465

TABLE 3 LNG Trade Routes (in nautical miles)

	Destination			
Source	U.S. East Coast	U.S. West Coast	Japan	Northern Europe
Caribbean	2,200			3,800
Algeria	3,600			1,300
Nigeria	5,100			3,900
Persian Gulf	12,000	12,000	6,800	
Northern Norway	3,900		12,900	1,150
Indonesia		8,300	3,200	
Northwest Australia		7,900	3,300	
Alaska		2,100	3,300	

Regasification facilities are based on a typical combination of seawater vaporizers with backup gas-fired vaporizers.

No provisions are made for recovery and/or utilization of the cold energy in the LNG.

In developing total plant investment, a factor of 40% of the estimated erected plant cost for the liquefaction plant and 25% of the estimated erected plant cost for the regasification terminal were added.

This accounts for various owners, costs such as interest during construction, cost of land, startup expenses, working capital, and camp and catering facilities.

The total system investment, including liquefaction, shipping and regasification, is given in Fig. 2.

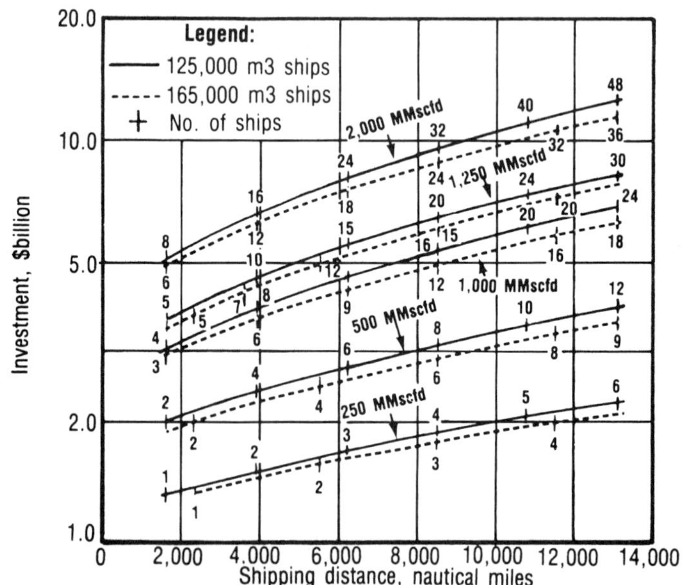

Mid 1982, $U.S., including liquefaction, shipping, and regasification facilities, typical LNG processing conditions.

FIG. 2. LNG project investment.

TABLE 4 Operating and Capital Cost Factors

	Annual Operting Cost, % EPC[a]	Annual Capital Cost % TPI[b]
Liquefaction	4.0	20.0
Shipping	[c]	16.0
Regasification	3.5	18.0

[a]Erected plant cost.
[b]Total plant (ship) investment.
[c]Calculated separately.

Operating and Capital Charges

Table 4 summarizes the annual operating and capital recovery factors used to determine total project revenues and hence unit product COS. Annual operating costs include payroll expense, maintenance costs, administration and general overhead expenses, and insurance and taxes.

For purposes of determining COS, it excludes liquefaction plant feed gas cost but does include ship fuel cost.

Capital charges include interest payments, debt retirement, depreciation, return on equity, and taxes. Specific financial arrangements such as debt-to-equity ratio, interest rates, return on investment, and tax structure have a major bearing on plant capital charges for a given project.

The capital recovery factors used are believed to be consistent with financial charges associated with a typical LNG project.

Project COS

The COS/unit of throughput for liquefaction and regasification facilities, exclusive of any internal fuel consumption, is shown in Fig. 3. Purchased power is included for seawater pumping associated with LNG vaporization. For gas-fired LNG vaporization, an additional charge of $0.09/MSCF is incurred during regasification.

Unit shipping cost data are depicted in Fig. 4 as a function of trade distance for 125,000 and 165,000 m^3 capacity ships. Ship boiloff is assumed to be fully utilized as supplemental ship fuel.

The fuel value of the boiloff gas is taken as $5.50/MMBtu (equivalent to $34.50/bbl fuel oil).

Total COS for the entire LNG system, less liquefaction plant fuel consumption, as a function of trade distance for various capacity projects is given in Fig. 5.

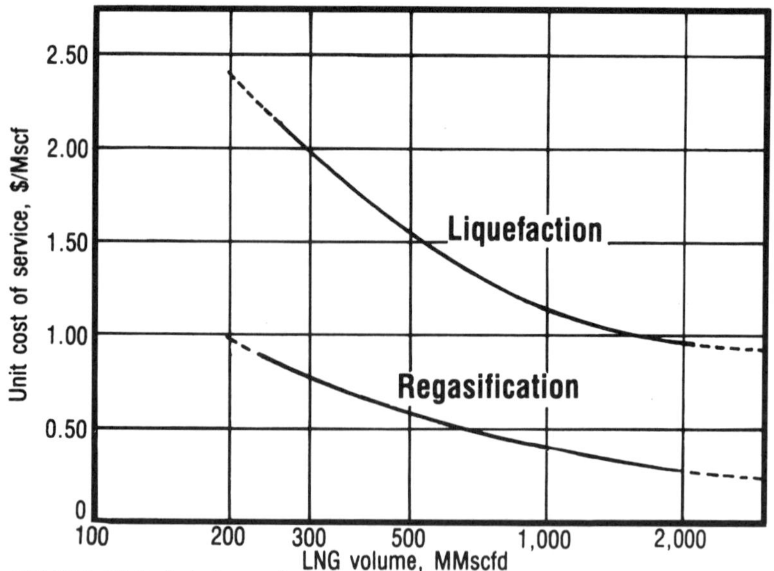

Mid 1982, $U.S., including capital and operating charges, excluding internal fuel consumption, seawater vaporization. For gas fired vaporization add $0.09/ Mscf.

FIG. 3. Unit cost of service.

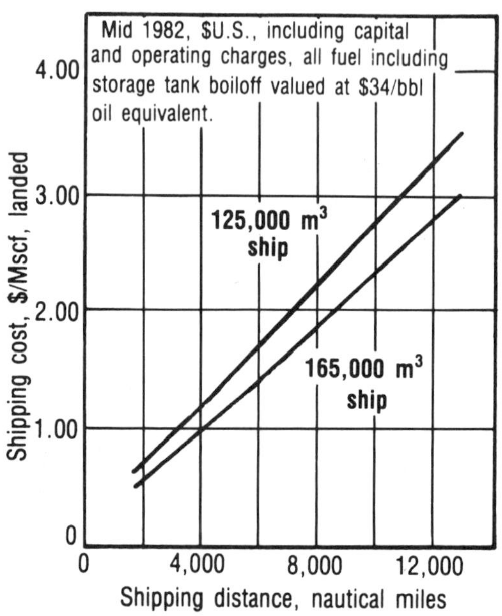

FIG. 4. LNG shipping cost.

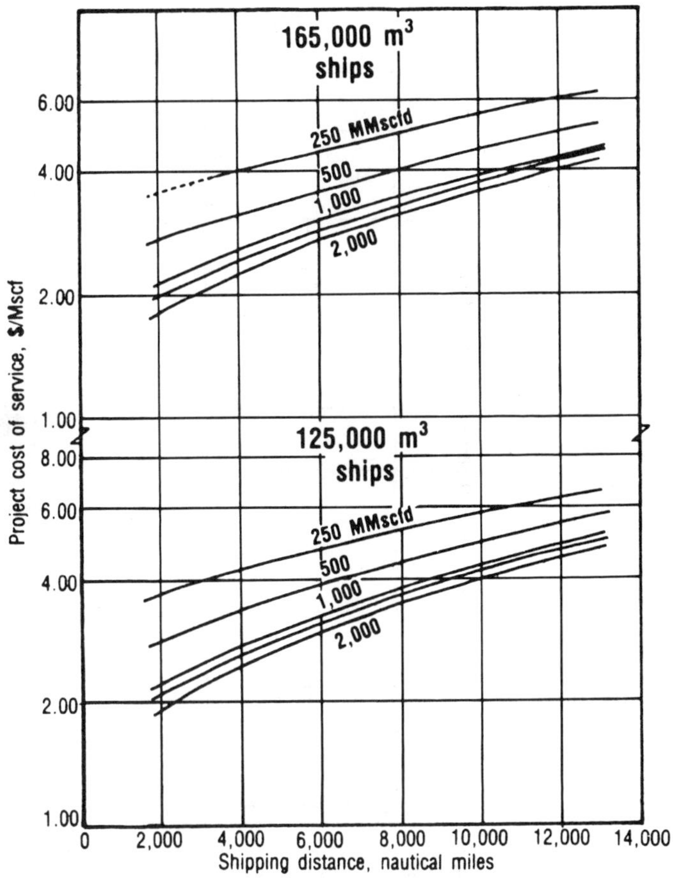

Mid 1982, $U.S., including capital and operating charges, excluding liquefaction plant internal fuel. Ship fuel, including boiloff, taken at $34/bbl oil equivalent.

FIG. 5. Project cost of services.

A cross plot of the data showing cost of service as a function of project capacity for various trade distances is given in Fig. 6.

To arrive at the total project unit COS for a specific project, the value of the fuel consumed in the liquefaction plant must be added.

The plant fuel cost, in turn, depends on the cost of the plant feed gas and the efficiency of the liquefaction process. Figure 7 gives the equivalent unit fuel cost as a function of plant feed gas cost for various internal plant fuel consumption rates.

The internal fuel consumption, called plant shrinkage, is expressed as a percentage of the gross LNG product heat content.

Although plant shrinkage values in the order of 15% were considered acceptable for a plant conceived and designed in the era of cheap energy values, the range of 8 to 10% is considered attainable for projects now under study. During marine transport, a slight enrichment of the LNG occurs in

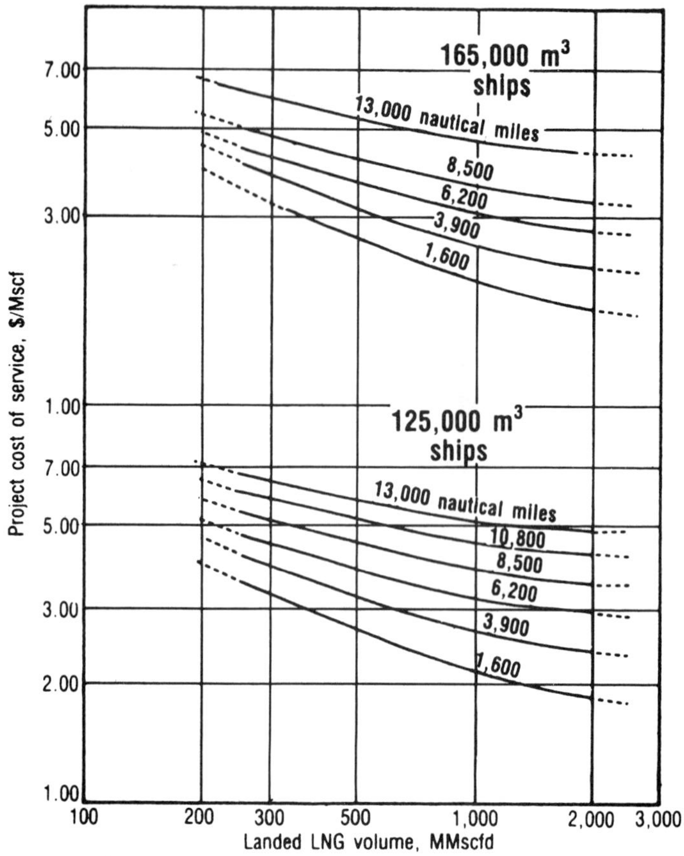

Mid 1982, $U.S., including capital and operating charges, excluding liquefaction plant internal fuel. Ship fuel, including boiloff, taken at $34/bbl oil equivalent.

FIG. 6. Project cost of service.

terms of heating value due to the preferential vaporization of the more volatile nitrogen and methane fractions. This factor, however, has been ignored for simplicity.

This material appeared in *Oil and Gas Journal*, pp. 47–51, February 20, 1984, and is reprinted with the permission of the editor.

References

1. R. N. DiNapoli, "LNG Costs Reflect Changes in Economy and Technology," *Oil Gas J.*, pp. 138–143 (April 4, 1983).

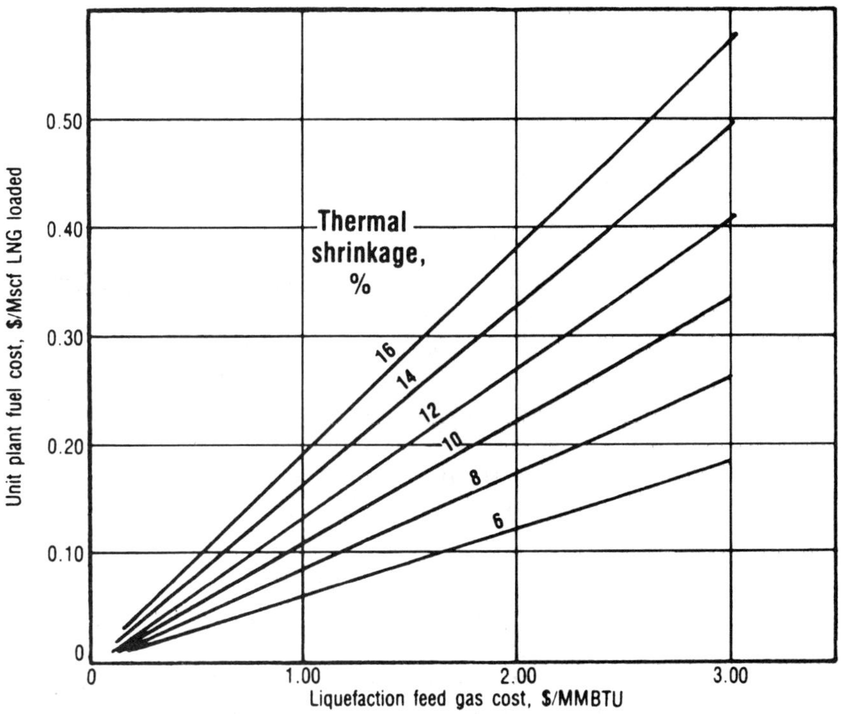

Mid 1982, $U.S., 1,000 BTU/scf HHV LNG product, thermal shrinkage given as % of gross LNG heating value.

FIG. 7. Liquefaction plant fuel cost.

2. R. N. DiNapoli, "Estimating Costs for Base-Load LNG Plants," *Oil Gas J.*, pp. 58–60 (November 17, 1975).
3. R. N. DiNapoli, "Costs Are Estimated for LNG Terminals," *Oil Gas J.*, pp. 83–84 (March 13, 1978).

ROBERT N. DiNAPOLI

Liquefied Natural Gas, Project Costs

Since its inception in the early 1960s, the liquefied natural gas (LNG) industry has grown from a single source trade supplying less than a million tons per year to a mature industry with a production capacity of over 50 million tons per year from some 10 locations in six countries. Total system facilities represent an investment of over $10 billion U.S. in dollars of the day. New facilities under construction or in the advanced planning stages will nearly double this investment figure.

Unique Features of LNG Projects

LNG projects can be characterized as highly capital-intensive projects requiring relatively long lead times for design, purchase, and erection of major facilities. For example, a 7 million tons per year (1000 MMSCFD) LNG project can represent a total investment of from U.S. $3–4 billion in today's dollars for liquefaction, shipping, and regasification facilities.

Several factors contribute to the resulting high capital costs of LNG projects as compared to those of more conventional energy-related projects. These include:

1. Location of the liquefaction facilities in a remote area requiring extensive camp and catering facilities during plant construction to maintain the construction labor force.
2. Extensive infrastructure required to support liquefaction plant permanent administration and operationing staff.
3. Rigid environmental and safety considerations associated with the storage and transfer of large quantities of liquefied natural gas.
4. Need for a large self-contained utility system to power the liquefaction plant refrigeration compression system.
5. Physical limitations in equipment sizes frequently requiring multiple or parallel units to meet required process flow conditions.
6. Large quantities of expensive stainless and high nickel steel needed because of the low-temperature processing conditions.
7. Extensive and complex drain and vent system required to dispose safely of flammable cryogenic fluids.
8. Specialized ship design required to transport large quantities of LNG at cryogenic temperatures safely.

A number of other considerations such as multinational financing tied to special equipment and service purchase agreements and local labor conditions can contribute to increased facility capital cost. Decisions in these areas, however, are most often made for political and/or financing reasons and are not necessarily subjected to full engineering analyses.

Liquefaction Plants

Liquefaction facilities typically can account for 50% or more of the overall project costs and are generally the most complex and time consuming to design and construct.

Project investment costs for liquefaction facilities have risen substantially since the first such plants were constructed in the mid to late 1960s. Because of the limited number of base-load liquefaction plants currently in operation and the diversity in designs, a definitive correlation of escalation in plant costs over this period is not evident. A summary of historical plant cost data is shown in Fig. 1 and illustrates the lack of consistency of such data but does show a rather dramatic increase in plant costs over the past 15 years.

In examining the data in Fig. 1 it should be noted that costs are expressed per unit of LNG production and as a function of the year of initial startup. The period of capital expenditure, however, occurs over the preceding three to four years. The effects of economy of scale should be considered, particularly with regard to plants built in the 1960s which are considerably smaller than plants currently considered to be economically viable.

Some consistency of cost data is evident for the large multitrain plants utilizing the propane-precooled, mixed refrigerant process built over the past

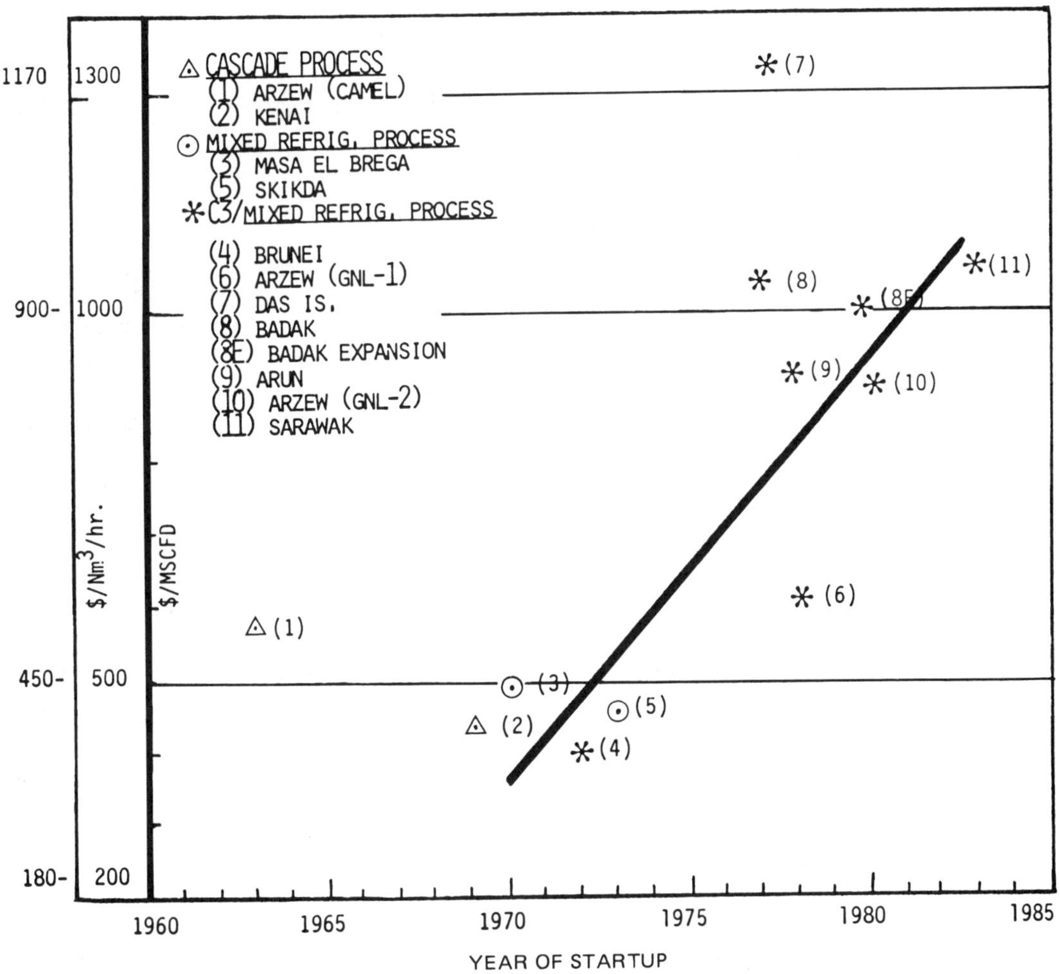

FIG. 1. Historical trend in capital cost for base-load LNG plants.

15 years. The origin of what is now considered to be a worldscale size LNG plant with a capacity in the range of 6 million tons per year can be traced to the construction of the Brunei plant in the late 1960s.

In the 10-year period since the startup of the first train at Brunei, unit cost for a worldscale size LNG plant has nearly tripled from approximately $400/MSCFD LNG production to about $1200/MSCFD LNG production. Most of this increase can be attributed to the effects of worldwide inflation coupled with the strong demand for energy-related goods and services evident during that period.

Capital costs for new LNG plants are expected to rise only moderately, at least for the near term, as a result of the sharp downturn in new plant construction and the intense competition which now exists for such projects. Continued improvements in technology together with more cost-effective construction techniques should aid in minimizing cost increases for new projects.

Areas of liquefaction technology which have the greatest potential impact for reductions in plant capital cost are:

1. The basic liquefaction technology selected and its resulting thermodynamic efficiency.
2. Choice of compressor drivers and the resulting efficiency of the power generation cycle.
3. Method selected for heat rejection.

Liquefaction Train Capacity

The trend to increased liquefaction train capacity has been evident since the first LNG plant was constructed at Arzew, Algeria, in the early 1960s. Since that time, individual train design capacities have increased sixfold, with present day designs capable of achieving LNG production rates in the range of 300–350 MMSCFD.

Within the limits of proven heat transfer technology and compressor/driver machinery, this trend has favored the use of precooled, mixed refrigerant processes. The two processes of this type considered to be of commercial importance are the propane, precooled mixed refrigerant process of Air Products and Chemicals Inc. and the precooled Tealarc process of Snam Progetti/Technip.

Increasing liquefaction train capacity from 150 to 300 MMSCFD reduces the unit cost ($/MSCF) for the liquefaction portion of the plant by some 16%. The effect on the total plant cost, however, is considerably less since costs of the other portions of the plant do not vary significantly with changes in liquefaction train capacity.

Driver Selection

The rapid escalation in the value of the natural gas feedstock to an LNG plant favors the use of high efficiency, aero-derivative gas turbines as drivers for the refrigeration compressors and the turbo-generators. Choice of gas turbines eliminates the necessity for an extensive high-pressure steam system and associated water treatment facilities. Cost of a steam system can range from \$100 to \$150 million for a 6 million ton capacity LNG plant.

Optimum thermal efficiency, however, is attained in a combined-cycle arrangement which retains a portion of the high-pressure steam system. Overall capital cost of the combined gas turbine-steam system, however, may exceed that of the straight steam system. Depending on the value of the fuel gas and the possibility of increased LNG production due to reduced plant shrinkage, however, the added capital cost can be more than offset by increased annual LNG sales revenues.

Heat Rejection

All of the LNG plants built to date utilize once-through seawater cooling or a closed loop cooling circuit and cooling tower as the primary means of heat rejection. Although extensive use of air cooling is used at one LNG plant, Arun, and to a lesser extent at other plant locations, a complex and costly cooling water system is still required.

Cooling water requirements for a typical LNG plant can vary from 70,000 to 270,000 m^3/h depending on the site environmental conditions, choice of power generation cycle, and basic process design requirements. Capital costs associated with such systems can range from \$70 to \$170 million depending to a great extent on the complexity of the water intake and outflow systems.

As noted above, it is possible to eliminate the need for the high-pressure steam system and its associated cooling water requirements through the use of gas turbines in a simple cycle arrangement as drivers for the compressors and turbo-generators. By utilizing air cooling for the refrigerant condensors and other process cooling loads, it is possible to eliminate the cooling water system totally with a substantial savings in capital costs.

This approach has been selected for the 6 million ton per year Northwest Shelf LNG plant now in the very early stages of construction on the northwest coast of Australia [1]. It will be the first LNG plant to rely solely on air cooling for total plant heat rejection.

Storage

The concern for safety has always been a major consideration in the design and construction of LNG facilities. This is due not only to the flammable nature of the process fluids but also the cryogenic conditions under which much of the processing takes place and the product is stored.

Nowhere has this concern for safety had a greater impact on facility cost than in the area of LNG storage. Until recently the majority of LNG storage tanks built in association with base-load liquefaction plants consisted of single containment tanks with a thin carbon steel outer wall for insulation protection. A low earthen dike or bund is provided in the event of an inner tank failure.

The consequences of a large LNG spill resulting from an inner tank failure have led to consideration of the double integrity concept of tank design. Several designs involving various combinations of low temperature steels and concrete tank walls have been proposed to satisfy such a requirement.

One such design developed by Shell has recently been installed at the Sarawak LNG plant in Malaysia and will be used in the Australian Northwest Shelf LNG plant. A similar double integrity design was used for the replacement tanks at the Das Island LNG plant.

Use of double integrity tank designs, however, results in installed storage costs of approximately $500/m^3 ($80/bbl) compared to a cost in the order of $250/m^3 ($40/bbl) for the older single containment, double wall tank designs. Other safety and design features, such as full hydrostatic testing of the inner tank and the use of in-tank pumps, add further to the installed tank cost.

Optimization of fleet carrier capacity and liquefaction plant storage capacity is also affected by the selection of the storage tank design. The higher cost of the double integrity design tends to minimize total installed plant storage capacity at the expense of increased flexibility in fleet transport capacity.

Capital Costs

In previous publications the author has presented a generalized procedure which permits the rapid estimation of the erected LNG plant cost [2, 3]. The procedure has been found of sufficient accuracy to permit order-of-magnitude and preliminary-type estimates to be developed rapidly. The basic procedure up-dated to reflect present-day costs and design requirements is summarized as follows.

Generalized Format

Table 1 summarizes the general format for buildup in total plant erected cost. For the major processing and utility areas, direct costs (major equipment, bulk items, subcontact items, and field installation labor) are given as a function of unit LNG production.

The direct cost of amine-type acid gas removal facilities is given as a function of unit feed gas flow rate in Fig. 2. Costs are given for a high (6%) and low (0.5%) limit of carbon dioxide concentration and assume removal to LNG processing specification of less than 100 ppm.

Figure 3 gives liquefaction unit direct costs, including dehydration, liquefaction, and refrigeration systems, as a function of unit LNG production. The upper curve reflects the higher costs associated with the use of gas turbines as drivers for the main refrigeration compressors.

Utility area direct costs are given in Fig. 4 as a function of total LNG production to storage. The steam turbine case includes power generation and distribution, cooling water systems, and all associated utility systems. The gas turbine case assumes a combined cycle arrangement with waste-heat recovery for either electric power generation or for driving one or more of the refrigeration compressors.

TABLE 1 Format for Base-Load Liquefaction Plant Capital Cost Buildup

Direct Cost Item	Source of Cost
Process (acid gas removal)	Figure 2
Process (liquefaction)	Figure 3
Utilities	Figure 4
Auxiliaries	Table 2
Storage	Table 2
Loading	Table 2
Site preparation	Table 2
Marine facilities	Table 2
Total direct costs	
Indirect costs	0.35 × direct costs
Bare plant cost	
Contingency	0.15 × bare plant cost
Total erected plant cost	

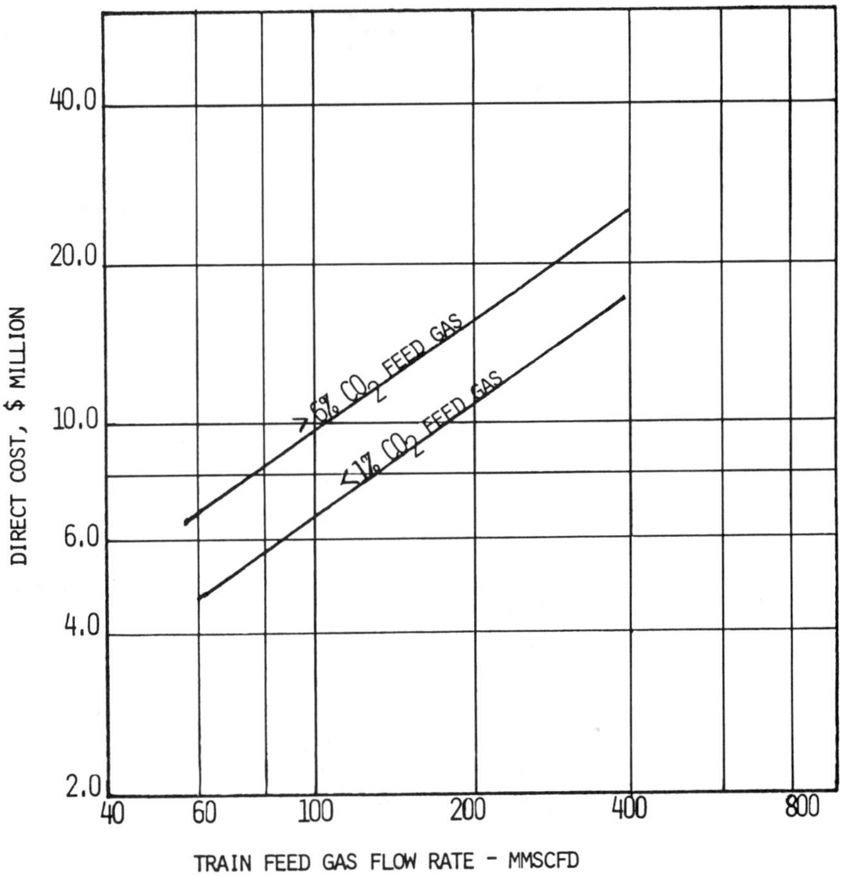

FIG. 2. Acid gas removal train cost. Basis: 1985 second quarter U.S. dollars, low H_2S content gas, amine-type process, 100 ppm CO_2 in treated gas.

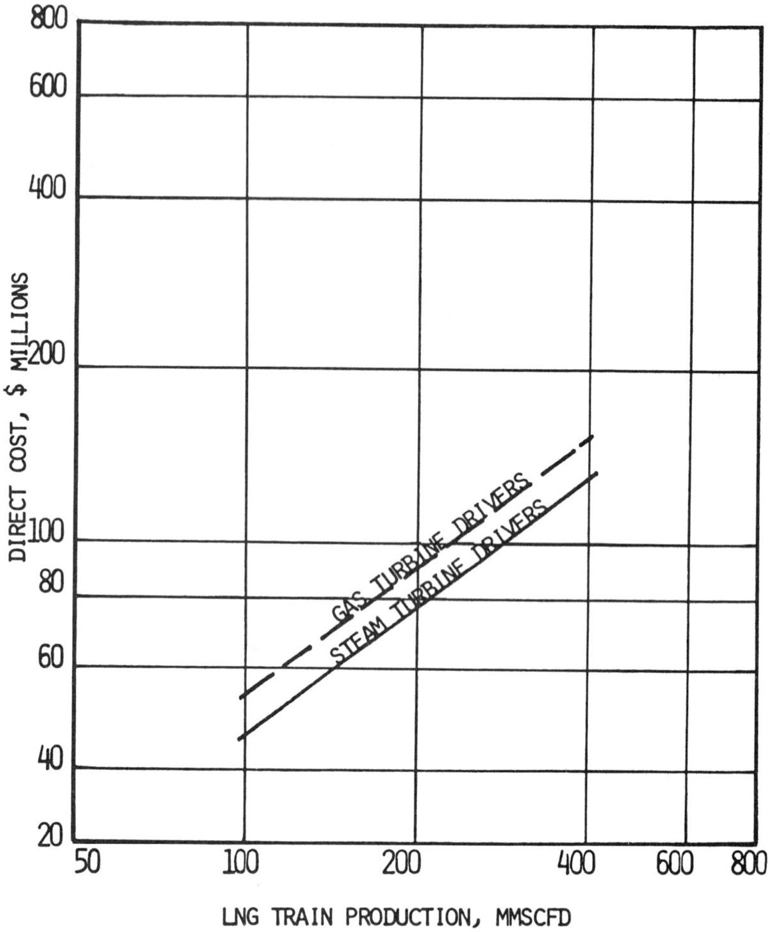

FIG. 3. Liquefaction train cost. Basis: 1985 second quarter U.S. dollars, single train; includes dehydration, liquefaction, and compression; typical feed gas conditions.

Table 2 gives typical cost data for the LNG storage and loading systems, auxiliary facilities such as relief and liquid disposal systems, fire protection, utility storage and various plant buildings and equipment, site preparation, marine facilities, and possible LPG extraction. These costs are not normally a direct function of plant capacity but more project and site related.

An example of the buildup in total erected plant cost for an LNG plant with a nominal production capacity of 7 million tons per year (1000 MMSCFD) is presented in Table 3. It assumes three acid gas and three liquefaction trains, all steam drivers for refrigeration and power generation, and conventional LNG storage tank design.

Indirect costs include construction and field-office costs, freight taxes and import duties, temporary camp and catering facilities, engineering, procurement, and administration, and contractor fee. These costs are taken as a percentage of the total plant direct cost.

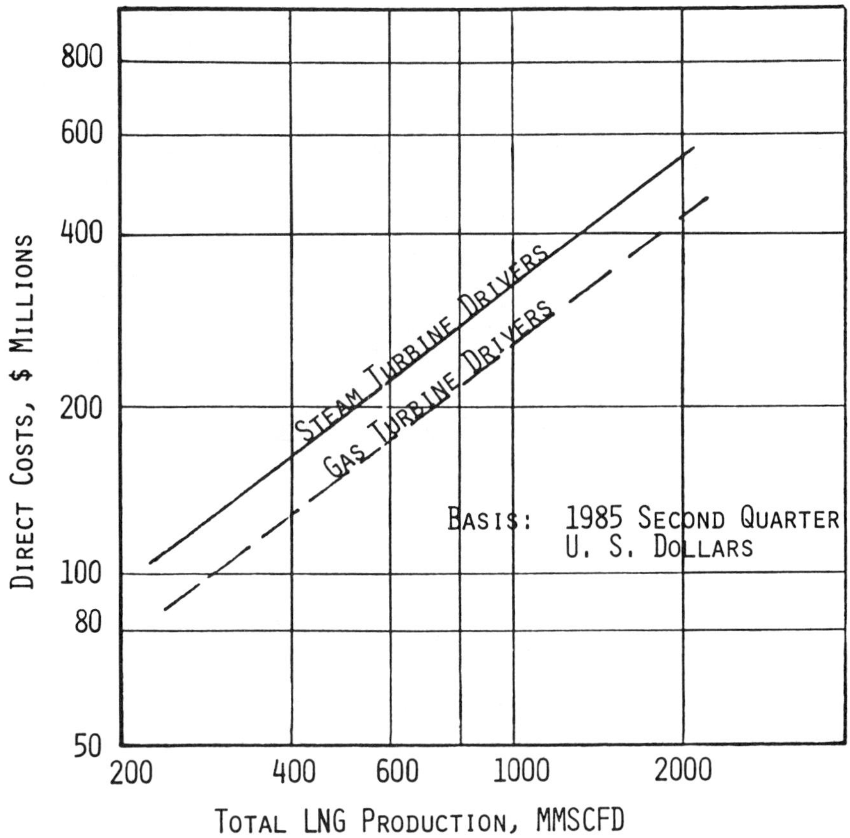

FIG. 4. Utility area cost. Includes power generations and distribution, cooling water, and other utility services.

TABLE 2 Direct Cost Data for Large Base-Load Liquefaction Plants[a]

Item		Typical Cost	Cost Range
Storage, $/bbl:			
Conventional		40	34–45
Double integrity		75	60–85
Auxiliary facility	$ million	80	60–100
Site preparation	$ million	25	20–40
LPG recovery	$ million	100	80–150
Loading	$ million	55	50–70
Marine facilities	$ million	50	40–90

[a]Direct costs. 1985 Second quarter cost basis: U.S. dollars.

TABLE 3 Example of Cost Estimate Buildup for Typical Base-Load Liquefaction Plant[a]

		Cost,[b] $ million
Process (acid gas removal)	3 × 16 MM	48.0
(liquefaction)	3 × 115.0 MM	345.0
Utilities		330.0
Auxiliaries		80.0
Storage, 40.0/bbl × 2 million bbl		80.0
Loading		55.0
Site preparation		25.0
Marine facilites		50.0
Total direct cost		1013.0
Indirect cost, 0.35 × 1013.0		355.0
Bare plant cost		1368.0
Contingency, 0.15 × 1368.0		205.0
Total erected plant cost		1573.0

[a]Basis: 1000 MMSCFD LNG production. 3 acid gas removal trains at 333 MMSCFD (1% CO_2). 3 liquefaction trains at 333 MMSCFD. 4 storage tanks at 500,000 bbl. All steam drivers. Typical site and marine facilities. No LPG production.

[b]1985 second quarter costs, U.S. dollars.

Shipping

Early LNG trades from North America and Europe utilized ships with capacities in the range of 25,000 to 40,000 m^3. Delivered price of these ships was in the order of $15 to $25 million. Trades developed in the late 1960s and early 1970s from Alaska and Brunei to Japan utilized larger ships with capacities in the range of 70,000 m^3 built at a cost of approximately $45 million per ship.

With the beginning of the Abu-Dhabi to Japan trade in the mid-1970s came the first of the 125,000 m^3 capacity LNG carriers. This class of ship (125,000–135,000 m^3) has become the industry standard for all succeeding LNG projects including the Australia to Japan Northwest Shelf LNG project schedule to begin shipments toward the end of 1989.

Figure 5 shows the increase in cost for 125,000 m^3 LNG carriers ordered from the mid-1970s to the very early 1980s. Little, if any, escalation in price for new ship orders is expected over the next few years. This is primarily due to the depressed state of the worldwide shipbuilding industry and the intense competition that can be expected for any new orders.

Little difference in ship cost can be expected due to differences in containment systems. All of the 125,000 m^3 class LNG carriers built to-date have utilized one of three proven containment systems. These are the

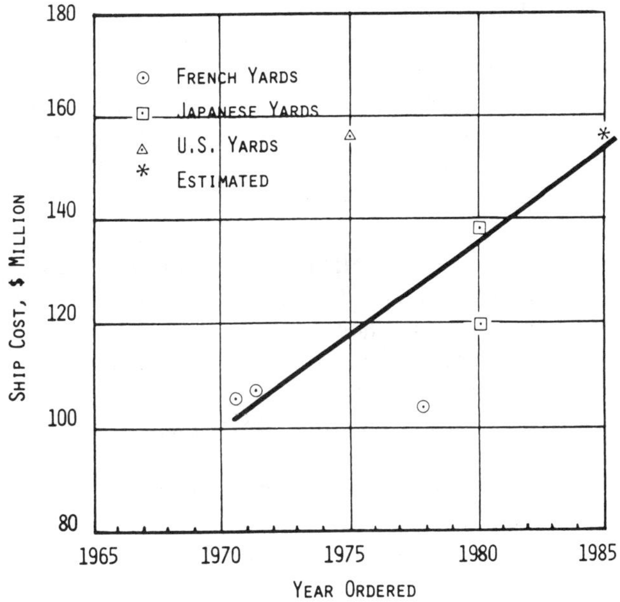

FIG. 5. Historical trend in LNG ship costs. Basis: 125,000 m³ capacity ships.

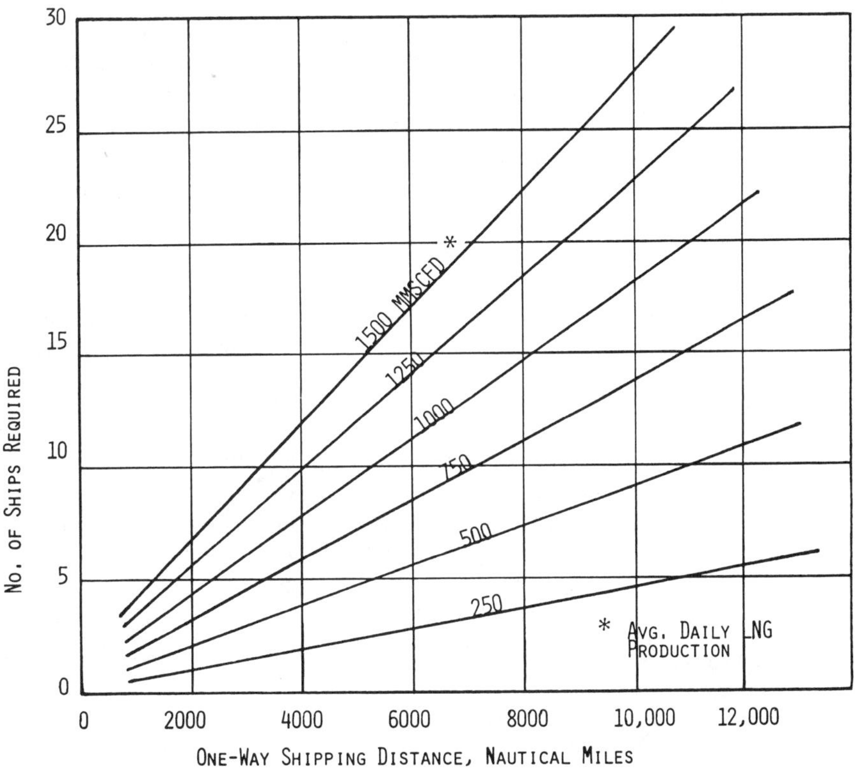

FIG. 6. Ship requirements for LNG projects. Basis: 24 h port time (each end), 18.5 knots average speed, 340 annual operating days, 125,000 m³ capacity ships.

Technigaz and Gas Transport membrane type systems and the Moss Rosenbergy sperical tank design. Variations in costs resulting from differences in containment systems are most often negated by competition between ship yards and/or various subsidies, either direct or indirect, provided by individual countries with experience in a particular type of containment system.

For estimating purposes a price of $150 million in current dollars can be taken for a 125,000 m^3 capacity ship ordered for delivery in the late 1980s to early 1990s. No new technology which could dramatically affect the cost of LNG ships is anticipated in the near future. Current technological developments are aimed at increasing operating efficiency and reducing product boiloff losses such as through the use of dual fuel diesel engines in place of less efficient steam turbine driven engines and the reliquefaction of boiloff vapors.

Figure 6 can be used to estimate rapidly the number of ships required for a given LNG production rate and shipping distance [3]. It is based on a 125,000 m^3 capacity ship and an average ship speed of 18.5 knots. As a rule of thumb, the number of ships can be considered to be inversely proportional to ship capacity and average ship speed.

Receiving Terminals

Although less complex and costly than either liquefaction or shipping facilities, LNG receiving terminals still represent sizable investments, typically in the range of $200 to $500 million in 1985 dollars. Like liquefaction and shipping facilities, capital costs for new receiving terminals have risen substantially since the initial LNG trades were begun in the mid-1960s. Facility costs since that time have increased from about $100/MSCFD of design throughput to somewhere in the range of $750/MSCFD for new facilities, expressed in dollars of the day.

In addition to the effects of worldwide inflation, a number of other factors have contributed to the increased capital cost for LNG receiving terminals. These include:

1. Higher safety standards, particularly with regard to LNG storage tank design.
2. Increased redundency in processing facilities to insure reliability of operation, particularly if the import terminal serves as the primary source of consumer gas supply.
3. Need for standby facilities to meet anticipated peak demand periods.
4. More stringent local safety and environmental regulations.

Storage

Hazards associated with the storage of LNG are of even more concern for receiving terminals which are often located in close proximity to industrial and/or populated areas. This has led to a greater acceptance of the double integrity storage tank design concept than is the case for liquefaction plants.

The installed cost for double integrity tank designs is again about twice that of the older, single containment type of design, i.e., \$500/m^3 vs \$250/m^3, as previously discussed for liquefaction plants. Further increases in storage area costs can occur if additional storage capacity is desired to insure continuity of supply and/or to meet peak demand requirements.

Vaporization

Other than the storage facilities, specification of the vaporization system probably has the greatest impact on capital costs of any other of the basic processing systems found in an LNG receiving terminal. Vaporization alternatives include either heat exchange with seawater or regasification in gas-fired heaters using a portion of the plant sendout, typically about 2.5%, as fuel.

While simple heat exchange with seawater minimizes utility consumption, installed costs are greater than with gas-fired heaters. Cost for seawater vaporization can be correlated at a function of sendout capacity depending on the seawater temperature drop specified [3]. Total installed cost for the vaporization of 500 MMSCFD of LNG using gas-fired heaters including sendout pumps and associated piping is estimated to be about \$45 million in 1985 dollars. Similar cost using seawater vaporization is between \$75 and \$95 million, depending on the seawater temperature difference specified.

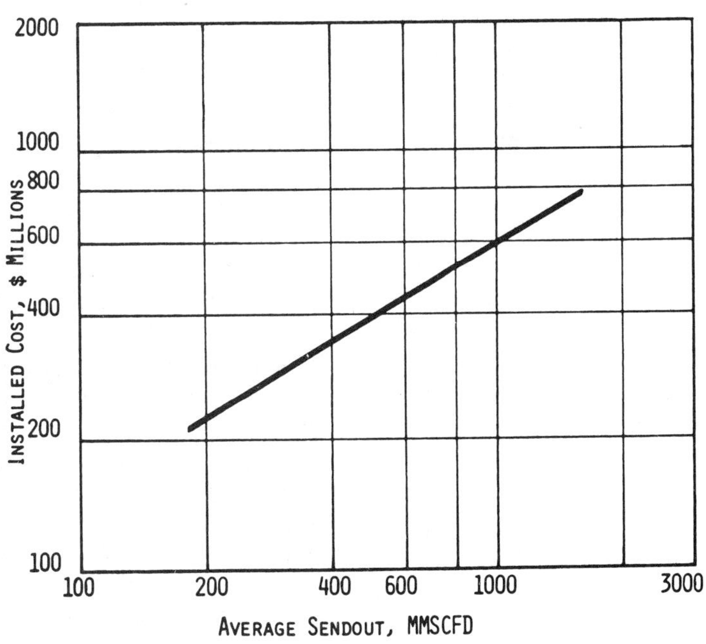

FIG. 7. Cost of LNG receiving terminals. Basis: 1985 second quarter U.S. dollars, conventional LNG storage.

Frequently a combination of seawater and gas-fired vaporizers is specified with the seawater vaporizers used for base-load sendout. The gas-fired vaporizers are then utilized during peak demand periods and also as partial backup for the base-load seawater vaporizers.

Facility Capital Cost

A generalized correlation of total facility installed cost as a function of average daily plant sendout is given in Fig. 7. These costs are based on conventional, single containment double-walled storage tanks and include a mix of seawater and gas-fired vaporization systems. The use of double integrity storage results in an increase in total facility costs of between 10 and 15%.

Innovative Cost Reduction Concepts

The greatest potential for cost reductions in conventional, land-based liquefaction plants due to improvements in processing technology would appear to lie in the area of the refrigeration compressor-driver selection and associated plant utility systems. As noted earlier, an all- gas turbine, aircooled processing arrangement has been selected for use in the Northwest Shelf LNG plant as part of an effort by the operator to reduce plant capital investment.

A number of more innovative design concepts have been advanced for LNG plants which offer the potential for major cost savings. Many of these, such as land-based modular construction techniques and barge-mounted facilities and various offshore floating and fixed based platform facilities, have been utilized in other less complex applications, such as oil and gas production, LPG recovery, and ammonia production.

Barge-mounted LNG facilities, either grounded or floating, offer the advantage of construction in the controlled, industrial environment of a shipyard and the ability to pretest and precommission certain critical sections of the process. Modular construction also offers potential savings in these areas but to a lesser degree since more field labor is required to assemble individual modules.

Fixed-based offshore plants offer less of a potential savings in the cost of the basic liquefaction facilities but could reduce offshort gas gathering and onshore transmission costs to the point of being economical, especially for fields far offshore or with a difficult sea bottom. Floating plants also might be attractive under these circumstances.

Figure 8 gives an approximation of the total facility costs for two types of barge-mounted liquefaction plants: (a) self-contained barge-mounted floating facilities including floating LNG storage, and (b) grounded barge-mounted facilities excluding storage and loading, buildings, etc.

Maximum capacity of a single barge is assumed to be approximately 250 MMSCFD. The cost for floating offshore storage and loading is estimated to

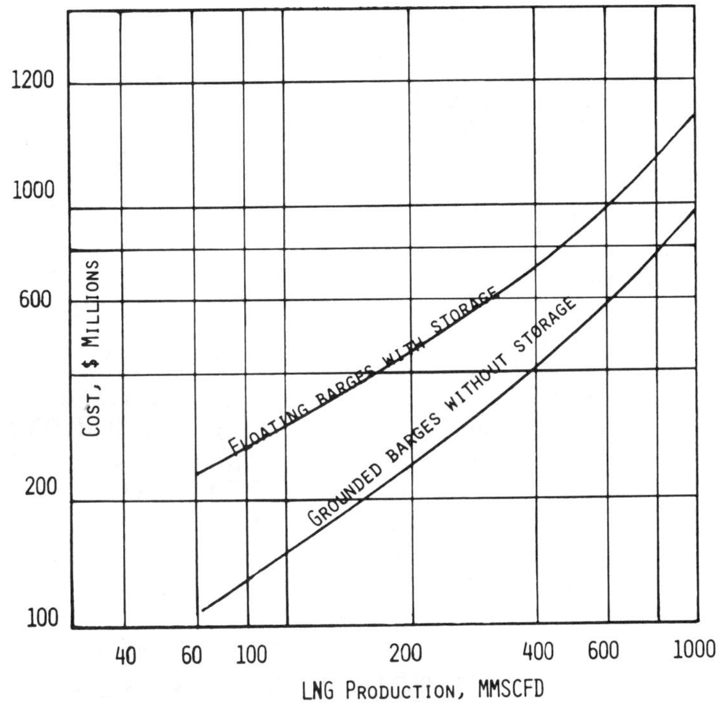

FIG. 8. Cost of barge-mounted LNG plants. Basis: 1985 second quarter U.S. dollars. Floating plants include all facilities and loading systems. Grounded barges include only AGR, liquefaction, and associated facilities.

be $900/m^3$ in 1985 dollars. This compares with a unit storage cost of about $1200/m^3$ for the cost of a 125,000 m^3 capacity LNG ship at current estimated shipyard cost.

Cost of an LNG liquefaction plant constructed on an offshore structure is estimated to cost from 25 to 50% more than a floating facility of similar capacity, depending on water depth and other local site conditions. Floating plants do, however, have the disadvantage of requiring an articulated loading arm or boom which permits movement at both ends. This concept has yet to be proven for the high-capacity transfer rates at cryogenic temperatures required for LNG ship loading.

Comparison of Design Concepts

An order-of-magnitude type comparison of total installed cost for the floating and grounded barge concepts with conventional land-based construction is given in Table 4. Comparisons are presented for a 1000 MMSCFD (7 million ton/yr) capacity project and a smaller 400 MMSCFD (2.8 million ton/yr) capacity project.

TABLE 4 Installed Cost

	Construction Concept (in millions of 1985 U.S. $)		
LNG Production Rate (MMSCFD)	Floating Barge	Grounded Barge	Conventional Land-Based
1000	$1650	$1480	$1570
400	$700	$790	$820

A comparison of this type indicates only a small potential savings of the order of 6% with the use of the grounded-barge concept as compared to conventional construction for a large 1000 MMSCFD capacity project. The floating concept is some 12% higher in cost.

For the smaller 400 MMSCFD capacity project, the floating barge concept shows some small cost savings due primarily to the savings in site-related costs for the grounded-barge and conventional land-based plant concepts. These costs constitute a greater percentage of the overall facility cost as the size of the project is reduced.

On an overall project basis the cost differential between the various construction techniques is too small to be meaningful and well within the accuracy of the estimation methodology. The various construction options must be carefully studied in detail for each specific project, and the influence of related factors, such as offshore development costs, site-specific labor costs, and the availability of subsidies and/or credit assistance from ship-building countries, carefully considered.

This material was originally presented at the Eighth International Conference on LNG, June 15, 1986, and is used with the permission of the Conference and the author.

References

1. "Contractors Named for Australian LNG Project," *Oil Gas J.*, *83*, 71 (July 29, 1985).
2. R. N. DiNapoli, "Estimating Costs for Base-Load LNG Plants," *Oil Gas J.*, *73*, 58–60 (November 17, 1975).
3. R. N. DiNapoli, "LNG Costs Reflect Changes in Economy and Technology," *Oil Gas J.*, *82*, 138–143 (April 4, 1983).

ROBERT N. DiNAPOLI

Liquefied Natural Gas, Refrigeration Cycles

Owners of liquefied natural gas (LNG) plants have to examine all offerings carefully to select a process that assures high on-stream factors, reliability of equipment, flexibility, ease of operations, and guaranteed capacities. Small differences in claimed thermodynamic efficiencies are unimportant, and usually are less than the uncertainties in equipment performance.

In selecting the liquefaction process and equipment for a new project, a proper choice must be made between the use of well-proven technology and the acceptance of innovations proposed to reduce capital costs and to improve efficiencies and reliabilities.

As of July 1987, 13 base-load LNG facilities had been built and one was under construction. They have a total liquefaction capacity of over 8 billion SCFD of natural gas. These facilities can be categorized according to the general type of refrigeration cycle used: classical cascade; mixed refrigerant; and propane precooled, mixed refrigerant. Variations exist within each category, depending on the process licensor and the specific requirements at each facility.

Classical Cascade

The first base-load LNG plants built, in Algeria and Alaska, used classical cascade refrigeration cycles. Three different refrigerants were cascaded: propane, ethylene, and methane. Two or three levels of evaporating pressures were used for each of the refrigerants. Multistage compressors were used, with different mass flows in each stage.

Figure 1 illustrates a cascade refrigeration cycle. For simplicity, the schematic shows only a single evaporating pressure and compression stage for each refrigerant.

In reality, refrigeration is supplied at eight or nine discrete temperatures. A simplified cooling curve for a typical cascade cycle (Fig. 2) shows that refrigeration is provided at successively lower discrete temperatures. In any gas liquefaction cycle, the total amount of heat which must be absorbed by the surroundings (cooling water or air) depends primarily on the amount of gas liquefied, and secondarily on the inefficiencies in the compressors and the heat-transfer process.

The cooling curves in Fig. 2 do not include the heat exchange within the "pure refrigerants": propane, ethylene, and methane, for the cascade system; and propane for the propane precooled, mixed-refrigerant system. In the mixed-refrigerant section it is not possible to separate the heat transferred to the high-pressure, mixed refrigerant and the natural gas.

Cascade refrigeration cycles are relatively easy to design. The properties of the refrigerants are well known, heat exchanger design is straightforward, and the cascade concept is easy to understand.

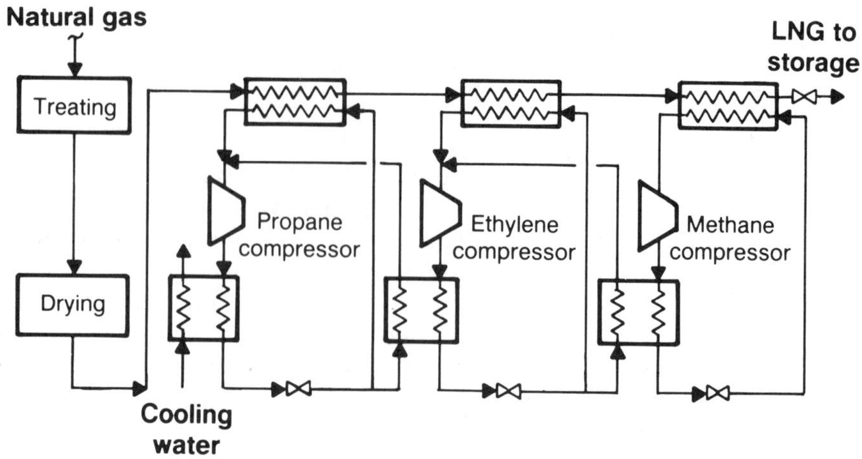

FIG. 1. Cascade cycle.

The initial decision to use well-known, easily understood refrigeration cycles for the emerging base-load LNG industry was sound. It was based on minimizing innovations, even though the process required a relatively large number of refrigerant compressors and heat exchangers.

Mixed Refrigerant

While the early cascade cycle plants were being placed in service, additional base-load LNG projects were being planned. The owners of the proposed plants were concerned with the potential difficulty of maintaining the many

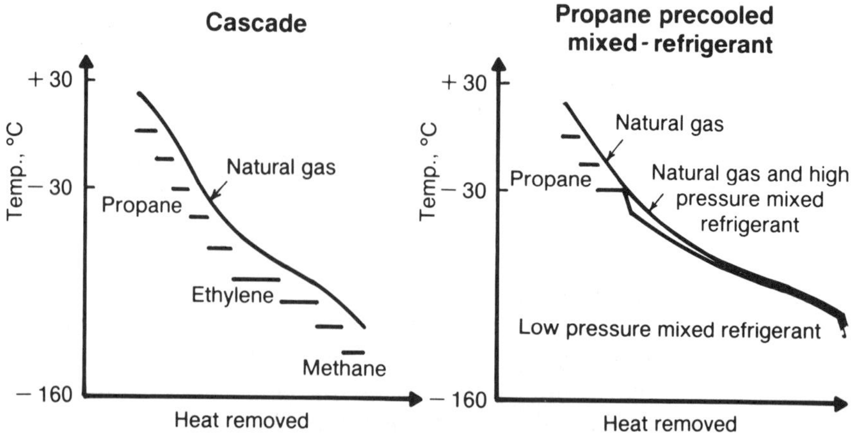

FIG. 2. Cooling curves.

machines needed for cascade cycles. New, mixed-refrigerant cycles were being developed. The principal capital and maintenance advantage of these cycles was that only a single compressor train was required.

In mixed-refrigerant cycles, the refrigerant usually consists of a mixture of nitrogen, methane, ethane, propane, butane, and pentane. The specific concentrations and operating pressures of the cycles varied with the details of each process.

The mixed-refrigerant cycle (Fig. 3) operates in a manner somewhat similar to a pure refrigerant system. Refrigeration is provided by liquids vaporizing at an essentially constant low pressure but over the entire range of temperatures at which the liquefied mixture evaporates (rather than at the constant temperature of a relatively pure refrigerant). The compositions and temperatures of the evaporating liquids change as vaporization progresses. The low-pressure, totally vaporized mixed refrigerant is compressed only to a pressure at which it is partially condensed.

By judicious selection of operating pressure and of the total composition of the circulating mixed refrigerant, and by proper arrangement of heat exchangers, efficient processes can be designed. In principle, they provide the required refrigeration at a selected continuum of temperatures from ambient to the boiling temperature of LNG, about −258°F. In reality, efficiencies are limited by the thermophysical properties of the mixtures and the machinery efficiencies. Furthermore, the ability to change refrigerant composition is a significant operating variable that allows efficient utilization of all available heat-transfer surface and actual compressor characteristics.

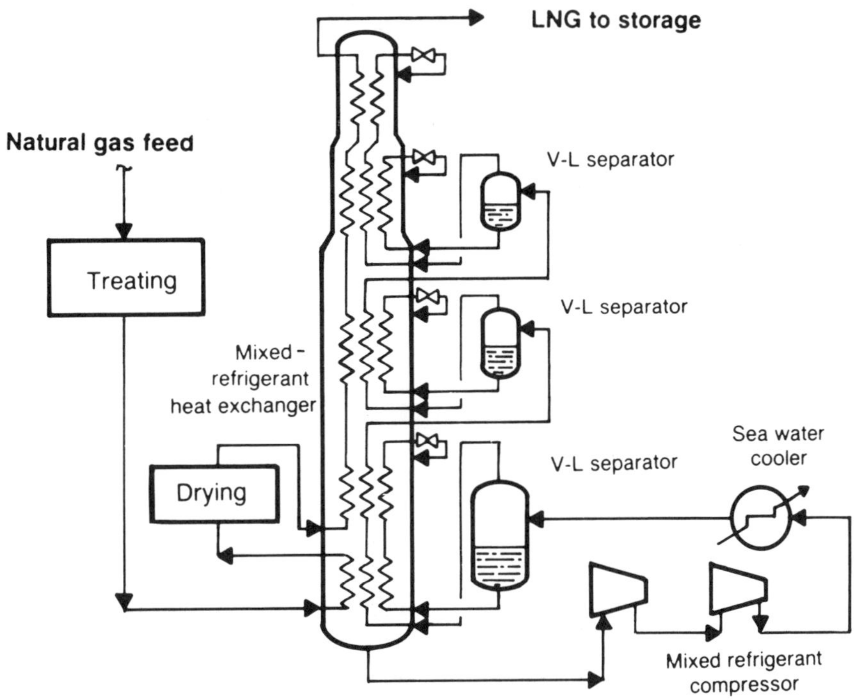

FIG. 3. Mixed-refrigerant cycle.

The first commercial mixed-refrigerant system was placed in service in Libya in 1970. The high-pressure, mixed refrigerant is partially condensed in seawater coolers and separated into a liquid fraction and a vapor fraction.

The natural gas feed and both high-pressure refrigerant streams are cooled in a single multifluid heat exchanger. Refrigeration is supplied over a range of temperatures by the vaporizing low-pressure mixed refrigerant.

The first vapor fraction is partially condensed in the heat exchanger. It is then separated into a second liquid fraction and a second vapor fraction, which are further cooled.

The first high-pressure fraction is flashed into the returning low-pressure vaporizing stream to provide the refrigeration for cooling the liquid and vapor fractions from the previous high-pressure separator, and to cool the natural gas. Separation and cooling steps are carried out at successively lower temperatures, with progressively lower-boiling fractions.

Propane Precooled, Mixed Refrigerant

The propane precooled, mixed-refrigerant cycle was developed later and was selected for all of the recent LNG plants. It combines the simplicity of a mixed-refrigerant cycle with the efficiency of the cascade cycle. This cycle is not used at nearly two-thirds of the base-load LNG plants. In the propane precooled, mixed-refrigerant cycle, propane refrigeration is usually provided at three temperature levels, to about −35°F. Precooling is followed by a mixed-refrigerant cooling system to provide the low-temperature refrigeration. The mixed refrigerant usually contains nitrogen, methane, ethane, and propane.

A single, large heat exchanger is used to provide refrigeration for the high-pressure mixed-refrigerant streams and the natural gas at a continuum of temperatures, from the lowest temperature propane evaporator to the final low temperature required for the liquefaction process. The composition of the mixed refrigerant can usually be selected to enable the propane precooled, mixed-refrigerant cycle to have efficiencies higher than those of cascade cycles.

Processes Available

As of July 1987, four companies offer process and equipment designs for precooled, mixed-refrigerant base-load LNG plants: Air Products and Chemicals of the United States, Linde AG of West Germany, and L'Air Liquide and Technip of France. Phillips offers its cascade cycles on a selective basis. The precooled, mixed-refrigerant processes (Figs. 4–7) are similar in that a precooled mixed refrigerant is used to provide the low-temperature refrigeration required for the final liquefaction of the natural gas. The processes differ,

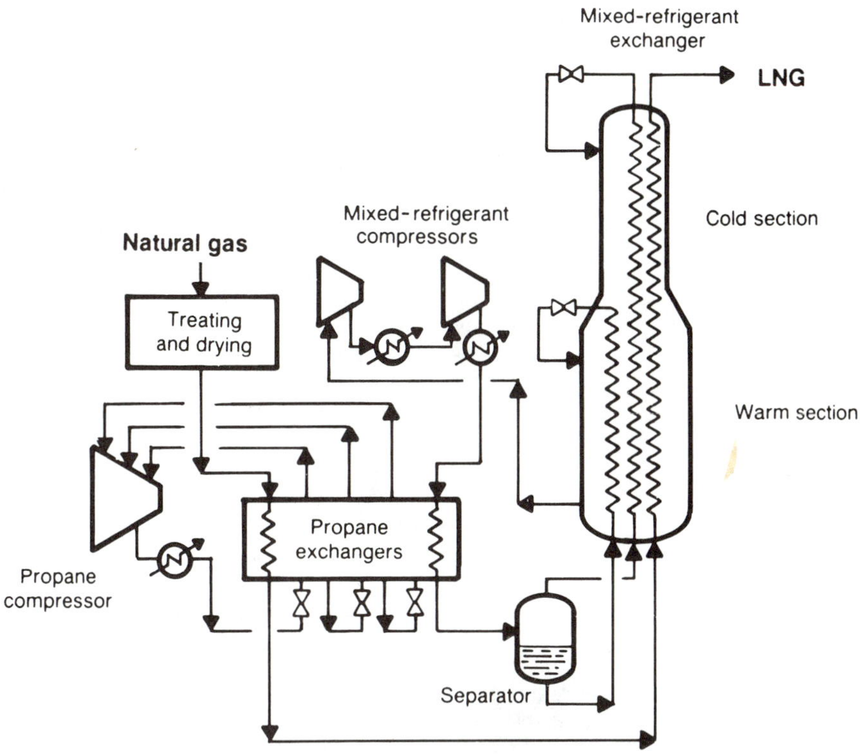

FIG. 4. Precooled, mixed-refrigerant process. Air Products.

however, in the refrigerant used for precooling the low-temperature, mixed refrigerant or in the heat exchangers which are used.

Air Products and L'Air Liquide precool their low-temperature, mixed refrigerant with propane evaporating at three pressure and temperature levels. Linde AG and Technip precool their low-temperature, mixed refrigerant with a high-temperature, mixed refrigerant of propane and ethane evaporating at three pressure levels, and over a range of temperatures which depends on the specific composition of the refrigerant mixture. Air Products has recently has proposed precooling by a mixed refrigerant for some locations.

L'Air Liquide's version of a propane precooled, mixed-refrigerant process provides propane precooling and mixed-refrigerant cooling in a single vertical, multisectioned plate-and-fin heat exchanger. Parallel exchangers are used to provide adequate plant capacity.

Propane evaporates at three different pressures and temperatures in three separate sections in the upper portion. The mixed refrigerant evaporates in the lower portion. The natural gas flows successively through each section. Each exchanger is balanced by controlling the flow of natural gas consistent with the refrigerant flows. This heat exchanger arrangement is useful for smaller plants, and is amendable to direct scale-up. One important limitation

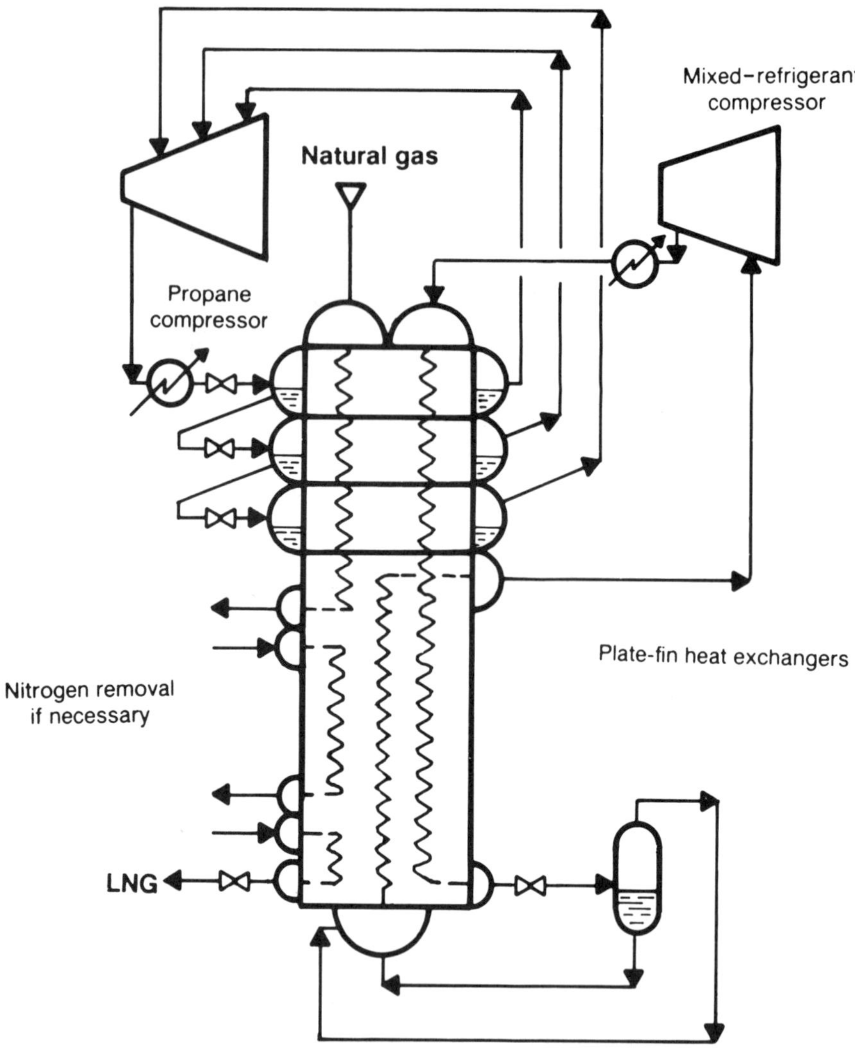

FIG. 5. Precooled, mixed-refrigerant process. L'Air Liquide.

in the overall process is the need for multiple heat exchangers and multiple control valves.

Technip's Precooled Tealarc process uses a mixture of ethane and propane to precool its low-temperature, mixed refrigerant. One modest advantage of using a mixture of ethane and propane rather than pure propane is that the cooling water in the condenser can undergo a higher temperature rise. Therefore, less cooling water is required. Another advantage, in some cases, is that identical drivers may be used.

A third possible advantage is that the low-temperature, mixed refrigerant can be precooled to lower temperatures. This may be advantageous in unique

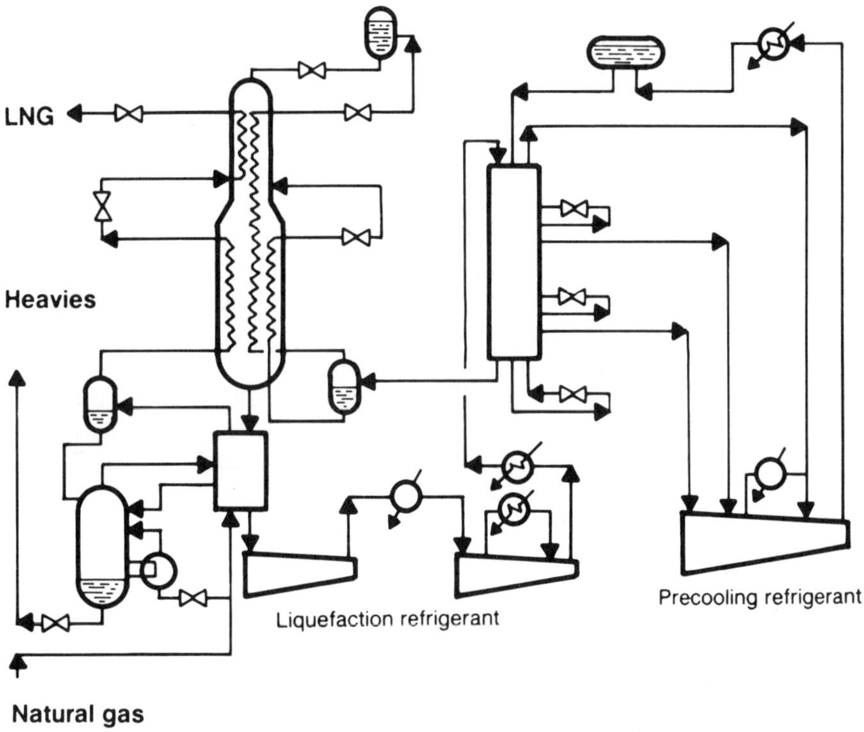

FIG. 6. Precooled, mixed-refrigerant process. Technip.

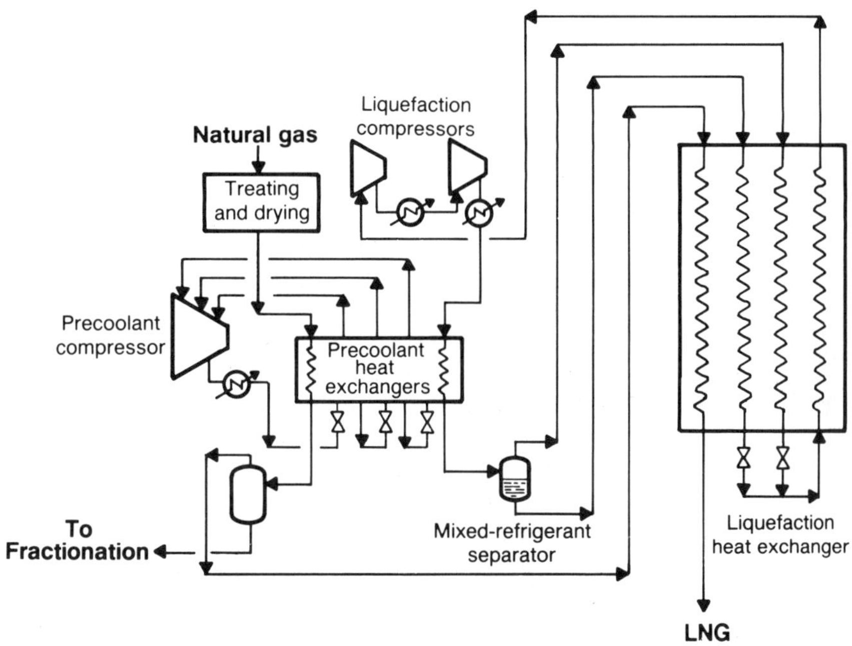

FIG. 7. Precooled, mixed-refrigerant process. Linde AG.

situations. In principle, compositions of the two mixed-refrigerant streams may be selected to obtain slightly higher calculated thermodynamic efficiencies. However, the overall heat exchange arrangement is more complex than in the propane precooled cycles, the control system for good distribution and prevention of hydrate formation more involved, and the differences in calculated efficiencies are small and unimportant.

Linde AG offers its dual flow process with two mixed-refrigerant circuits. It is probable that evaporating composition control will be more difficult in Linde's specific process, compared with Technip's.

Air Products' basic propane precooled, mixed-refrigerant process has been used at seven plant site and has been selected for a plant presently under construction. Modest modifications have been made to meet specific site requirements. Sufficient operating information has been gathered to demonstrate that the process meets its operating guarantees. A basic source of field information is available for the successful design of large, mixed-refrigerant, coil-wound heat exchangers.

Driver Selection

Nearly all of the installed plants use steam turbine drivers for the refrigerant compressor. However, one of the earliest plants located in Alaska, one of the more recent plants located in Indonesia, and the plant under construction in Australia found it advantageous to use gas turbine drivers.

The decision to use gas turbine drivers in the LNG plant located in Alaska was based on concern with possible freezing in steam condensate lines, coupled with the owner's good experience with gas turbines. The original decisions to use steam turbine drivers in most of the other plants was based on opinions that steam turbines would have fewer maintenance problems than gas turbines.

The operating records of the steam turbines in base-load LNG plants have been excellent; the operating records of gas turbines have also been excellent. Plants with steam turbine drivers require cooling water, usually seawater, for their steam condensers. They also require boiler feedwater make-up systems. The maintenance of the overall steam system must be taken into account when considering maintenance and on-stream factors. Gas turbines, on the other hand, require no such additional systems.

One advantage that steam turbine drivers have, compared to gas turbine drivers, is that the maximum power output is at least 10% higher and is usually more than 15% higher than the rated power output if the boilers have sufficient steam capacity. The additional available power, coupled with safety factors in process design, led to significant increases in plant capacities where there was adequate capacity in the natural gas pretreating systems. It is unlikely that future base-load LNG plants will have as much excess gas pretreating capacity as in the past. For gas turbines the available power is approximately inversely proportional to the ambient temperature (degrees absolute); it is usually 2–3% higher than the rated power at the normal site temperature.

Unless fuel efficiency is an overwhelming consideration at a specific location, it is likely that there will be an increasing use of gas turbine drivers in future base-load LNG plants. Industrial gas turbines have demonstrated their reliabilities and ease of operation. The reductions in capital related to air- or water-cooled heat exchangers, in cooling water requirements, and in the elimination of the need for boiler feedwater will be important factors to consider in overall plant design and operating decisions.

One unique combination of circumstances which could lead to the use of electric motor drivers is where hydroelectric power is plentiful and natural gas supply is limited. One proposed LNG project, which was recently canceled, considered LNG shipments from Canada to Japan. The Canadian government had limited the total amount of gas which could be consumed as a combination of both LNG product and fuel for the plant. Hydroelectric power is available in Canada. Even though electric motor-driven compressors do not have the flexibility of gas turbine or steam turbine-driven compressors, electric motors had been selected to increase the total amount of LNG which could be delivered.

Thermodynamic Efficiencies

Each of the suppliers of base-load LNG plants usually claims slightly higher thermodynamic efficiency. These claims are usually valid within the assumptions made for the calculations.

From a thermodynamic viewpoint, providing refrigeration at a continuum of temperatures, with smaller temperature differences at the lower temperatures, leads to a smaller increase in entropy or a smaller loss of energy or availability in the liquefaction process.

When making thermodynamic comparisons for different liquefaction processes, it is important that comparisons be made on the basis of realistic equipment specification and/or performance, and include the complete process. For example, the cooling curves shown for the cascade cycle include only the refrigeration provided to the natural gas, and do not include the heat interchange between refrigerants. The cooling curve for the propane precooled, mixed-refrigerant cycle includes the heat transferred between the mixed refrigerants as well as the heat transferred from the natural gas.

The differences in claimed thermodynamic efficiencies, which are usually made for a single operating point, are relatively unimportant and must be examined carefully. It is important to answer questions such as: Are compressors' powers being compared on the basis of the same expected polytropic efficiencies or on the expected power input to achieve expected flow conditions? Is it reasonable to obtain the temperature differences and pressure drops which are used in the design of the mixed-refrigerant heat exchangers? Finally, are energy analyses made for operating conditions which might not be achieved in actual plant operation?

JACOB M. GEIST

Liquefied Petroleum Gas. A. Description, Properties, Recovery, and Treating

Introduction

As the name suggests, liquefied petroleum gas (LPG) is petroleum gas supplied in the liquid state. LPG's are by- products easily obtained from natural gas (NG) separation plants and petroleum refineries, and consist essentially of propane/propylene (C_3's) and butane/butylene (C_4's) in various mixtures.

Under normal conditions, petroleum fractions like C_5's and higher are in the liquid state and used as solvents and motor gasoline fractions. C_2's and lighter require too high a pressure to make them versatile feedstocks/fuel. Hence, LPG's under moderate pressure have exhibited greater consumer acceptance. At atmospheric pressure but above freezing temperature, these substances would be gases. Other than propane/propylene, LPG is the lightest saleable petroleum product.

Uses

LPG is used as a domestic, industrial, and commercial fuel and as a chemical raw material. It is also used in internal combustion engines, and is being substituted for gasoline/diesel in trucks, buses, and tractors. Because of the low boiling point (−44 to 0°C) and high vapor pressure of these gases, their handling as liquids in pressure bottles is necessary.

LPG has a high octane rating, which makes it useful in engines having a compression ratio above 10 : 1. Another factor of importance in internal combustion engines is that LPG leaves little or no engine deposit in the cylinders when it burns [1].

Because LPG is considerably cheaper than diesel fuel in certain sections of the United States, some United States railroads have considered converting locomotives to operate on propane-rich LPG. For maximum saving in fuel cost, a locomotive should be able to function with any fuel, depending on which is cheaper in the area where the locomotives happen to be at that time. Indications are that dual-fuel operation may prove to be the key to successful use of LPG in locomotives [2]. If necessary, the antiknock performance of commercial LPG can be made to equal or exceed that of propane by the addition of tetramethyl lead (TML) antiknock compounds.

Residential and commercial demands represent nearly half of LPG sales. Home heating is by far the largest use of LPG in cold countries and especially in North America. Owing to demand from industries for butane derivatives,

LPG sold as fuel is made up largely of propane. The propane fraction only is supplied for residential fuel in northern winter climates because of its lower boiling point. The second largest use is in the manufacture of petrochemicals and propylene/intermediates [2].

Supply / Demand

The production of LPG is related mainly to oil exploitation and recovery from associated and nonassociated gas.

Although an increase in catalytic cracking and hydroconversion processes yields increased production of liquefied petroleum gas, the percent annual recovery from crude oil in the United States (Table 1) has constantly decreased due to increasing production of petrochemicals, behavior of pricing pattern, and the larger share of LPG flowing from natural gas.

The LPG (C_3's and C_4's) supply/demand situation for the United States is compared with that of the Free World in Tables 2A and 2B. As can be seen, predictions for the United States situation show an increasing deficit in the traditional demand and supply situation whereas there will be a surplus on the global basis. The global surplus, if it were to be entirely used by the United States, would leave a deficit.

Another interesting observation is that during 1973–1983, although the United States demand showed a constant increase, supplies showed a decrease, reflecting the impact of the OPEC oil price rise. As against this, the actual supply/demand scenario showed only a marginal variation.

Properties

LPG consists mainly of saturated and/or unsaturated C_3 and C_4 hydrocarbons meeting rigid safety and quality specifications. It has to be treated to remove sulfur [5] and/or its compounds such as hydrogen sulfide and mercaptans.

TABLE 1 Percent Annual Recovery of LPG's from Crude Oil in the United States [3]

Year	% Recovery	Year	% Recovery
1964	3.3	1979	2.4
1968	3.1	1980	2.3
1973	2.8	1982	2.7
1974	2.6	1983	2.6
1977	2.3	1984	2.9
1978	2.3	1985	2.8

TABLE 2A Free World and United States LPG Supply/Demand (in million m^3)[a]

	1973 [4]			1976 [18]			1980[a]			1985[a]		
	World	United States	United States/ World, %	World	United States	United States/ World, %	World	United States	United States/ World, %	World	United States	United States/ World, %
Supply	149.5	71.9	48.1	160.9	67.2	41.8	223.7	60.1	26.9	275.2	77.1	28.0
Demand	145.4	77.1	53.0	168.8	74.4	44.1	203.6	101.1	49.7	249.5	119.1	47.7
Surplus/ (deficit)	4.1	(5.2)	—	(7.9)	(7.2)	—	20.1	(41.0)	(22.8)	25.7	(42.0)	(19.7)
Supply/ demand	1.028	0.932	—	0.953	0.903	—	1.099	0.594	—	1.103	0.647	—

[a]Predictions.

TABLE 2B Free World and United States LPG Supply/Demand (in million m^3)

	1973 [4]			1976 [18]			1980			1985		
	World	United States	United States/ World, %	World	United States	United States/ World, %	World	United States	United States/ World, %	World	United States	United States/ World, %
Supply	149.5	71.9	48.1	160.9	67.2	41.8	167.2	90.3	54.0	173.8	91.8	52.8
Demand	145.4	77.1	53.0	168.8	74.4	44.1	160.1	98.4	61.4	165.3	99.8	60.4
Surplus/ (deficit)	4.1	(5.2)	—	(7.9)	(7.2)	—	7.1	(8.1)	—	8.5	(8.0)	—
Supply/ demand	1.028	0.932	—	0.953	0.903	—	1.043	0.918	—	1.051	0.920	—

In general, LPG specifications involve limits for physical properties. The composition of commercial grade products varies between wide limits.

Properties of the principal and trace compounds of LPG are given in Table 3, and the detailed specifications for LPG in Table 4. Since large quantities of C_4 components are used for enhancing motor gasoline production through the alkylation route, the data given in Table 5 on alkylate characteristics and yield factors and in Table 6 on products of isobutane alkylation with olefins find enormous use.

In any LPG recovery plant, the use of thermal equipment is an integral part. LPG is a nonfouling hydrocarbon. Its approximate fouling factors and heat transfer coefficients are given below [6]:

LPG fouling factor	0.001°F·ft²·h/Btu
LPG overall heat transfer coefficients:	
For steam-heated reboilers	155–160 Btu/h·ft²·°F
For water-cooled condensers	90–95 Btu/h·ft²·°F
For exchangers handling fouling hydrocarbons	30 Btu/h·ft²·°F
For exchangers handling nonfouling hydrocarbons	100 Btu/h·ft²·°F

LPG Recovery

LPG is a class of versatile petroleum products recovered from natural gas or derived from the refining of crude oil.

From Natural Gas

LPG recovered from natural gas (NG) is essentially free of unsaturated hydrocarbons (propylene and butylene). LPG is recovered from NG principally by (a) absorption, (b) compression, and (c) adsorption.

NG liquids must be extracted from the wet NG in sufficient quantities to eliminate the possibility of condensation in pipelines. NG liquids are usually propane and high hydrocarbons. Propane and butane are separated as LPG, whereas pentane and higher hydrocarbons are separated as natural gasoline.

From Refinery Gas

Removal of the LPG components from refinery fuel gas is equivalent to upgrading heavy fuel oil (HFO) to the most valuable product, LPG. Thus there is a great incentive for minimizing C_3^+ components in refinery fuel gas [9].

Recovery of LPG in a light ends recovery unit is a common feature of basic petroleum refineries (Fig. 1). LPG production is maximized using rather complex secondary conversion processes. Production can be further enhanced by recovery of propane and butane from the overhead off-gas of the platformer stabilizer (Fig. 2) through recirculation of LPG from the product rundown line as reflux. A typical refinery fuel gas composition is given in Table 7, and the analytical results of a plant test comparing off-gas and LPG

TABLE 3 Properties of the Principal and Trace Components of LPG [2, 6, 21]

No.	Name	Formula	Molecular Weight	Liquid Specific Gravity 60/60°F	Liquid, lbs/bbl	ft³ of Vapor[a]/bbl Liquid
			Saturates			
A-1	Ethane	C_2H_6	30.068	0.374[b]	149	1882
A-2	Propane	C_3H_8	44.094	0.5077[b]	178	1530
A-3	*n*-Butane	C_4H_{10}	58.120	0.5844[b]	205	1336
A-4	Isobutane	C_4H_{10}	58.120	0.5631[b]	197	1287
A-5	*n*-Pentane	C_5H_{12}	72.146	0.6312	221	1162
A-6	Isopentane	C_5H_{12}	72.146	0.6248	219	1151
A-7	*n*-Hexane	C_6H_{14}	86.172	0.6640	232	1024
A-8	Isohexane (2-methylpentane)	C_6H_{14}	86.172	0.6579	230	—
A-9	Neohexane (2,2-dimethylbutane)	C_6H_{14}	86.172	0.6540	228	—
			Unsaturates			
B-1	Ethene	C_2H_4	28.052	0.3500[b]	153	2072
B-2	Propene	C_3H_6	42.078	0.5220[b]	183	1647
B-3	1-Butene	C_4H_8	56.104	0.6013	210	1417
B-4	Isobutene	C_4H_8	56.104	0.6004	210	1422
B-5	*cis*-2-Butene	C_4H_8	56.104	0.6271	220	1486
B-6	*trans*-2-Butene	C_4H_8	56.104	0.6100	214	1444
B-7	1-Pentene	C_5H_{10}	70.130	0.6457	226	1224
B-8	1-Hexene	C_6H_{12}	84.156	0.6780	238	1071

[a]At 60°F and 1 atm as a perfect gas.
[b]At saturation pressure.

TABLE 4 Specification for LPG (ASTM D1835-76) [7]

Property	Special Duty Propane	Commerical Propane	Comercial Butane	Propane Butane Mixture
Distillation, 95% point, max, °C	−38.3	−38.3	2.2	2.2
Vapor pressure at 37.8°C, max, kPa	1430	1430	485	—
Propylene, max, vol.%	5.0	—	—	—
Butane and heavier, max, vol.%	2.5	2.5	—	—
Pentane and heavier, max, vol.%	—	—	2.0	2.0
Sulfur at 15.6°C, 101 kPa, max mg/m³	229	343	343	343
Residue on evaporation, 100 mL, max mL	0.05	0.05	0.05	0.05
Oil stain observation	Pass	Pass	Pass	Pass
Corrosion, copper strip, max no.	—	1	—	—
Hydrogen sulfide content	Pass	—	—	—
Moisture content	Pass	Pass	—	—
Free-water content	—	—	None	None

Normal bp, °F	Vapor Pressure at 100°F, lb/in.²abs	Freezing Point, °F	Critical Temperature, °F	Critical Pressure, lb/in.²abs	Latent Heat of Vaporization at Normal bp, Btu/lb	Low Heating Value, Btu/lb, gas
−127.53	—	−297.89	90.32	709.8	210.41	20,416
−43.73	190.0	−305.84	206.26	617.4	183.05	19,929
31.1	51.62	−217.03	305.62	550.7	165.64	19,665
10.89	72.21	−255.28	274.96	529.1	157.51	19,614
96.93	15.57	−201.50	385.92	489.5	153.59	19,499
82.13	20.44	−255.82	370.1	483.0	147.13	19,451
155.73	4.956	−139.63	454.5	440.0	143.95	19,391
140.49	6.767	−244.61	436.9	440.1	138.67	19,356
121.53	9.856	−147.77	421.2	450.7	131.24	19,299
−154.68	—	−272.47	49.82	742.1	207.57	20,276
−53.86	226.34	−301.45	197.4	667.0	188.18	19,683
20.73	63.08	−301.63	295.6	583.0	167.94	19,484
19.58	63.20	−220.63	292.51	579.8	169.48	19,367
38.70	45.53	−218.04	311.0	600.0	178.91	19,431
33.58	49.73	−157.99	311.0	600.0	174.39	19,397
85.94	19.115	−265.40	394.0	586.0	154.46	19,346
146.27	6.006	−219.67	463.0	500.0	155.00	19,100

TABLE 5 Alkylate Characteristic and Yield Factors, Using HF Catalyst [2, 8]

	Olefin Feed				
	1-Butane	*trans*-2-Butene	*cis*-2-Butene	Isobutene	Mixed Olefin
Alkylate properties:[a]					
Molecular weight	114.5	113.5	113.6	112.1	108.6
Reid vapor pressure, kPa	19	15	15	25	26
Density, g/cm³	0.707	0.706	0.705	0.697	0.698
ASTM end point, °C	181	164	164	177	177
RON + 0	94.4	97.8	97.6	95.9	93.7
MON + 0	91.6	94.6	91.4	93.4	90.8
RON + 0	106.5	111.6	111.3	108.5	105.6
MON + 3	106.4	100.6	109.4	108.3	105.7
Yield factors:					
Alkylate yield, vol./vol. olefin	1.73	1.77	1.81	1.73	1.79
i-C_4 consumption, vol./vol. olefin	1.10	1.11	1.17	1.15	1.28
C_3 yield, vol.% of propylene	0.0	0.0	0.0	0.0	16.10

[a]RON = Research Octane Number. MON = Motor Octane Number.

TABLE 6 Products of Isobutane Alkylation with Olefins [2, 8]

	Olefin Feed				
	1-Butane	*trans*-2-Butene	*cis*-2-Butene	Iso-butene	Mixed Olefin[a]
Feed ratio, isobutane/olefin	11	12	14	13	13
Product:					
Isopentane	3.31	1.84	1.79	5.44	5.85
n-Pentane	0.01	0.07	0.0	0.05	0.0
2-Methylpentane plus 2,3-dimethylbutane	1.47	1.37	1.39	2.88	2.89
3-Methylpentane	0.18	0.12	0.13	0.23	0.24
2,2- plus 2,4-Dimethylpentane	1.12	1.30	1.30	2.39	0.91
2,2,3-Trimethylbutane	0.03	0.0	0.0	0.0	0.10
2-Methylhexane	0.13	0.14	0.05	0.13	0.39
2,3-Dimethylpentane	0.72	0.63	0.68	1.18	14.42
3-Methylhexane	0.08	0.20	0.05	0.0	0.48
2,2,4-Trimethylpentane	41.30	48.71	48.93	50.21	32.49
2,5-Dimethylhexane	3.75	2.09	2.10	3.26	2.32
2,4-Dimethylhexane	6.41	2.87	2.88	3.56	2.99
2,2,3-Trimethylpentane	1.31	1.13	1.13	1.07	0.63
2,3,3-Trimethylpentane	10.38	12.92	12.86	9.35	7.98
2,3-Dimethylhexane	7.61	2.14	2.20	1.78	2.51
2-Methylhexane	0.18	0.0	0.0	0.0	0.0
3,4-Dimethylhexane	1.01	0.15	0.0	21.0	0.43
3-Methylhexane	0.18	0.0	0.78	0.0	0.0
2,2,5-Trimethylhexane	0.66	0.10	0.05	1.31	0.42
2,3,4-Trimethylpentane	12.77	21.39	20.39	10.69	10.95
Residue	7.02	2.83	2.75	6.29	5.99

[a]40.3% propylene, 58.2% butenes, 1.5% amylenes. Reaction conditions: feed propane, 2.75%; effluent propane, 3.11%; feed propylene, 2.25%.

compositions under normal operations and using LPG reflux are given in Tables 8 and 9. For a platformer stabilizer feed of, say, 250 t/d, which produces about 80% platformate and 10% LPG and 2% off-gas, LPG production can be increased to about 11% by reducing the off-gas from 2 to 1.5% of the feed.

Using Expander Cycle

Expander-type cycles are competitive with other gas recovery processes and are the most economical to use when:

"Free pressure drop" is available between feed and residue gas pressure
Product requires demethanization only
Feed is very lean and propane plus heavier components are required
A small, unattended and prefabricated unit for LPG recovery is needed
An offshore LPG facility is required

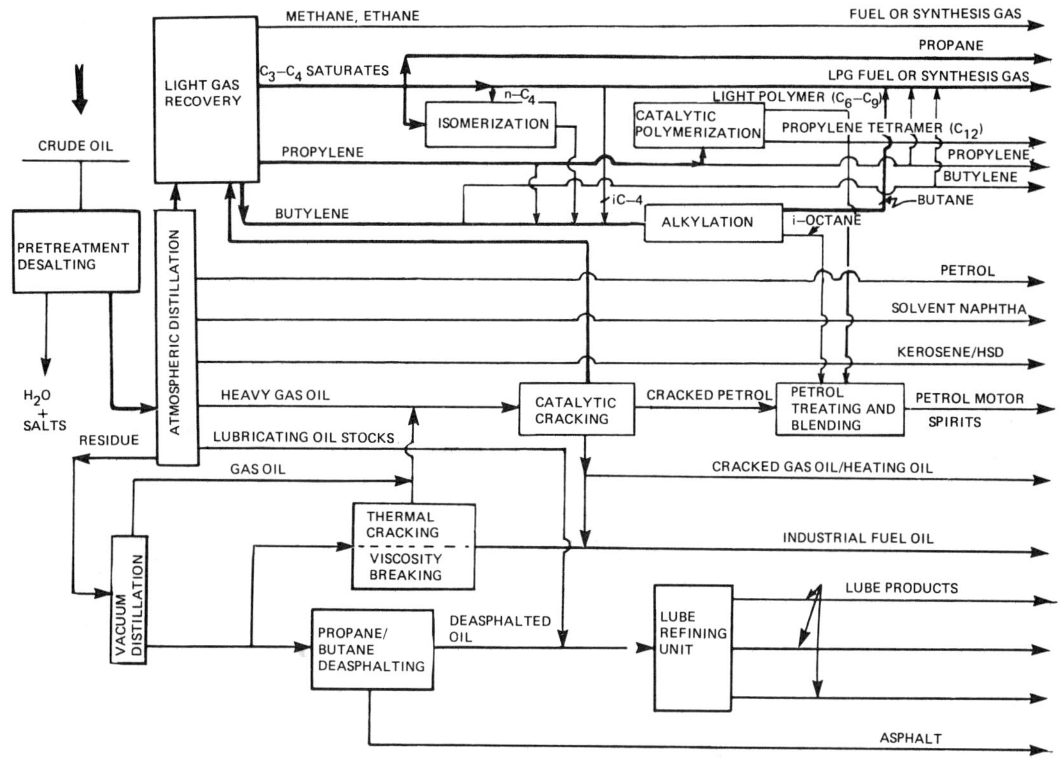

FIG. 1. Refinery operation showing separation of LPG and its components [14].

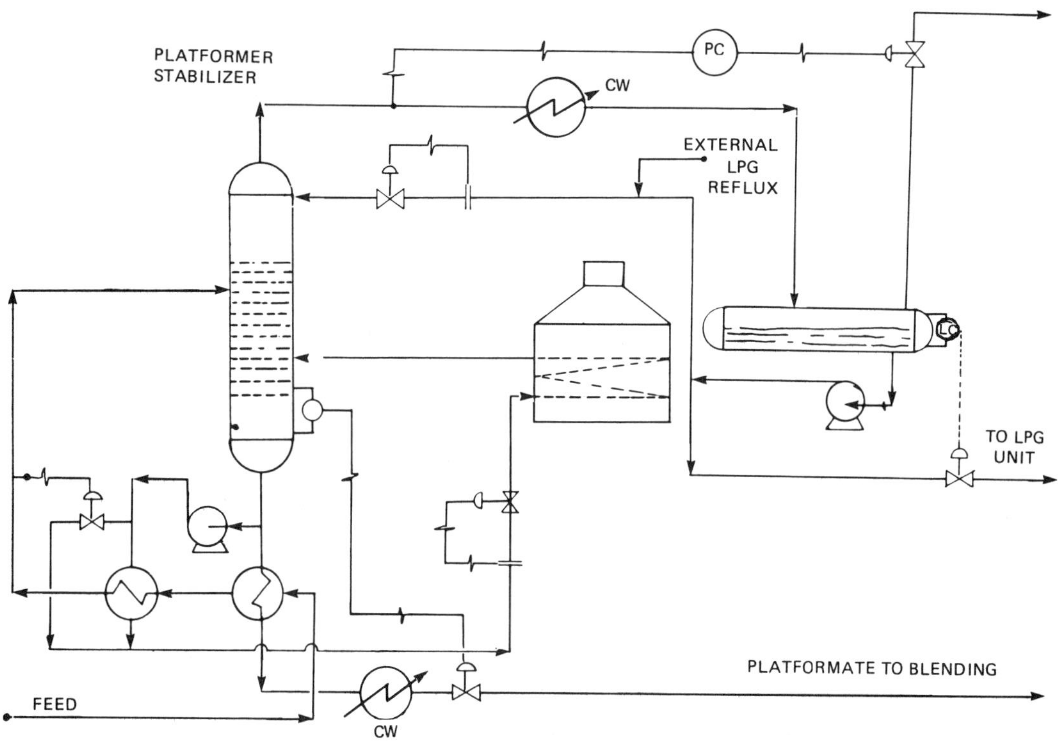

FIG. 2. LPG recovery from fuel gas ex-platformer stabilizer [9].

TABLE 7 Typical Refinery Fuel Gas Composition Variation (relative density: 0.4281-0.5741) [9]

	Range (vol.%)		Range (vol.%)
H_2	49.2–60.7	iC_5	0.5–0.9
C_1	18.3–26.4	nC_5	0.1–0.4
C_2	7.6–12.2	H_2S	0.5–0.8
C_3	5.5–8.6	CO_2	0.2–0.6
iC_4	1.3–4.3	O_2	0.6–1.0
nC_4	0.9–2.6		

TABLE 8 Composition of LPG and Gas Stream [9][a]

	Stabilizer Off-Gas		LPG (reflux and feed)		
	A	B	A	B	LPG Rundown
Specific gravity, 60/60°F	—	—	0.5215	0.5250	0.5429
Relative density	1.0603	1.0199	—	—	—
H_2, vol.%	16.8	20.0	Nil	Nil	Nil
C_1, vol.%	16.5	19.9	1.4	1.7	Nil
C_2, vol.%	30.1	27.0	15.9	15.6	6.9
C_3, vol.%	25.2	24.0	40.0	37.0	37.1
iC_4, vol.%	5.4	4.4	18.8	18.9	19.5
nC_4, vol.%	5.2	4.1	19.8	22.0	34.1
iC_5, vol.%	0.8	0.6	4.0	4.6	2.1
nC_5, vol.%	Nil	Nil	0.3	0.2	0.3

[a]A is the compositions of the off-gas and LPG at normal column operation. B is the compostions of the same streams with LPG recirculating to the reflux.

TABLE 9 Comparative Analysis of Off-Gas and LPG Absorbed [9]

	Composition of Off-Gas, Normal Operation			Composition of Off-Gas with 30% LPG in Reflux			LPG Absorbed,
Components	vol.%	wt.%	Mt/sd[a]	vol.%	wt.%	Mt/sd[a]	Mt/sd[a]
H_2	16.8	1.13	0.062	20.0	1.46	0.055	0.007
C_1	16.5	8.85	0.487	19.9	11.53	0.438	0.049
C_2	30.1	30.28	1.665	27.0	29.34	1.115	0.550
C_3	25.2	37.19	2.045	24.0	38.26	1.454	0.591
iC_4	5.4	10.50	0.578	4.4	9.24	0.351	0.227
nC_4	5.2	10.12	0.557	4.1	8.61	0.327	0.230
iC_5	0.8	1.93	0.106	0.6	1.56	0.059	0.047
nC_5	—	—	—	—	—	—	—
Total	100.0	100.0	5.500	100.0	100.0	3.799	1.701

[a]Thousand tons per stream day.

Three alternatives that can be considered are: (a) addition of facilities to reach 80% propane recovery using refrigerated oil, (b) using the expander cycle to match recovery of the oil plant, and (c) full use of the expander cycle to extract a significantly greater percentage of propane [10].

Propane recoveries can be increased to over 90% by adding external reflux facilities to the turboexpander cycle. The additional equipment required (Fig. 3) is a demethanizer reflux condenser, a demethanizer reflux accumulator, a reflux pump with spare, and replacement of the single-stage expander with a two-stage expander.

The expander cycles are normally a less expensive way of LPG recovery.

Using Secondary Conversion

LPG yield on crude normally varies from 1–2%. It can be more if the crudes are spiked with LPG or its components. In a refinery operation, in addition to virgin LPG obtained directly from crude, it can be obtained from secondary conversion processes based both on carbon rejection and carbon addition principles. The later is more expensive, essentially due to hydrogen requirements; e.g., in hydrocracking naphthas, about 25–30% of manufacturing cost is attributed to hydrogen manufacture alone.

Fluidized catalytic crackers using the heavy sidestreams of a vacuum tower as feedstock can increase the LPG yield by 2.5 to 3% on crude, and visbreakers using short residue as the feedstock can contribute another 0.1 to 0.3% LPG on refinery crude throughputs. However, the need for catalytic crackers and visbreakers never emerges from an LPG supply and demand situation; the justification flows from an upgrading of refinery fuel pool or getting the best out of the bottom of the barrel.

Vapor Pressure Control

The marketing requirements of some butane/LPG's include a specification for vapor pressure which is met by blending or spiking the butane with propane.

Complete linearization of vapor pressure (P) vs temperature (T) curves over a wide range may be realized by plotting log P vs $1/T$. For $\sqrt{P}$ vs T from −10 to 40°C, a straight line can be approximated. Based on this, four linearized curves are provided in Fig. 4 for n-butane, propane, and the upper and lower specification limits of spiked butane.

The control system (Fig. 5) used for C_4 spiking comprises (a) an absolute pressure transmitter range of 0 to 10 kg/cm^2, (b) a square-root relay, (c) a temperature transmitter range of −55 to +45°C, (d) a computing relay, and (e) a 2-term controller. The computing relay realizes the function $\sqrt{P} + t$ and hence has a defined constant output for any point on a given $\sqrt{P}$ vs t gradient [9].

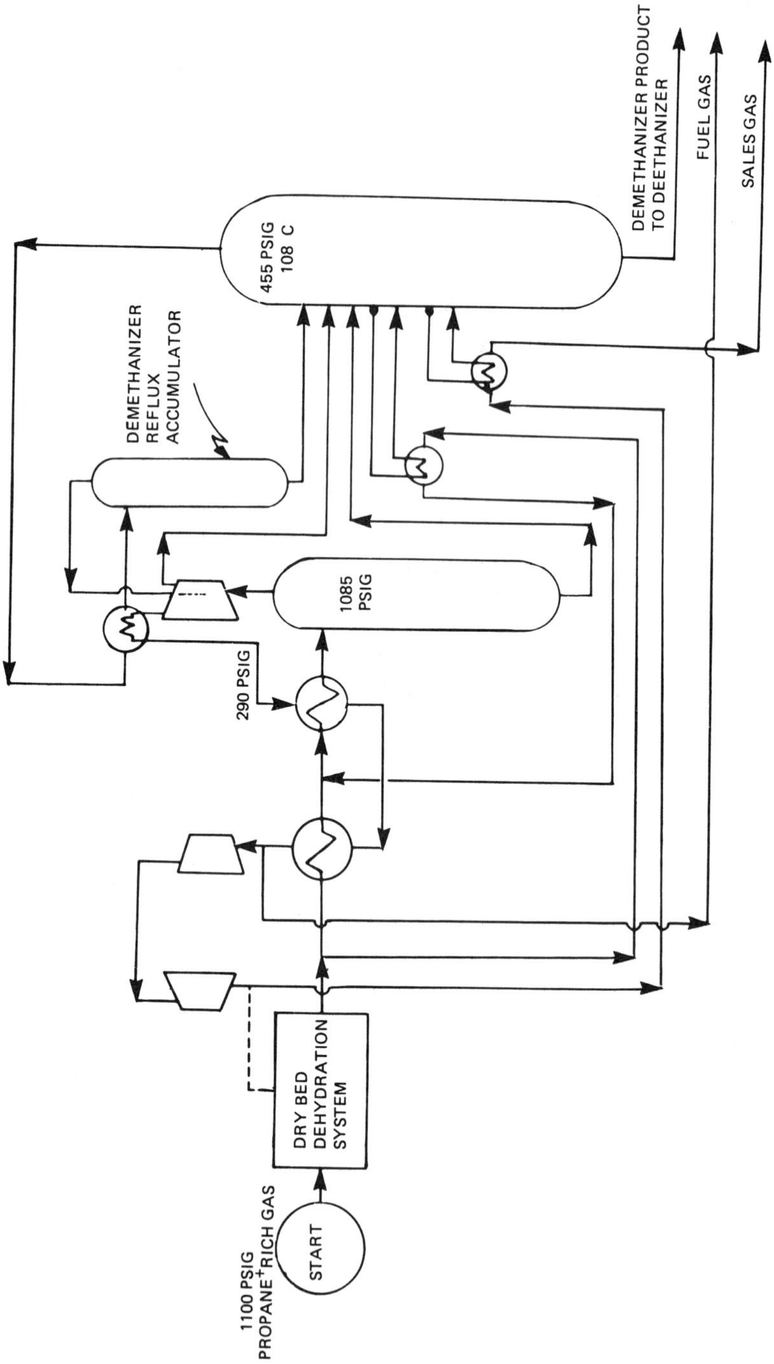

FIG. 3. Utilization of the expander cycle for LPG recovery [10].

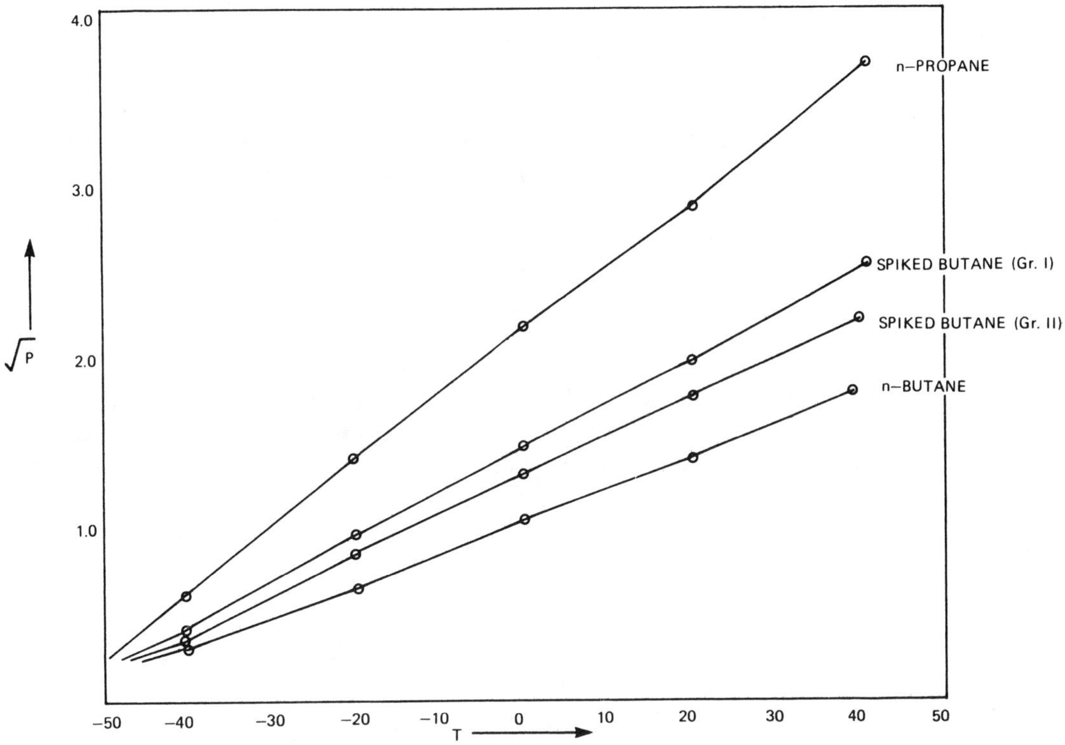

FIG. 4. Linearized vapor pressure curves [9]. Pressure in atmospheres and temperature in °C.

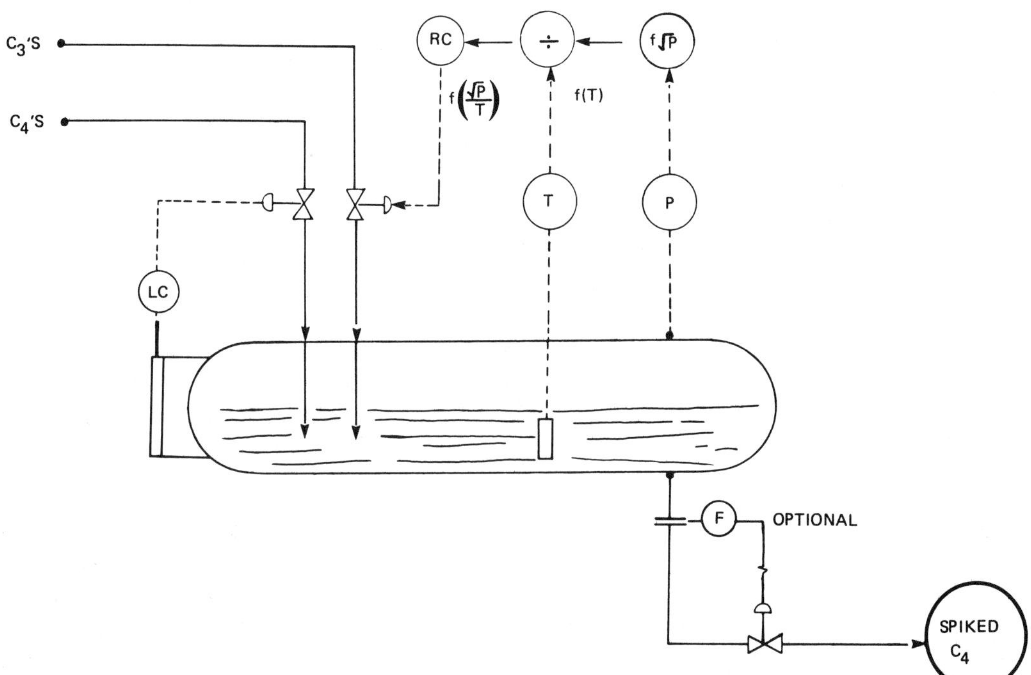

FIG. 5. Control system for C_4 spiking with C_3 [9].

LPG Spiking of Crudes

If excess light ends recovery capacity exists together with a market, it is generally more economical to spike crudes at the source or enroute with LPG or its components if they are available in surplus or at economic prices.

LPG Deasphalting

In an attempt to reduce the bottom of the barrel, several secondary conversion facilities are employed in a complex petroleum refinery. Cracker feed and/or blend stocks can be extracted out of vacuum residues using LPG, propane, or butane. The extraction process is known as deasphalting. The heavy asphalts can be visbroken to further upgrade the refinery product slate.

LPG Contamination

With Heavier Hydrocarbons (oily residues)

Most LPG supplies contain small amounts of heavier hydrocarbon liquids (above C_4). In normal supplies from refineries, this oil material is present in trace amounts of the order of 10–15 ppm having a boiling range of up to 350 or 400°C. Lubricating oils, gas oils, and kerosene can be present in LPG as contaminants. This can lead to field difficulties when trace quantities are greatly exceeded [9].

The method used for the determination of oily materials in LPG involves the following main steps [9, 11]:

A sample (100 mL) is allowed to weather at ambient temperature and is evaporated for 5 min at 100°F. The residue is dissolved in methyl ethyl ketone (MEK).

The MEK solution is transferred to a specially designed bottle and the oily residue is separated by adding sodium bisulfite solution.

The bottle is centrifuged. When the oil collects in the graduated neck, the volume is read to give the oily residue content.

Comprehensive tests can be designed to investigate the accuracy for different concentrations of oily residues and the effect of such variables as oily residue type (high or low boiling range), final evaporation temperature at the end of the weathering stage, the LPG type (butane or propane), etc. The correlation is best drawn for LPG samples containing oily residues of the kerosene/gas oil/lube oil type.

TABLE 10 Oily Residue Recovery from Propane/Butane [9]

	Oily Residue Recovery, % of Amount Added								
PPM Oily Residue Added:	25			100			250		
Temperature (°F):	100	140	212	100	140	212	100	140	212
Oily residue:									
n-Heptane	44	32	16	13	10	10	43	17	13
Gasoline	56	16	—	53	22	16	48	—	—
Kerosene	84	64	36	67	—	—	65	54	40
Gas oil	116	96	68	90	—	—	98	88	71
Lubricating oil	<40	<40	112	84	81	74	98	88	89

Some results for propane and butane are shown in Table 10. These show that if there is no initial weathering effect, the results are equally valid for propane or butane. Also, the higher the final evaporation temperature, the greater the loss of lighter material.

With Ammonia

One of the problems that the LPG industry has is contamination of LPG with ammonia (NH_3). NH_3 and LPG have approximately the same vapor pressure characteristics. Because of economic considerations, transportation and storage equipment are often used for NH_3 when not needed for LPG service [12].

With Other Contaminants

LPG may also be contaminated with fine iron oxide and other solids, water, caustic soda, free sulfur, and halogens.

LPG Sweetening

LPG treatment for the removal of mercaptans and/or hydrogen sulfide can be achieved by two distinct routes [9]:

Conventional wet treating using caustic soda solutions followed by an alumina dryer

A dry treating unit using molecular sieves to sweeten and dehydrate LPG simultaneously

Using Conventional Method

The desulfurization of olefinic hydrocarbons or paraffinic hydrocarbons containing appreciable amounts of olefins cannot be accomplished by the adsorption technique conventionally employed for the purification of saturated hydrocarbons.

The presence of about 2 wt.% H_2S in the C_4^- stream ex-debutanizer and the olefins in the C_4^- stream ex-platformer stabilizer gives rise to the formation of mercaptans in the deethanizer and in the depropanizer. Iron sulfide and iron oxide present in these columns are thought to be the catalysts for such mercaptan formation. The reduction obtained in mercaptan formation and the corrosion protection by Cronox-603 in the deethanizer/depropanizer is considered satisfactory [9].

Conventional sulfur-removal processes for light olefins treating include [13]:

Amine scrubbing: Suitable for bulk H_2S or COS removal.
Caustic wash: Efficient for removing H_2S. Desirable caustic soda solution concentration of 15–20% Bé.
Merox treating: Efficient for extracting mercaptans or converting them to noncorrosive disulfides.

Caustic soda wash can help remove small quantities of H_2S and large quantity of mercaptans (150 to 900 ppm as S) from butane, and H_2S up to 5000 ppm and mercaptans up to 1000 ppm from propane [9].

The strength of fresh caustic soda is usually about 7% (by weight). In a refinery operation, the spent caustic soda is used in the crude distilling units for HCl neutralization. Sodium sulfide and sodium mercaptide formed in the LPG/naphtha units pass to the crude distilling units, where the following reactions may occur [9]:

$$Na_2S + 2HCl \longrightarrow 2NaCl + H_2S$$

$$NaSH + 2H_2O \xrightarrow{250°F} NaOH + RSH$$

Thus, H_2S and mercaptans can be regenerated.

The high mercaptan level increases the concentration of sodium mercaptide in the treating solution, and thus increases the possibility of the oxidation of disulfides:

$$2RSNa + \frac{1}{2}O_2 + H_2O \longrightarrow RSSR + 2NaOH$$

The system can be set up as indicated in Fig. 6 for regenerating spent caustic ex-LPG treaters.

In conventional treatment with caustic soda solution (Fig. 7), the liquid propane is first contacted with diisopropanol amine (DIPA) in an extractor

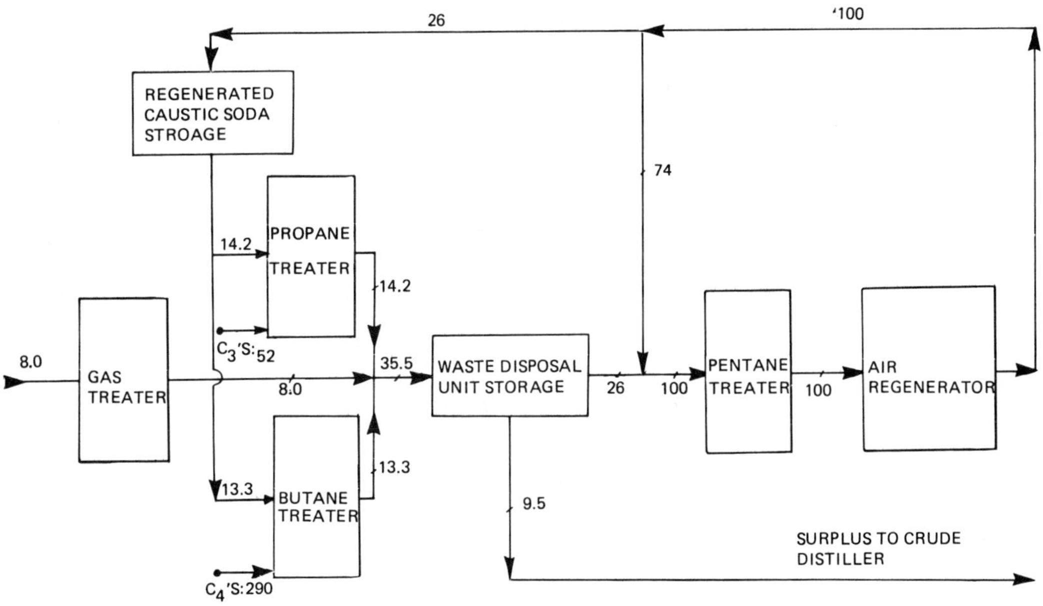

FIG. 6. Caustic soda cycle for LPG and other treating systems [9]. All values in tons/day.

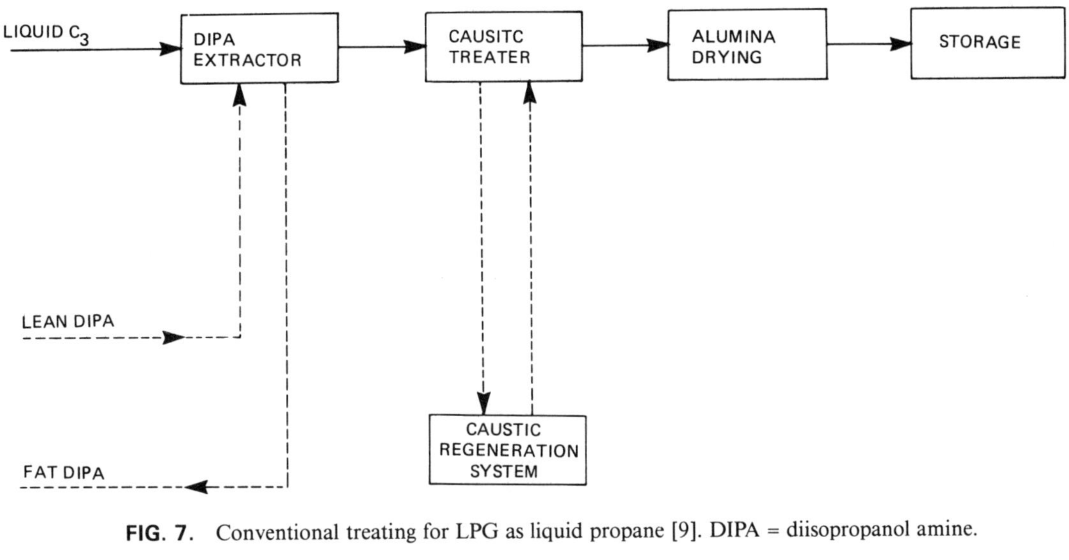

FIG. 7. Conventional treating for LPG as liquid propane [9]. DIPA = diisopropanol amine.

for the removal of bulk H_2S. It is then treated with caustic soda for mercaptans and/or trace H_2S removal [9].

The unit flow scheme depends on the nature of the crude oil processed, the type of secondary processing applied, and the type of LPG produced.

From nonhydrotreated feedstocks, the impurities are [9]:

Commercial propane: mercaptans and H_2S
Mixed C_3/C_4 LPG: mercaptans and H_2S (the amount of H_2S and mercaptans depends on the C_3 content and the quality of crude oil)
Commercial butane: mercaptans (essentially ethyl mercaptans)

From hydrotreated feedstocks, impurities are [9]:

Commercial propane: Water and H_2S
Mixed C_3/C_4 LPG: H_2S
Commercial butane: None

The treating schemes for various grades are given in Table 11.

Using Molecular Sieve

Molecular sieves are now used for sweetening and drying of LPG. The use of molecular sieves is not recommended for olefinic material because of the formation of polymers during hot regeneration. The overall block diagram of molecular sieve treaters is shown in Fig. 8.

TABLE 11 Treating Schemes for Various Grades of Virgin LPG's [9]

	Commercial Propane		Mixed C_3/C_4 LPG		
	Conventional Treating	Treating with Molecular Sieve	Conventional Treating	Treating with Molecular Sieve	Commercial Butane
Bulk H_2S removal	DIPA extraction	DIPA extraction	Not required[a]	Not required[a]	Treating not required[a]
Trace H_2S removal	Caustic treatment	Molecular sieve treatment	Caustic treatment	Molecular sieve treatment	Treating not required[b]
Drying	Alumina dryer	Molecular sieve treatment	Not required[c]	Not required[c]	Treating not required[b]

[a]May be justifiable when C_3 contents are more than about 20 mol%.
[b]A solid bed of caustic soda pellets is installed to remove minute quantities of H_2S that may occasionally appear.
[c]Unless stored at atmospheric pressure.

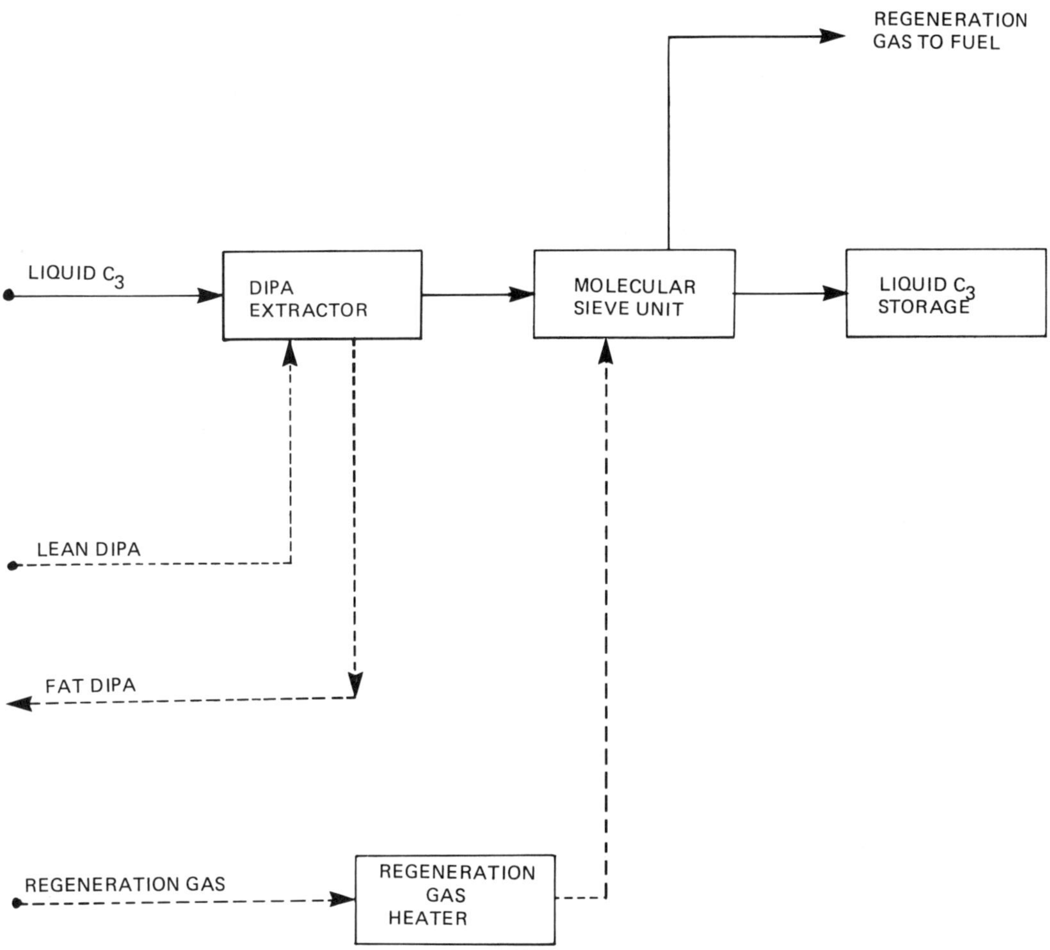

FIG. 8. Molecular sieve treating [9].

The liquid propane containing H_2S, mercaptans, and water is first treated with diisopropanol amine (DIPA) for removal of bulk H_2S. After DIPA treatment (a Shell process), the liquid propane is processed in a molecular sieve unit. Here the mercaptans, water, and the remaining trace H_2S are adsorbed by the sieve [9].

Separation by sieve entails a cyclic operation. The process gas or liquid is passed through a bed of molecular sieve material, usually at about ambient temperature. It may be necessary to provide three beds: one for adsorption, one for regeneration, and one for cooling. Normally, the recommended regeneration temperature is 260–315°C, although molecular sieves are capable of withstanding temperatures up to 600°C without damage [9].

Conventional wet treating is attractive for processing hydrotreated feedstocks for mixed C_3/C_4 LPG, but molecular sieve treating is more attractive for any other case [9]. The relative costs of LPG treating by the two methods are plotted in Fig. 9.

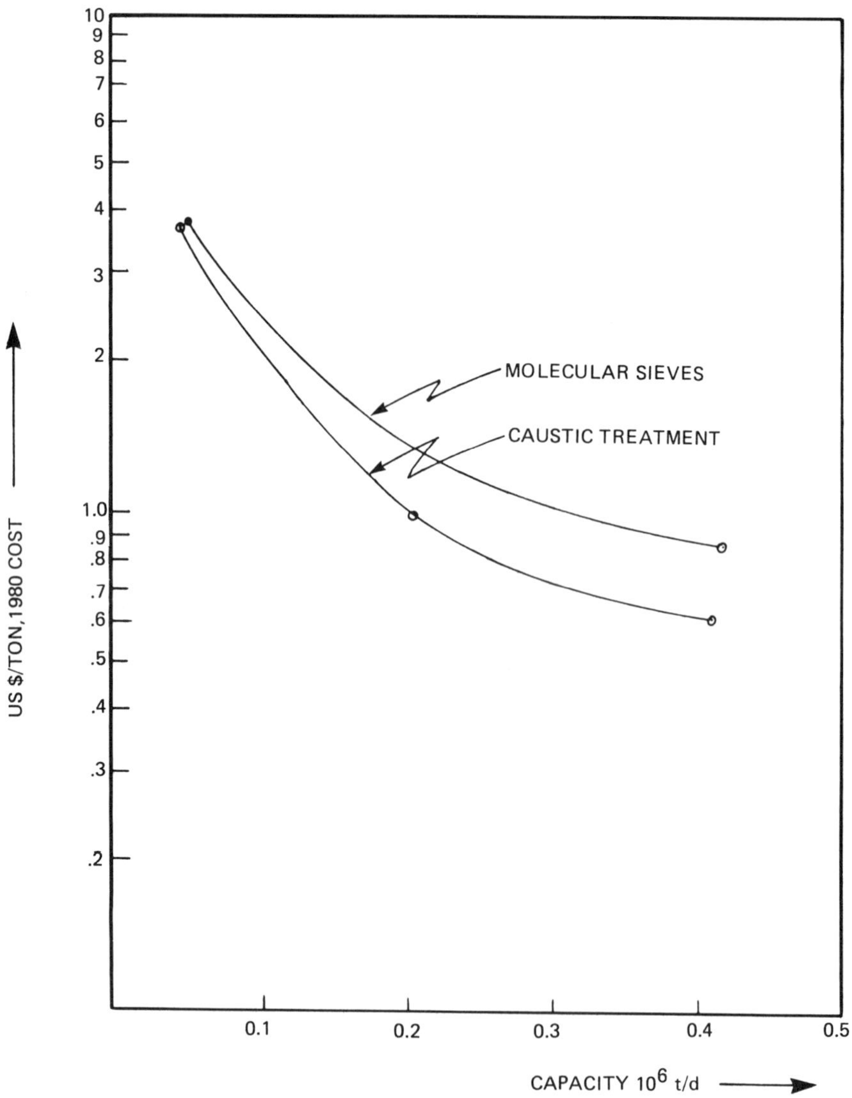

FIG. 9. Treatment of mixed C_3/C_4 LPG from Hydrotreated feedstocks [9].

Manufacture of Odorless LPG

The demand for odorless LPG has recently gone up, and stringent specifications have been drawn up. See Table 12 for typical properties of odorless LPG, and Fig. 10 for the treating and distilling equipment required for manufacture.

Neutralization with aqueous NaOH yields better results than acid treating with H_2SO_4 to remove odoriferous components from propane and butanes. Redistillation removes heavier reaction compounds.

TABLE 12 Typical Properties of Odorless LPG Components [9]

	ASTM Ref.	*n*-Butane	*i*/*n*-Butane	Propane
Specific gravity, 15/4°C	—	0.584	0.575	0.504
Composition, wt.%:				
Ethane	—	—	—	1.1
Propane	—	—	1.8	98.9
Isobutane	—	2.7	44.0	—
n-Butane	—	97.3	54.2	—
Isopentane	—	<0.1	<0.1	—
Vapor pressure, kg/cm^2 · g, 20°C	D 1267	1.1	1.6	7.7
Evaporation residue, ppm wt.	—	1	1	1
Volatile sulfur, ppm wt.	D 1266	1	2	1
Elemental sulfur, ppm wt.	SMS 282	<1	<1	<1
Copper strip corrosion	D 1838	1 A	1 A	1 A

The feedstocks used can be commercial-grade LPG: diethanol amine and caustic-treated propane and caustic-treated *i*/*n*-butane. The principle used is adsorption of odoriferous components on such solid adsorbents as activated charcoal, silica gel, and molecular sieve.

Treatment of propane and butane is performed in a block operation. The treatment is performed essentially by contact with 97% sulfuric acid followed by settling and coalescing. Subsequently, the acidic compounds, such as dissolved H_2SO_4, SO_2, and sulfonic acids, are removed with caustic soda of 100–130 NaOH/L by contact in a plant mixer. After settling and coalescing, LPG is redistilled in a 30-plate distillation column in order to remove alkylate-type material [9].

The "odor" of odorless LPG is rather difficult to assess. The treatment step applied is aimed at removal of foreign odoriferous compounds.

LPG from Alcohol

Alcohol feed can be converted to LPG and gasoline [15]. For ethanol conversion, a "pre-reaction" is carried out in a separate hot bed to avoid quenching at the entrance of the reactor. The products are mixed with recycle gas and fed to a fixed-bed conversion reactor, where exothermic reaction proceeds as with methanol to produce gasoline and LPG. After reaction, the products are cooled, LPG is flashed away, and the water is separated by gravity. Isobutane and propylene can be recovered from the gas product. The economics of such a conversion is rarely justified, for typical yields are 89% gasoline and 10% LPG.

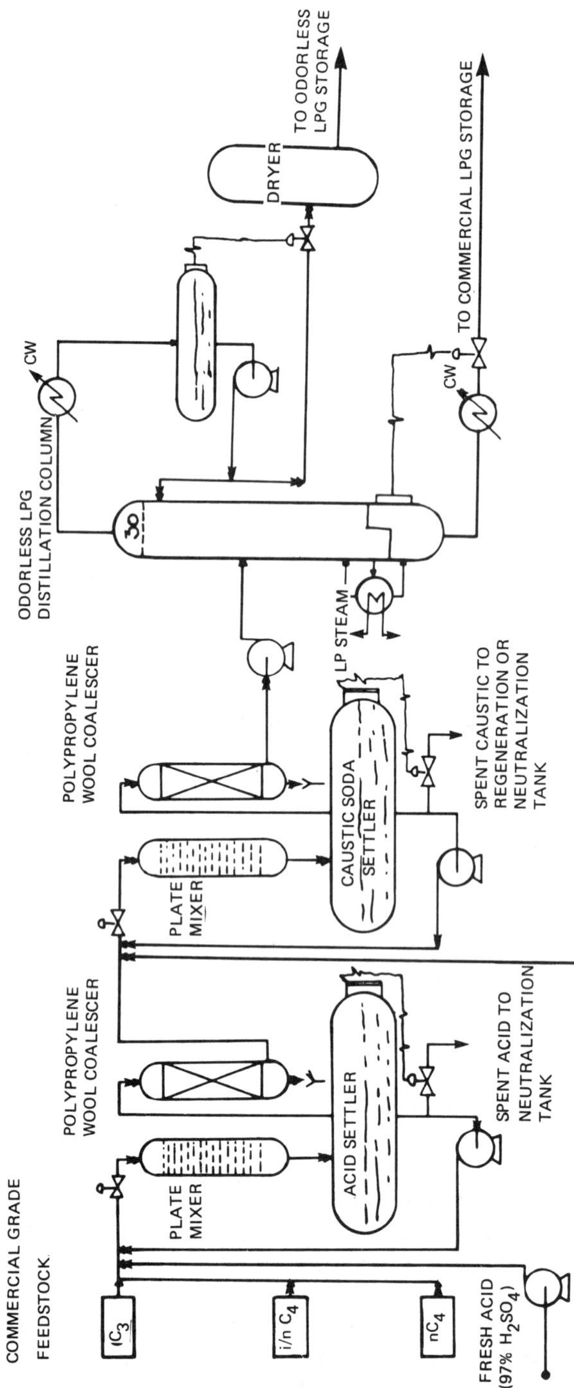

FIG. 10. Treating and distilling of odorless propane and butane [9].

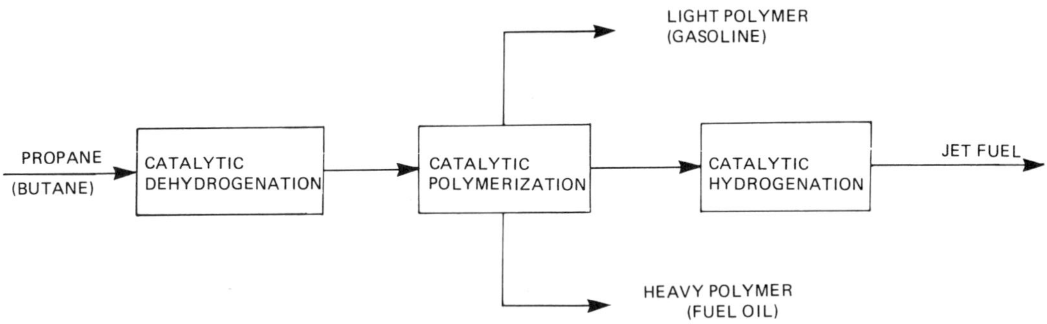

FIG. 11. Jet fuel from LPG [16].

Jet Fuel from LPG

The production of jet fuel (aviation turbine fuel) and/or diesel fuel from propane and/or butane [16] is economically viable in certain specific situations. A novel combination of processes is involved (Fig. 11):

Dehydrogenation of propane (and/or butane) to propylene (and/or butylene)—the monomer
Polymerization of this monomer to a substantial yield of the desired polymer by recycling the undesired polymer
Hydrotreating the polymer to saturate the double bonds

The ability to produce high-quality jet fuel by polymerization of propylene followed by hydrogeneration has been demonstrated in pilot-plant operation by at least one major oil company [16, 17]. Its economic analysis shows attractive rates of return in a range of reasonable production costs and product selling prices.

LPG Shipping

The LPG exports/imports industry is entangled in the most perplexing pricing dilemma of any segment of the volatile energy industry [18]. Political rather than market considerations continue to be the dominant determinants of LPG prices at both the supply and construction ends.

Various other relatively short-term factors have an ongoing effect on LPG shipping. The United States remains a major potential LPG growth area, particularly for industrial purposes. Demand for LPG ships depends directly on demand and supply of the product.

Safety Aspects

There are five common areas of risks [19] in handling LPG's.

1. *LPG Manufacturing and Storage*. Relates mainly to leaks developed in the process vessels and during transfer of the product due to carelessness or the inexperience of employees.
2. *General Liability*. Relates to bodily injury to the public and damage to property.
3. *Auto Liability*. Relates to vehicle accidents and loading and unloading operations.
4. *Workers Compensation*. Relates to handling of cylinders and tanks with resulting back injuries and hand and foot injuries.
5. *Product Liability*. These can be divided into three categories: (a) Losses caused by faulty–improper installation of equipment or inadequate servicing of customers' storage tanks. (b) Customer abuse of appliances. (c) Faulty equipment.

A new safety gauge, the gaslow gauge, can easily be fitted on LPG cylinders [19]. It can be used on gas grills, campers, trailers, and boats. The device detects hazardous leaks within 45 s and indicates if the supply is running low.

An LPG/water vapor system used at an initial water temperature of 362.7 K gives a peak mechanical work done of 140 kJ/kg of water at an LPG to water mass ratio of 1.2. This gives a peak work yield of 117 kJ/kg of LPG at a peak efficiency of 25%. The maximum explosion pressure attained is 40 atm, which is below the LPG critical pressure.

LPG Projects Worldwide

During 1983 [20] a number of LPG production/sweetening projects were underway all over the world. These amounted to 13.5 million T/yr for LPG production and 3.5 million T/yr for LPG sweetening.

The author appreciates the help received from Mr. V. K. Garg, Technical Assistant, Tecnagement Consultant, New Bombay, India.

References

1. Parker, *Concise Encyclopedia of Science & Technology*, McGraw-Hill, New York, 1985.

2. Kirk and Othmer, *Concise Encyclopedia of Chemical Technology*, Vols. 14 and 17, Wiley-Interscience, New York, 1985.
3. *Basic Petroleum Data Book*, API Refining Department, Washington, D.C., 1980.
4. M. P. Skillern, "The Future of LPG as a Petrochemical Feedstock," *CEP*, pp. 34–38 (October 1976).
5. M. B. Mick, *Hydrocarbon Process.*, p. 137 (July 1976).
6. Perry, *Chemical Engineers' Handbook*, 6th ed., McGraw-Hill, New York, 1984.
7. *Annual Book of ASTM Standards*, American Society for Testing and Materials, Philadelphia, 1980, Parts 23, 24, and 29.
8. T. Hutson Jr. and R. S. Logan, *Hydrocarbon Process.*, p. 107 (September 1975).
9. Consultations with Technical Staff of Maravan Refinery, Venezuela.
10. A. R. Valdes, "Use Expander Cycles for LPG Recovery," *Hydrocarbon Process.*, pp. 89–91 (December 1974).
11. *Test for Residues in LPG (end point index method)*, ASTM Standards D2, App. xiii, p. 1260.
12. *LP-Gas* (March 1985).
13. K. D. Manchada and R. H. Gilmour, "Drying and Desulfurizing Light Olefins with Molecular Sieve," *AIChE Symp. Ser. 134*, Vol. 69.
14. C. E. Dryden, *Outlines of Chemical Technology*, Affiliated East-West Press, New Delhi, 1965.
15. B. L. Maiorella, Fermentation Alcohol: Better to Convert to Fuel, *Hydrocarbon Process.*, pp. 95–97 (August 1982).
16. R. E. Maples and J. R. Jones, "Jet Fuel from LPG," *CEP*, pp. 55–58 (February 1983).
17. *Chevron Bulk Acid Polymerization Process*, Chevron Research Co., January 1972.
18. *The Future of LPG Shipping*, Presented at Gas Tech 78, LNG/LPG Conference, Monte Carlo, November 7–10, 1978.
19. R. Morby, "Acceptable Risks," *LP-Gas* (August 1985).
20. *Hydrocarbon Processing*, Section 2, June 1985.
21. J. B. Maxwell, *Data Book on Hydrocarbons*, Van Nostrand, New York, 1950.

OM P. GOYAL

Liquefied Petroleum Gas. B. Natural Gas Liquids Recovery Processes

General

Natural gas liquids (NGL) as recovered from produced gas are almost entirely composed of saturated normal paraffin series hydrocarbons in the C_2 to C_{10} range. Some napthenic compounds are in the C_6+ fractions, but only traces of olefins are present. Due to the fact that the majority of the light hydrocarbons

TABLE 1 End Usage of LPG and LRG Production for 1984 [3]

Usage	MM gal/yr	% of Total
Chemical feedstock	10.900	32.2
Motor gasoline blending	9.400	27.9
Residential and commercial fuel	5.200	15.4
Industrial fuel	2.900	8.5
Farm fuel	1.700	4.9
Gas utility distribution	1.100	3.3
Internal combustion engine fuel	1.000	2.8
Other (includes feedstock and oil field secondary recovery)	1.700	5.0
	32.300[a]	100.0

[a]Includes imports.

in refinery gas streams are present as a result of cracking or reforming operations, "light ends" generally contain significant amounts of olefins.

There were 861 operating gas processing plants in the United States at the end of 1984. These plants had a combined processing ability to handle almost 68 billion cubic feet of gas per day and were running at an average capacity of 60% [1]. These plants recovered slightly over 596 million barrels of NGL in 1984 from 18 trillion standard cubic feet of natural gas, or 33 bbl/MMCF [2, 3].

As of January 1, 1985, there were 191 operating refineries in the United States with a total run to stills for 1984 of 4408 million barrels. Although not all of these refineries had fuel treatment units, the liquefied refinery gas (LRG) recovery from these plants for that time was 133 million barrels, representing a volumetric recovery of 3.01% of the refinery feed [2, 3].

The end usage of LPG and LRG liquids in the United States for 1984 is illustrated in Table 1. Although these statistics are only for the United States, they clearly illustrate the magnitude and importance of LPG and LRG liquids to the chemical and refinery industry as well as to the domestic and industrial fuel markets. The recovery situation is very similar in Canada, Europe, Mexico, Venezuela, and Algeria. Significant recovery schemes are coming into being at a very rapid rate in all other areas of the world with oil and gas production.

Sources

Natural Gas Liquids (NGL)

As the name implies, natural gas liquids are recovered from natural gas streams. In oil and gas production terminology, there are three types of natural gas. In descending order of "richness" (content of NGL) they are: solution gas, associated gas, and nonassociated gas.

Solution gas is produced in conjunction with crude oil. At reservoir pressure and temperature, solution gas is dissolved in the crude oil. As the mixture is brought to the surface, the very high reservoir pressures are reduced and the gas comes out of solution. The GOR (gas–oil ratio) is expressed in units of standard cubic feet of gas per stock tank barrel of oil. The lower the GOR, the higher the content of NGL, which is expressed as GPM (gallons per 1000 standard cubic feet). For solution gas, the GOR usually ranges from 200 to 2000.

Associated gas refers to gas produced from underground reservoirs in which both oil and gas exist as separate phases. If the associated gas is produced from a well completed at or near the oil–gas interface, the well may also produce some oil and so be classified as a high GOR oil well rather than a gas well. The GPM (richness) of associated gas is lower than that of solution gas.

Nonassociated gas is produced from reservoirs which contain no oil. This type of gas is considered "dry" in that it generally consists mostly of methane and ethane with minimal amounts of propane and heavier components. As a rule, it is not economical to process this gas for liquid recovery unless it is available in large quantities and/or ethane recovery is desired.

Liquefied Refinery Gas (LRG)

The source of LRG is, by definition, refinery gas. Refinery gas stream volumes and compositions vary widely depending on the type of feedstock and the types of operations taking place in the refinery.

Small quantities of methane, ethane, and propane are contained in raw crude oil, and these constituents are distilled overhead in the primary crude still and are saturated normal paraffins.

Both catalytic and thermal cracking units produce off-gases that have significant amounts of ethylene, propane, and propylene, with smaller amounts of iso and normal butanes and butenes, along with some hydrogen and methane.

Reformers also produce off-gas with C_2 through C_4 fractions, larger amounts of hydrogen, and smaller amounts of methane. Hydrotreaters produce off-gas with large amounts of hydrogen, some hydrogen sulfide, and moderate amounts of both normal and olefinic C_2 through C_4 fractions.

Some refinery/chemical plant combinations have bleed purge streams to fuel from synthesis gas systems that are normally high in hydrogen and carbon dioxide but may contain enough C_2 to C_6 constituents to justify recovery treatment. These streams become very good candidates for liquids recovery if the recovery and recycling of hydrogen is considered.

Pretreatment

Pretreatment requirements for the gas stream to be processed necessarily vary in accordance with the composition of the gas stream, the desired recovery efficiency of the operation, and the disposition of the residue gas. Pretreatment steps usually are limited to dehydration, acid gas removal, diluent gas removal, and compression.

Dehydration

Virtually all of the natural gas that is processed for liquids recovery flows from the liquids recovery plant into natural gas transmission systems. The requirements of these systems nearly always dictate that the water vapor content of the gas be reduced to no more than 7 lb per one million standard cubic feet of natural gas (about 100 ppm). All of the recovery techniques to be described, except the ambient temperature absorption and the adsorption plants, require water removal to at least this level to avoid the formation of ice and/or solid hydrocarbon–water hydrates in the exchangers and vessels. In fact, the cryogenic processes require a water content of 0.1 ppm (or less) to maintain reliable operation.

Nearly all refinery gas streams wind up being utilized in the refinery fuel system at relatively low pressures. As such, they rarely require much if any dehydration.

Conventional triethylene glycol contact, ethylene glycol injection, or long cycle dry dessicant adsorption systems will provide adequate dehydration down to process temperature levels of −40°F. This is normally as cold as a conventional refrigeration system or a refrigerated absorption system will operate.

For operation down to about −100°F, economical dehydration can be obtained using a triethylene glycol contactor system that is azeotropically regenerated with isooctane, but the majority of operating systems in this temperature range are dehydrated with medium cycle dry dessicant adsorption.

All systems known to this writer that operate colder than −100°F are dehydrated using medium cycle dry dessicant adsorption employing molecular sieves as the adsorbant. This system is identical to the system shown in Fig. 8 except the regeneration cycle/adsorbing cycle is much shorter. Excellent engineering summaries of dehydration techniques are presented by Kohl and Riesenfeld (4) and Campbell (5).

Acid Gas Removal

Sulfur Compounds

LPG products for resale must contain no more than 3 ppm of hydrogen sulfide and 120 ppm of total volatile sulfur compounds [6]. In most instances this specification is met by treating the recovery plant feed gas with sweetening systems such as one of the alkanoamines or Sulfinol. In some cases the dehydration step and sulfur removal are accomplished jointly using mixed molecular sieve beds.

In plants where sulfur content of the inlet gas is low enough to not require treatment for the residue gas to meet sales gas specifications but is sufficient to make the products off specification, the product is treated in a liquid–liquid contactor using alkanoamines or sodium hydroxide solution, contact with solid pottassium hydroxide pellets, or, in some cases, by adsorption using molecular sieves [2].

Carbon Dioxide

Unless carbon dioxide is present in the feed gas in sufficient quantity to require its removal to meet residue gas specifications, there is no need to institute a pretreatment of CO_2 removal unless the process temperature will be below –75°F at pressures below 705 lb/in.^{2}abs, or if an ethane product is to be produced from the separated gas liquids [7].

If an ethane product is to be produced, the carbon dioxide must be removed to meet the product specification. This is normally accomplished by a liquid–liquid contact system or molecular sieve, as discussed above for H_2S removal.

Hydrogen Removal

Until recently, the recovery and recycling of hydrogen from refinery fuel gas streams has been a borderline to nonprofitable operation.

With the advent of reliable production quality semipermeable membrane units, the recovery of hydrogen has become an economically viable operation to consider in almost all plants that must manufacture or purchase hydrogen for operations. A "windfall" benefit of hydrogen removal from refinery gas streams is the combination reduction in the volume and enrichment of the fuel/flare stream that must be processed to recover liquids.

A second "windfall" is the fact that the hydrogen-rich stream must be compressed to the range of 700 lb/in.^{2} or greater to enable the recovery of the majority of the hydrogen. The permeate in this operation is hydrogen, hydrogen sulfide, carbon dioxide, and water vapor, with the majority of the hydrocarbon stream passing through as the high-pressure effluent. Due to the fact nearly all of the recovery techniques that will be presented later require an inlet pressure of 450 lb/in.^{2} or greater, hydrogen removal pretreatment absorbs a large segment of the investment cost (compression equipment) of the LRG recovery system.

Extraction Techniques

Of the 861 gas liquid extraction plants reported as being in operation in 1984, 42% were cryogenic, either turboexpander or refrigerated JT; 31% were absorption, ambient, and refrigerated; and 25% were straight refrigeration. The remainder were listed as adsorption or compression [1].

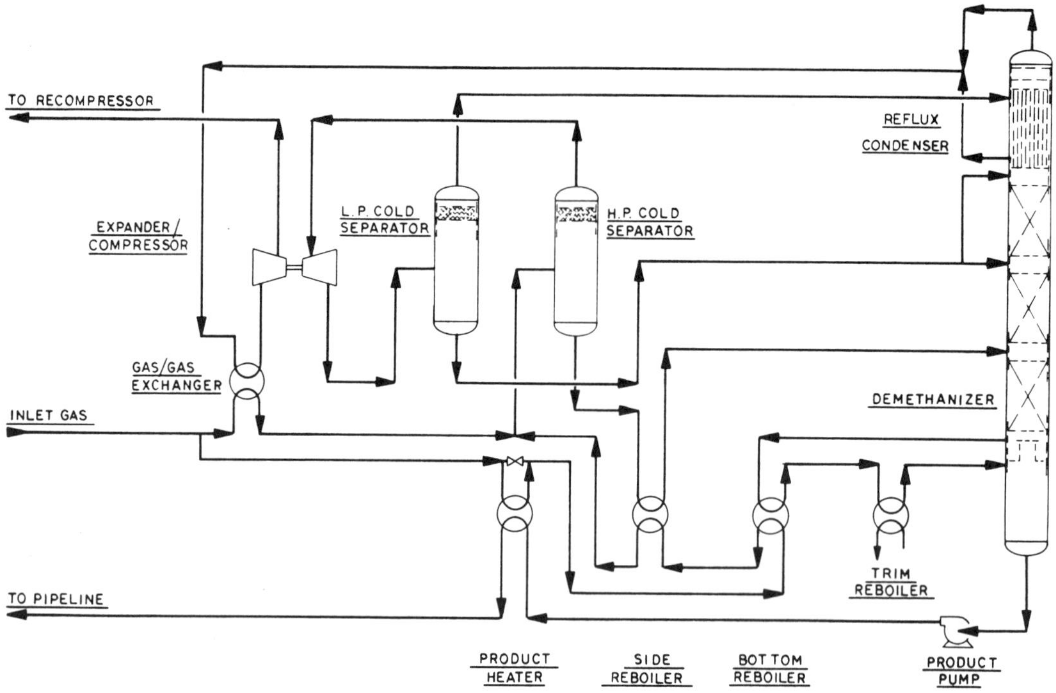

FIG. 1. Autorefluxed cryogenic deethanizer.

Cryogenic Turboexpander

The current technology in gas processing is geared almost exclusively to cryogenic separation. Since 1973, the overwhelming majority of new plants constructed have been of the turboexpander type. The "Ethane" article in this *Encyclopedia* is an extensive and authoritative reference for the turboexpander plant and is recommended reading [7].

For high ethane recovery, the cryogenic turboexpander extraction cycle is difficult to beat. The cryogenic plant becomes much more complex and expensive if the plant must be capable of maintaining high propane recovery levels while *not* recovering ethane. Either the demethanizer column must be designed to be capable of operation as a deethanizer column to reject recovered ethane back into the low-pressure residue gas stream, or a separate deethanizer column must be constructed to remove and return the ethane to the residue gas stream. Figure 1 is an example of a system that uses cold expander outlet to generate sufficient internal reflux to accomplish deethanization in one column.

Refrigerated JT Cycle

Production lease recovery of "gas well condensate" from very high pressure gas wells has long been accomplished by LTX (low temperature extraction)

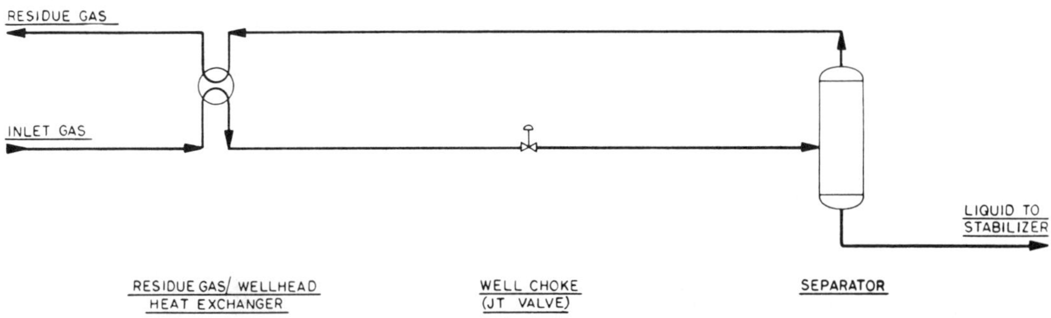

FIG. 2. LTX unit.

units. These units utilize the chilling effect of the choking of the produced gas from the high formation pressure down to the pipeline pressure. This "Joule-Thompson" throttling produces no work (is isenthalpic) unlike the expander (which is essentially isentropic), but does accomplish a significant temperature reduction. By back-exchanging the cool separator gas with the warm high-pressure wellhead gas ahead of the choke, the final resulting separator temperature produces a two-phase condition that results in sufficient stock tank liquid to justify the equipment. An example of this type of recovery equipment and representative calculated stream compositions are shown in Fig. 2 and Table 2.

Gas processing technology has carried this scheme from the simple wellhead unit and modified it into a reliable cryogenic gas liquids extraction system. The gas plant configuration is similar in layout to that of a turboexpander plant except that instead of a turboexpander/compressor, there is only an expansion (JT) valve. The heat extraction necessary to achieve the cryogenic processing level is accomplished by utilizing mechanical refrigeration prior to the expansion. This requirement for externally supplied work makes the JT plants significantly less thermally efficient than expander

TABLE 2 LTX Unit Recovery Compared to Choke Only Recovery

	Choke Only, % Recovery	LTX, % Recovery
C_3	18.1	64.2
iC_4	31.0	79.8
nC_4	36.9	84.5
iC_5	55.8	92.9
nC_5	67.1	94.5
C_6	80.5	97.6
C_7	90.9	100.0
Temperature, °F	+27.7	−24.4
Pressure, lb/in.^{2}abs	815	815

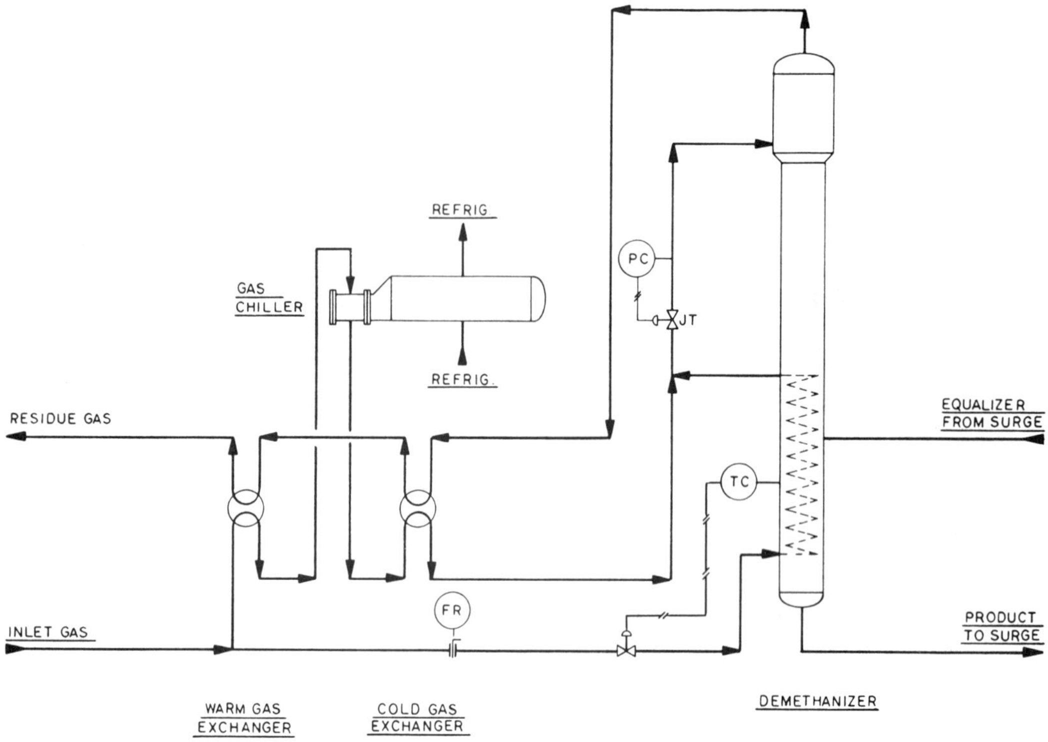

FIG. 3. Typical small refrigerated JT NGL recovery unit.

plants and limits their competitive position. However, in small to medium size plants they are usually competitive due to lower capital and maintenance costs and simplicity of operation. An example of a small JT plant design is shown in Fig. 3.

Metallurgy requirements for JT plants are the same as those for other cryogenic processes. Normalized A516-70 carbon steel can be used for plant sections down to −40°F, but most designers specify stainless steels A 304 or 316 for the cold sections, as even slight upsets can cause very low temperatures to occur throughout the plant.

The liquids recovery of these type of plants is only slightly lower than that of an expander plant if ethane is not recovered, and they have the same disadvantage previously discussed concerning expander plants; i.e., they are more expensive to install and operate if ethane is *not* to be recovered than if ethane is to be recovered.

Straight Refrigeration Plants

The straight refrigeration plant has been used for the recovery of LPG for over 35 years. It is mechanically similar to the refrigerated JT plant except that there is no pressure let-down effect for temperature reduction. The lowest temperature obtainable in the process is that reached in the chiller heat exchanger. Most of the early plants used ammonia absorption refrigeration systems, and were followed shortly by mechanical compression refrigeration utilizing ammonia, propane, or halocarbon compounds for refrigerants. As metallurgy and compression equipment improved, process temperature levels decreased. Currently, straight refrigeration plants are usually designed to run around −35°F, utilizing either propane or halocarbon refrigerants. Colder temperatures can be reached using cascade refrigerant systems, or various configurations of mixed refrigerants, but the economics of deeper refrigeration by mechanical means must be carefully examined on a case-by-case basis. Deeper refrigeration is very expensive and is generally only necessary for high recovery of ethane or ethylene, and the cost and reliability of the turboexpander system is usually more attractive.

A schematic for a straight refrigeration plant utilizing a single refrigerant is shown in Fig. 4.

Metallurgy requirements for straight refrigeration plants operating at −35 to −40°F do not require stainless steel. Normalized A 516-70 steel can be used almost throughout the cold plant. For sections where −50°F can be encountered, tempered nickel steel is adequate.

Such a plant is mechanically simple and easy to operate but has two unalterable limitations. One, its most economical recovery efficiency is obtained between 400 and 550 lb/in.^{2}gauge which is the pressure range where the equilibrium factors (y/x) of the LPG constituents are at their minimum. If the plant is operated at pipeline delivery pressures (800–1100 lb/in.^{2}gauge), the incremental recovery of propane and heavier is very costly on utilities and major equipment. The second limitation is that as the percentage of LPG constituents in the feed gas decreases (leaner gas), the percentage recovery of these constituents also decreases. An example of both these limitations is shown in Tables 3 and 4 for a typical refrigeration plant, comparing the chiller liquid recoveries at 450 and 1000 lb/in.^{2}gauge for a rich gas stream and a lean gas stream. As seen from Tables 3 and 4, the refrigeration requirements for

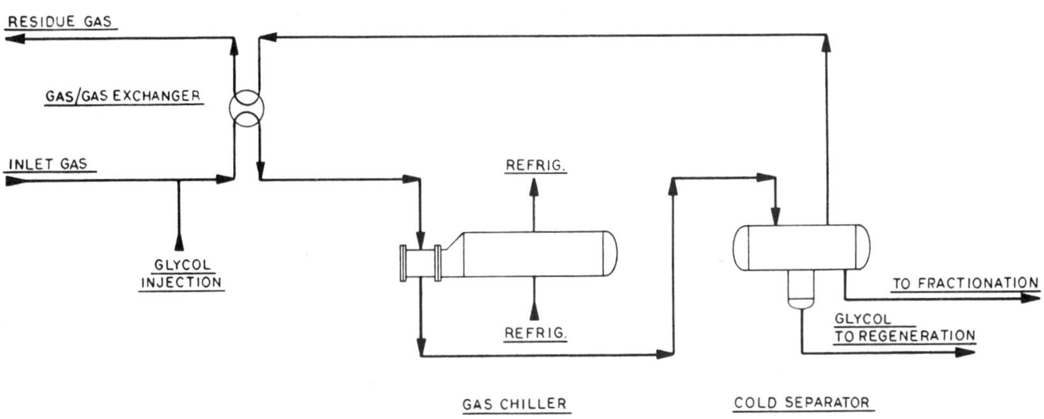

FIG. 4. Typical straight refrigeration NGL recovery unit.

TABLE 3 Comparative Chiller Product Recoveries for Rich Gas Streams (5000/MCF/d)

Component	Feed, mol%	HP Chiller, % Recovery	LP Chiller, % Recovery
N_2	3.69	25.10	2.82
CO_2	0.74	66.26	34.98
C_1	70.92	39.85	8.24
C_2	12.95	68.99	40.13
C_3	6.91	84.30	74.36
iC_4	1.37	90.80	89.10
nC_4	1.89	92.75	92.56
iC_5	0.64	96.05	97.45
nC_5	0.48	96.97	98.10
C_6	0.24	98.48	99.24
C_7	0.17	98.94	100.00
	100.00		
Chiller duty, MBtu/h		1489	966
Btu/lb C_3+		496	341
Pressure, lb/in.^{2}gauge		1000	450

TABLE 4 Comparative Chiller Product Recoveries for Lean Gas Streams (5000/MCF/d)

Component	Feed, mol%	HP Chiller, % Recovery	LP Chiller, % Recovery
N_2	3.69	9.83	1.23
CO_2	0.74	40.39	19.70
C_1	79.12	18.05	3.83
C_2	8.40	43.33	23.26
C_3	4.91	59.36	56.99
iC_4	0.91	78.00	78.80
nC_4	1.43	82.17	85.10
iC_5	0.28	89.61	94.16
nC_5	0.30	91.46	96.34
C_6	0.15	96.34	98.78
C_7	0.08	97.73	100.00
	100.00		
Chiller duty, MBtu/h		1217	753
Btu/lb C_3+		764	463
Pressure, lb/in.^{2}gauge		1000	450

the high-pressure cases are significantly higher than for the low-pressure cases due to the much greater amounts of methane and ethane that are also condensed. This also means higher cost of downstream equipment for larger demethanizer/deethanizer systems.

Oil Absorption Plants

The utilization of selective absorption of benzene and toluene from coke oven gas and manufactured gas was a simple but well-established unit operation before natural gas processing commenced [4]. The manufactured gas or coke oven gas was countercurrently contacted in an absorber column with lean straw oil (absorption oil) of about 180–200 molecular weight. The rich oil flowed or was pumped into a still vessel and was live steam stripped. The absorbed constituents and steam vapor were cooled and condensed by exchange with water. The noncondensable gases usually consisted of H_2 and CO, which were returned to the residue gas. The steam condensate was essentially nonsoluble in the benzene–toluene mixture, allowing the separation to take place by simple decanting.

The switchover of this system to processing natural gas and refinery gas streams required significant refinement. For one thing, the streams to be processed contain large amounts of absorbable material when compared to manufactured gas. Even the older plants, which were operated to recover gasoline range components, absorbed significant amounts of methane through butanes, resulting in "wild" high vapor pressure still product. Initially, these products were stored in weathering tanks to allow the undesired constituents to evaporate to the atmosphere. The obvious wastefulness, hazard, and environmental drawback of this practice soon required other solutions. To cut down on the amount of vent gas from the weathering tanks, a rich oil partial stripper column was added to the system between the absorber and the still. The early versions of this column were called "dephlegmators."

Later, as the market demand for butane and propane developed, fractionation of the still overhead product became required, and depropanizer and debutanizer columns had to be added. Along with this, greater recovery efficiency became a necessity. At about this point, the complexity of the design and operation of the plants had reached a point where practical rule-of-thumb methods were no longer economic and engineers acquired more authority and responsibility for gas plant design and operations. Although complex, the calculations for the design of absorption oil plants are straightforward and are well covered in several excellent texts [4–6].

The evolution of the oil absorption plant has developed almost entirely in response to market changes for the products produced. No new engineering procedures have been developed, but extremely accurate phase equilibrium data have been developed and utilized [6].

The initial absorbers operated at low pressure and ambient temperature. The absorption factor, L/KV (L = moles per hour of absorption oil, V = moles per hour of inlet gas, $K = y/x$ for the particular component) must be kept high to maintain recovery. See Fig. 5 [6] for a plot of factor A versus recovery

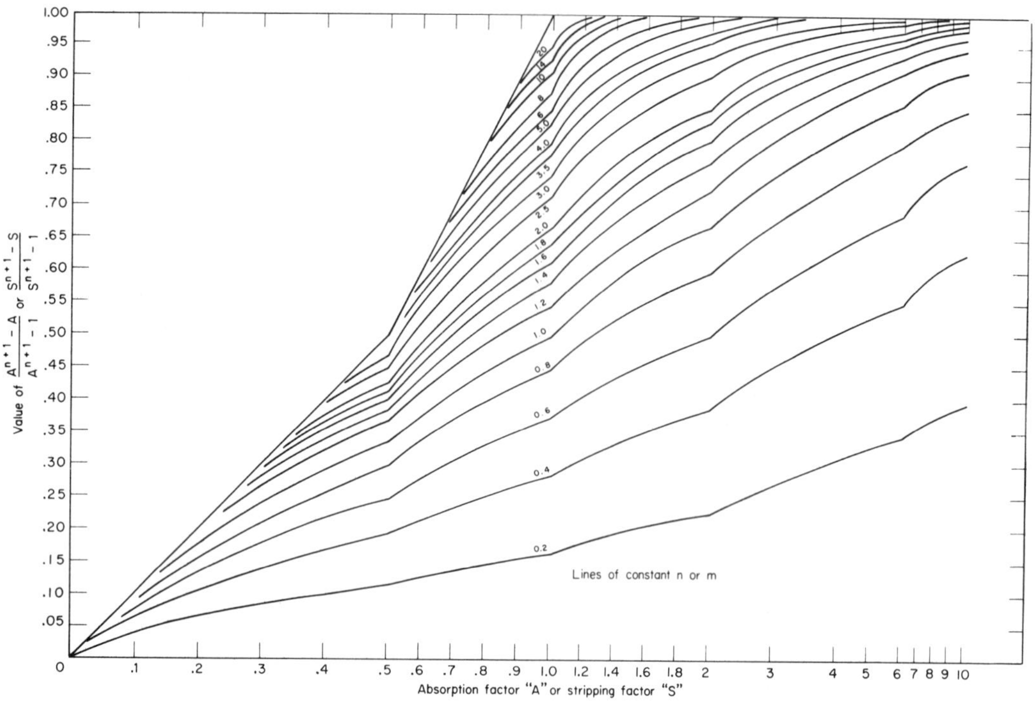

FIG. 5. Absorption factor A or stripping factor S.

efficiency. As absorber pressures increased, the component K's decreased, resulting in an increase in the absorption factor. However, at the higher pressures, a much larger amount of methane and ethane was also absorbed. Inasmuch as the heat of absorption is essentially the same as the heat of condensation, the bottom temperature of the absorber increased significantly, lowering the absorption factor. To overcome this effect, the designers added absorber intercoolers, taking rich oil out of the absorber at a trap tray, passing it through a water cooler, and returning it to the next tray down in the absorber. Depending on the richness of the gas being processed, some absorbers had up to three of these intercoolers removing the heat of absorption from the rich oil.

As market demand for propane increased, the next improvement required was to raise the still pressure so that the distillate could still be condensed using water or ambient air as the coolant. This raised the still bottoms temperature correspondingly, to the point that nominal boiler pressures were not adequate to supply the temperature with saturated steam. To bring these temperatures down, operators started to use lower molecular weight oil (160–180 MW), which had a lower boiling point. This had an added advantage of increasing the absorption factor A, because a given volume of oil circulation contains more moles per hour (L), if the MW is lower. It also had an immediate disadvantage of increased absorption oil loss into the residue gas because of the stripping factor $S = KV/L$. To overcome the increased lean oil loss, some plants were built with a five or ten tray "sponge" oil system at the top of the absorber. This system used a higher molecular weight (180–200) absorption oil to absorb the portion of the lower molecular weight oil that had been evaporated into the residue gas and required a separate still column and heater. The higher capital and operating costs of this system design were not particularly attractive and it was soon discarded.

The next move to more economical operation was to chill the absorption oil to the absorber. This reduced the absorber top temperature, reducing the lean oil loss and increasing the A factor. It also created an additional problem of hydrate formation because the lean oil was water saturated due to the still being steam stripped. At this point the designers gave up on steam-stripped stills and added the pump-around direct-fired system in use to this day. This simplified the still mechanical design by eliminating the requirements for steam condensate draw trays to extract water condensed within the column.

After the advent of chilled oil usage, the next major improvement was presaturation of the lean oil with methane and ethane prior to introduction of the oil to the absorber. This is accomplished by commingling the absorber residue gas and high-pressure lean oil in the lean oil chiller. This chiller effluent is separated into plant residue gas and presaturated oil which is pumped to the absorber. A design typical of most of today's operating oil absorption plants is shown in Fig. 6. These types of plants operate at –20 to –40°F, use 115 to 130 MW oil, and are capable of product recoveries in the following ranges:

Propane	85–95%
Butanes	97%+
Gasoline	99%+
Ethane	Up to 50%

The materials of construction are the same as for straight refrigeration plants.

There are still about 250 oil absorption plants in operation, but to this writer's knowledge, no grassroots plants of this type have been constructed since 1974.

Adsorption NGL Recovery Units

Utilization of selective adsorption to recover heavier hydrocarbon fractions from gas streams has been in use for as long or possibly even longer than selective absorption. The early units used charcoal as the adsorbent, and the current version, activated carbon, is still the most effective media used. Activated carbon, as a general rule, will adsorb approximately 2.5 gal of mixed hydrocarbon liquids per 100 lb of bed per exposure. The adsorbing and desorbing cycles for the system are dynamic, and the system is in essence chromatographic, with transition fronts of adsorbate moving through the bed in order of ascending molecular weight.

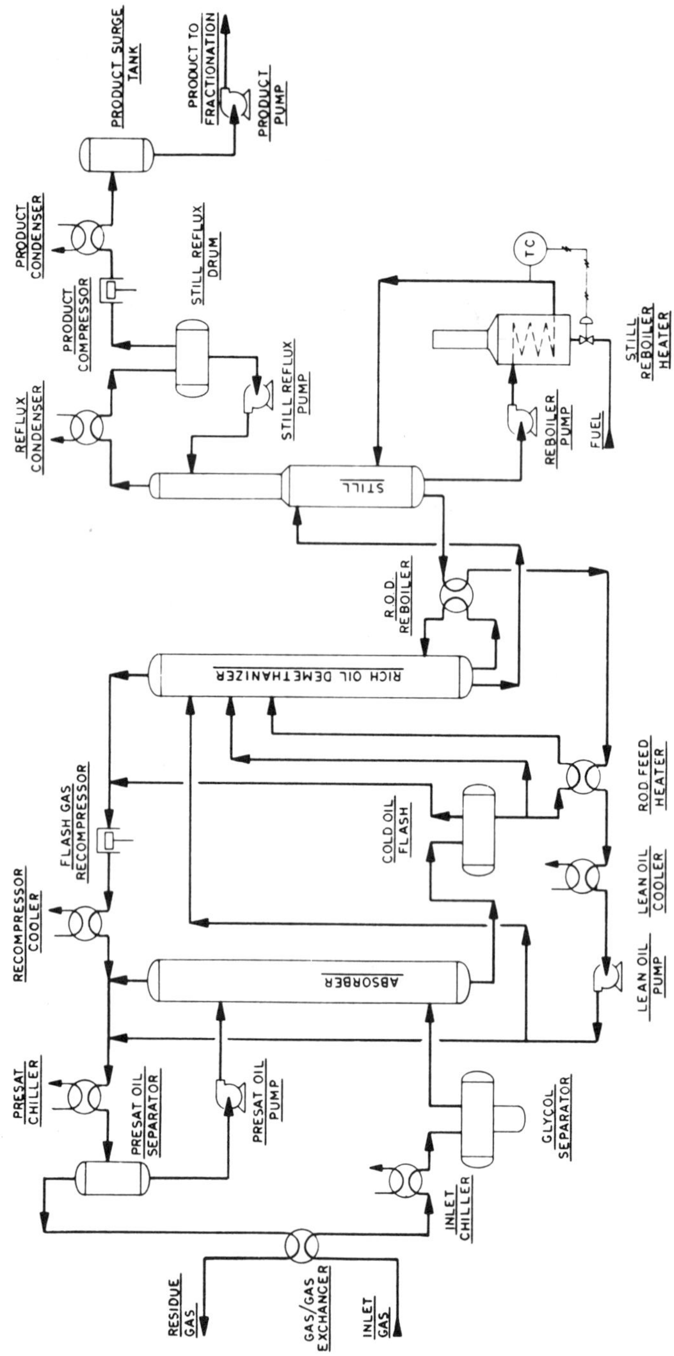

FIG. 6. Typical refrigerated oil absorption plant.

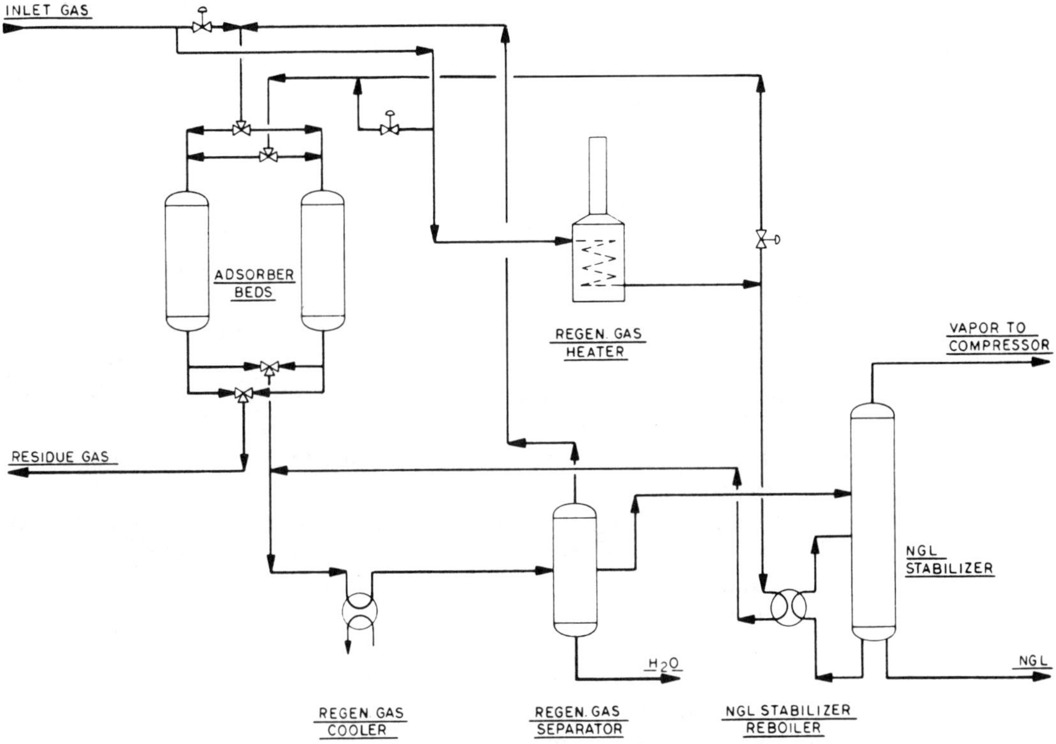

FIG. 7. Open cycle adsorption unit.

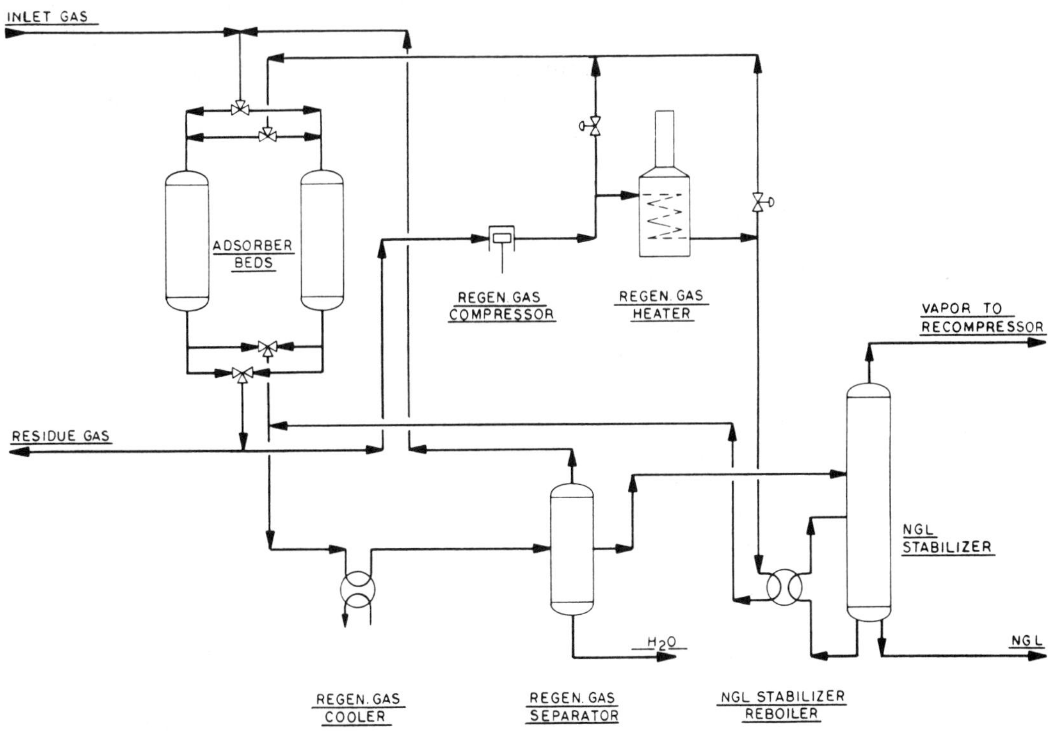

FIG. 8. Closed cycle adsorption unit.

The mechanical equipment is relatively simple, consisting of two or more adsorbent beds manifolded such that one group is adsorbing while the others are desorbing.

Desorption can be accomplished by pressure swing or by heating and cooling. With pressure swing, the saturated bed is rapidly depressured, utilizing the heat of adsorption contained that has warmed the adsorbent to promote the desorption that starts to take place with the equilibrium pressure change. This method is effective for the removal of low boiling constituents, but with the wide hydrocarbon range contained in gas streams, the adsorbent gradually fills up with heavies. Most hydrocarbon recovery units utilizing pressure swing also incorporate vacuum compressors to complete the regeneration. Rapid pressure swings cause significant breaking of the carbon media. The resulting fines increase the pressure drop in the bed and require regular replacement.

Heating and cooling desorbing can be carried out using either inlet gas or residue gas as the regeneration media. Figures 7 and 8 are examples of these configurations. The use of inlet gas involves taking a 20–25 $lb/in.^2$ pressure drop on the total gas stream to provide the driving force for the regeneration gas. It also has the disadvantage of preloading the bed during the cooling cycle. The use of residue gas does not preload the bed, and if used with a regeneration blower as depicted in Fig. 8, does not impose undue pressure loss in the gas stream, but it is more expensive to install and operate.

Due to the high utility cost per gallon recovered, the utilization of this type of equipment today is almost nonexistent for main line plants. The majority of such plants installed over the last few years have been small oil and gas lease units and tank vapor recovery systems [8]. The units do have the capability of recovery of C_4+ components at relatively low system pressures, and should not be overlooked for such applications. Several excellent design and operation texts are available for more detailed information [4–6].

References

1. *Worldwide Refining and Gas Processing Directory*, Pennwell, Tulsa, Oklahoma, 1986.
2. R. N. Maddox, *Gas and Liquid Sweetening*, 2nd ed., Campbell Petroleum, Norman, Oklahoma, 1974.
3. Sales of Natural Gas Liquids and Liquefied Refinery Gas, API Statistical Department Publication, Washington, D.C., October 1985.
4. A. Kohl and F. Riesenfield, *Gas Purification*, 3rd ed., Gulf Publishing Co., Houston, Texas, 1979.
5. J. M. Campbell, *Gas Conditioning and Processing*, Vol. 2, Campbell Petroleum, Norman, Oklahoma, 1979.
6. *Engineering Data Book*, 9th ed., Gas Processors Association, Tulsa, Oklahoma, 1979, pp. 15–46.
7. B. R. Randall, "Ethane," in *Encyclopedia of Chemical Processing and Design*, Vol. 19 (J. J. McKetta, ed.), Dekker, New York, 1983, pp. 402–431.
8. J. C. McGill and P. E. Kennedy, *Vapor Recovery Past and Present*, Paper Presented at Gas Processors Association East/North Texas Regional Meeting, Dallas, Texas, October 28, 1982.

CHARLES W. DRAKE

Lubricating Oils: Manufacturing Processes

Introduction

The manufacture of mineral lubricating oil base stocks consists of five basic steps: (1) distillation and (2) deasphalting to prepare the feedstocks, (3) solvent or hydrogen refining to improve viscosity index and quality, (4) solvent or catalytic dewaxing to remove wax and improve the low temperature properties of paraffinic lubes, and (5) clay or hydrogen finishing to improve color, stability, and quality of the lube base stock. Figures 1 and 2 are simplified processing diagrams illustrating some of the ways these processes are combined to manufacture paraffinic and naphthenic lube base stocks and byproducts, respectively. The finished lube base stocks are blended with each other and/or with additives using batch and continuous methods to prepare fully formulated lubricants. The most common route is the mixed processing route which consists of solvent refining, solvent dewaxing, and hydrogen finishing although a few refiners still use the solvent and clay processing route or the hydrogen refining and solvent dewaxing route. The all-hydrogen processing (lube hydrocracking—catalytic dewaxing–hydrorefining) route is used by two refiners for the manufacture of a limited number of paraffin base oils.

The effect of lube processes on the chemical constituents and physical properties of lube base stocks are summarized in Table 1. It should be noted that each process is generally used for one purpose and that any accompanying change must be accepted to obtain the desired change in physical properties or chemical composition. For example, solvent extraction is used to increase the viscosity index and to improve the quality of lube base stocks by extracting aromatics. Accompanying this change are a reduction in sulfur and nitrogen content, an increase in API gravity, a decrease in viscosity, and improvement in color.

Crude Oils

Crude oils are the source of the feedstocks used in the manufacture of mineral lube base oils and the hydrocarbons used in the manufacture of synthetic oils. Crude oils contain considerable quantities of carbon and hydrogen and small quantities of sulfur, nitrogen, and inorganic salts, and relatively smaller quantities of metals. The hydrocarbon compounds present in crude oils

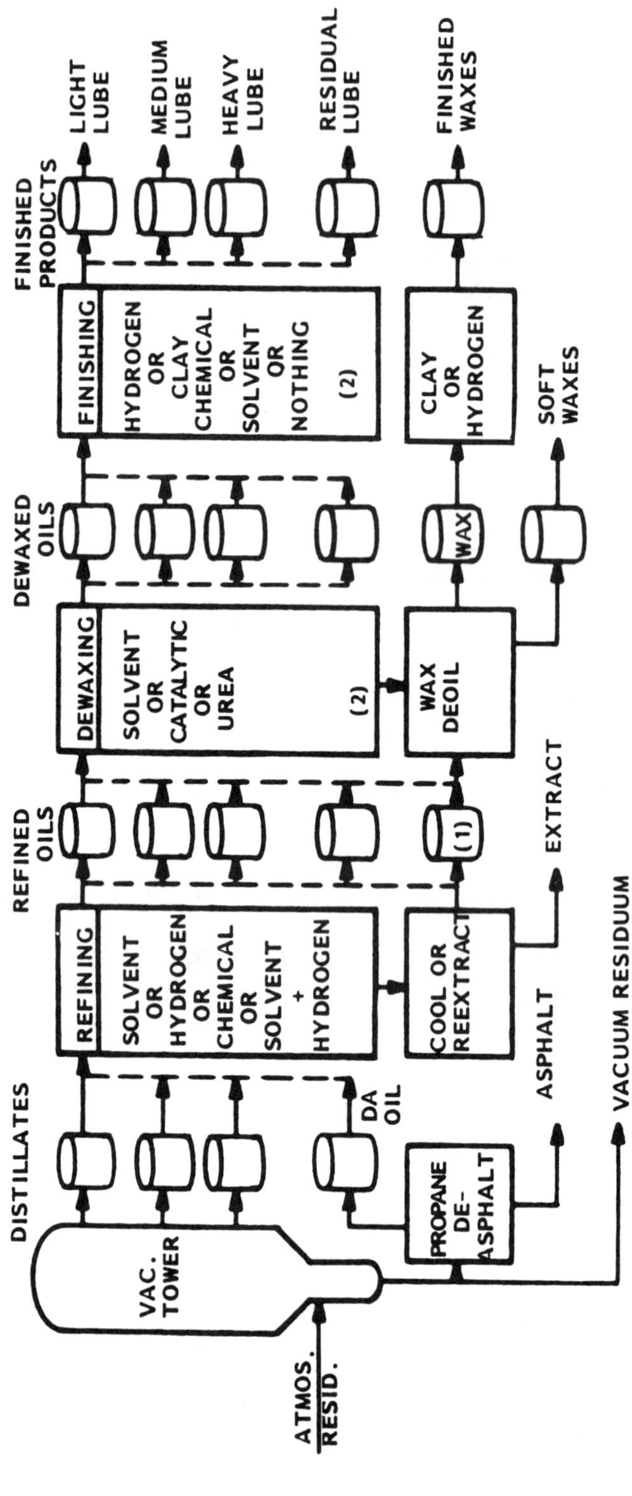

(1) CYCLE OILS USED AS MEDIUM VI OILS OR AS NAPHTHENE PALE OIL SUBSTITUTES.
(2) DEWAXING AND FINISHING PROCESSES ARE FREQUENTLY REVERSED.

FIG. 1. Process flow for manufacture of paraffinic lube oils.

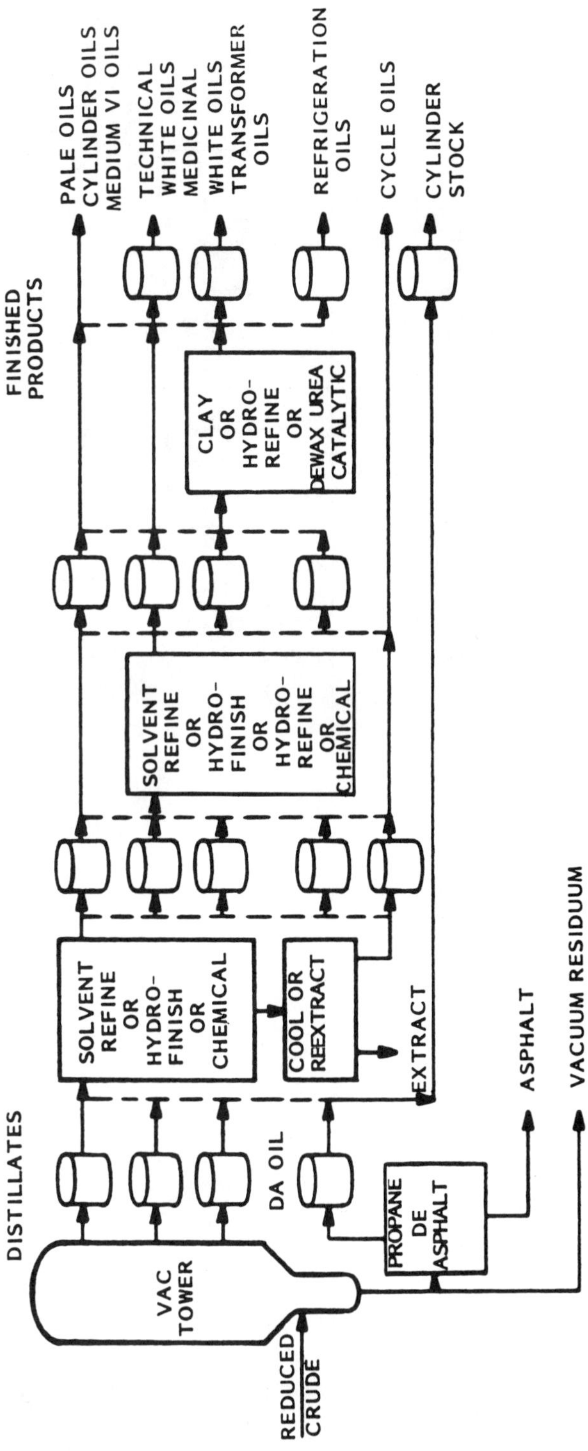

FIG. 2. Process flow for manufacture of naphthenic lube oils.

TABLE 1 Effect of Processes on Properties and Chemical Composition of Lubricating Oil Base Stocks[a]

		Process								
		Refining			Dewaxing			Finishing		
	PDA	Solvent	Hydrogen	Chemical	Solvent	Catalyst	Urea	Hydrogen	Acid	Clay
Property:										
API gravity	+	+	+	+	–	–	–	N	N	N
Flash point	N	N	N	N	N	N	N	N	N	N
Viscosity	–	–	–	–	+	+	+	N	N	N
Viscosity index	+	+	+	+	–	–	–	N/+	N/+	N
Pour point	+/–	+	+	+	–	–	–	N/+	N/+	N
Color	–	–	–	–	+	–	+	–	–	–
Thermal stability	+	+	+/–	+/–	N	N	N	+/–	+/–	+
Oxidative stability	+	+	+/–	+/–	N	N	N	+/–	+/–	+
Inhibitor response	+	+	+	+	N	+/–	N	+	+	+
Constituent:										
Asphaltenes	–	–	–	–	+	N/–	+	N/–	–	–
Resins	–	–	–	–	+	N/–	+	N/–	–	–
Aromatics	–	–	–	–	+	+	+	N/–	–	–
Naphthenes	+	+	+	+	+	+	+	N/+	+	+
Paraffins	+	+	+	+	–	–	–	N/+	+	+
Wax	+	+	+	+	–	–	–	N/+	+	+
Nitrogen	–	–	–	–	+	N/–	+	–	–	–
Oxygen	–	–	–	–	+	–	+	–	–	–
Sulfur	–	–	–	–	+	N/–	N	–	–	–

[a]N = nil (min), + = increase, – = decrease, +/– = depends on severity, PDA = propane deasphalting.

range in carbon number from 1 through 100 or more and from the very simple to the very complex.

Since the quantity and chemical composition of specific lube boiling range fractions vary widely from crude to crude, entirely different processing sequences and/or severities are used to produce lube base stocks which also vary in chemical composition. The manufacture of lube base stocks is further complicated in some refineries where as many as 15 to 25 different crude oils are processed. The refiner thus finds it necessary to segregate crudes based on their suitability for lubes manufacture. This information is developed using laboratory evaluation techniques which vary from simple distillations and a few physical and chemical tests to very complex evaluations involving distillation, processing in pilot plants which simulate the refiners lube plant (processing sequence), physical and chemical tests, product formulation, and bench or field testing.

Lube Distillation

The initial step in refining a crude oil is to separate the crude into a series of narrow boiling range fractions which are the raw stocks for the various products to be produced. After the water, salts, and sediment have been removed by desalting, this initial separation is carried out on a crude distillation unit (CDU) or vacuum pipe still (VPS) which is composed of at least two distillation sections generally referred to as the atmospheric distillation tower or unit (ADT or ADU) and a vacuum distillation tower or unit (VDT or VDU). Figure 3 is a simplified flow diagram for a lube crude still. The gases, naphtha, and kerosene fractions are removed in the ADU. The residuum from the ADU is distilled in the VDU. Although some fractions boiling at 500°F may be distilled on the ADU and used for the manufacture of low viscosity base oils, the majority of the lube distillates boiling between 580 and 1000°F are distilled in the VDU to the proper viscosity and flash specifications. A solution of caustic or lime is introduced into the feed to CDU or VDU for the purpose of neutralizing the organic acids present in some crude oils. Some refiners also use a circulating caustic-oil stream to neutralize these acids in the vapor phase and to prevent caustic from entering the vacuum residuum [1]. Neutralization of crude oils containing high contents of organic acids is used to reduce or eliminate corrosion in downstream processing units. It also improves the color, stability, and refining response of lube distillates.

The design and operation of the VDU is of utmost importance in the manufacture of lube base stocks because distillate properties, particularly boiling range and purity of the feedstocks, have a significant effect on processing response in the lube refining, dewaxing, and finishing units as well

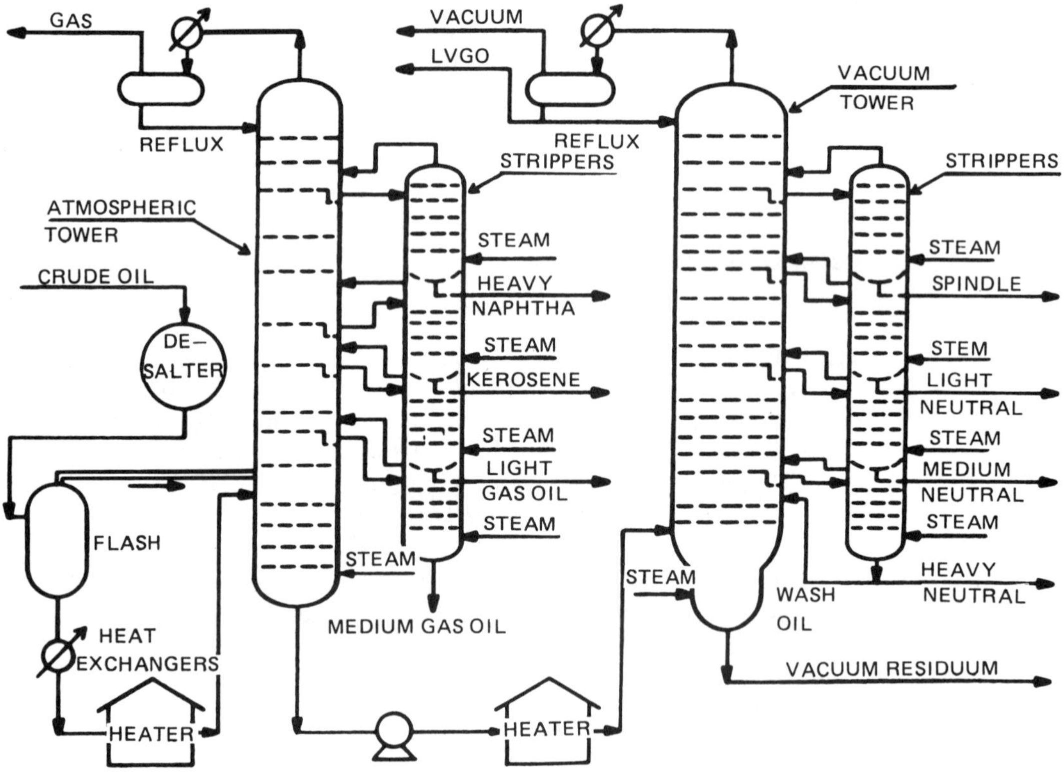

FIG. 3. Lube crude distillation unit flow diagram.

as the quality of the finished base stock. It is for these reasons that lube VDUs contain more fractionation stages, operate at lower pressure, and use more reflux than VDUs used to prepare fuels fractions for further processing. Refiners have in recent years installed a second VDT operating in series with the first VDT [2] and refurbished existing VDUs and/or installed new VDUs with high efficiency internals to reduce the flash zone pressure and improve the quality and yield of lube distillates. Information on crude oil distillation was reported by Atkins, McBride, and Owens [3] and Watkins [4].

Lube Deasphalting Processes

The vacuum residua contain a considerable quantity of high viscosity components useful in the manufacture of lubricating oils and asphaltenes and resins which contribute an undesirable dark color to the lube base stocks and form deposits of carbonaceous materials on heating. Refiners have employed many methods (adsorption, chemical treating, and precipitation with alcohols, ketones, and light hydrocarbons) to remove these undesirable constituents from vacuum residua and heavy distillates. Propane deasphalting [5–7] is most often used to remove these undesirable components which also impede the refining action of the downstream processes. Propane is preferred over the other liquefied gases used in the milder "deep" deasphalting (sometimes called decarbonizing) processes used to prepare feedstocks for fuels processing, because lube deasphalting requires removal of a greater quantity of the asphalts and resins present in the vacuum residuum.

The major process variables in deasphalting are dosage and temperature which range from about 500–1000 vol.% and 100 to 190°F, respectively. Pressure is a minor process variable which can be used to control the degree of separation. Deasphalted oil (DAO) yield is most dependent on crude source and will range from 30 to 90 wt.% basis vacuum residuum feed for most crudes currently being used. An increase in temperature decreases the yield and carbon residue of the DAO whereas an increase in solvent dosage increases the yield of deasphalted oil.

Heavy neutral distillates are sometimes produced by deasphalting the very high viscosity (wash oil) stream from vacuum fractionation of reduced crudes. The yield of DAO for use in bright stock and cylinder oil manufacture can be increased by including a higher than normal proportion of this wash oil in the vacuum residuum feed to the deasphalting unit.

Although mixer-settlers were used in the early deasphalting units and are still in use at a few locations, baffle towers of various designs and rotating disk contactors are used in modern deasphalting units. A simplified flow diagram for a propane deasphalting unit is shown in Fig. 4.

Single and dual effect evaporators are used to recover the solvent in the older deasphalting units with triple effect evaporation being used in modern or refurbished deasphalting units [5, 6]. Supercritical solvent recovery methods have also been developed [8, 9] and are being used in some deasphalting units.

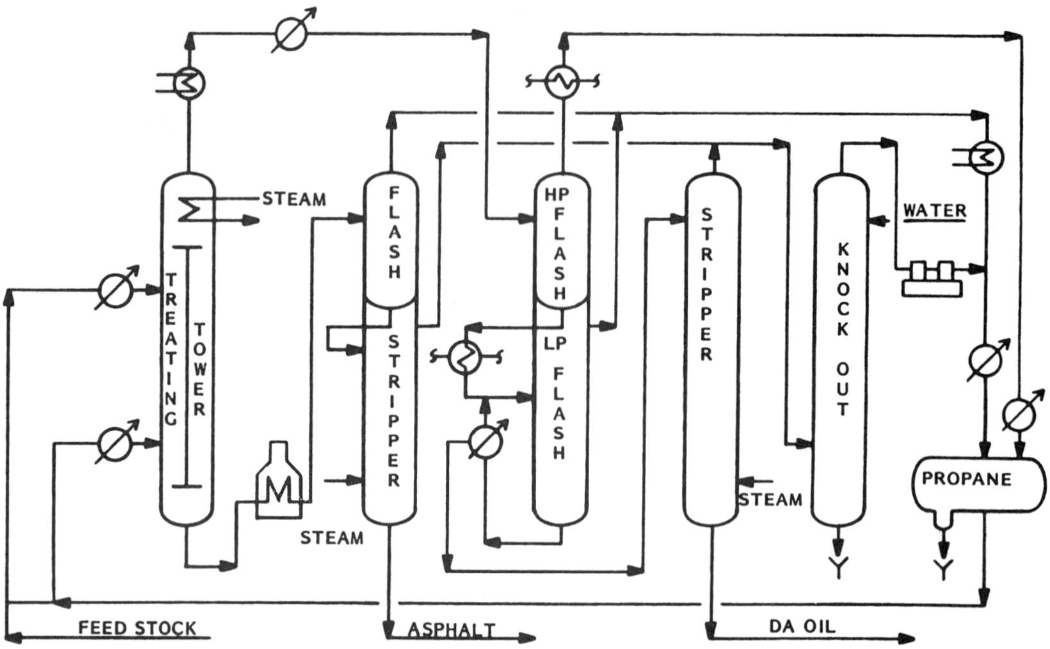

FIG. 4. Propane deasphalting unit flow diagram.

The Duo-Sol Process [1, 10, 11] is the only double-solvent process used to both deasphalt and extract lubricating oil feedstocks. Since it is both a deasphalting and extraction (refining) process, it does not conveniently fit into either the deasphalting or refining processes used for the manufacture of lube oils. Propane is used as the deasphalting or paraffinic solvent and Selecto (a mixture of phenol and cresylic acids) is used as the extraction solvent in this process. The Duo-Sol Process is most often used in the manufacture of bright stocks from vacuum residua. The process variables are temperature, solvent composition, and solvent dosage. The extraction is conducted in seven to nine batch extractors which are connected end to end followed by solvent recovery conducted in multistage flash distillation and stripping towers. The product raffinate requires no additional solvent or hydrogen refining for the manufacture of lubricating oil base stocks. Solvent dosages range from 100 to 400% Selecto and 150 to 500% propane basis feedstock. The temperature and solvent dosage used and yields of refined oil are highly dependent (like all refining processes) on the crude source being used and the quality of the base stock being manufactured. Since this process is capital intensive and phenol is toxic, no new units have been built since the mid-1950s and some units have been abandoned or replaced with deasphalting and/or solvent and hydrogen refining processes.

Lube Refining Processes

The vacuum distillates and deasphalted oils contain aromatics and other undesirable constituents which result in rapid darkening, oxidation, and sludging in service. Chemical, solvent, and hydrogen refining processes have been developed and are used to remove these undesirable components and to improve the viscosity index and quality of lube base stocks.

The classical chemical (sulfuric acid and clay refining) processes which were originally used for the refining of lube oil base stocks have been replaced by solvent extraction (solvent refining) and hydrotreating (hydrogen refining) processes because they are (1) more effective for the upgrading of feedstocks, (2) more cost effective, and (3) environmentally more acceptable. Although some refiners still use chemical refining processes, chemical refining is most often used for the reclamation of used lubricating oils or in combination with solvent or hydrogen refining processes for the manufacture of speciality lubricating oils and by-products.

Chemical Refining Processes

Acid-alkali refining [1, 10], also called "wet refining," is a chemical refining process in which lubricating oils are contacted with about 25 to 400 lb/bbl of 85–104 wt.% purity sulfuric acid followed by neutralization using aqueous or alcoholic alkali. Acid-alkali refining is conducted in a batch or continuous manner. In the batch process the oil to be treated is pumped to a treating agitator and mixed with acid of the desired strength. The oil and acid are mixed by mechanical means or by air blowing for a period of 10 to 30 min, after which time water may be added to assist in coagulation of the acid sludge. The sludge is removed or the oil decanted after settling for a period of several hours. More acid is added and the process repeated as needed. The acid or "sour" oil from this operation is then neutralized using an aqueous or alcoholic neutralizing agent followed by water washing and drying. Continuous acid refining involves the same steps as batch refining with the exception that (1) the acid, oil, "sour" oil, and neutralizing agent are mixed with pumps or static mixers; (2) excess acid, sludge, excess neutralizing agent, and soaps are removed by centrifuge or centrifugal extractors; (3) water washing is conducted using centrifugal extractors; and (4) brightening of the oil is conducted in continuous strippers. The advantages for the continuous process over the batch process are (1) higher yields of oil, (2) lower manpower requirements, (3) lower chemical consumption, (4) lower maintenance cost, (5) smaller space requirements, and (6) a reduction in air and water pollution.

Acid-clay refining [1, 10], also called "dry refining," is carried out in a manner similar to the acid-alkali refining process with the exception that clay and a neutralizing agent are used for neutralization of the "sour" oil. This process is used with oils that tend to form emulsions during neutralization, and it may be conducted in a batch or continuous manner. The neutralization products and bleaching clay are separated from the oil by using pressure filters. Continuous processes frequently employ the clay contacting methods used for the finishing of lubricating oils.

Neutralization [1] with aqueous and alcoholic caustic, soda ash lime, and other neutralizing agents is used to remove organic acids from some feedstocks. This type of treating can be conducted in a batch or continuous manner, as is done in sulfuric acid treating, or may be introduced into the crude distillation unit. Neutralization of feedstocks containing large quantities of organic acids is usually conducted to reduce organic acid corrosion in downstream units or to improve the refining response and color stability of lube feedstocks.

Hydrogen Refining Processes

Hydrogen refining, commonly called hydrotreating, was first used in the 1930s and discontinued because the then co-emerging solvent refining processes were more cost effective. A cheap source of hydrogen resulting from the use of catalytic reforming units and the need by some refiners to use "nonlube crudes" for lube oil manufacture led to reintroduction of the hydrogen refining processes in the late 1960s and early 1970s.

The hydrogen refining processes [12–26] are more severe than the mild hydrogen finishing processes (used as a replacement for the older chemical finishing processes). These processes consist of (1) the severe hydrotreating (lube hydrocracking) processes used as an alternative to solvent extraction and (2) the moderate severity hydrotreating (hydrorefining) processes used to prepare speciality products or to stabilize hydrocracked base stocks. A summary of process conditions for hydrogen refining processes is provided in Table 2.

The catalysts used in the lube hydrocracking processes are proprietary to the licensors of lube hydrocracking processes and are reported as various mixtures of cobalt, nickel, molybdenem, and tungsten on an alumina or silica–alumina-based carrier with nickel–tungsten probably used most often for manufacture of solvent neutral oils and bright stocks. Fluorides are sometimes incorporated in the catalysts or added to the feed to enhance catalyst activity. The frequency of catalyst regeneration is once every 1 to 3 years.

The catalysts used in the hydrorefining processes are proprietary but

TABLE 2 Process Conditions for Hydrogen Refining Processes

Process Variable	Hydrocracking	Hydrorefining
Pressure, lb/in.^{2} gauge	1500–3300	200–3000
Temperature, °F	600–850	480–850
Space velocity, V_0/V_c/h	0.25–1.5	0.3–5
Hydrogen recycle rate, SCF/bbl	3000–8000	550–8000
Hydrogen purity, mol%	70–90	90–100
Hydrogen consumption, SCF/bbl	500–3000	100–3000

TABLE 3 Investment Cost, Utilities, and Chemical Consumption for the Solvent and Hydrogen Processing Routes—Kuwait Crude [22]

	Processing Route	
	Solvent Refining (US $)	Hydrogen Refining (US $)
Investment cost (France 1981):		
Vacuum distillation	7,500,000	5,100,000
Propane deasphalting	5,600,000	6,900,000
Furfural refining	8,700,000	—
Hydrogen refining	—	18,200,000
Solvent dewaxing	15,500,000	15,500,000
Hydrogen finishing	3,500,000	2,200,000
Steam reforming	—	6,200,000
Total Investment	40,800,000	54,100,000
Utilities consumption:		
Fuel, ton/h	5.98	5.44
Electricity kWh/h	4,465	6,455
Steam, ton/h	36.1	36.8
Cooling water, m³/h	2,465	2,045
Chemicals consumption:		
Solvents, ton/yr	2,200	2,660
Hydrogen, ton/yr	357	See reformer
Catalysts, US $/yr	18,500	199,500
Reformer feed, ton/h	—	1.25
Steam production, ton/h	—	7

usually consist of nickel–molybdenum on alumina in the first stage and high nickel content or precious metal catalysts in the second stage.

A comparison of the investment costs and utilities and chemicals consumption for the manufacture of lube base stocks from Kuwait Crude using the solvent and hydrogen refining routes are summarized in Tables 3 and 4. Although these data [22] and other reported information [13, 15, 16] indicate that investment, utilities, catalysts, and chemicals costs are lowest for the solvent extraction route and highest for use of the hydrocracking route when processing the most widely used lube crudes, determination of the most cost-effective route requires a detailed study of the refiners available crude source and cost, available facilities, process combinations to be used, product quality level, and by-product use and value. The cost for addition of hydrogen refining to an existing lube plant will depend on the facilities available and if the existing solvent refining plant will be abandoned or used in parallel to pretreat the feed or posttreat the product from hydrogen refining.

Hydrogen refining processes are also used in combination with each other and with solvent extraction as summarized below.

1. Hydrocracking–hydrorefining
2. Hydrocracking–solvent extraction
3. Hydrogen finishing–solvent extraction (hydrogen starting)
4. Solvent extraction–hydrorefining (hydroextraction)

TABLE 4 Feedstock Requirements, Product, and By-products for the Solvent and Hydrogen Processing Routes—Kuwait Crude [22]

	Processing Route	
	Solvent Refining	Hydrogen Refining
Feedstock, ton/yr:		
Reduced crude (380°C)	1,021,989	609,480
Products, ton/yr:		
150 Solvent neutral	45,000	45,000
500 Solvent neutral	75,000	75,000
Bright stock	30,000	30,000
By-products, ton/yr:		
Vacuum gas oil	179,392	121,009
Vacuum residuum	328,860	0
Asphalts	151,602	217,889
Extracts	169,665	0
Waxes	39,415	39,415
Diesel and naphtha	2,055	74,115

The lube hydrocracking processes [12, 13, 15–18] are the most severe lube hydrogen refining processes and are most often used as a replacement for solvent refining or for viscosity reduction. These processes remove most of the nitrogen, oxygen, and sulfur present in lube oil feedstocks and convert the undesirable polynuclear aromatics and polynuclear naphthenes to mononuclear naphthenes, aromatics, and isoparaffins. The isoparaffins and mononuclear naphthenes and aromatics with multiple paraffinic side chains are generally recognized as the hydrocarbon structures in lube base stocks which have the desired viscometric properties (VI).

The advantages of lube hydrocracking as compared to solvent refining are (1) manufacture of lube base stocks from some (nonlube) crudes: (2) higher VI base stocks can be manufactured; (3) higher yield of lube base stock at a specified VI: (4) elimination of solvent extraction and finishing processes for some lube base stocks: (5) conversion of residual oils to distillate lube base stocks: (6) lube stocks of substantially better quality, in terms of VI and response to inhibition: and (7) production of high quality by-products, such as naphtha and middle distillate.

The disadvantages of lube hydrocracking as compared to solvent extraction are (1) lube base stocks darken and form sludge on exposure to air and light; (2) solvent refining, clay treating, or a second-stage hydrogenation is required to stabilize the hydrocracked base oils; (3) oils stabilized by hydrorefining are highly paraffinic and in some cases require a change in the additive package to overcome additive solubility problems; (4) severely hydrocracked lube stocks result in poorer solvent dewaxing filtration rates; (5) investment costs and operating costs are higher for hydrocracking; and (6) highly aromatic by-products suitable for use in carbon black or rubber extender oil manufacture are not produced.

The hydrocracking processes may be used alone or in series with single or dual reactors with the same or a different catalyst in each stage. Figure 5 is a

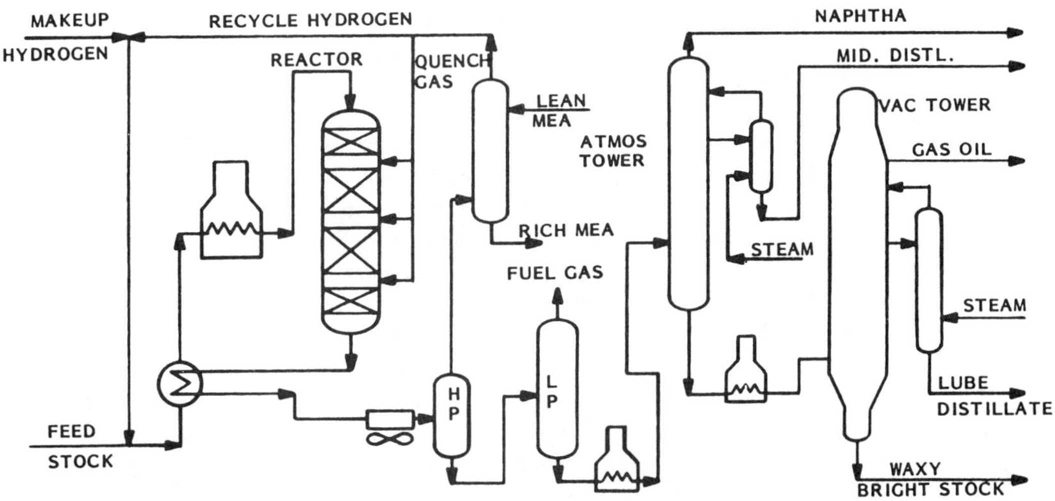

FIG. 5. Lube hydrocracker flow diagram.

simplified flow diagram for a single-stage lube hydrocracking unit in which the oil is mixed with hydrogen and processed downflow over a fixed bed of catalyst. Hydrogen quench is used to remove the heat generated and control the reaction temperature. The effluent from the reactor passes through a series of separators to remove the hydrogen and other light gases. The effluent product is then fractionated in atmospheric and vacuum distillation towers to provided the desired lube stocks and by-products. The effluent gas (mostly hydrogen) from the process is purified, if required, and recycled in the process.

These processes are generally operated in a blocked-out manner using narrow boiling range feedstocks because the VI of the low viscosity base oils is lower than desired and the VI of the high viscosity base oils are higher than desired if bulk (wide boiling range) feedstocks are used. These disadvantages can be overcome by recycle of the light lube fraction in the process or by subsequent hydrogen refining or solvent refining. The flow schemes covering the various modes of operation were reported by Bryson [15].

The feedstocks to the lube hydrocracking processes consist of (1) unrefined distillates and deasphalted oils, (2) solvent extracted distillates and deasphalted oils, (3) cycle oils, (4) hydrogen refined oils, and (5) mixtures of these hydrocarbon fractions. The use of slack wax as a feed to a lube hydrocracker for manufacture of very high VI base oils has been reported by Bull [16]. The composition and properties of the feedstocks to hydrocracking like the feedstocks to solvent extraction are dependent on the crude source and lube base stocks to be produced. Aromatic extracts from solvent refining can also be used as feedstocks for the manufacture medium VI base stocks.

Conventional VI base oil products obtained from the hydrocracking processes closely resemble those of solvent extracted oils with the exception that aromatic, sulfur, and nitrogen contents are usually lower and color is usually lighter at comparable VI levels. The composition of base oils produced by a combination of hydrocracking and solvent extraction is more like that of the solvent-refined base oils and do not require modification of the additive packages.

The yield, quality, and composition of lube base stock from hydrocracking processes are dependent on the quality of the feedstock, prior and postprocessing, catalyst, crude source, and VI of the base stock being produced. For a given feedstock, increased processing severity results in lower yield and viscosity and higher base oil viscosity index.

The operating conditions previously listed cover a wide range of temperature, pressure, and space velocity. Each of these variables has an effect on product characteristics which are also dependent on the mode of operation, catalyst used, nature of the feedstock, and products to be made.

Lube hydrocracking processes have been developed and are being used by several lube refiners. Shell France and Pennzoil currently use hydrocracking without a stabilizing process such as hydrogen, solvent, or clay treating. Pennzoil has also used a lube hydrocracker to convert surplus DA oil into distillate lube oils. The hydrocracking plant operated by EMP at Puertollano, Spain, was shut down in the late 1970s because it was less cost effective than furfural extraction for refining feedstocks derived from Arabian Light Crude. Chevron, Idemitsu Kosan, Petro Canada, and Ssangyong Oil use hydrorefining to stabilize the hydrocracked oils either immediately following hydrocracking or following fractionation and dewaxing. Quaker State used clay treating and Sun Oil uses furfural refining to stabilize the hydrocracked oils.

The hydrorefining processes [14, 20–24] operate at lower temperatures and at the same or somewhat lower pressures than the hydrocracking processes and are used to stabilize or improve the quality of lube base stocks from the lube hydrocracking processes and for manufacture of speciality oils.

Feedstocks to the hydrorefining processes are dependent on the nature of the crude source but generally consist of waxy or dewaxed solvent-extracted or hydrogen-refined paraffinic oils and refined or unrefined naphthenic and paraffinic oils from some selected crudes.

Figure 6 is a simplified flow diagram for a single-stage hydrorefining unit used for the stabilization of hydrcracked lube base stocks and manufacture of speciality lube base stocks and waxes. The two-stage process uses two single-stage hydrorefining units for the manufacture of medicinal grade white oils by removing essentially all of the sulfur, nitrogen, and aromatics in the first stage and elimination of the last traces of aromatics and impurities in the second stage.

The combination hydrogen and solvent refining processes result from the need to stabilize the hydrocracked lube base stocks and from the refiners desire to reduce the cost of lubes manufacture by elimination of the acid and clay refining of speciality products. Texaco and some of Texaco's affiliates have used and/or are using the Hydrogen Starting (mild hydrorefining to severe hydrogen finishing prior to solvent refining) route for the manufacture of lube base oils. Shell is using hydroextraction (mild furfural refining followed by severe hydrorefining) to manufacture lube base stocks [16]. Details concerning process conditions, catalysts, and economics for these processes have not been published. Vacuum gas oil, residual oil, and reduced crude desulfurizers and hydrocrackers are also sometimes used to provide feedstocks for the manufacture of lube oils using the solvent refining route.

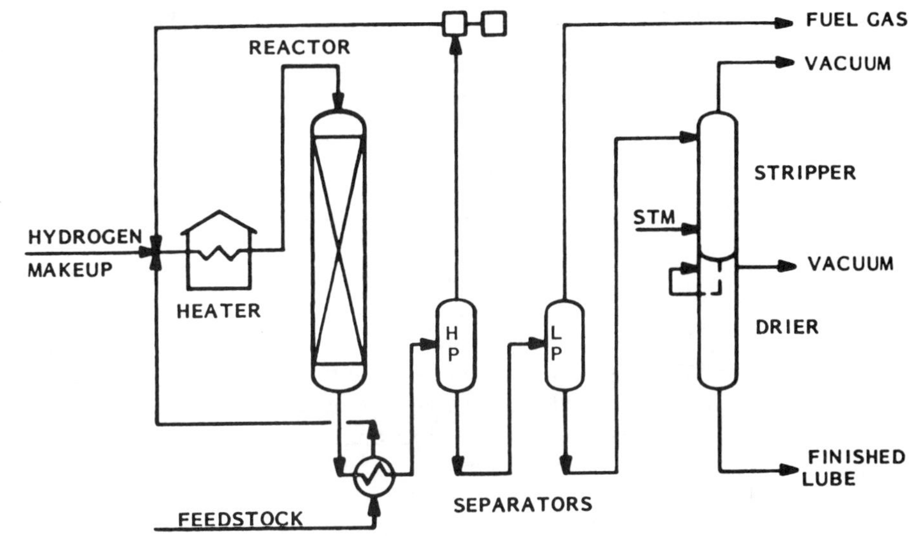

FIG. 6. Single-stage lube hydrorefining unit flow diagram.

Solvent Refining Processes

Petroleum refiners introduced solvent extraction (refining) processes in the late 1920s and early 1930s as an alternative to chemical and clay treating of lube base stocks for the removal of undesirable constituents and to improve the viscosity index of paraffinic lube base stocks [1]. Extraction has also been used to a lesser degree to improve the quality of naphthene pale oils and is now being more extensively used to reduce the toxicological aggressiveness of these base stocks.

The feedstocks to lube solvent extraction processes are (1) paraffinic and naphthenic distillates, (2) deasphalted oils, (3) hydrogen refined distillates and deasphalted oils, and to a lesser extent (4) cycle oils and (5) dewaxed oils. The products are (1) raffinates (refined oils) for further processing or (2) finished lube base stocks. The by-products are aromatic extracts which are used in the manufacture of rubber, carbon black, petrochemicals, FCCU feed, fuel oil, asphalt, etc.

Although no solvent meets all of the requirements of the ideal extraction solvent, a large number of solvents have been proposed and used commercially. The major solvents in use today are *N*-methyl-2-pyrrolidone (MP) and furfural, with phenol and liquid sulfur dioxide being used to a lesser extent. In addition to the quality of the crude being used, the main process variables are the processing temperature, solvent dosage, and solvent purity. These and solvent recovery methods each have an effect on process economics.

The extraction devices used in these processes are listed in Table 5.

Packed towers are generally used in the liquid sulfur dioxide process.

Since lube refining units must process a variety of different feedstocks of different viscosity and chemical composition from many crude sources in blocked operation at a variety of feed rates and processing conditions, design

TABLE 5 Extraction Devices Used in Solvent Refining Processes

Furfural	*N*-Methyl-2-pyrrolidone	Phenol
Centrifugal contactors	Baffle towers	Baffle towers
Packed towers	Centrifugal contactors	Centrifugal contactors
Rotating disk contactors	Packed towers	Packed towers
	Rotating disk contactors	

data for the proprietary extraction equipment is generally not available and can best be obtained from the designers of the extractors or the licensors of the processes. The report by Fiocco [27] presents an example of the long periods of time and experimentation (both laboratory and commercial) required to develop and improve the efficiency of lube oil extraction equipment.

Solvent recovery in the solvent refining processes is generally conducted in a series of multistage evaporators (commonly called flash towers) to reduce the energy requirements. Steam or inert gas strippers are used to remove the last traces of solvent, and a solvent purification section is used to remove water and other impurities. Additional information on the use of multistage evaporation and energy reductions which can be achieved from the use of additional evaporation stages or inert gas stripping is reported in the published literature [28–30].

The Edeleanu Process [1, 10], based on the use of liquid sulfur dioxide, was the first extraction process used by the petroleum industry and was introduced in 1907 to reduce the smoke point of kerosene. It was later applied to the extraction of lubricating oils and has been used in combination with benzene for the extraction and dewaxing of lubricating oil base stocks.

Although liquid SO_2 has good solvent power and selectivity for aromatic compounds, the requirement for low extraction temperatures limits its use to the extraction of naphthenic and low pour or dewaxed paraffinic feedstocks. The main disadvantages for use of liquid SO_2 are (1) toxicity, (2) air pollution control requirements, (3) moisture control to prevent corrosion, and (4) maintenance costs related to these items. No new units have been built for extraction of lube oils since the late 1950s and some units have been abandoned or replaced by solvent or hydrogen refining units. Although there are still some units in operation in Europe, currently it is being used at only one location in the United States for the extraction of naphthene oils.

The Furfural Refining Process [1, 10, 31, 35], the most widely used lube refining process on a worldwide basis, was first used commercially in the early 1930s and has been most extensively developed by Texaco. It is also used for the extraction of straight run gas oils and light and heavy cycle oils from catalytic cracking operations.

In addition to the quality of the feedstock, the main process variables are temperature, solvent dosage, purity of the solvent, and the quantity of extract recycled to the feed or below the feed in the extraction device. The yield of refined oil (selectivity) of furfural is equivalent to or better than that of the other refining solvents. The temperatures and solvent dosages used are highly dependent on the quality of the feedstock, crude source, and quality level of base stocks being produced. Although the normal ranges are 100 to 250°F and 100 to 500 vol.% furfural basis feed, higher and lower temperatures and dosages are used in some cases.

A simplified flow diagram for a furfural refining unit is shown in Fig. 7. RDCs are the currently favored extraction devices because of their excellent turn-down ratios, rapid change-over of feedstocks, and the elimination of the need to shut down for cleaning (decoking) which is experienced with packed towers.

The Phenol Refining Process [1, 33] was introduced in the early 1930s and has for the most part been replaced by the MP refining processes in the United States and to a lesser degree in Europe.

Phenol is a highly selective and highly toxic solvent which was first used for the extraction of lubricating oil feedstocks in 1930. The selectivity of phenol is good but generally lower than that of furfural or MP. In addition to the quality of the feedstock, the main process variables are temperature, dosage, the quantity of water or oil in the circulating solvent, and the dosage of wet solvent or water injected into the feed or extractor below the feed. The preferred extraction devices are packed towers and baffle towers.

N-Methyl-2-pyrrolidone (MP) Refining Processes [29, 30, 34–37] were developed by Exxon (EXOL N Extraction) and Texaco (Texaco MP Refining Process). MP has replaced furfural and phenol as the major extraction solvent in recent years and is beginning to replace these solvents on a worldwide basis. Figures 8 to 10 are representative of a few of the simplified flow diagrams for these processes. The process flow for these processes is similar to that of the furfural and phenol refining processes. The main differences in these processes are the different techniques used in the drying of the solvent, the use of wet MP in the Exxon EXOL N Process and the preference for anhydrous MP in the Texaco MP Refining Process. Cooling and/or water injection into the extract mix leaving the extractor can be used to produce cycle oils for the manufacture of medium VI base oils and to control the aromatic content of the extract. Preferred extraction devices are packed towers and trayed towers.

In addition to the quality of the feedstock, the main process variables are temperature, dosage, purity of the solvent, and the amount of water or wet solvent injected into the feed or treating solvent or into the extraction device below the feed. MP is nontoxic and has excellent solvent power and selectivity which is equivalent to that of furfural. Although the water content of the solvent should be minimized to maximize solvent power and minimize the solvent circulation, there are some feedstocks (crude source dependent) where water is used to improve the selectivity of MP. Since the limitation in most lube extraction units is solvent turnover, increases of 25 to 60% in feed rate have been obtained from the conversion of furfural and phenol refining units to MP.

The investment, operating, and energy costs are lower for the use of MP as compared to the use of furfural or phenol because the higher solvent power (lower treating dosage) of MP results in the need for smaller units and less energy consumption for a given size lube plant. Comparative investment costs and utilities consumption for the use of furfural and MP are shown in Table 6 [34].

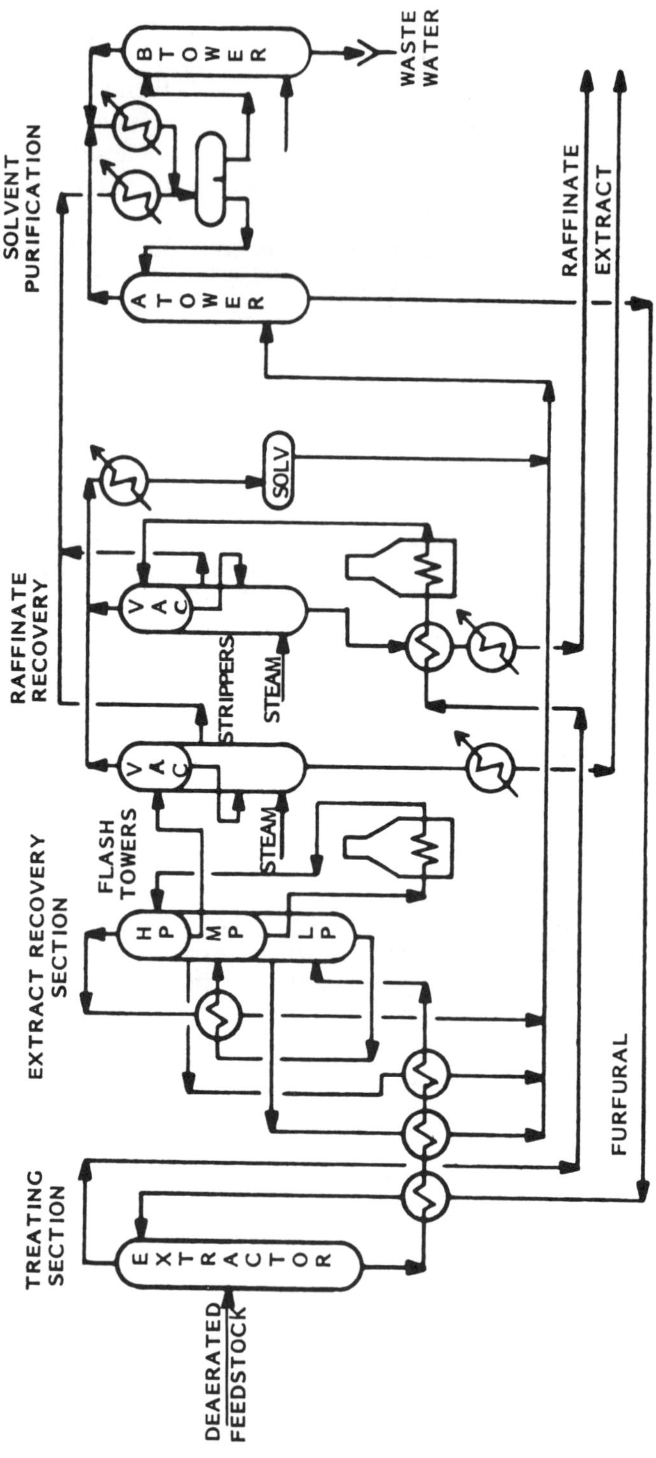

FIG. 7. Texaco furfural refining flow diagram.

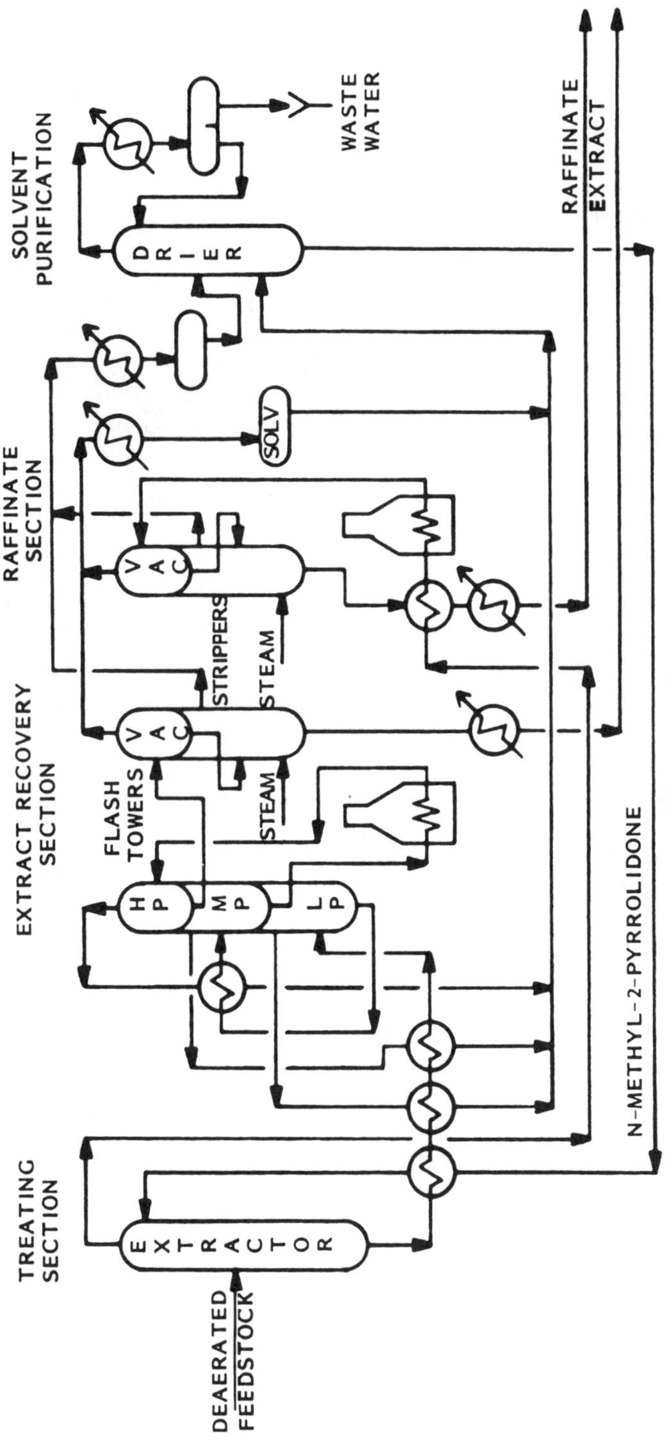

FIG. 8. Texaco MP refining unit flow diagram.

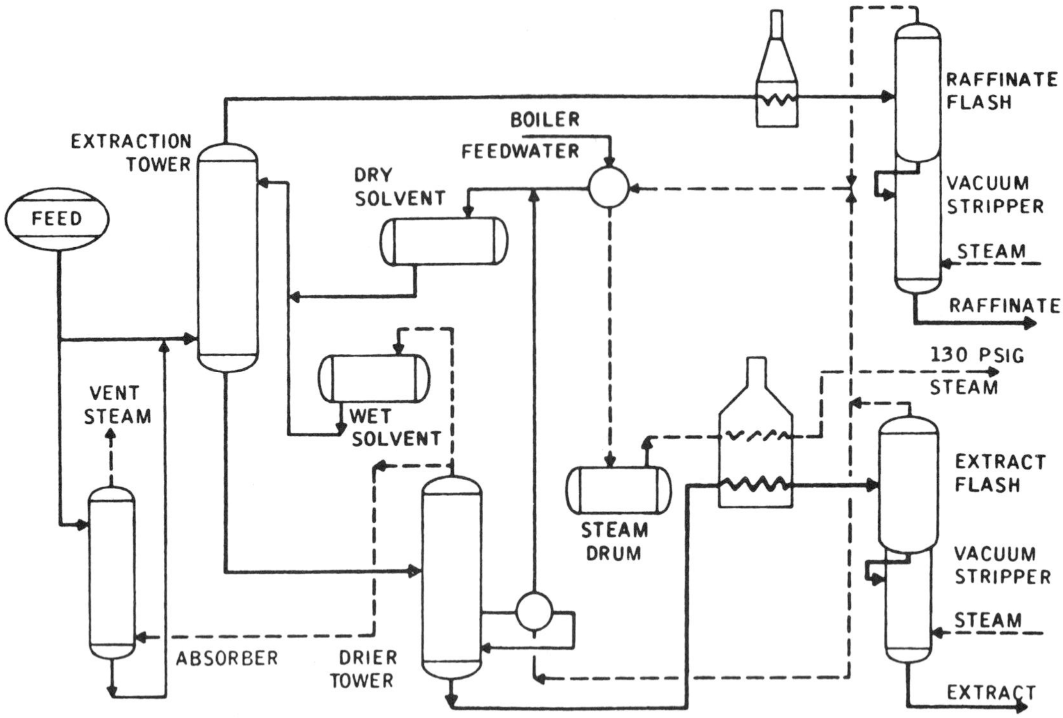

FIG. 9. EXOL N extraction unit using steam stripping.

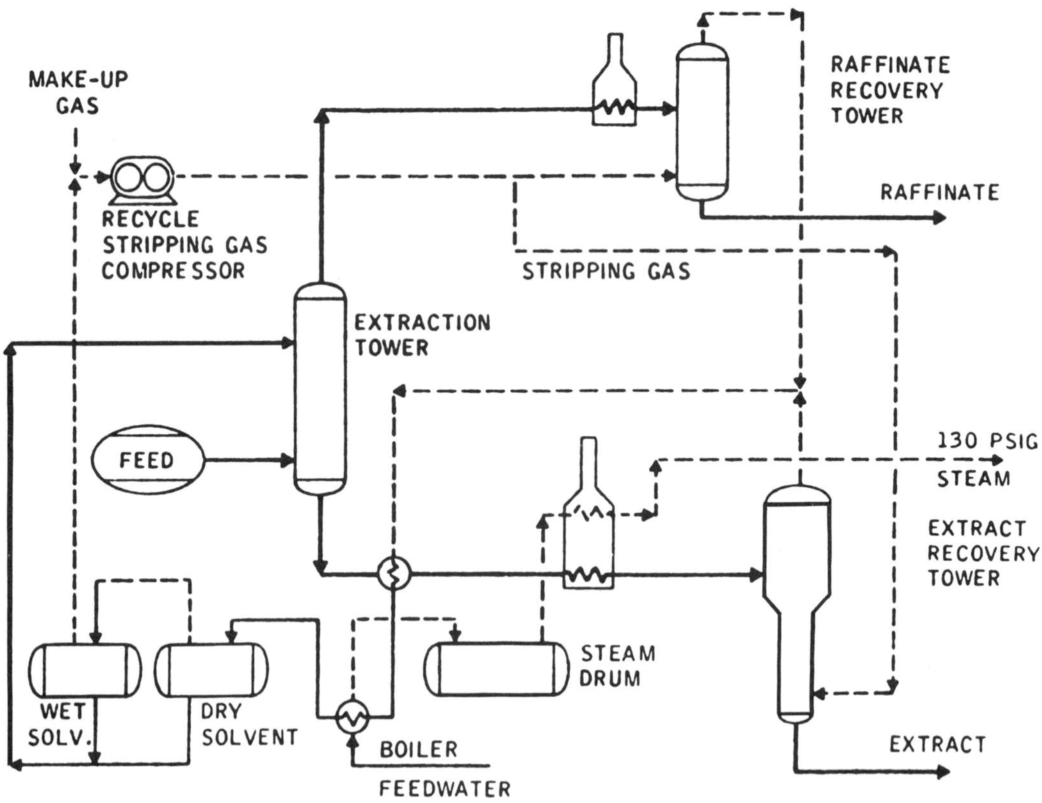

FIG. 10. EXOL N extraction unit using recycled stripping gas.

TABLE 6 Investment, Utility, and Chemical Costs for Solvent Refining Arabian Light Feedstocks [34]

		MP Refining		Furfural Refining	
Nominal Feed Rate, BPSD		10,000		10,000	
kg/h		63,000		63,000	
Investment cost (1986 US Gulf Cost), $		13,600,000		17,200,000	
Utilities and Chemicals Cost	$/Unit	Rate	Cost, $	Rate	Cost, $
Fuel (heat absorbed), MM · kcal/h	16.5	8.18	135.0	12.9	212.9
High pressure steam, kg/h	0.014	7864	110.1	5745	80.4
Low pressure steam, kg/h	0.012	1117	13.4	696	8.4
Cooling water, m^3/h	0.024	472	11.3	720	17.3
Electrical power, kW	0.05	267	13.4	402	20.1
Solvent, kg/h	2.9/1.5	2.5	7.3	38	57.0
Na_2CO_3, kg/h	—	0.2	—	1.6	—
Nitrogen, kg/h	—	8	—	8	—
Total cost, $/h			290.4		396.0
$/metric ton			4.65		6.34

Lube Dewaxing Processes

The raw paraffin distillates and residual oils leaving the crude stills contain wax and are normally solids at ambient temperature. The deasphalting and refining processes increase the wax content of lube feedstocks. Removal of wax from these fractions is necessary to permit manufacture of lubricating oils with the desired low temperature properties. Catalytic dewaxing, solvent dewaxing, and urea dewaxing processes have replaced the older cold settling, pressure filtration, and centrifuge dewaxing methods in the manufacture of lubricating oils.

Catalytic Dewaxing Processes

The removal of wax from lubricating oil base stocks by solvent dewaxing is expensive from the standpoint of investment, operating costs, and production of low pour point (below about −35°F) oils is generally not practical. Several petroleum refiners have patented various selective hydrocracking (catalytic dewaxing) processes for the manufacture of lube oil base stocks. The processes which have been commercialized to date were developed by British Petroleum [38], Chevron [19, 26], and Mobil [39–42]. Modified versions of the BP and Mobil processes are used to dewax fuels fractions. These processes are more cost effective and permit obtaining lower pour point products than the solvent dewaxing processes. Viscosity index is generally lower at the same pour point for catalytic dewaxed as compared to solvent dewaxed neutrals prepared from the same feedstock. Dewaxed oil yields are in some cases lower and in others higher than that obtained by solvent dewaxing. Products formulated from the lower VI catalytically dewaxed oils are equivalent to the solvent dewaxed oils and have demonstrated better low temperature properties [42]. However, more severe extraction or hydrogen refining of the distillate feedstocks to catalytic dewaxing is required to produce lube base stock of the same VI as that obtained by solvent dewaxing. The BP process can be used to dewax a wide range of naphthenic feedstocks and waxy or partially dewaxed feedstocks. However, it is not suitable for the manufacture of high VI paraffinic lube base oils. The Mobil MLDW process can be used to process all grades of lube base stocks. The Chevron Process has to date been used to dewax hydrogen refined 100 and 240 neutral oils and is believed suitable for dewaxing the full range of hydrogen and solvent extracted feedstocks.

The process flow of the BP process is essentially that of the hydrorefining unit shown in Fig. 6 with the exception that hydrogen quench (not needed with the Chevron or Mobil processes) is required to control the reaction temperature. Finishing, if required for purification and color improvement, requires an additional processing step unless a hydrogen finishing reactor is added. The BP Catalytic Dewaxing Process uses a proprietary synthetic mordenite containing platinum as the dewaxing catalyst.

The simplified process flow for the Mobil MLDW process is shown in Fig. 11 and consists of two reaction stages. The first reactor contains a proprietary ZSM-5 based dewaxing catalyst, and the second reactor contains an amorphous hydrogen finishing catalyst used to saturate olefins that are created by the dewaxing catalyst and to improve oxidative stability, color, and demulsibility of the finished lube oil.

The simplified process flow of the Chevron process is like that of the MLDW process. This process also uses a proprietary dewaxing catalyst in the first stage and a hydrogen finishing type catalyst in the second stage. Catalysts

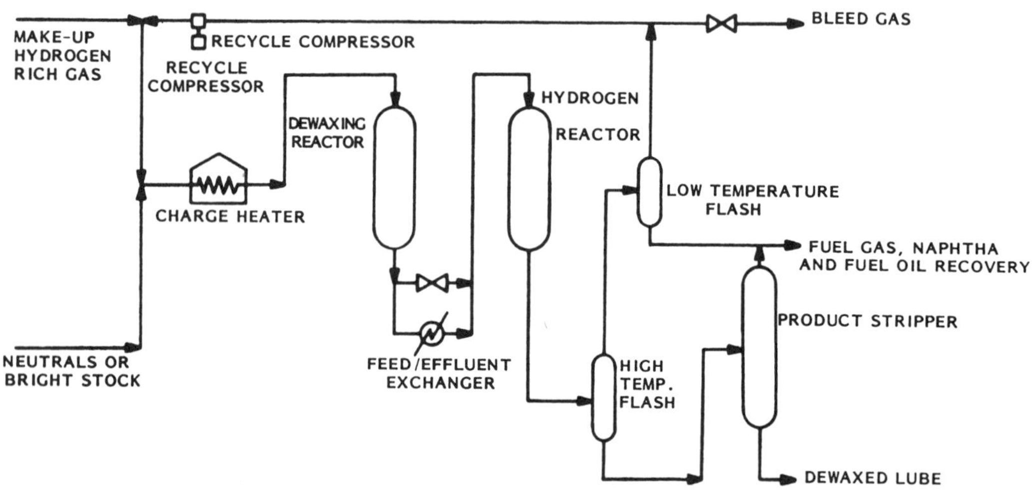

FIG. 11. MLDW process flow diagram.

TABLE 7 Process Conditions

	Process		
	British Petroleum	Mobil	
	Dewaxing	Dewaxing	Finishing
H_2 partial pressure, lb/in.^{2}	300–1500	250–3000	
Space velocity, V_0/V_c/h	0.5–5.0	Depends on feedstock	
Temperature, °F	550–750	525–675	475–550
H_2 circulation, SCF/bbl · d	2000–5000	500–5000	

used in this process have not been disclosed but are probably similar to the ZSM-5 zeolite containing a small quantity of a hydrogeneration metal in the dewaxing reactor and a conventional hydrogen finishing catalyst in the second reactor.

The processing conditions and hydrogen consumption are dependent on the (1) boiling range, (2) wax content, (3) pour point of the dewaxed oil, (4) viscosity, and (5) chemical composition of the feed. Generalized process conditions [38, 40] are summarized in Table 7.

Process conditions for the Chevron process have not been reported.

Technical information and details concerning process conditions and design for the catalytic dewaxing processes are currently only available through secrecy agreements with the licensors of the processes.

The first BP unit (a converted hydrotreating unit) was brought on stream in 1977 and a grassroots unit was brought on stream in 1983 with additional units in the planning stage. The Mobil Lube Dewaxing Process was demonstrated in 1978. Commercial MLDW units in operation include two Mobil units (one each in Australia and the United States) and two licensed units. Additional units are in the planning stage. The Chevron unit was brought on stream in 1985 at their Richmond California Refinery.

Solvent Dewaxing Processes

A considerable number of solvent-based processes have been developed over the years for the dewaxing of lubricating oils [1, 10, 43]. These processes can be divided into three basic sequential steps: (1) crystallization, the dilution and chilling of the feedstock with solvent; (2) filtration of the wax from the solution of dewaxed oil and solvent; and (3) solvent recovery from the wax cake and filtrate for recycle in the process by flash distillation and stripping. This processing sequence is depicted in Fig. 12 for a ketone dewaxing unit. The major process variables include (1) the nature of the feedstock, (2) the solvent and solvent composition, (3) the solvent dilution procedure, (4) the chilling procedure, (5) the filtration procedure, and (6) the solvent recovery method. The manner in which the above variables are controlled can have a significant effect on (1) the production rate, yield of dewaxed oil; (2) the pour point of the dewaxed oil; (3) the oil content of the wax; and (4) the investment and operating costs.

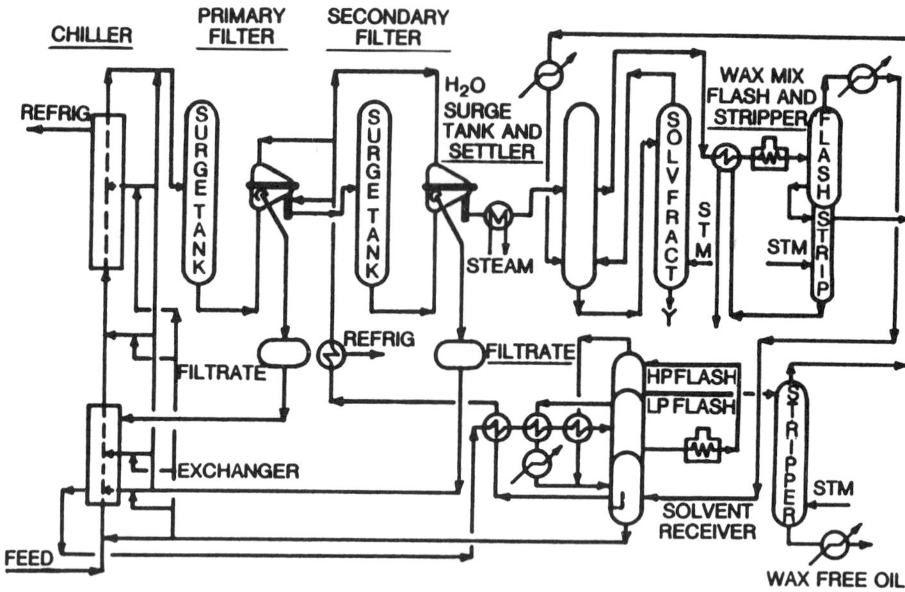

FIG. 12. Texaco solvent dewaxing unit flow diagram.

The major processes in use today are the ketone dewaxing processes. Processes used to a considerably lesser degree are the Di/Me Process and the propane dewaxing process.

The ketone dewaxing processes are based on improvements which have been made in the original solvent dewaxing process, the Acetone-Benzol Process (A-B process), which was first used commercially in 1927 [1, 10, 44, 45]. The original A-B or "classical" solvent dewaxing process was a single dilution single-stage filtration process. It has been modified to use various mixtures of acetone, benzene, methyl ethyl ketone (MEK), methyl isobutylketone (MIBK), toluene, and other aromatic hydrocarbons. The solvent mixtures used most often are MEK–toluene and MEK–MIBK with neat MIBK being used in some cases. Improvements made to the ketone dewaxing processes over the years include (1) replacement of batch chillers with scraped-surface exchangers/chillers and crystallizers; (2) rotary vacuum filters as replacements for the pressure-type filters; (3) synthetic filter cloth replaced cotton canvas for longer on-stream time; (4) controlled shock chilling, multiple dilution, and filtration techniques; (5) multiple effect evaporation for solvent recovery; (6) inert gas in place of steam for stripping; (7) cold backwashing as a replacement for hot washing of the filters; and (8) improved refrigeration plants and techniques [29, 45–47]. These processes and modifications of these processes are also used to prepare low oil content hard and finished waxes. Although some refiners use the older double-dilution single-stage filtration procedures or modifications of these processes described in the literature, the most widely used ketone dewaxing processes in use today are the Texaco Solvent Dewaxing Process and the Exxon Dilchill Process, respectively.

The Texaco Solvent Dewaxing Process [1, 7, 10, 43, 44], generally called the MEK process, normally uses a mixture of MEK and toluene as the dewaxing solvent and sometimes uses mixtures of other ketones and aromatic solvents.

Figure 12 is a simplified flow diagram for this process. The waxy feedstock is heated to 10–15°F above the cloud point of the oil and diluted with solvent while chilling at a controlled rate in double-pipe scraped-surface exchangers and chillers. Two to four volumes of solvent using an incremental dilution procedure for low to medium viscosity stocks and a double-dilution controlled shock chilling procedure for high viscosity stocks are used in the more modern MEK units with the older double-dilution single-stage filtration used in some units. About 60% of the chilling is obtained by heat exchange between the feedstock and solvent with the cold filtrate from filtration in the annulus of the double-pipe exchangers. The remainder of the refrigeration required for chilling is obtained by indirect heat exchange with a refrigerant in the annulus of the double-pipe chillers. The slurry leaving the chillers at a temperature of 5 to 20°F below the desired pour point is filtered using rotary vacuum filters and the wax cake is washed with a spray of cold solvent before being discharged by an inert gas blow back. The filtrate from these primary filters is used to prechill the feedstock and solvent mixture in the scraped-surface exchangers. The filtrates from these filters may be separated into a primary (oil-rich) filtrate used as the chilling medium and the wash (oil-lean) filtrate used as dilution solvent. The wax cake from the primary filter is diluted with additional solvent and filtered in a second (repulp) rotary vacuum filter with cold solvent washing of the wax cake to reduce the oil content of the wax. The filtrate from the repulp filter is normally used as feedstock dilution solvent in the crystallization train but may also be separated into an oil-rich filtrate for use as feedstock dilution solvent and an oil-lean filtrate for dilution of the wax from the primary filter. The solvent is recovered from the resultant dewaxed oil filtrate and wax cake by dual- or triple-effect flash vaporization and recycled in the process.

The wax recrystallization and wax warm-up deoiling procedures are used in those cases in which the lube refiner also manufactures a hard or finished wax. The Edeleanu Spray Deoiling Process [48] and older wax sweating processes [1] are also used to manufacture low oil content waxes.

The Exxon Dilchill Dewaxing Process [10, 45, 46, 49, 50] uses direct cold solvent dilution-chilling technique with a high degree of mixing in a special crystallizer in place of the scraped-surface exchangers. The high degree of mixing is used to overcome the poor filtration rates obtained with the conventional shock chilling techniques. A solvent drying step must be added to remove the last traces of water from the solvent to prevent the icing of the solvent chillers during chilling of the solvent to the low temperatures required for direct chilling of the feedstock. Indirect refrigeration and scraped-surface chillers are used to complete the chilling cycle. Filtration and multiple effect evaporation for solvent recovery are conducted in the usual manner.

Data have been reported which show that the filtration rates oil content of the slack wax produced by this process are better than those obtained using the conventional (single-dilution single-stage filtration) ketone dewaxing processes [50]. Although comparative commercial data on the same waxy feedstock using the Dilchill procedure and multidilution or controlled shock chill procedures are not available, laboratory comparisons have shown that filtrations rates are comparable when the same dilution ratios and filtration procedures are used. In addition, filtration rates comparable to those reported for the Dilchill process have been obtained in some commercial ketone dewaxing processes using the conventional incremental dilution and controlled shock chill procedures.

The warm-up wax deoiling procedure is used with the Dilchill Process in the manufacture of hard or finished wax.

The Di/Me Dewaxing Process [45, 51] uses a mixture of dichloroethane (Di) and methylene dichloride (Me) as the dewaxing solvent. This process, developed by Edeleanu Gellschaft, is used by a few refineries in Europe for the dewaxing of lubricating oil base stocks and the manufacture of low oil content wax. The process flow is essentially the same as that of the ketone dewaxing processes except that the oil-lean wash filtrate is used as dilution in the chilling train. The wax cake from the primary filter is diluted with the oil-lean wash filtrate from the second-stage filter and the repulped mixture filtered in the second-stage (repulp) filter to produce hard or finished wax. The second stage is omitted if hard wax production is not desired.

The Propane Dewaxing Process [1, 10, 45] was developed and first used in 1932 by Standard Oil Company of Indiana and further improved by the JUIC (Standard Oil of New Jersey, Union Oil Co., Standard Oil of Indiana, and M. W. Kellog patent combine). Process flow is essentially that of the ketone dewaxing processes with the exception that higher pressure equipment is required, and chilling is done in evaporative chillers by vaporizing a portion of the dewaxing solvent. Filtration is conducted using rotary filters and washing of the wax cake with cold propane. Solvent is recovered for recycle in the process using two or more evaporators and by stripping. Advantages for this process are (1) the solvent is cheap and readily available, (2) evaporative chilling greatly reduces the adhesion of wax to the crystallizer walls and eliminates the need for expensive crystallizers, and (3) wax cloud points of propane dewaxed bright stocks are usually lower as compared to ketone dewaxed bright stocks. The main disadvantages for the use of propane are that (1) the differential between the dewaxed oil and filtration temperature (25–45°F) is considerably higher than that of the ketone dewaxing or Di/Me dewaxing processes, (2) control of batch chilling is difficult because the compressors are underutilized during the initial chilling phase of the process, and (3) dewaxing aids are required to obtain good filtration rates.

The use of ketone solvents as a wax antisolvent to improve the economics of the propane/propylene dewaxing process using a mixture of propylene and acetone as the dewaxing solvent was tested commercially [49]. Although this test was reported to be successful, it is not known if the modified process is being used commercially.

Lube Urea Dewaxing Processes

The formation of crystalline complexes (adducts) between urea and straight-chain hydrocarbons was discovered by Bengen in 1940 and has been used as a basis for lube oil dewaxing processes and for the manufacture of normal paraffins. No new urea dewaxing units have been constructed and some existing units have been abandoned in recent years. Those interested in additional information should review Hoppe [52] and Scholten [53].

Lube Oil Finishing Processes

Although acid and clay are still used to some extent for the finishing of lubricating oil base stocks and wax, these processes have for the most part been replaced with hydrogen finishing processes.

Sulfuric acid treating [1, 10] is the original or "classical" refining and finishing process for the manufacture of lubricating oils. Although it is still used for this purpose by a few refiners, it finds it main use in the manufacture of specialty oils and the reclamation of used lubricating oils. The treating of lubricating oils with sulfuric acid is conducted in a batch or continuous manner as was described in the section on acid refining. The main difference in acid finishing as compared to acid refining is that the quantity of acid used is usually low (10 or less lb/bbl) in comparison to the large quantities (25 to 400 lb/bbl) used in the acid refining processes.

Clay contacting [1, 10] involves the intimate mixing of oil with fine bleaching clay at elevated temperature for a short period of time followed by separation of the oil and clay. This process is frequently combined with the acid treating process for the finishing and neutralization of lube base stocks. The process improves color and chemical, thermal, and color stability of the lube base stock. The process variables include the clay dosage and treating temperature. Clay dosages are usually relatively low (4 to 20 lb/bbl) and treating temperature ranges from about 220 to 650°F or just below the flash point of the oil being treated. Use of excessively high temperatures can result in darkening of the oil.

Clay percolation [1, 10, 54] is a static bed absorption process used to purify, decolorize, and finish lube base stocks and waxes. This process has in large part been replaced by hydrogen finishing but is still in limited use for the manufacture of refrigeration oils, transformer oils, turbine oils, white oils, and waxes. Although Attapulgus clay can be used, the most frequently used clay is Porocel, an activated bauxite. The process variables include temperature, flow rate, throughput, and type of clay.

Hydrogen finishing processes [56–60] are mild hydrogeneration processes used in place of the older and more costly acid and clay finishing processes for the purpose of improving color, odor, thermal, and oxidative stability, and demulsibility of lube base stocks. They are fixed-bed catalytic hydrogeneration processes used for neutralization, desulfurization, and denitrification of lube base stocks. Unlike the hydrogen refining processes, hydrogen finishing processes do not saturate aromatics nor break carbon—carbon bonds.

Process flow is essentially identical to the hydrorefining process shown in Fig. 6. The operating conditions are dependent on feedstock composition (related to crude source as well as type and severity of prior processing), catalyst, and product specifications. General operating conditions for these processes are listed in Table 8.

TABLE 8 Operating Conditions

Hydrogen partial pressure, $lb/in.^2$	200–1500
Temperature, °F	450–650
Liquid hourly space velocity, V_0/V_c/h	0.5–3.0
Hydrogen rate, SCF/bbl feed	100–5000
Hydrogen purity, mol%	50–100
Hydrogen consumption, SCF/bbl feed	50–200

Hydrogen finishing catalysts are usually cobalt–molybdenum, nickel–molybdenum, or iron–cobalt–molydenum on alumina. The catalysts are received in the oxide form and must be sulfided before use. They provide long service life and are regenerated using a controlled oxygen burn. Metal poisoning of the catalysts is usually not a problem with lube feedstocks because the metals are removed in the deasphalting and refining processes.

Feedstocks to these processes are usually naphthenic or dewaxed paraffinic oils which may be or may not have been chemically, solvent, or hydrogen refined. These processes sometimes (1) precede solvent dewaxing to improve the quality or processing respones of the wax by-product from solvent dewaxing or (2) precede solvent extraction (hydrogen starting) to improve the yield of refined oil or reduce the sulfur content of aromatic extracts. When used in this manner, the size of the units, hydrogen consumption, and operating costs are increased in comparison to hydrogen finishing following solvent dewaxing. However, the size of the extraction unit may be reduced, and installation of finishing units for the manufacture of wax or desulfurization of extracts (if needed) are eliminated or reduced in size.

The effect of hydgen finishing temperature and pressure is highly dependent on the quality of the feedstock and the type of catalyst used. An increase in temperature or pressure will normally improve neutralization, desulfurization, denitrification, product color, and product stability. However, increasing the temperature above some maximum which is related to the catalyst and feedstock quality will degrade the color, oxidation stability, and other properties of the base oil.

The hydrogen finishing processes used by most of the lube oil refiners are properietary processes such as Ferrofining (British Petroleum), Gulfinishing (Gulf), Hydrofining (Exxon), Hydrogen Finishing (Texaco), and Lube Oil Hydrotreating (IFP).

The hydrorefining processes previously discusses are sometimes used as finishing processes for the stabilization of hyrocracked oils and as a replacement for the acid and clay finishing of specialty products such as transformer oils, white oils, and waxes.

References

1. V. A. Kalichevsky and K. A. Kobe, *Petroleum Refining with Chemicals*, Elsevier, London, 1956, pp. 72–122, 319–456.

2. R. G. Brand, "Mobil's New 100,000 bbl/day Crude Distillation Unit," *Heat Eng.*, pp. 98–101 (January-February 1960).
3. G. T. Atkins, E. O. McBride and L. W. Owens, "Crude Oil Distillation," in *Encyclopedia of Chemical Processing and Design*, Vol. 13, Dekker, New York, 1981, pp. 238–260.
4. R. N. Watkins, *Petroleum Refining Distillation*, 2nd ed., Gulf Publishing, Houston, 1981.
5. J. A. Bonilla et al., "FW Solvent Deasphalting," in *Handbook of Petroleum Refining Processes*, McGraw-Hill, New York, 1986, pp. 8.19–8.51.
6. C. P. Chang and J. R. Murphy, "Deasphalting," in *Encyclopedia of Chemical Processing and Design*, Vol. 14, Dekker, New York, 1983, pp. 149–166.
7. W. P. Gee and H. H. Gross, "Dewaxing and Deasphalting," in *Advances in Chemistry Series*, No. 5 (Progress in Petroleum Technology), American Chemical Society, Washington, D.C., 1951, pp. 160–176.
8. S. R. Nelson and R. G. Roodman, *ROSE: The Energy Efficient Bottom of the Barrel Alternative*, Paper Presented at the 1985 Spring AIChE Meeting, Houston, March 24–28, 1985.
9. J. R. Salazar, "UOP Demex Process," in *Handbook of Petroleum Refining Processes*, McGraw-Hill, New York, 1986, pp. 8.61–8.70.
10. D. Klamann et al., "Production of Petroleum Based Lubricating Oils," in *Lubricants and Related Products*, Verlag Chemie, Weinheim, 1984, pp. 51–83.
11. M. H. Tuttle, "The Performance and Flexibility of the DUOSOL Process," in *Proceedings—Fifth Mid-Year Meeting, API*, Vol 16M, No. III, 1935, pp. 112–123.
12. A. Billion et al., "Consider Hydrorefining for Lubes," *Hydrocarbon Processing*, September 1975, pp. 139–144.
13. A. Billion et al., "Procede D'Hydroraffinage Pour La Production D'Huiles Lubrifiantes," in *Proceedings—Tenth World Petroleum Congress*, Vol. 4, 1980, pp. 211–220.
14. A. Billon et al., Improvements in Waxes and Special Oil Refining," in *1980 Proceedings—Refining Department, API*, Vol. 59, pp. 168–177.
15. M. C. Bryson et al., "Gulfs Lubricating Oil Hydrotreating Process," in *Proceedings—Division of Refining, API*, Vol. 49, 1969, pp. 439–443.
16. S. Bull and A. Marmin, "Lube Oil Manufacture by Severe Hydrotreatment," in *Proceedings—Tenth World Petroleum Congress*, Vol. 4, 1980, pp. 221–228.
17. V. P. Burton and L. E. Hutchings, *Production of Quality Lubricants by the HDC Unibon Process*, Paper Presented at the PetroPeru's Lube Oil Manufacturing Operations Seminar, Lima, May 8–12, 1978.
18. T. R. Farrell and J. A. Zakarian, "Lube Facility Makes High-Quality Lube Oil from Low-Quality Feed," *Oil Gas J.*, pp. 47–51 (May 19, 1986).
19. R. W. Geiser and L. E. Hutchings, "Quality Lubricants from Pennsylvania Grade Crude Oil by the Isomax Process," in *1973 Proceedings—Division of Refining, API*, Vol. 53, pp. 738–757.
20. J. B. Gilbert and R. Kartzmark, "Advances in the Hydrogen Treating of Lubricating Oils and Waxes," in *Proceedings—Seventh World Petroleum Congress*, III, 1967, pp. 193–205.
21. J. B. Gilbert et al., "Hydroprocessing for White Oils," *Chem. Eng.*, pp. 87–89 (September 15, 1975).
22. *IFP Technology for the Refining of Lube Base Oils, White Oils and Waxes*, Reference 29676, Institut Francais Du Petrole, France, November 1981.
23. H. C. Murphey et al., "High Pressure Hydrogenation—Route to Specialty Products," in *Proceedings—Division of Refining, API*, Vol. 49, 1969, pp. 817–904.
24. M. K. Rausch and G. E. Tollefsen, *DUOTREAT Process*, Presented at the 1972

National Fuels and Lubricants Meeting of the NPRA, New York, September 14–15, 1972, Paper No. F&L-72-44.
25. D. H. Shaw, "Recent Developments in Oil Refining," in *Proceeding of the Eleventh World Petroleum Congress*, Vol. 4, 1984, pp. 345–357.
26. J. A. Zakarian et al., *All Hydroprocessing Route for High-V.I. Lubes*, Paper Presented at the AIChE Spring National Meeting, New Orleans, April 6–10, 1986.
27. R. J. Fiocco, "Development of the Cascade Weir Tray for Extracton," in *AIChE New Developments in Liquid-Liquid Extractors: Selected Papers from ISEC '83, AIChE Symposium Series, 238*, Vol. 80, 1984, pp. 89–93.
28. P. Taylor, *Operating Lube Plants Efficiently*, Paper Presented at the AIChE Spring National Meeting, New Orleans, April 6–10, 1986.
29. A. Sequeira Jr. et al, "Return To Basics—How to Reduce Energy Requirements in Lube Oil Solvent Extraction and Dewaxing Processes," in *1980 Proceedings—Refining Department, API*, Vol. 59, pp. 133–150.
30. J. D. Bushnell and R. J. Fiocco, "Engineering Aspects of the EXOL N Lube Extraction Process," in *1980 Proceedings—Refining Department, API*, Vol. 59, pp. 133–150.
31. L. C. Kemp, G. B. Hamilton, and H. H. Gross, "Furfural as a Selective Solvent in Petroleum Refining," *Ind. Eng. Chem.*, *40*(2), 220–227 (1948).
32. R. E. Manley et al., "Refining of Lubricating Oils with Furfural," in *Proceedings—Fourteenth Mid-Year Meeting American Petroleum Institute*, Vol. 16M, No. III, 1936, pp. 39–46.
33. R. K. Stratford et al., "The Use of Phenol as a Selective Solvent in the Production of High-Grade Lubricating Oils," in *Proceedings—Fourteenth Annual Meeting American Petroleum Institute*, Section III (Refining), Chicago, October 23–26, 1936, pp. 90–95.
34. F. C. Jahnke, *Solvent Refining of Lube Oils—The MP Advantage*, Paper Presented at the AIChE Fall National Meeting, Miami Beach, November 2–7, 1986.
35. B. M. Sankey et al., "EXOL N: New Lubricants Extraction Process," in *Proceedings of the Tenth World Petroleum Congress*, Vol. 4, 1979, pp. 407–414.
36. A. Sequeira, P. B. Sherman, J. U. Douciere, and E. O. McBride, "MP Refining of Lubes," *Hydrocarbon Processing*, pp. 155–160 (September 1979).
37. A. Sequeira et al., *Conversion of Furfural Refining Units to N-Methyl-2-pyrrolidone (MP) Refining Units*, Paper Presented at the AIChE Spring National Meeting, New Orleans, April 6–10, 1986.
38. J. D. Hargrove, "Dewaxing, Catalytic," in *Encyclopedia of Chemical Processing and Design*, Vol. 15, Dekker, New York, 1983, pp. 346–352.
39. R. G. Graven and J. R. Green, *Hydrodewaxing of Fuels and Lubricants Using ZSM-5 Type Catalysts*, Paper Presented at the Australian Institute of Petroleum 1980 Congress.
40. F. A. Smith, *Mobil Lube Oil Dewaxing (MLDW) Technology*, Paper Presented at the Texaco Lubricating Oil Manufacturing Licensee Symposium, White Plains, New York, May 18–20, 1982.
41. K. W. Smith et al., "New Process Dewaxes Lube Base Stocks: Mobil Lube Dewaxing," in *1980 Proceedings—Refining Department, API*, Vol. 59, pp. 151–158.
42. W. C. Starr and J. W. Walker, *Quality of Hydrodewaxed Base Stocks*, Presented at the 1981 National Fuels and Lubricants Meeting of the NPRA, Houston, November 5–6, 1981, Paper No. F&L-81-85.
43. S. Marple Jr. and L. J. Landry, "Modern Dewaxing Technology," in *Advances in Petroleum Chemistry and Refining*, Vol. 10, Wiley-Interscience, New York, 1965, pp. 192–216.
44. F. X. Govers and G. R. Bryant, "Solvent Dewaxing of Oils with Benzol and

Acetone," in *Proceedings of the American Petroleum Institute*, Vol. 14, No. III, May 1933, pp. 7–15.
45. G. G. Scholten, "Solvent Dewaxing," in *Encyclopedia of Chemical Processing and Design*, Vol. 15, Dekker, New York, 1983, pp. 353–370.
46. J. D. Bushnell and J. F. Egan, *Commercial Experience with Dilchill Dewaxing*, Presented at the NPRA Annual Fuels and Lubricants Meeting, Houston, 1975, Paper No. F&L-75-50.
47. J. M. Scalise et al., "Solvent Dehydration System Cuts Energy Use, Improves Dewaxed Oil Yield," *Oil Gas J.*, pp. 84–86 (August 27, 1984).
48. G. W. Wirtz, *Spray Deoiling Process*, Paper Presented at the Texaco Lubricating Oil Manufacturing Licensee Symposium, White Plains, New York, May 18–20, 1982.
49. J. F. Eagen et al., "Successful Development of Two New Lubricating Oil Dewaxing Processes," in *Proceedings—Ninth World Petroleum Congress*, Vol. 5, 1975, pp. 345–357.
50. D. A. Gudelis et al., "Improvements in Dewaxing Technology," *API Proceedings—Division of Refining*, Vol. 53, 1973, pp. 724–737.
51. S. Norbert, "German Unit Gives Dewaxing Data," *Hydrocarbon Processing Pet. Refiner*, pp. 104–106 (December 1963).
52. A. Hoppe, "Dewaxing With Urea," in *Advances in Petroleum Chemistry and Refining*, Vol. 8, Wiley-Interscience, New York, 1964, pp. 193–234.
53. G. G. Scholten, "Dewaxing, Urea," in *Encyclopedia of Chemical Processing and Design*, Vol. 15, Dekker, New York, 1983, pp. 353–370.
54. Englehard Minerals & Chemicals Corp., *Hydrocarbon Refining with Static-Bed Percolation*, EM-9349, Revised, Menlo Park, New Jersey, April 1986.
55. R. M. Butler and R. Kartzmark, "Chemical Changes in Lubricating Oil on Hydrofining," in *Proceedings—Fifth World Petroleum Congress*, Vol. III, 1959, pp. 151–160.
56. H. F. Dare and J. Demeester, *Ferrofining—First Commercial Unit on Stream*, Paper No. Tech. 62-15 Presented at the Annual Meeting of the NPRA, April 2–4, 1962, San Antonio, Texas.
57. J. B. Gilbert et al., "Hydrogen Processing of Lube Stocks," *J. Inst. Pet.*, *53*(526), 317–327 (October 1967).
58. E. O. Kindschy et al., "Lubricating Oil Hydrotreatment to Improve Quality and Yields," *Preprint 35C, 55th National Meeting of AIChE*, Houston, February 1965.
59. R. L. Menzl and W. L. Webb, "Hydrotreating of Lubricating Oil Stocks for Industrial Oils," in *Proceedings—American Petroleum Institute*, Section III, Refining, 1965, pp. 48–53.
60. F. Tsuneyoshi et al., "Hydrogen Treating of Some Lubricating Oil Fractions," *Bull. Jpn. Pet. Inst.*, *6*, 1–10 (June 1964).

AVILINO SEQUEIRA, Jr.

Lubricating Oils, Solvent Refining with *N*-Methyl-2-pyrrolidone

Introduction

Today, solvent refining is used throughout the lube oil industry to improve lube oil quality as measured by the viscosity index, color, and stability, and, more recently, to remove carcinogenic aromatic materials. The main solvents currently in use in lube oil refining are *N*-methyl-2-pyrrolidone (MP), furfural, and phenol (see the *Lubricating Oils, Manufacturing Processes* articles). The current trend is toward MP as the preferred solvent. Economics, of course, is the driving force for this trend. In the case of phenol, the conversion to MP has been further helped by the high toxicity of phenol.

This article provides a brief background on solvent refining and an economic analysis of MP vs furfural refining which demonstrates the current basis for the trend toward MP refining. For more details on the history and operation of the solvent refining process, refer to the references listed at the end of this paper.

Properties

The properties of MP are the basis of its economic advantage. Table 1 shows a comparison of MP, furfural, and phenol properties.

The key property, the one that makes MP so attractive, is the solvent power. Figure 1 shows solvent reduction using MP instead of furfural or phenol at constant refined oil quality. As can be seen, the amount of solvent reduction varies with a particular feedstock and with the product produced. Generally, however, a 25–55% reduction in required solvent dosage is typical. Figure 2 gives an indication of the size of the solvent dosages needed.

The selectivity of the solvent is another important property. A comparison of solvents based on selectivity is shown in Fig. 3. As seen from the figures, the selectivity (i.e., yield at given product quality) of refined oil is better for furfural than for phenol. In comparing MP to furfural, we see that the selectivity is essentially the same if proper operating conditions are used. The selectivity can be varied for all solvents by changing the solvent dosage and extraction temperature. In addition, the selectivity and/or solvent power of MP and phenol can be modified by water injection.

The stability of the solvent is important from a solvent make-up and maintenance standpoint. Fouling of fired heaters and exchangers is greatly reduced when operating with MP as compared to furfural operation. This results in an increased on-stream factor for MP.

TABLE 1 Comparison of Properties of MP, Furfural, and Phenol

	MP	Furfural	Phenol
	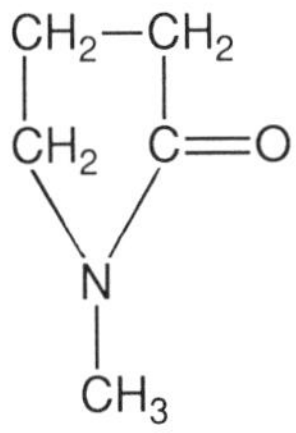	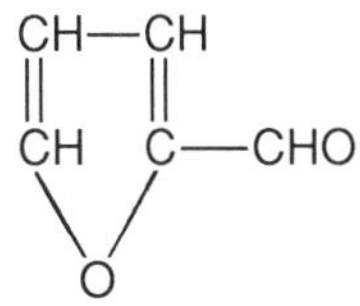	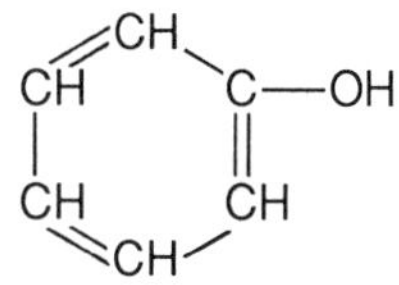
Relative cost, 1985	1.9	1.0	0.55
Density, 25/4°C	1.03	1.15	1.07
Boiling point, °C	202	162	182
Melting point, °C	–24	–37	41
Latent heat at 101 kPa (1 atm):			
kJ/kg	493	451	479
J/m^3	508	519	513
Solvent power	Excellent	Good	Very good
Selectivity	Very good–Excellent	Excellent	Good
Stability	Excellent	Good	Very good
Biodegradability	Good	Good	Good
Toxicity	Low	Moderate	High

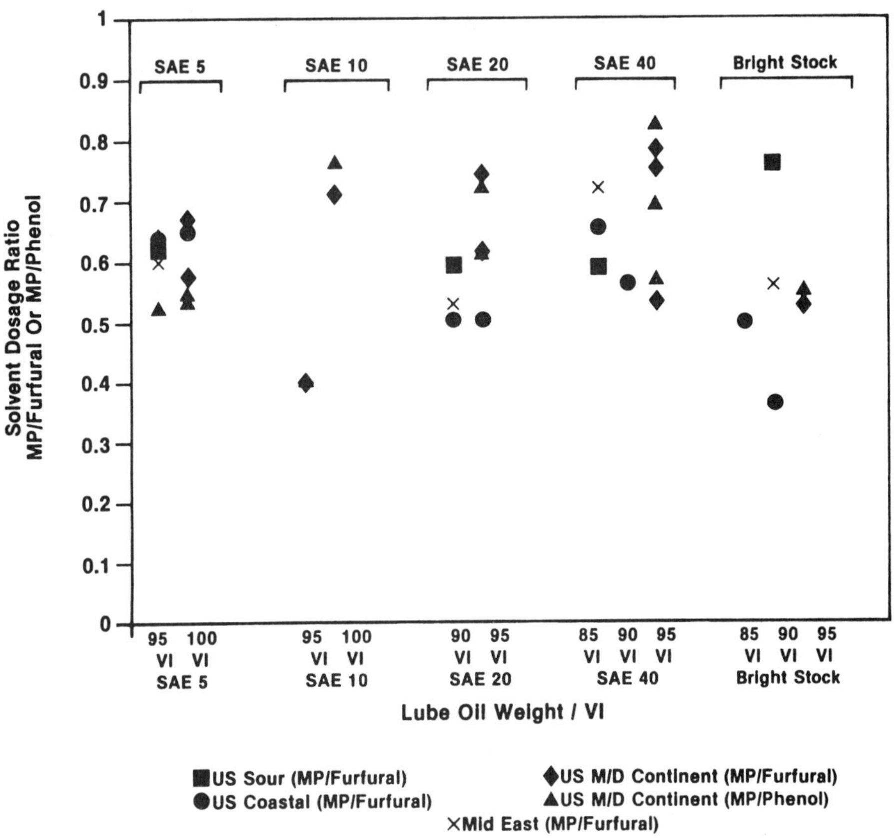

FIG. 1. Solvent refining dosages: MP vs other solvents.

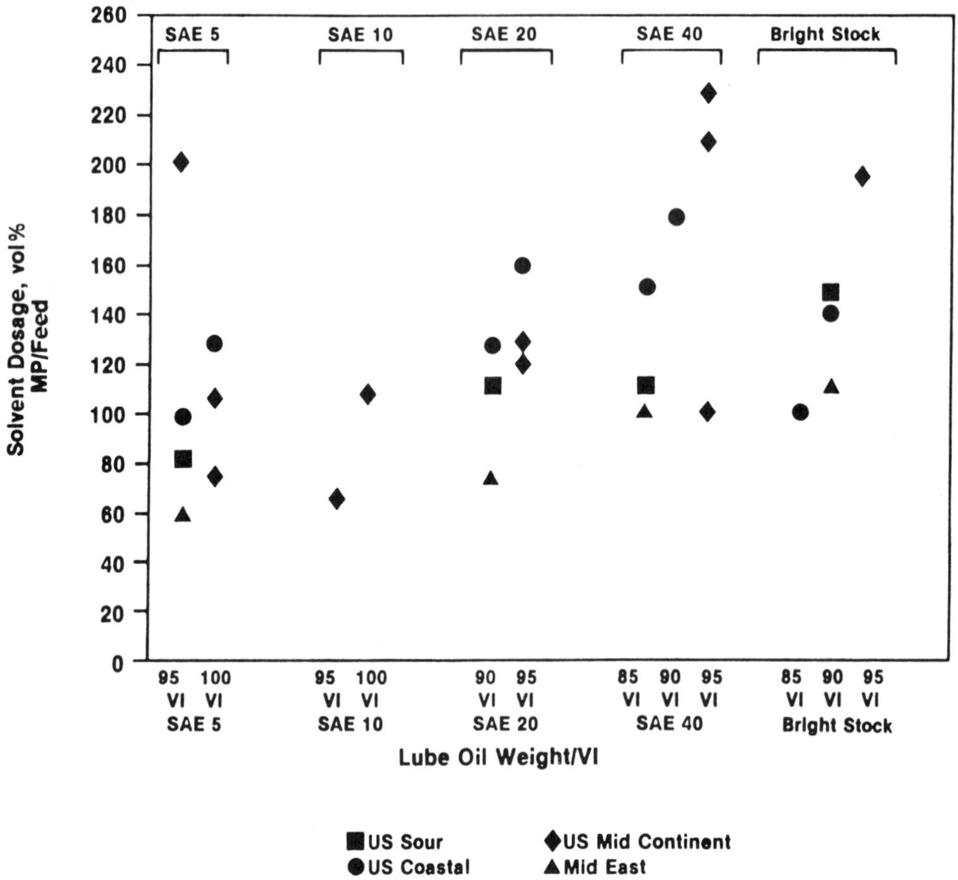

FIG. 2. Solvent refining dosages: MP dosage.

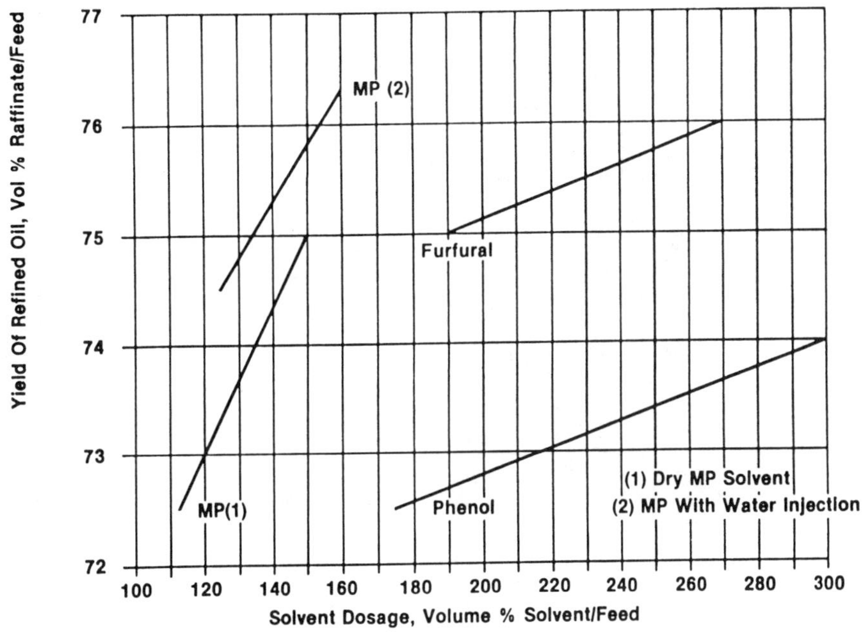

FIG. 3. Selectivity vs dosage comparison for SAE 10 weight 0.1 at 95 viscosity index and °F pour point.

Biodegradability and toxicity are important from environmental, health, and safety aspects. MP has by far the lowest toxicity of the common solvents. This is likely to become more significant as environmental regulations are tightened. MP also maintains the good biodegradability of the other solvents. Refer to Rowe's paper for detailed biodegradability data [6].

One other property which should be noted is the boiling point of the various solvents. The higher boiling point of MP as compared to furfural allows operation of the solvent recovery system at a higher temperature. This is an advantage as higher operating temperatures help heat integration. On the other side, a reasonable gap between the solvent boiling temperature and the lighter components of the oil being refined is needed to allow good solvent recovery. This is normally not significant unless one is refining a very light boiling range oil.

Flow Schemes

Figure 4 shows a simplified flow scheme of the Texaco MP Refining Process. The process can be divided into four sections: the treating section, the raffinate recovery section, the extract recovery section, and the solvent purification section.

In the treating section, the feed and the solvent are contacted in a rotating disk contactor, packed tower, trayed tower, or other suitable liquid–liquid contacting device. The raffinate product, along with 10 to 20% solvent in the raffinate, exits the overhead of the contactor and flows to the raffinate recovery section. The bulk of the solvent (80–95%) and the extract are taken

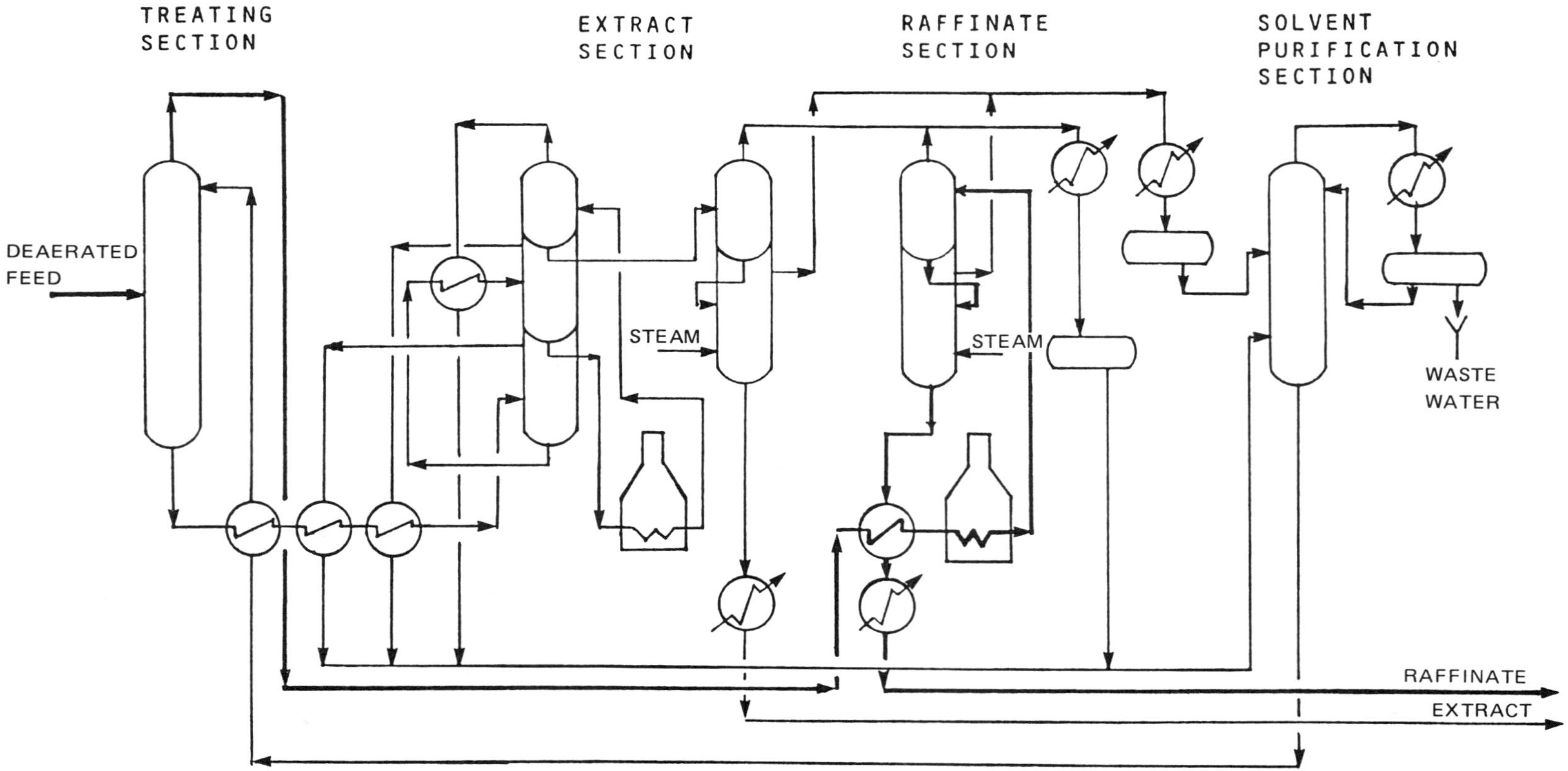

FIG. 4. Texaco MP Refining Process.

from the bottom of the contactor to the extract recovery section. The extract contains the aromatic materials which have a low viscosity index and are likely to be carcinogenic.

The raffinate recovery section is normally a single-effect evaporation recovery system with a one-flash column followed by a steam stripper. Due to the low utility cost in this section, corresponding to the low amount of solvent, the equipment here is minimized to minimize costs.

The extract recovery section uses either double or triple effect evaporation. At current energy costs, triple-effect evaporation is the most economical system for this section. In this section the solvent is vaporized in three flash columns, with the flash vapors from the higher pressure/higher temperature flash used to provide the heat for the lower pressure flashes. After the final flash, the extract product is steam stripped for removal of traces of solvent.

Excess water from the steam stripping, water used to moderate solvent power (if any), and water in the feed must be purged from the system to prevent a water buildup. This is accomplished in the solvent purification section. For MP refining, this is simply a fractionation column which takes water overhead and dry solvent from the bottom of the tower. Uncondensed vapor from the high pressure flash is typically used to drive the water out of the solvent, reducing or eliminating the need for a reboiler.

The flow scheme for furfural refining is shown in Fig. 5. The only difference between the furfural and MP flow scheme is in the solvent purification section. Furfural and water form an azeotrope which requires the use of a dual column system to remove water from the unit. For a given capacity unit, a furfural unit will require larger equipment for the extract recovery section and often for the treating section due to the higher solvent dosage required.

The typical phenol solvent refining unit is shown in Fig. 6. Again, the flow scheme is very similar to the MP flow scheme. The two major variations are (1) a feed absorber system to eliminate any phenol contamination in the waste stream and (2) the installation of a preflash or dryer column on the extract recovery system. This dryer replaces the solvent purification column. Due to the significant amount of water injection typically used with phenol extraction, the dryer is located at the front of the extract recovery rather than at the end.

Figure 7 shows a typical furfural unit converted for MP solvent. The major change here is in the solvent purification section where the "B" tower of the furfural system is repiped to take into account the fact that no azeotrope is formed and water is removed from the overhead rather than from the bottom of this column. In addition, typically, debottlenecking changes are made to the raffinate recovery section to allow increased capacity. The reduced solvent dosage will offset the increased feed rate in the extract recovery section and usually also the treating section. However, the raffinate recovery section, which recovers oil with a fraction of solvent, requires increased capacity with increased feed rate.

Figure 8 shows a typical phenol unit which has been converted to MP solvent. The flow scheme is essentially unchanged from the phenol flow scheme, but again, miscellaneous equipment will require debottlenecking, particularly in the raffinate section, the same as would be required in converting a furfural refining unit.

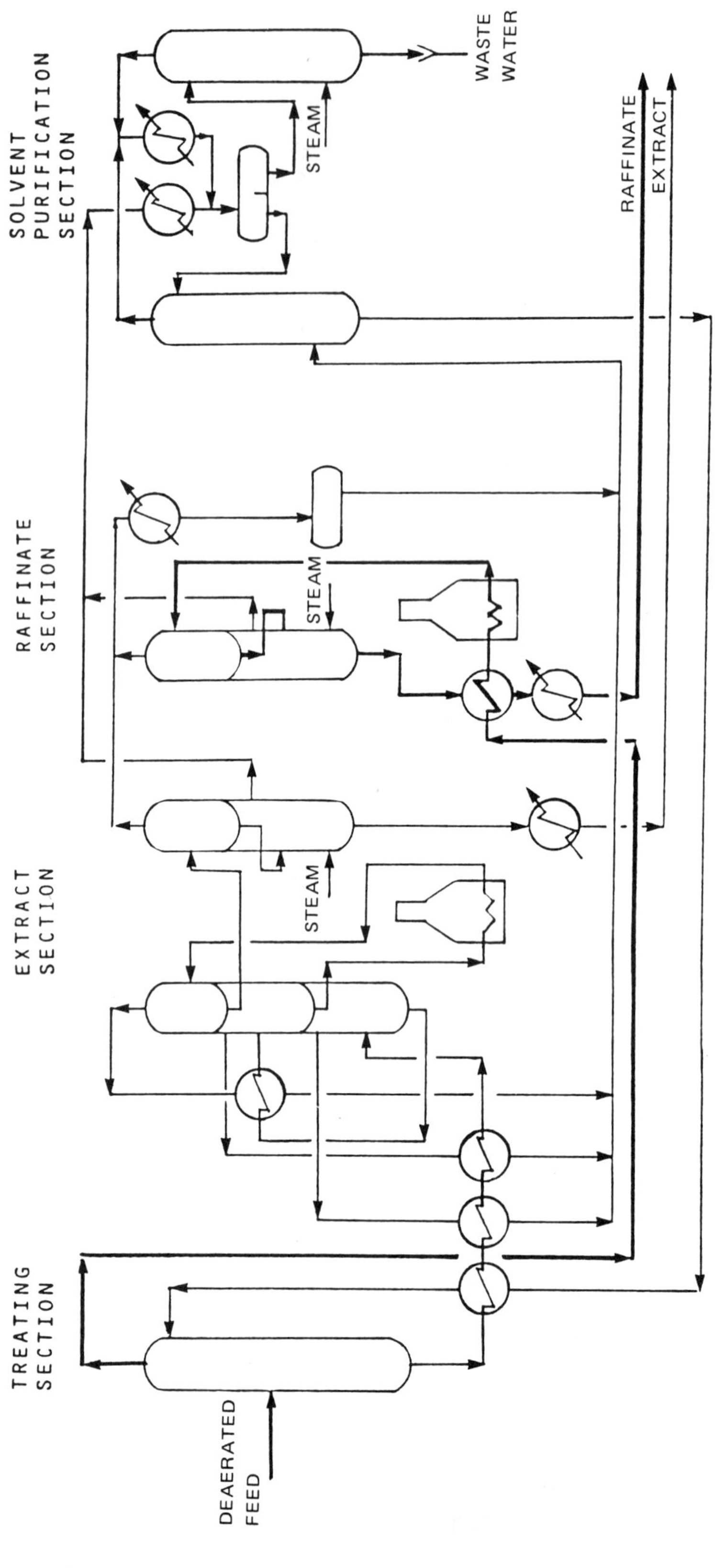

FIG. 5. Texaco Furfural Refining Process.

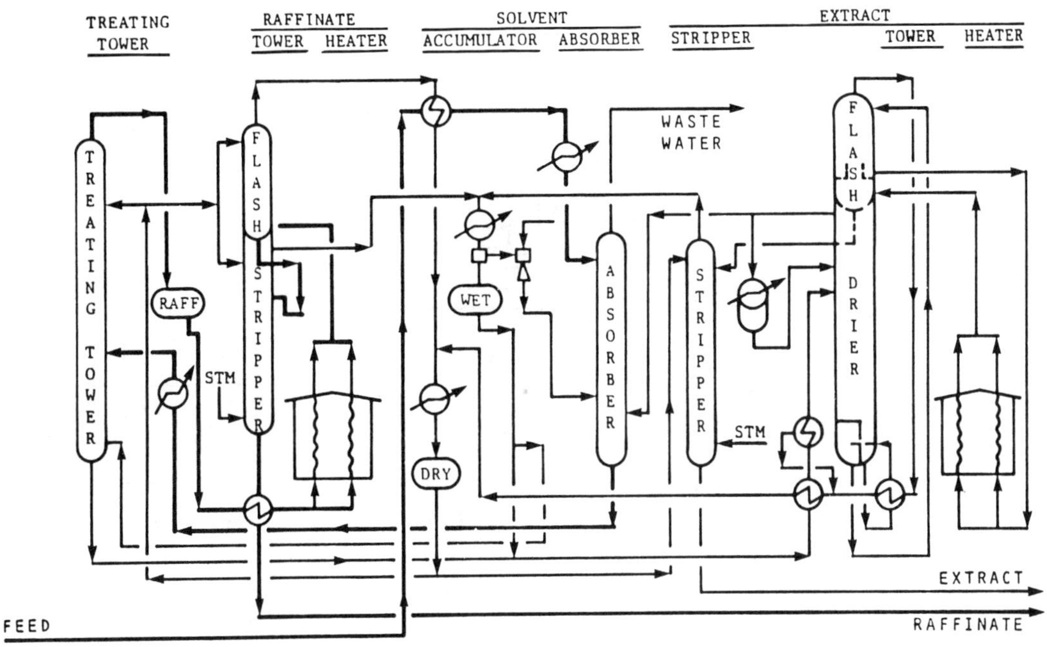

FIG. 6. Phenol refining unit flow diagram.

Costs

A capital cost comparison between furfural and MP refining for a nominal 10,000 BPD grassroots solvent refining unit is shown in Table 2. As expected, the number of equipment items required for each case is essentially the same. The substantial savings on investment obtained using MP solvent is due to the reduced equipment size, particularly in the extract recovery section, resulting from the reduced solvent dosages.

The cost of converting an existing furfural unit to MP solvent varies depending on the exact unit configuration and upon the capacity increase attained in parallel with the conversion. Typical costs for conversion of a 6000-BPD unit to MP are shown in Table 3. Conversion costs are labor intensive and are less sensitive to capacity than a grassroots unit. Therefore, larger units would be even more attractive for conversion to MP. Conversions are generally accompanied by a capacity increase which enhances the economics. Further information on conversion of a furfural unit may be found in Ref. 3. This reference covers the conversion of the Motor Oil Hellas solvent refining unit to MP solvent. This unit is somewhat atypical in that it uses steam for furfural recovery and hot oil for MP recovery.

Operating costs are also significantly reduced with MP solvent. Table 4 compares utility cost, including solvent makeup costs, for MP and furfural. As can be seen, MP solvent would be expected to save on the order of 25% in operating costs.

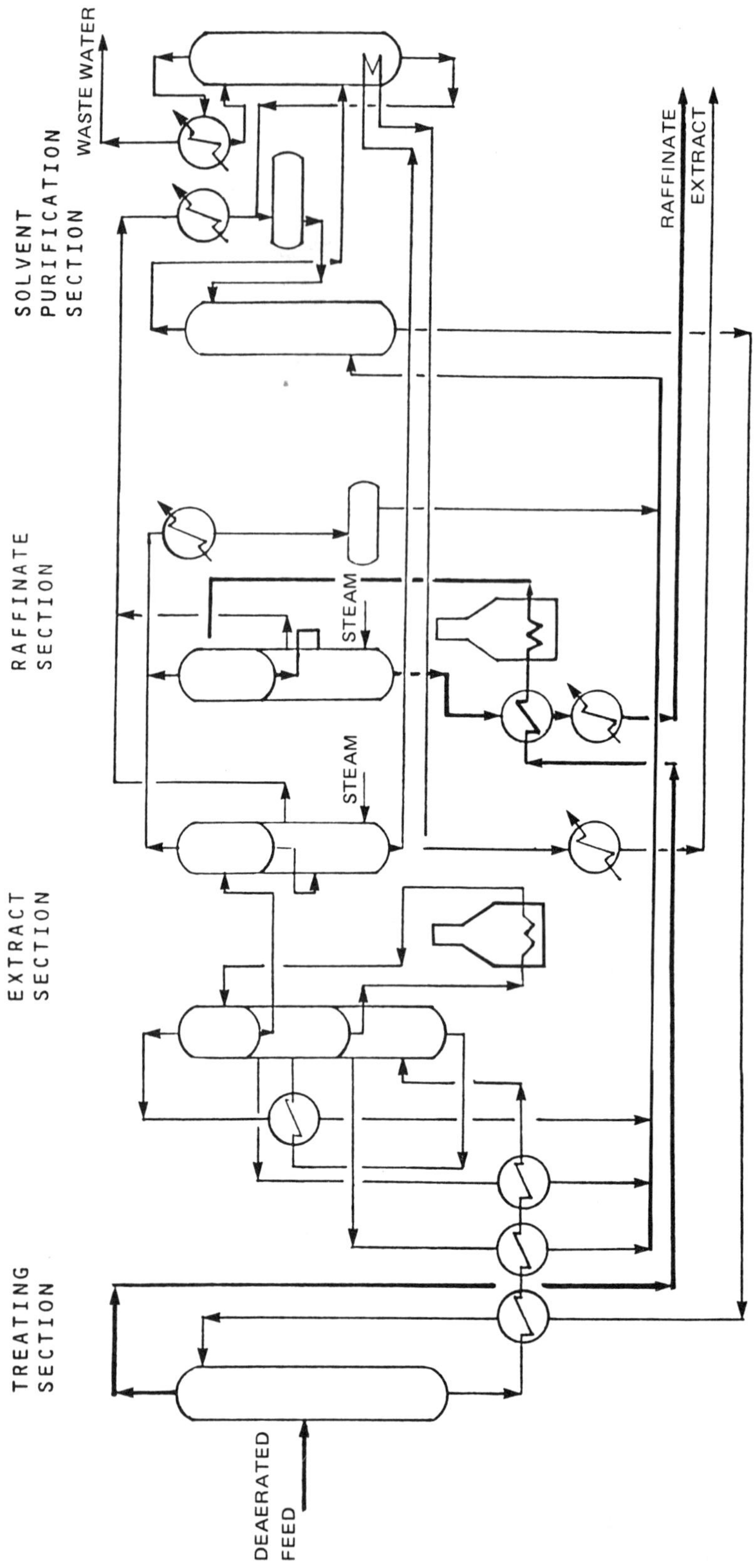

FIG. 7. MP refining unit converted from furfural unit.

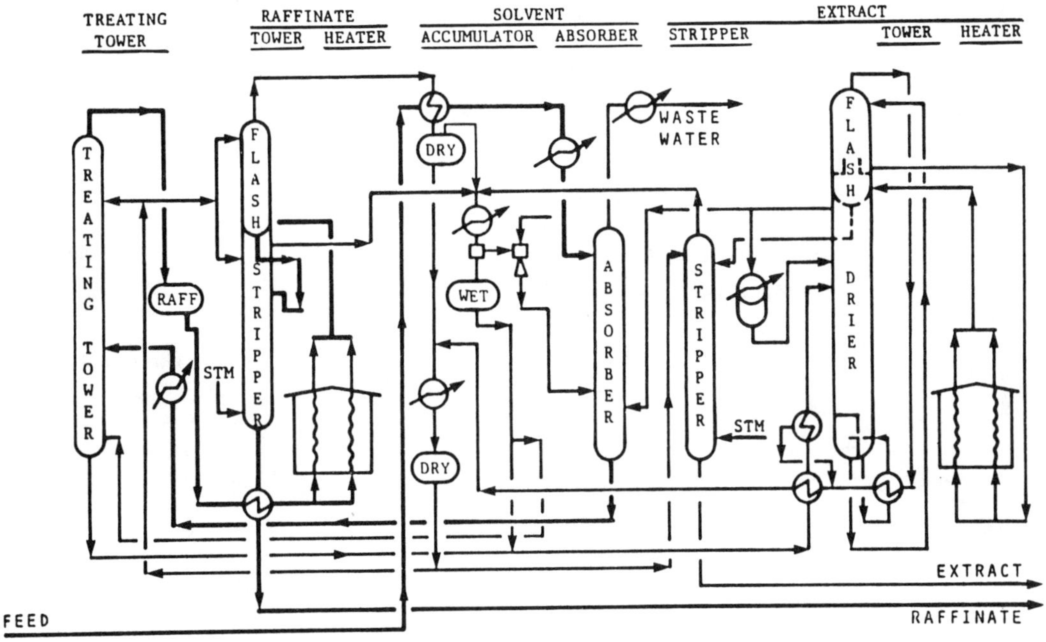

FIG. 8. MP refining unit converted from phenol unit.

Using the capital and operating costs of Tables 2, 3, and 4, a cash-flow analysis was made to determine the overall advantage of using MP for solvent refining. Table 5 lists the assumptions used for the analysis; Tables 6, 7, 8, and 9 show the furfural and MP analysis, including present values and payout times. Case A is the base case with the subsequent cases varying the various key parameters such as product margin, operating cost, interest rate, capital inventment, and on-steam time.

TABLE 2 Grassroots Capital Costs, MP vs Furfural [nominal 10,000 BPSD (63,000/kg/h) unit]

	Solvent	
	MP	Furfural
Equipment count:		
Towers	11	12
Drums	5	5
Exchangers	20	21
Pumps (including spares)	26	30
Heaters	2	2
Miscellaneous	3	3
Costs:		
Unit construction[a]	$12,700,000	$16,600,000
Solvent inventory	870,000	600,000
Total	$13,600,000	$17,200,000

[a]January 1, 1986, mid construction, United States, Gulf Coast.

TABLE 3 Conversion Costs [nominal 6000 BPSD (37,800 kg/h) unit before conversion]

	No Capacity Increase	Capacity Increase to 50,400 kg/h Included
Equipment modernization ($)	1,300,000–1,900,000	1,600,000–2,400,000
Downtime[a] ($)	300,000	300,000
Solvent inventory ($)	500,000	700,000
Total ($)	2,100,000–2,700,000	2,600,000–3,400,000
Capacity increase (%)	0	33 (12,600 kg/h)

[a]Basis: 6 weeks downtime at $50,000/week.

TABLE 4 Utility Costs

		MP		Furfural	
Nominal feed rate: BPSD		10,000		10,000	
kg/h		63,000		63,000	
	Cost ($/unit)	Rate	Cost	Rate	Cost
Fuel, gJ/h	3.95	34.2	135.0	53.9	212.9
High-pressure steam, kg/h	0.014	7864	110.1	5745	80.4
Low-pressure steam, kg/h	0.012	1117	13.4	696	8.4
Cooling water, m^3/h	0.024	472	11.3	720	17.3
Electric power, kW	0.05	267	13.4	402	20.1
Subtotal			283.1		339.1
Solvent, kh/h	2.9/1.5	2.5	7.3	38	57.0
$NaCO_2$, kg/h	—	0.2	—	1.6	—
N_2, kg/h	—	8	—	8	—
Total cost: $/h			290.4		396.1
$/mt			4.65		6.34

TABLE 5 Assumptions for Discounted Cash Flow Analysis

20 year life
5-year depreciation with benefit of 48% of value due to reduced taxes
Investment over 3-year period for grassroots investment over short period for revamp
No inflation
8000 h/yr for furfural operation; 8382 h/yr for MP operation
Continuous payment discount
Other as noted in Tables 6–13

TABLE 6 Grassroots Furfural Refining Analysis: Base Case

		Present Worth Payout Calculations, Furfural Unit				
Year	Cash Flow ($)	Discount Factor	Present Value ($)	Cumulative Present Value ($)	Payout Years	
0	—	1.0000				
1	(4,300,000)	0.9333	(4,013,035)	(4,013,035)	1.00	0.00
2	(8,600,000)	0.8115	(6,979,191)	(10,992,226)	1.00	0.00
3	(4,300,000)	0.7057	(3,034,431)	(14,026,657)	1.00	0.00
4	6,015,840	0.6136	3,691,537	(10,335,120)	1.00	1.00
5	6,015,840	0.5336	3,210,032	(7,125,088)	1.00	1.00
6	6,015,840	0.4640	2,791,332	(4,333,755)	1.00	1.00
7	6,015,840	0.4035	2,427,246	(1,906,510)	1.00	1.00
8	6,015,840	0.3508	2,110,648	204,139	0.90	0.90
9	4,364,640	0.3051	1,331,589	1,535,728	0.00	0.00
10	4,364,640	0.2653	1,157,903	2,693,631	0.00	0.00
11	4,364,640	0.2307	1,006,873	3,700,504	0.00	0.00
12	4,364,640	0.2006	875,541	4,576,045	0.00	0.00
13	4,364,640	0.1744	761,340	5,337,385	0.00	0.00
14	4,364,640	0.1517	662,035	5,999,421	0.00	0.00
15	4,364,640	0.1319	575,683	6,575,103	0.00	0.00
16	4,364,640	0.1147	500,594	7,075,697	0.00	0.00
17	4,364,640	0.0997	435,299	7,510,996	0.00	0.00
18	4,364,640	0.0867	378,521	7,889,516	0.00	0.00
19	4,364,640	0.0754	329,148	8,218,665	0.00	0.00
20	4,364,640	0.0656	286,216	8,504,881	0.00	0.00
	65,254,880		8,504,881	8,504,881	7.90	4.90

Capital, $	17,200,000 (including inventory)
Discount rate, %	15.00
Cash flow, $/yr	4,364,640 (excluding tax benefits)
Cash flow basis:	
Product margin,[a] $/mt	15.0
Operating h/yr	8000
Operating cost, $/h/mt	6.34
Feed rate, mt/h	63.0

[a]Product margin is (value of raffinate) + (value of extract products) − (value of feed).

TABLE 7 Grassroots Furfural Refining Analysis: Summary of Parameter Variation[a]

Case	Capital (MM$)	Discount Rate (%)	Product Margin ($/mt)	Operating Hours (h/yr)	Operating Cost ($/h/mt)	Present Value (MM$)	Payout from Start-Up (yr)
A (base)	17.2	15	15	8000	6.34	8.5	4.9
B	18.9	—	—	—	—	7.5	5.6
C	—	10	—	—	—	17.6	4.0
D	—	—	10	—	—	(2.2)	—
E	—	—	—	7000	—	6.2	5.9
F	—	—	—	—	6.97	7.1	5.5

[a]All values are the same as the base case except where specified.

TABLE 8 Grassroots MP Refining Analysis: Base Case

Year	Cash Flow ($)	Discount Factor	Present Value ($)	Cumulative Present Value ($)	Payout Years	
		Present Worth Payout Calculations, *N*-Methyl-2-pyrrolidone (MP) Unit				
0	—	1.0000				
1	(3,400,000)	0.9333	(3,173,097)	(3,173,097)	1.00	0.00
2	(6,800,000)	0.8115	(5,518,430)	(8,691,528)	1.00	0.00
3	(3,400,000)	0.7057	(2,399,318)	(11,090,845)	1.00	0.00
4	6,771,083	0.6136	4,154,982	(6,935,864)	1.00	1.00
5	6,771,083	0.5336	3,613,028	(3,322,836)	1.00	1.00
6	6,771,083	0.4640	3,141,763	(181,073)	1.00	1.00
7	6,771,083	0.4035	2,731,968	2,550,895	0.07	0.07
8	6,771,083	0.3508	2,375,624	4,926,519	0.00	0.00
9	5,465,483	0.3051	1,667,440	6,593,960	0.00	0.00
10	5,465,483	0.2653	1,449,948	8,043,908	0.00	0.00
11	5,465,483	0.2307	1,260,825	9,304,732	0.00	0.00
12	5,465,483	0.2006	1,096,369	10,401,101	0.00	0.00
13	5,465,483	0.1744	953,364	11,354,466	0.00	0.00
14	5,465,483	0.1517	829,013	12,183,479	0.00	0.00
15	5,465,483	0.1319	720,881	12,904,359	0.00	0.00
16	5,465,483	0.1147	626,853	13,531,212	0.00	0.00
17	5,465,483	0.0997	545,089	14,076,301	0.00	0.00
18	5,465,483	0.0867	473,991	14,550,291	0.00	0.00
19	5,465,483	0.0754	412,166	14,962,457	0.00	0.00
20	5,465,483	0.0656	358,405	15,320,862	0.00	0.00
	85,841,213		15,320,862	15,320,862	6.07	3.07

Capital, $	13,600,000 (including inventory)
Discount rate, %	15.00
Cash flow, $/yr	5,465,483 (excluding tax benefits)
Cash flow basis:	
Product margin,[a] $/mt	15.0
Operating h/yr	8382
Operating cost, $/h/mt	4.65
Feed rate, mt/h	63.0

[a]Product margin is (value of raffinate) + (value of extract products) − (value of feed).

TABLE 9 Grassroots MP Refining Analysis: Summary of Parameter Variation[a]

Case	Capital (MM$)	Discount Rate (%)	Product Margin ($/mt)	Operating Hours (h/yr)	Operating Cost ($/h/mt)	Present Value (MM$)	Payout from Start-Up (yr)
A (base)	13.6	15	15	8382	4.65	15.3	3.1
B	15.0	—	—	—	—	14.5	3.4
C	—	10	—	—	—	26.6	2.6
D	—	—	10	—	—	4.1	6.6
E	—	—	—	7000	—	11.5	3.7
F	—	—	—	—	5.12	14.3	3.2

[a]All values are the same as the base case except where specified.

By comparing Tables 6 and 8, one can see a $7 million overall advantage using MP solvent and a reduction in the payout time from startup of from 4.9 to 3.1 years. Comparing Case C of Tables 7 and 9, which reflect reduced profit margins, one can see that payout and value of the MP process is much less sensitive to reduced operating margins. The on-steam factor using MP solvent would be expected to be better due to reduced maintenance from elimination of coking in the heaters and exchangers as reflected in the base case operating hours per year.

TABLE 10 Conversion to MP with Capacity Increase: Base Case

		Present Worth Payout Calculations, Unit Converted to MP with Capacity Increase				
Year	Cash Flow ($)	Discount Factor	Present Value ($)	Cumulative Present Value ($)	Payout Years	
0	(3,000,000)	1.0000	(3,000,000)	(3,000,000)	1.00	0.00
1	2,012,802	0.9333	1,878,476	(1,121,524)	1.00	1.00
2	2,012,802	0.8115	1,633,457	511,933	0.69	0.69
3	2,012,802	0.7057	1,420,398	1,932,331	0.00	0.00
4	2,012,802	0.6136	1,235,128	3,167,460	0.00	0.00
5	2,012,802	0.5336	1,074,025	4,241,484	0.00	0.00
6	1,753,602	0.4640	813,667	5,055,151	0.00	0.00
7	1,753,602	0.4035	707,536	5,762,687	0.00	0.00
8	1,753,602	0.3508	615,249	6,377,936	0.00	0.00
9	1,753,602	0.3051	534,999	6,912,935	0.00	0.00
10	1,753,602	0.2653	465,216	7,378,151	0.00	0.00
11	1,753,602	0.2307	404,536	7,782,687	0.00	0.00
12	1,753,602	0.2006	351,770	8,134,458	0.00	0.00
13	1,753,602	0.1744	305,887	8,440,345	0.00	0.00
14	1,753,602	0.1517	265,989	8,706,334	0.00	0.00
15	1,753,602	0.1319	231,295	8,937,629	0.00	0.00
16	1,753,602	0.1147	201,126	9,138,755	0.00	0.00
17	1,753,602	0.0997	174,892	9,313,647	0.00	0.00
18	1,753,602	0.0867	152,080	9,465,727	0.00	0.00
19	1,753,602	0.0754	132,244	9,597,971	0.00	0.00
	31,614,447		9,597,971	9,597,971	2.69	1.69

Capital and inventory, $	2,700,000
Downtime costs, $	300,000
Discount rate, %	15.00
Cash flow, $/yr	1,753,602 (excluding tax benefits)
Cash flow basis:	
Product margin,[a] $/mt	15.0
Operating h/yr	8382 (8000 base, 382 increase)
Operating margin benefit, $/h/mt	1.69
Operating cost, $/h/mt	4.65
Feed rate, total mt/h	50.4
Feed increase, mt/h	12.6

[a]Product margin is (value of raffinate) + (value of extract products) − (value of feed).

TABLE 11 Conversion to MP with Capacity Increase: Summary of Parameter Variation[a]

Case	Capital (MM$)	Discount Rate (%)	Product Margin ($/mt)	Operating Hours (h/yr)	Operating Cost ($/h/mt)	Present Value (MM$)	Payout from Start-Up (yr)
A (base)	2.7	15	15	8382	4.65	9.6	1.7
B	3.0	—	—	—	—	9.4	1.8
C	—	10	—	—	—	13.4	1.6
D	—	—	10	—	—	5.6	2.5
E	—	—	—	8000	—	8.3	1.9
F	—	—	—	7000	—	7.0	2.2
G	—	—	—	—	5.12	9.6	1.7

[a]All values are the same as the base case except where specified.

Table 10 shows an analysis based on conversion of an existing furfural unit to MP with a capacity increase from 6000 to 8000 BPSD. Generally, when converting to MP solvent, the capacity is also increased. This takes advantage of the larger capacity of most of the existing equipment due to reduced solvent rates. Note the short 1.7 year payout for this conversion. Table 11 shows the impact of variation in key parameters.

In some cases the solvent refining unit has become the lube oil plant bottleneck due to lower quality feed. In such cases the capacity increase benefits will be even larger, since downstream capacity already exists and increased benefits would be based on overall lube plant product margin rather than just solvent refining unit product margin.

Tables 12 and 13 show the same analysis for a conversion without an increase in capacity.

TABLE 12 Conversion to MP (no change in capacity): Summary of Parameter Variation[a]

Case	Capital (MM$)	Discount Rate (%)	Product Margin ($/mt)	Operating Hours (h/yr)	Operating Cost ($/h/mt)	Present Value (MM$)	Payout from Start-Up (yr)
A (base)	2.1	15	15	8382	4.65	2.7	3.5
B	2.3	—	—	—	—	2.6	3.8
C	—	10	—	—	—	4.2	3.2
D	—	—	10	—	—	2.2	4.0
E	—	—	—	8000	—	1.7	4.6
F	—	—	—	7000	—	1.3	5.3
G	—	—	—	—	5.12	3.0	3.3

[a]All values are the same as the base case except where specified.

TABLE 13 Conversion to MP (no capacity increase): Base Case

		Present Worth Payout Calculations, Unit Converted to MP with Capacity Increase				
Year	Cash Flow ($)	Discount Factor	Present Value ($)	Cumulative Present Value ($)	Payout Years	
0	(2,400,000)	1.0000	(2,400,000)	(2,400,000)	1.00	0.00
1	862,106	0.9333	804,572	(1,595,428)	1.00	1.00
2	862,106	0.8115	699,628	(895,800)	1.00	1.00
3	862,106	0.7057	608,372	(287,427)	1.00	1.00
4	862,106	0.6136	529,019	241,592	0.54	0.54
5	862,106	0.5336	460,017	701,609	0.00	0.00
6	660,506	0.4640	306,473	1,008,082	0.00	0.00
7	660,506	0.4035	266,498	1,274,580	0.00	0.00
8	660,506	0.3508	231,737	1,506,317	0.00	0.00
9	660,506	0.3051	201,511	1,707,828	0.00	0.00
10	660,506	0.2653	175,227	1,883,055	0.00	0.00
11	660,506	0.2307	152,371	2,035,426	0.00	0.00
12	660,506	0.2006	132,497	2,167,923	0.00	0.00
13	660,506	0.1744	115,214	2,283,137	0.00	0.00
14	660,506	0.1517	100,187	2,383,324	0.00	0.00
15	660,506	0.1319	87,119	2,470,442	0.00	0.00
16	660,506	0.1147	75,755	2,546,198	0.00	0.00
17	660,506	0.0997	65,874	2,612,072	0.00	0.00
18	660,506	0.0867	57,282	2,669,354	0.00	0.00
19	660,506	0.0754	49,810	2,719,165	0.00	0.00
	11,157,611		2,719,165	2,719,165	4.54	3.54

Capital and inventory, $	2,100,000
Downtime cost, $	300,000
Discount rate, %	15.00
Cash flow, $/yr	660,506 (excluding tax benefits)
Cash flow basis:	
Product margin,[a] $/mt	15.0
Operating h/yr	8382 (8000 base, 382 increase)
Operating margin benefit, $/h/mt	1.69
Operating cost, $/h/mt	4.65
Feed rate, total mt/h	37.8
Feed increase, mt/h	0

[a]Product margin is (value of raffinate) + (value of extract products) − (value of feed).

Summary

Table 14 summarizes the economic driving forces for conversion to MP, showing a discounted cash flow return on investment from 40 to 95%. On the bases of the strong economic incentive, we expect the conversion to MP refining to continue at a strong pace.

TABLE 14 Summary of Data

	Grassroots		Converted Unit	
	MP	Furfural	Increase Capacity	No Capacity Increase
Unit capacity (nominal):				
BPSD	10,000	10,000	8,000	6,000
kg/h	63,000	63,000	50,400	37,800
Investment, $	13,600,000	17,200,000	2,700,000	2,100,000
$/kg/h feed	216	273	214 (incremental feed)	—
Downtime cost, $	—	—	300,000	300,000
Operating cost, $/1000 kg feed	4.65	6.34	4.65	4.65
Present value, $	15,300,000	8,500,000	9,600,000	2,700,000
Payout period, yr:				
From start-up	3.1	4.9	1.7	3.5
From start of investing	6.1	7.9	2.7	4.5
Discounted cash flow return on investment, %	34	25	95	41

Other Considerations

While we have made a good general comparison to help guide refineries considering changing or building MP solvent refining units, the overall specific refining system, including upstream and downstream units, must be considered. Also, as seen by the scatter of the date in Figs. 1 and 2, the performance of MP is sensitive to feedstock and product specifications; thus specific performance must be accounted for.

The downstream MEK dewaxing unit and wax deoiling unit may also be modernized using the newest Texaco technology which includes multidilution, repulp filtration, and warm-up deoiling. This technology can add to the profitability of a revamp by increasing the yield of dewaxed oil, reducing the oil content in the slack wax, and increasing the units capacity.

This article was presented at the AIChE Meeting in Miami, November 3, 1986, and is used here with the permission of the publisher of the *AIChE Journal*.

References

1. A. Sequeira et al., *MP Refining of Lubricating Oils*, Presented at the NPRA 1979 Annual Meeting, March 25–27, 1979, San Antonio, Texas.

2. A. Sequeira et al., *Return to Basics—How to Reduce Energy Requirements in Lube Oil Solvent Extraction and Dewaxing Processes*, Presented at the 45th Mid-Year QPI Refining Meeting, May 14, 1980, Houston, Texas.
3. C. W. Harrison et al., *Conversion of a Furfural Refining Unit to MP Refining of Lube Oils*, Presented at the NPRA 1983 Annual Meeting, March 20–22, 1983, San Francisco, California.
4. M. R. McClure et al., *Recent Improvements to Lube Oil Solvent Refining and Dewaxing Process and Their Effect on Design of Large Modern Lube Plants Such as The Jubail Lube Oil Refining*, Presented at the 2nd Symposium on Arab and International Lubricating Oils Industry, June 27–28, 1981, Oran, Algeria.
5. A. Sequeira et al., *Conversion of Furfural Refining Units to N-Methyl-2-pyrrolidone (MP) Refining Units*, Presented at the AIChE Meeting, April 6–10, 1986, New Orleans, Louisiana.
6. E. A. Rowe et al., "Lube Solvent No Threat to Waste Treatment," *Hydrocarbon Process*., pp. 63–65 (October 1980).

FRED C. JAHNKE

Lubricating Oils, Rerefining

Introduction

Rerefining of used lubricating oil has been practiced extensively for many years, especially in North America and Europe. The extent of this activity in the United States has varied widely (both up and down) from time to time in response to developing technology, changing petroleum refining and marketing economics, and government policies. The latter factor has included excise taxes, labeling requirements, and environmental protection regulations.

Large rerefining installations typically segregate charge stocks into two or three separate categories of used oil, such as: (1) oil collected from service stations, garages, and other sources known to consist principally of drained crankcase oil from gasoline and diesel engines; (2) segregated crankcase oil to be custom rerefined for fleet users, such as railroad diesel lubricating oil; and (3) straight mineral oils and lower additive content industrial oils. The selection of processing steps, and the degree of treatment in each step, may then be optimized for each feedstock category.

The most sophisticated processing is required for the drained crankcase lubricating oil from internal combustion piston engines, both gasoline and diesel, of Categories (1) and (2). As formulated by manufacturers and marketers, new crankcase lubricating oils usually consist of a highly refined lube base stock with an equivalent atmospheric boiling range within limits of about 650 to 1000°F, compounded with various chemical additives designed to improve certain lubrication and stability properties. The used oil as collected for rerefining is comprised of (1) much of the original base stock and additives, which have survived the usage substantially unchanged, in admixture with (2) components of the engine fuel from "piston blow-by"; (3) decomposition products of the original base stock and additives, including some materials boiling below 650°F, and some above 1000°F; (4) condensed moisture and dirt and engine wear metal not removed by the circulating oil filter; and (5) miscellaneous foreign material inadvertently picked up in the collection system, including water, grease and gear lubricants, solvents, and other liquids and solids.

Removal of water, solids, and engine fuel components or "crankcase dilution" is normally accomplished by mechanical means and simple "atmospheric" distillation. The extent of removal of fine solids, immiscible materials, and unstable heavy components necessary in this "pretreating" step depends largely on the type of vacuum distillation or evaporation equipment subsequently used. If any material is present which would cause plugging or fouling of such equipment, it must be removed or, alternately, the vacuum equipment must be capable of operating without excessive fouling on the type of material charged to it, and the disposition of the vacuum residue must tolerate all heavy contaminants in the rerefining feed.

No rerefining procedures have been devised for recovering components of the additive package for reuse for their original purposes. The basic objective of most rerefining operations has been (a) to remove the low boiling contaminants listed in Items (2)–(5) along with solids and immiscible materials as is necessary to insure operability of subsequent steps, and then (or simultaneously) (b) to effect as complete a separation as possible of the remaining lubricating oil base stock from the additives, residues, and lube oil boiling range decomposition products. Thus the principal product of a rerefining procedure is a lube oil fraction, or fractions, corresponding as closely as possible to the base stock from which the original lubricating oil was compounded.

Although treatment with sulfuric acid to remove additives and contaminants was the principal processing step in most United States rerefining plants for many years, this procedure has now (1987) been eliminated entirely in the United States because of problems of disposal of the acid sludge. Most rerefining processes now in use involve variants of three essential steps:

1. Settling, flashing, stripping, in-line filtering, and/or pretreating to remove sediments, insolubles, water, and low boiling petroleum fractions
2. Vacuum distillation or evaporation (or solvent treatment) to separate lube oil from heavy decomposition products, additives, and residues
3. Finishing by hydrotreating or clay contacting to improve product quality, particularly with respect to color and color stability

General

Definitions

The terms "waste oil," "used oil," and "spent oil" have been applied somewhat interchangeably to both crankcase drainings and discarded industrial oils. An even more general term, "slop oil," includes with these materials discarded hydrocarbon streams and emulsions from the petroleum production, transportation, storage, refining, and petrochemical manufacturing industries. In this discussion, "used lubricating oil" refers to any discarded oil with potential for rerefining (or less sophisticated processing for recycling to produce a reusable lube oil product).

"Recycling" of used lubricating oil is a general term covering the processing of such oils to produce usable petroleum products, including both rerefined (or "reclaimed") lubricating oils and fuel (or burning oil) products.

"Rerefining" of used lubricating oil describes the processing of such oil to remove all materials which have been purposely or inadvertently added to the original lube oil base stock. Rerefining is a form of recycling, but recycling of, for example, a straight mineral oil to its original use by simple dehydration and screening would not be considered as "rerefining," but rather is called "reclaiming."

Historical Background

Lube oil rerefining expanded substantially during the 40s, 50s, and 60s. By 1965 there were about 160 commercial installations in the United States (and many more very small facilities) with a combined capacity of some 300 million gallons per year, or about 15% of the total United States lubricating oil consumption. The average plant capacity was under 2 million gallons per years, and most plants were operated batchwise rather than continuously. Most of these plants used a processing scheme based principally on sulfuric acid treating, followed by clay contacting. Other plants returned to the lube oil supply pool a product which had undergone much less extensive "cleanup" than that afforded by acid and clay.

During this period, sulfuric acid sludge and spent contact clay were usually disposed of in landfills, or even open pits, and environmental pressures on the small plants, though significant, were generally not prohibitive. The plants were built at relatively low cost, frequently with used equipment, and a modest profit could be made in picking up feedstocks with no payment (or at most a few cents per gallon) to its "generators," and in marketing the rerefined products in relatively low priced lube product formulations. Freedom of rerefined oil from a 6¢/gal federal excise tax on new lubricating oil was an important factor until the mid-60s, when changes in the application of this excise tax began to erode this economic benefit.

In 1987 the number of rerefining companies operating and under construction in the United States had shrunk to about half a dozen, with total input capacity of approximately 80 million gallons per year. The high cost of disposing of the acid sludge in an environmentally acceptable manner caused most acid-treating plants to become uneconomic, and the capital investment required for continuous vacuum distillation or evaporation equipment made it unfeasible to replace the small acid-treating plants with such facilities. All plants presently in operation in the United States are based on the vacuum distillation or evaporation procedure to separate additives and other high boiling materials, followed by final clay contacting or hydrotreating. A typical processing train has a feed capacity of about 10 million gallons per year, and up to 20–30 million gallons per year is now gathered at the largest rerefining locations. All these plants operate on a continuous 24-h basis rather than "batchwise."

An analysis of *Composition and Management of Used Oil Generated in the United States* prepared for the U.S. Environmental Protection Agency in 1984 [4] indicated the following approximate volumes of United States lubricating oil in 1983 (all figures in millions of gallons):

	New Oil Sales	*Used Oil Generated*
Automotive	1251	699
Industrial	1061	507
Total	2312	1206

Of the the approximately 1.2 billion gallons of used lube oil generated, only about 85 million gallons (principally crankcase drainings) entered the rerefining industry, and from this approximately 63 million gallons of rerefined lube oil, or about 2.7% of new lube sales, was produced. Several additional small rerefining plants have ceased operating since this balance was developed, and current rerefining volume is estimated to be about 70 million gallons per year, with one 10 million gallon plant being constructed. Thus additional charge stock could be made available for quite a substantial increase in the quantity of used lube oil rerefined. As a practical matter, however, the volume of feedstock which can be collected economically at any potential rerefining location is limited, and there is pressure on the "waste management" industry to divert to rerefining feedstock materials such as chlorinated solvents which are basically not suitable for this use, as discussed below.

Collection of Used Lube Oil Streams

Careful monitoring and control of feedstock collection is a very important aspect of rerefining operations, although this would not normally be considered a part of the processing procedure. With the exception of custom rerefining for large fleet users such as railroad diesel lubricants, all rerefiners do most of their own gathering of feedstocks, supplementing this with oil purchased from other gatherers or collectors.

Oil gathered to be rerefined for lube oil must be selected from sources which include principally lubricating oils as opposed to other hydrocarbon materials which would be satisfactory only for reprocessing for burning oil and fuel products. Moreover, the type and degree of processing required for various types of used lubricating oils differ, so that most rerefiners provide segregated storage for different feedstocks. When a movement (usually a "truck-load") of used oil is brought into the plant, it is given screening tests before being commingled with other feedstocks. One truck-load containing waxy material or components with a large quantities of resins or petrochemical by-products could contaminate a large amount of otherwise usable feedstock. In some plants, small holding tanks are employed into which a truck-load shipment is discharged and held while being tested. The inspection tests normally run on such feedstocks include:

BS&W
Density
Viscosity, at one or two temperatures
Distillation (ASTM D86-Atmospheric)
Organic chlorides (a qualitative "hot wire" colorimetric screening test or X-ray fluorescence analysis

In some instances a test is made for saponifiable material (to detect animal or vegetable fats).

Distillations are run on the rerefining feedstock to determine the extent of crankcase dilution etc. Much of the used lube oil accumulated will have a closed cup flash point above 140°F, which means it would be satisfactory for burning oil without any further stripping of light ends. Contaminants which render a material unsuitable for rerefining include tank bottoms, particularly from cleaning crude oil tanks, some barge cleaning slops, crude oil production slops, and many others. Greases increase the rerefining difficulty, but are generally not a major component of a used oil stream. Chemical plant wastes, restaurant grease, etc. are generally unsuitable, and strenuous efforts are made to eliminate these materials from the feedstock supply.

The results of these tests will allow the rerefiner to judge whether the material is suitable for his processing procedures, and to which of the alternate feedstock systems it should be transferred.

If the material has been purchased from another collector, a deduction will normally be made for the nonhydrocarbon materials indicated in the BS&W test. Also, most rerefiners set a maximum BS&W of 25 or 30%, above which the feedstock will be rejected outright and returned to the supplier. A large water content greatly increases the amount of heat required for evaporation, and if an attempt were made to settle out the bulk of this water for discharge to the environment as a liquid, extensive treating and monitoring of water quality would be required.

Analysis of Rerefining Feedstocks

In the manufacture of lubricating oils, petroleum refineries normally charge the atmospheric residuum from a selected crude oil to a lube vacuum distillation unit, where two or three distillate streams and a vacuum residuum are produced. The distillate streams are processed on a segregated basis through the various lube manufacturing steps such as dewaxing, solvent extraction, and hydrofinishing, to yield finished "neutral oils" of different viscosities. If a "bright stock" or higher viscosity lube oil is required, this is produced from the vacuum residuum. The purpose of this segregation of lube streams through the various manufacturing stages is twofold: (1) to provide

TABLE 1 Typical Paraffinic Mid-Continent Base Oils

	ASTM Method	100 Neutral	250 Neutral	600 Neutral	150 Bright
Gravity, API	D287	33.7	30.8	30.0	27.0
Flash, Open Cup, °F	D92	380	440	505	580
Pour, °F	D97	−5	+5	+5	+5
Viscosity: SUS at 100°F	D2161	101	260	620	2570
SUS at 210°F	D2161	39.0	49.9	70.0	155.0
Viscosity index	D2270	96	96	97	96
Color	D1500	L0.5	L0.5	L1.5	L3.5
Vacuum distillation at 760 mmHg	D1160[a]				
IBP, °F:		620	720	709	761
5% distilled, °F		675	794	836	886
10%		680	812	885	958
20%		710	832	912	985
30%		725	840	929	1002
40%		740	849	942	1015
50%		760	857	956	1029
60%		775	864	974	Cracked
70%		790	873	988	
80%		805	885	1002	
90%		825	901	1022	
95%		840	911	1037	

[a]Run at 10 mm pressure and converted to the equivalent temperature at 760 mm.

flexibility in lube oil product blending by having a variety of different blend stocks, and (2) to permit optimizing operating conditions in the dewaxing step and treating severity in the solvent extraction step.

Additional types of blend stocks may be produced by processing lube streams from various types of crude oils and by varying the type and severity of the downstream processing steps. For example, naphthenic lube oils are produced from selected naphthenic base crude oils without solvent extraction and usually without dewaxing.

Table 1 lists characteristics of typical base oils produced from mid-continent crude oil. These base stocks are blended together and compounded with additives as required to produce lubes meeting the various SAE and military viscosity and service classifications. Table 2 shows typical formulations of several single grade and multigrade motor oils formulated from the base stocks described in Table 1.

The principal additives now used in automotive engine lubricants consist of the following [2]:

1. Detergents and dispersants to disperse insoluble contaminants and prevent deposition of solids, varnish, etc. in the engine at high temperatures. Typical compositions include barium, calcium, and magnesium phenolates or organic phosphates and sulfonates as detergents, and polymeric

TABLE 2 Typical Motor Oil Formulations from Mid-Continent Lube Stocks

		Single Grade					Multigrade		
SAE Grade		SAE 20	SAE 30			SAE 40	10W/30	10W/40	
SAE Service Classification		SE	SD	SE	SF	SE	SE	SE	SF
Base stocks (vol.%):									
100 Neutral		13.0					46.4	20.6	20.4
250 Neutral		80.2	29.5	29.0	28.0		41.1	61.9	61.1
600 Neutral			65.0	64.2	65.0	85.0			
150 Bright						7.5			
Subtotal base stock		93.2	94.5	93.2	93.0	92.5	87.5	82.5	81.5
Additive (vol.%):									
Detergent/dispersant		6.8	5.5	6.8	7.0	7.5	7.0	9.0	10.0
Viscosity index improver, vol.%							5.5	8.5	8.5
Subtotal additives		6.8	5.5	6.8	7.0	7.5	12.5	17.5	18.5
Physical tests:									
Gravity, API	D287	29.8	29.1	29.0	29.0	28.5	30.0	28.5	28.3
Flash, Open Cup, °F	D92	440	470	470	470	475	410	415	415
Pour, °F	D97	−20	0	0	0	0	−40	−45	−45
Viscosity: SUS at 100°F	D2161	350	530	532	532	838	336	447	450
SUS at 210°F	D2161	55.2	65.2	65.5	65.5	82.0	64.5	83.5	84.0
Viscosity index	D2270	97	97	97	97	97	140	143	144
Color	D1500	L3.5	L3.0	L4.0	L4.0	L4.0	L4.0	L4.5	L4.5

alkyldithiophosphonates and alkyl succinimides as dispersants. These were among the first additives used in motor oils, and the compounded oils were originally known as "detergent" motor oils, as distinguished from straight mineral oils.

2. Pour points depressants which control wax crystal formation. Typical materials include polymethacrylates, alkylated naphthalenes, chlorinated paraffins, and phenolic polymers.
3. Antioxidants, including zinc dithiophosphates and aromatic amines. Use of antioxidants became more extensive as improvement of base stock quality by solvent extraction (with phenol or furfural) removed natural oxidation inhibitors from the lube distillates.
4. Friction modifiers which are surface-active materials forming a bond with a metal surface. Typical components are fatty acids and amines, organic phosphorous compounds, phosphoric acid esters, and molybdenum disulfide.
5. Antiwear and extreme pressure agents are used to reduce friction and prevent wear in metal-to-metal contact. Typical compositions include zinc dithiophosphates, phosphates, organic sulfur and chlorine compounds, sulfurized fats, and sulfides.
6. Corrosion and rust inhibitors, including magnesium or calcium sulfonates, metal phenolates, and alkenyl-succinic acids.
7. Miscellanous: Additives such as seal swell agents and antifoams.

All of the above materials are generally combined into a mixture known as the "detergent/dispersant additive package." If this mixture is too viscous to be blended readily with the base stock, it is sometimes premixed with a small amount of a suitable lube oil to reduce its viscosity. Typical "dosages" of the detergent/dispersal additive package in high performance oils run in the range of 5 to 10 vol.%.

The other principal category of additives is the viscosity index (VI) improver, which minimizes viscosity changes with temperature fluctuations. These are principally polymers and copolymers of methacrylates, butadienes, olefins, and alkylated sytrene. Typical concentrations of VI improver run up to 7–8% for polymethacrylates and 8–10% for polyisobutylene. Thus, total additives for multigrade oils may now comprise up to 15–20% of a lube blend, and typical average composite materials picked up for rerefining generally contain at least 10–12 vol.% additives (based on lube fractions plus additives).

It will be noted that many of these additive compounds contain metals, which contribute to the ash content of the oil. The extent of their removal from lube oil being rerefined by sulfuric acid treating in the past was usually monitored by simple determination of the "ash" of the treated oil. Also, while most of the additive materials are reasonably stable, there is some decomposition during service. Most of these materials are higher boiling than most lube oil fractions (with the exception of heavy ends in formulations which contain a substantial amount of bright stock) and would be expected to remain in the vacuum bottoms where a distillation cut point equivalent to at least 1000°F is made between the distillate recovered lube oil and the by-product vacuum bottoms.

In general the trend for several years has been toward more severe service designations and increased use of multigrade oils, especially 10W/40. As indicated in Table 2, increased use of multigrade oils results in increased use of the lighter neutral oils and less use of heavier neutrals and bright stock. Overall, the boiling point of the heaviest components of the average lube base stock is now generally lower than the initial boiling point of the chemical additives. This trend in lube oil manufacture has contributed to the growth of high vacuum distillation or evaporation as the most widely used technique for removal of used additives in rerefining, as discussed below.

Table 3 shows estimated inspections, trace metals content, etc. on the typical 10W/40 SF lube blend described in Table 2: (1) before the additives are added and (2) after the addition of the additives. The third column in this table develops the estimated analysis of the used lubricating oil which would be expected to result from normal use of this material in crankcase service. This indicates all the various materials picked up by the engine oil during use, such as dirt, wear metal, decomposition products, and the heavy ends from the fuel which "blows by" the engine piston. In the case of gasoline engines, the fuel has in the past contained some tetraethyl lead or other "antiknock" agents. This accounts for the presence of lead in the used lube oil, even though lead is not normally a component of any of the additives. As use of tetraethyl lead is being phased out of gasoline, the amount of lead contaminant in rerefining feedstocks has been reduced over the years and will continue to be reduced further in the future.

The estimated used oil analysis developed in Table 3 based on use of a 10W/40 lube oil is, of course, only one component of a typical composite used oil stream collected for rerefining. Typical characteristics of such a mixture have been estimated and are presented in the final column of Table 3. This is based on a mixture of various crankcase lubricant grades including the 10W/40 with 18.5% additives. Some of the used lube oil is, of course, straight mineral oil (including some rerefined oil) without addition of detergents or other additives. In addition to the used lube oil, waste solvents containing organic chlorides and extraneous materials may be picked up to some extent in the collection and transportation system, along with a certain amount of water. PCB has also been found as a component of used lube oils, although this is being flushed from the waste collection systems because no PCB has been used in electrical transformer cooling for many years. While hydrochloric acid formed by decompositions of organic chlorides could cause corrosion of overhead equipment, materials picked up through established channels generally do not cause excessive overhead corrosion in rerefining equipment. The dehydration and stripping equipment is normally made of carbon steel, as are the clay-contacting facilities. (The vacuum still heaters and the vacuum evaporators are built principally of stainless steel.)

Current regulations permit use of high halogen content gasoline and liquid fuels as rerefining plant fuel, and most of the chlorine entering with the feedstock is handled in this manner. Currently the gas oil by-product not used as plant fuel may contain up to 4000 ppm of chlorides, with certain monitoring and reporting requirements, and higher if sold to an industrial burner. Of course, this may be made more restrictive in the future.

No actual experimental data are available on inspections of a particular lube oil both before and after compounding with the additive package, along

TABLE 3 New and Used Lube Oil Inspections

	10W/40 SF Lube Oil			Typical Composite Rerefining Feedstock
	Base Stock Blend	Compounded Oil, (with 18.5 vol.% total additives)	Estimated Characteristics of Used Oil	
BS&W, %	—	—	1.0	8.0
Inspections (dry basis):				
Gravity, °API	31.5	28.3	28.6	29.0
Flash, Closed Cup, °F	400	400	140	120
Flash, Open Cup, °F	415	415	340	300
Pour point, °F	–45	–45	–40	–30
Viscosity: SUS at 100°F	210	450	300	340
SUS at 210°F	47	84	60	59
Viscosity index	96	144	130	120
Color	L0.5	L4.5	Dark	Dark
Distillation (conversion to 760 mmHg) IBP, °F:	660	680	450	400
5%	705	730	680	620
10%	740	760	750	685
20%	785	800	790	745
30%	815	825	815	785
40%	835	840	835	810
50%	845	860	855	835
60%	860	875	870	860
70%	870	895	895	885
80%	885	925	935	925
90%	900	—	—	1020
95%	910	—	—	—
Ash, wt.%	0.01	0.90		1.3
Sulfur, %	0.05	0.50		0.6
Ramsbottom carbon, %	—	1.05		—
Conradson carbon, %	0.05	—		2.3
Total acid no.	0.02	3.7		—
Total base no.	—	7.5		—
Trace elements (ppm):				
Nitrogen	—	1000		1500
Chlorine	—	—		500
Sodium	—	—		100
Phosphorus	—	930		900
Calcium	—	—		1200
Barium	—	—		200
Zinc	—	1100		1000
Magnesium	—	1000		400
Iron	—	—		700
Lead	—	—		700
Aluminum, Arsenic, Boron, Cadmium, Chromium, Copper, Silicon, Tin, Titanium	—	—		5–50 ppm each

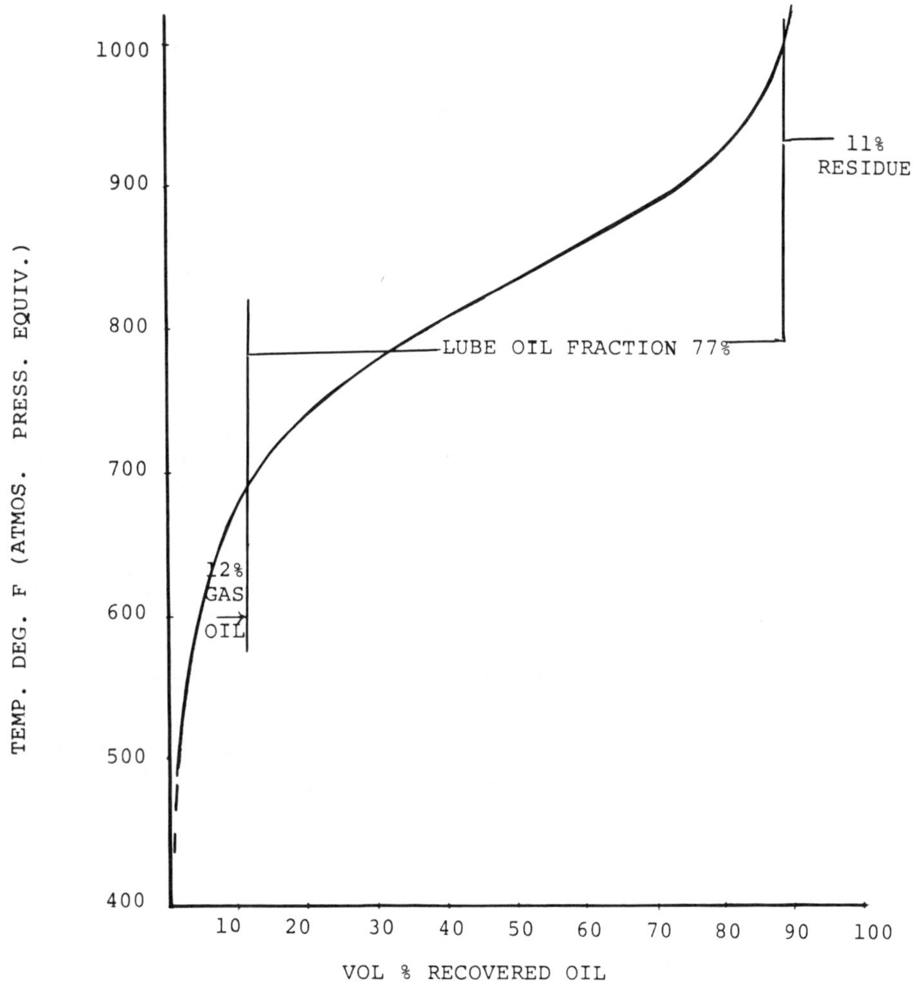

FIG. 1. Boiling point distribution of typical used lubricating oil (dry basis).

with tests on the corresponding used oil after typical service, as has been estimated in Table 3. The estimated representative average inspections of used lubricating oil charged to a rerefining facility as developed in Table 3 will be used as a basis for subsequent discussions on processing of this material with the predominant United States rerefining technology of vacuum distillation and clay contacting. This typical feedstock "analysis" represents a synthesis from various data obtained from the literature for the past 10–15 years, adjusted in accordance with recent and anticipated trends. This is believed to be as representative as possible of typical feedstock obtainable in the late 1980s. It is recognized, however, that individual feedstock samples may vary substantially, even after screening out totally unsuitable materials.

Figure 1 shows a plot of equivalent atmospheric distillation of the typical feedstock from the last column of Table 3, after dehydration. The key distillation "cut points" are:

	Dry Basis	*Including 8% BS&W*
% at 212°F	0	8.0
% at 700°F	12.0	19.0
% at 1000°F	89.0	89.9

Current United States Processing Schemes

Overall Processing Plan

Elimination of sulfuric-acid-treating procedures and switching of the rerefining industry to vacuum distillation (or evaporation) as the basic processing operation has resulted in a substantial simplification of the overall processing scheme. With sulfuric-acid treating it was necessary to dehydrate the feedstock completely before subjecting it to acid treatment to prevent dilution of the strong sulfuric acid. On the other hand, there was no need to remove crankcase "dilution" or fuel components ahead of the acid-treating step, since these could be conveniently stripped from the hot oil in the subsequent clay contacting step. Their presence during acid treating reduced the viscosity of the oil and thereby increased the ease of separating the acid sludge.

With the imposition of more stringent air quality controls, as well as more rigorous control of plant effluent water quality, most plants now arrange their procurement and collection practices to avoid bringing relatively large amounts of water in with the feedstock, and depend principally on dehydration by evaporation. The total water flashed overhead in the initial processing is not condensed but is vented to an incineration chamber (usually one of the plant furnaces) along with vacuum jet discharge and other wet vapors. Here it is subjected to a high temperature before being discharged to the atmosphere. This takes care of both the water effluent and air quality problems except for situations in which excessives amounts of chlorides, sulfur compounds, or metals might be present in the water vapor, and thus discharged to the air. These do not normally present a major problem, even though many rerefineries are located within the city limits of major cities, and thus are subject to the most restrictive air quality regulations.

The sulfuric-acid-treating procedure resulted in most of the dirt, insolubles, and polymerizable components of the feed being removed from the oil with the acid sludge. Hence it was usually unnecessary, from a strictly operational standpoint, to remove such materials ahead of acid treating. (In some cases, however, used oils with a very large content of VI improver were difficult to acid treat because of a gel formation binding oil with the sludge.) Extensive experimental work and plant investigations were, however, conducted over the years in efforts to improve upon the overall economics in the acid-based rerefining operation by removing certain components of the used oil ahead of the acid-treating step. This included heating and treating with solvents, and breaking emulsions through use of chemical agents, use of coagulants such as sodium silicate, and other means. Many of these procedures, which complicated the processing, resulted in additional by-product and waste streams for disposal. The only by-products from the present sequence involving wiped film evaporation as described below are a light gas oil, the residual or tar fraction, and spent contact clay.

A generalized block flow diagram of typical processing sequences is shown in Fig. 2. This indicates some of the principal processing alternatives, particularly with regard to (1) the production of multiple viscosity grades of the final lube product as opposed to a single composite lube stream, (2) a vacuum distillation "still" as an alternative to a wiped film evaporator, and (3) final hydrofinishing vs clay contacting.

These vacuum distillation plants, having a relatively high throughput rate, are run continuously on a 24-h basis. Sometimes regular shutdowns are scheduled, such as scheduling on a 6-d operating week. This is a distinct change from the former practice of small plants processing "batches," principally on a daytime only (or two shift) basis. Clay contacting of segregated streams is still operated batchwise in certain instances.

Settling and Screening

Assuming no separation of an aqueous layer from the feedstock is to be attempted, the feed may still be settled, preferably at an elevated temperature, to remove as much dirt and sediment as possible. In addition, the feed is often pumped through an in-line filter with a fine mesh screen (100-200 mesh) to eliminate solid materials as far as possible. However, these materials, even including some dirt, cause no particular problem if they pass through the entire processing sequence and wind up in the evaporator residue, as described below. The pretreatment step need only provide for centrifuging or other means to remove polymerizing or fouling materials, if such are present, in the event that the type of vacuum distillation facilities employed does not have the necessary tolerance for such fouling contaminants. Any settled materials or solids removed by a screen filter may be discarded along with spent contact clay.

Dehydration and Stripping

Crankcase dilution by components of the engine fuel, both gasoline and diesel, consists principally of materials boiling above 300–325°F. This represents the heavy ends of gasoline and material in the diesel fuel boiling range. Where vacuum distillation is to be employed, in order to facilitate operation at relatively high vacuum conditions, it is necessary to boil off all water and any light gasoline boiling range fractions. Generally, however, the used oil contains little material boiling below about 325°F, and the quantity of such, or the opportunities to obtain higher than plant fuel value for it, would not justify extensive efforts to recover this heavy gasoline component as a separate product. Therefore, most processing sequences will provide for flashing water overhead, along with the lightest gasoline boiling range fractions, to a combustion chamber and then subsequently to strip out diesel fuel boiling range material up to the lightest lube oil components.

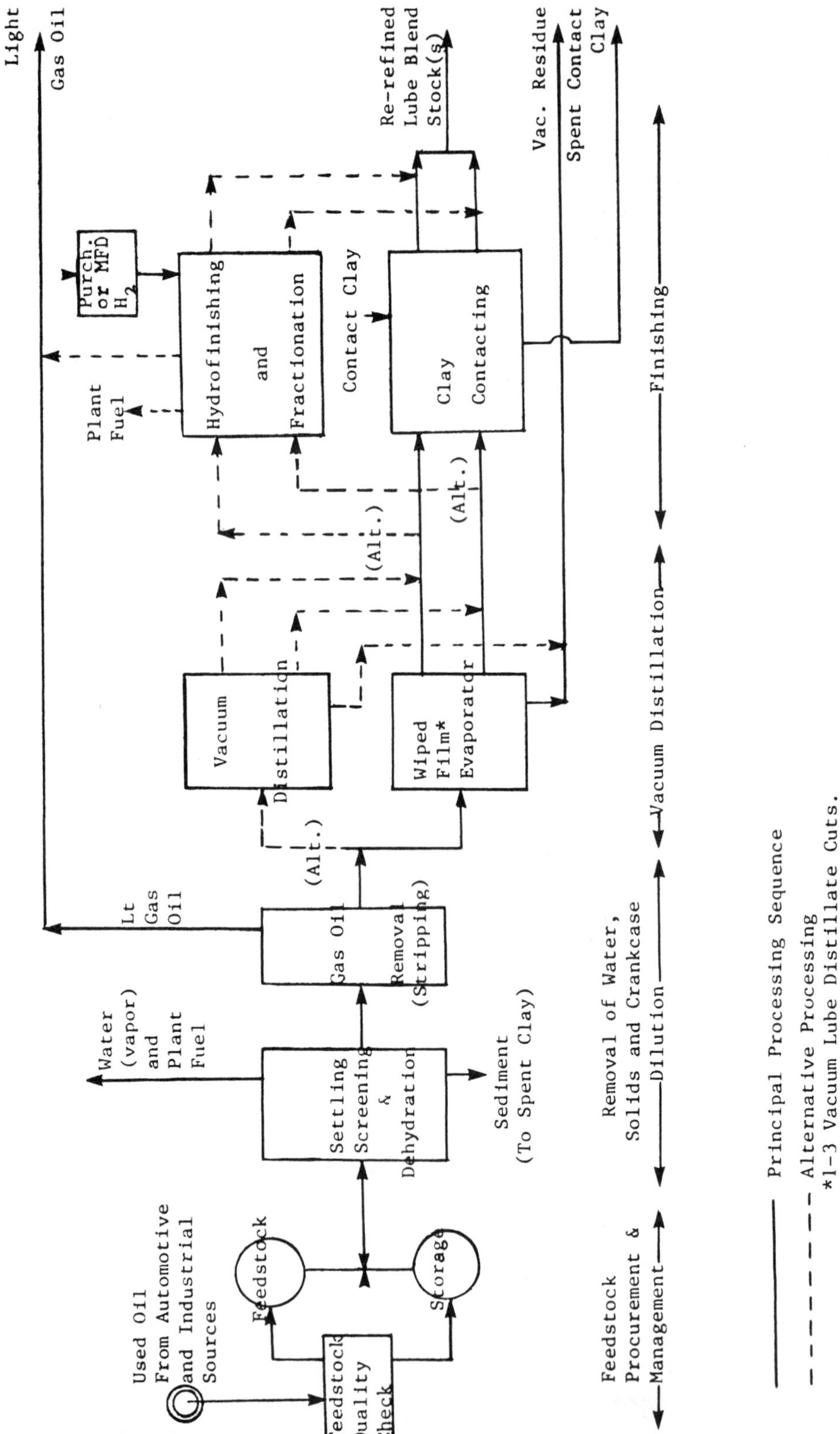

FIG. 2. United States lubricating oil rerefining.

Since most used lube oil will meet the 140°F minimum closed cup flash point even before stripping of naphtha fractions, the total hydrocarbon mixture could be charged to vacuum distillation after dehydration. In this case the gas oil would be stripped from the lube fractions at the final hydrofinishing or clay-contacting step.

These settling, dehydration, and stripping steps of the processing present no special processing requirements, and no special alloy equipment is required. The only by-product stream (other than solids strained from the feed) is the single "crankcase dilution" cut. This material may be used to supplement plant fuel or may be disposed of to petroleum refiners or blenders, who produce principally diesel fuel from it. Increased monitoring of this stream for hazardous components (principally chlorides) may be required in the future.

Vacuum Distillation or Evaporation

Vacuum distillation or evaporation is the "heart" of all existing United States rerefining installations. The feed to this step contains both the recoverable lube oil fractions and a mixture of high boiling materials which can be removed as a single residual product. There may be, of course, some light gas oil boiling range hydrocarbon if the processing sequence provides for removing this during or after the vacuum distillation step. The distillation could be carried out either in equipment substantially duplicating a conventional refinery vacuum unit as designed for the production of raw lube distillate streams (if fouling is not excessive) or in a high vacuum wiped filmed evaporator. As discussed previously, the trend in lubricating oil formulations in recent years has been to blend lube oils from lighter distillate feedstocks thickened with viscosity index improvers as opposed to former formulations of straight mineral oils and detergent single grade oils from heavier distillates, including some bright stock. While much of the bright stock cannot be distilled overhead even under very high vacuum conditions, the distillates used in present multigrade lube oil formulations contain little material boiling higher than about 900–1000°F atmospheric equivalent (see Tables 1 and 2). This material can be distilled overhead under readily obtainable vacuum conditions.

Use of a conventional vacuum still in this service presents certain problems: (1) the relatively low yield of residual material, which has an extremely high viscosity is difficult to remove from the still; (2) localized overheating occurs, causing coking, polymerization, and further degradation of additives and the lube oil fractions; and (3) fouling of the equipment which plugs tray vapor passages and other restricted flow areas. Depending, of course, on the contaminants present in the rerefining feedstock, these fouling problems usually render the distillation of used lubes in conventional vacuum equipment (either wet or dry) impractical without extensive pretreatment to remove the fouling precursors.

The wiped filmed vacuum evaporator (WFE) presents a practical alternative to a conventional vacuum distillation system for this critical step of lube oil rerefining processes, even without any special pretreatment to remove equipment fouling components [3]. This type of equipment has been used widely in the chemical processing industry for many years in the evaporation of heat sensitive, relatively high boiling materials. It is particularly useful where the bottoms fraction is very viscous and/or represents only a small fraction of the feedstock. During the past 10–15 years, many WFEs have been installed in lube oil rerefining plants in the United States and throughout the world.

A "cutaway" view of a typical WFE is shown as Fig. 3. This equipment consists of a vertical heated cylinder fitted with internal rotating wiper blades acting on the inside of the shell. Preheated feed material is distributed around

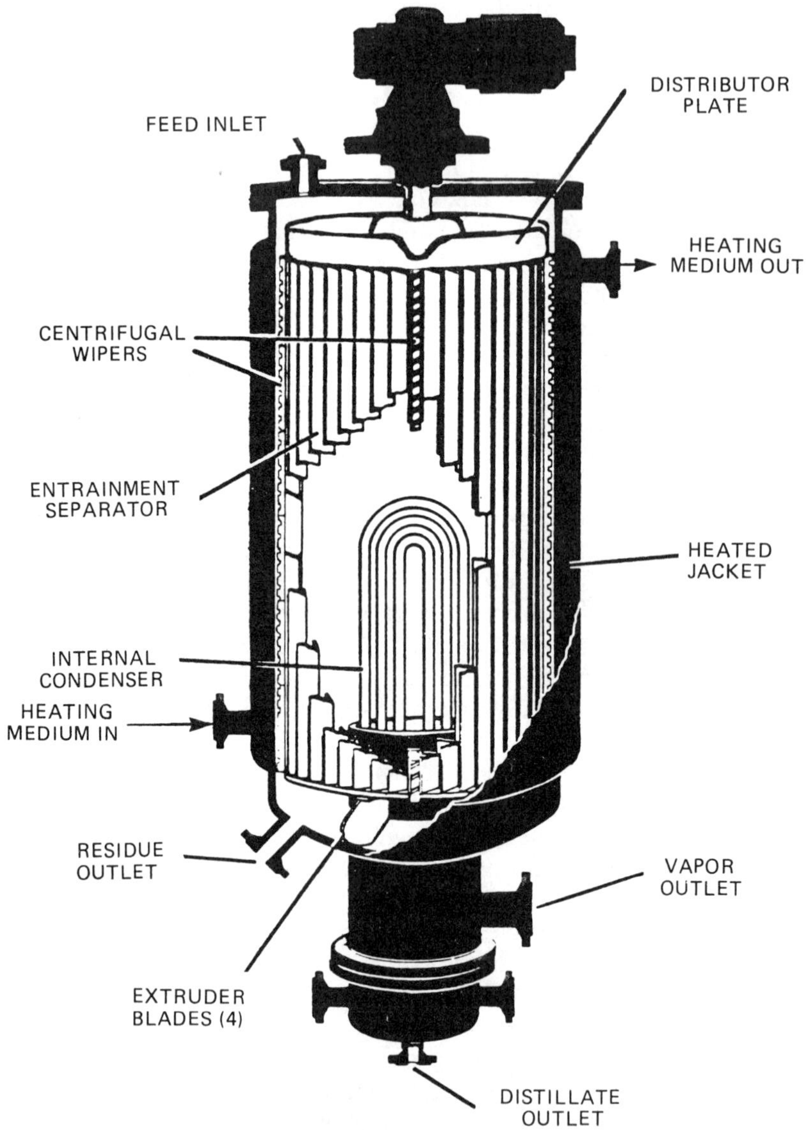

FIG. 3. Wiped film evaporator. (Courtesy Pfaudler Corp.)

the inside of this cylinder near the top, and under the influence of gravity, centrifugal force, and the mechanical "scraping" action of the rotating wiper blades, it flows downward as a thin film along the inside surface of the cylinder. The cylinder surface is heated by an external jacket containing steam or other suitable heating medium, and the inside of the cylinder is maintained under vacuum conditions. The speed of the rotor blades is such that the wiping edge travels at a speed of approximately 15 ft/s. Under these conditions the film of oil on the heated inside surface of the cylinder is between 0.02 and 0.04 in. thick. In the application to lube oil rerefining, a heating medium such as Syltherm (a product of Dow Chemical Co.) is used at a temperature of the order of 650–700°F to provide the desired oil film temperature inside the cylinder. This may be higher than 600°F, depending on the boiling point of the heaviest material being evaporated and the level of vacuum available. The heating medium temperature and the rate at which this material is pumped through the shell can be adjusted to increase the oil film temperatures as desired. Multistage steam jet vacuum eductors are used to bring the absolute pressure in the cylinder to within a range of 1–2 mmHg.

The oil vapor leaving the heated surface inside this wiped film evaporator passes through an entrainment separating screen or baffle and onto the surface of internal condensers where a part of it is condensed and the liquid withdrawn from the system. The remaining vapor may pass outside the unit to external condenser coils, in which case lighter oil is condensed at this point. Thus two lube streams of two separate viscosities can be produced from a single unit (three, if a preliminary flash evaporator is added ahead of the WFE), or these may be combined or condensed as a single lube product. In some rerefineries, two WFEs are used in series to effect recovery of several lube cuts of different viscosities.

This type of equipment has been supplied to oil rerefining installations by the Pfaudler Co. of Rochester, New York, and the Luwa Corp. of Sherwood, North Carolina. Both companies manufacture equipment in sizes up to 40 m^2 (430 ft^2) of wiped heating surface, although most of the units in rerefining service are somewhat smaller. This equipment is ordinarily provided in stainless steel to minimize corrosion.

The operational advantages of the WFE over conventional vacuum distillation are that heavy lube oil fractions can be distilled out of very viscous residues with minimum entrainment and that it is a good approach to equilibrium conditions between the residual liquid and separated vapor. With careful design and the use of the heat-transfer medium, localized overheating, which might lead to decomposition, polymerization, coking, and fouling of the equipment, can be minimized. Although the WFE equipment is rather expensive in terms of the conventional cost of constructing rerefining facilities based on acid and clay treatment, its use has become widespread in the United States rerefining industry, and it appears likely that most installations in the future will be based on this operation.

Hydrofinishing or Clay Contacting

Even with careful control of the vacuum distillation to minimize entrainment of bottoms into the distillate streams through use of entrainment eliminators (both in conventional vacuum stills and wipe film evaporators,) the overhead lube distillate streams need a final processing step to improve and stabilize color. When the pretreating and distillation steps have been properly conducted, this finishing step can be accomplished through use of a clay-contacting step. However, an alternative providing more flexibility would be to finish the lubes with a mild catalytic hydrogenation step similar to the hydrofinishing processes employed almost universally in the manufacture of new lubricating oil base stocks. Such hydrogenation generally involves operating pressures of the order of 800–900 lb/in.^{2} and temperatures in the range of 600–700°F. Several catalyst manufacturers license specific operating conditions for this procedure.

In the clay-contacting step the finely divided contact clay is mixed intimately with the oil, and the mixture heated to a temperature usually in the range of 400–450°F. A relatively short contact time may be used (generally 15–45 min is adequate), after which the clay is filtered out of the oil. This is usually done by the plate and frame presses, with a final blotter filter step. It is necessary to cool the oil to 325°F or less before filtering, depending on the filtering medium used. Oil lost to clay soakage is about 30–35% by weight in the spent clay, or around 2% of the lube oil being contacted. Overall contacting loss generally runs 3–4% of the feed to this step.

If a continuous rotary precoat filter is used, filtration may be done at higher temperatures and the soakage loss cut at least in half. This equipment was widely used in contact finishing of new lubes before hydrofinishing displaced contacting. It is not widely used in rerefining, probably because of the high investment per unit of capacity for relatively small filters.

The clay–oil mixture is usually agitated with open steam to prevent any settling of clay ahead of filtering. This facilitates stripping of any light material from the oil, if necessary.

A principal disadvantage of hydrofinishing over clay contacting is the higher investment cost. The cost of hydrogen is, in normal circumstances, essentially equal to the cost of contact clay. The advantages include improved lube yields and quality, and freedom from by-product disposal problems. Currently no plants use hydrogenation in the United States, although one recently constructed in the San Francisco area uses purchased liquid hydrogen, obtained at a cost of about $15/MCF. Typical hydrogen consumption is 150–200 cubic feet per barrel of lube oil treated, so the raw hydrogen cost is of the order of 6–7¢ per gallon of lube. On the other hand, typical contact clay dosages are of the order of 0.2–0.35 pounds per gallon of Filtrol 20 clay, costing about $300–$350 per ton delivered. This represents a clay cost of 5 to 6¢ per gallon of finished lube, or about the same magnitude as the purchased hydrogen. The fact that clay contacting has been most widely employed may have been influenced to some extent by the fact that most rerefining plants had clay-contacting facilities which were used in former acid and clay operations before they switched to the WFE.

If a rerefining plant were able to obtain by-product hydrogen from a refinery by pipeline delivery, the hydrofinishing costs might be reduced significantly. No plant in the United States is now able to purchase relatively low cost impure hydrogen from an oil refinery, although in normal refinery accounting the cost of hydrogen is considered as not much greater than its heating value. This would be at least an order of magnitude less than the liquid hydrogen price of $15/MCF. Refineries are unwilling to commit their hydrogen to a long-term sale to a customer like a lube rerefiner since the hydrogen might be needed at any time for some refinery processing modification. Some refineries even manufacture hydrogen by reforming natural gas or other feedstocks for desulfurization and other hydrogen-consuming processes. Also, in order to use hydrogen purchased by pipeline from a refinery, a rerefiner would probably have to be located near the refinery, and refiners are usually unwilling to provide or assist the rerefiner in obtaining such a site.

The choice between hydrofinishing and clay contact finishing in the future will probably depend largely on the continued ability of rerefining plants to dispose of spent contact clay to ordinary landfills. No change in this situation seems imminent although, of course, regulations could be tightened with respect to spent clay disposal to the point where the added cost of hazardous waste-type landfill or other permissible disposal might make the hydrofinishing alternative more attractive in some instances. Oil does not tend to leach from this type of waste material, as is demonstrated in the case of large dumps of spent contact clay from new lube manufacture which have been exposed to weathering for over 50 years. A 10 million gallon rerefining plant would have to dispose of approximately 5 to 6 tons per day of spent clay. The bulk density of the wet clay is usually 90 to 95 pounds per cubic foot.

Fractionation of Rerefined Product Lube Oils

As indicated in the preceding discussion, the vacuum distillation or evaporation step can be conducted to produce a single lube distillate or adjustments can be made to produce two or more separate distillates of different viscosity grades. In the case of clay contacting, these materials would be contacted in a blocked operation so that the final lube product would consist of separate grades for blending. In the case of hydrofinishing, the single lube distillate would normally be hydrofinished and the final product rerun under vacuum to produce the required separate blend stocks. A trace of additional light gas oil may be yielded at this stage (Fig. 2).

KTI Relube Process

Kinetics Technology International (KTI) of Monrovia, California, provides a single source package wherein facilities for the combination of the manufacturing operations as described in Fig. 2 can be purchased by a rerefiner for shipment in packaged modules to a rerefining site. The "Relube" process provides all of the facilities described in Fig. 2, including the WFE and hydrofinishing options. This includes hydrofinishing of the recovered lube based on either purchased liquid hydrogen or hydrogen manufacturing from available feedstocks. By having a wiped film evaporator, the facility is completely flexible with regard to the type of feedstock it can handle. The first commercial installation of this process combination was in Greece and has been operating successfully for several years.

TABLE 4 By-Products from Lube Rerefining

	Typical Feedstock (Table 3)	Water and Plant Fuel Gas	Gas Oil	Lube Product	Residue	Spent Clay Soakage and Loss
BS&W, %	8.0	—	—	—	—	—
Vol.% of feed:						
Wet basis	100.0	9.0[a]	10.0	68.1	10.2	2.7
Dry basis	100.0	1.1	10.9	73.9	11.0	3.1
Inspections (dry basis):						
Gravity, °API	29.0		37.0	30.6	14.5	
Flash, Closed Cup, °F	120		140	400	—	
Flash, Open Cup, °F	300		—	410	575	
Pour point °F	−30		—	−20	—	
Viscosity: SUS at 100°F	340		—	300	—	
SUS at 210°F	59.0		—	52.0	8000	
Viscosity index	120		—	95	—	
Color	Dark		—	L0.5	—	
Distillation (atm):						
10%	685		550	740	—	
50%	835		600	840	—	
90%	1020		680	900	—	
Ash, % (D482)	1.3		0.01	0.1	10.0	
Sulfur, %	0.6	Trace	0.01	0.06	0.3	
Conradson carbon, %	2.3		0.02	0.2	17.0	
Chlorine, ppm	1000	[b]	2000[b]	—	—	—
Metals, ppm	5200		—	30	4.5%	Trace

[a]8% water plus 1.04% uncondensed heavy gasoline.
[b]Chlorine in feed goes principally to gaseous and liquid plant fuels.

Disposition of By-Products

Table 4 shows the estimated analysis of the product streams and by-product streams for the typical feedstock as developed in Table 3. In addition to showing that the bulk of contaminants are removed from the lube oils, this indicates that substantially all of the metals will be collected in the distillation or evaporator bottoms stream. This material has been disposed of by most existing plants as an asphalt blend stock. It is expected that the residual material will be considered as a "hazardous waste material" in the future, thus requiring close monitoring and control of its use. Commercial asphalt blenders have had no problems in blending this in road building and roofing formulations, and it is anticipated that essentially all rerefining vacuum bottoms will be used in this manner in the future.

This disposition avoids the problem of air pollution on burning the residual stream or blending it into fuel oils. The residue must be kept hot until blended, and it is transported in insulated trucks.

Waste oils containing large amounts of chlorinated solvents are kept out of the used lube charged to rerefining insofar as possible. However, such materials have limited other disposal possibilities, and they frequently find their way to the lube rerefining feedstock. While the organic chloride content of a typical used lube oil is significant, most of this goes to the overhead incinerator. The recovered light gas oil fraction may contain up to 4000 ppm of chlorides and can be used as a supplementary rerefining plant fuel or, with prescribed monitoring and reporting, as a refinery or blending plant feedstock for the manufacture of diesel fuel or No. 2 heating oil.

Other Processes

Propane Clarification

Separation of asphaltenes and resins by treatment of a vacuum residuum with propane is used in the manufacture of bright stock. The additive and other heavy materials in a used lube oil can be rejected similarly from propane solution. The ratio of propane to oil required is high relative to treating conditions for bright stock manufacture. A rerefining process based on propane has been commercialized in Europe by Institut Francais du Petrole (IFP). The procedure would presumably be environmentally acceptable for a United States installation, and the propane "clarified" oil could then be finished by hydrotreating or clay contacting. The precipitated material would be expected to be quite similar to the evaporator or vacuum distillation bottoms.

Acid Treating

Conventional acid treating–clay contacting operations are still feasible in some parts of the world, but appear to be losing ground, as in the United States. Development of some environmentally acceptable disposition for acid sludge, which is not now commercially feasible, could lead to reactiviation of some modification of this operation, but there appears to be no activity in this direction at present.

Phillips Re-Refined Oil Process

The Phillips Re-Refined Oil Process (PROP), which was developed by Phillips Petroleum Co., provides for demetallization of the used oil by treatment with an aqueous solution of diammonium phosphate. The precipitated metals are then removed by filtration with absorbent clay and charcoal. The oil is not required to be distilled overhead, but is then hydrofinished. While this process had been demonstrated to be technically feasible in full-scale installation, no installations are now operating in the United States.

DOE Solvent Pretreatment Distillation

The Bartlesville Energy Technology Center (BETC) of the U.S. Department of Energy, now National Institute for Petroleum and Energy Research (NIPER), developed a process for treatment of waste oil with a mixture of alcohols to remove a "sludge" containing many metallic additive components. The treated mixture was then vacuum distilled and hydrofinished [1].

The pretreating steps contributed to the practicality of conventional vacuum distillation, so that use of the WFE was not required. This process was ready for commercialization about the time that WFEs were beginning to be installed as a replacement for acid treating, and the success of WFE evaporation has apparently superseded further efforts to build a demonstration BETC process plant.

Bibliography

Booz, Allen & Hamilton, Inc. (K. D. Weinstein, T. D. Myers, and S. R. Craft), *Enhanced Utilization of Used Lubricating Oil Recycling Process By-Products*, DOE/BC/10059-19, March 1982, 166 pp.

Cotton, F. O., Whisman, M. L., Goetzinger, J. W., and Reynolds, J. W., "Analysis of 30 Used Motor Oils," *Hydrocarbon Process.*, *56*(9), 131–140 (1977).

GCA Corporation, *The Fate of Hazardous and Non-hazardous Wastes in Used Oil Disposal and Recycling*, DOE/BC/10375-1, October 1983, 249 pp.

NBS Special Publication 488, U.S. Department of Commerce/National Bureau of Standards, Issued August 1977.

Proceedings of Conference Held at National Bureau of Standards, Gaithersburg, Maryland, October 23–26, 1979 on Measurement and Standards for Recycled Oil.

Temple, Barker & Sloane Inc., *Regulatory Impact Analysis of Proposed Standards for the Management of Used Oil*, Prepared for U.S. Environmental Protection Agency, November 1985.

Weinstein, N. J., *Waste Oil Recycling and Disposal* (PB 236 248), Prepared for the U.S. Environmental Protection Agency by Recon Systems, Inc., and Response Analysis Corporation.

Whisman, M. L., Reynolds, J. W., Goetzinger, J. W., Cotton, F. O., and Brinkman, D. W., "Re-refining Makes Quality Oils," *Hydrocarbon Process.*, *57*(10), 141–145 (1978).

References

1. F. O. Cotton, D. W. Brinkman, J. W. Reynolds, J. W. Goetzinger, and M. L. Whisman, *Pilot-Scale Used Oil Re-refining Using a Solvent Treatment/Distillation Process*, BETC/R1-79/14, January 1980.
2. Richard J. Bigda & Associates, *Review of All Lubricants Used in the U. S. and Their Re-refining Potential*, DOE/BC/30227-1, June 1980, 84 pp.

3. Pfaudler Co. (A. Bellavia and H. Hartley), *Pfaudler Oil Re-refining System at CAM-OR*, Paper Presented at 5th International Conference on Used Oil Recovery, Las Vegas, Nevada, November 14–17, 1983.
4. Franklin Associates Ltd., *Composition and Management of Used Oil Generated in the United States*, Prepared for U.S. Environmental Protection Agency, November 1984 (PB/85-180-297).

JAMES L. WALKER

Lubricating Oils, Synthetic

For more than 50 years synthetic fluids have been used as lubricants for a variety of specialized applications. In most cases, specific fluids have been developed with physical and chemical properties tailored to the severe demands of equipment operating under temperature extremes or in other hostile environments. Typical examples are the use of synthetic esters for aviation gas turbines, polyalkylene glycol fluids for automotive brake systems, and phosphate esters for fire-resistant hydraulic fluid applications. In each case, success has been achieved by proper selection of a synthetic fluid having properties best suited to the application and design of the equipment concerned.

This article is limited to a review of the type of synthetics used by industry. A brief discussion explores the advantages of synthetics over mineral oils, provides general guidelines for their use, and elaborates on product performance and limitations. [1–4].

Definition

The American Society for Testing Materials' (ASTM) tentative definition for synthetic lubricant is "A synthetic lubricant is a product with consists of stocks manufactured by chemical synthesis and containing necessary performance additives." According to this definition, the base stocks for synthetic lubricants, unlike those of mineral oil, must be products of discrete chemical reactions. The base stocks are tailored through molecular restructuring to meet predetermined physical and chemical qualities.

The finished synthetic lubricant will contain a base stock, additives to impart certain performance characteristics, and may contain a carrier for the additives. Should the carrier be a mineral oil, the mineral oil content should be no higher than 10 to 15% of the lubricant if it is to be considered a true synthetic product.

ASTM has developed a classification system for synthetic base fluids as follows:

Synthetic hydrocarbons:
- Alkylated aromatics
- Olefin oligomers
- Cycloaliphatics

Organic esters:
- Dibasic acid esters
- Polyol esters
- Polyesters

Other:
- Halogenated hydrocarbons
- Phosphate esters
- Polyglycol ethers
- Polyphenyl ethers
- Silicate esters
- Silicones

Blends:
- Mixtures of the above

Note that this classification system specifically omits such materials as molybdenum disulfide, graphite, plastics (such as polyethylene, Teflon, nylon), inert or liquid gases, liquid metals, exotic natural oils, and surfactant chemical concentrates.

Basic Chemistry of Synthetic Lubricants

General

Crude oil is a complex mixture of hydrocarbons. While crudes vary in chemical composition, they all possess the same basic elements. Light hydrocarbon gases, such as ethane, methane, butane, and propane, are removed by atmospheric distillation. Gasoline, diesel fuel, and other fuel oil fractions are all distilled from the crude, leaving residuum, from which mineral lubricating oil stocks are derived. Unique refining techniques are used for the removal of undesirable components such as asphalts, waxes, and sulfur compounds.

There are literally thousands of undesirable compounds present in crude oil, and while most of them are removed by refining, some will remain in the lubricating oil stocks.

In contrast, synthetic products normally are produced by chemical reactions in which pressure, temperature, and the percentage of component elements can be carefully controlled. The path of the reaction up to the desired end product frequently includes several steps, each of which necessitates a purification of the intermediate products. It is this resulting freedom from catalyzing compounds that gives synthetic lubricants their distinctive characteristics. It also contributes to their higher cost compared to mineral oils.

The raw materials for synthetics are, for the most part, obtained from the refining of petroleum and extraction of desired hydrocarbons from natural gas. Ethylene and its derivatives are among the most important petrochemical feedstocks. Several of the most important synthetic lubricants can be produced from this basic material by means of specific reaction steps. These steps are shown in Fig. 1.

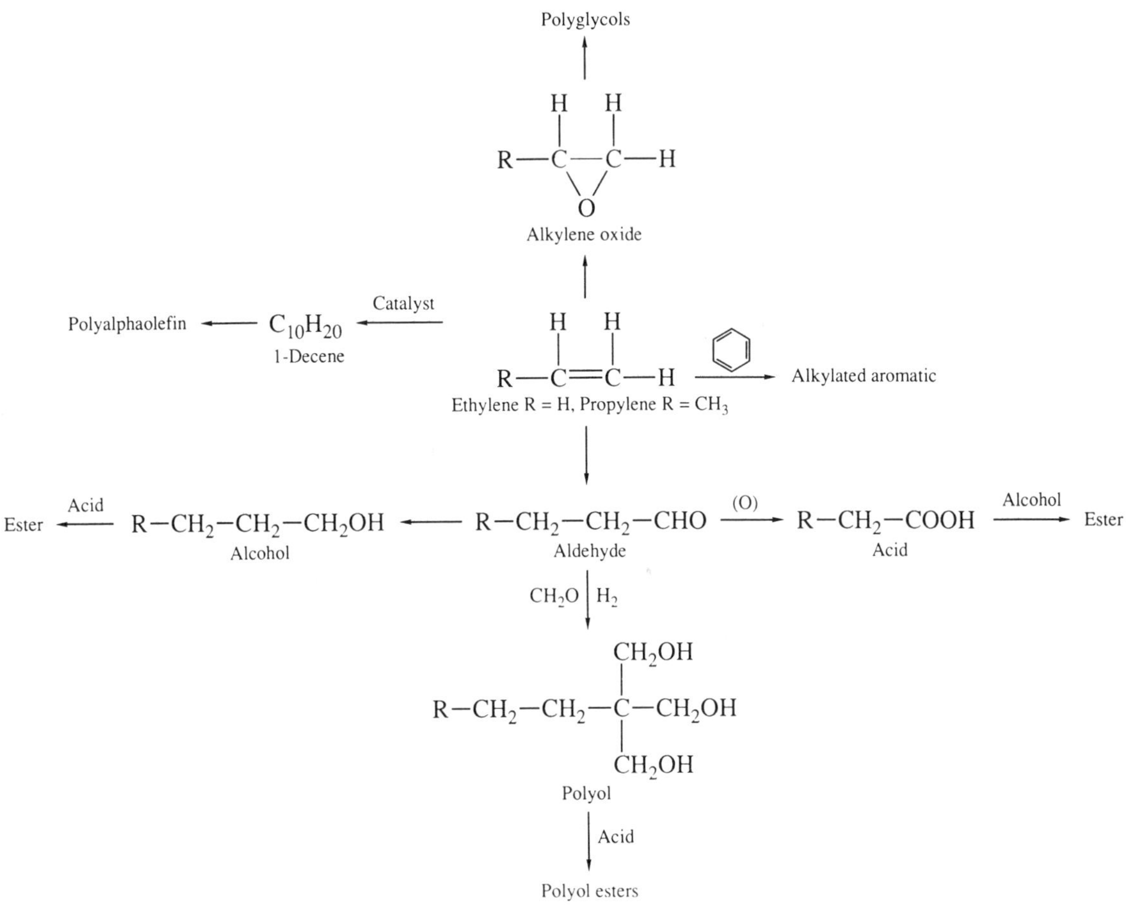

FIG. 1. Synthetic lubricant derived from ethylene. Copyright © by Mobil Oil Corp.

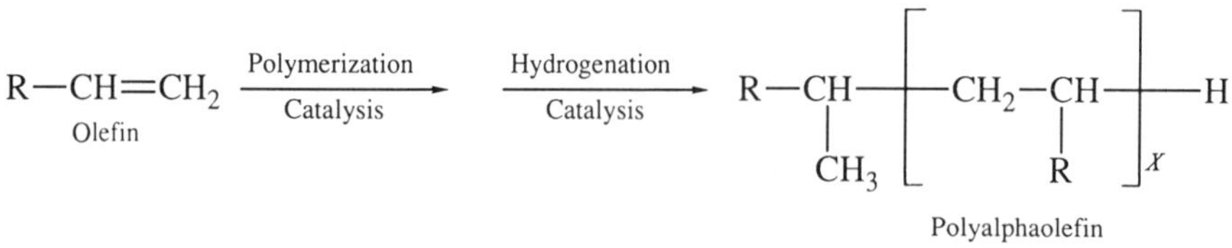

FIG. 2. Basic chemistry involved in the production of polyalphaolefins. Copyright © by Mobil Oil Corp.

Figures 2 and 3 show one of several methods for the production of polyalphaolefins, a synthesized hydrocarbon.

The essential steps in the process are as follows: Ethylene is distilled from oil, coal, or natural gas and reacted to form the basic building block of the polyalphaolefin, decene or C_{10}, an alphaolefin in the liquid state. The decene is polymerized in the presence of a catalyst, yielding dimers (two decene molecules in length), trimers (three), tetramers (four), and some heavier fractions. For the most part, the trimer and tetramer fractions are used for synthetic base stocks. However, both dimers and pentamers are used to obtain either the very low or very high viscosities required for some applications. The others are recycled to the reaction process.

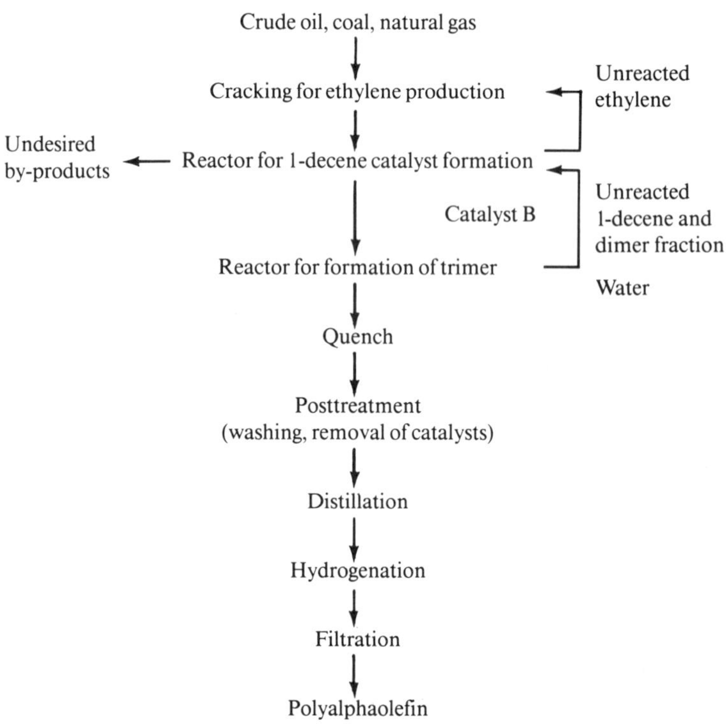

FIG. 3. Steps in the production of polyalphaolefins. Copyright © by Mobil Oil Corp.

To improve thermal and oxidative stability, the remaining double bonds in the molecules must be removed. This is accomplished through hydrogenation, the addition of hydrogen, which saturates the molecule and eliminates all double bonds. As shown in Fig. 3, there are intermediate steps: Washing for catalyst removal and distillation to achieve the desired viscosity.

Characteristics of Synthetic Lubricants

Fully 98% of the worldwide synthetic lubricants market is in four generic groups: Polyglycols, approximately 38%; synthesized hydrocarbons, 33%; organic esters, 22%; and phosphate esters, 5%. For this reason this article is devoted exclusively to these groups of products.

Synthetic lubricants are problem solvers and are used for special applications where petroleum products are inadequate (e.g., extremely high and low temperatures, extreme wear conditions) or where the lubricant must have special characteristics (e.g., fire resistance). The use of synthetic lubricants is always advisable when they can have a positive cost-efficient effect on machine reliability, oil life, energy consumption, and safety, in spite of their relatively high price.

The characteristics of synthetic lubricants come from the properties of the base fluids and from the effect of the additives used. The physical and chemical qualities of the base fluids include such things as viscosity–temperature behavior, low temperature fluidity, boiling point, compatibility with paints and sealants, miscibility with petroleum, hydrolytic stability, and the ability to dissolve chemical additives.

Additives are used to influence oxidation stability, load-bearing ability, corrosion protection, and evaporative loss.

Table 1 shows the relative performance characteristics of some synthetic lubricants compared with mineral oil.

Following is a brief summary of the important properties of the four generic groups of synthetics mentioned above.

Synthesized Hydrocarbons (SHF)

This general class is composed of polyalphaolefins, alkylated aromatics, polybutenes, and cycloaliphatics. Particular emphasis is placed on polyalphaolefins in this article because they are the fastest growing segment of the synthetic lubricants market.

Polyalphaolefins are prepared by the polymerization of alphaolefins, such as butene or 1-decene—see Figs. 2 and 3 and the discussions of them.

TABLE 1 Performance of Synthetic Lubricants Compared to Mineral Oils

	Synthetics							
Properties	Mineral Oil Paraffinic	Polyalpha-olefin	Dialkylated Benzene	Dibasic Acid Ester	Polyol Ester	Poly-glycol	Phosphate Ester	Silicone Fluid
Viscosity index	Fair	Good	Fair	Good	Good	Very good	Poor	Excellent
Low temperature[a]	0 to −25°F	−50 to −80°F	−50 to −80°F	−40 to −60°F	−30 to −60°F	−20 to −60°F	0 to −50°F	−100°F, very low
High temperature[b]	250–350°F	375–500°F	375–500°F	375–550°F	425–625°F	400–500°F	325–400°F	Over 500°F, very high
Oxidation stability	Fair	Good	Good	Good	Excellent	Good	Fair	Good
Volatility	Fair	Excellent	Good	Excellent	Excellent	Good	Fairly good	Good
Hydrolytic stability	Excellent	Excellent	Excellent	Fair	Fair	Good	Fair	Good
Additive response	Excellent	Good	Excellent	Very good	Very good	Fair	Good	Poor
Compatibility with mineral oil	Excellent	Excellent	Excellent	Good	Fair	Poor	Poor	Poor
Compatibility with most paints and finishes	Excellent	Excellent	Excellent	Poor	Poor	Good	Poor	Good

[a]Depends on starting torque.
[b]Intermittent service.

Table 2 shows a comparison of the viscosities of a synthetic hydrocarbon (SHF) based on a polyalphaolefin and a conventionally refined mineral oil with a comparable viscosity at 100°C. Note that the viscosity of an SHF can be measured at low temperatures. The pour point of the SHF is much lower than that of the mineral oil because the SHF contains no wax. The SHF also has a lower volatility than the mineral oil, as indicated by its higher flash point and lower percentage distilled at 400°C.

A unique advantage of an SHF (polyalphaolefin fluid) is that it possesses a lower traction coefficient than mineral oils.

> Traction is defined as unit fluid friction resulting from the very high oil viscosity in the Hertzian load zone in gears, rolling bearings, and other mechanisms subject to elastohydrodynamic (EHL) conditions. It is distinct from both viscous churning effects, which occur outside of the lubricated area, and surface frictional losses, which require asperity interaction in the lubricated area. Thus, tractional properties describe a fluid's resistance to shear at the point of highest pressure. Traction coefficient defines the relationship between tangential and normal forces acting on the oil film in EHL contacts. It is analogous to coefficient of friction under sliding conditions, but applies specifically to highly loaded machine elements separated by a lubricant film. Oils with a low traction coefficient save energy in gears and rolling contact bearings [5].

Laboratory and field tests have shown that oils with low traction coefficients, like polyalphaolefins and polyglycols, can save up to 20% of the inefficiencies in worm gear units operating under heavy loads.

Another advantage of polyalphaolefins of measureable benefit is their inherent oxidation stability.

Figure 4 illustrates the oxidation stability of an SHF and a mineral oil distillate stock and their responses to oxidation inhibitor additives. In this test, air is bubbled through the lubricant in a glass tube at 162.8°C in the presence of iron, copper lead, and aluminum catalysts. Increased viscosity is recorded as a function of time throughout the test. As shown, the viscosity of the SHF remained relatively unchanged after 80 h whereas the mineral oil viscosity began to increase significantly after 20 h, indicating that oxidation was taking place.

TABLE 2 Synthesized Hydrocarbon Physical Properties

	SHF	Mineral Oil
Viscosity, cST:		
at 100°C	5.7	5.2
at 40°C	29.0	29.5
at −17.8°C	1010	[a]
at −40°C	7790	[a]
Viscosity index	140	102
Pour point, °C	−54	+20
Flash point, °C	235	218
Distillation,		
% overhead at 400°C	2	20

[a]Too viscous to measure.

Polyglycols

Polyalkylene glycols, commonly known as polyglycols, are one of the oldest of the commercially used synthetic lubricants. Even though they were developed in the mid-19th century, they did not become commercially viable until World War II.

Polyglycols are linear polymers synthesized by the addition of an alkylene oxide to a hydroxyl-containing compound. The hydroxyl compound may be water, alcohol, ethylene glycol, propylene glycol, or glycerine. The final fluid viscosity is a function of the molecular weight of the polymer and is controlled by the selection of the chemicals used in the reaction.

Polyglycols can exhibit a variety of desirable lubricant properties, as Table 3 shows. These include excellent lubricity, high flash point and viscosity index, low volatility and pour point, and good thermal stability. However, their incompatibility with mineral oils limits their usefulness in many applications.

They are used to lubricate large high temperature gears and bearings such as those found in the plastic, rubber, and paper industries. They are also used to lubricate hydrocarbon gas compressors due to their insolubility with hydrocarbon gases.

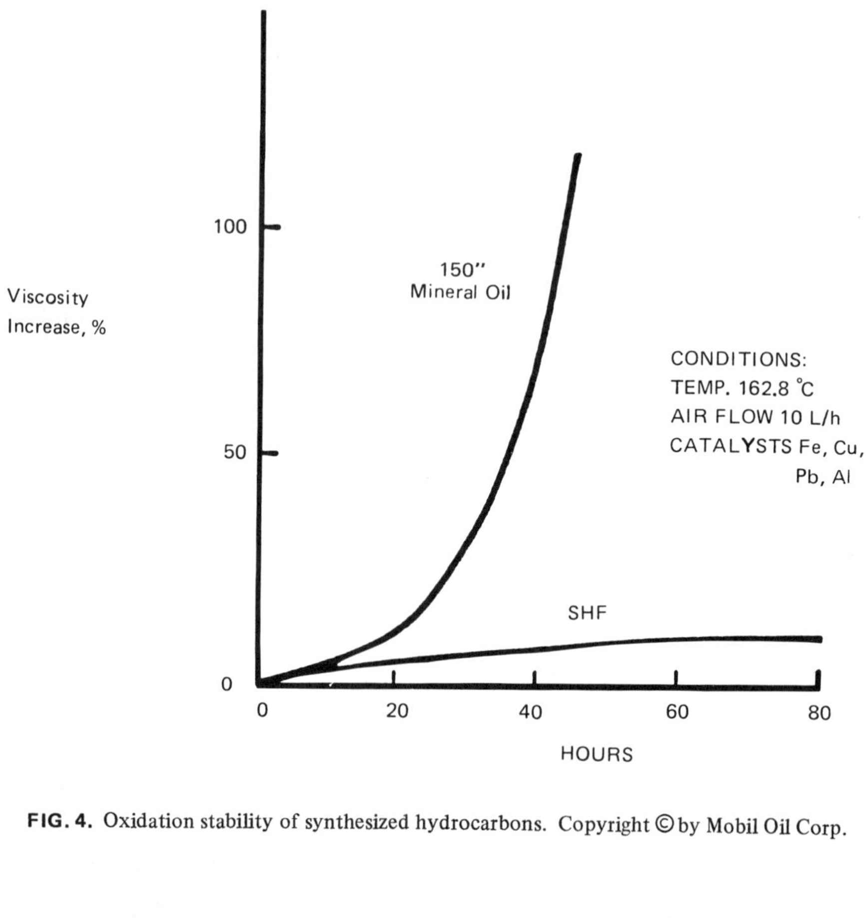

FIG. 4. Oxidation stability of synthesized hydrocarbons. Copyright © by Mobil Oil Corp.

TABLE 3 Properties of Polyglycols

Lubricity	Excellent
Flash point, °C	200 to 280
Viscosity index	150 to 200+
Volatility	Low
Pour point, °C	−23 to −57
Thermal stability	Good
Mineral oil compatibility	Very poor

Organic Esters

Organic esters came into importance as lubricants during World War II. They were first used in Germany in mineral oil blends to improve low temperature properties and to supplement scarce supplies of petroleum. They have been used as jet engine lubricants since the early 1950s, and they are now the base for essentially all aircraft jet engine oils.

An ester is an organic, oxygen-containing material formed by the reaction of an alcohol and an organic acid. Esters used in lubricants have excellent physical properties compared with an SAE 10 weight grade mineral oil (Table 4). The ester and the mineral oil have similar viscosities at 100°C. The ester, however, has a very low pour point because it contains no wax, so it retains its fluidity at much lower temperatures. It has a much higher viscosity index, which is indicative of its excellent viscosity temperature characteristics. The ester also has very low volatility, apparent from the high flash point and low percentage distilled at 400°C. It readily dissolves most additives and helps retain deposit precursors in solution. This solvency property renders ester-based lubricants unsuitable for use with various compounds commonly found in paints and elastomers.

TABLE 4 Organic Ester Physical Properties

	Ester	Mineral Oil
Viscosity, cST:		
at 100°C	4.6	5.2
at 40°C	21.0	29.5
at −17.8°C	474	[a]
at −40°C	5465	[a]
Viscosity index	140	102
Pour point, °C	−57	+20
Flash point, °C	243	218
Distillation, % overhead at 400°C	3	20

[a]Too viscous to measure.

TABLE 5 Organic Ester Compatibility Guide Copyright © by Mobil Oil Corp.

Suitable	Marginal	Unsuitable
Elastomers		
Nitrile rubber (Buna-N, NBR), only if nitrile exceeds 36%	Nitrile rubber (Buna-N, NBR), with nitrile content 30–36%	Nitrile rubber (Buna-N, NBR), with nitrile content below 30%
Fluorilicone rubber	Polyurethane	Natural rubber
Polysulfide (Thiokol)	Ethyl propylene terpolymer	Styrene–butadiene rubber
Fluorocarbon (Viton, Teflon)	Epichlorohydrin	Butyl rubber
	Polyacrylate rubber	Chlorosulfonated polyethylene
	Silicone rubber	Neoprene
Paints		
Epoxy	Alkyds	Acrylic
Baked phenolic	Phenolic	Latex (household)
Two-component urethane	Single-component urethane	Vinyl
Moisture-cured urethane	Industrial latex	Varnish
		Lacquer
Plastics		
Nylon	Polyurethane	Polystyrene
Fluorocarbon (PVC)	Polyethylene	Polyvinyl chloride
Polyacetal (Delrin, acrylonitrite-butadiene, Celcon)	Polypropylene	
		Styrene (ABS)
	Polycarbonate (Lexan)	
	Acrylic (Lucite, Plexiglas)	
	Polysulfone	
	Phenylene oxide (Noryl)	
Metals		
Steel and alloys	Cadmium	Lead
Aluminum and alloys	Zinc	
Copper and alloys	Magnesium	
Nickel and alloys		
Titanium		
Silver		
Chromium		
Tin		

Table 5 summarizes the precautions that should be observed in the selection of seals, finishes, and structural materials used in the presence of lubricants made from organic esters.

Phosphate Esters

Three types of phosphate esters are used as lubricants: triaryl phosphate ester, trialkyl phosphate ester, and mixed alkylaryl phosphate ester.

The triaryl phosphate esters are commercially used today as fire-resistance hydraulic fluids, in turbines (for governor control purposes), and in a wide variety of other fire-prone applications.

These esters are produced by catalyzed reactions of phenols with phosphoroxytrichloride at 150–200°C. Hydrogen chloride is removed by blowing with an inert gas or by chemical means. The crude phosphate ester is distilled to remove cresylic acid, washed with aqueous alkali and with water, and then dehydrated under vacuum. Filtration completes the process.

Phosphate esters are flammable. They will burn if the source of energy is sufficiently great and the conditions are favorable. The oxidation stability of phosphate esters, in general, is fair to good and can be improved with antioxidant additives. Hydrolytic stability is only fair. In hydraulic equipment, phosphate esters not only act as the fluid power medium, they also provide wear protection in pumps and valves.

As in the case with all esters, the phosphate esters are powerful solvents for certain elastomers. It is therefore essential that suitable materials be used for seals and hoses. Some elastomers that can be used with these fluids are butyl rubber, silicone rubber, ethylene propylene rubber, polytetrafluorethylene, and fluorocarbon rubber.

Selection and Application of Synthetics

Generally, all lubricants are called upon to reduce friction, temperature, and wear, to control corrosion, and to remove contaminants. In addition, lubricants perform specialized functions such as to transmit power, as in hydraulics, and as seals, as with grease.

Synthetic lubricants can be justified when one or more of the above functions is no longer performed suitably by mineral oils. For example, operating temperatures are either too high or too low and the conventional lubricant will not flow (cold) or will deteriorate (hot). The low temperature fluidity and/or high temperature stability of synthetic lubricants will have cost justification in these instances.

Major applications of synthetic fluids in today's environment are as follows:

Polyalphaolefins: Engine, gear, turbine and compressor oils, greases, hydraulic and power steering fluids.
Dialkylbenzenes: Engine, gear, turbine and hydraulic oils and greases.
Organic Esters: Engine, gear, turbine, compressor, hydraulic and jet engine oils and greases.
Polyglycols: Fire-resistance fluids, brake fluids, gear oils, circulating oils, gas compressor oils and greases.
Phosphate Esters: Fire-resistant fluids.

Automotive Application

Automotive engine oils are one of the largest potential uses for synthetic fluids. Polyalphaolefins and organic esters are widely employed as base fluids for engine lubricants.

The superior qualities of these synthetics form the basis for these diverse engine lubricants and provide the following benefits:

Fuel savings between 2.8 and 4.3%
Outstanding engine wear protection and cleanliness in both gasoline and diesel passenger car engines
Excellent results in turbocharged passenger car engines
Easier cold starting and faster oil flow to critical parts during start-up
Good engine response and smooth running operation
Provides outstanding engine protection for up to 25,000 miles or 1 year oil changes.

The synthetic oil properties which provide these benefits are:

Very high natural viscosity index (7/50)
Very low pour points, -54°C
Excellent thermal and oxidation stability with additives
Good rust and corrosion protection
High load-carrying capability
Fully compatible with conventional mineral oils

Synthetic engine oils, based on synthesized hydrocarbon technology, are being manufactured to exceed the engine performance requirements of service classification API SF/CD, the European builders CCMC specification, the VW/Audi 500.00 fuel efficient engine oil specification, and the VW/Audi 505.00 turbocharged diesel engine oil specification. They are fully compatible with conventional petroleum-based engine oils and will provided the maximum protection in well-maintained engines. These oils have been fully accepted for all seasons use by all major United States and European vehicle manufacturers.

Industrial Application

Synthetic lubricants have captured about 2% of the worldwide industrial lubricant market. They are available for many different applications in industry:

Extreme-temperature bearing and circulating systems
High-severity gears
High-temperature air compressors

High-pressure hydraulic pumps
Fire-resistant applications
Critical grease-lubricated equipment

Even though synthetic lubricants could be used to lubricate every piece of equipment in industry, their use cannot always be justified economically on either a performance basis or a price-per-gallon basis. Mineral oils should be used to lubricate most plant equipment.

Synthetic lubricants are problem solvers. Applications where synthetics demonstrate significant advantages over mineral oils include:

Where operating temperatures continually exceed 200°F. Synthetic lubricants offer excellent high-temperature oxidation and thermal stability that reduce the formation of deposits.

Where ambient temperatures are below 0°F (low temperature fluidity is required). The excellent low-temperature characteristics of synthetics improve cold weather flow properties. They exhibit a relatively small change in viscosity over a wide range of operating temperatures to allow the use of lower viscosity oils for improved mechanical efficiencies.

Overloaded equipment. The low-traction coefficient of synthetics reduces energy requirements and increases operating efficiency.

Low bulk oil temperatures, high bearing temperatures. The excellent viscosity/temperature properties and shear stability of synthetics provide improved protection against wear.

Long service life. Synthetics offer three to five times longer oil life than the best mineral oils, and their low volatility reduces consumption in applications subject to high temperatures.

Greases

Research in the 1930s and 1940s revealed that certain ester-based greases far outperformed mineral oil-based greases in low temperature properties, lubricity, and evaporation rate. Not much was done with these greases until the late 1960s when a synthetic grease, Mil-G-81322A, based on a polyalphaolefin thickened with colloidal clay, was developed. Because of its exceptional multiservice capability, this synthesized hydrocarbon (polyalphaolefin) grease has a wide range of applications in air transport equipment, including landing wheel assemblies, control systems and actuators, screwjacks, sealed bearing motors, oscillating bearings, variable pitch propellers and helicopter rotor bearings, etc.

There are a number of other types of synthetic greases currently in use, including ester-based, silicone-based, and perfluoroalkyl ester-based. The ester-based greases are used in ball, roller, and needle bearings, gears, and on sliding and rolling surfaces of equipment, such as instruments, cameras, and aircraft control systems. Silicone greases are used primarily in lightly loaded rolling element bearings and cover wide temperature ranges.

Polytetrafluorethylene-thickened perfluoroalkyl ether greases are used in aerospace rolling element bearings and other applications where fuel, oil, and liquid oxygen resistance is needed and where low volatility and high temperature stability are primary considerations.

Miscellaneous Comments on Synthetics

Compatibility

Are synthetic lubricants compatible with conventional mineral oils? The manufacturer should always be consulted for assurance in this regard.

Disposal

Depending upon the chemistry of the fluid, there could be disposal questions and these should, likewise, always be addressed to the supplier.

Conclusion

Currently, synthetic lubricants serve many important application needs. The use of these superior lubricants will grow to conserve energy and meet the requirements of higher temperature and stress experienced in modern machinery. Synthetic lubricants solve application problems at both high and low temperature extremes. They can be justified by lasting longer and protecting parts from early failure.

Design and plant lubrication engineers are continually searching for better products to permit machinery to operate more efficiently and trouble-free. As more experience is gained throughout industry, there is every reason to believe that the use of synthetics will grow vigorously over time. Should more information be desired on synthetic lubricants, see Ref. 5.

References

1. E. L. Armstrong and D. S. Taber, *Synthesized Hydrocarbon Lubricant Review*, Presented to the Synthetic Lubricants Session, American Chemical Society National Meeting, Atlantic City, New Jersey, September 12, 1974.
2. G. R. Jordan, *Electric Bills and the Traction Fraction (Synthetic vs Mineral Lubricants)*, Presented to the American Society of Lubrication Engineers 37th Annual Meeting, Cincinnati, Ohio, May 10–13, 1982.
3. L. W. Manley and R. M. Jublot, *New Developments in Synthetic Lubricants*, Presented to the Tenth World Petroleum Congress, Bucharest, Romania, September 9–14, 1979.
4. L. E. Tedrow, *Synthetic Lubricants—Their Use and Performance in the Pulp and Paper Industry*, Presented to the Technical Association for Pulp and Paper Industry 1985 Engineering Conference, Atlanta, Georgia, September 16–19, 1985.
5. *Mobil Synthetic Lubricants*, Mobil Oil Corp., 1985.

L. E. TEDROW

Lubricating Oils: Significance of Tests

Since prehistoric times man has recognized the existence of friction, even though he couldn't put it in analytical terms. But he found that mud made dragging skids easier and that animal fat on axles made wheels turn more easily. Over the years other natural lubricants, such as vegetable oils and sperm oils, were found to be useful in reducing friction. These lubricants, while still useful, are not adequate for our industrialized society, either in volume or in desirable properties. The major quantities of lubricants base stocks are now "mineral" oils produced from petroleum crude oil. Used in lesser amounts are vegetable and animal oils and synthetic base stocks.

The primary function of lubricating oils is to impose a slippery, protective film between moving parts. This film, which separates the moving parts from direct contact, reduces friction and wear. There are a number of other functions, some of which are related to the type of equipment being lubricated and some of which are common to all applications. These functions include removal of heat from the system, prevention of rust and corrosion, prevention of excessive deposits, dispersion and removal of contaminants produced in the system, water separation, prevention of emulsification, maintenance of sealing where it is critical, and resistance to degradation by molecular shear, heat, oxidation, and other chemical reactions.

Animal or Vegetable Oils

Historically, animal and vegetable oils provided the first widely used lubricating oils. The term "oil" is probably derived from "olea," the olive. These oils were produced by rendering animal fats and by extracting the oils from vegetable seeds. They are, however, subject to oxidation and are thus somewhat unstable. This plus higher cost led to the use of petroleum mineral oils for lubricant base stocks. They are still used as compounding agents which enhance the lubrication properties of some petroleum-based lubricants. The article on *Fats and Fatty Acids* in Volume 21 of this *Encyclopedia* provides additional information on the manufacture and use of these materials.

Synthetic Lubricating Oils

Synthetic lubricating oils are relatively pure compounds made by chemical synthesis, most often from petroleum-based hydrocarbons. While the use of synthetic lubricants as motor oils in the retail market is fairly new, synthetics have been used for many years in special aviation and industrial applications where the oils are subjected to extremely high temperatures or a flammable environment. Mineral oils would not be suitable for these applications. Synthetic lubricants are generally much more costly than mineral lubricating oils. The base fluids can be classified as follows:

1. Synthesized hydrocarbon fluids (SHF)
   a. Olefin oligomers
   b. Alkylated aromatics
   c. Polybutene
   d. Cycloaliphatics
2. Esters
   a. Dibasic acid esters
   b. Polyol esters
   c. Phosphate esters
   d. Silicate esters
3. Ethers
   a. Polyethylene glycol ether
   c. Polyphenyl ethers
4. Other
   a. Silicones
   b. Halogenated fluids

Primary applications for synthetic lubricants are listed in Table 1. Additional information on synthetic lubricants is to be found in the article entitled *Lubricating Oils, Synthetic*.

Mineral Lubricating Oils

The low cost and available large volume of mineral oils (generally called "lubricating oils") derived from petroleum crude oil makes them the most widely used of all lubricants. The lubricating oil base stocks contain a mixture of the many different hydrocarbons naturally present in crude oil. These base

TABLE 1 Primary Applications for Synthetic Lubricants

Field of Service	Synthetic Fluids Used
Industrial:	
Circulating oils	Polyglycol, SHF, organic ester
Gear lubricants	Polyglycol, SHF
Hydraulic fluid (fire resistant)	Phosphate ester, polyglycol
Compressor oils	Polyglycol, organic ester, SHF
Gas turbine oils	Organic ester, SHF
Greases	SHF
Automotive:	
Passenger car engine oil	SHF, organic ester
Commercial engine oil	SHF, organic ester
Gear lubricant	SHF
Brake fluids	Polyglycols
Aviation:	
Gas turbines	Organic ester
Hydraulic fluids	Phosphate ester
Greases	Silicones, organic ester, SHF

stocks can be placed into three general classes: (1) Paraffinic, having a high viscosity index (90–100) with a pour point of 0 to 20°F; (2) Naphthenic, with a low viscosity index (0–40) and a low pour point of –50 to –20°F; and (3) Lube base stocks having an intermediate viscosity index prepared from paraffinic–naphthenic mixed base crude oils with inherent qualities between the two extremes of paraffinic and naphthenic crudes.

Petroleum crude oils have an infinite variation in their compositions. No two crudes are alike. In fact, crudes produced from adjacent wells are frequently dissimilar as are crudes produced from different zones in the same field. In the early days of the petroleum industry, crude fractions of appropriate gravity and viscosity were obtainable only from Pennsylvania grade crudes. Only these were considered to be suitable for use in automobile engines and other machines operating at high speed. This crude required only dewaxing and acid or clay treatment to produce suitable base stocks with a viscosity index (VI) of about 95 and a pour point of 0 to 10°F. Subsequently, several other crudes were discovered with similar properties and which required a minimum of processing. These crudes are very paraffinic. The virgin lube distillate fractions from other grades of crude generally contain more aromatics and naphthenes, and thus have an inherently lower viscosity index which detracted from their use as lube base stocks. As the demand for lubricating oils increased, petroleum refiners developed many chemical treating and solvent extraction processes which would upgrade many of these less desirable crude fractions into suitable lube oils. Refiners have more recently developed hydrogenation processes which are being used in place of or to supplement the chemical and extraction processes. Hydrogen refining (sometimes called hydrotreating or hydrocracking) processes are of particular interest because they can be used to upgrade the lube fractions from less desirable crude oils. In fact, high quality lubricating oils now can be produced from almost any but not all crude oil by a combination of hydrogenation and solvent extraction or by hydrogenation alone. Various combinations of these processes are also used to make naphthenic and specialty oils such as refrigeration, transformer, and white oils. Additional information on lubricating manufacturing processes can be found in the preceding article.

Types of Lubricants

There are many different types of lubricants. Following is a partial list. As discussed later, the properties of each lubricant are designed to meet the needs of each service.

1. Automotive and aviation lubricants
   a. Crankcase oils—Passenger cars and light trucks
   b. Crankcase oils—Heavy duty service
   c. Crankcase oils—Two-stroke cycle engines
   d. Crankcase oils—Aircraft
   e. Automatic transmission fluids
   f. Torque fluids

   g. Power steering fluid
   h. Automotive gear oils
   i. Hydraulic fluid
   j. Shock absorber fluid
   k. Greases
2. Railroad lubricants
   a. Diesel engine oils
   b. Gas engine lubricants
   c. Journal oils
   d. Greases
3. Marine lubricants
   a. Marine diesel oils
   b. Steam turbine oils
   c. Reciprocating steam engine lubricants
   d. Hydraulic oils
   e. Refrigerator oils
   f. Gear oils
   g. Greases
4. Industrial products
   a. Turbine oils
   b. Circulating oils
   c. Hydraulic oils
   d. Air compressor oils
   e. Refrigeration oils
   f. Cylinder oils
   g. Gas engine oils
   h. Paraffinic mineral oils
   i. Naphthenic mineral oils
   j. Textile oils
   k. Rock drill oils
   l. Transformer oils and other electrical insulation oils
   m. Paper machine oils
   n. Gear oils
   o. Process oils
   p. Spray oils
   q. Heat transfer oil
   r. Roll oils
   s. Cutting oils
   t. Soluble oils
   u. Way lubricants
   v. Metal working fluids
   w. Quenching oils
   x. Rust proofing oils

Properties and Tests

Within the content of this publication it is not possible to include all the properties of all the lubricants listed previously and to discuss all the tests required to define the properties. The principle properties and tests are discussed in a little detail. If the reader wants more detail he should go to lubricant handbooks published by most lubricant manufacturers or to books, such as *Lubrication Fundamentals* by J. G. Wills (Dekker) and *Lubricants and Related Products* by D. Klamann.

Aniline Point

The aniline point determination measures the solvent power of a petroleum product. It is measured as the temperature at which solvency is complete. Solvency is increased as temperature is increased. Paraffinic hydrocarbons have the least solvency for aniline (and therefore, the highest aniline point temperature), and aromatics have the highest solvency (thus, lowest aniline point). Naphthenic oils are intermediate. For a lubricating oil or hydraulic oil, the aniline point is an indication of its tendency to cause swelling of rubber parts, such as seals, that are contacted by the oil. The lower the aniline point, the greater the swelling tendency. Therefore, for automotive lubricants a high aniline point (low aromatics content) is desirable. With certain other oils, such as spray oils, cleaning solvents, ink oils, and thinners, a higher degree of solvency, and thus a lower aniline point, is required.

Ash and Sulfated Ash

The ash content of a lubricating oil is related to the quantity of incombustible materials present. These materials are, for the most part, derived from the metallic additives present in the oil. In used oils it is also an indication of the dirt and wear metals with which the oil has become contaminated. For new oils of unknown formulation, ash has been used as an indicator of detergent level. However, with the current trend toward ashless detergents, this test is of somewhat dubious value.

Color, ASTM D1500

The color of the oil is normally no indication of its lubricating properties. It is, however, a guide to the presence of contaminants or to the degree of deterioration in storage. It is also an indication of the intensity of refining. Absence of color (water white) is important in certain applications such as in textile machinery lubrication to avoid indelible staining of the textile. Absence of color is also important to users of waxes, petrolatums, and white oils where extremely high purity is required.

Copper Strip Corrosion

Industrial equipment commonly has parts that are made of copper or alloys of copper. It is essential that any oil in contact with these parts be noncorrosive to them. Straight mineral oil of high quality is essentially free of corrosive materials. However, certain oils contain extreme pressure (EP) agents that might be corrosive to copper. For these applications, such as automotive hypoid rear axles, care is taken to have no copper parts present.

Demulsibility

Emulsions of water–oil mixtures are related to the composition of the oil, the presence of contaminants or added ingredients, and to the degree of agitation of the mixture. A highly refined mineral oil resists emulsification. After agitation the water and oil break quickly into separate phases.

Depending upon the use of the lubricant and some fire-resistant hydraulic fluids, the tendency to form emulsions can be either good or undersirable. For example, soluble cutting fluids require good emulsibility and have special emulsifying agents added to them to promote this property. On the other hand, crankcase oils and turbine oils require good demulsibility. Crankcase oils are exposed to water from the atmosphere and to water from the combustion of hydrocarbons. A portion of this water can condense and form an emulsion. With turbine oils there is exposure to condensing steam, which can also form an emulsion. The water in these emulsions promotes rusting of ferrous parts and accelerate oxidation of the oil.

Dielectric Strength

Many types of electrical apparatus, such as transformers and high-voltage switchgear, are filled with lubricating oils having a high resistance to electrical conductivity. The dielectric strength is a measure of the insulating ability of the oil. Very small amounts of contaminants, such as water, dust, metal soaps, and organic acids, destroy the insulating properties. New highly refined oils with low water content are nonconductors. In service, however, the oil eventually becomes contaminated. Water, condensed from atmospheric moisture, is the principal offender. A small amount of dissolved water (maximum of 35 ppm) can be tolerated, but free water has a pronounced effect. The presence of solid particles, which provide a nuclei about which water droplets form, tends to keep the water dispersed in the oil. Products of oxidation also impair the insulating capability of the oil.

A drop in the dielectric strength is an indication of the deterioration of oil in service. This test is therefore used to evaluate used oils. If the drop in dielectric strength is due to water, the oil can generally be reclaimed by drying. However, if it is due to oxidation, the oil may have deteriorated beyond a safe limit. In order to evaluate the oil for continued service, the dielectric strength test is supplemented with tests for power factor, neutralization number, and interfacial tension.

Flash and Fire Points

The flash and fire points are measurements of the flammability of a petroleum product. The flash point is the temperature at which enough vapor is produced to be burned in an instantaneous flash when exposed to a source of ignition. The fire point is the temperature at which combustion will be sustained when exposed to a source of ignition. The fire point temperature is, of course, higher than the flash point temperature, usually about 50°F.

Normally, these tests are used to determine the storage and operating temperatures and the type of storage that will preclude the possibility of a fire.

Flash and fire points are also useful in evaluating used oils. A drop in flash or fire point indicates contamination by dilution of motor oils with unburned fuel. An increase indicates evaporation of the oil. These tests of lubricating oils are determined by the open-cup method, usually called Cleveland Open Cup, and abbreviated COC. Normally, only the flash point is specified on new oils.

Gravity

Gravity is an expression of the weight of a given volume of product. It can be expressed as specific gravity, density, or API. Specific gravity is defined as the ratio of the mass (weight) of a given volume of product to the mass of an equal volume of water, usually at 60°F for each. The density is the absolute value and can be expressed as lb/gal or lb/ft^3 in English units or as kg/m^3 in the SI system of units.

In the petroleum industry the API gravity scale is almost universally used as the measure of the density of a petroleum product. API gravity is an arbitrary scale, calibrated in degrees and related to the specific gravity by

$$\text{API gravity (degrees)} = \frac{141.5}{\text{specific gravity at } 60/60°\text{F}} - 131.5$$

The higher the specific gravity or density, the lower the API gravity. Water, by definition, has an API gravity of 10°.

Interfacial Tension

The interfacial tension (IFT) test measures the tension at the interface of two immiscible liquids, oil and water. At the interface each liquid exerts its own surface tension so that for a new oil of known quality a definite interfacial tension exists with water. Contaminants, and particularly oxidation products, reduce the interfacial tension. The test is used to check the quality in prolonged service of transformer oils, turbine oils, and paper-machine oils.

Load-Carrying Ability

Lubricants must be capable of maintaining a film that prevents metal-to-metal contact. Otherwise, scoring of the surfaces and possible failure of the parts will result. For machine parts that encounter high unit loadings, special extreme pressure (EP) lubricants are required.

In an attempt to approximate field conditions a lubricant will encounter, several laboratory machines and test procedures have been developed. Widely used tests are the Timken machine, the FZG test, the 4-Ball EP test, and the 4-Ball friction and wear test. In all of these tests, the loads are gradually increased and the pressures determined at which scoring, failure of parts, seizing, and welding take place.

Neutralization Number

The neutralization number measures the organic acid content of base oils and the acids produced by oxidation in storage or service. The acid numbers are expressed in milligrams of potassium hydroxide (KOH) needed to "neutralize" a gram of sample. The neutralization number is important in oils of critical service, such as turbine oils and insulating oils. With new oils it is a check on the consistency of product quality. With used oils, neutralization test results serve as a guide to mechanical condition, change in operating conditions, or product deterioration due to oxidation.

Oxidation Stability

All petroleum products are subject to chemical attack by oxygen. It is promoted by high temperatures, catalysts, and the presence of water or acids. Oil oxidation results in two general classes of degradation products:

1. Oil-insoluble materials, i.e., resins, varnish, or sludge
2. Oil-soluble products, primarily acids and peroxides

Resistance to oxidation is important in the performance of a lubricant. Acids formed may be corrosive to metals. Varnish may deposit on sliding surfaces, causing them to stick or wear. Sludge may plug screens or passages or the rings on cylinders, causing them to be ineffective. Resistance to oxidation is highly important for a steam-turbine oil because of the serious consequences of a bearing failure. Transformer oils, gear oils, hydraulic fluids, heat transfer oils, and crankcase oils also require a high degree of oxidation stability to ensure a satisfactory service life.

There are several accelerated tests which are designed to correlate with field performance.

Pour and Cloud Points

As a lubricating oil is chilled, it eventually reaches a point where it will no longer flow under the influence of gravity. This condition is brought about either by the thickening (more viscous) that always accompanies a reduction in temperature or by crystallization of wax dissolved in the oil, restricting the flow of the liquid portion. The lowest temperature to which an oil can be chilled and still be poured from a container is called the "pour point."

When certain oils are chilled, the dissolved waxes precipitate as tiny wax crystals. This crystal formation gives the oil a cloudy appearance. The temperature at which this cloud becomes noticeable is called the "cloud point."

The pour point is related to the ability of the oil to start lubricating when a cold machine is placed into operation. Engines that are stopped and started under low-temperature conditions require an oil that will flow readily when cold.

Waxy crystals that form at the cloud point could plug the wick through which oil feeds some lubricating devices or it could accumulate and plug circulating oil systems that operate below the cloud point but above the pour point. In general, however, pour point is a much more significant specification than cloud point.

Viscosity

Viscosity is the most significant property of a lubricating oil. The primary purpose of a lubricant is to reduce friction and minimize wear by separating lubricated surfaces with an oil film. At the same time it is desired not to impose unnecessary energy-consuming viscous drag.

Viscosity is a measure of resistance to flow. It decreases with increasing temperature and increases with large increasing pressure.

There are two measures of viscosity: kinematic and absolute. Kinematic viscosity is the more common and is measured by the time for an oil at a specified temperature to flow through a capillary tube. Absolute (dynamic) viscosity is a measure of the tangential forces needed to shear one parallel plane of fluid over another parallel plane of fluid. It is measured with a rotating viscometer.

The units of viscosity are centipoise (cP) and centistoke (cSt). The absolute viscosity in centipoises at any given temperature is equal to the kinematic viscosity in centistokes times the specific gravity at the same temperature. The SI unit corresponding and numerically equal to the centipoise is the millipascal second (mPa · s), and the SI unit numerically equal to the centistoke is square millimeters per second (mm^2/s). Another expression of viscosity is Saybolt Universal seconds (SUS) which may be measured directly but is usually converted from centistokes.

Test temperatures are usually 40 and 100°C for centistokes and 100 and 212°F for Saybolt Universal Seconds.

Lubricants that can operate at low temperature conditions, such as hydraulic oils, automatic transmission fluids, and gear oils, may be measured in the 0 to –40°C range.

Viscosity is usually the primary consideration for the selection of a lubricating oil for a specific application. In order to provide the most effective lubrication, the viscosity must conform to the speed, load, and temperature conditions of the parts to be lubricated.

Systems with higher speeds, lower temperatures, or lower pressures require an oil of lower viscosity because a higher viscosity oil introduces excessive fluid friction and unnecessary drag.

Lower speeds, higher temperatures, and higher pressure require a higher viscosity oil. An oil that is too low in viscosity lacks the film strength necessary to support the load and to provide adequate lubrication of the wearing surfaces.

Viscosity Index

All lubricating oils thin out or have lower viscosity as the temperature is increased. Likewise, oils become thicker or more viscous as the temperature is reduced. However, not all oils respond to the same degree to temperature changes. The relationship of the viscosity at a low temperature to the viscosity at a higher temperature is called the viscosity index (VI). Oils having a high VI change less with temperature than do oils with a lower VI.

Lubricating oils are subjected to wide variations of temperatures in service. At high temperatures the viscosity can drop to a point where the oil is so thin that the oil film is broken, allowing metal surfaces to touch, resulting in excessive wear. At the other extreme, the temperature can be so low that the oil becomes viscous and does not allow proper circulation to the parts being lubricated.

Take an automobile, for example. During startup the oil can be quite cold, particularly during winter. But the oil must not be so viscous that the drag on the engine makes starting difficult. During warm-up the oil must be able to flow to all the moving parts. Finally, after the engine has reached its normal operating temperature, the oil must not be so thin that oil consumption is high or the lubricating film can no longer carry the load. Most motor oils have a viscosity index of 100 or higher. Where temperature variations are less or for continuous operation at constant temperature, viscosity index is less critical.

Automotive Lubricants

Classifications of Engine Oils

Engine oil quality is defined by performance in laboratory or full-scale engines as well as in laboratory tests, all designed to represent the performance of the oil in actual field service. The two most widely accepted systems of engine oil classification are:

1. The SAE (Society of Automotive Engineers) Viscosity Classification System which classifies oils according to their viscosity at 100 and −18°C. The high temperature viscosity relates to oil consumption and wear; the low temperature viscosity to cold-starting performance. Oils with a high viscosity index are better able to perform efficiently at both high and low temperatures.
2. The API (American Petroleum Institute) Engine Service Classification System which rates oils based upon their performance in critical engines operating under carefully controlled conditions designed to simulate severe service in the field.

TABLE 2 Engine Oil Viscosity Classification, SAE J300d

SAE Viscosity Grade	Viscosity Range		
	Centipoise (cP) at −18°C (ASTM D2602), Maximum	Centistokes (cSt) at 100°C (ASTM D445)	
		Minimum	Maximum
5W	1,250	3.8	
10W	2,500	4.1	
20W	10,000	5.6	
20		5.6	Less than 9.3
30		9.3	Less than 12.5
40		12.5	Less than 16.3
50		16.3	Less than 21.9

SAE Viscosity Classification

The ranges for viscosity grades are shown in Table 2. In these classifications, grades with the suffix W are intended primarily for use where low ambient temperatures will be encountered whereas grades without the suffix letter are intended for use where the lowest ambient temperature encountered will not be critical with respect to oil viscosity.

Oils can be formulated that will meet the −18°C and 0°F limits of one of the W grades as well as the 100°C or 212°F limits for the non-W grades. For example, an oil can be formulated to meet the −18°C limits for the 10W grade and the 100°C limits for 40 grades. It can then be designated as SAE 10W-40 grade and is referred to as a multigrade or multiviscosity oil. Oils of this type generally require the addition of VI improvers to the petroleum or synthetic lubricating oil base stock.

This SAE system is used by automobile manufactures to designate suitable oil viscosities for their engines and by oil marketers to label their various grades.

SAE Service Classifications

A large number of engine tests are used for evaluating the performance of engine oils. These involve a variety of engine types, both laboratory and full-scale engines. The oils are usually further evaluated in fleet tests in actual service. For an engine oil intended to be used for a specific service to be sold, it must pass all the appropriate tests. These tests can be conveniently grouped into six catagories:

1. Tests for oxidation stability and bearing corrosion protection
2. Single cylinder high temperature tests
3. Multicylinder high temperature tests
4. Low operating temperature tests
5. Rust and corrosion protection tests
6. Preignition tests

ASTM Sequence Engine Tests

The tests through which the engine oil go are called "ASTM Sequences," namely, Sequences IID, IIID, and VD. Sequence IID is primarily a rust test for military specifications MIL-L-46152 and MIL-L-2104C and for SF oils. Sequence IIID is chiefly concerned with oil thickening (viscosity increase) under very hot engine conditions but it also evaluates valve-train wear plus ring and lifter sticking for MIL-L-46152 and SF oils. Sequence VD test evaluates low-temperature sludge and varnish control, plus intake-valve tip wear.

API Engine Service Classifications

After going through the tests, the oils are classified as being suitable for specified services:

SB for Minimum Duty Gasoline Engine Service. Service typical of older gasoline engines operated under such mild conditions that only minimum protection is afforded. Oils designed for this service provide only antiscuff capability and resistance to oil oxidation and bearing corrosion. They should not be used in any engine unless specifically recommended by the engine manufacturer.

SD for 1968 Gasoline Engine Warranty Maintenance Service. Service typical of engines in 1968 through 1970 models of passenger cars. It may also include some 1971 or later models as specified in the owners manuals. These oils provide more protection against high- and low-temperature engine deposits, wear, rust, and corrosion than oils designed to meet SC classification.

SE for 1972 Gasoline Engine Warranty Maintenance Service. Service typical of gasoline engines in passenger cars and some trucks beginning with 1972 models and continuing through 1979. Oils designed for this service provide more protection against oil oxidation, high-temperature engine deposits, rust, and corrosion than oils designed to meet the Engine Service Classifications SC and SD and may be used when either of these classifications is recommended.

SF for 1980 Gasoline Engine Warranty Maintenance Service. Service typical of gasoline engines in passenger cars and some trucks beginning with the 1980 models operating under operating procedures recommended by engine manufacturers. Oils developed for this service provide increased oxidation stability and improved antiwear performance relative to oils meeting minimum requirements for API Service Category SE. The oils also provide protection against engine deposits, rust, and corrosion. Oils meeting API Service Classification SF may be used where service categories SC, SD, and SE are recommended.

CA for Diesel Engine Service. Service typical of diesel engines operated in mild to moderate duty. Oils designed for this service provide protection from bearing corrosion and from ring belt deposits in some naturally aspirated diesel engines. This classification was used in the 1950s but

TABLE 3 Typical Inspections of Different Grades of Crankcase Oils

Physical Properties	Viscosity, cSt, 40°C	Viscosity, cSt, 100°C	Viscosity, SUS, 100°F	Viscosity, SUS, 210°F	VI	Pour (°F)	Flash, COC (°F)
SAE SW-30	55.8	9.5			155	−37	430
SAE 10W-30	61.9	9.6	334	60	137	−32	440
SAE 10W-40	96.7	14.4	494	76	154	−32	430
SAE 10W	37.1	6.1	191	46.5	108	−27	405
SAE 20W	68.8	9.0	352	56.5	104	−17	440
SAE 30	111.0	12.1	580	68.0	98	−6	450
SAE 40	114.8	14.5	760	77.5	98	0	470
SAE 50	210.7	18.6	1112	95.0	98	+10	480

should not be used in any engine unless specifically recommended by the equipment manufacturer.

CB for Diesel Engine Service. Service typical of diesel engines operated in mild to moderate duty with lower quality fuels which necessitate more protection from wear and deposits. Oils designed for this service provide necessary protection from bearing corrosion and from ring belt deposits in some naturally aspirated diesel engines with higher sulfur content fuels. Introduced in 1949.

CC for Diesel Engine Service. Service typical of certain naturally aspirated, turbocharged, or supercharged diesel engines operated in moderate to severe service and certain heavy-duty gasoline engines. Oils with this classification provide protection from high-temperature deposits and bearing corrosion in diesel engines and from rust, corrosion, and low-temperature deposits in gasoline engines. These oils were introduced in 1961.

CD for Diesel Engine Service. Service typical of certain naturally aspirated, turbocharged, or supercharged diesel engines where highly effective control of wear and deposits is vital, or when using fuels of a wide quality range including high sulfur fuels. Oils designed for this service were introduced in 1955 and provide protection from bearing corrosion and from high-temperature deposits in these diesel engines.

The API Engine Service Classification is an open-ended system which permits addition, as needed, of new categories without changing or deleting existing categories.

Table 3 presents typical inspections of the various grades of automotive crankcase oils.

Two-Stroke Cycle Engine Oil

Two-cycle engine oil is a high quality oil that is mixed with gasoline fuel. It is sometimes solvent diluted for easy mixing with the gasoline, even at low temperatures. As with other crankcase oils, it is designed to provide reduced spark plug fouling and surface ignition, protection against rust, wear, corrosion, exhaust port plugging, and ring sticking. It passes tests prescribed by the National Marine Manufacturers' Association (NMMA). This oil is for two-cycle engines such as those used in some small passenger cars, scooters, lawn mowers, small tractors, chain saws, and many two-wheeled vehicles.

Aircraft Reciprocating Engine Oil

Aircraft engine oils are formulated from highly refined mineral base stocks to which are blended ashless dispersant additives. Some grades of aircraft engine oils are straight mineral oil with no additives; these oils are generally used as break-in oil for new or rebuilt engines.

The viscosities of aircraft engine oils may be designated by SAE viscosity grade or by a grade number which is approximately the viscosity in SUS at 212°F for the base oil.

Various specifications for aircraft engine oils are given in Table 4. It will be noted that the United Kingdom grade designations for ashless dispersant oils are one grade lower than the common grade designation. The dispersant thickens the oil so that one grade lower in the base oil is required to make a designated finished oil. For example, a 100-grade base oil makes a 120-grade finished oil.

Automatic Transmission Fluids (ATF) and Torque Converter Fluids

Automatic transmission fluids are made of low viscosity (10W), highly refined base oils blended with specially balanced additive combinations. These products have high temperature oxidation resistance, dispersency and detergency, anticorrosion and rust protection, and compatibility with transmission parts such as elastomeric seals and plastics. They have a very high viscosity index so that they can be used over a wide temperature range.

TABLE 4 Specifications for Aircraft Engine Oils

Common Grade Designation	Approximate SAE Grade	U.S. Specifications		U.K. Specifications	
		Straight Mineral MIL-L-6082	Dispersant MIL-L-22851	Straight Mineral DERD 2472	Dispersant DERD 2540
65	30	1065	None	None	None
80	40	None	Type III(a)	A/O	D65
100	50	1100	None	B/O	D80
120	60	None	Type II(a)	None	D100

Currently, automatic transmission fluids are manufactured to meet specifications developed by equipment manufacturers, mainly General Motors Corporation and Ford Motor Company. The General Motors specification is called Dexron II. The Ford Motor specification, called Type F, is applicable to all Ford models prior to 1977 as well as some of the 1977 through 1980 models. More recently, Dexron II is also recommended for some Ford cars.

The Dexron II and Type F fluids differ chiefly in friction properties, reflecting differences in transmission design and shift feel preferences. Both fluids have similar friction properties at high sliding speeds. However, as sliding speed approaches zero (clutch lockup), General Motors wants a decrease in friction coefficient (more slipperiness) for a smooth, jerk-free shift feel. Ford, on the other hand, uses fewer clutches with a high lockup pressure and desires an increase in friction coefficient at low sliding speeds.

Dexron II and Type F fluids are compatible but mixing them should be avoided since this changes the frictional properties. This could result in poor shifting or, in extreme cases, failure of the transmission.

Only the transmission fluid recommended by the car manufacturer should be used.

Passenger cars that have a common housing for the torque converter and the automatic transmission use automatic transmission fluid for both. However, transit coach drives and some passenger car and construction equipment drives have separate housing. In this case the torque converter fluid is an oxidation inhibited fluid of about 100 SUS (20.5 cSt) at 100°F (38°C).

Automotive Gear Oils

In automotive equipment there are various types of gears to be lubricated in addition to automatic transmissions. These include manual transmissions, gear boxes, differentials, and universal joints. Because of difference in design and in service conditions, there are a number of gear lubricants, each formulated to satisfy a specific requirement.

TABLE 5 SAE J306c Gear Oil Viscosity System

SAE Viscosity Grade	Maximum Temperature for Viscosity of 150,000 cP (°C)	Viscosity at 212°F (100°C) (cSt)	
		Minimum	Maximum
75W	−40	4.1	
80W	−26	7.0	
85W	−12	11.0	
90		13.5	<24.0
140		24.0	<41.0
250		41.0	—

One of the most important characteristics of a gear lubricant is its load-carrying capacity. This is its ability to prevent or minimize wear, scuffing, or scoring of gear-tooth surfaces. Some gears are operated under light loads, in which case an oxygenation-inhibited mineral oil is adequate. But other services, for example trucks, tractors, and earth-moving equipment, operate under such heavy loads that additives are used to provide higher load-carrying capacity. Lubricants of this type are generally referred to as extreme pressure (EP) lubricants. API has prepared five different service classifications which describe the type of lubricant to be used for different service conditions.

The viscosity of a gear lubricant has some effect on load-carrying capacity, leakage, and gear noise. At low temperatures, viscosity determines the ease of gear shifting and has considerable influence of the flow of the lubricant to bearings and to gear-tooth surfaces. SAE viscosity grades are established for gear oils in the same manner used for engine oils. Grades of gear oils that are best suited for cold-weather use are defined by viscosity limits at low temperatures and minimum viscosities at 212°F (100°C). Higher viscosity grades, which are expected to operate at higher temperatures and do not require as good cold-fluidity properties, are defined by viscosity ranges at 212°F (100°C). The SAE J306c Gear Oil Viscosity System is given in Table 5.

In addition to providing the proper lubrication properties, the additives used in gear oils provide protection against deterioration in storage, oxidation, foaming, corrosion, and rusting.

E. OWEN McBRIDE

Lubricating Oils, Molecular Weight Estimation

According to the ASTM Standard D-2878-70, the approximate value of lubricating oil molecular weight may be estimated on the basis of evaporation loss under specified conditions.

The method is performed as follows: 10 grams of oil are heated to an appropriate temperature (usually 400°F), air is passed through the oil sample (in special cases nitrogen may be used), and the evaporation time is arranged so that 5 ± 1% of evaporation loss is obtained. (The detailed description of the test method may be found in ASTM D-972 and D-2878.)

Using the data found by means of this test, the approximate molecular weight of the lubricating oil may be calculated.

The above-mentioned standards propose four different equations:

1. For all lubricants in general
2. For polyol esters
3. For dibasic esters
4. For mineral oils

From these four equations, two have been chosen: Nos. 1 and 4.

These equations are:

$$\text{Log } M_G = 3.028 - 0.164 \log (10{,}335PW/t) \quad (1)$$

$$\text{Log } M_M = 2.848 - 0.106 \log (10{,}335PW/t) \quad (2)$$

where M_G and M_M = average molecular weights of lubricant vapors for general lubricants (M_G) and for mineral lubricants (M_M)

P = ambient atmospheric pressure, torr (mmHg)

W = weight of lubricant evaporated, g

t = evaporation time, s

These equations served as a basis to construct a single nomograph which allows *both* equations to be solved using only two movements of a ruler, and saves a lot of time by eliminating troublesome calculations.

Note: Although, strictly speaking, the molecular weight found relates to only the evaporated part of the lubricating oil, it may also be taken as an approximate molecular weight of the total lubricating oil.

The Nomograph

In order to use the nomograph (Fig. 1), it is necessary to know:

1. The ambient pressure (atmospheric) (torrs)
2. The quantity of oil evaporated (grams)
3. The time in which the evaporation occurs

Although the time in the original formula is expressed in seconds, the appropriate scale of a nomograph is graduated in hours and minutes for greater convenience.

The method of use of the nomograph is as follows:

1. Connect the known values of W and P on the appropriate scales with a ruler. Mark (A) the intersecting point of a ruler with the Reference Line.
2. Connect Point A with a ruler to the known value of t on the appropriate scale. Read the final result M on the intersection point of a ruler with the M scale.

Note: You may read at once *two* results of M on both sides of the M scale. On the left-hand side the values of M_G are plotted (for lubricants in general); on the right-hand side the values of M_M for mineral lubricating oils only.

Typical Example. A lubricant is evaporated at 400°F according to ASTM 2878-70. The evaporated weight W = 0.5 g, the evaporation time t = 10 h, and the ambient atmospheric pressure P = 770 torr.

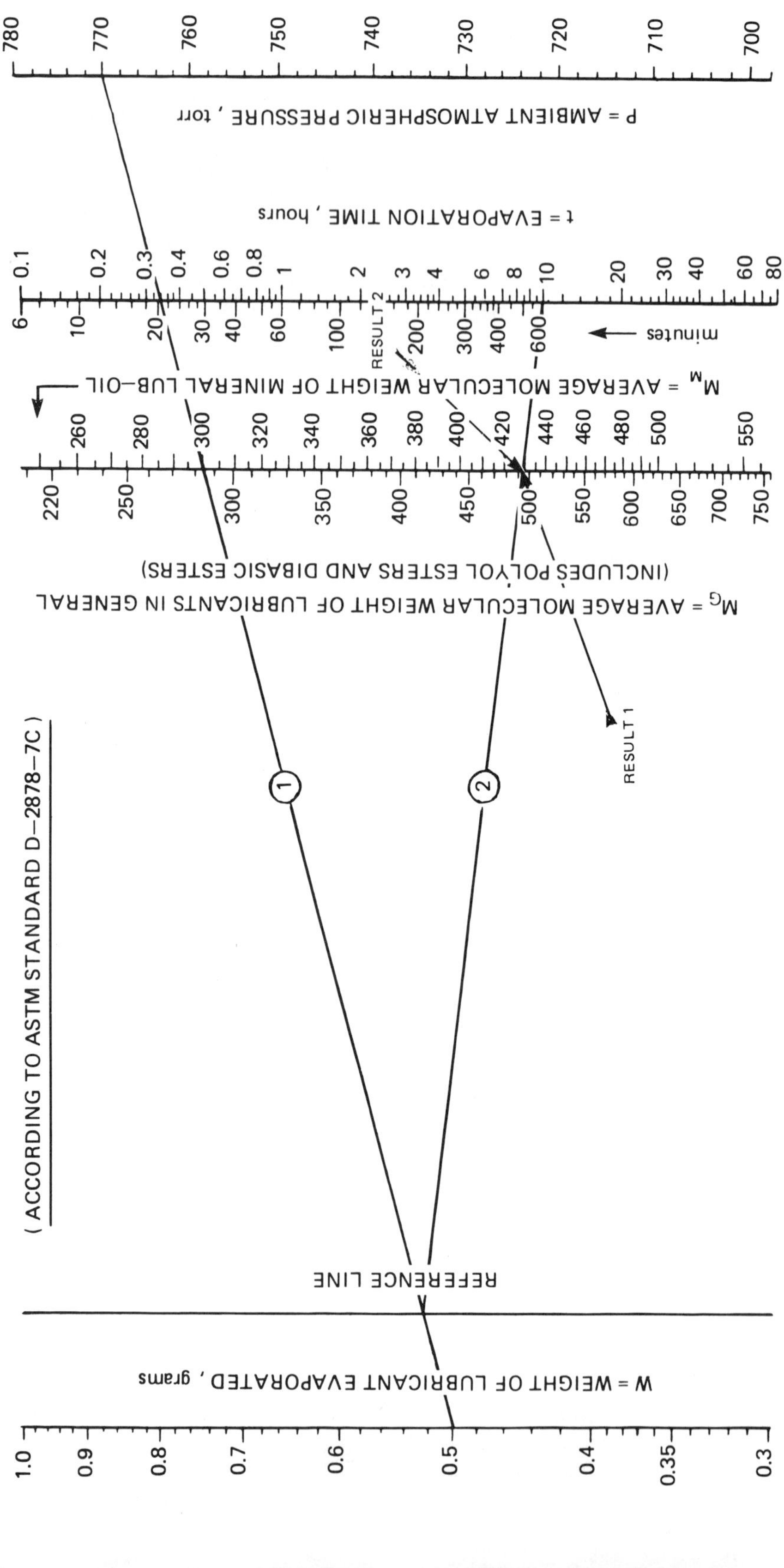

FIG. 1. Estimation of molecular weights of lubricating oils based on evaporation loss.

It is required to calculate the molecular weight of lubricant for the cases: (a) for lubricant in general, of unknown composition (M_G); (b) for mineral lubricating oil (M_M).

Solution: Use Eqs. (1) and (2). The results for both the equations and the nomograph are $M_M = 428$ (mineral) (Result 2) and $M_G = 493$ (general) (Result 1).

This material appeared in *Hydrocarbon Processing*, January 1973, and is reprinted with the permission of the editor.

ADAM ZANKER

Lubricating Oils, Viscosity Index Estimation

The basic lubricating crankcase oils have viscosity indexes in the range between 70 and 110 viscosity index units. Two nomograms have been prepared for this kinematic viscosity index range for all lub-oils having a kinematic viscosity between 2 and 25 cSt at 210°F. This corresponds to SAE grades of oil SAE 5W, 10W, 20W, 20, 30, 40, and 50.

In order to increase the accuracy of reading to 0.1 viscosity index units, the viscosity scale has been divided into three curves, namely: Low, Medium, and High. The Low and Medium range curves are shown in Fig. 1 and the High range curve in Fig. 2.

These nomograms are constructed according to standard I.P.-73/53, which corresponds to ASTM-D-2270 (Section A for viscosity indexes above 100). The desired viscosity index is found by connecting with a ruler the known kinematic viscosities at 100°F and at 210°F. The intersecting point of the ruler with the viscosity index scale shows the result.

This material appeared in *British Chemical Engineering*, *14*(2), 207 (1969) and *14*(3), 359 (1969), and is reprinted with the permission of the editor.

ADAM ZANKER

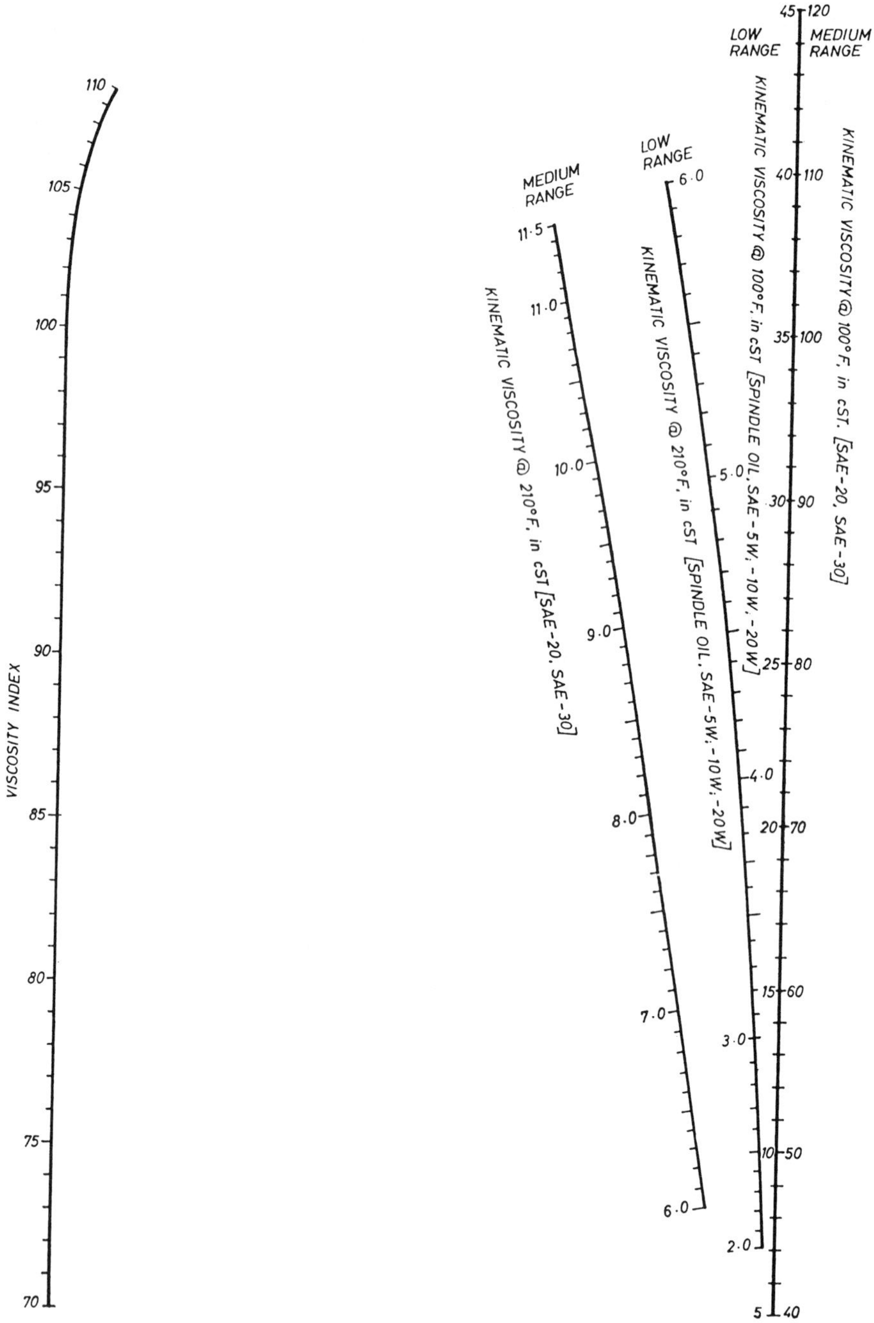

FIG. 1. Viscosity index of lubricating oils in the low and medium range.

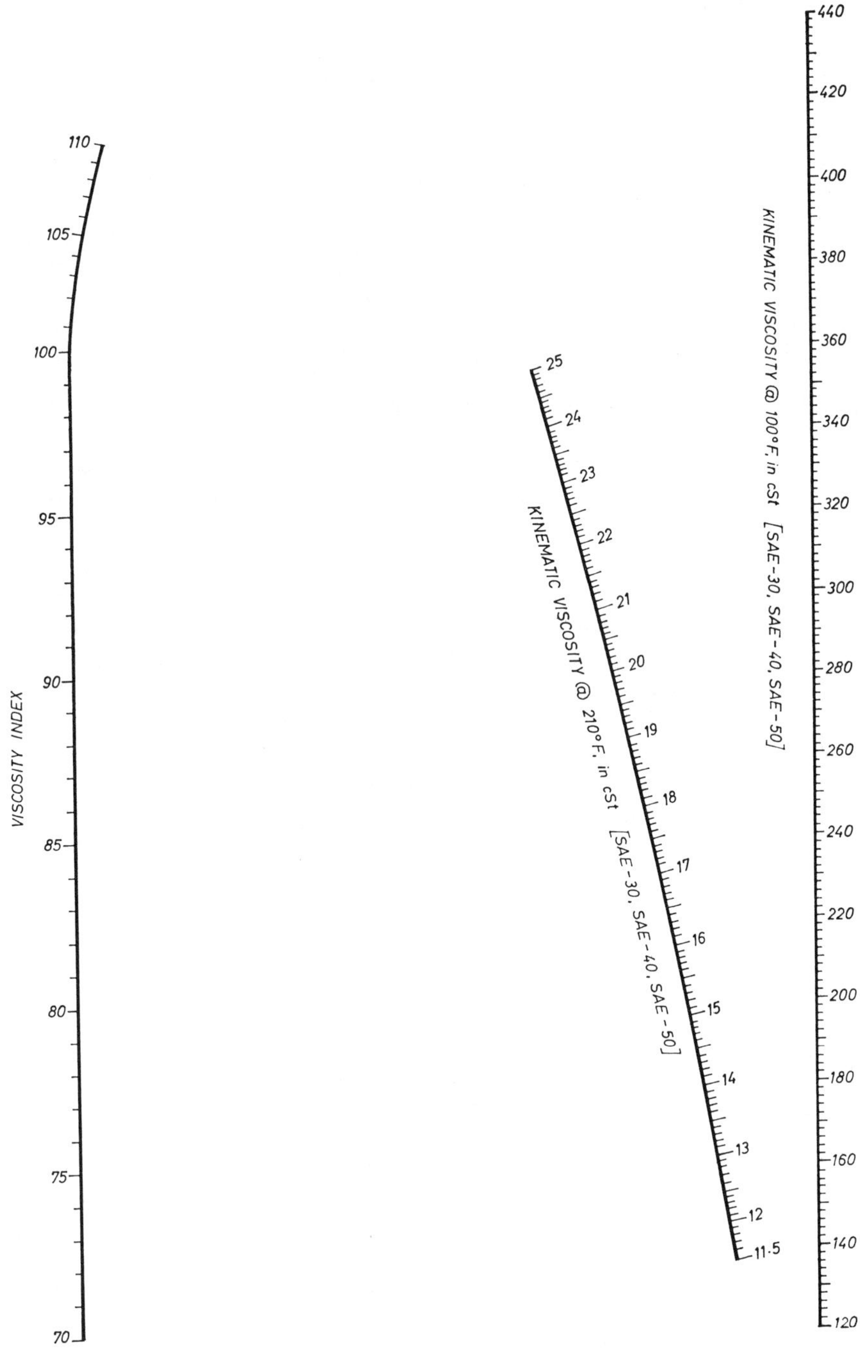

FIG. 2. Viscosity index of lubricating oils in the high range.

Masonry, Chemical-Resistant

Definition and Characteristics

Chemical-resistant masonry may be defined as nonmetallic construction used as structural material or support, or as a protective layer over a nonchemical-resistant support (either with a liquid barrier layer or without) in chemical or corrosive environments. Such materials are employed as protection for floors, walls, gutters, trenches, and sumps, and as linings for process equipment, ducts, and chimneys, or as independent structures such as self-supporting chimney liners, footings, piers, or other supports set in contaminated soil or ponds or other containments of corrosive chemicals, or nonmetallic piping carrying acid or other chemical corrosive wastes.

Though thought of primarily as "acid-brick," composed of hard burned masonry units cemented together with a chemical-resistant mortar, such constructions may include carbon brick, glass block, granite, basalt, tile, ceramic plates, blocks, pipe sections, or odd shapes assembled in the same manner, and as monolithic surfacing materials and as polymer concretes. The latter, when one considers the aggregate as the ceramic units and the binder as the mortar that cements them together, are really variations of the same principles, differing only in the ways in which they are applied.

For some reason, engineering courses in most colleges and universities neglect the study of these items, and their characteristics—both strengths and limitations—are little understood by many designers. Properly employed, they can provide years of satisfactory service in severe chemical environments at a cost far less than that of the special alloys that might otherwise be selected, and in many cases they far out-last such metallic designs. Where installed by inexperienced craftsmen, or to an unsuitable design, or using materials that have been incorrectly chosen for the exposure, failure can be quick and costly.

Consider carefully the following characteristics of chemical-resistant masonry.

Excellent in *compression*, but proportionally weaker in *tension* and *shear*. Remember that the units (brick, blocks, stone, etc.) can be very strong individually, but they are cemented together with a mortar (or adhesive). Failure in the bond between the blocks takes place at a far lower tension than in the *cohesion* of the blocks themselves or in the layers of mortar between them. Tension failures of monolithics and polymer concrete, though still usually in the adhesion to the aggregates, is at a far higher strength level than in block structures since surfaces are intricate and bond lines are discontinuous.

All such structures have a measureable absorption, higher in block and mortar type construction than in monolithics and polymer concrete, but still a measureable amount, so that liquids and gases can diffuse through them. The diffusion through well-designed resin polymer concretes is often very small so that only small molecules—such as HCl—can penetrate slowly through them, but eventually they too can be penetrated. In addition, the shrinkage that takes place on cure of mortars and the binders of monolithics and polymer concretes can eventually open cracks in the structures—perhaps tiny, perhaps larger—which lower the strength of the composite and through which liquids and gases can pass.

All these structures are more brittle and less flexible than metallic structures. Therefore, they can accept far less bending and vibration than their metallic counterparts.

Chemical-resistant masonry structures have, in general, low heat conductivity. (The exception is one composed of carbon or graphite units.) The amount of thermal insulation of linings made of these materials can be varied by the selection of the block, brick, or other unit from closed cell foamed borosilicate glass block (with K factor of 0.6 Btu · in./ft^2/h/°F) to (for instance) fireclay brick (with a K factor of 9 Btu · in./ft^2/h/°F).

Chemical-resistant masonry structures (with the exception of those made of carbon units) have nil electrical conductivity.

American "acid bricks," which are made from hard burned clays, have a tendency to grow or swell irreversibly over a period of time, perhaps one year, perhaps longer, by varying amounts, usually found to be in the range of 0.16% of any dimension. This factor has been widely noted and the subject of many studies, but the mechanism, limits, and the relationship of clay source and analysis and the temperature and duration of firing to the observed effect have not been determined. In designing a structure involving acid brick, this factor must be provided for.

Where Used

Considering the above characteristics, it should be clear that these materials are useful as self-supporting structures only in a few limited cases, such as independent chimney liners, where there is exposure to corrosive gases and moisture, as footings or supports for other masonry structures where the footing is exposed to corrosive contaminated soil or to chemical spills, or as barrier walls subject to corrosive splash or spray, or in contact with corrosive contaminated materials.

The most common uses of these materials are as surface protection of substrates that would otherwise be exposed to corrosive environments for which the substrate is unsuitable. Thus, a concrete (or other type) floor may be protected from damage from chemical spills by the use of a suitable monolithic surfacing, a polymer concrete overlay, or an "acid brick" or tile wearing surface. A trench carrying chemical wastes or a concrete waste collection pit or neutralizing tank can be similarly protected.

Carbon steel process tanks have been lined with sheet rubber linings since before the beginning of this century, but as process temperatures were increased, the thermal limits of those linings were exceeded, and the service lives of the linings became uneconomically short. By the end of the second decade of this century, the B. F. Goodrich Co. was taking advantage of the insulating effect of an "acid-brick" lining to bring the temperature of the rubber lining down to an acceptable level. This type of lining also provided protection against wear and mechanical abuse. The brick lining could not be used successfully alone because liquids can penetrate it, as noted above, and therefore, without the rubber membrane, the chemicals would reach the steel. (See Fig. 1.)

With the development of stainless steel in the third decade, there was a movement by engineers to return to all-metal design until cost figures were compared and it was discovered that even with the added costs of the installation of the rubber and brick, the alloy was more expensive than the

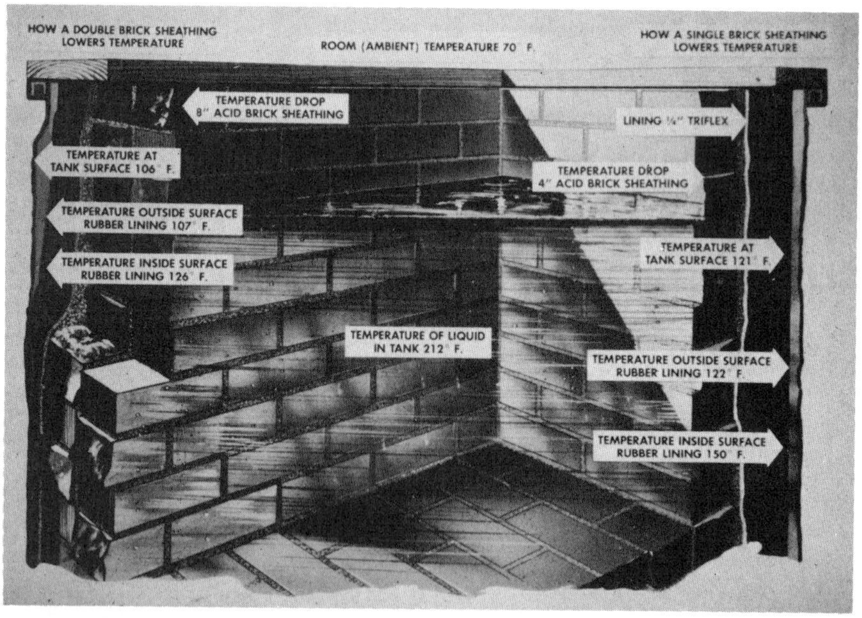

FIG. 1. Illustration of thermal drop through 4″ and 8″ of acid-proof brickwork. From W. L. Sheppard Jr., "Materials of Construction of Pickling Tanks," in *Blast Furnace and Steel Plant*, 1968. (Courtesy B. F. Goodrich Co.)

composite design. As temperatures were further increased, the additional thicknesses of acid brick required to provide the necessary insulation in many cases increased costs to the point where this type of lining became less economical, and interest shifted back to the alloys and lighter vessels with thinner walls. But as more exotic processes were developed and temperatures for some of them were increased into the refractory ranges, in some cases the process temperatures carried the surface temperature of the alloy beyond the acceptable limits of corrosion rates for the alloy in exposure to the contained chemicals. Now, again, the "acid-brick" lining design could help by providing sufficient insulation to bring the shell temperature back down to an acceptable level. (See Fig. 2.)

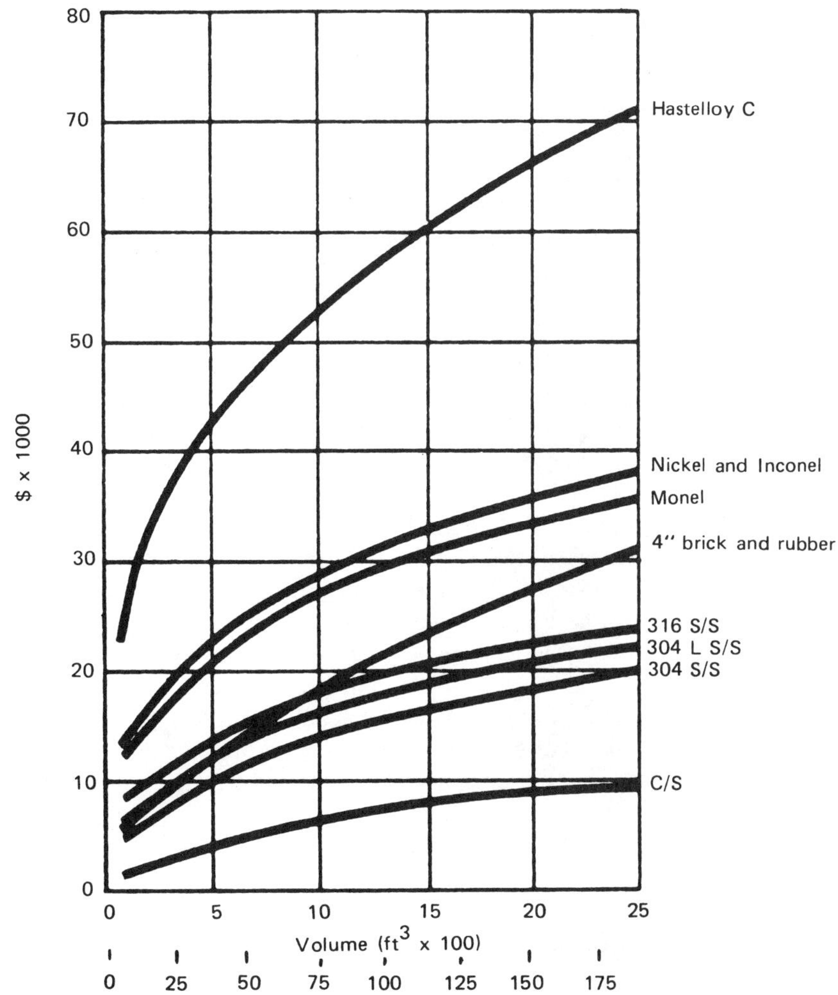

FIG. 2. Shop-fabricated tank costs (1971). Data based on ¼" thick walls. (From R. R. Pierce, "Engineering Brick-Lined Process Vessels," *Mater. Prot. Perform.*, December 1972.)

Floors

In the chemical process industries the most frequent uses of chemical-resistant masonry are in floors, trenches, and concrete containment vessels, and in ceramic pipe joined with chemical-resistant jointing materials and having chemical-resistant masonry-lined concrete manholes carrying chemical wastes. The selection of the type of chemical-resistant masonry for the application should be made *before* design is determined, based on (1) chemical and thermal exposures (including idle time and clean-up), (2) traffic and load-bearing considerations, (3) ease of access to the area for inspection and maintenance, (4) consideration of production costs should a shutdown for repair or maintenance become necessary, and of the possibilities of continuing to operate while repairs or maintenance is under way, and (5) the frequency and type of expansion joints that will be required with the type of material selected.

Monolithics vary widely in acceptable thermal limits depending on type of material and in resistance to wear, abrasion, and mechanical damage, but in all cases, polymer concretes and "acid-brick" design will accept higher thermal limits and more abuse. Monolithics should be bonded directly to the substrate to obtain the optimum in physical strength, so a membrane cannot normally be installed below them and over the surface of the substrate. Therefore, very few surfacing materials applied monolithically can provide economical service life if exposed to a liquid head of a corrosive chemical. Under normal conditions in floors, stress relief or expansion joints, every 20′ or less, are required in monolithic floor surfacing materials or other surfacing bonded directly to the substrate, and over *all* expansion joints, control joints, and all other points of movement in the substrate.

Polymer concretes also vary in acceptable thermal limits, with sulfur concrete limited to 190–200°F as the lowest temperature limit of these. Polymer concretes, as thick and often well-reinforced surfacings, can be applied over a membrane. But expansion joints must be installed closer—the spacing in accordance with the manufacturers' recommendations for that specific material, and continuous from surface down to membrane.

The longest lived surfacing and the one providing the widest range of acceptable exposures is properly installed "acid brick." The specific components must be selected in accordance with the anticipated exposure—both chemical and thermal—placed over a suitable liquid-tight membrane, and with expansion joints located not more than 20′ apart, preferably closer, from surface to membrane, and within one brick of the location of all expansion joints or other points of movement in the substrate, around all fixed points except drains, and adjacent to all changes in direction, such as trench walls.

Vessels

The requirements and limitations of the materials used as floor surfacings become even more critical when they are considered as linings for vessels where the fluid contact is continuous and often under a liquid head, rather than simply wet/dry as in the case of a floor, and in the process industries often under considerable pressure and at a sustained elevated temperature. Here the limitations of each type—monolithic, polymer concrete, or acid brick—must be considered against all exposure factors, and with the added consideration that the substrate may be concrete or metallic. If concrete, it is essential that a membrane be used since concrete has a high absorption, and if without a membrane, internal pressures—even just the weight of a standing head—can force contained liquids through the lining and on into and perhaps even through the concrete. If the vessel is steel and a dense monolithic lining or coating is used, contained liquids can still be forced into and eventually through the monolithic, but much slower than would be the case with the more absorbent concrete below it, so that the monolithic may here have an economical life expectancy.

When used as linings for trenches or pits, the severity of the exposure falls between those of floor and process vessel, and should be assessed individually.

Design Requirements

Monolithics. It is important to remember that all monolithics shrink to some degree on cure. Therefore, if the finished structure is to function properly, the concrete substrate surface should be strong enough not only to provide an anchor for the bond of the surfacer to the concrete but also for the stresses that will occur in the surfacer as the monolithic pulls itself together (that is, shrinks) as it cures. It is common practice to specify a clean 3000 $lb/in.^2$ concrete with the surface float finished, then brush blasted or acid etched free of surface contaminants, release agents, or additives that can react with the hardening agent or the binder of the monolithic selected.

In addition, the surface should be sloped continuously to drains or trenches, at a minimum 1/8″ per foot, nominally 1/4″ per foot. The best test is to flood the finished surface of the concrete and then mark all puddles and correct them before proceeding with the topping. Standing puddles will eventually cause problems with a monolithic.

The need for and frequency of expansion joints were mentioned above.

Polymer Concretes. Liquid-tight membranes can and should be placed over the substrate before placing the polymer concrete. They have a dual function: first, as the liquid-tight seal to seal off any fluids that get through the polymer either as a result of porosity (as in silicate concretes) or shrinkage cracks which occur in almost all polymers and, second, to separate the polymer concrete from the substrate and allow it to move as a unit, sliding on the membrane over the substrate as it shrinks, or expands or contracts with temperature changes, closing or opening the expansion joints that must be designed into it as previously stated.

Because the design must provide for this differential and independent movement, it is important that the substrate surface be smooth and that penetrations through the polymer concrete be centered between expansion joints or surrounded by expansion joints.

Acid-Resistant Brick. Liquid-tight membranes are also a must where

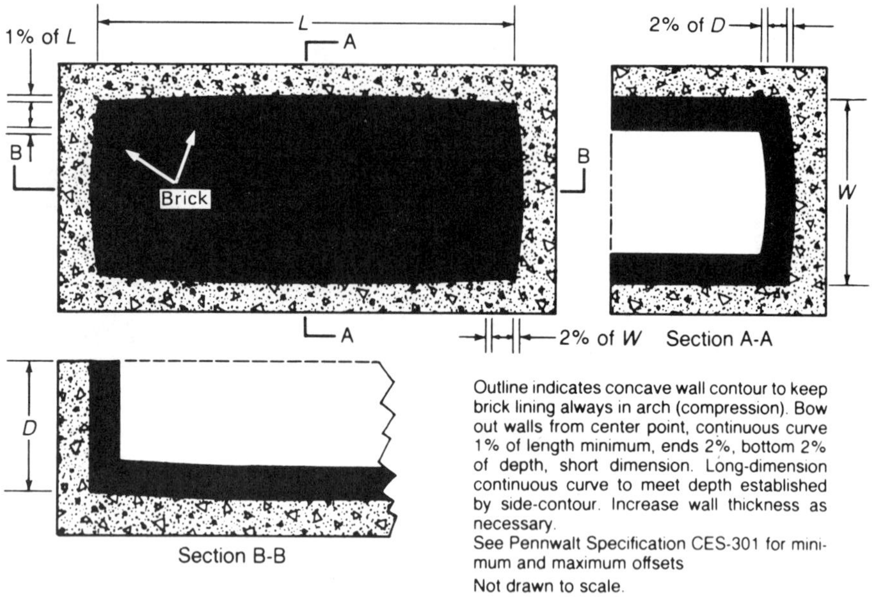

FIG. 3. Sketch of a typical contoured tank. (Courtesy Pennwalt Corp.)

acidbrick is to be installed, and they function in the same dual capacity as they do with polymer concretes. Since the brick (or other block) and the substrate always have different coefficients of thermal expansion and since acid bricks are subject to the irreversible growth discussed earlier, they should never be bonded to the substrate.* The expansion joints (which are *necessary*) have already been discussed.

It should be borne in mind that when solvent materials that can attack expansion joint sealants are present in a vessel's contents, expansion joints cannot be used successfully. In such cases a different design must be employed to prevent failure of the lining. This is accomplished by contouring. All straight lines become curves, and the lining, being in an "arch" configuration, is restrained. The more it wants to grow, the tighter the brickwork fits inside the substrate. (See Fig. 3.)

The thickness of the lining is also important. Since the lining, except in those cases where it is contoured, is designed to slide on the membrane when it is installed on walls in straight-walled vessels, the lining must be sufficiently thick to be self-supporting on its own base. See Table 1 for design recommendations.

Where a vessel or trench lining or floor undergoes an outside angular direction change, expansion joints must be placed approximately two bricks from that direction change to prevent the brick lining at the corner from being pushed off the substrate at that point. Outside curves must be totally avoided since a brick lining will always be pushed off such substrates regardless of expansion joint locations.

*An exception to this rule is floor construction involving very thin brick or tile less than 1" thick. In such cases, "stress relief" joints must be incorporated into the design.

TABLE 1 Rule-of-Thumb Suggested Thickness of Acid-Resistant Brick Linings

Depth (ft)	Length (ft)	Brick Thickness (in.)
≤1	≤30	2½
≤2	≤15	2½
1–2	15–30	4
2–6	≤15	4
	≥15	8
>6	Any length	8 or more

Where expansion joints cannot be used (such as when the lining is exposed to a strong solvent for which no suitable expansion joint is available), thrust blocks may be employed to prevent the brickwork from being pushed off the corners. (See Fig. 4.)

The reader is referred to the Bibliography for information required to avoid error in producing a satisfactory and long-lived construction. In order to show the importance of selecting the proper materials, the correct design, an experienced installer, and competent inspection, the following examples are presented.

Unsatisfactory Design or Construction

1. In late 1947 a storage tank for 93% sulfuric acid was built. Since the process lines running from the tank were to be fed by gravity rather than by pumps (eliminating pump maintenance), it was decided to build the tank on the factory roof, and because steel could not be obtained, a cylindrical tank was cast out of concrete with a lead-lined outlet located in the center of the bottom, lined with a ⅜″ thick reinforced hot-applied unfilled oxidized asphalt

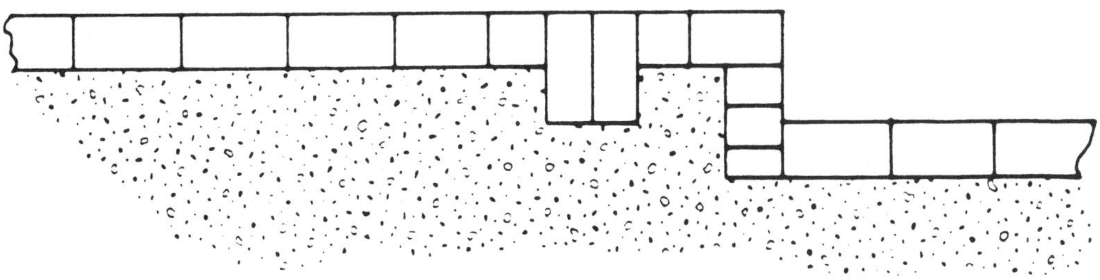

FIG. 4. Note “thrust block” to prevent brick at step from pushing away from corner. From W. L. Sheppard Jr., *Chemically Resistant Masonry*, 2nd ed., Dekker, New York, 1982; see pp. 44, 45, 66.

membrane, and 4″ of "acid brick" laid in hot sulfur cement. (See the design detail in Fig. 5.)

Within a month after the tank was filled with acid, acid drops were noted on the roof under the tank, and these were traced back to the elbow under the outlet. Acid was found to be slowly running down the *outside* of the lead pipe, and the whole underside of the ceramic block through which the pipe passed was wet with acid.

The designer had failed to note that the design as he had drawn it up made the membrane discontinuous. The sulfur mortar in which the block was set was exposed on the top to the acid, and the contact face was under pressure from head of acid in the tank. The mortar had an absorption in the vicinity of 0.25%, and so the acid was being slowly forced into and through the sulfur joint, and so slowly collecting on the underside of the joint, running across the face of the ceramic block and down the *outside* of the lead pipe.

Fortunately, this mal-design could be corrected without extensive repair as shown in Fig. 3. Note that the flange at the top of the lead pipe was extended around the block containing the pipe and under the adjacent brick, sandwiched into the membrane.

2. In another case, a decade and a half ago, a large steel tank which was to contain acid chemical wastes containing some petroleum products was designed. The steel vessel was inner lined with a glass fabric-reinforced furan resin membrane, and inner-lined with "acid brick." Shortly after it was put in service, the tank started to leak. The brick was removed opposite the leak, the membrane repaired, the brick replaced, and it was returned to service only to leak again elsewhere. After this cycle was repeated three or four times, they called in someone experienced in this type of construction. Investigation disclosed that the steel tank had been assembled by skip-welding the plates together. The movement between the unwelded areas of the plates tore the membrane as quickly as it was repaired. This kind of a shell does not provide continuous support and is completely unacceptable for such linings. Before installing *any* membrane in any vessel, it should be tested water-tight. Ship-lap construction is also unacceptable since it does not provide a smooth inner surface to line. The tank was abandoned and a new one built.

3. At about the same time a concrete "equalizer" tank, roughly 60′ × 25′ × 11′ deep with straight walls, a hot asphalt membrane, and a brick lining laid in

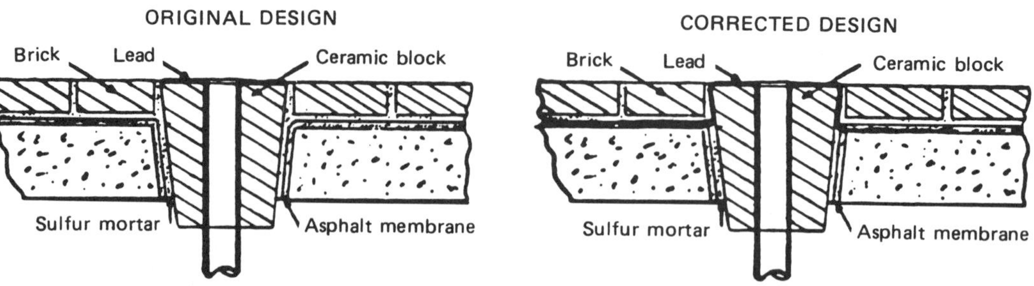

FIG. 5. From W. L. Sheppard Jr., *Chemically Resistant Masonry*, 2nd ed., Dekker, New York, 1982.

a phenolic resin mortar, without indicating the thickness of the brick desired, was built. The tank was to receive acid wastes from explosive manufacture, primarily sulfuric acid, but with traces of nitric. The low bidder installed the specified asphalt membrane and a 2¼″ thick brick lining was laid, as specified, in a phenolic mortar, both in November. In late January, though the tank had not even been in service, all the brick along one long wall had fallen into the tank and the rest of the lining was bulged and in imminent danger of collapse.

A check of the concrete walls by an engineer disclosed that the concrete contractor had insufficiently supported his forms, so that when he poured his concrete the forms had moved slightly inward under the weight of the concrete and so, instead of dead straight walls, they bowed slightly inward. As the brick swelled, due to their slow irreversible growth, they expanded and pushed away from the wall and fell into the tank. A 2¼″ thick brick wall was far too thin for stability in this size vessel anyway, but even the 8″ wall, which *should* have been specified, would eventually have failed under such a maldesign. It is far safer to contour all flat walls so that all brick are kept in arch and so in compression. If the floor is not slightly dished or *dead* flat, the brick laid over it can bulge and heave upwards.

Unsatisfactory Application

Design Alteration—Some Examples

1. It is readily apparent that it costs more money to form up and pour concrete to build a vessel with bowed walls than it would be if the walls were straight. All too often when a big job comes up and many contractors bid on it, the low, and successful, bidder will have based his bid on omitting something that was in the design. An expensive item such as bowed walls is just such an item, and being forced to do it may make the difference between profit and loss on a job that has been figured very closely. The author has seen instances where a contractor tried to install straight walls when his specifications and drawings clearly required bowed ones, and then when stopped by an inspector try to argue the client out of forcing the issue by offering to split the savings with him and saying that the curved walls are not needed—that they are just for appearance. Sometimes he gets away with this, and this can be the direct cause of a failure *after* the time on the contractor's warranty has expired.

2. Another well-known contractor makes a habit of bidding a floor in which a bed joint of ⅛ to 3/16″ thickness is specified between the membrane and the bottom of the brick by omitting that bed joint, and at installation he applies a paper-thin coating of the mortar over the membrane, then sets the brick directly on this, buttering the ends of the brick but not the bottoms, so in effect without a bed joint. This saves him the cost of a pound to a pound and a half of expensive mortar per square foot, so he can get a profit out of an excessively low bid. This change in design will result in rough surface floor (which he will probably blame on the designer or the concrete contractor) and air voids under the brick. If there are traces of organics or growth salts in the environment, they will collect in the air voids and eventually cause trouble—but after the warranty expires.

If the floor is unacceptable to the owner due to roughness, he may offer to grind the surface to make it smooth enough to be acceptable. Acid bricks have hard-burned skins or surfaces, but are softer inside the skin, so they wear faster in areas where the skin is ground off. In addition, they are not the same color inside as on the surface. Such surface grinding is *not* recommended, and the contractor should be required to take out low brick, build up the bed, and replace them.

3. The laying of tile with an adhesive bed to anchor them to the substrate is often done by contractors using a serrated trowel which spreads ribbons of epoxy bedding mortar (or adhesive) on the concrete. The tile (if they are ribbed, with the ribs buttered and filled with the mortar) are then pressed down into the bed, and the pressure is supposed to spread the ribbons until they become a single continuous flat surface or bed, and all the air squeezed out. If this is done properly, the tile are properly bedded and adhered. However, many contractors fail to butter the backs of the tile or to fill all the grooves in the tile back, and often use a serrated trowel with very shallow grooves, and these only partly filled, so that the ribbons never spread out, and the concrete is never completely covered. Thus, liquids can penetrate through the bare spots into the concrete, and the tile may be adhered to the concrete in only a few places—resulting in poor bond and early disbondment. The author prefers to avoid this potential problem by banning all serrated trowels from the workplace.

Contractor Substitutions for Specified Materials

The world is full of cheap materials which are *claimed* by the vendor to do the same thing as the material the designer specified. A contractor who is supplying his own materials obviously wants to substitute them, if you will let him, and save money.

1. Some contractors have tried to substitute silicate cements for furan or phenolic mortars. Though silicates are suitable in acid solutions except those containing hydrofluoric acid or acid fluorides, they will be destroyed by acid fluorides, and by alkalis, resulting in failure if these materials happen to be in the environment to which the structure is later exposed.

2. Applicators may substitute an amide-hardened, decorative, easily applied, and much cheaper floor topping for the amine-hardened epoxy floor surfacer specified for chemical exposure, resulting in failure—probably shortly after the guarantee expires.

3. A contractor will sometimes try to substitute roofers' asphalt for the hot-applied, unfilled, high temperature oxidized asphalt often used for membrane with acid brick. Roofers' asphalt flows at far lower temperatures than does that specified and can sag or flow away from the area on which it is applied, causing bare spots through which leakage can take place and damage to the substrate. In addition, any oxidizing material, such as bleach or nitric or chromic acids, can penetrate it—causing failure.

Unsatisfactory Installation

1. There are many ways in which an installer/contractor can produce an unsatisfactory installation. A poor craftsman is paid less than a good or an experienced one, but he produces damaged materials—like badly cut brick. But throwing away the damaged brick is wasteful and costs the contractor more in materials. Therefore, instead of throwing away the damaged material, it is used, resulting in a sloppy installation that is doomed to fail.

2. Using insufficient mortars for joints and setting beds is a common practice with some contractors. These materials are the most expensive ones in the contract, and any material saving increases profits. Of course, this will result in voids in the masonry, which in turn will lead to failure of the construction, though the contractor hopes that will not occur until the guarantee has expired.

Failure of Inspection

1. The quality of the finished work also depends on the quality of the inspection. Acid brick and tile work are usually part of much larger contracts, and many inspectors have no experience with this work. On one occasion, as an example, the Corps of Engineers inspector following the construction at an Army hospital, observing the installation of a 9″ × 9″ quarry tile floor in the kitchen, ignored the quality of the workmanship (which was superior) to condemn the floor because the joints were not exactly 1/4″ wide, measured with his steel rule. He wanted the entire floor removed and relaid to provide the *exact* measurement, even after he was shown that the manufacturers' tolerance on dimensions of the tile made an *exact* and totally uniform joint impossible. The work was held up until an order from the Chief of Engineers was handed down instructing him to approve it.

2. With tile floors bonded tightly to a graded and sloped concrete substrate, it should be obvious that if a concrete substrate is accepted that is not flat and uniformly smooth, any tile floor that is cemented to it will reflect the same unevenness. But since the concrete slabs are often poured by the general contractor, and a subcontractor lays the tile, it is sometimes found that the general contractor has pressured the tilesetter to lay his tile on an unacceptable substrate, with the result that an uneven and unacceptable tile surface has resulted.

Improper Operation

After the construction work is completed and the finished unit is put in service, it is sometimes found that the unit suffers damage or failure due to operators' error. One example should suffice to illustrate this.

A chemical company lined an 18′ tall, 3′6″ diameter process tank with a fiberglass-reinforced furan resin membrane and inner lined it with 9″ of fireclay acid brick, laid in furan resin mortar. The vessel was to receive organic solvents to be treated with hydrochloric acid under 200 lb/in.^{2} pressure and at 220°F, a suitable lining for this service. However, within a few weeks of putting the unit in service, inspections disclosed the flaking off or destruction of the faces of the interior brick lining, so that the mortar joints were higher than the brick faces—in a "waffle" pattern. The brick manufacturer claimed that the damage was due to the presence of acid fluorides in the hydrochloric acid, but the chemical company and the mortar manufacturer both said this could not be the case because the acid was made by the reaction of chlorine with hydrogen, and no fluorine whatever was present in any of the raw materials. The mortar manufacturer sent an observer to watch the operator running the unit. The operator closed and sealed the unit, charged the solvent into it, then the hydrochloric acid under pressure, and started heating up the unit. After building up to operating temperature and pressure (in a quarter to a half an hour), it was held under those conditions for 3 h with the 9″ masonry lining saturated and in equilibrium. Then the operator stopped the process, cut off the heat, and at the same time opened the valve, bringing the pressure down to atmospheric in 1 or 2 s. The dense brick surface could not release the pressure built up in the brick that rapidly, and it popped off the face of the brick. Now that the cause was known, it was easy to correct. A 2½″ thick carbon brick lining, laid in a furan mortar, was placed inside the 9″ fireclay brick lining. This type of brick is more porous, so that the pressures could be released more rapidly through them while preventing the spalling of the fireclay brick under the carbon brick.

Changes in Environment after the Equipment Is Installed

If materials are selected to handle specific conditions, and after construction these conditions are changed to create an environment for which the selected materials are not suitable, failure will result. Most process engineers and plant managers are aware that if they alter processes without making certain that the materials to which the process chemicals will be exposed are suitable for this new exposure, they are taking a chance on damage to or failure of the equipment. However, few people ever think of the similar damage that may occur when cleaning crews change their cleaners.

A large Canadian dairy advised that the joints in several of their floors, dairy brick recently installed, laid with furan resin mortar joints and bed, showed damage. Many of the joints were receding. Since furan mortars have been successfully employed for over 40 years in dairy floors—with no such problems reported—the manager of the dairy was asked what cleaners were being used on the floor. He phoned back a few hours later with the trade names of three cleaners. A check with the cleaner manufacturer disclosed that one of these cleaners was sold *only* to use in cleaning the stainless steel equipment in the dairy, and contained nitric acid. The cleaning crew had decided to use it regularly on the floor because it removed dirt rapidly. Nitric acid rapidly damages furan mortars and epoxy mortars and, somewhat less rapidly, phenolic mortars. It does not affect vinyl ester or polyester mortar until it is over a 30% concentration. However, most of the cleaners used in dairies are alkaline, and these can attack vinyl ester and polyesters and are best handled with furan mortars.

Failure Analysis

The Bibliography provides the titles of three articles designed to help the user in determining the causes of failures that are observed in acid-brickwork, in monolithic surfacings, and in expansion joints in both types of structures. Also given are the titles of articles to assist the user in the inspection of new installations for maintaining an acid-resistant floor.

This article was excerpted from a lecture entitled "Uses and Misuses of Chemical-Resistant Masonry" presented September 24, 1986, and repeated by special request October 7, 1987, at the Liberty Bell Corrosion Course, and some of this article was published in *Chemical Engineering*, December 8, 1986, copyright © 1986, by McGraw-Hill, Inc., New York, New York 10020, and is reprinted by special permission.

Bibliography

General

Pierce, R. R., "Engineering Brick-Lined Process Vessels," *Mater. Prot. Perform.*, December 1972.

Sheppard, W. L., Jr., *Chemically Resistant Masonry*, 2nd ed., Dekker, New York, 1982.

Sheppard, W. L., Jr. (ed.), *Corrosion and Chemical Resistant Masonry Materials Handbook*, Noyes, Park Ridge, New Jersey, 1986.

Maintenance

Sheppard, W. L., Jr., "Plant Floors Thrive on Preventive Maintenance," *Food Eng.*, September 1974.

Inspection

Sheppard, W. L., Jr., "Inspecting Chemically-Resistant Masonry," *Plant Eng.*, March 19 and April 16, 1981.

Failure Analysis

Sheppard, W. L., Jr., "Spotting and Avoiding Problems with Acid-Resistant Brick," *Chem. Eng.*, May 3, 1982.

Sheppard, W. L., Jr., "Failure Analysis of Chemically-Resistant Monolithic Surfacings," *Chem. Eng.*, July 23, 1984.

Sheppard, W. L., Jr., "Expansion Joints for Chemically Resistant Masonry," *Chem. Eng.*, August 19, 1985.

WALTER LEE SHEPPARD, JR.

Masonry, Chemical-Resistant, Expansion Joints

Three general types of expansion joints are used in construction work: hard or rigid board, such as asphalt or asbestos board; accordion-type metal or metal-and-fabric joints; and compressible or deformable seals.

The first type are really not joints at all; rather, they are merely separators of doubtful value put in between two slabs or other components (usually in concrete structures). Such joints cannot expand or compress with changes in the concrete. Accordion-type joints—the second type—are used primarily in ductwork and piping.

The third type is of concern here. Although the focus will be on the use of these joints in chemical-resistant masonry, the discussion also applies to ordinary concrete construction.

Construction of Joints

Recommended practice can be found in *Guide to Joint Sealants for Concrete Structures*, Report 504R-77, published by the American Concrete Institute, Detroit, 1977. Figure 1 is from that report and shows why most manufacturers specify that the joint should be filled with deformable sealant to a depth (from the exposed surface) equal to one-half the width of the joint (see Parts 1–3 of Fig. 1).

The balance of the joint should be filled with a compressible material such as a closed-cell foam or loose fiber. An exception to this is in a joint in the floor, gutter, or trench of a food plant, where food products can penetrate the top sealant and enter open spaces in the compressible material. The food can ferment and become rancid. In this case, the entire joint should be filled with deformable sealant.

Another exception: Consider an expansion joint in a monolithic topping over a construction joint in a concrete substrate, where the monolithic joint is shallow (e.g., 1/4 in. deep). The joint must be wide enough so that the allowable elongation of the sealant in it will not be exceeded. Here, again, fill completely with deformable sealant.

From Fig. 1, note that as the joint opens, the deformable sealant, if it properly adheres to the sides of the joint, must stretch and become thinner at its waist (center). If the sealant also bonds to the joint bottom, it cannot assume this shape as the joint opens. This adhesion creates a tearing stress on the sides of the joint; stress is greatest at the top of the joint. This can be prevented by installing a bond breaker at the bottom of the joint (see the figure).

A compressible, rather than deformable, material can be used to fill the bottom of the joint space (see Parts 4B and 4Bi). A compressible substance supports the deformable sealant above it, yet, as the joint closes, allows the

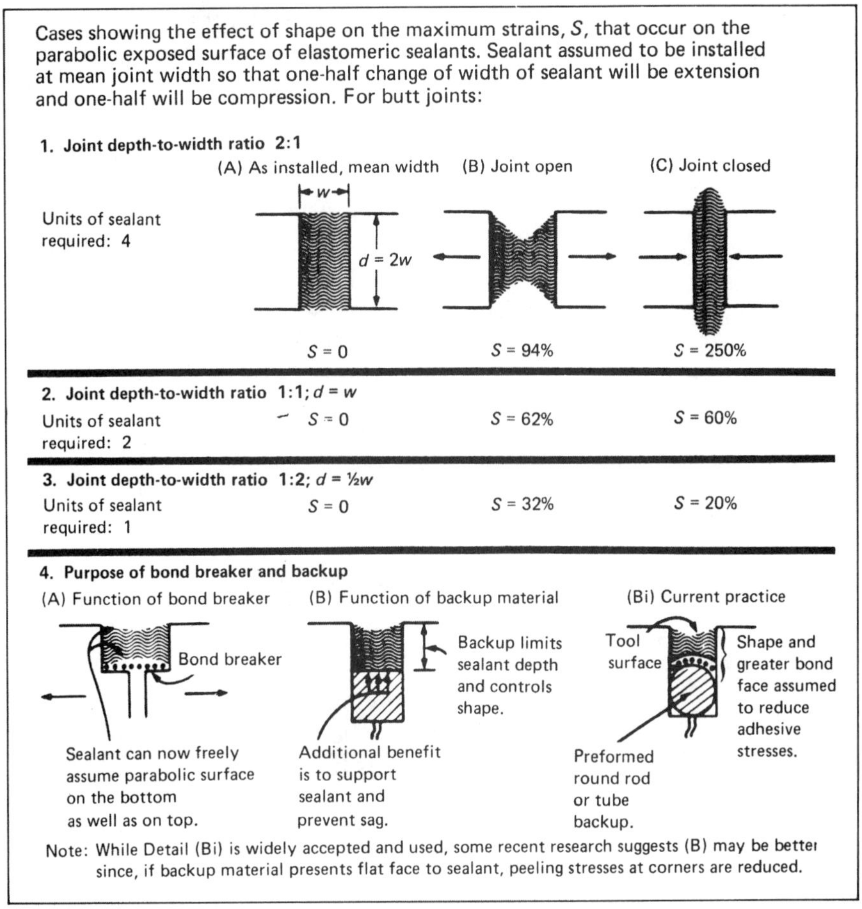

FIG. 1. Guidelines for construction of expansion joints. (From American Concrete Institute Report 504R-77. Used with the permission of the Institute.)

resulting bulge to push down into it. Usually, a bond breaker is unnecessary if such a material lies under the sealant, since the material is stretchy and flexible enough to allow the sealant to assume the desired shape. Table I of the report (not reproduced here) presents data on many common sealants.

See the report for determination of joint width, joint design for concrete, and sketches of types of failures.

Sealants

The sealant not only must have chemical resistance but be extensible enough to maintain a tight seal between the two sides of the joint. Over the expected temperature range, the bond must be maintained and the sealant must not crack. This is true for idle time and cleaning operations, too.

If elongation of the sealant is less than 50%, the joints will have to be excessively wide for the sealant to function properly. If the sealant is too elastic—200% elongation or more—it will be too soft to support wheeled vehicles. Thus, forklifts and other equipment will pound the joint's edges, resulting in chipping and breakdown. Such damage always results in disbonding.

Since elasticity drops at low temperatures, ask the manufacturer what the elongation of the sealant is at the minimum expected temperature. This will help to set the frequency, location, and width of the expansion joints.

In computing joint width, use a safety factor of 2. This means that, after determining the maximum amount of movement, one should select a joint width that will give compression and extension of the sealant of less than one-half its maximum elongation. If an expansion joint is anchored at its end (e.g., set in concrete or mortar), these ends cannot move. The masonry will eventually crack and heave.

Failure Analysis of Expansion Joints

I. Loss of Bond

1. Surfaces of sides of joint were wet (and a special damp-surface primer had not been used) when sealant was installed. Water was standing in joint during or shortly before installation, or flooding took place before the sealant has cured.
2. If the joint is in concrete, a monolithic, or a castable material (e.g., polymer concrete): (a) Concrete mix may have contained an additive that reacted with the resin or hardener, depleting the mix or otherwise preventing full cure and bonding; (b) Joint may have been finished or smoothed with tools that had been coated with a release agent (e.g., a silicone) or the bond breaker or release-pad on the bottom of the joint may intrude into the side of the joint; (c) If there is no, or an inadequate, membrane below the concrete, then water or other liquid may have penetrated from below, causing bond loss at the joint's sides by wetting bond surfaces before sealant could cure. Sometimes, subsurface water-pressure can cause disbondment; (d) Installer may have failed to clean sides of joint, leaving dust, dirt, or particles of weak material (laitance); or (e) Installer may not have primed or surface-treated joint.
3. If joint is in brick or other chemical-resistant masonry: (a) Installer may have failed to clean sides of joint; (b) Installer may not have primed or surface-treated joint; (c) If there is no, or an inadequate, membrane below the brick or block, then water, etc., may have penetrated from below; and (d) For tile on a bed of portland cement, if the cement has not dried out fully, moisture can rise before the sealant is fully cured, causing disbonding.
4. If the joints are too narrow for the sealant, or too far apart, excessive movements may be beyond the elasticity of the sealant. Measure the

joint size and distance between joints, compute maximum movements, and compare these with manufacturer's data for maximum elongation. Also, irregular joints (wide in some places, narrow in others) may fail for the same reason—stresses transmitted to and from wide and narrow sections.

5. Failure to use release agent or pad at the bottom of the joint can result in disbonding from joint sides.
6. Mixes of improper sealant-component proportions can cause overhardening, with loss of elasticity or excessive cure shrinkage. See also III-1, III-2, and III-3.
7. Installation at too low a temperature may result in incomplete cure and inadequate bond.
8. Exposure to rapid thermal cycling or abrupt temperature changes (see No. 11).
9. Exposure to a chemical that affects the sealant's bond strength.
10. Service in low temperatures may so reduce elongation of sealant that it may not function according to design, resulting in disbonding or cracking.
11. Very abrupt thermal changes, such as using hot water or steam to thaw ice, can result in movements too rapid for sealant to respond.
12. Joint sides are not at right angles to masonry edges or edges are not squared. If sides are not truly vertical, the pull during opening, or pressure during closing, of the joint is not at right angles to movement. Stresses are in shear instead of tension or compression, resulting in disbonding.

II. Excessive Hardening, Cracking, or Breaking Up of Sealant, or Sealant Collapses into Joint

1. Excess hardener in mix, or other incorrect proportions in mix. See I-6.
2. Manufacturing problem with sealant that causes curing to continue past its normal time, resulting in excessive hardening or shrinking. Check the batch number and have the manufacturer look at a retained sample.
3. Overheating—exposure to radiant heat or hot liquids above limit set by manufacturer.
4. Freezing or temperatures below those that the sealant can tolerate.
5. Chemicals in environment may cause overcure or remove plasticizer.
6. Joint too narrow for anticipated movement. See I-4.
7. No bond breaker used on bottom of joint. See I-5.
8. Excessive filler added to mix of a three-part sealant.
9. Installation at too high or low a temperature or during rapid thermal cycling. See I-7, I-8, I-10, and I-11.
10. Sealant collapsing into joint can be due to destruction of backing material. See IV-5. Cause can also be due to backing material that is incompatible with sealant.

III. Sealant Excessively Soft and Does Not Harden to Meet Manufacturer's Specifications

1. Failure to add proper amount of hardener or curing material. See I-6.
2. Wrong hardener used or wrong cans selected in making up mix. (In one case, two cans of resin were used instead of one resin/one hardener.) See I-6.
3. Hardener left out by mistake. See I-6.
4. Installation at too low a temperature, resulting in improper cure. See I-7 and I-8.
5. Joint wet during installation or became wet before cure. See I-1.
6. Chemical present, causing sealant to soften. See II-5.
7. In some cases, excessive primer can puddle, preventing complete cure.

IV. Sealant Appears to Show Chemical Attack

1. Temperatures may exceed design specifications. Drainage may be improper—make sure that liquids do not puddle and stand on the floor. And, of course, unexpected chemicals may be present.
2. Material used different from that specified, or wrong filler used (e.g., a carbon filler is required for hydrofluoric acid).
3. Check installation inspection reports to make sure that proper mix has been used. Had sealant cured properly after installation?
4. Water or solvents intruding from underneath. See I-2.
5. If a compressible cellular or fibrous filler has been used in the bottom of the joint, make sure that it is still there. Check also that the filler (a) has been packed tightly enough to prevent traffic from breaking loose the sealant and pushing it into the bottom of the joint, (b) has been selected properly for the chemical environment (e.g., polyesters are unsuitable for strong caustics), and (c) has not become wet or soaked with chemicals before the sealant is installed.
6. The damage may be mechanical—traffic can wear or tear out the sealant. See whether the edges of the joint are broken.

V. Sealant Soft in Some Areas, Hard in Others

1. The sealant has not been mixed uniformly.
2. Chemicals may have spilled on some parts of the joint, leaving others unharmed.
3. During installation, parts of the joint have become wet. See if there are roof leaks. Also, high humidity may result in condensation, with moisture dripping from walls and the ceiling, or water or cleaners spilled before cure complete.
4. Radiant heat or hot spills may cause localized overheating.
5. During installation, drafts or breezes can cause thermal changes and carry moisture. Also, are hard or soft areas in continuous or little sunlight?

6. Damage may be from manufacturing errors. Test a sample from the batch.

VI. Blisters and Bubbles in Sealant

1. Strong breezes were present during installation and curing.
2. Intense, concentrated sunlight present, causing blisters.
3. May result by applying sealant over concrete of pH greater than 9, especially when concrete is not fully cured or is still moist.
4. Sealant components were mixed at a high speed (over 350 r/min), resulting in air being beaten into mix.
5. Sealant applied over wet substrate or in joint that becomes wet by seepage under sealant, especially when temperatures are rising during application.
6. After placement and before cure, air voids (such as in porous concrete, below sealant) are subjected to rising temperatures.

VII. Sealant Bulging Out of Joint or Shrinking Down into It, Without Loss of Bond at Sides

During joint closing, movement of sides of joint pushes sealant up and out. During opening, sealant is sucked down. This is what should happen!

1. However, if joint does not close and sealant is extruded upward: Sealant may be pressed upward by pressure underneath, e.g., subsurface fluid-penetration.
2. Due to rising temperatures, air pressure results from air voids underneath the sealant.
3. Poor compaction of insufficient fiber or cellular filler in the joint gives inadequate support. This permits sealant to subside into joint, even if joint does not open.
4. Backing material that is incompatible with sealant has been used in bottom of joint. See II-10.
5. Backing material is porous, and is invaded by sealant, preventing backing from compressing. Sealant pushes upward.

VIII. Failure of Expansion Joint to Function as Designed

Manifested by heaving of floor on both sides of joint while joint does not close up; or floor may crack on one or both sides near joint, but joint does not open up.

1. Failure to close up, accompanied by floor's heaving, means either (a) something hard is in the joint that keeps it from closing or (b) the joint is anchored in a solid rather sliding on a surface.

Examples of (a): Bedjoint under a brick floor continues through expansion joint or encroaches most of way into it; contractor has failed to sweep out rubbish and dirt from joint before filling it with sealant; material used to fill bottom of joint is incompressible or packed too tightly; and sealant has become too hard to function properly.

Examples of (b): Failure to match expansion joint in brickwork exactly to expansion joint in substrate; or where there is no expansion joint in substrate, failure to place membrane or bondbreaking sliding joint between brick, tile, etc., and substrate. If surface is anchored to substrate without an expansion joint in it, the joint in the surface cannot open or close. Such joints are used only to relieve compression or tensile stresses in the surface material and are not expansion joints. As such, joints should be filled to full depth with sealant.

2. Failure to open with cracking of floor on one or both sides of joint can only result from anchoring surface brick, tile, monolithic, or castable to substrate (see No. 1b) with excessive shrinkage in substrate and shrinkage cracks developing in surface that match developing cracks in substrate. This can also be caused by an expansion (construction or control) joint that lies under surfacing adjacent to the expansion joint, but not directly under it as it should be.
3. Failure of designer to end each expansion joint in another expansion joint, or in a sliding joint, will immobilize joint so it cannot function.

WALTER LEE SHEPPARD, JR.

Mechanical Seals (see also O-Rings)

This is a comprehensive approach for selecting mechanical shaft seals to ensure high reliability at reasonable cost. In addition to information on developing and analyzing bid packages, several seal designs are analyzed for advantages and weaknesses.

Processing plants are confronted with an increasing number of available mechanical seal designs. The user must choose from among inexpensive standard seals and exotic, highly engineered seal models. We have seen seal costs range from less than $200 to over $6000 for pumps which didn't seem all that different to superficial observation. Each of these has its place, although it may prove difficult to determine which seal should be used for maximum long-term effectiveness in a given application or service.

This article outlines a selection strategy that makes maximum use of the capabilities of knowledgeable seal manufacturers. The strategy avoids unnecessary proliferation of different designs and leads to the selection of high quality seals for the largest possible number of pumps in a given installation. While primarily developed for grass-roots plants, this approach can also be used to upgrade mechanical seals systematically in existing installations.

Pump mechanical seal failure incidents outnumber any other rotating mechanical component failure event in typical petrochemical plants. Very often, 65 to 70% of pump maintenance expenditures must be allocated for mechanical seal repair and replacement [1].

Until now, seal selection generally has been left to the *pump* vendor. In many instances, this practice has resulted in low initial cost, but maintenance-intensive and failure-prone mechanical seal installations. In contrast, optimum selection practices make extensive use of *seal* vendor experience. However, to advise the pump user properly, seal vendors require full information on product composition, process conditions, crystallization temperatures, solids entrainment, and the like. All of these data are highly relevant if proper selection is to be assured, and withholding data for "security" reasons may cost the owner more than such protection is worth.

This is not to suggest that seal selection simply be turned over to the seal manufacturer. On the contrary, the owner's engineer must take the lead in mechanical seal optimization efforts. However, he needs guidance; a "road map" to seal selection. This "road map" should direct him to seals that embody more than initial cost advantages. The emphasis clearly should be toward standardization without sacrificing reliability. Seals should be simple to install and maintain; they should not be vulnerable to minor deviations in pumps operation or properties of pumpage. Indeed, a given seal should suit the needs of many pumping services to reduce spare parts inventory, streamline training requirements, and leave little room for maintenance errors.

These goals can be met with a well-defined selection strategy that starts with development of a suitable bid request package and leads to a bid evaluation that stresses technical features instead of lowest possible bid price. Such a strategy may well result in the added bonus of greatly increased seal reliability and considerably lower maintenance expenditures for most plants. Many major manufacturers of mechanical seals have indicated their support and willingness to cooperate in the implementation of our selection strategy. Specifically, this strategy requires development of bid request information that asks the seal vendor to assign severity categories to the various pumping services disclosed by the user. The user then screens the seal vendors' proposals to identify optimum seal configurations. Principal features of optimum seals are highlighted later in this article.

Development of Bid Request Package

The development of bid request information is a key element in a selection strategy leading to the procurement of mechanical seals which comply with the user needs outlined above. Bid requests must be forwarded to several experienced seal manufacturers and must make it clear that the manufacturer should submit cost proposals for only those services where his seal selection is backed by solid experience. His inability to furnish seals for some services should in no way disqualify him from submitting bids for those services where he is competent to provide a good product.

To begin, the user should assemble API data sheets for the various pumps that need mechanical seals. These data sheets must be forwarded to the seal vendors and the vendors asked to recommend classification categories for each pump (Table 1). Classification categories range from 1 to 10 in increasing severity. Category 1 would be reserved for pumping services that are easiest to seal, or where potential seal distress would not be of serious concern. Category 10 would comprise services or conditions where seal failures could result in extreme hazards and consequential damage. Category 10 seals merit special designs and expert attention through all stages of design, fabrication, quality control, installation, and operation. Verification of flawless operation would be assisted by state-of-art instrumentation and auxiliaries.

Classification categories can be assigned only after the user or purchaser provides the seal manufacturer with a comprehensive list of pumps that have been tentatively selected. Also, this pump tabulation must disclose all of the fluid properties and operating parameters known to the user. With disclosure thus going beyond the typical contents of API data sheets, the seal manufacturer can be requested to list the "operating windows" within which the proposed seal will function reliably in the pump tentatively selected. It is to be understood that the "operating window" refers to the *actual* seal with the chosen balance ratio, flush plan, stuffing box layout, etc. Notice also that we have opted to designate the pumps as "tentatively selected" because we should anticipate that even a capable seal vendor may be unable to offer his optimum seal for a given pump. Should this be the case, it might be appropriate to consider a more suitable pump model for the intended service. Making the seal the weakest link in pump selection should not be considered an acceptable alternative.

TABLE 1 Seal Selection Strategy

Seal Type	A	B	C	D
General characteristics of pump or pumpage	Nontoxic, low pressure, moderate temperature, no limitations on pump size, but primarily AVS and ANSI pumps	Moderate pressure, abrasive inclusions, low and moderately high temperatures. Primarily API pumps	Severe service, high pressure and/or extreme temperature, high loss potential. Exclusively API pumps	Extreme hazard and consequential damage risk. Special construction pumps
Service example and classification	Filter backwash pump, 5 hp, 20 gpm. 2 to 38 psig, 90°F, 1760 rpm Classification 1	Caustic transfer pump, 15 hp, 25 gpm, 0.3 to 105 psig, 100°F, 3550 rpm Classification 4	Synthetic tar pump, 200 hp, 280 gpm, 13 to 280 psig, 520°F, 3550 rpm Classification 7	Nuclear waste pump/reactor emergency pump. Last resort safety pump Classification 10
	Sour water pump, 20 hp, 310 gpm, 1 to 72 psig, 230°F, 3550 rpm Classification 2	Kerosene feed pump, 125 hp, 310 gpm, 0.1 to 250 psig, 90°F, 3550 rpm Classification 5	Intermediate synfuel pump, 500 hp, 930 gpm, 7 to 625 psig, 720°F, 1760 rpm Classification 8	
	Slop oil pump, 40 hp, 100 gpm, 0 to 79 psig, 150°F, 3550 rpm Classification 3	HC solvent reflux pump, 250 hp, 1310 gpm, 65 to 270 psig, 300°F, 3550 rpm Classification 6	Ethylene product pump, 1250 hp, 820 gpm, 390 to 1745 psig, −50°F, 3550 rpm Classification 9	

Next, the seal vendor should propose a seal Type "A" from his manufacturing program that would satisfy the requirements of all pumps with service classifications 1, 2, and 3; a seal Type "B" that would satisfy the purchaser's guideline requirements for all pumps with classifications 4, 5, and 6; and finally a seal Type "C" for classifications 7, 8, and 9. Bid invitations for service classification 10 are thought to merit special handling and should go to companies whose special expertise and competence have been verified by in-depth experience checks.

Seal vendors proposing seals may elect to narrow their offer to only two seal types, say Type "A" for categories 1, 2, and 3, and Type "C" for categories 4 through 9; or Type "B" for categories 1 through 6, and Type "C" for categories 7, 8, and 9; etc.

As mentioned earlier, it is recommended to mail the bid request information to three or four capable mechanical seal manufacturers. Their response should be analyzed critically to flush out significant deviations among the various proposals. These deviations may range from materials of construction to different API flush plans and from differences in basic configuration to differences in application philosophy of stationary vs rotating seal members. Reconciling the deviations or differences will assist the engineer responsible for final selection in determining whose seal offer has the best chance of meeting the user criteria highlighted earlier and amplified later.

To assist the purchaser in development of bid request information and later in evaluation of bids received, we have developed the selection matrixes shown in Table 2. The upper matrix is concerned with general seal selection considerations. This matrix is easy to use and interpret. Under the heading "Basic type seal," the matrix explains that low and moderate temperatures, pressures, speeds, etc. can be accommodated by the majority of basic configurations. From the second heading we would infer that Type "A" seals are probably identical to "basic" seals. They should not be applied in high pressure or high speed services, but could very well serve in high temperature environments as long as heat resistant secondary seals or effective auxiliary cooling were applied. Type "B" seals would go one step further by featuring high speed capability, as long as the design is of the stationary type (Fig. 8, later). Finally, Type "C" seals would add high pressure capability as long as two-ply bellows and/or stress resistant face mountings were incorporated in the design.

The lower matrix points to specific seal design or material considerations and ranks their relative significance in applications that have to cope with high abrasives content, poor lubricity, extreme temperature, etc. For instance, a bellows seal could represent a significant improvement in applications where seal failure due to clogging of springs might lead to costly losses. The same seal should be considered excellent for high temperatures. Or, we could examine double seals and see that this design has no influence on high speed capability or ease of installation; however, it might significantly improve pump reliability under high temperature conditions and should be rated excellent for sealing against pumpage with high abrasives content, poor lubricity, low vapor pressure, low viscosity, hazardous or toxic properties, and high risk resulting from seal failure. The next column describes tandem seals and might alert us to the fact that the less expensive tandem seals embody the same design advantages as double seals, except for ability to seal against high abrasives content and poor lubricity of pumpage. Thus, if the pumpage is without abrasives and has good lubricity, it would be appropriate to select tandem seals instead of double seals. Another advantage of tandem seals is that they will not require the buffer fluid system to operate at pressures in excess of stuffing box pressure.

The remaining columns in the lower matrix of Table 2 should be used in the same fashion by the engineer specifying or evaluating mechanical seals for pumping services in processing plants.

Desirable Design Features

Evaluation of the various bids is made easier by recognizing desirable design features incorporated in mechanical seals. Some of these merit closer consideration.

Cartridge Construction

Cartridge seals are designed for rapid installation and removal. The cartridge seal is an arrangement of seal components on a shaft sleeve and in a seal gland constituting a single unit which is usually assembled and preset at the factory. Both bellows and spring-type seals can be cartridge arrange if the pump stuffing box is large enough.

Cartridge seal units offer major maintenance advantages. Replacement is rapid and there is far less risk of assembly error and assembly damage than with conventional mechanical seal mounting. For these reasons we prefer cartridge seals for typical pumps. Cartridge arrangements are routinely available for horizontally split pumps. Overhung pumps are not often supplied with cartridge seals due to space and general pump design constraints.

One note of caution: Metallic gaskets under shaft sleeves may take a permanent set and cannot be reused.

"Symmetrical Package" and "Unitized" Seal Construction

Stuffing box size and general dimensional constraints have impeded for years the application of advanced or high performance mechanical face seals in many overhung, AVS, and ANSI-type pumps. After the needs of the petrochemical industry were again discussed at a fluid sealing forum [2], experienced seal manufacturers addressed the issue and developed "Symmetrical Package" and "Unitized" seals incorporating the principal components shown in Fig. 1. These preassembled package seals are now available as single or double mechanical seals. They will completely replace the stuffing box of many pumps whose hydraulic end would be adequate, but whose stuffing box dimensions are judged unsuitable for reliable long-term seal operation or for utilization of optimum seal designs.

TABLE 2—GENERAL SEAL DESIGN CONSIDERATIONS

	Basic type seal			A type seal			B type seal			C type seal		
	L	M	H	L	M	H	L	M	H	L	M	H
Temperature	X	X (1)		X	X	X (1)	X	X	X (1)	X	X	X (5)
Pressure	X	X (9)		X	X		X	X		X	X	X (8)
Speed	X	X		X	X		X	X	X (6)	X	X	X (6)
Corrosives	X	X	X (2)	X	X	X (2)	X	X (2)	X (3)	X	X (2)	X (3)
Abrasives	X	X (4)		X	X (4)		X	X (4)		X	X (4)	

Specific seal design or material considerations

Equipment or product deviations	Stationary design	Metal bellows design	Isolated springs	Hydraulic balance	Double seal	Tandem seal	Cartridge mounting	Tungsten carbide	Silicon carbide	Carbon graphite
Extreme temperature	N	E/10	S	S	S	S	N	S	E	E
Coking/flashing	S	E/11	E	N	E	S	N	E	E	N
High abrasive cont.	S	S	S	N	E	N	N	S	S	N
Poor lubricant	N	N	N	S	E	N	N	S	E	E
Corrosive	N	N	E	N	N	N	N	N	E	E
Hazardous	N	N	N	N	E	E	N	N	N	N
Low viscosity	N	N	N	E	E	E	N	S	E	E
High vapor pressure	S	N	N	E	E	E	N	S	E	E
Congealing	S/12	S/12	E	N	S	N	N	E	N	N
High loss potential	S	S	N	N	E	E	N	N	S	N
Installation ease	N	N	N	N	N/7	N/7	E	N	N	N
High speed	E	N	N	E	N	N	N	S	E	E

Explanation of Symbols Used in Table 2

1. Heat resistant secondary seals and/or auxiliary cooling.
2. Moderate upgrading of metallurgy to provide corrosion resistance.
3. Maximum upgrading of metallurgy to provide corrosion resistance.
4. Abrasion resistant faces.
5. Metal bellows design.
6. Stationary design.
7. Cartridge mounted assembly recommended.
8. Two-ply bellows and/or stress resistant face mounting.
9. Stepped shaft or sleeve to achieve hydraulic balance.
10. Metal, asbestos, or graphite secondary seals.
11. External steam quench in gland.
12. Heat the sealing area before rotating shaft.

L = Low	N = No significant improvement
M = Moderate	S = Significant improvement
H = High	E = Excellent

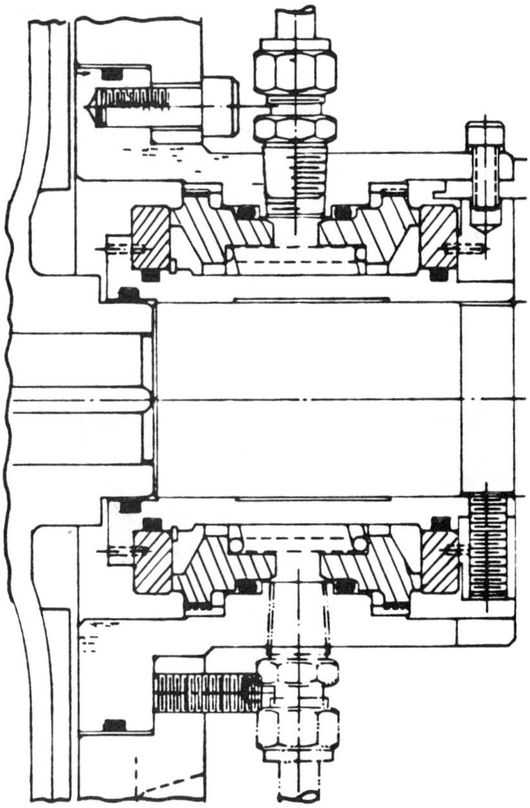

FIG. 1

Proper application of these self-contained seals could lead to the procurement of suitably configured hydraulic portions of centrifugal pumps from the pump manufacturer, and procurement of optimized package seals from the seal manufacturer. Symmetrical Package or Unitized seals would be mounted to the pump casing by the seal manufacturer; as a minimum, the seal manufacturer's mounting instructions would have to govern at final assembly.

In any event, Symmetrical Package and Unitized seals open up untold possibilities for reliability improvements and cost reduction on a wide spectrum of centrigual pumps and pumping services.

Hard Face Material and Preferred Rotating Member

Heat generated at seal faces must be rapidly conducted away if fluid vaporization and resulting problems are to be avoided. Depending on service conditions and pump design, either the rotating or stationary seal ring must dissipate as much frictional heat as possible. Considerably greater hardness, shock resistance, and better wear properties make silicon carbide the preferred seal face material in many of the more severe applications.

In applications where carbon is used as one of the seal faces, most of the heat will be dissipated through the higher conductivity silicon carbide or tungsten carbide mating ring. Heat dissipation will be enhanced if this component is rotated instead of the carbon. Thus, it would be advantageous to rotate the high conductivity component whenever effective heat dissipation is of critical importance.

Placement of O-Rings

An advantageous seal design recognizes that O-ring life can be reduced by close proximity to the heat source, by swelling due to chemical attack, and by operation in a dynamic mode, especially in the presence of erosive materials. Going to PTFE chevrons or wedges may allow operation at higher temperatures and reduced risk of chemical attack, but will very often lead to fretting of metal surfaces in contact with it. Bellows seals eliminate many of these problems by using static secondary sealing. Seals with spring-loaded running faces are forced to use dynamic means of secondary sealing which could, in some instances, be more prone to failure.

Mechanical Design Considerations

Important differences can exist in the mechanical designs of competing vendors. For instance, execution "E" of Fig. 2 shows the method of clamping rotating hard face (1) against shaft sleeve (2) of a stationary bellows seal assembly. This clamping method ensures perpendicularity between shaft centerline and rotating seal faces. However, this clamping method also invites distortion at the running faces. Execution "F" tends to avoid distortion by mounting the rotating hard face in a resilient backing ring (3) and by pulling mounting ring (4) against collar (5).

Two different clamping methods are shown in Fig. 3. Both of these methods were devised to eliminate distortion of running faces which, incidentally, is still a possibility unless careful engineering and material selection keep the shrink-fitted hard face and mating ring carrier together throughout the anticipated temperature range. However, in execution "G" the collar is set-screwed to the shaft or shaft sleeve, whereas in execution "H" the mating ring carrier is set-screwed to the shaft or shaft sleeve. Experience shows that on some seal models perpendicularity and seal setting accuracy are more difficult to achieve with the clamping method indicated as execution "G" in Fig. 3. As shown, the seal requires very careful adjustment of cap screws inserted through the collar. This problem can be overcome if the design allows collar and carrier faces to butt-up solidly.

Another interesting difference exists in the carbon holders of the more conventional mechanical seals. The upper half of Fig. 4 shows a lock ring (1) executed with a set screw (2) which engages a slot in carbon holder (3). Under certain service conditions, contact between set screw and slot may cause a

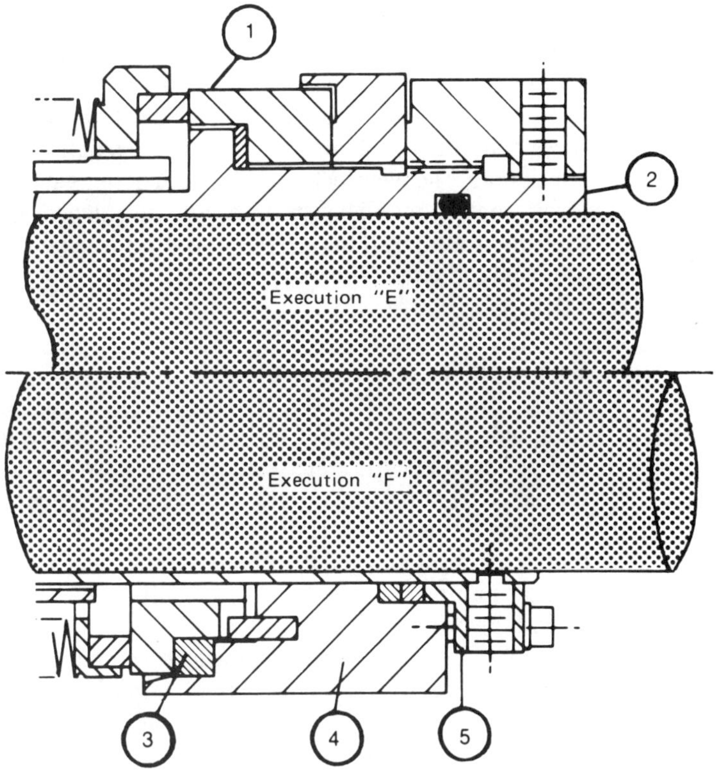

FIG. 2. Competing methods of mounting hard face against shaft sleeve.

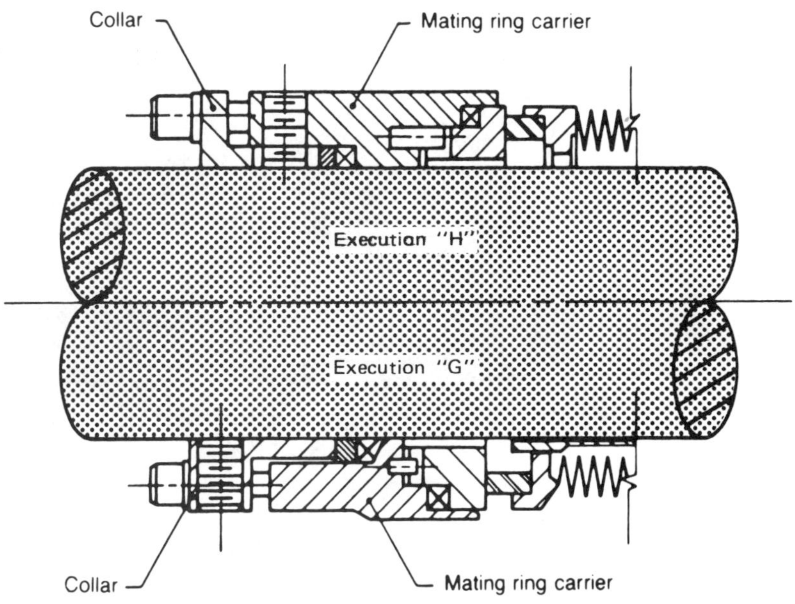

FIG. 3. Competing clamping methods.

wear pattern which may prevent proper seal operation. Moreover, tightening of the set screw can distort the relatively thin lock ring and cause contact or interference between lock ring OD and carbon holder ID. The construction features shown in the lower half of Fig. 4 would tend to eliminate both of these potential problems by providing an axially oriented drive pin (4) and a considerably heavier lock ring (1). Both designs shown in Fig. 4 deserve credit for presenting relatively smooth, low turbulence surfaces to their respective fluid environment. This is largely accomplished by locating the springs on the atmospheric side of the seal.

Seal Type "A"

Although the user would be wise to look for desirable design features in competing offers, the seal selection strategy would allow a Type "A" seal to be furnished by many seal manufacturers. Experience shows that the majority of pumping services with classification 1, 2, or 3 would employ AVS or ANSI-type centrifugal pumps. It will often not be possible to fit cartridge-type seals in these pumps. Balanced seals normally should not be required for Type "A" seals. However, if a balanced seal is chosen, the balance should be achieved internal to the seal instead of using stepped shafts or sleeves. Figures 1 through 8 all show seals which can incorporate this design advantage.

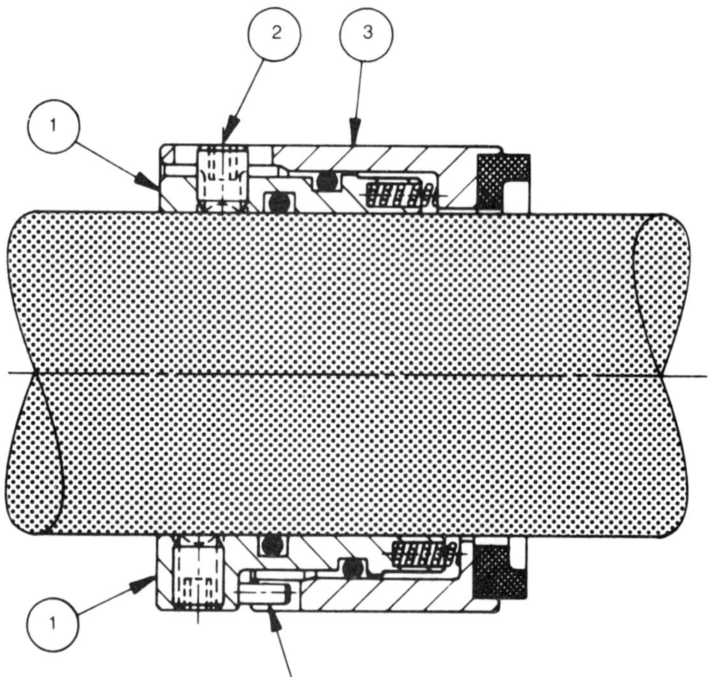

FIG. 4. Carbon holders.

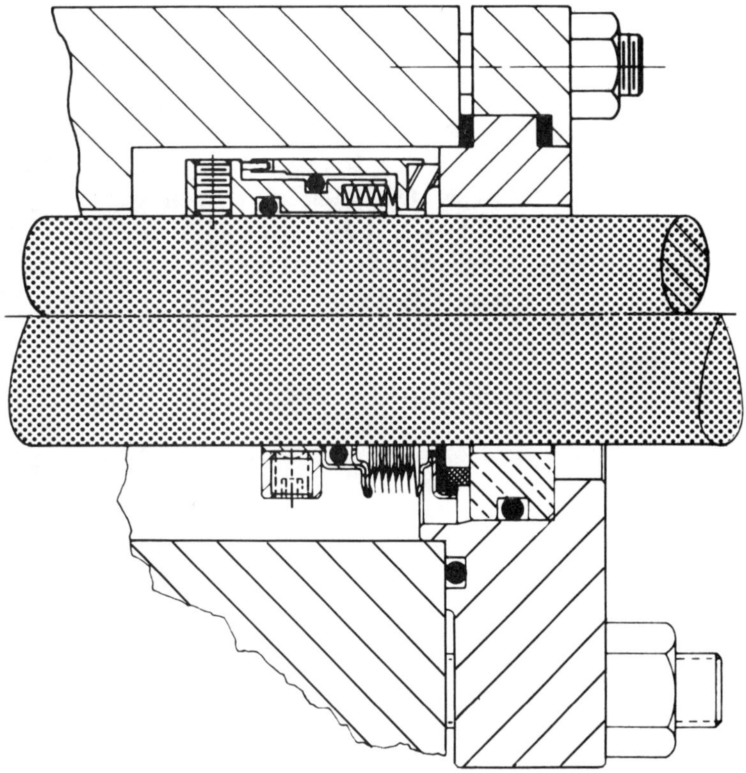

FIG. 5. Typical "A" seals.

Simplicity of maintenance may be of somewhat greater importance for the Type "A" seal than compliance with every one of the desirable features cited earlier. Figure 5 illustrates two of several seals we would expect to be offered as Type "A" seals. Notice that the stationary hard faces are reversible and probably can be reconditioned several times. The top half of Fig. 5 depicts a "T-clamped" stationary seat ring using gaskets which are difficult to keep evenly compressed at assembly. Also, the application of excessive clamping pressure may cause distortion at the seal faces.

The bottom half of Fig. 5 shows a recently introduced low-cost bellows seal with an O-ring equipped, reversible stationary seal ring. Both seat and O-ring are available in several materials. However, neither of the two seal executions shown here should be expected to serve as an effective throttle bushing in case of catastrophic seal failure. Throttle bushings should be made from a nonsparking material, have only a small shaft clearance, and be fitted into the gland plate. This requirement is given in the 6th edition of API Standard 610, Para. 2.7.1.12, but not always observed by the vendor.

In a specific procurement situation, we would probably ask the manufacturer who proposed a Type "A" seal with the "T-clamped" stationary to re-bid on the basis of using the stationary seat execution shown in conjunction with the bellows seal at the lower half of Fig. 5. When selecting a low-cost, Type "A" seal for corrosive pumpage, we would want to verify the suitability of the bellows material for satisfactory long-term operation.

Seal Type "B"

Type "B" seals must be selected for satisfactory operation in pumping service classifications 4, 5, and 6. Most pumps meeting these classifications probably would be API-type, and our preference would be cartridge seals, even though overhung-type process pumps are not routinely furnished with design features that make it easy to use cartridge arrangements. Type "B" seals should avoid having the spring (or springs) immersed in fluid. Figure 6 shows two of several seals that very probably would give excellent service in many service classifications and are thought to meet the cost/benefit criteria envisioned for Type "B" service severities. These seals use one or more stationary springs and incorporate a number of desirable features. A cartridge arrangement for ease of installation, the single nonrotating spring shown with the design in the top half of Fig. 6 is arranged to operate away from the product, bronze spring retainer (1) serves as a throttle bushing, and the

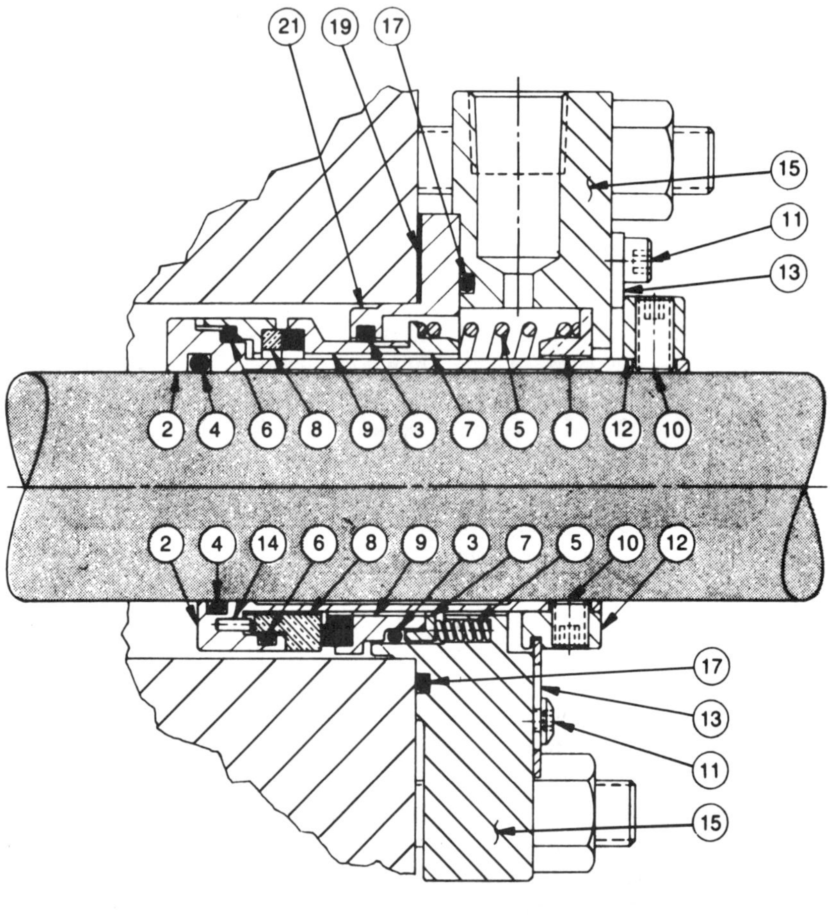

FIG. 6. Typical "B" seals.

relatively clean profile inside the stuffing box reduces seal drag. (Note that rotating components are identified with even numbers and stationary components with odd numbers.)

Except for utilizing several springs, the seal design shown in the bottom half of Fig. 6 is quite similar to the design shown in the top half. Both seals incorporate the desirable features of many similar stationary seal designs:

Self-squaring faces. This feature may result in appreciably better seal life for pumps with excessive shaft deflection or pumps operating with nominal shaft deflection at high speeds.

Nonflexing springs. Spring life extension and long-term, uniform pressure can be expected.

Preassembled cartridge construction. These seals can be shipped with the gland plate in place. No field measurements or settings will be required.

However, a closer look will show functional differences in the arrangement of O-ring (3). It could be argued that progressive wear of the seal faces shown in the upper half of Fig. 6 will cause the O-ring to make sliding contact with a clean portion of part (9), whereas advancing the stationary seal face in the lower half of Fig. 6 will cause O-ring (3) to slide over a wetted and potentially contaminated portion of gland place (15).

Functionally similar features can also be found in an intermediate range of bellows seals as shown in Fig. 7. Of course, these should also be considered for Type "B" services. Rotating bellows seals tend to be self-cleaning by virtue of centrifugal action. As mentioned earlier, they do not incorporate sliding (dynamic) elastomers. Instead, they use static secondary sealing means. Stationary *bellows* seals will exhibit the same advantages as given for stationary *spring* seals, above. Generally, stationary-type seals should be preferred in applications encountering face peripheral velocities in excess of 4500 ft (1372 m) per minute, serious shaft deflection, or coking after the pumpage has crossed the seal faces.

When applying bellows seals in light hydrocarbons, we should look for design features that prevent torsional windup of the bellows in case the seal faces undergo slipstick motion relative to each other. If the design does not alleviate these concerns, the user may favor spring-type mechanical seals for light hydrocarbon services.

Seal Type "C"

Severe duty, high pressure, extreme temperature, and high loss potential are the predominant factors making up service categories 7, 8, and 9. The slate of experienced vendors and acceptable configurations narrows considerably for Type "C" seals, which deserve to be called High Performance Seals. Every *pump* in these service categories should comply with the most stringent requirements of applicable API specifications. Similarly, Type "C" seals would originate from manufacturers with outstanding reputation only.

One of perhaps three possible Type "C" seals is illustrated in Fig. 8. This high temperature seal uses stationary bellows, eliminates O-rings, and

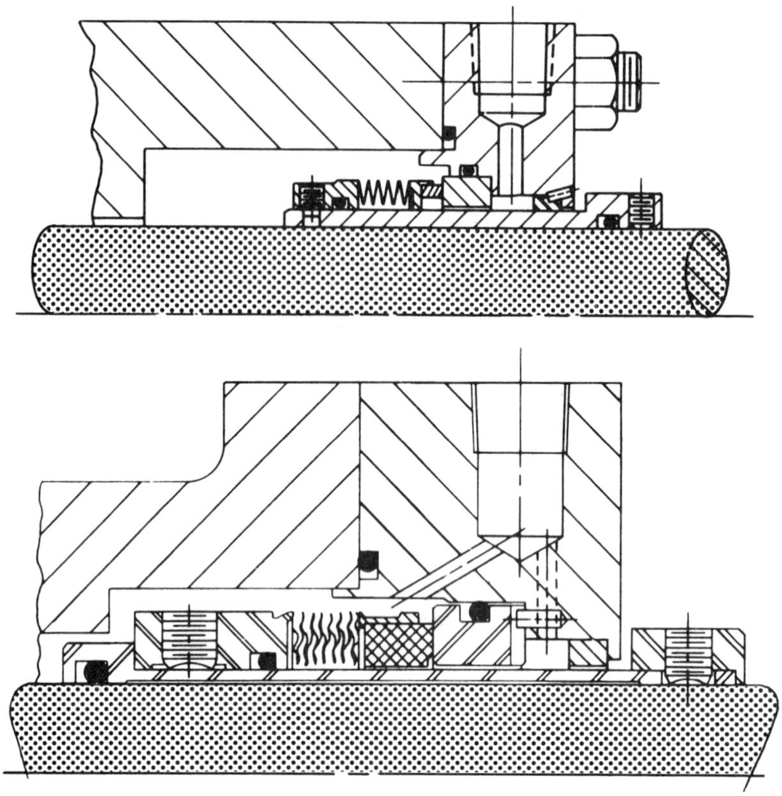

FIG. 7. Typical "B" bellows seals.

employs high temperature graphite foil gasketing. Only proven materials of construction and highly sophisticated fabrication and quality control techniques should be used to produce these seals. Qualified vendors have successful experience with 2-ply bellows construction to handle higher pressures and will be able to produce these seals free from harmonic resonance which, in earlier seals of this type, caused distress.

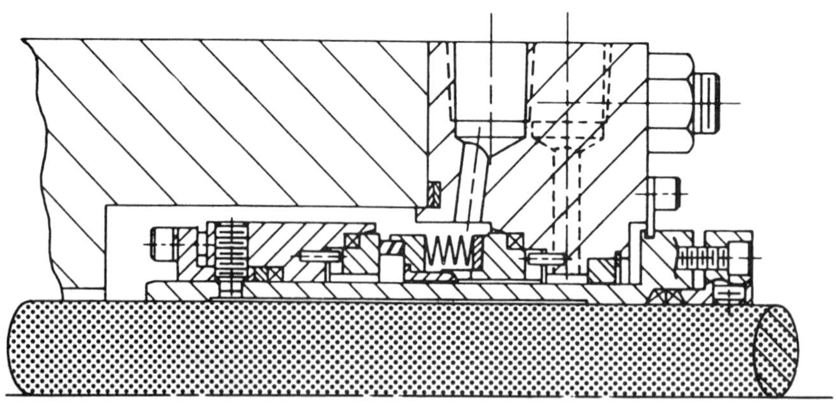

FIG. 8. Typical "C" seal.

TABLE 3 Bid Comparison for Mechanical Seals

Service data: Kerosene feed pump — Item: P-28 A/B

Driver rating:	125 hp (92 kw)	Viscosity at P.T.:	1.9 cSt
Diff. head:	704 ft (214 m)	Vapor press at P.T.:	1.0 psia (0.069 bar)
Suct. pressure:	14.8 psia (1.02 bar)	Specific gravity:	0.82
Disch. pressure:	265 psia (18.3 bar)	Temperature:	90°F (32°C)
		Speed:	3560 rpm

	Bidder		
Service classification assigned by bidder	Apex Seal 5	Custom Seal 6	Superb Mfg. Co. 5
Seal type assigned by bidder	B	C	B
API seal code	BTTFL	BDTFL	BTTFN
Seal model	Apex 1010	CS-500	Silicarb-X
Seal design option	Standard	Cartridge	Stationary type
API flush plan	13	13	13
API auxiliary seal plan	52	54	52
Stuffing box pressure (est)	39 psig	35 psig	40 psig
Operating window (allowable deviations):			
Temperature	±130°F (73°C)	±125°F (69°C)	+110/+160°F
Discharge pressure	−110, +220 psi	−50, +200 psi	−100, +200 psi
Viscosity	−1, +500 cSt	−1.2, +200 cSt	−1, +400 cSt
Seal balance ratio	79%	84%	82%
Seal drawing number	578-23122	8563CDA	C-802BF-20
Special features and/or remarks	Universal gland	Floating throttle bushing	Grafoil backup
Cost, incl. gland and sleeve	$899	$995	$1070
Cost, seal only	$472	$510	$532
Deviations from specified requirements			

High performance seals usually incorporate a cushion-type stationary mating ring to avoid distortion transmitted through the gland by axial forces and to allow optimum flatness control at assembly.

Bid Comparison

After the bids are received, they have to be tabulated and compared. The format shown in Table 3 facilitates this comparison. The reviewing engineer should look for significant differences among competing bids and determine which offer incorporates a majority of desirable design features. Special features beyond those specified by the purchaser may have been proposed by some bidders and deserve extra credit for reducing the risk of catastrophic failure incidents. Each special feature must be given a separate assessment of value. Alternatively, the purchaser may decide that bidder X's offer is less expensive than, but nevertheless technically equal to, the offer made by bidder Y. He may now wish to upgrade his selection by asking X to furnish the seals with optional, although not previously specified features. Floating bushings in the gland ring are only one of many available options which may prove attractive to an experienced purchaser. Auxiliary packing is perhaps another low-cost option which may be offered by some vendors, although this author agrees with the favorite saying of a wise old machinery engineer in California: "Old packings never die, they just drip away."

This material appeared in *Hydrocarbon Processing*, pp. 75–81. January 1983, and is reprinted with the permission of the editor.

References

1. J. H. Ingram, *Pump Reliability—Where Do You Start?*, Paper Presented at the 37th Petroleum Mechanical Engineering Workshop and Conference (ASME), Dallas, Texas, September 13–15, 1981.
2. H. P. Bloch, *A User's View of Fluid Sealing Economics*, Paper Presented at the 45th Annual Meeting of the Fluid Sealing Association, Sun Valley, Idaho, October 10–13, 1978.

HEINZ P. BLOCH

Microemulsions

Introduction

A microemulsion may be defined as a thermodynamically stable isotropic solution of two immiscible fluids, generally oil and water, containing one or more surface-active species. The surface-active species or surfactants are mostly located at the interface between the domains of polar and nonpolar fluids. Historically, microemulsions were first described by Schulman and coworkers [1, 2] as transparent or translucent systems formed spontaneously by mixing oil and water with relatively large amounts of an ionic surfactant together with a cosurfactant. Microemulsions need not be transparent and are not required to contain cosurfactants or cosolvents and electrolytes. Many systems of practical interest do contain a cosolvent such as a medium chain alcohol and also electrolytes. It is also possible to formulate microemulsions using very polar solvents instead of water. Currently, there is no universally accepted definition of microemulsions. The above definition is a rather broad one which includes among microemulsions the classical ones with cosolvents, reverse micellar solutions, and also "swollen" or "solubilized" micellar solutions. This definition also does not identify a specific structure for microemulsion aggregates. Different types of microstructures are possible, and for some systems the structure is still debated, as discussed later. Microemulsions are to be distinguished from coarse emulsions (macroemulsions) which are kinetically stabilized two-phase systems. The size of the dispersed phase in emulsions is typically one to two orders of magnitude larger than in microemulsions.

The utilization of microemulsions preceded their introduction into the scientific community by Schulman and coworkers [1, 2]. For example, microemulsions formulated with eucalyptus oil, water, soap, and white spirit were used more than a century ago to wash wool efficiently. Several industrial products such as lubricating oils, liquid waxes, and detergent formulations were patented during the 1930s [3]. Microemulsions have received considerable attention in recent years because of their interesting thermodynamics, physicochemical behavior, and applications. The importance of microemulsions for enhanced oil recovery [4] has played a key role in the development of extensive theoretical and experimental research on microemulsions.

Some of the interesting features of microemulsions include (1) spontaneous formation and thermodynamic stability, (2) intricate phase behavior, (3) large interfacial area per unit volume, (4) a wide range of interfacial curvature, (5) ultralow interfacial tensions and critical phenomena, and (6) large solubilization in both organic and aqueous phases.

A detailed review of microemulsions is beyond the scope of this article. However, there are several recent reviews [5–8] and proceedings [9–11]. Only salient features of the thermodynamics and phase behavior of microemulsions will be presented. A few selected applications will be described briefly.

Thermodynamics

The thermodynamic stability of microemulsions is intriguing in view of the small aggregate size (on the order of 100 Å) and hence very large interfacial area per unit volume. Early workers [1, 2] postulated a transient negative interfacial tension in an effort to explain the spontaneous formation of microemulsions. It is now recognized that thermodynamically stable systems will form spontaneously if the interfacial tension is low enough (even though positive) that the increase in interfacial free energy due to dispersion of one phase in the other is less than the free energy decrease due to the entropy of dispersion. Ruckenstein and coworkers [12, 13] treated the thermodynamic stability by taking into account contributions to the free energy due to the adsorption of surfactant, the van der Waals and electrostatic interaction forces between particles, and the entropy of dispersion. A negative minimum in the plot of free energy of formation versus droplet radius corresponds to a stable microemulsion. Miller and coworkers [14, 15] included the effect of bending on the droplet size. For a given surfactant concentration, the bending effect leads to a larger number of droplets having a size smaller than the "normal" radius which the surfactant film assumes at an oil–water interface. This occurs because the decrease in free energy associated with the increased entropy of dispersion due to more droplets exceeds the energy necessary to bend the surfactant film beyond its natural radius.

Microemulsions are not always dispersions of droplets. The packing of surfactant molecules at the interface plays an important role in determining the structure and shape of the aggregates. A packing parameter has been defined as v/a_0l_c where v is the volume of the surfactant hydrophobe, a_0 is the optimal cross-sectional area per polar head, and l_c is approximately 80–90% of the fully extended length of the surfactant chain [16]. Although limitations exist, this parameter is a simple guide in determining whether microemulsions will be water-in-oil type ($v/a_0l_c > 1$) or oil-in-water type ($v/a_0l_c < 1$). This is illustrated in Fig. 1(a) and 1(b). A roughly planar interface exists when v/a_0l_c approaches 1. Such a situation is favored by the addition of a cosolvent such as a short-chain alcohol (Fig. 1c). Under conditions of small or zero net curvature, microemulsions may be bicontinuous [17] with an interpenetrating network of organic and aqueous domains separated by the surfactant film, or lamellarlike with defects due to thermal fluctuations [18, 19]. Bicontinuous microemulsions are not yet properly understood although several models have been proposed [20–22].

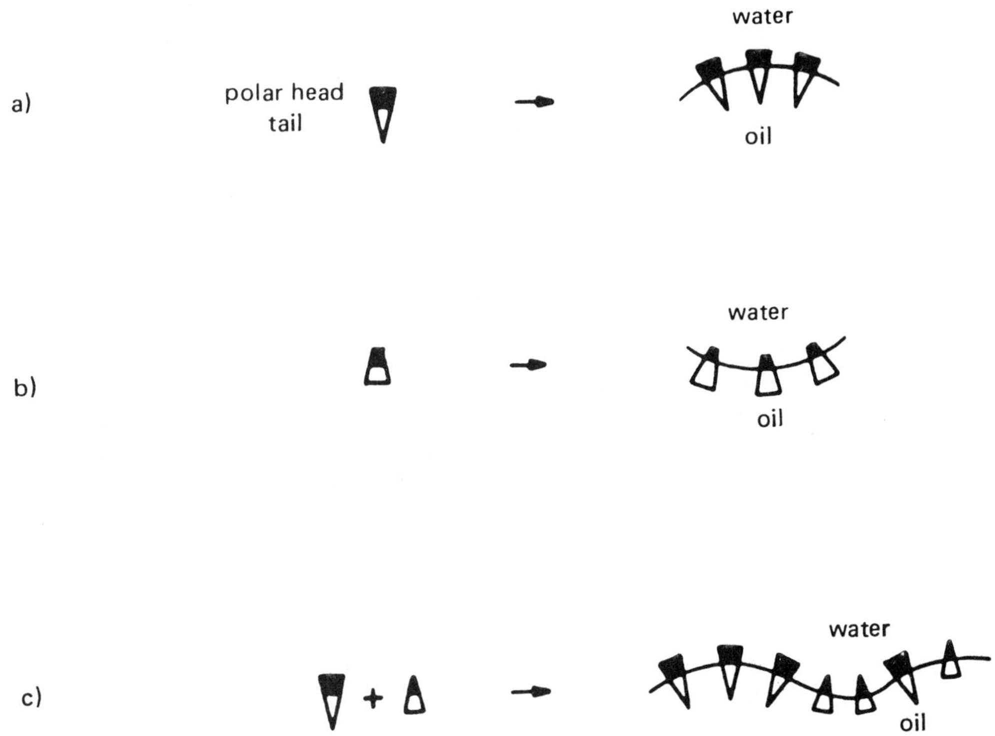

FIG. 1. A schematic showing the effect of surfactant packing on the curvature of the interfacial film: a) bulky polar head favors oil-in-water microemulsion; b) bulk hydrophobic tails favor water-in-oil microemulsion; c) if the surfactant is balanced or in the presence of a cosolvent as shown, the net curvature is very small or zero, and bicontinuous microemulsions are possible.

Phase Equilibria, Solubilization, and Interfacial Tensions

Physicochemical aspects of the phase behavior of microemulsions have been extensively studied, particularly because of their importance in applications such as enhanced oil recovery. The phase behavior exhibited by microemulsions is very rich. In addition to being single phases, microemulsions can exist in equilibrium with excess oil, water, or both. Winsor [23] referred to these equilibria as Types I, II, and III, respectively. Such transitions occur when an appropriate variable such as salinity is changed. Microemulsions containing a few percent of an anionic surfactant (e.g., petroleum sulfonates), a cosurfactant such as a short-chain alcohol, and equal volumes of oil and NaCl brine have been extensively studied [4]. The phase behavior is termed "simple" [24] when the microemulsions behave as though composed of three pure components having ternary diagrams as shown in Fig. 2. Figure 2(a) at low salinities illustrates a two-phase region in which microemulsions along the binodal curve exist in equilibrium with oil containing molecularly dispersed surfactant. The surfactant is partitioned predominantly into the aqueous phase. This microemulsion system, which corresponds to Winsor's Type I, is often called a "lower" phase and is water-continuous. Figure 2(c) at high salinities indicates a two-phase region in which microemulsions exist in equilibrium with excess brine, i.e., Winsor's Type II. Such microemulsions are commonly named "upper" phase and are oil continuous. Figure 2(b) at an intermediate salinity illustrates Winsor's Type III microemulsion in the

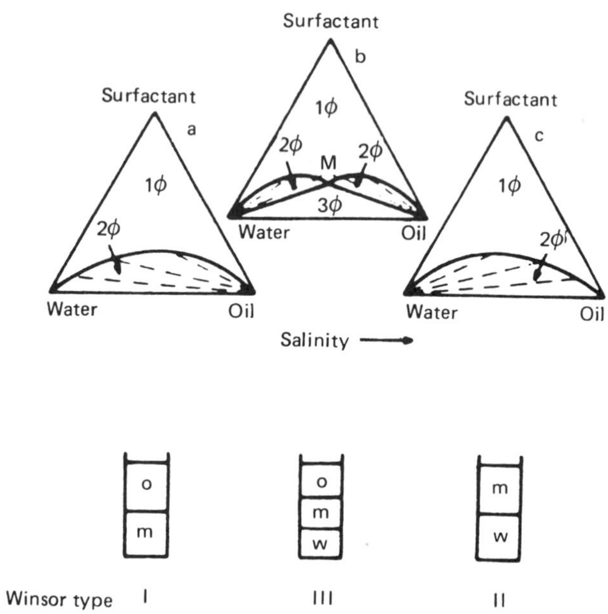

FIG. 2. Illustration of "simple" phase behavior and Winsor I, III, and II systems.

lower triangle. Three phases exist in equilibrium: a microemulsion corresponding to composition M, excess brine, and excess oil. Type III microemulsions have been designated as "middle" phase [24] and also "surfactant" phase [18].

Although not all microemulsions conform qualitatively to Fig. 2, "simple" behavior appears to be a good first approximation for many systems of practical importance. A notable difference between real and simple systems is the locus of middle phase compositions rather than a single point. It is also possible to have four coexisting phases, two of which may be microemulsions in equilibrium with one another, or a microemulsion in equilibrium with a liquid crystalline phase. A liquid crystalline phase may also exist in equilibrium with only brine and oil. It should be noted that the pseudoternary diagrams are slices at constant salinity of the tetrahedron necessary to display the phase boundaries of a four-component system.

Factors which affect the phase behavior of microemulsions include salinity, surfactant type and concentration, cosolvent type and concentration, pH, oil composition, temperature, and pressure. As salinity increases, there is a steady progression from lower phase to middle phase to upper phase microemulsions. This reflects a continuous evolution of the preferred curvature of the surfactant film, and corresponds to an increased hydrophobicity with added salts like NaCl.

At low salinities the droplet size in the water-continuous lower phase increases with increasing salinity. This corresponds to an increase in solubilization of oil and is reflected in increased scattering. As salinity increases further, the middle phase appears and is initially water-continuous. The microemulsion is apparently bicontinuous over an intermediate salinity range. The middle phase becomes oil-continuous at higher salinities. After the transition from three to two phases, the microemulsion remains oil-continuous with drop size decreasing with increasing salinity.

Table 1 summarizes the qualitative changes in phase behavior of anionic surfactants. Some details of the effects of different variables can be found in Ref. 4. The phase transitions can generally be understood in terms of relative strengths of hydrophilic and hydrophobic properties of the surfactant film in the microemulsions. The phase behavior depends strongly on the type and

TABLE 1 Effect of Several Variables on the Phase Behavior of Anionic Microemulsions

Variable	Phase Transitions
Salinity ↑	lower ⟶ middle ⟶ upper
Oil: alkane carbon number ↑	upper ⟶ middle ⟶ lower
Oil: aromaticity ↑	lower ⟶ middle ⟶ upper
Alcohol concentration ↑ (low MW)	upper ⟶ middle ⟶ lower
Alcohol concentration ↑ (high MW)	lower ⟶ middle ⟶ upper
Surfactant: hydrophobic chain length ↑	lower ⟶ middle ⟶ upper
Temperature ↑	upper ⟶ middle ⟶ lower
pH ↑ (for carboxylic acids, amines, and other pH-sensitive surfactants)	upper ⟶ middle ⟶ lower

structure of the surfactant. For example, microemulsions containing nonionic surfactants are less sensitive to salinity, but are more sensitive to temperature. The partitioning of cosolvents such as alcohols between the surfactant film, the organic phase, and the aqueous phase also affects the phase behavior. It is generally possible to tailor microemulsions for specific applications by changing an appropriate variable. For example, as evident from Table 1, the effect of salinity on the phase behavior can be counterbalanced by an increase in the pH of an appropriate microemulsion.

There are two bulk interfaces in the middle phase and one in the lower or upper phase microemulsion system. Thus, one or three values of interfacial tension (IFT) may be measured depending on system composition: (1) γ_{mo} between microemulsion and excess oil phase, (2) γ_{mw} between microemulsion and excess brine phase, and (3) γ_{ow} between excess oil and brine phases. Phase volumes and, consequently, the volumes of oil (V_o) and brine (V_w) solubilized in the microemulsion depend on the variables which control the phase behavior. The solubilization parameters are defined as V_o/V_s and V_w/V_s, where V_s is the volume of the surfactant in the microemulsion phase. These parameters can be easily determined from phase volume measurements if it is assumed that all the surfactant is in the microemulsion phase.

A typical example of the variation of IFT and solubilization parameters with salinity is shown in Fig. 3 [4]. The magnitude of γ_{mo} decreases as V_o/V_s increases, i.e., as more oil is solubilized. Similarly, the magnitude of γ_{mw} decreases as V_w/V_s increases. The salinity at which the values of γ_{mo} and γ_{mw} are equal is called the optimal salinity based on IFT. Similarly, the intersection of V_o/V_s and V_m/V_s defines the optimal salinity based on phase behavior. The optimal salinity concept is very important for enhanced oil recovery, as discussed later.

Miller et al. [25] suggested a model for phase separation in microemulsions which accounts for the salient features observed experimentally. The oil-in-water microemulsion droplets are attracted to one another by van der Waals forces and, if ionic, repelled by electrical double-layer forces. The repulsion term dominates at low salinity. The droplet size increases and the double-layer thickness decreases with increasing salinity. Hence the droplets can approach one another more closely and attractive forces become more important. Eventually, attraction dominates and the microemulsion separates into two water-continuous phases, a middle phase rich in drops and an excess brine phase lean in drops. This is analogous to a gas–liquid transition. The model predicts that interfacial tension values between two water-continuous phases can be ultralow (less than 10^{-2} dyn/cm) even when the system is not close to the consolute point.

Near-critical conditions are observed at compositions corresponding to transitions from lower to middle phase and middle to upper phase. The correlation length diverges at the critical point, causing critical opalescence which is observed experimentally. The interfacial tensions between the middle phase and the new excess phase are extremely low. Near the optimal salinity both γ_{mo} and γ_{mw} are influenced by respective critical end points. In addition to salinity, other variables, e.g., temperature, which produce phase transitions in the neighborhood of a consolute point will also cause critical behavior.

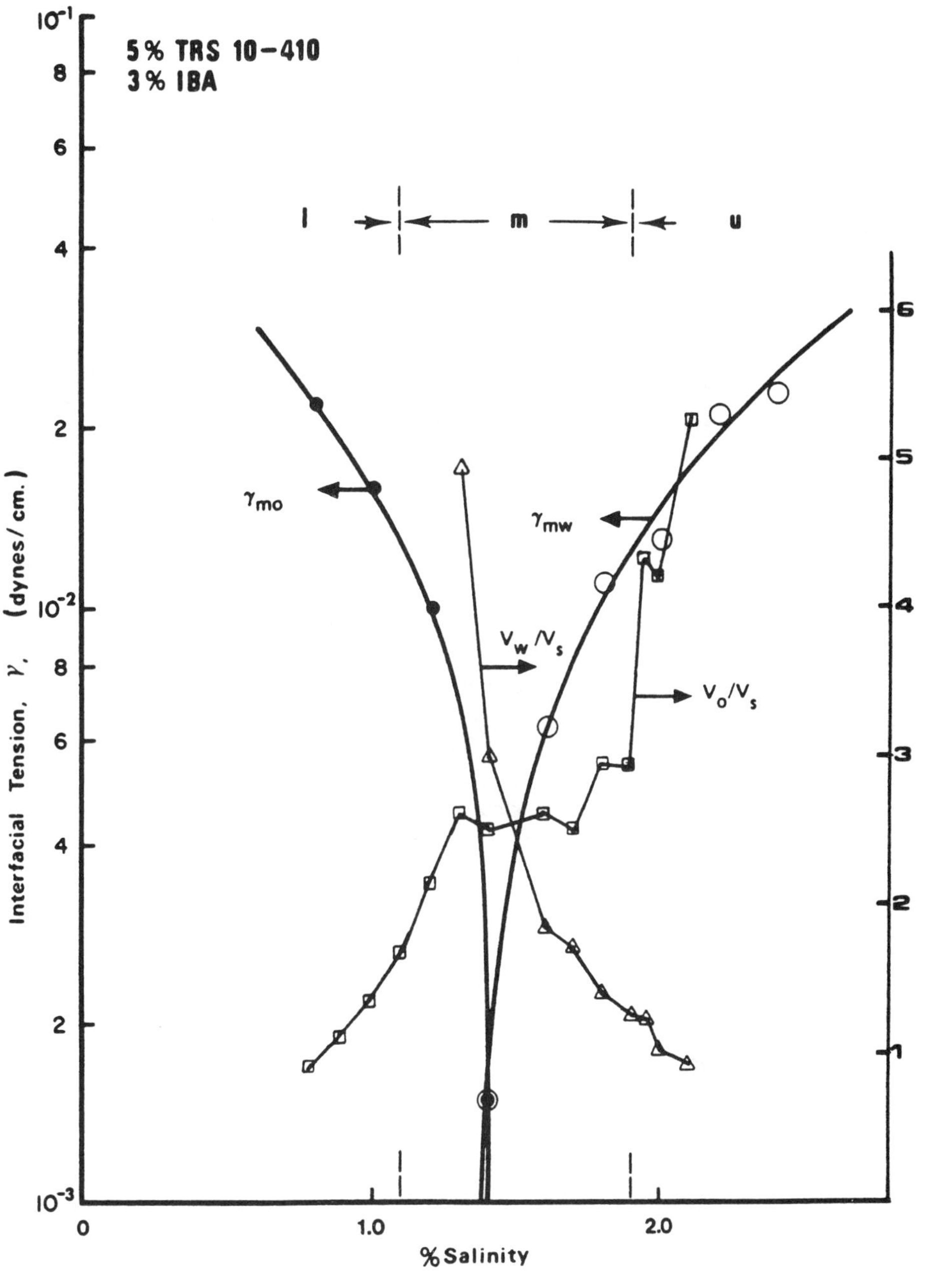

FIG. 3. Variation of interfacial tensions and solubilization parameters with salinity for a microemulsion system containing a petroleum sulfonate, TRS 10-410. An aqueous solution containing 5 wt.% TRS 10-410 (Witco), 3 wt.% isobutanol, and varying salinity was equilibrated with an equal volume of *n*-dodecane at 22°C to obtain the microemulsion.

Characterization

The phase behavior, microstructure, aggregate size, interactions, interfacial tensions, rheology, and other properties are important both in terms of fundamental understanding and applications. A variety of techniques may be used to obtain such information. Generally, a combination of different techniques is warranted to reduce ambiguity in characterizing microemulsions. Phase diagrams are useful in understanding the behavior of microemulsions, although experimentally it is tedious to locate the phase boundaries even on a pseudoternary diagram. A polarized light screen [26] provides information about the macroscopic phase behavior of solutions in terms of isotropy, birefringence, scattering, and also interfacial phenomena such as critically diffuse regions. Equilibration is fast in middle phase microemulsions, but may take a few weeks to months far from the optimal salinity.

Dilution of microemulsions is desirable for several characterization techniques, e.g., light scattering. Unfortunately, it is generally difficult to ensure that the microemulsion characteristics are not affected by dilution. However, dilution is possible for certain microemulsion systems with well-defined droplets and when the interactions are weak [7].

Scattering techniques are widely used in characterizing microemulsions. The tools include static and dynamic light scattering, small-angle neutron scattering, and X-ray scattering. In principle it is possible to obtain detailed information about the structure, size, and shape of the droplets or domains. However, caution must be exercised in interpreting scattering data. For example, the diffusion coefficient measured by dynamic light scattering can be related to the aggregate size using the familiar Stokes-Einstein equation only under very restricted conditions. One normally needs to account for interactions, polydispersity, critical phenomena, etc. Nevertheless, the scattering techniques are finding more usage in the characterization and fundamental understanding of microemulsions.

Other techniques for structural characterization include sedimentation and ultracentrifugation, electron microscopy, fluorescence methods, as well as electrochemical techniques like voltammetry. Dynamic properties related to the exchange processes of molecular constituents may be obtained using NMR, electron spin resonance, ultrasonic absorption, and electric birefringence, among other techniques.

Rheological measurements indicate that microemulsions generally behave as Newtonian fluids. This is not unexpected in view of the very small characteristic size of the aggregates in oil-in-water or water-in-oil microemulsions. However, middle phase microemulsions behave differently and may show viscoelastic behavior. The rheology is dependent on hydrodynamic and colloidal interactions.

Electrical conductivity is a classic tool to distinguish between oil-in-water and water-in-oil systems. However, even at low concentrations of the dispersed phase (<15%), water-in-oil systems may show an increased conductivity as an indication of "percolation" phenomenon. Dielectric measurements also provide similar information. Other bulk characterization techniques for microemulsions include density and heat capacity measurements.

Low interfacial tensions are characteristic of microemulsions (Fig. 3). Measurement of such low tensions require special techniques such as the spinning drop, sessile drop, and surface light-scattering methods.

Applications of Microemulsions

The special features of microemulsions provide the basis for a wide variety of applications. Commercial applications are increasing and the scope is tremendous, as evident from the increasing number of papers and patents on microemulsions. Some of the important applications are described below.

Model Colloids

From a purely scientific standpoint, microemulsions are model colloids which serve to test theories for a wide variety of topics. Thus microemulsions have been used as model systems to study stability, properties of hard and soft sphere fluids, hydrodynamic and colloidal interactions, critical and percolation phenomena, and rheology of dispersions.

Enhanced Oil Recovery

Conventional production methods for crude oil do not recover the total amount of oil present in the reservoirs. During the primary recovery stage immediately following drilling, oil is driven to individual wells by natural forces in the reservoir. Waterflooding is a common practice after primary recovery. This secondary recovery process involves injecting water into some wells to drive oil through the reservoir to other wells. Even after secondary recovery about one-half of the original oil remains underground in the form of immobile, discrete globules or "ganglia." The oil ganglia are trapped in the small pores by capillary forces. Enhanced or tertiary recovery methods are aimed at recovering this oil efficiently. The capillary forces have to be reduced drastically in order to recover the residual oil. This requires the interfacial tension to be reduced by several orders of magnitude, typically from about 30 dyn/cm between crude oil and brine to "ultralow" values on the order of 0.001 to 0.01 dyn/cm. Such lowering of interfacial tension is possible with microemulsions, as previously discussed (Fig. 3). The potential of enhanced oil recovery with microemulsions is enormous. Considerable research has been done and is on-going, and several field tests have been conducted [4].

A typical surfactant flooding process involves sequential injections of (1) a preflush of low salinity brine, (2) a surfactant slug, (3) a dilute aqueous polymer solution, and (4) brine. The surfactant slug may take the form of a "soluble oil" containing the surfactant and an alcohol cosolvent but little or no brine, a microemulsion having substantial contents of both oil and brine, or an aqueous solution of the surfactant and alcohol containing little or no added oil. Economic factors dictate the use of as little surfactant as possible and hence a relatively small slug. The use of water-continuous slugs with little oil has the advantage that it minimizes injection of expensive oil along with the expensive surfactant (typically 2–10% by weight).

One of the challenges of surfactant flooding is to develop processes which will be effective under diverse conditions. Large composition differences exist among crude oils and reservoir brines. Reservoir temperatures may exceed 100°C in deep reservoirs. Porosity, permeability, and chemical composition of the rocks vary widely. Hence, the importance of understanding and manipulating the phase behavior of microemulsions. The effects of surfactant, cosolvent, oil, temperature, pressure, and other variables on microemulsion flooding are well documented [4, 27].

The optimal salinity corresponds to the composition where middle phase microemulsions exist and both γ_{mo} and γ_{mw} are ultralow. The displacement of oil by the microemulsion is governed by γ_{mo}, and the displacement of the microemulsion by the water phase is governed by γ_{mw}. Both these tensions should be ultralow to prevent plugging and achieve effective displacement of oil. Thus the optimal salinity is a useful guide in developing surfactant formulations. In addition to phase behavior studies, core tests are necessary to optimize microemulsion formulations for specific field conditions. Methods to maintain ultralow tensions during surfactant flooding have been reviewed in Ref. 4 along with the present problems (e.g., adsorption, polymer–surfactant interactions) and future prospects. Perhaps the most important factor determining the future of microemulsion flooding is the price of oil!

Microemulsions as Media for Reactions

A rapidly growing field of microemulsion application is as media for a variety of chemical reactions including electrochemical, photochemical, enzymatic, and polymerization reactions. Chemical reactions are also important from a characterization point of view. For example, diffusion coefficients and hence size may be estimated via cyclic voltammetry of electroactive species solubilized in microemulsions.

The existence of microdomains or droplets with large interfacial area per unit volume allows the possibility of controlling the reaction rates, pathways, and stereochemistry, as well as the morphology of the precipitation products. Catalysis of various chemical reactions has great potential for industrial applications [28, 29]. One factor in the rate enhancement is the tremendous increase of contact surface between the reactant molecules which may be adsorbed at the interfacial film or solubilized inside the dispersed phase. The rate enhancement may far exceed the value predicted by simple partitioning of substrates between the dispersed phase and the continuous phase. The pathway of a reacting system and the stereochemistry may be controlled by the local environment of the microdomains. For instance, in the case of enzymatic reactions the microenvironment may mimic the active sites, and certain configurations or orientations could be favorable for the bound substrate.

Some factors to be considered in utilizing microemulsions as reaction media include the dynamics of the surfactant molecules, the collisions between the droplets, the flexibility of the interfacial film, and the partitioning of the reactants. The average lifetime of a surfactant molecule in the interfacial film is on the order of microseconds while the exchange time between droplets is on the order of milliseconds [30]. The number of "sticky" collisions which allow exchange between droplets decreases with increasing rigidity of the interfacial film. When the reaction rates are faster than the exchange times as in electron and proton transfers, the droplets may be treated as virtually isolated or "frozen". On the other extreme, when the rates are very slow, the dispersed phase can be regarded as "continuous" from the reaction kinetics point of view, allowing regular rate expressions to apply. For the intermediate case, statistical distributions and interdroplet exchange will affect the reaction rate [31].

Holt [5] and Mackay [6] reviewed several types of chemical reactions in microemulsions including acid-base reactions, formation of metalloporphyrins and other complex ions, hydrolysis of esters, and several photochemical and electrochemical reactions. Some of the studies are important in terms of a better understanding of interfacial chemistry and novel synthesis. *Photochemical* investigations have been primarily focused on light energy conversion, i.e., artificial photosynthesis. It has been demonstrated that microemulsions can be used for photoionization and photoinduced charge separation [32, 33]. Further research and development may lead to commercial feasibility.

Enzymatic reactions can be carried out with the enzymes located in the droplets of water-in-oil microemulsions. The enzyme activity is retained or even enhanced in microemulsions [31, 34, 35]. As pointed out earlier, the microenvironment in microemulsions mimics the *in vivo* biological situation better than simple aqueous solutions. The reactivity of enzymes depends on the pH and the water content. There appears to be an optimum water content where maximum reactivity is obtained. Both water-soluble and oil-soluble substrates (e.g., steroids) have been successfully studied, indicating a wide scope for enzymatic reactions in the "microreactors" of microemulsions.

Polymerization in microemulsions has been demonstrated to produce latex particles of small size (100–500 Å) and uniform size distribution. Such small and uniform particles cannot be obtained from conventional emulsions. Also, photochemical induction is not feasible for emulsions because of the turbidity but can be applied to microemulsions systems. Both oil-soluble and water-soluble types of monomers have been polymerized in microemulsions [36–40]. However, problems due to phase separation have been observed in some studies. Further work is needed in order to understand the kinetics of polymerization as a function of microemulsion characteristics and mode of initiation. Nevertheless, polymerization in microemulsions is a highly promising field.

Microemulsions have been used not only to prepare microlatex particles but also metal particles for catalysts, ferrofluids, photographic emulsions, etc. Particles that have been prepared include iron chlorides [41], iron borides [42], Pt, Pd, and Ir [43], and silver chloride [44]. One difficulty with the classical preparation of ultrafine particles is sintering, which may be avoided by using microemulsions. One of the precursor reagents (A) may be solubilized into the droplets. The other reagent (B) may also be solubilized into the droplets but separately, and then the microemulsions mixed for the reaction to occur through collisions of the droplets. Alternatively, reagent B may be added directly and allowed to contact A by diffusion. Nucleation and growth of the particles occur inside the droplets. The kinetics of growth and particle size may be modified by adjusting the size and number of droplets, the flexibility of the interfacial film, the reactant concentration, etc.

Separations Using Microemulsions

Microemulsions may be used in liquid–liquid extraction processes to recover minerals from low-grade ores. Also, a new class of separation techniques is possible using microemulsions as liquid membranes rather than coarse emulsions. Some of the advantages of using microemulsions include reversible phase behavior which allows membrane formulation and product recovery to be simpler, the control of leakage to very low values, and very fast separation rates due to reduced globule size and internal droplet mixing. Microemulsion membranes have been successfully used to separate organics and metal ions.

Other Applications

One of the earliest applications has been as Carnauba wax floor polishes [3] prepared as a high temperature water-in-oil microemulsion, which then is inverted into an oil-in-water type. Many pharmaceutical and cosmetic formulations are microemulsions. Microemulsions are also relevant to the detergent and lubricant industries. Many agricultural and horticultural sprays employ microemulsions. Some other applications being investigated include use as blood substitute and organ preservation fluid, drug delivery, corrosion inhibition, and heat transfer medium.

In conclusion, microemulsions are fascinating from a scientific standpoint and also offer a wide variety of applications. Microemulsions have a lot more to contribute to both science and technology.

References

1. J. P. Hoar and J. H. Schulman, *Nature, 152*, 102 (1943).
2. J. H. Schulman and E. G. Cockbain, *Trans. Faraday Soc., 36*, 651 (1940).
3. L. M. Prince, *Microemulsions*, Academic, New York, 1977.
4. C. A. Miller and S. Qutubuddin, "Enhanced Oil Recovery with Microemulsions," in *Interfacial Phenomena in Non-Aqueous Media* (H. F. Eicke, ed.), Dekker, New York, 1986.
5. S. L. Holt, *J. Dispersion Sci. Technol., 1*, 423 (1980).
6. R. A. Mackay, *Adv. Colloid Interface Sci., 15*, 131 (1981).
7. A. M. Bellocq, J. Biais, P. Bothorel, B. Clin, G. Fowcke, P. Lalanne, B. Lemaire, B. Lemanceau, and D. Roux, *Adv. Colloid Interface Sci., 20*, 167 (1984).
8. S. E. Friberg, *J. Dispersion Sci. Technol., 6*, 317 (1985).
9. I. D. Robb (ed.), *Microemulsions*, Plenum, New York, 1982.

10. K. L. Mittal and B. Lindman (eds.), *Surfactants in Solution*, Plenum, New York, 1984.
11. D. O. Shah (ed.) *Macro- and Microemulsions: Theory and Applications*, ACS Symposium Series 272, 1985.
12. E. Ruckenstein and J. C. Chi, *J. Chem. Soc., Faraday Trans. II, 71*, 1690 (1975).
13. E. Ruckenstein, *Chem. Phys. Lett., 5*, 517 (1978).
14. C. A. Miller and P. Neogi, *AIChE J., 16*, 212 (1980).
15. S. Mukherjee, C. A. Miller, and T. Fort Jr., *J. Colloid Interface Sci., 91*, 223 (1983).
16. D. J. Mitchell and B. W. Ninham, *J. Chem. Soc., Faraday Trans. II, 77*, 601 (1981).
17. L. E. Scriven, *Nature, 267*, 333 (1976).
18. K. Shinoda and S. Friberg, *Adv. Colloid Interface Sci., 4*, 281 (1975).
19. C. Huh, *J. Colloid Interface Sci., 71*, 408 (1979).
20. Y. Talmon and S. Prager, *J. Chem. Phys., 69*, 2984 (1978); *76*, 1535 (1982).
21. J. Jouffroy, P. Levinson, and P. deGennes, *J. Phys., 43*, 1241 (1982).
22. B. Widom, *J. Chem. Phys., 81*, 1030 (1984).
23. P. A. Winsor, *Solvent Properties of Amphiphilic Compounds*, Butterworths, London, 1954.
24. R. L. Reed and R. M. Healy, in *Improved Oil Recovery by Surfactant and Polymer Flooding* (D. O. Shah and R. S. Schechter, eds.), Academic, New York, 1977.
25. C. A. Miller, R. N. Hwan, W. J. Benton, and T. Fort Jr., *J. Colloid Interface Sci., 61*, 554 (1977).
26. W. J. Benton, J. Natoli, S. Qutubuddin,. S. Mukherjee, C. A. Miller, and T. Fort Jr., *Soc. Pet. Eng. J., 22*, 53 (1982).
27. D. O. Shah (ed.), *Surface Phenomena in Enhanced Oil Recovery*, Plenum, New York, 1981.
28. J. H. Fendler and E. J. Fendler, *Catalysis in Micellar and Macromolecular Systems*, Academic, New York, 1975.
29. J. H. Fendler, *Membrane Mimetic Chemistry*, Wiley, New York, 1982.
30. M. Zulauf and H. F. Eicke, *J. Phys. Chem., 83*, 480 (1979).
31. P. L. Luisi and B. E. Straub (eds.), *Reverse Micelles*, Plenum, New York, 1984.
32. J. Kiwi and M. Gratzel, *J. Phys. Chem., 84*, 1503 (1980).
33. S. S. Atik and J. K. Thomas, *Chem. Phys. Lett., 79*, 357 (1981).
34. C. Balmy and P. Donzou, *Biochemie, 61*, 445 (1979).
35. P. Meier and P. L. Luisi, *J. Solid-Phase Biochem., 5*, 269 (1980).
36. J. O. Stoffer and T. Bone, *J. Dispersion Sci. Technol., 1*, 37 (1980).
37. Y. S. Leong, G. Riess, and F. Candau, *J. Chim. Phys., 78*, 279 (1981).
38. F. Candau and Y. S. Leong, *J. Polym. Sci., Polym. Chem. Ed., 23*, 193 (1985).
39. L. M. Gan, D. H. Chew, and S. E. Friberg, *J. Polym. Sci., Polym. Chem. Ed., 19*, 1581 (1983); *21*, 513 (1983).
40. A. Jayakrishnan and D. O. Shah, *J. Polym. Sci., Polym. Lett. Ed., 22*, (1984).
41. K. Kon-no, M. Gobe, K. Kandooni, and A. Kitahara, *J. Colloid Interface Sci., 93*, 293 (1983).
42. N. Lufimpadio, J. B. Nagy, and E. G. Deroune, in *Surfactants in Solution*, Vol. 3 (K. L. Mittal and B. Lindman, eds.), Plenum, New York, 1984, p. 1483.
43. M. Boutonnet, J. Kizling, P. Stanius, and G. Maire, *Colloids Surf., 5*, 209 (1982).
44. M. J. Hou and D. O. Shah, Paper presented at the 50th National Symposium of Colloid and Surface Science, Atlanta, Georgia, June 15–18, 1986.

SYED QUTUBUDDIN

Microprocessors, Use in Distributed Control Systems

Recent developments in microprocessor technology have made it possible to design control schemes far different from the traditional ones. Instead of large control rooms whose walls are lined with instruments, displays, annunciators, and so on, major plants can now be run by a few operators seated at video display terminals. Instead of trying to keep track of hundreds of instruments, these operators are concerned mainly with process parameters that are out of limits, or are trending in that direction. The control system selects these items and calls the operators' attention to them, using color, flashing displays, etc.

This article explains what the plant design engineers must provide to the control-system supplier, so that it can put together a complete control system, and provide the plant designers with a proposal and bid. The article then goes into the procedures by which plant designers can evaluate the proposals from various control-system suppliers and choose the one best suited for them.

Defining Requirements

The basic project documents that the plant designers start with in defining the process requirements are the process and engineering flow diagrams. These diagrams contains the following information:

The type(s) of process(es) to be controlled—namely, continuous, batch, or a combination of the two.

Number of process trains and number of process units per train—namely, reactors, distillation columns, storage vessels, pumps, compressors, etc.

Process units common to all process trains—e.g.: compressor(s), vent scrubbing columns, solvent recovery systems, raw-material distribution.

Quality control means and procedures: on- or offline.

Utilities production and distribution—e.g.: steam, compressed air and cooling water; also, waste collection and treatment.

Heat-balance and material-balance requirements for each process unit, for the entire plant, or both.

Type and number of process-parameter-sensing elements (digital, analog, pulse, etc.) that constitute the inputs to the control system.

Type and number of process controlled-variables (analog, digital, pulse, etc.) applied to on/off valves, pumps, control valves, pulsed stepping motors, etc., that constitute the outputs from the control system to the field devices.

A thorough engineering evaluation of the above data, combined with detailed knowledge of process operations and geographic distribution of main process equipment, will allow definition of the following:

Modes of operation—manual, semiautomatic (automatic with operator's intervention at critical operational points), or fully automatic. In selecting the appropriate mode for the entire process, or separately for a specific portion of the process, one must consider the past operational experience: Is the process well established (how long ago, licensed or not?), or if new, how much operational flexibility is required to optimize its parameters while running?

Degree of control redundancy required to make the process operation safe, minimize the loss of production due to interruptions, and provide for adequate equipment maintenance, without affecting throughput.

Definition of the number and structure of product recipes, and the procedures for changing them, while ensuring consistent quality.

Process startup and shutdown procedures.

Definition of the number and types of control points, considering full or partial operator attendance and mode(s) of operation chosen. One must select: (1) one central control room; (2) several independent control rooms, each one controlling a well-defined portion of the process, with no control communication required between control rooms; or (3) several control rooms (satellites) connected via a communication network with a central control room.

Definition of plant/operator interface; control and monitoring procedures; operator training procedures.

One must take into consideration (for future expansion of operations) optimizations of various procedures that might be implemented with only minimum additional cost or interference with operations.

During the definition of the process requirements stage, frequent additions or deletions to the engineering flow diagrams will be necessary for such things as:

Adding/deleting/relocating process-parameter-sensing elements.

Adding/deleting/relocating control devices, such as pumps, valves, etc.

Reconfiguring piping.

Redefining certain control functions, measurements, alarms.

Defining necessary local controls.

Functional Specification

Definition—The functional specification defines a control system, in board terms (function blocks), in accordance with all requirements that have been determined via process and operation analysis.

A control-system manufacturer will generate its proposal–quotation for the control system that it considers best suited for the particular project, on the basis of this document.

Scope; battery limits; terminology—The document should define, in general terms, the project for which a control system is to be provided, with the battery limits clearly stated.

Carefully define all terms, such as control system, manufacturer, user, consultant, etc., that are frequently referred to.

Environmental conditions—The environmental conditions that must be defined are: temperature limits, humidity limits, contaminants in the ambient atmosphere, and area classification (as defined by the National Electrical Code).

Installation of equipment—Break down the control system into subsystems that will constitute independent enclosures containing fully assembled hardware, completely wired and factory tested. Describe separately, hardware, cables, documentation, and personnel support necessary for total integration of the control system at the jobsite.

Wiring methods, codes and certification—Define all wiring methods in accordance with the requirements given in the National Electrical Code for the specific area-classification.

Intrinsic safety requirements and proper certification must be determined in detail.

Interfacing with foreign equipment—Prior knowledge of available hardware components and their characteristics is essential. As the control system specification is generated, the engineer will be able to anticipate offerings of systems in which one or more pieces of equipment are *not* made by the control system vendor–bidder (i.e., foreign equipment).

List all foreign equipment by manufacturer's name, including model, type, and interfacing model.

Expandability—Clearly state the limits within which the control system can be expanded (I/Os, processors, memory, auxiliary memory, operating system software).

These restrictions are usually imposed in order to maintain guaranteed system performances after various expansions are implemented. The main concerns are to maintain the same real-time system response, and to maintain an adequate traffic load within the communication network after expansion.

Exemptions/alternatives—Itemize any exemptions from the functional specification, or alternative solutions.

For instance, there are cases where the specification calls for remote installed inputs and outputs—features that some vendors cannot supply. Such a vendor will state in its bid that it takes exception to this requirement.

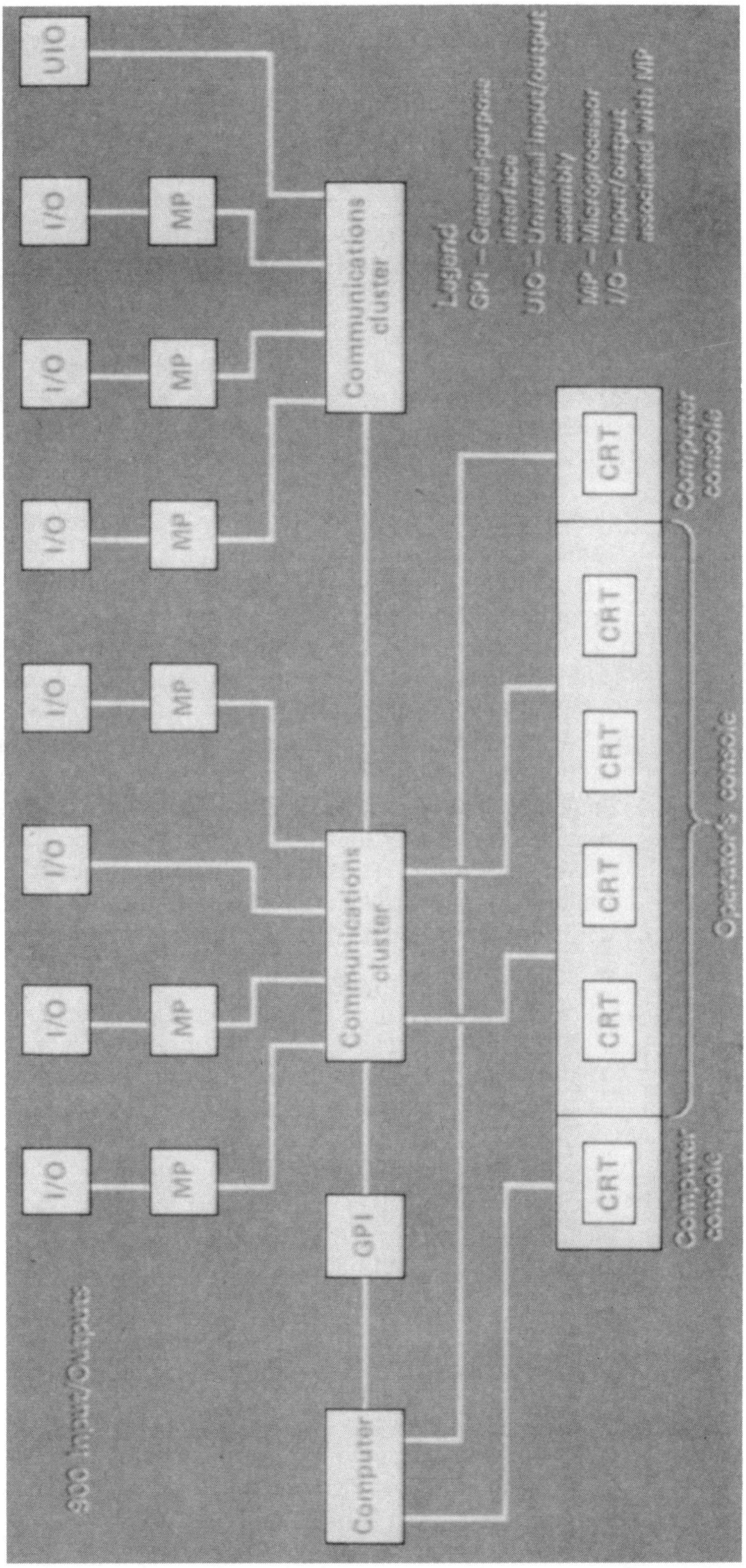

FIG. 1. Functional block diagram of a distributed control system.

Sometimes, for example, a special communication interface is offered in lieu of one requested in the specification. This alternative solution may be a better or more economical choice.

Control-system block diagram—Figure 1 shows a functional block diagram of a distributed control system. The system includes foreign equipment and corresponding functional interfaces.

System Structure (function blocks)

Control equipment (local control)—A primary control device in a distributed control system can be chosen from (but is not limited to) the following: a microprocessor-based multiple-loop controller; a programmable logic controller; a minicomputer; a combination of the above three.

The choice is made based on the type and number of control functions that must be performed at the local level, and the level of intelligence (processor power, flexibility) and security that is required. In general terms, a large number of logical and sequential functions will dictate choosing a programmable logic controller.

The programmable-controller software and operation are essentially structured to handle discrete (on/off) logical functions, such as those used for interlocks and sequential control.

A concentration of analog control loops will generally dictate choosing a multiple-loop controller. A balanced combination of sequential control, analog control, and data acquisition concentrated in a particular area may require a very powerful microprocessor-based local unit, or a minicomputer.

As an example, let us assume that our choice is a microprocessor-based multiple-loop controller. In this case, the functional specification must define:

All I/O hardware modules, their configuration and signal performances (electrical characteristics, accuracy, resolution, noise immunity, etc.)

The software set of algorithms configurable by the user to build the control requirements for a specific area. The software set must comprise PID control, including all variations (feedforward, adaptive, cascade, etc., computation module and logic functions.)

The level of redundancy and security checks.

Method of control system configuration.

Method of configuration storage, loading, and downloading.

In the case of a programmable controller, one should define:

The I/O type and distribution (if remote I/Os are required).

A detailed list of functions (logical, numerical, data formatting, etc.) that a particular PLC (programmable logic controller) should be required to perform in order to meet a specific application.

Size of internal memory and expansion capability.

Communication interfacing with other PLCs, or with a host computer.
Memory utilization efficiency with respect to I/O processing, application programming, communication, etc.
Means of interfacing with an operator's console that is based on a CRT (cathode ray tube).

There are powerful microprocessor-based local units that can easily accommodate continuous/regulatory analog control with a substantial amount of interlock/sequential control within the same unit, and be able to address over 2000 I/Os of various types (analog, digital, pulse, etc.). Obviously, when generating the specification requirements of those units, one should keep in mind this wide range of capabilities.

Process I/O equipment—Process I/O devices must be available to provide the data acquisition of a wide variety of noncontrol (monitoring only) parameters that include analog and digital signals (inputs and outputs).

These devices will be provided with various signal-conditioning cards—thermocouple, RTD (resistance temperature detector), pulses from counters, contacts from switches, etc.—a time multiplexer, associated power supplies, and the corresponding communications interface to the network.

Communication network—The communication network should be based on an industrial-grade digital communication link, preferably using coaxial cable, that provides a high-speed data path between all control and I/O devices, multiple operator interfaces, and foreign equipment interfaces. The requirements are:

The link must accommodate as many devices as possible. The design of the communication network determines the maximum number.
The link should be at least 10,000 ft.
The network must accept multiple-master operations (i.e., a master can always initiate communication).
The throughput should be sufficient to ensure fast updating of process parameters and fast response to command field devices. Communication speeds of 0.5–1 megabaud (megabit/s) are presently used. Throughput is a function of speed (measured in bauds) and the quantity of data statistically exchanged among various devices connected to the network.
The network should be 100% redundant (cable, equipment, power supply), with automatic switchover in case of failure. The network should operate with a well-accepted communication protocol—e.g., SDLC (synchronous data link control) or HDLC (high-level data link control)—and error-checking data transfer. Each manufacturer uses a particular protocol that sometimes derives from either SDLC or HDLC. There are no industry standards.

Operator Console(s)

Console structure, displays—An operator console generally uses video color displays for monitoring, and a functional or standard keyboard (or both) for commands. Video color-displays are generated by color CRTs, driven by processors. The keyboards are connected to the processors, which are connected to the communication network.

Functional keyboards are designed specifically for plant operation. The keys are dedicated to specific control operations such as auto/manual, setpoint, ramp up/down, acknowledge alarm, open/close devices, etc. A numerical keypad is used for operator data entries.

Standard keyboards are similar to a regular typewriter keyboard, but also have a numerical keypad.

Auxiliary information devices provided on a console are: hardcopy peripherals, video copier, stripchart recorders, hard-wired annunciator panels, and floppy-disk drives.

In principle, all CRTs should have access to all plant process parameters, and their functions should be the same. This allows the operators to bring up on different screens the same display, or to interchange functions among CRTs. All displays should be of preformat type and be linked to actual process parameters with "fill in the blanks" programming procedures.

A preformat display has its skeleton programmed by the manufacturer and cannot be altered by the user. The process parameters that constitute the dynamic part of this type of display are entered by the user via a CRT-based procedure that requires answering questions displayed on the screen, and filling in the blanks with appropriate data.

A system of display hierarchy was recently adopted by manufacturers of distributed control systems. The hierarchy is based on three levels of information:

Overview (status and alarm of at least 300–400 parameters).
Group (status and alarm of at least 30 parameters).
Loop (detailed control, status, alarm per parameter, and access for modifications).

Various control parameters, configured using the fill-in-the-blanks procedure described above, should be protected from being accessed and changed indiscriminately. This protection is implemented by locking procedures using hardware (by switch) or software (with a password usually determined by the user).

Alarming—Alarms should be displayed on all CRTs on all three hierarchical levels, using video flashing and color changing, and be logged automatically on a dedicated printer. Return to normal condition should also be automatically logged. Alarm limit settings should be configurable for each individual point.

Trending—Two types of trending should be provided:

Video trending—Each CRT should be able to simultaneously display up to four real-time trends on optional trend-rates; all data related to those trends should appear on the screen—process parameter identifier (tag), engineering units, present value, and alarm status.

For example, simultaneous trending of a cascade control loop (2 process variables, 2 outputs) is extremely important for fine control timing.

Historical trending—Up to 24 h should be stored on a magnetic medium, retrievable on a video copier at the operator's request.

Real-time trend-recording on multiple-pen stripchart recorders.

Diagnostics and system-security display—These types of displays should present the status (on-off, malfunction) of all devices with which the operator console communicates, indicating malfunctions that may have occurred:

Status of primary and backup communication links.
Status of primary and backup control devices.
Status of primary and backup power supplies.
Status of peripherals.
Continuous indication of throughput traffic on the communication link.

Control data-base configuration—Data-base configuration is done through the operator console by using the CRT and its associated keyboard. An interactive program supported by standard display and employing a conversational fill-in-the-blanks technique allows the operator to construct the system's data base. All data are stored on disks and, by simple commands, data bases can be downloaded or uploaded, to or from the disks. Also, via the data highway, the same procedure is used for downloading and uploading local-control-unit data bases.

Functional Specification Writing

Experience has shown that a single loop will require, on average, a hundred words to describe.

The data base for a typical microprocessor-based distributed control system normally contains information for 500-plus loops.

The power, range, speed, and economics of these systems warrant that the more mundane information-gathering, alarming, trending, and logging also be made part of the data base. Thus, the specifications and engineering data document of a medium-sized system will require about 50,000 to 75,000 words.

A recommended guide for the structure of such a document is: 1.0 Project organization; 2.0 Correspondence; 3.0 Project schedule; 4.0 System development/support; 5.0 Documentation; 6.0 Control system specification; 7.0 Engineering data; 8.0 System testing; 9.0 Training; 10.0 Maintenance agreement proposal; 11.0 Drawing attachments; 12.0 Spare parts; 13.0 Component descriptions and I/O index; 14.0 Accounting sheets; and 15.0 Document schedule.

Equitable Basis for Comparing Systems

The nature of the equipment involved makes comparisons difficult at best. Each supplier embraces a different philosophy and, therefore, has its own packaging and proposal methods. Hence, it is necessary to devise a functional basis by which one can relate the quotations to one another. A cross-reference to supplier item-numbers is useful in finding items in their respective proposals.

In comparing quotations, items should be added to offset apparent economies. These represent required equipment that certain vendors have failed to include. Preferably, all bids should be complete, with buy-out item cost given for goods not made by the supplier itself.

Each vendor should meet specifications to an acceptable level, e.g., 95%. It is impossible to write a specification that all could meet, due to the nature of the equipment. If a specification were written such that one vendor could meet it fully, it would be unfair to the others.

After a vendor is chosen, the purchase specification should be written around its equipment line. At that point, the economies of packaging peculiar to that line can be evaluated. Those that do not conflict with project standards should be embraced. High-density packaging is false economy.

In addition to accumulating the foregoing facts, one must also form opinions on:

The most expensive equipment.
The least expensive equipment.
Whether all the proposed vendors are capable of supporting this equipment in the site area.
Whether the computer interface is 100% redundant, and if so, of what importance is this fact.

At this time, a committee should be formed to evaluate the proposed vendors. Visits to vendor manufacturing facilities, demonstrations of equipment, and hands-on experience should be scheduled. After these visits, a meeting might be held to define a method for evaluation of the distributed control system (DCS).

The engineer should present a tabulation of commercial aspects, with recommended adjustments required to put all vendors on an equal quantitative basis.

The committee should configure a matrix consisting of:

Objective concerns:
- Commercial aspects.
- Interface aspects.
- Schedule aspects.
- Other equipment-cost factors.
- Discounts/service.
- Discounts in effect.

Subjective concerns:
- Present site-support capabilities.
- Operator training.
- Operator interface.
- Reliability/redundancy.

TABLE 1 Vendor Analysis Matrix

	Ranking					
	1st	2nd	3rd	4th	Weight	Points
	Objective Items					
System cost	A	B	C	D	55	
Computer interface cost	A	C	B	D	15	
PLC replacement	B	—	—	—	10	
Related equipment discount	C	B	A	D	5	
Commercial terms	—	—	—	—	1	
Delivery	—	—	—	—	2	
						88
	Subjective Items					
Present site support	A	B	C	D	4	
Operator training	A	B	C	D	2	
Computer interface	A	B	C	D	1	
Reliability	B	A	C	D	2	
Operator interface	C	A	B	D	1	
Flexibility	B	C	A	D	1	
Schedule	A	B	C	D	1	
						12
Total						100

Position factor: 1st = 1.00; 2nd = 0.75; 3rd = 0.5; 4th = 0.25.

Vendor	Weighted points
A	83.25
B	72.0
C	50.5
D	21.75

Example of weighted points calculation for Vendor A: $(55 \times 1) + (15 \times 1) + (5 \times 0.5) + (4 \times 1) + (2 \times 1) + (1 \times 1) + (2 \times 0.75) + (1 \times 0.5) + (1 \times 0.75) + (1 \times 1) = 83.25$

Computer interface experience.
Flexibility of vendor to accommodate changes, etc.

The matrix could be configured according to the example in Table 1.

Human-Engineering the Control Center

Advances in electronics have brought about microprocessors with functions that allow the configuration of advanced control schemes onto programmable, compact packages.

The advent of these control processors, coupled to video monitors, has given the operator the opportunity to have many process variables under immediate control.

The human engineering aspect is to present these to the operator so that control can be effectively managed. The elements required in designing control centers with control panels are the basis of developing the "window" to the process in a DCS. A large-sized control panel, which would formerly have required six operators, can easily be handled by two operators working at a video control console.

A large system can be readily controlled by requiring the operator to monitor only necessary information. Superfluous data are not presented, thereby minimizing confusion. The operator reacts primarily to off-normal conditions, rather than trying to control and monitor a panel containing lights, buttons, and dials.

Most DCSs employ standard CRT screens, which allow an operator to monitor an entire facility by using overview displays. These typically provide the operator with deviation from setpoint, and alarm displays showing the status of all points within the plant area associated with the workstation. Other display formats allow the operator, via the keyboard, to view group displays that show several variables in more detail, as well as individual loops that give essential loop data.

While the basic format of overview, group, and loop displays are standard ones provided by most DCS manufacturers, the most efficient control of the plant can best be achieved with a well-designed data base configuration. Prior to data base formatting, the instrument loop identification-tag numbers are assigned to ease association with areas within the plant.

The layouts of the overview and group displays, which show loop tag numbers, are formatted so that they can be readily identified and associated with their plant area. When a plant has dual equipment trains with similar instrumentation in each train, the loop tag numbers are assigned the same numerical suffix; i.e., a plant having two reactor trains, each with identical temperature controls, would be tagged as follows:

TC 1001 for Reactor 1
TC 2001 for Reactor 2

Note that the first digit of the tag number identifies the reactor train.

An adequate number of video screens is essential for optimum operation of the video workstation. The video console operator must be able to both monitor the plant overview and work at the loop level during normal plant operating conditions. During upset conditions, several operators must be able to assume responsibility for specific plant areas. Thus, an intimate knowledge of the process and its controls is needed to adequately determine the number of video stations required for a particular plant.

System Compatibility

Compatibility between the communication network and foreign devices represents the most challenging undertaking in control system design (see Fig. 2 and Refs. 1 and 2). Unfortunately, there are no accepted comprehensive standards, in terms of hardware and software, that govern the details of communication compatibility.

There are two directions from which this issue is approached:

1. First come the characteristics that support the distributed control systems:

Transmission rate.

Master/slave relationship (predefinition or polling). In the case of master/slave transmission, it is necessary to determine which device initiates the communication (master) and which are the devices that must solely respond to external messages (slaves). In the case of a polling precedure, each device is polled on a time basis; within the time interval allocated, the device can act as a master that initiates transmissions. Outside that interval, the device acts as a slave, only responding to external messages.

Type of transmission (asynchronous, synchronous, duplex, half-duplex).

Type of protocol (HDLC, SDLC, ASCII, etc.).

Communication security: (1) hardware and coaxial cable redundancy and automatic switchover, and (2) error checking on data transfer and recovery from a fault during message transmission.

2. Second is the device that must talk or listen to the communication network. The characteristics:

Type of device (computer, programmable controller, analysis equipment, a foreign data-highway, an intelligent terminal).

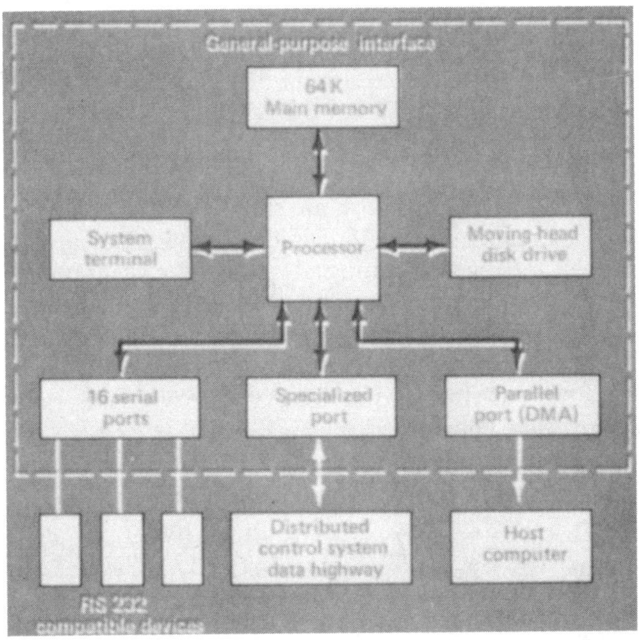

FIG. 2. General purpose interface used to overcome incompatibility among items of equipment.

Type of communication port (serial or parallel) [1].
Transmission rate at port entry.
Type of transmission supported by the port (synchronous, asynchronous).

After all data described above have been gathered—and assuming that in our case we have to interface a host computer, analysis equipment, and PLCs—our first option is to specify a general-purpose interface (GPI) as part of the microprocessor distributed system and request bidders to include it in their specifications. A GPI may consist of the following:

Processor (16-bit words, minimum).
64K main memory.
Auxiliary memory: 5-million-byte moving-head disk.
GPI system terminal.
Communication ports: Specialized port that is compatible with the distributed-control-system data highway. Parallel ports for high-speed communication to and from a host computer. Serial ports for communication to and from compatible devices.

These requirements cover a spectrum of communication procedures that can be easily accommodated with known hardware and software; the design of the specialized port becomes an integral part of the design of the distributed control system communication network. This specialized port puts realtime data into (and takes such data out of) the GPI processor's main memory, based on a program that services all the communication ports of the distributed-system communication network.

The parallel-communication-port design used for synchronous high-speed communication with a computer must be firmed up with respect to the particular make of the computer provided in the project. The timing, the control line designations, and the specifics of protocol and message formatting must be defined by both manufacturers.

The serial ports are simpler in design in terms of servicing data transfers, and require the foreign-device manufacturer to conform to the protocol and message formatting adopted by the serial-port designer.

One must be aware that the GPI is a communication system in itself and requires a correct specification and coordination of all communication aspects to ensure proper operation.

Obviously, the size of memory (main and auxiliary) and the number of serial ports can vary.

A unit of data exchange between the GPI and the foreign devices constitutes a message. A complete information transfer consists of a request message from the initiator (example: foreign device), followed by a reply message from the responder (example: GPI, which simultaneously talks/listens to the distributed-control-system communication network).

The request message is made up of a "header," used to coordinate message flow, indicate error conditions, and describe function to be performed; "data" come after the header, and then an "error check" message follows. The reply message is similar to the request message and is made up of the same three elements.

The auxiliary memory and the terminal are necessary to program the GPI according to the specific foreign devices designated to be serviced for a certain project, as well as to perform maintenance and diagnostics.

The most important advantage of the GPI is that it unburdens foreign devices from the time-consuming task of supporting their own communication. The most important device connected to the GPI is the computer. One of the computer tasks is to control the proper operation of the GPI through commands that can check its status of connect/disconnect it to/from the network.

The GPI communicates with a host computer and off-line analysis equipment. The main control functions of a particular process plant reside in the distributed control system, which is designed with sufficient redundancy to operate continuously. A failure of the GPI does not take the process plant out of control, and therefore does not endanger the operation. The result of a GPI failure is temporary loss of data in and out of the computer or from analysis equipment.

An alternative solution, where a GPI is not required, is shown in Fig. 3. In this case the control system has two independent communication networks—one that is internal to the microprocessor-based control system, and a second that services the programmable logic controllers. In fact, the microprocessor distributed-control-system consoles are emulating a PLC so far as communication signals and protocol are concerned.

The manufacturer of the microprocessor-based control system implements a communication software package called "the driver," which supports

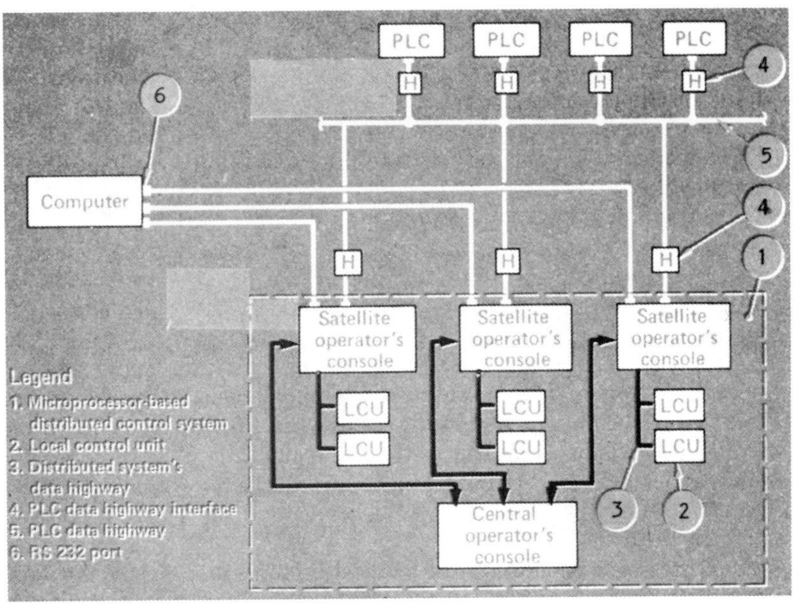

FIG. 3. Another way of handling equipment incompatibility.

the PLC's data-highway port in terms of protocol, message formatting, and error checking. A similar "driver" program is developed for the port connected to the computer, based on a different protocol, message format, and error checking set.

In this configuration the GPI is eliminated. The price one pays is loss of speed. A parallel interface can move data at a speed of 1–5 megabits/s, but in the latter configuration the speed cannot exceed 57K bits/s on the PLC data highway, and 9600 bits/s in and out of any serial port. It is the project engineer's task to make a thorough analysis of data-transfer-speed impact on the total response time required to control the actual process. In some cases a high speed of response may not be required; thus, a dedicated interface processor (GPI) may not be necessary.

Distribution of Control / Communications

A system configuration that is conceived to meet all the control requirements dictated by a particular process must be enhanced further after analyzing how it responds to practical installation, maintenance, and expansion procedures.

Installation—The modularity of the system with respect to process units and process trains allows a step-by-step installation, according to the general plant-installation schedule. Let us assume that a plant has three chemical reactors. Each is treated as an independent control entity; thus, sensors, control devices, and the corresponding control units are installed, wired, checked out, tested, and started up independently.

Concurrently, each plant has common process elements that service the above-mentioned process units. These are: Center(s) of raw-material storage and distribution, center(s) of utilities production and distribution, and centers(s) of waste collection and treatment. Dedication of control resources to the common process-elements must allow installation and full operation prior to startup of the process unit, the process trains, or both.

Installation of the data highway should precede local control-units installation. The control-room equipment installation should follow. Then, in parallel or sequentially, the local control equipment should be put in place. This sequence allows testing by using the data highway as early as possible, and increasing the data-transfer load as more local control units are connected. Any noise problems or impedance mismatch can be detected, and corrective measures taken. Testing local equipment, by employing the operator's console, allows the use of diagnostics and testing software, which increases the efficiency of field installation and checkout.

Extreme care must be taken in choosing the right environment for the local control equipment. Good accessibility and protection from mechanical damage, rain and snow and excessive heat are the main factors.

The control system configuration must allow the connecting and disconnecting of control units (local or central) in such a way that the impact on process operation will be minimal. The design follows two principles:

1. In cases where operations cannot be interrupted, 100% hot-equipment redundancy is provided. Manufacturers are offering control units and communication equipment provided with two microprocessors. Separate power supplies back up one another. One microprocessor is controlling while the second is tracking the operation off-line. In case of failure, the off-line microprocessor becomes active and an alarm is triggered.
2. In cases where operations allow limited interruption in case of failure, the control unit disconnects itself from the data highway, and a corresponding alarm is triggered. The impact is limited to only a reduced portion of the plant, with acceptable impact on the overall operations.

However, provision of 100% redundancy is costly. One must judiciously assess when this feature must be applied.

Maintenance—Basically, good design practices provide for efficient maintenance and thus ensure smooth plant operation. Examples of good control-system design practices are: For input/output and associated multiplexers:

Optical indication of input and output point status—light-emitting diode (LED).

Fuses on all output points.

I/O card replacement should be possible without power shutdown and disconnection/reconnection of wires. Only card extraction and insertion should be required.

Multiplexer failure should be detected and isolated automatically.

Redundant power supplies should be provided to all I/O cabinets and multiplexers.

For local control units:

These should be provided with 100% redundancy or should automatically fail into a predetermined safe state (whichever process requirements dictate).

Remote transfer of control from one microprocessors to the other must be provided for.

Remote diagnostics on the off-line microprocessor should be possible while the other one is on-line.

For general control-room equipment:

CRTs should be driven by two independent processors to prevent any loss of plant monitoring.

An adequate number of CRTs should be provided, considering plant operation and monitoring requirements, allowing simultaneous operation, diagnostics, and maintenance procedures.

For communication:

A redundant data-highway network is essential, and monitoring its integrity is of paramount importance to the system's operation.
Disconnecting equipment from the data highway, or reconnecting it, should not influence the highway's normal operation in any way. Communication should not be affected by a malfunction in any device physically connected to the network.

A control system design based on the above practices will allow the operators to detect and intervene quickly in case of failure, and also aid in scheduling a program of preventive maintenance.

Implementation—Responsibilities

It is essential that the engineers in charge of the plant project be responsible for the control system implementation as well.

The primary reasons:

1. Inclusion of the control-system implementation schedule into the overall project schedule; this allows total control of all phases of the project from a single management team that can monitor and resolve scheduling conflicts and set up current and long-range objectives, based on items that are present on the critical path.
2. Coordination of the inflow and out of engineering information between the client and the suppliers and subcontractors.
3. Strict control of proprietary information.
4. Coordination of the documentation generated by different sources of the control system (i.e., microprocessor vendor, computer vendor, local panel vendors, etc.).
5. Delivery and cost control.

To exercise effective control on all phases of the control system implementation, selected suppliers of the major control elements (microprocessor system, computer(s), programmable logic controllers, analysis equipment) should receive from the project engineer a proposed schedule as part of the functional specification. The vendors submit, as part of their quotation, a detailed schedule that includes engineering, manufacturing, integration, software generation, testing.

The interrelated tasks that take place between the project engineer and the vendor are shown in the same schedule. The vendor's schedule, when reviewed and approved by the project engineer becomes one of the purchase-order documents. Agreed-upon milestone dates are established for progress payments on the equipment to ensure compliance with the schedule.

In the total schedule of the control system, the consultant engineer activities are interleaved with vendors' activities.

Those activities are:

1. Front-end engineering:
   System configuration, control philosophy, functional specification.
   Evaluation of quotations and vendor(s) selection.
   Purchasing specification, negotiations, and purchase-order issuance.
2. System engineering:
   Field instrumentation, interfacing.
   Control room(s) design.
   Electrical design (including wiring, cable routing, and terminations).
   I/O list and data-base generation.
   Application software programming.
   Design of logs, reports, and CRT displays.
   Detailed specification of acceptance-test procedures.

A control system, as shown in Fig. 2, requires two years from engineering start to shipment to the jobsite. The overall responsibility of a control system implementation is that of the project engineer. However, this responsibility is shared with all suppliers. Alert supervision and creative solutions to interfacing conflicts are constantly required from the project, or consultant, engineer.

Because data-base generation and application software programming are included in the project or consultant engineer's scope of work, the need for proprietary process information by equipment vendors is limited. In addition, all the changes incurred during engineering of different specialties (structural, piping, electrical, process) can be absorbed by a control/instrument team assigned to the project who, in turn, modify the data base or the application programs accordingly.

Coordination of the system's documentation is essential in the engineering phase of the project and, later, during installation, startup, and plant operation.

During the engineering phase, the vendor must supply, on a scheduled basis, documentation related to data base generation, logs and reports, and CRT displays. In addition, drawings of equipment components (dimensions, wiring, grounding, etc.) are needed for detailed system design. In principle, all documents (schematics, drawings, lists) must be prepared and approved in accordance with the schedule. Ultimately, a revised set of documentation marked "as-built" should be submitted to the client. This will constitute the basic information to be used for startup and operation.

Monitoring of delivery and cost-control avoids misunderstandings and misinterpretations of specification requirements while components are in the manufacturing process or staging.

Most important in implementing a system of high-technology complexities is the human factor. The caliber of the person(s) involved in control projects will ultimately be reflected in the quality of the overall system. Therefore, it is the project engineer's responsibility to continuously train engineering personnel. In selecting control-equipment vendors it is essential to assess the personnel who will support the equipment to be provided.

System Testing Requirements

All subsystems should undergo a minimum of three levels of testing, which should be witnessed and approved by the client and the consultant engineer's representatives.

The first level is the testing done prior to any major subsystem being shipped for system integration at the vendor's local factory.

The second level is the testing after system integration, before the vendor certifies that the system is fully operational. This is termed the "factory acceptance test." The test should include simulation of all inputs and outputs on a loop basis. Each analog input should be tested by imposing 4- to 20-mA input to the input card, completing the software tie resident in the processor (micro, PLC, mini), and reading the value of the controller output by means of a test meter at the output card. All software—as well as hardware links, such as cascade, ratio feedforward, calculations, etc.—should be checked at this time. A similar test should be conducted for digital inputs and outputs, the associated interlock/sequential control, and any other I/O signal levels or types associated with control or monitoring.

In addition, all system software should be tested at this time, including, but not limited to, all operating system software, logs, displays, failure modes, advanced control, and optimization. The test should be performed using the data base for this project. During the factory acceptance test, the complete system should undergo an operability check, and remain fully operational for a minimum of 100 consecutive hours, with no hardware or software failures.

Operator Training Program

Early training of personnel who will be involved in the operation and maintenance of microprocessor-based control systems is essential to a successful plant startup and operation.

When the training plan is formulated, it would be preferable to have the DCS vendor quote reserved spaces for operating and maintenance training classes. The time slot allocated for training should fit in properly with the project schedule.

Training of operating personnel should take place in three stages. The first would occur at the vendor's training facility. The second stage should take place while the consultant engineer is developing the system's data base, and the third during system checkout.

A plant should possess suitably trained personnel to maintain and improve its software as knowledge of the plant grows. This will afford opportunities to innovate useful control experiments (which should be carefully documented).

Standardization

For the control-system project engineer, the task of configuring a system becomes more and more difficult because the control product market constantly receives new systems that are advertised and marketed as "the total system," "the universal system," "the most powerful system." These systems are supposedly good for any application and will respond to all present and future process needs.

A thorough analysis of the market and of industry needs tells us that an optimum control system consists of products from different manufacturers, and the task of system integration becomes more and more difficult, due primarily to the lack of standardization in data communications. Tremendous efforts are underway to overcome these barriers in the following areas:

Hardware interface (IEEE standards, EIA standards).
Protocols (HDLC, SDLC).
Message format (no standards at the present time).
Control data representation (TC12A Committee of the International Purdue Workshop).
Data base structure and access techniques (no standards).

Organizations involved in this effort are:

International organizations:
ISO—International Standards Organisation.
CCITT—Consultative Committee on International Telegraphy and Telephony.
United States organizations:
ANSI—American National Standards Institute.
ISA—Instrument Society of America.
International Purdue Workshop.
IEEE—Institute of Electrical and Electronics Engineers.

In the organization described, manufacturers, users, and government groups are all represented.

Due to the neutral position of the consultant engineer firms as service providers to users and as continuous scanners of the control market, their participation and contributions to the standardization effort should be increased substantially.

The goal of the standardization effort should be: Compatible and optional solutions with respect to interfacing and protocols, preferably in forms of interchangeable firmware adapted to the variety of control devices that constitute the building blocks of any control system.

Standardization may create a good environment for free competition in the international control market, and the efforts toward this goal will certainly enhance international cooperation in this highly technological field.

Conclusion

The man/process interface has changed substantially with the advent of CRTs and keyboards as replacements for conventional panels. The engineering of a microprocessor-based distributed control system is a complex task involving parallel thinking concerning details and integration aspects of the system with respect to hardware and software.

Plant-operation history, event gathering, and anticipation are involved on a continuous basis in the decision-making procedures. Thus, control-system engineering not only deals with hardware, but creates intelligent systems that must respond effectively to tight quality parameters within the economic constraints of our times. It is a challenge facing the engineering profession worldwide.

Abbreviations and Acronyms

ANSI	American National Standards Institute
AASCII	American Standard Code for Information Interchange
CCITT	Consultative Committee on International Telegraphy and Telephony
CRT	cathode ray tube
DCS	distributed control system
EIA	Electronic Industries Association
GPI	general-purpose interface
HDLC	high-level data link control
IEEE	Institute of Electrical and Electronics Engineers
I/O	input/output
ISA	Instrument Society of America
ISO	International Standards Organisation
LED	light-emitting diode
PID	proportional, integral, derivative control
PLC	programmable logic controller
RTD	resistance temperature detector
SDLC	synchronous data link control

References

1. J. Martin, *Telecommunications and the Computer*, Prentice-Hall, Englewood Cliffs, New Jersey, 1976.
2. H. I. Hertanu, "Using Communication Techniques in Distributed Control," *Intech*, December 1980.

GABRIEL J. CORDOVA
HEROLD I. HERTANU
GEORGE T. DOYLE

Molecular Sieves, Silicon Enriched

Introduction

Union Carbide has developed a family of framework-silicon-enriched zeolite molecular sieves with the faujasite (type-Y) zeolite crystal structure called LZ-210 (n), where "n" refers to the silica/alumina ratio of the product. These materials exhibit properties which distinguish them from conventional Y zeolite products, including ammonium Y, stabilized Y and Y zeolites which have been subjected to various aluminum extraction techniques. The latter two are currently employed in various premium FCC octane catalysts. United States and foreign patents have been obtained on LZ-210, its method of manufacture, and use in FCC.

The new LZ-210 zeolite compositions are prepared by a novel chemistry discovered by Skeels and Breck [1] for the substitution of silicon for aluminum in the crystal framework of conventional Y zeolite materials, e.g., NH_4Y. The resulting framework-silicon-enriched LZ-210 zeolites display many properties which are particularly important in FCC catalyst applications. Perhaps the most important attribute is the broad flexibility of the framework-silicon-enrichment process to produce a zeolite product composition tailor made for the specific FCC service requirement. For example, the process permits control of the zeolite framework silica/alumina ratio, and consequently the unit cell size of the LZ-210 product. In addition, it allows the reduction of the zeolite sodium content to unusually low levels. In the LZ-210 manufacturing process, dealumination and silicon substitution in the zeolite framework are accomplished without creation of significant defects in the crystal lattice or alumina and/or silica/alumina "debris," which are known to form in the zeolite crystal when conventional steam stabilization techniques are employed to prepare aluminum-depleted crystal framework structures (e.g., USY). The various aluminum extraction techniques employed to prepare modified USY zeolites (e.g., dealuminated USY) do not quantitatively remove this nonframework "debris," nor can they restore the structure loss suffered in the "stabilization" step.

The silica/alumina ratio of the LZ-210 used to make an FCC catalyst, the extent of rare earth exchange, and other FCC catalyst manufacturing steps affect the composite unit cell size and zeolite sodium content of the equilibrium catalyst. These zeolite parameters in the equilibrium catalyst are known to strongly influence the relative rates of hydrogen transfer and cracking, the key factors in FCC catalysis affecting gasoline octane [2]. With LZ-210 zeolite base it is possible to formulate superior catalysts matching the specific requirements of any performance-oriented FCC market segment.

The silicon-enriched essentially defect-free structure imparts a substantial enhancement in thermal and hydrothermal stability to the LZ-210 zeolites.

The exceptional hydrothermal stability of LZ-210, coupled with the extent of rare earth cation exchange employed, permits a high degree of control over the activity distribution (and unit cell size distribution) of equilibrium FCC catalysts. Appropriate selection of the LZ-210 silica/alumina ratio and degree of rare earth exchange also allows substantial reduction and control of the amount of nonframework alumina and silica/alumina "debris" that is formed in the equilibrium catalyst. The result of the combined benefits of enhanced hydrothermal stability and control over nonframework "debris" is that the FCC product selectivity and gasoline octane are favorably affected [3].

Low unit cell size in equilibrium catalysts are generally associated with production of high octane FCC gasoline. Using LZ-210, maximum octane FCC catalysts can be manufactured which permit zeolite unit cell (a_0) shrinkage to levels below those generally associated with high octane USY based maximum octane catalysts. These maximum octane catalysts based on LZ-210 produce gasoline octanes above those produced by USY catalysts. This superior octane performance is accomplished without the activity penalty and gasoline yield loss normally associated with USY catalysts.

This article presents information on the chemistry of the framework-silicon-enrichment process and the properties of the resultant LZ-210 zeolites. Comparisons are made with the properties of various type Y and modified Y zeolites. The unique performance response to rare earth cation exchange, as determined in MAT, is presented for a representative LZ-210 and compared to that of USY. Companion papers presented by Katalistiks International, Inc. and Katalistiks b.v. provide extensive pilot plant data on the performance of LZ-210 based FCC catalysts compared to competitors' catalysts, and data on the performance of LZ-210 based catalysts in commercial FCC units.

Chemistry and Characteristics of Framework Silicon Enriched LZ-210 Zeolites

Chemistry

A major discovery in zeolite chemistry was made by Skeels and Breck [1], who found that the replacement of zeolite framework aluminum atoms by silicon atoms can be achieved by the application of aqueous solutions of silicon-containing reagents at mild reaction temperatures. The reagents are characterized by their ability to form aluminum complexes that are thermodynamically favored compared to framework aluminum, and by their ability to generate monomeric silicon species in solution. A favored reaction scheme applied to Y zeolite is given as follows:

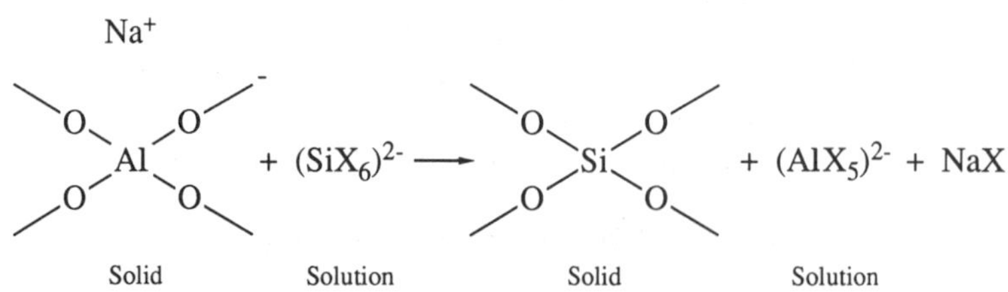

The overall reaction is believed to proceed through two consecutive steps. It is conceived that first framework aluminum atoms are removed from the Y zeolite by the hydrolized $(SiX_6)^{2-}$ solution. Subsequently, silicon atoms are inserted in a slower reaction step. Substantial dealumination without silicon insertion may cause crystal collapse, while the silicon-enriched product becomes more stable relative to the starting zeolite. It is also clear from the equation that exchanged sodium is a reaction product (as NaX) when the silicon-enriched product is formed. This favors the preparation of low Na_2O zeolites for octane catalysts, a well-known advantage for octane enhancement [2].

A variety of chemical, physical, and crystallographic evidence demonstrates that the silicon atoms are inserted into Y zeolite framework sites vacated by aluminum atoms. For example, material balance of the reaction system shows essentially perfect stoichiometry between aluminum removed and inserted silicon. Crystallographic information and particularly the gradual changes in lattice parameter, a_0, observed with incremental reagent additions indicate good distribution of the inserted silicon atoms throughout the zeolite crystal. According to Skeels, for example, 60% replacement of aluminum by silicon is readily achieved while maintaining nearly full faujasite crystal integrity [1]. Measurement of the cation balance indicates aluminum remaining after silicon insertion retains its tetrahedral coordination (shown in Table 1 as M^+/Al).

Hydrothermal Properties of LZ-210 Zeolites

In order to study the stability of framework-silicon-enriched LZ-210 zeolites in the presence of steam, a series of Y samples with a silica/alumina ratio of 5.0 were treated with silicon-containing reagent to achieve product silica/alumina ratios ranging from 6.5 to 19.7. Following the washing step to remove occluded by-product solution, the samples were characterized for chemical composition and crystallinity (see Table 1). Recognizing the detrimental effect of sodium on crystal retention in the presence of steam at elevated temperatures, the sodium content of all samples (including both LZ-210 and reference Y materials) was reduced via NH_4^+ exchange to below 0.4 wt.% (see Table 2).

The chemical and physical characteristics of the silicon-enriched LZ-210 products shown in Tables 1 and 2 follow closely the characteristics reported earlier by Skeels. The LZ-210 samples show very high retention of crystallinity. The retention of the residual aluminum in the tetrahedral position is indicated by M^+/Al ratios of approximately 0.9. The M^+/Al ratios somewhat smaller than unity are justified here because of the extensive washing of the samples, resulting in partial Na cation hydrolysis. The crystal retention of the products has been examined by three independent measurements including X-ray diffraction, surface area, and oxygen adsorption capacity measurements. In order to arrive at the best estimate, the average of these three determinations was calculated in terms of percent crystal retention relative to untreated reference NH_4Y (Na_2O = 2.25%). The only exception from essentially full crystal retention is the LZ-210 sample with a silica/alumina ratio of

TABLE 1 Properties of LZ-210

Zeolite	SiO_2/Al_2O_3[a]	Na_2O (wt.%)	$(NH_4)_2O$ (wt.%)	M^+/Al Ratio	O_2[b] Capacity (wt.%)	Surface[c] Area (m^2/g)	X-Ray[d] Crystallinity (%)	Unit Cell Size (Å) Measured[e]	Unit Cell Size (Å) Calculated[f]	DTA Collapse Temperature (°C)
NH_4Y, Reference	5.1	2.25	9.5	1.02	34.1	875	100	24.73	24.66	884
LZ-210	6.5	2.30	6.8	0.91	33.8	915	—	24.62	24.58	973
LZ-210	7.4	1.28	6.3	0.85	31.2	890	107	24.56	24.54	1016
LZ-210	8.4	1.13	6.1	0.88	31.5	814	95	24.53	24.51	1058
LZ-210	9.1	1.20	6.2	0.98	33.7	855	110	24.51	24.49	1064
LZ-210	11.0	0.39	5.1	0.87	31.0	840	98	24.46	24.44	1110
LZ-210	19.7	0.18	3.7	0.99	30.1	767	93	24.41	24.34	1175

[a] $SiO_2Al_3O_3$ ratio determined by bulk chemical analysis.
[b] Wt.% O_2 absorbed at −183°C and 100 torr.
[c] Determined by 3-point BET method with nitrogen.
[d] X-ray diffraction pattern peak areas relative to reference to NH_4Y, Reference.
[e] Determined from X-ray diffraction pattern d-spacings.
[f] Calculate from the chemical Si and Al content according to Breck, *Zeolite*, *Molecular Sieves*, 1974, p. 94. As discussed in the literature, the calculated values obtained with cation exchanged or chemically modified Y zeolites serve as approximate values.

TABLE 2 Properties of Low-Soda LZ-210

Zeolite	SiO_2/Al_2O_3[a]	Na_2O (wt.%)	$(NH_4)_2O$ (wt.%)	M^+/Al Ratio	O_2[b] Capacity (wt.%)	Surface[c] Area (m^2/g)	X-ray[d] Crystallinity (%)
NH_4Y, Reference	5.1	2.25	9.5	1.02	34.1	875	100
Low-soda[e] NH_4Y	5.0	0.36	10.7	0.98	33.0	935	105
LZ-210	6.4	0.38	8.6	0.94	35.1	949	
LZ-210	7.6	0.26	7.7	0.92	34.7	927	99
LZ-210	8.4	0.05	7.6	0.98	33.8	923	
LZ-210	11.7	0.05	5.4	0.88	30.7	863	103
LZ-210	19.7	0.18	3.7	0.99	30.1	767	93

[a] SiO_2/Al_2O_3 ratios determined by bulk chemical analysis.
[b] Wt.% O_2 absorbed at −183°C and 100 torr.
[c] Determined by 3-point BET method with nitrogen.
[d] X-ray diffraction pattern peak area relative to NH_4Y, Reference.
[e] DTA crystal collapse temperature = 852°C for low-soda NH_4Y.

19.7, which retained about 90% crystallinity. The DTA crystal collapse temperatures for the LZ-210 crystals show very large increases in thermal stability, from 852°C for low soda reference NH_4Y to 1175°C for the LZ-210 product at a silica/alumina ratio of 19.7. The difference between the reference Y and the most silicon-enriched LZ-210 product is 323°C. This is a very large difference, indeed, and it is consistent with the early publication [1].

While the effect of soda on the thermal stability of Y zeolite is usually small, in the presence of steam its effect is large, accelerating crystal collapse. Therefore, in order to allow a fair comparison, samples of the LZ-210 zeolites as well as the reference NH_4Y used in the steaming study were ammonium-exchanged to reduce Na_2O content below 0.4 wt.%. The steaming treatment, particularly the high temperature, 870°C, was chosen as a discriminatory tool to distinguish between zeolite products of varying steam stability. The steam partial pressure (175 mm) and the treatment time, 5 h, were selected for relevance to FCC process conditions.

Following steam treatment, the zeolite samples, including the steamed Y reference, were examined for crystal retention using X-ray diffraction, surface area, and oxygen sorption capacity, as described above. An average of these three values was calculated for each material, and the crystal retention relative to the NH_4Y reference material was established in percent (see Table 3).

The data in Table 3 show that, similar to the thermal stability results, the silicon-enriched LZ-210 zeolite products display greatly enhanced hydrothermal stability, relative to low-soda NH_4Y (Na_2O = 0.36 wt.%). For example, the low-soda NH_4Y (Na_2O = 0.36 wt.%), following the steam treatment, retains only about 15% crystallinity, while the LZ-210 product with a silica/alumina ratio of 11.7 retains about 90% crystallinity. It is important to note that the 6.4 silica/alumina ratio product retains about 58% crystallinity. Also, it should be noted that for the LZ-210 products the crystal losses indicated in Table 3 include any losses occurring in the silicon-insertion and steaming steps.

TABLE 3 Crystallinity Retention Following Severe Steam Treatment[a] of Low-Soda LZ-210

Zeolite	SiO_2/ Al_2O_3	Na_2O (wt.%)	$(NH_4)_2O$ (wt.%)	O_2 Capacity[c] Retention (%)	Surface Area[d] Retention (%)	% X-Ray Crystallinity[e] Retention (%)	Average[f] Retention (%)
NH_4Y, Reference	5.1	2.25	9.5	2.6	9.0	0.0	3.9
NH_4Y, low-soda	5.0	0.36	10.7	25.8	12.5	7.7	15.3
Low-soda LZ-210	6.4	0.38	8.6	57.4	59.0		58.2
Low-soda LZ-210	7.6	0.26	7.7	68.6	72.4	64.3	68.4
Low-soda LZ-210	8.4	0.05	7.6	71.9	75.7		73.8
Low-soda LZ-210	11.7	0.05	5.4	77.7	77.2	109.4	88.1
Low-soda LZ-210	19.7	0.18	3.7	69.8	73.4	99.2	80.2

[a] 870°C, 23% H_2O in air for 5 h.
[b] SiO_2/Al_2O_3 ratio determined by bulk chemical analysis.
[c] O_2 capacity of steamed zeolite/ O_2 capacity of fresh NH_4Y, Reference X100.
[d] Surface area of steamed zeolite/surface area of fresh NH_4Y, Reference X100.
[e] X-ray peak areas of steamed zeolite/X-ray peak area of fresh NH_4Y, Reference X100.
[f] Average of O_2 capacity, surface area, and X-ray crystallinity retention data.

It is well known that an enhancement of the silica/alumina ratio of the Y crystal framework can also be achieved by alternative methods such as steam stabilization and by extraction of the aluminum. Therefore, it is relevant to compare these materials with LZ-210 zeolite products. For this reason, two aluminum-depleted Y zeolites were prepared by EDTA (ethylenediaminetetraacetic acid) extraction [4–6] and by steam stabilization followed by HCl acid extraction. Both materials were prepared to have a silica/alumina ratio of about 8 and were subsequently NH_4^+ exchanged to reduce soda content to below approximately 0.4 wt.%. A third sample was prepared by a steam stabilization treatment without additional aluminum extraction, commonly referred to as a USY type zeolite. This material was also ammonium exchanged to reduce soda content. All zeolite samples were subsequently steam treated using the conditions described above.

The characteristics of the samples before and after steaming are given in Table 4. The table also presents comparable data for LZ-210 products.

Characterization of the "steam stabilized" Y, the EDTA-extracted Y, and the "steam-stabilized" and acid-extracted Y products shows that they all lose considerable crystallinity in the extraction or steaming steps. However, they all show increased DTA collapse temperature resulting from the dealumination of their crystal framework. Following steam treatment, described above, their crystal retention, relative to the original NH_4Y reference, in decreasing order is: steam-stabilized Y > EDTA-extracted Y >> steamed, acid-extracted Y. It should be noted that the crystal retention of steam-stabilized Y, a material previously steam treated at preferred steaming conditions, was about the same as the LZ-210 with a silica/alumina ratio of 6.4. Also, it should be noted that the latter product received no prior steam stabilization. The EDTA and acid-extracted products show lower crystallinity retention upon steam treatment relative to any of the silicon-enriched LZ-210 products. The differences in crystal retention between the low-soda NH_4^+ exchanged EDTA-treated Y, and even a moderately silicon-enriched LZ-210 product with a silica/alumina ratio of 8.4 is already very large, 52 versus 74%, in favor of the LZ-210 product. With further silicon enrichment at a silica/alumina ratio of 11.7, the difference is even larger, 52 versus 88%.

The outstanding crystal stability of LZ-210 products has been demonstrated here under severe steaming conditions. Clearly, these materials at silica/alumina ratios greater than 6.4 display superior hydrothermal stability relative to modified H-Y type zeolite products obtained by aluminum extraction (EDTA), steam stabilization followed by HCl acid extraction, or steam stabilization alone.

Illustration of Improved Crystal Retention for LZ-210

Figure 1 presents a stylized drawing depicting the morphology of a series of fresh and steamed Y zeolites and LZ-210 (9.0). Actual TEM pictures taken of samples of zeolite crystal sections cut at approximately 500 to 1000 Å

TABLE 4 Crystallinity of Low-Soda Aluminum Deficient Y Zeolite Products Following Severe Steam Treatment[a]

Zeolite	Properties of Unsteamed Materials								Relative Crystallinity Retention Following Severe Steaming				
	SiO_2/ Al_2O_3	Na_2O (wt.%)	$(NH_4)_2O$ (wt.%)	M^+/Al Ratio	O_2[c] Capacity (wt.%)	Surface[d] Area (m^2/g)	% X-Ray[e] Crystallinity	Unit Cell Size Measured	DTA Collapse	O_2[f] Capacity Retention	% Surface[g] Area Retention	% X-Ray Crystallinity Retention	Average[i] Retention
"Steam stabilized Y" (USY)	5.8	0.17	4.0	0.38	27.8	734	73	24.55	1010	59.4	59.1	—	59.3
Al extracted using EDTA	8.2	1.02	7.0	0.96	31.9	803	88	24.55	980	24.3	17.8	17.0	19.7
Low-soda Al extracted using EDTA	8.1	0.42	7.2	0.93	31.2	812	67	24.62	980	51.4	56.1	49.0	52.2
Steamed, acid-extracted Y	8.8	0.76	0.05	0.08	19.9	579	48	24.30	1055	28.7	30.4	26.0	28.4
Low-soda steamed acid-extracted Y	9.1	0.33	1.8	0.26	19.9	527	50	24.30	1085	23.2	30.3	28.0	27.2
Low-soda LZ-210	6.4	0.38	8.6	0.94	35.1	949	—	24.69	940	57.4	59.0	—	58.2
Low-soda LZ-210	7.6	0.26	7.7	0.92	34.7	927	99	24.56	998	68.6	72.4	64.3	68.4
Low-soda LZ-210	8.4	0.05	7.6	0.98	33.8	923	—	24.58	1031	71.9	77.2	75.7	73.8
Low-soda LZ-210	11.7	0.05	5.4	0.88	30.7	863	103	24.42	1105	77.7	77.2	109.4	88.1
Low-soda LZ-210	19.7	0.18	3.7	0.99	30.1	767	93	24.41	1175	69.8	73.4	99.2	80.8

[a]870°C, 23% H_2O in air for 5 h.
[b] SiO_2/Al_2O_3 ratio determined by bulk chemical analysis.
[c]Wt.% O_2 absorbed at −183°C and 100 torr
[d]Determined by 3-point BET method with nitrogen.
[e]X-ray diffraction pattern peak areas relative to NH_4Y, Reference.
[f] O_2 capacity of steamed zeolite/ O_2 capacity of fresh NH_4Y, Reference X100.
[g]Surface ara of steamed zeolite/surface area of fresh NH_4Y, Reference X100.
[h]X-ray peak areas of steamed zeolite/X-ray peak area of freash NH_4Y, Reference X100.
[i]Average of O_2 capacity, surface area, and X-ray crystallinity retention data.

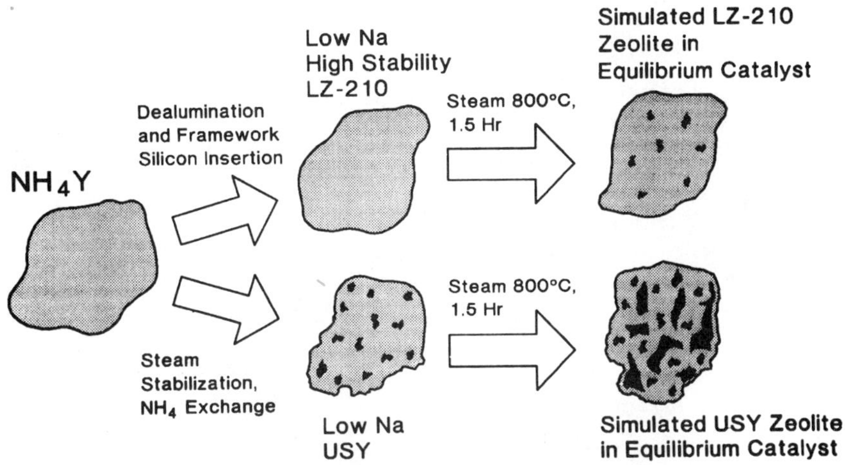

FIG. 1. Illustration of improved crystal retention for LZ-210.

thickness are presented in Figs. 2 through 8. All the samples discussed here are nonrare earth exchanged. The fresh starting material is NH_4Y. Steam stabilization followed by ammonium ion exchange produces low sodium stabilized Y or USY. The stabilization process results in the creation of highly crystalline regions that contain a framework structure which is depleted of aluminum relative to the starting NH_4Y, and defect regions which constitute void space created by coalescence of atomic defects formed when framework aluminum is hydrolyzed. Nonframework alumina and silica/alumina created during the stabilization process may be present in the intracrystalline voids as well as occluded in the retained crystalline framework structure. In contrast, the LZ-210 (9.0), which has undergone a sufficient degree of silicon substitution from the same starting NH_4Y to render the product LZ-210 more stable (both thermally and hydrothermally) than USY, retains the same defect-free crystal structure of the starting NH_4Y. As a result, the LZ-210 has a higher surface area and a higher O_2 capacity than USY.

The steamed samples depicted in Fig. 1 (actual TEM's given in Figs. 4, 6, and 8) have been exposed to steaming conditions (800°C for 1.5 h) to simulate the condition of zeolite contained in equilibrium FCC catalyst particles that have seen typical average service. Clearly, the "equilibrium" USY sample has undergone considerably more loss of crystal structure than the comparable LZ-210 sample. The more crystalline, comparatively defect-free LZ-210 "equilibrium" sample should retain more of the performance benefits generally associated with crystalline zeolite FCC catalysts, e.g., higher activity retention and superior product selectivity, compared to the "equilibrium" USY sample which has lost a high degree of the fresh catalyst crystallinity.

In light of these considerations, the LZ-210 zeolites are expected to show benefits as cracking components in FCC catalysts. These materials have less aluminum and more silicon atoms in their crystal at the start. Therefore, upon steaming and concurrent hydrolysis of the framework aluminum, these materials have less defect sites and consequently less intracrystalline micro-

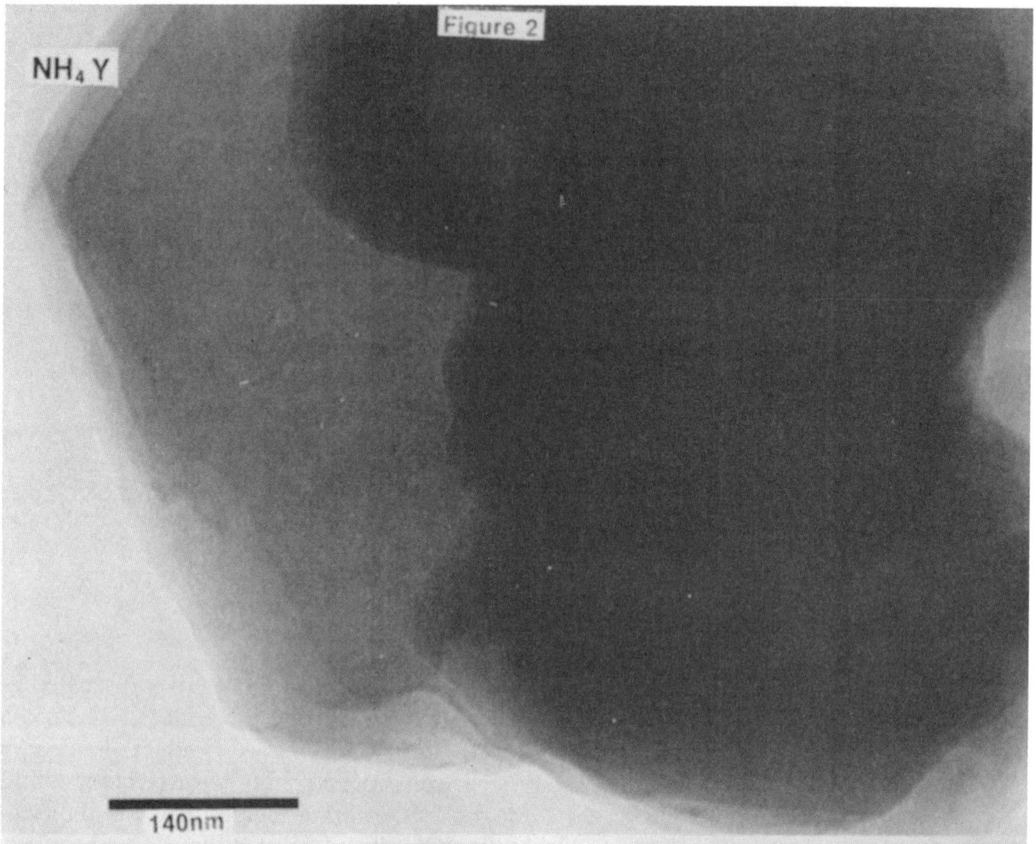

Figure 2

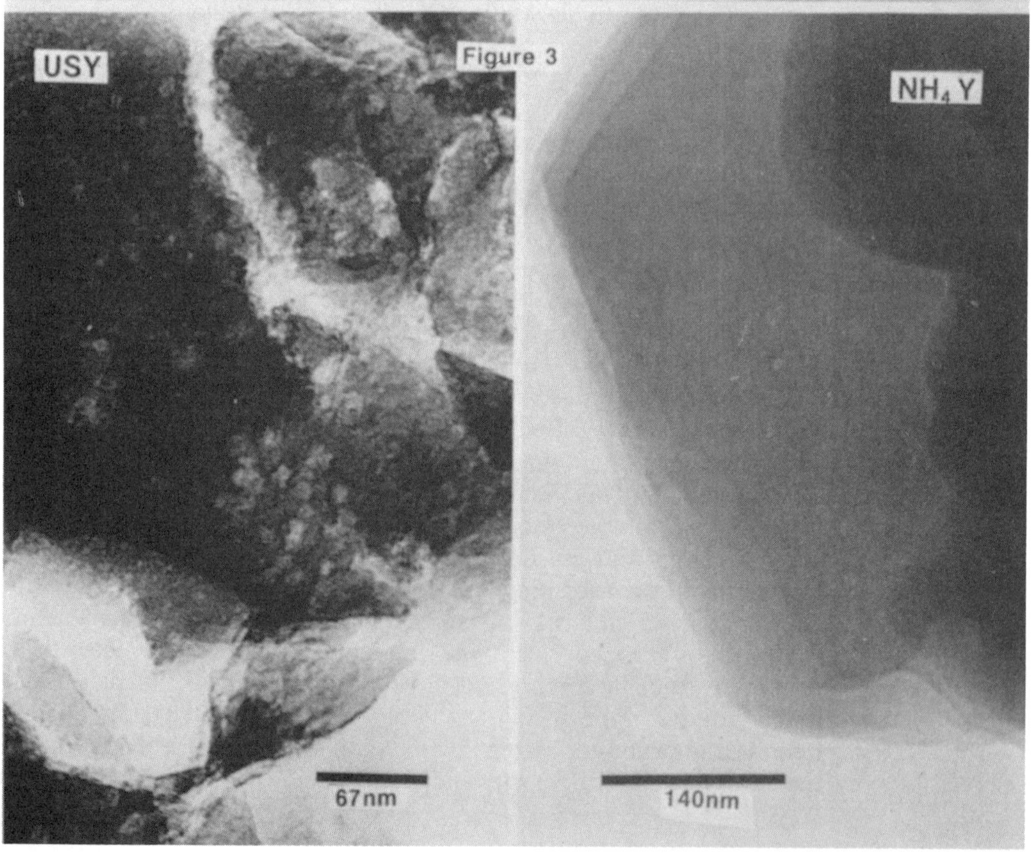

Figure 3

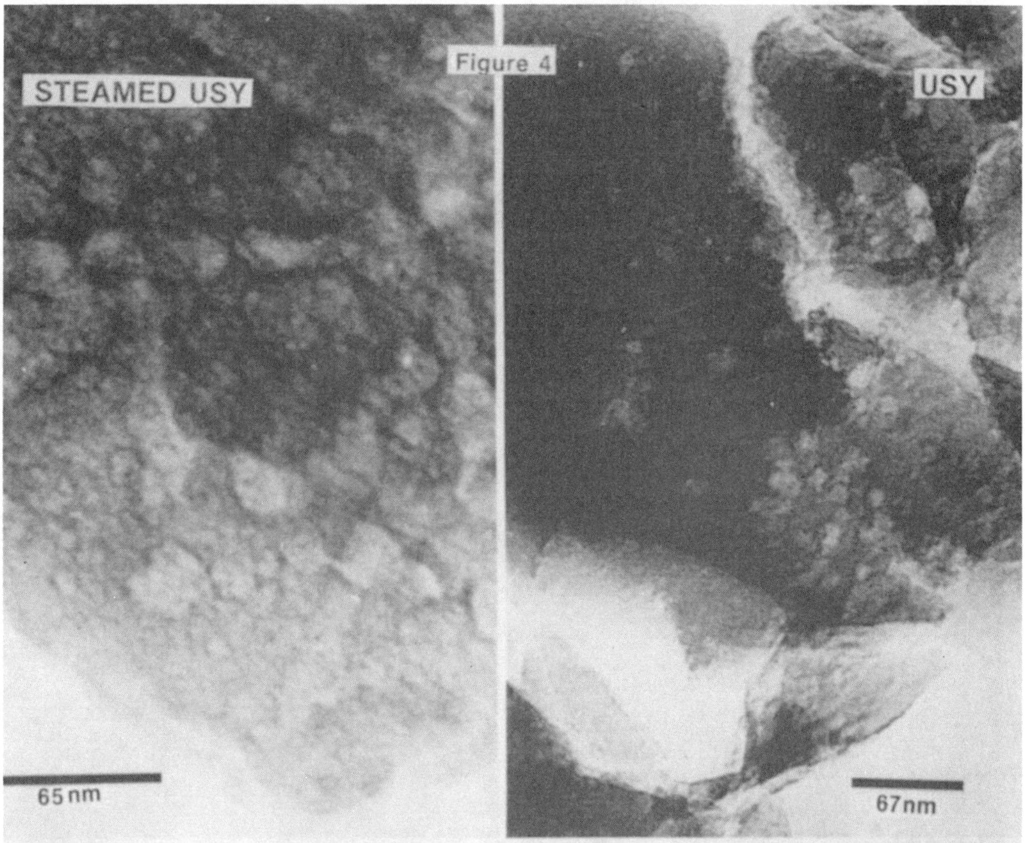
Figure 4
STEAMED USY
USY
65 nm
67nm

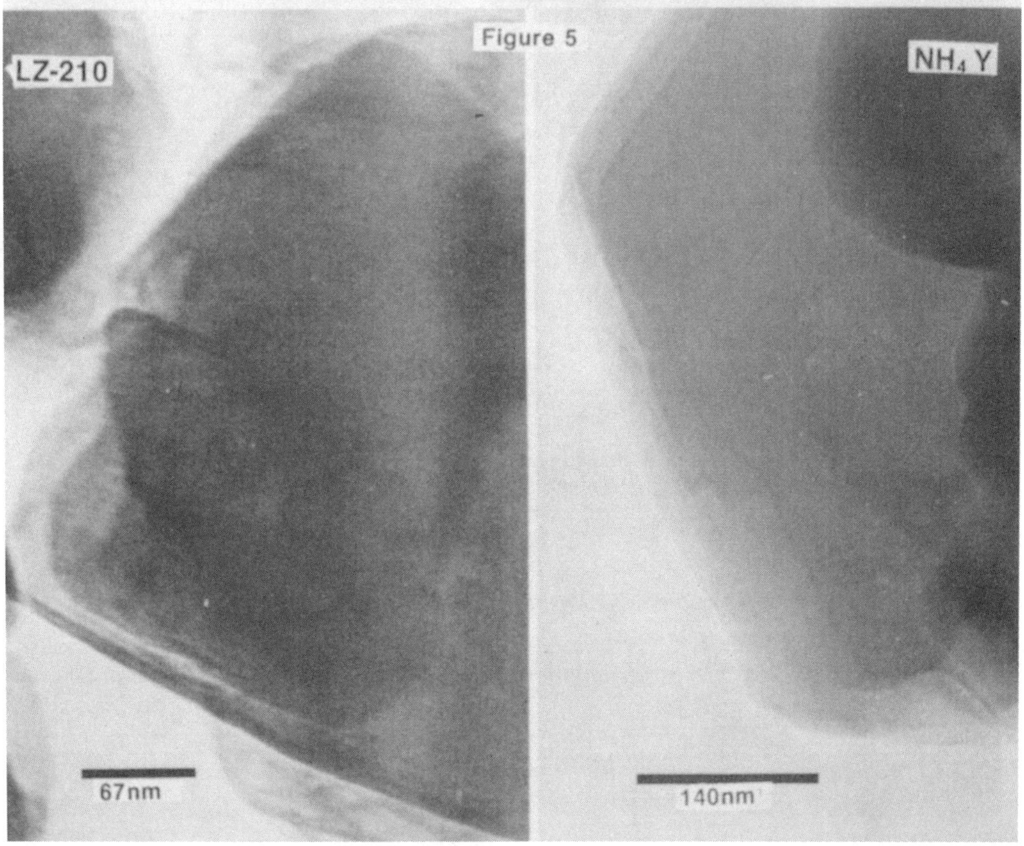
Figure 5
LZ-210
NH4 Y
67nm
140nm

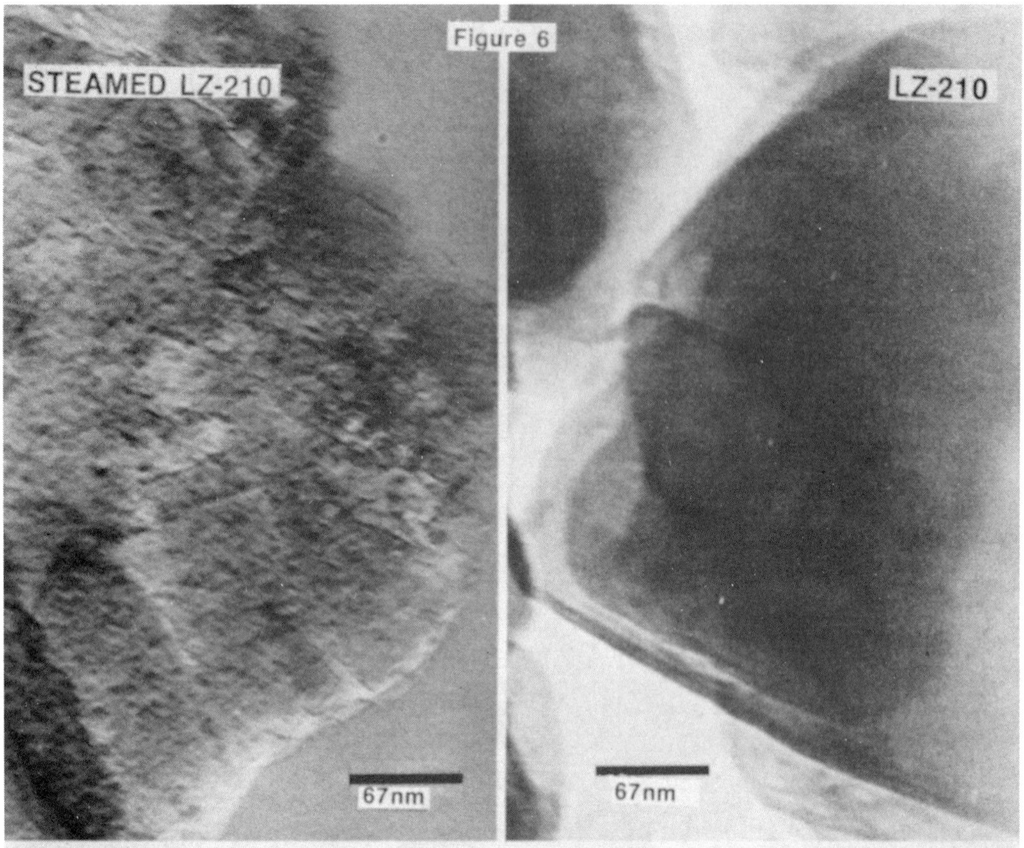

Figure 6

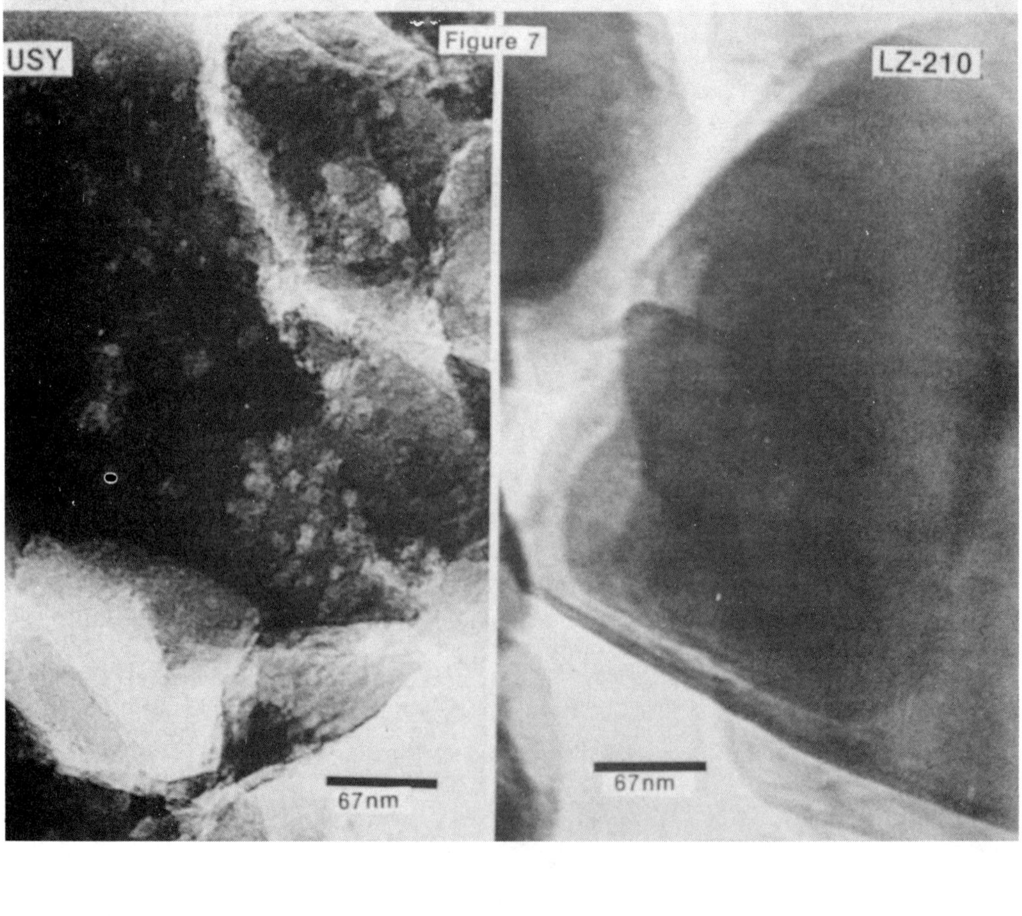

Figure 7

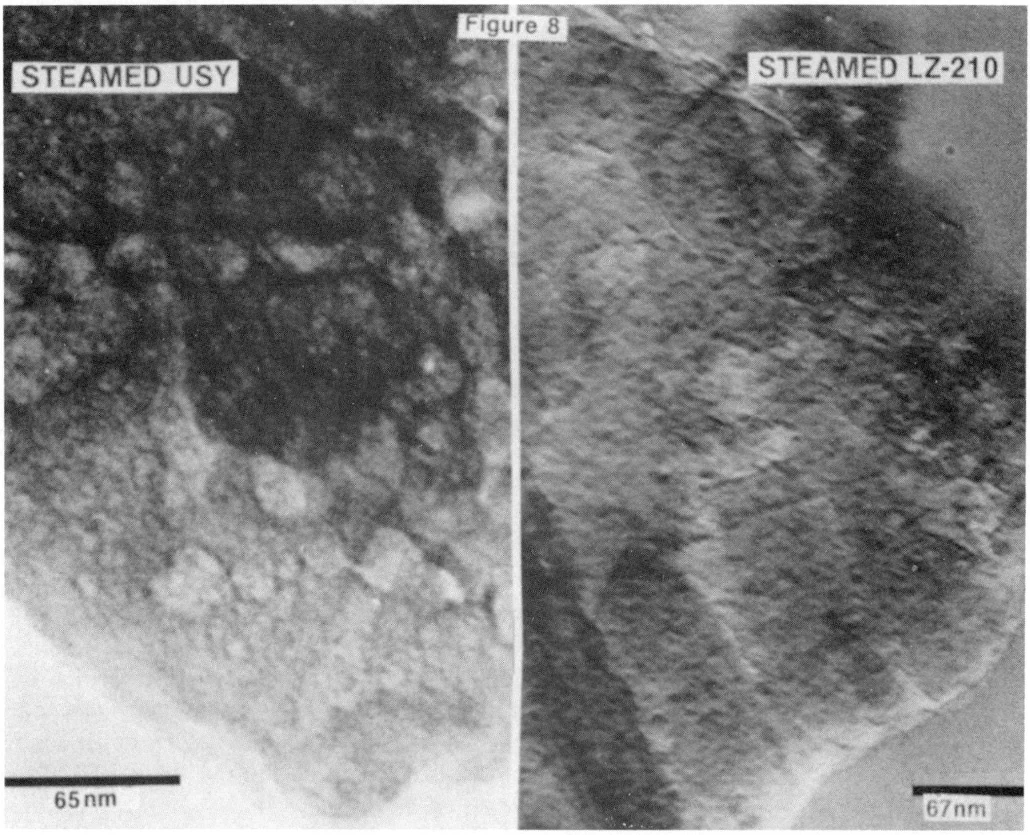

porosity. Therefore, their crystal decomposition is slower relative to conventional stabilized zeolites. Higher intrinsic crystal stability and the resulting higher crystal retention results in enhanced cracking activity retention in service. The intrinsically higher crystal stability and the reduced initial aluminum content should slow down the formation of alumina and silica-alumina debris created within the Y crystal upon loss of crystallinity, following exposure to steam at high temperatures. With a higher fraction of selective zeolite acid sites and less "debris acid" sites, noted for low selectivity, improved product selectivities may be expected relative to those obtained with alternative modified H-Y products.

Unique Response of LZ-210 to Rare Earth Exchange

Rare earth cation exchange enhances Y zeolite stability and increases equilibrium catalyst unit cell size. An undesireable consequence of rare earth exchange is increased hydrogen transfer activity relative to cracking activity, resulting in less olefinic gasoline which is lower in octane than that obtainable with USY catalysts. Several high-octane or octane-barrel FCC catalysts are currently offered by various FCC catalyst manufacturers based on partially rare earth exchanged USY or dealuminated USY. Depending on the extent of rare earth exchange, these catalysts trade-off octane for activity when compared at constant zeolite content. Alternatively, some rare earth exchange of USY permits the use of less zeolite in the catalyst formulation at constant activity. However, rare-earth-exchanged USY catalysts invariably produce lower octane than nonrare-earth-exchanged USY catalysts.

Use of LZ-210 offers new degrees of freedom in FCC catalyst formulation because its response to rare-earth exchange is uniquely different from that of USY. To illustrate, a representative member of the LZ-210 family was used in a series of FCC catalysts, all with the same zeolite content and all using the Katalistiks Sigma catalyst matrix. Each member of the series was prepared with a different rare earth content. A similar series of catalysts was prepared based on USY, with identical zeolite content and matrix as the LZ-210 series. All of the catalysts had low sodium content. Both the LZ-210 and USY series were subjected to steam deactivation at 816°C for 2 h at 1 atm and then tested in MAT with a West Texas VGO at 930°F (499°C), 3.0 cat/oil, and 16 WHSV.

Figure 9 presents three sets of data from the study for both the RE LZ-210 catalyst series and the RE USY catalyst series. Conversion, olefin-to-total C_4 ratio, and iso/normal ratio for C_4 paraffins are presented as a function of rare earth loading. Several features distinguish the RE LZ-210 system from the RE USY system.

There is a rare earth loading level, Point A, below which the RE USY system displays higher activity than the RE LZ-210 system. It is believed that this higher activity is due to the higher silica/alumina ratio, by bulk chemical analysis, of the USY. A substantial fraction of the alumina in the USY system is believed to be catalytically active nonframework material, which contributes to the overall activity of the catalyst. However, other workers have attributed this active nonframework material to an undesirable increase in light gas make. The steamed LZ-210 based catalysts contain far less nonframework material and therefore are lacking its contribution to activity. Higher activity in the zero and very low rare earth regions, at equal rare earth levels, is not considered an advantage for the RE USY system, since this activity boost is most probably caused by nonselective nonframework material. In this region the maximum relative activity advantage for the RE USY system is 12% higher (by pseudo-second-order kinetics) than the particular RE LZ-210 system presented here. It should be noted that the relative catalyst activities in this low rare earth loading region have been observed to vary with silica/alumina ratio of the RE LZ-210 used and the steaming conditions selected. There are reasonable conditions under which RE LZ-210 displays equal or even higher activity compared to RE USY at equal, low rare earth loadings.

At rare earth loadings greater than that for Point A, the RE LZ-210 system displays higher activity than the RE USY system. As rare earth loading increases, both of the catalyst systems level off in activity, with the RE LZ-210 system giving about 27% higher catalytic activity (by pseudo-second-order kinetics) than the RE USY system. In this region, rare earth apparently produces greater activity retention with the LZ-210 zeolite than with USY, and the zeolite catalytic activity dominates the activity contribution of nonframework active material.

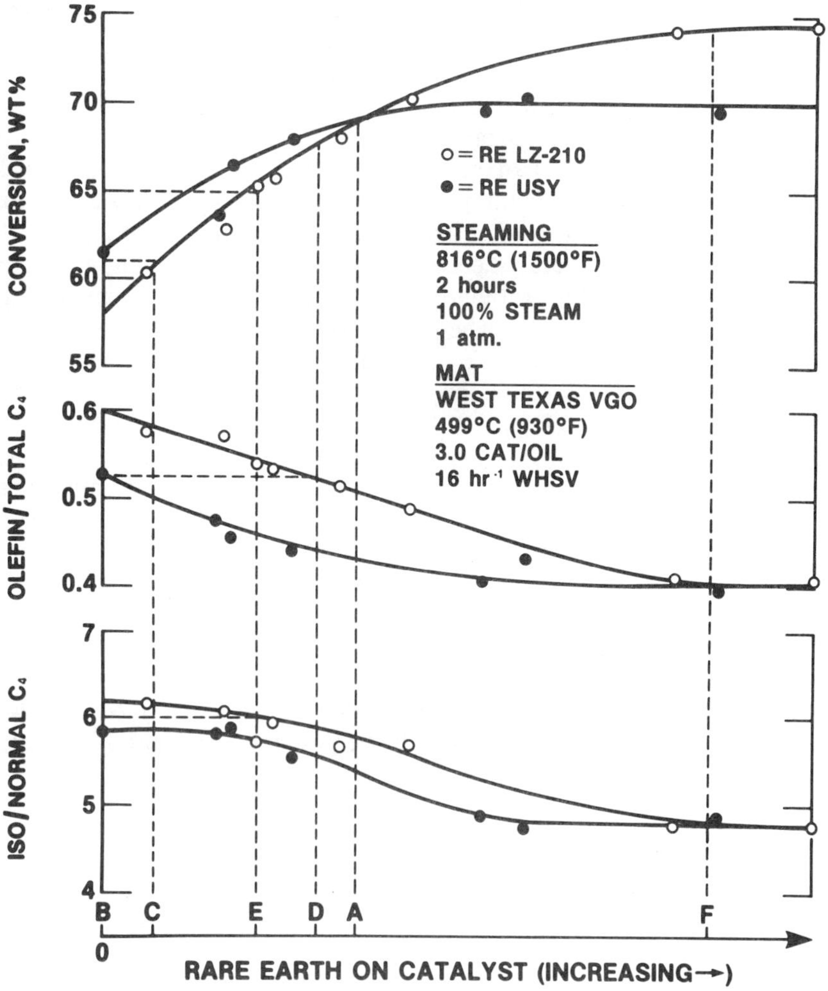

FIG. 9. Response to rare earth.

Other workers [2] have observed a relationship between increased C_4 olefin content in total C_4's and gasoline octane (both research number and motor number) for the RE USY system. It therefore seems reasonable to generalize that catalysts producing higher olefin content in the C_4 products are likely to also produce higher gasoline research and motor octane numbers. This line of reasoning enables the use of GC analyses of MAT vapor-phase products (specifically, C_4's) to gain at least a qualitative view of the expected trend in gasoline octane as a function of rare earth loading. Figure 9 clearly shows that up to the rare earth loading of Point D, the RE LZ-210 system produces a higher olefin/total C_4 ratio than the maximum octane version of the RE USY system; the USY formulation containing zero rare earth. This is a very important observation since nonrare earth USY catalysts are known to produce the highest gasoline octanes of all zeolite-based FCC catalysts. Yet, here, there are data to suggest the potential for even higher octane with RE LZ-210.

Assuming that rare earth loading E in the RE LZ-210 system gives gasoline with octane equal to the zero rare earth USY formulation, Point B, the result would be a RE LZ-210 formulation with 19% higher catalytic activity than the zero rare earth USY catalyst with equal octane performance. (Independent pilot plant data support the assumption.) The rare earth loading on RE LZ-210 required to match the activity of the zero rare earth USY catalyst corresponds to Point C. Between rare earth levels C and E, RE LZ-210 formulations can trade-off higher activity for higher olefinicity (and potentially higher octane) without any performance debit relative to the zero rare earth USY formulation. It is clear by inspection of Fig. 9 that any RE USY formulation can be matched or exceeded in activity by an appropriately chosen RE LZ-210 formulation, and that the olefinicity of C_4's will simultaneously be matched or exceeded. Not until the rare earth loading reaches Point F do the olefinicity curves converge, at which point the activity curves show the greatest activity enhancement for RE LZ-210.

Figure 9 shows an additional octane-related improvement with the enhancement of the iso/normal ratio for C_4 paraffins produced by the RE LZ-210 series compared to the RE USY series. Again, there is a window of rare earth loadings that permits equal or higher C_4 iso/normal ratios at equal or higher activity levels for the RE LZ-210 system. This datum directly suggests higher isobutane yields can be expected with the RE LZ-210 system, and is indicative that the gasoline range paraffins will also contain higher levels of branched isomers.

Summary and Conclusions

Framework-silicon-enriched LZ-210 zeolites provide the opportunity to greatly enhance the effective zeolitic crystallinity of the FCC catalyst remaining in the FCC process environment. High silica/alumina ratio LZ-210 products exhibit higher thermal and hydrothermal stability than any known stabilized Y zeolites.

The increased crystal stability and related activity retention afforded by the framework silicon enrichment process is believed to be due to (a) the substantial reduction of crystal defects compared with dealuminated structures, (b) their high and controllable silica/alumina ratio, and (c) their inherently low Na_2O content.

The process by which LZ-210 is manufactured produces zeolites of low to very-low Na_2O level (as low as 0.05 wt.%) with benefits both in zeolite activity retention and gasoline product octane.

LZ-210 zeolites retain a higher degree of the original crystal structure after steaming relative to stabilized Y zeolite products. They also contain less intracrystalline alumina and silica/alumina nonframework debris after steaming than stabilized Y zeolites. These features result in superior FCC activity retention and product selectivity.

LZ-210 offers wide flexibility to select the silica/alumina ratio of the zeolite in fresh FCC catalyst to match FCC performance objectives.

LZ-210 displays a unique response to rare earth loading compared to USY. Increased catalyst activity and product olefinicity can be achieved with RE LZ-210 compared to any RE USY formulation, including USY with no rare earth added. These RE LZ-210 formulations have potential for producing higher gasoline octane than USY catalysts.

This article was presented at the Katalistik's 7th Annual Fluid Cat Cracking Symposium, Venice, Italy, May 12–13, 1986.

References

1. G. W. Skeels and D. W. Breck, "Zeolite Chemistry V—Substitution of Silicon for Aluminum in Zeolite via Reaction with Aqueous Fluorosilicates," *Proc. Sixth Int. Zeolite Conf.*, pp. 87–96 (1984).
2. L. A. Pine et al., "Prediction of Cracking Catalyst Behavior by a Zeolite Unit Cell Size Model," *J. Catal., 85*, 466–476 (1984).
3. J. A. Rabo et al., *High Stability Zone Zeolites in Octane Catalysts—New Products from Union Carbide Corporation and Katalistiks International, Inc.*, 1986 NPRA Annual Meeting, AM-86-30.
4. C. V. McDaniel et al., "Zeolite Stability and Ultrastable Zeolite," *ACS Monograph 171*, 285–331 (1976).
5. G. T. Kerr, *J. Phys. Chem.*, 2594 (1968).
6. G. T. Kerr, *J. Phys. Chem.*, 2780 (1969).

G. N. LONG
R. L. CHIANG
R. J. PELLET
J. A. RABO

Natural Gas Liquids and Natural Gasoline

Background, History and Development

In the early part of the twentieth century near Sisterville, West Virginia, someone discovered that if the gas produced from wells was compressed and cooled, a clear hydrocarbon liquid would condense. The liquid was too "wild" to be used for motor fuel, but if allowed to age in an atmospheric tank for a day or so, it could be used alone or blended with naphtha or kerosene and used to fuel the horseless carriages that were beginning to appear. An increase in the demand for this liquid precipitated the birth of the gas processing industry.

Natural gas is composed primarily of methane, with smaller amounts of ethane, propane, iso and normal butanes, iso and normal pentanes, hexanes, and components heavier than hexane. While the earliest recovery of constituents from natural gas mentioned above were mostly butanes and heavier, eventually recovery to some degree was effected for ethane and heavier. The products recovered from natural gas have been referred to as liquified petroleum gas (LPG) and more recently as natural gas liquids (NGL). The terms mean essentially the same, and NGL will be used to apply to the ethane and heavier components removed from the gas stream.

Early Plants

The first gas processing plants were quite simple in concept. "Casinghead" gas was typically compressed to 300 lb/in.^{2}gauge and cooled to condense the liquids. Early modifications of this process involved flashing the condensed liquids to atmospheric pressure, or vacuum, and recycling the resulting vapor.

Attempts were made early to extract work from the gas by driving a reciprocating steam engine with gas instead of steam (the first expander plant). These more sophisticated systems were plagued with freezing and lubrication problems and were never really successful.

Probably the most important step in the development of NGL processes occurred about 1915 (focusing on natural gasoline recovery) with the development of the oil absorption process. This process consisted of two main vessels, the absorber and the still, and remains fundamentally unchanged today. Although the incidental recovery of the light ends, i.e., propane and lighter, was regarded as a nuisance, recovery of the gasoline fraction was increased by employing several innovations.

These included the application of bubble cap trays in the columns and two-stage stripping in the still (50–60 and 15 lb/in.^{2}gauge). It must be remembered that "recovery" was a meaningless term at that time, as no analytical procedures existed for accurately determining the gasoline content of natural gas.

Recovery of liquids from charcoal adsorption facilities on the residue gas streams alerted operators of oil absorption plants to the fact that their recoveries were not as good as they thought. This provided incentive for the development of processing knowledge necessary to improve plant operations and facilitate better designs. In the mid-1920s the demand for lighter hydrocarbons began to increase as a market for bottled gas and chemical feedstocks developed. These developments were augmented by an improvement in the ability to design, construct, and operate fractionation equipment.

The phenomenon of retrograde condensation was discovered in the gas distillate reservoirs at about the same time. It was well known from gas compression plants that when the pressure was raised, liquid condensed out. It was a great surprise, therefore, to discover that when the pressure of some gas reservoirs was reduced, liquid condensed in the formation. Since the gas was of little value and a large part of the liquid condensed in the reservoir was lost forever, the gas cycling plant was developed. This process extracted liquids on the surface and reinjected the gas to maintain the reservoir pressure.

The retrograde condensation phenomenon demonstrated that the properties of hydrocarbon mixtures at high pressures, particularly the vapor–liquid equilibrium "constants," deviated in strange ways from Henry's law theory which had been successfully used at low pressures. Although some research was carried out to determine the thermodynamic properties of hydrocarbon mixtures at high pressures, there was no unified effort in the early years on the part of the industry to support such programs.

After the development of the fractionating column and the cycling plant, the technical progress of the industry became slower and less spectacular for a period of time. The early 1940s saw the development of the rich oil stabilizer, which not only reduced the amount of recycle gas but also simplified the design of the still and related equipment. The use of low molecular weight absorption oil was recognized as desirable, but could not be practiced because of excessive loss of the oil by vaporization.

The use of low molecular weight oil became viable only when low-temperature absorbers were introduced. Refrigerated oil had been recognized as desirable, but earlier attempts at low-temperature absorption had failed because of the formation of ice or hydrates in the absorption system. It was not until satisfactory methods of dealing with hydrate formation in gas were perfected, such as solid dessicants or glycol, that low-temperature processing became practical.

By the 1950s the use of refrigerated lean oil absorption was increasing rapidly. The temperature levels of the process continued to drop, reaching the −40°F level by the late 1950s. This proved to be a practical limit both for metallurgical reasons and the use of propane as a refrigerant in most plants. At this point, many plants were being designed for 90+% propane recovery and 25+% ethane recovery (often referred to as incidental ethane recovery, as the amount normally attained associated with the required propane recovery).

Throughout the 1960s many large gas processing plants were built on major pipelines, referred to as "straddle" plants. The refrigerated lean oil plant reached its highest development level during this time. The use of a two-oil system was employed to reduce the total oil circulation. This was effectively two plants in series, with the first plant using a low molecular weight oil to achieve the NGL recoveries, and the sponge oil used to recover the low-weight oil. Recoveries of 70+% ethane were close to the practical limits of −40°F lean oil plant designs.

As the demand grew for higher level recoveries of ethane, new process schemes were developed. Two concurrent developments combined to dramatically change the then predominant NGL recovery process. In the mid-1960s a practical turboexpander was developed for use in a gas processing plant. The first applications were in situations where "free" pressure drop was available. The economics in these applications provided a high incentive for owners to experiment with a new technology. The second item made it practical to apply the turboexpander process even when free pressure drop was not available. The gas turbine was a source of high horsepower at a relatively low cost, particularly when compared to low speed integral engines. The combination of the turboexpander with the gas turbine for recompression provided the right results to efficiently produce the low temperature levels required for high ethane recovery levels, and this basic scheme essentially displaced the refrigerated oil plant in new applications by the mid-1970s.

The cryogenic turboexpander plant is the dominant NGL recovery process throughout the world today. While there are still isolated cases where one of the other NGL recovery processes is a logical choice, only a few plants will be built that do not follow this pattern.

Selection of an NGL recovery process involves consideration of a number of variables. It is necessary to have the basis of design defined with the inlet gas composition, pressure, and temperature. Residue gas conditions must be defined, as well as product specifications. Economic parameters should also be defined to allow the optimum process design selection, as well as optimum recovery of the NGL components. Any lack of definition of the foregoing list will diminish the design engineer's ability to select the best overall process.

NGL Recovery Processes

In order to acquaint the design engineer with the various processes used in processing natural gas for NGL recovery, a brief description will be discussed for the following processes:

1. Stage separation
2. Refigeration
3. Adsorption
4. Absorption
5. Expander
6. Product fractionation

Under each of the main processes, numerous variations can be employed. Combinations of the laws of thermodynamics, interlocked with the economic world, permit an almost endless number of major and minor variations. There is no one "best" design among gas process plants unless all parameters are constant. This is a rare, or improbable, occurrence.

Stage Separation

Frequently it is necessary to make a separation in the producing field at, or near, the wellhead. Depending on the gas composition and reservoir conditions, liquids may be separated at flowing conditions. If it is impractical to have a complete gas processing facility at this point, it may be desirable to

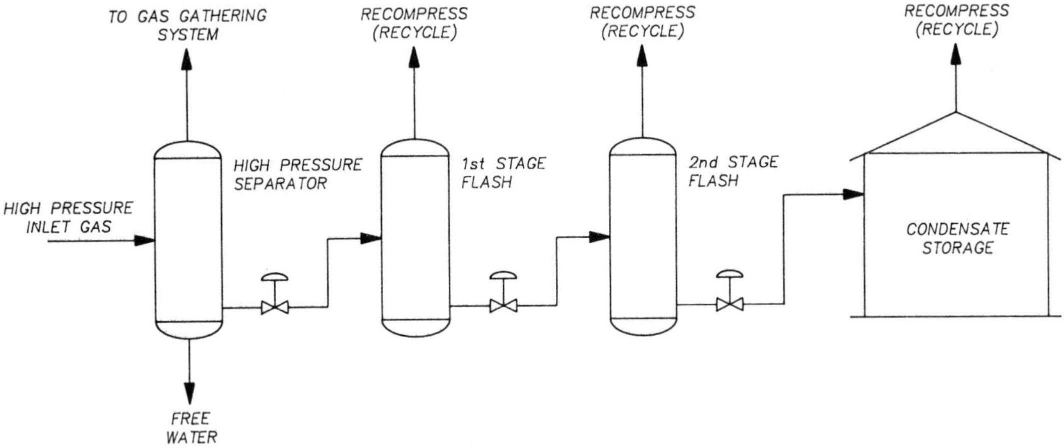

FIG. 1. Stage flash liquid recovery.

provide a stage flash separation scheme to produce a salable liquid. A simple stage flash arrangement is shown in Fig. 1. Flashing the liquid in stages to atmospheric pressure will yield a higher net NGL production than if the expansion were accomplished in a single step. Frequently the staged flash separation includes recompression of the flash vapors, and recycling them to the prior flash stage. This further maximizes the NGL production. The different stages act as a partial fractionator in the process.

If a large pressure drop is available at the wellhead, this can be used to increase field recovery of NGL. Since the adiabatic (Joule-Thompson, J-T) expansion of the wellhead gas generally produces a cooling effect, a common process scheme exchanged cold residue gas with the gas before expansion, resulting in an even lower temperature in the separator after expansion. This scheme, referred to as an LTX unit, again increased the NGL recovery for the simple flash recovery type of process. This is illustrated in Fig. 2. The cooling and exchange of the gas streams will usually result in process temperatures

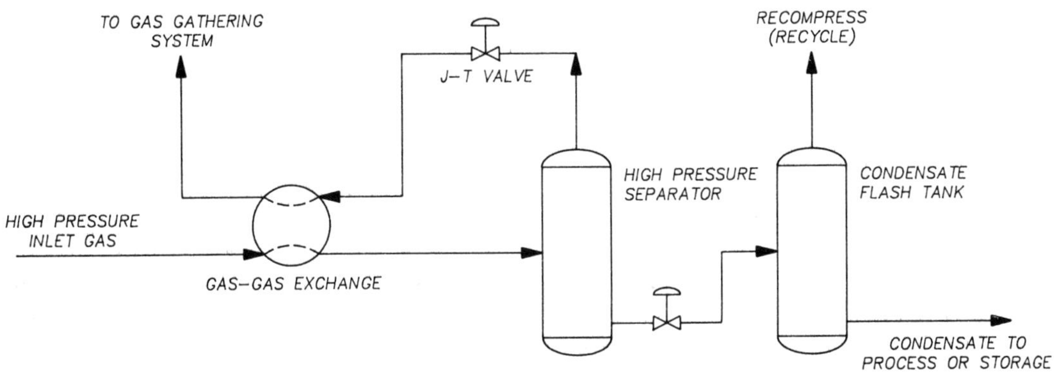

FIG. 2. Simple LTX recovery NGL process.

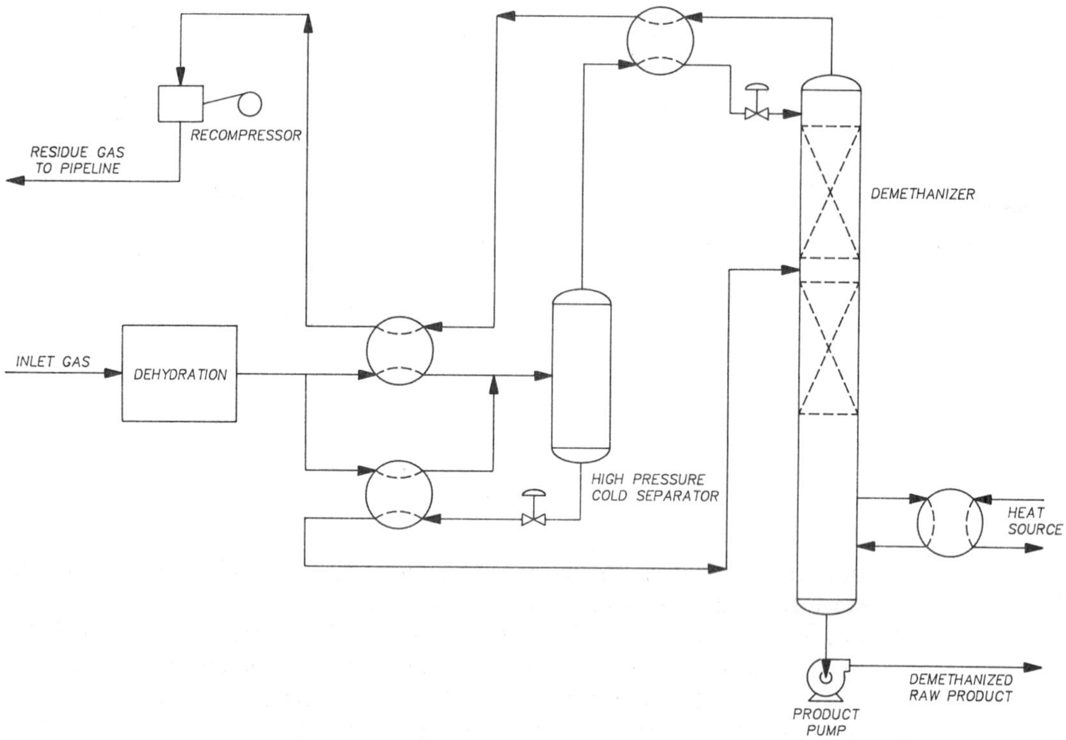

FIG. 3. Joule-Thompson NGL recovery process.

below the gas hydrate point, therefore some provisions must be incoporated for preventing hydrate formation or removing the hydrate continuously.

The process concept of using the cooling effect of adiabatic gas expansion can be carried much further. The process scheme shown in Fig. 3 can be very effective to produce small streams, typically less than 5 million SCFD, for moderately high ethane (or high propane) recovery. While the process is thermodynamically less efficient than a process utilizing a turboexpander, it may provide the optimum economic solution. This scheme is often modified by incorporating external refrigeration to achieve lower temperatures in the process than can be achieved with the J-T expansion alone.

Refrigeration

Refrigeration has been extensively utilized in the recovery of NGL from natural gas almost from the inception of gas processing. Depending on the pressure at which the gas is processed, some liquids will usually be condensed. A critical word of caution must be expressed regarding the creation of liquids when cooling a gas. Natural gas, containing methane and the heavier com-

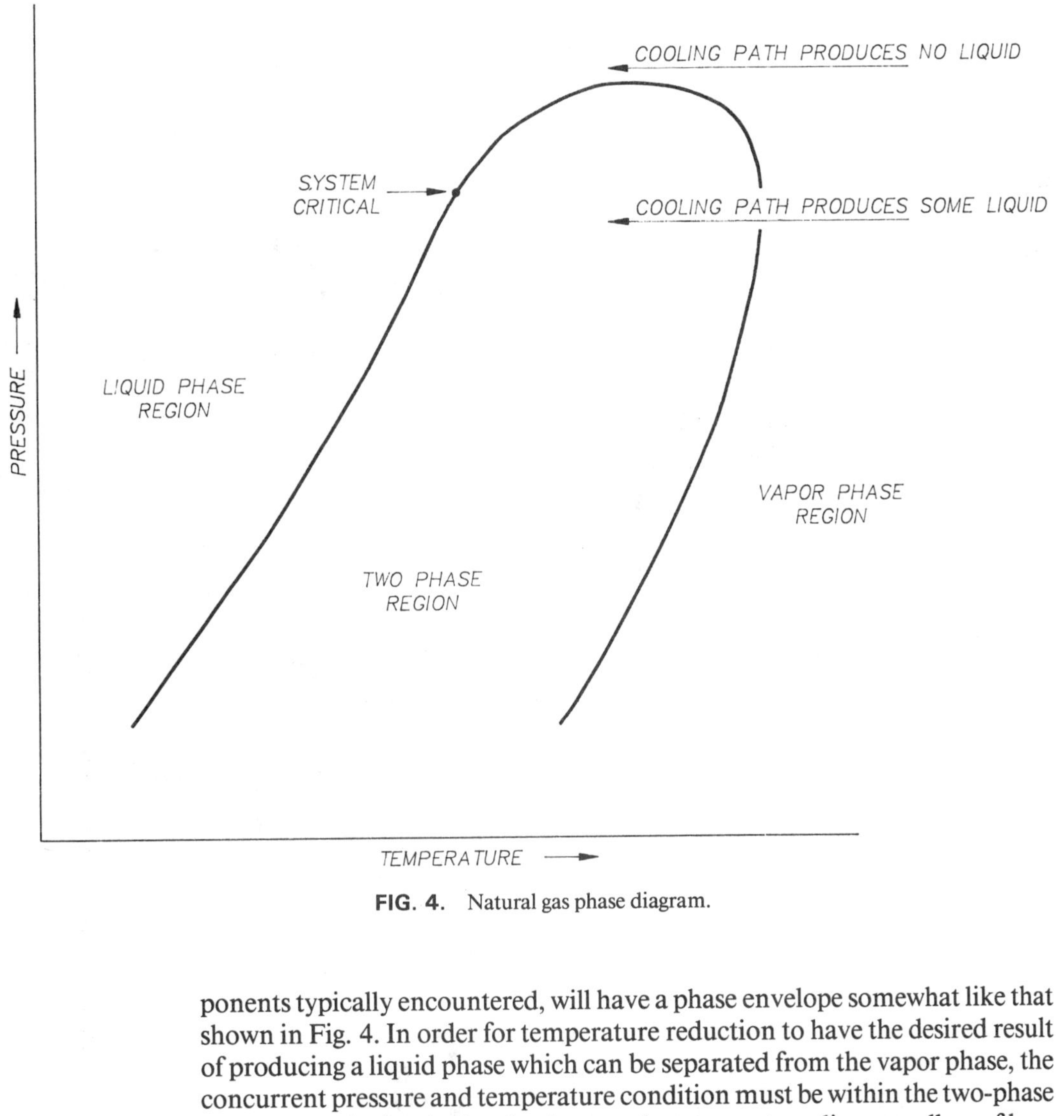

FIG. 4. Natural gas phase diagram.

ponents typically encountered, will have a phase envelope somewhat like that shown in Fig. 4. In order for temperature reduction to have the desired result of producing a liquid phase which can be separated from the vapor phase, the concurrent pressure and temperature condition must be within the two-phase envelope. This simple, but fundamental, statement applies regardless of how cold the system is. The gas may be cooled at pressures above the phase envelope, but separation can only occur at temperatures inside the envelope.

Refrigeration processes can be applied on a practical basis for recovery levels of only butanes and heavier, all the way to high ethane recovery. The factors particularly significant are the gas richness (NGL content), refrigeration level(s), and the operating pressure. Refrigeration processes are better suited to rich gases and moderate pressures. Optimum process pressures are 450 to 550 lb/in.^{2}gauge for propane or ethane recovery. The process may employ a single refrigerant or cascade refrigeration if cryogenic levels are justified. Figure 5 illustrates a simple refrigeration process using a single refrigerant. Figure 6 illustrates a cascade refrigeration scheme utilizing propane and ethane refrigerants to achieve high ethane recovery from the inlet

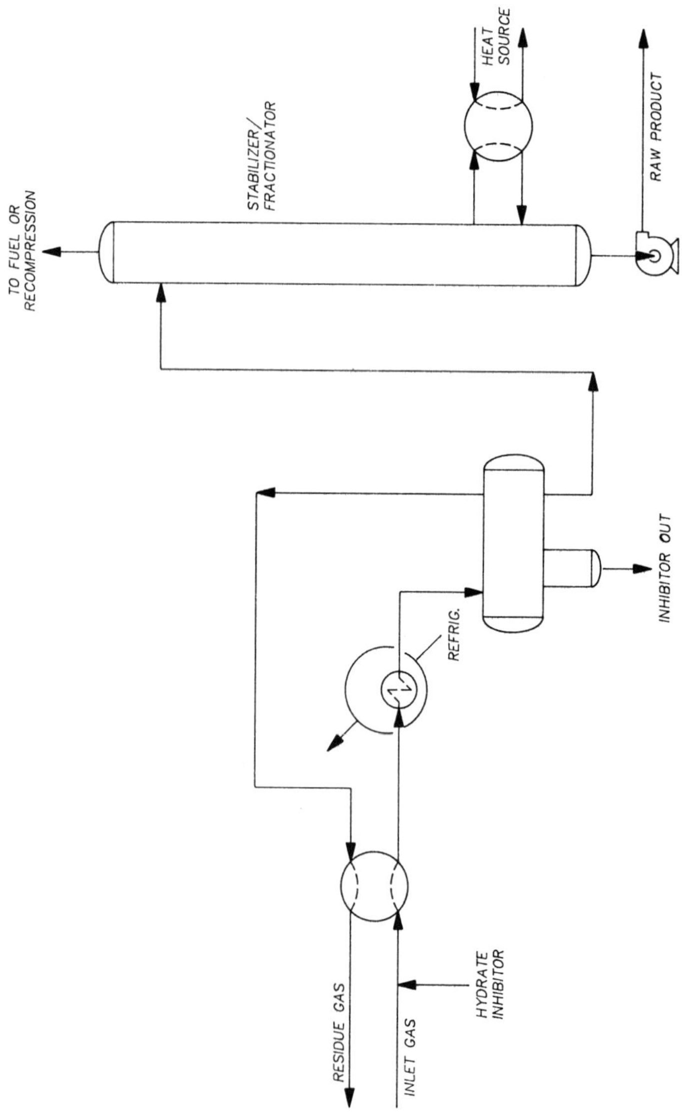

FIG. 5. Simple straight refrigeration NGL recovery scheme.

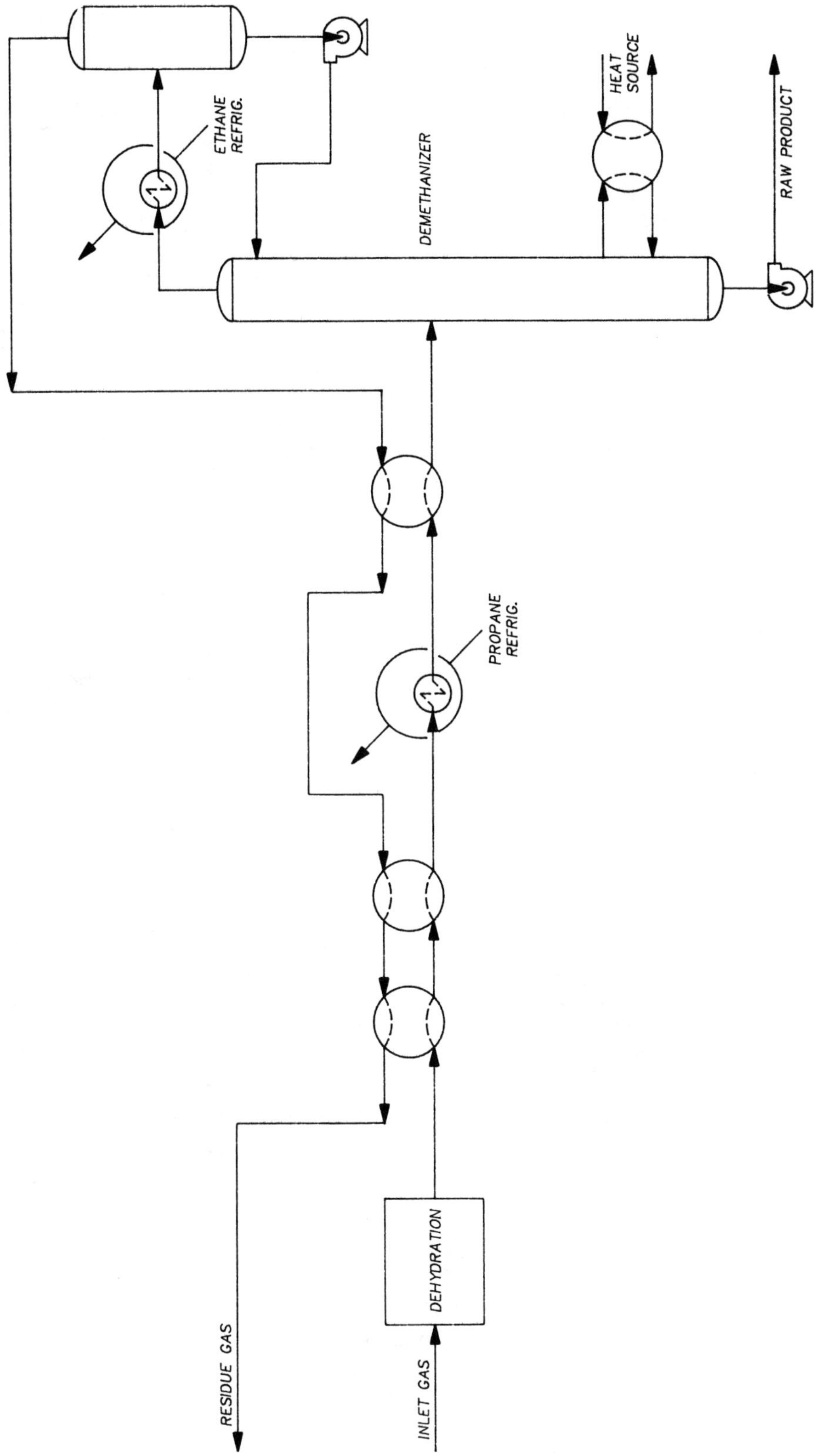

FIG. 6. Cascade refrigeration NGL recovery scheme.

gas. The cascade refrigeration process is optimally utilized when the inlet gas pressure is in the 500–600 lb/in^{2}gauge range. This allows operation in a region of the phase envelope to allow use of ethane as the low level refrigerant.

Modifications of the cascade refrigeration scheme include the substitution of a multicomponent refrigerant for the propane and ethane refrigerants. The multicomponent refrigerant is thermodynamically more efficient, but is more complex and harder to operate. Its application has to be economically justified with compression horsepower reduction and lower utility costs.

Adsorption

The process of adsorption of components onto a fixed-bed adsorbent has been used in the gas processing industry almost from the inception of the industry. While it has been used over a long period of time and in many different applications, it has never become a major NGL recovery scheme.

The earliest uses of adsorption were to recover gasoline components from the natural gas stream. This was often done in combination with the need to dehydrate the gas stream. The removal of both water and heavy hydrocarbons gave some measure of dew point control of the gas stream, which became more necessary as the use of natural gas increased and the gas began to be moved by pipeline some distance from its point of production to the point of consumption. The adsorption process was used without much refinement or technical design improvements until a renewed interest occurred in the 1950s. At that time the adsorption process for NGL was modernized for more efficient operation, and design data were improved to better size the units.

A typical adsorption cycle is shown in Fig. 7. This illustrates a three-bed unit. In this scheme, one bed is adsorbing hydrocarbons from the raw inlet stream, the second bed is desorbing the recovered hydrocarbons by having a hot regeneration gas flow through, and the third bed is in the process of cooling before being switched back to the adsorbing of NGL from the raw inlet stream. The illustrated three-bed system has the advantage of having a continuous flow of inlet gas, regeneration gas, and cooling gas. A two-bed system can be employed, but the flows are somewhat less continuous. The recovered NGL is separated from the regeneration gas in the raw make tank, and then must be demethanized or deethanized, as the case may be.

The adsorption process is a combination of batch and continuous processing. The quantity of NGL adsorbed from the raw gas stream is a function of:

1. Quantity of adsorbent
2. Temperature and pressure of the gas stream
3. Affinity of the adsorbent to retain the NGL components
4. Quantity of NGL in the gas steam
5. Length of time of contact

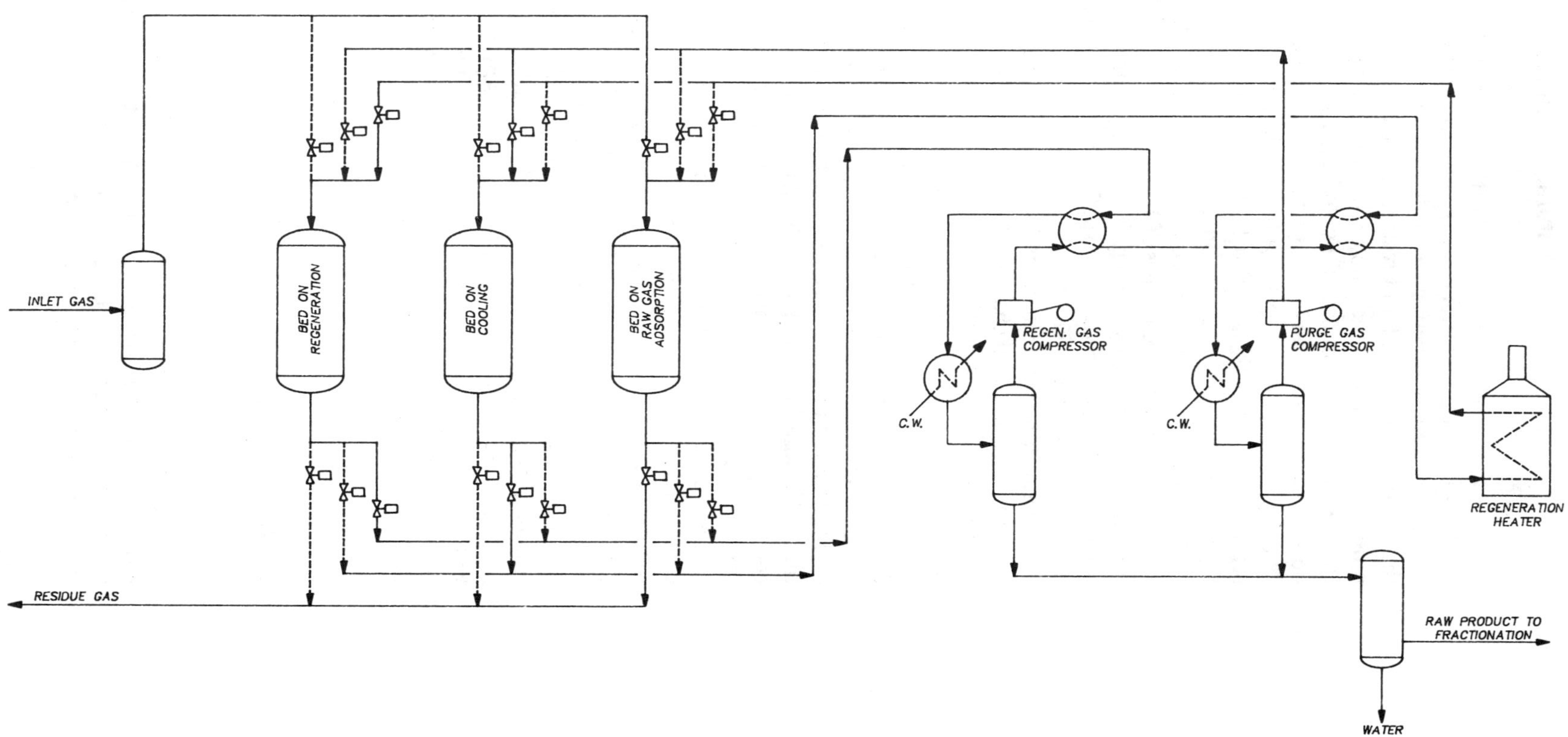

FIG. 7. Three-bed adsorption NGL recovery process.

Once the adsorbent is saturated with the key NGL component, additional gas flowing over the adsorbent will be unaffected and the NGL will stay in the gas. Therefore it is necessary to switch the inlet gas from a saturated bed at that time to a fresh bed and restart the adsorbing process. The loaded bed must be regenerated and cooled before cycling back to inlet gas again. Regeneration is accomplished by flowing a small amount of gas (such as a portion of the residue gas) through a heater and then over the saturated bed. The regeneration gas at 650°F (+/–) will desorb the NGL components. The regeneration gas is then cooled to condense the NGL components. These liquids are recovered and fractionated to meet necessary specifications.

Bed size is generally kept small to minimize the heating and cooling systems. Adsorption cycle times of 20 minutes were used in numerous designs (referred to as quick cycle plants), but longer and shorter cycles were also used. The adsorbent beds were usually internally insulated to help minimize the regeneration requirements.

Several different adsorbents have been used in this process, including silica gel, alumina, and charcoal. While molecular sieves are frequently used in various adsorbent processes, they have not been used extensively in NGL recovery systems. As the adsorbent process peaked in application in the 1950s and 1960s, activated carbon was the most widely used adsorbent. Plants were designed for 70–80% propane recovery, and are plant, at least, was designed for 50% ethane recovery. As the recovery level of NGL increased, the regeneration gas scheme became more complex in order to efficiently retain the NGL adsorbed from the inlet gas. Complex heat exchange systems, coupled with refrigeration and even lean oil, were used to recover the NGLs from the regeneration gas.

Several factors favor the use of an adsorption system, particularly in comparison to a lean oil system. Plant cost for a adsorbent NGL process is more closely related to the quantity of product recovered than the volume of gas processed. Therefore, on very lean streams there were cost advantages for the adsorbent process. It is suitable to small streams. It can be simpler, and therefore easier to automate, at moderate NGL recovery levels. It will simultaneously dehydrate and remove hydrocarbons.

The most probable application for an adsorption NGL process today would be for field processing to achieve water and hydrocarbon dew-point control. It could be a viable choice if only heavy hydrocarbon recovery were desired from a large gas stream.

Lean Oil Absorption

The lean oil adsorption process has been widely used in the gas processing industry. It was the predominant design for new plants until the mid-1970s when the turboexpander process became dominant. There are almost an infinite number of variations of this process that have been employed. Only a

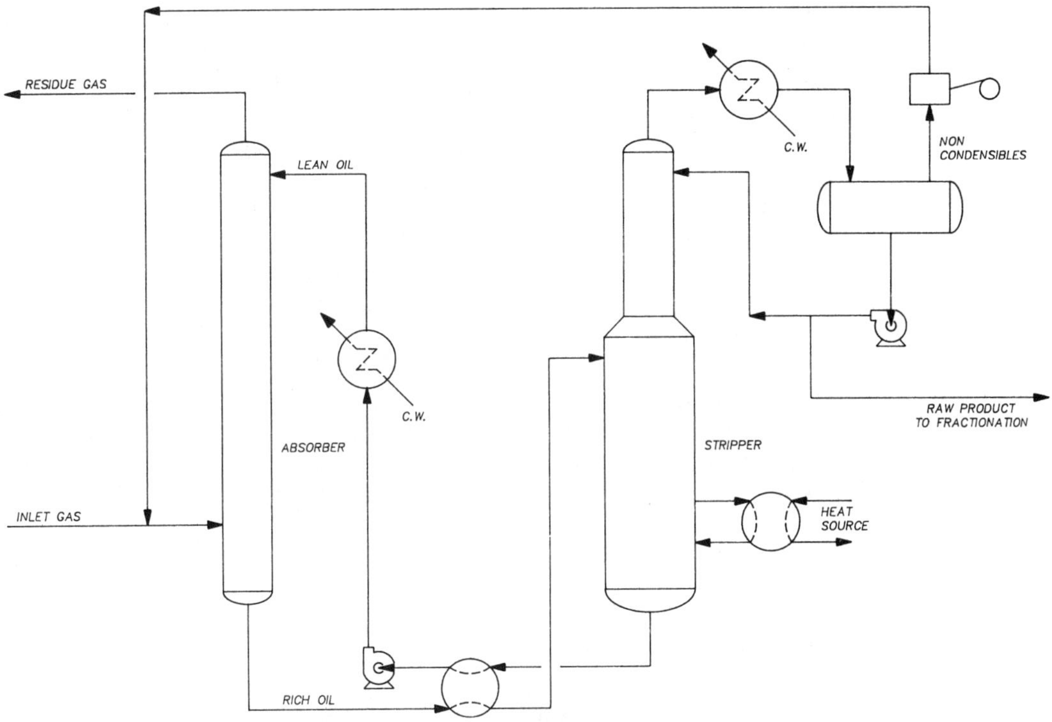

FIG. 8. Simple absorption and stripping process.

few of the basic schemes will be discussed as this is now a semiobsolete process design for new plants to recover NGLs.

Lean oil absorption is actually a combination of absorption and stripping. In the simplest form, raw inlet gas is contacted in a multistage contacting device (absorber) with a circulating hydrocarbon absorption medium (lean oil) to remove the desired NGL components from the gas (see Fig. 8). The absorbed light hydrocarbon components are then stripped from the liquids (rich oil) from the absorber. Raw product is condensed overhead and must be then fractionated to meet product specifications. Vapors not condensed are recompressed and either recycled to the inlet or flow to the residue.

The scheme as shown leaves a lot to be desired in terms of process recovery efficiency, but it does represent the basic aspects of the oil absorption process. These are the minimum units to the process, but as will be seen later, substantial complexity was added to the oil absorption process as it was extended for higher NGL recoveries and more efficient operation.

The early applications of lean oil absorption were based on the absorber operating at essentially ambient conditions. Actually the absorber operating temperature would be dictated by the heat rise due to the latent heat of absorption for the absorbed gas components in the lean oil, which had been cooled to the lowest optimum temperature available from either cooling water or air cooling.

Lean oil characteristics were based on an optimum balance between a low molecular weight to minimize the actual mass of circulation and a high molecular weight to minimize lean oil losses. The vaporization losses from the absorber are a function of the equilibrium ratio (*K* value) at the top of the absorber. This is determined by the lean oil molecular weight, the temperature, and the pressure on the absorber top tray. Typically a lean oil molecular weight of 220 was used in ambient lean oil absorbers.

Because of the need to have a fairly high boiling point oil to minimize absorber losses, operation of the still in ambient absorption plants required steam stripping. It is advantageous to operate the still at the highest practical pressure to maximize raw product condensation. If the lean oil were to be heated to its vaporization temperatures at this pressure, thermal cracking of the lean oil would occur. Consequently, the still was designed to be stripped using superheated steam.

The ambient lean oil plant design prevailed as the dominant NGL recovery process until the mid-1950s. Several factors contributed to a need for improvement in the process efficiency. Use of natural gas was rapidly expanding due to the increase of natural gas pipelines from the Gulf Coast to other parts of the country. The need for extracted hydrocarbons was also increasing for the LPG markets and as chemical feedstocks. The simplest way to increase NGL recovery was to lower the process temperatures in the absorber. This was achieved by chilling the inlet gas and the oil to the absorber.

Retrofits to existing plant designs were practical, but only to a moderate amount. Since steam was used to strip the lean oil, the lean oil was water saturated, imposing limits on how low a process temperature was practical before freezing or hydrates were encountered. Dehydration of the inlet gas was not generally a part of the design, therefore potential hydrate formation restricted inlet gas chilling. Retrofits were limited to 60–70°F as a result of these limitations.

By the second half of the 1950s, new plants were being designed incorporating the advantages of reduced operating temperatures in the absorber. The progression was in steps as more knowledge was gained and problems were overcome. Temperatures rapidly dropped to the −20°F level, which represented an operational limit for normal carbon steel. The end of the 1950s saw process designs pushed to −50°F, which represented the limit of Charpy-impact-tested carbon steel. The economic barrier to use nickle alloy steels, permitting temperatures below −50°F, seemed to be too great. A second practical limitation was in the use of propane as a single refrigerant in the design. The atmospheric boiling point of propane is approximately −44°F. Most operators chose not to have a subatmospheric system due to concerns of air leakage into the propane. Only a few oil absorption plants were built to operate below −50°F.

Along with the emergence of refrigerated oil processes and direct refrigeration processes, the need for reliable dehydration methods increased. This is referred to briefly later in this section.

Even though refrigerated oil absorption is not considered for most new plant designs, it still represents a large portion of current gas processing capacity in the United States and the world. As applied to a large main line gas processing operation, the process could be complex as a result to minimize oil circulation rate and reduce fuel consumption.

Figure 9 illustrates schematically the basic process design for a large main line gas processing plant. Some units of the plant are common to all designs and some are optional enhancements for optimum specific applications.

Absorber Arrangement

Several alternative configurations for the absorption portion of the process can be considered.

1. Simple countercurrent flow of cold gas to cold oil can be used. This scheme may or may not include a sponge oil section, depending on factors discussed later. Typically the main absorber will contain 20 to 24 actual trays, equivalent to 8 to 12 theoretical trays.
2. An absorber presaturator chiller can be added to the absorber circuit to reduce the total lean oil circulation rate. The presaturator chiller reduces oil circulation in two ways. First, the presaturator chiller provides a final contact between lean oil and gas at the lowest possible process temperature, hence a lighter lean oil can be used. Second, because of the removal of latent heat of absorption external to the absorber, heat rise in the absorber is reduced and the average absorption temperature is lower. This improves the absorption factor for the key component.
3. A preabsorber chiller can be added to the absorber circuit to reduce the lean oil circulation rate. The preabsorber chiller, like the presaturator chiller, removes heat external to the absorber with the same benefit stated above.

Both Steps 2 and 3 add one theoretical contact stage at the lowest available process temperature.

Rich Oil Partial Demethanization

Partial demethanization of the absorber rich oil can be utilized to minimize or eliminate recompression of flash gas. Considerations require to determine degree of demethanization are:

1. Quantity of fuel to be consumed in the plant.
2. Quantity of rich oil demethanizer (or deethanizer) effluent gas which can be absorbed by the absorber portion of the lean oil in a presaturator utilizing the overheads from the rich oil demethanizer (or deethanizer).

When Items 1 and 2 above have been determined, it is then possible to calculate the degree of partial rich oil demethanization required. Generally this must be determined for the worst of several operating conditions, including maximum absorber pressures, minimum fuel consumption, and

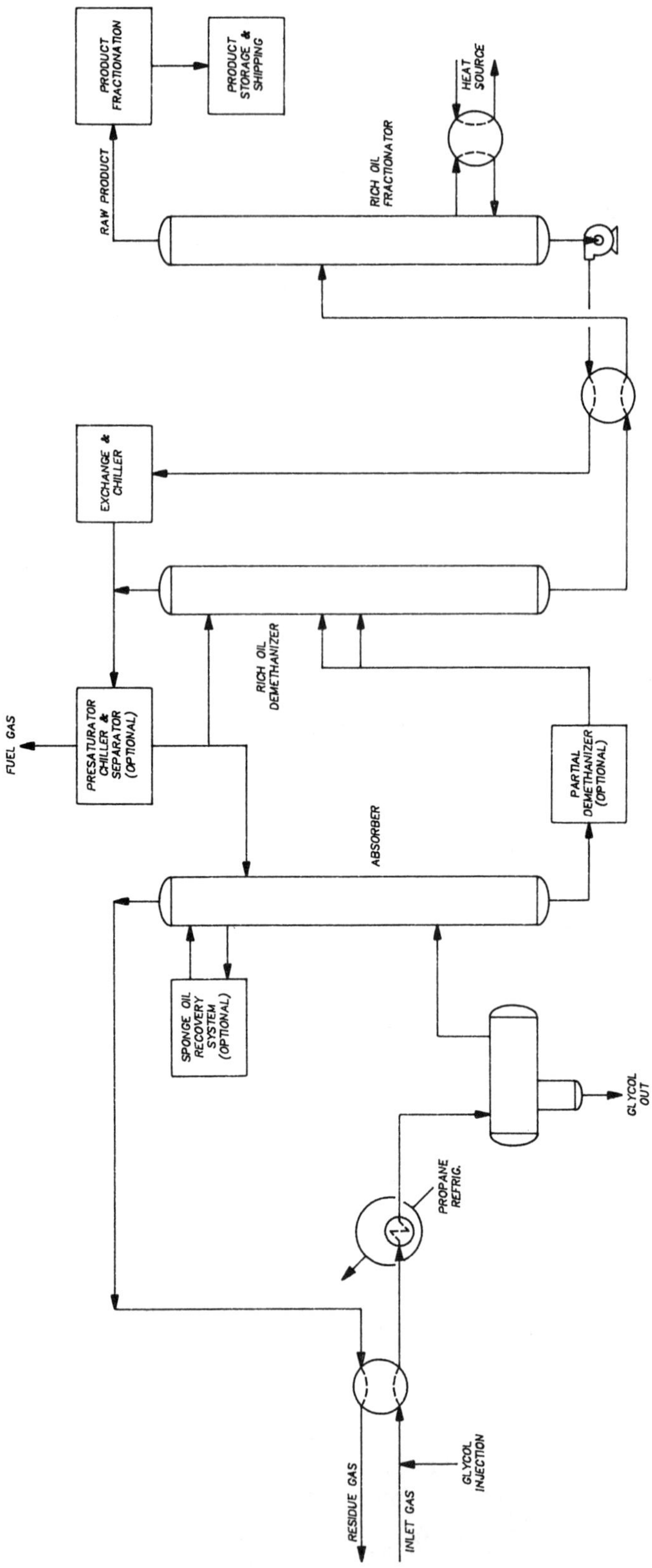

FIG. 9. Main line refrigerated oil absorption process plant.

the lowest pressure which may be required for the rich oil demethanizer (deethanizer).

Rich Oil Demethanizer (Deethanizer)

The rich oil demethanizer (deethanizer) consists of a stripping section for the removal of methane (or methane and ethane) from the rich oil and a reabsorber section for recovery of the key light component. Operating pressure will be set as high as possible, as limited by the available heat medium temperature for reboiler input. The highest operating pressure is chosen to reduce the absorption oil requirements in the reabsorber and to increase the amount of gases absorbed in a presaturator chiller if utilized. The maximum operating pressure for a rich oil demethanizer will be from 400 to 550 lb/in.^{2}gauge, and for a rich oil deethanizer 250 to 450 lb/in.^{2}gauge. The maximum pressure is influenced by the inlet gas richness, absorption oil molecular weight, refrigeration temperature, and temperature level of the heating medium.

Rich Oil Fractionator

The rich oil fractionator separates products lighter than the lean oil from the lean oil. Preferably a lean oil will be selected which can be produced from the inlet gas in quantities in excess of lean oil vaporization losses so that lean oil itself becomes a product. Normally the excess lean oil is blended with the raw product or product gasoline as it is produced.

Conditions in determining the rich oil fractionator operating conditions include:

1. Vapor pressure of the raw product for high propane recovery plants is in the range of 100 to 140 lb/in.^{2}gauge at 100°F. The rich oil fractionator pressure should, if possible, be set high enough to allow total condensation of the raw product with air- or water-cooled condensers. Normally this pressure is 120 to 150 lb/in.^{2}gauge. For ethane recovery plants, a chiller can be utilized to condense the raw product not condensed in the reflux condenser. Alternately, noncondensed product can be compressed to the raw product delivery pressure.
2. If steam is used as the heating medium, reboiling temperature of the rich oil fractionator at 150 lb/in.^{2}gauge, together with required steam pressures, are as presented in Table 1.

From Table 1 it is obvious that steam-heated rich oil fractionation reboilers should be limited in application to use with very light lean oils. By corollary, it is also obvious that if steam is specified as the power producing and heat supply source, then a light lean oil is required and consequently a sponge oil system is probably applicable.

TABLE 1

Lean Oil Molecular Weight	Boiling Temperature (in °F) of Lean Oil at 150 lb/in.^{2}gauge	Pressure (in lb/in.^{2}gauge) of Saturated Steam Required for 25° MTD
90	360	195
100	400	315
110	440	475
120	485	740
130	530	1200

Alternative heat sources for heat input to the rich oil fractionator are a direct fired heater or waste heat recovery (with refire if necessary) on the exhaust of the process plant prime movers.

Sponge Oil System

Some of the items to be considered in a sponge oil system design, such as illustrated in Fig. 10, are:

1. A sufficient number of sponge section trays must be used to recover the vaporized light lean oil efficiently. Approximately 8 to 10 are commonly used. This number of trays will recover approximately 90% of the vaporized light lean oil when sponge oil circulation is about 6 to 8% of light lean oil circulation.
2. Sponge oil itself must be substantially lower in volatility than the light absorption oil or its vaporization loss will be excessive. The sponge oil molecular weight used in conjunction with a 100 molecular weight lean oil would be at least 140 molecular weight. This combination of lean oil and sponge oil will give total vaporized losses, including both the light oil and sponge oil, of around 4 gallons per million standard cubic feet of gas processed at −35°F and 900 lb/in.^{2}gauge.
3. The rich sponge oil contains the light lean oil plus methane and ethane. This mixture cannot be demethanized by simple means at pressures corresponding to the main lean oil system, consequently the overhead product from the sponge oil fractionator will not be totally condensing due to the presence of methane and ethane. The off-gas from this condensing system is quite rich with light lean oil and gasoline vapors, and it cannot be used for fuel without further processing. One processing arrangement to reduce gasoline loss from the sponge oil fractionator is to use a reabsorber as illustrated in Fig. 10.
4. In order to maintain and effectively control a substantial difference in molecular weight between the lean oil and the sponge oil, it is necessary to remove an intermediate cut oil. This can be accomplished by adding a reboiled side cut stripper to the sponge oil fractionator as indicated in Fig. 10.

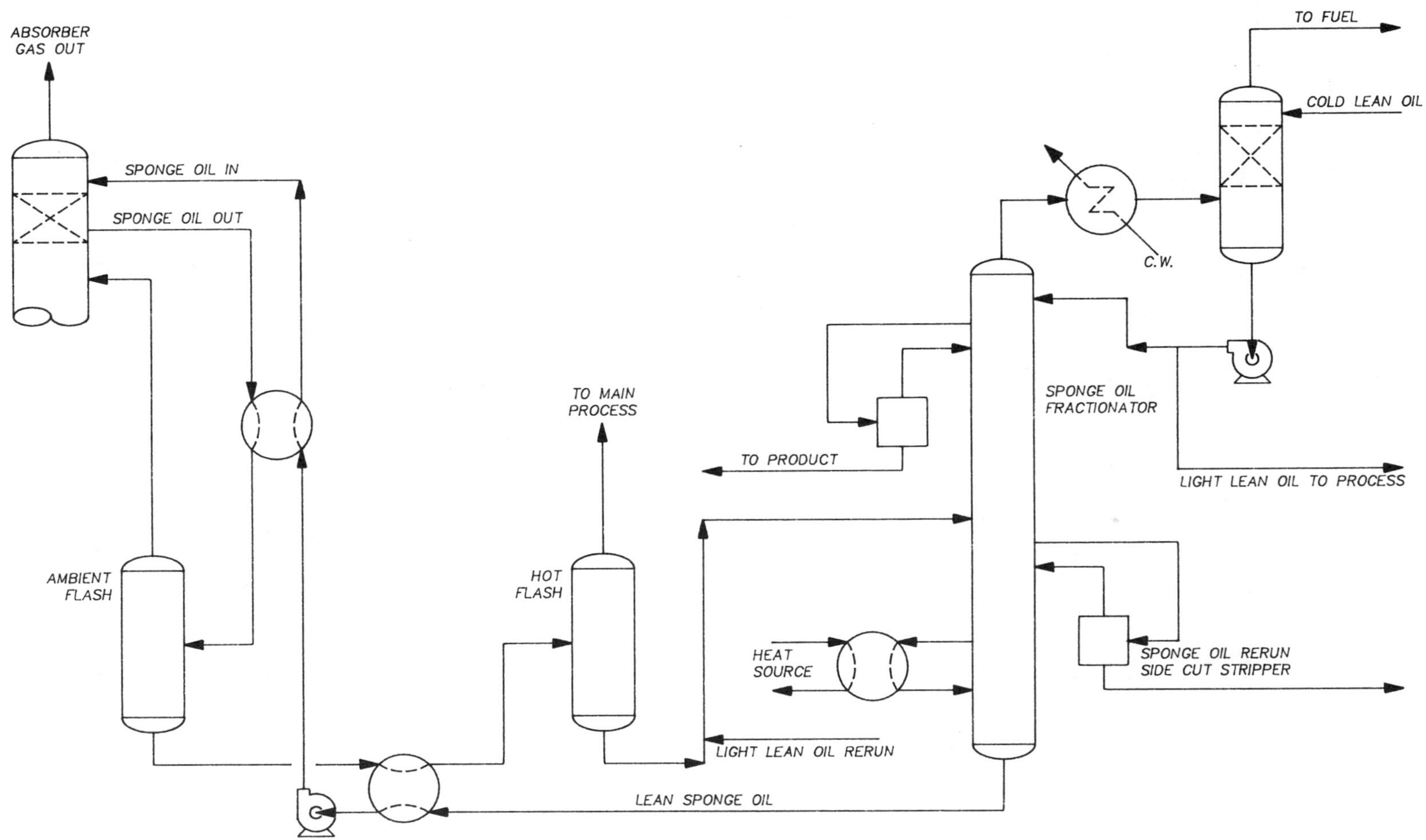

FIG. 10. Typical sponge oil system.

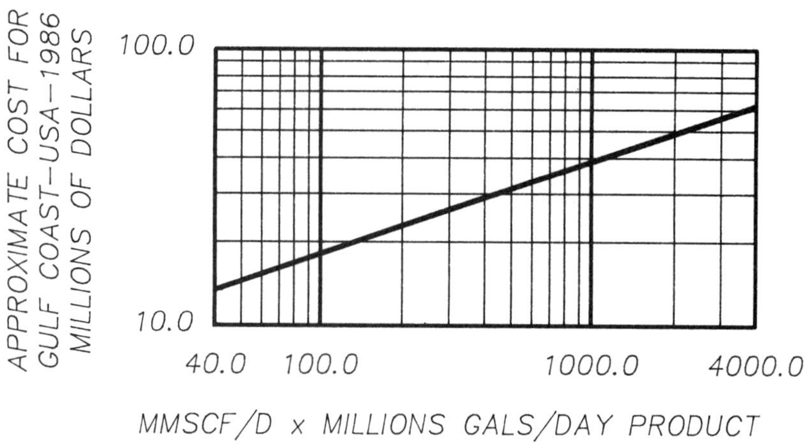

FIG. 11. Main line lean oil absorption plant cost.

5. In order to control the quantity of heavy ends in the sponge oil and hence minimize wax deposition in the absorber sponge oil section, provision should be made to rerun the sponge oil. This can be accomplished by using a reboiling side cut stripper operating in the bottom section of the sponge oil fractionator. This operation will require that the side cut stripper reboiler outlet temperature be higher then the sponge oil fractionator bottoms temperature.

Experience has shown that a sponge oil system becomes economical in the range of 300 to 500 MMSCFD inlet volume.

Plant Costs

A generalized cost curve is shown in Fig. 11 for larger refrigerated lean oil absorption plants. The cost is shown as a function of the plant gas volume and the quantity of products recovered. Figure 11 is for a grass roots plant for 90% propane and 25% incidental ethane recovery, including product fractionation, 5 days product storage for propane and heavier products, and necessary utility systems to be independent of outside utilities. The actual costs can vary fairly widely from project to project depending on actual site location, specifications, required flexibility, etc.

Fuel Gas Consumption

Fuel gas is normally the largest single cost in the operating expenses of a gas processing plant. Selection of prime mover is tied closely with the value of fuel. For example, typical fuel consumption of a 90% propane recovery plant from a gas containing 0.6 to 0.7 gallons per thousand cubic feet of gas of

TABLE 2

Prime Mover	% Residue Gas Used as Fuel
Gas turbine + centrifugal compressors + heat recovery	0.60
Reciprocating engines and compressors	0.63
Reciprocating engines and centrifugal compressors	0.67
Steam turbine and centrifugal compressors	0.91

propane and heavier, producing three products and using various prime movers is shown in Table 2.

Relative richness of the gas affects plant fuel consumption. Figure 12 indicates the relative fuel consumption as a function of the propane and heavier components in the inlet gas.

High Pressure Gas Processing

Processing of high pressure gas, 1300 lb/in.^{2}gauge and higher, that is to be recycled to a reservoir, would probably justify a lean oil plant design. The NGL can be recovered from the gas stream without pressure reduction of the gas stream. Oil absorption has been used to process gas streams at pressures up to 2000 lb/in.^{2}gauge.

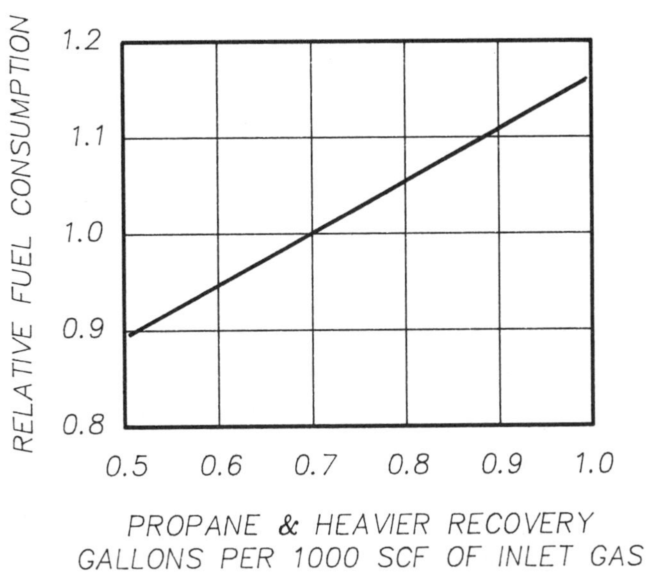

FIG. 12. Relative fuel consumption vs gas richness.

Turboexpander (cryogenic) Processes

As previously stated, the main process design scheme used currently for major NGL recovery plants is based on the use of a turboexpander in the process. The first practical NGL recovery plant in the United States to utilize a turboexpander was built in the mid-1960s. The design was for a high level of propane recovery. As a matter of interest, the first plant was built to utilize the expander process scheme for reasons that did not apply to the subsequent proliferation of plants that followed.

The first plant was built at the delivery point of a pipeline to a city, where a significant pressure drop in the gas was normally taken through pressure regulation valves. This pressure drop was being wasted. By utilizing the turboexpander to take the pressure drop instead of control valves, an impressive amount of energy could be recovered. Simply stated, this pressure drop was translated into a refrigeration effect that allowed recovery of a high percentage of the propane and heavier components in the pipeline gas. Original perceptions were that the expander process would be primarily applicable only in situations where some "free" pressure drop was available. This was quickly put aside as several factors combined, over the next few years, to bring the expander design to prominence.

A turboexpander is a device designed to allow gas to expand along an approximate isentropic path. Steam turbines are turboexpanders designed with steam as the expanding gas. The concept of expanding a gas for power recovery was not new to the gas processing industry. The availability of a practical, radial inflow, widely variable flow, efficient machine capable of coping with liquid forming in the process was one of the keys to the application to a gas processing facility. The other important feature was the direct shaft connected compressor to absorb the power produced in the expander. Since the usual process scheme maintains a fixed flow relationship between expanded gas and compressed gas, the turboexpander-compressor operates with a balanced load over a wide range of inlet gas rates. Control of the system is straightforward and system operability is very good.

Real hydrocarbon gases cool significantly with isentropic expansion. This becomes an efficient source of low temperature refrigeration (−100 to −150°F range). While this was lower than required for efficient propane recovery, it was ideal for ethane recovery plants. And the need for higher ethane recovery, for petrochemical feedstock, was rapidly increasing.

The expander process requires a large pressure drop (usually with an expansion ratio between 2 and 4). The pressure must be restored if the gas being processed is a pipeline stradle plant, or if the gas is being delivered at pipeline pressure. This requires a significant amount of horsepower—more than the horsepower required for refrigeration in a refrigerated lean oil plant. But, along with the availability of the practical turboexpander-compressor, large gas turbine prime movers were becoming available to the industry at moderate dollars per horsepower on an installed basis. The basic simplicity of the expander plant equipment, coupled with the competitive installed cost of the prime mover, combined to make the expander process a lower cost when

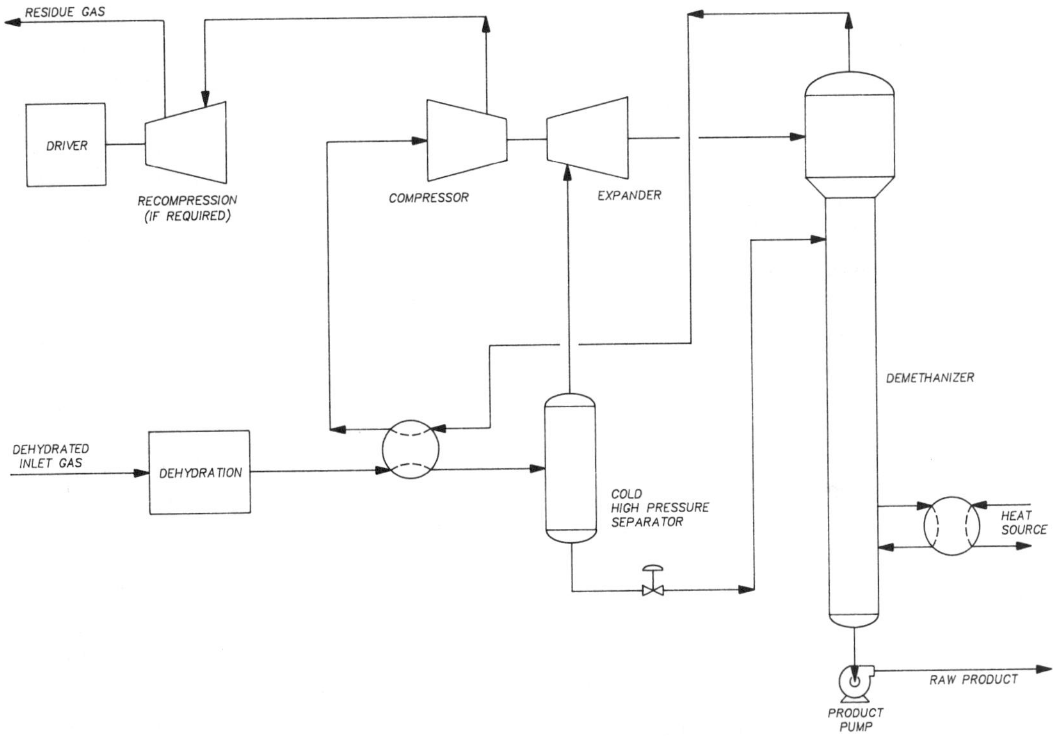

FIG. 13. Simple turboexpander NGL recovery process.

applied to ethane recovery than a refrigerated lean oil plant. With efficient recovery of the gas turbine waste heat, the expander process could also be operated for less fuel. These factors all contributed to the rapid shift toward the expander process as the preferred NGL recovery scheme.

Development of the Process Complexity

As is common with the development of most new process schemes, they evolve into more complex and efficient models to achieve higher recoveries and lower overall costs. The earliest designs employing the expander were very simple, as is illustrated in Fig. 13. Compared to an equivalent refrigerated lean oil plant, this expander plant would have less than half as many pieces of equipment. The plant was simpler to operate and required less space for the facility. But, due to the low operating temperatures and the high operating speed of the expander, it was critical that the inlet gas be properly dehydrated and filtered before flowing to the main process. Severe operating problems surfaced when these factors were not properly handled.

In addition to the necessity of proper dehydration and filtering which were easily recognized as important, some new design problems emerged as the process designs were more widely utilized. The thermophysical properties generally available in the industry were inadequate for accurate prediction of performance. While this problem had also occurred in the application of low temperature lean oil absorption, underdesign could be partly overcome by increasing lean oil circulation. No such flexibility was available in the expander process. A second problem emerged in predicting capacities of separators and trayed towers operating at the low temperatures ahead of and after the expander. New design procedures and criteria developed to overcome these problems.

Along with the development of a practical machine for the expander, a new (to the gas processing industry) heat exchanger type was being applied in many plants to reduce plant cost. The brazed aluminum type exchanger provided a very cost effective design, suitable for the low process temperatures and providing a high density surface to allow close approaches for good thermodynamic efficiencies. To effectively solve the problems in the low temperature portion of the demethanizers related to predicting allowable tray loadings, the use of packing became common. By the late 1970s, reliable design was available from a large number of suppliers. The concept of a "standard" design was popular, and the inherently compact equipment led to a large number of plants to be built as skid mounted. Complete plants were available from supplier "inventory" during the early 1980s, and operating companies would occasionally buy multiple plants at a time for installation at locations not yet identified. The loss of efficiency in using a generic design was more than offset by an earlier installation and start-up.

Expander plant designs rapidly developed to ethane recovery levels of 70 to 80%, without extensive complications. The conventional simple process scheme that uses the liquids from the outlet of the expander as reflux to the demethanizer is satisfactory for recovery levels of approximately 80+% for ethane. Above approximately the 85% level of ethane recovery, some sort of methane reflux is required for most inlet gas compositions. The methane-rich reflux can be generated in a variety of ways, varying from using a portion of the lean high pressure gas which has been "condensed" by exchange to recycling a portion of the residue gas which is also condensed to provide the reflux.

Referring to Fig. 13, the simple process scheme represents the basic parts of the expander process for NGL recovery. Inlet gas (after dehydration) is exchanged against low pressure, low temperature residue gas. After exchange the liquids condensed from the inlet gas are separated in a high pressure separator. This separator typically operates at a 25 lb/in.^{2}gauge lower pressure than the inlet pipeline pressure, and at a temperature between -50 and -80°F. Liquids from the separator are flashed and fed to the demethanizer. Vapors from the separator flow to the expander where they are expanded down to the pressure of the demethanizer. This expansion produces useful work, which is used in residue gas compression. The expanded gases are cooled to -130 to -160°F, and some liquids are condensed. The combined stream is fed to a separator on the top of the demethanizer. Liquids from the separator flow to the top of the demethanizer to provide reflux to the tower. The demethanizer is operated as a stripper, with reboiler heat being supplied to provide sufficient heat to adequately demethanize the raw product from the bottom of the tower. The demethanizer typically has 6 to 10 theoretical trays. Cold residue vapor is exchanged with the inlet gas and is then compressed in the compressor which in integral with the turboexpander, thereby absorbing the work produced in the expander. This compression is generally insufficient to deliver the residue gas to its final pressure, therefore supplemental compression must be provided to restore the residue gas to the required level.

Depending on pressure levels, gas richness, recovery levels, etc., it may be practical to use the inlet gas to provide reboiler heat input to the demethanizer as shown in Fig. 14. This is thermodynamically more efficient than the preceding simple scheme, and was one of the first enhancements used in the expander process design. Figure 15 adds additional enhancements to improve plant efficiency. A side reboiler improves the thermodynamic recovery of refrigeration from the process, and a flash tank upstream of the demethanizer reduces the load on the tower. Figure 16 shows the addition of external refrigeration which may be advantageous for richer gases or higher recoveries. An additional low pressure flash tank and demethanizer feed exchange have been added. The next sophistication is shown with the use of two expanders in the process in Fig. 17. This flow scheme includes two side reboilers on the demethanizer, low pressure separation, and external refrigeration. While this can improve the thermodynamic efficiency of the process, it adds significant operating complication that must be considered.

Plant and Horsepower and Cost

A generalized curve for plant cost is shown for the expander process NGL plant, similar to that shown for refrigerated lean oil absorption. The plant cost in Fig. 18 is shown as a combined function of inlet gas volume and plant products. An approximation of recompression horsepower to restore the residue gas to inlet gas pressure is shown in Fig. 19. Both curves represent the generalized case, and significant deviation can be expected for variations from typical conditions.

Product Fractionation

Fractionation of the products from an NGL plant may be accomplished at the same plant with the NGL recovery process, or they may be shipped by pipeline as a single raw product to be separated at a remote product fractionation facility. This decision is made by the plant owner depending on market locations, availability of a raw product pipeline, and savings for scale in larger, centralized fractionation facilities. Typically NGL products can include:

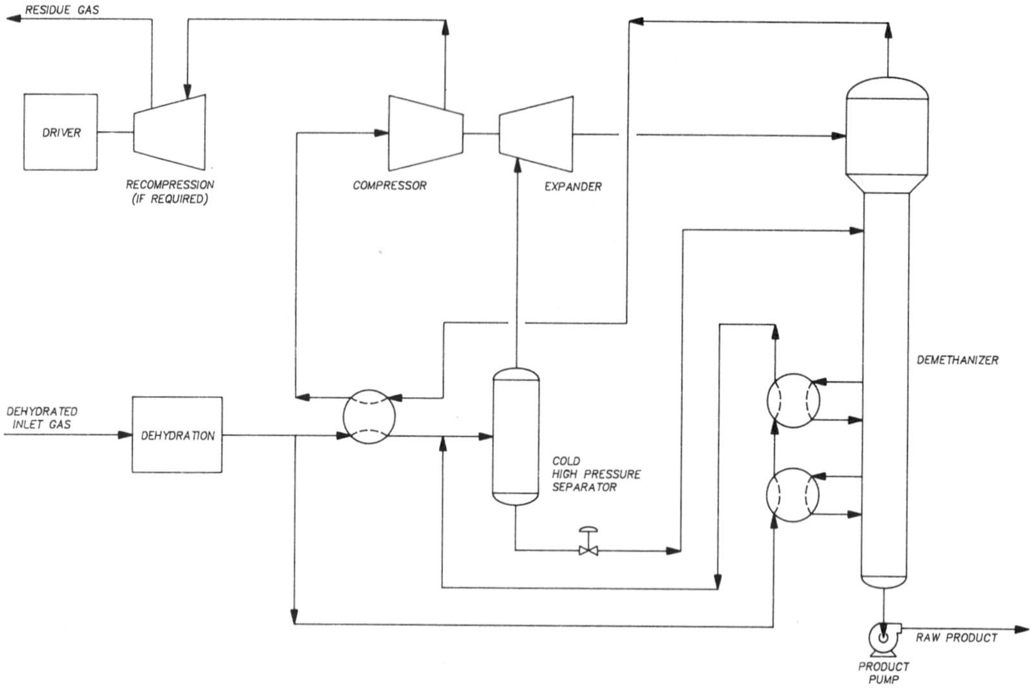

FIG. 14. Turboexpander scheme with inlet gas reboiler.

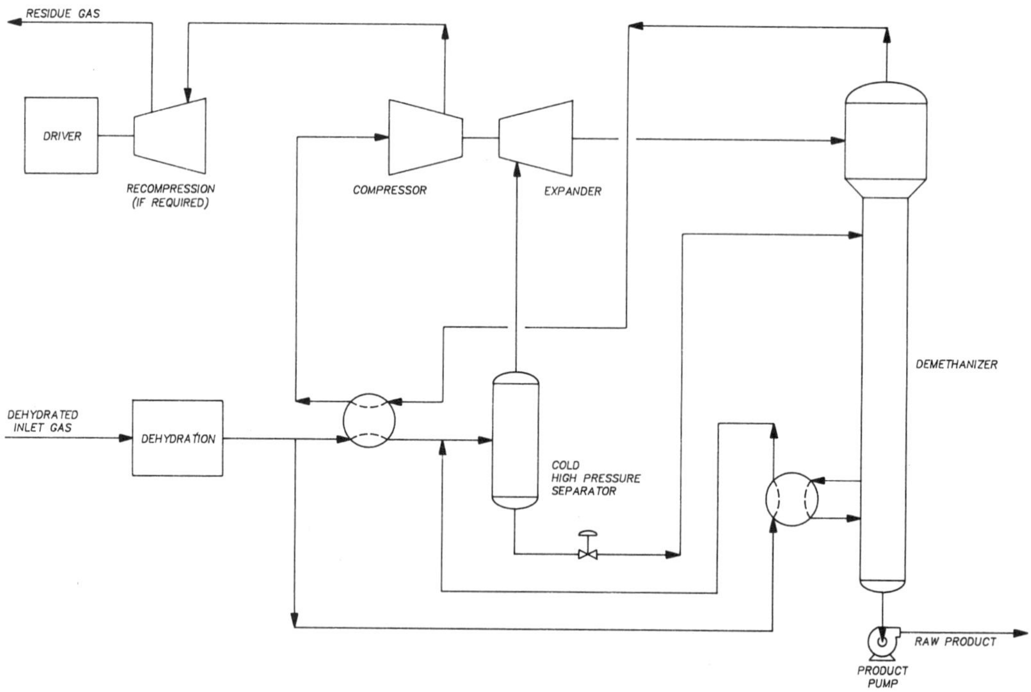

FIG. 15. Turboexpander scheme with demethanizer side reboiler.

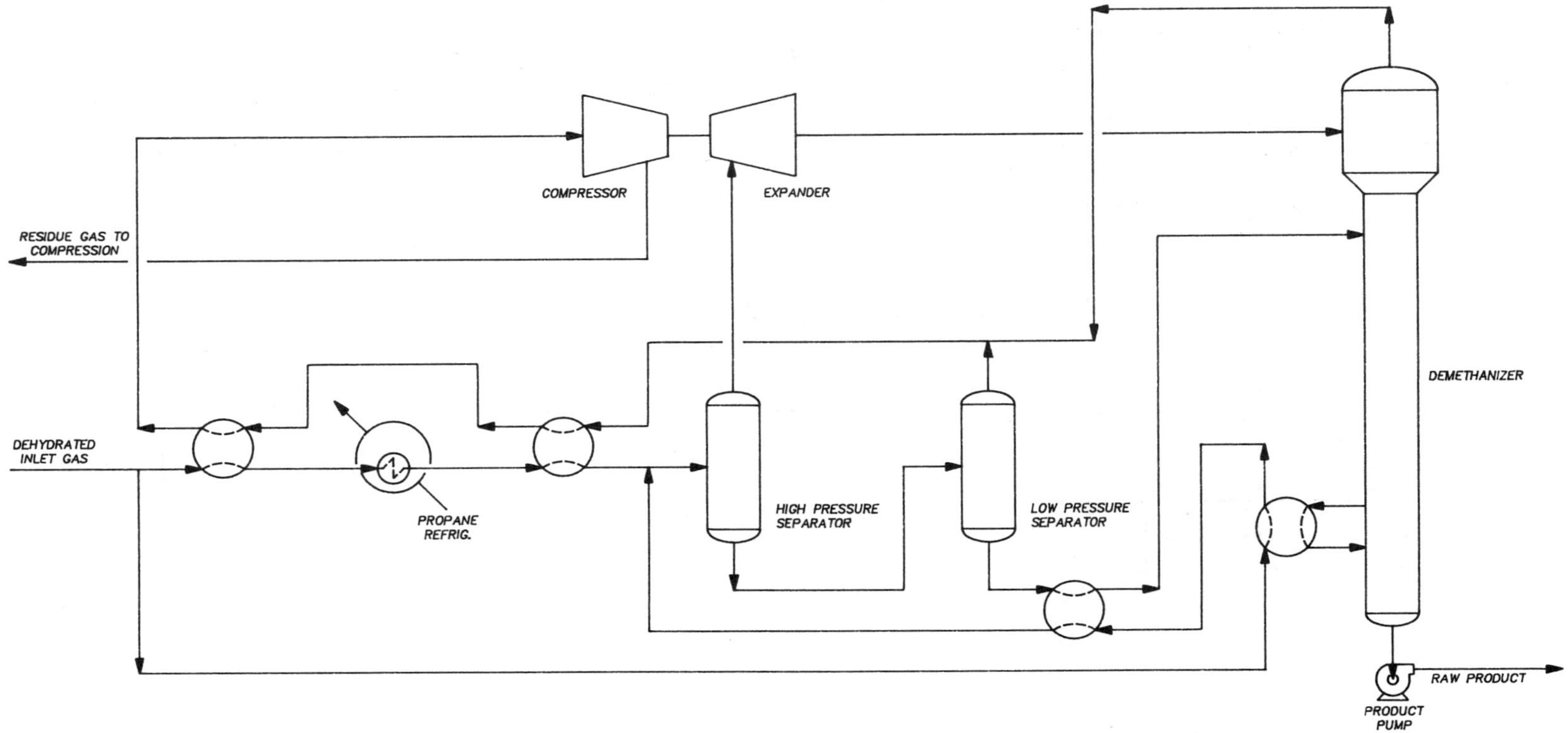

FIG. 16. Turboexpander process with external refrigeration.

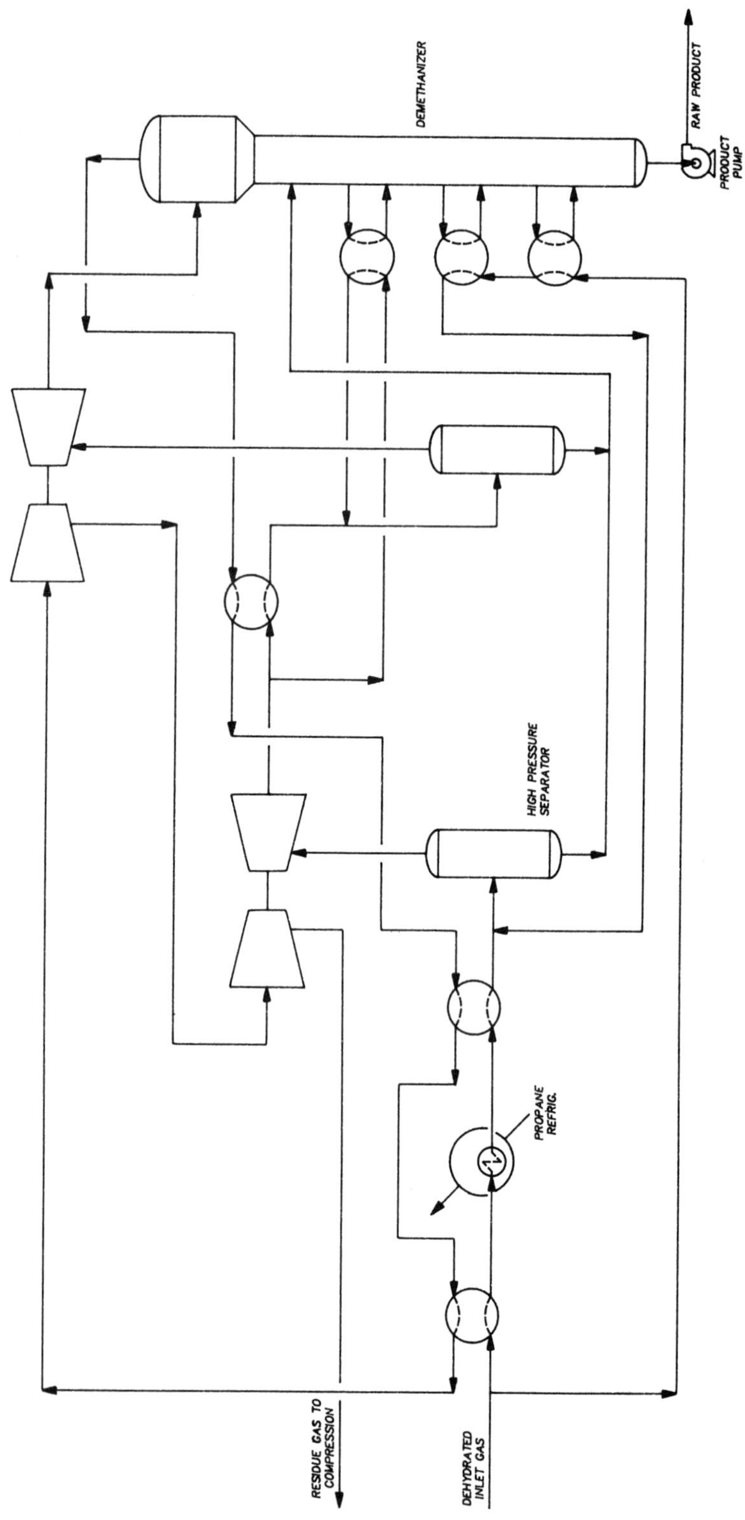

FIG. 17. Turboexpander process with two expanders and external refrigeration.

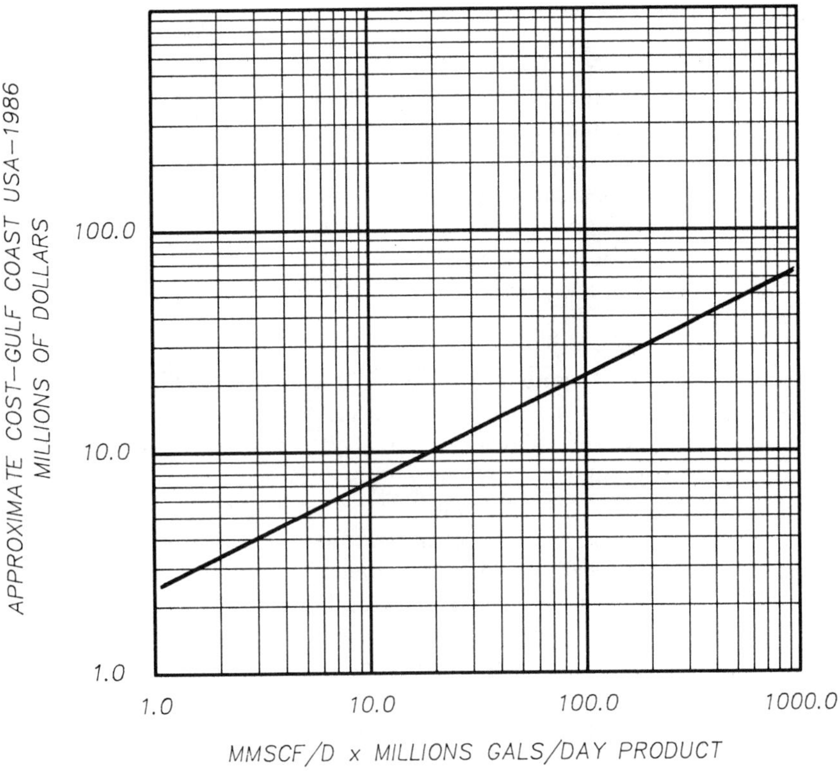

FIG. 18. Plant cost for turboexpander process.

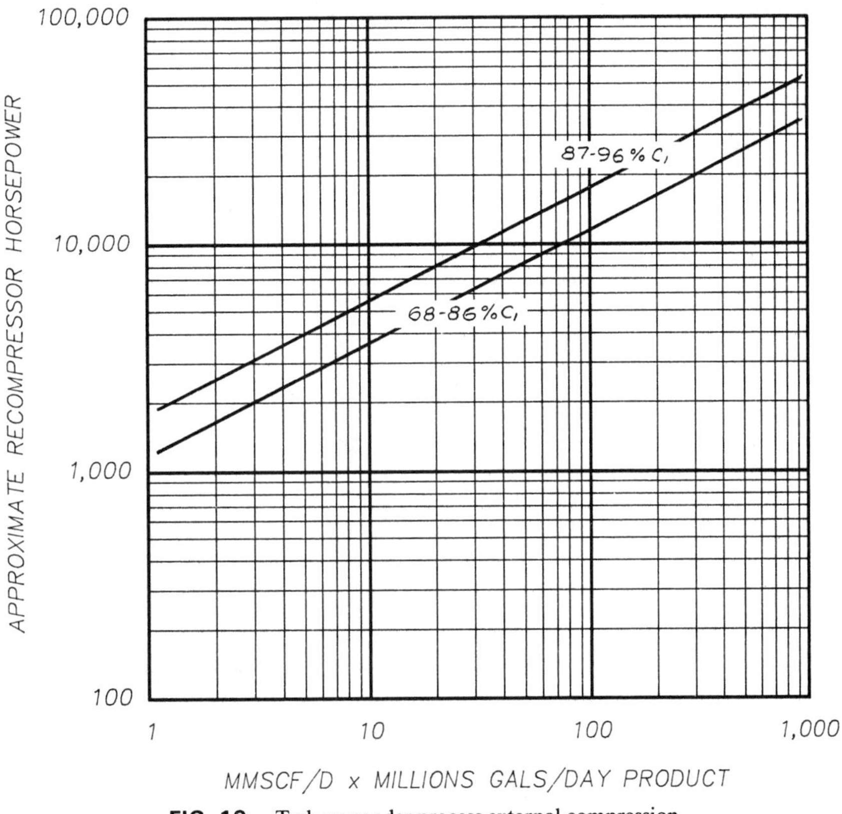

FIG. 19. Turboexpander process external compression.

Ethane: liquid or vapor, 95+% purity,
Ethane/propane mix: from 70/30 to 30/70 spread
Propane: liquid, 95+% purity
Mixed butanes: liquid, 95+% purity
Isobutane: liquid, 95+% purity
n-Butane: liquid, 95+% purity
Natural gasoline: liquid, 12# Reid vapor pressure

A conventional arrangement for fractionation of the NGL products is shown in Fig. 20. Some variation in sequence of separation will be found between plants, particularly when built in conjunction with a NGL recovery plant.

Utilities consumption is a major concern in the fractionation of products, consequently several modifications have been incorporated in some plants to reduce heating and cooling requirements. This is particularly true in fractionation between the iso and normal components of butane and pentane. It is fairly common to operate a debutanizer at a high enough pressure so that the debutanizer condenser can provide part of the reboiler heat to a de-isobutanizer. This reduces cooling water requirement for the debutanizer condenser and fuel for reboiler heat to the de-isobutanizer. Various heat pump cycles have been employed whereby a fluid is evaporated to provide condensing duty, then compressed and condensed to provide reboiler heat input. Application of utility-saving schemes are a matter of economic tradeoff between higher capital cost and operation complexity versus lower utility costs.

Dehydration and Treating

No discussion of NGL recovery processes would be complete without reference to several ancillary and necessary operations. Gas dehydration is integral to essentially all NGL recovery plants built since the 1950s. Removal of acid gas constituents (carbon dioxide and hydrogen sulfide) from the inlet gas or products is also frequently necessary. A very brief description of these schemes is given for reference.

Dehydration

Natural gas from a formation will almost always contain water, up to saturation limits at reservoir or separator conditions. If gas is cooled to the point that free water is present, hydrates of gas and water will form depending on the temperature, pressure, and composition of the gas. These hydrates cannot be tolerated in most NGL recovery schemes in use today. The NGL process must be protected either by inhibition of the hydrates or removal of

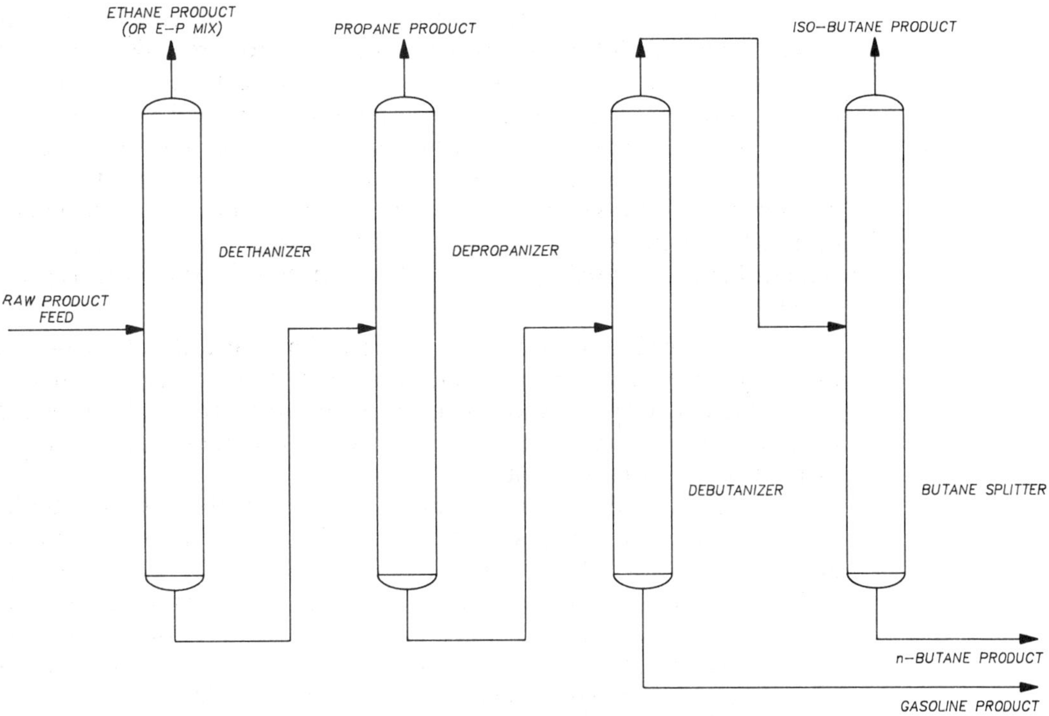

FIG. 20. Typical fractionation arrangement.

the water from the gas stream before processing. The most common schemes in use are:

1. Glycol injection
2. Glycol contactor
3. Alcohol injection
4. Fixed-bed dehydration

Glycol injection has been used extensively in refrigerated lean oil plants. A mixture of ethylene glycol and water (70 to 80 wt.% ethylene glycol) is injected in the inlet gas stream to the gas-gas exchanger and gas chiller. The glycol solution acts as an inhibitor to prevent the formation of hydrates at operating conditions. The glycol solution, with absorbed water, is removed from the gas stream and reconcentrated. The solution is recycled as a continous process. This scheme is susceptable to problems such as inadequate distribution in the exchangers, difficulty to remove from the gas, foaming, and mutual solubility between the hydrocarbon liquids and the glycol solution.

Dehydration of gas using a trayed contactor, similar to an oil absorption flow scheme, is frequently used even when a NGL plant is not involved.

Triethylene glycol is normally used, concentrated to various strengths depending on the degree of dew-point depression required. While 60° dew-point depression may be common for field dehydration, it is feasible to achieve dew-point depression of up to 150°F by using highly concentrated glycol, 10 or more trays in the contactor, and keeping the circulation rate high relative to water content of the gas. For high depression operation, it is necessary to either gas strip the lean glycol in conjunction with the reboiler or operate the regeneration at vacuum conditions. High dew-point depression systems have been used upstream of low temperature NGL recovery processes.

Alcohol injection is similar to glycol injection in that the alcohol–water mix inhibits the formation of hydrates. Methanol is most frequently used due to cost, but ethanol is also used when low temperatures are involved. Usually if alcohol injection is used, it involves only small quantities and no attempt is made for recovery of the alcohol.

Fixed-bed dehydration is the most common method of dehydration associated with expander-type NGL recovery facilities. Adsorbents employed are alumina, silica gel, and molecular sieves. Molecular sieves are most widely used, and provide water contents of less than 1 ppm. Many different regeneration schemes are used, but typically a portion of the dry residue gas is heated to regenerate the beds. Attention has to be paid to the regeneration scheme to avoid excessive spikes of water in the residue gas. A similar problem of concentration spikes can occur for small amounts of carbon dioxide or hydrogen sulfide in the inlet gas.

Acid Gas Removal

Several problems can be associated with the presence of carbon dioxide and hydrogen sulfide in the gas to a NGL recovery plant. The removal of hydrogen sulfide is mandatory in most cases from a hazard point of view. If the H_2S is present in significant quantities, then a Claus-type sulfur recovery plant may be required. If the H_2S is present in trace quantities, then only treatment of products will be required.

The necessity for the removal of CO_2 requires some investigation. If H_2S removal is required, generally some or all of the CO_2 will be removed in the same system. It may be necessary to remove CO_2 if the concentration is high enough to cause solid CO_2 formation in the low temperature section of the NGL recovery process. If restrictions on the residue gas heating value would restrict NGL recovery due to the presence of CO_2 (and nitrogen), it may be advantageous to remove all or part of the CO_2.

The subject of acid gas removal is very complex. A short list of the common schemes encountered in NGL recovery plants is as follows:

1. Amine systems
2. Physical solution absorption

3. Fixed bed adsorption (molecular sieve)
4. Membranes
5. Nonregenerative chemical reaction

The amine systems are most widely used, and can be applied to acid gas removal from the gas phase or the liquid phase. The flow scheme is similar to a simple oil absorption system. The acid gases are removed by a weak reversible chemical reaction in the amine/water solution. The reaction is reversed by heating the solution.

The physical absorption systems are very similar to the oil absorption process, and some operate at ambient temperatures while other operate at low temperatures. Absorption of heavy hydrocarbons is one of the drawbacks to the physical absorption systems.

Molecular sieves can be designed to selectively remove acid gases. This is normally not applicable to large concentrations. The scheme is essentially analogous to dehydration with molecular sieves.

Membranes have been used to separate high concentrations of acid gas from hydrocarbon gases. The process involves the permeation of the acid gases through a membrane, with large pressure drop through the membrane as the driving force. The process is very simple but requires large amounts of horsepower if the acid gas must be recompressed for disposal.

Nonregenerative chemical reactions are used when the acid gas content is small and chemical costs are acceptable. Iron sponge is used for H_2S removal. Caustic, dry or liquid, can be used to remove H_2S or CO_2.

NGL Recovery with Inert Gas

Over the past few years, the use of nitrogen and carbon dioxide for injection into the reservoir has become a major activity to increase the oil removed from the reservoir. This use of an inert gas to drive the crude oil and increase the recovery from a field is also resulting in a new type of gas processing plant. As the inert gas sweeps the field, it will eventually become part of the associated gas produced in the operation, requiring recovery and recycle. The subject of enhanced oil recovery using inert gas is too broad to cover here, but the impact of this technique on NGL recovery will be briefly considered.

The concentration of nitrogen or carbon dioxide in gases naturally produced would typically be in the range of 0 to 2 mol%. In the case of nitrogen, it is completely inert and can be left in the gas under normal conditions. The presence of CO_2 may be acceptable, and CO_2 is usually not removed unless potential freezeup might be encountered in low-temperature NGL recovery processes. The presence of these components in moderate concentrations is acceptable for normal pipeline gas services, and their major detriment is the reduction of the heating value of the gas.

This situation changes dramatically when the inert gases are used for enhanced oil recovery and eventually break through the reservoir to be produced with the naturally occurring hydrocarbon gases. When this occurs, the composition of the gas from the field to be processed undergoes a dramatic change in composition. This may occur over a period of years, but in some cases has been only a matter of months. Once the breakthrough has occurred, the concentration of inert gases continues to increase over the life of the project. This means that a plant designed to process gas from an enhanced oil recovery (EOR) program must be designed to operate with a continuously changing composition. The inert gas may grow to represent 80% of the gas to be processed.

It is practical to design a plant to process gas from an EOR project for NGL recovery, but obviously the design must take into account the presence of the inerts and the change in composition over years of operation. One of the uncertainties relates to the prediction of what the actual inlet gas composition will be over a period of time. Plant designs should include a great deal of flexibility in order to cope with these uncertainties. Since the composition changes may occur over a period of years, the plant may be designed to be added to in discreet stages in order to delay capital investment until it is actually required.

Processing high content inert gas from an EOR field may be done to recover NGL liquids, to recover the inert gases for reinjection into the reservoir, to produce a salable pipeline gas, or any combination of the above. As the quantity of inerts increases in the gas, it may eventually become uneconomic to process the gas for any purpose other then recycle to the reservoir.

Processes for recovering NGL from high content inert gases can vary significantly from plant to plant. They can incorporate any of the recovery schemes already described in this article, singularly or in combination. If NGL recovery only is the intent, then the plant will be about as complex as if processing a conventional hydrocarbon gas. If the inert gas is to separated, then the plant becomes fairly complex. Recovery of inert gas is accomplished in a cryogenic or low temperature process scheme if the inert gas is nitrogen. Processes similar to those used in air separation plants can be used, including multiple fractionation towers thermally linked and heat pump schemes for very low temperature refrigeration production. If the inert gas is carbon dioxide, the CO_2 can be recovered with an acid gas removal process or with a cryogenic process. Concentration and volume of the CO_2 will influence the process selection. Any plant designed to recover the inert gas will involve large amounts of compression horsepower to accomplish separation from the hydrocarbon constituents and return the inert gas to injection pressure. It is very difficult to generalize the cost of high content inert gas processing plants because the cost is a function of too many significant parameters that vary from plant to plant.

WARREN E. WHITE, Jr.

Nylon Salts and Nylon Intermediates

Diamines and dicarboxylic acids are important intermediates for the synthesis of polyamides. The products of neutralization of diamines with dicarboxylic acids are known as nylon salts. Preparation of the salt either as a pure product or as an aqueous solution prior to polymerization is normally the first step in the synthesis of polyamides by direct condensation of diamines with diacids.

In early work on polyamide synthesis the need was recognized for high purity of monomers and for use of the diamine and diacid in proportions corresponding to an exact equivalence of the amide-forming functions [1, 2]. Salt preparation as a first step in the polymerization process can serve as a final step in monomer purification and can also provide an accurate stoichiometric monomer balance which is essential for the preparation of polymers with high molecular weight.

Salt Preparation

The dicarboxylic acid salts of many aliphatic diamines can be easily isolated in pure crystalline form. Diamines and diacids are generally soluble in alcohols, including methanol, ethanol, and butanol, or in mixtures of alcohols and ether whereas nylon salts have low solubility in these solvents [1, 3]. A general method useful for the preparation of a variety of nylon salts involves a combination of alcohol solutions of the diacid and diamine and crystallization of the nylon salt from the reaction mixture. Diacids for which the two dissociation constants are approximately equal tend to combine with diamines to form crystalline salts with stoichiometric composition and high purity. Nearly stoichiometric composition is obtained with these salts even if the molar equivalence of monomers in the solution is not exact [1, 4]. A salt with an exact balance can be approached by recrystallization. Diacids with significantly different dissociation constants often form noncrystalline polymeric salts of nonstoichiometric composition [4].

If monomers of high purity are available, a salt solution can be prepared and used directly for polymerization without isolation of the crystalline salt. Treatment of salt solutions with decolorizing carbon can be used to remove traces of colored impurities. Monomer equivalence in the salt solution can be established by accurate measurement of solution pH. The equivalence pH for a nylon salt, i.e., the pH of a solution containing exactly equal molar concentrations of diamine and diacid, can be determined by titration of a

TABLE 1 Properties of Nylon Salts

Salt	Melting Point (°C)	Equivalence pH	Refs.
24	190		4
26	130–131		4
46	204		1
47	138		1
49	175		1
510	129	7.5	1
64	191–192		4
66	196–197	7.6	3
610	170–172		1, 3, 4
N,N′-Diisobutyl, 610	137–138	7.5	3

solution of the diacid with a solution of the diamine or by calculation using the following equation if the acid and base constants are known [5]:

$$\mathrm{pH} = 7 + \frac{1}{2}p_a - \frac{1}{2}p_b$$

where p_a and p_b are the negative exponents of the acid and base constants, respectively. The two functional groups for both the diamine and diacid will have slightly different dissociation constants. The second dissociation constant in each case must be used to calculate the pH at the equivalence point.

For best accuracy in establishing the salt balance in an aqueous solution by pH measurement with a glass electrode, the salt concentration should be in the range of 1 to 10%. While the pH of a solution of the salt of a weak acid and weak base is independent of salt concentration [5], high salt concentrations affect the response of the glass electrode.

Properties of Nylon Salts

Although a great many polyamides have been prepared by condensation of diamines with diacids, very little information has been reported on the properties of nylon salts. Solubilities at 25°C of 49% in water, 0.4% in absolute methanol, and 0.02% in absolute ethanol have been reported for hexamethylene diammonium adipate [1]. In general, nylon salts with low hydrocarbon content are water soluble. With increased hydrocarbon content, water solubility decreases and solubility in alcohols increases. Crystal structure data have been reported for 46 [6], 66 [6, 7], and 610 [7] salts.

Melting point and equivalence pH values for a number of nylon salts are given in Table 1. Nomenclature codes for the salts are the codes for the corresponding polymers [8].

References

1. D. D. Coffman, G. J. Berchet, W. R. Peterson, and E. W. Spanagel, *J. Polym. Sci.*, *2*, 306 (1947).
2. W. H. Carothers, *Trans. Faraday Soc.*, *32*, 39 (1936).
3. W. R. Sorenson and T. W. Campbell, *Preparative Methods of Polymer Chemistry*, Wiley-Interscience, New York, 1968. Chap. 3.
4. R. W. Lenz, *Organic Chemistry of Synthetic High Polymers*, Wiley-Interscience, New York, 1967, Chap. 4.
5. I. M. Kolthoff and H. A. Laitinen, *pH and Electro Titrations*, Wiley, New York, 1941, Chap. 1.
6. S. Hirokawa and T. Ashida, *Mem. Def. Acad., Jpn.*, *2*, 95 (1962).
7. C. J. Brown, *Acata Crystallogr.*, *21*, 185 (1966).
8. M. I. Kohan, *Nylon Plastics*, Wiley, New York, 1973, Chap. 1.

I. K. MILLER

Oil, Crude, World Reserves, Production, and Refining Capacity

Many readers are interested in knowing the world reserves, production, and refining capacities of crude oil. These data are presented here in tabular form, but they should be updated annually since there are changes consistently. The *Oil & Gas Journal, World Oil*, and other magazines annually publish these updated data. In addition to the summary data shown here, these magazines publishes many pages of detailed data showing names of fields, discovery dates, depth of wells, producing wells, nonproducing wells, yearly production, °API gravity of fluid, number of refineries (see also the article "Petroleum Refining, World Capacity" in this *Encyclopedia*), and processes used.

JOHN J. McKETTA

Worldwide Oil and Gas at a Glance[a]

	Estimated Proved Reserves, January 1, 1988		Oil Production	
	Oil	Gas	Producing Wells[b]	Estimated 1987
Country	(1000 bbl)	(10^9 cu ft)	December 31, 86	(1000 b/d)
Asia-Pacific				
Australia	1,691,960	18,610	869	566.1
Bangladesh	500	12,720	10	0.5
Brunei	1,420,000	7,010	609	133.7
Bruma	58,000	9,460	450	24.0
China, Taiwan	5,400	890	90	2.6
India	4,250,000	17,550	2,670	608.7
Indonesia	8,400,000	73,000	5,774	1,185.8
Japan	56,790	1,030	387	12.1
Korea, South	—	—	—	—
Malaysia	2,900,000	52,200	452	467.4
New Zealand	160,000	5,200	38	28.3
Pakistan	96,000	22,400	44	41.6
Papua New Guinea	200,000	1,000	—	—
Philippines	16,000	10	10	5.1
Singapore	—	—	—	—
Sri Lanka	—	—	—	—
Thailand	99,000	3,720	167	31.3
Total Asia-Pacific	19,353,650	224,800	11,570	3,107.2

% Change from 1986	No. of Refineries	Refining Capacity (b/cd), January 1, 1988 Crude	Thermal Operations	Catalytic Cracking	Catalytic Reforming
+10.3	10	637,100	—	184,800	154,800
—	1	31,200	—	—	1,650
−8.5	1	10,000	—	—	—
−20.0	2	26,300	1,700	—	—
+35.7	2	600,000	15,000	25,000	62,500
−2.8	12	1,058,742	113,900	133,470	26,690
−5.6	6	714,200	92,500	12,600	62,100
−2.2	43	4,566,850	82,800	557,150	533,940
—	5	820,000	30,000	—	59,450
−4.4	4	212,300	—	—	21,410
−4.2	1	81,700	—	—	21,700
+1.4	3	130,050	—	—	5,450
—	—	—	—	—	—
−25.6	4	286,000	—	23,100	40,200
—	5	858,000	137,700	—	54,300
—	1	50,000	12,500	—	3,750
−9.7	3	191,860	9,600	9,250	25,300
−2.5	103	10,274,302	495,700	945,370	1,073,240

Country	Estimated Proved Reserves, January 1, 1988: Oil (1000 bbl)	Estimated Proved Reserves, January 1, 1988: Gas (10^9 cu ft)	Oil Production: Producing Wells[b] December 31, 86	Oil Production: Estimated 1987 (1000 b/d)
Western Europe				
Austria	105,000	420	1,177	21.6
Belgium	—	—	—	—
Cyprus	—	—	—	—
Denmark	440,000	4,400	40	94.0
Finland	—	—	—	—
France	212,620	1,170	583	63.5
Germany, Federal Republic	316,000	6,400	3,129	73.8
Greece	21,600	20	16	24.4
Ireland	—	1,900	—	—
Italy-Sicily	739,000	10,200	239	50.0
Netherlands	195,000	64,100	550	91.3
Norway	14,800,000	105,940	202	973.3
Portugal	—	—	—	—
Spain	38,600	600	48	32.8
Sweden	—	—	—	—
Switzerland	—	—	—	—
Turkey	380,000	1,030	564	52.0
United Kingdom	5,200,000	22,000	710	2,445.9
Total Western Europe	22,447,820	218,180	7,258	3,922.6
Middle East				
Abu Dhabi	92,205,000	183,500	517	969.4
Bahrain	140,550	6,900	279	43.2
Dubai	4,000,000	6,000	150	381.2
Iran	92,850,000	489,400	361	2,341.7
Iraq	100,000,000	26,300	615	2,095.8
Israel	700	30	9	1.0
Jordan	12,000	—	10	4.0
Kuwait	91,920,000	36,400	363	1,095.8
Lebanon	—	—	—	—
Neutral Zone	5,210,000	12,300	491	399.2
Oman	4,012,000	9,500	789	565.0
Qatar	3,150,000	156,700	174	284.4
Ras al Khaimah	400,000	2,000	6	10.0
Saudi Arabia	166,980,000	139,900	588	4,054.2
Sharjah	1,500,000	12,000	20	66.9
Syria	1,750,000	1,500	963	231.7
Yemen, North	550,000	1,600	45	10.0
Yemen, South	—	—	—	—
Total Middle East	564,680,250	1,084,030	5,380	12,553.5

% Change from 1986	No. of Refineries	Refining Capacity (b/cd), January 1, 1988 Crude	Thermal Operations	Catalytic Cracking	Catalytic Reforming
+2.8	1	204,000	17,000	24,000	32,000
—	4	630,500	62,800	102,000	80,300
—	1	16,000	—	—	3,400
+27.2	3	177,000	70,670	—	31,100
—	2	241,000	46,300	41,800	42,900
+7.2	14	1,940,600	163,550	288,800	258,700
−6.8	16	1,647,800	286,400	174,700	307,100
−7.9	4	384,500	41,120	50,500	51,300
—	1	56,000	—	—	11,000
+2.0	19	2,563,100	388,400	277,400	289,600
+2.5	7	1,381,000	151,560	125,500	157,400
+16.0	3	240,000	85,500	—	29,150
—	3	294,300	—	10,100	35,400
−13.1	10	1,305,000	178,000	143,500	189,100
—	5	436,500	68,000	27,000	72,700
—	2	132,000	20,000	—	26,000
+3.9	5	675,595	4,500	34,100	65,370
−3.0	15	1,802,700	152,000	392,000	367,500
+2.0	115	14,127,595	1,735,800	1,691,400	2,050,020

+3.0	2	180,000	—	—	30,055
+9.1	1	250,000	19,000	36,000	17,100
+14.0	—	—	—	—	—
+26.7	4	530,000	80,800	—	63,845
+24.0	7	318,500	—	—	43,500
—	2	180,000	70,000	20,000	26,000
—	1	100,000	—	4,410	8,640
−11.9	4	628,000	—	30,000	51,000
—	2	37,000	—	7,250	7,492
+16.4	—	—	—	—	—
+1.2	1	76,932	—	—	15,386
−14.6	1	62,000	—	—	12,030
+9.0	—	—	—	—	—
−16.8	7	1,375,000	27,000	76,000	178,900
+9.4	—	—	—	—	—
+19.4	2	228,790	41,199	—	19,348
—	1	10,000	—	—	2,500
—	1	170,000	—	—	12,000
+0.5	36	4,146,222	237,999	173,660	487,796

Country	Estimated Proved Reserves, January 1, 1988 Oil (1000 bbl)	Gas (10^9 cu ft)	Oil Production Producing Wells[b] December 31, 86	Estimated 1987 (1000 b/d)
Africa				
Algeria	8,500,000	105,900	840	647.9
Angola-Cabinda	1,149,000	1,760	381	341.3
Benin	100,000	–	6	12.0
Cameroon	520,000	3,880	176	170.0
Congo	720,000	2,470	286	118.0
Cote d'Ivoire	–	–	–	–
Egypt	4,300,000	10,240	724	899.3
Ethiopia	–	–	–	–
Gabon	645,000	600	295	155.8
Ghana	1,000	–	–	–
Ivory Coast	120,000	3,530	14	16.0
Kenya	–	–	–	–
Liberia	–	–	–	–
Libya	21,000,000	25,700	661	1,019.7
Madagascar	–	–	–	–
Morocco	2,700	70	4	0.3
Mozambique	–	2,200	–	–
Nigeria	15,980,000	84,000	1,253	1,238.6
Senegal	–	–	–	–
Sierra Leone	–	–	–	–
Somalia	–	210	–	–
South Africa	–	980	–	–
Sudan	300,000	–	–	–
Tanzania	–	4,100	–	–
Togo	–	–	–	–
Tunisia	1,800,000	2,960	150	104.3
Zaire	112,000	30	104	31.8
Zambia	–	–	–	–
Total Africa	55,249,700	248,630	4,894	4,755.0

	Refining Capacity (b/cd), January 1, 1988				
% Change from 1986	No. of Refineries	Crude	Thermal Operations	Catalytic Cracking	Catalytic Reforming
+4.0	4	464,700	—	—	55,600
+21.0	1	32,100	—	—	1,900
+55.8	—	—	—	—	—
−5.6	1	43,000	—	—	6,500
+2.6	1	21,000	—	—	2,000
—	2	60,000	—	—	16,600
+10.6	7	452,110	16,470	—	30,940
—	1	18,000	—	—	2,200
−3.2	1	23.000	7,200	—	1,500
—	1	28,000	—	—	5,550
−7.9	—	—	—	—	—
—	1	90,000	—	—	9,000
—	1	15,000	—	—	2,000
−1.1	2	329,400	—	—	14,582
—	1	16,350	—	—	2,600
−5.0	2	154,600	—	5,600	26,800
—	—	—	—	—	—
−15.5	3	270,000	—	47,000	39,700
—	1	29,800	—	—	2,870
—	1	10,000	—	—	—
—	1	10,000	—	—	—
—	4	433,500	63,500	84,400	62,800
—	1	21,440	—	—	1,700
—	1	13,500	—	—	3,000
—	1	20,000	—	—	4,400
−2.9	1	34,000	—	—	3,300
−2.0	1	17,000	—	—	3,000
—	1	23,750	—	5,040	5,040
−1.7	42	2,630,250	87,170	142,040	303,582

Country	Estimated Proved Reserves, January 1, 1988 Oil (1000 bbl)	Gas (10^9 cu ft)	Oil Production Producing Wells[b] December 31, 86	Estimated 1987 (1000 b/d)
Western Hemisphere				
Argentina	2,270,000	23,600	8,389	419.1
Barbados	3,620	10	75	1.4
Bolivia	156,000	5,040	296	18.5
Brazil	2,340,000	3,600	4,880	562.8
Canada	6,825,000	98,000	35,246	1,508.3
Chile	290,000	4,200	347	28.3
Colombia	1,590,000	3,600	2,770	387.8
Costa Rica	—	—	—	—
Dominican Republic	—	—	—	—
Ecuador	1,615,000	4,020	922	157.2
El Salvador	—	—	—	—
Guatemala	41,500	20	12	3.9
Honduras	—	—	—	—
Jamaica	—	—	—	—
Martinique	—	—	—	—
Mexico	48,610,000	76,530	3,768	2,537.8
Netherlands Antilles	—	—	—	—
Nicaragua	—	—	—	—
Panama	—	—	—	—
Paraguay	—	—	—	—
Peru	511,860	650	3,438	166.7
Puerto Rico	—	—	—	—
Suriname	27,000	—	56	2.2
Trinidad & Tobago	567,000	10,390	3,211	163.1
Uruguay	—	—	—	—
Venezuela	56,300,000	95,000	9,797	1,591.9
Virgin Islands	—	—	—	—
United States	25,270,000	186,700	636,475	8,276.7
Total Western Hemisphere	146,416,980	511,360	709,682	15,825.7
Total Non-Communist	808,148,400	2,287,000	738,784	40,164.0
Communist Areas				
China	18,400,000	30,700	34,000	2,647.0
USSR	59,000,000	1,450,000	128,000	12,486.5
Other[d]	1,800,000	29,300	NA	422.0
Total Communist	79,200,000	1,510,000	162,000	15,555.5
TOTAL WORLD	887,348,400	3,797,000	900,784	55,719.5

[a]All reserves figures except those for the USSR (and gas for Canada) are reported as proved reserves recoverable with present technology and prices. USSR figures are "explored reserves" which include proved, probable, and some possible. Canadian gas figure, under criteria adopted by Canadian Petroleum Association in 1980, includes proved and some probable.

	Refining Capacity (b/cd), January 1, 1988				
% Change from 1986	No. of Refineries	Crude	Thermal Operations	Catalytic Cracking	Catalytic Reforming
−1.1	11	689,500	120,800	112,450	39,600
−9.1	1	3,000	—	—	—
+5.3	3	46,930	—	—	14,158
−1.9	13	1,407,300	33,800	350,500	24,800
+2.5	27	1,868,900	78,150	385,550	368,650
−15.3	2	141,000	18,400	37,000	5,300
+29.1	4	226,000	60,000	91,000	6,000
—	1	16,200	6,500	—	1,200
—	2	48,500	—	—	7,900
−45.2	3	122,000	25,200	16,000	2,780
—	1	17,000	—	—	3,800
−20.6	1	16,000	—	—	3,000
—	1	14,000	—	—	1,800
—	1	35,500	—	—	3,540
—	1	12,800	—	—	7,410
+4.5	9	1,354,000	82,000	267,000	157,800
—	2	320,000	67,000	42,000	15,000
—	1	14,500	—	—	2,800
—	1	100,000	—	—	7,500
—	1	7,500	—	—	—
−7.1	6	182,018	—	21,305	1,680
—	2	123,000	—	12,000	5,800
+13.4	—	—	—	—	—
−3.4	2	300,000	18,000	25,000	31,000
—	1	45,000	—	5,000	3,000
−3.2	6	1,201,100	138,000	193,100	6,000
—	1	545,000	80,000	—	125,000
−4.6	187[c]	15,288,274[c]	1,789,088[c]	5,014,195[c]	3,595,532[c]
−2.4	291	24,145,022	2,516,938	6,572,100	4,441,050
−1.0	587	55,323,391	5,073,607	9,524,570	8,355,688
+1.0	40	2,200,000	NA	NA	NA
+1.5	39	12,260,000	NA	NA	NA
−1.2	45	3,150,000	NA	NA	NA
+1.4	124	17,610,000	NA	NA	NA
−0.4	711	72,933,391	5,073,607	9,524,570	8,355,688

[b]Does not include shut in, injection, or service wells.

[c]Estimates based on capacity as of January 1, 1987, plus known 1987 closures and expansions.

[d]Includes Albania, Bulgaria, Cuba, Czechoslovakia, East Germany, Hungary, Mongolia, North Korea, Poland, Romania, Viet Nam, and Yugoslavia.

O-Rings

In hydrocarbon processing plants, mechanical seals for pumps and compressors, tube fittings, and pipe flanges often use O-rings to prevent fluid flow or leakage. According to application, O-rings can be categorized as static (seal between flange facings) and dynamic (subjected to movement or wobble) (see Fig. 1). Table 1 lists the commonly available O-ring materials and their characteristics.

Chemical compatibility of O-rings with a process fluid and temperature limits will define the method of O-ring production, using full-circle molding, ambient adhesive bonding, and hot bonding or vulcanizing. Having no joint, hence no weak point, reliable in operation, full-circle, molded O-rings are the most common. Available in a wide range of stock sizes and materials, O-rings of this type also can be custom-molded. Ambient adhesive bonded O-rings of any diameter can be quickly and easily made, using cord stock of most materials except silicone rubber. A simple jig used for cutting square ends and aligning them for bonding gives a smooth joint, which can sometimes be

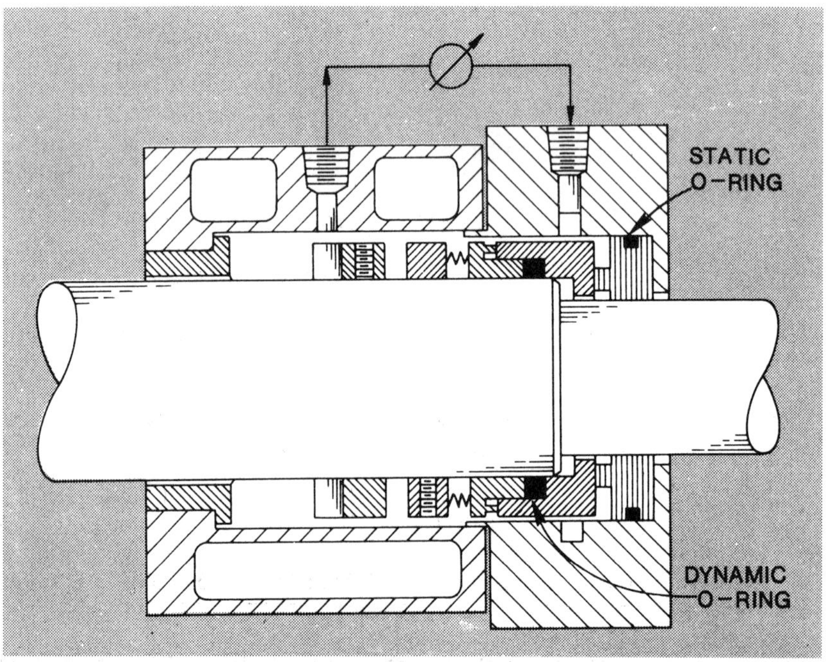

FIG. 1. Mechanical seal installation with static and dynamic O-rings.

made in place without machine disassembly. Vulcanizing is considered to be an intermediate method in terms of nonstock O-ring delivery, chemical and temperature resistance. Thermal and chemical resistance of the hot, bonded O-rings are superior to the adhesive-bonded but inferior to the molded.

O-ring failure analysis can be instructive to prevent machine failure. There are several common causes of O-ring failure.

Deterioration in Storage

Some synthetic rubbers such as neoprene and buna N are sensitive to ultraviolet radiation, others to heat and ozone. Storage in a cool, dark environment, away from electrical equipment, is therefore recommended.

Temperature

Exceeding an allowable temperature is a common cause of O-ring failure (see Fig. 2). The largest O-ring failed from overheating because of blockage of seal flush. The inner one did not recover from compression set at high temperature, remaining "flattened out" as shown. The two lower rings failed because of overheating or chemical attack. Table 1 lists temperature limits for common O-ring materials. These limits can often be exceeded for short periods. Process fluid temperature may not be equal to O-ring temperature. A cool flush may reduce O-ring temperature, as may heat dissipation through a barrier structure. On the other hand, localized frictional heating may increase the O-ring temperature. If high or low temperatures are suspected as causing

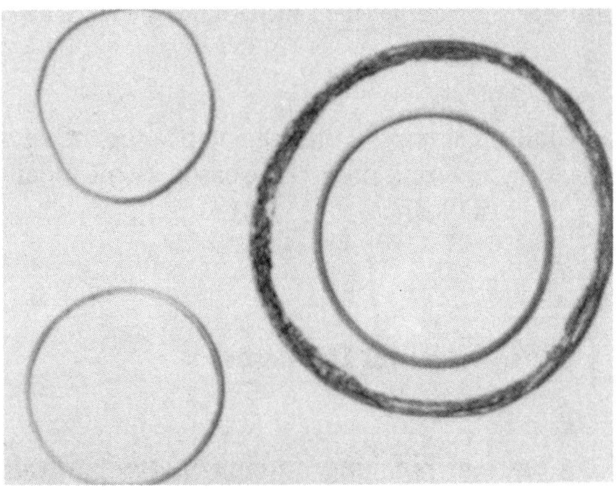

FIG. 2. Failed O-rings.

TABLE 1 O-Ring Material

Property	Neoprene	Buna N	Fluorocarbon DuPont Viton	Ethylene Propylene EPDM	Polyacrylate
	Material				
Service temperature limits, °F	−65 to +300	−60 to +300	−10 to +450 for continuous, dynamic service. Intermittent service to 600. Static service to −50	−60 to +350	−20 to +350
Specific gravity	1.25	0.98	1.8–1.9	0.86	1.09
Chemical resistance	Good for common refrigerants and lube oils	Good for most petroleum oils	Good for broad range of hydrocarbons and acids. Not recommended for ammonia or amines	Good for phosphate ester base hydraulic fluids. Not recommended for petroleum oils	Used extensively for auto transmissions and power steering
Sunlight resistance	Poor	Poor	Good		
Compression set resistance	—	Good	Good to excellent	—	Fair
Abrasion resistance	Fair to good	Fair to good	Fair to good	—	—
Remarks	—	Poor ozone resistance	The best general purpose O-ring material for refineries and chemical plants. Has largely displaced neoprene and buna N for such plants. O-rings made from DuPont E60C Viton provide major improvement in high temperature compression set resistance over the older Vitons[a]	—	—

[a]To identify Viton, drop the material into carbon tetrachloride. If it sinks, it is probably Viton. If it floats, it is not. Kalrez perfluoroelastomer also sinks, but this material is uncommon and seldom unidentified by other means.

failure, it may be practical to change the environmental temperature or the O-ring material. In extreme cases, an all-metal bellows seal may permit elimination of O-rings.

Mechanical Damage

Tearing, pinching, foreign matter embedment, dry rubbing, and various other mechanical damage can occur during installation, operation, and removal. A sharp steel tool used for O-ring removal can scratch the groove or

Material				
Silicone	Urethane	Perfluoroelastomer DuPont Kalrez (formerly ECD-006)	Composite—Synthetic Rubber Inside, DuPont Teflon Outside	Fluorosilicone
−178 to +450 (to +700 for short periods)	−65 to +240	−36 to +550 continuous. To +600 intermittent	To +400	−90 to +400
1.1–1.6	1.25	2.01	—	1.4
Good for dry heat in static applications	Good for hydrocarbons. Poor in acids, ketones, chlorinated hydrocarbons	Excellent overall fuel and chemical resistance, similar to Teflon	Inert to most chemicals	Good for dry heat plus exposure to hydrocarbons
Good	Good	Good	Good	Good
Good	Fair to good	Fair to good. Good below 500°F	Superior to Teflon used alone. This is its main selling point	—
Poor	Excellent	Fair to good	Fair	Fair
Can often be identified by red color, or failure to bond with cyanoacrylate adhesive	High tensile strength and extrusion resistance. Some types of ants like to eat some types of urethane rubber, so best to provide ant-proof storage	A comparatively new material. O-rings made from it are available only from DuPont. When its unique properties are required, however, it can easily be worth its price	Has chemical resistance of Teflon with better compression set resistance. Not recommended for certain applications—consult manufacturer. For the future, it appears possible that this type of O-ring may become obsolete, as the Kalrez O-rings come into more common use	—

sealing surface and cause leakage. Brass, wood, or plastic tools can be used without risk of scratching.

Chemical Attack

Table 1 is useful in selecting O-ring materials compatible with various fluids. Experimental verification is sometimes worthwhile. Complications may occur because of different properties of supposedly identical O-rings produced by various manufacturers. Also, a loss of identification in storage and handling is possible. To minimize unpleasant surprises for critical service such as hot xylene, we routinely discard new O-rings which come with new and rebuilt seal assemblies, and replace them with O-rings of known material from a single manufacturer considered reliable. To check whether an unknown, used O-ring is Viton or something else, use the carbon tetrachloride test described in Table 1.

This material appeared in *Hydrocarbon Processing*, pp. 191–192, April 1976, and is reprinted with the permission of the editor.

MALCOLM G. MURRAY Jr.

Paints and Coatings

Four key factors assure proper coatings performance. Surprisingly, engineers ignore one or more of them most times, they are involved in a painting project. That is why there are so many failures and expensive repairs later.

Surface preparation, paint selection and specification, paint application, and inspection are the four key ingredients of a successful painting program. Leave out any of these and one will get the unwanted ingredient of a paint job, namely, paint failure.

In the CPI (Chemical Process Industries) (Table 1) the corrosive nature of the materials being handled leads to more reasons for failure than in other industries. Consequently, there is more reason to spend time in implementing a coatings specification, preparation and application, and inspection program. Cost engineering studies prove that painting costs can be reduced by as much as 40% when a properly implemented painting plan is carried out. It also implies a basic understanding of what makes up a coating in the first place (Appendix 1).

Whether a project is grass roots, retrofit, revamp, or repaint, Weismantel International recommends the use of PMP—Preventive Maintenance Painting. This means that painting will take place before the metal, wood, or other substrate is subjected to potential damage or corrosion. This premise is based on the fact that CPI equipment and structures are expensive investments and must be protected or they will have to be replaced. Such a maintenance program does not consider planned obsolescence, planned failure, or the other alternative—simply not painting. We do not normally recommend these latter alternatives, but if engineers are faced with them, the technical staff should consider rate-of-return calculations, the time-value of money, the significant cost of replacing equipment (even if it is written off the books), and the considerable danger and safety hazards that come with equipment corrosion of most process equipment or structural supports and piping, much of which is high pressure or handling toxic, flammable, or hazardous materials.

TABLE 1 Definition of the Nineteen Segments That Make Up the Chemical Process Industries (CPI)[a] by U.S. Government Standard Industrial Classification (SIC) Code

Industrial Segments	SIC Codes
1. Chemicals	
Alkalis and chlorine	2812
Industrial gases	2813
Industrial inorganic chemicals	2819
Synthetic rubber and elastomers	2822
Gum and wood chemicals	2861
Cyclic crudes and intermediates	2865
Industrial organic chemicals	2869
Chemicals and chemical preparations	2899
2. Drugs and cosmetics	
Biological products	2831
Medicinal chemicals and botanicals	2833
Pharmaceutical preparations	2834
Perfumes, cosmetics, and other total preparations	2844
3. Explosives and ammunition	
Explosives	2892
Small arms ammunition	3482
Ammunition, except for small arms	3843
Ordnance and accessories	3489
4. Fats and oils	
Cottonseed oil mills	2074
Soybean oil mills	2075
Vegetable oil mills	2076
Animal and marine fats and oil	2077
Shortening, table oils, margarine, and other edible fats and oils	2079
5. Fertilizers and agriculture chemicals	
Nitrogenous fertilizer	2873
Phosphatic fertilizers	2874
Fertilizers, mixing only	2875
Pesticides and agricultural chemicals	2879
6. Foods and beverages	
Condensed and evaporated milk	2023
Wet corn milling	2046
Cane sugar, except refining only	2061
Cane sugar refining	2062
Beet sugar	2063
Malt beverages	2082
Malt	2083
Wines, brandy, and brandy spirits	2084
Distilled, rectified, and blended liquors	2085
Flavoring extracts and syrups	2087
Roasted coffee, includes instant coffee	2095
Food preparations	2099
7. Leather tanning and finishing	3111

(continued)

TABLE 1 (*continued*)

Industrial Segments	SIC Codes
8. Lime and cement	
Cement, hydraulic	3241
Lime	3274
9. Man-made fibers	
Cellulosic man-made fibers	2823
Synthetic organic fibers, except cellulosic	2824
10. Metallurgical and metal products	
Electrometallurgical products	3313
Primary smelting and refining of copper	3331
Primary smelting and refining of lead	3332
Primary smelting and refining of zinc	3333
Primary production of aluminum	3334
Primary smelting and refining of nonferrous metals	3339
Secondary smelting and refining and alloying of nonferrous metals and alloys	3341
Enameled iron and metal sanitary ware	3431
Electroplating, plating, polishing, anodizing, and coloring	3471
Coating, engraving, and allied services	3479
11. Paints, varnishes, pigments, and allied products	
Inorganic pigments	2816
Paints, varnishes, lacquers, enamels, and allied products	2851
12. Petroleum refining and coal products	
Petroleum refining	2911
Paving mixtures and blocks	2951
Asphalt felts and coatings	2952
Lubricating oils and grease	2992
Coke and by-products	3312
13. Plastics materials, synthetic resins, and nonvulcanizable elastomers	2821
14. Rubber products	
Tires and inner tubes	3011
Rubber footwear	3021
Reclaimed rubber	3031
Fabricated rubber products	3069
15. Soap, glycerin, cleaning, polishing, and related products	
Soap and other detergents except specialty cleaners	2841
Specialty cleaning, polishing, and sanitation preparations, except soap and detergents	2842
Surface-active agents, finishing agents, sulfonated oils, and assistants	2843
16. Stone, clay, glass, and ceramics	
Flat glass	3211
Glass containers	3221
Pressed and blown glass	3229
Brick and structural clay tiles	3251
Ceramic wall and floor tiles	3253

(continued)

TABLE 1 *(continued)*

Industrial Segments	SIC Codes
Clay refractories	3255
Structural clay products	3259
Pottery and related products	3261, 3262, 3263, 3264, 3269
Gypsum products	3275
Abrasive products	3291
Asbestos products	3292
Steam and other packing, and pipe and boiler covering	3293
Miscellaneous minerals and earth	3295
Mineral wool	3296
Nonclay refractories	3297
Nonmetallic mineral products	3299
17. Wood, pulp, paper, and board	
Wood preserving	2491
Pulp mills	2611
Paper mills, except building paper mills	2621
Paperboard mills	2631
Paper coating and glazing	2641
Building paper and board mills	2661
18. Other chemically processed products	
Part of broad woven fabric mills, wool; including dyeing and finishing	2231
Finishers of broad woven fabrics of cotton	2261
Finishers of broad woven fabrics made of man-made fiber and silk	2262
Dyeing and finishing textiles	2269
Artifical leather, oilcloth, and other impregnated and coated fabrics, except rubberized adhesives	2295
Printing ink	2893
Carbon black	2895
Carbon and graphite products	3624
Storage batteries	3691
Primary batteries (dry and wet)	3692
Photographic equipment and supplies	3861
Lead pencils, crayons, and artists materials	3952
Carbon paper and inked ribbons	3955
Linoleum, asphalted felt base and other floor coverings	3996
Manufacturing industries	3999
19. Semiconductors and related devices including electronic chemicals	3674

[a]Petrochemicals are included in various CPI segments. By definition, petrochemicals are:

2821 Plastic materials	2865 Cyclics and aromatics
2822 Synthetic rubbers	2869 Acrylics and aliphatics
2824 Synthetic fibers	2873 Nitrogenous fertilizers
2843 Surfactants	2895 Carbon black

Selecting the Paint System

Given the above prelude, we turn to paint selection. Given a properly prepared surface and application, paint performance is directly related to the type of coating chosen. Selection depends on knowing the nature of the corrosive atmosphere, how it may change, and determining the temperature, humidity, and related environmental conditions (pH, salinity in the air, etc.) that relate to coating exposure.

For very mildly corrosive conditions in which relative humidity is rarely above 50% and the corrosion rate is less than 25 mdd (milligrams per square decimeter per day, or 0.19 lb steel per square foot per year), it would be difficult to justify painting from the standpoint of corrosion. However, such mildly corrosive conditions are rarely found in industrial plants. Severe corrosion rates of 300 mdd are not uncommon in industrial and marine situations. Carbon steel and many other metals should be protected from such exposures.

To this point we have not considered the price of the paint. Generally, the price per gallon comes into play after determining the generic painting system deemed appropriate for exposure conditions. Then one can "shop" among the vendors, but even then the actual cost of the paint is often not the largest part of a total paint job.

Top-quality coatings should be compared generically, but identification by generic name *per se* is no guarantee of quality. Coatings should be purchased on specifications from reliable coatings manufacturers. It is false economy to purchase a protective coating without knowing its solids content and resin content.

This is not to say that cost is not important. Engineers or specification engineers should specify the system that gives the best performance even a defined time period. If, for example, a coating system performs adequately for 6 years and costs $0.60/ft^2, a system costing $1.20/ft^2 cannot be justified if it gives the same service unless the more expensive coating offers some additional advantage that will become more important later. But, in these conditions, the time-value of money (Appendix 2) must be considered.

Regardless, the standards for selecting the coating system for CPI plants boils down to certain basic criteria of which the most important are: weather resistance, stress and impact qualities, abrasion resistance, adhesion properties, flexibility, temperature resistance, drying qualities, application criteria, chemical resistance (to acids and alkali of various types and concentrations plus solvents of both alaphatic and aromatic nature), and other factors (Appendix 3).

Table 2 gives an overview of qualities of typical paints used for the CPI. The engineer should be particularly cautious, however, of making generalities. Why? Because a certain coating may show excellent resistance to 20, 30, or 50% sulfuric acid, yet may fail miserably in 10% acetic acid. Whenever possible, specifications should rely on known exposure data and/or swatch tests painted on the precise equipment on which the coating system will be asked to perform.

TABLE 2 General Evaluation of Basic Resins Used in CPI Coatings Formulations[a]

	Type[b]					
Exposure	Vinyl	Epoxy	Urethane	Phenolic	Alkyd	Oil
Alkali	10	8	8	2	6	1
Acid	10	10	9	10	6	1
Solvents	5	8	6	10	4	2
Salts	10	10	10	10	8	6
Water	10	10	10	10	8	7
Heat	7	9	9	10	8	7
Abrasion	7	6	6	5	6	4
Humidity and UV	10	9	9	8	8	8
Stress and impact	8	3	7	2	4	4
Oxidation	10	6	6	7	3	1
	87	80	80	74	61	41

[a]Source: Weismantel International, Kingwood, Texas.
[b]Perfect rating equals 10.

Note: The words "coating system" are used for describing selection criteria. It is the interaction of surface preparation, primer and one or more top coats of the proper film thickness application, and drying time (or curing time) that proves satisfactory. Substitutions for one item in a system can lead to failure. The concept of "or equal" clauses in paint specifications is often a way for purchasing agents to supplement a cheaper paint than the one really wanted. Most coatings are *not* equal in weight per gallon, pigment loading, resin used, viscosity, or other qualities. At times the engineer may have to specify the coating required by company name, product name, and even batch number. (If the latter number is used, don't be surprised if the manufacturer changes other batch numbers to the batch that you want. At times it may become necessary to have third party inspectors present for batch manufacturing and to keep records of amounts of paint ordered and used to assure batch renumbering is not taking place.)

It is not necessary to be this cautious in routine coating projects, but the need for quality control (QC) and inspection for critical jobs cannot be overemphasized.

Primer

A primer should meet as many as possible of the following requirements.

Provide good adhesion when the surface has been cleaned or prepared according to specifications.
Have appropriate flexibility-distensibility.
Assure satisfactory intercoat bonding-surface for the next coat.

Have the ability to stifle or retard the spread of corrosion from discontinuities such as pinholes and breaks in the coating film.
Have chemical and weather resistance qualities to protect the surface for a time period in excess of that anticipated before application of the next coat in the system.
In some cases, notably tank lining, have chemical resistance equivalent to the rest of the system.
Have adequate film thickness
Create a uniform bond between the primer and the top coat (tie coat).
Be a superior barrier with respect to aggressive chemicals in the environment.

One aspect of priming has changed remarkably during the past few years: the use of conversion primers. Normally, these are rust-converting liquids containing small amounts of an appropriate mild acid or other chemicals mixed with a film-forming resin. The conversion process neutralizes or binds the rust. In some cases, mild rust may actually enhance the adhesion. The jury is still out on long-term, widespread use of rust-conversion primers, but they are gaining in popularity and can be considered in some CPI applications (Appendix 4).

Before closing the book on primers, add a special note of caution to priming and topcoating CPI equipment that normally comes with an original equipment manufacturer coating. This would include blowers, compressors, conveyors, cranes, extruders, fans, hoists, pumps, and exchangers. Obviously, an engineer should not rely on a vendor's standard paint for an application that requires special coating. For example, an operating engineer at a large fertilizer warehouse complained that the vendor's standard coating on forklifts and conveyors was deteriorating, causing the equipment to rust and corrode. To avoid this, special painting instructions and specifications became part of the ordering specification for this kind of equipment. If the problem is very serious, inspectors should be on-site to inspect the equipment before it is painted (for surface cleanliness, etc.) and to assure that the correct coating (as specified by the operating company) has been used. There are many cases where the painting contractor deliberately or inadvertently used the wrong paint. In cases where repainting is necessary, the job can become expensive and subject to litigation.

Intermediate and Topcoats

As with primers, intermediate coats must provide a satisfactory bond with succeeding coats to provide pinhole-free surfaces (as required). They also act as a barrier to a corrosive atmosphere should the topcoat break down.

The topcoat itself is the first barrier to corrosion and weathering as well as being the surface seen by management and the public. However, in some situations the barrier to the environment is primarily a function of the body of the prime coat, while the finish coat provides a pleasing appearance, a nonskid surface, a matrix for antifouling agents, or other specialized purposes. Obviously, the chemical resistance of the finish coat in such a situation must be sufficient to assure there is no failure.

The above discussion identifies key problem areas and general "choice" considerations; however, there are thousands of different chemical environments and dozens of basic types of coatings. The job now is to reduce this number complex into some form of matrix that makes specification possible. To start, one should look at the various types of coatings available.

Inorganic Zinc

This is the workhorse coating of the CPI. Because of its cathodic qualities, it provides excellent corrosion resistance on carbon steels, and damaged surfaces still maintain some degree of resistance to rusting under the coating surface. Some zinc-rich systems still provide adequate protection after 25 years. The basic functioning of inorganic zinc-rich paints (Appendix 5) has not changed in recent years; however, the zinc-loading has changed. Two component inorganic zinc-rich primers now contain as little as $11^1/_2$ pounds of zinc dust per gallon compared to historical highs of 14 pounds per gallon or more. The newer versions can give adequate protection depending on the amount of binder used because the amount of zinc in the final film may actually be more (as much as 91%) than the higher loaded predecessor paints.

Inorganic zinc-silicate coatings have an excellent history in hot, dry services, such as on the exterior of mufflers and stacks. Used alone, they can be successfully employed at temperatures to 800°F (427°C). When topcoated with a high-heat silicone coating (Appendix 6), they can be used at temperatures up to 1000°F (538°C). In the latter case it is imperative that the silicone be applied to the inorganic coating prior to the inorganic film being heated to any temperature above 300°F (149°C).

Organic Zinc

Primers made from zinc dust plus an organic elastomer are not as widely used as inorganic zinc coatings. Organic binders such as epoxies, vinyls, acrylics, etc. can encapsulate the metal particles, thus inhibiting the cathodic protection qualities that are the prime reason for using zinc-rich paints.

Urethanes

These products are finding much wider acceptance in the CPI, especially for high build applications on tanks and similar equipment. Polyurethane coatings have been successfully applied for a number of years. 100% solids polyurethane coatings (Table 3) are used as linings over steel or concrete in large storage tanks that hold crude oil, jet fuel, diesel fuel, unleaded gasoline, caustic solutions, and other refined product storage tanks. Polyurethane coatings, in contrast to more brittle coatings, are less likely to suffer from cracking and separation because they retain their flexibility and abrasion resistance. They have several benefits (Table 4).

TABLE 3 100% Solids Polyurethane Coatings[a]

Excellent corrosion resistance
Superior flexibility and impact strength
Excellent chemical and abrasion resistance
Fast room temperature cure
Superior dielectric strength
Excellent adhesion
Excellent tensile strength and elongation
Applied with conventional two-component equipment
Up to 200 mils per pass
Solvent free
Avoid pinholing with 100% solids

Two-Component Polyurethane Coatings

Chemical properties:	
Raw material base	Isocyanate/Polyol
Solids	100%
Application/storage considerations:	
Pot life (2 fl oz)	30 s to 30 min[b]
Tack-free time (30 mils)	20 to 30 min at 77°F
Blending ratio	2:1 ratio by volume
Storage life	6 months in original unopened containers
Application temperature	20–140°F
Film build	In excess of 200 mils in one application or vertical surface
Physical properties:	
Color	Blend–ivory
Weight/gallon	9.1–9.4 lb/gal
Hardness (Shore D), ASTM D-2240-75	65–75 D[b]
Tensile strength, ASTM D-638-56T	2000–3000 lb/in.^{2} [b]
Elongation, ASTM D-638-56T	50–75%[b]
Impact, ASTM G-14	Up to 160 in./lb[b]
Compressive, ASTM D-695-63T	Up to 30,000 lb/in.^{2} [b]
Tear strength, ASTM D-624-54T	Up to 500 lb/in.^{2} [b]
Flexibility	180° bend over 1/8 in. at 30 mils
(Federal Test Standards, 141 Method 6221)	Mandril
Performance characteristics:	
High temperature resistance	Intermittent to 350°F, long term 200°F
Chemical resistance	Excellent in most cases
Moisture vapor transmission, ASTM E-398	0.005 perms
Cathodic disbondment, ASTM G-3	Very good to excellent
Abrasion resistance	47 mg loss, CS-17, Tabor Abrader Wheel, 1000 g load, 1000 cycles
Adhesion	Excellent up to 2500 lb/in.^{2}

[a]Source: Thanecoat Inc., Houston, Texas.
[b]Coating systems available within these ranges.

TABLE 4 The Benefits of Using Polyurethane Coatings[a]

Ease of application:
Reduced labor and staging due to single coat application
Sag-free vertical and overhead application
Time-saving one step coating
Up to 200 mils per pass without running or sagging
Minimum production loss due to reduced downtime
Equally suited over steel, concrete, and other construction materials
Excellent chemical and corrosion resistance:
Resists most acids, oils, fuels, and other products associated with pertrochemical processing
Withstands extreme pH changes
Superior flexibility and elongation properties:
Flexibility to withstand stress movement of floaters and riveted seam tanks
Ability to adjust to wide temperature fluctuations
Excellent for reconditioning tanks:
Tanks can be put back into service much more quickly using fast-cure urethane systems compared to other lining systems
Highly corrosive and abrasive environments are the standard operating service of polyurethanes. Adding to their superior moisture sealant characteristics, they become the most logical choice for those impossible solution problems
Excellent for tube sheet and water box sealant:
Rapid turn around on emergency repairs

[a]Source: Thanecoat Inc., Houston, Texas.

Epoxies

Various types of epoxies are currently available: Catalyzed, baking-type, and oil modified. The latter have qualities inbetween conventional alkyd enamels and truly chemical resistant coatings.

Outside weatherability of epoxy coatings has improved considerably over the past 5 years. They now display better chalk resistance than the first generation materials and offer good resistance to many organic and inorganic chemicals. Catalyzed epoxies come in four varieties. Amine-cured systems display the best solvent and acid resistance of coatings of this generic type. Polyamide-cured epoxies have less general chemical resistance, but are superior to amine-cured types in water resistance, weather resistance, and ability to adhere to difficult surfaces.

Amine-adduct-cured materials are based on the prereaction of a portion of the catalyst with the epoxy resin. Such materials are less sensitive to climatic conditions than amine-cured epoxies and are considered the equal of either amine or polyamide variations.

High-baked epoxies display the best chemical and solvent resistance of any type of epoxy but, as their name implies, require very-high-temperature baking to achieve complete polymerization. Use of this type of epoxy is normally limited to the interior of tanks handling concentrated caustics or solvents. Some epoxy-based materials are extremely weak in acid and water service, and they also show a marked tendency to discolor and chalk.

Coal Tar Epoxies

These are a combination of thermosetting and thermoplastic resins usually containing about 35% epoxy. The product produces film with good acid and water resistance.

Vinyl

When considering resistance to wide savings in pH, vinyl-based coatings excel. The films are thermoplastic and thus can be recoated easily. Vinyl-resin coatings are limited in solvent and heat resistance (they are temperature-sensitive above 150–180°F or 66–82°C). In addition, they display a marked tendency to be sensitive to intercoat contamination. The films have greater strength in tension than in adhesion, and this can lead to widespread peeling in sheets if surface preparation specs are not followed closely.

Given this overview, the paint specifier has to establish whether a job should be shop primed and coated or field primed and coated. There are certain advantages to each, especially when it comes to straight run piping (see *Paint Handbook*, by Guy E. Weismantel, McGraw-Hill, New York, 1981). Shop application and economics are also discussed in various NACE (National Association of Corrosion Engineers) publications.

For general maintenance painting, or for grassroots projects, many coatings selections will be the same although repainting may only require addition of "X" mils of top coat. For some equipment and structures, Table 5 offers selection criteria.

Surface Preparation

It is false economy for any plant of significant size to be without copies of basic SSPC (Steel Structure Painting Council) and NACE (National Association of Corrosion Engineers) specifications for surface preparation and coatings. These specifications and/or guidelines offer excellent surface preparation procedures. Appendix 7 highlights some of the key points covered under SSPC, and Appendix 8 covers NACE information. See Appendix 9 for blasting guidelines.

It is common to run into a variety of types of surfaces to be painted in a CPI plant; however, the two most often found in these facilities are metal and concrete. The following two sections cover the general surface preparations used for metal and concrete.

TABLE 5 Some Typical Paint Selection Guidelines[a]

Surface	Surface Preparation	Example of One System That Can Be Recommended	Mils
Structural steel	Commercial blast	Inorganic zinc	3
		Epoxy-polyamide	4
Steel pipe (above ground)	Commercial blast	Inorganic zinc	3
		Epoxy coal tar	8
Steel pipe (below ground)	Near-white blast	Epoxy coal tar	8
		Epoxy coal tar	8
Galvanized metal	Solvent or etch preparation	Self-priming copolymer	4
General service tanks	Commercial blast	Modified vinyl primer	2
		Vinyl topcoat	3
	Commercial blast	Chlorinated rubber	2
		Chlorinated rubber	3
	Commercial blast	Inorganic zinc	1½
		Vinyl	4
Water tanks	While metal blast	American Water Works specifications	
Process equipment	Commerical blast	Inorganic zinc	3
		Appropriate chemical resistant topcoat	4
Incinerators	Commercial blast	Inorganic zinc	3
	Modified silicone		2
Steel cooling towers	Near-white metal blast	Epoxy coal tar	8
		Epoxy coal tar	8
	White metal blast	Inorganic zinc	1
		Epoxy coal tar	8
		Epoxy coal tar	8

[a]Source: Weismantel International, Kingwood, Texas.

Metal Preparation for Product Finishes*

Why Metal Preparation Has Become Increasingly Important

Many factors contribute toward producing the optimum end results from industrial coatings. One of the most important of these is surface preparation. This section deals with the most common metals used in today's industrial products and covers the most generally accepted metal cleaning processes of industrial finishers.

*Reprinted with permission from The Sherwin-Williams Co., copyright © 1982.

It is almost impossible to read trade and finishing journals which do not contain at least one article on the subject of metal preparation. It may be asked—"Why?" Products have been painted for years and it is comparatively recent that such emphasis has been placed on the subject.

An obvious cause is the trend toward increased and varied metal fabrication. Greater use of aluminum, magnesium, zinc, and other metals has created new problems. The fundamental reason is continued demand for better paint performance. Not only has this fact, in itself, necessitated higher standards in each step of a finishing process, but it has also brought about many basic changes in paint formulations.

In the era of long-oil, slow-drying type paints, oil on the surface was often compatible with the paint and absorbed by the paint film without any appreciable loss of adhesion. The newer, fast-drying resins unfortunately are, in general, incompatible with rustproofing oils, drawing compounds, etc. If these paints are applied over such foreign substances, proper adhesion is impossible.

Metal preparation covers two steps in the finishing process, *cleaning* and *treatment—cleaning* being the removal of foreign substances, and *treatment* that operation performed to improve adhesion and ultimate durability by etching, depositing other substances, or otherwise changing the surface character of the metal. In some instances, both of these steps are performed in one operation, though generally to a limited degree.

Metal Cleaning

Purpose. To remove dirt, rust, rustproofing, and drawing oils and compounds, fingerprints, mill scale, and many other foreign substances, both visible and invisible, thereby improving adhesion and reducing the tendency to blister and corrode on exposure.

Methods: 1. Solvent Cleaning

A. Wiping. This consists of simply washing off the surface with petroleum or aromatic solvents, using rags or sponges. The method is widely applicable, but because rags and solvent are immediately contaminated with grease and dirt, a complete cleaning is practically impossible, and the method is recommended only as a last resort. Unless noninflammable solvents are used, fire hazard is an additional objection.

B. Solvent-Jet Cleaning. In its simplest form, this method consists of spraying solvent, generally naphtha or mineral spirits, or xylol or mixtures thereof, on the surface in a washing action. A spray gun with the fan turned down makes a good "jet." The method can be likened to hosing leaves and dirt off the sidewalk.

This method is applicable on large units not easily put through washing machines. Partially concealed surfaces are more readily reached. Solvents are not re-used, eliminating recontamination. The volume of solvent used is generally not large. Excessively heavy grease deposits can be removed, preceding other cleaning methods. The chief objection is the fire hazard.

C. Vapor Degreasing. This is a common, solvent-type cleaning method. The use of chlorinated solvents such as trichlorethylene and perchlorethylene in closed-cycle degreasing systems has found widespread application where further treatment is not necessary, although occasionally a vapor degreaser will precede a phosphatizing process. These degreasers may employ vapor or liquid-phase cleaning with or without spray scrubbing action.

Most commonly, the cold article to be cleaned is placed in the vapors which condense and run off until the metal has reached the temperature of the vapors. On removal, it is dry and grease-free.

The solvents used are not particularly effective in removing soaps, oxidized lanolin, tightly adhering dirt, rust, etc.

Costs are generally somewhat higher than alkaline cleaning.

2. Alkaline Cleaning

The alkaline cleaners are the most common cleaners in use. They are low in cost and generally effective. Available under numerous proprietary names, they consist of alkaline salts, soaps, detergents, etc., and vary in composition depending on the type of equipment used and cleansing requirements. They are used both in power washers and in soak or dip tanks. Sometimes an electric current is added for faster and more complete cleaning. The method, much more common in the plating industry, is known as electrolytic cleaning and can be either cathodic or anodic.

Alkaline cleaners are generally used as hot solutions, at strengths ranging from 1/8 to 16 oz/gal. Temperatures of the solution run from 170 to 212°F.

Cleaning action results from emulsification or saponification of oils and dirt. Efficiency is dependent on agitation in dip or soak tanks and on the scouring action of the sprays in power washers.

Rinsing is of extreme importance in using alkaline cleaners. Alkali left on the surface attacks the paint film, causing early failure by loss of adhesion and blistering. In extreme cases, particularly where pigments (some reds, blues, and greens) susceptible to alkali are used, actual discoloration occurs.

Since the rinse water is rapidly contaminated by the alkali being "dragged-over." it is necessary to overflow the rinse tank by continuous addition of fresh water. As a rule, the rinse water should be hot—180–212°F—both to obtain more efficient rinsing and faster drying off of cleaned parts.

In practice, sufficient heat is not always available to keep the tank hot and overflowing rapidly. In such cases, as well as where "drag-over" is abnormally high, it may be desirable to use two rinses—the first cold and the second hot. The cold tank can then be overflowed more rapidly, the hot tank at a slower rate.

In many plants the water is very hard. As there are numerous objections to excessively hard water, softened water or steam condensate may be necessary. The calcium and magnesium salts in hard water may break down at the high temperature and leave deposits on the work.

Reducing the temperature of the water may tend to eliminate these deposits, but even when in solution, some of the salts will remain on the metal. If these are subsequently painted over, early failure by blistering can be expected.

Since aluminum is readily attacked by alkali, use alkaline cleaning on this surface with caution and always in accordance with the manufacturer's directions.

3. Emulsion Cleaners

These are made up of soaps, detergents, and grease solvents. When mixed with water—from 10 to 100 parts of water to 1 part cleaner—they form neutral to slightly alkaline emulsions. Some are mixed with higher boiling naphthas.

Emulsion cleaners are generally used in the same way as alkali cleaners—in power washers or soak tanks followed by rinsing. It is claimed that they are more efficient in removing certain contaminates like carbon smut, drawing compound fillers, etc. They may also be faster with certain oils. Being more nearly neutral, they are somewhat less hazardous to use.

Alkali cleaners will attack such metals as tin, aluminum, and zinc. Where this is not permissible, less alkaline emulsion cleaners may be successfully used.

Some emulsion cleaners are claimed to have rust inhibitive properties to prevent rust formation after cleaning and before painting. These are not usually rinsed off, or a small amount of the cleaner is added to the rinse tank.

Where adhesion and good durability are critical, this method of rustproofing is not satisfactory, since it is dependent on a film of rustproofing oil or other equally objectionable matter.

4. Acid Cleaners

A. Pickling. This method is used primarily to remove rust and scale. If the metal is greasy, pickling generally follows another form of cleaning, such as alkaline cleaning.

Pickling acids vary in strength with the severity of rust and scale. An 8–10% solution of sulfuric acid, at 140–160°F, will remove heavy deposits. Solutions of commercial hydrochloric acid are effective removers of lighter rust deposits. Because of hazards involved in the use of this and other acid solutions, metal-cleaning and treatment specialists must be consulted for proper instructions.

Proprietary pickling solutions contain inhibitors to limit the attack on the base metal. After pickling, thorough rinsing is necessary. Acid pickled steel is in a very active state and rusts readily; painting or other treatment should follow immediately. This flash rusting can be controlled by rinsing in weak phosphoric and/or chromic acid solution. Fumes from hot sulfuric and hydrochloric acids are very corrosive, and surrounding equipment must be properly protected. Nonfuming proprietary pickling solutions are available.

B. Phosphoric Acid Type Cleaners. Proprietary cleaners based on phosphoric acid and grease solvents which will remove moderate amounts of surface contamination are available. These are actually combination cleaners and treatments, since they etch and form protective iron-phosphate salts, giving improved paint adhesion and corrosion resistance.

The most common of these are the "wipe-on" cleaners which are very effective when properly used. Others are used in similar fashion to alkali and emulsion cleaners. These are often the most effective cleaners for use in the two-stage washers, although, for best results, 3 stages are recommended. Under this title, Met-L-Mate or Dual Etch may be used.

5. Burn-Off

By passing the article through an oven, usually heated with open gas burners to a relatively high temperature, residual oils are driven off or ignited. The method, at one time quite common, has been mostly replaced by chemical cleaning processes. Some forms of soil, particularly pigmented drawing compounds, are not removed and, as used in the past, the metal was in a rather active state and rusted readily unless further treated or immediately painted.

A modern version of the burn-off process was recently introduced. By using special burners, the metal is heated to the blue stage. The steel under these conditions does not rust readily and, its is claimed, makes a good painting surface.

6. Flame Cleaning

This method is used chiefly on structural steel to remove scale. A flame is directed at the steel, causing rapid heating and cooling when the flame is removed. Differences in expansion cause the scale to break away. Flame cleaning may also be used to remove condensed moisture.

7. Mechanical Cleaning

Scraping, wire brushing, or sanding by hand or with power tools can be effective if properly done. As a rule, only rust and loose mill scale are so removed. Complete removal of mill scale by these methods often increases the activity and tendency to corrode.

8. Blasting

Blasting with sand, shot, or grit is a very common method for cleaning large machines, railroad equipment, structural steel, etc. Blasting produces a chemically clean surface and, because of the surface roughness, gives excellent adhesion. Blasted surfaces rust very rapidly and painting should be done immediately. If this is not possible, washing with weak chromic acid solution will control rusting for moderate periods. (See Appendix 9.)

General: Precleaning

Where the article to be cleaned is very dirty, it is often possible to effect definite operation economy by including a precleaning stage to remove most of the dirt before going into the normal cleaning cycle. This avoids excessive contamination of the final cleaning bath and often permits use of lower cost chemical cleaners in the first stage.

Rustproofing

In many finishing cycles, there is a lapse of time between cleaning and subsequent painting. It is an unfortunate circumstance that clean metal often rusts more rapidly than dirty metal. As a result, some means of controlling flash rusting is necessary. Where cleaning is followed by a metal treatment in a continuous system, no problem exists, but if no subsequent treatment is used, it is necessary to passivate or protect the metal.

A frequent method following alkali or emulsion cleaning is to add chromic or chromic and phosphoric acid to the second rinse. Whether one or both are used will depend somewhat on the water condition involved.

Not only is the metal temporarily passivated, but corrosion resistance of the paint film is definitely improved.

There are numerous proprietary compounds available for this purpose. Many contain emulsifiable oils which, while effective in preventing flash rust, do impair adhesion. They are recommended only for less critical uses where long life of the paint is not expected.

Chemical Treatments

It is now standard practice to chemically treat metals after cleaning to further improve adhesion, corrosion, and humidity resistance. The most common chemical treatments are based on phosphoric acid and may be classified into two groups: Crystalline and Amorphous.

1. Crystalline Phosphate

There are several patented systems employing the phosphate principle which include proper cleaning followed by chemical treatment. The phosphating solutions consist of phosphoric acid and metal phosphates which react with and deposit complex crystals on the metal.

The crystalline, somewhat porous surface is excellent as a paint base, giving improved adhesion, corrosion, and corrosion creep resistance.

Most commonly, the treatment consists of three stages:

1. Phosphating solution
2. Hot water rinse
3. Hot, dilute chromic acid rinse

The three stages may be either spray or dip, with spray being preferred since it permits better control of the crystal size. Large crystals reduce gloss of the finishing paint and may be excessively brittle.

2. Amorphous Phosphate

Except as already discussed under "Acid Cleaners," the amorphous types are used in much the same way as the crystalline types.

While generally they do not contribute quite as much to the ultimate durability of the paint finish, they do have a number of advantages. They are generally lower in cost and, being noncrystalline, they have less effect on gloss.

The amorphous chemical treatments are recommended for use both with and without the final chromic acid rinse. For best results, the chromic acid rinse is desirable since it has been proved that where the final rinse is neutral (clean water), the resistance to corrosion is much lower. In fact, under certain conditions, a cleaning cycle with a chromic acid rinse is preferable to using a cleaning-phosphating cycle without the final acid rinse.

Treatment of Various Metals: Zinc

Paint adheres poorly to new zinc, possibly due both to the smooth surface and to chemical reaction between the metal and the paint. This is sometimes known as "alkaline peeling."

Weathering, mechanical roughening, or simple etching of zinc surfaces improves paint adhesion. However, for added corrosion resistance, a chemical treatment is desirable. Best results are generally obtained with the crystalline phosphate types, although the amorphous types are ample for many uses.

Zinc-coated steels with phosphate treatment are marketed under various trade names. These usually give good paint performance without the need for additional cleaning or treatment unless contaminated during fabrication.

Since zinc is reactive to alkalis and acids, care must be exercised in choosing the proper cleaner to avoid excessive attack of the metal.

Aluminum

Aluminum is, in itself, very resistant to corrosion since on exposure a tight film of oxide forms which protects the base metal from further corrosion. Intermediate treatments are unnecessary except under extreme humidity or salt air conditions.

Most paints, however, do not adhere well to aluminum, and treatments are generally necessary to prevent embrittling and loss of adhesion.

For many purposes, phosphoric acid type treatments are satisfactory. These may be either the wipe-on, spray, or dip type. Hot, dilute chromic acid gives similar results.

Where exposure conditions are more severe, anodizing or alkaline dichromate give better results. These processes form protective coatings which are excellent bases for paint. Both processes are slow, requiring up to 30-min immersions. Since aluminum is readily attacked by alkali, use alkaline cleaning on this surface with caution and always in accordance with the manufacturer's directions.

Proprietary aluminum treatments are available which give about equal results with much shorter reaction times. Costs are usually considerably lower.

When aluminum is assembled in contact with steel, it is generally recommended that both surfaces be primed before the final operation. Unless so insulated, electrolysis takes place at the joint, causing galvanic corrosion of the aluminum.

Magnesium

Paint applied to magnesium is subject to "alkaline peeling" similar to that experienced with zinc.

Most magnesium products are finished with a protective chemical coating, even before final fabrication of the product. This coating is intended to protect the metal during storage, shipment, and manufacture. The chrome pickle process, knows as Dow No. 1, is used for this purpose. The treatment is a short immersion in a solution of nitric acid and sodium dichromate.

The coating is suitable as a paint base but cannot be used where close tolerances are required, due to etching of the metal. The dichromate process, known as Dow No. 7, is the best for corrosion resistance and is widely used as a base for painting. Owing to certain hazards involved, manufacturer's recommendations must be followed implicitly. Under no circumstances should the process be undertaken without proper investigation.

Magnesium can also be anodized, producing a coating which has excellent corrosion resistance.

Cleaning-Treatment Systems

Factors Affecting Choice

The proper choice of cleaning and treatment systems must be made by the manufacturer of the articles to be processed. Not only do the various methods vary in efficiency, but the number of stages through which the work is put will affect the final results.

Some of the many factors that must be considered, are:

1. The kind of metal (steel, aluminum, etc.)
2. The kind of soil (rust, dirt, grease, drawing compounds, etc.)
3. Ultimate durability required of the finish
   (a) Will the article be exposed to high humidity, salt atmosphere, etc.?
   (b) Is it a short- or long-life article?
   (c) Is the finish purely decorative, or must it also protect?
4. Initial cost
5. Operation space available
6. Competitors' methods

These points are of such scope and involve basic policy to such an extent that only those responsible for the manufacture and sale of the article in question can give them proper weight and consideration.

Types of Cleaning-Treatment Systems

It would be impossible within the scope of this section to consider all the possible cleaning-treatment systems. They may consist of simply one stage or operation, or 10 to 12 stages. Only some of the more commonly encountered are considered below.

One-Stage Operation—Types

1. Burn-off
2. Blasting
3. Mechanical cleaning
4. Solvent cleaning
5. Acid cleaning (occasionally)

Within the scope of their applicability, these systems give satisfactory results. Single-stage alkali, emulsion, and some acid cleaners cannot generally be considered satisfactory prepainting preparations. Deposits left on metal are often more harmful than the soil they remove.

Two-Stage Operation

Two-stage power washers are quite common in industry. Usually an alkali or emulsion cleaner is used in the first stage, followed by a rinse.

One of the major objections to a two-stage washer is the lack of control of flash rusting if the work is not immediately painted. Since steel in an alkaline state will rust more slowly than when neutral, and since some emulsion cleaners have rust inhibitors added, it is an all too common practice to allow the rinse tank to become contaminated by the cleaner. Most often the rinse could then just as well have been omitted entirely.

If the soil is such that it can satisfactorily be removed by one of the available acid cleaners, these are generally preferable for use in two stages. (Heavy grease and certain drawing compounds are effectively removed.) By using these acid cleaners, moderate contaminations of the rinse tank will have less adverse effect on adhesion, etc. than will even slight alkali contaminations.

Three-Stage Operation

Three stages should be considered the minimum for general fabrication:

1. Cleaning—alkali, emulsion, or acid
2. Rinse

3. Rinse with dilute chromic acid ($^1/_{16}$—$^1/_{10}$%) (for certain water conditions, some phosphoric acid may be used)

The first rinse must be thorough to prevent any cleaner, particularly alkali, from being dragged into the final rinse and neutralizing the acid.

This system rustproofs the steel sufficiently to prevent flash rust for short periods. The final acid rinse adds some corrosion resistance, but since, at the strength used, there is no acid etching, adhesion is promoted only to the extent that the metal is clean.

Four-Stage Operation

1. Alkali or emulsion cleaning
2. Rinse
3. Phosphating solution
4. Rinse

A moderately good system with improved adhesion due to the phosphating solution which may be either the crystalline or amorphous type. The main objection is the lack of a final acid rinse. Normal tap water is usually slightly alkaline, and some of the corrosion and blister resistance gained from the third operation is lost in the fourth stage.

1. Vapor degrease
2. Phosphating solution (crystalline or amorphous)
3. Rinse
4. Chromic acid rinse

Where the soil present is such that vapor degreasing will remove is sufficiently, so that the phosphating action can proceed without hindrance, this system is equal to the more generally applicable five- and six-stage operations systems.

Five- and Six-Stage Operations

1: Clean—alkali or emulsion. 2 or 2 and 3: One or two rinses. 3 or 4: Phosphating—crystalline or amorphous. 4 or 5: Rinse. 5 or 6: Chromic acid rinse.

Whether one or two rinses must be used after cleaning will depend on local conditions, efficiency of the rinse, drag-over, etc. This type of system is generally used—particularly with the crystalline phosphate—for such items as washing machines and refrigerators, where maximum paint performance is required.

Additional modification of this basic system could include precleaning where excessively heavy soil, rust, etc. exist.

Summary

1. The object of cleaning the metal is:
   a. To condition it for subsequent metal treatment.
   b. To remove all contamination, dirt, oil drawing compounds, etc. which prevent proper adhesion of paint.
   c. To remove all soluble salts, sulfates and chlorides in particular, which promote blistering by osmosis and incite rust on exposure. Hardness of the rinse water must be considered since the salts present may themselves cause premature blistering.
2. When using chemical cleaners, thorough rinsing is mandatory. A cold overflowing rinse is generally preferable to a hot still rinse. The final rinse in any system should never be alkaline. Preferably, it should be acidified with chromic or chromic-phosphoric acid.
3. Metal treatment is used to:
   a. Improve adhesion.
   b. Improve durability by increasing corrosion resistance.
4. Chemical cleaning can be done either in power-spray washers or dip tanks. Different chemicals are usually used and the manufacturer's recommendation should be followed.
5. Rustproofing compounds which leave alkaline, soluble salt, or oily deposits are not satisfactory to paint over.
6. To provide a barrier between the metal and subsequent paint coats which will prevent a possible reaction between the metal (e.g., zinc) and the paint vehicle which results in loss of adhesion.

Concrete Preparation for Product Finishes*

Cement, which in concrete is combined with water, sand, gravel, and crushed stone, is essentially a powdered mixture of complex calcium silicates, aluminates, and aluminum ferrites. These compounds bind with water to form monolithic stone via hydration. The first stage of the hardening process is curing, which takes about 28 d; further hardening will continue for years. During the initial hardening of the concrete, a certain amount of free lime is separated and is gradually converted into calcium carbonate by reaction with carbon dioxide from surrounding air—or water, if the concrete is submerged. This reaction enhances concrete strength.

Concrete composition and properties can vary considerably, even in pours made on the same day, by the same crew, using the same raw materials. Variations may result from fluctuations in raw-material uniformity, incomplete mixing, differences in the amount of working during placement, and weather changes affecting the rate of hydration.

*By Dean M. Berger. Excerpted by special permission from *Chemical Engineering*, p. 141 ff., October 25, 1976, copyright © 1976 by McGraw-Hill, New York, New York 10020.

Remedying Reinforcement Corrosion

The pH of concrete is normally 12 or 13. Steel used in reinforcement rods becomes passive when pH rises above 11.5. However, in some environments, such as in the ocean, the pH of concrete may drop to 6 to 7, a range in which steel corrodes readily. Chlorine-free concrete has a high resistance to the flow of electric current; but when chlorides are added, this resistance is lowered 5 to 10 times, advancing the corrosion of the reinforcing steel. When reinforcing rods corrode, their corrosion products increase their volume, resulting in cracking of the concrete.

Two other factors affecting the corrosion of reinforcing steel are concrete cover and porosity. The closer the steel is to the surface and the higher the porosity, the greater the susceptibility to corrosion.

The most popular remedies for corrosion of reinforcing steel are the use of: (1) coatings—both metallic and dielectric ones such as coal tar and epoxy powder; (2) nonsacrificial coatings—steel can be clad with copper and nickel, an expensive but successful tactic as long as a break does not occur; and (3) sacrificial coatings, such as zinc-rich galvanizing. The addition of corrosion inhibitors to reinforced concrete is widely thought to weaken it.

Concrete Types

The ASTM standard C-150 [1] defines portland cement as a hydraulic cement manufactured from pulverized clinker that consists mainly of hydraulic calcium silicates, and contains one or more calcium-sulfate forms as an interground addition (Table 6). Air-entraining cements are portland cements to which air-entraining substances such as greases, tallow, salts, or alkalis are added. Hydraulic cements are cements that set quickly and do not shrink while curing; such cements will cure underwater.

TABLE 6 Eight Types of Portland Cement Have Been Defined in ASTM C-150 [1]

Type	Application
I	Used when the special properties specified for any other type are not required. This type is called "natural" cement and is defined as a hydraulic cement produced by calcining a naturally occurring argillaceous limestone at a temperature below the sintering point and then grinding to a fine powder.
IA	Air-entraining cement for the same uses as Type I, where air entrainment is desired.
II	For general use; more especially when moderate sulfate resistance or moderate heat of hydration is desired.
IIA	Air-entraining cement for the same uses as Type II.
III	Offers high early strength.
IIIA	Air-entraining cement for the same uses as Type III.
IV	For use where a low heat of hydration is preferred.
V	For use where high sulfate resistance is preferred.

Coating Application Practices

For best results, concrete surfaces that are to be coated should be clean, dry, and well-cured. In general, poured concrete should be cured for at least 30 d at temperatures over 70°F before film-forming coatings are applied. This curing period enables the concrete to attain sufficient hardness and cuts down on coating blistering by permitting excess water to evaporate. Recommended curing time varies from 28 d to 6 mo, depending on service conditions and coating type. Concrete slabs, block, and pipe are generally steam cured during manufacture and can be coated at any subsequent time if they are clean and dry.

Whenever curing agents are used to retard the release of water, they should be selected carefully. Chlorinated rubber or vinyl solutions have been popular for such applications and satisfy the general requirements of ASTM C-309-73. Recently, two-component epoxy coatings have been recommended for use both as curing membranes and as form-release agents. These coatings eliminate the need for sandblasting or acid-etching, and consequently lower the application cost of epoxy coating systems [5].

Other curing compounds, such as mineral oils or wax, must be removed (often by blast cleaning) before a permanent, adhesive coating is applied.

Chemical Resistance of Coatings

Coatings become necessary whenever the surface is exposed to an environment that includes chemical fumes, splashes, and immersion.

Such environments occur in catch basins and sewage pipe, which may be subject to attack and deterioration in acids. For example, H_2S-containing sewer gas condenses on the walls of sewers and on the undersides of tank covers in waste treatment plants. Weak hydrogen-sulfide acid forms water-soluble lime salts that can be leached out of concrete. In contact with air, these salts oxidize to calcium sulfate—destructive because it combines with the alumina found in all cements to form calcium aluminum sulfate.

This double salt crystallizes with 30 molecules of water and expands to burst the concrete. Once the concrete has been split open, water can enter the crack and react with unstable calcium aluminum sulfate to yield aluminum hydroxide and gypsum. Gypsum crystallizes out, and the aluminum hydroxide separates as a slimy, cheesy mass—positive proof that the concrete is disintegrating. It should be recognized that this type of disintegration takes place mainly above the water level; below the water level, H_2S attack is not as serious as leaching is [4].

Products that destroy concrete are sulfates of sodium, magnesium, and ammonium—as found in seawater, factory wastes, and some groundwater. Other chemical solutions that attack concrete include sugar, fermenting liquids, ammonium chloride, magnesium chloride, ferric chloride, ammonium nitrate, vegetable and animal fats and oils, and mineral oils that contain free acids.

Concrete coatings also help to guard against physical attack from moisture. Moisture penetrates concrete by capillary action. In cold weather the moisture freezes in pores, swells up, and causes spalling. Coatings and other protective treatments are designed to prevent moisture from entering concrete pores.

Coatings provide a tank lining that protects the concrete from stored solutions by preventing the liquid from leaking through the concrete via capillary action.

Coatings also provide a surface that will prevent product contamination. Linings forestall the leaching of concrete constituents into solution.

In the design of small concrete tanks, expansion joints should be avoided, since they are often the target of chemical attack. In larger tanks, chemical-resistant joints composed of PVC, polysulfide, or asphalt-epoxy have been used successfully. Joints in the tank form must be made as smooth as possible so as to provide a flat surface for the coating or liner. A strong, dense concrete mix with ample steel reinforcement to reduce movement and cracking of the tank is advised.

Recently developed monomers such as methyl methacrylate or styrene-butadiene can be entrained in poured concrete to augment chemical resistance. Polymer-impregnated concrete (PIC) absorbs 90–98% less moisture than conventional concrete and sharply reduces penetration by salt solutions [6].

Surface Preparation before Coating

The overall performance of any coating depends on the surface of the concrete to be coated. All foreign matter must be removed completely to ensure good bonding. To protect concrete against chemical attack, the coating should be porefree.

Potential troublemakers in applying coatings to concrete are laitance, efflorescence, form oils and waxes, air pockets, and concrete hardeners.

The best surface for coatings is one that has the texture of medium-grade sandpaper but is not powdery. Heavy-duty epoxy surfacers may require a broom-stroked finish to improve adhesion if sandblasting has not been used to roughen the concrete surface.

Laitance and Efflorescence

Laitance is an incompletely hydrated cement scum which floats up and clings loosely to the surface of a pour. The resulting powder is found on all poured work and prevails on floors and on the insides of centrifugally spun pipe. Since the bonding and strength of laitance are poor, any coating applied over it will eventually peel. For the best coating performance, laitance should be removed by whip sandblasting, dry abrasion, vacuum blasting, abrasive blasting with water injection, high-pressure water blasting (with or without abrasive), or acid-etching. Concrete that is to be coated should be finished with a wooden float rather than steel trowels which induce glazing .

In general, acid-etching is most effective for preparing horizontal surfaces such as floors. Sandblasting is better suited to walls.

Efflorescence results from the deposition of water-soluble salts. During curing, moisture moves from the interior of the concrete to the surface, from which it evaporates. Even after coating, if water continues to enter concrete, efflorescence can develop and disrupt a paint film. Efflorescence on concrete or brickwork (retaining walls) can be removed with muriatic acid. Its recurrence can be prevented with sound waterproofing.

If it is suspected that an underground or below-grade concrete surface is subject to excessive capillary moisture or hydrostatic pressure, a simple check should be run. The condition can be spotted by placing a rubber mat or plastic sheet over the finished concrete surface for a period of 10 h. If moisture collects under the cover, consult a coating supplier for specific recommendations on which penetrating compound to use. Obtain detailed instructions as to surface preparation and coating schedule.

Form Oils and Curing Compounds

In recent years a major source of coating failure in concrete tanks has been nonadherence caused by a film of form grease or oil that has been transferred from the forms to the concrete surface. Such films are used as freeing agents that facilitate the removal of forms; because even acid-etching does not clean form films satisfactorily, they should not be matched with surfaces that are to be protectively coated for chemical immersion [2].

Form oils containing large amounts of wax or soap are used because they strip easily. However, a residuum of these compounds remains on the concrete surface and is removed only by drastic measures such as sandblasting, detergent scrubbing, or flame volatilizing. The effect of these waxes or soaps on coatings is the same as on forms: the finished coating peels away readily from the surface. (Waxes used as curing compounds produce the same effect.) If concrete is to be coated for corrosion protection, it is preferred that the form be coated with a lacquer or hard epoxy that remains on the form when it is dismantled. Also, curing compounds should not be applied to tank bottoms, floors, and other areas that are to be coated later on.

Evidence of form-oil problems shows up quickly as cratering or "fish eyes" in the finished coating. Because the coating cannot wet the oil, it flows away from the oil-saturated area.

Recent use of nonmigrating epoxy-polyamide form-release agents and curing compounds has helped to eliminate this difficulty and yields concrete surfaces for which no further surface preparation is necessary. Epoxy topcoats may be applied immediately after curing.

Concrete Surface Characteristics

Air pockets or bubbles persist in the surface of all concrete, although good vibration and working techniques will minimize the number of surface imperfections that result.

Small surface holes and pits can be covered with a coating applied by spray, brush, or roller, but many will remain uncoated because air or solvent within the hole expands to cause blistering. If the coating at first bridges the void-space, the film literally dries from both sides and shrinks, leaving a hole. Subsequent coats meet the same fate.

Spray-squeegee-spray techniques have been adopted for applying high-solid epoxy surfacers. Such surfacers can be coated in extremely thin films—less that 5 mils—to provide an economical, "nuclear grade" coating system that can sustain decontamination. In less-critical applications, water-base epoxy surfacers offer excellent nonsagging characteristics as well as easy application and cleanup.

When air pockets reside beneath a thin layer of cement that has little strength, coatings applied over this layer can fail from either mechanical damage or from loss of adhesion. These pockets should be opened up by mechanical means or by whip sandblasting. The open pockets are then filled with cement plaster, thick organic coatings, or cement-latex coatings applied by brush, trowel, or squeegee.

"Sacking" a surface—i.e., dressing it with a carborundum stone and cement grout to fill voids—is useful if the procedure is performed soon after the forms are removed; timing is crucial in order to ensure that the pour surface and grout have roughly equal hydration times. Proper sacking begins with the brushing on of a coarse mortar, followed by rubbing with a clean, wet sack to remove surface scum and film.

(About the quickest way to ruin a concrete surface is to permit workmen to dress it up with a cement wash just prior to painting. Cement washes bond poorly to concrete because of their different hydration rates, and eventually powder or flake off, taking top paint with them.)

Concrete hardeners are sometimes used to increase surface hardness, decrease permeability to liquids, and provide added resistance to mild chemical attack. These hardeners are made from sodium silicate and magnesium, zinc, or lead fluorosilicates. Hardeners should *not* be used when coatings are to be applied, because hardeners migrate or float to the pour surface, embuing it with a glossy, greyish-brown appearance. Organic coatings will not adhere to the inorganic hardeners, and the latter cannot be removed by acid-etching. The only way to properly prepare a hardened concrete surface to receive paint is to sandblast it.

Before a solvent-based coating can be applied to a concrete surface, the surface should be dry throughout at least the top $^1/_{16}$ in. of depth. Dry concrete will appear to be light grey. In cases where there is a question about dryness, a commercial, probe-type moisture meter can be used.

Never encapsulate concrete that is incompletely dried with a nonbreathing film coating. Moisture trapped within will ultimately find its way out, and in doing so will dislodge the impermeable film. Ideally, one coating surface should be a "breather film" if the other is to be impermeable.

Types of Concrete Work

Different types of concrete work have inherently different surface characteristics. The most commonly encountered surface types are those of concrete blocks, poured-concrete walls, precast slabs, concrete floors, Gunite, packer-head pipe, tamped pipe, spun pipe, and hand-layup pipe components.

Concrete blocks present a uniform surface with round holes. The surface is strong because it is steam cured during processing. Although blocks themselves need no aging, the mortar lines between block construction do require aging before coating. Before the coating can be applied, the block must be cleaned of dust, dirt, and loose mortar. Painting with low-viscosity decorative topcoats without prior sealing leaves a very unsatisfactory appearance, because the paint is absorbed by the porous surface. A surfacing coat is recommended to plug all holes and kill porosity. Sealing by brushing, rolling, or spraying of thin-bodied sealers provides a porefree but not smooth surface. Smooth surfaces can be obtained on concrete block by troweling or squeegeeing onto it heavy-bodied thixotropic surfacing materials. The surfacing or sealing material should be compatible with the intended topcoat.

Poured-concrete walls have air bubbles and holes of various sizes and shapes at or near the surface. The difficulties with such imperfections have been mentioned already. Actual surface preparation depends on the desired chemical and physical characteristics of the finish. Immediately after the forms are stripped, and while the concrete is green, repairs on voids larger or deeper than 1/4 in. should be made with cement-sand grout smoothed flush with the surface. Grouted areas should be kept damp for 2 or 3 d to assure adhesion and strength. Laitance and dust should be removed by blasting or etching.

Sacking can be performed soon after the forms are stripped. Before the application of any surfacing material, holes and voids should be opened by blasting or power sanding. Sacking is not recommended for tank linings, however. For tank linings or immersion service, high-solid organic mastics can be squeegeed into voids; the lining should then be a coat of the same material. Although this type of sealing is a little more expensive, it is the best for chemical immersion service, which requires a nonporous, nonflaking surface finish.

Gunite and *sprayed concrete* display surfaces that are hard, dense, and free from air bubbles and cement laitance. Usually the only treatment needed before coating is to remove foreign matter, dirt, or dust that could impair coating adhesion. If a Gunite surface is too smooth because of after-troweling, acid-etching or blasting can be used to obtain a texture similar to medium-grade sandpaper.

Precast slabs have surface characteristics similar to poured walls. The slabs usually require grinding treatment of the joints. Steam curing during processing eliminates the need for aging.

Concrete floors do not contain major surface irregularities because of the use of hand or mechanical tool-working. Concrete floors are finished with steel, wood, or rubber trowels, or given a broomed finish, depending on the smoothness required. (A broomed finish is usually specified whenever heavy-duty epoxy surfacers are applied to concrete floors; the broomed finish promotes adhesion of the surfacer.) Regardless of the method used to finish floors, cement laitance will always remain on the surface; blasting or etching will remove it.

Packer-head pipe and *tamped pipe* have a dense finish akin to Gunite.

Hand-layup pipe, used for irregular shapes, has a finish that varies with the tools that have been used to work it—steel, wood, or rubber trowels. *Spun pipe* usually has surface characteristics intermediate between those of precast slabs and packer-head pipe.

To facilitate production, most pipe is steam cured and therefore requires no aging. It must, however, be dry before coating.

Inspection

One of the most overlooked duties of any concrete construction job is inspection. To ensure proper surface preparation and application of coatings, the American Society for Testing and Materials Committee DO1.43 has set down guidelines in its *Proposed Manual of Coating Work for Nuclear Power Plant Primary Containment Facilities*. The committee has written sections on concrete surface preparation, on qualification of journeyman painters for containment coatings, and on inspection of concrete coatings.

The inspector should be provided with a checklist for the various hold-points during concrete-surface preparation. He should identify curing compound, hardeners, form oil, spackling compounds, and grouts and caulking compounds.

The inspector should record the condition of the concrete, noting the following:

Honeycomb or porosity
Roughness or smoothness
Cracking
Efflorescence
Laitance
Looseness
Contaminants
Temperature and humidity
Excessive moisture
Type of cleaning method and abrasive used (sweep-blasting, sand-blasting, acid-etching, etc.)

The adherence of coatings to concrete can be monitored with an adhesion tester (such as the commercially available Elcometer), using epoxy glue to hold the test dolly in place. When the dolly is pulled free, the type of failure and the tensile strength of the adhesion should be recorded.

Performance of all coating application work should comply with Federal Law 29 CFR Part 1910 and Part 1926, the Occupational Safety and Health Act. OSHA Material Safety Data Sheets will be furnished by the coating supplier upon request. These are required where certain materials are applied in confined work areas.

References

1. *ASTM Annual Standards*, Vols. 13, 14, and 27, American Society for Testing and Materials, Philadelphia, Pennsylvania, 1975.
2. *Coatings and Linings for Immersion Service*, National Association of Corrosion Engineers, Houston, Texas, 1972.
3. *Proposed Manual of Coating Work for Nuclear Power Plant Primary Containment Facilities*, ASTM DO1.43, American Society for Testing and Materials, Philadelphia, Pennsylvania, 1975.
4. C. G. Pauli, *Coating of Concrete*, Koppers Co., Pittsburgh, Pennsylvania, 1975.
5. J. Prible, *Concrete Surfacers*, Ameron, Monterey Park, California, 1975.
6. Mehta, Menson, Chen, and Vanderhoff, "Polymer Impregnated Concrete: Field Studies," *Transp. Eng. J.*, February 1975.
7. W. H. Kuenning, "Characteristics of Masonry," *Off. Dig., Fed. Soc. Coating Technol.*, pp. 584–593 (June 1963).
8. R. C. Mielenz, "Concrete as a Substrate for Paint," *Off. Dig., Fed. Soc. Coating Technol.*, pp. 563–583 (June 1963).
9. *Textured Finishes for Slabs, Concrete Information*, Portland Cement Association, Skokie, Illinois.
10. *Concrete Finishes—Tolerances for Blemishes*, International Council for Building Research, Studies and Documentation, Rotterdam CB Report 24.

Paint Application

There are three considerations under paint application: First, there are certain coatings calculations estimating procedures that are part of any paint job. Second, the application should be done properly in accordance with the specification. Third, the whole painting program—especially application—should include specific procedures for inspection and quality control.

Coating Calculations

A number of shortcut procedures are available to the paint specifier in calculating paint required and application guidelines. Typical of these are nomograph estimates for coating tanks (Appendix 10). Many of the paint manufacturers offer handy reference data to assure accurate methods of estimating cost and application. Tables 7–18, Figs. 1–3, Appendixes 11 and 12 provide calculations and conversion specifics.

TABLE 7 Length

Inches	Feet	Yards	Miles	Millimeters	Meters
1	0.0833333	0.0277778	0.0000157828	25.4000508	0.0254000508
12	1	0.3333333	0.0001893939	304.8006096	0.30480061
36	3	1	0.0005681818	914.4018288	0.91440183
63360	5280	1760	1	1609347.219	1609.3472187
0.039370	0.00328083	0.00109361	0.0000006214	1	0.0001
39.270	3.2808333	1.0936111	0.0006213699	1000	1

TABLE 8 Area

Square Inches	Square Feet	Square Yards	Acres	Square Miles	Square Centimeters	Square Meters	Hectares
1	0.00694444	0.000771605			6.451625806	0.00064516258	
144	1	0.1111111	0.0000229568		929.0341161	0.09290341	0.0000092903
1296	9	1	0.0002066116	0.0000003228	8261.307045	0.83613071	0.000083613
6272640	43560	4840	1	0.0015625	40468726.10	4046.872610	0.40468726
4014489600	27878400	3097600	640	1		2589998.470	258.999847
0.1549997	0.00107639	0.000119599			1	0.0001	
1549.9969	10.7638673	1.1959853	0.0002471044	0.0000003861	10000	1	0.0001
15499969	107638.673	11959.8526	2.4710439	0.0003861006		1000	1

TABLE 9 Various Size Elevated Water Tanks[a]

Capacity (thousand gallons)	Riser (Diameter, ft)	Inside Area (ft^2)	Outside Area[b] (ft^2)
50	4	3,150	6,500
100	4	4,300	8,000
150	4	5,100	9,900
200	4	5,900	11,100
250	4	6,700	12,700
500	5	10,000	19,600
750	Dry 8	13,600	29,100
1000	Dry 8	17,000	36,900

[a]Low water level 100 ft above grade.
[b]Includes supporting columns.

TABLE 10 Various Sizes of Cylindrical Tanks

Capacity (bbl)	Tank Dimensions (ft and in.)		Roof Area (ft^2)	Shell Area (ft^2)
	Diameter	Height		
150	10-0	10-3	80	315
300	12-0	15-0	115	565
500	20-0	10-0	315	630
1,000	20-0	18-0	315	1,130
2,000	25-0	24-0	490	1,885
3,000	25-0	36-0	490	2,890
5,000	30-0	40-0	705	3,770
5,000	35-0	30-0	960	3,300
10,000	42-6	40-0	1,415	5,340
10,000	45-0	36-0	1,590	5,090
15,000	48-0	48-0	1,810	7,240
15,000	52-0	40-0	2,125	6,535
20,000	60-0	40-0	2,825	7,540
25,000	67-0	40-0	3,525	8,420
30,000	67-0	48-0	3,525	10,100
30,000	73-4	40-0	4,230	9,335
35,000	80-0	40-0	5,025	10,055
45,000	90-0	40-0	6,360	11,310
55,000	100-0	40-0	7,855	12,565
80,000	110-0	48-0	9,500	16,590
80,000	120-0	40-0	11,310	15,080
100,000	134-0	40-0	14,100	16,840
125,000	150-0	40-0	17,670	18,850
150,000	150-0	48-0	17,670	22,620
180,000	180-0	40-0	25,470	22,620
268,000	200-0	48-0	31,415	30,160

TABLE 11 Spheres

Diameter (ft)	Capacity (bbl)	Surface of Sphere (ft^2)
20	746	1,257
25	1,457	1,963
30	2,518	2,827
35	3,998	3,848
40	5,969	5,027
45	8,498	6,362
50	11,657	7,854
55	15,515	9,503
60	20,142	11,310
65	25,608	13,273
70	31,984	15,394

TABLE 12 Flat Plates[a]

Thickness (in.)	Weight (in pounds) per Square Foot	Square Feet per Ton, One Side Only
1/16	2.55	784
1/8	5.10	392
3/16	7.65	261
1/4	10.20	196
3/8	15.30	131
1/2	20.40	98
5/8	25.50	78
3/4	30.60	65
7/8	35.70	56
1	40.80	49

[a]If 2 surfaces are desired, multiply the right column by 2.

TABLE 13 Standard Steel Shapes[a]

Designation	ft²/lineal ft
W Shapes	
W 36 × 300 (36 × 16½)	11.51
× 280	11.47
× 260	11.42
× 245	11.38
× 230	11.34
W 36 × 194 (36 × 12)	9.99
× 182	9.96
× 170	9.92
× 160	9.89
× 150	9.86
× 135	9.81
W 33 × 240 (33 × 15¾)	10.73
× 220	10.68
× 200	10.63
W 33 × 152 (33 × 11½)	9.33
× 141	9.30
× 130	9.26
× 118	9.21
W 30 × 210 (30 × 15)	9.97
× 190	9.92
× 172	9.87
W 30 × 132 (30 × 10½)	8.46
× 124	8.44
× 116	8.41
× 108	8.37
× 99	8.34
W 27 × 177 (27 × 14)	9.13
× 160	9.08
× 145	9.04
W 27 × 114 (27 × 10)	7.81
× 102	7.76
× 94	7.73
× 84	7.69
W 24 × 160 (24 × 14)	8.71
× 145	8.66
× 130	8.61
W 24 × 120 (24 × 12)	7.99
× 110	7.96
× 100	7.92
W 24 × 94 (24 × 9)	6.98
× 84	6.94
× 76	6.91
× 68	6.87
W 24 × 61 (24 × 7)	6.22
× 55	6.19
W 21 × 142 (21 × 13)	7.84
× 127	7.80
× 112	7.75
W 21 × 96 (21 × 9)	6.44
× 82	6.38
W 21 × 73 (21 × 8¼)	6.23
× 68	6.21
× 62	6.18
× 55	6.14
W 21 × 49 (21 × 6½)	5.58
× 44	5.55
W 18 × 114 (18 × 11¾)	6.93
× 105	6.89
× 96	6.86
W 18 × 85 (18 × 8¾)	5.91
× 77	5.88
× 70	5.84
× 64	5.82
W 18 × 60 (18 × 7½)	5.49
× 55	5.47
× 50	5.44
× 45	5.41
W 18 × 40 (18 × 6)	4.94
× 35	4.90
W 16 × 96 (16 × 11½)	6.48
× 88	6.44
W 16 × 78 (16 × 8½)	5.49
× 71	5.46
× 64	5.43
× 58	5.40
W 16 × 50 (16 × 7)	5.00
× 45	4.98
× 40	4.95
× 36	4.92
W 16 × 31 (16 × 5½)	4.44
× 26	4.40
W 14 × 730 (21 × 17½)	9.19
× 665	9.02
× 605	8.86
× 550	8.71
× 500	8.58
× 455	8.45
W 14 × 426 (17 × 16)	8.37
× 398	8.29
× 370	8.21
× 342	8.12

(continued)

TABLE 13 *(continued)*

Designation	ft²/lineal ft	Designation	ft²/lineal ft
× 314	8.04	W 12 × 58 (12 × 10)	5.31
× 287	7.96	× 53	5.29
× 264	7.89	W 12 × 50 (12 × 8)	4.66
× 246	7.84	× 45	4.63
W 14 × 237 (14 × 16)	7.81	× 40	4.61
× 228	7.78	W 12 × 36 (12 × 6½)	4.18
× 219	7.75	× 31	4.15
× 211	7.73	× 27	4.12
× 202	7.70	W 12 × 22 (12 × 4)	3.35
× 193	7.67	× 19	3.32
× 184	7.64	× 16.5	3.30
× 176	7.62	× 14	3.27
× 167	7.59	W 10 × 112 (10 × 10)	5.24
× 158	7.56	× 100	5.19
× 150	7.54	× 89	5.14
× 142	7.51	× 77	5.08
W 14 × 320 (16¾ × 16¾)	8.06	× 72	5.06
W 14 × 136 (14 × 14½)	7.26	× 66	5.03
× 127	7.23	× 60	5.00
× 119	7.21	× 54	4.97
× 111	7.18	× 49	4.94
× 103	7.15	W 10 × 45 (10 × 8)	4.30
× 95	7.12	× 39	4.27
× 87	7.10	× 33	4.23
W 14 × 84 (14 × 12)	6.30	W 10 × 29 (10 × 5¾)	3.59
× 78	6.27	× 25	3.56
W 14 × 74 (14 × 10)	5.65	× 21	3.53
× 68	5.62	W 10 × 19 (10 × 4)	3.01
× 61	5.59	× 17	2.98
W 14 × 53 (14 × 8)	4.95	× 15	2.96
× 48	4.92	× 10.5	2.93
× 43	4.90	W 8 × 67 (8 × 8)	4.17
W 14 × 38 (14 × 6¾)	4.56	× 58	4.11
× 34	4.54	× 48	4.05
× 30	4.51	× 40	4.01
W 14 × 26 (14 × 5)	3.95	× 35	3.98
× 22	3.92	× 31	3.95
W 12 × 190 (12 × 12)	6.44	W 8 × 28 (8 × 6½)	3.48
× 161	6.33	× 24	3.45
× 133	6.23	W 8 × 20 (8 × 5¼)	3.07
× 120	6.18	× 17	3.05
× 106	6.12	W 8 × 15 (8 × 4)	2.65
× 99	6.09	× 13	2.63
× 92	6.06	× 10	2.60
× 85	6.04	W 6 × 23 (6 × 6)	3.04
× 79	6.01	× 20	3.00
× 72	5.98	× 15.5	2.96
× 65	5.96	× 16 (6 × 4)	2.34

(continued)

TABLE 13 *(continued)*

Designation	ft²/lineal ft	Designation	ft²/lineal ft
× 12	2.30	S 10 × 35 (10 × 5)	3.22
× 8.5	2.26	× 25.4	3.17
W 5 × 18.5 (5 × 8)	2.48	S 8 × 23 (8 × 4)	2.65
× 16	2.46	× 18.4	2.62
W 4 × 13 (4 × 4)	2.00	S 7 × 20 (7 × 3⅝)	2.38
		× 15.3	2.35
M Shapes		S 6 × 17.25 (6 × 3⅜)	2.11
		× 12.5	2.07
M 14 × 17.2 (14 × 4)	3.63	S 5 × 14.75 (5 × 3)	1.85
M 12 × 11.8 (12 × 3⅛)	2.99	× 10	1.80
M 10 × 29.1 (10 × 5¾)	3.55	S 4 × 9.5 (4 × 2⅝)	1.54
× 22.9	3.52	× 7.7	1.52
M 10 × 9 (10 × 2¾)	2.54	S 3 × 7.5 (3 × 2⅜)	1.28
M 8 × 37.7 (8 × 8)	3.96	× 5.7	1.25
× 34.3	3.94		
× 32.6	3.93	*HP Shapes*	
M 8 × 22.5 (8 × 5¼)	3.07		
× 18.5	3.05	HP 14 × 117 (14 × 14½)	7.20
M 8 × 6.5 (8 × 2¼)	2.07	× 102	7.15
M 7 × 5.5 (7 × 2⅛)	1.84	× 89	7.11
M 6 × 33.75 (6 × 6)	3.00	× 73	7.05
× 22.5	2.96	HP 12 × 74 (12 × 12)	5.99
× 20	2.94	× 53	5.91
M 6 × 4.4 (6 × 1⅞)	1.60	HP 10 × 57 (10 × 10)	4.98
M 5 × 18.9 (5 × 5)	2.45	× 42	4.91
M 4 × 16.3 (4 × 4)	1.96	HP 8 × 36 (8 × 8)	3.98
× 13.8	1.95		
× 13	1.94	*American Standard Channels*	
		C 15 × 50 (15 × 3⅜)	3.62
S Shapes		× 40	3.59
S 24 × 120 (24 × 8)	6.55	× 33.9	3.57
× 105.9	6.52	C 12 × 30 (12 × 3)	2.97
S 24 × 100 (24 × 7)	6.29	× 25	2.95
× 90	6.27	× 20.7	2.93
× 79.9	6.25	C 10 × 30 (10 × 2⅝)	2.57
S 20 × 95 (20 × 7)	5.60	× 25	2.54
× 85	5.58	× 20	2.52
S 20 × 75 (20 × 6¼)	5.36	× 15.3	2.49
× 65.4	5.33	C 9 × 20 (9 × 2½)	2.31
S 18 × 70 (18 × 6)	4.96	× 15	2.28
× 54.7	4.92	× 13.4	2.27
S 15 × 50 (15 × 5½)	4.29	C 8 × 18.75 (8 × 2½)	2.09
× 42.9	4.27	× 13.75	2.06
S 12 × 50 (12 × 5½)	3.71	× 11.5	2.05
× 40.8	3.67	C 7 × 14.75 (7 × 2⅛)	1.86
S 12 × 35 (12 × 5)	3.62	× 12.25	1.85
× 31.8	3.61	× 9.8	1.83

(continued)

TABLE 13 *(continued)*

Designation	ft²/lineal ft
C 6 × 13 (6 × 2)	1.65
× 10.5	1.63
× 8.2	1.61
C 5 × 9 (5 × 1¾)	1.41
× 6.7	1.37
C 4 × 7.25 (4 × 1⅝)	1.19
× 5.4	1.16
C 3 × 6 (3 × 1½)	0.97
× 5	0.96
× 4.1	0.94
Miscellaneous Channels	
MC 18 × 58 (8 × 4)	4.28
× 51.9	4.27
× 45.8	4.25
× 42.7	4.24
MC 13 × 50 (13 × 4)	3.51
× 40	3.47
× 35	3.45
× 31.8	3.44
MC 12 × 50 (12 × 4)	3.24
× 45	3.22
× 40	3.20
× 35	3.18
MC 12 × 37 (12 × 3½)	3.10
× 32.9	3.08
× 30.9	3.08
MC 12 × 10.6 (12 × 1½)	2.47
MC 10 × 41.1 (10 × 4)	2.97
× 33.6	2.94
× 28.5	2.91
MC 10 × 28.3 (10 × 3½)	2.75
× 25.3	2.78
× 24.9	2.74
× 21.9	2.76
MC 10 × 8.4 (10 × 1½)	2.14
MC 10 × 6.5 (10 × 1⅛)	2.02
MC 9 × 25.4 (9 × 3½)	2.59
× 23.9	2.58
M 8 × 22.8 (8 × 3½)	2.43
× 21.4	2.42
MC 8 × 20 (8 × 3)	2.28
× 18.7	2.27
MC 8 × 8.5 (8 × 1⅞)	1.76
MC 7 × 22.7 (7 × 3½)	2.28
× 19.1	2.26
MC 7 × 17.6 (7 × 3)	2.10
MC 6 × 18 (6 × 3½)	2.10
× 15.3	2.11
MC 6 × 16.3 (6 × 3)	1.94
× 15.1	1.93
MC 6 × 12 (6 × 2½)	1.78
MC 3 × 9 (3 × 1⅞)	1.13
× 7.1	1.09
Structural Tees—Cut from W Shapes	
WT 18 × 150	5.84
× 140	5.80
× 130	5.78
× 122.5	5.76
× 115	5.73
× 97	5.06
× 91	5.04
× 85	5.02
× 80	5.00
× 75	4.98
× 67.5	4.96
WT 16.5 × 120	5.44
× 110	5.40
× 100	5.38
× 76	4.72
× 70.5	4.70
× 65	4.68
× 59	4.65
WT 15 × 105	5.05
× 95	5.02
× 86	4.99
× 66	4.28
× 62	4.27
× 58	4.26
× 54	4.24
× 49.5	4.21
WT 13.5 × 88.5	4.63
× 80	4.59
× 72.5	4.57
× 57	3.96
× 51	3.92
× 47	3.91
× 42	3.89
WT 12 × 80	4.41
× 7.25	4.38
× 65	4.35
× 60	4.05
× 55	4.02

(continued)

TABLE 13 *(continued)*

Designation	ft²/lineal ft	Designation	ft²/lineal ft
× 50	4.00	× 213	4.34
× 47	3.53	× 199	4.29
× 42	3.51	× 185	4.24
× 38	3.50	× 171	4.21
× 34	3.47	× 160	4.19
× 30	3.15	× 157	4.14
× 27	3.13	× 143.5	4.09
WT 10 × 71	3.97	× 132	4.05
× 63.5	3.95	× 123	4.01
× 56	3.92	× 118.5	4.00
× 48	3.27	× 114	3.98
× 41	3.23	× 109.5	3.96
× 36.5	3.16	× 105.5	3.95
× 34	3.15	× 101	3.93
× 31	3.12	× 96.5	3.91
× 27.5	3.10	× 92	3.89
× 24.5	2.82	× 88	3.88
× 22	2.81	× 83.5	3.87
WT 9 × 57	3.52	× 79	3.84
× 52.5	3.50	× 75	3.83
× 48	3.47	× 71	3.82
× 42.5	3.00	× 68	3.69
× 38.5	2.98	× 63.5	3.67
× 35	2.94	× 59.5	3.66
× 32	2.94	× 55.5	3.64
× 30	2.78	× 51.5	3.62
× 27.5	2.77	× 47.5	3.60
× 25	2.75	× 43.5	3.59
× 22.5	2.74	× 42	3.69
WT 8 × 48	3.28	× 39	3.68
× 44	3.26	× 37	2.87
× 39	2.79	× 34	2.84
× 35.5	2.77	× 30.5	2.83
× 32	2.76	× 26.5	2.51
× 29	2.73	× 24	2.49
× 25	2.53	× 21.5	2.48
× 22.5	2.52	× 19	2.31
× 20	2.51	× 17	2.29
× 18	2.48	× 15	2.28
× 15.5	2.24	× 13	2.00
× 13	2.22	× 11	1.98
WT 7 × 365	4.85	WT 6 × 95	3.31
× 332.5	4.75	× 80.5	3.25
× 302.5	4.65	× 66.5	3.18
× 275	4.56	× 60	3.15
× 250	4.47	× 53	3.11
× 227.5	4.39	× 49.5	3.10

(continued)

TABLE 13 (*continued*)

Designation	ft²/lineal ft
× 46	3.08
× 42.5	3.06
× 39.5	3.05
× 36	3.03
× 32.5	3.01
× 29	2.69
× 26.5	2.68
× 25	2.36
× 22.5	2.35
× 20	2.33
× 18	2.12
× 15.5	2.10
× 13.5	2.08
× 11	1.70
× 9.5	1.68
× 8.25	1.67
× 7	1.65
WT 5 × 56	2.68
× 50	2.66
× 44.5	2.62
× 38.5	2.58
× 36	2.57
× 33	2.56
× 30	2.53
× 27	2.52
× 24.5	2.50
× 22.5	2.18
× 19.5	2.17
× 16.5	2.15
× 14.5	1.82
× 12.5	1.80
× 10.5	1.77
× 9.5	1.53
× 8.5	1.51
× 7.5	1.50
× 5.75	1.48
WT 4 × 33.5	2.14
× 29	2.10
× 24	2.06
× 20	2.04
× 17.5	2.02
× 15.5	2.00
× 14	1.76
× 12	1.75
× 10	1.56
× 8.5	1.55
× 7.5	1.35
× 6.5	1.33
× 5	1.32
WT 3 × 12.5	1.55
× 10	1.52
× 7.75	1.50
× 8	1.19
× 6	1.17
× 4.25	1.14
WT 2.5 × 9.25	1.28
× 8	1.25
× 6.5	1.02
Structural Tees—Cut from M Shapes	
MT 7 × 8.6	1.83
MT 6 × 5.9	1.51
MT 5 × 14.55	1.81
MT 5 × 14.55	1.81
× 11.45	1.78
× 4.5	1.28
MT 4 × 18.85	2.01
× 17.15	2.00
× 16.3	1.99
× 11.25	1.57
× 9.25	1.54
× 3.25	1.05
× 2.75	0.93
MT 3 × 16.875	1.54
× 11.25	1.51
× 10	1.49
× 2.2	0.81
MT 2.5 × 9.45	1.25
MT 2 × 8.15	1.00
× 6.9	1.00
× 6.5	0.99
Structural Tees—Cut from S Shapes	
ST 12 × 60	3.27
× 52.95	3.26
× 50	3.15
× 45	3.14
× 39.95	3.13
ST 10 × 47.5	2.82
× 42.5	2.79
× 37.5	2.68
× 32.7	2.67

(*continued*)

TABLE 13 *(continued)*

Designation	ft²/lineal ft	Designation	ft²/lineal ft
ST 9 × 35	2.48	ST 3.5 × 10	1.19
× 27.35	2.46	× 7.65	1.17
ST 7.5 × 25	2.14	ST 3 × 8.63	1.06
× 21.45	2.13	× 6.25	1.04
ST 6 × 25	1.86	ST 2.5 × 7.375	0.92
× 20.4	1.84	× 5	0.90
× 17.5	1.81	× 4.75	0.77
× 15.9	1.80	× 3.85	0.76
ST 5 × 17.5	1.61	ST 1.5 × 3.75	0.64
× 12.7	1.58	× 2.85	0.62
ST 4 × 11.5	1.33		
× 9.2	1.31		

[a]This table reflects the usual way plans designate steel members. The letter preceding the numerals indicates the "shape," the first number or numbers indicate the depth of the web in inches, the last number (following "×") indicates the weight in pounds per lineal foot—thus W 36 × 300 is a wide flange beam 36″ in depth weighting 300 pounds per lineal foot. The nominal web depth and flange width are shown in parentheses. Sources for this information: *AISC Steel Construction Manual* and Painting and Decorating Contractors of America.

TABLE 14 Areas of Pipe Products

Inside Diameter (in.)	Square Feet Per Linear Foot, Exterior	Inside Diameter (in.)	Square Feet Per Linear Foot, Exterior
½	0.13	14	3.67
1	0.34	16	4.20
2	0.62	18	4.92
3	0.92	20	5.24
4	1.18	24	6.48
5	1.46	30	7.85
6	1.73	36	9.42
8	2.26	40	10.47
10	2.81	48	12.56
12	3.35	60	15.71

TABLE 15 Rooms with 9-Foot Ceilings (figures include side walls and ceilings in square feet)

Wall Dimensions	3	4	5	6	7	8	9	10	11	12	13	14	15
3	117	138	159	180	201	222	243	264	285	306	327	348	369
4	138	160	182	204	226	248	270	292	314	336	358	380	402
5	159	182	205	228	251	274	297	320	343	366	389	412	435
6	180	204	228	252	276	300	324	348	372	396	420	444	468
7	201	226	251	276	301	326	351	376	401	426	451	476	501
8	222	248	274	300	326	352	378	404	430	456	482	508	534
9	243	270	297	324	351	378	405	432	459	486	513	540	567
10	264	292	320	348	376	404	432	460	488	516	544	572	600
11	285	314	343	372	401	430	459	488	517	546	575	604	633
12	306	336	366	396	426	456	486	516	546	576	606	636	666
13	327	358	389	420	451	482	513	544	575	606	637	668	699
14	348	380	412	444	476	508	540	572	604	636	668	700	732
15	369	402	435	468	501	534	567	600	633	666	699	732	765
16	390	424	458	492	526	560	594	628	662	696	730	764	798
17	411	446	481	516	551	586	621	656	691	726	761	796	831
18	432	468	504	540	576	612	648	684	720	756	792	828	864
19	453	490	527	564	601	638	675	712	749	786	823	860	897
20	474	512	550	588	626	664	702	740	778	816	854	892	930

TABLE 16 Theoretical Coverage in Square Feet per U.S. Gallon[a]

Solid Content by Volume (%)	Required Dry Film				
	1	2	3	4	5
100	1604.00	802.00	534.66	401.00	320.80
95	1523.80	761.90	507.93	380.95	304.76
90	1443.60	721.80	481.20	360.90	288.72
85	1363.40	681.70	454.46	340.85	272.68
80	1283.20	641.60	427.73	320.80	256.64
75	1203.00	601.50	401.00	300.75	240.60
70	1122.80	561.40	374.26	280.70	224.56
65	1042.60	521.30	347.53	260.65	208.52
60	962.40	481.20	320.80	240.60	192.48
55	882.20	441.10	294.06	220.55	176.44
50	802.00	401.00	267.33	200.50	160.40
45	721.80	360.90	240.60	180.45	144.36
40	641.60	320.80	213.86	160.40	128.32
35	561.40	280.70	187.13	140.35	112.28
30	481.20	240.60	160.40	120.30	96.24
25	401.00	200.50	133.66	100.25	80.20
20	320.80	160.40	106.93	80.20	64.16

[a]Coverage (at 1 mil dry) = % volume solids × 1604.

$$\text{Coverage (at recommended dry mils)} = \frac{\text{coverage at 1 dry mil}}{\text{recommended dry mils}}.$$

16	17	18	19	20	21	22	23	24	25
390	411	432	453	474	495	516	537	558	579
424	446	468	490	512	534	556	578	600	622
458	481	504	527	550	573	596	619	642	655
492	516	540	564	588	612	636	660	684	708
526	551	576	601	626	651	676	701	726	751
560	586	612	638	664	690	716	742	768	794
594	621	648	675	702	729	756	783	810	837
628	656	684	712	740	768	796	824	852	880
662	691	720	749	778	807	836	865	894	923
696	726	756	786	816	846	876	906	936	966
730	761	792	823	854	885	916	947	978	1009
764	796	828	860	892	924	956	988	1020	1052
798	831	864	897	930	963	996	1029	1062	1095
832	866	900	934	968	1002	1036	1070	1104	1138
866	901	936	971	1006	1041	1076	1111	1146	1181
900	936	972	1008	1044	1080	1116	1152	1188	1224
934	971	1008	1045	1082	1119	1156	1193	1230	1267
968	1006	1044	1082	1120	1158	1196	1234	1272	1310

Thickness Per Coat

6	7	8	9	10
267.33	229.14	200.50	178.22	160.40
253.96	217.68	190.47	169.31	152.38
240.60	206.22	180.45	160.40	144.36
227.23	194.77	170.42	151.48	136.34
213.86	183.31	160.40	142.57	128.32
200.50	171.85	150.37	133.66	120.30
187.13	160.40	140.35	124.75	112.28
173.76	148.94	130.32	115.84	104.26
160.40	137.48	120.30	106.93	96.24
147.03	126.02	110.27	98.02	88.22
133.66	114.57	100.25	89.11	80.20
120.30	103.11	90.22	80.20	72.18
106.93	91.65	80.20	71.28	64.16
93.56	80.20	70.17	62.37	56.14
80.20	68.74	60.15	53.46	48.12
66.83	57.28	50.12	44.55	40.10
53.46	45.82	40.10	35.64	32.08

TABLE 17 Wet Film Thickness Requirements[a]

Solid Content of Material %	Required Dry Film Thickness									
	1	2	3	4	5	6	7	8	9	10
100	1	2	3	4	5	6	7	8	9	10
95	1.1	2.1	3.1	4.2	5.3	6.3	7.4	8.4	9.5	10.5
90	1.1	2.2	3.3	4.4	5.6	6.7	7.8	8.8	10.0	11.1
85	1.2	2.4	3.5	4.7	5.9	7.0	8.2	9.4	10.6	11.8
80	1.3	2.5	3.8	5.0	6.2	7.5	8.7	10.0	11.2	12.5
75	1.4	2.7	4.0	5.3	6.7	8.0	9.3	10.7	12.0	13.3
70	1.5	2.9	4.3	5.7	7.1	8.6	10.0	11.4	12.9	14.3
65	1.6	3.1	4.6	6.1	7.7	9.2	10.8	12.3	13.8	15.4
60	1.7	3.3	5.0	6.7	8.3	10.0	11.7	13.3	15.0	16.7
55	1.8	3.6	5.4	7.2	9.1	10.9	12.7	14.5	16.4	18.2
50	2.0	4.0	6.0	8.0	10.0	12.0	14.0	16.0	18.0	
45	2.2	4.4	6.7	8.9	11.1	13.3	15.6	17.8		
40	2.5	5.0	7.5	10.0	12.5	15.0	17.5			
35	2.8	5.7	8.6	11.4	14.3	17.1				
30	3.3	6.7	10.0	13.3	16.7					
25	4.0	8.0	12.0	16.0						

[a]Wet mil thickness $= \frac{\text{dry mil thickness}}{\text{\% volume solids}}$.

Dry mil thickness = wet mil thickness × % volume solids.

TABLE 18 Dew Point Chart (percent relative humidity above which moisture will condense on metal surfaces)

Metal Surface Temperature (°F)	Surrounding Air Temperature (°F)																
	40	45	50	55	60	65	70	75	80	85	90	95	100	105	110	115	120
35	60	33	11														
40		69	39	20	8												
45			69	45	27	14											
50				71	49	32	20	11									
55					73	53	38	26	17	9							
60						75	56	41	30	21	14	9					
65							78	59	45	34	25	18	13				
70								79	61	48	37	29	22	16	13		
75									80	64	50	40	32	25	20	15	
80										81	66	53	43	35	29	22	16
85											81	68	55	46	37	30	25
90												82	69	58	49	40	32
95													83	70	58	50	40
100														84	70	61	50
105															85	71	61
110																85	72
115																	86

CORRUGATED METALS

2½" Corrugated Sheet—To find width before corrugation multiply the width after corrugation by 1.08. Assume depth to be ⅝".

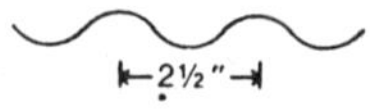

1¼" Corrugated Sheet—To find width before corrugation multiply the width after corrugation by 1.11. Assume depth to be ⅜".

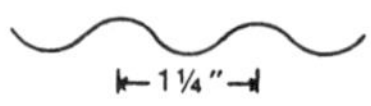

ROOF DECK

If the roof deck has a cross-section view similar to that shown, first figure the square foot area then multiply by 2.42 to obtain the actual surface area.

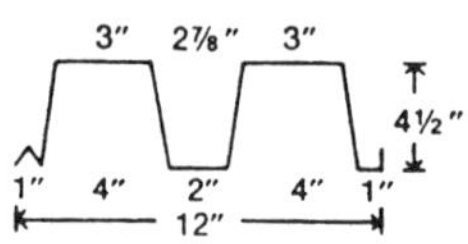

If the roof deck has a cross-section view similar to that shown, figure the top side as just the square foot area of surface. Figure the underside as follows—

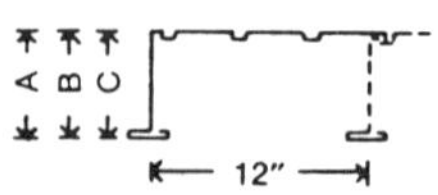

A For each square foot area multiply by 1.63 for actual surface area.

(A) 4½" (B) 6" (C) 8"

B Multiply by 1.75.

C Multiply by 1.92.

SIDING

If the siding has a cross-section view similar to that shown multiply each square foot of area by 1.5 for actual surface area. Double for both sides.

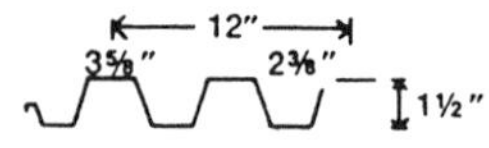

If the siding has a cross-section view similar to that shown multiply each square foot of area by 1.42 for actual surface area. Double for both sides.

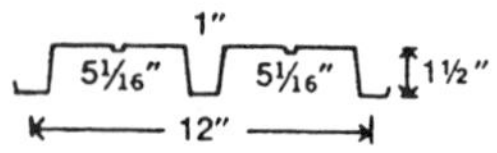

If the siding has a cross-section view similar to that shown multiply each square foot of area by 1.75 for actual surface area. Double for both sides.

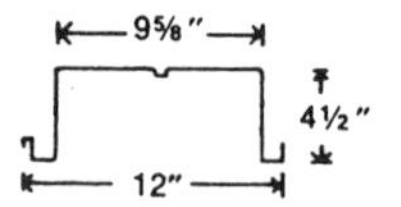

If the depth is 3" multiply by 1.5. Double for both sides.

STACKS

To compute the square foot area of a stack multiply height (B) by the average diameter (A) and multiply that total by 3.

EXAMPLE: Diameter of stack at the top—5 feet. Diameter of stack at the bottom—15 feet. Average diameter—10 feet (2 | 5+15). Height 60 feet. 60×10=600. 600×3=1800 square feet of surface area.

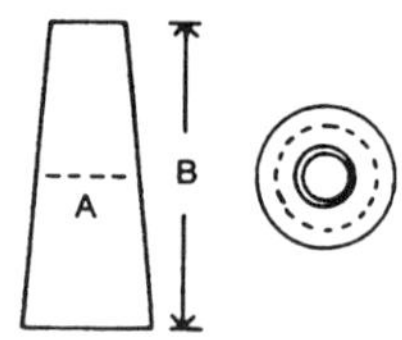

FIG. 1. Surface area calculations.

TRIANGLE

To find the number of sq. ft. in any shape triangle or 3 sided surface, multiply the height by the width and divide the total by 2.

40′ height
×50′ width
2,000 sq. ft.

1,000 sq. ft.
2⟌2,000

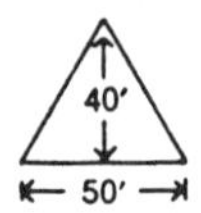

SPHERE

To find the number of sq. ft. of a sphere or ball, multiply the diameter (distance across) by itself and then multiply this total by 3.1416. If you haven't the diameter, you can find it by measuring the circumference and multiplying it by .31831.

50′ diameter
×50′ diameter
2,500

2,500
×3.1416
7,854.0000 sq. ft.

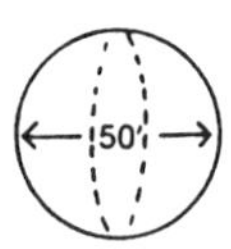

CIRCLE

To find the number of sq. ft. in a circle, multiply the diameter (distance across) by itself and then multiply this total by .7854.

50′ diameter
×50′ diameter
2,500

2,500
×.7854
1,969 sq. ft.

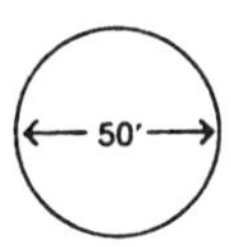

SQUARE

Multiply the base measurement in feet times the height in feet.

40′ × 40′ = 1600 sq. ft.

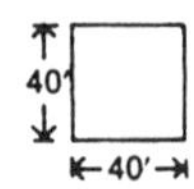

CYLINDER

When circumference (distance around cylinder) is known, multiply height by circumference.

157′ circumference
×100′ height
15,700 sq. ft.

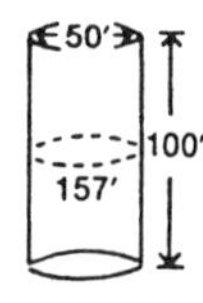

When diameter (distance across) is known, multiply diameter by 3.1416. This gives circumference. Then multiply by height.

3.1416
×50 diameter
157.0800 feet

157′ circumference
×100′ height
15,700 sq. ft.

Note: Figures do not include end area. See circle.

RECTANGLE

Multiply the base measurement in feet times the height in feet.

20′ × 40′ = 800 sq. ft.

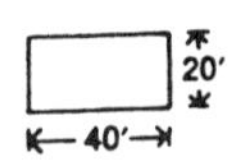

FIG. 2. How to estimate square foot coverage for different shapes.

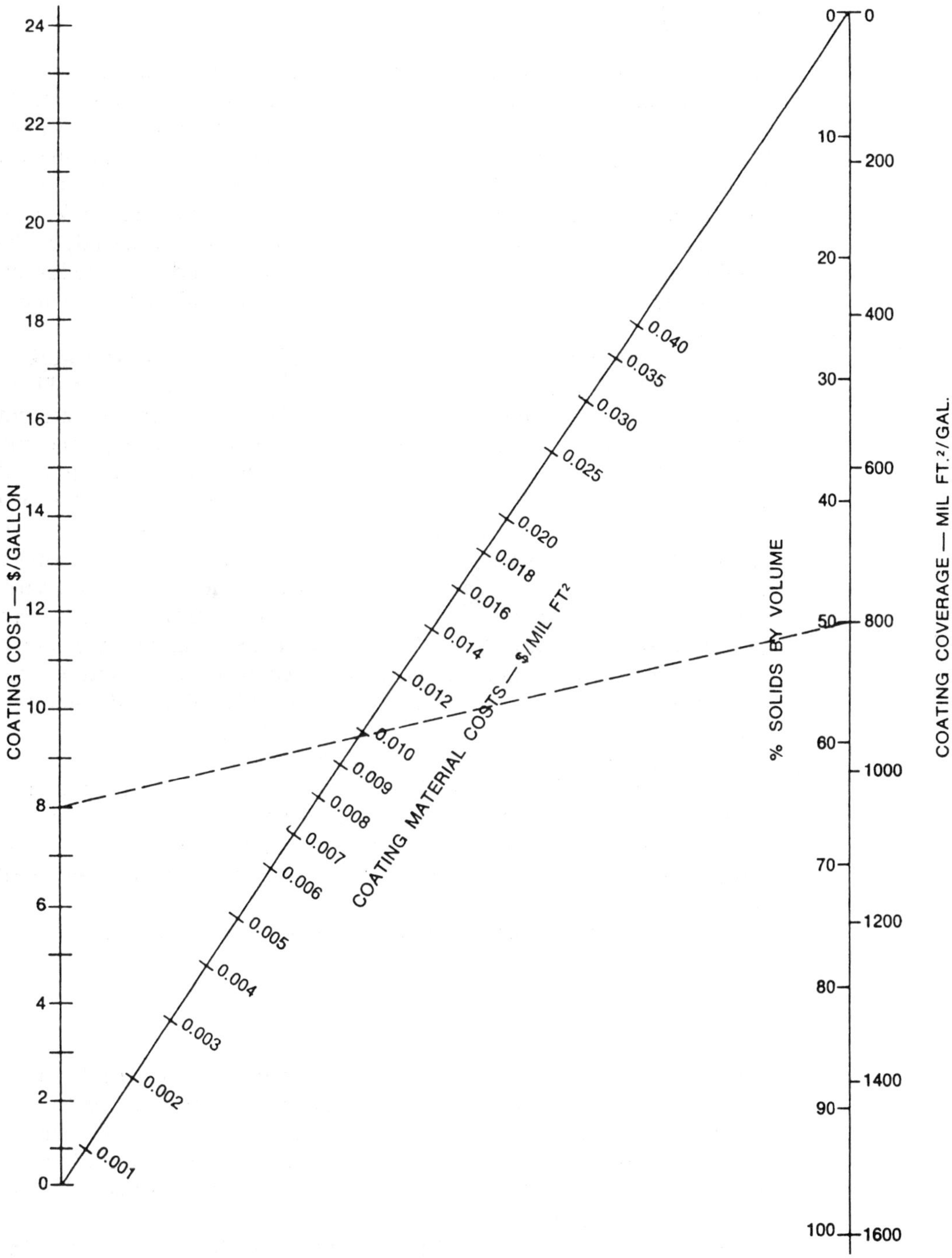

FIG. 3. Cost per mil ft² determination. With the price per gallon and total solids (pigment + vehicle solids) by volume of the coating given, simple alignment of these values with a straight edge will determine the coating material cost per mil ft². This will allow an accurate comparison between different materials which is not possible from the price per gallon alone. *Example*: A material selling for $8.00/gal and containing 50% total solids would cost $0.01/mil ft².

Proper Application

Underscoring proper application is proper surface preparation and includes the anchor pattern of the area to be painted. For metal surfaces, this relates to the surface profile. The surface profile, or roughness, of the blast-cleaned surface depends on the type of abrasive used and the force with which it impacts on the surface. Although there is some question as to the best surface profile for a given coating system, it is generally recognized that too deep an anchor pattern will result in peaks and may not be covered sufficiently by the coating system, causing corrosion-initiation sites. Similarly, too shallow an anchor pattern will result in a smooth metal surface to which paint will not adhere.

The key to obtaining the right surface profile is to relate field work to actual surface profile recommendations of the paint manufacturers. Firms that cannot give you those recommendations, or applicators that are not familiar with various methods to obtain and measure surface profile and anchor pattern, are really not keyed into CPI painting needs. Keep in mind that the greater the surface to which the coating adheres, the greater the total adhesive strength compared with the tensile strength of the system. A uniform anchor pattern is vitally important to adhesion. It is obtained by using a clean, well-graded, and sized abrasive. Generally, in a field operation, a hard, sharp, and correct-sized silica sand will produce the desired results at the least possible cost. In comparison, a soft, round, ungraded bank sand will not cut steel fast, will cut it with uneven etch, and will require large amounts of sand.

Proper selection of an abrasive implies knowledge of how abrasion size relates to anchor pattern, abrasion shape relates to surface finish, and abrasion hardness relates to cleaning speed and job cost.

While paint application procedures should be spelled out by the manufacturer (to include application gauges, spray pressures, and suitable equipment), some special problems can crop up with zinc-rich paints (Appendix 13) and two- or three-component systems. Here, use only an experienced applicator.

Appendix 14 gives general helpful information for paint application.

Inspection

Inspection procedures have not changed much over the past 10 years, although some new, more-accurate instruments have reached the marketplace and coatings themselves are different. For example, high solids coatings are commonplace in today's marketplace, brought about by the U.S. Environmental Protection Agency's desire to control volatile organic emissions (solvent emissions) to reduce air pollution.

Visual inspection is considered a minimum procedure, and this should be supplemented by instrumentation and test equipment that includes comparators and dry and wet film thickness gauges. Other equipment includes: Nozzle orifice gauge, needle air-pressure gauge, anchor pattern standards, visual comparators, surface magnifier, humidity gauge, wet-film gauge, dry-film gauge (for example, the Mikrotest, Inspector, Elcometer, or Tinsley magnetic tape devices), and U.S. Standard Film Thickness cards for verification of gauge readings. The most common inspection devices are the surface-profile comparator (KTA-Tator Associates, Inc., Coraopolis, Pennsylvania) and the Clemtex anchor-pattern standards, CAPS (Clemtex, Ltd., Houston, Texas). These devices are designed for quick field inspection of a blast-cleaned surface.

Do not underestimate the simple value of having an inspector present during application. The eye of an experienced inspector is a most useful tool. An inspector can quickly examine the work and arrive at a very accurate appraisal of quality. In addition, he can pick out points or areas requiring close, detailed inspection. Backing up visual inspection with actual tests avoids many common paint failures. Keep in mind that use of inspection gauges is only as good as the person using the equipment. For example, the Inspector gauge mechanism is counterbalanced so there is no effect on its readings with the gauge held in different positions. Apparently the Elcometer mechanism is not counterbalanced; when it is held in different positions, the readings vary.

Paint Failures

Even the best specified properly applied paint can fail when external forces are applied to the coating. This can be damage from welders in the area, lift trucks or cranes running into tanks, or a host of other unforeseen examples. Of course, using the wrong paint, the wrong application technique, or the wrong surface preparation is a sure way to failure. Appendixes 15–18 provide troubleshooting remedies. For further problem-solution guidelines, refer to the *Paint Handbook* (McGraw-Hill, New York, 1981) and to the July and August 1982 series of articles on "Paint Failures" appearing in the *American Paint Journal*.

Special Painting Situations

Extensive use of coatings takes place in CPI-related processing plants, e.g., wastewater treatment plants and nuclear power plants.

Wastewater treatment plants offer a particularly hostile environment due to the constant humidity and the off-gases that are given off from the treatment process. Anaerobic digesters offer particular problems in that area. Typical recommendations in this area are: (1) enhance the sludge digestion process; (2) safely contain the gases produced, and (3) satisfy regulatory requirements to eliminate pollution and odor. There are general maintenance and retrofit programs that can extend the life of digesters by 5 or more years. These include:

Combination water- and sandblast to remove all loose paint, caulking, corrosion, and concrete.
Flood all cracks, joints, seams, and other openings where leaking occurs with 100% solids polyurethane or epoxy until an area is flush with the adjacent concrete.
Use of packing and elastomeric seals compatible with surface coatings.
Spray complete exterior of the digester with the same 100% polyurethane and have a finished coat averaging 50 mils of product on steel and 65 mils on concrete.

The ultimate solution for extending the life of digesters is to follow a prescribed program for both inside and outside the digester. Depending on digester conditions, the cost would generally range from \$2.65/ft^2 (for outside reconditioning only) up to \$7.90/ft^2 (for internal and external reconditioning). Recommendations generally call for extensive use of 100% polyurethane and epoxy coatings and sealants due to their success in handling corrosive environments.

Table 19 is a general painting guide to painting these kinds of facilities.

Nuclear power plants require complex approved coatings that must give long life. Failures involve painting over or removal of contaminated surfaces. Workers must be adequately protected and are only permitted in the nuclear area for short periods. Repair costs reach upward to \$25 to \$50/ft^2. ASTM (Committee DO1.43) has prepared a 188-page manual of approved coatings for primary containment areas for nuclear plants.

Appendix 1. Basic Paint Principles

Understanding what makes up the contents of a paint in a can will alleviate some coating failures. Paints, whether decorative or protective in nature, are usually made up of these basic ingredients: the solvent, the pigment, and the resin. In the case of clear finishes, the pigment portion is often eliminated. It is often the "volume relationship" between these three components that makes a paint glossy or flat, durable or nondurable. Up to a certain volume ratio, the addition of pigment actually reinforces and improves film-forming properties. With continual pigment addition, a paint formula passes through a critical value called the critical-pigment-volume-concentration. When this critical volume relationship is exceeded, the resistance properties of the paint rapidly deteriorate.

The solvent (sometimes water) in paint film evaporates as the film dries, leaving only the pigment and the resin on the film as it lies on the surface. The amount of solvent will relate to the measurements or readings one gets when using a wet film thickness gauge. Solvents are known contributors to air pollution—particularly photochemical smog. Solvents fall into the category of volatile organic compounds (VOC's) that are being reduced in most

TABLE 19 Water and Waste Pollution Control Plant and Equipment Painting Guide[a]

Surface	Exposure	Type Coating
Aeration Basins, Tanks, and Mechanical Aerators		
Steel	Non-immersion	Aliphatic polyurethane
	Immersion or non-immersion	Epoxy-polyamide
		High-solids epoxy-amine
		Vinyl copolymer
	Immersion	Coal tar-epoxy
Concrete	Non-immersion	Modified epoxy texture
		Acrylic latex
	Immersion or non-immersion	Epoxy-polyamide
		High-solids epoxy-amine
	Immersion	Coal tar-epoxy
Alum Tanks		
Steel	Exterior	Aliphatic polyurethane
		30% silicone-alkyd
		Alkyd gloss
	Interior	Epoxy-polyamide
		High-solids epoxy-amine
Buildings		
Concrete	Exterior below grade	Asphalt
		Coal tar
	Interior floors	Epoxy-polyamide
Concrete and dense masonry	Exterior	Modified epoxy texture
	Interior	Epoxy-polyamide
		Water-borne acrylic-epoxy
		Acrylic latex
Porous masonry	Exterior	Modified epoxy texture
	Interior	Epoxy-polyamide
		High-solids epoxy-amine
		Acrylic latex
Plaster and wallboard	Interior	Acrylic latex
		Water-borne acrylic-epoxy
Steel doors, trim	Exterior	Alkyd gloss
	Interior—mild	Alkyd semigloss
	Interior—severe	Epoxy-polyamide
		Water-borne acrylic-epoxy
Wood doors, trim	Exterior	Alkyd gloss
	Interior	Alkyd semigloss
		Epoxy-polyamide

(continued)

TABLE 19 (*continued*)

Surface	Exposure	Type Coating
	Chemical Feeders and Mixing Tanks	
Steel and equipment	Exterior	Aliphatic polyurethane
		Vinyl copolymer
	Interior	Epoxy-polyamide
		High-solids epoxy-amine
		Coal tar-epoxy
	Chlorine Contact Basins	
Steel	Non-immersion	Aliphatic polyurethane
	Immersion or non-immersion	Epoxy-polyamide
		High-solids epoxy-amine
	Immersion	Coal tar-epoxy
Concrete	Non-immersion	Modified epoxy texture
	Immersion or non-immersion	Epoxy-polyamide
		High-solids epoxy-amine
	Immersion	Coal tar-epoxy
	Chlorine Rooms	
Concrete walls and ceilings	Interior	Epoxy-polyamide
		High-solids epoxy-amine
		Water-borne acrylic-epoxy
		Acrylic latex
Concrete floors	Interior	Epoxy-polyamide
	Clarifiers	
Steel	Non-immersion	Aliphatic polyurethane
	Immersion or non-immersion	Epoxy-polyamide
		High-solids epoxy-amine
		Vinyl copolymer
	Immersion	Coal tar-epoxy
Concrete	Non-immersion	Modified epoxy texture
	Immersion or non-immersion	Epoxy-polyamide
		High-solids epoxy-amine
	Immersion	Coal tar-epoxy
	Clear Wells	
Steel	Non-immersion	Aliphatic polyurethane
	Immersion or non-immersion	Epoxy-polyamide
		High-solids epoxy-amine
		Vinyl copolymer
Concrete	Non-immersion	Modified epoxy texture
	Immersion or non-immersion	Epoxy-polyamide
		High-solids epoxy-amine

(*continued*)

TABLE 19 *(continued)*

Surface	Exposure	Type Coating
	Coagulation Basins	
Steel	Non-immersion	Aliphatic polyurethane
	Immersion or non-immersion	Epoxy-polyamide
		High-solids epoxy-amine
		Vinyl copolymer
Concrete	Non-immersion	Modified epoxy texture
	Immersion or non-immersion	Epoxy-polyamide
		High-solids epoxy-amine
	Control Chambers	
Concrete	Immersion or non-immersion	Epoxy-polyamide
		High-solids epoxy-amine
	Immersion	Coal tar-epoxy
	Digesters	
Steel and equipment	Immersion or non-immersion	Epoxy-polyamide
		High-solids epoxy-amine
	Immersion	Coal tar-epoxy
Steel covers	Top	Aliphatic polyurethane
		30% silicone-alkyd
		Alkyd gloss
	Underside	Epoxy-polyamide
		High-solids epoxy-amine
		Coal tar-epoxy
Concrete and covers	Non-immersion	Modified epoxy texture
		Acrylic latex
	Immersion or non-immersion	Epoxy-polyamide
		High-solids epoxy-amine
	Immersion	Coal tar-epoxy
	Effulent Channels	
Steel	Immersion or non-immersion	Epoxy-polyamide
		High-solids epoxy-amine
	Immersion	Coal tar-epoxy
Concrete	Immersion or non-immersion	Epoxy-polyamide
		High-solids epoxy-amine
	Immersion	Coal tar-epoxy
	Elutriation Tanks	
Steel and equipment	Non-immersion	Aliphatic polyurethane
	Immersion or non-immersion	Epoxy-polyamide
		High-solids epoxy-amine
	Non-immersion	Coal tar-epoxy

(continued)

TABLE 19 (*continued*)

Surface	Exposure	Type Coating
Concrete	Non-immersion	Modified epoxy texture
	Immersion or non-immersion	Epoxy-polyamide
		High-solids epoxy-amine
	Immersion	Coal tar-epoxy
	Ferric Chloride and Ferric Sulfide Tanks	
Steel	Exterior	Aliphatic polyurethane
		30% silicone-alkyd
		Alkyd gloss
	Interior	Epoxy-polyamide
		High-solids epoxy-amine
		Coal tar-epoxy
	Filter Beds and Troughs	
Steel	Immersion or non-immersion	Epoxy-polyamide
		High-solids epoxy-amine
Concrete	Immersion or non-immersion	Epoxy-polyamide
		High-solids epoxy-amine
	Flocculators	
Steel and equipment	Non-immersion	Aliphatic polyurethane
	Immersion or non-immersion	Epoxy-polyamide
		High-solids epoxy-amine
		Vinyl copolymer
Concrete	Non-immersion	Modified epoxy texture
	Immersion or non-immersion	Epoxy-polyamide
		High-solids epoxy-amine
	Floor Plates	
Steel	Exterior or interior	Epoxy-polyamide
		High-solids epoxy-amine
	Gas Holders	
Steel and covers	Exterior	Aliphatic polyurethane
		30% silicone-alkyd
		Alkyd gloss
	Interior	Epoxy-polyamide
		High-solids epoxy-amine
		Coal tar-epoxy
Concrete	Exterior	Modified epoxy texture
		Acrylic latex
	Interior	Epoxy-polyamide
		High-solids epoxy-amine
		Coal tar-epoxy

(continued)

TABLE 19 *(continued)*

Surface	Exposure	Type Coating
	Green Houses	
Steel	Exterior	Aliphatic polyurethane 30% silicone-alkyd Alkyd gloss
	Interior	Epoxy-polyamide Water-borne acrylic-epoxy
Concrete	Exterior	Modified epoxy texture Acrylic latex
	Interior	Epoxy-polyamide Water-borne acrylic-epoxy
	Grit Chambers	
Steel and equipment	Immersion or non-immersion	Epoxy-polyamide High-solids epoxy-amine
	Immersion	Coal tar-epoxy
Concrete	Non-immersion	Modified epoxy texture Acrylic latex
	Immersion	Coal tar-epoxy
	Lift Stations	
Steel and equipment	Immersion or non-immersion	Epoxy-polyamide High-solids epoxy-amine
	Immersion	Coal tar-epoxy
Concrete	Non-immersion	Modified epoxy texture Acrylic latex
	Immersion	Coal tar-epoxy
Concrete wet walls	Immersion or non-immersion	Epoxy-polyamide High solids epoxy-amine
	Immersion	Coal tar-epoxy
	Machinery	
Steel	Non-immersion: Severe	Aliphatic polyurethane Epoxy-polyamide
	Mild	30% silicone-alkyd Alkyd gloss
	Immersion or non-immersion	Epoxy-polyamide High solids epoxy-amine
	Immersion	Coal tar-epoxy
	Manholes and Covers	
Concrete, brick	Interior below grade	Epoxy-polyamide High-solids epoxy-amine
Steel covers	Top and underside	Epoxy-polyamide High-solids epoxy-amine

(continued)

TABLE 19 *(continued)*

Surface	Exposure	Type Coating
	Parshall Flumes	
Steel	Immersion or non-immersion	Epoxy-polyamide
		High solids epoxy-amine
	Immersion	Coal tar-epoxy
Concrete	Immersion or non-immersion	Epoxy-polyamide
		High solids epoxy-amine
	Immersion	Coal tar-epoxy
	Pipes	
Steel	Immersion or non-immersion	Epoxy-polyamide
		High-solids epoxy-amine
	Immersion	Coal tar-epoxy
	Non-immersion: Severe	Aliphatic polyurethane
		Epoxy-polyamide
	Mild	30% silicone-alkyd
		Alkyd gloss
Galvanized	Immersion or non-immersion	Epoxy-polyamide
		High solids epoxy-amine
	Immersion	Coal tar-epoxy
	Non-immersion: Severe	Aliphatic polyurethane
		Epoxy-polyamide
	Mild	30% silicone-alkyd
		Alkyd gloss
PVC	Non-immersion—severe	Epoxy-polyamide
Concrete	Non-immersion	Acrylic latex
	Immersion or non-immersion	Epoxy-polyamide
		High solids epoxy-amine
	Immersion	Coal tar-epoxy
Insulated	Non-immersion	Acrylic latex
	Presedimentation Basins and Tanks	
Steel	Non-immersion	Aliphatic polyurethane
	Immersion or non-immersion	Epoxy-polyamide
		High solids epoxy-amine
		Vinyl copolymer
Concrete	Non-immersion	Modified epoxy texture
	Immersion or non-immersion	Epoxy-polyamide
		High-solids epoxy-amine
	Primary Tanks	
Steel and equipment	Non-immersion	Aliphatic polyurethane
		Vinyl copolymer
	Immersion or non-immersion	Epoxy-polyamide
		High-solids epoxy-amine
		Vinyl copolymer
	Immersion	Coal tar-epoxy

(continued)

TABLE 19 *(continued)*

Surface	Exposure	Type Coating
Concrete	Non-immersion	Modified epoxy texture Acrylic latex
	Immersion or non-immersion	Epoxy-polyamide High-solids epoxy-amine
	Immersion	Coal tar-epoxy
	Pumping Stations	
Steel and equipment	Immersion or non-immersion	Epoxy-polyamide High-solids epoxy-amine
	Immersion	Coal tar-epoxy
Concrete	Non-immersion	Modified epoxy texture Acrylic latex
	Immersion	Coal tar-epoxy
Concrete wet walls	Immersion or non-immersion	Epoxy-polyamide High-solids epoxy-amine
	Immersion	Coal tar-epoxy
	Pumps and Valves	
Steel	Non-immersion: Severe	Aliphatic polyurethane Epoxy-polyamide High-solids epoxy-amine
	Mild	30% silicone-alkyd Alkyd gloss
	Railings	
Steel or galvanized	Interior or severe exposure	Epoxy polyamide
Steel	Exterior or interior	Aliphatic polyurethane 30% silicone-alkyd Alkyd gloss
Galvanized	Exterior or interior	Aliphatic polyurethane 30% silicone alkyd Alkyd gloss
	Rakes	
Steel	Immersion or non-immersion	Epoxy-polyamide High-solids epoxy-amine
	Receiving Wells	
Concrete	Immersion	Epoxy-polyamide High-solids epoxy-amine Coal tar-epoxy

(continued)

TABLE 19 *(continued)*

Surface	Exposure	Type Coating
	Reservoirs	
Concrete	Immersion or non-immersion	Epoxy-polyamide High-solids epoxy-amine
	Screening, Secondary, Sediment, and Skimming Tanks	
Steel and equipment	Non-immersion	Aliphatic polyurethane
	Immersion or non-immersion	Epoxy-polyamide High-solids epoxy-amine Vinyl copolymer
	Immersion	Coal tar-epoxy
Concrete	Non-immersion	Modified epoxy texture Acrylic latex
	Immersion or non-immersion	Epoxy-polyamide High-solids epoxy-amine
	Immersion	Coal tar-epoxy
	Screw Pumps	
Steel	Immersion or non-immersion	Epoxy-polyamide High-solids epoxy-amine
	Immersion	Coal tar-epoxy
	Sludge Beds, Elevators, Conveyors, and Collectors	
Steel	Immersion or non-immersion	Epoxy-polyamide High-solids epoxy-amine Vinyl copolymer
	Immersion	Coal tar-epoxy
Concrete	Immersion or non-immersion	Epoxy-polyamide High-solids epoxy-amine
	Immersion	Coal tar-epoxy
	Sluice Gates	
Steel	Immersion or non-immersion	Epoxy-polyamide High-solids epoxy-amine
	Immersion	Coal tar-epoxy
	Storage Tanks	
Steel	Exterior	Aliphatic polyurethane Vinyl copolymer 30% silicone-alkyd Alkyd gloss
	Interior	Epoxy-polyamide High-solids epoxy-amine Coal tar-epoxy

(continued

TABLE 19 *(continued)*

Surface	Exposure	Type Coating
Concrete	Exterior	Modified epoxy texture
		Acrylic latex
	Interior	Epoxy-polyamide
		High-solids epoxy-amine
		Coal tar-epoxy
	Structural Steel	
	Exterior—Severe	Aliphatic polyurethane
		Vinyl copoloymer
	Interior—Severe	Epoxy-polyamide
		High-solids epoxy-amine
	Exterior or interior—mild	30% silicone-alkyd
		Alkyd gloss
	Trickling Filters	
Steel and equipment	Non-immersion	Aliphatic polyurethane
		High-solids epoxy-amine
		Epoxy-polyamide
	Immersion	Coal tar-epoxy
Concrete	Non-immersion	Modified epoxy texture
		Acrylic latex
	Immersion or non-immersion	Epoxy-polyamide
		High-solids epoxy-amine
	Immersion	Coal tar-epoxy
	Vacuum Filters	
Steel	Immersion or non-immersion	Epoxy-polyamide
		High-solids epoxy-amine
	Immersion	Coal tar-epoxy
	Venturi Tubes	
Steel	Exterior or interior	Epoxy-polyamide
		High-solids epoxy-amine
	Washwater Tanks and Troughs	
Steel	Immersion or non-immersion	Epoxy-polyamide
		High-solids epoxy-amine
	Waste Gas Burner	
Steel	High temperature	Silicone
Concrete	Exterior	Modified epoxy texture
		Acrylic latex

[a]Source: TNEMEC Inc., Kansas City, Missouri.

formulations to assure compliance with U.S. EPA regulations as well as VOC requirements set by many of the states. Specifiers should be particularly familiar with California regulations, especially those in the Los Angeles area.

Generally, topcoat paints used in CPI applications will not be heavily loaded with pigments because striking increases, the film becomes porous and, as a result, weathers faster, is less washable, and loses abrasion resistance and flexibility.

Appendix 2. The Time-Value of Money Related to Painting

Discounted cash flow (DCF) and rate of return is well covered in the literature. In summary, it is the algebraic summation of all savings and expenses (cash flow) for each year of investment life. Cash flow is converted to the present value of money using a discount factor. The discount factor that reduces the present value of all cash flows to zero is the percent return on a project.

Given this background, one can compare various systems and investments. For example, if one were to compare surface preparation methods prior to applying a gloss enamel to steel structures and equipment, the exhibit of Table 20 might apply.

Appendix 3. Typical Coating Characteristics

Abrasion Resistance. The ability to stand up to physical traffic and abuse from people or equipment.

Adhesion. The ability of the coating to adhere to the substrate.

Chemical Resistance. Resistance to breakdown by acids, bases, salts, and other chemicals.

Color and Glass Retention. Determines how long the coating maintains its original appearance. Varies widely by type.

Corrosion Resistance. The capacity to neutralize or keep oxygen and water away from a substrate. Requires good adhesion and low moisture vapor transmission. Can be enhanced by inhibitive pigments or by galvanic protection which sacrifices zinc to save the substrate.

Drying Time. The time it takes to dry for handling or recoating. Important for early topcoating and quick turnaround.

Immersion Capability. Requires very strong adhesion and resistance to penetration by water or chemicals. The coating also must not contaminate the solution.

TABLE 20 Comparison of Surface Preparation Methods Using DCF for a Gloss Enamel[a]

Year of Expenditure	(A) Cost of Wire-Brush System ($)	(B) Cost of Sandblast System ($)	(C) Cost of Column (A) Over (B) Savings ($)	(D) Depreciation on Added Investment ($)	(E) Taxable Income (C) + (D), ($)	(F) Income Tax, –52% of (E), ($)	(G) Cash Flow after Taxes (C) + (F), ($)	(H) Discount Factors at 10% Rate	(I) Discounted Cash Flow at 10% Rate (G) × (H), ($)	(J) Discount Factors at 15% Rate	(K) Discounted Cash Flow at 15% Rate (G) × (I), ($)
0	214,000	314,000	–100,000				–100,000	1	–100,000	1	–100,000
1	0	16,000	–16,000	–10,000	–26,000	+13,500	–2,500	0.909	–2,300	0.870	–2,200
2	0	16,000	–16,000	–10,000	–26,000	+13,500	–2,500	0.826	–2,100	0.756	–1,800
3	314,000	16,000	+298,000	–10,000	+288,000	–150,000	+148,000	0.751	+110,000	0.658	+97,000
4	16,000	16,000	0	–10,000	–10,000	+5,200	+5,200	0.683	+3,500	0.572	+3,000
5	16,000	174,000	–158,000	–10,000	–168,000	+87,500	–70,500	0.621	–43,700	0.497	–35,000
6	16,000	16,000	0	–10,000	–10,000	+5,200	+5,200	0.564	+2,900	0.432	+2,300
7	174,000	16,000	+158,000	–10,000	+148,000	–77,000	+81,000	0.513	+41,500	0.376	+30,500
8	16,000	16,000	0	–10,000	–10,000	+5,200	+5,200	0.464	+2,400	0.327	+1,700
9	16,000	16,000	0	–10,000	–10,000	+5,200	+5,200	0.424	+2,200	0.284	+1,500
10	16,000	0	+16,000	–10,000	+6,000	–3,100	+12,900	0.386	+5,000	0.247	+3,200
									Sum of discounted cash flows = +19,400		–200

By interpolation between 10 and 15%, the discounted rate of return on added investment for sandblasting = 14.8%

[a]Source: Weismantel International, Kingwood, Texas.

Low Odor, Toxicity. Important for worker safety, especially in confined areas. Also a factor in meeting air pollution regulations.

Method and Ease of Application. Application options available: Brush, roller, spray, and dipping. Also includes the restrictions air temperature and air moisture content may place on application.

Moisture Vapor Transmission (MVT). The penetration of moisture vapor through the coating to the substrate. No coating provides an impermeable barrier, but the lower the MVT, the better the corrosion protection.

Penetration. The ability to flow into the microscopic pores and crevices of the substrate for good adhesion.

Pot Life. The length of time the coating remains workable once it is opened and mixed.

Recoatability. The compatibility of a coating with a variety of topcoats. Also, the time limitations on recoating.

Scrubability. Resistance to abrasion and cleaning agents used in repeated washdowns.

Solvent Resistance. The ability to resist a variety of process solvents when cured.

Surface Preparation Requirements. The degree of surface cleaning and depth of profile that is required.

Volatile Organic Compounds (VOC's). Solvents and other organic chemicals that evaporate into the atmosphere and lead to air pollution.

Weather Resistance: Resistance to ultraviolet radiation from sunlight, oxidation, hot/cold and wet/dry cycles, acid rain.

Appendix 4. Rust Converting Primers*

During the past 2 decades the quality of paint systems available for the protection of steel surfaces against corrosion has improved dramatically. The availability of coatings that are highly resistant to corrosive environments has resulted in renewed emphasis on proper surface preparation to extend the service life of the protective top coat. Even the best paint systems will not provide effective protection, however, if applied to steel surfaces that are not free of rust.

Rust-converting primers are a proven answer, even though many corrosion control contractors are not familiar with their use. The primers provide economical and other advantages compared to sandblasting or the use of phosphoric or other acids, red lead–linseed oil primers, and mechanical surface treatments.

*Reprinted by permission from *Gas Industries Magazine*, March 23, 1987.

Problems with Other Methods

The most widely accepted treatment for effective trust removal is sandblasting, since it offers the best surface preparation for painting. Although sandblasting to white metal provides an excellent base for priming and painting the surface, the newly exposed steel surface will start rusting within hours if exposed to high humidity, rain, or condensation. Unless the protective coating is applied before the new rust forms, the service life of the coating system will be reduced. In addition, sandblasting is not completely effective on deeply pitted rust, or where the surface has welded seams, nuts, bolts, and other areas that are not easily accessible.

Sandblasting can also be ruled out for a variety of other reasons in many applications. These include:

Cost effectiveness.
Field service work restrictions.
Difficulties in coordination of sandblasting and painting cycles.
Hazards from sparks.
Contamination due to dust.
Availability of trained personnel.
Environmental considerations.
Situations where removal of steel along with the rust is detrimental.

Another solution has been the use of phosphoric and similar acids to chemically neutralize rust. Although acid treatments offer an economical alternative to sandblasting, there are a number of limitations to effective treatment. Phosphoric acid may not completely neutralize all of the different chemical rust formations. Acid neutralization is also ruled out because of environmental and safety considerations, as well as difficulties in field applications. After treatment, residual acid salts can cause blistering of the protective coating if not removed from the pores of the steel, and the treated surface may need washing to remove the acid salts.

A third option has been mechanical surface treatments such as power cleaning, scraping, or wire brushing. It is virtually impossible to remove all rust by using these methods. The presence of residual rust will result in a continuation of the corrosion process, and will result in premature failure of the protective coating.

Another standard of rust treatment has been the use of red lead–linseed oil primers. Linseed oil easily penetrates rust layers, and this type of primer offers good resistance to corrosion after curing. The primary drawbacks are safety and environmental considerations, as well as slow drying times. There are also limitations on the temperature and humidity conditions required for effective curing.

Since mechanical surface treatments can cause premature coating failure due to residual rust, and acid cleaning or use of toxic primers are cause for both health and environmental concerns, the advancements in the area of rust-converting primers offer an economical, safe alternative for effective treatment of rusted steel surfaces.

Rust-Convertible Primers

What exactly are rust-converting primers, and how do they work? Basically, a rust-converting primer is a mixture of small amounts of low-toxicity acids with a film-forming resin, usually a vinyl-acrylic latex. When these primers are applied to rusted metal surfaces, the acids chemically react with the rust to form a stable chemical complex. As the primer dries, a tough black polymer coating forms, which bonds tightly to the steel surface.

There are a number of benefits from using rust-converting primers. The primer is often in a latex base, and does not have large quantities of toxic solvents present. Thus, overall toxicity levels are very low. They are safer to use than concentrated acid rust removers or primers containing large amounts of toxic solvents or pigments.

Since rust neutralization and priming occur with one application, one step is eliminated from the treatment process. In addition, surfaces do not need to be completely rust-free. In fact, the presence of some rust on the surface is actually beneficial when using these systems, says Walter Gorbunow, President of Great Northern Research. The time restrictions, as well as the expense of white metal sandblasting, are also eliminated when using rust-converting primers.

Rust-converting primers differ markedly from other primers, Gorbunow says. When applied to rusted steel surfaces, standard primers can do no better than surround the rusted particles. This often leads to improper adhesion to the steel surface and still leaves rust particles embedded in the film. With the presence of rust in and under the primer, underfill corrosion is more likely to occur. Rust-converting primers penetrate through the rust to the steel surface and the chemically converted rust is not subject to further corrosive action.

In addition, many rust-converting primers form a dry film that is much more flexible than standard primer films. This flexibility helps prevent the cracking or crazing that can lead to primer and top coat failure, and which in turn would expose the steel surface to further corrosion.

Application

Rust-conversion primers are applied by brushing, spraying, or with a roller, as with conventional primers. Brushing is the preferred method for small jobs, and spraying with conventional paint spray equipment is recommended for larger areas. Specific details on equipment use are available from the manufacturers of the primers.

A question is sometimes raised about whether rust-conversion primers containing a latex resin may be sensitive to moisture after drying. Most conversion primers have resins that are very low in moisture vapor transmission. In other words, they resist water vapor penetration to the treated surface. This resistance is further improved by selection of a top coat suitable for the environment. There is a limitation when the primer film is immersed in water or any other liquid. Generally, rust-conversion primer systems are not recommended for this type of application.

Because the primers contain water, applications cannot be made when temperatures are below 40 to 45°F. There are also some minor limitations on the types of top coats that may be applied, although most types of industrial paints will adhere well to conversion primers.

Surface Preparation

The type of surface preparation used will vary depending on each application, based on job site limitations and financial considerations. Table 21 outlines procedures for each common type of surface condition.

Many of the manufacturers of rust-conversion primers have technical and field representatives to advise on application and process options for each particular application. On small jobs the instructions provided in technical literature and on container labels are usually sufficient. Where a large job is involved, or where unique conditions exist, it is wise to consult with the primer's manufacturer before application.

Sandblasting is recommended for surface preparation in some cases. This does not eliminate the cost savings in the use of rust-conversion primers, since light sandblasting is used. The cost of this is about 25% that of white metal sandblasting, normally required before treating corroded surfaces with conventional primers and top coats. The difference in cost is associated directly to labor. Light sandblasting takes about a quarter of the time that is required to white metal sandblast the same surface area. There are also additional benefits to light sandblasting, such as minimizing the total time for completion of the job, and thus reducing downtime.

On large jobs the greatest overall savings occur when rust-conversion primers are used on a lightly sandblasted or power-washed surface in place of the more expensive and time-consuming white metal sandblasting. Table 22 shows the cost advantages in such an application.

In addition to the potential savings that occur from power washing or light sandblasting, followed by the use of rust-conversion primer, the total time required to complete the job is considerably less than with white sandblasting. Where downtime in the area affects productivity, the rust-conversion primer option will add further to overall savings.

Power washing would appear to be the most economical option in the example shown in the cost table. However, power washing is limited to situations where there are not rust formations present under tightly adhering paint films. If paint blistering is present, due to underfill rust, power washing may not adequately expose the rusted areas for neutralization when the primer is applied.

Extended Corrosion Resistance

Surfaces treated with rust-conversion primers versus a standard metal primer applied directly over rusted steel should have a two- to fourfold increase in service life, Gorbunow says. As an example, if a standard metal primer

TABLE 21 Choosing a Treatment for Corroded Steel Surfaces (in sequence: from the lowest level of surface corrosion to the most difficult surface conditions)[a]

Surface Condition	Wire Brush	Water Rinse[b]	Light Sandblast	Power Wash	Apply Rust-Conversion Primer[c]	Dry 24 h	Apply Suitable Topcoat for Environment
Light rust, no paint					×	×	×
Heavy rust, no paint	×	×			×	×	×
Large area, option				×	×	×	×
Light rust, loose paint	×	×			×	×	×
Large area, option #1			×		×	×	×
Large area, option #2				×	×	×	×
Heavy rust with loose paint or rust under paint blisters	×	×			×	×	×
Large area, option #1			×		×	×	×
Large area, option #2				×	×	×	×

[a]Source: *Gas Industries Magazine*, March 23, 1987.
[b]Water rinse: Water rinsing is necessary only when water soluble surface contaminates or excess dusting of rust occurs during the wire brushing process.
[c]Applying conversion primer: Where the treated surface is still very rough after initial preparation work, two light coats of rust-conversion primer may be required to insure good film formation over high spots. If a second application of primer is required, it may be applied within 30 to 60 min (after the first coating has dried to touch).

TABLE 22 Cost Comparison of Methods

Power washing:	$0.15–$0.20/ft^2
Light sandblasting:	$0.45–$0.65/ft^2
White metal sandblasting:	$1.60–$2.75/ft^2
Surface to be treated:	5000 ft^2
Condition of surface:	30% rust, 20% loose paint, 10% bare metal, 40% tightly adhered paint

Work Step Costs	Power Wash Preparation	Light Sandblast Preparation	White Metal Sandblast Preparation
1. Cost of powerwashing at $0.15/ft^2	$750.00		
Rust conversion primer at $40.00/gal, 25 gal (1 coat)	$1000.00		
Labor: 1 Man at $20.00/h. Total: 12 h (priming)	$240.00		
2. Cost of light sandblasting at $0.45/ft^2		$2250.00	
Rust conversion primer at $40.00/gal, 25 gal (1 coat)		$1000.00	
Labor: 1 Man at $20.00/h. Total: 12 h (priming)		$240.00	
3. Cost of white metal sandblasting at $1.60/ft^2			$8000.00
Standard metal primer at $18.00/gal, 18 gal (1 coat)			$324.00
Labor: 1 Man at $20.00/h. Total: 12 h (priming)			$240.00
Total cost[b]	$1950.00	$3490.00	$8564.00

[a]Source: *Gas Industries Magazine*, March 23, 1987.
[b]Total cost does not include cost of materials, labor, or paint for the top coat since costs for each type of job would be the same for this step.

applied to a rusted metal surface gave 1 year of protection, a rust-conversion primer would provide 2 to 4 years of protection on the same surface. These estimates are based on proper surface preparation. Depending on the labor costs and the cost of downtime for each maintenance cycle, savings can be substantial.

Rust-conversion primers can also be used on galvanized metal. Where rust formation from the exposed steel is present, the primers are effective and may be used over the entire area to be treated.

Not all paint contractors use rust-conversion primers, even though the primers are well proven. It is possible, however, to find contractors in a geographical area that are familiar with the use and application of the system by contacting the various manufacturers of rust-conversion primers.

Rust-conversion primer systems are fast becoming a specified alternative when effective treatment of rust on steel surfaces is required. The low toxicity and nonflammability of the systems allow use without shutting down operations in most circumstances, and the systems have proven themselves as cost-effective alternatives to conventional sandblasting/painting systems.

On small jobs, maintenance personnel can effectively treat corrosion with the primer. Where larger areas are to be treated, or where technical expertise is required to assist in proper surface preparation, manufacturers can provide guidance.

Example: Utility Uses Rust-Conversion Primer. A common problem was faced by maintenance personnel at one utility using rust-conversion primers. Spot rusting on piping throughout the facility required treatment to prevent the spread of rust formation. Corrosion was present on about 5% of the piping. To reduce overall costs, it was necessary to have company maintenance personnel perform the work.

The surfaces along the pipes were prepared by light wire brushing, to remove loose paint and to expose rust. A dry wipe on each area was made to remove loose rust after wire brushing. Since there were no contaminants on the pipes, such as water-soluble chemicals, oil, and so on, it was not necessary to wash the surfaces.

Two coats of rust-conversion primer were applied, allowing 30 min drying time between coats. With this short drying time, the initially treated areas were ready for the second primer coat by the time the last areas had been treated with the first coat.

After the second primer coat had dried for 24 h, each area was painted by brushing on a general-purpose industrial alkyd enamel. This top coat was chosen because the atmosphere did not contain any harsh chemicals or solvents.

After 2 years, no signs or rusting exist on any of the treated surfaces. Maintenance personnel continue to use the same process when corrosion occurs along other sections of pipe.

Appendix 5. Basics of Inorganic Zinc-Rich Paints

Zinc-rich paints (normally used as primers) offer a variety of advantages for coating CPI equipment made of steel. To begin with, it offers *cathodic protection capabilities*. It is also *compatible* with a variety of topcoats to include vinyls, epoxies, silicones, and acrylic latex. Inorganic zinc *does not deteriorate* under severe exposure and is relatively *easy to apply*. It is easy to *touch up* and many offer *good heat resistance* up to 600°F. When properly specified and applied, they often offer economic advantages over other types of priming.

Appendix 6. Silicone-Based Coatings*

High-temperature silicone-based coatings are specialized materials. Understanding how they work and how to specify and apply them will help to ensure proper service and eliminate such problems as disbondment, discoloration, and early failure.

*By Paul E. France. Excerpted by special permission from *Chemical Engineering*, pp. 61–63, June 27, 1983, copyright © 1983 by McGraw-Hill, Inc., New York, New York 10020.

Basics of Formulation

For high-temperature applications, the coating system is expected to retain its appearance and integrity while protecting metal substrates at temperatures above 300°F (150°C).* Also, the coating may be subjected to corrosives.

In general, coatings are made up of a resin (or vehicle), pigments, and solvents. Conventional coatings, such as alkyds, use organic vehicles as pigment binders. However, these vehicles may decompose under heat, and this can cause premature failure.

To overcome this problem, high-temperature coatings use heat-resistant silicone resins. Silicones are organosilicon compounds that contain organic groups attached to inorganic ones. The inorganic groups have Si–O–Si bonds. Silicones have excellent thermal stability and resistance to oxidation. They are also essentially transparent to, and resistant to degradation by, ultraviolet radiation.

The combination of heat-resistant properties and weathering characteristics makes silicone resins ideal for formulation into heat-resistant maintenance coatings. Unmodified silicone resins can be combined with organic resins to reduce costs or improve properties such as adhesion, abrasion resistance, and curing time.

The pigments used must be compatible with the silicone and should not decompose at high temperatures. Pigments must also be color-stable over the entire working-temperature range of the coating.

Thermally stable inorganic pigments keep their color over time, unlike organic pigments, and so are used in silicone coatings. Traditionally, only black and aluminum-colored heat-stable pigments were available. Now, there is a wide range of colors, including earth tones.

Analyzing Operating Conditions

In specifying a high-temperature coating, the factors affecting performance must first be assessed. In addition to temperature, these include the nature of the substrate, its structure, stress due to thermal cycling, weathering, application limitations, corrosives, and life expectancy of the coating.

Two common pitfalls are made in specifying: (1) assuming that a single high-temperature coating will be right for all applications and (2) "overspecifying" the coating. Too often, the substrate skin temperature is guessed at, and the guess is made on the high side for safety. Thus, the coating system specified may be suitable for operating temperatures much higher than those that will be encountered.

Also, in overspecifying, the coating may not cure properly. Coatings based on unmodified resins require curing at elevated temperatures to achieve optimum film properties—i.e., a threshold temperature must be reached before the silicone resin reacts with pigments and extenders to crosslink or polymerize. For this reason, a coating rated for 1000°F (540°C) will not perform satisfactorily at a temperature below 450°F (230°C). Curing will never take place.

*Conversions from °F to °C are rounded off to two significant figures.

Measuring the Temperature

Correct temperature determination is critical to writing a specification. Both the temperature range and the maximum temperature need to be found. So should thermal cycling and the rate of heat rise.

Surface thermometers and pyrometers are the most accurate ways to take temperature measurements. However, they must contact the surface. Equipment may not be easily accessible—or it may be so hot that it cannot be approached safely.

Also, temperature readings taken at the most accessible locations can be misleading. For example, at ground level a stack may be heavily lined with refractories. It will have skin temperatures much lower than at its upper reaches where the lining is thinner.

When contact measurements cannot be made, other methods must be used. One is infrared-emissivity measurement. An infrared scan provides accurate temperature profiles of such equipment as smelters, blast furnaces, and kilns.

For stacks, the stack-gas inlet temperature can be determined from the process-control temperature recorder. Once this temperature is known, the exit gas temperature can be found for an unlined stack of known height and diameter. This determination is done by using Fig. 9-40 in the *Chemical Engineers' Handbook*, 5th ed. (R. H. Perry and C. H. Chilton, eds.), McGraw-Hill, New York, 1973.

Range of Applications

There are two broad categories of high-temperature silicone-based coatings: those for service below 500°F (260°C), and those for service above 500°F to 1200°F (650°C). In the former case, coatings are usually based on silicone-modified resins, which contain about 25–30% silicone. In the latter case a higher percentage of silicone is required. As temperature is increased, more silicone is needed.

(Silicone-ceramics withstand temperatures to 1400°F (760°C), but these are ceramic coatings; they will be briefly mentioned later.)

If the maximum skin temperature is under 500°F, then a single coating system is needed. However, if a broader range of temperatures exists, two different systems are required. This is typically true for complex equipment such as units in chemical-processing plants and kilns.

In cases where there is an extremely rapid temperature rise, it is unlikely that any coating will work. This is because of the thermal stresses caused by the difference in coefficients of expansion between the substrate and the coating.

Design and Maintenance Factors

In writing a specification for a high-temperature coating, the equipment design and its condition must be considered. Usually, design changes can be made only on new construction, and only when a coatings specialist is consulted before fabrication begins.

If proper measures are not taken, premature coating failure can be caused by items such as bolts, rivets, corners, edges, inverted channels, and poorly treated weldments. Sharp protrusions should be ground off, and welds power-brushed. Such areas should be spot-primed with a suitable silicone-zinc-dust heat-resistant primer.

The metallurgical makeup of the substrate must be considered, since not all equipment is made of carbon steel. Stainless steel that is to be insulated should be coated to prevent externally induced chloride stress-corrosion-cracking. The coating system must be chloride-free.

Any type of zinc-containing coating should be kept away from stainless steel, because subsequent welding might result in destructive alloying of the steel. Here, it is necessary to specify a coating that is free from chlorides, metallic zinc, and any other harmful contaminants.

Prerusted or "weathering" steel may need painting. All products of oxidation must be removed from it before coatings are applied.

Mill scale must also be removed from any metal or alloy. Upon heating, the scale eventually shatters, disbonds, and separates from the parent metal.

When refractories are used, their condition must be considered. Obviously, a gross failure of a refractory lining will result in overheating of the equipment's surface, destruction of the coating, and rapid fatigue-type failure of the steel casing.

Lesser refractory failures—e.g., thinning or cracking—may cause hot-spot failures of the coating. Local discolorations result, and are followed by disbonding, peeling, and flaking.

Surface Preparation

Once the conditions of application are known, the coating can be specified. However, no coating—no matter how well specified—will perform properly if it is not applied properly.

First, the surface must be correctly prepared. All organic contaminants must be removed completely, since they can cause poor adhesion and premature film failure. The procedures of the Steel Structures Painting Council should be followed for each type of substrate.

For carbon steel, abrasive blasting is the preferred method. It removes contaminants and creates a mechanical anchor pattern to hold the coating. The profile should not exceed 1 to 1.5 mils, since high-temperature coatings are applied in thin films to reduce internal thermal stresses.

For stainless steel, the removal of oil, grease, and cutting and drawing compounds can be done by either steam-detergent cleaning or wiping down with a high-flashpoint nonchlorinated solvent.

Priming

To avoid recontamination, priming should be done as soon as possible after surface preparation is finished. For carbon steel subjected to weathering and chemicals, use a silicone-zinc-dust primer. Topcoats are not always able to prevent under-film corrosion of the substrate. For indoor exposure in nonaggressive environments, a two-topcoat application offers a viable option.

When high-temperature equipment is to be painted, the nature of the previously applied coatings must be considered. Silicone-based topcoats should be applied only over either clean, dry, silicone-based primers or coatings of known composition. Inexpensive shop primers are not suitable.

Such primers and other coatings that are not heat-resistant must be removed. If this is not done, the previously applied coating will fail, and so will the heat-resistant coating. If the composition of the existing coatings cannot be determined, remove all of them.

During priming, the dry-film thickness of the primer should not exceed 1.5 mils for temperatures to 300°F (150°C), and less for higher-temperature service. Primers should be allowed at least a 24-h wait before topcoating to ensure complete drying and "flashoff" of entrapped solvents (for curing, it is necessary for the coating to reach a threshold temperature). Brushing and rolling topcoats over an uncured primer can cause lifting of it.

Field-Application Methods

Equipment should be allowed to cool to ambient temperature before it is painted. (The only exception is coatings that are made to be applied to hot surfaces.) If equipment is warm—say 120°F (50°C)—rollers and brushes will produce excessively thick films, which can fail prematurely via disbonding, cracking, and flaking caused by thermal stresses in the film.

Spray applications on hot surfaces can result in a condition similar to "dry spray." The film will not adhere properly, and will be extremely porous due to bubbling that results from rapid solvent evaporation.

Surface contamination is often a problem, especially for primers. Zinc dust is reactive and can give rise to surface contaminants that will produce poor adhesion. Any industrial "fallout dust" may be problematical; apply the topcoat as soon as possible after the primer is cured. If too much time passes after the primer is applied, remove any contaminants from its surface before putting on the topcoat.

Avoid prolonged exposure to wet weather, salt fog, or other corrosive conditions before a high-temperature coating is cured. Work should be scheduled so that equipment exposed to such environments can be put back into service as quickly as possible.

Poor control of film thickness can be a problem. If the film is too thick, it can check ("alligator"), crack, and lift. The total system dry-film thickness should be about 2.5–3 mils maximum for temperatures to 500°F (260°C), and 1.5–2 mils for higher temperatures.

Applying Coatings to Hot Surfaces

As already noted, most high-temperature coatings are made to be applied to surfaces at ambient temperature. What about equipment that either is rarely shut down or cannot be scheduled for painting due to short turnaround times?

For such problems, special coatings can be used. These materials—i.e., Dampney Co.'s Thurmalox 260 series—are made for in-service painting of equipment as hot as 400°F (200°C), and are rated for continuous temperatures to 500°F (260°C). Uses include coating of process vessels, piping, and heat exchangers.

These coatings are based on a copolymerized silicone resin that contains a heat-activated catalyst. Heat triggers the catalyst, crosslinking the coating and producing a chemically resistant finish similar to one created by an oven cure in a factory. Thurmalox 260 coatings are self-priming and resist corrosion.

Their use removes abrasive blasting and painting from the turnaround schedule. One major benefit of this is elimination of the threat of blast particles contaminating equipment that has been opened up for inspection or repair.

For application, surfaces are blasted to a commercial grade. Usually, one coat of the material is applied by airless spray to a minimum dry-film thickness of 1.5 mils. For surfaces previously coated with a silicate-based inorganic zinc-rich primer, one coat is sufficient.

Performance Limitations

Although typical silicone-based heat-resistant coatings work well, they do have some limitations.

They are not intended for immersion service. Splash zones, mists, and fumes can be a problem, too. Even when cured properly, these coatings are softer than most organic finishes. Adhesion is good, but the substrate must be free as possible from grease and dirt.

When silicone-based coatings are modified with organic resins, heat resistance is reduced at the high-temperature end, and gloss and color-retention suffer somewhat. However, film properties (such as flexibility, chemical resistance, and toughness) and curing are improved.

Colored enamels based on unmodified silicone resins withstand temperatures of 500–800°F (260–430°C). Black formulations perform up to 1000°F (540°C), and aluminum combinations up to 1200°F (650°C).

Heat-resistant paints containing ceramic frits operate successfully to 1400°F (760°C). Here, the silicone resin thermally decomposes, and the frits fuse into a substrate-Si-O-frit bond. The resultant finish is very durable and heat-stable.

Finally, heat-resistant coatings require maintenance. They must be inspected, and repaired if damaged.

Appendix 7. The Importance of SSPC Specifications

With NACE, the Steel Structures Painting Council offers the most detailed set of specifications for surface preparation and coatings for steel currently available. Individual membership to SSPC is $40/yr and includes copies of their *Journal of Protective Coatings and Linings*.

SSPC has a number of Task Forces whose goals coincide with proper painting practices in the CPI. An example of just some of these Task Forces activities follows.

Industrial Blast Cleaning. The Task Group on "Industrial Blast Cleaning," a new standard covering SSPC-SP 6 and SSPC-SP 7.

Power Tool Cleaning. The Task Group on Power Tool Cleaning resolved comments and negatives from a ballot on the new Power Tool Cleaning Specification, which is expected to be formally adopted by the Council in 1987.

Abrasives. The Abrasives Task Group approved the scope and format of a draft specification of nonmetallic abrasives and commented on the details of the specification. A revised draft will be circulated for comment prior to the SSPC Annual Meeting in November 1987. Also reviewed in the meeting was a proposal by SSPC to test a number of abrasives using the test methods called for in the specification to determine their viability. In addition, the Task Group reviewed the outline of a proposed SSPC videotape on abrasives.

Wet Blast Cleaning. The Wet Blast Cleaning Task Group reviewed two draft specifications, one on wet blasting with and without abrasives and one on air/water/abrasive blasting. In addition, the committee discussed the need for education about the wet blast process and its viability as an alternative to dry abrasive blasting.

Latex Coatings. The Committee reaffirmed the need for revision to three SSPC latex specifications on the basis of developing performance criteria. Results of a survey on performance testing requirements were considered, and experiences with performance testing were reviewed.

Coal Tar Epoxy. The Committee discussed SSPC taking responsibility for military specifications on coal tar epoxy. Two coal tar epoxy specifications, "Coal Tar Mastic, Cold Applied" and "Bituminous Emulsion, Coal Tar Based," were submitted to SSPC for final action.

Water-Borne Epoxies. The Committee agreed to renew work, which had been dormant since 1984, on development of a specification for water-borne epoxies. The previously developed draft was reviewed and will be mailed to develop additional comments.

Epoxy Polyamide. The Committee heard a special technical seminar on the performance capabilities of rust tolerant epoxies and agreed on the need for additional work to develop specifications, guides, and reports about these materials.

Maintenance Painting. Draft 5 of a Guide to Maintenance Painting was reviewed and revised. Several presentations were given on procedures for conducting condition assessment surveys. The Committee will also consider preparing a manual of maintenance painting and pictorial standards to judge the quality of surface preparation over previously paneled surfaces.

New Specifying Methods. The committee reviewed and revised Draft 4 of a Guide for Preparing Specifications. Participants also discussed the need for pilot specifications and the relative value of accelerated test equipment.

Protective Linings. The committee heard presentations on lining work in petrochemical facilities, lining ductile iron pipe, and cleaning contaminated surfaces for lining application. The results of a questionnaire on the scope of the Committee's work was also reviewed.

Paint Application Methods. In four task group sessions, the Committee considered pre-application procedures, application methods, applying thick film coatings, and dealing with hazardous wastes.

Regulations and Litigation. The Committee heard case histories and personal experiences about blasting hazards, VOC regulations, lead and chromate removal, and possible regulations on coal tar. Task groups were formed on VOC compliance and on removal and disposal of hazardous materials.

Inspection. The Committee reviewed the status of chapter drafts for the Inspection Manual planned for publication by SSPC. A revised schedule was developed for outlining chapter drafts and reviews.

Safety. The Committee heard three presentations on respirator safety and developed Task Groups to prepare a list of potential hazards in surface preparation and painting work, to revise SSPC-PA Guide 3 on safety, and to develop a guide to the safe use of respirators.

Paint Thickness. The Committee was reactivated to review and revise SSPC-PA 2 on measurement of paint thickness. Among the areas of revision will be calibration of pull-off gauges and the incorporation of new thickness gauges, such as those with LCD readouts, into the procedures described in the specification.

In addition, in the *Steel Structures Painting Manuals*, Volumes 1 and 2, John D. Keane, research director for the Steel Structures Painting Council, has assembled what is probably the finest collection of experts anywhere to show how to protect steel as thoroughly as circumstances require and economics dictate.

Appendix 8. A Guide to NACE Guidelines

The National Association of Corrosion Engineers is concerned with all methods of corrosion prevention and control. NACE members work in varied industries, including metals, refining, petroleum production, chemical processing, plastics, marine environments, pipelines, aerospace, coatings and linings, cathodic/anodic protection, mining, nuclear, oil and gas production, plastics, pulp and paper, water treatment, waste treatment, food processing, electronics, engineering and construction, consulting services, communications, inhibitors, education, research, mass transit, and many others.

Currently NACE offers specific documents and handbooks in the area of protective coatings. These include:

NACE Coatings and Linings Handbook. Contains the latest NACE Standards and TPC Reports on atmospheric coatings and immersion service.

Corrosion Prevention by Protective Coatings. This is a book containing practical information about high performance coatings, the problems involved in their use, and ways in which they can be used most effectively.

NACE Surface Preparation Handbook. Extremely useful soft cover handbook containing current information on proper surface preparation prior to coating application.

Corrosion Control by Organic Coatings. A classic compilation of the papers highlighted at the International Conference on Corrosion Control by Organic Coatings at Lehigh University.

Coatings and Linings for Immersion Service. Prepared by Technical Committee T-6 on Protective Coatings, this manual is a composite of factual and quantitative data on the performance of various materials which are commonly in use in coatings and linings.

Bibliography on Chemical Cleaning of Metals. A comprehensive bibliography on the chemical cleaning of metals from 1960 through 1982.

Appendix 9. Blasting Guidelines

While most of this information is covered in detail in SSPC and NACE specifications and guidelines, a general overview is considered here.

White Blast Metal Cleaning. "A White Metal Blast Cleaned Surface Finish is defined as a surface with a gray-white, uniform metallic color, slightly roughened to form a suitable anchor pattern for coatings. The surface, when viewed without magnification, shall be free of all oil, grease, dirt, visible mill scale, rust, corrosion products, oxides, paint, or any other foreign matter. The color of the clean surface may be affected by the particular abrasive medium used."

Near-White Blast Cleaning. "A Near-White Blast Cleaned Surface Finish is defined as one from which all oil, grease, dirt, mill scale, rust, corrosion products, oxides, paint, or other foreign matter have been completely removed from the surface except for very light shadows, very slight streaks, or slight discolorations caused by rust stain, mill scale oxides, or slight, tight residues of paint or coating that may remain. At least 95% of each square inch of surface area shall be free of all visible residues, and the remainder shall be limited to the light discoloration mentioned above."

Commercial Blast Cleaning. "A Commercial Blast Cleaned Surface Finish is defined as one from which all oil, grease, dirt, rust scale, and foreign matter have been completely removed from the surface and all rust, mill scale, and old paint have been completely removed except slight shadows, streaks, or discolorations caused by rust stain, mill scale, oxides, or slight, tight residues of paint or coating that may remain."

Brush-Off Blast Cleaning. "A Brush-Off Blast Cleaned Surface Finish is defined as one from which all oil, grease, dirt, rust scale, loose mill scale, loose rust, and loose paint or coatings have been removed completely, but tight mill scale and tightly adhered rust, paint, and coatings are permitted to remain provided that all mill scale and rust have been exposed to the abrasive blast pattern sufficiently to expose numerous flecks of the underlying metal fairly uniformly distributed over the entire surface."

Appendix 10. Nomogram and BASIC Microcomputer Program Estimate Coating Material Quantity for Vertical Cylindrical Tanks*

Several factors are involved in estimating the amount of material required to apply a protective coating to the exterior of a vertical cylindrical tank: number of coats to be applied, dry film thickness wanted, and volume percentage of solids in the coating.

Two of the values—number of coats and dry film thickness—can be arbitrarily established. It is considered good practice to apply three coats. Coverage to be applied should be expressed in square feet per gallon at a given mil thickness.

Percentage of nonvolatile solids, by volume, must be known to estimate the required amount of material to cover a given number of square feet of surface.

Coating manufacturers designate this percentage on the label of their coating containers.

*By Bill Sisson. Reprinted by permission from *Oil and Gas Journal*, June 1985.

The nomogram (Fig. 4) will estimate gallons required to coat a vertical cylindrical tank (walls and one end), and is based on the formula

$$G = \frac{0.7854D^2 + \pi DH}{\frac{1604S}{T}}$$

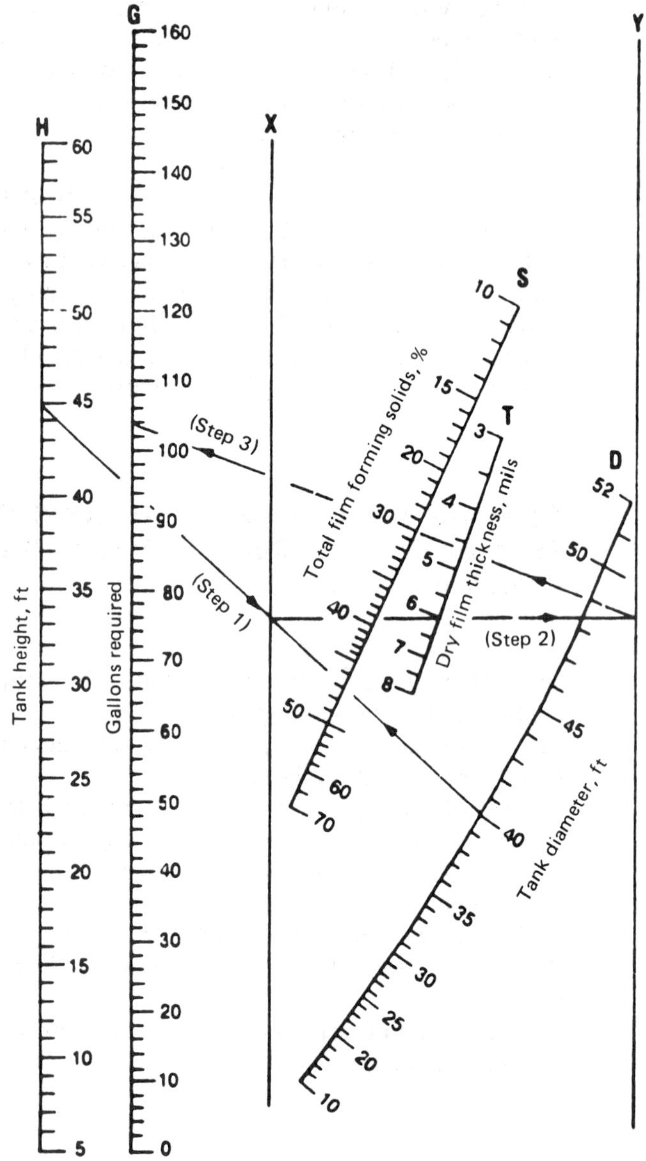

FIG. 4. Coating quantity for vertical cylindrical tanks.

where G = gallons required; H = height of tank, ft; D = diameter of tank, ft; S = total film-forming solids, percentage by volume; T = total dry film thickness, mils (0.001 in.); $\pi = 3.1416$; 1604 = square feet of coverage per gallon at 1-mil thickness (100% solids); and $0.7854 = \pi/4$.

Example. How much material is required to coat the outside walls and one end of a vertical tank 40-ft in diameter and 45 ft high?

The covering material contains 25% film-forming solids; thickness is to be 6.0 mils.

Solution: Step 1, connect 45 ft on the H scale with 40 ft on the D scale and mark at intersect with the X scale.

Step 2, line this marked point with 6.0 on the T scale and extend to the Y scale.

Step 3, line point found on the Y scale with 25% on the S scale, extend line to the G scale, and read about 103.5 gal required.

Calculation of formula: Given H = 45 ft, D = 40 ft, T = 6.0 mils, and $S = 25\%$.

$$G = \frac{0.7854 \times 40^2 + 3.1416 \times 40 \times 45}{\frac{1604 \times 0.25}{6}}$$

$$= \frac{1256.64 + 5654.867}{\frac{401}{6}}$$

$$= \frac{6911.5068}{66.833}$$

$$= 103.414 \text{ gals required}$$

Appendix 11. Frequently Used Metric Conversions for the Coatings Industry*

Film Thickness

Mils to microns (μm): Mils × 25.4 = μm
Inches to millimeters (mm): Inches × 25.4 = mm

Coverage Rate

Square feet per gallon (ft^2)/gal) to square meters per liter (m^2/L): ft^2/gal × 0.0245 = m^2L
Square feet (ft^2) to square meters (m^2): $ft^2 \times 0.0929 = m^2$

*Reprinted with permission of Porter Coatings, Louisville, Kentucky.

Thinning

1 fl. oz/gal = 30 mL/gal
¼ pt/gal = 118 mL/gal
½ pt/gal = 237 mL/gal
1 pt/gal = 473 mL/gal
1½ pt/gal = 710 mL/gal
1 qt/gal = 946 mL/gal

Volume Measure

1 fl. oz = 30 mL or 0.03 L
¼ pt = 118 mL or 0.12 L
½ pt = 237 mL or 0.24 L
1 pt = 473 mL or 0.47 L
1 qt = 946 mL or 0.95 L
1 gal = 3.8 L
5 gal = 18.9 L
55 gal = 208 L

Cubic feet (ft^3) to cubic meters (m^3): $ft^3 \times 0.0283 = m^3$

Weight Measure

Pounds per gallon (lb/gal) to kilograms per liter (kg/L): lb/gal × 0.1198 = kg/L
Pounds to kilograms: lb × 0.04536 = kg
Pounds per square foot (lb/ft^2) to grams per square meter (g/m^2): $lb/ft^2 \times 4882 = g/m^2$

Hose Sizes: Diameter (approximate conversions)—Inches to Centimeters (cm)

Inches	Centimeters	Inches	Centimeters
⅛ = 0.125	0.3	½ = 0.5	1.3
¼ = 0.25	0.6	¾ = 0.75	2.0
5/16 = 0.3125	0.8	⅞ = 0.875	2.2
⅜ = 0.375	1.0	1.0	2.5

Feet to meters (m): ft × 0.3048 = m

Conventional (air) Spray: Fluid Tip Sizes (approximate conversions)—Inches to Millimeters (mm)

Inches	Millimeters	Inches	Millimeters
0.040	1.0	0.090	2.3
0.050	1.3	0.100	2.5
0.060	1.5	0.110	2.8
0.070	1.8	0.120	3.0
0.080	2.0	0.130	3.3

Airless Spray: Tip Sizes (approximate conversions)—Inches to Microns (μm)

Inches	Microns	Inches	Microns	Inches	Microns
0.007	178	0.019	483	0.031	787
0.009	229	0.021	533	0.033	838
0.011	279	0.023	584	0.035	889
0.013	330	0.025	635	0.037	940
0.015	381	0.027	686	0.039	991
0.017	432	0.029	737	0.041	1041

Conversion factor: In. × 25,400 = Microns

Pressure and Flow Rate

Pounds per square inch (PSI) to kilograms per square centimeter (kg/cm^2):
PSI × 0.0703 = kg/cm^2
Cubic feet per minute (CFM) to liters per second (L/s): CFM × 0.472 = L/s
Gallons per minute (GPM) to liters per second (L/s): GPM × 0.0631 = L/s

Appendix 12. Coatings Calculations*

$$\text{Percent solids (by volume)} = \frac{\text{volume solids}}{\text{total volume}}$$

Dry film thickness (D.F.T.) = wet film thickness (W.F.T.) × % volume solids

*Reprinted with permission of Porter Coatings, Louisville, Kentucky.

$$\text{Wet film thickness} = \frac{\text{D.F.T.}}{\text{\% volume solids}}$$

$$\text{Spread rate} = \frac{1604\ \text{ft}^2}{\text{W.F.T.}}$$

$$\text{Coverage} = \text{\% volume solids} \times 1604\ \text{ft}^2$$

$$\text{Effects of thinning: New volume solids} = \frac{\text{total solids}}{\text{new total volume}}$$

$$\text{Cost/mil ft}^2 = \frac{\text{cost/gal}}{\text{coverage}}$$

Example. What is the cost/mil ft^2 of a coating having 45% volume solids and a cost of $17.50/gal?

$$\text{(Volume solids) } 45\% \times 1604 = 721.80 \text{ (coverage)}$$

$$\frac{\text{(Cost/gal) } 17.50}{\text{(Coverage) } 721.80} = 2.42 \text{ cents (cost/mil ft}^2\text{)}$$

Appendix 13. Guide to Zinc-Rich Paint Application*

The use of zinc in coatings to protect iron and steel substrates goes back to at least 1836, when the French engineer Sorel suggested in a patent that iron rusting could be controlled by treatment with zinc.

The most popular method of applying zinc to steel continues to be hot-dip galvanizing, which protects steel surfaces very well. In highly corrosive environments, however, topcoating is often desirable to guard zinc galvanize from eroding too quickly.

The selection of corrosion-resistant topcoats for galvanized surfaces has presented difficult problems regarding adhesion. Moreover, not all surfaces can be easily galvanized. The construction industry, therefore, welcomed the development of zinc-rich coatings.

These coatings fall into two major classes: those based on inorganic vehicles and those based on organic ones. The best-known example of an early inorganic type is the sodium-silicate-based, zinc-rich paint applied to an aboveground pipeline between Whyalla and Morgan in South Australia. This coating was applied in 1941 and was guaranteed for 20 years. According to a report given more than 30 years later [1], it remains in excellent condition.

The coating consists of a simple mixture of zinc dust and sodium silicate solution and had to be baked for half an hour to be converted to an insoluble

*By Dean M. Berger. Excerpted by special permission from *Chemical Engineering*, p. 147 ff., March 14. 1977, copyright © 1977 by McGraw-Hill, Inc., New York New York 10020.

film. Since then, numerous modifications to improve handling, film formation, and durability have been described in the patent and trade literature.

Uses in the CPI

Because zinc is anodic to steel, galvanize and zinc-rich primers act as sacrificial coatings to protect steel structures in aggressive environments, such as are found in refineries, petrochemical plants, paper mills, and many other process plants. These primers are generally matched with a topcoat suited for the specific chemical conditions.

In instances where the economics of the project preclude the use of galvanize, zinc-rich primers have been successfully adopted. The breakpoint varies with the accessibility of hot-dipping facilities, the pricing schedule, available vat size, lot size, and local shop efficiency. Factors favoring the use of zinc-rich primers include:

No restriction on the size or shape of the item to be coated.

Selective application. Since zinc galvanize is applied by immersion, the entire piece must be coated. Zinc-rich primers may be applied to just one side or to a specific section. Areas to be welded can easily be marked off.

Scheduling flexibility. Zinc-rich primed steel may be coated at a convenient interval and does not require a waiting period, which might be part of a galvanizer's shop schedule.

Absence of warpage, a problem that may be encountered with galvanize.

Several petrochemical plants have adopted zinc-rich coatings as their standard primers. Where possible, bare steel is coated with inorganic zinc-rich primers prior to construction. The primer is applied directly to the steel after automatic blast-cleaning to a near-white metal surface. The steel stands during installation with just the primer on it. After erection, finish coats of vinyl, epoxy, chlorinated rubber, coal-tar epoxy, polyurethanes, or latex are applied to a total of 8 mils minimum dry-film thickness.

Zinc-rich systems are particularly effective in coastal areas, and have frequently been the preferred method for offsetting the effects of the salt air common to marine environments. Other paints break down due to sporadic rust attack, whereas the zinc-rich primer provides sacrificial galvanic protection for the steel substrate.

Water-Based Inorganic Zincs

Various changes have been made to water-based inorganic zinc coatings to improve application, curing, and overall performance. Recent products contain a pigment that is substantially zinc dust of specially blended superfine grades with high metallic zinc content produced by the distillation process.

Additives such as red lead, lead peroxide, lead chromate, and lead sulfides have been used to lengthen pot life by delaying or preventing hydrogen evolution and retarding the tendency to thicken. The addition of lead compounds can also improve corrosion resistance while increasing the hardness of the cured coating.

Water-based lithium silicate solutions, which yield stable vehicles and paints, self-cure readily upon exposure to the atmosphere and produce films having good abrasion resistance and durability.*

Ethyl or Alkyl Silicates

This important class of self-curing zinc-rich coatings, falling between the inorganic and organic primers, is based on alkyl silicates. Although these compounds are normally grouped in the inorganic category (they exhibit all of the film properties of the inorganic silicates), they have been modified with partially hydrolyzed members of the series methyl through hexyl or glycolether silicates. The ethyl silicate type is widely used.

Hydrolyzed ethyl silicate in various states of hydrolyzation has been used as a binder for paints, and especially for heat-resistant paints, for some time. Upon partial hydrolysis, some of the epoxy groups in the ethyl orthosilicate are replaced by hydroxyl groups, thereby liberating ethanol. Some of the hydroxyl groups react with each other, giving off water and tying silicon atoms together with oxygen bridges.

The partially hydrolyzed, polycondensed ethyl silicate contains about 40% SiO_2 and continues of hydrolyze upon atmospheric exposure. It has been reported that zinc-dust paints made with this vehicle apply easily with either brushing or spraying, adhere well to iron and steel, and give excellent protection against rusting—even when immersed in salt solution [2].

According to the patent for an ethyl silicate paint,† partial hydrolysis of tetraethyl orthosilicate may be carried out by dissolving the alkyl silicate in a suitable organic solvent, adjusting the pH to between 1.5 and 4.0 by the addition of any conventional acid, and adding a quantity of water less than that required for complete hydrolysis. The reaction is then allowed to run its course, while the mixture is stirred until a homogeneous, oily liquid has been obtained. This liquid is then mixed with filler component consisting essentially of finely divided metal.

This product, a partial ester of polysilicic acid, can be used as the silicate portion of a zinc-rich paint. However, since by virtue of the silanol OH groups the material is a polysilicic acid, it will react with heavy metals and cannot be packaged with the zinc. In fact, it must be packaged in metal-free containers and is usually supplied in plastic bottles. When the paint is finally mixed and

*U.S. Patent 3,180,746 describes this water-based, self-curing inorganic zinc-rich coating, and U.S. Patent 3,130,061 details the original technology. Many paint companies are licensee producers.

†One of the most widely used zinc-rich paints based on ethyl silicate is described in U.S. Patent 3,056,684, dedicated to the public in 1972.

applied, moisture from the atmosphere completes the hydrolysis to silica, inducing the formation of a typical silica/zinc-silicate coating.

The first butyral-modified, ethyl silicate zinc-rich paint was patented in 1968 (U.S. Patent 3,392,130). The final film produced by this paint displays extremely good flexibility; it is easy to apply and to topcoat.

Colored zinc-rich paints are also available and have become quite popular recently. One-coat protection is offered and topcoating is not required.

One-Package Primers

The most promising recent developments involve preconstruction primers. These products are normally applied 0.75 to 1.0 mil over sandblast-cleaned steel. A single coat of the one-package zinc-rich primer is applied; the plate is then handled immediately and stored. After fabrication, the final coating is applied.

Weld-through primers (such as Hooker Chemicals and Plastics Corp.'s Ferrophos) are being developed to provide better welding characteristics. These coatings may be added in amounts up to 30% of the zinc content without diminishing the protective qualities of the zinc-rich primer. They exhibit good welding qualities and show little tendency toward gas evolution during welding.

In the newer single-packaged paints the use of amines (such as cyclohexylamine or triethanolamine) offers a hydroxyl source that does not react with the organic polysilicate vehicle. When a coating is applied, the amine reacts with atmospheric moisture to yield OH^- ions. The alkyl polysilicate then undergoes basic hydrolysis to form a colloidal polysilica matrix; the resultant alcohol by-product is lost by vaporization.

In addition to the above-mentioned primers, a polyol silicate and a polyol hydrocarbon ether silicate are also available. These vehicles provide virtually unlimited stability as well as good flexibility and welding characteristics.

Organic Zinc-Rich Primers

The three main organic binders used to formulate zinc-rich paints are chlorinated rubber, epoxy-polyamide, and phenoxy.

Phenoxy resins are high-molecular-weight, thermoplastic materials that combine the applicating and handling characteristics of a thermoplastic with many of the outstanding physical and chemical properties of a thermosetting resin. Phenoxy resins are made from Bisphenol-A and epichlorohydrin, and their basic chemical structure is similar to that of epoxy resins.

A major difference between organic and inorganic zinc-rich primers relates to the adhesion of topcoat to primer. Epoxy, vinyl, chlorinated rubber, and other topcoats adhere to the inorganic zinc-rich primer mainly by mechanical or polar bonding, whereas the organic primer may soften and reharden when exposed to solvents used in the topcoat.

Care should be taken, therefore, in topcoat selection. Vinyls are incompatible with phenoxy and require modifications with acrylic to adhere. Wash-primer tiecoats are frequently recommended.

Organic zinc-rich primers have no critical application requirements. They are commonly applied over blast-cleaned steel to a dry-film thickness of 2.5 to 5.0 mils by brush, air spray, or airless spray. Any reasonable thickness, however, can be applied without risk of cracking or flaking.

Organic zinc-rich primers come close to being ideal in that they combine a high order of permanence, easy application characteristics, and economy.

The most effective type is based on an epoxy-polyamide vehicle. This versatile primer (offered by many manufacturers) can be applied to a variety of substrates and offers maximum adhesion and protection. In addition, it is easily topcoated with a variety of chemical-resistant finishes.

Other organic vehicles find special uses for temporary protection and are not recommended for high performance. These include such oil-modified vehicles as alkyds, phenolics, and epoxy esters.

Zinc Chemistry

In aggressive environments the metal must be topcoated. Zinc is amphoteric and reacts quickly with chemicals. Numerous salts, many of which are insoluble, are formed.

Most chemical reactions with zinc occur in the presence of moisture. In such environments as coastal areas, one reaction that occurs might be described in a simplified form as

$$2Zn + 2NaCl + 3H_2O \longrightarrow ZnOZnCl_2 + 2NaOH + 2H_2$$

(Many other reactions may occur, however.) Because this reaction liberates sodium hydroxide, such paint vehicles as alkyds, which are alkali sensitive, should never be specified as topcoats over zinc in marine environments.

Reliability Factors

The reliability of a good zinc-rich coating system depends upon many important factors:

1. Adequate surface preparation, using an appropriate anchor pattern. (Specified by the Steel Structures Painting Council as a near-white, sandblasted metal surface.)
2. Proper film thickness (3.0 mils minimum).
3. Use of a high-quality zinc-rich primer.
4. Application of a tiecoat over the cured primer.
5. Selection of a chemical-resistant topcoat.
6. Total film thickness (8 mils minimum).

The world shortage of zinc dust is expected to prevail for many years. Considerable effort is being made to conserve the available supply. When zinc is topcoated with chemical-resistant finishes, it is reasonable to lower the zinc content of the primer from 85 to 75%, based on total film weight. Another option is to use zinc-flake pigments, which provide good sacrificial protection of low zinc content.

The Steel Structures Painting Council (SSPC) has developed an extensive specification for zinc-rich primers. The principal categories are:

SSPC PS12.01: One-coat zinc-rich paint systems.
SSPC PS12.02: Topcoated inorganic zinc-rich paint systems.
SSPC PS12.03: Topcoated organic zinc-rich paint systems.

ASTM Subcommittee DO1.46.09 is studying the adhesion of topcoats over zinc-rich primers. This committee is also examining the problems of pinholing and blistering of topcoats applied to zinc-rich primers after various time intervals. These phenomena usually occur when such topcoats are applied too soon; inorganic zinc must be allowed sufficient time to cure [3]. In some instances, steam curing may be required.

The formation of salts caused by H_2SO_4, H_2SO_3, and H_2S is believed to be responsible for the lack of topcoat adhesion in some coating systems. These zinc salts are formed as a result of chemical exposure. Moisture and chemical fumes penetrate the topcoat, causing it to peel off.

References

1. C. G. Munger, *Inorganic Zinc Coatings—Past, Present and Future*, Presented at the NACE Protective Coatings Symposium, April 1975.
2. A. C. Elm, *Zinc Dust Metal Protective Coating*, New Jersey Zinc Co.
3. W. Patton, *Performance Characteristics of Zinc-Rich Coatings Applied to Carbon Steel* (NASA TN D 7336), Kennedy Space Center, Florida, July 1973.

Appendix 14. Helpful Application Information*

Spreading Rate and Application

Putting on too little paint by overspreading or putting on paint unevenly will give you poor hiding and require additional coats regardless of quality. However, the higher quality products have less tendency toward overspreading than lower quality paints.

*Reprinted with permission of Fuller-O'Brien Corporation, South San Francisco, California.

Application Rate Example. A high quality paint will completely cover an undercoat without showing any holidays. A poor hiding paint will show flaws or colors in the undercoat.

Proper Application. Figure 5 shows the "V" method of applying an even roller coat at the often recommended 400–450 ft^2/gal. In the "V" method, pick a 2-ft^2 section of wall and make a "V," as shown in the example. Follow this with horizontal strokes, then finish with vertical strokes over the area and refill your roller for the next section. Apply even pressure when rolling or brushing, and avoid excessive roller pressure or overbrushing. Make your first stroke upward to avoid dripping. As you progress, always start in a dry area, and paint toward a freshly painted area, blending the laps. The nap of your roller should be matched to the texture of your surface.

Applicator Choice and Quality

Know your surface. Select applicators designed for your surface texture—rough to smooth. Also, use only applicators designed for latex paint. Proper selection of quality applicators can make your job easier and 30% faster.

Rollers. Use short nap rollers for smooth surfaces and longer naps for rougher surfaces.

Lower Quality Cover	"Best" Quality Cover
Holds less paint	Holds maximum amount of paint
Produces uneven hiding	Applies paint more evenly for better hiding
Increases painting time	Greatly reduces painting time.
Takes more work to produce acceptable finish	Takes less work to produce best finish

Brushes. The "best" quality brush picks up more paint and releases more paint with less chance for brush marks. Choose a brush designed for latex paint with firmly set, flagged (split tip) bristles.

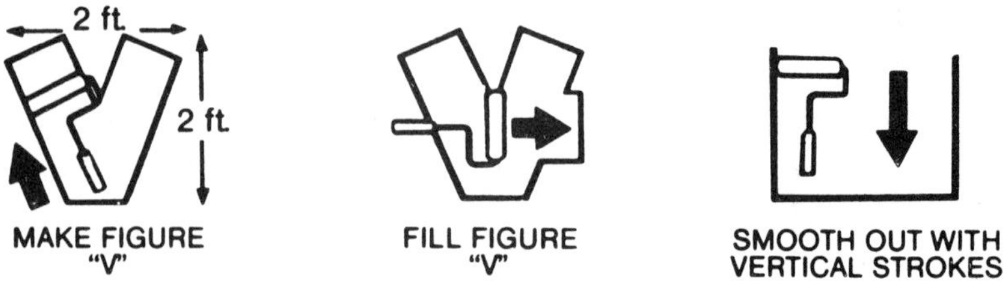

FIG. 5. Application with "V" method.

Paint Terminology

Adhesion and Surface Condition. High and average quality products will adhere well to properly prepared surfaces. Glossy surfaces, high moisture conditions, and surfaces with many older coats of paint can pose special problems. Discuss surface preparation with your dealer for best results.

Applicator. When using a roller, it is a good idea to first paint a narrow bordering edge with the "best" quality trim brush. Roll out the roller in the corrugated section of the tray to distribute the paint evenly over the entire surface of the roller and to remove excess paint.

Painting with the brush will be made easier by dipping the brush about halfway to the ferrule (metal band). Then, tap the brush lightly against the top of the can. This will shake off paint drippings and allow you to use both sides of the brush.

Application Ease. Average and high quality paints should apply easily without excessive dripping or running and without craters or blisters resulting from frothing or bubbling.

Enamel Holdout. Primer coats of good quality latex flat paints will assure that you get good gloss from enamel topcoats.

Leveling. Latex flat paints, in general, do not level as well as enamels or glossy paints. High temperature and low humidity will increase this problem, as will highly absorbent surfaces. Higher quality products generally perform better in this feature, showing fewer brush marks and roller stipples. Your applicator choice and quality also affect the leveling performance.

Paint Label Analysis. Label analyses that list major ingredients can help you get the most paint value of your money. However, quality and type of ingredients do not tell the whole story. Good formulating skills, which provide the best balance of major and minor ingredients, contribute to the quality of the product.

It should be added that a number of excellent paint manufacturers do not list components on their labels. In these instances, the reputation of the manufacturer and the confidence you have in your paint dealer will have to be sufficient for paint quality selection.

Water Resistance. Latex interior flat paints, as a class, will absorb spots of standing water, sometimes becoming soft and easily damaged. See your dealer for a suitable product for windowsills or shelves that carry potted plants. The more durable film of the higher quality products resists this damage and shows good performance.

Appendix 15. Causes of Common Finishing Difficulties and Their Remedies*

This is a check sheet for determining the causes of difficulties most often encountered in finishing operations and their remedies.

The majority of problems usually result from very simple causes which minor adjustments will correct. The causes are often so simple that they are overlooked, resulting in lost production and considerable expense.

Cause	Remedy
Breaking of Liquid (partial precipitation, out of solution, of film-forming solids)	
A. Wrong solvent used.	A. If the break is slight, the slow addition of the proper solvent, along with constant agitation, may effect a good result.
B. Subjected to unusual conditions of heat or cold.	B. Keep material at a temperature from 70 to 75°F. If break occurs because of extreme of either heat or cold, the treatment is similar to Correction E.
C. Over-reduction.	C. Follow directions for proper reduction. If material is already over-reduced, addition of fresh material will often bring entire batch back to proper state.
D. Reducer added too fast without sufficient stirring.	D. Add reducer slowly, stirring constantly.
E. Natural oxidation of the material if allowed to remain open to the air over a period of time.	E. Addition of proper amounts of solvent, plus infusion of fresh material, will put batch into condition if oxidation has not proceeded too far. It is usually well to choose a reducer of greater solvent strength than originally recommended.
F. Addition of incompatible paint or varnish	F. Very often there is no remedy. It is best to prevent it by first making the addition in a small way or, better, contacting your Technical Service Department with samples and details.

Note: If the break is too pronounced, it may not be possible to put the material back into condition satisfactory for use.

Cause	Remedy
Skinning of Liquid	
A. While it has been possible (to a large extent) to minimize skinning, it is something which will occur to a varied degree whenever any air-drying enamel is exposed to the air. Skinning can be almost entirely eliminated in baking enamels where tank conditions are reasonably good.	A. Make sure that containers in which the material is stored are air-tight. Dipping tanks should preferably have an oil- or water-sealed cover, and cover should be in place whenever tank is not in use. Whenever conditions are such that skinning cannot be overcome by normal means, consult your finishing representative.

Note: To avoid skinning during storage of open containers, or during long disuse of dip tank:

a. Oil-Type Materials. Cover remaining contents of partially filled container with small amount of turpentine before sealing.

b. Synthetic Type. Cover remaining contents of partially filled container with small amount of synthetic reducer before sealing.

Cause	Remedy
Sagging of Film (curtaining)	
A. Sagging is caused by either over-reduction or by use of too slow a solvent.	A. Use the proper solvent consistent with the general nature and temperature of the surface to be coated.
B. Application of too heavy a coat.	B. Do not apply so much material to the surface.
C. Draft condition.	C. Eliminate draft.
D. Strong sunlight causing top drying and consequent later slippage of film on vertical surfaces.	D. Avoid application in strong sunlight.
E. Uneven distribution of spray coating.	E. More careful application by proper handling of spray gun.
F. Jerky operation of mechanical equipment for withdrawal from dip tank.	F. Repair of redesign equipment.
G. Cold weather.	G. Use faster evaporating reducing thinner or bring room temperature up to 75°F.

Cause	Remedy
Lack of Flow	
A. Insufficient reduction.	A. Reduce according to instructions.
B. Use of solvent with too fast an evaporation rate.	B. If fast evaporation is due to local weather conditions, choose a slower evaporating solvent than originally recommended.
C. Improper atomization of spray gun.	C. Adjust spray equipment.
D. Application of too thin a film.	D. Apply more material to surface.
E. Draft condition.	E. Find reducing solvent or blend to provide proper flow in a draft or eliminate the draft.
Washing of Film	
A. In some dip operations, faulty ventilation in the hood above the dip tank allows a concentrated collection of solvent vapors. This reduces the film on the object which has just been withdrawn from the dip tank, thereby causing the film to wash or flow off the finishing surface.	A. Provide proper ventilation over dip tank.
B. Faulty ventilation in oven causes concentration of vapor.	B. Provide proper ventilation.
C. Wash caused by cleaning solvents remaining in crevices.	C. Be sure surface is clean, as well as all crevices. Change angle of drain.
Nondrying or Poor Drying	
A. Humid weather.	A. If possible, place in heated drying room.
B. Cold weather.	B. Maintain a temperature of a least 65°F. 75°F is desirable for normal drying.
C. Absorption of drier by paint material.	C. While it is a problem of formulation to avoid possibility of drier absorption, there are occasions when the best formulated products are apt to face that difficulty. Remedy is to add up to 3% of the proper drier.

Cause	Remedy
D. Greasy, waxy, or otherwise unclean paint surface.	D. Clean surface carefully with volatile solvents. If metal, use special metal treatment, such as Metalprep, Galvaprep, Lithoform, etc.
E. Failure to stir all pigment of pigmented finishes into proper suspension before application. Failure to stir properly unbalances formula of applied material and often will cause poor drying.	E. Stir the material thoroughly so that liquids and pigment will be evenly dispersed.
F. If application is over a stained surface, there may be some dye in the stain used which tends to prohibit drying.	F. Use the proper stain.
G. Improper ventilation.	G. Provide ventilation.
H. An attempt to fill rough wood or metal by applying a heavy coat retards through drying.	H. Do not attempt to use finish coat as a surfacer. Apply only a full covering coat.
Spotty Drying	
A. Unclean surface.	A. Clean carefully with volatile solvent or, if metal, with a commercial metal cleaner.
Lack of Hiding	
A. Over-reduction	A. Add fresh, unreduced material to that which has been reduced.
B. Application on very hot, smooth surface which tends to cause film to flow off.	B. Use a faster evaporating solvent.
C. Pigment not properly stirred into suspension.	C. Stir thoroughly to properly distribute pigment.
D. Too-slow evaporating solvent, causing too much flow.	D. Use faster evaporating solvent.
E. Improper atomization.	E. Adjust spray equipment.
F. Low film thickness.	F. Apply more paint via more passes with spray gun, higher solids (less reduction), faster thinner.

Cause	Remedy
Lack of Adhesion	
A. Certain types of metal such as galvanized iron, cadmium, and zinc are difficult surfaces.	A. If normal methods of metal preparation do not overcome adhesion difficulties, then send full particulars, with samples of metal, to your finishing representative.
B. Unclean surface.	B. Clean carefully with volatile solvent, or if metal, with a commercial metal cleaner.
C. Lack of film toughness, produced by over-addition of drier.	C. Check results against fresh material to which no drier has been added.
D. Mar-proofer or wax in previous finish or in first coat.	D. If refinishing over mar-proofed old finish, clean carefully with strong, volatile solvent. If mar-proofer is in the first coat just applied, it will be necessary to choose another type of undercoater or else a mar-proof finish which will allow application of another coat over without loss of adhesion. (Consult your finishing representative.)
E. Sometimes the finish coat and the primer used are not meant to be used together, and the solvent in the finish coat practically lifts the primer from the surface. Even though film will dry and have good appearance, primary adhesion has been ruined.	E. Make sure that the proper recommended primer and finish coat are used together.
F. Overbaking, which accelerates loss of flexibility in the film.	F. Check oven and bake according to instructions.
Lack of Adhesion between Coats	
A. Primer and enamel not recommended for use together.	A. Use properly recommended system.
B. Primer dries too hard—or glossy—due to inherent drying quality or long aging prior to application of finish coat.	B. Roughen primer with sandpaper or steel wool. It may even be necessary to use a reducer of higher solvent strength in the finish coat in order that a tooth can be obtained in the primer film.

Cause	Remedy
Brittleness	
A. It is often difficult to differentiate between "lack of adhesion" and brittleness in evaluating some film failures. Other than inherent brittleness or lack of adhesion in a finish, the cause for either difficulty will be the same.	A. See "Lack of Adhesion."
B. Improper baking. If complete polymerization of film has not been effected, brittleness may follow.	B. Check oven operation and follow baking instructions.
Flat Spots	
A. An absorbent-type putty has not been sealed in and, accordingly, causes top coat to strike in.	A. Seal the putty.
B. In some types of ovens, the temperatures may not all be uniform, causing overbaking at some portions of the finished object.	B. Ventilate the oven and circulate the air within it. Have oven checked by competent engineer.
C. There may be chemical substances upon the surface which would tend to dull the gloss. In the case of urea formaldehyde enamels, the action of trichlorethylene degreaser fumes causes flatting.	C. Make sure that surface is carefully cleaned before finishing. In case of fumes attacking film, remove the source of fumes from close contact with oven.
D. Foul ovens.	D. Provide proper oven ventilation.
E. Slight wrinkle in spots caused by addition of too much drier.	E. Use less drier.
F. Oily or dirty surfaces.	F. Provide clean painting surface.
G. Certain types of metal, such as Galvanneal and terneplate may cause flatting in spots during baking operations.	G. The flat spots, resulting from improper pickling or other causes, can usually be eliminated quickly by proper cleaning.
Too Much Spray Dust	
A. Wrong solvent blend.	A. Usual remedy is to choose a slower evaporating thinner.
B. Excess spray pressure.	B. Reduce pressure.

Cause	Remedy
C. Over-reduction of material.	C. Use less reduction. Add fresh material to that which has already been over-reduced.
D. Gun held too far from surface.	D. Hold gun at proper distance from work (usually 6 to 10 in.).

Excessive Body

Cause	Remedy
A. Any material which will dry in the presence of air at normal temperatures will tend to take on body by virtue of the oxidation which takes place.	A. If bodying of the material has not proceeded to the point where there is livering action, it is often possible to bring the thickened particles back into solution by addition of a stronger solvent of the same general type or class.
B. Even a straight baking-type enamel will tend to take on additional body due to evaporation of solvents.	B. Add proper solvent to bring liquid to proper viscosity and body.
C. In the more advanced stages of oxidation, a livering action often occurs which is aggravated by the too-swift addition of extra thinner. It should be remembered that thinner should always be added slowly and the mixture stirred at the same time.	C. If a definite livering has occurred, it is not easily feasible to reclaim material. Sample should be submitted to your finishing representative.
D. Use of improper solvent.	D. Use recommended thinner.

General: The primary cause of excessive bodying is, in most cases, improper handling of dip tank or other storage facilities. A method for keeping all storage tanks tightly sealed should be arrived at and carefully adhered to.

Cracking or Crazing of Film

Cause	Remedy
A. Application of long-oil material over a very short one, or vice versa.	A. Make sure that materials used comprise a definite approved system.
B. Application of too-heavy coats.	B. Apply only sufficient material to accomplish full covering.

Excessive Marring

Cause	Remedy
A. Film not completely dried.	A. Allow for more complete air-drying or baking.

Cause	Remedy
Discoloration	
A. Overbaking in either time or temperature.	A. Check oven temperature carefully.
B. Presence of foreign vapors.	B. Investigate the nature of any vapors which might be present. It will then be necessary to shield off the vapors from contact with the finish. If contact is unavoidable, contact your finishing representative for proper recommendation to meet the hazard.
Excessive Print	
A. Insufficient drying time.	A. Allow longer air-drying.
B. Underbaking	B. Bake more thoroughly.
C. Too heavy a coat.	C. Apply lighter coats.
D. In some cases, the addition of too much drier actually retards drying of film.	D. Cut down on drier addition. Check to be sure that correct drier is being used.
E. Slow drying due to poor drying conditions.	E. See reference to "Nondrying or Poor Drying."
F. Selection of improper quality.	F. Consult your finishing representative for suitable recommendation.
Dirty or Seedy Finish	
A. Unclean conditions of application. 1. Dust in paint room. 2. Dirt in air or paint lines of spray apparatus.	A. Cleanliness. Rearrange equipment so that any spray dust from booths does not reach drying chambers.
B. Improper solvent which tends to throw resin out of solution.	B. Use the proper recommended thinner.
C. Material has been subjected to extreme cold which tends to throw some particles out of solution.	C. Allow material to reach 75° F before applying. If still seedy, consult your finishing representative.
Orange Peel	
A. Use of improper solvent for prevailing temperature condition.	A. Choose a solvent which will allow greater flow.

Cause	Remedy
B. Improper handling of spray equipment.	B. Adjust air pressure and fluid flow and be sure that gun is held at proper distance from work.
C. Application of too thin a film not allowing proper flow.	C. Apply heavier coating.
Blushing (of lacquers)	
A. Separation of cotton due to: 1. Humid weather. 2. Drafts. 3. Poor thinner. 4. Lacquer sprayed when cold. 5. Damp spray rooms (generally concrete floors at ground level). 6. Moisture in spray equipment.	A. Combination of factors tends to cause blushing and, likewise, a combination of factors may be used to remedy the difficulty. 1. Close windows, and add retarder to thinner or use a better one. 2. Bring the lacquer to room temperature. 3. Blushing caused by condensation of water and subsequent evaporation from cold spray rooms can be avoided by warming up the room.
Gum Blush or Haze (of lacquers)	
A. Incorrect thinner (not necessarily a cheap one).	A. Use correct thinner as recommended by manufacturer of the lacquers.

Note: Both blushing and gum blush can almost always be removed on finished articles by spraying reflow thinner over the affected parts.

Cause	Remedy
Oil Bloom (of lacquers)	
A. Rubbing down with oil before lacquer is thoroughly dry. Absorbed oil floats to surface later.	A. Allow long drying time. Bloom can sometimes be removed by washing with gasoline or spraying thin coat of clear. Allow to dry and rerub.
White Spots	
A. Water mixing with the lacquer either through the "separator" or by not having the surface dry.	A. Clean air line and "separator." Be sure surface to be finished is dry. Bleed the line at least once every shift, or every 8 h.

Cause	Remedy
Brown Spots	
A. Oil coming through "separator" of spray line.	A. Cleanliness. Bleed the line at least once every shift, or every 8 h.
Pinholes or Bubbling	
A. Drafts which cause surface drying and force the solvent to break through that surface film in order to evaporate.	A. Avoid drafts.
B. Fine drops of moisture coming through separator in spray apparatus.	B. Clean spraying equipment.
C. In the case of wood finishing either the solid wood or the veneer may be improperly kiln dried, or may have absorbed excessive moisture.	C. Only solution is to cure or dry wood properly.
D. Thinner evaporates too fast.	D. Use slower thinner.
E. Porous surfacer or fillers.	E. Use tighter surfacers or else seal it before applying finishing coat.
F. Incomplete drying of filler. Strong solvent in finishing coat tends to react with undried filler.	F. Use a faster drying filler or allow greater drying time or arrange to dry at elevated temperatures.
G. Spots of grease on surface.	G. Clean surface carefully.
H. Material applied while frothy, following violent agitation.	H. Allow froth to subside before applying.
I. Lack of wetting of the surface by the enamel.	I. Wipe surface to be sprayed with a solvent-saturated cloth before application of the next coat.
Wrinkling of a Smooth Enamel—Gas Checking	
A. Too heavy a coat.	A. Apply light coat.
B. Addition of too much drier.	B. Use less drier.
C. Some materials may not be applied satisfactorily in the sun.	C. Apply in shade.
D. Foul ovens cause some materials to gas check.	D. Improve ventilation of oven and adjust the gas and air mixture.

Cause	Remedy
Bleeding	
A. Organic red pigments or various dyes used in stain or undercoats have not been sealed properly.	A. Best remedy is to avoid use of bleeding colors. Where bleeding colors have been used, a shellac-type sealer usually tends to seal the bleeding better than varnish or lacquer-type sealers.
Raising or Blistering	
A. Sometimes strong solvents tend to react with preceding coat.	A. Be sure that the undercoats are thoroughly dry. Use primer recommended. Use thinner with lowest solvent strength which will still act as steady diluent.
Excessive Settling	
A. Over-reduction or improper thinner.	A. Follow thinning instructions.
B. Too rapid thinning.	B. Add thinner gradually, stirring constantly.
Excessive Chalking	
A. Finish coat applied over porous surface which absorbs the binder and leaves unprotected pigment at surface.	A. Seal porous surface thoroughly before application of finish coat.
Cratering	
A. Silicone contamination.	A. Locate source of contamination and eliminate it. Check wipers, belt dressings, lubricating greases and oils, hand creams, metal and wood polishes, etc. as possible sources.

Appendix 16. How to Estimate Chemical Coating Requirements for Covering Product Surfaces*

The following examples are given as an aid in overcoming the problems involved in determining the area of the product surfaces to be coated.

Many complicated forms can be broken down into simple geometric figures such as the following. The surfaces to be coated can then be determined by using the following formulas.

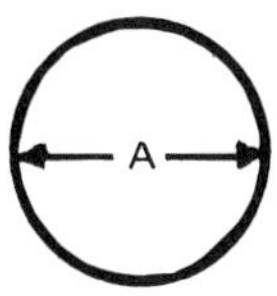

CIRCLE

Area = 0.785 × square of the diameter = 0.785 × $(A)^2$ = 0.785 × A × A

Example: The circle is 4″ in diameter. Area = 0.785 × $(4)^2$ = 0.785 × 4 × 4 = 12.56 $in.^2$

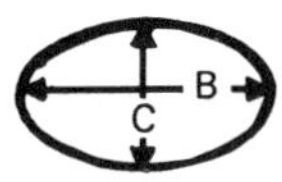

ELLIPSE

Area = 0.785 × long diameter × short diameter = 0.785 × B × C

Example: Ellipse 4″ × 3″. Area = 0.785 × 4 × 3 = 9.42 $in.^2$

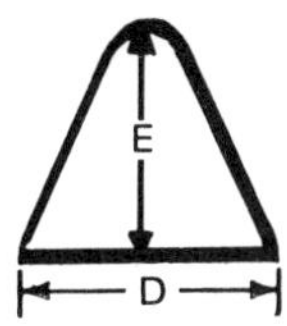

PARABOLA

Area = $\frac{2}{3}$ base × height = $\frac{2}{3}$ × D × E

Example: Base is 3″ and the height is 5″. Area = $\frac{2}{3}$ × 3 × 5 = 10 $in.^2$

SPHERE

Area = 3.14 × square of diameter = 3.14 × $(F)^2$ = 3.14 × F × F

Example: Sphere is 5″ in diameter. Area = 3.14 × $(5)^2$ = 3.14 × 5 × 5 = 78.5 $in.^2$

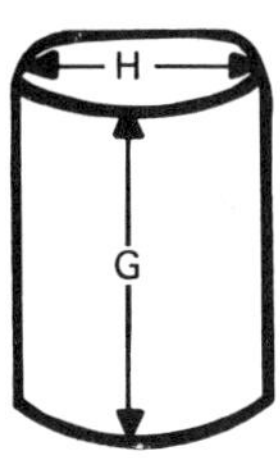

***CYLINDER**

*1. Hollow

Area = circumference × length = 3.14 × H × G

Example: Tube 4″ in diameter and 12″ long. Area = 3.14 × 4 × 12 = 150.7 $in.^2$

2. Solid

Area = circumference × length plus twice cross-sectional area = 3.14 × H × G + 1.57 × H × H = Area to be covered

Example: Round bar is 4″ in diameter and 12″ long.

Area = 3.14 × 4 × 12 = 150.7
+ 1.57 × 4 × 4 = 25.1
175.8 $in.^2$

*On all cylinders, cones, and frustrums of cones that are hollow and where it is desired to know the area that must be covered, if outside and inside areas are to be determined the average of the outside and inside diameters should be used in the formulas and the result doubled.

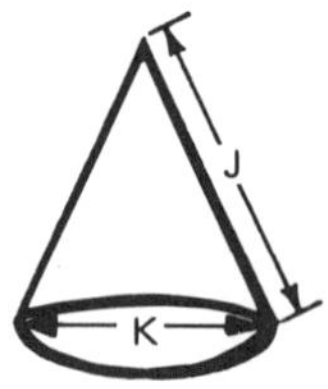

***CONE**

*1. Hollow

Area = $\frac{1}{2}$ of circumference of base × slant height 1.57 × K × J

Example: Cone is 4″ in diameter at base and 6″ slant height. Area = 1.57 × 4 × 6 = 37.68 in.^{2}

2. Solid

Area = $\frac{1}{2}$ circumference of base × slant height + area of base = 1.57 × K × J + 0.785 × K × K

Example: Same as above. Area = 1.57 × 4 × 6 + 0.785 × 4 × 4 = 37.68 + 12.56 = 50.24 in.^{2}

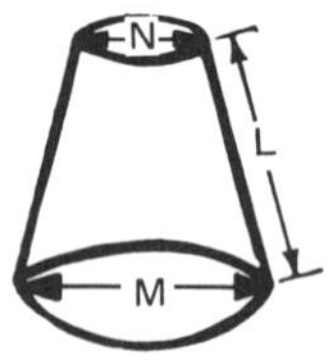

FRUSTRUM OF CONE

*1. Hollow

Area = $\frac{1}{2}$ sum of circumference of bases × slant height = 1.57 × (M + N) × L

Example: A tapered tube 4″ diameter at small end, 6″ diameter at large end, and 6″ slant height. Area = 1.57 × (6 + 4) × 6 = 94.2 in.^{2}

2. Solid

Area = $\frac{1}{2}$ sum of circumference of bases + slant height + sum of areas of bases. 1.57 × (M + N) × L + 0.785 × (M^2 + N^2) = in.^{2}

Example: A tapered bar 4″ diameter at small end, 6″ diameter at large end, and 6″ slant height. Area = 1.57 × (6 + 4) × 6 + 0.785 × (6 × 6 + 4 × 4 = 94.2 + 40.8 = 135 in.^{2}

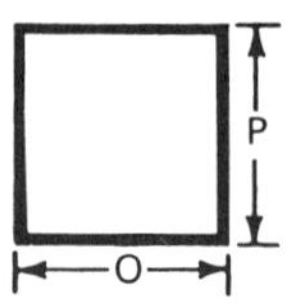

SQUARE

Area = O × P

Example: Square 5″ on a side, Area = 5 × 5 = 25 in.^{2}

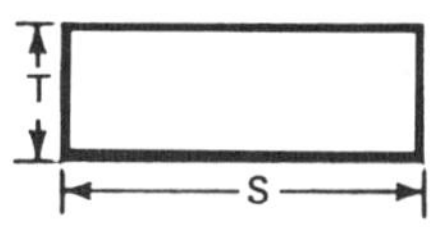

RECTANGLE

Area = S × T

Example: Rectangle 5″ × 3″. Area = 5 × 3 = 15 in.^{2}

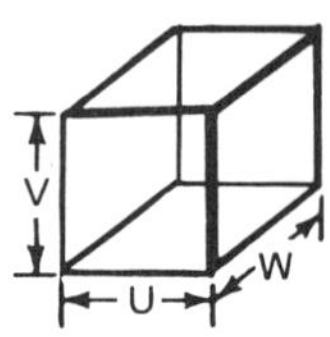

CUBE

(All sides equal)

Area = 6 × square of one side

Example: Cube 6″ on one side. Area = 6 × $(6)^2$ = 216 in.^{2}

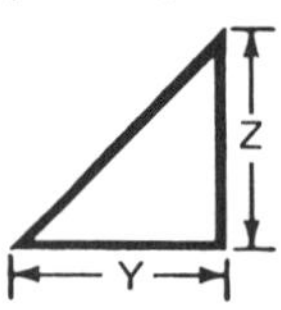

TRIANGLE

$\frac{1}{2}$ × base × altitude

Area = $\frac{1}{2}$ × Y × Z

Example: Base of triangle is 8″ and height is 6″. Area = $\frac{1}{2}$ × 8 × 6 = 24 in.^{2}

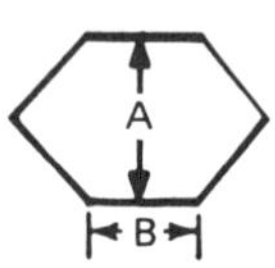

HEXAGON

(Six equal sides—all angles equal)

Area = $\frac{3}{2}$ × length of one side × distance between any two parallel sides = $\frac{3}{2}$ × B × A

Example: Hexagon 2″ on a side and 4″ between flats. Area = $\frac{3}{2}$ × 2 × 4 = 12 in.^{2}

*On all cylinders, cones, and frustrums of cones that are hollow and where it is desired to know the area that must be covered, if outside and inside areas are to be determined the average of the outside and inside diameters should be used in the formulas and the result doubled.

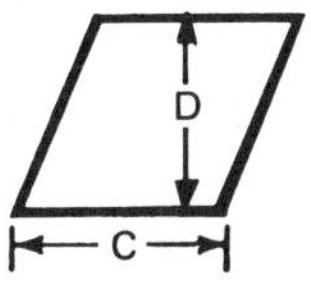

PARALLELOGRAM
(Opposite sides parallel)
Area = length of side × vertical distance to parallel side = C × D
Example: A parallelogram with one side of 6″ and a distance of 4″ between this side and the parallel side. Area = 6 × 4 = 24 in.^{2}

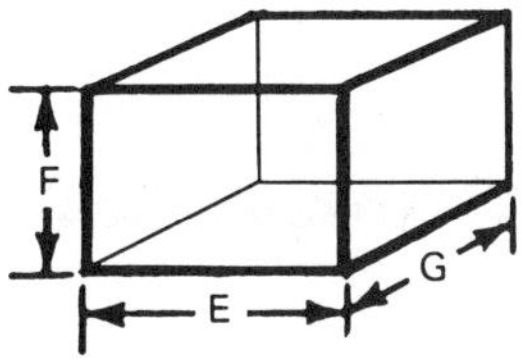

RECTANGULAR PARALLELOPIPED
(Opposite sides parallel)
Area = 2 × (E × F + F × G + G × E) = Surface
Example: A block having sides 4″, 6″, and 8″ long, respectively. Area = 2 × (4 × 6 + 6 × 8 + 8 × 4) = 208 in.^{2}

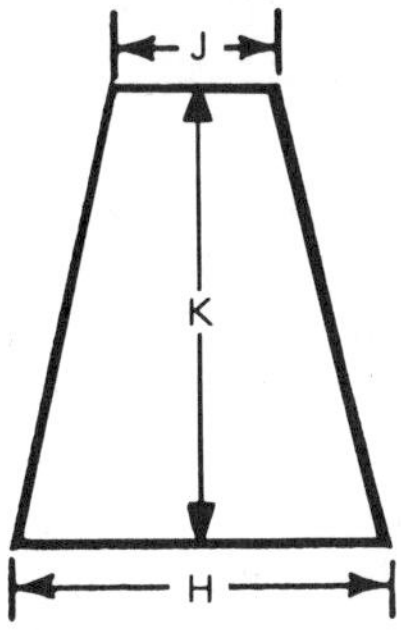

TRAPEZOID
(One pair of opposite sides parallel)
Area = ½ sum of the parallel sides × vertical distance between them = ½ × (H + J) × K
Example: A trapezoid having parallel sides 6″ and 4″ long, respectively, distance between them being 4″. Area = ½ × (6 + 4) × 4 = 20 in.^{2}

Appendix 17. 10 Basic Finishing Rules for Avoiding Common Products Finishing Problems*

1. Be sure the material you are using is adequate for the purpose intended. Proper testing of finished samples or pilot lots will offset future complaints.
2. Make routine inspection of material for working properties before throwing on production line. This prevents shutdowns.
3. Keep equipment in working order. Daily inspections should be made. Dip tanks should be checked daily for viscosity, gravity, performance; spray lines should be kept clear; etc.
4. Be sure that the product surface is properly cleaned and in suitable condition for painting.
5. Reduce paint in accordance with manufacturer's instructions. Strain reduced material into spray tank or other production line equipment.
6. Practice routine inspection. Faulty production should be apprehended quickly to prevent accumulating rejects.
7. Use good housekeeping measures. A clean shop produces clean work and reduces lost time caused by rejects, accidents, fire, etc.
8. Be aware that changes in weather often require adjustments in handling procedure, such as change of reducer, drying time before packing, etc.

9. Check on stock rotation. Use lots in order received to prevent leaving extremely old materials in stock.
10. In refilling leftover material, strain into clean containers, fill containers to the top, and close tightly so that there will be no air leakage into the package. Label and date.

Appendix 18. Troubleshooting Chemically-Resistant Monolithics*

I. Failure to Cure—Material Either Remains Soft or Hardens Only Partially; Alternatively, There May Be Both Hard and Soft Spots

1. Moisture (e.g., rain, spillage) or another liquid has settled on the surface. This may be due to inadequate weather protection, flooding of the surface from one or more sides, cooling of the air below its dewpoint on the substrate, or cold-air drafts over the surface (from external doors, etc.).
2. Surface was wet or chemically contaminated when the surfacing was applied. Cause may be inadequate cleaning, drying, or neutralization.
3. Concrete mix contained an admixture (such as an air-entrainment agent, water reducer, or curing agent) that either reacted with and depleted the hardener in the surface material or inhibited the cure of the surfacing.
4. Concrete may have contained too much water (i.e., it did not dry enough), so that when the topping was applied, water collected under it to inhibit curing. (Thin sections may fail to cure completely.)
5. Resin and hardener were not mixed in correct proportions, or not mixed uniformly. (If cure is spotty, incomplete mixing is often the cause.)
6. Substrate or materials were too cold to cure properly, or the temperature of the substrate was allowed to fall below the curing temperature after its placement.
7. Overheating beyond their thermal limits will soften some monolithic toppings. If so, these toppings may appear to be partly cured, and show marks and indentations. They will usually reharden when they are cooled. (See also Item II-11 and Item IV-3.)
8. The material was exposed to intense sunlight.

II. Disbondment—Material Separates from the Substrate or Does Not Adhere

1. Surface was inadequately cleaned and dried. The bond is to dirt on the surface. (If dirt is on the surface, it can often be seen adhering to the underside of the delaminated surfacing material.)

*Reprinted by permission of Sherwin-Williams Co., Chicago, Illinois.

2. For new concrete, the contractor may have used a curing agent or sealer that acted as a bond breaker.
3. For new concrete, cement finishers may have dipped trowels in, or wiped them with, a silicone cleaner.
4. See also Item I-4.
5. Where the day-to-night thermal gradient is ±50°F, water under—not in—the slab may have been drawn up under the topping from as far as 15 ft down. If this happens, apply the monolithic on the 4 P.M. to midnight shift. The cure will be advanced enough to prevent such a problem by the time the temperature rises in the morning.
6. Oils, other release agents, or foams were used, and these left residues on concrete surfaces.
7. Concrete has inadequate surface strength. This can be the result of: (1) inadequate design specifications, (2) failure of the bulk plant to follow design instructions, (3) too much water in the mix, (4) excessive troweling in finishing the concrete, (5) failure to clean the surface or remove "laitance" (fine particles of lime or portland cement that come to the surface upon finishing). The surface of the concrete may be cleaned by brush blasting or by etching with hydrochloric acid. Proper design strength calls for a compressive strength of 3000 lb/in.^{2} at the time of application and a bond strength of 300 lb/in.^{2} using the specified surfacing material as a bonding agent.
8. Either the resin and the hardener were mixed to incorrect proportions or mixing was incomplete.
9. Substrate was too cold for adequate cure, but air temperature was high enough to cure surface.
10. Materials were used that were partly set.
11. Top temperature was exceeded. Topping has a higher coefficient of expansion than does the concrete. When the bond strength is exceeded, the topping will disbond, bulge, then crack. Cleaning by boiling water or steam can produce this. (See also Item I-7 and Item VI-3.)

III. Cracking

1. Topping was applied over an expansion joint, construction joint, or other point of movement in the substrate. (An expansion joint in the topping is required in such areas.)
2. The distance between expansion joints or stress-relief joints was too great. (Cure shrinkage results in accumulation of stresses in the topping. When these exceed the bond strength, the topping disbonds and cracks.)
3. For larger sections of concrete substrate, stress-relief joints were not placed at 20-ft or smaller intervals. (See comment under No. 2.)
4. Materials were improperly proportioned or incompletely mixed.
5. Materials were applied after working life had expired.
6. Note that if disbonding occurs, cracking due to stresses from cure shrinkage will almost certainly follow.
7. If overheating happens, disbondment will take place. If the topping is hard and does not soften appreciably at higher temperatures, it will crack.

8. Area had been frozen at particularly low temperatures. The material becomes more brittle and develops excessive shrinkage stresses at very low temperatures.
9. During cure, materials were exposed to intense sunlight—this is especially seen in spotty areas.

IV. Penetration

All resinous, siliceous or sulfur cements, toppings and monolithics are porous to some degree. Diffusion through these surfacings is faster for small molecules. Expect eventual penetration in continuously wet conditions (e.g., puddling, retaining sumps and trenches is continual use). All areas surfaced with such cements, toppings and monolithics should be sloped to prevent puddling.

Penetration will result successively in: (1) disbondment if the penetrant is a chemical that attacks the substrate at all rapidly, (2) cracking of the topping, and (3) curling upward of the edges of the crack. After disbondment and cracking occur, the substrate will show signs of chemical attack. To verify this, peel off an adjacent topping that appears sound, and check the substrate's surface with pH paper.

V. Chemical Attack

Evidence of chemical attack can be: (1) surface softening; (2) surface discoloration that cannot be removed by cleaning; and (3) surface etching, by either destruction or removal of the aggregate (e.g., silica aggregate removed by HF exposure). For etching, the surface can remain hard and porous or become powdery and crumbly. Discoloration is followed by deterioration. Other signs are softening and swelling.

VI. Blisters or Bubbles

Part A. Appearing After Application and While the Material Is Still Soft and Before It Has Hardened. Bubbles or Blisters Are Small; Some May Break, Leaving Small Indentations

1. Materials have been mixed with a high-speed mixer, entrapping air in the resin. After the surface has been troweled in place and finished, air bleeds out as blisters or tiny bubbles. A paddle mixer moving at more than 350 rev/min can cause this.
2. A breeze over 10 mi/h can cause this.
3. A highly alkaline surface (pH > 10) can result in "gassing" and subsequent blisters.
4. Application on porous concrete: Air in the pores expands as the daytime temperature rises, and pushes through the topping, resulting in blisters. This can be avoided by applying the monolithic after 4 P.M.

5. Application over concrete that has moisture in it or below it. The effect is the same as in No. 4, but here the underside of the topping also fails to cure properly. (See also Item II-5.)
6. Exposure to varying intense sunlight, heat, or cold during installation and cure.

Part B. Appearing Weeks After Cure Has Taken Place. Bubbles or Blisters Are Thick-Skinned and Usually Rather Large

1. Possible diffusion of corrosives through topping attacked the substrate at the bond surface and caused gassing or concrete "growth," with resulting delamination.
2. Possible chemical attack from underneath. Corrosives may have entered the substrate elsewhere and traveled along the rebars.
3. Overheating may have caused disbonding and bulging, similar to blistering, if the topping softened when overheated. (See also Item II-2 and Item I-7.)

VII. Expansion Joint Failure

1. Loss of bond to sides of joint. This can be due to: (1) poor design—edges of joint were not at right angles to the surface; (2) sealant bonded to bottom of joint–joint opened and material was dragged off its sides; (3) sides of joint were dirty or specified primer was not used when joint was filled; (4) low-level chemical attack occurred—usually caused by a solvent; (5) elastic limit of the sealant was exceeded; (6) sealant was heated beyond its thermal limit; (7) subfreezing of the surface took place; and (8) material suffered thermal shock, resulting in too-rapid movement of adjacent surfaces.
2. Swelling of joint. The causes can be: (1) chemical attack, which results in swelling or gassing—this is detectable by presence of crumbling, a porous condition, or spongy cavitation and loss of strength; and (2) failure to use a compatible material under the sealant—as joint closed, noncompressible material below it extruded upward, pushing the sealant out of the joint.
3. Breakup of joint filler, usually due to either (1) excessive movement beyond the elastic limits of the sealant, (2) chemical attack, or (3) excess hardener in mix.
4. Brittleness, hardness, crumbling, and loss of elasticity, due to (1) chemical attack or (2) overheating beyond the maximum service temperature.
5. Uneven cure. This is usually due to (1) exposure to moisture during cure, but can also due to (2) wind blowing over the surface, (3) excessive sunlight, or (4) nonuniform mixing of the ingredients.

GUY E. WEISMANTEL

Paper Manufacture

Paper manufacture is one of the largest industries in the civilized world, and its usage is still growing rapidly. The major applications are, first, in communications—newspapers, magazines, books, pamphlets, and in computer readouts. The second major use is in packaging—wrapping paper, bags, cartons, corrugated cardboard, and the like. There are also a host of smaller applications such as insulation, lightweight structures, sporting goods, cleaning, and medical items.

The growth in demand could well outstrip the earth's supply of the basic raw material, trees, except for two mitigating tendencies: the use of thinner grades of paper and the substitution of plastics for paper. The latter are usually made from petroleum or natural gas raw materials. Recycling wastepaper and more efficient processing are also helpful.

Nearly all paper is now made from wood cellulose pulp. The pulping process is described in a separate section, and it varies somewhat depending on the type of wood being converted. Basically the process accomplishes the separation of the source material into fine fibers with more or less removal of lignin or other nonfibrous adjuncts. Some specialty papers are made from sources of cellulose other than wood, such as rice hulls, hemp, bagasse, etc.; but a pulping process similar to that used for wood chips is still necessary. In the very early days of papermaking, raw materials were used which were already substantially pure cellulose, such as rags. In these cases, pulping as such could be omitted and the source material merely mechanically chopped up, washed, and bleached. Very high grade writing paper is sometimes still made from rag stock. Manufacture of the cheapest newsprint also skips the normal pulping operation, i.e., removal of lignin from cellulose. In this case a high grade of wood is mechanically ground, washed, and bleached to provide newsprint feedstock.

After pulping, the papermaking process may be subdivided into the following operations.

A. Stock Preparation

Included in this operation are preparation of a thick slurry of pulp in water, "beating," hydropulping or refining to reduce the thickness of fibers (disintegrating thick clumps or bundles to fine individual fibers or fibrils), addition of various chemicals to modify properties of the finished paper, a final cleaning to remove dirt, sand, lumps, etc., and dilution with more water.

B. Sheet Formation

This is a key step in papermaking, and on a commercial scale is carried out at high speed on a moving filter medium such as a wire or cloth on a Fourdrinier machine or on rotating cylinders or moving belts. Multi-ply sheets can be made by repeated deposition of fibers. In this step a very dilute slurry (less than 1% in solids content) is run onto the filter medium, and water is rapidly drained through the support to yield a sheet of somewhat interlocked fibers. The gravity dewatering action is aided by vacuum, pressure from an adjacent sheet, or even centrifugal force.

C. Drying and Calendering

The moist sheet leaving the forming area has little strength until it is dried from an initial moisture of 70 to 80% by weight to approximately 4 to 10% by weight.

The wet sheet may be picked up from the forming section on a carrier felt and transferred to a series of heated steel rolls, where moisture is removed by evaporation. The initial rolls may provide for blowing hot air through the wet paper. The steam heated rolls or "drying cans" are staggered so that both sides of the paper are dried. At tne end of the drying train there will usually be one or more pairs, or a stack, of calender rolls which smooth and densify the paper with a pressure of several hundred pounds per inch. The calendered paper is generally received on a large roll holding several tons of paper.

D. Finishing

Finishing of paper is a concept which may include several different steps along the process. It may include the special additives such as dyes and pigments added to the pulper or beater to enhance color and opacity, or strength additives and fillers, also added in the stock preparation area.

It may include resin or latex dipping or spraying steps included part way along the drying train. Or it may include the application of finish coatings at the calendering stage.

In any case, the roll of paper on the take-up reel is first trimmed to exact width with cutting knives at the edges, and then generally taken to a separate station for cutting into smaller widths for specific uses.

It may be subjected to "creping" where the sheet is jammed against a mechanical resistance as it is unwound and rewound. It may be further treated with resins or surface finishing agents.

Finally, the product is "converted" into specific types of end products.

Details of Papermaking Process

A. Stock Preparation

In most paper mills the cellulose pulp is stored in the form of large sheets, either dry for purchased material or moist ("wet lap") for pulp produced on site. It is generally handled on pallets, and when ready to be used, is dumped from pallets into a machine for quickly breaking up the sheets (about 40 $in.^2$ and 1/8-in. thick) and slurrying the fibers in water.

A typical machine for accomplishing this task is the Beloit hydropulper shown in Fig. 1. A powerful agitator is driven from the bottom. Its curved knife-like blades provide vigorous agitation for the whole contents of the vessel as well as impelling sufficiently fine fibers through the slotted bottom

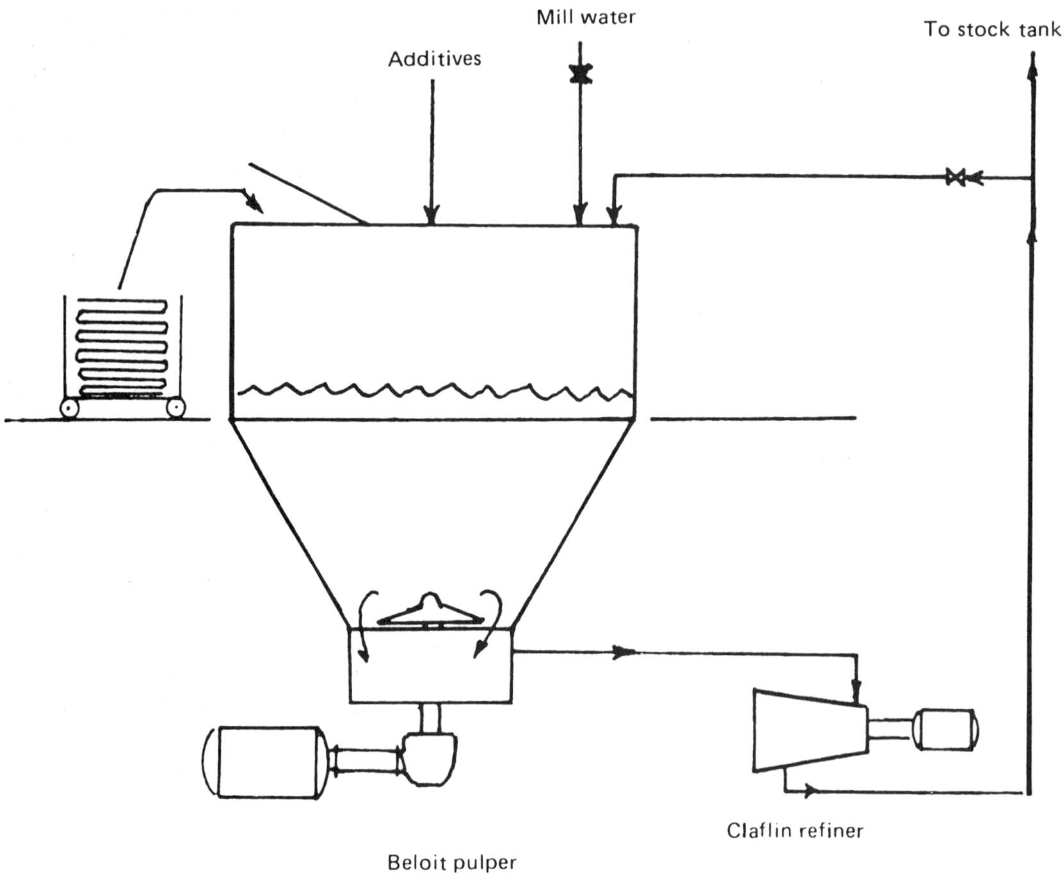

FIG. 1. Pulper system.

into the small chamber below. Agitator power may be as high as 100 hp per thousand gallons of charge capacity. The charge capacity would be of the order of 3000 to 6000 gal, and the run time, 15 min to 1 h, part of which time is devoted to circulating the slurry through the refiner, a high-speed rotating device in which internal conically disposed knives move past stationary knives or bars. A tight clearance is maintained by axial pressure against the rotating cone. The concentration of pulp in water, known as consistency, leaving this system is generally of the order of 1 to 2%, depending on fiber length. The longer the fibers, the lower the consistency must be in order to maintain a reasonable flowability. Besides cellulose pulp (or other fibers) loaded into the pulper, many other additives are generally introduced at this stage. These may be strength additives such as urea–formaldehyde resins, melamine–formaldehyde resins, rosin, or various natural gums. Synthetic gums such as polyethylene oxide derivatives and carboxymethyl cellulose may be used. Pigments and dyes are added for control of transparency, smoothness, and color. The cheapest of these is calcium carbonate or clay.

For effective whiteness, titanium dioxide is used in smaller quantities. Alum is used in many cases to promote adhesion of the other additives. Biocides may be added to prevent slime or mold growth. The total quantity of additives may be as much as 30% of the weight of the pulp, but is generally much less, of the order of 3 to 5%.

The thick slurry from the pulper is dumped into a "dump chest" for storage, then transferred to a "machine chest" for continuous feed to the paper machine area. It is diluted with "white water" or recycled liquid which drains through the paper machine screen and suction boxes into a silo or receiving tank. This system of recycling liquid not only conserves the water used in large quantities on the paper machine (slurry concentrations entering the machine are as low as 0.3% or even less) but also reclaims much of the additives which are not trapped on or adsorbed by the fibers on the machine. Thus, the additives put into the pulper are the *net* amounts taken up by the paper, while a substantial amount may circulate with the "white water." The diluted stock is generally filtered through a "barrier screen," a long rotating perforated cylindrical screen, and also passed through one or two "cleaners" in series (see Fig 2). These are long conical vessels into which the thinned slurry enters tangentially near the top; the slurry spins around rapidly, its radius of gyration decreasing as it moves downward in the cone, finally turning around near the bottom and passing up through the central core of the cone to an outlet at the top center. Meanwhile, any material such as sand, grit, bits of tramp metal, or wood are thrown out to the side of the cone and slide down into a chamber at the bottom, from which these contaminants may be continuously or batchwise discharged. The cleaned slurry is adjusted in consistency and fed to the "head box" of the paper machine, as described in the next section.

In older paper mills or in highly specialized mills where relatively short runs of a wide variety of products are made, the pulping operation may be carried out in "beaters" or "Hollanders" as shown in Fig. 3. These are long elliptical tubs, with a paddle wheel mounted on one long leg of the ellipse. The "paddles" are actually iron or other metal bars rotating against a bed plate

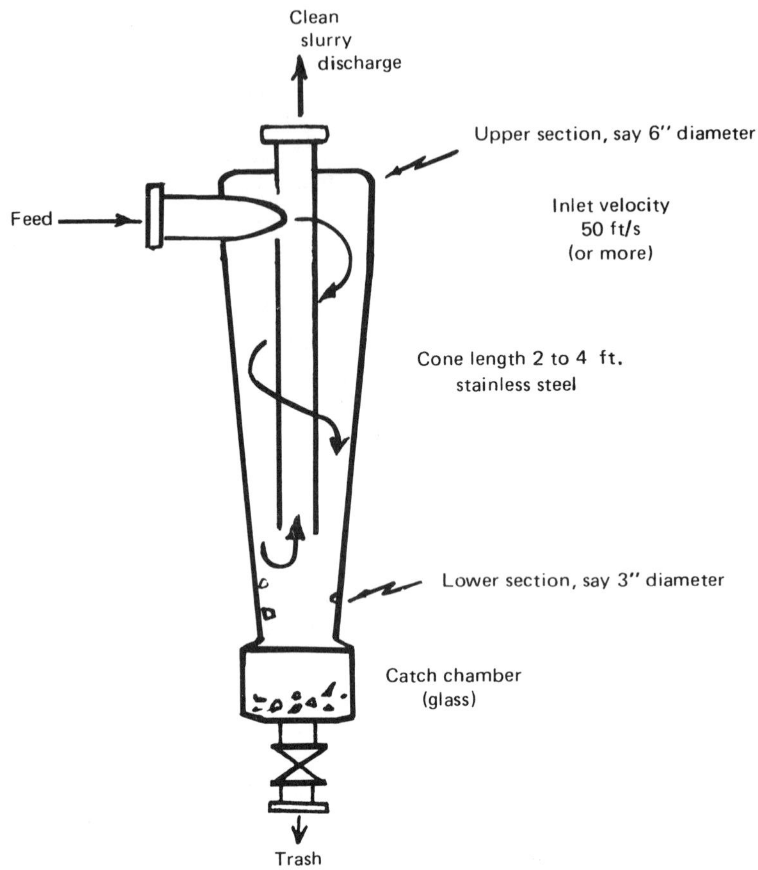

FIG. 2. Hydroclone-type cleaner.

with a sharp knife mounted to give a narrow but adjustable clearance from the bars. The assembly may be provided with a spring or counterweight system designed to allow widening of the clearance in the event of a blockage or oversized lump of hard material coming into the clearance area. The beaters are slow compared to the hydropulper, but provide for good visual observation of the fibrillating action and for holdup of batches pending testing or chemical reaction of additives.

B. Sheet Formation

The basic equipment used for sheet formation is still the Fourdrinier moving wire. Originally the feed end of the wire was mounted on an oscillating track, and the whole feed end was shuttled from side to side a distance of several inches. With the advent of high speed, wide machines, with screens traveling as much as 3000 ft/min, the shaking mechanism became too troublesome to

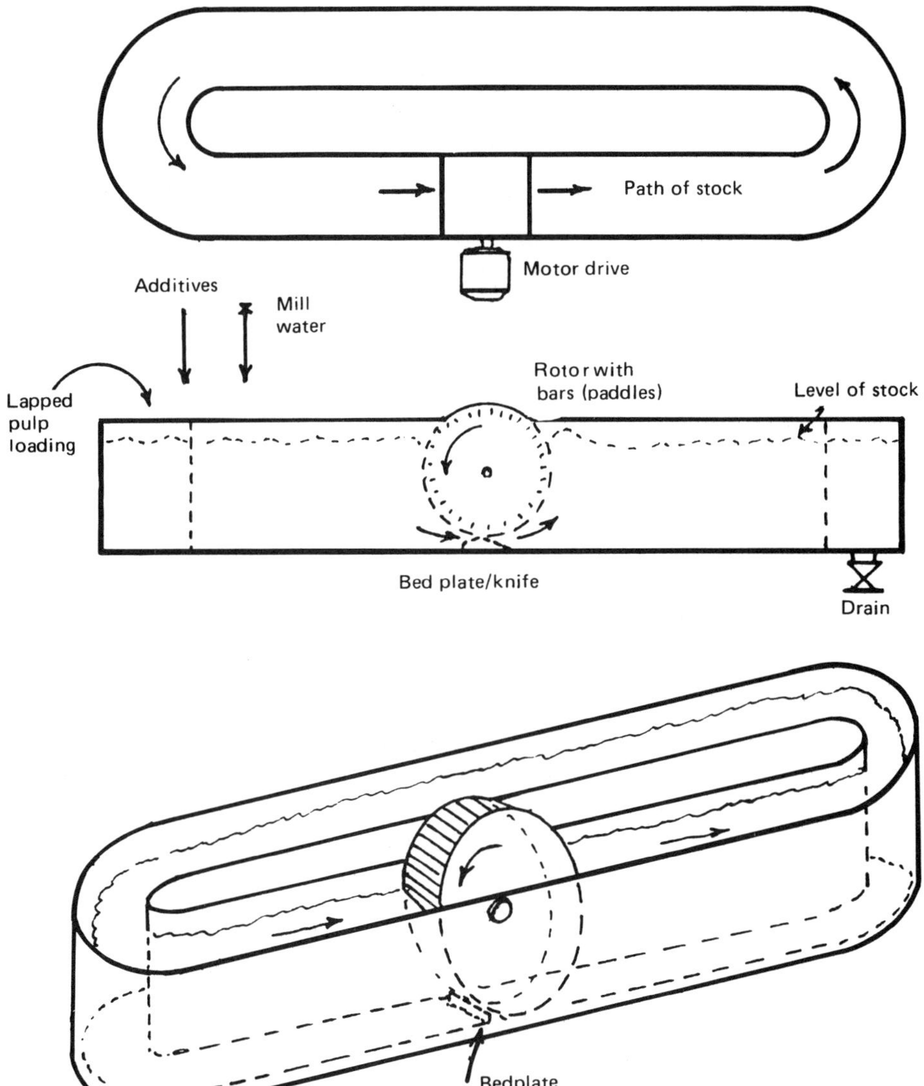

FIG. 3. Beater (Hollander).

be maintained; it has been abandoned in favor of more accurate control of the feeding of the thin slurry onto the moving wire. The slurry feeding the machine enters through a head box which is, in turn, fed through a carefully designed manifold of piping to insure uniform flow and pressure. The head box discharges through a "slice" or chute onto the surface of the moving wire, as shown in Fig. 4. The head box is contoured and baffled so that the slurry is maintained in moderately turbulent flow so as to maintain a random distribution of fibers in uniform consistency with a combination of static and hydraulic head uniform with respect to machine width and time. The "slice"

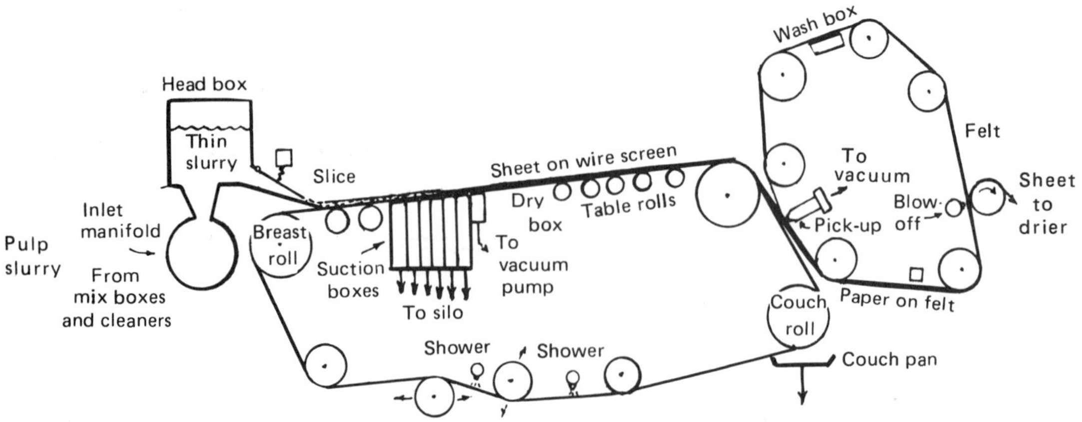

FIG. 4. Fourdrinier sheet former.

is so designed that the slurry leaves the lip at a velocity close to that of the moving screen. A slight excess of slurry velocity is known as "rush" and a slight deficiency is known as "drag." The amount of rush or drag will affect the character of sheet formation. To provide adequate hydraulic impetus, sometimes head boxes are pressurized in the vapor space above the liquid level.

The slurry as it is laid down on the wire should be uniform in depth, consistency, free of waves or ripples, and free of bubbles. Shortly after leaving the slice, the screen passes over a series of "suction boxes," or chambers with perforated tops connected to a knock-out pot and a uniform vacuum system. The boxes may be 3 to 8 in. wide, of length equal to the full width of the screen, and carefully gasketed so as to draw in water but not air. The water in the slurry should be drawn off uniformly across the width of the machine. Generally there are 3 to 6 wet suction boxes arranged close to each other in series along the wire, and they suffice to draw the free water from the surface of the newly formed sheet. Each box has its vacuum individually controlled so as to achieve uniform proportional draw-off of water from the sheet. The water from the boxes discharges into the "silo" or white water receiver tank, which is generally maintained under some vacuum. The water from the silo is returned to the slurry mixing boxes ahead of the head box via large centrifugal pump ("fan" pump) to maintain constant slurry feed and approximately constant level in the silo.

After the free water is drawn off the surface of the newly formed sheet, air will start to pass through as additional water is drained through. The screen therefore passes over one or more "dry" suction boxes, i.e., suction boxes designed to handle appreciable quantities of air along with water. Such boxes drain into a separator, the vapor space of which is piped to a high capacity wet vacuum pump such as a Nash pump. The water from the dry box separator will still drain into the silo.

After the last suction box, the sheet is ready to be removed from the wire. This is usually accomplished by transferring it to a felt, a moving band of high quality fabric which acts as a blotter to remove more moisture and as a supporting carrier, moving the sheet to the drying section of the machine.

Pick-up from the screen to the felt is accomplished by the felt passing over a "pick-up slot" vacuum source, which draws air through a narrow slot, through the felt, and through the wet sheet, lifting it off the wire and onto the moving felt. The felt will be moving at the same speed as the wire. The wire continues around over a "couch roll" where adhering water is removed into a "couch pan" for recycle. The wire then returns to the "breast roll" at the feed end, just under the head box. Between the couch roll and the head roll are several rolls which adjust the tension and alignment of the wire, and which seal off water sprayed onto the wire by high pressure jets to keep the wire clean. Under the wire just ahead of, and after, the suction boxes are several small supporting rolls called "table rolls."

For special heavy duty materials, modern paper machines are available which can lay down not only one but two or more layers of wet sheet, one over the other. Often a top layer of thinner but more special quality stock can be laid down over a bottom or base layer of heavier stock. In such cases the forming section of the Fourdrinier is made slightly longer and a second headbox and slice are added to lay down the top layer before the bottom layer is fully drained. Care must be taken that the entering top layer slurry does not disrupt the partially formed bottom layer.

For heavy sheet made at high speeds, a considerably different design of paper machine can be used. The wet sheet is formed under pressure between two wires, one on one side, the other on the other side of the sheet, with the feed injected between the two. The clearance between the wires decreases as the sheet moves along, the water being squeezed out into chambers on each side of the wire. To avoid the complication of a multitude of table rolls, one side of the pair of wires may run on a large cylindrical roll, and the other side stretched over it. The action can be repeated with any desired number of head boxes and forming cylindrical rolls.

Returning to the basic simple Fourdrinier operation, the sheet being carried on the felt is moved a relatively short distance (5 to 15 ft) to the first of several drying devices, either of squeeze roll, through drier, or "can" type, as described further on. The sheet is removed from the felt at the point of entry to this drying device by "blowing off." The "blow-off" is a slotted pipe placed at the appropriate point behind the felt, through which air is blown at a modest pressure to remove the wet paper. The felt continues on around its cycling loop, generally past a water wash station and squeeze rolls, and a vacuum box to dry the felt.

Felts used on paper machines must be of a high degree of uniformity in porosity, mechanical strength, stretch qualities, and thickness.

C. Drying and Calendering

The wet sheet as transferred from the carrier felt to the drying system is more than 70% by weight water, and a good deal of thermal energy would be required if all the moisture were to be removed via the conventional steam-heated "can" driers. In many mills a rubber-coated pair of squeeze rolls is used to mechanically remove as much water as possible. One of the rolls may be porous to facilitate taking the water away from the surface of the paper. A high degree of water removal by squeezing through rolls is limited by the poor mechanical strength of the sheet at this point in the process, and also by the disadvantage of excessive compression of the wet sheet, making it less amenable to evaporative drying.

An alternative method of removing the large initial content of water in the sheet is to use a "through drier," as shown in Fig. 5. The through drier is a large diameter perforated metal drum which rotates, carrying the sheet around under a large, closely fitting metal hood. Hot combustion gases pass from the hood through the moist sheet, vaporizing water. The vapors pass through the paper sheet and the perforations of the drum into the interior of the drum which is maintained under a moderate vacuum (say 4–8 in. water). The connection to the source of vacuum is a stationary shoe inside the rotating drum, so placed that the sheet is under vacuum from the moment it reaches the drum until shortly before it reaches the point of discharge (see Fig. 5). At the discharge a short stationary shoe provides a modest blast of compressed air to ensure removal of the sheet from the perforated drum.

The moist air coming from the sheet passes into the suction of a large fan, which circulates the air past a chamber where natural gas or LPG is burned to quickly heat the air to a controlled temperature well above the boiling point of water (say 300–500°F). The upper limit of temperature depends upon the residual moisture in the sheet leaving the drier—the greater the moisture content, the higher the allowable temperature. Moisture balance in the circulating air system is controlled by bleeding moist air out after the blower, before the combustion chamber. The rejected moist air may be passed through an economizer to recover its heat, transferring it to cold make-up air required to keep the circulation volume in balance. Operation of a through-drier system is usually controlled by a microcomputer.

Final drying of the paper is usually accomplished by use of the time-honored "can" driers which are simply cylindrical drums over which the paper passes, with alternating sides facing the drum surface. The cans are heated internally by steam at a moderate pressure (say 10 to 50 lb/in.^{2}), admitted through rotary "Johnson joints." The condensate is similarly removed, being picked up at the bottom of the rotating drum by a stationary pickup siphon or manifold. The cans are built with as thin a shell as possible to withstand pressure and mechanical requirements, to facilitate heat transfer. They are highly polished and accurately aligned. A typical can-drier arrangement is shown in Fig. 6.

After the paper has been dried to about 3 to 5% moisture it is ready for the final steps in the ordinary papermaking process. The paper passes through one or more calendering rolls which are highly polished, precision squeeze rolls which provide for densification and a smooth finish on the paper. The pressure on the rolls is hydraulically controlled to give a total load of many tons across the width of the moving sheet. To ensure against differences in pressure across the width of the calender, elaborate internal compensating devices are built into the rolls.

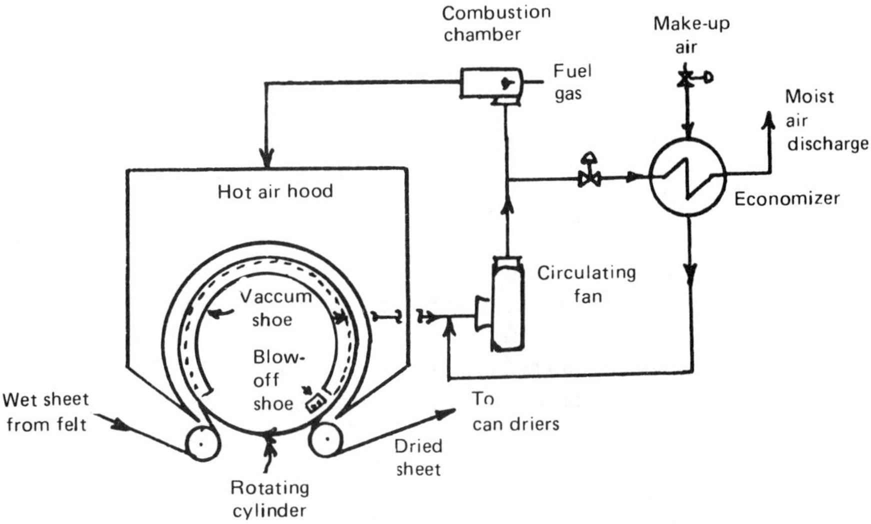

FIG. 5. Through drier.

As the mechanical and chemical properties of paper are extremely sensitive to final moisture content, it is sometimes desirable to use sophisticated means to control it. One such means is the use of a "moisturizer," which applies a controlled amount of a fine mistlike spray of water onto the surface of the paper after the calender. A high voltage may be utilized to direct the spray specifically to the paper surface. The can drier system is operated so as to overdry the paper, and the final moisture is established by use of the moisturizer.

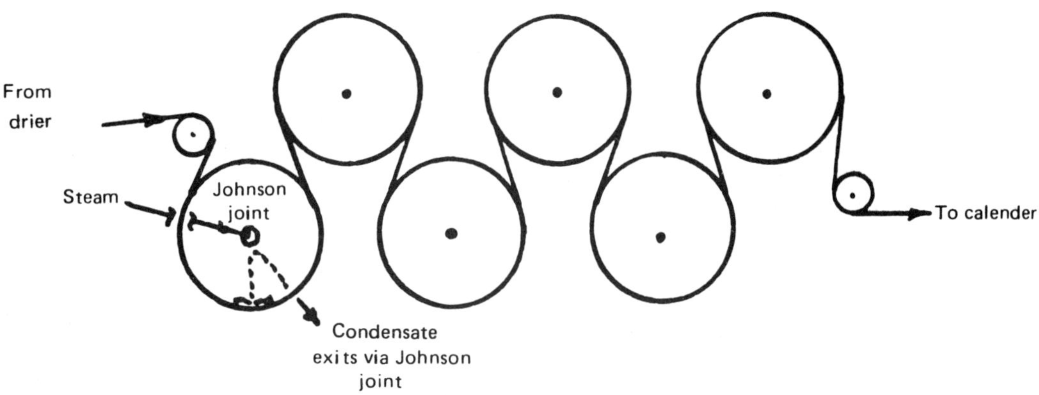

FIG. 6. "Can" driers.

D. Finishing

The paper leaving the forming and drying section of the mill is normally wound up, under controlled tension, on a "jumbo roll" which covers the full width of the machine and may be wound to 5 ft in diameter or more. This heavy roll is then removed (while a new roll is started) and taken to a cutting/slitting machine, where the jumbo roll is unwound and rapidly run past a series of circular knives set at the proper spacing to cut the sheet into whatever widths may be desired.

For may purposes a highly glossy finish may be preferred, in which case a separate calendering operation can be carried out whereby a layer of resin or plastic material is sheeted through a pair of calender rolls and then immediately laid onto the paper as it passes through another pair of rolls. A pattern may be embossed on the plastic surface during such an operation.

For special strength additives to the paper, such as vinyl acetate emulsions, viscose solutions, rubber latex, and a wide variety of other materials, a dipping plus squeeze-roll arrangement may be inserted into the drying train part of the plant. For example, after a half-dozen drying cans, the paper with a moisture content of 5–10% is dipped and squeezed to yield an impregnated paper with 20–30% reinforcing agent and perhaps another 20–30% water. This sheet then passes over another 6–12 drying cans or even a through drier to work the moisture back to 3–5%.

A creping operation has already been described.

Miscellaneous Auxiliary Equipment

In this brief description a large number of auxiliary items have been skipped, but perhaps deserve passing mention.

1. The white water circulation system takes advantage of gravity to a considerable degree. The Fourdrinier wire with its suction boxes is located on a floor of the mill well above the basement, while the white water silo is well below the machine. This provides a natural drainage suction, and vacuum pumps are needed only to trim the pressure in the vapor space of the silo. Of course, the dry vacuum boxes do need Nash vacuum pumps.
2. Because of many small sources of water around the paper machine (wire-cleaning sprays or "showers") and felt cleaning showers, wet end paper trimming jets, water seals, etc., a fair amount of excess white water is developed (beyond what can normally be recycled to the machine). This excess white water passes into a "save all" filter, a large rotary vacuum filter which recovers most of the fibers in the excess water, and even some of the pigments (which are present only in small amounts). The save all product is recycled to the pulpers.

3. When starting up a machine, or when operational upsets occur, a large amount of damaged sheet "broke" is generated. This broke is also usually recycled to the pulpers unless it is contaminated, in which case it may be burned.
4. To facilitate startup with a minimum of scrap or "broke," a usual practice is to cut only a narrow "tail" of sheet leaving the Fourdrinier wire (the rest being recycled wet to the mix boxes). This "tail" is passed under a rope at one side of the machine which threads over and under all the equipment the sheet must pass through on its way through the drying end. If the tail makes its run successfully, the tail is quickly widened to full sheet width and the drying system thus becomes fully threaded. The edge of the sheet that passed under the rope is trimmed away at the wet end, and the rope no longer carries a "tail."
5. Since can driers are bulky, they are arranged close together in staggered fashion. As water vapors emanate from the paper passing over the closely stacked cans, it is advantageous to provide good ventilation between successive cans to provide dry air and to remove hot, moist air.
6. As through driers handle very hot gases and since occasionally some paper may be trapped in the through-drier ductwork, it is desirable to provide adequate fire prevention measures. These include automatic shutoff of the combustion system, shutoff of the fresh air intake, and replacing the air with a steam snuffing system.
7. The paper, as it passes through the drying system, shrinks, and the speed of the rolls handling it must be correspondingly adjusted. This is not a simple task but is accomplished by providing many individually speed controlled motor drives along the length of the machine. The speed is adjusted to maintain constant tension in the moving sheet.
8. Occasionally it will happen that there is uneven shrinkage across the width of the machine, a condition that can cause serious tracking problems and sheet breakage. This problem can be alleviated by judicious placement and adjustment of Mount Hope rolls. These are rubber (or elastomer) covered bowed rolls, the degree and direction of bowing being controllable by simple adjustments which can be made while the machine is running. The internals of these rolls are made up of a multitude of short cylindrical sections, all rotating on a common small diameter flexible axis.

Instrumentation

The instrumentation of a modern paper machine has become highly sophisticated. Generally the machine is subdivided into a number of separate control stations, each of which is monitored and controlled by a microcomputer. These stations then feed information to a master computer and control station which keeps the whole machine under the specified operating conditions.

Sensing instruments include flow to the head box, consistency, flow through each suction box, vacuum, wire speed, wet and dry sheet thickness, moisture content, porosity, presence of holes or contaminants, and many other variables. Many of these are monitored across the width of the sheet, and a degree of uniformity is controlled.

Some Paper Product Properties

Some key properties of typical grades of paper as made today may be listed as follows.

*Basis Weight (in grams per square meter)**

Tissue	15–20
Towel	50–60
Newsprint	45–50
Grocery bag	50–100
Fine papers	60–150 (loaded)
Kraft linerboard	125–440
Boxboard	190–585

Caliper (thickness) (in micrometers)

Capacitor tissue	7.6
Facial tissue	65
Newsprint	85
Offset bond	100
Linerboard	230–600
Book cover	770–7600

Tensile Strength (in kg/cm width or sometimes in breaking length, i.e., length which is self-supporting)

Newsprint	2
Linerboard	12
Aluminum foil	20–25

The strength in the machine direction will be 1.5 to 2.5 times that in the cross direction. The strength in thickness direction is even less than in the cross

*In older terminology, lb/3000 ft^2 ream; 1 lb/ream = 1.62 g/m^2.

direction. A practically used measure of strength is the Mullen burst pressure, namely the pounds pressure required to burst an unsupported disk of paper 30.5 mm in diameter. (Pressure may run 10 to 100 lb.)

Other Properties Measured

Depending on the ultimate use, properties measured may include:

Moisture
Moisture vapor permeability
Liquid permeability
Elongation
Tear strength
Opacity, brightness, gloss, color stability
Taste, odor
Electrical resistance, dielectric strength

ERNEST O. OHSOL

Paper and Pulp, Energy Management

Energy management is a vital concern throughout the paper industry. Regulations requiring decreased consumption per unit of production, increasing costs per Btu, and threats of curtailment have made it imperative that mills find and implement means of increasing energy efficiency and of using alternative sources. The control technology applicable to accomplishing energy efficiency improvements in the pulp and paper industries is discussed. Computer implementation of energy-saving techniques offer outstanding opportunities because of the accuracy with which individual units can be regulated, and the coordination which can be enforced over entire complexes for broad-based optimization.

Early energy management efforts in paper mills and other industrial plants were focused on electrical load control. Savings were achieved in many cases without affecting production. Attention is now being turned toward steam generation and distribution systems, because these relate directly to the consumption of expensive purchased fuels. This can be particularly beneficial in pulp and paper applications because of the large amounts of steam used for direct and indirect heating needs in the processes and for conversion to mechanical shaft work or electricity.

Boiler Load Allocation

The power houses in most large mills have a number of power boilers, in parallel, to meet steam demand. Bark and recovery boilers are typically base-loaded, while fossil-fuel units on the plant master are used as swing boilers to meet variations in demand (Fig. 1). A field-proven boiler load allocation optimizer offers significant boiler fuel savings [1]. This technology is applicable to a number of parallel swing boilers which satisfy plant steam demand. The boiler load allocation optimizer programs determine the load setpoint for each boiler (e.g., Boiler P1 through P4 shown in Fig. 1) on line to provide minimum steam generation cost.

The optimization routine contains the Nelder/Mead Optimum Search Algorithm [2]. The objective function to be minimized by the Nelder/Mead algorithm is the total cost (C_T) of operating a set of N boilers. The total cost of N boilers can be expressed as

$$C_T = \sum_{i-1}^{N} C_{bi}$$

Here the cost on each individual boiler (C_{bi}) is computed from the equation

$$C_{bi} = \frac{L_i K_i C_{ci}}{h_{ci} \mathrm{EFF}\,|L_1|} + C_{pi}$$

where* L_i = the independent variable and is the steam flow for boiler i
K_i = constant expressing the Btu/lb of steam
C_{ci} = cost of the fuel for boiler i (\$/unit of fuel)
h_{ci} = enthalpy of fuel for boiler i (Btu/unit of fuel)
EFF $|L_i|$ = efficiency of boiler i as a function of the load (L_i) on boiler i
C_{pi} = cost of peripheral equipment on boiler i

Four-Boiler Example

Load allocation among parallel boilers is not an obvious decision in which an operator can arrive at the least-cost solution intuitively. Therefore, most power boilers, such as that shown in Fig. 1, take swings at an equal increment in response to steam demand. Let us consider an example.

There are four boilers with these capacities: No. 1 (120,000 lb/h); No. 2 (80,000 lb/h); No. 3 (80,000 lb/h); and No. 4 (120,000 lb/h). We have

*Conversion factors for units used in this article: Btu × 1056 = J; Btu/h × 0.2931 = W; Btu/lb × 4184 = J/kgK; lb/h × 0.4536 = kg/h.

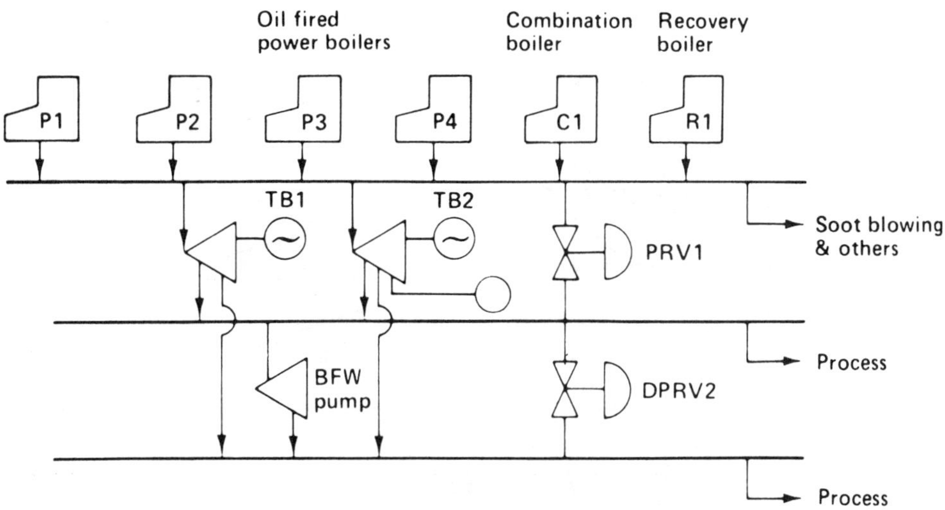

FIG. 1. Typical mill steam balance diagram.

calculated and plotted boiler efficiency (Fig. 2) based on the plant steam generation log sheet. Boiler data were further regressed to obtain a set of four equations representing each boiler:

No. P1

$$e(L)_1 = -3.618 \times 10^{-10} L_1^2 + 1.733 \times 10^{-5} L_1 + 86$$

No. P2

$$e(L)_2 = -3.656 \times 10^{-10} L_2^2 + 9.187 \times 10^{-6} L_2 + 85$$

No. P3

$$e(L)_3 = -8.14 \times 10^{-10} L_3^2 + 9.125 \times 10^{-5} L_3 + 85$$

No. P4

$$e(L)_4 = -6.0 \times 10^{-10} L_4^2 + 0.5 \times 10^{-5} L_4 + 84$$

Fuel cost for each boiler and the preceding four equations become the basis for generating the boiler operating cost for each boiler. Then, application of the Nelder/Mead method provides optimum load allocation as discussed in the previous section.

The optimization program searches for the load that each boiler should carry for a given plant steam demand. These conditions are given: User-specified allocation is 62,500 lb/h per boiler for a total of 250,000 lb/h, and fuel cost is \$2/10⁶ Btu.

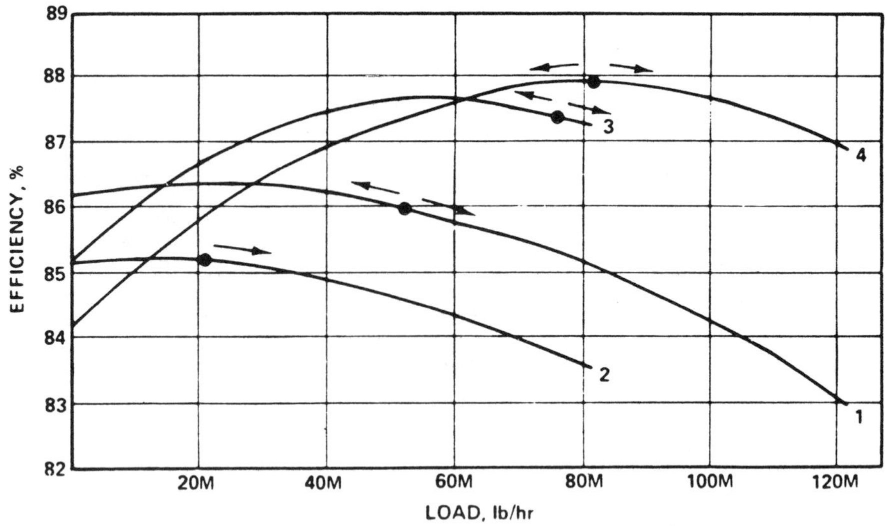

FIG. 2. Boiler performance characterization.

The tally for least-cost and user-specified load allocations appears in Table 1. Based on 350 operating days per year, the potential savings for this example come to $36,000 (Table 1). Our experience indicates that the potential fuel cost reduction by use of this allocation optimizer ranges from 1 to 2% of the total fuel cost.

Steaming Efficiency

For any particular boiler, there are fundamental limits imposed by configuration, materials, and other factors which determine how efficiently the latent energy in a fuel can be recovered as Btu's of steam. Operating conditions within the boiler then pose constraints on how closely the design efficiency can be approached.

TABLE 1 Comparison of Load Allocation Methods

Boiler	Least Cost	User Specified
No. 1, lb/h of steam	51,698.1	62,500
No. 2, lb/h of steam	21,485.7	62,500
No. 3, lb/h of steam	75,722.2	62,500
No. 4, lb/h of steam	101,094.0	62,500
Totals, lb/h of steam	250,000.0	250,000
Cost, $/h	575.60	579.98
Savings, $/h	4.38	

In conventional combustion control systems, fuel flow is measured and used to calculate the primary regulatory actions. This is appropriate in oil- or gas-fired boilers and to some extent in coal-burning units, because the Btu value of the fuel is relatively constant so that mass flow rate is a good indicator of energy input. Other quantities, including parameters of the combustion chamber and exhaust stack, are also measured and used to trim the controller settings.

In the pulp and paper industries, there are opportunities to minimize use of oil and maximize use of coal and waste fuels. Although the resulting steam is less expensive than that generated using traditional fuels, optimization is still valuable because it reduces the need to fire the more costly or scarce commodities. A problem has been that waste fuel composition is highly variable and difficult to measure. Btu value and moisture content are, therefore, unavailable as signals, and calculating compensatory action is not straightforward.

Bark Boilers

Bark or hog fuel boilers burn wood wastes in many pulp mills and lumbering operations. These units typically provide steam from wood wastes valued at \$5-10/ton—1/4 to 1/6 the cost of oil or gas at current prices.

Most of the functions needed to optimize bark boilers for steam generation can be readily provided using conventional electronic instrumentation. The decision and other specialized tasks associated with the air breakthrough, and with the empirical relations between measured excess oxygen and resultant steaming efficiency, can be implemented using handwired logic and function generator modules—compatible at the hardware and signal levels with analog transmitters, controllers, and transducers. Computer control has also been applied to bark boilers.

Black Liquor Recovery Boilers

Black liquor recovery boilers are essential units in kraft pulp plants and provide another illustration of opportunities to improve steaming efficiency through enhanced control. The original incentives for these boilers were to burn an effluent that was difficult to dispose of otherwise and to recover chemicals for use in the digesters. But the boilers can produce large amounts of steam, and this has now become an important operating criterion.

Strategies based on controlling excess oxygen in the stack have been used successfully in computer control systems to optimize the operation of black liquor recovery boilers [3]. As with hog-fired units, boiler efficiency is greatest at a point just above that at which combustibles disappear from the flue gas. The relationship between efficiency and oxygen for a simulated recovery boiler is shown in Fig. 3 for an assumed carbon monoxide concentration. The mathematical model on which this simulation is based has been developed to investigate recovery boiler sensitivity to process-parameter variation.

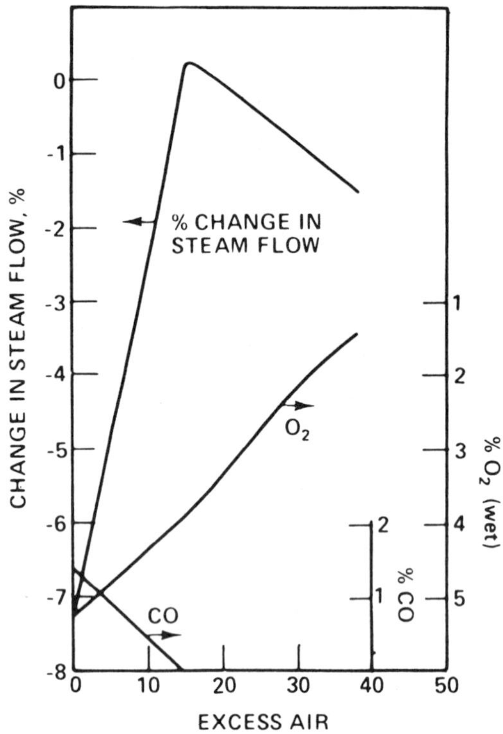

FIG. 3. Relationship of steaming efficiency to excess air for an assumed carbon monoxide concentration in the flue, based on a model of a black liquor recovery boiler.

Steam Network Management

There are often opportunities to exercise discretion in the use of generated steam in a plant. These may occur on short notice if process demand drops, or boiler capacity may be sufficient to routinely generate steam beyond process and space-heating requirements. Management of the steam network offers opportunities for savings by satisfying absolute as well as discretionary needs for heat and work in some optimal fashion.

Typical installations have boilers that generate steam at high pressure; this is expanded to several different pressure levels for use in the plant. The expansions may occur through units such as turbines or heat exchangers, in which case work or heat is extracted. The expansion may also occur through reducing valves, in which case all of the enthalpy is available at the lower pressure. Expansion policies can be established and enforced which ensure the most effective use of the work availability and heat energy in the steam as it flows through the various headers. This requires that the state of the steam be known at the entrances and exits of all units and pressure reduction stations and that calculations be performed which assign relative values to potentials for providing heat and work under given mill operating conditions.

Turbogenerator management offers an opportunity for potential savings in operating expenses. By constraining the steam flows to satisfy both the process steam requirements and, through the turbogenerators, the kWh demand requirements, the turbogenerator network will, at the minimum, fulfill the needs of the process. Upon optimization, the cost of operation will be the least among the infinite combinations of process variables that satisfy the process requirements.

Turbogenerators

Three types of turbogenerators are commonly used: extraction, backpressure, and extraction/condensing. A diagram of the extraction turbogenerator appears in Fig. 4. Any other turbogenerator or, for that matter, any PRV (pressure reducing valve) may be included in what follows with minor modifications. The extraction turbogenerator was chosen for example purposes. The instrumentation that appears on the drawings is deemed necessary so as to implement the calculations that follow.

In order to determine the kW for a particular turbogenerator, one must usually obtain the manufacturer's specification charts and determine a correlation equation between the throttle, extraction flow, and the kW.

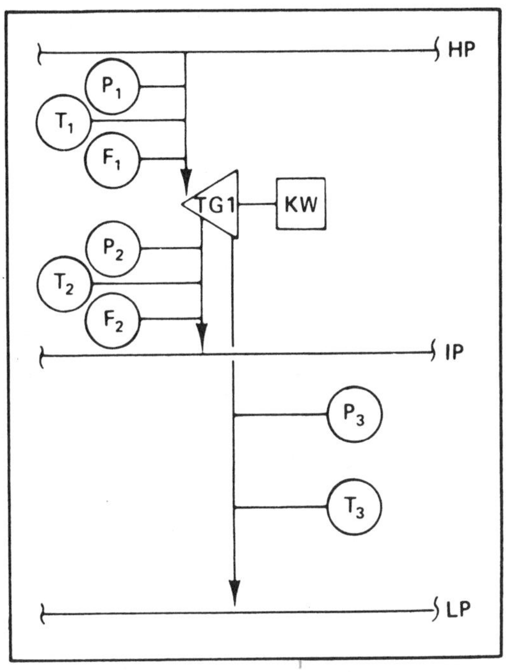

FIG. 4. Extraction turbogenerator.

$$\text{kW} = a_1F_1 + a_2F_2 + a_3$$

where F_1 = throttle flow
F_2 = extraction flow
a_1, a_2, a_3 = coefficients based on manufacturer's specification charts

The enthalpy and entropy for each stream will be calculated. These values are used for calculating actual and ideal heat rates, in addition to supplying thermodynamic information about the steam stream themselves. By definition, the ideal heat rate is that which would exist if the turbogenerator generates power isentropically. As an example, the heat rate equations for the extraction turbogenerator are

$$\text{Heat rate} = |h_1F_1 + \Delta h_2(F_1 - F_2)|(\text{kWh})$$

$$\text{Ideal heat rate} = |\Delta h_1 F_{1\,(\text{ideal})} + \Delta h_2(F_1 - F_2)_{\text{ideal}}\,|/(\text{kWh})$$

These are calculated using the flow rate and enthalpies of the streams entering and leaving the turbogenerators, as shown in Fig. 4. Turbine steam path efficiency, which measures the deviation from the thermodynamically ideal performance of the turbogenerator, is evaluated by dividing the actual heat rate by the ideal heat rate.

System Consideration

For each of the various turbogenerators and PRVs, it is necessary to write a mass and energy balance. As an example, consider the extraction turbogenerator in Fig. 4. Its balance is given by

$$F_1 = F_2 + F_3$$

where F_3 is calculated by $F_1 - F_2$ and is the steam flow into the low pressure header. Similarly, the energy balance will be given by

$$F_1h_1 = F_2h_2 + \text{kW}3412.7n + (F_1 - F_2)h_3$$

where n is mechanically efficiency and h_1, h_2, and h_3 are determined using the equation for the enthalpy and temperatures T_1, T_2, and T_3 and pressures P_1, P_2, and P_3, respectively.

To further define the system, we must determine the overall balances. The fact that the kWh generated $\Sigma(\text{kWh}_i)$ plus the kWh bought (kWh_b) must satisfy the kWh demand (kWh_d) of the plant generates one such overall balance. One may consider this as an equality constraint; i.e., the various terms must satisfy the constraint.

$$\text{kWh}_\text{d} = \sum_i^x (\text{kWh}_i) + \text{kWh}_\text{b}$$

where x = the number of turbogenerators.

Another overall balance of equality constraint that needs to be satisfied is the one defined by the steam header demand. We require that each particular steam header satisfy the needs of the plant for that steam pressure.

There is only one inequality constraint to be satisfied. The peak kW_b for the month or some average of a few peak kW_b for the month must be between certain values or else a penalty is paid. What the penalty is depends in which range the peak kW_b falls. The particular penalties and ranges are dependent upon the contract terms. Based upon the above, we notice that there is an incentive for making certain that the peak kW_b is not large. We may, by placing the above inequality constraint into the objective function, implement a policy that is consistent with a peak shaving control strategy.

Optimization

In order to optimize the performance of a system, it is necessary to define an objective function so that we have a quantitative means of gauging this performance. The objective function proposed here will contain the following elements:

The cost of steam input into the turbogenerator network (\$/Btu).
The cost of kWh generated for each turbogenerator ($\$/kWh_i$). Thus, if we can sell the kWh at \$/kWh, that is its cost on a unit basis.
The cost of kWh bought from an outside utility company ($\$/kWh_b$).
The cost associated with the peak $kW_{peak,\ b}(C_i)$ is in a certain range (U_i, W_i).

If the utility contract states that at various levels of the kW_b there are various penalties, we merely incorporate that information as an inequality constraint in the objective function.

The objective function symbolically may be represented as:

$$J = \sum_{i}^{y} F_1 h_1(\$/\text{Btu}_i) - \sum_{i}^{x}(\text{kWh}_i)(\$/\text{kWh}_i) + (\$/\text{kWh}_b)(\text{kWh}_b) + \sum_{i}^{z} \text{kW}_{\text{peak, b}} C_i(U_i \leqslant \text{kW}_{\text{peak, b}} \leqslant W_i)$$

where y = number of input streams
z = number of peak kW levels in the contract
F_i = flow of input stream i, lb/h
h_i = enthalpy of stream i, Btu/lb
kWh_i = kWh generated by turbogenerator i
kWh_b = kWh bought from utility company
C_i = cost/kW for a $kW_{peak,\ b}$ that was between U_i kilowatts and W_i kilowatts and W_i kilowatts

The previously mentioned objective function is modified appropriately depending upon the specific contract terms. We determine the optimum by manipulating the throttle and extraction valves (which are our independent variables) and thus we affect the kWh. Through our balance equations we define the F_i, kWh_b, and $kW_{peak, b}$. We thus have defined all the terms in J (the objective function) and attempt to determine the set of throttle and extraction valve settings that measure J and thus optimize plant operation.

Steam Balancing

The steam distribution system typical of those found in pulp and paper mills is shown in Fig. 1. Some methods of monitoring the steam usage at various points in systems of this complexity are necessary to provide the data for effective management strategies [4].

Steam balances are relatively straightforward calculations, which show the material flows at the battery limits of the mills for given demand under various operating conditions. Overall accuracy of 2 to 3% is usually sufficient, so conventional electronic instruments are appropriate.

The balances can be used directly to identify and investigate losses. If there are no leaks, and metering instruments are properly calibrated and maintained, steam balances should be within 3% in each header. Venting is often the most easily corrected loss mechanism in pulp and paper mill steam distribution systems. Steam balances provide the data needed to establish operating policies which minimize venting.

Steam accounting tasks includes mass and energy balancing, and Btu usage monitoring for various process areas. Systems performing such accounting functions would ideally include means to detect sudden or gradual deviations from previous operating values as indications of possible leaks, heat exchanger fouling, or process problems. The historical data would also be useful for future planning.

Instrumentation

Energy management for pulp and paper mills will typically be achieved using computers with analog instruments in supervisory control system configurations. This provides the benefits of advanced computation and centralization for coordinating and optimizing individual units, while taking the greatest advantage of existing instrumentation and allowing upgrading in stages.

Most of the individual control functions associated with the boilers in pulp and paper mills can be achieved using state-of-the-art analog controls. The broad-based coordination and the complex strategies necessary for optimization require capabilities such as memory, calculations, logic, and operator interfaces well beyond those that are feasible with traditional instrumentation. Computer-based systems appear to be essential for managing operations in a manner that will maximize the profitability and productivity of production plants [5].

Conclusion

The basic aim of this article is to demonstrate savings opportunities in utility costs through energy management applications in the mill powerhouse, with special emphasis in steam generation and distribution optimization. There is attractive economic justification for the areas discussed. The optimization technique described is one approach to parallel unit control. Other techniques, based on real-time performance measurement, are also being applied. Most pulp and paper mills are considering a building block approach with phased systems implementation, starting with the most attractive ROI projects. Eventually, each mill should have a well-integrated energy management system which permits mill utility personnel to enforce and achieve the best possible energy efficiency and utilization by an optimum millwide total energy allocation program.

References

1. C. H. Cho, *Instrum. Technol.*, *25*(10), 55 (1978).
2. J. A. Nelder and R. Mead, *Comput. J.*, *7*(1), 303 (1955).
3. J. Conner and T. L. Blevins, *Pulp Pap.*, *52*(6), 140 (1978).
4. A. E. Opel and L. F. Gilbert, *Closed Loop Source Monotoring Saves Energy and Money*, Presented at the ASME Winter Meeting, December 10–15, 1978.
5. C. H. Cho, *Let's Examine the Role of the Computer in a Plant Energy Conservation Program*, ISA/74-524, October 1974.

CHUN H. CHO
TERRY L. BLEVINS

Pharmaceutical Intermediates, Sourcing Strategies

Chemical intermediates used in the manufacture of pharmaceutical active ingredients, the active ingredients themselves, and other pharmaceutical intermediates are becoming more and more available in the international marketplace (Table 1). Pharmaceutical and specialty chemical companies in Europe and the Far East are manufacturing and marketing such bulk materials as 6-aminopenicillanic acid, 7-amino-cephalosporanic acid, methyldopa, diazepam, ibuprofen, and salicyclic acid at prices that are very competitive with traditional sources (Table 2).

The increasing availability of various pharmaceutical and chemical intermediates, coupled with fluctuations in the value of international currencies, has disrupted the traditional distribution network used by pharmaceutical manufacturers to obtain these materials. Manufacturers—domestic and foreign, multinational in scope or small in size—are implementing a global sourcing strategy as part of their overall efforts to manufacture their products in the most cost-effective manner.

TABLE 1 Pharmaceutical and Chemical Intermediates, and Pharmaceutical Active Ingredients Available Today

Chemical Intermediates	Final Drug Product
Isobutylbenzene	Ibuprofen
Phenylacetic acid	Penicillin G
2,4-Dichlorobenzoic acid	Furosemide
Salicyclic acid	Aspirin
2-Amino-5-chlorobenzophenone	Diazepam
Pharmaceutical Intermediates	
7-Aminocephalosporanic acid (7-ACA)	Cefaloglycin, Cefazolin
6-Aminopenicillanic acid (6-APA)	Amoxicillin, Ampicillin
7-Deacetoxycephalosporanic acid (7-ADCA)	Cefalexin
Penicillin G, nonsterile	Penicillin G
Oxytetracycline	Doxycycline
Pharmaceutical Active Ingredients	Brand Name Product (Company)
Ibuprofen	Motrin (Upjohn)
Acetaminophen	Tylenol (Johnson & Johnson)
Propranolol HCl	Inderal (Ayerst)
Diazepam	Valium (Roche)
Methyldopa	Aldomet (Merck)

TABLE 2 Foreign Companies That Manufacture Pharmaceutical and Chemical Intermediates

Europe	Far East
Alchymars (Italy)	Chemexcil (India)
ANSA Antibiotics (Turkey)	C. Itoh (Japan)
Antibioticos S.A. (Spain)	G. Amphray Laboratories (India)
Cilag A.G. (Switzerland)	Gujarat Lyka (India)
Farmos Group Ltd. (Finland)	Heni Chemical Industries (India)
Lark S.p.A. (Italy)	Kimia Farma (Indonesia)
Pierrel S.p.A. (Italy)	Priya Chemicals (India)
Proses (Turkey)	Shanghai Pharmaceutical Industrial Corp. (People's Republic of China)
Star Ltd. (Finland)	SPIC (People's Republic of China)
Zambon Chimica S.p.A. (Italy)	Tanabe (Japan)
	Yodogawa (Japan)

Traditionally, large multinational pharmaceutical companies used to build and operate manufacturing facilities in major worldwide geographic market areas. Offshore facilities were usually managed by the firm's international division. Each geographic market area tended to operate autonomously, with few transfers of pharmaceutical intermediates and/or finished pharmaceuticals between them. Furthermore, the international division had limited contact with domestic operations. Multinational companies tended to captively manufacture in bulk most of their active ingredients and key chemical intermediates.

Smaller, domestically based pharmaceutical companies with only final dosage form manufacturing capabilities usually purchased their bulk active ingredients from the chemical or pharmaceutical divisions of United States-based multinational pharmaceutical companies. Their finished goods product lines were generic (off-patent), patented products sold under a licensing agreement (with the supplier of the bulk active ingredient), and/or patented products (patent owned by the smaller firm) where the active ingredient was custom manufactured. There were only a limited number of sources that these smaller companies could turn to for bulk active ingredients.

All this has changed. The number of specialty chemical companies that offer pharmaceutical chemicals and/or bulk active ingredients for sale in the United States has skyrocketed. In 1981, only 24 firms were listed in the *OPD Chemical Buyer's Directory* under the category "Pharmaceutical Intermediates." In 1987 some 80 firms were listed under the categories "Pharmaceutical Intermediates" and "Pharmaceutical Chemicals." This represents a 333% increase in just 4 years. If one adds in the pharmaceutical companies that also offer pharmaceutical intermediates, the number increases to well over 100 firms. A sizable number of these firms either have offshore manufacturing facilities or represent companies that are foreign-based. There are also a

TABLE 3 Companies That Offer Pharmaceutical Intermediates[a]

Company	Intermediate Manufacture	Traders[b] Brokers	Custom Synthesis Tolling
S.S.T.		×	
Upjohn	×		×
Pierrel	×		×
Chemie Linz	×		
Fallek	×	×	
R. W. Greeff		×	
Knoll	×		
Lonza	×		
Ciba Geigy	×		
Aceto		×	×
Napp	×		
DeGussa	×		
Hexcel	×		×
Gyma Labs		×	
Ganes	×		×
American Roland		×	
Helm		×	
Hexagon	×		×
Pfizer	×		×
Acic		×	
Chemical Dynamics		×	

[a]As of 1986.
[b]They often represent firms that also offer services in intermediate manufacture and custom synthesis.

growing number of firms that will custom-manufacture pharmaceutical intermediates either on a contract or toll basis (Table 3).

Global sourcing is the procurement of bulk active ingredients and/or pharmaceutical intermediates from a number of sources—domestic or foreign, in-house or from the outside—in a manner that minimizes the cost of goods sold for finished pharmaceuticals manufactured from these substances.

Flexibility is the key to a successful global sourcing strategy. Its success depends on the ability to rapidly reconfigure a company's pharmaceutical manufacturing resources to take advantage of favorable economic conditions. Since worldwide economic conditions are constantly changing, a company's sourcing strategy should give manufacturing managers the latitude to react to these changes in the most advantageous manner.

Pharmaceuticals Manufacture

The manufacture of finished goods pharmaceuticals (or pharmaceuticals in their final dosage form) can be divided into two basic steps: the manufacture of the active ingredient(s) and the manufacture of the final dosage form (Fig. 1).

Active ingredients are usually manufactured in bulk, using various combinations of chemical process equipment. These ingredients may be synthesized biologically (fermentation), synthesized chemically (organic chemical synthesis), or extracted from animal or plant tissue or some combination of these techniques. Raw materials and chemical intermediates used in active ingredients manufacture are usually available in regular commerce. In some cases, however, a chemical intermediate may not be readily available and it will be custom manufactured (either in-house or by a contract manufacturer).

Dosage form manufacture consists of the formulation and blending of active and inert ingredients, followed by the preparation and packaging of the finished product. It can be a liquid, powder, tablet, capsule, or ointment. Pharmaceuticals and specialty chemical companies manufacture chemical intermediates, active ingredients, and/or inert ingredients depending on their processing capabilities, marketing strategy, and/or the vagaries of the marketplace.

Many of the larger multinational pharmaceutical companies have the capability to manufacture a large portion of their chemical and pharmaceutical intermediates in-house while smaller firms with limited manufacturing capabilities must rely on outside sources for a large number of their pharmaceutical intermediates. Therefore, a large multinational firm with a sizable number of manufacturing facilities located throughout the world will view global sourcing from a different perspective than a smaller firm with a limited number of manufacturing plants.

Benefits of Global Sourcing

Global sourcing can provide a pharmaceutical manufacturer with major economic benefits depending on its size and manufacturing capabilities. Some of the more important benefits include:

- Less expensive sources for bulk active and inert ingredients, and chemical intermediates
- Greater bargaining power with domestic sources of pharmaceutical ingredients that are available from foreign sources
- Proximity to major geographic market(s)
- Financial and tax incentives in exchange for locating a manufacturing facility in a particular country or location
- Making available additional manufacturing capacity for new pharmaceutical and chemical intermediates by purchasing older, captively manufactured intermediates from outside sources
- Expanding one's finished goods product line for a small capital investment via outside purchase of active ingredients
- The ability to rapidly establish a manufacturing presence in a foreign location by erecting a final dosage form manufacturing unit there and purchasing bulk ingredients locally

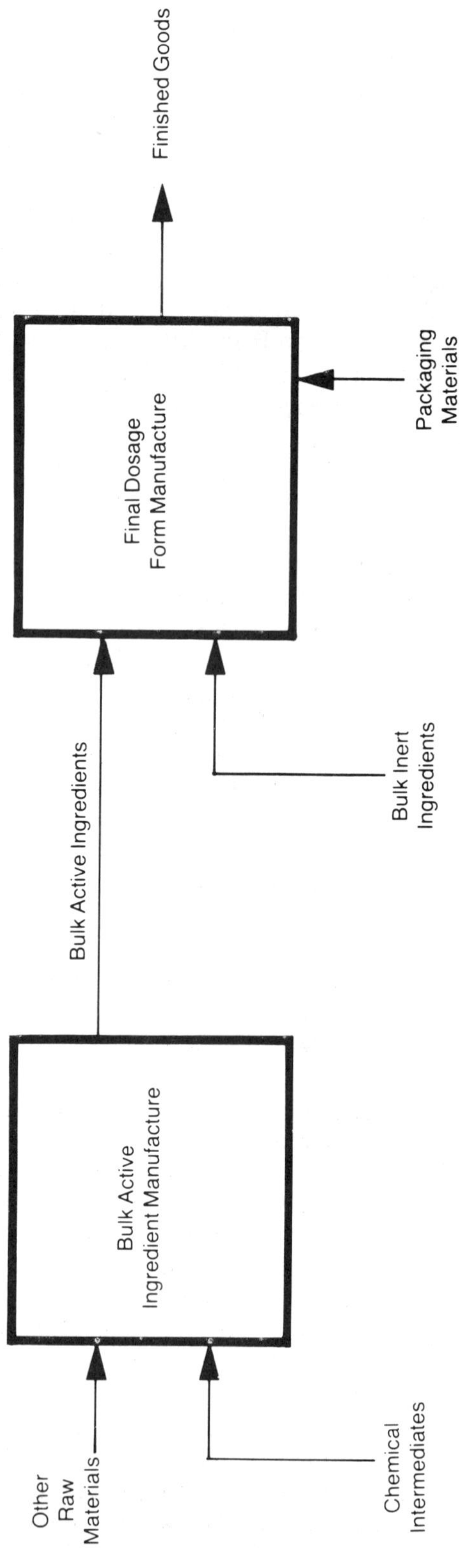

FIG. 1. Manufacture of finished goods pharmaceuticals.

TABLE 4 Cost of Selected Pharmaceutical Intermediates

Pharmaceutical Intermediate	Price ($/kg) 1980	Price ($/kg) 1987	Average % Decrease in Price
Potassium pencillin G, nonsterile	35–40	25–30	27
6-Aminopenicillanic acid	75–85	65–75	13
Lysine	4.50	2.90	36
Riboflavin, USP	53–56	42–49	16
Erythromycin base, USP	120	110–130	0
Streptomycin sulfate, USP	47	47	0
Phenylacetic acid	4.50	4.50	0
Biotin, USP	750–850	500–550	34

Both multinational companies and smaller companies are reaping the benefits of increased availability of many pharmaceutical intermediates by paying lower prices for them. The prices of many bulk active ingredients and pharmaceutical intermediates, including many of the antibiotics, various semisynthetic antibiotic starting materials, some amino acids, and most vitamins, have either decreased or remained the same over the past 5 years. For example, bulk potassium penicillin G, nonsterile, that cost between $35 and $40 per kilogram in 1980 can now be obtained for $25 to $30 per kilogram in 1987—a 27% decrease. At the same time, the price of phenylacetic acid (used in the manufacture of penicillin) has remained constant at $4.50 per kilogram (Table 4).

Lower prices for pharmaceutical intermediates translate into lower costs for bulk active ingredients manufactured from them, which in turn lowers the cost of goods sold for final finished pharmaceuticals. Even when prices remain constant in actual dollars, they are actually decreasing in real dollars due to inflationary effects. In many cases these lower manufacturing costs have helped maintain profit margins for various pharmaceutical products.

With the proliferation of foreign pharmaceutical intermediate suppliers operating plants certified by the Food and Drug Administration (FDA), which allows them to export pharmaceutical substances to the United States, smaller domestically based pharmaceutical companies have been able to exert some leverage on the traditional, domestically based sources of supply. Those companies that traditionally bought bulk active ingredients from multinational pharmaceutical companies can obtain the same active ingredients at a lower price overseas (even after shipping costs are factored in).

Marketing and Sales

To defend their market position, traditional pharmaceutical intermediate suppliers have altered their pricing and trade terms in such a way as to make their bulk active ingredients more competitive with material derived from foreign sources. They have also attempted to make improvements in their overall manufacturing process to lower the cost of the intermediates. Those few suppliers who have retained their original pricing and trade terms have slowly lost market share to overseas competitors.

In terms of sales, the largest pharmaceutical marketplaces are located in Western Europe, the United States, and Japan. These there marketplaces had combined pharmaceutical sales of $75 billion in 1986, representing 62% of the worldwide total. To be competitive in these marketplaces, pharmaceutical companies must locate manufacturing facilities in each of these geographic locations. In some countries, government regulation may also require local manufacture.

Two types of companies participate in the marketplaces: small firms that market pharmaceuticals within a country's borders and the large multinational companies that market pharmaceuticals to an entire region. The smaller companies usually market generic products, over-the-counter preparations, and/or licensed products, and do not have bulk active ingredient manufacturing capabilities. These firms utilize global sourcing in the context of active ingredient procurement as discussed earlier.

Multinational pharmaceutical companies have a number of considerations in determining sources. Many of them have bulk active ingredient and/or pharmaceutical intermediate manufacturing capabilities at one or more locations within a given geographic region. To make a logical sourcing decision, these companies must determine their costs to manufacture these intermediates at each one of these locations and compare them to the price of obtaining the same material from outside sources.

Needless to say, other considerations must be factored in a sourcing decision such as prior contractual arrangements, regulatory constraints, and labor agreements. However, multinational pharmaceutical companies strive to attain the goal of purchasing pharmaceutical intermediates at the lowest cost possible.

TABLE 5 Countries That Offer Financial Incentives to a Manufacturing Facility within Their Borders

Country or Region	Income Tax Holiday	Repatriation of Profits	Duty-Free Exports	Subsidized Worker Training	Industries Zones	Grants, Low-Interest Loans
Puerto Rico	—	×	×	Trained workers exist	×	×
Bahamas	×	×	×	×	×	×
Ireland	Limited	—	×	×	×	×
Scotland	—	—	×	×	—	×
Singapore	Unknown	Unknown	×	×	×	×
Barbados	×	×	×	×	×	×
Hong Kong	Low tax rate	×	×	×	×	—

Overseas Manufacturing Opportunity

An increasing number of countries offer pharmaceutical companies (and other "high technology" firms) a package of financial incentives in exchange for locating a manufacturing facility within their borders. These incentives usually include an income tax holiday for a number of years, the ability to repatriate profits, property tax exemptions, low interest loans, subsidized worker training programs, an industrial zone (with good transportation links, energy sources, land, etc.), and the right to export finished products to a given market area tariff-free. A list of key countries and the incentives they offer are shown in Table 5.

These incentives are initially offset by the expenses associated with plant construction, start-up worker training programs, expatriate labor, etc. However, pharmaceutical companies have been able to recover these expenses within 1 to 3 years. Then they have a manufacturing operation that is extremely competitive in terms of cost of goods sold.

Countries that offer these financial incentives also hope to benefit. They are looking to strengthen their economies by providing their citizens with jobs (specifically those requiring skills and/or professional training), industrializing rural "underdeveloped" areas, creating sources of hard currency via exports of finished goods, and developing a group of direct and indirect services and/or industries to support these new facilities.

A pharmaceutical manufacturer can choose to erect a fully integrated manufacturing facility including pharmaceutical intermediate synthesis and dosage form manufacture, a facility with limited manufacturing capabilities, or a major distribution center. This decision is often based in part on the availability of pharmaceutical and/or chemical intermediates from nearby sources.

As a company's new products come out of research and into the marketplace, demands for additional manufacturing capacity often occur for active ingredient synthesis and/or dosage form preparation. Depending on the quantities needed and the processing requirements, additional manufacturing capacity can be made available by building new facilities and/or by a readjustment of production schedules to accommodate the new products.

How to Utilize Global Sourcing

However, global sourcing can also be utilized. Selected pharmaceutical and chemical intermediates that are currently being manufactured in-house could be purchased from outside sources, especially those intermediates used to formulate older "off-patent" pharmaceuticals (see Appendix). Assuming that the manufacturing technology for the new intermediate is similar to that of the older intermediate(s) and that the older intermediate(s) is readily available at a competitive price(s), additional manufacturing capacity can be obtained for a negligible capital investment and in a relatively short period of time.

Smaller generic pharmaceutical companies, which have limited bulk active ingredient manufacturing capability or plan to expand into the growing generic pharmaceuticals market, can utilize global sourcing in conjunction with their existing formulation and blending capabilities to rapidly expand their finished goods product lines. Soon after a highly successful brand-name product comes off patent, its active ingredient becomes available for purchase in the open market. Products such as Merck's Aldomet, Pfizer's Diabinase, and Upjohn Motrin that have recently gone off patent are readily available in generic form. Also their active ingredients are being manufactured in bulk by a growing list of pharmaceutical intermediate suppliers. Table 6 lists current suppliers of selected active ingredients used in the formulation of leading pharmaceutical products whose patents have expired.

TABLE 6 Current Suppliers of Active Ingredients[a]

Methyldopa (Aldomet, 1984) Acic Agvar Chemicals, Inc. Borge International Chemworth Chugai International Inc. Gyma Labs Lark S.p.A. Medimpex North America Sitco Vichem Chlorpropamide (Diabinese, 1984) Acic Agvar Chemicals American Overseas Marketing Inc. Gyma Labs Roussel Corp. Diazepam (Valium, 1985) Accurate Chemical Agvar Chemicals, Inc. Gyma Labs Interchem Corp. S.S.T.	Ibuprofen (Motrin, 1985) Acic Accurate Chemical Algon Borge International Chem Imports Chugai International Conray Chemicals Ethyl Corp. European Manufacturers Assoc. Flavine International Henley & Co. Hexagon Interchem Corp. Isogenics Lark S.p.A. Mitsubishi International MWM Chemical Corp. Plantex Sitco S.S.T. Flurazepam (Dalmane, 1984) Gyma Labs Interchem Corp. Roussel Corp.	Propranolol HCl (Inderal, 1984) Acic Aceto Chemical Arrow Chemical Byron Chemical Chemical Imports European Manufacturers Assoc. Flavine International Gyma Labs Interchem Corp. Knoll Pharmaceuticals Mitsubishi International Napp Chemicals Orsynex Inc. Pfanstiehl Laboratories Plantex U.S.A. Sipsy Chemical Sitco S.S.T. Vichem Cephalexin (Keflex, 1987) Acic Borge International Flavine International Interchem Corp. Lark S.p.A. Mitsubishi International S.S.T. Vichem

[a]The branded product which utilizes the active ingredient in its formulation and the date its patent expired is shown in parentheses.

With the increased availability of a wide range of pharmaceutical active ingredients, a pharmaceutical company can rapidly establish a manufacturing presence in a foreign location. For a relatively small capital investment, a pharmaceutical company can erect and operate a dosage form manufacturing unit within 12 to 18 months. The facility would be staffed with an appropriate mix of expatriate and indigenous labor and purchase its bulk active ingredients from outside sources. This strategy may not be appropriate in developing countries that are looking to become self-sufficient in the manufacture of essential drugs (and their active ingredients). Some sort of arrangement would need to be made with government agencies and local producers to assist them in acquiring the technology for the manufacture of these active ingredients. If such an arrangement can be made, the company would have an advantage over other firms looking to enter the country.

Nevertheless, the operation of such a facility does have its disadvantages:

Only a limited pool of people are trained to operate and maintain pharmaceutical processing equipment.
Service infrastructure for pharmaceutical facilities needs to be established.
Pharmaceutical inert ingredients and packaging materials are scarce.
It is difficult to communicate with company headquarters.
Political environment is unpredictable.
Government that is insensitive to the needs of pharmaceutical manufacturers.

Most of these disadvantages are associated with the difficulties of operating in a country not accustomed to pharmaceutical processing. Except for such established overseas locations as Puerto Rico and Ireland that manufacture pharmaceuticals, most locations are better suited to manufacture products that require assembly and that use semiskilled labor.

In Conclusion

The increasing availability of bulk active ingredients and pharmaceutical intermediates on a worldwide basis has changed the traditional distribution network used by pharmaceutical manufactures to obtain these materials. Pharmaceutical companies are implementing a global sourcing strategy as part of their overall efforts to manufacture their products more efficiently. The key to a successful global strategy is flexibility, which gives manufacturing managers the latitude to react to changes in worldwide economic conditions in the most favorable manner. Larger multinational pharmaceutical companies view global sourcing from a different perspective than a smaller firm with a limited number of manufacturing units. The economic benefits that can be derived from global sourcing vary and can be used to enhance a company's manufacturing strategy.

Appendix. Generic Drug Industry

The United States generic drug industry is attracting the nation's attention due to the incredible impact that its growth has had on the structure and profitability of the pharmaceutical industry in general. It has shown a historic growth of 25% over the past 5 years—a rate twice that of the prescription pharmaceutical industry. Total sales of generic drugs are expected to reach $7.2 billion in 1989 based on an annual real growth rate of 15%. The generic drug industry currently represents 21% of the United States prescription drug industry and close to 60% of the total worldwide generic drug sales of $6.0 billion. Currently, generic drug substitution in Europe and Japan is between 5 and 10%. However, the trend in the growth of generic drugs is expected to continue worldwide due to cost containment pressures in these countries and the extension of essential drug programs in developing nations. Overall, this growth will only be proportional to the growth of generic drugs in the United States and, therefore, will not shift the proportion of sales drastically.

The single most important factor affecting the growth of this industry over the next 5 years is the expiration of a number of innovative, single-entity, high-volume products which currently represent close to $3 billion of revenue for the large research-based companies. After 1989, the growth of generics should drop off to between 8–10% due to a decreasing number of off-patent drugs becoming available to duplicate and other adaptive strategies that will be utilized by large research-based firms to fend off competition including patent restoration and extension.

FREDERICK G. HARRISON

Plastics, Fiberglass Composite Materials

After several false starts and some dramatic failures, fiberglass-reinforced plastic (FRP) technology has reached a level of sophistication and reliability such that it not only stands alone in certain applications, but is competing successfully with steels in others. A whole family of fabrication processes has grown up, and standards are being set to protect the quality of the finished product.

Commercial composite materials for corrosion-resistant equipment mainly use fiberglass* reinforcements with polyester or epoxy resin matrices (binders). The principal fabrication process is contact molding, although more and more machine-made parts are being produced.

The purpose of this review is to compare the properties, performance, and economics of the principal materials systems, and to compare some of the fabrication processes used for the construction of corrosion-resistant equipment.

Economics

The manufacture of composite materials for chemical process equipment has grown into a billion-dollar annual-sales industry over the last 25 to 30 years. The annual growth rate still approaches 20%. While a major part of the business is in pipe and tanks, a significant portion is in ducts, scrubbers, and wastewater treatment facilities. Markets are developing for pumps, valves, and support structures.

The success of any new material (or materials system, in the case of composites) depends upon the cost/performance ratio of the material compared with competing materials. The current position for composites is very favorable, and the outlook bright. In Table 1 a cost comparison [1] for a

TABLE 1 Price of a 4000-gal Vertical Tank[a]

Material	Sales Price ($)
Polyester/fiberglass	1,650
Carbon steel	1,500
304 Stainless	5,000

[a]These Jan 1991 prices are for a tank with six nozzles and one manway.

*"Fiberglas" is the registered trademark of Owens-Corning Fiberglas Corp. In this article, glass-fiber material is generically referred to, and is spelled fiberglass.

4000-gal storage tank shows the attractive economics of composites in relation to carbon-, stainless-, and rubber-lined-steel vessels. Further, a cost comparison for chemical plant piping showed that a system of fiberglass pipe and fittings ranked very close to carbon steel in cost and was far cheaper than a stainless steel system [2].

And for many environments (e.g., halogen acids or salts), the corrosion resistance of reinforced plastics is superior to that of the best stainless steels.

Polyester Resins

Let us initially note some fundamentals about polyesters.

An ester is a reaction product (a salt) of an alcohol and an acid. One simple ester is ethyl acetate, the product of combining ethyl alcohol and acetic acid.

For thermosetting polyesters, propylene glycol is the usual alcohol, while phthalic and maleic anhydrides (in various ratios) provide the acids. The reaction product is a low-melting-point solid that must be dissolved in a low-molecular-weight monomer to achieve further polymerization. Styrene is the most common monomer; the normal level is 45–55% styrene in the polyester.

The most-used resin in reinforced-plastic corrosion-resistant structures is isophthalic polyester; primarily because of low cost, easy handling, good acid resistance, and fast cure time. More expensive resins provide special properties. The approximate costs of polyester resins for corrosion-resistant equipment ($/lb, Jan 1991) are as follows:

Orthophthalic polyester	0.97
Isophthalic polyester	1.06
Bisphenol A fumarate	1.44
Vinyl ester	1.44

Curing of the polyester requires a catalyst—normally, an oxygen supplier such as an organic peroxide. When the organic peroxide decomposes (either from heat or the chemical action of a promoter), the double bond of the styrene molecule opens up and reacts with the polyester molecules, achieving a crosslinked thermoset polymer (in contrast to the linear linkage of thermoplastic polymers). The resulting solid plastic may be thought of as a single giant molecule, because all of the atoms are chemically linked to one another.

Monomers

Styrene is a benzene derivative and is classed as an aromatic solvent. It may also be called vinyl benzene or phenyl ethylene. The chemical formula is $C_6H_5CH{:}CH_2$. The price is about $0.27/lb (June 1979).

The effects of an increase in styrene content on polyester resins are: viscosity decreases; gel time decreases [except for the benzoyl peroxide/dimethylamine (BPO/DMA) system]; heat-distortion temperature approaches that of polystyrene (may increase or decrease, depending on polyester type); shrinkage increases linearly from 3–4% at 0% styrene (from extrapolation) to 14% at 100% styrene; corrosion resistance increases (especially acid resistance); refractive index increases; brittleness increases. Other mechanical properties and ultraviolet yellowing are not affected by styrene content.

Since styrene accounts for nearly all of the monomer usage in polyester, other monomers are generally used only for special purposes. Some of these other monomers and their characteristics are: *vinyl toluene*—lower shrinkage, next cheapest to styrene; *diallyl phthalate*—less shrinkage, lower exotherm (exothermic polymerization reaction); *methyl methacrylate*—ultraviolet stability (best mixed with styrene); *divinyl benzene*—higher heat-distortion temperature, better chemical resistance.

Curing of Polyesters

Inhibitors

Polyesters (with styrene) are inherently unstable and can auto-cure in storage from the action of heat or sunlight. A minute amount of an inhibitor (a hydroquinone compound) is therefore added to the resin by the manufacturer to prevent this. Further inhibitor addition is sometimes desirable for certain heat-cured applications.

Catalysts

There are a large number of peroxide compounds on the market for catalyzing. Three commonly used catalysts in the fabrication of corrosion-resistant equipment are:

Methyl ethyl ketone peroxide—Normally sold as a 60% solution in dimethyl phthalate. This is the most commonly used catalyst.

Benzoyl peroxide—Sold as powder (pure) or paste (50%). It is normally dissolved in a small amount of styrene before being added to the polyester.

Tertiary butyl peroxyoctoate—This is used alone or in combination with other peroxides for heat-cured systems.

Promoters

Promoters accelerate the curing process by reacting with the peroxide compounds. *PROMOTERS MUST BE KEPT OUT OF CONTACT WITH*

CONCENTRATED PEROXIDES, OTHERWISE VIOLENT REACTIONS WILL RESULT.

The principal promoters are:

Cobalt (*or other metallic*) *soaps* such as cobalt naphthenate, cobalt octoate, manganese naphthenate, and so on.
Dimethylamine. This may be used alone or with cobalt in a double-promoted BPO catalyst system.
Other compounds such as *lauryl mercaptan.*

Exotherm

The reaction of styrene and polyester generates heat to form a solid polymer (exothermic reaction). It is mass-sensitive (a large mass contains more exothermic energy per unit of surface than does a small mass). On very thin sections, curing may be very slow; in large masses, the exothermic heat can cause cracking, or even charring and fire. In hand layup with about 30% glass content, the maximum thickness that can be produced in a single step, with a normal catalyst system, is about ⅜ in.; thicker sections should be made in multiple layers.

Fillers and glass fibers act to soak up some of the exothermic heat. The peak exotherm temperature for a given system may be compared to other systems by the "SPI Exotherm Test." Details may be obtained from the Society of the Plastics Industry (New York City).

Gel Time

In the first stage of cure, the polyester becomes a gelatine-like material that will no longer flow as a liquid. The time to reach the gel stage is important, for it establishes the working time available for "wet out" (the wetting of the glass reinforcement) and fabrication. The variables affecting the gel time (sometimes called "pot life") are: polyester formulation (catalyst, promoter, and inhibitor levels); ambient temperature; and mass of material.

A useful rule-of-thumb for processes where the resin pot is continuously replenished is: The usage rate of material must be twice the mass of material in the pot, divided by the pot life.

Example. A resin pot (wet-out bath, holding pot) contains 15 lb of resin that will gel in 30 min. If the usage rate (fresh resin being added continuously or at frequent intervals) is at least 30 lb per ½ h, the resin pot will not gel, and a continuous operation can be sustained—assuming the fresh resin is mixed thoroughly with the old resin.

The same rule-of-thumb can be used to size the resin pot or to establish a usable gel time for continuous layup, filament winding, or pultrusion fabrication.

Temperature versus Time

The ambient temperature is more important for establishing a complete cure than is the time involved. The maximum Barcol hardness (45–50) is achieved only with heat cure; room-temperature curing yields a Barcol hardness of 25–30.

Heat Curing

If heat curing can be used (it is sometimes not feasible for large structures), the promoter content can be reduced or eliminated. Some producers prefer to use a low level of promoter with a heat cure. The promoted resin will serve to complete the cure (over a period of several days) in the event of an oven malfunction.

Inhibition

Curing is inhibited by exposure of the polyester resin to air. Some resins (notably the Bisphenol A type) are seriously affected by this phenomenon. If a film cannot be placed over the part, a resin that contains wax should be used. The resin manufacturer's literature will note the resins containing wax, as well as the amount and technique to be used.

Moisture also inhibits the curing of polyester resins. So do many sulfur-containing compounds such as rubber and neoprene.

Shrinkage

Shrinkage of a polyester part is caused by heat expansion and contraction, or resin shrinkage during polymerization. The shrinkage of resin can create several difficulties: internal stresses, possibly causing cracks; the part sticking in the mold; and warping (from uneven internal stress).

Shrinkage can be reduced by: higher filler and/or glass content; reduced styrene content; reduced exotherm (lower curing temperature); and thermoplastic additives. In a cylindrical part, curing from the inside out will reduce the shrinkage stresses as compared with curing from the outside in.

Safety

In this day of increasing government regulations, safety precautions are not only desirable but mandatory. The use of safety shields, respirators, and other devices must be considered for each operation.

Resin manufacturers' literature will ordinarily give guidelines as to what to expect with toxic chemicals, but regulations about levels change frequently, so it is essential to keep up to date. The following subjects should be considered: styrene fumes; resin flammability; peroxide handling; peroxide/promoter/resin storage; amines (can cause skin problems); and exotherm.

Isophthalic and Orthophthalic Polyesters

The essential difference between these lies in the aromatic benzene-type ring of the phthalic anhydride molecule. The chemical formula of an isophthalic compound is the same as that of an orthophthalate, but the molecular arrangement is different (see Fig. 1).

Orthophthalic polyesters (often called general-purpose polyesters) are not as resistant to chemical attack as are isophthalic resins. Thus, the isophthalic polyesters are more often used in corrosion-resistance applications.

Bisphenol A Polyester Resins

Bisphenol A (a benzene-like compound) is reacted with propylene oxide to form a glycol (an alcohol compound). This glycol is reacted with fumaric acid to form the resin Bisphenol A fumarate. Most producers sell this latter compound in a flake form or as a solution in styrene.

Early studies of this resin disclosed that, although it had exceptional corrosion resistance, it was brittle. A modified version having high elongation was developed. The optimum resin was found to contain 10% of the flexibilized resin mixed with the standard Bisphenol A.

In the corrosion-resistant-equipment market, the Bisphenol A fumarate has a well-established reputation, and it is widely specified.

Vinyl Ester Resin

Vinyl ester is a reaction product of an epoxy resin with a polyester (such as methyl methacrylate). It shares many of the attributes of polyesters—acid resistance, fast curing with peroxide catalysts, and dilution with styrene. In addition, the vinyl ester retains the high strength and elongation aspects of

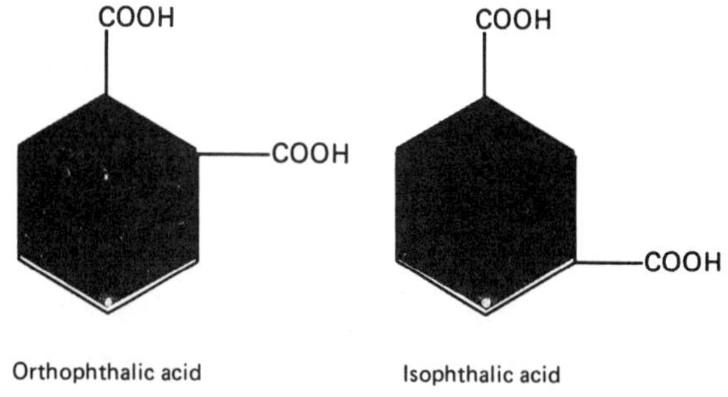

FIG. 1 Structure of phthalic acid isomers.

an epoxy, along with some of the epoxy's resistance to solvent attack. Since there are many types of epoxies, there are several vinyl esters now on the market, such as high-temperature versions, fire-retardant types, and resins having high toughness.

Vinyl ester is the only polyester competing in the high-pressure-pipe market, long dominated by epoxy resins. It has demonstrated excellent cyclic pressure performance.

Additives

Additives are substances blended into the polyester resin to provide a special property. Fillers and pigments are not included in this section.

Fire-Retardant Additives

A considerable measure of fire retardancy can be achieved with relatively high (near 50%) levels of hydrated alumina, $Al(OH)_3$. This combination increases the viscosity; ordinarily, it is used only in compression molding.

Antimony oxide (at a 5–15% level) is used to enhance the nonflammability of halogenated polyester resins. This additive is only effective in the presence of chlorine or bromine compounds.

Thixotropy

In hand-layup work, resin drainout is sometimes a problem. To combat this, a colloidal silica (made from silicone compound decomposition) is often used as a thixotropic agent to increase resin viscosity.

Conductivity

In some applications (such as explosive-vapor ducts or chimney liners), static charges will build up in the nonconductive fiberglass-reinforced plastic (FRP). To reduce the danger of electrostatic sparks, conductive layers are added to the laminate. The conductivity can be achieved by additions of certain types of graphite, carbon black, graphite fibers, and metal-coated glass fibers.

Low Profile

To reduce shrinkage in molded articles, a small percentage of a thermoplastic powder can be added. Several types are used, such as polyethylene and polystyrene.

Resin Thickening

Certain compounds (notably calcium or magnesium oxides) when added to polyester cause a gelation reaction that does not affect the double bonds and does not create any appreciable crosslinking. These compounds are used to produce sheet or bulk molding compounds for high- or moderate-pressure molding. The gelled material is tackfree and can be handled; when heated to 200°F or more, the compound reverts to the low-viscosity state and flows readily.

Fillers and Pigments

Fillers

The primary purposes for using fillers are to reduce cost and reduce exothermic heat. The principal fillers are: calcium carbonate (ground limestone), talc, aluminum silicate (kaolin clay), and silica (sand). While calcium carbonate is favored for many noncorrosive applications, it cannot be used in corrosion-resistant equipment. Clay is the filler favored for most molded corrosion-resistance applications.

Reinforced-plastic mortar (RPM) systems (usually in filament-wound pipe or tanks) consist of approximately 30% resin, 30% fiberglass, and 40% sand. The sand is usually 50 to 100 mesh, with all fines removed. Coarse-filler systems (such as used in RPM) can be loaded to a higher level than fine-filler ones such as clay or talc. Needless to say, in corrosion equipment the filler must resist the environment expected in service. Some fillers are treated with silane compounds to enhance shear strength (and chemical resistance) at the resin–filler interface.

Pigments

Pigments are used for color, but more importantly (in corrosion applications) for ultraviolet resistance. It has been conclusively shown that polyesters (and most other organics) deteriorate from weathering, but the damage is essentially a surface phenomenon. Even after several years of exposure, with glass fibers showing all over the surface, strength properties are retained. In corrosion-resistant equipment, it is desirable to retain the resin-rich surface layer. A pigmented resin or surface coating (gel coat) can effectively block ultraviolet rays and keep the resin-rich surface. Many types of pigments are available: Two that are commonly used are carbon (black) and titanium dioxide (white).

Gel Coats and Surface Coatings

As mentioned before, gel coats are often used to protect surfaces from weathering. A gel coat is a highly pigmented polyester. The name stems from the method of application; the coating is applied to the mold. When the coating reaches a gel state, the remainder of the laminate is applied.

In corrosion-resistant equipment, most specifications require an inner resin-rich layer, using a C glass veil or a polyester surface mat (mats will be discussed in a later section). The purpose of the resin-rich layer is to provide protection for the glass fibers comprising the structural portion of the laminate.

Postfabrication coatings (paints, gel coats, or surface mats) may be used to provide extra corrosion resistance in exposed areas. The nature of the coating may be quite different from the body of the laminate. A pigmented urethane or silicone coating, for example, can provide better ultraviolet resistance than an ordinary polyester gel coat.

Special Resins

Fire-Retardant Resins

The principal means of fire-retarding a polyester (or epoxy) resin is to replace hydrogen atoms in the molecule with halogen (chlorine or bromine) atoms. Thus, chlorendic anhydride replaces phthalic anhydride in a polyester, and brominated compounds may be used for an epoxy resin.

The fire retardancy of halogenated resins is enhanced by the addition of a small percentage (3–5%) of antimony oxide (Sb_2O_3). This filler does not add fire retardancy to plain resins, only to the halogenated variety.

Although not in general use, furan resins have considerable promise for the corrosion-resistant-equipment market. Their corrosion resistance to acids and alkalis is outstanding; resistance to solvents is also superior to that of most other resins. In addition, furan resins are low-smoke organic compounds and are inherently fire-retardant.

The furfuryl alcohol molecule has a five-sided ring with a methyl alcohol molecule attached at one point. In the presence of a strong acid, a methyl linkage bonds the rings together with the OH groups, forming water. Acid type and acid level are critical. A postcure is necessary to eliminate water by-products.

Because of the high exothermic temperature, the water from the condensation reaction, and the brittle nature of the resin, the danger of cracking is high. In addition, furan resins have a short working time (10–30 min). For these reasons, most fabricators do not like to work with them.

Epoxy Resins

Epoxies are not a single class of resins but rather describe a family of resin types. The common factor is the epoxy linkage: an oxygen molecule linked to two carbon atoms in the organic chain. This reactive group can join to an amine or an acid to make a strong and durable bond.

Since the epoxy and hardener join together in the polymerization reaction, the choice of hardener can have a strong effect on the properties of the polymer. The crosslinking action evolves no by-products, and the exothermic temperature is low.

Epoxies are the strongest of the common polymers, with tensile strengths of 12,000–15,000 lb/in.^{2}. Some formulations with postcuring have high heat resistance. Adhesion to most inorganics (and some organics) is excellent, and epoxies have been the first-choice resin for most high-pressure fiberglass pipe, especially when accompanied by high-temperature requirements.

Epoxies are attacked more readily by strong acids than are polyesters, but alkali resistance and solvent resistance are superior.

The most common epoxy is made from Bisphenol A; other types are epoxy novolac (a reacted combination with phenolic) and cycloaliphatics. Hardeners include aliphatic amines and polyamides for room-temperature curing (mostly used in adhesives). Aromatic amines and acid anhydrides are ordinarily used for filament winding, molding, or other heat-cured-resin processes. Several latent hardeners are used for making epoxy preimpregnated fabrics.

Thermoplastic/Thermoset Combinations

Combination or hybrid structures have been made from thermoplastic/thermoset combinations for enhanced corrosion resistance. The thermoplastics normally used include polypropylene, polyvinyl chloride (PVC), chlorinated polyvinyl chloride (CPVC), and FEP (fluorinated ethylene-propylene) Teflon.

One procedure is to *heat-bond a fiberglass cloth to a thermoplastic sheet.* The side of the cloth away from the thermoplastic is left dry to provide a bonding surface for the thermosetting resin.

This combination of cloth and thermoplastic may be cut, heat-softened, formed, and welded into the proper shape and dimensions (such as a tank, scrubber, Venturi, or other piece of equipment). After forming, the thermosetting plastic and fiberglass structure is built up on the glass-cloth side of the structure (usually on the outside). This buildup is usually accomplished by hand layup, but filament winding, sprayup, and compression molding can be used.

Another approach is the *adhesive bonded thermoplastic/thermoset.* Filament-wound pipe is being made by overwrapping PVC or CPVC (the only polymers used at this time) with resins that can bond tightly to the thermoplastic substrate. In one instance, an epoxy resin is used, which bonds tightly to the thermoplastic. In another case, a specially modified polyester is used as a primer coat, then a standard polyester completes the overwrap.

The most serious problem with thermoplastic/thermoset hybrids arises from a thermal mismatch. The thermoplastic liner has an expansion rate several times higher than the reinforced thermoset's. Low temperatures can create stresses at the interface. In addition, thermal cycling can cause cracks to develop in some structures.

The current cost of the hybrid structures is about double that of a reinforced thermoset, without the thermoplastic liner. In some severe corrosion-service applications, however, the hybrid is cost-effective.

Reinforcements

The history of reinforced plastics dates back many years. High-pressure NEMA (National Electrical Manufacturers Association) laminates of phenolic, epoxy, melamine, and other resins, some dating back to the early 1900s, are made with paper, cotton, linen, and glass cloth.

In the present era of reinforced plastics for the corrosion market, glass-fiber reinforcements are used almost exclusively. Many types of reinforcements have been developed in continuous strands, woven fibers, and chopped fibers. The level of reinforcements ranges from less than 10% to above 80% by weight in some filament-wound structures.

Types of Glass Fibers

Four basic glass compositions are presently used in plastics reinforcement.

The lowest-cost type is *A (alkali) glass,* similar in composition to ordinary window or bottle glass. Several firms make mats from A glass, but its use is not widespread.

The most common reinforcement is *E glass,* a boroaluminosilicate containing normally small percentages of calcia (CaO) and magnesia (MgO). The alkali metal (sodium and potassium) content is kept very low. The product's combination of good water resistance and reasonable cost has not been excelled in its 40-year existence.

C glass, a calcium aluminosilicate, has exceptional acid resistance and is useful in surface mats, glass flakes for coatings, and yarns for acid-resistant cloth. C glass has poor water resistance and has not been used as a major reinforcement.

S glass is used in high-strength aerospace applications. It is several times costlier than E glass. Although there are no known applications of S glass in the corrosion market, it has exceptional resistance to acids (approximately equal to C glass) and excellent resistance to water.

Approximate glass-fiber-reinforcement prices are shown in Table 2.

Fiberglass Nomenclature

Fiber filament diameter and weight are standardized and related by letter designations, as shown in Tables 3 and 4.

TABLE 2 Fiberglass-Reinforcement Prices[a]

Type of Reinforcement	Price ($/lb)
Unsplit rovings (forming packages)	0.75
Unsplit rovings (conventional)	0.75
Split rovings for chopping	0.85
Chopped-strand mat	1.15 (1½ to 3 oz)
Continuous-strand mat	1.32 (1½ to 3 oz)
Woven roving	0.96 (24 oz)
Chopped strands	0.75
Milled fibers	0.75

[a]Published list prices from Certainteed Corp. (Jan 1991), for delivered truckload or carload.

Glass fibers are grouped into "strands" with a specific number of fibers, which may be in the hundreds or even thousands. Strands are combined into "rovings," which contain a specific number of strands, usually between 8 and 120. The weight of fiberglass is referred to as "yield," which is the number of yards of strand (or roving) that weighs one pound. Notice that yield is *inversely* proportional to weight. A heavy strand will have a low yield, since it doesn't require a great length to make up a full pound weight (see Table 4).

In order to find the yield of a roving, therefore, it is necessary to *divide* the strand yield by the number of strands in the roving. For example, a roving with 8 strands of K filament with 408 fibers per strand will have a yield of $3700 \div 8 = 463$ yd/lb.

Conversely, the filament diameter can sometimes be determined from the roving yield (which is printed on the package) and the number of strands in the roving. For example, if a roving has 16 strands and its yield is 225 yd/lb, the yield of each strand is $16 \times 226 = 3600$ yd/lb. Since there are only two standard filaments with this approximate yield (see G-816 and K-408 in Table 4), the roving probably consists of one of these two filaments.

TABLE 3 Glass-Filament Diameter

Letter Designation	Average Diameter Range (in.)
A	0.00006–0.00010
B	0.00011–0.00015
C	0.00016–0.00020
D	0.00021–0.00025
E	0.00026–0.00030
F	0.00031–0.00035
G[a]	0.00036–0.00040
H	0.00041–0.00045
J	0.00046–0.00050
K[a]	0.00051–0.00055
L	0.00056–0.00060
M[a]	0.00061–0.00065
N	0.00066–0.00070
P	0.00071–0.00075
Q	0.00076–0.00080
R	0.00081–0.00085
S	0.00086–0.00090
T[a]	0.00091–0.00095
U	0.00096–0.00100
V	0.00101–0.00105
W	0.00106–0.00110
X	0.00111–0.00115
Y	0.00116–0.00120
Z	0.00121–0.00125

[a]Fiber diameters most commonly used in reinforcements.

TABLE 4 Relation of Strand Size and Yield (common standard products)

Filament Designation	Number of Fibers in Strand	Approximate Strand Yield (yd/lb)
G	204	15,000
	408	7,500
	816	3,600
K	204	7,500
	408	3,700
	816	1,800
M	2,080	675
	2,080	450
	4,080	225
T	2,080	225
	4,080	113

Fiberglass Sizes

In the parlance of textile-fiber producers, a "size" is a material applied to the fibers in the forming process. With only a few exceptions, sizes are emulsions of organic compounds in water (certain S glass sizes are not). For reinforcement glass fibers (rovings or mats), the size applied in the forming process contains elements for compatibility with the end-process and the matrix resin. Ordinarily, sizes are used for general-purpose compatibility with epoxy or polyester resins, but special-purpose sizes have been developed for individual uses (such as for filament-wound vinyl-ester pipe).

Sizes have three components: coupling agents, film formers, lubricants and emulsifiers. Here follows a brief discussion of each component.

Coupling Agents

The purpose of the coupling agent is to provide a bridge between the fiberglass surface and the polymeric matrix binder. Since the chemistry of polyesters is quite different from epoxies, an optimum coupling agent for epoxy applications is quite different from the optimum for polyesters. Coupling agents may interact unfavorably with film formers and with the fabrication process, so numerous compounds have been used to find the best combinations.

The earliest coupling agents (still used in some applications) were organic chromium compounds. Most of the current coupling agents are rather complicated silicone compounds, called silanes; recently, certain titanate compounds have been developed for some applications.

Experience has shown that epoxy resins have greater tolerance for size variability than do polyester resins. Polyester-compatible reinforcements (rovings or mats) can be used with an epoxy resin; it is not advisable to use an epoxy-compatible roving with a polyester resin—a very low-strength product is likely.

Film Formers

Film formers give a leathery toughness to the glass fibers while holding them together for subsequent processing. If there were no film formers, the filaments would "balloon" due to static electricity and would have a harsh feel.

Compounds used for film formers include solid and liquid epoxies and polyesters, polyvinyl acetate, and other thermoplastic emulsions.

The film former can make a great difference in the strength of the fabricated product, although its contribution is not so great as that of the coupling agent. In certain sensitive tests, such as fatigue performance, the type of film former is important. In some instances, interaction effects have been found between the film former, coupling agent, and the type of matrix resin employed in a structure.

Lubricants and Emulsifiers

Generally speaking, lubricants are water-soluble oils (polyalcohols, for example) that help decrease fiberglass damage during fabrication into rovings or during other processing methods. Often, the size emulsifiers (detergent-type compounds) also serve as lubricating elements.

Forms of Reinforcement, and Uses

Rovings

Two types of rovings are available.

An unsplit type, used as a continuous reinforcement in filament winding, pultrusion, or woven roving.

A split-strand roving, which is used for chopping into lengths of ⅛ to 2 in. One type is factory-chopped and sold in ⅛- or ¼-in. lengths as chopped strands for mixing into bulk molding compounds (BMC). The split-strand rovings are also used in sprayup, in making chopped-strand mat, or in preforms (a contoured mat).

In the past few years, a newer type of continuous-strand product has become available—a thick-walled cylindrical forming package which can be dried and wrapped immediately after forming. This product is normally sold at a slightly lower price than conventional roving.

Chopped-Strand Mat

Chopped-strand mat is made by chopping split-strand fibers from forming cakes (or rovings) in 2-in. lengths, gathering the fibers on a conveyor chain, coating the mat with a binder, drying and heat-setting the binder, and rolling up the mat. Two types of binders are used: soluble and insoluble (in polyester resin).

Chopped-strand mat is available in a number of widths (up to 76 in. wide); weights range from ¾ to 3 oz/ft^2. The principal application is in hand layup for tanks, pipes, and other structures. Other applications are in translucent panels, filament-wound tanks, and molded structures.

Continuous-Strand Mat

Continuous-strand mat is made in the United States only by Owens-Corning Fiberglas (an imported French mat is sold by Certain-Teed). It is made in a patented process by swirling fibers (directly from the bushing) onto a conveyor chain. A binder agent is added just as in chopped-strand mat. The mat is available in widths up to 76 in. and weights from ¾ to 3 oz/ft^2.

Continuous-strand mat has greater tensile strength, but greater springback in the wet state; it is seldom used in hand layup because it will not conform as easily as chopped-strand mat. The high strength makes continuous-strand mat useful in compression molding and in pultrusion.

Chopped Strands

Chopped fiberglass strands have a high percentage (1½–2%) of an insoluble binder. Fiber lengths are ⅛ to ½ in. The strands are sold for mixing with polyester or epoxy resins and fillers to make bulk molding compounds (sometimes called dough molding compounds or premixed compounds). The high content of insoluble binder is necessary for the strands to withstand the mixing process. If individual filaments are mixed in a compound, they tend to ball up and separate from the mixture. The compounds are used in compression molding, transfer molding, and injection molding.

Milled Fibers

Fiberglass strands are ground up by a hammer mill to produce milled fibers. Four sizes are manufactured (depending on the hole size in the hammer mill screen): 1/32, 1/16, ⅛, and ¼ in.

Milled fibers have been used in a number of molding compound formulations. Recently, these fibers have found a potentially large market in reinforcing molded urethanes for automotive applications.

Woven Rovings

A woven roving is a heavy cloth normally made from 218-yield rovings in an approximately square weave pattern. Two common weights of fabric are:

24 oz/yd^2 (5 × 4 with 218 yield) and 18 oz/yd^2 (5 × 4 with 300 yield) where 5 × 4 indicates 5 strands/in. in the warp direction and 4 strands/in. in the fill direction.

Other weights have been developed for special purposes, and other warp and fill ratios, besides 5 × 4, have found particular applications. The 24-oz fabric is by far the most popular. Woven roving is made only with polyester-compatible sizes in widths up to 10 ft, usually with the same rovings sold for filament winding or pultrusions.

The greatest use of woven roving is to provide a structural backbone for hand-layup (contact-molded) structures. The usual construction method (discussed in the process section following) is to interweave woven rovings with mat layers.

Processing Methods

Contact Molding

Contact molding is defined as a zero-pressure molding method in which only one side "contacts" the mold surface. There are two principal techniques—hand layup and sprayup. Both have higher labor costs but lower tooling costs than other molding processes.

Hand Layup

Mat or mat-and-woven-roving layers are wetted out with resin (normally polyester, but sometimes epoxy) and laid up on a male or female mold (Fig. 2a). Wetting should take place from bottom to top to help eliminate air bubbles. Resin is poured onto the working surface, and mat is laid on top of the resin. The best practice uses alternate layers of mat and woven roving. Often a gel coat is applied to the mold surface prior to layup of the reinforcement. Strong and excellent structures have been made by this process. It is unbeatable for one-of-a-kind or limited-production structures. There is no restriction on size, from very small to very large. A wide variety of resins can be used.

A degree of automation (an impregnating machine) has been introduced in recent years for assembly-line structures such as boats. Formerly, impregnation was accomplished by pouring resin from a bucket and working it in with a hand roller. The impregnator consists of two motor-driven rolls with a pool of resin between the rolls. The mat and woven roving pass between the rolls and the resin is squeezed into the glass reinforcement. The rolls can wet out 50 ft or more of laminate per minute. Molds for hand layup are often made from FRP. Coated plaster, cast metal, sheet metal, wood, and silicone rubber also are used.

Sprayup

By chopping the glass in a mechanism that also "throws" the chopped fibers (and at the same time sprays polyester resin), a structure can be built up

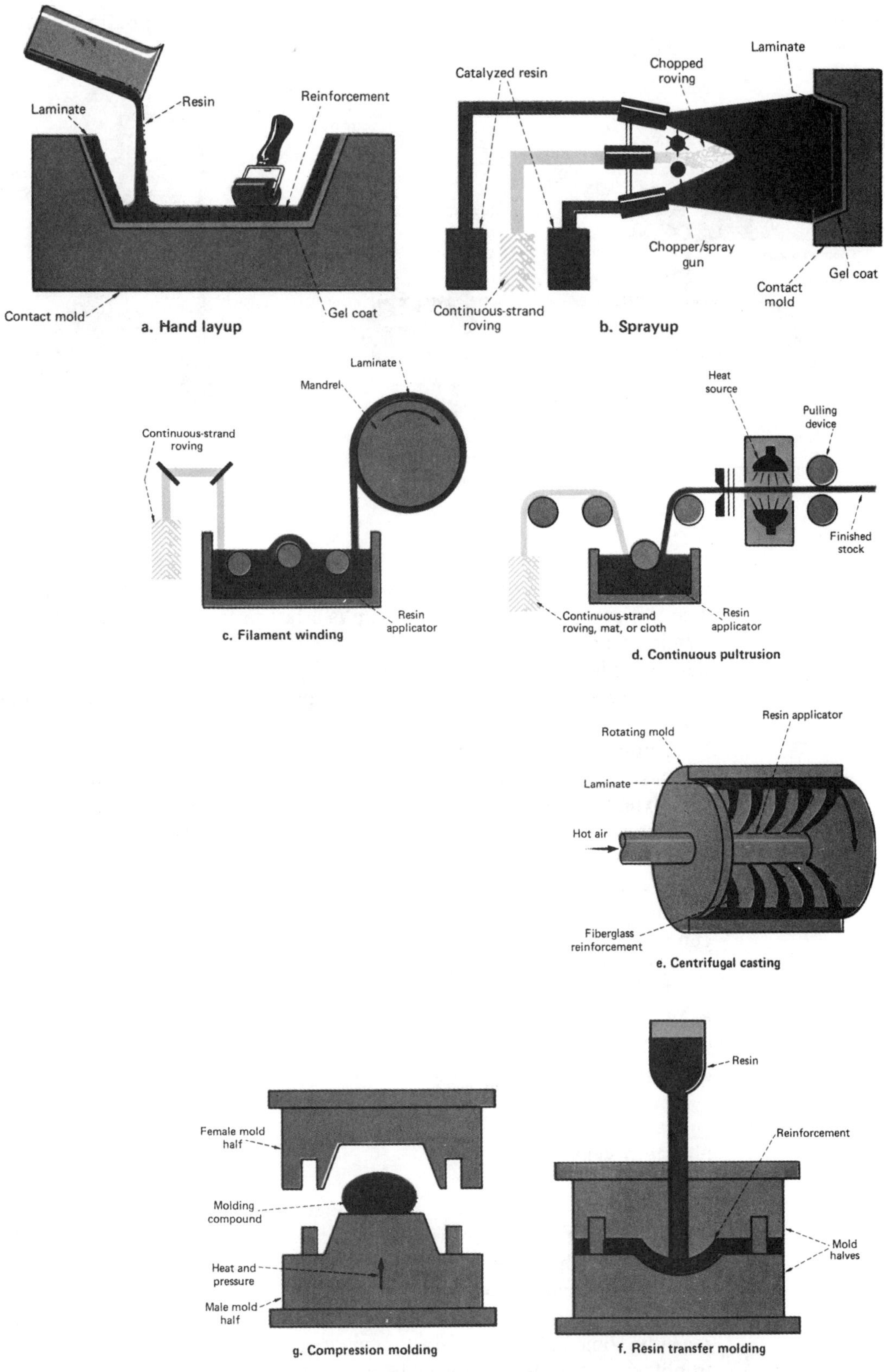

FIG. 2 Schematic diagram of FRP processing methods.

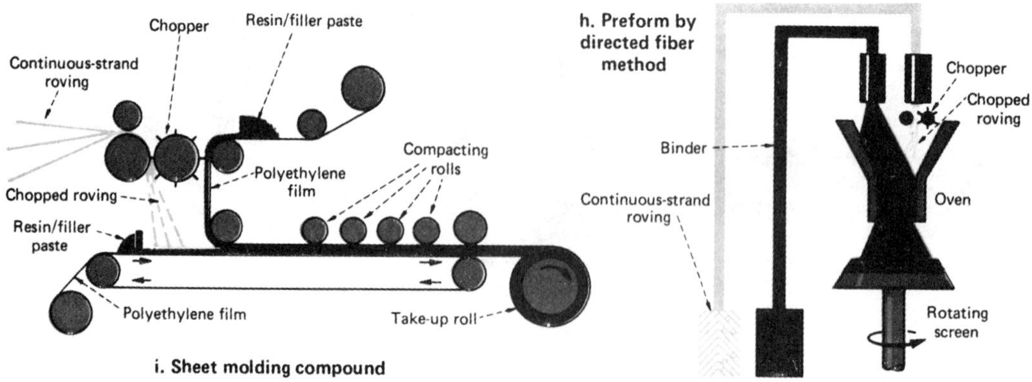

FIG. 2 (*continued*).

layer by layer in a matlike style (Fig. 2b). Following deposition of fiber and resin, it is necessary to roll-out the structure (compacting the resin and glass) with a special rolling wheel. Sprayup is a fast process, with rates of 20–30 lb/min of product possible. Like hand layup, the chopped glass and resin can be applied over a gel-coated mold.

A typical structure is the one-piece shower stall or tub-shower combination.

A number of chopping and spraying guns are on the market. There are two basic types of spray guns—one with internally mixed resin and the other with externally mixed resin. The internal-mix system has the reputation for achieving a more thorough mixing, but the external mix avoids the buildup of cured resin on the gun and the necessity for immediately flushing the mixer after spraying. There are also two types of spray nozzles—airless and air atomized. Because of the need for reducing styrene vapors, the airless gun has gained favor in recent years.

Sprayup is often used in combination with other processes, especially hand layup and filament winding. Automated, tape-controlled machines have been developed that produce complex shapes, such as end-caps for tanks, large-diameter pipe fittings, and other structures that are required in quantity.

Filament Winding

This process is most important in producing low-cost, high-strength, corrosion-resistant equipment (Fig. 2c). Filament-wound shapes combine the highest-strength fiberglass composite with the lowest-cost raw materials and a highly automated process.

Structures normally have only one smooth side (as in contact molding); recently, some have been made that incorporate a molding step after winding to obtain a smooth exterior and provide exterior attachments (bosses, undercuts, odd curvatures).

The filament-winding process had its beginning in the aerospace industry for producing structures with a high strength/weight ratio. Most solid-fueled rocket motors are still made by the filament-winding process. In the rocket motor development, a great deal of glass sizing research, stress analysis techniques, and resins development became available for adaptation to commercial structures.

Table 5 illustrates some advantages and limitations of filament winding for making pipe, tanks, ducts, and other corrosion-resistant structures.

Winding-Angle Effects

There are two basic types of filament winding—helical and biaxial.

Consider a cylindrical structure. In *helical winding,* a constant angle (traditionally measured from the rotational axis), alternately plus and minus, is maintained. Each pair of angles constitutes one layer, even though the layer may be constructed in steps. The required hoop/axial stress ratio is accomplished by winding at an optimum angle. For example, it has been mathematically shown (and confirmed by experiment) that a winding angle of 54¾ degrees will result in a 2/1 hoop-to-axial strength ratio. This is the optimum for an internal pressure requirement with no restraints (such as in a closed-end cylindrical tank).

In *biaxial winding,* the required strength ratio is accomplished by combinations of 0- and 90-degree windings. The total thicknesses of the 0- and the 90-degree layers determine the strength ratio (assuming equal glass content in each layer). For example, the 2/1 hoop-to-axial strength ratio would consist of twice as many windings at 90 degrees as those at 0 degrees.

Materials

The principal reinforcement is fiberglass roving; aramid yarns (an aromatic polyamide fiber) and graphite rovings have also been employed. In aero-

TABLE 5 Features of Filament Winding

Advantages
Automatable
High-strength products
Versatile in size range
Low-cost raw materials
Room-temperature or heat curing
High production rates possible
Strength orientation possible
Limitations
Reverse curves difficult
Low-angle (parallel to principal axis) winding difficult
Complex (double-curvature) shapes difficult
Air-pollution problems

space structures, preimpregnated epoxy tapes are often used; the tapes are made from fiberglass, aramid, graphite, and boron fibers.

Polyester resins probably account for more than half of the total business in filament winding, principally in tanks and large-diameter pipe. For small-diameter, high-pressure pipe, epoxy is the predominant resin, although vinyl ester is used by some producers. Other resins used include furans (for corrosion resistance) and polyimides (for high-temperature performance).

Impregnation Baths

There are many techniques (in wet-filament winding, which is the most common form) for wetting the strands prior to emplacement on the mandrel. The purpose of the impregnation bath is to wet the fiberglass strands (or other reinforcement) and remove excess resin. The excess resin can be squeezed out at the mandrel by the winding tension and resulting pressure, but it is economically preferable to remove as much resin as possible at the bath.

The dip bath system is the most common. The glass strands are guided over and under bars submerged in the resin. For ease in threading, it is desirable to have all the top bars (the ones that the strands pass under) fastened to side-rails so that all the bars can be lifted out of the bath simultaneously.

Rollers can be used to reduce the tension, but "roll wraps" can occur if strands break; this will eventually shut down the equipment. Some designers have used immersed rollers with the strands passing over the top of the rollers. This is effective, but results in less "working" of the glass to obtain complete wet-out.

The usual method of removing the excess resin is by passing the wet strands between a metal bar and a rubber (or urethane) bar, which are pressed together. Other methods incorporate slots, dies, or rollers.

Winding Machines

The most common machine has gears and roller chain drives to link the mandrel and carriage. Other types include cam-driven and electronic-drive machines. The latter is a recent development that incorporates a variable-speed drive continuously adjusted to maintain the desired speed ratio between mandrel and carriage.

Many fabricators have designed and built their own equipment, and there are a number of special-purpose machines. One machine that provides a continuous winding operation for large-diameter pipe has a cantilevered steel-ribbon mandrel that advances as it rotates, and disassembles at the free end. The endless steel ribbon returns through the hollow core to the beginning.

Cost Factors

The high production rates possible on filament-winding equipment (linear speeds of 300–500 ft/min are common in medium to large sections), plus highly automated handling equipment, have reduced costs in making filament-wound products. Recent surveys [2] have shown that polyester (and even epoxy) filament-wound pipe can compete favorably against plain carbon steel in some circumstances. Recent price increases for steel may make filament-wound fiberglass even more competitive.

Future Trends in Filament Winding

Combinations with pultrusion for more-automated systems
Automated handling of raw materials and products, with greater use of fillers (such as currently used in making RPM pipe)
Combinations with thermoplastics

Pultrusion

Pultrusion is a truly continuous process (Fig. 2d). With an automated cutoff saw, a pultrusion unit can run with virtually no attention, except for occasional checking for glass breakouts and resin levels.

Ordinarily, two layers of mat encapsulate each roving layer, with rovings spaced about four per inch of width. The cured thickness of a single layer of mat and rovings is about 0.040 in.

Materials and Process

Pultrusion resins are predominantly polyester, but epoxy is used in a few special-purpose applications. The range of polyester types is from lowest-cost orthophthalic to premium grades such as vinyl ester or Bisphenol A. The limit on fillers is the resin viscosity; at high filler loadings, the rovings will not wet adequately. Pigments are often added for coloration and ultraviolet resistance. An internal mold release is a must.

Resin impregnation baths are usually 3 to 6 ft long. In a way this is strange, since filament winders (whose speeds are 50 to 100 times higher) normally use much shorter resin baths. In filament winding, much of the wet-out occurs on the mandrel and tensile forces tend to squeeze out air. In pultrusion, as soon as the rovings reach the die cavity, any remaining air is trapped in the laminate, which at this point is cured by the heat source.

Surface mats are sometimes added to provide a resin-rich appearance. Fiberglass surface mats have no strength in the wet state. They should be fed into the structure as close to the curing die as possible. Polyester surface mats (unwoven cloth) have greater strength and will survive the trip through the impregnation bath; unfortunately, they are more expensive than glass.

The hot dies for curing are normally 2 to 4 ft long and should have as high a polish as possible. They are made from hardened steel, polished, and then hard-chrome-plated. Ordinarily, the die is split longitudinally. Surface smoothness is critical.

The relationships of glass, resin, filler, and stripping-die area are mathematically solvable on a volume basis.

The total amount of roving can be calculated from the relationship

$$Y_{tot} = 1 + W_g(\rho_m/\rho_g - 1)/36W_g\rho_m A$$

where Y_{tot} = total yield of glass rovings in yd/lb; W_g = weight fraction of glass in the composite; ρ_m = density of resin and filler mixture in lb/in.^{3}; ρ_g = intrinsic fiberglass density in lb/in.^{3}; A = curing-die area in in.^{2}.

From this, the number of roving packages can be determined from

$$N = Y_g/Y_{tot}$$

where N = number of packages of fiberglass; Y_g = yield of individual package in yd/lb.

Centrifugal Casting

The centrifugal casting process for making fiberglass pipe is one of the oldest FRP processes (Fig. 2e). A cylindrical mold is spun about its long axis. A mat or mat-and-cloth reinforcement is laid in the mold, resin is poured in, and the mold is turned. The laminate is compressed against the mold.

In a more recent development, sprayup glass is chopped and resin sprayed inside while the mold is spinning. In other operations, a low-viscosity premixed compound is dispensed into the rotating mold.

Centrifugal casting requires a modest investment and produces parts having smooth surfaces and low void content. The process, which has shape limitations, is used for making tubes, pipes, and tanks.

Resin Transfer Molding (RTM)

This is a relatively new process, sometimes called resin injection molding, which appears to have a large potential for producing complex shapes, using woven roving, mats and surface mats, or gel coats. See Fig. 2f.

The process uses matched molds, male and female, made from reinforced plastic or metal. The dry reinforcements (mat, cloth, woven roving, etc.) are placed in the mold, which is then closed. Tight seals, usually O-rings, are necessary at all mold joints. A vacuum pulls some of the air out of the mold, and then resin, promoted and catalyzed for a pot life of about 30 min, is pumped in at the bottom. When resin flows out at the top of the mold, pumping is stopped. After the resin has hardened, the mold can be opened and the part removed.

In comparison to *hand layup,* RTM gives two molded sides, dimensional accuracy, and faster production cycles—but requires higher capital investment.

In comparison to *compression molding,* the RTM process has a lower capital investment but a higher labor factor and slower cycle, so that for runs of more than about 10,000 parts, compression molding is cheaper. Some fairly large parts have been built via RTM, and the process has considerable potential.

Compression Molding

Many mass-produced parts for corrosion-resistant equipment are being made by one of the several forms of compression molding (see Fig. 2g). These include pipe flanges, pipe fittings, manholes, and small tanks.

All of these parts have a complex shape and must be produced in large quantities. Compression molding is a process using two matched molds, male and female. The molds are preferably made from high-carbon steel hardened on the surface after machining. The mold faces are then polished to a high gloss, and chrome-plated for wear resistance. They usually will last for 10,000 parts before requiring stripping and replating. Molds may be made from FRP or filled epoxy, depending on: type of part and shape, mold material (and cost), number of parts to be produced, type of reinforcement and resin.

Many of the variations in compression molding depend on the type of material being molded. Several innovations in materials systems have occurred in recent years. The types of materials now being used are bulk molding compound, mats or preforms with liquid resins, and sheet molding compound.

Bulk Molding Compound

This material is sometimes called "dough molding compound" or "premix." Bulk molding compounds (BMC) are made from polyester or epoxy resin having relatively low glass contents (10–15%) and high filler contents (30–40%). The ingredients are charged into a heavy-duty mixer, such as a dough mixer, and blended. The fiberglass is either ⅛- or ¼-in.-long chopped strand with a high amount of insoluble binder (1½ to 2%) to prevent it from filamentizing. Experience has shown that filamentized strands ball up and separate out in the mixing process. With higher glass contents, this separation also occurs.

The polyester or epoxy resin is catalyzed for high-temperature cure to achieve a long life at room temperature. Heat activates the catalyst system and allows the polymerization to occur quickly.

Bulk-molding-compound parts have moderate tensile strengths (around 15,000 $lb/in.^2$) with better impact resistance than a filled resin. They are used in many low-stressed applications.

Mats or Preforms with Liquid Resin

Continuous strand mats are often used with liquid resin in compression molding where the draw (depth) is not too great. In more-complex sections, a preform is used (Fig. 2h). This is made of chopped glass fibers (1–2 in.) blown against a screen shaped like the part. The screen has a vacuum pulled on the opposite side. After sufficient fiber buildup, a binder is sprayed onto the preform, and the matlike structure is dried.

The preform is placed in the mold in the same manner as the mat. The exact quantity of filled resin is poured over the preform, and the mold is closed. The high pressure of the press pushes the liquid resin into the fiberglass. When curing is complete, the part is strong and durable, with 20–25% glass content.

Sheet Molding Compound

A quantity of approximately 0.5–1% magnesium or calcium oxide will cause polyester resins to thicken to a viscosity of about 18–20 million cP. This is a level at which the material is essentially nontacky and has a leather-like stiffness. If the thickened polyester is heated, the resin becomes liquid again and will cure, under the influence of a catalyst, in a normal manner.

The sheet molding compound (SMC) is made by continuously laying down liquid resin, mixed with fillers, thickening additives, and a catalyst, on a traveling polyethylene film (Fig. 2i). Glass fibers (2 in. long) are chopped and sprinkled onto the resin layer. A second layer of resin is laid down onto another film that is pressed down on top of the glass fibers.

The sandwich of films, glass, and resin passes under rollers, or a pair of chain belts, that massage the layers and work the resin into the fiber bundles. The SMC is then rolled up and set aside for "maturation," a period of several hours during which thickening occurs. At the end of maturation, the sheet can be cut into sections to make a weighed charge for the molding process. The film can be stripped off since the SMC is nontacky.

The charge can be varied in both weight and shape, as required for the part. While the hot mold halves are open, the charge is placed in the mold. Emplacement may be manual or mechanical. The mold is closed and the charge flows to fill the mold cavity. Pressure may reach 1500–2000 lb/in.^{2} from the hydraulic press before and during the curing cycle, which lasts 1 to 2 min.

A variation of sheet molding compound, SMC-II, uses an adjusted chemical system to thicken the resin to a viscosity level approximately half as high as the standard SMC. This resin is still nontacky, but it will flow to fill the mold at a lower pressure. This lower pressure allows the use of reinforced plastic or aluminum molds that are much lower in cost than the hardened steel molds required for standard SMC.

The properties of the SMC parts are equivalent to preform parts (20,000–30,000 lb/in.^{2} tensile at about 30% glass content) but with flow properties, reproducibility, and cost similar to BMC parts.

Mold Releases

Mold releases are used in one of two ways, or a combination of both—internal, mixed in the resin, or external, applied to the mold. The common *internal* mold releases are: lecithin; zinc, calcium, or other stearates; organic phosphate compounds. *External* mold releases include: fluorocarbons (dispersions of a solid fluorocarbon, in a volatile solvent); silicone oils; waxes.

The silicone oils are good releases but cannot be used if any secondary bonding is planned. Some filament winders use fluorocarbon; some prefer waxes or silicones. In pultrusion, only an internal release can be used; in compression molding, it is common to use both internal and external mold releases.

Miscellaneous Molding Methods

There are also a number of minor molding methods that are infrequently used in the manufacture of corrosion-resistant structures. Among these are the following.

Autoclave

A laminate shaped over a mold, usually male, is placed in a heated pressure tank and cured. This process is used mostly in the aerospace industry for cloth/epoxy laminates.

Cold Molding

This is a form of compression molding that uses a promoted polyester resin and requires no heat for curing. It is slower than normal hot-compression molding. The investment required and the product obtained are similar to those for resin transfer molding.

Vacuum-Bag Molding

This is similar to the autoclave molding system but uses a vacuum bag. It involves less investment and is a lower-pressure system.

Injection Molding

This is a high-investment, mass-production process mostly used for small thermoplastic items, both unreinforced and with up to 40% glass fibers. The nature of the process involves high-pressure pumping and movement of materials through small orifices; the glass fibers are reduced to a very short length, probably less than 1/32 in.

In recent years, techniques have been developed for molding thermoset resins, primarily reinforced ones. Because of high investment and high mold cost, the process is limited to large production runs.

Rotational Molding

This process slowly rotates a closed, split mold on two axes. A dry powder or a liquid tumbles inside the heated mold and gradually builds up a shell. The process is limited to hollow shapes but can produce closed-end structures without the use of a core mold. Thermoplastic resins, reinforced and unreinforced, are most commonly used, but some liquid thermosets have been molded by this process.

Other Processes

These include: cold stamping of reinforced thermoplastic sheets; fiberglass/polyester-backed thermoplastic sheet (vacuum-formed); encapsulation; and continuous lamination.

Standards and Specifications

The production of corrosion-resistant composites is a rapidly growing business, and there have been numerous failures due to misapplication, poor craftsmanship, or underdesign.

The most active standards group by far is ASTM Committee D-20.23 "Reinforced Plastic Piping Systems and Chemical Process Equipment." There are nine sections, dealing with various products and test methods. See Table 6.

At present, the various sections of D-20.23 are working on approximately 30 different draft standards or revisions to standards. These include specifications, test methods, or recommended practices for:

Underground petroleum-storage tanks
Contact-pressure-molded chemical-resistant tanks
Contact-pressure-molded ducts
Corrosion resistance of molded fittings
Manholes
Underground chemical tanks
Sewer and industrial pressure pipe

Some of the principal ASTM standards that pertain directly or indirectly to chemical equipment made from composite materials are listed in Table 7.

TABLE 6 Active Sections in ASTM Committee D-20.23

Section No.	Title
D-20.23.10	Reinforced thermosetting resin pipe
D-20.23.11	Reinforced plastic mortar pipe
D-20.23.12	Mechanical test methods
D-20.23.13	Chemical and environmental test methods
D-20.23.14	Pipe fittings, flanges and joints
D-20.23.15	Tanks and process equipment
D-20.23.16	Underground tanks and structures
D-20.23.17	Fume handling equipment
D-20.23.18	Reinforced thermosetting resin materials of construction

TABLE 7 Principal Relevant ASTM Standards

Standard No.	Title
ANSI/ASTM C581-74	Chemical resistance of thermosetting resins used in glass fiber reinforced structures
ANSI/ASTM D1599-74	Short-time rupture strength for plastic pipe, tubing, and fittings
ANSI/ASTM D2143-76	Standard test method for cyclic pressure strength of reinforced thermosetting resin pipe
ANSI/ASTM D2562-70	Standard recommended practice for classifying visual defects in parts molded from reinforced thermosetting plastics
ANSI/ASTM D2584-72	Standard test method for ignition loss of cured reinforced resins
ASTM D2992-71	Standard method for obtaining hydrostatic design basis for reinforced thermosetting resin pipe and fittings
ASTM D2996-71	Standard specification for filament wound reinforced thermosetting resin pipe
ASTM D3299-74	Standard specification for filament wound glass fiber reinforced polyester chemical resistant tanks
ASTM D3681-78	Test for determining chemical resistance of reinforced thermosetting resin pipe in a deflected condition

Four other standards should be mentioned in connection with corrosion-resistant equipment:

U.S. Department of Commerce NBS PS15-69, "Custom contact-molded reinforced-polyester chemical-resistant process equipment"
British Standard BS 4994: 1973 "Specification for vessels and tanks in reinforced plastic"
British Standard BS 5480: Part 1: 1977 "Specification for glass fiber reinforced plastics (GRP) pipes and fittings for water supply or sewerage
American Petroleum Institute Standard 5 LR

References

1. John Decker (Westerman Companies), Private Communication, January 1991.
2. S. P. Marshall and J. L. Brandt, "Installed Cost of Piping," *Chem. Eng.,* 68–82 (August 23, 1971).

J. ALBERT ROLSTON

Plastics, Fiberglass, Reinforced

Fiberglass-reinforced plastic (FRP) has been used for various types of equipment in the chemical process industries (CPI) since the early 1950s, and its use continues to grow. Process vessels of all shapes and sizes, columns, scrubbers, hoppers, hoods, ducts, fans, stacks, piping, filter-press frames, pumps, pump bases, valve bodies, elevator buckets, heat-exchanger shells and tube sheets, mixer drive shafts, mist-eliminator blades, floor toppings, and vessel and tank lining systems, are just a few examples of equipment made of FRP.

The chief reason for the popularity of these materials is their excellent resistance to corrosion, as well as their ability, when the appropriate additives have been incorporated, to resist heat and/or fire. This article will discuss these properties and other important factors that determine a particular material's applicability under certain conditions. But first, we will discuss a few of the basics of FRP.

What Is FRP?

FRP stands for, most commonly, *fiberglass-reinforced plastic,* although since the introduction of other fiber reinforcements, FRP is also used to mean simply *fiber-reinforced plastic.* Terms used interchangeably with FRP are *reinforced thermoset plastic* (RTP) (which should not be confused with *reinforced thermoplastic*), *reinforced thermoset resin* (RTR), and *glass-reinforced plastic* (GRP). *Laminate* refers to the material that is manufactured from thermosetting resin and reinforcement fibers at the time of equipment fabrication.

FRP is a composite material consisting of a thermosetting polymer, often a type of polyester, reinforced with glass (or other) fibers. Reinforcements and processing methods are discussed in detail in Ref. 1.

There are six types of FRP resins: isophthalic, orthophthalic, chlorendic, Bisphenol A fumarate, furan, and vinyl ester. Each is described briefly below. Their properties are compared in Table 1, and some actual applications in corrosive environments are summarized in Table 2.

Isophthalic Resins

Isophthalic resins are nonfire-retardant, either rigid or flexible unsaturated polyester resins based on isophthalic acid and glycols of various types.

These resins are used for moderate corrosion resistance applications up to 180°F. At temperatures not exceeding 180°F, they generally exhibit excellent resistance to water, weak acids, and alkalis, and good resistance to solvents and petroleum products such as gasoline and oil. The flexible isophthalics exhibit a lesser degree of chemical resistance than the rigid isophthalics of higher molecular weight and are limited to 150°F (maximum).

TABLE 1 Comparison of Properties of Various Types of FRP[a]

	Isophthalic	Orthophthalic	Chlorendic	Bisphenol A Fumarate	Furan	Vinyl Ester	Carbon Steel	Stainless Steel
Corrosion resistance:								
Acids	B	C	A	A	A	B	C	B
Alkalis	B	C	C	A	A	A	B	B
Peroxides	C	C	A	B	C	B	C	C
Hypochlorites	C	C	A	B	C	B	C	C
Solvents	B	C	B	B	A	B	A	A
Flame retardance	C	C	A	C	B	C	A	A
Structural strength	A	B	A	A	A	A	A	A
Thermal insulation	A	A	A	A	A	A	C	C

A = high, B = moderate, C = low.

TABLE 2 Summary of Actual Applications of FRP in Corrosive Service

Equipment	Corrosive Environment	Type of Resin[a]
Venturi cooler	160°F boiler flue gas	C
Stacks, chimney liners 500 ft and higher	Flue gas at 350–375°F, with peaks to 500–700°F	C
	Lined stacks for 310°F (continuous) flue gas	C, B
Scrubbers: Cross-flow; ionizing; cyclone; co-current; countercurrent; spray; packed tower; vertical; parallel flow; horizontal	300–350°F bagasse flue gas, trash burner flue gas	C
	Acidic inert gas at 120–140°F	C
	Coal dust containing fluoride up to 350°F	C
	340°F flue gas and scrubbed carbonate liquor	C
Circulating tanks and piping	Acidic fluids up to 180°F	C
Mist eliminators, grating support beams	Sulfurous acid to 350°F and thiosorbic lime	C
	Coke quenching at 200°F	F
Fans and blowers	350°F flue gas	C
Electrostatic precipitators vibrator housings	H_2S and SO_2 fumes at 280–360°F	C
Piping with abrasion-resistant lining	Scrubbing-liquor slurry	C
Desulfurizing units	H_2S, SO_2, and citric acid	C
	H_2S, SO_2, and monoethanolamine to 270°F	F
Incinerator duct, stack, scrubbers	Trash, garbage, chemicals (no damage after short-duration exposures to 600°F)	C
Smelter duct, stack scrubbers	Copper, lead, zinc to 280°F	C

[a]C = chlorendic, B = Bisphenol A, F = furan.

Orthophthalic Resins

The difference between orthophthalic and isophthalic resins is in the position of the two —COOH groups in the phthalic acid molecule: they are on adjacent carbons (e.g., in the *ortho*-position) in orthophthalic acid, and are separated by one carbon (e.g., in the *meta*-position) in isophthalic acid. Orthophthalic resins (often called general-purpose polyesters or ortho resins) provide only a minimum of corrosion resistance, and thus are not usually used in instances where corrosion resistance is needed.

Chlorendic Resins

Chlorendic resins are unsaturated halogenated polyester resins based on HET (hexachlorocyclopentadiene) acid or chlorendic anhydride reacted with a stable glycol (such as neopentyl glycol).

They are particularly well suited for use at elevated temperatures, up to 350°F, because the chlorendic backbone is highly resistant to distortion by heat.

They are able to handle aggressive, highly oxidizing environments, concentrated acids, and some solvents very well, but are poor in alkaline service.

Chlorendic resins can be formulated to achieve Class I fire rating (based on the standard test, discussed later). The only material with a better rating (of 0) is asbestos.

Bisphenol A Fumarates

These are unsaturated, rigid polyesters made by reacting Bisphenol A with propylene oxide to form a glycol, then reacting the glycol with fumaric acid to produce the resin.

Bisphenol A fumarate resins exhibit excellent corrosion resistance to both aggressive acid and alkali environments up to 250°F, but are not suitable in strong oxidizing conditions or solvent applications. They are substantially better than the isophthalics in severe corrosion applications.

Fire-retardant varieties of Bisphenol A resins are available.

Vinyl Esters

Vinyl ester resins are methacrylated epoxies that are very similar to polyester, although they are classified separately. They offer excellent physical strength and, in general, much better impact strength than rigid polyester resins. While the standard vinyl ester resins are limited to 200–225°F in most applications, other versions with higher crosslink density are suitable for up to 250°F.

These resins exhibit excellent resistance to acids, alkalis, hypochlorites, and many solvents. They are preferred for filament winding, especially for machine-made piping.

Brominated versions of vinyl esters are available for fire-retardant applications.

Furan Resins

Furan resins are based on a furan polymer derivative of furfuryl alcohol. They exhibit excellent resistance to strong alkalis and acids containing chlorinated organics, and are superior to polyesters and vinyl esters in solvent resistance. Furan laminates are good up to about 250°F for many corrosive applications. However, the furan material is not suitable for oxidizing chemicals, and should not be used for chromic or nitric acids, peroxides, or hypochlorites. Most furans offer some degree of fire retardance.

Generally, the furan resins are considered to be the best materials for all-around corrosion resistance. Unfortunately, they are one of the most difficult resins to work with and cure at room temperatures. Only qualified fabricators—those with proven performance—should be used for furan applications.

Evaluating Corrosion Resistance

As shown in Table 1, FRPs do not resist all environments, nor do they respond equally to specific corrosives. Unless a successful installation exists to serve as a guide, testing and evaluation must be done on an application-by-application basis. This is the more common situation.

Because of the many variables that can affect chemical resistance, it is often somewhat difficult to evaluate the results of chemical resistance tests and to select an economically serviceable material. This section describes the parameters that must be evaluated, factors that affect performance, some testing methods, and how to evaluate test results.

Chemical Attack

Chemical attack on FRP is a complicated phenomenon that can occur in a number of different ways, which may be broadly classified as follows:

Resin attack. This includes: (1) degradation and disintegration of a physical nature due to absorption, permeation, or solvent action which, under mild conditions, may manifest itself as reversible or irreversible swelling; (2) oxidation; (3) hydrolysis; (4) radiation, including nuclear; (5) thermal attack; or (6) combinations of these.

Glass attack. Certain environments might not attack the resin itself, but upon absorption will attack the glass reinforcement. Fluorides, alkalis, hot water and its vapor, and hydrochloric acid under certain conditions are typical examples of glass-attacking agents.

Glass–resin interface attack. The glass–resin interface can be attacked by many substances, even though the resin itself might be reasonably resistant to attack. Wicking (degradation of the reinforcement due to an inadequate resin cover) and delamination are typical effects of this type of attack.

As a result of exposure to an environment, the FRP can respond in a number of different ways. It might not be affected at all, or it might be embrittled, softened, discolored, charred, crazed (developing a network of fine cracks), weakened, delaminated, dissolved, or blistered, or it might exhibit any combination of these effects.

Although all FRP materials will exhibit attack in fundamentally the same manner in a particular environment, certain types—chlorendic, Bisphenol A, and vinyl ester—are significantly more resistant. This is due to their somewhat unique structures, which have a built-in steric protection of ester groups. However, knowledge of the chemical or molecular structure of such resins *does not* eliminate the need for actual testing to determine suitability for a particular application. For example, certain vinyl esters are reasonably resistant to alkaline environments under some conditions; others are only fairly so.

Temperature and Concentration Effects

Changing the temperature of an environment will influence the response of FRP laminates. An increase in temperature will accelerate the rate of attack, in some instances to the point where degradation can be extremely rapid.

However, FRP laminates are heterogeneous and, in contrast to homogeneous metals and alloys, do not react at a predictable rate when exposed to a corrosive environment. The rule of thumb (often used for metals and alloys) that the corrosion rate will double for each 10°F rise in temperature is not applicable to FRP materials. Temperature effects cannot be extrapolated reliably to predict material response at different temperatures; an FRP material may be severely attacked by a substance at 180°F but possess excellent resistance up to 150°F.

A decrease in temperature will almost always reduce the degree of attack. However, phase separation or precipitation of one of the components of the environment as a result of the drop in temperature can completely alter the mode of attack.

There are similar problems in attempting to predict response based on concentration of the environment. A decrease in concentration generally results in decreased attack, but not in all instances, particularly when the material is exposed to corrosive organics. An increase in concentration will not necessarily accelerate attack on FRP—for example, 10% sodium hydroxide is *more* aggressive than a 50% solution.

Impurities or very small amounts of a substance can also significantly influence the response of FRP laminates and can often accelerate attack. Hydrochloric acid, for example, is not the same as hydrochloric acid contaminated with small amounts of chlorobenzene or other organics. In addition, certain conditions may cause a minor component to separate out of solution into a concentrated layer or phase and result in significantly increased attack in that region.

For reliable corrosion-resistance results, FRP must be tested under controlled, known conditions and under conditions that very closely simulate the actual environment in which the material would be used.

Laminate Cure

Cure plays one of the more important parts in the chemical resistance developed by FRP materials.

Theoretically, the curing reaction should go to completion at room temperature, with all double bonds reacted, to achieve the complete cure or crosslinking shown schematically for polyester in Fig. 1. However, complete crosslinkage is rarely achieved at ambient temperature, with only about 95% of the unsaturation typically being converted. This accounts for reduced chemical resistance and, in general, for the inability of a resin to achieve full property potential. On the other hand, maximum chemical resistance and certain other improvements can be expected if an elevated temperature is used to more fully react the resin.

It is extremely important that, for FRP materials to perform at full potential, as complete a cure as possible must be achieved.

This also indicates that candidate materials must be tested at essentially the same level of cure. A comparison cannot be made of one material cured at room temperature with another cured at an elevated temperature, because an elevated-temperature cure is not representative of most industrial-equipment fabrication techniques, where room temperatures are used almost exclusively.

The degree of cure can be determined by various methods, the simplest of which is the Barcol hardness test, or ASTM Method D-2583 [2]. A hardness value, on a scale of 0–100, is obtained by measuring the resistance to penetration of a sharp steel point under a spring load with an instrument called the Barcol Impressor. Standards and specifications generally accept at least 90% of the resin manufacturers recommended Barcol hardness value, which indicates that full property potential, including sufficient (though not necessarily maximum) chemical resistance, has been achieved.

Some FRP laminate surfaces that are exposed to air will not cure well, resulting in reduced chemical resistance. Barcol hardness readings may not detect this condition in all cases, so an acetone sensitivity test should also be used to check surfaces. If the surface feels tacky or soft after the appli-

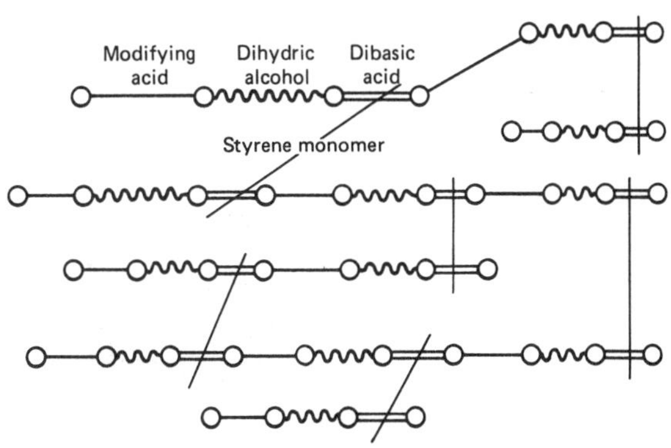

FIG. 1 Complete crosslinking in polyester resin.

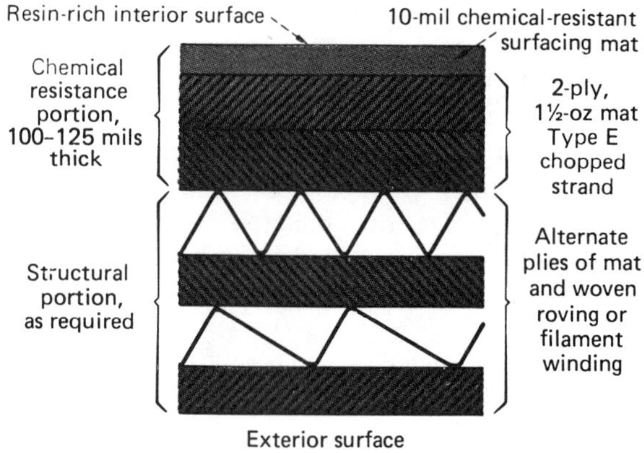

FIG. 2 Typical laminate construction to provide chemical resistance.

cation of acetone, it is not properly cured, and a postcure at elevated temperature (up to 250°F) may be required before exposure of the material to a corrosive environment.

Laminate Construction

Fabrication techniques also contribute to corrosion resistance.

Equipment for chemical-resistance applications must have a resin-rich surface containing a chemical-resistant surfacing veil or mat, whose purpose is to isolate the fiberglass reinforcement from attack that would result in wicking and blistering. The corrosion barrier should be about 125 mils thick and fabricated with two or three plies of Type E chopped strand mat. The structural portion of the laminate (the outer shell of the wall of a vessel or the interior of an I-beam) is high in glass fiber content; for the maximum strength/thickness ratio, chopped glass mat, cloth, woven roving, or, for very high strength, filament-wound reinforcement can be used.

Figure 2 illustrates the typical laminate construction required for chemical-resistant equipment. Figure 3 shows the standard laminate currently used for chemical resistance tests by ASTM Method C-581 [3]; this simulates the interior chemical-resistant barrier surface of the actual construction in Fig. 2.

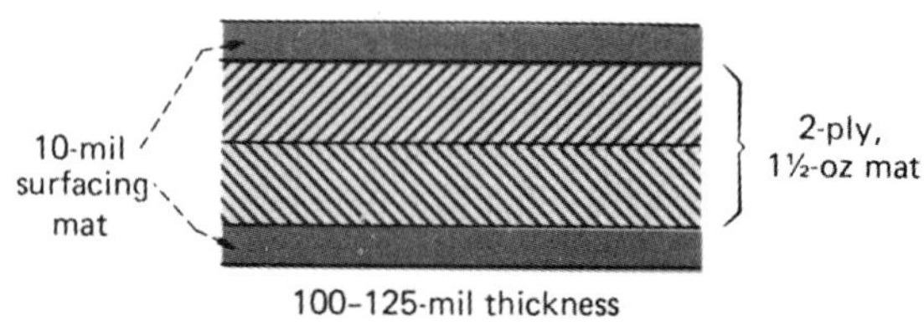

FIG. 3 Standard laminate construction for chemical resistance testing.

Candidate materials must be tested at the same nominal thickness and construction. While this is a relatively simple concept, there are some ¼-in.-thick laminates in the field that were submitted for comparative testing with the standard ⅛-in.-thick specimens, as well as laminates with two or more surfacing veils. The response of the thicker laminate or the one with two veils will always be better than that of the standard laminate. Curves F and G in Fig. 4 point out very well how this can be misleading. The thicker laminate (Curve F) appears to be significantly better than the thinner one (Curve G), even though they are constructed in the same way and of the same material. Castings are not representative of an actual fabrication and should not be used to assess chemical resistance of reinforced laminates.

Test Methods

The ideal method for determining the response of FRP materials to a corrosive environment is to expose one 10-mil-surfaced face of the standard laminate shown in Fig. 3 to the environment under stress, with the magnitude of the load and the direction of the force corresponding to what would be encountered in actual service. Unfortunately, although this method is used by a number of investigators, it is somewhat complex and not practical for evaluating a large number of laminates or materials under field conditions.

Another excellent test method is to totally immerse the standard laminate in the environment, again under stress. This is more representative of actual service conditions, since stress and chemical exposure are simultaneous. However, this method is also rather difficult and is not practical either for in-the-field testing or for testing a large number of laminates.

A more practical method is to totally immerse standard laminates (as shown in Fig. 3) according to ASTM Method C-581 procedure. Although not as representative of actual conditions, it has been proven over the years and does successfully predict response and stability. It also provides an added safety factor, since it involves a significantly more severe exposure than actual service conditions, where only one surface would be exposed.

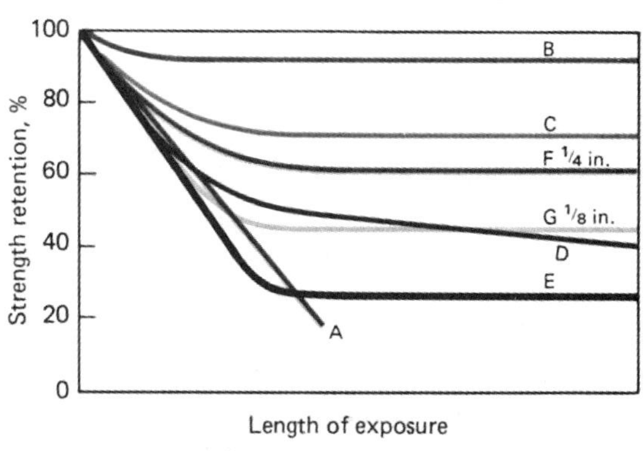

FIG. 4 Flexural strength retention as a function of exposure.

This total immersion method consists of the simultaneous exposure of a minimum of three test laminates to the environment, either in the laboratory under simulated conditions or under actual field conditions, in such a way that all surfaces are freely in contact with the test environment. A water condenser prevents loss of the solution; in other tests, the glass container would be insulated to control temperature. Certain solutions, e.g., sodium hypochlorite, should be changed frequently to ensure that the laminates are exposed to maximum concentration at all times.

Test laminates are usually removed after 1, 2, and 3 months (at the minimum). After each exposure period, changes in flexural strength and modulus, as well as in Barcol hardness and in visual and microscopic appearance, are recorded.

The entire test can be completed in 3 months; however, specimens generally are exposed for 12 months or more. What is important is to follow the course of attack by plotting hardness, flexural strength, and modulus retention to determine serviceability. It is always best, of course, to expose a sufficient number of samples to obtain duplicate results in any one time period, with at least three time periods required to establish an acceptable curve.

Thickness, weight, and color changes can be disregarded. Significant weight and thickness changes resulting from exposure will always be accompanied by significant changes in physical properties or hardness and are meaningless in themselves; changes in laminate color have also been found meaningless in corrosion-resistance testing.

In certain processes it is important to know whether the FRP material will change the color of the solution and, particularly, whether discoloration persists with time. Tests to determine this must be run using the actual surface-area-to-volume ratio and expected residence time. It has been found that discoloration usually does not continue after the first exposure. Thus, a surface preconditioning, i.e., subjecting the surface to hot water or atmospheric steam for about 4 hours, or to the actual product for about 4 hours at the appropriate temperature, will often prevent discoloration.

Evaluation of Test Results

Evaluating the test results is the most difficult part of any material-selection program, and is much more complicated for nonhomogeneous structures such as FRP laminates than for metals. It is impossible to correlate property changes to a rate of deterioration, but experienced assessment of the property-change/time curves, such as Fig. 4 showing flexural-strength retention vs months of exposure, can be used with a high degree of confidence to predict resistance and serviceability.

Rapid harmful reactions, represented by Curve A in Fig. 4, and those that are so slow as to produce only a minimum property change, Curves B and C, can be assessed quite easily. Obviously, Material A is unsuitable, while Materials B and C should, for most applications, be satisfactory for essentially an indefinite service life. However, if the laminate surface exhibits relatively bad blistering or crazing or is subject to other attack, the material's service life may not be satisfactory, even though Curves B and C indicate otherwise. In such cases, experience must serve as a guide.

Borderline cases, such as Curves D and E, often present problems. The flexural-strength retention of Material E levels off at a relatively low value over time. Depending on the material's retention of other properties, its visual appearance and its resistance in similar environments, it might still be economically serviceable if a greater-than-ordinary thickness were used to provide the typical 5–10 to 1 safety factor. An economic evaluation of competitive materials must be done before a decision can be made. For Material D, testing should continue, since strength retention did not level off over the length of the test. If the material continues to lose flexural strength at a rate of no more than about 0.5% per month, it can be used quite successfully, with an expected service life of from 10 to 20 years.

Some investigators believe that the attack of FRP materials generally occurs at a decreasing rate approximated by a logarithmic function, and that if the retention data are plotted on log-log coordinates, the resulting straight lines can be extended to predict service life and property retention at some future time. However, such a log-log plot rarely results in a straight line. Also, because the lines are so close to each other and because of normal data fluctuations, it is quite difficult to confidently extend the lines to the 5-, 10-, or 20-year time frame.

It should be emphasized that none of these property changes correlates with another or with degradation of the material, and that no one or two properties should be or can be used as a basis to accept or reject a material. Selection must be based on a combination of the test results. A conservative approach, rather than an overly optimistic one, is warranted, since it is better to err in that direction than to risk early failure.

Fire Retardancy

All plastics are based on organic constituents. As such, most are inherently flammable and, once ignited, will burn profusely until completely consumed. However, there are several methods for making many of the thermoset resins fire-retardant.

In an estimated 20% of all chemical-resistant FRP applications, there is a need for some degree of fire retardancy. In addition, many of these applications are associated with higher operating temperatures—from 250 to 450°F—and require a material having high heat resistance as well. An example is a boiler duct handling wet SO_2 flue gas at 310°F.

Developing Flame Retardancy

Flame retardancy can be achieved by using numerous chemical additives, both organic and inorganic. Because most of these have a negative effect on mechanical and/or chemical-resistance properties, only the most widely used system for attaining optimum fire retardancy in a chemical-resistant FRP will be discussed here—a halogenated thermosetting resin system into which the inorganic synergist antimony oxide (Sb_2O_3) has been added.

This additive is referred to as a synergist because it enhances the natural fire retardancy of halogenated resins. Yet, if Sb_2O_3 were added to a nonhalogenated resin, it would have no effect on that laminate's burning characteristics.

The general practice is for the FRP equipment fabricator to add and mix powdered Sb_2O_3 into the liquid uncured halogenated resin, then add the curing catalyst to the resin/Sb_2O_3 mix. This is combined with the glass fibers to form the FRP laminate. Since the Sb_2O_3 is a white powder, it colors the laminate an opaque white, which is not necessarily a needed characteristic. However, Nyacol 1540 (a colloidal suspension of antimony pentoxide) allows some translucency and permits visual inspection of a laminate.

Fire Retardancy Tests and Ratings

The most commonly used test for ignition and flammability is the National Fire Protection Association's NFPA 255 [4], or ASTM Method E-84 [5]. It is frequently referred to as the "tunnel test," and its purpose is to determine the comparative burning characteristics of a material by evaluating the flame spread (FS) over its surface, which is exposed to a test fire in a forced-air chamber or tunnel. A flame-spread classification which considers both the ignition time and the distance the flame front advances down the tunnel during the 10-min duration of the test is determined for the test material. The FS is then compared with those for asbestos-cement board and select-grade red oak flooring, which have FSs that have been established arbitrarily as 0 and 100, respectively.

An FS of "25 or less" is generally required to meet most fire codes, although there are some notable exceptions. An FRP fabrication with an FS of 35 might have a significantly lower cost than one with an FS of 20; if the intended application can be safeguarded in another manner, such as with sprinklers or by being remotely located, the use of the FRP with the 35 FS would probably be permitted.

Heat Resistance

The various thermosetting resin technologies have different heat-resistance properties. Table 3 compares the continuous-operation temperature limits of four common laminates. Since the type and amount of reinforcement used also affect laminate performance under exposure to high temperature, a comparison of heat-deflection temperatures (HDTs) for the clear cast resins containing no reinforcement is made too.

The engineer designing equipment for high-temperature operation should also be aware of the reduction in mechanical properties of the laminate at higher temperatures, and incorporate this into the design for both normal and anticipated excursions.

TABLE 3 Heat-Resistance Characteristics of FRP Laminates and Resin Castings

	Isophthalic	Vinyl Ester	Bisphenol A Fumarate	Chlorendic
Continuous operating temperature of FRP laminate system containing 65% glass, °F	150–180	225–250	250	250–350
Heat-deflection temperature of clear cast resin containing no glass reinforcement, °F	206	212	270	302

An illustration of the need for both high heat resistance and fire retardancy is the use of FRP composites in power generation. Here, the more heat-resistant and acid-resistant chlorendic polyester resins are used in the construction of scrubbers, mist-eliminator blades, breeching ducts, and chimney liners in contact with hot, corrosive fossil-fuel gases.

Because of the low thermal conductivity of FRP laminates—about 1.5 Btu/h·ft^2·°F·in., compared with 150 Btu/h·ft^2·°F·in. for stainless steel—a low external temperature (for example, in the annulus of an FRP liner insert in a chimney) can result in a median wall temperature in a relatively thick laminate section that is considerably below that of the hot material (i.e., the gas inside the chimney liner).

Choosing a Material

To compare FRP with other materials (e.g., metals and alloys) for use in CPI equipment, a fairly detailed analysis of the specific application must be conducted. While economics may well be the controlling influence, other factors also must be considered:

All chemicals to which the equipment will be exposed—feedstocks, intermediates, products and by-products, waste materials, and cleaning agents
Normal operating concentrations of chemicals, and maximum and minimum concentrations
The pH range of the system
Normal operating temperatures of the equipment, and maximum and minimum temperatures
Abrasion resistance and/or agitation requirements
Fire retardancy and heat resistance requirements
Thermal insulation requirements

FRP vs Selected Other Materials

FRP offers corrosion resistance equal to that of stainless steel to both internal and external exposed surfaces. However, carbon steel and other low-alloy metallics oxidize and require protective coatings to make them fully corrosion-resistant, whereas FRP does not. Carbon steel vessels require extensive surface preparation and application of corrosion-resistant liners, e.g. flake-glass-filled polyesters or vinyl esters and/or other materials, to provide adequate protection; FRP, on the other hand, is resistant throughout.

FRP can be fabricated into intricate one-piece shapes, requiring fewer joints than other materials, with more continuous, unobstructed surface area.

FRP is inherently nonconductive—an excellent electrical insulator, as well as a very good thermal insulator and a good noise barrier.

References

1. J. A. Rolston, "Fiberglass Composite Materials and Fabrication Processes," *Chem. Eng.*, pp. 96–110 (January 28, 1980).
2. ASTM Method D-2583, *Standard Test Method for Indentation Hardness of Rigid Plastics by Means of a Barcol Impressor,* ASTM, Philadelphia, Pennsylvania, February 27, 1981.
3. ASTM Method C-581, *Standard Practice for Determining Chemical Resistance of Thermosetting Resins Used in Glass Fiber Reinforced Structures Intended for Liquid Service,* ASTM, Philadelphia, Pennsylvania, November 28, 1983.
4. NFPA 255, *Method of Test of Surface Burning Characteristics of Building Materials,* National Fire Protection Association, Quincy, Massachusetts, 1984.
5. ASTM Method E-84, *Standard Test Method for Surface Burning Characteristics of Building Materials,* ASTM, Philadelphia, Pennsylvania, June 26, 1981.

ROBERT C. TALBOT

Plastics, Fiberglass, Reinforced, for Chloralkali Industry

Premium-grade corrosion-resistant resins have long been recognized as the material of choice for fiberglass reinforced plastic (FRP) equipment for hot wet chlorine electrolytic cell processes.

Case histories over the past 25 years have clearly demonstrated that such FRP equipment provides better than average service life for hot wet chlorine headers, brine feed line piping, tanks, and other associated equipment required in the process.

The more recent introduction of the "membrane"-type electrolytic cell relies heavily on FRP process equipment to handle high purity brine feed to the cells, as well as depleted brine laden with chlorine in the recycle system.

The purpose of this paper is to present several case histories of successful installations where these resins are used effectively to satisfy the requirements of the chlorine producing industry.

Introduction

The use of FRP in the chloralkali process industry apparently began during the late 1950s when an experimental FRP chlorine cell header was placed in service handling hot wet chlorine gas, contaminated with organics, from impregnated graphite anodes.

Prior to this use of FRP, chemical-resistant stoneware was typically used for such service. Stoneware was available only in short lengths of pipe, making the installation difficult to handle and support properly. Stoneware was heavy, required extra supports spaced at close distances, and was very difficult to seal properly with cell putty at the numerous joints required in a typical chlorine cell circuit. Stoneware was also fragile and susceptible to breakage from thermal shock and impact. Early electrolytic chlorine cell rooms required constant maintenance to maintain the system and prevent hazardous chlorine gas leakage into the surrounding areas.

The chemical process industry, pulp and paper industry, as well as municipal sewage and water treatment plants use chlorine in very large quantities. Chlorine certainly is by far one of the most basic and important chemicals produced in the world today, and a product that could not be easily replaced in our present-day society.

History shows that the first practical chlorine cell was introduced in 1886. At the turn of the century, the Hooker Electrochemical Company was formed and in the mid-1920s introduced the then newly developed Townsend electrolytic diaphragm cell. At this time chlorine was primarily used to produce sodium hypochlorite "bleach" solutions for cleaning purposes and later was used for water purification, etc.

As the industry continued to grow, the need for more efficient, lighter weight, corrosion-resistant materials with greater resistance to thermal and mechanical shock became apparent. The FRP polyester resins became the acclaimed, next generation standard material of construction to handle hot wet chlorine gas and brine feed systems. These resins have been used successfully for the past 25+ years to meet the challenges in installations of the large multiton capacity chlorine plants constructed in the 1960s and 1970s. During this period of time, the modified Bisphenol A fumarates were also found to offer suitable resistance to hot wet chlorine, whereas the standard Bisphenol A fumarates and vinyl ester resins were found to be less corrosion resistant.

Chlorine is produced by the electrolysis method, where a saturated solution of either NaCl or KCl brine is fed into the electrolytic cell (either diaphragm, mercury, or the new membrane-type cells). These brines are electrolytically converted to produce chlorine gas, hydrogen gas, and sodium or potassium hydroxide (10–15% hydroxide for a typical diaphragm cell and up to 33% hydroxide for the new membrane cells). These chlorine cells operate at 180–220°F, and the chlorine gas therefore is "hot and wet," requiring further cooling and drying (passed through H_2SO_4), and then passing on to a liquifier and storage (see Fig. 1).

The chloralkali industry has been bombarded with claims of superior corrosion resistance for various generic types of polyester and/or vinyl ester resins. But in reality, the secret of success is in the proper combination of resin/glass and high quality workmanship by the fabricator using the proper lay-up techniques and design criteria to handle the environmental conditions (Fig. 2).

This article is a review of such proven fabrication techniques and successful case histories.

FRP Materials of Construction for Chlorine Plant Service

Chlorine Gas Handling

Fire-retardant chlorendic acid based resins have been used successfully for the past 25–30 years to handle hot wet chlorine gas at up to 220°F. History has shown that all "mat" hand lay-up laminate construction with an additional corrosion allowance provides the longest service life, whereas past installations using standard corrosion barrier construction with a filament wound structural overlay with *no corrosion allowance* have resulted in early failure in hot wet chlorine piping.

Hot wet chlorine reacts with the inner resin-rich surface of the FRP laminate and forms a chlorinated resin or "chlorine butter" layer. This chlorination or degradation attack mechanism continues to penetrate into the FRP substrate during the first years of operation and eventually reaches a maximum depth of penetration. This depth of penetration is often past a normal corrosion barrier of one ply of Type C veil and two plies of 1½ oz chopped strand Type E mat. Therefore the lay-up sequence, type of resin selected, and degree of resin cure achieved in the fabrication process becomes very important for a successful application. Laboratory tests and actual plant service tests have shown that the higher the density and/or hardness of the chlorine butter formed within the FRP pipe or equipment, the slower the rate of penetration into the FRP laminate substrate (see Table 1 and Fig. 3).

This mode of attack initiated specification of an additional corrosion allowance during the early 1960s in addition to a standard corrosion barrier as prescribed in NBS 15-69 or ASTM C-582 (see Table 2). This corrosion allowance compensates for a projected loss of sound laminate material and

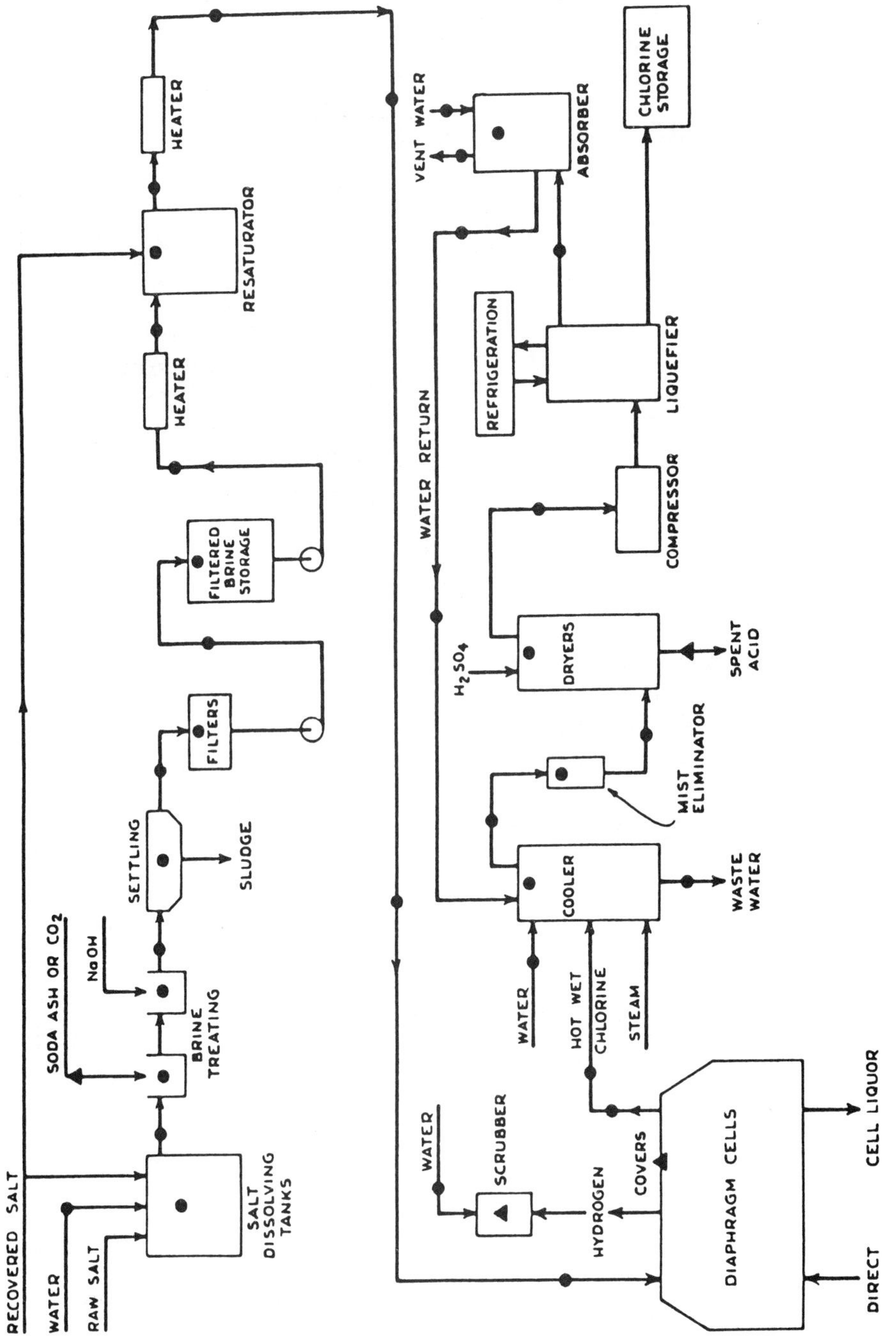

FIG. 1 Flow diagram of a typical diaphragm cell chlorine plant. (●) FRP being used successfully or could be used. (▲) FRP would be expected to perform satisfactorily.

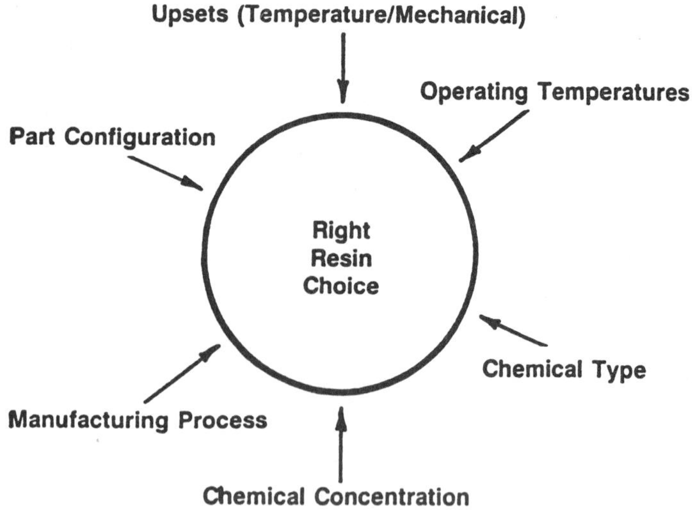

FIG. 2 Variables to consider when specifying FRP.

allows for a given depth of permeation/penetration into the laminate substrate. This combination of a standard corrosion barrier and corrosion allowance should provide a minimum of 250 mils thickness or greater (up to 375 mils) which can be further enhanced by specifying all mat construction for the structural outer reinforcement of chlorine piping (see Fig. 4). However, many large diameter headers require the use of either woven roving or filament wound, continuous fiber layer in the outer structural reinforce-

TABLE 1 Summary of Comparative Evaluations (corrosion-resistant FRP resin laminates; hot wet chlorine)[a]

Hooker Chemical Corporation, North Tonawanda, New York

Selected Resin Brand Tested	Temperature (°F)	"Chlorine Butter" Description	Penetration (mils), in Years		
			1	2.5	7
Chlorendic	203–220	Hard	9	51	109
Vinyl ester	210–220	Soft	22	69	—[b]
Bisphenol A	203–210	Soft	—[b]	59	—[b]

220 *Wyandotte Chemical Corporation, Wyandotte, Michigan*

Selected Resin Brand Tested	Percent Retention of Flexural Strength	Exposure Temperature (°F)
Chlorendic	60	210–220
Vinyl ester	15–20	210–220
Bisphenol A	20	210–220

[a]Summary by Ashland Chemical Company.
[b]Not reported.

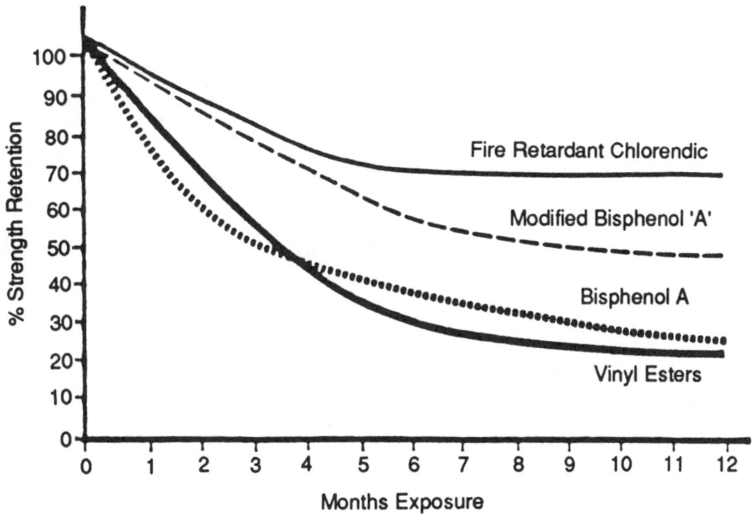

FIG. 3 Strength retention of various resin laminates in hot wet chlorine service.

ment for strength. Experience has shown that these materials are acceptable if used only on the outer structural portion of the laminate. Specifications should require at least 0.375 in. of all mat construction before adding high glass content continuous fiber to the laminate structure. Likewise, all cut edges of laminates should be adequately overwrapped with mat and Type C veil to achieve optimum service life. The inner resin-rich surfaces must have at least one ply, and preferably two plies, of Type C veil for good corrosion resistance.

The outer layer of the laminate should be opaque to minimize the potential hazards of Cl_2/H_2 photocatalytic explosive reaction. The use of ultraviolet screeners, incorporated into the exterior layer of the laminate, is recommended, especially for chlorine ducting exposed outdoors and subjected to ultraviolet and weathering degradation. This outer layer should be of mat construction and resin rich for good resistance to external attack.

FRP is used for various types of chlorine handling equipment such as headers, coolers, strippers, heat exchangers and cooler shells, tube sheets and heat exchanger bonnets, butterfly valves, seal tanks and mist eliminators, etc.

Diaphragm Cell Covers

FRP construction has in most cases completely replaced the concrete cell top/covers during the past 10–15 years. While concrete offered greater weight advantages in holding a positive seal at the cell flange face without clamping, the rapid rate of degradation and spalling of the concrete aggregate into the diaphragm cell chamber resulted in unnecessary shutdowns and replacement of damaged diaphragms.

TABLE 2 Partial List of Standards in the Corrosion-Resistant Plastic Industry

Description	Title	Comments
	Domestic	
ASTM C-581-83	Standard specification for chemical resistance of thermosetting resins used in glass fiber reinforced structures	Latest revision 1983
ASTM C-582-84	Standard specification for reinforced plastic laminates for self-supporting structures for use in a chemical environment	Latest revision 1984
ASTM D-4097-82	Specification for contact molded glass-fiber reinforced thermoset resin chemical resistant tanks	Latest revision 1982
ASTM D-3299-81	Standard specification for filament wound glass fiber reinforced polyester chemical resistant tanks	Latest revision 1981
ASTM D-2996-83	Standard specification for filament wound reinforced thermosetting resin pipe	Latest revision 1983
NBS 15-69	Historical document—voluntary product standard—custom contact molded reinforced polyester chemical resistant process equipment	Latest revision 1969–discontinued by NBS—copies available through SPI
	Foreign	
BS-4994: 1983	Specification for vessels and tanks in reinforced plastics	Latest revision unknown
CS 41 GP22	Standard for process equipment reinforced polyester chemical resistant custom contact molded	Latest revision 1969–under revision at this time

FRP, while much lighter in weight, has eliminated the spalling of aggregate and therefore extended the cell service life sufficiently to offset the added cost of FRP. Generally, the modified Bisphenol A and standard Bisphenol A resins have been used for cell cover construction. Chlorendic resins are not resistant to caustic when present at the flange face tie down area, but showed no evidence of attack with cell heads exposed to chlorine wetted with the cell feed brine solution.

When fire retardance is required by some end-users, the outside layers of the lay-up sequence in the cell cover are fabricated with either a chlorinated or brominated corrosion-resistant resin. The addition of antimony trioxide (Sb_2O_3) acts as a synergist with these halogenated resins for improved fire retardancy of the FRP laminates.

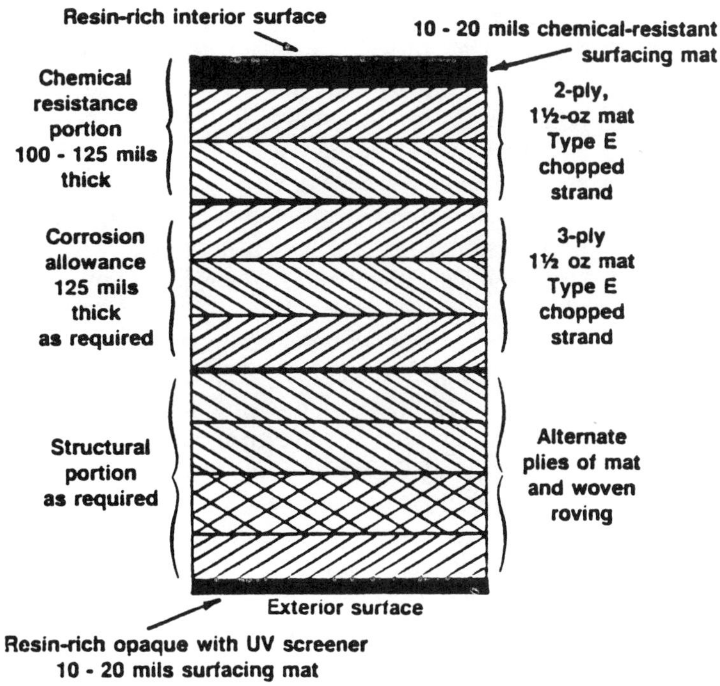

FIG. 4 Typical laminate construction to provide chemical resistance for hot wet chlorine service.

New Technology for Cell Covers

For improved dimensional stability and resistance to internal craze cracking of resin-rich surfaces, a major chlorine producer in the Gulf Coast area has fabricated cell covers with a highly crosslinked, high temperature resistant vinyl ester. The high (>5%) tensile elongation of this resin allows for much improved impact strength and resistance to thermal cycling effects when compared to the rigid resins previously used for cell covers. There is also less shrinkage and warpage of the cell cover during fabrication. These units have been in service for approximately 3 years and are expected to last for several more years of dependable service.

Brine Handling

During the past 25 years the chloralkali industry has made significant changes in the selection of materials of construction to handle saturated NaCl and KCl brine feed systems.

Brine feed systems in the 1950s were generally handled in black iron (carbon steel) piping, which at that time offered the best initial installed economics. However, the long-term repair costs were rarely factored into the total cost of justifying materials of construction during those days. Carbon steel failed by a selective corrosion pitting-type attack and also contributed to excessive metal-ion contamination of the downstream sodium or potassium hydroxides solutions produced.

Cyprus wood staved tanks were also used for make-up feed brine since cyprus exhibits excellent resistance to saturated salt solutions. Unfortunately, the carbon steel retainer rings required constant maintenance and brine leakage was a common occurrence, with severe corrosive attack to structural steel members and to surrounding concrete floors contributing to high maintenance costs.

The total brine system became one of the greatest new opportunities for FRP equipment in the early 1960s. Certainly the brine area was a natural adjunct to hot wet chlorine and was considered equally as important for materials engineers to solve an age-old corrosion problem with the new FRP technology. FRP evolved as the preferred material of construction to handle brine as well as for chlorine.

The fire-retardant chlorendic-acid-based resins were evaluated under actual plant conditions by using test spool sections of hand layed-up FRP piping, inserted into existing steel pipe lines, and also as fiberglass reinforced linings on steel for brine storage tanks. These FRP test sections were exposed to the make-up saturated alkaline brine feed solutions, to depleted chlorinated and dechlorinated brine solutions, to highly errosive salt slurry from centrifugal filters, etc.

From these series of extensive evaluations, the fire-retardant chlorinated polyesters were selected to construct an entire brine handling system for a new mercury cell circuit at the Hooker Chemical Company, Niagara Falls, plant. It went on-stream in 1961 and continued in operation until approximately 1983 when the plant was shut down.

This installation included approximately 2 miles of FRP pipe, the largest FRP installation of its time, handling NaCl and KCl alkaline brine at 175°F temperature, at a pH of 8–11, with pressures up to 80 lb/in.^{2}gauge at a brine velocity of 10 ft/s. FRP was also used to handle the 200°F depleted chlorinated brine coming from the cells and for pressure equalizing header tanks in the system to maintain constant pressure. The same FRP materials were used to construct 5000 gal deionized water storage tanks at elevated storage temperatures.

The use of FRP in this mercury cell circuit not only provided a chemically pure brine system with virtually no metal-ion contamination, but also the resultant downstream purity of the sodium and potassium hydroxide products (50% concentrations) met the high quality, light color standards required for the industry.

This installation was the one most important major confidence builders for FRP usage in the chloralkali industry and has since repeatedly proven the material's superiority over other materials of construction throughout the industry, both domestic and foreign.

FRP has since been used extensively to handle acidified feed brine systems, which are significantly more corrosive to steel, making FRP even more desirable for such service.

Most premium-grade high temperature polyesters or vinyl esters are suitable for brine service, but special care must be taken in handling depleted chlorinated brine solutions at temperatures above 200°F.

Specifications should include heavy wall construction for extended service life and allow for a full corrosion barrier with Type C veil for acidified brine and synthetic surfacing materials for alkaline brine. Hand lay-up or filament wound construction is usually acceptable for most installations.

Proper tie down and support of FRP piping is a must and should be considered as a standard installation procedure for successful applications.

FRP is now used extensively in the feed and depleted brine systems for piping, tanks, brine boxes, heat exchanger shells, tube sheets and bonnets, tank covers (large diameters), filters, salt chutes, saturators, manifolds, vacuum flesh strippers, raw salt conveyer housings, and also for structural materials such as grating, safety rails, ladders, and siding materials. More recently, all FRP pumps and pump bases have become available for brine handling.

New Membrane Cell Technology

The new "membrane" cell technology offers numerous advantages to the chloralkali producer as compared to either the diaphragm or mercury cell technology. Reportedly the membrane cells are more energy efficient and are operated at a significant savings in power costs. They are also more environmentally desirable and eliminate the use of asbestos and mercury from the cell operation.

The chloralkali industry has made a significant contribution to cleaning up our environment by eliminating gas emissions from existing plants. The use of FRP has contributed to this improved condition, thus greatly reducing the corrosion problems to structural steel and other associated equipment in the plants. Here again the membrane technology promises to be even better and much easier to control with further improvements to the environmental surroundings.

Since the membrane cells require high purity saturated feed brine solutions free of any metal-ion contamination, FRP once again becomes the preferred nonmetallic material of construction for these new installations.

Recent installations of membrane cell circuits include chlorendic resins for the hot wet chlorine headers. Also extensive use of FRP for the entire brine systems including saturated NaCl brine, depleted highly corrosive chlorinated brine up to 200°F, and depleted dechlorinated recycle brine solutions. Also FRP resins are used for storage tanks handling concentrated HCl and sodium sulfite used to adjust the brine solutions. The brine system included FRP tanks, piping, pump bases, floor grating, etc. where, depending on the specific environment, the resins were either chlorendic base, vinyl ester, or highly crosslinked vinyl ester resins.

The high purity sodium hydroxide cell liquor (33–35% NaOH) is handled with polypropylene-lined vinyl ester FRP structurally reinforced piping.

While these circuits are relatively new, it is premature to claim extensive service life for such membrane cell operations. However, based on past experience with FRP in mercury cell circuits, FRP will continue to be the performance leader for the future.

Conclusions

After 25 years of successful installations in the chloralkali industry, it can be concluded that FRP equipment has achieved industry recognition for its dependability as the most cost-effective material of construction for this service.

In hot wet chlorine service, it is not uncommon for FRP headers incorporating chlorendic acid-based resins to last for 12–15 years and in some cases up to 20 years. Service life in hot wet chlorine is very dependent on laminate design and quality of workmanship by the fabricator.

FRP offers advantages in ease of installation. It is light weight and can be readily pre-spooled to allow for a minimum of shutdown time, should replacement be required.

Likewise, in highly saturated NaCl or KCl brine solutions, FRP has achieved equal acceptance as a cost-effective material of construction for tanks, pipe, and associated equipment.

As we enter a new era in the chloralkali industry with the introduction of the new "membrane" cell technology, the need for higher purity feed brine solutions, free of metal-ion contamination, makes FRP a natural choice for such service. Also, handling chlorine-contaminated depleted brine from the membrane cells is very practical with either a highly crosslinked high temperature vinyl ester resin or a chlorendic acid resin based on over 20 years of service life in a mercury cell circuit in the Northeast, where the conditions are very similar to those found in the membrane circuit.

For extended service life, thermoplastic-lined FRP piping is being used in the depleted brine lines. Such dual laminate construction is also used to handle the 33% sodium hydroxide solutions from the membrane cells.

It can truly be acclaimed that FRP has evolved as a major material of construction to handle hot wet chlorine and brine solutions in the chloralkali industry based on over 25 years of successful installations. It can be predicted that FRP will remain the material of choice as the chloralkali industry converts to the lower energy consumption membrane cell technology during the next decade.

Much of this article was presented at the 42nd Annual Conference of the Society of the Plastics Industry, February 2, 1987, and is used with the permission of the Society.

References

1. W. A. Szymanski and R. C. Talbot, *Application of Polyester Fabrications in the Chemical Process Industry,* 19th Annual NACE Conference, March 1963.
2. *Salt and Water, Power and People—A Short History of Hooker Electrochemical Company,* 1955.

ROBERT C. TALBOT

Plastics, Fiberglass, Reinforced, for Construction Industry

Reinforced plastic (RP) panels have been used in the construction industry for about 30 years. These panels offer a number of advantages over other materials of construction. RP panels are corrosion resistant to many chemical environments. They are light in weight and easier to install than other systems. They require no special handling or equipment. RP panels can be made translucent to allow natural light to enter a building. RP panels do not reflect radio waves and, therefore, can be used in the electronic industry where equipment is tested that generates radio signals.

One area where fire-retardant unsaturated polyester RP panels have needed improvement is in weather resistance. Some of the traditional halogenated resin systems have had poor resistance to UV light. The halogen source in these prior art resins tended to cause yellowing and chalking after exposure to sunlight. By changing the halogenated raw material used in synthesizing the resin, it was possible to greatly improve the weather resistance of building panels. By extreme testing of many light stabilizing additives, additional improvements have been attained. This combination of carefully selected chemical building blocks and custom-tailored additives allows fire-retardant resin systems to resist weather comparably to nonfire-retardant systems.

These high performance weather-resistant resins retain the advantages of other resin systems. Information on physical properties, liquid properties, cure, corrosion resistance, and fire retardancy, as well as weathering data, will be presented.

A number of installations utilizing these new resin systems will be reviewed. The flexibility in design and other advantages of using RP panels will be discussed.

History

Fiberglass reinforced plastic (RP) corrugated building panels were first introduced to the construction industry during the late 1940s to compete with conventional roofing and siding materials. At that time, the chemical process industry was desperately trying to combat corrosion's devastating effects to the roofing and siding materials used on chemical process buildings and similar problem areas.

It soon became apparent that the industrial grades of nonflame-retardant RP materials exhibited improved chemical resistant properties and retained a high percentage of their original structural integrity even when exposed to rather severe corrosive conditions. However, where the same materials were exposed to more aggressive chemical media under splash, spill, and fume conditions, a need for further improvement in materials became evident. Since many of the conventional building materials, such as galvanized steel and/or asbestos, exhibited inherent fire-retardant properties, the need for a good flame-retardant polyester resin was also apparent.

Recognizing this need for improved chemical resistance coupled with the requirement for flame retardance, the Hooker Chemical Company, Niagara Falls, New York, developed the first halogenated polyester resins based on chlorendic acid technology and introduced these new resins in the early 1950s.

The Resolite Division of H. H. Robertson introduced their first flame-retardant RP corrugated panels during 1954, incorporating chlorendic base resins and thereby initiating the acceptance of the "halogenated" flame-retardant polyester resins by the construction industry for industrial building applications.

These materials provided the necessary chemical resistance to withstand most of the splash, spill, and fume conditions they were exposed to, with the added protection of flame retardancy.

These earlier flame-retardant resin formulations suffered some degree of ultraviolet radiation degradation in the form of laminate surface discoloration along with chalking and fiber bloom. This initiated further research and development of more color-stable materials with improved overall weatherability for enhanced appearance.

During this evolutionary period of the past three decades, the halogenated flame-retardant resins have continued to demonstrate their superiority over other building materials, especially when exposed to severe industrial environments and often containing aggressive chemical fumes under splash/spill conditions at elevated temperatures exceeding 120°F.

Resin Development

During the development of the new high performance resins, it was found that by changing the base halogenated raw materials along with careful selection of the chemical building blocks used to synthesize the new resins, significant improvements in the weathering characteristics were achievable.

Extensive field and laboratory testing was conducted to evaluate the effects of many different ultraviolet additives along with the combined improvements attained with an acrylic modification of the resin formulations. The visual appearance of the laminates was greatly enhanced.

The new systems are carefully formulated to meet the custom fabricator's specific manufacturing requirements for cure, glass wet out, and general handling characteristics, with consideration given to providing adequate corrosion resistance for most industrial applications.

Today's halogenated resin formulations are truly much improved over the older original halogenated products introduced 30+ years ago and are comparable in many respects to the much improved general purpose resins used by the panel industry today.

The new flame-retardant resins are formulated with sufficient halogen content to provide ASTM E-84 Class I flame retardancy with <25 Flame Spread (FS) with smoke generation of <450. Actual values depend on the weight of the panel and formulation used by the fabricator. They can be used for both translucent and opaque panels in up to 12 oz-weight/ft^2 without the addition of antimony oxides (trioxide or pentoxide).

The typical liquid properties of the resin along with typical physical strength properties of commercial grade laminates are shown in Tables 1, 2, and 3, respectively.

Weathering Tests

The effects of ultraviolet light on most materials are well known and a major hurdle for the RP panel industry to overcome.

The use of halogenated resins presents a problem with discoloration of RP flame-retardant panels. This phenomenon usually occurs as a surface effect and the discoloration is usually limited to less than a mil (0.001 in.) thickness. The use of ultraviolet, screeners in halogenated resins effectively retards the discoloration. However, such UV additives do not guarantee that RP laminates will never discolor.

For accelerated laboratory testing, the QUV weathering test apparatus (fluorescent ultraviolet/water condensation—ASTM G53-77) was used to simulate the effects of sunlight and water as rain or dew. This test method is a suitable means for screening candidate resin formulations. The better

TABLE 1 Typical Liquid Properties for Hetron FR1525 Series Resins

Nonvolatile, %	63
Brookfield viscosity, cPs	350
Gardner color	3 Max
Appearance	Clean/clear
Refractive index	1.529

TABLE 2 Typical Physical Strength Properties of a Commercial Corrugated 8 oz/ft³ Panel, 27–30% Glass Content at 77°F

Tensile strength, lb/in.^{2}	14,000
Tensile modulus, lb/in.^{2} × 10^{-6}	0.75
Tensile elongation, %	2.2
Flexural strength, lb/in.^{2}	27,000
Flexural modulus, lb/in.^{2} × 10^{-6}	0.73
Barcol hardness	45

appearing candidates were then selected on the basis of gloss retention, resistance to discoloration, and so forth. These resins were then further fine tuned, and the formulations were adjusted to maximize the weathering properties.

Final candidate resins were then submitted for field outdoor weathering test to South Florida Test Service where the various RP test laminates are exposed on test racks at a 45° angle facing the equator for a period of one year, per ASTM G7-37A "Atmospheric Environmental Exposure Testing on Non-Metallic Materials."

The results of these outdoor weathering tests were significant and clearly demonstrated a major advancement in color stability of this new halogenated resin system.

Both laminates were fabricated using clear resin (unpigmented) with UV additives as required for each resin system and cured to an optimum Barcol hardness. As can be seen, after one year of actual outdoor exposure, the flame-retardant resin is essentially as good as the GP orthophthalic.

Chemical Resistance

The chemical resistance properties of the RP panels are extremely important to the projected life of the material. History has shown that the high-per-

TABLE 3 Typical Physical Strength Properties of a High Strength, High Glass Content Commercial Grade Laminate, Glass Content 47% at 77°F

Tensile strength, lb/in.^{2}	55,290
Tensile modulus, lb/in.^{2} × 10^{-6}	2.66
Tensile elongation, %	2.4
Flexural strength, lb/in.^{2}	60,535
Flexural modulus, lb/in.^{2} × 10^{-6}	2.2
Compressive strength, lb/in.^{2}	32,200
Barcol hardness	50

TABLE 4 Retention of Physical Properties at 120°F for 6 Months Exposed under Vapor Phase with Splash and Spill Conditions

	Hetron FR1525 Resin	Hetron 29355 Resin
5¼% Sodium hypochlorite:		
Flex strength, %	89	91
Flex modulus, %	84	85
Barcol hardness	30	30
5% Sodium hydroxide:		
Flex strength, %	45	34
Flex modulus, %	51	53
Barcol hardness	25	27
5% Sulfuric acid:		
Flex strength, %	81	83
Flex modulus, %	102	78
Barcol hardness	30	23
Saturated sodium chloride:		
Flex strength, %	84	109
Flex modulus, %	82	80
Barcol hardness	40	35
15% Phosphoric acid:		
Flex strength, %	81	94
Flex modulus, %	86	79
Barcol hardness	35	25
15% Hydrochloric acid:		
Flex strength, %	64	71
Flex modulus, %	65	70
Barcol hardness	30	25
5% Alum:		
Flex strength, %	91	85
Flex modulus, %	106	59
Barcol hardness	35	30
5% Nitric acid:		
Flex strength, %	62	83
Flex modulus, %	79	73
Barcol hardness	30	25

formance flame-retardant resins used by the panel industry for industrial applications last much longer than most protected steel-based building materials.

For the purpose of evaluating the relative chemical resistance of these new resins, the standard ASTM C-581 test procedure was modified to simulate splash, spill, and fume conditions.

Test coupons were cut from commercial produced panels. Unlike standard corrosion laminates, no surfacing veil or mat materials were used. These coupons were placed in the vapor phase of closed containers, with the respective corrodents as tested.

The containers were held in temperature-controlled ovens at 120°F for 6 months and each container was handshaken twice each work day to splash the corrodent onto the exposed test coupons. The corrodents were changed periodically to maintain the concentration of the test solutions. As in ASTM C-581, the corrosive effect is accelerated by exposing both sides of the test laminates. The test procedure is generally considered to be far more severe as compared to one-sided immersion testing.

Likewise under the testing conditions, the effects of chemical attack were more severe than those normally encountered under actual service applications, where siding and roofing materials are usually subjected to good ventilation and are rarely totally wetted by the corrosive media.

Upon completion of the 6 months of testing, the coupons were visually examined. There was little evidence of any attack to the coupons other than some slight discoloration and some slight surface attack in the sodium hydroxide and hypochlorite coupons.

Of particular importance, the original flexural strength values for the new resin were significantly higher when compared to the older chlorendic-based laminates. Therefore, the tests show that the new resin physical strength retention properties are better after prolonged exposure to chemical environments. While the percent retention values are similar for both resins, the actual strength of the exposed laminates are in fact greater than the older product.

The physical strength retention values are shown in Table 4.

Much of this article was presented at the 41st Annual Conference of the Society of the Plastics Industry, January 27, 1986, and is used with the permission of the Society.

ROBERT C. TALBOT
MYRON D. DALLUGE
CARL E. COATS

Plastics, Fiberglass, Acoustic Emission Testing

Acoustic emission has become an important nondestructive test method in the process industry. The technique is broadly accepted for testing glass fiber reinforced plastic (FRP) pipe, tanks, and vessels, and its use for testing metal equipment is growing.

The early work in acoustic emission was directed toward testing of new metal vessels and pipelines. For many reasons, both technical and economic, the efforts met with only limited success. In recent years, emphasis has been on in-service metal vessels and application of the method to FRP. Research and experience have led to a better understanding of the behavior of pipelines and new metal vessels, and it is now possible to test metal equipment using standard test procedures and defined evaluation criteria.

Early Detection of Defects

Acoustic emission complements other nondestructive examination methods. While methods such as radiography and ultrasonics are used to define the type, geometry, and orientation of defects in a small, localized area, acoustic emission is used to assess the structural integrity of an entire item of equipment under operating loads. Of particular importance is the ability to test in-service vessels with process fluids. In many cases it is unnecessary to shut down the unit for this test, since it incurs only minor disruption of plant operations. Acoustic emission testing also reduces the need for internal inspection. These features make acoustic emission particularly suitable for testing in the chemical process industry.

The sensitivity of acoustic emission test equipment can be set to provide an early warning of defect growth and incipient failure. The method is able to detect certain types of defects that are not detectable by other methods: e.g., early-stage stress corrosion cracking, deficiencies in FRP equipment, and oxygen and nitrogen contamination of zirconium and titanium welds. Compared to many other nondestructive test methods, acoustic emission has predetermined, objective evaluation criteria that are not open to the subjective interpretation of operators. Recent research has shown that certain defects have unique acoustic emission signatures which can be used to define the type, as well as the presence, of a structural deficiency.

Over the past few years there have been many successful case histories. As the technique has become more reliable, the chemical process industry has turned more and more to acoustic emission for equipment inspection for cost savings and safety. In the early days a number of exaggerated claims were made for acoustic emission testing, and successes were accompanied by some well-publicized failures. As with any new technology, there is a temptation to apply the method beyond its current state of technical development. However, major applied research and development programs carried out since 1975 have provided a basic understanding of acoustic emission and have helped stimulate its use for vessel testing.

Proof-Testing New Equipment

Acoustic emission has been used for proof-testing of new equipment; for periodic inspection of in-service tanks, vessels, and piping; for continuous monitoring; and for requalification testing. Early chemical process industry applications of acoustic emission were confined to new vessels [1–5]. However, in recent years periodic inspection of in-service vessels and piping has assumed greater importance than proof-tests of new equipment.

The early pioneering work with new metal vessels [2, 3] provided an important foundation for future application of the technology. Proof-tests are normally carried out in conjunction with the hydrostatic test specified by the governing code. Acoustic emission supplements the hydrotest and other nondestructive examination methods specified by such codes as the *ASME Boiler and Pressure Vessel Codes* [6]. Conventional nondestructive test methods, such as radiography, ultrasonics, and dye penetrant, have proved satisfactory for inspection of new metal vessels. Even though acoustic emission provides an additional level of refinement and better detection of certain types of critical structural defects, it is often difficult to justify the additional cost. Until the code-formulating bodies accept acoustic emission as an alternative to conventional inspection methods, the technique is unlikely to find widespread use for new vessels.

In certain situations, however, acoustic emission provides a unique capability not available with other nondestructive examination methods.

Zirconium and Titanium Vessels. Welding of these materials is difficult and requires a 100% inert gas purge to avoid oxygen and nitrogen contamination. Contaminated welds are brittle and prone to crack. Conventional nondestructive test methods are unable to detect this brittleness, and the only indication of contamination is a bluish tinge to the weld. Color is not always a reliable indication of contamination and provides no information about the interior of the weld. In contrast, acoustic emission not only indicates weld contamination as soon as stress is applied, but detects tungsten inclusions in zirconium. In zirconium, tungsten inclusions tend to remain as angular particles which, even when small, act as stress risers, and it is difficult for radiography to detect around nozzles and reinforcing pads.

Multiwall Vessels. Inspection of the welds in internal layers is difficult with conventional nondestructive methods. Acoustic emission can detect defects in those welds, assess the severity of the defects, and periodically monitor to see if such defects are growing.

Other Vessels. Acoustic emission also makes it possible to detect brittle welds, high residual stresses, and unsatisfactory stress relief.

For these situations there are overriding technical reasons for using acoustic emission, and the technique is frequently specified in such cases. Acoustic emission is also used to inspect new production line vessels, such as oil well blowout preventers. New vessels for critical service conditions, such as those containing lethal, flammable, or otherwise hazardous fluids, and large field erected storage tanks are also routinely tested with acoustic emission. In these cases the serious consequences resulting from a failure justify the additional cost of the acoustic emission inspection.

In-Service and On-Line Tests. The ability of acoustic emission to test on-line and in-service brings about significant economic benefits and permits more frequent inspection of equipment. With periodic on-line tests, the extent of new damage since the previous test can be estimated. It detects typical in-service problems such as corrosion, stress-corrosion cracking, mechanical damage, and thinning, as well as a measure of the defect severity. Early identification of defects permits a follow-up with other nondestructive tests and planned shutdown for inspection and repair.

Acoustic emission is a reliable and practical nondestructive test method which is widely used for structural evaluation of FRP tanks, vessels, and piping. It is also used for structural integrity monitoring of FRP components in such industries as electric utilities, automotive, and aerospace.

There have been cases where acoustic emission testing failed to detect significant structural defects of metal vessels. One such instance occurred during a November 1979 acoustic emission test of a 55-ft-diameter (17-m-diameter) carbon steel sphere, in which the sphere was tested by overpressurizing with product immediately prior to shutdown. The consultant carrying out the test reported that no defects were present since no acoustic emission events had been recorded during the pressurization of the sphere. Internal inspection of the sphere, however, revealed over 250 cracks in the weld areas. The shallow surface cracks ran across the welds and were present in most areas of the sphere. Investigation of the test and the instrument configuration showed that real-time checks had been incorporated into the equipment to eliminate "invalid" data. Unfortunately, these checks, which were based on time of arrival assumptions for a flat plate, eliminated all valid event data from a doubly curved surface such as a sphere.

All data striking all sensors must be measured and recorded for post-test study. Spurious data can be eliminated by post-test filtering during data analysis. Eliminating data in real time is risky, because genuine data can be mistaken for false data and irretrievably lost.

Source Location

An acoustic emission test is normally used to monitor the entire vessel, and any defect, anywhere in the vessel, will emit under stress. Techniques for determining the position of a defect are referred to as "source location." Among various methods of source location, time of arrival, zone, and hit sequence are most commonly used. Time of arrival uses the relative arrival times of a stress wave striking a set of sensors. From this information it is possible to use triangulation methods to determine the location of the source of the stress wave. Implicit in this method are the assumptions that the stress wave travels through the material at a constant known velocity and that enough sensors are hit to enable triangulation calculations to be carried out. In practice, both of these assumptions break down. Zone location is a more approximate method and assumes that defects are located in the region surrounding sensors recording the highest energy emissions. Hit sequence is a refinement of the zone method, in which the zone is localized based on the energy of subsequent hits on the sensors surrounding the most energetic sensors.

Source location schemes can result in loss of important data. Many of the older acoustic emission systems are designed around real time, time of arrival source location schemes. Although this method works very well on flat plates in the laboratory, it gives very poor results on actual vessels under field conditions. One of the problems with instruments that use time of arrival source location is that they reject data which fails to meet predetermined locatability criteria. This can lead to loss of most of the valid acoustic emission data. Current practice is to record all data with real-time zone location and to follow up with a more accurate source location method during post-test analysis.

An acoustic emission test is done primarily to determine if defects exist in the item of the equipment under test; the instrument is used to measure and record data. More important than source location are data from non-locatable sources, which must be considered when evaluating the test data.

Time of arrival source location is based on triangulation and the difference between sensor arrival times of a stress wave from a given event. The early instruments used arrays of sensors, and a locatable event was required to strike a minimum number of sensors in a particular array. Once a sensor is hit, it is shut down for a predetermined time or until the other sensors in the array receive a hit from the same event. During the dead period, events striking the sensor are not recorded. Sometimes, adjacent arrays are locked out to prevent the same event from being located twice by two different arrays. A lockout means that an adjacent array will not accept data while the first array is searching for a locatable event. To avoid lockouts that can result in loss of data, some systems have adopted a method in which sensors are not broken into specific arrays, but all events are recorded with an associated microsecond time and the first three sensors hit by an event are used for location.

In the time of arrival source location, most significant events are assumed to be locatable. On the contrary, data from field tests of metal vessels have shown [7] that the number of locatable events range from 0 to 20% of the total number of hits. Among the many reasons why such a small percentage of events are locatable are: attenuation of the stress wave as it travels in the metal, stress wave distortion at welds and other discontinuities, shielding due to nozzles and manways, geometric configuration of the vessel, and wave-mode transformations.

Moreover, with time of arrival source location, poor quality data may be obtained. In many instances, calculated locations show major deviations from actual locations. Time difference location calculations are based on assumptions of geometry, sensor placement, constant wave speed, and the ability of the instrument to measure the arrival time of the same point of a stress wave at different sensors. In many cases, small deviations from these assumptions result in major errors in the calculated location of the source. Other causes of source location error are multiple sources, background noise, wave dispersion, reverberations, multipath propagation, and different frequency wave modes. Assumptions about the geometry of the vessel are also a major cause of inaccuracy. Frequently, time of arrival calculations assume that the stress wave is traveling in a flat plane. This is seldom the case, as most vessels are fabricated with single- and double-curved shells.

Zone Location

Zone location is a method for locating the approximate source of an event utilizing individual sensor activity. Figure 1 shows the sensor layout for a typical tank, with the zones around each sensor marked. The zones of adjacent sensors are made to overlap to ensure complete detection of emissions by more than one sensor. The approximate location of the defect can be determined by recording which sensor or sensors detect the emission. Zone location is used frequently in real time to determine the approximate source of an event. In post-test analysis a more accurate approximation of the source of the event is obtained by using the hit sequence or time of arrival method.

The hit sequence method (or Stuart's method) is based on the order that a given event strikes a group of sensors. Stuart's method reduces and refines the zones defined in the single sensor zone location method. Rather than provide an exact location, the method defines a subzone from which the event originated. The greater the number of sensors that are hit, the smaller the resulting subzone and more accurate the location. Field experience has shown that hit sequence source location accurately locates the position of a growing defect. As discussed previously, only a small percentage of the total

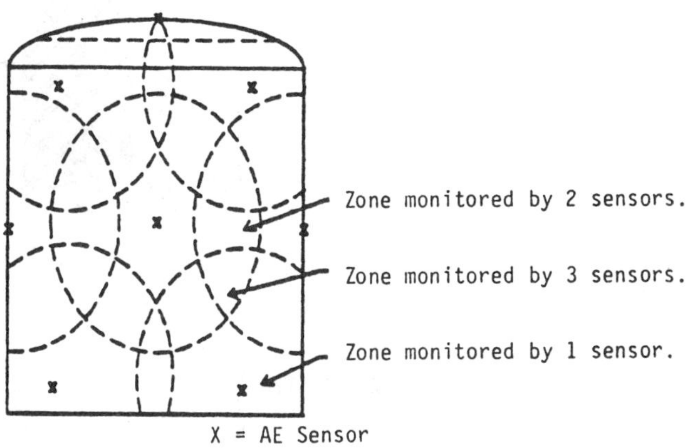

FIG. 1 Sensor and zone location for a tank.

events strike more than one sensor. Accordingly, the hit sequence technique pinpoints zone location for only a portion of the data that may or may not represent all data originating from a given zone.

The principle of hit sequence location in Fig. 2 shows how a zone is refined as additional sensor hits are recorded. The event strikes the center sensor first, thereby defining the primary zone. The right-hand sensor of the center row is struck second and this defines the first subzone. This subzone is further refined by the next hit that strikes a sensor below and between the two hit previously. Each zone and subzone is bounded by bisectors between sensors. Experience has shown that Stuart's method is robust against errors from sensor placement or wave velocity assumptions.

It is often difficult to distinguish which hits should be associated together to define an event, particularly when a large number of hits occur in a short time period, as would be the case with bursts of emission, noisy environments, low attenuation structures, or certain types of spurious emission. A Stuart's method, recently refined, uses energy-based severity analysis to group adjacent sensor hits into specific events.

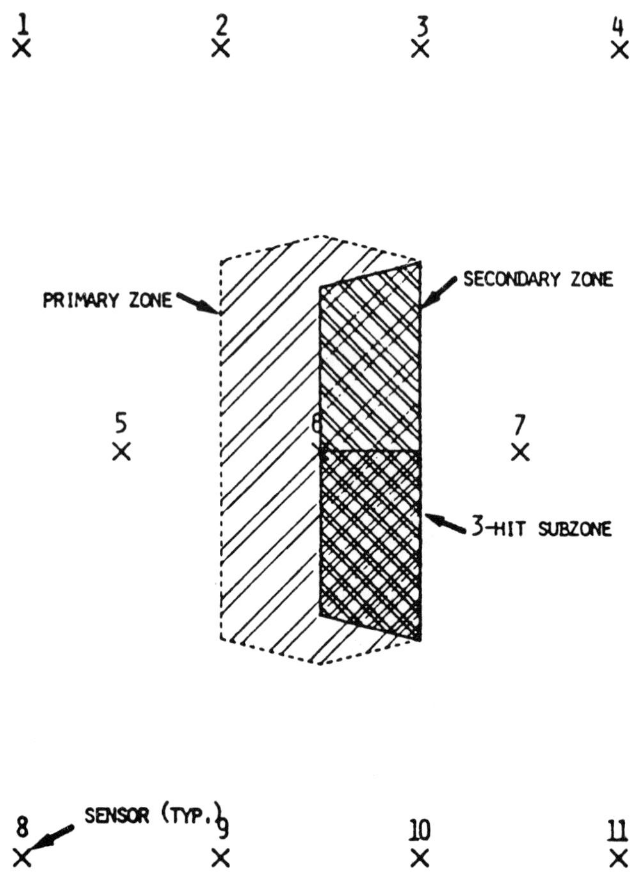

FIG. 2 Hit sequence source location.

Kaiser and Felicity Effects

The Kaiser effect is defined as the absence of detectable emission until previously applied stress levels are reached. In contrast, the Felicity effect (or the breakdown of the Kaiser effect) is defined as the presence of significant acoustic emission at stress levels below those previously applied. Initially, it was postulated that the Felicity effect was unique to reinforced plastics and that the Kaiser effect would always hold for metals. Recent work has shown that this is not the case and that damaged metal equipment also exhibits the Felicity effect. During many in-service tests, acoustic emission is detected at stress levels below those present during normal operation.

The Felicity effect in data from a metal vessel, Fig. 3, was demonstrated during a destructive test of a 5-ft-diameter (1.52-m-diameter) by 14-ft 4-in. (4.37-m) straight side horizontal vessel. The initial portion of the data is shown in Fig. 3 with unload/reload cycles at 200 and 325 lb/in.^{2}gauge (1.4 and 2.2 MPa) pressures. The Felicity effect occurs during both cycles. The ultimate failure was due to a cracked weld that began to leak at 462 lb/in.^{2}gauge (3.2 MPa). Accordingly, the Felicity effect was observed at a load of less than half the ultimate load.

In metal equipment the presence of the Felicity effect indicates a relatively severe defect. It should be noted that the Kaiser effect is based on the assumption that energy release from a material is irreversible. The presence of the Felicity effect does not violate this assumption, but it indicates

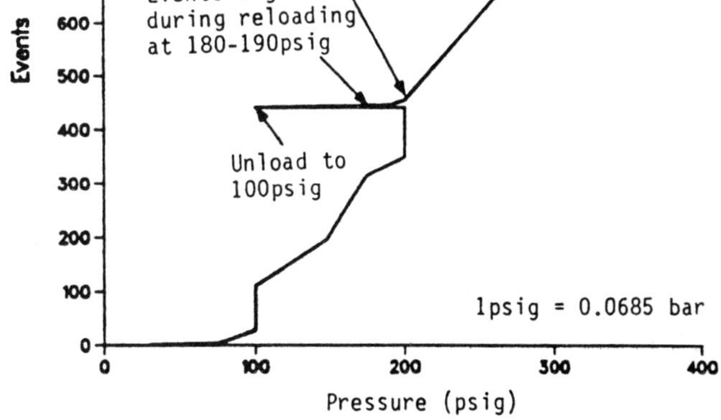

FIG. 3 Felicity effect during loading of a metal vessel.

additional damage occurring during each load cycle. For this low-cycle fatigue situation to occur, major damage (such as cracking or yielding) must be present.

Background Noise

Metals are good transmitters of stress waves. Background noise is a much bigger problem in metal vessels and piping than in fiber-reinforced plastic equipment. Therefore, particular care must be taken to eliminate known sources of background noise. Certain types of background noise, such as electromagnetic interference (EMI) and radio frequency interference (RFI), cannot be entirely eliminated. For these situations, narrow band filtering of the preamplifiers and instrument can help.

Some systems use guard sensors to eliminate background noise transmitted into the vessel through piping, supports, and other external connections. This practice is not recommended. The purpose of guard sensors is to detect incoming noise so that nearby vessel sensors can be shut down until the background noise has died out. Shutting down sensors can cause loss of genuine acoustic emission data. As discussed previously, all emissions should be recorded and genuine emissions separated from background noise during post-test analysis.

In recent years, analysis techniques, such as cross correlation of the acoustic emission parameters, have been successful in distinguishing genuine emission from extraneous noise. Correlation plots are particularly helpful in identifying sources of background noise which, in many instances, have a unique signature. Once identified, background noise can be filtered out during the post-test analysis.

Correlation plots in Fig. 4 can be used to identify and eliminate false emissions. The three correlation plots show unfiltered data collected during pressurization of a 55-ft-diameter (16.76-m-diameter) carbon steel sphere. The log counts vs amplitude correlation, Fig. 4(a), is an important plot. Genuine data will normally fall within the bounds shown. In this case, high count nonstructural data fall outside this range. A large number of low-amplitude events can also be seen in the 100–500 count range, again suggesting background noise. A number of events are in the 40–45 dB amplitude range, even though the threshold was set to 50 dB. This plot, however, does not reveal when the nonstructural and low-amplitude events occurred: it cannot be determined whether they occurred as a single emission burst or whether they were scattered throughout the entire test period. In Figs. 4(b) and 4(c), the log counts vs time correlation clearly reveals distinct bursts of high count data and the amplitude vs time correlation reveals that the 40–45 dB events occurred early in testing. It was found that the test threshold had been lowered below the 50 dB nominal threshold 2816 seconds into the test. This time period corresponds to the large group of low-amplitude events in Fig. 4(c).

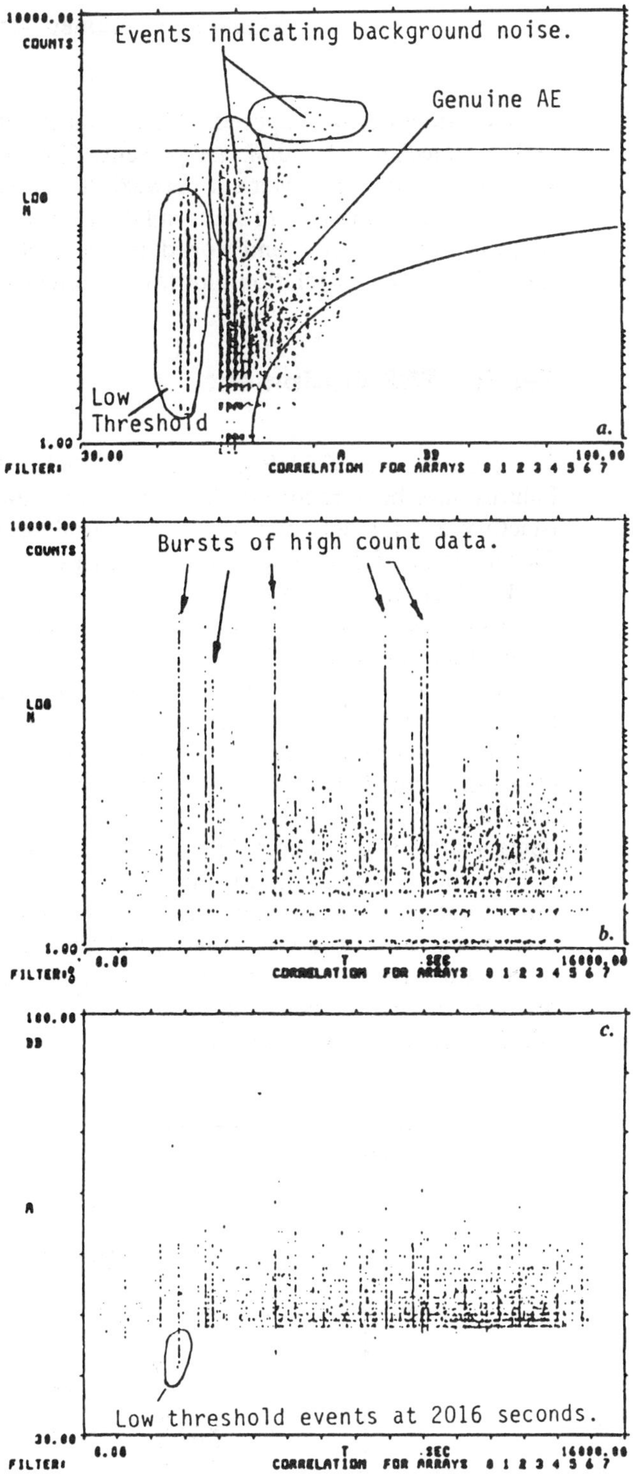

FIG. 4 Data correlated from a 55-ft-diameter (16.76-m) sphere. (a) Log counts vs amplitude correlation. Events indicating background noise and low thresholds are present. (b) Log counts vs time. Distinctive bursts of high count data can be seen. (c) Amplitude vs time correlation. Most low events occurred during the initial data burst.

The bursts of low-amplitude, high-count events are known to occur when leaks or mechanical sliding are present. The bursts in this particular case were due to sliding movement between the vessel and supporting piping.

In analyzing these test results, all data at the time of the bursts, including some genuine acoustic emission data, were eliminated by using exclusive time filters. The correlation plot for the filtered data is shown in Fig. 5.

Testing FRP Equipment

The performance of FRP pipe and vessels has been poor, and numerous failures have been reported. Apart from acoustic emission, there is no satisfactory test for determining the structural adequacy of FRP equipment. This technique fills an important need that cannot be met by the previously used hydrostatic overload test. For metal vessels, hydrotesting of tanks and vessels offers many advantages beyond testing their integrity, including relieving high residual weld stresses and inducing favorable stress patterns in high-stress areas. With FRP, hydrotesting tanks and vessels can induce permanent damage, leading to reduced long-term life of the equipment.

Early work on composite rocket casings [8] cast doubt on the suitability of acoustic emission for composites. However, the need for a nondestructive test for fiberglass tanks prompted research programs with a view to developing a simplified low-cost field test. In August 1975, a FRP process vessel at Monsanto's Sauget, Illinois, plant was tested by using acoustic emission prior to start-up. Routine testing of new vessels began in 1977 and was extended to in-service vessels in early 1978.

Since acoustic emission has been accepted as an important nondestructive test for FRP components, approximately 8000 tank and vessel tests and 10,000 pipe tests have been run.

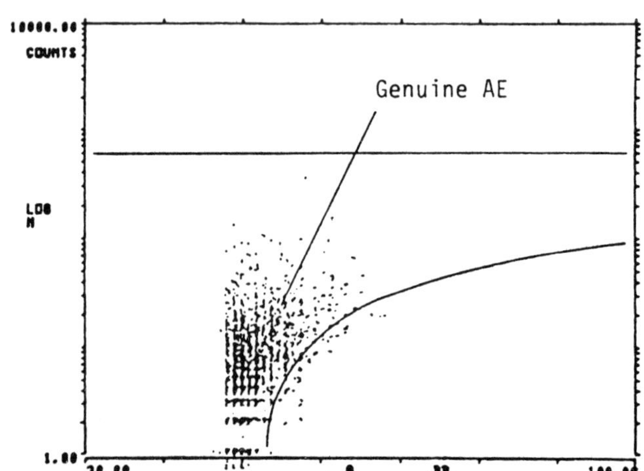

FIG. 5 Data in Fig. 4 with spurious emissions removed.

The *Recommended Practice for Testing RP Vessels* [9] of January 1982 was established as a standard test method for chemical process industry equipment. The practice was followed by a second *Recommended Practice for Testing Pipe* [10], ASTM [11], and ASME [12] standards for tanks and vessels, and an ASTM standard for manlift booms [13]. ASTM Committee E7 is close to issuing a *Standard Practice for Pipe*. A draft API standard for downhole tubing [14] includes provisions for quality control and acceptance testing with acoustic emission. In addition, the standard includes design provisions that are in part based on acoustic emission laboratory tests. The latter provisions are still the subject of some controversy, and the extent and final form of these provisions have not been resolved. A subcommittee of the *ASME Boiler and Pressure Vessel Code* is rewriting the Section X to allow unique FRP pressure vessels. An acoustic emission test will be a mandatory requirement of this code.

Figure 6 shows catastrophic FRP tank failures of Monsanto vessels during the period 1972–1986. In addition to the two major failures per year experienced during the 1970s, there had been numerous minor failures such as leaks, cracks at nozzles, breakage of holddown lugs and attachments, internal surface cracking, and blistering. As a result, many tanks became unsuitable for their intended function.

The dramatic reduction in catastrophic failures coincides with the introduction of company-wide acoustic emission testing in 1979–1980. Other factors, such as improved design methods, better control of fabrication quality, and a greater understanding of the nature of composites, also contributed to the reduction in failures.

The 1982 and 1984 failures occurred in tanks that had undergone acoustic emission testing. In both cases the test showed the tanks likely to fail under

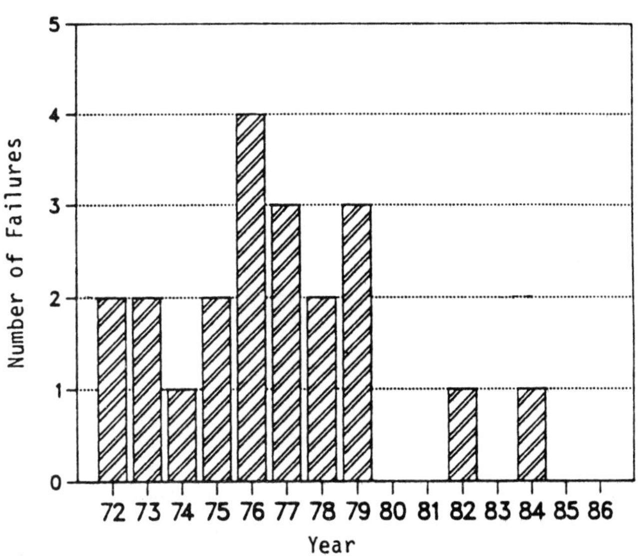

FIG. 6 FRP tank failure history.

continued operation; in one case, a replacement tank was ordered. Both tanks were operated at reduced levels, and appropriate precautions were taken to mitigate the consequences of failure.

At Monsanto, approximately 1700 acoustic emission tests of FRP tanks have been conducted together with some 1400 FRP pipe tests. For both tanks and piping, all defects identified by acoustic emission have been confirmed by follow-up visual or ultrasonic inspection. There is no known case of a structurally significant defect escaping detection by acoustic emission.

Evaluation Criteria

Predetermined objective evaluation criteria have been developed for assessing the condition of both FRP and metal equipment. For metals, the general format of the evaluation criteria is shown in Table 1. The first loading of pressure vessels, tanks, and piping systems tends to be noisy because of local yielding and stress redistribution. As a consequence, if an item of equipment fails the test under initial loading, it is reloaded and the data from the reload evaluated against a more severe set of criteria.

Specific numbers for the evaluation criteria depend on:

The material of construction
Whether the loading is first time, reload following hydrotest, or in-service
The type of equipment—pressure vessel, tank, or piping system
The intended service of the equipment
The load at which emissions occur relative to the operating load (Felicity effect)

The criteria in Table 1 are simple to use and easily applied in the field. Recently developed data analysis methods use statistical and regression analysis based on maximum energy and history of the emission as a function of load. These methods may also normalize the energy data to account for differences in sensors, type of equipment, insulation and coatings, equipment geometry, and material of construction.

Evaluation criteria for FRP equipment are contained in a number of the codes and standards [9–13]. A typical example is Table 2 [9].

In Conclusion

Application of the acoustic emission technique has been growing rapidly and it is being accepted as a major nondestructive test method for structural evaluation of tanks, vessels, and piping. It also offers cost savings and increased safety.

TABLE 1 Metal Vessel Evaluation Criteria[a]

Pressure Vessels and Tanks	Emission during Load Hold	Count Rate	Number of Hits	Large-Amplitude Hits	Relative Energy or Amplitudes	Activity	Evaluation Threshold (dB)
Pressure vessels without full postweld heat treatment (first loading)	Not more than E_H hits beyond time T_H	Not applied	Not applied	Not more than E_A hits above a specified amplitude	Do not increase with increasing load	Do not increase with increasing load	V_{TH}
Other pressure vessels and tanks	Not more than E_H hits beyond time T_H	Less than N_T counts per sensor for a specified load increase	Not more than E_T hits above a specified amplitude	Not more than E_A hits above a specified amplitude	Do not increase with increasing load	Do not increase with increasing load	V_{TH}

[a] E_H, N_T, E_T, E_A = specified acceptance criteria values.
V_{TH} = specified evaluation threshold.
T_H = specified hold time.

TABLE 2 FRP Evaluation Criteria

	Tanks		
	First Loading	Subsequent Loadings	Pressure Vessels
Emission during load hold	None beyond 2 minutes		
Felicity ratio	Not applicable	Greater than 0.95	
Total counts	Less than N	Less than $N/2$	Not excessive
Large amplitude events	Less than 10	Less than 10	Less than 10

References

1. M. P. Kelly, D. O. Harris, and A. A. Pollock, *Detection and Location of Flaw Growth in Metallic and Composite Structures,* ASTM Special Technical Publication 571, 1975.
2. D. O. Harris and H. L. Dunegan, "Acoustic Emission. 5. Applications of Acoustic Emission to Industrial Problems," *Nondestructive Testing,* June 1974.
3. H. L. Dunegan, "Acoustic Emission Testing of 12-Nickel Maraging Steel Pressure Vessels," *International Conference on Pressure Vessel Technology, Part 11, Materials Fabrication and Inspection,* ASME.
4. B. Woodward, N. R. McDonald, and M. J. Hincksman, "Application of Acoustic Emission Monitoring to Pressure Tests of a Steam Receiver Vessel with Flawed Nozzle Welds," *Aust. Weld. Res.,* December 1977.
5. T. Tsukikawa et al., "Accoustic Emission Testing during a Burst Test of a Thick Walled $2\frac{1}{4}$Cr-1Mo Steel Pressure Vessel," *Pressure Vessels and Piping Conference,* San Francisco, June 1979, ASME Paper 79-PVP-94.
6. *ASME Boiler and Pressure Vessel Code,* ASME, July 1983.
7. T. J. Fowler, "Acoustic Emission Testing of Chemical Process Industry Vessels," in *Progress in Acoustic Emission, Proceeding of the 7th International Acoustic Emission Symposium,* The Japanese Society for Non-Destructive Testing, Tokyo, Japan.
8. E. C. Jessen, H. Spanheimer, and A. J. De Herrera, *Prediction of Composite Pressure Vessel Performance by Application of the Kaiser Effect in Acoustic Emissions,* ASME Paper H300-12-2-037, June 1975.
9. *Recommended Practice for Acoustic Emission Testing of Fiberglass Tanks/Vessels,* SPI, January 1982.
10. "Recommended Practice for Acoustic Emission Testing of Fiberglass Reinforced Plastics Piping Systems," *International Symposium on Acoustic Emission from Reinforced Plastics,* SPI, July 1983.
11. *Standard Practice for Acoustic Emission Examination of Fiberglass Reinforced Plastic Resin (RF) Tanks/Vessels,* ASTM E1067-85, 1985.
12. "Acoustic Emission Examination of Fiber Reinforced Plastic Vessels," in *ASME Boiler and Pressure Vessel Code,* Section V, Article 11, June 1985.

13. *Standard Test Method for Acoustic Emission for Insulated Aerial Personnel Devices,* ASTM F914-85, 1985.
14. F. H. Pickering, "Design of High Pressure Fiberglass Downhole Tubing: A Proposed New ASTM Specification," *International Symposium on Acoustic Emission from Reinforced Plastics,* SPI, July 1983.

T. J. FOWLER

Platinum Group Metals

The Republic of South Africa remained the leading producer of platinum and the USSR remained the leading producer of palladium in 1989 (Table 1). In the future, most new production capacity for platinum-group metals (PGM) is expected to come from the Republic of South Africa.

Environmental legislation and concern over clean air continued to be a major factor driving PGM demand in the United States and Western Europe. With political changes sweeping Eastern Europe, it remains to be seen whether these countries will use catalytic converter technology to reduce automobile emissions. While the need is clear, the required capital to pay for clean air remains a problem.

Legislation and US Government Programs

A bill authorizing the minting of a palladium commemorative coin was not approved by the US House of Representatives. The staff of the US Mint testified that the coins would be difficult to produce. In addition, domestic sources of palladium are limited, and it is possible that some of the metal for the coin would have to come from sources originating in the USSR or the Republic of South Africa.

TABLE 1 Salient Platinum-Group Metals Statistics (kilograms)[a]

	1985	1986	1987	1988	1989
United States:					
Mine production:[b,c]					
Platinum	W	W	780	1,240	1,430
Palladium	W	W	2,330	3,730	4,850
Value[d] (thousand $)	W	W	44,686	67,622	85,318
Refinery production:					
Primary refined	227	135	191	297	339
Secondary:					
Nontoll-refined	8,043	11,016	5,117	4,787	3,954
Toll-refined	32,293	35,924	44,935	46,403	46,253
Total refined metal	40,563	47,075	50,243	51,488	50,546
Stocks, yearend:					
Industry (refined)	35,106	40,187	38,412	35,515	32,543
National Defense Stockpile:					
Platinum	14,079	14,079	14,079	14,079	14,079
Palladium[e]	39,259	39,334	39,334	39,334	39,334
Iridium	920	920	920	920	920
Exports:					
Refined[f]	16,369	11,879	13,423	20,301	23,082
Total	27,640	23,349	22,031	28,787	38,128
Imports for consumption:					
Refined[g]	106,928	115,924	98,879	110,948	111,107
Total	124,090	139,256	118,397	124,324	113,278
Imports, general	124,090	136,824	118,397	124,324	113,278
Consumption (reported sales to industry)	70,650	64,705	60,280	70,998	78,439
Consumption, apparent[h]	104,511	109,904	95,457	103,302	101,230
Net import reliance[i] as a percent of apparent consumption	92	90	91	91	90
Price, dealer, average, per ounce:					
Platinum	$291	$461	$553	$523	$507
Palladium	$107	$116	$130	$123	$144
World: Mine production[j]	246,988[r]	260,192[r]	273,582	281,854[p]	283,643[e]

[a]The platinum-group comprises six metals: platinum, palladium, iridium, osmium, rhodium, and ruthenium. e = estimated, p = preliminary, r = revised, w = withheld to avoid disclosing company proprietary data.
[b]By-product of copper refining plus production from Stillwater Mining Co. for 1987–89.
[c]Estimates from published sources.
[d]Value based on dealer prices.
[e]Includes 75 kg purchased in 1985, but not added to inventory in that year.
[g]Excludes ores, scrap, and platinum grains and nuggets.
[h]1985–1986 mine production excluded to avoid disclosing company proprietary data. 1987–1989 includes mine production plus nontoll-refined production plus refined imports for consumption minus refined exports plus or minus changes in government and industry stocks.
[i]Refined imports for consumption minus refined exports plus or minus changes in government and industry stocks.
[j]1985–1986 totals exclude United States mine production in order to avoid disclosing company proprietary data.

The US Administration's proposed Clean Air Bill called for decreasing the hydrocarbons limit for automobiles from the current 0.41 g/mi to 0.24 g/mi.

Strategic Considerations

While domestic production of platinum and palladium from the Stillwater Mine increased, domestic mine production was refined in Belgium and in 1989 accounted for only 3% of United States imports of refined platinum and 9% of United States imports of refined palladium (Table 2). Even though the US Federal Government stockpiled platinum, palladium, and iridium, there were no government programs engaged directly in the development or exploitation of mineral deposits. Exploration, development, and mining were considered to be functions of the private sector.

Import dependence on the Republic of South Africa and the USSR remained an area of concern for the United States. The threat of disruption from South Africa appeared more related to mining labor unrest than any other factor. A disruption in supplies from the USSR appeared unlikely given improvement in relations with that country and the need of the USSR to generate foreign currency.

The US Department of Defense, which oversees the National Strategic Stockpile, recommended to Congress that the government purchase 933 kg rhodium and 2022 kg ruthenium for the Stockpile [1]. In 1988 an advisory panel of the American Society of Metals also recommended the purchase. Stockpile goals remained unchanged at 40,746 kg platinum, 93,311 kg palladium, and 3048 kg iridium.

Production

The only PGM mine in the United States, southwest of Billings, Montana, was operated by the Stillwater Mining Co. (SMC), owned 50% by Chevron Corp. and 50% by Manville Corp. Estimates from published sources showed that production of platinum at the Stillwater Mine in 1989 was about 1430 kg and production of palladium was about 4850 kg. Small amounts of PGM were recovered as by-products of domestic copper refining.

In 1989, SMC shipped its concentrates to Belgium for smelting and refining, but applied for permission to construct a $6 million smelter to process its PGM concentrates. The company hoped to complete construction

TABLE 2 Platinum-Group Metals Refined in the United States (kilograms)

	Platinum	Palladium	Iridium	Osmium	Rhodium	Ruthenium	Total[a]
Primary metal:							
Nontoll-refined:							
1985	16	108	—	—	—	—	124
1986	19	116	—	—	—	—	135
1987	32	158	—	—	—	—	191
1988	46	248	2	—	[b]	—	297
1989	47	289	2	—	—	2	339
Toll-refined:							
1985	34	—	—	—	—	68	103
1986	—	—	—	—	—	—	—
1987	—	—	—	—	—	—	—
1988	—	—	—	—	—	—	—
1989	—	—	—	—	—	—	—
Secondary metal:							
Nontoll-refined:							
1985	1,629	6,263	8	—	97	46	8,043
1986	2,204	8,627	9	—	134	41	11,016
1987	1,180	3,743	4	19	123	49	5,117
1988	1,133	3,545	4	—	104	2	4,787
1989	1,149	2,670	6	—	94	35	3,954
Toll-refined:							
1985	15,259	15,270	218	[b]	1,130	415	32,293
1986	20,977	12,388	111	44	1,792	613	35,924
1987	22,580	19,169	102	25	1,895	1,164	44,935
1988	22,884	20,923	252	19	1,826	499	46,403
1989	24,058	20,037	219	1	1,565	373	46,253
1988 Totals:[a]							
Total primary	46	248	2	—	[b]	—	297
Total secondary	24,017	24,468	256	19	1,930	501	51,191
Total refined metal	24,062	24,717	258	19	1,930	501	51,488
1989 totals:							
Total primary	47	289	2	—	—	2	339
Total secondary	25,207	22,707	225	1	1,659	408	50,207
Total refined metal	25,254	22,996	227	1	1,659	410	50,546

[a]Data may not add to totals shown because of independent rounding.
[b]Less than ½ unit.

by the end of 1990. Final refining of the precious-metal matte probably would still be done in Belgium.

Consumption and Uses

Platinum, palladium, and rhodium were used in emission catalysts for light trucks (trucks weighing 14,000 lb or less, gross weight) and automobiles (Table 3). A typical emission catalyst in 1989 contained approximately 1.77 g platinum, 0.47 g palladium, and 0.2 g rhodium, for a total of 2.44 g PGM. These average quantities have not changed since 1985. There was variation in the quantities of PGM contained in each catalyst for any given year, depending on the year the vehicle was manufactured, the engine size, the normal operating temperature of the vehicle's engine, and the manufacturer of the catalyst. In 1989 there were 10.6 million vehicles produced in the

TABLE 3 Platinum-Group Metals[a] Sold to Consuming Industries in the United States[b] (kilograms)

Year and Industry	Platinum	Palladium	Iridium	Osmium	Rhodium	Ruthenium	Total
1985	31,905	32,980	332	28	2,745	2,662	70,650
1986	30,513	27,681	382	21	2,906	3,203	64,705
1987	25,471	30,956	250	29	2,692	882	60,280
1988:							
Automotive[c]	19,346	5,101	[d]	—	2,084	—	26,532
Chemical	3,184	3,669	117	—	109	604	7,683
Dental and medical	581	6,622	2	21	2	3	7,231
Electrical	3,494	13,049	190	—	123	1,067	17,923
Glass	681	11	[d]	—	85	1	779
Jewelry and decorative	385	196	20	—	177	14	792
Petroleum	1,072	1,438	75	—	1	—	2,587
Miscellaneous	2,383	4,156	89	2	710	132	7,471
Total	31,125	34,241	495	23	3,292	1,821	70,998
1989:							
Automotive[c]	18,774	4,886	—	—	1,982	—	25,643
Chemical	2,424	1,923	95	—	189	26	4,657
Dental and medical	632	8,424	105	57	1	15	9,233
Electrical	3,894	17,352	112	—	272	1,778	23,408
Glass	1,130	181	—	—	177	1	1,489
Jewelry and decorative	418	179	7	—	205	6	814
Petroleum	2,859	2,543	—	—	27	—	5,429
Miscellaneous	3,566	3,786	81	—	273	61	7,766
Total	33,698	39,273	400	57	3,126	1,886	78,439

[a]Comprises primary and nontoll-refined secondary metals.
[b]Data may not add to totals shown because of independent rounding.
[c]1985–1989 platinum, palladium, and rhodium sales to the automotive industry are estimated based on United States light truck sales and automobile production.
[d]Less than ½ unit.

United States that were subject to emissions control and outfitted with catalytic converters, of which about one-third were light trucks.

In electronic applications, ruthenium was the principal PGM used in thick film resistors, and palladium was the principal PGM used in thick film conductors, multilayer ceramic capacitors, and connectors. Platinum "targets" were used for sputtering thin films on circuit boards. Platinum-rhodium alloys were used for manufacturing thermocouples for precise temperature measurement.

For glass manufacturing applications, most of the PGM, specifically platinum, rhodium, and palladium, were used in bushings for the extrusion of textile or continuous filament glass fiber.

The nonautomotive catalyst applications of PGM were numerous. The petroleum refining industry used PGM, principally platinum, in reforming, cracking, and isomerization reactions. Chemical catalysts containing platinum and rhodium were used in inorganic syntheses of nitric acid and hydrogen cyanide. Palladium was used in the production of hydrogen peroxide. A wide variety of organic chemicals and pharmaceuticals were produced using PGM catalysts.

The US Bureau of Mines does not collect data on domestic investor demand for platinum, but according to Johnson Matthey PLC, projected investor demand for 1989 in North America was expected to be about 1866 kg, down from 2644 kg in the previous year [2]. A summary of the typical uses for each PGM is shown in Tables 4 and 5.

Stocks

In addition to the reported stocks held by refiners, importers, and dealers, end users of PGM held sizable quantities of PGM that were not reported to the US Bureau of Mines.

TABLE 4 Typical Uses of Platinum, Palladium, and Rhodium

Platinum	Palladium	Rhodium
Automobile catalyst	Automobile catalyst	Acetic acid catalyst
Cancer drugs	Dental alloys	Automobile catalyst
Coins	Hydrocracking catalyst	Glass bushings
Cracking catalyst	Hydrogen peroxide catalyst	Nitric acid catalyst
Crucibles	Multilayered capacitors	Thermocouples
Fuel cell electrode	Thick films pastes	
Glass bushings	Vinyl acetate catalyst	
Hydrogen cyanide catalyst		
Isomerization catalyst		
Jewelry		
Nitric acid catalyst		
Reforming catalyst		
Targets for thin films		
Thermocouples		

TABLE 5 Typical Uses of Ruthenium, Iridium, and Osmium

Ruthenium	Iridium	Osmium
Caustic soda electrode	Caustic soda electrode	Biological staining
Chlorine electrode	Chlorine electrode	Pharmaceutical catalyst
Resistor circuits	High-temperature crucibles	
	Reforming catalyst	

Prices

In March 1989, two scientists from the University of Utah announced that they had fused deuterium nuclei at a relatively low temperature using a palladium cathode immersed in heavy water. The process was regarded by some as a potential breakthrough in the decades-long search for a way of generating electricity from controlled nuclear fusion. While results of the experiment were being evaluated by other scientists, news of the announcement produced a flurry of speculation in palladium and caused dealer prices to increase from $135/oz in January to a high of $166/oz in April. As speculation tapered off, prices declined to about $137/oz by October.

The dealer price of rhodium began increasing sharply in November and continued increasing in December, with spot prices approaching $2000/oz. The increase was attributed to the reported technical difficulties at Johnson Matthey's newly commissioned Rustenburg refinery in Bophuthatswana. Also contributing to the price rise was the absence of rhodium sales by the USSR, the second largest supplier of rhodium after the Republic of South Africa.

World Review (Tables 6–11)

In July 1989, the European Community (EC) voted to require that all member nations comply with automobile exhaust emissions limits, comparable to those in the United States, by January 1, 1993, for cars with engine

TABLE 6 Refiner, Importer, and Dealer Stocks of Refined Platinum-Group Metals in the United States, December 31 (kilograms)[a]

Year	Platinum	Palladium	Iridium	Osmium	Rhodium	Ruthenium	Total[b]
1985	17,783	14,152	527	9	1,466	1,170	35,106
1986	20,426	16,958	611	12	1,475	705	40,187
1987	19,004	17,356	506	1	996	549	38,412
1988	18,438	14,837	432	8	1,165	634	35,515
1989	14,791	15,182	522	36	1,096	916	32,543

[a]Includes metal in depositories of the New York Mercantile Exchange (NYMEX); on December 31, 1989, this comprised 5,152 kg platinum and 2,815 kg palladium.
[b]Data may not add to totals shown because of independent rounding.

TABLE 7 Average Producer and Dealer Prices of Platinum-Group Metals (dollars per troy ounce)[a]

	Platinum		Palladium		Rhodium		Iridium		Ruthenium	Osmium
	Producer	Dealer	Producer	Dealer	Producer	Dealer	Producer	Dealer	Dealer	Dealer
1985	475	291	127	107	915	929	600	438	101	915
1986	519	461	131	116	1,196	1,157	600	414	73	704
1987	600	553	150	130	1,239	1,222	532	363	70	633
1988:										
January	600	492	150	124	1,275	1,187	420	333	67	602
February	600	452	150	119	1,275	1,238	420	326	65	610
March	600	491	150	121	1,275	1,235	420	310	62	603
April	600	492	150	124	1,275	1,230	420	315	62	509
May	600	545	150	122	1,275	1,231	420	310	60	580
June	600	576	150	127	1,275	1,266	420	309	61	590
July	600	543	150	124	1,275	1,185	420	304	65	625
August	600	529	150	124	1,275	1,214	420	302	45	625
September	600	506	150	119	1,275	1,218	420	305	67	625
October	600	522	150	120	1,275	1,191	420	286	63	580
November	600	566	150	125	1,275	1,232	420	287	60	580
December	600	557	150	131	1,275	1,190	420	287	60	580
Average	600	523	150	123	1,275	1,218	420	306	61	592
1989:										
January	600	528	150	135	1,275	1,247	420	295	64	580
February	600	530	150	141	1,275	1,254	420	293	62	580
March	600	534	150	145	1,275	1,271	[b]	295	62	580
April	600	538	150	166	1,275	1,274	[b]	300	62	570
May	600	515	.30	152	1,275	1,280	[b]	303	62	550
June	600	494	150	152	1,275	1,275	[b]	305	61	550
July	600	500	150	150	1,275	1,269	[b]	305	61	550
August	600	483	150	134	1,275	1,247	[b]	305	61	550
September	600	476	150	137	1,275	1,265	[b]	305	62	550
October	600	483	150	137	1,275	1,269	[b]	305	63	529
November	600	504	150	138	1,275	1,302	[b]	307	63	500
December	600	502	150	137	1,275	1,644	[b]	313	63	500
Average	600	507	150	144	1,275	1,300	NA	303	62	549

[a]Average prices calculated at the low end of the range and rounded to the nearest dollar.
[b]Producer prices discontinued March 22, 1989.

displacements less than 1.4 L. Until now, most automobile catalytic converters in the EC were on cars with engine displacements greater than 1.4 L. Consequently, the major producers of catalytic converters planned to expand capacity to meet the demand of what is potentially the world's largest automobile market. About 13 million new cars are sold per year in the EC. Plant expansions of autocatalyst facilities were anticipated in the Federal

TABLE 8 NYMEX Trading Volume for Futures Contracts, December 31 (number of contracts)

	1986	1987	1988	1989
Platinum[a]	1,624,635	1,361,546	1,460,455	1,190,529
Palladium[b]	145,562	160,284	139,883	200,892

[a]50 troy ounces per contract.
[b]100 troy ounces per contract.

TABLE 9 United States Exports of Platinum-Group Metals for 1989 by Country (kilograms)[a]

Country	Platinum	Palladium	Rhodium	Iridium, Osmium, Ruthenium	Waste and Scrap	Total Quantity	Total Value (thousands)
Australia	73	42	—	19	—	134	$1,477
Austria	2	116	—	—	—	118	624
Belgium	85	543	—	11	2,808	3,447	20,109
Brazil	143	22	35	1	—	201	5,803
Canada	1,902	644	197	17	443	3,203	45,814
China	150	907	36	28	—	1,121	7,919
France	128	62	—	1	100	291	3,829
Germany, Federal Republic of	140	499	250	143	2,703	3,735	41,639
Hong Kong	27	16	1	—	3	47	622
Italy	55	313	1	—	902	1,271	12,698
Japan	3,652	4,027	387	25	292	8,383	100,962
Korea, Republic of	348	40	70	1	1	460	8,364
Netherlands	—	1,497	—	—	—	1,497	9,941
Singapore	6	182	—	8	—	196	1,608
Sweden	—	22	—	79	144	245	2,057
Switzerland	615	216	16	—	125	972	13,629
Taiwan	359	393	3	8	—	763	6,579
USSR	—	1,565	—	92	—	1,657	8,704
United Kingdom	645	1,647	159	24	7,514	9,989	103,237
Other	84	252	1	50	11	398	2,494
Total	8,414	13,005	1,156	507	15,046	38,128	398,109

[a]Source: Bureau of the Census.

Republic of Germany, the Republic of Korea, Belgium, and France to meet the increased demand in Europe [3].

According to the interim 1989 review on platinum published by Johnson Matthey, world investment demand for platinum decreased from 19,600 kg to only about 5000 kg in 1989. Higher interest rates and less fear of a disruption in supply from South Africa contributed lower investor interest in platinum.

The International Precious Metals Institute (IPMI) of Allentown, Pennsylvania, sponsored a seminar on platinum-group metals January 29–31 in Las Vegas, Nevada. Presentations centered around the use of PGM in autocatalysts, industrial pollution control, fuel cells, jewelry, electronics, and health applications. Proceedings of the meeting are available for purchase through IPMI.

Capacity

Capacity for PGM is generally cited in terms of platinum capacity. The data in Table 12 represent rated capacity, defined as the maximum quantity that can be produced on a normally sustainable long-term operating rate, based on the physical equipment of the plant and routine operating procedures for labor, energy, materials, and maintenance. Capacity includes both operating plants and plants temporarily closed that in the judgment of the author can be brought into production within a short period of time with minimum capital expenditure.

TABLE 10 United States Imports for Consumption of Platinum-Group Metals in 1989 by Country (kilograms)[a]

Country	Platinum	Palladium	Rhodium	Ruthenium	Iridium	Osmium	Waste and Scrap	Ores	Total Quantity	Total Value (thousands)
Australia	5	—	—	—	—	—	3	—	8	$160
Belgium	1,326	6,410	337	—	—	—	249	1	8,323	61,207
Canada	1,198	1,094	—	—	—	—	562	8	2,862	36,389
Dominican Republic	1	34	—	—	—	—	—	—	35	552
France	10	817	—	—	—	—	—	—	827	3,838
Germany, Federal Republic of	1,976	263	194	54	101	4	—	—	2,592	40,541
Hong Kong	—	1	—	1	—	—	551	—	553	8,402
Italy	—	1	19	—	—	—	24	—	44	1,189
Japan	286	2,241	1	—	1	—	2	—	2,531	9,649
Mexico	1	—	—	—	—	—	45	—	46	371
Netherlands	94	289	14	7	4	—	—	—	408	3,990
Norway	179	411	26	—	—	—	—	—	616	5,138
South Africa, Republic of	34,109	17,270	2,580	2,027	502	54	—	—	56,542	755,638
Switzerland	2,123	1,016	438	1	—	—	17	—	3,595	63,307
Taiwan	90	973	—	—	—	—	1	—	1,064	6,794
USSR	792	11,327	2,169	—	—	—	21	—	14,309	159,658
United Kingdom	6,928	8,920	1,256	793	80	—	432	—	18,409	217,841
Other	120	68	71	—	—	—	252	3	514	7,029
Total	49,238	51,135	7,105	2,883	688	58	2,159	12	113,278	1,381,693

[a]Source: Bureau of the Census.

TABLE 11 Supply and Demand for Platinum, Palladium, and Rhodium in the Market Economy Countries in 1989 (kilograms)[a]

	Platinum	Palladium	Rhodium
Supply			
Mine production:			
South Africa, Republic of[b]	82,838	35,308	4,070
Canada	4,461	4,669	415
United States[c]	1,430	4,850	—
Other	2,167	1,521	—
Total	90,896	46,348	4,485
Secondary from old scrap:			
Japan	1,700	620	280
United States	1,149	2,670	94
Total	2,849	3,290	374
Soviet sales to market economy countries	13,680	53,650	3,580
Total	107,425	103,288	8,439
Demand			
Industrial:			
Japan	48,680	47,120	3,000
United States	33,698	39,273	3,113
Western Europe	17,260	18,660	2,000
Other	8,090	5,910	160
Total	107,728[d]	110,963	8,273

[a]Sources: Principally Johnson Matthey PLC, and CPM Group Ltd.
[b]Estimated by the Bureau of Mines.
[c]Estimates for public sources.
[d]Excludes approximately 5,130 kg of investment demand.

TABLE 12 Platinum Annual Mine Capacity of Major Producing Companies as of December 31, 1989 (kilograms)

	Capacity
North America:	
Inco Ltd.	3,800
Falconbridge Ltd.	1,300
Stillwater Mining Co.[a]	1,430
Total	6,530
Africa:	
Rustenburg Platinum Mines Ltd.[b]	44,000
Impala Platinum Holdings (Pty.) Ltd.[c]	34,000
Western Platinum Ltd.	7,800
Barplats Mines	1,000
Total	86,800
World total (rounded)	93,300

[a]Jointly owned by Chevron Corp. and Manville Corp.
[b]Owns Lebowa Platinum Ltd.
[c]Owns the Karee Mine and Messina Mine.

South Africa, Republic of

Barplats Mines (formerly Lefkochrysos Ltd.) produced 933 kg platinum at the Crocodile River Mine. Barplats is controlled by Rand Mines. All of Barplats' production was from the UG-2 reef, rather than from the more easily processed Merensky reef [4]. In the past, platinum producers have overcome the metallurgical problems of treating UG-2 ores by blending them with Merensky ores. It appears, however, that technical problems for treating pure UG-2 ores have been overcome.

Rustenburg Platinum Mines Ltd. decided not to develop the Maandagshoek platinum mine in the eastern Transvaal because of its inability to obtain tax concessions from the South African Government. The costs of developing the mine would have been too high without the tax concessions.

USSR

The USSR began marketing and selling a 1-oz palladium coin honoring Russian Ballet. The Ballerina palladium bullion coin is the world's first palladium bullion coin. Owing in part to the difficulties in minting, only about 30,000 coins were sold in 1989 [5].

Current Research

Nippon Mining Co. announced that it had developed a new corrosion-resistant platinum magnet that contains 70% platinum and 30% iron. Its major application was expected to be in precision motors for use in ultravacuum and ultraclean environments.

Platinum–silicide was being investigated as a material that substitutes for cadmium–mercury–telluride in infrared detectors. Platinum–silicide performs better and is cheaper to produce than the traditional cadmium–mercury–telluride. Platinum–silicide detectors are made by depositing a layer of platinum only a few molecules thick over silicon integrated circuits. Infrared detectors made with platinum–silicide are used in military applications such as heat-seeking missiles [6].

The US Bureau of Mines investigated leaching PGM from scrapped automobile catalysts using a solution of sodium cyanide. Recovery rates for platinum, palladium, and rhodium were over 90% and the process was environmentally safe. Work on the process to reduce recovery costs was progressing through 1990 at the Bureau's Reno Research Center.

Outlook

World Supply of Platinum

The Republic of South Africa and the USSR were the most important countries supplying platinum. Because of the planned opening of new mines and the expansion of existing ones, production of platinum in South Africa was projected to increase by one-third from about 83,000 kg in 1989 to about 111,000 kg by 1994 [4]. For the USSR, sales of platinum to market economy countries was expected to decline because the Soviets are expected to boost their own consumption and/or increase sales to Eastern Europe, where platinum can be used to produce unleaded gasoline and reduce automobile emissions. Over the next 5 years, Canadian production of platinum should remain flat, while United States production could grow another 25% from expansion of the Stillwater Mine in Montana (Table 13).

Jewelry demand for platinum in Japan should grow about 25% to 44,000 kg by 1994. Investment demand for platinum is probably the most volatile end use, subject to wide swings in either direction, depending on economic conditions, exchange rates, and interest rates.

World Demand for Platinum

Demand for platinum in automobile catalysts, particularly 3-way catalysts that use platinum and rhodium, was expected to be strong over the next 5 years.

In the United States, the number of cars and trucks outfitted with catalytic converters has remained between 10 and 11 million vehicles from 1987 through 1989. While production of cars and trucks was expected to remain flat, overall consumption of platinum was expected to rise because of the greater amounts of platinum expected to be used in each catalytic converter. As mentioned earlier, the proposed Clean Air Bill called for reducing hydrocarbon and nitrogen oxide emissions. Another proposal being debated was extending the certification period for catalytic converters from 50,000 to 100,000 mi. All these measures, if enacted, would require about one-third more platinum per converter than currently used.

The decision of the Economic Community (EC) in 1989 to adopt emissions limits for cars with engines smaller than 1.4 L will result in a large increase in demand for platinum. By 1994, demand for platinum used in autocatalysts in the EC is expected to double from about 9300 kg in 1989 to 18,000 kg.

Autocatalysts are currently required in Australia, Canada, Japan, South Korea, the United States and most of Western Europe. Other countries, such as Brazil, Mexico, and Taiwan, were expected to begin requiring autocatalysts in the early 1990s. World demand for platinum in autocatalysts could increase from about 40,000 kg in 1989 to 56,000 kg in 1994.

Background

Products for Trade and Industry

The basic commercial forms of PGM were sponge or powder, which may be converted to other forms such as bars, pastes, or chemicals. The catalyst

TABLE 13 Platinum-Group Metals: World Production by Country (kilograms)[a]

Country[b]	1985	1986	1987	1988[p]	1989[e]
Australia, metal content, from domestic nickel ore:[c]					
Palladium	476	428	490[e]	410[e]	400
Platinum	95	115	130[e]	105[e]	100
Canada: Platinum-group metals from nickel ore	10,485	12,190	10,930	12,541	10,375
Colombia: Placer platinum	362	447	638	810	964[d]
Ethiopia: Placer platinum[e]	2[r,e]	2	1	1	2
Finland:					
Palladium	35	96	89	106	100
Platinum	35	120	120	54	60
Japan, metal recovered from nickel-copper ores:[f]					
Palladium	1,359	1,453	1,417	1,170	846
Platinum	691	663	753	647	999
South Africa, Republic of: Platinum-group metals from platinum ore[e,h]	115,100	123,200	131,300	133,300	135,800
USSR: Placer platinum and platinum-group metals recovered from nickel-copper ores[e]	118,200	121,300[r]	124,400[r]	127,500[r]	127,500
United States: Platinum-group metals from palladium ores and gold-copper ores:[e,i]					
Palladium	W	W	2,330	3,730	4,850
Platinum	W	W	780	1,240	1,430
Yugoslavia:					
Palladium	95	85	132	142	140
Platinum	3	33	24	23	22
Zimbabwe:					
Palladium	30	35	29	46	35
Platinum	19	26	18	28	20
Total[j]	246,988[r]	260,192[r]	273,582	281,854	283,643

[a]Table includes data available through April 25, 1990. Platinum-group metal production by the Federal Republic of Germany, Norway, and the United Kingdom is not included in this table because the production is derived wholly from imported metallurgical products and to include it would result in double counting. e = estimated, p = preliminary, r = revised, W = withheld to avoid disclosing company proprietary data; excluded from "Total."

[b]In addition to the countries listed, China, Indonesia, Papua New Guinea, and the Philippines are believed to produce platinum-group metals, and several other countries may also do so, but output is not reported quantitatively, and there is no reliable basis for the formulation of estimates of output levels. However, a part of this output not specifically reported by country is presumably included in this table credited to Japan. (See footnote g.)

[c]Partial figure; excludes platinum-group metals recovered in other countries from nickel ore of Australian origin; however, a part of this output may be credited to Japan. (See footnote g.)

[d]Reported figure.

[f]Data are for years ending June 30 of that stated.

[g]Japanese figures do not refer to Japanese mine production, but rather represent Japanese smelter-refinery recovery from ores originating in a number of countries; this output cannot be credited to the country of origin because of a lack of data. Countries producing and exporting such ores to Japan include (but are not necessarily limited to) Australia, Canada, Indonesia, Papua New Guinea, and the Philippines. Output from ores of Australian, Indonesian, Papua New Guinean, and Philippine origin are not duplicative, but output from Canadian material might duplicate a part of reported Canadian production.

[h]Includes osmiridium produced in gold mines.

[i]Estimates for the Stillwater Mine, from published sources.

[j]Data may not add to totals shown because of independent rounding.

industry employs an extensive number of chemical compounds containing PGM. A typical PGM catalyst may consist of a platinum–rhodium gauze woven from wire. The electronics industry purchases PGM pastes and the dental industry uses wire and a variety of alloys.

Industry Structure

In North America, PGM are recovered by a small number of scrap refiners, as shown in Table 14. Other companies collect scrap materials such as catalysts and PGM-bearing solutions and process them to increase the grade. These upgraded secondary materials are then sold to or treated on toll by refiners. For example, in addition to its refining operations, Mulit-Metco, Anniston, Alabama, produces a 90% PGM concentrate from scapped autocatalysts, which in turn is refined by another company. World Resources Co., McLean, Virginia, collects electroplating solutions, upgrades them, and sells the concentrate to another refiner. Most companies specialize in refining or upgrading a particular type of scrap, such as petroleum catalysts, autocatalysts, or electronic scrap.

Refiners often charge a consumer a fee to have scrap toll refined, but ownership of the scrapped catalyst remains with the consumer. A refiner replaces a wornout catalyst with a fresh catalyst and charges the consumer for the refining and fabrication costs. In some cases, refiners simply refine scrap and sell it to other companies to fabricate catalysts.

Geology—Resources

PGM deposits are associated with magmatic intrusions of mafic and ultramafic rocks. They also occur to a lesser extent in placer deposits. Layered deposits associated with stratiform complexes are the only ones mined prin-

TABLE 14 Selected North American Platinum-Group Metals Refiners and Fabricators

Company	Type	Plant Location	Specialty
AT&T/Nassau Metals	Refiner	Gaston, South Carolina	Electronics
	"	Staten Island, New York	"
Degussa/Metz	Refiner, fabricator	South Plainfield, New Jersey	All
	Fabricator	Burlington, Ontario	Autocatalysts
Dupont Corp.	"	Wilmington, Delaware	Electronics
Engelhard Corp.	Refiner, fabricator	Carteret, New Jersey	All
	Fabricator	Seneca, South Carolina	Catalysts
Gemini Industries	Refiner	Santa Ana, California	"
Handy & Harman	Refiner, fabricator	South Windsor, Connecticut	Electronics
	"	South Plainfield, New Jersey	"
Johnson Matthey Inc.	"	West Deptford, New Jersey	All
Martin Metals Inc.	Refiner	Los Angeles, California	Electronics
Multi-Metco Inc.	"	Anniston, Alabama	Autocatalysts
Noranda Ltd.	"	Montreal, Quebec	Electronics
PGP Industries Inc.	Refiner, fabricator	Santa Fe Springs, California	"

cipally for the PGM, with nickel, copper, and cobalt sometimes produced as by-products. These are found in the Bushveld Complex, Republic of South Africa, and the Stillwater Complex, United States. In other PGM deposits, such as those found in the Sudbury Complex, Canada, and Noril'sk, USSR, the PGM are produced as by-products of nickel and copper mining [7].

In South Africa, it is interesting to note that base metals such as nickel and copper are important in generating revenues from the Merensky and Platreef ores. This is not the case at the Stillwater Mine in the United States, where platinum and palladium contribute nearly 100% of revenues [8].

World reserves of PGM are about 56 million kilograms, with 89% contained in the Bushveld Complex, Republic of South Africa, and most of the remaining 11% located in the USSR, Canada, and the United States.

Technology

Assaying

Fire assay techniques have long been used to determine the presence of precious metals. The use of lead as a collector for fire assays is suitable for gold and silver, but not for the PGM. For the PGM, nickel sulfide or copper sulfide is the preferred collector. In addition to fire assays, PGM can be determined by chemical methods and instrumental methods such as X-ray fluorescence and spectrochemical methods [9].

A list of independent PGM assayers is shown in Table 15. The list is meant to be a sampling rather than a complete list of assayers.

Primary Processing

The processing of PGM entails four general steps: mining, concentrating, smelting, and refining. After mining, platinum ore is crushed, ground, and concentrated by froth flotation. The concentrates are dried, roasted, and smelted to form a sulfide matte containing the PGM. The matte is treated in a refinery using solvent-extraction techniques to separate and purify the six PGM.

Recycling

Because of their high value, PGM are routinely recovered from petroleum catalysts, chemical catalysts, automobile catalysts, glass fiber bushings, elec-

TABLE 15 Independent Platinum-Group Metals Assayers

Company	Location
Accredited Laboratories Inc.	Carteret, New Jersey
Alex Stewart (Assayers) Ltd.	Merryside, England
Alfred H. Knight Laboratories Ltd.	Pompton Lakes, New Jersey
Bondar-Clegg	Ottawa, Canada
International Testing Laboratories	Newark, New Jersey
Ledoux & Company	Teaneck, New Jersey
Umpire & Control Services Inc.	West Babylon, New York

tronic scrap, laboratory equipment, dental materials, and jewelry. Johnson Matthey estimated that 4510 kg platinum and 2333 kg palladium were recovered from scrapped catalytic converters in North America in 1989. Small quantities of rhodium were also recovered.

Major collectors and refiners of autocatalysts are shown in Table 16. In the United States, only Multi-Metco, the successor of Texas Gulf Corp., refined any substantial quantities of PGM. Multi-Metco's output required further processing by other companies to produce commercial grade metal. The other major refiners of scraped automobile catalysts are in Canada, Belgium, and Japan.

Economic Factors

Prices

A time series of historical prices for each of the six PGM and a brief discussion of factors influencing prices is given in a Bureau of Mines publication entitled *Nonferrous Metal Prices in the United States through 1988.* [10].

In the first quarter of 1990, the price of rhodium exceeded $2000/oz, a record high for this metal. In 1989, the average price of rhodium was only $1300. The immediate cause of the price rise was attributed to technical production difficulties at a newly commissioned refinery in the Republic of South Africa.

Futures contracts are traded on the New York Mercantile Exchange (NYMEX) and the Tokyo Commodity Exchange for Industry (TOCOM), and to a lesser extent on the MidAmerica Exchange [11]. Futures contracts help consumers of platinum and palladium lock in prices and allow speculators an opportunity to make profits. By comparing the current price with the price for future delivery, one can surmise whether speculators expect prices to rise or fall.

Platinum and palladium futures contracts, specifying 99.9% metal content, were traded on the NYMEX in units of 50 and 100 troy ounces, respectively. Table 8 shows the number of contracts traded, yearend, for 1986 through 1989.

Trading of platinum futures contracts on the TOCOM began in 1984.

TABLE 16 Collectors and Refiners of Autocatalysts

Company	Type	Plant Location
A-1 Specialized Services & Supplies Inc.	Collector	South River, New Jersey
Bowden Industries Inc.	"	Covington, Tennessee
Brown Recycling & Manufacturing	"	Somerville, Alabama
Catalytic Converter Refining Co.	"	Northlake, Illinois
INCO Ltd.	Refiner	Sudbury, Canada
Metallurgie Hoboken Overpelt/SGM	"	Hoboken, Belgium
Multi-Metco	"	Anniston, Alabama
Nissan Group/Ikeda	"	Japan
Parkans International Inc.	Collector	Houston, Texas
Sumitomo Metal Mining Co.	Refiner	Japan
U.S. Scrap Co.	Collector	Los Angeles, California

The contract unit was 500 g, the quality specifications were 99.9%, and prices were quoted in Japanese yen per gram.

In London, physical prices of platinum and palladium bullion are set each day in the morning and afternoon for the wholesale professional market. The eight companies participating in establishing prices were members of the London-Zurich Good Delivery Agreement that sets standards for platinum and palladium trading in Europe. London and Zurich are the two most important European trading centers for platinum and palladium.

References

1. U.S. Department of Defense, *Report to the Congress on National Defense Stockpile Requirements 1989,* p. 8.
2. J. S. Coombes, *Platinum 1989 Interim Review,* Johnson Matthey PLC, p. 11.
3. "Catalytic Converter Producers Gear Up for EC Demand," *Met. Week, 60*(39), 2 (September 25, 1989).
4. *Precious Metals Supplement, Min. J.* (*London*), *313*(8047), 8 (November 24, 1989).
5. "Precious Metals News and Review," *Int. Precious Met. Inst. Newslett., 13*(12), 5 (1989).
6. "Platinum Silicide's Growing Challenge," *Lasers Optronics, 8*(10), 63–67 (1989).
7. D. Sutphin and N. J. Page, *International Strategic Minerals Inventory Summary Report—Platinum-Group Metals,* U.S. Geological Survey Circular 930-E, 1986.
8. D. J. D. Russell, Anderson & Co. Inc., South Africa, *Platinum Supply—Enough to Go Around?,* Speech Given at the 2nd NYMEX International Platinum Dinner, New York, September 27, 1989.
9. S. Kallmann, "A Survey of the Determination of the Platinum Group Elements," *Talanta, 34*(8), 677–698 (1987).
10. U.S. Bureau of Mines, Branch of Nonferrous Metals, *Nonferrous Metal Prices in the United States through 1988.*
11. G. Findlay, *Trading in Platinum,* Woodhead-Faulkner Ltd., 1988.

J. ROGER LOEBENSTEIN

Index

The lightface page numbers refer to Volume 1 and the **boldface** page numbers refer to Volume 2.